Nineteenth-Century Literature Criticism

Guide to Thomson Gale Literary Criticism Series

For criticism on	Consult these Thomson Gale series
Authors now living or who died after December 31, 1999	*CONTEMPORARY LITERARY CRITICISM (CLC)*
Authors who died between 1900 and 1999	*TWENTIETH-CENTURY LITERARY CRITICISM (TCLC)*
Authors who died between 1800 and 1899	*NINETEENTH-CENTURY LITERATURE CRITICISM (NCLC)*
Authors who died between 1400 and 1799	*LITERATURE CRITICISM FROM 1400 TO 1800 (LC)* *SHAKESPEAREAN CRITICISM (SC)*
Authors who died before 1400	*CLASSICAL AND MEDIEVAL LITERATURE CRITICISM (CMLC)*
Authors of books for children and young adults	*CHILDREN'S LITERATURE REVIEW (CLR)*
Dramatists	*DRAMA CRITICISM (DC)*
Poets	*POETRY CRITICISM (PC)*
Short story writers	*SHORT STORY CRITICISM (SSC)*
Literary topics and movements	*HARLEM RENAISSANCE: A GALE CRITICAL COMPANION (HR)* *THE BEAT GENERATION: A GALE CRITICAL COMPANION (BG)* *FEMINISM IN LITERATURE: A GALE CRITICAL COMPANION (FL)* *GOTHIC LITERATURE: A GALE CRITICAL COMPANION (GL)*
Asian American writers of the last two hundred years	*ASIAN AMERICAN LITERATURE (AAL)*
Black writers of the past two hundred years	*BLACK LITERATURE CRITICISM (BLC)* *BLACK LITERATURE CRITICISM SUPPLEMENT (BLCS)*
Hispanic writers of the late nineteenth and twentieth centuries	*HISPANIC LITERATURE CRITICISM (HLC)* *HISPANIC LITERATURE CRITICISM SUPPLEMENT (HLCS)*
Native North American writers and orators of the eighteenth, nineteenth, and twentieth centuries	*NATIVE NORTH AMERICAN LITERATURE (NNAL)*
Major authors from the Renaissance to the present	*WORLD LITERATURE CRITICISM, 1500 TO THE PRESENT (WLC)* *WORLD LITERATURE CRITICISM SUPPLEMENT (WLCS)*

ISSN 0732-1864

Volume 169

Nineteenth-Century Literature Criticism

Criticism of the
Works of Novelists, Philosophers, and Other
Creative Writers Who Died between 1800
and 1899, from the First Published Critical
Appraisals to Current Evaluations

Jessica Bomarito
Russel Whitaker
Project Editors

THOMSON
GALE

Detroit • New York • San Francisco • New Haven, Conn. • Waterville, Maine • London • Munich

Nineteenth-Century Literature Criticism, Vol. 169

Project Editors
Jessica Bomarito and Russel Whitaker

Editorial
Kathy D. Darrow, Jeffrey W. Hunter, Jelena O. Krstović, Michelle Lee, Thomas J. Schoenberg, Noah Schusterbauer, Lawrence J. Trudeau

Data Capture
Frances Monroe, Gwen Tucker

Indexing Services
Factiva

Rights and Acquisitions
Margaret Abendroth, Emma Hull, Jackie Jones

Imaging and Multimedia
Dean Dauphinais, Robert Duncan, Leitha Etheridge-Sims, Lezlie Light, Michael Logusz, Dan Newell, Kelly A. Quin, Denay Wilding

Composition and Electronic Capture
Carolyn Roney

Manufacturing
Rhonda Dover

Associate Product Manager
Marc Cormier

LIBRARY OF CONGRESS CATALOG CARD NUMBER 84-643008

ISBN 0-7876-8653-0
ISSN 0732-1864

Printed in the United States of America
10 9 8 7 6 5 4 3 2 1

Contents

Preface vii

Acknowledgments xi

Literary Criticism Series Advisory Board xiii

Preface

Since its inception in 1981, *Nineteeth-Century Literature Criticism* (*NCLC*) has been a valuable resource for students and librarians seeking critical commentary on writers of this transitional period in world history. Designated an "Outstanding Reference Source" by the American Library Association with the publication of is first volume, *NCLC* has since been purchased by over 6,000 school, public, and university libraries. The series has covered more than 450 authors representing 33 nationalities and over 17,000 titles. No other reference source has surveyed the critical reaction to nineteenth-century authors and literature as thoroughly as *NCLC*.

Scope of the Series

NCLC is designed to introduce students and advanced readers to the authors of the nineteenth century and to the most significant interpretations of these authors' works. The great poets, novelists, short story writers, playwrights, and philosophers of this period are frequently studied in high school and college literature courses. By organizing and reprinting commentary written on these authors, *NCLC* helps students develop valuable insight into literary history, promotes a better understanding of the texts, and sparks ideas for papers and assignments. Each entry in *NCLC* presents a comprehensive survey of an author's career or an individual work of literature and provides the user with a multiplicity of interpretations and assessments. Such variety allows students to pursue their own interests; furthermore, it fosters an awareness that literature is dynamic and responsive to many different opinions.

Every fourth volume of *NCLC* is devoted to literary topics that cannot be covered under the author approach used in the rest of the series. Such topics include literary movements, prominent themes in nineteenth-century literature, literary reaction to political and historical events, significant eras in literary history, prominent literary anniversaries, and the literatures of cultures that are often overlooked by English-speaking readers.

NCLC continues the survey of criticism of world literature begun by Thomson Gale's *Contemporary Literary Criticism* (*CLC*) and *Twentieth-Century Literary Criticism* (*TCLC*).

Organization of the Book

An *NCLC* entry consists of the following elements:

- The **Author Heading** cites the name under which the author most commonly wrote, followed by birth and death dates. Also located here are any name variations under which an author wrote, including transliterated forms for authors whose native languages use nonroman alphabets. If the author wrote consistently under a pseudonym, the pseudonym will be listed in the author heading and the author's actual name given in parenthesis on the first line of the biographical and critical information. Uncertain birth or death dates are indicated by question marks. Single-work entries are preceded by a heading that consists of the most common form of the title in English translation (if applicable) and the original date of composition.

- The **Introduction** contains background information that introduces the reader to the author, work, or topic that is the subject of the entry.

- A **Portrait of the Author** is included when available.

- The list of **Principal Works** is ordered chronologically by date of first publication and lists the most important works by the author. The genre and publication date of each work is given. In the case of foreign authors whose works have been translated into English, the list will focus primarily on twentieth-century translations, selecting those works most commonly considered the best by critics. Unless otherwise indicated, dramas are dated by first performance, not first publication. Lists of **Representative Works** by different authors appear with topic entries.

- Reprinted **Criticism** is arranged chronologically in each entry to provide a useful perspective on changes in critical evaluation over time. The critic's name and the date of composition or publication of the critical work are given at the beginning of each piece of criticism. Unsigned criticism is preceded by the title of the source in which it appeared. All titles by the author featured in the text are printed in boldface type. Footnotes are reprinted at the end of each essay or excerpt. In the case of excerpted criticism, only those footnotes that pertain to the excerpted texts are included. Criticism in topic entries is arranged chronologically under a variety of subheadings to facilitate the study of different aspects of the topic.

- A complete **Bibliographical Citation** of the original essay or book precedes each piece of criticism.

- Critical essays are prefaced by brief **Annotations** explicating each piece.

- An annotated bibliography of **Further Reading** appears at the end of each entry and suggests resources for additional study. In some cases, significant essays for which the editors could not obtain reprint rights are included here. Boxed material following the further reading list provides references to other biographical and critical sources on the author in series published by Thomson Gale.

Indexes

Each volume of *NCLC* contains a **Cumulative Author Index** listing all authors who have appeared in a wide variety of reference sources published by Thomson Gale, including *NCLC*. A complete list of these sources is found facing the first page of the Author Index. The index also includes birth and death dates and cross references between pseudonyms and actual names.

A **Cumulative Nationality Index** lists all authors featured in *NCLC* by nationality, followed by the number of the *NCLC* volume in which their entry appears.

A **Cumulative Topic Index** lists the literary themes and topics treated in the series as well as in *Classical and Medieval Literature Criticism, Literature Criticism from 1400 to 1800, Twentieth-Century Literary Criticism,* and the *Contemporary Literary Criticism* Yearbook, which was discontinued in 1998.

An alphabetical **Title Index** accompanies each volume of *NCLC*, with the exception of the Topics volumes. Listings of titles by authors covered in the given volume are followed by the author's name and the corresponding page numbers where the titles are discussed. English translations of foreign titles and variations of titles are cross-referenced to the title under which a work was originally published. Titles of novels, dramas, nonfiction books, and poetry, short story, or essay collections are printed in italics, while individual poems, short stories, and essays are printed in roman type within quotation marks.

In response to numerous suggestions from librarians, Thomson Gale also produces an annual paperbound edition of the *NCLC* cumulative title index. This annual cumulation, which alphabetically lists all titles reviewed in the series, is available to all customers. Additional copies of this index are available upon request. Librarians and patrons will welcome this separate index; it saves shelf space, is easy to use, and is recyclable upon receipt of the next edition.

Citing *Nineteenth-Century Literature Criticism*

When citing criticism reprinted in the Literary Criticism Series, students should provide complete bibliographic information so that the cited essay can be located in the original print or electronic source. Students who quote directly from reprinted criticism may use any accepted bibliographic format, such as University of Chicago Press style or Modern Language Association style.

The examples below follow recommendations for preparing a bibliography set forth in *The Chicago Manual of Style*, 15th ed. (Chicago: The University of Chicago Press, 2003); the first example pertains to material drawn from periodicals, the second to material reprinted from books:

Franklin, J. Jeffrey. "The Victorian Discourse of Gambling: Speculations on *Middlemarch* and *The Duke's Children*." *ELH* 61, no. 4 (winter 1994): 899-921. Reprinted in *Nineteenth-Century Literature Criticism*. Vol. 168, edited by Jessica Bomarito and Russel Whitaker, 39-51. Detroit: Thomson Gale, 2006.

Frank, Joseph. "*The Gambler*: A Study in Ethnopsychology." In *Freedom and Responsibility in Russian Literature: Essays in Honor of Robert Louis Jackson,* edited by Elizabeth Cheresh Allen and Gary Saul Morson, 69-85. Evanston, Ill.: Northwestern University Press, 1995. Reprinted in *Nineteeth-Century Literature Criticism*. Vol. 168, edited by Jessica Bomarito and Russel Whitaker and Russel Whitaker, 75-84. Detroit: Thomson Gale, 2006.

The examples below follow recommendations for preparing a works cited list set forth in the *MLA Handbook for Writers of Research Papers,* 6th ed. (New York: The Modern Language Association of America, 2003); the first example pertains to material drawn from periodicals, the second to material reprinted from books:

Franklin, J. Jeffrey. "The Victorian Discourse of Gambling: Speculations on *Middlemarch* and *The Duke's Children*." *ELH* 61.4 (Winter 1994): 899-921. Reprinted in *Nineteenth-Century Literature Criticism*. Eds. Jessica Bomarito and Russel Whitaker. Vol. 168. Detroit: Thomson Gale, 2006. 39-51.

Frank, Joseph. "*The Gambler*: A Study in Ethnopsychology." *Freedom and Responsibility in Russian Literature: Essays in Honor of Robert Louis Jackson.* Eds. Elizabeth Cheresh Allen and Gary Saul Morson. Evanston, Ill.: Northwestern University Press, 1995. 69-85. Reprinted in *Nineteenth-Century Literature Criticism*. Eds. Jessica Bomarito and Russel Whitaker. Vol. 168. Detroit: Thomson Gale, 2006. 75-84.

Suggestions are Welcome

Readers who wish to suggest new features, topics, or authors to appear in future volumes, or who have other suggestions or comments are cordially invited to call, write, or fax the Associate Product Manager:

Associate Product Manager, Literary Criticism Series
Thomson Gale
27500 Drake Road
Farmington Hills, MI 48331-3535
1-800-347-4253 (GALE)
Fax: 248-699-8054

Acknowledgments

The editors wish to thank the copyright holders of the criticism included in this volume and the permissions managers of many book and magazine publishing companies for assisting us in securing reproduction rights. Following is a list of the copyright holders who have granted us permission to reproduce material in this volume of *NCLC*. Every effort has been made to trace copyright, but if omissions have been made, please let us know.

COPYRIGHTED MATERIAL IN *NCLC*, VOLUME 169, WAS REPRODUCED FROM THE FOLLOWING PERIODICALS:

Anglia: Zeitschrift für Englische Philologie, v. 134, September, 1971 for "The Handling of Time in *Vanity Fair*" by John A. Sutherland. Reproduced by permission of the author.—*Cithara,* v. 9, November, 1969. Copyright © 1969, St. Bonaventure University. Reproduced by permission.—*College Language Association Journal,* v. 31, September, 1987; v. 37, March, 1994. Copyright © 1987, 1994 by The College Language Association. Both used by permission of The College Language Association.—*ELH,* v. 32, September, 1965; v. 42, fall, 1975. Copyright © 1965, 1975 The Johns Hopkins University Press. Both reproduced by permission.—*English,* v. 43, spring, 1994. Copyright © The English Association 1994. Reproduced by permission.—*ESQ: A Journal of the American Renaissance,* v. 23, 2nd quarter, 1977 for "Elizabeth Palmer Peabody's Views of the Child" by Bruce A. Ronda; v. 23, 3rd quarter, 1977 for "Elizabeth Palmer Peabody and the Philosophy of Language" by Philip F. Gura. Copyright © 1977 *ESQ: A Journal of the American Renaissance.* Both reproduced by permission of the publisher and the author.—*Études Irlandaises,* v. 12, June, 1987. Copyright © 1987 by Presses Universitaires du Septentrion. Reproduced by permission.—*Genre,* v. 8, June, 1975 for "*Melmoth the Wanderer*: Gothic on Gothic" by David Eggenschwiler. Copyright © 1975 by the University of Oklahoma. Reproduced by permission of *Genre,* the University of Oklahoma, and the author.—*The Keats-Shelley Review,* autumn, 1989. Copyright © 1989 by The Keats-Shelly Review. Reproduced by permission.—*Literature and History,* v. 11, autumn, 2002. Copyright © by Manchester University Press 2002. Reproduced by permission.—*Massachusetts Studies in English,* v. 9, 1984 for "Feeling and Conception of Character in the Novels of Charles Robert Maturin" by Diane D'Amico. Copyright © by Diane D'Amico. All rights reserved. Reproduced by permission of the author.—*Pacific Coast Philology,* v. 4, April, 1969 for "Myth and the Gothic Dream: C. R. Maturin's *Melmoth the Wanderer*" by Veronica M. S. Kennedy. Copyright © 1969 by Pacific Ancient and Modern Language. Reproduced by permission of the publisher and the author.—*Papers on Language & Literature,* v. 13, spring, 1977; v. 35, fall, 1999. Copyright © 1977, 1999 by The Board of Trustees, Southern Illinois University at Edwardsville. Both reproduced by permission.—*Philological Quarterly,* v. 77, winter, 1998. Copyright © 1998 by The University of Iowa. Reproduced by permission.—*Publications of the Arkansas Philological Association,* v. 8, fall, 1982. Copyright © 1982 by Arkansas Philological Association. Reproduced by permission.—*Research Studies,* v. 45, March, 1977. Copyright © 1977 by Washington State University. Reproduced by permission.—*Studia Anglica Posnaniensia,* v. 40, 2004. Copyright © 2004 by Adam Mickiewicz University Press. Reproduced by permission.—*Studies in English Literature, 1500-1900,* v. 8, autumn, 1968; v. 11, autumn, 1971; v. 17, autumn, 1977; v. 21, autumn, 1981. Copyright © 1968, 1971, 1977, 1981 William Marsh Rice University. All reproduced by permission.—*Studies in Romanticism,* v. 25, winter, 1986; v. 36, winter, 1997. Copyright 1986, 1997 by the Trustees of Boston University. Both reproduced by permission.—*Studies in the American Renaissance,* 1992. Copyright © 1992 University of North Carolina. Reproduced by permission.—*Studies in the Novel,* v. 11, summer, 1979; v. 26, summer, 1994. Copyright © 1979, 1994 by North Texas State University. Both reproduced by permission.—*Tennessee Studies in Literature,* v. 20, 1975. Copyright © 1975 by The University of Tennessee Press. Reproduced by permission of The University of Tennessee Press.—*Victorians Institute Journal,* 1977. Copyright © 1977 by Victorians Institute. Reproduced by permission.—*The Wordsworth Circle,* v. 21, summer, 1990. Copyright © 1990 Marilyn Gaull. Reproduced by permission of the editor.

COPYRIGHTED MATERIAL IN *NCLC*, VOLUME 169, WAS REPRODUCED FROM THE FOLLOWING BOOKS:

Alcott, Amos Bronson. From "Journal Entry Dated December 24, 1865," in *The Journals of Bronson Alcott.* Edited by Odell Shepard. Little, Brown and Company, 1938. Copyright © 1938 by Odell Shepard. Renewed 1965 by Odell Shepard. All rights reserved. Reproduced by permission.—Alcott, Amos Bronson. From "Letter to Elizabeth Palmer Peabody, May 24, 1874. (Letter 74-30)," in *The Letters of A. Bronson Alcott.* Alcott-Pratt Collection, Harvard College Library. MS Am

Thomson Gale Literature Product Advisory Board

The members of the Thomson Gale Literature Product Advisory Board—reference librarians from public and academic library systems—represent a cross-section of our customer base and offer a variety of informed perspectives on both the presentation and content of our literature products. Advisory board members assess and define such quality issues as the relevance, currency, and usefulness of the author coverage, critical content, and literary topics included in our series; evaluate the layout, presentation, and general quality of our printed volumes; provide feedback on the criteria used for selecting authors and topics covered in our series; provide suggestions for potential enhancements to our series; identify any gaps in our coverage of authors or literary topics, recommending authors or topics for inclusion; analyze the appropriateness of our content and presentation for various user audiences, such as high school students, undergraduates, graduate students, librarians, and educators; and offer feedback on any proposed changes/enhancements to our series. We wish to thank the following advisors for their advice throughout the year.

Charles Robert Maturin
1780-1824

(Also wrote under the pseudonym Dennis Jasper Murphy) Irish novelist and playwright.

The following entry provides an overview of Maturin's life and works. For additional information on his career, see *NCLC,* Volume 6.

INTRODUCTION

A prominent Gothic novelist and playwright, Maturin was a clergyman as well as an author. He strove to explore profound religious themes in his writings, examining the complex relationship between transgression and guilt and investigating the impact of spiritual despair on the individual conscience. He remains best known for his novel *Melmoth the Wanderer* (1820), the story of a scholar who barters his soul to the Devil. The novel is founded on a number of literary and religious myths, including the legend of Doctor Faustus, the biblical allegory of Cain, and the tale of the Wandering Jew, and it remains striking for the complexity of its protagonist and the poetic quality of its language. *Melmoth the Wanderer* has earned comparisons with the most distinguished Gothic novels of its era, among them Horace Walpole's *The Castle of Otranto,* Ann Radcliffe's *The Mysteries of Udolpho* and *The Italian,* and Matthew Lewis's *The Monk.* Although remembered primarily as a novelist, Maturin also authored three plays, one of which—the verse tragedy *Bertram* (1816)—enjoyed moderate success on the London stage. While Maturin received little popular or critical acclaim during his lifetime, he remains important, not only for his mastery of the Gothic form, but also for his deep, philosophical examinations of the nature of the human psyche. The mythic figure of Melmoth has claimed a place alongside Johann Wolfgang von Goethe's Faust and Lord Byron's Manfred as one of the most powerful literary characters of the nineteenth century. In many respects, Maturin's work forms a bridge between the supernatural horror novels of the Gothic movement and the poetical innovations of Romanticism. Maturin influenced such diverse writers as Charles Baudelaire, Honoré de Balzac—who published a sequel to *Melmoth the Wanderer* entitled *Melmoth réconcilié* (*Melmoth Reconciled*) in 1835—and Oscar Wilde.

BIOGRAPHICAL INFORMATION

Maturin was born in Dublin on September 25, 1782, to William Maturin and Fidelia (Watson) Maturin; he was

one of six children. His ancestors were French Huguenots—Protestants expelled from France during the reign of Louis XIV. Maturin's grandfather, Gabriel Jasper Maturin, was a distinguished clergyman who succeeded Jonathan Swift as the Dean of St. Patrick's Cathedral. At the age of fifteen, Maturin entered Trinity College. After earning his B.A. in 1800, he studied to become an Anglican minister, receiving his ordination in 1803. That year he married Henrietta Kingsbury, and the couple moved to Loughrea, Galway, where Maturin served as curate of a rural parish. In 1805 he returned to Dublin to become curate of St. Peter's Church, a position he held for the rest of his life.

Struggling to support his wife and family on his meager salary, Maturin turned to writing in the hope of paying his numerous creditors. He published his first three novels—*The Fatal Revenge; or, The Family of Montorio* (1807), *The Wild Irish Boy* (1808), and *The Milesian Chief* (1812)—at his own expense, unable to find a publisher for them. Due to the exotic, often horrific nature of these early works, Maturin wrote under the pseudonym Dennis Jasper Murphy to avoid provoking scandal within his parish. None of the novels earned any money, however, and Maturin's financial difficulties persisted. His problems were exacerbated in 1809 when his father lost a position at the post office amid false corruption charges, placing a greater financial burden on Maturin and his family. While most contemporary reviewers savaged his early works, Maturin managed to elicit praise from Sir Walter Scott, who wrote an anonymous review praising the imaginative power of *The Fatal Revenge.* An extensive correspondence ensued between the two authors, and they became life-long friends. In 1816, with the assistance of Scott and Lord Byron, Maturin produced his first play, *Bertram,* at London's Drury Lane Theatre, acknowledging himself as the author for the first time. Although the work proved a financial success, Maturin soon squandered his earnings from the play, driving himself deeper into debt. His subsequent plays, the tragedies *Manuel* (1817) and *Fredolfo* (1819), could not match the success of *Bertram.* During the same period Maturin published *Women; or, Pour et contre* (1818), a novel set in France at the end of the Napoleonic era.

In 1820 Maturin published his most famous novel, *Melmoth the Wanderer.* Although some reviewers praised the novel as a representative work of Gothic fiction, it alienated many contemporary readers with its labyrinthine plot and dark themes, and earnings for the book were minimal. Unable to achieve lasting success as a writer, Maturin spent his final years in abject poverty. He was never able to rise above the level of minor curate in the church because of both the sensational subject matter of his writings and his eccentric personality. In the last year of his life, Maturin published *The Albigenses* (1824), his sole work of historical fiction, and *Five Sermons on the Errors of the Roman Catholic Church* (1824), in which he outlined his critique of Roman Catholic practices. He died in Dublin on October 30, 1824.

MAJOR WORKS

Maturin's most significant work remains his 1820 novel *Melmoth the Wanderer.* The story revolves around the title character, a scholar who offers his soul to the Devil in exchange for an additional 150 years of life. As part of the agreement, the Devil offers Melmoth the opportunity to reclaim his soul by finding another human being willing to accept the same bargain. Thus begins Melmoth's arduous journey around the world and his continual striving to find someone to share his fate. A penetrating glimpse into the nature of sin, the novel depicts Melmoth's struggles to come to terms with his transgressions and his increasing horror at his own inner nature. In many respects, *Melmoth the Wanderer*

represents the quintessential Gothic novel, incorporating the imagery and many of the trademark motifs of the genre, including ruined castles, foreboding landscapes, and an evil protagonist. At the same time, the work surpasses the limitations of the Gothic form in a number of key aspects, notably in its psychological and theological depth and in the powerful originality of its central character.

Although none have elicited the same level of critical interest as *Melmoth,* Maturin's other novels and plays are still noteworthy for their explorations of Gothic and Romantic themes. His play *Bertram,* which enjoyed moderate success and was arguably his most popular work during his lifetime, follows the adventures of a fallen nobleman, Bertram, who becomes a notorious highwayman after he is dishonored. At once a villain and a hero, Bertram fit squarely within the Byronic tradition of the Romantic man-of-action, whose bravery and charm make up for an ambiguous morality. Such novels as *The Fatal Revenge* and *The Milesian Chief,* though largely ignored today, remain interesting examples of the Gothic genre. *The Albigenses,* a historical novel, examines the religious controversy surrounding Pope Innocent III's crusade against the Manichean sect in thirteenth-century France. Although *The Wild Irish Boy* is widely considered Maturin's least important book, in recent years scholars have taken an interest in it for its themes of Irish nationalism, as well as its debt to such Irish women authors as Lady Morgan and Sydney Owenson.

CRITICAL RECEPTION

Maturin's works confounded many contemporary reviewers, who objected to the seemingly chaotic structures of his novels and plays, as well as to the author's preoccupation with dark themes. Writing in 1921, a reviewer for the *Quarterly Review* described *Melmoth the Wanderer* as "a clumsy confusion which disgraces the artist and puzzles the observer." Some critics, including Samuel Coleridge, objected to Maturin's work on moral and religious grounds; Coleridge viewed *Bertram* as "melancholy proof of the depravation of the public mind." Lord Byron, on the other hand, highly praised the play and played an important role in bringing it to the stage. The most prominent early champion of Maturin's writings was Sir Walter Scott, who lauded the potential of Maturin's first novel, *The Fatal Revenge,* citing in particular Maturin's "great command of language" and the originality of his imagination.

Maturin's work remained largely ignored until the middle of the twentieth century, when scholars began to take renewed interest in the psychological and religious themes in his writings. One of the first book-length studies of his career, Niilo Idman's *Charles Robert Maturin,* appeared in 1923. In the 1950s and 1960s critics began to examine the various mythological foundations of *Melmoth the Wanderer,* identifying parallels between Melmoth and Faust, Prometheus, Milton's Satan, Cain, and the Wandering Jew, among others. In his 1956 study *The Romantic Agony,* Mario Praz praised *Melmoth the Wanderer* as a "masterpiece of the 'tales of terror' school." Praz identified distinct aspects of Romanticism in the protagonist, who he saw as both a mythic hero and an individual tormented by feelings of guilt and despair. Other writers from these years, notably H. W. Piper and A. Norman Jeffares, recognized elements of both literary Romanticism and Irish nationalism in Maturin's body of work. In the 1970s and 1980s scholars David Eggenschwiler and Mark M. Hennelly, Jr. offered existentialist interpretations of Melmoth's character. Other critics during this period began to pay closer attention to the structural aspects of Maturin's novels. Writing in the journal *Papers on Language and Literature,* Jack Null argued that the book's convoluted plot was designed to serve as a mirror of Melmoth's troubled psyche, an argument reiterated by G. St. John Stott in a 1987 essay. In his 1988 study *Horror Fiction in the Protestant Tradition,* Victor Sage examined the strong anti-Catholic stance in *Melmoth,* arguing that Maturin's contempt for Catholic ritual formed part of a distinct strain of Protestantism during his era. Since the 1990s a range of new critical perspectives has emerged, examining Maturin's work within the context of British colonialism, Irish nationalism, and nineteenth-century theology.

PRINCIPAL WORKS

The Fatal Revenge; or, The Family of Montorio. 3 vols. [as Dennis Jasper Murphy] (novel) 1807

The Wild Irish Boy. 3 vols. [as "The Author of *Montorio*"] (novel) 1808

The Milesian Chief: A Romance. 4 vols. [as "The Author of *Montorio*"] (novel) 1812

Bertram (play) 1816

Manuel (play) 1817

Women; or, Pour et contre. 3 vols. [as "The Author of *Bertram*"] (novel) 1818

Fredolfo (play) 1819

Sermons (prose) 1819

Melmoth the Wanderer: A Tale. 4 vols. [as "The Author of *Bertram*"] (novel) 1820

The Albigenses: A Romance. 4 vols. (novel) 1824

Five Sermons on the Errors of the Roman Catholic Church (prose) 1824; revised edition, 1826

CRITICISM

Edinburgh Review (review date July 1821)

SOURCE: Review of *Melmoth the Wanderer. Edinburgh Review* 35, no. 70 (July 1821): 353-62.

[*In the following review, the anonymous critic faults* Melmoth the Wanderer *as excessive and unrestrained, both in its prose style and its imaginative exuberance.*]

It was said, we remember, of Dr. Darwin's Botanic Garden—that it was the sacrifice of Genius in the Temple of False Taste; and the remark may be applied to the work before us [**Melmoth the Wanderer**], with the qualifying clause, that in this instance the Genius is less obvious, and the false taste more glaring. No writer of good judgment would have attempted to revive the defunct horrors of Mrs. Radcliffe's School of Romance, or the demoniacal incarnations of Mr. Lewis: But, as if he were determined not to be arraigned for a single error only, Mr Maturin has contrived to render his production almost as objectionable in the manner as, it is in the matter. The construction of his story, which is singularly clumsy and inartificial, we have no intention to analyze:—many will probably have perused the work, before our review reaches them; and to those who have not, it may be sufficient to announce, that the imagination of the author runs riot, even beyond the usual license of romance;—that his hero is a modern Faustus, who has bartered his soul with the powers of darkness for protracted life, and unlimited worldly enjoyment;—his heroine, a species of insular goddess, a virgin Calypso of the Indian ocean, who, amid flowers and foliage, lives upon figs and tamarinds; associates with peacocks, loxias and monkeys; is worshipped by the occasional visitants of her island; finds her way to Spain, where she is married to the aforesaid hero by the hand of a dead hermit, the ghost of a murdered domestic being the witness of their nuptials; and finally dies in the dungeons of the Inquisition at Madrid!—To complete this phantasmagoric exhibition, we are presented with sybils and misers; parricides; maniacs in abundance; monks with scourges pursuing a naked youth streaming with blood; subterranean Jews surrounded by the skeletons of their wives and children; lovers blasted by lightning; Irish hags, Spanish grandees, shipwrecks, caverns, Donna Claras and Donna Isidoras,—all opposed to each other in glaring and violent contrast, and all their adventures narrated with the same undeviating display of turgid, vehement, and painfully elaborated language. Such are the materials, and the style of this expanded nightmare: And as we can plainly perceive, among a certain class of writers, a disposition to haunt us with similar apparitions, and to describe them with a corresponding tumor of words, we conceive it high time to step forward and abate a nuisance which threatens to become a besetting evil, unless checked in its outset.

Political changes were not the sole causes of the rapid degeneracy in letters that followed the Augustan era of Rome. Similar corruptions and decay, have succeeded to the intellectual eminence of other nations; and we might be almost led to conclude, that mental as well as physical power, after attaining a certain perfection, became weakened by expansion, and sunk into a state of comparative imbecility, until time and circumstance gave it a new progressive impetus. One great cause of this deterioration is the insatiable thirst for novelty, which, becoming weary even of excellence, will 'sate itself in a celestial bed, and prey on garbage.' In the torpidity produced by an utter exhaustion of sensual enjoyment, the Arreoi Club of Otaheite is recorded to have found a miserable excitement, by swallowing the most revolting filth; and the jaded intellectual appetites of more civilized communities will sometimes seek a new stimulus in changes almost as startling. Some adventurous writer, unable to obtain distinction among a host of competitors, all better qualified than himself to win legitimate applause, strikes out a fantastic or monstrous innovation; and arrests the attention of many who would fall asleep over monotonous excellence. Imitators are soon found;—fashion adopts the new folly;—the old standard of perfection is deemed stale and obsolete;—and thus, by degrees, the whole literature of a country becomes changed and deteriorated. It appears to us, that we are now labouring in a crisis of this nature. In our last Number, we noticed the revolution in our poetry; the transition from the lucid terseness and exquisite polish of Pope and Goldsmith, to the rambling, diffuse, irregular, and imaginative style of composition by which the present era is characterized; and we might have added, that a change equally complete, though diametrically opposite in its tendency, has been silently introduced into our prose. In this we have oscillated from freedom to restraint;—from the easy, natural, and colloquial style of Swift, Addison and Steele, to the perpetually strained, ambitious, and overwrought stiffness, of which the author we are now considering affords a striking exemplification. 'He's knight o' the shire, and represents them all.' There is not the smallest keeping in his composition:—less solicitous what he shall say, than how he shall say it, he exhausts himself in a continual struggle to produce effect by dazzling, terrifying, or surprising. Annibal Caracci was accused of an affectation of muscularity, and an undue parade of anatomical knowledge, even upon quiescent figures: But the artist whom we are now considering has no quiescent figures:—even his repose is a state of rigid tension, if not extravagant distortion. He is the Fuseli of novelists. Does he deem it necessary to be energetic, he forthwith begins foaming at the mouth, and falling into convulsions; and this orgasm is so often repeated, and upon such inadequate occasions, that we are perpetually reminded of the tremendous puerilities of the Della Cruscan versifiers, or the ludicrous grand eloquence of the Spaniard, who tore a certain portion of his attire, 'as if heaven and earth were coming together.' In straining to reach the sublime, he perpetually takes that single unfortunate step which conducts him to the ridiculous—a failure which, in a less gifted author, might afford a wicked amusement to the critic, but which, when united with such undoubted genius as the present work exhibits, must excite a sincere and painful regret in every admirer of talent.

Whatever be the cause, the fact, we think, cannot be disputed, that a peculiar tendency to this gaudy and ornate style, exists among the writers of Ireland. Their genius runs riot in the wantonness of its own uncontrolled exuberance;—their imagination, disdaining the restraint of judgment, imparts to their literature the characteristics of a nation in one of the earlier stages of civilization and refinement. The florid imagery, gorgeous diction, and Oriental hyperboles, which possess a sort of wild propriety in the vehement sallies of Antar the Bedoween chieftain of the twelfth century, become cold extravagance and doundering fustian in the mouth of a barrister of the present age; and we question whether any but a native of the sister island would have ventured upon the experiment of their adoption. Even in the productions of Mr Moore, the sweetest lyric poet of this or perhaps any age, this national peculiarity is not infrequently perceptible; and we were compelled, in our review of his *Lalla Rookh,* a subject which justified the introduction of much Eastern splendour and elaboration, to point out the excessive finery, the incessant sparkle and efflorescence by which the attention of the reader was fatigued, and his senses overcome. He rouged his roses, and poured perfume upon his jessamines, until we fainted under the oppression of beauty and odour, and were ready to 'die of a rose in aromatic pain.'

Dryden, in alluding to the metaphysical poets, exclaims 'rather than all things wit, let none be there:'—though we would not literally adopt this dictum, we can safely confirm the truth of the succeeding lines—

> Men doubt, because so thick they lie,
> If those be stars that paint the Galaxy:—

And we scruple not to avow, whatever contempt may be expressed for our taste by the advocates of the toiling and turgid style, both in and out of Ireland, that the prose works which we have lately perused with the greatest pleasure, so far as their composition was concerned, have been Belzoni's *Travels,* and Salame's *Account of the Attack upon Algiers.* Unable, from their insufficient mastery of our tongue, to rival the native manufacture of stiff and laborious verbosity, these foreigners have contented themselves with the plainest and most colloquial language that was consistent with a clear exposition of their meaning;—a practice to which Swift was indebted for the lucid and perspicuous character of his writings, and which alone has enabled a great living purveyor of 'twopenny trash' to retain a certain portion of popularity, in spite of his utter abandonment of all consistency and public principle. If the writers to whom we are alluding will not condescend to this unstudied and familiar mode of communing with the public, let them at least have the art to conceal their art, and not obtrude the conviction that they are more anxious to display themselves than inform their readers; and let them, above all things, consent to be intelligible to the plainest capacity; for though speech, according to the averment of a wily Frenchman, was given to us to conceal our thoughts, no one has yet ventured to extend the same mystifying definition to the art of writing. It will be expected that we should support our animadversions upon Melmoth by a few extracts from its pages; and, as an illustration of the unmeaning rant which we have just deprecated, we select, amid many of similar sound and fury, signifying nothing, the following passage.

> 'But I feel another pride,' answered Melmoth, and in a proud tone he spoke it; 'a pride which, like that of the storm that visited the ancient cities, whose destruction you may have read of, while it blasts, withers, and incrusts paintings, gems, music and festivity, grasping them in its talons of annihilation, exclaims, Perish to all the world, perhaps beyond the period of its existence, but live to me in darkness and in corruption! Preserve all the exquisite modulation of your forms! all the indestructible brilliancy of your colouring! but preserve it for me alone!—me the single, pulseless, eyeless, heartless embracer of an unfertile bride—the brooder over the dark and unproductive nest of eternal sterility—the mountain whose lava of internal fire has stifled, and indurated, and enclosed for ever, all that was the joy of earth, the felicity of life, and the hope of futurity!'
>
> Vol. III. p. 307

Of extravagant fustian upon trifling occasions, the following is a sample, uttered by a monk, because he is displeased with the preternatural lustre of Melmoth's eyes.

> Who is among us? Who? I cannot utter a blessing while he is here. I cannot feel one. Where he treads, the earth is parched! where he breathes, the air is fire! where he turns, his glance is lightning. Who is among us? Who?
>
> Vol. I. p. 77

After this, let us no longer smile at the furious hyperboles of Della Crusca upon Mrs. Robinson's eyes. In the same strain we are told of a convent whose 'walls sweat, and its floors quiver,' when a contumacious brother treads them;—and when the parents of the same per-

sonage are torn from his room by the Director of the convent, we are informed that 'the rushing of their robes as he dragged them out, seemed like the whirlwind that attends the presence of the destroying angel.' In a similar spirit, of pushing every thing to extremes when he means to be impressive, the author is sometimes offensively minute; as when he makes the aforesaid persecuted monk declare, that 'the cook had learned the secret of the convent, (that of tormenting those whom they had no longer hopes of commanding), and mixed the fragments he threw to me with ashes, hair, and dust;'—and sometimes the extravagance of his phrases becomes simply ludicrous. Two persons are trying to turn a key—'It grated, resisted; the lock seemed invincible. Again we tried with cranched teeth, indrawn breath, and fingers stripped almost to the bone—in vain.' And yet, after they had almost stripped their fingers to the bone, they succeed in turning that which they could not move when their hands were entire.

We have said that Mr Maturin had contrived to render his work as objectionable in the matter as in the manner; and we proceed to the confirmation of our assertion. We do not arraign him solely for the occasional indecorousness of his conceptions, or the more offensive tone of some of his colloquies, attempted to be palliated by the flimsy plea, that they are appropriate in the mouths that utter them. Dr Johnson, as a proof of the total suppression of the reasoning faculty in dreams, used to cite one of his own, wherein he imagined himself to be holding an argument with an adversary, whose superior powers filled him with a mortification which a moment's reflection would have dissipated, by reminding him that he himself supplied the repartees of his opponent as well as his own. In his waking dreams, Mr Maturin is equally the parent of all the parties who figure in his Romance; and, though not personally responsible for their sentiments, he is amenable to the bar of criticism for every phrase or thought which transgresses the bounds of decorum, or violates the laws that regulate the habitual intercourse of polished society. It is no defence to say, that profane or gross language is natural to the characters whom he embodies. Why does he select such? It may be proper in them; but what can make it proper to us? There are wretches who never open their lips but to blaspheme; but would any author think himself justified in filling his page with their abominations? It betrays a lamentable deficiency of tact and judgment, to imagine, as the author of Melmoth appears to do, that he may seize upon nature in her most unhallowed or disgusting moods, and dangle her in the eyes of a decorous and civilized community. We shall not stop to stigmatize, as it deserves, the wild and flagrant calumnies which he insinuates against three-fourths of his countrymen, by raking in the long-forgotten rubbish of Popery for extinct enormities, which he exaggerates as the inevitable result, rather than the casual abuse of the system, and brands with an intolerant zeal, quite as uncharitable as that which he condemns. These faults are either so peculiar to the individual, or in their nature so obviously indefensible, as to repel rather than invite imitation. But there is another peculiarity in the productions of this gentleman which claims a more detailed notice, because it seems likely to have extensive effects in corrupting others:—we mean his taste for horrible and revolting subjects. We thought we had supped full of this commodity; but it seems as if the most ghastly and disgusting portion of the meal was reserved for the present day, and its most hideous concoction for the writer before us,—who is never so much in his favourite element as when he can 'on horror's head horrors accumulate.' He assimilates the sluggish sympathies of his readers to those of sailors and vulgar ballad readers, who cannot be excited to an interest in the battle of the Arethusa, unless they learn that 'her sails smoked with brains, and her scuppers ran blood;'—a line which threatens him with formidable competitors from before the mast. Mere physical horror, unalleviated by any intense mental interest, or redeeming charities of the heart, may possess a certain air of originality, not from the want of ability in former writers to delineate such scenes, but from their deference to the *'multaque tolles ex oculis'* of Horace; from the conviction of their utter unfitness for public exhibition. There is, however, a numerous class of inferior caterers to the public, ready to minister to any appetite, however foul and depraved, if they be once furnished with a precedent; and we foresee an inundation of blood and abomination if they be not awed or ridiculed into silence. We have quietly submitted to these inflictions from two or three distinguished writers, whose talents may extenuate, though they cannot justify, such outrages upon feeling. When regular artists and professors conduct us into their dissecting room, the skill with which they anatomise may reconcile us to the offensiveness of the operation; but if butchers and resurrection-men are to drag us into their shambles, while they mangle human carcases with their clumsy and unhallowed hands, the stoutest spectators must turn from the exhibition with sickness and disgust.

Were any proof wanting that this Golgotha style of writing is likely to become contagious, and to be pushed to a more harrowing extravagance at each successive imitation, Mr Maturin would himself supply it. Lord Byron, in his *Don Juan,* had described a set of sailors, strangers to one another, reduced to the dreadful necessity of destroying one of their number to supply food for the rest; an incident sufficiently horrible in itself, but which the monstrous imagination of the present author instantly seizes to invest with a new, more loathsome, and absolutely incredible hideousness. The scene of his cannibal repast is a subterranean dungeon, where a beautiful woman and her lover are buried alive, by monkish cruelty, to perish by starvation: of which pro-

cess, the following circumstantial account is given by a fiend in human form, who was stationed at the door, and relates the dread catastrophe with a hellish delight.

It was my penance (no,—my delight) to watch at the door, under the pretence of preventing the possibility of their escape (of which they knew there was no possibility); but, in reality, not only to inflict on me the indignity of being the Convent gaoler, but of teaching me that callosity of heart, and induration of nerve, and stubbornness of eye, and apathy of ear, that were best suited to my office.—But they might have saved themselves the trouble. I had them all before ever I entered the Convent. Had I been the superior of the Convent, I should have undertaken the office of watching the door. You will call this cruelty; I call it curiosity,—that curiosity which brings thousands to witness a tragedy, and makes the most delicate female feast on groans and agonies. I had an advantage over them,—the groan, the agony I feasted on were real. I took my station at *the door*—that door which, like that of Dante's Hell, might have borne the inscription, "Here is no hope,"—with a face of mock penitence, and genuine cordial delectation. I could hear every word that transpired.—For the first hours they tried to comfort each other,—they suggested to each other hopes of liberation,—and as my shadow, crossing the threshold, darkened or restored the light, they said—"that is he!"—then, when this occurred repeatedly, without any effect, they said, "No, no, it is not he!" and swallowed down the sick sob of despair, to hide it from each other. Towards night a monk came to take my place, and to offer me food. I would not have quitted my place for worlds; but I talked to the monk in his own language, and told him I would make a merit with God of my sacrifices, and was resolved to remain there all night with the permission of the superior. The monk was glad of having a substitute on such easy terms, and I was glad of the food he left me, for I was hungry now; but I reserved the appetite of my soul for richer luxuries. I heard them talking within. While I was eating, I actually lived on the famine that was devouring them, but of which they did not dare to say a word to each other.' . . . 'All that night, however, I heard their groans,—those groans of physical suffering that laugh to scorn all the sentimental sighs that are exhaled from the hearts of the most intoxicated lovers that ever breathed.'—'Then the agony of hunger increased; they shrunk from the door, and grovelled apart from each other. *Apart!*———how I watched that.—They were rapidly becoming objects of hostility to each other. Oh, what a feast to me!———The second night they raved and groaned (as occurred); and, amid their agonies (I must do justice to women whom I hate as well as men), the man often accused the female as the cause of all his sufferings; but the woman never—never reproached him. Her groans might indeed have reproached him bitterly, but she never uttered a word that could have caused him pain. There was a change which I well could mark, however, in their physical feelings. The first day they clung together, and every movement I felt was like that of one person. The next, the man alone struggled; and the woman moaned in helplessness. The third night—how shall I tell it?—but you have bid me go on. All the horrible and loathsome excruciations of famine had been undergone; the disunion of every tie of the heart, of passion, of nature, had commenced. In the agonies of their famished sickness, they loathed each other;—they could have cursed each other if they had had breath to curse. It was on the fourth night that I heard the shriek of the wretched female;—her lover, in the agony of hunger, had fastened his teeth in her shoulder;—that bosom, on which he had so often luxuriated, became a meal to him now.

II. 234

We have omitted this miscreant's flippant allusion to Madame de Sevigné and his own damnation, uttered in a spirit which (to use the author's own words upon another occasion), 'mingled ridicule with horror, and seemed like a Harlequin in the infernal regions flirting with the furies:'—But we must not forget to mention, as little characteristic touches in this scene of preposterous horrors, that the monster who describes it was also a parricide, and that the female, on whose dying agonies he had feasted, was his only sister! After this appalling extract, we need not pursue our quotations from pages which, as more than one of the personages say of themselves, seem to swim in blood and fire; and we shall conclude with the following passage from a dream.

> The next moment I was chained to my chair again,—the fires were lit, the bells rang out, the litanies were sung;—my feet were scorched to a cinder,—my muscles cracked, my blood and marrow hissed, my flesh consumed like shrinking leather,—the bones of my leg hung two black withering and moveless sticks in the ascending blaze;—it ascended, caught my hair,—I was crowned with fire,—my head was a ball of molten metal, my eyes flashed and melted in their sockets:—I opened my mouth, it drank fire,—I closed it, the fire was within,—and still the bells rang on, and the crowd shouted, and the king and queen, and all the nobility and priesthood looked on, and we burned and burned! I was a cinder, body and soul, in my dream.

II. 301

These, and other scenes equally wild and abominable, luckily counteract themselves;—they present such a Fee-fa-fum for grown up people, such a burlesque upon tragic horrors, that a sense of the ludicrous irresistibly predominates over the terrific; and, to avoid disgust, our feelings gladly take refuge in contemptuous laughter. Pathos like this may affect women, and people of weak nerves, with sickness at the stomach;—it may move those of stouter fibre to scornful derision; but we doubt whether, in the whole extensive circle of novel readers, it has ever drawn a single tear. The Society for the Suppression of Mendicity has fortunately cleared our streets of the offensive vagrants who used to thrust their mangled limbs and putrid sores into our faces to extort from our disgust what they could not wring from our compassion:—Be it *our* care to suppress those greater nuisances who, infesting the high ways of literature, would attempt, by a still more revolting exhibition, to terrify or nauseate us out of those sympathies which they might not have the power to awaken by any legitimate appeal.

Let it not be imagined, from any thing we have now said, that we think meanly of Mr Maturin's genius and abilities. It is precisely because we hold both in respect that we are sincerely anxious to point out their misapplication; and we have extended our observations to a greater length than we contemplated, partly because we fear that his strong though unregulated imagination, and unlimited command of glowing language, may inflict upon us a herd of imitators who, 'possessing the contortions of the Sybil without her inspiration' will deluge us with dull, turgid, and disgusting enormities;—and partly because we are not without hopes that our animadversions, offered in a spirit of sincerity, may induce the Author himself to abandon this new Apotheosis of the old Raw-head-and-bloody-bones, and assume a station in literature more consonant to his high endowments, and to that sacred profession to which, we understand, he does honour by the virtues of his private life.

***New Monthly Magazine and Literary Journal* (essay date May 1827)**

SOURCE: "Conversations of Maturin—No. 1." *New Monthly Magazine and Literary Journal* 19, no. 77 (May 1827): 401-11.

[*In the following essay, the anonymous critic offers an analysis of Maturin's character, while examining the impact of his life circumstances on the development of his art.*]

Gentle reader, you and I have met to talk of Maturin. You have known him in print, as I have at the social table: you have communed with him in the embodied imaginings of his spirit—and I when the workings of that spirit were upon him: you have conversed with him at the dim distance of a poetic vision—and I when he was invested with its reality. We are both, therefore, under our different knowledge of him, equally entitled to devote an hour to his memory; so, without parade, let us begin.

There were few men of real ability more subject to vicissitudes of temperament than Maturin. The circumstances of his private fortune, which generally harassed his spirit, worked visible changes in the tone of his writings, and can be identified in that over-wrought excitement under which he sought to escape their influence. He chose the track of the marvellous and the terrible because they afforded an ideal refuge from the positive ills that surrounded him; and having freely indulged in the cup of romantic terrors and extravagant delusions, he was forced to continue the stimulants to keep up the tone of his mind. It is folly to say that our minds do not take the colour of the channel in which we permit our thoughts to flow: it cannot be otherwise. He who devotes his genius to the conjurations of romance, finally either believes in their horrors, or becomes irritable and nervous. So it was with Maturin. Without imbibing the superstition, he yielded to the effects, of a course of wild and abstract invention, and became in consequence credulous and uncalculating. Indeed Maturin's greatest fault was weakness: but it was a weakness that circumscribed its operations to his own actions and impulses. He had much of that amiable and reckless kindness which you anticipate from the ardent hero of a legend; who feels with oppressive sensibility the sorrows he cannot heal, and is duped by his easy submission to every tale that has a sprinkle of mystery or innocence in it. The diversity of Maturin's character, too, has naturally enough been visited by the censure and surprise of those who knew him, and would scarcely be credited by those who did not. But the cynical, who have no merits of their own, should be tardy in pronouncing judgment upon the talented and the ambitious: they cannot understand or develope the machinery by which such spirits are moved. No doubt, he weakened his powers by associating with inferior intellect, and prostrated his imagination before the unprofitable and the flippant. But as some men require to be provoked into exertion, so others require to be indulged; and Maturin was of the latter class. His foibles were common-place, and would, in another, never have attracted observation: but every thing Maturin said and did was converted into tea-table speculation, because the society in which he moved was composed of everyday people, to whom genius was unintelligible, and who attributed his peculiarities to the follies and the madness of the voluntary pursuits he adopted. Had it been his fate to have been cast among kindred beings—to have mixed with the intelligence of the day—the necessity of appearing, what he really was, a man of talent, would have placed his character in its proper light, and redeemed him from the frivolities he negligently permitted to gain an ascendency over him. But he never had that opportunity. Living in a quarter of the kingdom where literary fellowship cannot be obtained, his habits were assimilated to the idle company that courted him; and his pliability of temper and amenity of disposition contributed to confirm the modes to which his communion subjected him. But it is a question, after all, whether we have a right to draw aside the veil that conceals the private errors of those who have contributed to our enjoyments or our instruction; and whether we should take advantage of the prominent position in which their intellectual supremacy has placed them, and which exposes all those feelings that in obscure men are unnoticed. The purest poets are not poets at all moments: they do not speak in rhapsodies, or live amongst beings of air; they are men like ourselves, governed by the same domestic feelings, and liable to the same influences: we are not justified in contrasting their lives with their works, or in demanding why a strict parallel has not been preserved between them. On the other hand, it is rather a recompense to the common condition of mankind to know that the great and favoured amongst them are moved by the same weaknesses, and guilty of the same dereliction; and that high attainments are not always a protection against the current errors of humanity: and it must be some source of instruction to the best of us to read in the foibles of a distinguished genius the humiliating lessons of human weakness and imperfection. If a man lives for the public, the public have a right to him—they possess a copyhold in him—he is theirs; and if, when he is dead, it be considered that he was affected by any peculiar moral disorder, the public have a right to send him to the general anatomy-house, where he may be dissected for the improvement of the science of human nature, and the common benefit of all mankind.

Maturin's early circumstances strongly conduced not only to his becoming a writer, but to the character of his writings. He began his literary course under the pressure of pecuniary difficulties; and he followed it with little alleviation to the close. An incident, too, of rather a mysterious nature connected with his descent, gave a romantic turn to his mind, and the impressions it made upon him from childhood were never effaced. He often dwelt upon it with enthusiasm, and indulged in the dream of tracing, at one day or another, the mystery to its developement. Some twenty or thirty years before the French revolution, a lady of rank attached to the court is said to have been driving through a retired street in Paris, when the cries of an infant child caught her attention. The singularity of the circumstance in so lonely and remote a spot naturally induced her to inquire into the cause, and she drew up her horses, desiring her servant to ascertain from whence the cries proceeded. The man returned, after a very short search, with a basket containing a child newly born, which he found in an obscure corner of the street. The infant was dressed in the richest clothing, and seemed to belong to parents of distinction, whose motives for that inhuman abandonment there may be no great difficulty in guessing at; but although many exertions were afterwards made to discover who they were and the causes of their conduct, the whole matter still remains, and is likely to continue, an impenetrable mystery. The street in which the child was found was called the Rue de Mathurine, in honour of a convent which then stood in it dedicated to a French saint of that name; and the foundling, consequently, was called Mathurine, *Anglicè* Maturin. The lady to whose maternal fosterage the child was thus providentially committed, sent it at a proper age to the convent to be educated, and never neglected an opportunity of promoting the future objects for which she designed it. But the boy, born under the caprice of Fortune, grew up under its inflictions, and was doomed to the trials of a very fluctuating life. He had scarcely reached manhood, when he became a victim to the political fury of the times, and was thrown into the Bastille, from which, after a long incarceration, he escaped into England at the period of the Revolution. Here he married and naturalized. From this individual, with whom the name of Maturin originated, the poet descended.

This incident formed an important feature in the exciting sources of Charles Robert Maturin's ambition. He long and devotedly cherished the thought that his ancestry, to whom he assigned places of rank and distinction, and whom he invested in his poetic ardour with all the pomp and paraphernalia of chivalry, would ultimately be discovered; and so deeply engaged was his mind upon the subject, that a short time before his death he actually wrote a tale upon the slight materials afforded by the circumstance above related. That tale has never been published, although hopes were entertained amongst the immediate circle to whom its composition was communicated, that it would appear shortly after his decease. The conduct of that tale was, I have some reason to think, governed by his own firm belief that the lady of rank who rescued the foundling was actually its mother: in which belief he persevered to the hour of his death.

Maturin's family in Ireland were respectably connected, and he was himself related to a dignitary of the Protestant church. His father was a man of sound understanding and refined taste in literature, to which it was his desire to have devoted his attention had not the death of a distinguished character arrested the patronage to which he looked forward, and blighted his expectations. This disappointment damped his enthusiasm, and diverted him from the pursuit of objects upon which he feared to launch without encouragement and support. Other prospects and other interests engaged his talents, and he was induced to forego the enjoyments of literary expectancy for the less brilliant, but more solid, occupation of a government office, to which he was appointed through the influence of his relatives. Years of arduous application were finally rewarded by an honourable advance to a station of high respectability in the Post-office, Dublin, where he latterly filled the rank of clerk to one of the provincial roads, I believe the Leinster. I should not have adverted so particularly to these circumstances, but that they are intimately connected with the first causes of young Maturin's authorship. At an advanced age, Mr. Maturin lost his situation in the Post-office, and became, with a small family, destitute in the winter of life. The poet, who was the seventh child, the pet, and the hope of the old couple, was roused to poetry by disappointment, and from that hour devoted himself to what a friend of mine, a punster, once called the black art—black in three senses—wit, legerdemain, and despair.

As I have spoken of a punster, I must mention that Maturin had a nervous dislike to punning: he had little of the grinning pleasantry of Aristophanes or Rabelais about him; and his antipathies, which were few, but vivid, might be fairly represented in the Commons of the House of Correction by a bad pun, which I have no doubt would do full justice to its constituents. I have heard him declare that he considered punning to have been originally introduced into society as a system of annoyance against those who were irascible or petulant, because puns, he considered, materially affected the nerves. But, however much he reprobated the crime of originating a pun, he thought that the guilt of repeating a pun, as you would an anecdote, for the amusement of your company, was infinitely more vexatious and unpardonable. Of course, he never made puns himself, either in his writings or his conversation; yet in both, he occasionally fell into that species of conceit which resembles them very closely, and only want pungency to make them puns.

Maturin was essentially a poet. He possessed the great materials of poetry, and preserved an ascendent tone of inspiration through all his writings: yet it is to be remarked, that he did not always write in the same character of style, or keep legitimately to the standard which he seemed to have himself set up. This is partially to be attributed to the variations of animal spirits, and principally to his desultory mode of study. Raphael is distinguished by his brilliancy of colouring—Morland by his pigs: who could mistake the redundant regularity of Johnson—the dilated correctness of Addison—the elaborate energy of Gibbon? It was not so with Maturin. He cultivated himself less than the example of others, and permitted the impressions of what he read to displace the memory of what he thought. He wrote less from permanent principle than immediate impulse, and too often sacrificed what he had to say to the consideration how he should say it. Like Rousseau, who was in love with the last petticoat he saw until he had seen another, Maturin unconsciously adopted something of the last book he read until its recollection was obliterated by the next. His passion for poetry was lofty and pure: he pursued it with an ardour that could not be restrained by the usages of composition; and drank at the very spring-head of Helicon until he became intoxicated with the draught. But it was imagination, not thought: sparkling illustrations—fantastic descriptions—the lineaments of the horrible, the mysterious, and the unreal—were the materials upon which he worked: the externals of character he sketched graphically, perhaps too minutely: but the solid qualities of mind, the powerful operation of the passions, he rarely touched, and seldom successfully. Where he has succeeded, you find that, although the development of the fiction engrosses your attention, the hero has been all along treading on the confines of the marvellous, with just enough of mortality in his changes to show that he is not quite superhuman. His characters are commonly in masquerade: sometimes depicted with a natural force and freedom, but in the next scene plunged into an enigma, and spun out into an interminable labyrinth of improbability. All this, however, if we can once abstract it from the notion of reality, is well and effectually done. That he possessed an original genius, we have sufficient testimonies; but these testimonies are only the indications of genius, not its fruits. He would not permit the blossoms to ripen, but forced them into sudden expansion by a too luscious and overheated cultivation. Nor did he always select with taste what he performed with ability; and hence we frequently turn with loathing from the figures he presents, while we carry with us a pleasurable recollection of the drapery in which he has clad them. Poetry was certainly his ruling passion; but it was the poetry of embellishment and the senses—wild, diffuse, and voluptuous. Conscious of the difficulty of confining himself to limits, he shrunk from the labour of versification, and rioted in the boundless region of romance. Two or three instances of this, singular enough, occur to my recollection.

A gentleman of musical ability, a relative and an intimate of Maturin, proposed that the poet should plan a lyrical work like the *Irish Melodies,* giving to him the department of adapting the songs to appropriate music. Maturin entered upon the project with enthusiasm: a spark from Moore's lyre kindled up his soul, and with a desire too hot for constancy, he commenced the composition in ardent anticipation of fame and profit. But, alas! the licence that Maturin's genius demanded was a *carte blanche*: his versification was perfect revelry: it knew no restraints; and was almost in form and substance a re-animation of the lyrist of the Olympic games. He just wrote enough to discover that he could write no more. The composer despaired of "marrying" to congenial music, verse that was so disastrously "immortal;" and ultimately the design was abandoned, to the great loss of the public.

Another instance is connected with the last novel he published, ***The Albigenses.*** When he conceived the plan of that work, he found that it would admit, or, perhaps, require the introduction of occasional pieces in verse; and unwilling to encounter a second time the chances of failure, he accepted the promises of some literary friends, who were eager to have a corner in his pages. They, of course, performed their undertaking, for they were ambitious to "see themselves in print:" but, as Maturin proceeded in his work, circumstances occurred which led him to change his mind, and he determined to fill up the blanks himself. He certainly did fill them up, but not with verse; that labour he evaded by the substitution of Ossianic prose, or rather an impassioned imitation of Rousseau, tricked out in the most gaudy and glittering habiliments. A song of this description, he makes some musical maidens sing to his heroine.

On one occasion, shortly after the publication of ***Melmoth*** [***Melmoth the Wanderer,***], the King's visit to Ireland inspired the patriotism of her poets with grateful sensibilities, and Maturin, amongst the rest, thought the opportunity a good one for a poetical compliment to the monarch. Accordingly he set about his poem, but was at a loss to fix upon a measure that would equally suit the purpose and his own taste. A continuous stanza would never answer: it should be something at least alternate, that would preserve him from the labours of perpetual rhyme;—he fixed upon the alternate octosyllable measure. But Maturin's skill in this species of composition was certainly very inferior to his genius. In vain he endeavoured to check the exuberance of his fancy, and chain it down to eight syllables: the difficulty of producing four perfect lines alternately was insurmountable; and he at length determined on dropping the rhyme between the first and third, so that only the second and fourth should harmonize: ultimate, or pen-ultimate, or ante-pen-ultimate were all one to Maturin; he despised the jingle, and could not accomplish it. He completed three lines; and a friend, who assures me that Maturin communicated the fact to him, has given them to me: they are,

> Stars of Erin, shine out! shine out!
>   The night of thy sorrow is past,
> And the dawn of a joyous day—

Thus far the poet proceeded: and it may appear perhaps incredible that he could proceed no farther. After many attempts he produced two final lines, but rejected them both. One was

> Rises upon thee at last.

But the measure was incomplete, and he changed it to

> Rises on thee and for thee at last.

And here the measure was superabundant. In a transport of rage he flung the paper into the fire. It is worthy of remark, too, that his principal reason for being dissatisfied with the last line was that its termination too closely resembled Moore, who, he said, had established a sort of copyright in the expression.

It was not inability to conquer the difficulties of rhyme that produced this aversion to it: it was rather a rooted aversion to it that produced the difficulties. He had a natural distaste to the constant return of sound arising from the restraints it threw upon his luxuriant fancy; and he required more preparation for a stanza than he would for a chapter of romance. I have heard that the chorus in ***Bertram*** cost him many sleepless nights, although it consists of but eight or ten lines, and contains nothing worth the labour of an hour. He was at length determined to overcome this disrelish, which he became persuaded was only a caprice; and sketched the materials of a poem to which he intended to devote much time and labour. The plan was grounded upon that of Lalla Rookh and the Queen's Wake, for the purpose of affording him the means of varying that which he most dreaded, and of adapting the work to the humours in which he wrote. The scene was to be laid in Ireland during the period of harps and minstrels, and to be diversified by an occasional relief from the clansmen of the North. But he did not live to fulfil his project; and nothing remains of it, but the knowledge of his intention. I should mention, however, that on one occasion he effected a splendid victory over this antipathy. Trinity College, Dublin, had offered an honorary prize for the best poem on the event which then engaged the attention of Europe, the battle of Waterloo; and Maturin, without much difficulty, carried off the prize in a poem of great power and beauty. He presented it in a most handsome manner to one of his pupils, Shea, who published it; and Maturin disinterestedly declined to accept any portion of the profits of the publication, which had a very successful sale.

Maturin's opinions of poetry, as of every thing else, were to be inferred rather than gathered. It was very difficult to draw him into literary conversation: like Congreve, he wished to be an author only in his study. Yet he courted the society of men of letters when it was to be had: but would at any time have sacrificed it to dally an hour in the drawing-room, or at the quadrille. Sometimes, however, amongst friends (particularly if he was in a splenetic mood) he freely entered into a discussion upon the living authors of England, and delivered his opinions rapidly, brilliantly, and with effect. On one occasion a conversation of this description took place, in which I had the pleasure of participating: I will recall the substance of it as well as I can. Do not expect from Maturin the turgidity of Boswell's great man, or the amiable philosophy of Franklin: you will be disappointed if you anticipate any thing profound or speculative from him; for at the best of times he was exceedingly fond of mixing up the frivolity of a fashionable converzatione with the most solid subjects.

I met him in the county of Wicklow on a pedestrian excursion in the autumn; a relaxation he constantly indulged in, particularly at that season of the year. It was in that part of the vale of Avoca, where Moore is said to have composed his celebrated song: a green knoll forms a gradual declivity to the river, which flows through the vale, and in the centre of the knoll there is the trunk of an old oak, cut down to a seat. Upon that venerable trunk, say the peasants, Moore sat when he composed a song that, like the Rans de Vache of the Swiss, will be sung amidst those mountains and valleys as long as they are inhabited. Opposite to that spot I met Maturin, accompanied by a young gentleman carrying a fishing-rod. We were at a distance of thirty miles from Dublin: in the heart of the most beautiful valley in

the island: surrounded by associations of history and poetry, with spirits subdued into tranquillity by the Italian skies above, and the peaceful gurgling of the waters below us. Never shall I forget Maturin's strange appearance amongst these romantic dells. He was dressed in a crazy and affectedly shabby suit of black, that had waxed into a "brilliant polish" by over zeal in the service of its master; he wore no cravat, for the heat obliged him to throw it off, and his delicate neck rising gracefully from his thrice-crested collar gave him an appearance of great singularity. His raven hair, which he generally wore long, fell down luxuriantly without a breath to agitate it; and his head was crowned with a hat which I could sketch with a pencil, but not with a pen. His gait and manner were in perfect keeping; but his peculiarities excited no surprise in me, for I was accustomed to them. In a short time we were seated on the banks of the Avoca, the stream cooling our feet with its refreshing spray, and the green foliage protecting us from the sun.

"Moore is said to have written his song in this place."

"I don't believe a word of it," replied Maturin. "No man ever wrote poetry under a burning sun, or in the moonlight. I have often attempted a retired walk in the country at moonlight, when I had a madrigal in my head, and every gust of wind rang in my ears like the footsteps of a robber. One robber would put to flight a hundred tropes. You feel uneasy in a perfectly secluded place, and cannot collect your mind."

"But Moore, who is a poet by inspiration, could write in any circumstances."

"There is no man of the age labours harder than Moore. He is often a month working out the fag end of an epigram. 'Pon my honour, I would not be such a victim to literature for the reputation of Pope, the greatest man of them all."

"Don't you think that every man has his own peculiarity in writing, and can only write under particular excitements, and in a particular way?"

"Certainly. Pope, who ridiculed such a caprice, practised it himself; for he never wrote well but at midnight. Gibbon dictated to his amanuensis, while he walked up and down the room in a terrible passion; Stephens wrote on horseback in a full gallop: Montaigne and Chateaubriand in the fields: Sheridan over a bottle of wine; Moliere with his knees in the fire: and Lord Bacon in a small room, which he said helped him to condense his thoughts. But Moore, whose peculiarity is retirement, would never come here to write a song he could write better elsewhere, merely because it related to the place."

"Why omit yourself in the list? you have your own peculiarity."

"I compose on a long walk; but then the day must neither be too hot, nor cold: it must be reduced to that medium from which you feel no inconvenience one way or the other; and then when I am perfectly free from the city, and experience no annoyance from the weather, my mind becomes lighted by sunshine, and I arrange my plan perfectly to my own satisfaction."

"From the quantity of works our living poets have given to the public, I would be disposed to say that they write with great facility, and without any nervous whim. . . ."

"But Lord Byron—he must write with great ease and rapidity."

"That I don't know; I never could finish the perusal of any of his long poems. There is something in them excessively at variance with my notions of poetry. He is too fond of the obsolete; but that I do not quarrel with so much as his system of converting it into a kind of modern antique, by superadding tinsel to gold. It is a sort of mixed mode, neither old nor new, but incessantly hovering between both."

"What do you think of *Childe Harold*?"

"I do not know what to think of it, nor can I give you definitively my reasons for disliking his poems generally."

"You have taken up a prejudice, perhaps from a passage you have since forgotten, and never allowed yourself patience to examine it."

"Perhaps so; but I am not conscious of a prejudice."

"No man is. . . ."

"And which of the living poets fulfils your ideal standard of excellence?"

"Crabbe. He is all nature without pomp or parade, and exhibits at times deep pathos and feeling. His characters are certainly homely, and his scenes rather unpoetical; but then he invests his subject with so much genuine tenderness and sweetness, that you care not who are the actors, or in what situations they are placed, but pause to recollect where it was you met something similar in real life. Do you remember the little story 'Delay is Danger?' I'll recite you a few lines describing my favourite scene, an autumn-evening landscape:—

> On the right side the youth a wood survey'd,
> With all its dark intensity of shade;
> Where the rough wind alone was heard to move,

> In this, the pause of nature and of love,
> When now the young are rear'd, and when the old,
> Lost to the tie, grow negligent and cold—
> Far to the left he saw the huts of men
> Half hid in mist that hung upon the fen;
> Before him swallows, gathering for the sea,
> Took their short flights, and twitter'd on the lea;
> And near the bean-sheaf stood, the harvest done,
> And slowly blacken'd in the sickly sun;
> All these were sad in nature, or they took
> Sadness from him, the likeness of his look,
> And of his mind—he ponder'd for a while,
> Then met his Fanny with a borrow'd smile.

"Except Gray's *Elegy,* there is scarcely so melancholy and touching a picture in English poetry."

"And whom do you estimate after Crabbe?"

"I am disposed to say Hogg. His *Queen's Wake* is a splendid and impassioned work. I like it for its varieties, and its utter simplicity. What a fine image is this of a devoted vessel suddenly engulphed at sea:

> Some ran to the cords, some kneel'd at the shrine,
> But all the wild elements seem'd to combine;
> 'Twas just but one moment of stir and commotion,
> And down went the ship like a bird of the ocean!

"But do not altogether take me at my word in what I say of Crabbe and Hogg. They have struck the chord of my taste; but they are not, perhaps, the first men of the day. Moore is a writer for whom I feel a strong affection, because he has done that which I would have done if I could: but after him it would be vain to try any thing. . . ."

"Is it your opinion that the swarm of minor poets and writers advance the cause of literature, or that the public taste would be more refined and informed, if those who administered to it were fewer and better?"

"I object to prescribing laws to the republic of letters. It is a free republic, in which every man is entitled to publicity if he chooses it. The effect unquestionably of a swarm of minor poets is the creation of a false taste amongst a certain class; but then that is a class that otherwise would have no taste at all, and it is well to draw their attention to literature by any agency. In the next age their moral culture will improve, and we shall go on gradually diminishing the contagion."

"I object *en masse* to the caterers for Magazines; if they were capable of better things, they would throw off the security of disguise, and announce themselves singly. . . ."

I am quite sure that many of his opinions will appear strangely contradictory of the character of mind to be inferred from his works; but Maturin wrote, as I have before remarked, not from a permanent and deep sympathy, but from immediate feeling; and some of his opinions were whims adopted without reflection, and grown inveterate by indifference. There is a strong, I should be disposed to say, remarkable resemblance between *Manfred* and **Bertram**: the same gloomy imagery and mysterious management of the passions: the same intermixture of the beautiful and the repulsive, by which nature is made to adapt and mould herself to the very excesses of poetry: and the same light of indistinct revelation in which the machinery is placed, where the tempters pass dimly yet visibly before us. From this extraordinary similarity, it would be inferred at once that Maturin admired if he did not imitate Lord Byron; yet, marvellous as it may seem, he could not read him! A closer examination, however, will enable us to discover the great points of difference, which are lost on the surface, and lie in the depths and sources of their poetical perception. *Manfred* is exuberantly metaphysical, and develops one by one the sensations that are produced by a particular state of mind, operated upon by circumstances of highly-wrought, imaginative and unearthly horror. But this is done in such an elevated strain of poetry, and inanimate nature is made so to mingle in, and contribute to, the workings of the agonized spirit, that the superficial effect of *Manfred* is one unbroken impression of beauty and awe. In **Bertram** a fierce passion is wildly sketched: it breaks out like a torrent—interrupted, abrupt, overwhelming. All things yield to its power: it gains a master sway over your sympathies. Heaven and earth are invoked in their most desolate aspects to aid its course, and you retire with the same impression of undefined terror and beauty. But there is nothing abstract in **Bertram**: it possesses scarcely a touch of deep feeling: its pathos is language and situation; and they are powerful. The likeness is external, but the internal characters exhibit that sort of dissimilarity that exists between thought and imagination.

Of Sir Walter Scott I have heard Maturin speak in terms of rapture. He considered his extraordinary productions the greatest efforts of human genius, and often said that in the poetry of universal nature he considered him equal to Shakespeare. Indeed so sensibly imbued was he with the characteristics of those magic fictions, that he apprehended the publication of his last work, **The Albigenses,** would expose him to the accusation of an intentional imitation of Ivanhoe. I believe the public, however, never perceived any imitation beyond that into which every novelist falls who happens to write after Sir Walter; a disadvantage, by the way, for which reviewers ought to make some allowance. It was generally understood, but how justly I cannot say, by Maturin's relatives after his decease, that Sir Walter Scott had undertaken the task of his biography, which was to be published with a full edition of his works, for the benefit of his widow and family. Two years have now passed away, and that expectation has not been realized; and I am disposed to suspect that the *Life of Na-*

poleon has become too laborious a project to admit time for the humble memoirs of an Irish dramatist. This disappointment is to be lamented for the sake of the amiable survivors, and the interests of Irish literature; but the materials of such a life would be slender indeed, and perhaps offer little variety to their compiler. His transitions of station, and change of scene and circumstance were few: his literary associations equally barren; in truth, his life would be little more than a thread upon which to hang the fictions it produced.

There was something exceedingly impressive and tender in his private character. It was coloured by the softest tints of domestic affection, and was full of amiability and kindness; tempered by a dash of romantic devotedness, and solitary fidelity to the objects of his attachment. His love was a direct sentiment that borrowed no hue from the medium through which it passed, but came direct from the heart, warm and sincere. Of this singleness and purity was his long-cherished passion for Miss Kingsbury, sister to the present Archdeacon of Killaloe, to whom after years of attachment he was married while yet going through his college course. It was the first love of boyhood, and full of ardour and truth. His marriage, no doubt, gave the final turn to his speculations, and determined him to enter the Church, in the hopes that the interest of his wife's brother would advance him to future independence. On taking orders he was appointed to the curacy of Loughrea, where he had little to cheer or animate his spirits, and which to a man like Maturin was a moral expatriation. He endured it, however, for the sake of that dear partner of his affection, for whose sake he would have suffered and did suffer much: and to the honour of those glorious feelings of home and its sweet, sweet links, he retained that sentiment undiminished to the last hour of his life. He was not long in Loughrea: the unconscious efforts which a man in an uneasy position will make to extricate himself, procured for Maturin an exchange into Dublin, where he was nominated to the curacy of St. Peter's. In that situation he remained—a clergyman and a poet; his profession drawing him one way—his genius another— and necessity both!

Mario Praz (essay date 1951)

SOURCE: Praz, Mario. "The Shadow of the 'Divine Marquis.'" In *The Romantic Agony,* translated by Angus Davidson, 2d edition, pp. 93-186. 1951. Reprint, New York: Meridian Books, 1956.

[*In the following essay, Praz examines Maturin's extreme depictions of cruelty and suffering in* Melmoth the Wanderer.]

[T]he majority of English writers of this period do not seem to have realized the nature of their predilection for cruel and terrifying spectacles. Maturin, for example, who in *Melmoth the Wanderer* (1820) produced the masterpiece of the 'tales of terror' school, and who professed to 'depict life in its extremities, and to represent those struggles of passion when the soul trembles on the verge of the unlawful and the unhallowed', puts into the mouth of one of his characters this analysis of the feelings of 'amateurs in suffering'[1]:

> It is actually possible to become *amateurs in suffering.* I have heard of men who have travelled into countries where horrible executions were to be daily witnessed, for the sake of that excitement which the sight of suffering never fails to give, from the spectacle of a tragedy, or an *auto-da-fé,* down to the writhings of the meanest reptile on whom you can inflict torture, and feel that torture is the result of your own power. It is a species of feeling of which we never can divest ourselves,—a triumph over those whose sufferings have placed them below us, and no wonder,—suffering is always an indication of weakness,—we glory in our impenetrability. . . . You will call this cruelty, I call it curiosity,—that curiosity that brings thousands to witness a tragedy, and makes the most delicate female feast on groans and agonies.[2]

As is to be expected, there appears also in *Melmoth* [*Melmoth the Wanderer*] the figure of the maiden born beneath an unlucky star; but she is a younger sister of Goethe's Margaret rather than a direct descendant of Clarissa, just as in *Melmoth* also the Byronic type ends by becoming confused with the Mephistopheles of the German master. Balzac, Baudelaire, and Rossetti, among others, were admirers of Maturin, which should suffice to justify a longer analysis of the novel than economy of space will permit. We shall limit ourselves to the points which are most relevant to the present discussion.

Melmoth has made a bargain with Satan, by which, in exchange for his soul, his life is to be prolonged; but he can still escape damnation if he succeeds in finding some one to share his fate. He wanders thus for more than a hundred years from country to country, spreading terror with his eyes, which no one would wish ever to have seen, for, once seen, it was impossible to forget them. Wherever there is a man reduced to desperation, there appears Melmoth to haunt him, in the hope of persuading him to entrust him with his fate: he explores the asylum, the prison, the frightful dungeons of the Inquisition, the houses of the wretched. Like a tiger in ambush, he peers in search of evil and sin; he has something of Goethe's Mephistopheles, something of the Byronic hero, something of the Wandering Jew, something of the vampire:

> Melmoth, as he spoke, flung himself on a bed of hyacinths and tulips. . . . 'Oh, you will destroy my flowers,' cried she. . . . 'It is my vocation—I pray you pardon me!' said Melmoth, as he basked on the crushed flowers, and darted his withering sneer and scowling glance at Isidora. 'I am commissioned to trample on and bruise every flower in the natural and moral world—hyacinths, hearts, and bagatelles of that kind, just as they occur.'[3]

Here it is Mephistopheles who speaks, but in the following passage it is the mocking grin of a brother of Schedoni or Lara:

> The stranger appeared troubled, an emotion new to himself agitated him for a moment, then a smile of self-disdain curled his lip, as if he reproached himself for the indulgence of human feeling even for a moment. Again his features relaxed, as he turned to the bending and averted form of Immalee, and he seemed like one conscious of agony of soul himself, yet inclined to sport with the agony of another's. This union of inward despair and outward levity is not unnatural. Smiles are the legitimate offspring of happiness, but laughter is often the misbegotten child of madness, that mocks its parent to her face.[4]

The central episode of the novel (which is made up of several stories one inside the other, like the *Thousand and One Nights* or the masterpiece of Cervantes, works which Maturin quotes) consists of the love-affair of Melmoth, who here conforms to the type of the enamoured fiend in Oriental tales, with a girl who has been brought up in the primitive simplicity of a tropic isle: a creature who begins life with the name of Immalee and a character like that of Haidée in Byron's *Don Juan,* and finishes it with the name of Isidora and a destiny which relates her to Goethe's Margaret. Beside Immalee, the innocent child of Nature, the accursed wanderer feels as though relieved of the weight of his horrible destiny; he is on the point of confiding to her his ghastly secret; but then his hatred for all forms of life seizes upon him again, and he torments the pure virgin with threats, peals of Satanic laughter, and other Byronic-Mephistophelian terrors. Immalee, now become Isidora and transplanted to Spain, consents to unite her fate with Melmoth's; the lovers are joined in matrimony at dead of night by the spectre of a monk, among the ruins of an ancient monastery. Meanwhile Isidora's father imposes upon her a betrothed chosen by himself, and the girl, who already carries in her womb the fruit of her guilt, flies with Melmoth; her brother Fernan pursues and is killed in a duel by Melmoth, as Valentin was by Faust. Melmoth is recognized by the spectators, Isidora flings herself, desperate, upon her brother's body and refuses to follow her demon lover; she is shut up in the prisons of the Inquisition—as could be foreseen—and the infant girl who is born in the meantime is destined for the cloister. Finally the child is found dead in its mother's arms, and the mother dies of a broken heart after refusing for the last time the offer of Melmoth, who has visited her in prison and conjured her to accept liberty at a terrible price (a scene parallel to the one in Margaret's prison; Isidora's last cry is also for her wretched lover: 'Paradise!' she says to Fra José who attends her in her last moments, *'will he be there?'*). Melmoth, after wandering the earth for a hundred and fifty years, returns to his ancestral castle, and there is seized upon by devils who hurl him into the sea; in fact he has the classic end of those who are possessed of the Devil—Marlowe's Doctor Faustus, Byron's Manfred, Lewis's Monk.

The novel abounds in frightful descriptions of tortures both physical and moral. There is a long story of a forced monastic vow derived from Diderot's *Religieuse*[5] and elaborated with a subtlety of penetration into the terrors of the soul such as is elsewhere only found in Poe; there is a parricide who recognizes his own sister in the woman whom he has been pleased to starve to death with her lover; there is a mother who pretends that her son is the fruit of an adulterous union, in order to avoid his marrying a poor cousin whom he is thus persuaded to think is his sister; there is a trial of the Inquisition, a mysterious personage being present, as in Mrs. Radcliffe's *The Italian*; there is a whole family reduced to desperation and hunger through the avarice of the priests, and a youth who sells his own blood to support them. As for the latter, he is found one night in a pool of blood caused by the imperfect ligature of a vein, and the author paints this picture of cadaverous beauty:[6]

> . . . a kind of corse-like beauty, to which the light of the moon gave an effect that would have rendered the figure worthy of the pencil of a Murillo, a Rosa, or any of those painters, who, inspired by the genius of suffering, delight in representing the most exquisite of human forms in the extremity of human agony. A St. Bartholomew flayed, with his skin hanging about him in graceful drapery—a St. Laurence, broiled on a gridiron, and exhibiting his finely-formed anatomy on its bars, while naked slaves are blowing the coals beneath it,—even those were inferior to the form half-veiled, half-disclosed by the moonlight as it lay.

Already, in another passage,[7] Maturin had lingered over the description of the tortures inflicted upon an extremely beautiful young monk, and had declared the group of torturers and victim to be worthy of Murillo: 'A more perfect human form never existed than that of this unfortunate youth. He stood in an attitude of despair—he was streaming with blood. . . . No ancient sculptor ever designed a figure more exquisite and perfect than that they had so barbarously mangled.'

Notes

1. Vol. ii, p. 62 of the 1892 London edition (R. Bentley and Son).

2. Sade's explanation of this phenomenon may be found in a note to vol. iv of *Justine*:

   'Nos places publiques ne sont-elles pas remplies chaque fois que l'on y assassine juridiquement? Ce qu'il y a de fort singulier c'est qu'elles le sont presque toujours par des femmes; elles ont plus de penchants que nous à la cruauté et cela parce qu'elles ont l'organisation plus sensible. Voilà ce que les sots n'entendent pas.'

3. Vol. ii, p. 309.

4. Vol. ii, p. 243.

5. The story of Alonzo de Monçada as told in *The Tale of the Spaniard* is copied from that of Marie-Suzanne Simonin in the convent of Longchamp. Alonzo is destined by his parents for the cloister because of his irregular birth; Suzanne because she is the child of an adulterous union. Both resist the will of their parents, both are inveigled and threatened by priests in the same way and finally yield, after a moving scene with their respective mothers. Both seek an annulment of their vows from the civil tribunal, and make use of the same stratagem to obtain the paper on which to write their petition. They suffer the same cruel persecutions, are examined, as being possessed of an evil spirit, by a special ecclesiastical commission, and found innocent; but they lose their cases, and for the same reason. All these incidents, as well as many secondary details, were taken by Maturin from the *Religieuse,* often with the same words, and always with exaggerations and amplifications for the purpose of 'darkening the gloomy' and 'deepening the sad', as was the usual practice of this anti-Catholic and 'terrible' writer. A more detailed analysis of the relation between the two works was given by me in *The Review of English Studies* of Oct. 1930. Any one who wishes to examine some of the passages in which Maturin's imitation really becomes plagiarism, should compare pp. 284 et seq. of vol. i of *Melmoth* with pp. 80 et seq. of the *Religieuse,* in *Œuvres complètes,* ed. cit., vol. v (the episode of the visit of the bishop is the counterpart of the visit of the 'grand vicaire' in Diderot). The episode of the imprisonment in the dungeons of the Inquisition, of the escape and the taking refuge in the Jew's house derives partly from Godwin's *St. Leon;* see N. Idman, *Charles Robert Maturin, his Life and Works (a Dissertation)* (Helsingfors, Centraltryckeri, and London, Constable, 1923), pp. 230-1. For the analogies between *The Tale of the Indians* and *Faust,* see W. Müller, *Ch. Rob. Maturin's Romane 'The Fatal Revenge' und 'Melmoth the Wanderer', Ein Beitrag zur Gothic Romance* (Weida, 1908), pp. 98-9.

6. Vol. iii, p. 120.

7. Vol. i, p. 179.

H. W. Piper and A. Norman Jeffares (essay date May 1958)

SOURCE: Piper, H. W., and A. Norman Jeffares. "Maturin the Innovator." *Huntington Library Quarterly* 21, no. 3 (May 1958): 261-84.

[*In the following essay, Piper and Jeffares analyze aspects of Irish nationalism and literary Romanticism in Maturin's oeuvre. According to the critics, Maturin's significance lies as much in his portrayals of early-nineteenth-century Irish society and culture as in his accomplishments as a Gothic novelist.*]

Charles Robert Maturin (1782-1824) is chiefly remembered as one of the followers of "Monk" Lewis and Mrs. Radcliffe, and he deserves his place in the history of the Gothic novel, for his **Melmoth the Wanderer** (1820) is an impressive example of the kind. Nevertheless, this reputation obscures his equally important place as a serious novelist of interest to the student of cultural history.[1] It is the purpose of this article to show him as one of the earliest distillers of that blend of nationalism and romanticism which was to be so potent in the nineteenth century.

He is not the less interesting because his blend was of Irish nationalism and Wordsworthian romanticism. Certainly Scott's poetry and Irish ballads played their part in Maturin's development, but his first novel, **Fatal Revenge; or, The Family of Montorio** (1807), makes it clear that the *Lyrical Ballads* and its preface gave his variety of romantic nationalism its foundation. It is perhaps unusual to think of that volume as a special incitement to nationalism, but it led Maturin to see Irish resistance to English rule as part of a clash between two cultures, one nationalistic and romantic, based on a Gaelic folk tradition and the "natural" emotions of a native population living in close contact with nature, and the other cosmopolitan and neoclassical, making nature conform to the habits and tastes of society.

When this theme appears in **Fatal Revenge,** it is only incidental to a very Gothic plot. It is, however, introduced through one of the two heroines, who, under the name of Cyprian, has disguised herself as a young man in order to be near the object of her affections, Ippolito. The two soon discuss poetry, and when Ippolito says, "Nature must indeed be the object of poetical representation but it must be nature modified and conformed to the existing habits and tastes of society," Cyprian replies to this in romantic terms, "I would invert your rule, and admit the influence of prevailing manners into my strains, so far as they were conformable to nature." When she has discoursed for a time in this way, Ippolito suggests that she should study "the poesy of the heretic English which has a spirit of simple appeal to the strong and common feelings of our nature, often made in such language as the speakers of common life clothe their conceptions in." The subjects of English poetry, says Ippolito, are "the indigent peasant weeping over her famished babes—the maniac who shrieks on the nightly waste—age pining in lonely misery—honest toil crushed in the sore and fruitless struggle with oppression and adversity."

Maturin linked this spirit with that of the native Irish, for he makes Ippolito move from these obvious references to *Lyrical Ballads* to ballads in general and claim that Irish poetry is richer in its harmony and more melting than English. As an example, and perhaps not a very happy one, Ippolito quotes a ballad of Maturin's own composition, **"Bruno-Lin, the Irish Outlaw."** The poem itself is not particularly nationalist in spirit, but the strength of Maturin's national feeling is shown by a curious piece of sarcasm, perhaps directed at the Union. Ippolito cannot even recall the name of Ireland, and remarks, "I have forgot their name, but of a people so endowed the name will not always be obscure."

Before Maturin began his career, two women novelists had started their exploration of Irish subjects, Maria Edgeworth in *Castle Rackrent* (1800) and Lady Morgan (Sydney Owenson) in *St. Clair; or, The Heiress of Desmond* (1803) and in *The Wild Irish Girl* (1806).[2] Maria Edgeworth was virtually the creator of the regional novel. *Castle Rackrent,* she thought, might convey a specimen of manners and characters perhaps unknown in England. Her story is told by an old peasant, whose speech she created with a skill anticipating the later work of Lady Gregory and Synge; but the subject is the lively life of the landed proprietors in Ireland before the Union. Her motives in capturing and echoing peasant speech were based more upon a genuine delight in its turns, locutions, and vocabulary, in its sense of exaggeration and of anticlimax, and in its sheer liveliness, than upon any wish to demonstrate any superiority of past or present Gaelic culture. The peasants were incidental to the squirearchy; she saw them through no Wordsworthian belief in the intrinsic significance primitive people should possess for civilized people; she was, after all, an eighteenth-century rationalist in spirit, and could not envisage primitive people possessing any superiority over those who were civilized.[3]

Lady Morgan, however, seized on the romantic possibilities of Ireland. The priggish hero of her first novel arrives in a "castle in Connaught where you find the character, the manner, the language, and the music of the native Irish in all their primitive originality." This locale led her hero to expect to find literary traditions, because the native Irish had been driven to this area by religious and political persecution and secluded there until after the Restoration. But *St. Clair*'s series of letters busy themselves mainly with recording the minutiae of the hero's platonic affair with Olivia, an Irish girl, modeled not a little on Lady Morgan's own character. The two exchange poems, lend and give each other books, including the inevitable Goethe and Rousseau, and read Guarini together. But in the midst of *St. Clair,* supposedly written to illustrate the dangers of rhapsodies upon passionate love, of contempt for self-restraint, the heroine sings Irish songs to her own harp accompaniment, discusses the birthplace of Ossian, and introduces the hero to her grandfather, "the only gentleman in these parts who cultivates Irish wit, or appears anxious to rescue from total oblivion the poetry and music of his country: he is in every respect the true type of the old Irish chieftain, implacable in his resentments, making decision the criterion of his wisdom." Irish manuscripts, his harper, and his ruins hold the next place in his heart to his family.

Most of the Irish material in *St. Clair* was incidental to the exploration of the lovers' sensibilities. After Lady Morgan had been to England and realized the attitude of people there toward Ireland, she wrote *The Wild Irish Girl* as a patriotic gesture, as an essay in propaganda, more self-conscious than *Castle Rackrent* or, probably, than any other novels that preceded it, excepting those of Godwin. *The Wild Irish Girl* contains developed versions of the previous heroine and the chieftain, this time attended by a cultivated priest as chaplain. Many passages of the earlier novel are simply recapitulated, but the hero is a vast improvement on the priggish nonentity who romanticized his way through platonic mazes in *St. Clair.* This one has a Byronic touch; he has "lived too fast in a moral as well as a physical sense." However, he is reclaimed from his enervation by the attraction of everything Irish, aided by Glorvina's charms. The novel is packed with information upon many and diverse aspects of Irish life: language and literature, legends and antiquities, music and dancing, topography and modes of life in both peasant's hut and chieftain's castle.[4] Indeed, footnotes frequently occupy far more space than does the text.

Maturin had these three novels by his two countrywomen to use as examples when he began writing. He must also have been affected by the rapidly increasing interest in Irish music (as well as in the customs and manners of the Irish), which was occurring in Ireland at the end of the eighteenth century, a probable concomitant of the successful bloodless revolution of 1782 and the establishment of the short-lived yet brilliant Irish parliament in Dublin. Joseph Cooper Walker had published his *Historical Memoirs of the Irish Bards* in 1786[5]; Charlotte Brooke, her *Reliques of Irish Poetry* in 1789; and Edward Bunting, his *General Collection of the Ancient Irish Music* in 1796. The last work resulted from the famous festival arranged in Belfast in 1792 by Dr. James McDonnell at which the last ten harpers met and played.[6] The vogue for Irish music spread to England when Lady Morgan's *Twelve Original Hibernian Melodies, with English Words, Imitated and Translated, from the Works of the Ancient Irish Bards* appeared in 1805, a work that Thomas Moore thought of using in the preparation of his *Irish Melodies,* the first collection of which was published three years later. These melodies were partly due to Moore's work with Edward Hudson, a fellow undergraduate at Trinity College Dublin, condemned to exile for his part in the 1798 rebellion.

Sylvester O'Halloran's *Introduction to the Study of the History and Antiquities of Ireland* of 1772 was followed by his *General History of Ireland from the earliest accounts to the close of the twelfth century* in 1778. His work had an effect upon the growing national self-consciousness of Irish writers after the Union. Another sphere of writing which helped to create a climate of interest in the Gaelic-speaking world outside the neo-classical culture of Dublin and the country houses was the work of travelers[7] like Arthur Young[8] and Charles Topham Bowden,[9] not to mention the illiberal reflections of Richard Twiss, whose effigy afterward appeared on the bottoms of a popular line of chamber pots.[10] The most likely and obvious influence upon Maturin must have been his own experience of the "hidden Ireland," to borrow Professor Daniel Corkery's phrase, which he obtained sometime during 1804-1806 when acting as a curate in Loughrea, a market town in the west of Ireland.[11] He visited the seat of the O'Moore family, Cloghan Castle, during this time and thus came in contact with an ancient Irish family's mode of life.

What distinguished Maturin from the two novelists who preceded him was that his interest in Irish subjects, such as folk song and harp music, was so affected by Wordsworth's romanticism. Maria Edgeworth was anti-romantic in tone; Lady Morgan owed more to continental than English sources. Though Maturin's own ballad in *Fatal Revenge* acknowledged Scott's influence, which was certainly neither "democratic" nor revolutionary, his romanticism, like Wordsworth's, looked to the present and the future. Indeed, he had absorbed from Wordsworth not only a faith in the strong "natural" feelings common to all men, but also a belief in the power of Nature herself. When the dialogue in *Fatal Revenge* between Cyprian and Ippolito ends, Ippolito, who is given to fashionable dissipation, is reassured by Cyprian: "Be assured that these cool and healthful moments of reproving thought snatched from the fevering turmoils of the world, will have an effect that shall not be unfelt or forgotten there."[12]

It is interesting, for reasons which will appear, that Maturin should have introduced these ideas through his love story. But they are only an interlude in this novel, for, despite a misleading assurance, an "adieu to dungeons and poisons and monks," the rest of the story is a creaking display of the Gothic paraphernalia, its scenery, unlike that in his other novels, glowing with colors borrowed from Mrs. Radcliffe's palette.

These passages between Cyprian and Ippolito constitute the only originality in the novel, and it is not surprising that they should reappear in various forms as the themes of the works which give Maturin his place as a regional novelist: *The Wild Irish Boy*; *The Milesian Chief*; *Women*; and, to a certain extent, *Melmoth the Wanderer.* But before we leave *Fatal Revenge,* there is a further passage which casts a good deal of light on the importance of these ideas to Maturin, and on why he laid so much stress on emotion. At one point the plot of the novel called for poems written by a nun to express her forbidden love for a man. Maturin, as we have seen, was in the habit of using up his own poetry, but, of course, he would hardly have on hand poems written from a woman's point of view. What he did use were his own poems describing a man's guilty love for a woman:

> Enough for me the joy to view
> Thy purer beauties glow,
> Bid unrestrained those odours rise
> Whose sweets I ne'er must know.

The second poem makes the nature of the relationship clearer:

> I wish I were a blushing flower,
> Within thy breast one hour to reign,
> Then I might live without a crime
> Then I might die without a pain.

The third is most explicit:

> . . . And I'll quench in the nectar that bathes thy red
>   lip
> The fever that's burning in mine.
> And lapt in a dream, I'll forget that a voice
> Would recall, that a fear would reprove—
> Till I start as the lightning is lanced at my head
> And wonder there's guilt in our love.
>
>   (p. 131)

There is no suggestion in any of the biographies of Maturin of any guilty passion which might have given birth to these poems. Though young, he was in Holy Orders when he married, but there seems nothing in his marriage with Miss Henrietta Kingsbury, the daughter of the Archdeacon of Killala, which would call down lightning from heaven. He always stressed domestic bliss as the highest attainable human happiness, and his marriage was spoken of as very happy. His wife, a pupil of Madame Catalini, was one of Dublin's best singers, and had an appetite for social life the equal of his own. The poems suggest either a fresh attraction felt by an affianced young man (such as he depicts in *Women*) or one already bound by marriage vows (as in *The Wild Irish Boy*). Certainly he wrote in the preface to *The*

Milesian Chief, "If I possess any talent, it is that of darkening the gloomy, and of deepening the sad; of painting life in extremes, and of representing those struggles of passion when the soul trembles on the verge of the unlawful and the unhallowed."[13]

In his novels Maturin usually contrasts two heroines, one cultivated and intellectual, the other simple in her emotions. For the first heroine love nearly always ends in tragedy, though only in his play *Bertram,* a story of adultery, can the love between men and women be described as guilty. All this, with the poems, makes it a reasonable conjecture that some important personal experience reinforced Maturin's interest in romantic passion and his interest in what may be called the spiritual differences between Ireland and England. Be that as it may, Maturin's power of emotional analysis and his ability to contrast Irish and English types of nationalism, as revealed by the new values which romanticism was finding in popular tradition, gives his novels a peculiar confidence and strength.

His second work, *The Wild Irish Boy* (1808), was written primarily out of a desire and a need to make money, which it signally failed to do. Its title suggests at once its affinities with Lady Morgan's *The Wild Irish Girl,* published two years earlier. Maturin obviously hoped that the similarity of title and, to a certain degree, of subject, would push his novel into the slipstream of Lady Morgan's successful work. From her he had learned several useful things: that a regional novel based on Ireland could be romantically colored in the style of the Gothic romances upon which he had greedily fed his youthful and impressionable imagination; that a good plot could be made by bringing a sophisticated and *ennuyé* stranger into suitably romantic Irish surroundings and then hurling this character into a love affair (more passionate than that used by Maria Edgeworth in *Ennui*) with a natural and individualistic Irish character; and that an Irish (or Milesian) chieftain complete with chaplain could prove a dignified and unusual character, and a further means of using the almost anthropological lore about the Irish which was to his hand.

He used some of these ideas in *The Wild Irish Boy.* Unsuccessful potboiler though this is, it does demonstrate Maturin experimenting with various approaches to a regional Irish novel and continuing to develop the relationship between Wordsworthianism and other phases of romanticism already suggested in *Fatal Revenge.* The wild Irish boy, Ormsby Bethel, has spent three years as the pupil of an indolent clergyman amid "the most wild and aerial scenery of the lakes," and the effect of this scenery on his character has been "powerful and almost creative"; his three years in the lake district, "a species of romantic intoxication." He traversed the solitude of the lakes and mountains in the day and read the books his tutor had brought with him from Oxford, which had never been opened since, amid "the evening murmur of winds and dashing of waterfalls." He became "an incurable visionary."

After experiencing *Ossian,* his infatuation was complete; but he had an "exercise of mind" which blended all this Wordsworthianism directly, and curiously, with Irish nationalism:

> Amid the spots of quiet clouds that lay scattered over the evening sky, like islands on the great deep; I have imagined some fortunate spot, some abode peopled by fair forms, human in their affections, their habits, in every thing but vice and weakness; to these I have imagined myself giving laws, and becoming their sovereign and their benefactor.
>
> The idea was sufficiently chimerical, for in a state of innocence there was no occasion for restraint; and in the equality produced by universal excellence, there was no room for sovereign or superior. I was therefore compelled to admit some shades into the character of my imaginary community; but I resolved they should be such as held a latent affinity with virtue, or could be easily reconciled to it by legislative discipline and cultivation. I therefore imagined them possessed of the most shining qualities that can enter into the human character, glowing with untaught affections, and luxuriant with uncultivated virtue; but proud, irritable, impetuous, indolent, and superstitious; conscious of claims they knew not how to support, burning with excellencies, which, because they wanted regulation, wanted both dignity and utility; and disgraced by crimes which the moment after their commission they lamented, as a man laments the involuntary outrages of drunkenness. I imagined a people that seemed to stretch out its helpless hands, like the infant Moses from the ark, and promise its preserver to bless and dignify the species.
>
> When I had conceived this character, such was its consistency, its *vraisemblance,* that I immediately concluded it to be real. I was satisfied there existed such a people—with the hesitation of one who fears his purpose is suspected, I mentioned the character I had conceived to my tutor, and asked if he thought it possible that any people were distinguished by such features. He answered immediately, that I had accurately described the Irish nation.[14]

After a time spent in Trinity College Dublin, where he falls under the spell of Calvinistic society, Ormsby is summoned by his mysterious father to the west of Ireland, and there he meets the old Irish chieftain De Lacy, becoming "acquainted with modes of life which appear to the inmates of England like the visions of romance." Around the chieftain's castle are sallow, meager, and ill-clad people; but even the faces of the meanest indicate the influence of the chief whom they love and who loves them. The castle in which he lives is surrounded by bogs, its gate out of repair, access to its kitchen is by means of a cart laid across a gap, and the kitchen itself is thronged with a horde of idle followers.

De Lacy himself is modeled upon Inismore of *The Wild Irish Girl,* but he is toned down. He does not wear native costume but an out-of-fashion English dress cov-

ered with a scarlet cloak. He is dignified "in a wild and original way," speaks French, Italian, and Spanish, and is acquainted with continental literature and politics. He keeps to the customs of his fathers, thinks in Irish, and when he speaks in English uses "strong and peculiar phrases." He is a puritanical nationalist, a *laudator temporis acti* who declares: "He who shakes my belief in the antiquity of my country, must first shake my belief in the beatitude of the immaculate Virgin Mary" (p. 194). What is more important, he is made to denounce England: "Is it for those who have desolated the country, and razed every mark of power or of resistance from the face of it, to demand where is the proof of power, or of resistance, and after beating down with the savageness of conquerors, the monuments of our strength and greatness, to ask with the insolence of conquerors, what monuments of strength and greatness are left to us?" (p. 193)

Maturin also tried his hand at a piece of Edgeworthian material, not even thinly disguised:

> . . . a castle-rack-rent, an house of disorder and riot, where a bad dinner, vilely dressed, and attended by careless servants, was washed down by floods of wine, that were swallowed with the precipitation of men who were in haste to forget themselves. His mistress sat at the table, some of his illegitimate children by his servants attended at it; the company were some vulgar and worthless wretches, who were permitted to live there to excite laughter, and to swallow wine. The conversation was such as not even young Hammond could give a colouring of decency to, and the jests such as buffoons or schoolboys would substitute for wit.
>
> (p. 221)

This type of treatment of Irish material is unique in Maturin's work, for in this lighter vein he handles the peasantry with a touch of the lively farce which marks the novels of Lover and Lever. The hero passes by Montrevor House when the family arrives from London. A sound arises that he can compare to "nothing human," and a crowd of peasants surrounds the carriages. Ormsby prevents one from being pushed over the verge of a hill by the terrified horses, and is shot by an outrider in the confusion. Later he gets an explanation of what happened from one of the tenants: they had decided to go out and give the new lord a shout of joy on his arrival. They had come too early, stepped into Paddy Donnellan's and taken a drop of whiskey, emerged, fallen in the ditch, fought, and then heard the carriages approaching: "And we all rolled out as bad as we could, and when we all began to shout, hell to the soul of us that could open our mouths, and my lord's servants knocked down some of us, and the rest of us knocked down ourselves . . ." (p. 287). After the melee, the tenant and his friends had explained to Lady Montrevor the reasons for what they had done, the servants had pushed them away, and a gentleman had given them a power of money in her ladyship's own sweet name, and then we gave a shout in earnest, that would have brought her in from the other world if we had murdered her. But may I never die in sin, if when I heard of you, and of that blundering rogue that put a bullet in your arm, if I did not determine to go drown myself in the bog, and never come out of it again till I heard you were well and alive.

(p. 288)

Well as the last passages catch the Synge-song of the peasants, the rapid flow of their exaggerated speech, it was not what Maturin wanted to get across to his readers. He sought something much more dignified than what verges upon the stage Irish character of the eighteenth century, the blundering Paddy. He wanted to impress the rulers of England with the reliability of the Anglo-Irish and their ability to run Ireland, however much he disapproved of their apparent desertion of it after the Union.

Ormsby is therefore translated from the country to the dissipations of Dublin, thence to London, having inherited De Lacy's fortune (an unusual touch, that the old chieftain was wealthy), and being ambitious "to show that Irishmen were not the degraded beings that Englishmen have a right of concluding from their scandalous desertion of their duties and their country." He is filled with an intense nationalism; he speaks of Ireland's depressed trade, a sign perhaps of the increasingly middle-class nature of Dublin after the Union, her neglected populace, her renegade nobility, her dissipated, careless, and "unnational" gentry; and he is made anxious by the country's being "deteriorated by a religion, which, in every country where it had prevailed, had extinguished all spirit but the spirit of superstition." The need was for national education. He attacks the Union, the fatal measure which "could not probably be recalled but might certainly be alleviated." The Union had not even given the internal security from commotion and danger which had been promised by its sponsors, for in July 1803 "a troop of rebels had marched within half a furlong of the Castle of Dublin, the seat of a Military Governor."

This reference to the enormity of rebellion makes it clear that Maturin is placing respectable arguments in the mouth of his hero. There is no question of independence from the crown (Maturin was a protestant clergyman, a member of the Established Church of Ireland); this is a plea for a return of the Irish parliament, or, failing that, some degree of what might be called home rule. The English statesman to whom he addresses these remarks makes use of the information but does nothing, and Ormsby continues to squander his substance in the fashionable world of London. He is emerging from a passionate devotion to his wife's mother when he becomes ensnared and ruined by the gently insinuating Lady Delphina Orberry.

Once Ormsby has rejected this lady's advances, she contrives his financial ruin along with the loss of his reputation. During his attempts to pull himself out of the ensuing morass, he regards Ireland as an antithesis to London's profligate world of fashion. He can escape there and recover. Here is the implicit doctrine Cyprian had advanced in *Fatal Revenge,* that Nature can refresh and restore the jaded or debauched sophisticate. Lady Montrevor, Ormsby's mother-in-law, promises to go back with him and her daughter. Her sophistication appears not utterly sunk into puritanical gloom; that would be altogether too sudden and unconvincing a transformation: "*Allons donc a l'Ireland,* you know, it is the *Island of Saints,* so we shall be quite in character, by being out of all *human* character." But she does make it clear to the youth that this artificiality is but a mask:

I protest I only fear we shall be too perfect; so lest I should rise too rapidly in my own estimation, I will go talk nonsense to all the world for another hour—once more let's "mock the midnight bell." Oh, my dear Ormsby, don't despise me for this levity—it is not levity—a glow of natural feeling pervades my whole heart and soul, and if I don't laugh, I must certainly cry.

(p. 367)

We are now back, most obviously, to the conversations of Cyprian and Ippolito in *Fatal Revenge.* Lady Montrevor is subtly indicating her change from one type of character to the other. She is beginning to turn to the world of natural feeling, to leave the cosmopolitan world of neoclassical convention. Her return from London to the west of Ireland is symbolic of the change. Once more Ireland has conquered spiritually.

All this use of Irish material in *The Wild Irish Boy* is not tightly integrated with the structure of the novel. It indicates what Maturin meant when he wrote in the preface, "He who is capable of writing a good novel ought to feel that he was born for a higher purpose than writing novels." He wanted, obviously, to write about Ireland. He wrote better about it than about a fashionable London of which he knew nothing. He felt that a fashionable novel would sell better, and its materials should be "a lounge in Bond Street, a phaeton tour in the park, a masquerade with appropriate scenery, and a birth-day or birth-night, with dresses and decorations, accurately copied from the newspapers." This cynicism about the making of a novel did not suit him—though it is possible that he thought he might combine the Irish material of Lady Morgan with the social satire of Maria Edgeworth's *Belinda,* which Ormsby Bethel praises fulsomely. He was too romantic for satire. He lamented he had not time to write more about Ireland; his heart was full of it. His head was apparently full of London newspaper reports. But he was compelled, he asserted, to consult the pleasures of his readers, not his own.

The Milesian Chief, written four years later, was a more conscious attempt to gain literary laurels. In it he was being truer to his inclinations and the result is a far better novel. He was now much more skilled in his method of contrasting English and Irish national character (for that, ultimately, is what Cyprian and Ippolito were also rehearsing in *Fatal Revenge,* though no reader but an Irishman might have suspected it at the time) as well as comparing "natural" with sophisticated character. In *The Wild Irish Boy* he had merely produced the commonplace Irish remarks about the difference between the English and the Irish character. The Irish were formed to give more delight, the English to give more tranquil and rational happiness; the Irish were more ardent as lovers, the English better as husbands; and, a detached piece of generalization, the Irish, while better acquainted with the modes of pleasing, attained their success by some sacrifice; they have less dignity, stability, and force of character than those who live for other purposes. But Maturin, despite his apparent detachment, contrived, like Dr. Johnson with the Whig dogs, that the English did not get the best of it.

The contrast is achieved more subtly in *The Milesian Chief* by means of opposing characters. Here Maturin uses Lady Morgan's device of placing a sophisticated stranger in Ireland. He gives the idea a twist by making the stranger a beautiful talented girl, Armida Fitzalban, who has had a *succès d'estime* in Europe, and is engaged to Wandesforth, an English officer. Her father, Lord Montclare, brings her to Ireland. Her sensibility has previously been affected by the "sombrous imagery and luxurious melancholy" of Ossian, yet she trembles at the thought of the savage country she is to visit, and her heart is desolated by the "bleak waste of bog, scarce seen through the rain that beat heavily against the carriage windows" as she travels across the flatness of the central plain toward the west.

Once arrived, she falls violently in love with Connal O'Riordan, the Milesian chief, a member of an old and once powerful Irish family, who lives with his old grandfather in a ruined watch-tower, the castle proper and the estates having been sold to Lord Montclare. This is another vestigial idea probably taken from *The Wild Irish Girl,* where the Milesian chieftain's lands had been confiscated by the Saxon hero's family in Cromwellian times. Both writers realize that the possession of land is the basic element in the racial antagonisms of Irish and English. The old grandfather plans a rebellion to free Ireland, with Connal as its leader. Connal, however, thinks the venture is impossible, endeavors to check it, but is foiled in his attempts by the treachery of Wandesforth (who has arrived in Ireland with his regiment), and is furious that Armida has rejected him. After various agonizing misunderstandings, jealousies, and suspicions which lead to a renewal of her engagement with Wandesforth, Armida eventually throws in her lot with Connal and goes to an island off the coast with the retreating rebels. She later returns to the castle, where her mother tricks her into agreeing to a marriage with Connal's brother Desmond, and she dies through a self-administered poison. Connal, meanwhile, has surrendered, been mercilessly flogged at Wandesforth's command and released. He shoots Wandesforth and is finally executed by a firing squad.[15]

Maturin is, in part, investigating the reasons why an intelligent young Irishman would consider rebellion against English rule, and discovering reasons why such an attempt was bound to fail without adequate assistance from continental Europe. Maturin was not only a post-revolutionary romantic, he was a post-'98-rebellion, post-Robert-Emmet-rebellion romantic. He had none of the earlier Wordsworthian idealism about the virtues of the lowly born. He said in one of his sermons: "God knows, and all the world knows, that there is more evil among the lower classes than among any other in society, and that, not because they are *lower,* but because they are more destitute of the benefits of knowledge, and the blessings of religion—because they are more ignorant—and of ignorance the almost certain companion is vice."[16]

On the whole, *The Milesian Chief* depicts the unsuitability of the peasantry as revolutionary troops. They are not amenable to any discipline, though they fight courageously against hopeless odds; they are brutal, the people are terrified of them, and their leader's heart "swelled with agony at the thought of the high born Armida being seen by the eyes of rebel peasantry." He is himself murderously attacked by some of his own men, one of whom later informs against him. He thinks gloomily of what would happen to his forces if they were to survive victorious: they would receive the curses of their countrymen; they would see the desolation of their own native land. He had himself decided, before the rebellion was forced into being by Wandesforth's breach of faith, that it would be impossible for Ireland to subsist as an independent country, to exist without dependence upon continental powers or a connection with England. These views are reinforced when he returns from a vain journey to Dublin to explore the possibilities of obtaining pardon for his troops and discovers that the "few brave men penitent for their crime" he had left behind are now transformed into a "ferocious band, mutinous to their leader, hostile to Government, and formidable to the country" and with the "inflamed passions and unruly habits of a rabble mad for rapine." Connal's experience and disillusionment are sadly akin to those of Beauchamp Bagenal Harvey, one of the gentlemen who led the Wexford rebels in 1798.

But the rebellion is only part of Maturin's design to portray his native country to the world; he had a larger plan in mind: "I have chosen my own country for the scene, because I believe it the only country on earth, where, from the strange existing opposition of religion, politics and manners, the extremes of refinement and barbarism are united, and the most wild and incredible situations of romantic story are hourly passing before modern eyes."[17] He fulfilled that larger plan by creating an intense drama out of the tragic and passionate love of Armida and Connal, and that of Connal's brother Desmond and Armida's half-sister Endymion, or Ines. Desmond is introduced as a contrast to Connal. He is no nationalist, joins Wandesforth's regiment, but finally deserts to the rebels and dies with Connal.

Armida's ostensible tragedy is that she is overcome by love for this proud savage, Connal. He rescues her from death three times but resists her attraction for him. His is a masochistic love doomed to despair, just as his love of his country leads him to what he knows will be ultimate defeat. She fails fully to understand or appreciate his world, and he tells her he will never be happy out of it. He despises her spiritual home, Italy, which, characteristically, he has never seen, in comparison with his western world. She understands nothing of the history of, or the political situation in, Ireland. And because of both history and politics he hates her presence in the castle of his ancestors, hates all she stands for; yet despite these differences, or because of them, Armida and Connal become infatuated, incompatible in every way as they are. The blind harper's burst of song foretelling death symbolizes the future course of their relations, a series of constant misunderstandings and misinterpretations of each other's actions. Yet their passion is genuine, as genuine as Connal's passion for the antiquities of his race and for Irish music, on which he lectures Armida constantly.

Maturin's insistence upon bringing Irish culture before his readers derives (though he uses less footnoting) from Lady Morgan's informative technique, but he contrives to weld his material to the story more neatly. Connal's proud character would be insupportable if he did not have this lofty love of a Gaelic culture utterly unknown to Armida's world. As Idman (p. 70) has pointed out, *The Milesian Chief* ultimately records the triumph of a weaker country, since Armida, standing as a symbol of the civilized world, abandons it for the product of this wild, romantic, ancient race, who has, for all his barbarism, a dynamic attraction lacking in the more stolid (if more convincingly drawn) Wandesforth.

The lesser love affair is curiously like that of Cyprian and Ippolito in *Fatal Revenge*. In each case Maturin has thrown two ostensible males together and they develop feelings of what almost amounts to homosexual attachment for each other, before one of the two is conveniently discovered to be female.[18] To give Desmond his due, he runs away from Endymion because he is afraid of the possibility of an unnatural relationship, while Endymion regards him as an elder brother and

can't understand her feelings for him, as she thinks herself a boy. He has, besides, been renowned for "local gallantry" before he meets her, and after escaping from what he regards as an intolerable situation he lives in sin in Dublin with Gabriella, a well-born young lady who has unsuccessfully pursued Connal. The preface to *The Milesian Chief* already alluded to may indeed refer to such struggles of passion as these, "when the soul trembles on the verge of the unlawful and the unhallowed."

The other two spheres in which Maturin thought his talents might lie, darkening the gloomy and painting life in extremes, are amply explored in *The Milesian Chief,* the best portions of which are the descriptions of Irish scenery. He uses nature to reinforce the novel's mood of impending disaster throughout; rain, storm, tempest add to the wildness of the western scenery. Seascapes, solitary islands, ruins, bogs, barren mountains, all play their part in creating the atmosphere of wildness and brooding melancholy, which informs his interpretation of Irish nationalism.

Maturin's next novel, **Women,** is a study of inner life, a novel too advanced for its age,[19] and a sensitive portrayal of young love. In it Maturin continues his exploration of regionalism. He sets the novel in Dublin and exposes the life of one of its Methodist circles. De Courcy, a young Trinity College undergraduate of excessive sensibility, falls in love with Eva, whom he has rescued from mysterious assailants; she is a passively lovely girl in a theologically minded and dreary household. After becoming engaged to her, he is attracted by a woman who is her opposite, Zaira, an opera singer, a development of Lady Montrevor and Armida Fitzalban.[20] Though overflowing with the conversational gush of the bluestocking, she is less fantastic than her dilettante predecessors. De Courcy runs away with her; she teaches him too much, and too obviously, and as a result he has a typical young man's flirtation with another woman, Eulalie. The logical result of all this is his return to Eva. When he leaves Zaira, her passion increases, and the second half of the novel is a protracted though penetrating analysis of her mental state. When De Courcy returns to Eva, she is dying of consumption brought on by his earlier desertion of her; his declination into death follows on hers; and then Zaira discovers that she has been responsible for bringing about the death of her own daughter. A mysterious old peasant woman, who has been moving in and out of the story with some of the omniscience of Meg Merrilies, turns out to be Zaira's mother, Eva's grandmother. This, then, is another anatomy of romantic love; but it is also, paradoxically, an advanced piece of realistic psychology.

Women takes up and gives fuller treatment to several of the ideas of *The Wild Irish Boy.* The Methodist home of the Wentworths, which De Courcy visits and endures for Eva's sake, corresponds to the Calvinist circles in which Ormsby Bethel found himself as a student, with the absurd Macowen's ranting thrown in for good measure. De Courcy's vacillations between an intellectually brilliant mother and a religiously respectable daughter develop the situation in which Ormsby had found himself: married to a pale, delicate daughter while enraptured by the brilliance of her mother. In each case the obvious discrepancies of age assert themselves and the hero eventually realizes he is really in love with the daughter.

Women has fewer of the improbabilities that marred the earlier novel. For instance, Hammond, the worthy counselor of **The Wild Irish Boy,** lacked life, whereas the dour Northern Montgomery, himself in love with Eva, is convincing: he is too human to resist the temptation of telling Zaira that De Courcy is engaged to Eva or of commenting sourly upon Zaira's failings to De Courcy. The realism can be measured by Maturin's dwelling upon an apparently unpromising milieu. It was, however, one which he knew and understood. He describes the social life of Dublin with a satiric eye, and a much more satisfactory picture he makes of it, too, than of fashionable London at fifth hand. For his *mise en scène* he selects the immediate neighborhood of Dublin. He is not looking for the wilder effects of the west that he had used in **The Milesian Chief,** but he is none the less determined to use nature for his purposes. As the story develops, the mad old peasant woman's wild appearances, her speeches, and songs in Irish add their mystery; and her entrances are led up to by the changing aspects of nature. The Gothic spirit raises its head in a description of a city fire, an anticipation of Lady Morgan's transference of that type of romantic treatment into urban scenes in *The O'Briens and the O'Flahertys* (1827). Zaira displays "the theology of the heart" in her raptures over the beauties of nature. And for them Dublin had suitable scenery near at hand. There is a description of an equestrian picnic which Zaira arranges in Wicklow, in which the picnickers explore the wild and mountainous scenery of Luggelaw. A storm breaks out and this allows De Courcy to contrast Eva's earlier terrified, almost superstitious, behavior under the same conditions with Zaira's intellectually stimulated fortitude. Montgomery, with a surly ungraciousness, points her out as "quite a female Plato lecturing on the promontory of Sunium, lecturing away amid a storm that terrifies every other female."

This storm[21] is a means of building up the tension, which discharges with the sinister utterances of the mad old woman: "The clouds, rising slowly above the Killina hills, soon spread far south; Bray-Head was enveloped from its summit to its base; and the long sweeping folds of leaden-coloured vapour passed from hill to hill southward, like giant spectres gliding over their summits, and leaving the folds of their mysterious mantles linger-

ing and darkening on the track of their progress."[22] But the scenery's effect upon the soul could also be described in Wordsworth's tones (adapted, admittedly, to the purposes of romances):

> Beneath them, to right and left, lay the bays of Dublin and Killina, still as if in the first moment of their creation, before they had felt the rush of the breeze, or the ripple of the tide. The low murmur of the waves, that scarce reached their ears, seemed to send a voice of deep, lonely tranquillity to the heart, where its tones were addressed. It seemed to say—"Listen to us, and be at peace." The grey hill, smooth to its summit, the rude obelisk against which they leaned, and which appeared rather like a thing placed there by Nature than by man, all around them seemed to mark the boundary between the world of Nature and of man. They felt themselves alone, and they felt, what those who love alone can feel, that such moments of abstraction are moments of the most exquisite enjoyment.
>
> (pp. 62-63)

Scott's novels as well as his poetry had their effect on Maturin. Not only does the old peasant woman remind us of Meg Merrilies, with her uncanny ability to arrive on the scene of action, but the supernatural is also present. The appearance of the figure of Eva upon Killina Hill is a symbolical warning incident parallel to but more intense (because of its occurrence in a "natural" setting) than the earlier melodramatic occasion on which De Courcy clasped Eva to his bosom:

> Her long, light hair (of a different colour from Zaira's) diffused its golden luxuriance over his bosom; her white slender fingers grasped his with the fondling helplessness of infancy, and twined their waxen softness round and round them; her pure hyacinth breath[23] trembled over his cheeks and lips. In clasping her closer to his heart, he felt something within his vest; he drew it out; it was the flower Zaira had given him the night before, and which he had placed there; *it was withered;* he flung it away.
>
> (pp. 22-23)

There was only one peasant character in **Women.** Paradoxically, in his next novel, **Melmoth the Wanderer,** which is the quintessence of the tale of terror and a return to his earlier and lasting delight in the Gothic phenomena, Maturin begins the introductory tale with his most realistic characterizations of peasants. This first unit of the novel's sixfold plot, with its Chinese-box continuity, is a superb piece of storytelling. There is a steady increase in suspense achieved in two ways, through the realistic rendering of the peasant character which keeps the imaginative soaring of the story firmly rooted, and through the use of emotive descriptions of nature which set a suitable scene wherein Maturin's brooding eerie imagination could display its power.

Young John Melmoth, yet another undergraduate from Trinity College Dublin, travels to the house of his dying miserly uncle in County Wicklow; the atmosphere of the place gets on his nerves and prepares us for the horrors to follow:

> The weather was cold and gloomy; heavy clouds betokened a long and dreary continuance of autumnal rains; cloud after cloud came sweeping on like the dark banners of an approaching host, whose march is for desolation. As Melmoth leaned against the window, whose dismantled frame, and pieced and shattered panes, shook with every gust of wind, his eye encountered nothing but that most cheerless of all prospects, a miser's garden—walls broken down, grass-grown walks whose grass was not even green, dwarfish, doddered, leafless trees, and a luxuriant crop of nettles and weeds rearing their unlovely heads where there had once been flowers, all waving and bending in capricious and unsightly forms, as the wind sighed over them. It was the verdure of the church-yard, the garden of death.[24]

Maturin's last novel, **The Albigenses,** was to form part of a trilogy dealing with ancient, medieval, and modern manners in Europe. It owed its inception to the popularity of Scott's historical novels. And it might be argued that Maturin was using as a basis Irish material translated into another place and time. Lady Morgan had done this in her novel of Provence, *The Novice of St. Dominick* (1805).[25] Maturin was using for background the situation of a religious community under the threat of attempted domination by superior power, which brought out the heroic qualities of the oppressed. The novel was highly praised by contemporary critics, but cannot be thought successful in comparison to some of his earlier work. It has two dissimilar heroines, Isabelle, a nobly-born lady, and Genevieve, probably modeled upon Rebecca in *Ivanhoe,* who is modest, self-denying, and not of exalted origin. But there is no sensitive yet proud hero torn between these two ladies, who experience Radcliffean escapes through secret passages, doors, and vaults, all for the sake of two of the most unrelentingly dull paragons ever wished upon fiction. Whereas in **The Milesian Chief** Armida and Connal addressed each other histrionically, struck attitudes, and often seemed stilted, they were full of life in comparison to all the characters of this novel. **The Albigenses** is ruined by its melodramatic style which not even the descriptions can overcome. And the best of the descriptions derive from Maturin's Gothic rather than his Wordsworthian genre.

It is easy to find faults in Maturin's novels. They are full of them: sometimes excessively complicated in structure, usually brought to a hasty finish, with frequent errors in syntax and grammar, containing manifest absurdities in character and plot, and overflowing with melodramatic excesses. Throughout them, however, Maturin showed his ability to make innovations in the novel such as those suggested in this paper. That these remained unnoticed was part of his tragedy, a tragedy much akin to that of another Irish eccentric and

writer, James Clarence Mangan, who wrote of Maturin with sympathy. Maturin could write compellingly; indeed, language occasionally took on a plastic quality in his hands; he invested the least likely of situations with a passionate intensity and a comprehension of human emotions, particularly those of young lovers, which stemmed from the conviction he expressed in one of his sermons: "Man is unhappy, not because the world is hostile to his happiness, but because he is a guilty creature—and no guilty creature can be happy while he remains in that state."[26]

Notes

1. His novels are: *Fatal Revenge; or, The Family of Montorio,* 1807; *The Wild Irish Boy,* 1808; *The Milesian Chief,* 1812; *Women; or, Pour et Contre,* 1818; *Melmoth the Wanderer,* 1820; *The Albigenses,* 1824. His plays are: *Bertram,* 1816; *Manuel,* 1817; *Fredolfo,* 1817.

2. A Dublin edition of 1802 is supposed to have existed, but no copies survive. See Lionel Stevenson, *The Wild Irish Girl* (London, 1936), p. 317.

3. Maria Edgeworth regarded the peasants as dependents, her father's and later her own responsibility. Both she and her father wished that the English and the Anglo-Irish would not despise the Gaelic Irish peasantry as savages. They themselves proved that decent treatment would be reciprocated, for very few of Mr. Edgeworth's tenants had not remained loyal in the rebellion of 1798. Maria Edgeworth's views were akin to those of Sir Jonah Barrington, *Personal Sketches and Recollections* (1876), p. 341: "No people under Heaven could be so easily tranquillised and governed as the Irish; but that desirable end is alone attainable by the personal endeavour of a liberal, humane and resident aristocracy." The peasants, once educated, were to remain in a subordinate position in society.

4. A letter of Mr. Edgeworth's, dated Dec. 23, 1806, quoted by Mona Wilson, *These Were Muses* (London, 1924), pp. 70 ff., refers to the "just character" given by Lady Morgan to the "lower Irish."

5. He, as well as Edward Lysaght, assisted Lady Morgan with information and encouragement.

6. Cf. Donal O'Sullivan, *Irish Folk Music and Song* (Dublin, 1952), p. 10.

7. See for general discussion and particular references Constantia Maxwell, *The Stranger in Ireland* (London, 1954), pp. 125-135, 209-221. See also her *Dublin under the Georges* (London and Dublin, 1946), pp. 247-277.

8. *A Tour in Ireland; With General Observations on the Present State of That Kingdom; Made in 1776,*

1777 and 1778 and Brought Down to the End of 1779 (London, 1780).

9. *A Tour Through Ireland* (Dublin, 1791). For the depressed condition of the peasantry see p. 159, and for their native music, pp. 105, 165, 219. For discussion of conditions in the countryside see Maxwell, *Country and Town in Ireland under the Georges* (London, 1940), passim.

10. This enterprising line in hardware prompted the circulation of a motto attributed to Lady Clare, wife of the Lord Chancellor:

> Here you may behold a liar,
> Well deserving of hell-fire:
> Every one who likes may p - - -
> Upon the learned Doctor T - - - -.

Cf. Maurice Craig, *Dublin 1660-1860* (Dublin and London, 1952), p. 210, and Maxwell, *Dublin under the Georges*, p. 276.

11. Cf. Niilo Idman, *Charles Robert Maturin, His Life and Works* (Helsingfors and London, 1923), p. 12.

12. *Fatal Revenge*, 4th ed. (London, 1840), p. 24.

13. *The Milesian Chief* (London, 1812), p. iv.

14. *The Wild Irish Boy*, 2nd ed. (London, 1814), p. 102.

15. The hero's death is perhaps a development of the noble savage's inevitable fate at the hands of civilization; cf. the end of Oroonoko in Mrs. Behn's novel.

16. *Sermons* (London, 1819), p. 364.

17. *The Milesian Chief*, p. v.

18. Cf. *Fatal Revenge* (1807), Ch. iv, p. 61: "When the talents and taste of Cyprian failed, even the pensiveness of the little monitor would yield to the solicitude for his pupil; in the graceful petulance of airy command, he would wind his slender arms around Ippolito and with female blandishments declare he should not quit the palace, blandishments to which he bowed with the pouting smile of reluctance."

Cf. also Ch. vii, p. 118: "The obscurity of his introduction, the peculiarity of his manners, gave even a hovering shade of awe to impressions, of which the character had otherwise been faint and fugitive. Not of a sex to inspire love, and still too female for the solid feelings of manly friendship, Cyprian hovered around his master, like his guardian sylph, with the officiousness of unwearied zeal and the delight of communicated purity."

In Ch. ix Cyprian is reading letters, asks Ippolito to kiss him, and then faints.

19. Alaric Watts called it a "horrible anatomy of the moral frame," *The New Monthly Magazine, and Universal Register*, XI (1819), 167.

20. Scott thought her to be originally derived from Madame de Stael's *Corinne* (*The Quarterly Review*, June 1818). See also Willem Scholten, *Charles Robert Maturin the Terror-Novelist* (Amsterdam, 1933), p. 64.

21. The storm scene possesses humor, as did the scene with Macowen in the Wentworth house. Maturin unfortunately reserved his wit and humor for his own conversations.

22. *Women* (Edinburgh and London, 1818), II, 38.

23. Hyacinth breath always seems to have been exuded by Maturin's heroes or heroines when they were in close physical contact with their lovers. There was an element of the commercial copywriter lost in him.

24. *Melmoth the Wanderer* (Edinburgh and London, 1820), I, pp. 51-52.

25. Cf. Stevenson, *The Wild Irish Girl*, p. 65: "The praises of Provençal minstrelsy, and the elaborate account of how the language and culture of Provence survived in defiance of oppression, could be transferred to Ireland by any alert reader. The sufferings of the poor, under a system of absentee landlordism, were shown with similar insinuation. Even more prominent was the insistence on the evils of a religious antagonism which filled otherwise admirable people, Catholics and Protestants alike, with prejudice, hatred, and vengeance, leading to the horrors of civil war. The eloquent pleading for tolerance and cancellation of ancient feuds had as much relevance to contemporary Ireland as to France of two centuries before."

26. *Sermons* (1821), p. 81.

Leven M. Dawson (essay date autumn 1968)

SOURCE: Dawson, Leven M. "*Melmoth the Wanderer*: Paradox and the Gothic Novel." *Studies in English Literature, 1500-1900* 8, no. 4 (autumn 1968): 621-32.

[*In the following essay, Dawson examines the paradoxical elements in Maturin's* Melmoth the Wanderer. *Dawson asserts that the prevalence of paradox in the Gothic genre represents a concerted effort to come to terms with diverse, often contradictory aspects of human existence. Dawson also claims that Gothic fiction shares qualities with Romanticism, particularly its emphasis on the vital role of psychology and art in the individual's understanding of his or her own experience.*]

In the following discussion, using *Melmoth the Wanderer* as my example, I will show the numerous ways in which paradox is a central part of Gothic fiction and finally attempt to show that it is just here, in the use of paradox, that Gothic fiction has its greatest philosophical depth and value, and makes contact with what is most valuable in romanticism. Since paradox is a difficult word to define, some discussion of its meaning is necessary before one considers its importance to the Gothic novel. A paradox is a statement or combination of words which appears at first glance to be patently false or to imply a contradiction but which is found, on closer examination, to be true in fact. The apparent absurdity of the assertion often is a result of the language employed in stating it; the contradictory nature of reality in relation to our initial evaluation of this statement often reveals a certain crudeness or inaccuracy in the way we use language or in the abstractions on which we base our language and therefore our thought. At the initiation of logical thought in history, Aristotle, in his typical, disarmingly elementary way, described the dangers latent in language as the vehicle of thought: "It is impossible in a discussion to bring in the actual things discussed; we use their names as symbols instead of them; and therefore we suppose that what follows in the names, follows in the things as well, just as people who calculate suppose in regard to their counters. But the two cases (names and things) are not alike."[1]

As a result of this disparity between "words and things," paradox—over and above being a common device for exhibiting ingenuity—can be a philosophical tool for destroying traditional and erroneous ways of thinking and for shedding light on the dangers latent in words themselves. W. V. Quine in a recent discussion of paradox and its effect on the history of thought concludes that "Of all the ways of paradoxes, perhaps the quaintest is their capacity on occasion to turn out to be so very much less frivolous than they look."[2] He further asserts that: "The argument that sustains a paradox may expose the absurdity of a buried premise or of some preconception previously reckoned as central to physical theory, to mathematics or to thinking process. Catastrophe may lurk, therefore, in the most innocent-seeming paradox. More than once in history the discovery of paradox has been the occasion for major reconstruction at the foundations of thought."[3]

The paradoxes which are philosophical tools in the way described above, which bring on crises in thought, are antinomies and are to be distinguished from veridical paradoxes, which are true at both a verbal and factual level, and falsidical paradoxes which are false at both a verbal and a factual level. Quine distinguishes among the three types of paradoxes in the following way: "A veridical paradox packs a surprise, but the surprise quickly dissipates itself as we ponder the proof. A falsidical paradox packs a surprise, but it is seen as a false alarm when we solve the underlying fallacy. An antinomy, however, packs a surprise that can be accommodated by nothing less than a repudiation of part of our conceptual heritage."[4]

Hence, paradox, and from now on by paradox I mean antinomy, is a method of moving from language and traditional ways of judging events—from our "conceptual heritage"—to fact. As the hero of *Melmoth the Wanderer* must admit—in regard to the first strange and paradoxical event of the novel, the death of his practical and miserly uncle through "a ridiculous fright that a man living 150 years ago is alive still"—"facts will confute the most stubborn logician," (*Melmoth,* [*Melmoth the Wanderer*] p. 14). This movement, the movement of paradox from logic to experience, from language to reality, is basic to the period of the Gothic romance, to the Gothic novel generally, and to Charles Maturin's Gothic masterpiece, *Melmoth the Wanderer* especially.

To say that Gothic fiction includes such a movement seems a rather grandiose claim for this genre, which is generally considered to be a kind of "pulp" literature. Admittedly the goal of Gothic literature in its early stages was usually easy popularity through sensationalism, but in this regard, also, paradox was suited to the Gothic writers. No matter how enthusiastic and cerebral one becomes about paradox it must be kept in mind that its primary characteristic is a pleasing, theatrical display of cleverness. Paradox is a verbal version of the rabbit in the hat and derives its appeal from those reliable attractions—surprise and strangeness. Thus it is certainly an appropriate characteristic of the Gothic novel, which seldom ignores strangeness, surprise, cleverness, and theatrical "high-jinks."

Various critics have recognized paradoxical qualities in some of the conventions of the Gothic novel, without using the term or attempting to exploit the concept of paradox to unify these conventions. Most critics recognize the essentially paradoxical character of the Gothic hero, hero-villain, or Byronic hero. Lowry Nelson in an article, "Night Thoughts on the Gothic Novel," goes so far as to assert that the Gothic hero is a part of a pervasive paradoxical confusion of conventional good and evil basic to Gothic literature.[5] J. M. S. Tompkins in *The Popular Novel In England 1770-1800* [(1932)] emphasizes the effective incongruency of the interaction, and almost equation, of terror and beauty in the Gothic tale, notably in Ann Radcliffe's romances. William Axton in his introduction to *Melmoth the Wanderer* approaches an association of the function of paradox to Gothic fiction when he implies that the tales basically seek the "inapparent relations and qualities of things."[6] Mr. Nelson in the article cited above comments that the Gothic novel manipulates and examines a basic problem of all great literature, the disparity between appearance and reality. He confronts the basic ways in which Gothic fiction reveals the reality behind appearance when he states that the Gothic writers prepared the way for later "psychological" writers who "demonstrated that sadism, indefinite guiltiness, mingled pleasure and pain (Maturin's "delicious agony"), and love hate were also deeply rooted in the minds of the supposedly normal."[7]

Extremely revealing and provocative is Devendra Varma's quotation from Macaulay cited in *The Gothic Flame* [(1956)]. Macaulay states that the wit of Horace Walpole—the author of the first great Gothic tale, *The Castle of Otranto*—"was, in its essential properties, of the same kind with that of Cowley and Donne. Like them, Walpole perpetually startles us by the ease with which he yokes together ideas between which there would seem at first to be no connection."[8] Here Macaulay has noted a connection with the masters of verbal paradox, the metaphysicals, and with their central type of paradox, as described by Samuel Johnson, the "yoking" of dissimilars or opposites.

The most obvious and also the most easily overlooked instance of the relation of paradox to the Gothic novel is associated with the consistent and striking commercial success of this type of fiction. It would seem that the primary reason for this success is the paradoxical fact that we, the readers, enjoy being frightened and horrified. The characters within Gothic fiction are themselves acutely aware of this apparently contradictory association of emotions. In *Melmoth the Wanderer* John Melmoth is described as listening to the old crone's relation of the story of his strange ancestor with "varying and increasing emotions of interest, curiosity, and terror, to a tale so wild, so improbable, nay, so actually incredible, that he at last blushed for the folly he could not conquer" (*Melmoth*, p. 18). The villainous tool of the Inquisition in the Spaniard's narrative, which constitutes a large part of Maturin's novel, seeks the opportunity of hearing a condemned couple starve to death and refuses to eat, saying that he "reserved the appetite of his soul for richer luxuries," the luxuries of hearing the man and woman's last agonies (*Melmoth*, p. 164). The Spaniard himself admits in his description of the horrible death of this villain and parricide that "It is a fact, Sir, that while witnessing this horrible execution, I felt all the effects vulgarly ascribed to fascination. I shuddered at the first movement—the dull and deep whisper among the crowd. I shrieked involuntarily when the first decisive movements began among them: but when at last the human shapeless carrion was dashed against the door, I echoed the wild shouts of the multitude with a kind of savage instinct," (*Melmoth*, p. 196). It is undoubtedly with this odd mingling of "interest, curiosity and terror" that we allow Gothic tales to effect their paradoxical fascination on us.

Another basic and central way in which the Gothic romance is related to paradox originates from a necessary characteristic of events designed to evoke horror in a reader. If a tiger attacks a small boy and devours him, this event is certainly frightening, but the emotion elicited by the description of this action does not compare with the power exerted over the mind by the contemplation of the same child being attacked and intricately mutilated by its mother. We expect some cruelty from tigers, but we conventionally expect affection between parent and child. Evil or naturally terrible creatures engaged in evil deeds are not nearly so disturbing as good or naturally meek and kind creatures committing evil acts; there is something natural and predictable about the former, and therefore less terrifying, and something unnatural and strange about the latter, and therefore more terrifying. Melmoth, if we keep in mind his perverted feelings, exemplifies this strange characteristic of human psychology. His enjoyment of the calm sea is in contemplating the possibility of "a gaudy and gilded pleasure barge" containing a "Rajah and the beautiful women of his haram" being "overturned by the unskillfullness of their rowers" since "their plunge, and dying agony, amid the smile and beauty of the calm ocean, produce one of those contrasts in which his fierce spirit delighted," (*Melmoth,* p. 230). For Melmoth, and for each reader, the horror of an event is in inverse proportion to its naturalness.

In this relationship of horror to unnaturalness or "contrast," we have one reason for the savage, evil, and satanic women, monks, and nuns, and the incestuous crimes, both sexual and homicidal, of the Gothic stories. In the scene described above in which the parricide working for the Inquisition delights in the agonies of the starving pair, it is revealed that the woman is actually his sister. The heroine of Maturin's novel is forced by despair to find happiness in the cruel death of her own infant; she says "It moaned all night—towards morning its groans grew fainter, and I was glad—at last they ceased and I was very—happy!" (*Melmoth,* p. 404). Earlier in the novel there is the deathbed confession of the monk "of a temper and manners remarkably mild and attractive," who explained his motivation for doing evil in this way: "'I was a monk, and worked for victims of my imposture to gratify my pride! and companions of my misery, to soothe its malignity.' He was convulsed as he spoke, the natural mildness and calmness of his physiognomy were changed for something that I cannot describe—something at once derisive, triumphant, and diabolical," (*Melmoth,* pp. 84 and 87).

We find, again, the exploitation of the horrible effects of contrast, incongruity, and unnaturalness in the imaginative description of the vaults beneath the convent; "the horror of being among those who are neither the living nor the dead—those dark and shadowless things that sport themselves with the reliques of the dead, and feast and love amid corruption,—ghastly, mocking, and terrific," (*Melmoth,* p. 144). It is not enough that these imagined creatures live among the dead or commit violent acts there; the paradoxical effect of their "sporting" and "loving" in such a place must be exploited.

This mention of love among the dead in a discussion of the Gothic novel brings us naturally to a discussion of love in the Gothic romances and how it becomes involved in paradox. "Love in a sepulchre," an idea exploited by Shakespeare, becomes a stock "gimmick" in Gothic romances. A good example of this paradoxical, subterranean romance is the famous "seduction" scene from Matthew Lewis's *The Monk,* in which Monk Ambrosio asserts, as he ravishes the heroine, Antonia, in the burial vaults beneath St. Claire's convent, that "This sepulchre seems to me Love's bower." This strange appeal of love hate or love horror is present in Maturin's hero's relationship to the innocent Indian maid—"Amid this contrasted scene of the convulsive rage of nature, and the passive helplessness of her unsheltered loveliness, he [Melmoth] felt a glow of excitement, like that which pervaded him when the fearful powers of his 'charmed life' enabled him to penetrate the cells of a madhouse or the dungeons of an Inquisition," (*Melmoth,* p. 241). Later he contemplates her and his eyes "flash" upon her "the brightest rays of mingled fondness and ferocity," (*Melmoth,* p. 248).

Possibly this association of fondness and ferocity—this association of love with violence, terror and destructive forces—derives from the traditions of amorous lyric poetry of the preceding two centuries. These traditions can be easily perceived in the satirical treatment of the convention in the following sonnet from Thomas Nashe's *Unfortunate Traveler* [(1594)]:

> If I must die, O let me choose my death
> Sucke out my soule with kisses cruell maide,
> In thy breasts christall bals enbalme my breath,
> Dole it all out in signs when I am laide.
> Thy lips on mine like cupping glasses claspe,
> Crush out my winde with one strait girting graspe,
> Stabs on my heart keepe time whilest thou doest sing.
> Thy eyes lyke searing yrons burne out mine,
> In thy faire tresses stifle me outright,
> Let our tongs meete and strive as they would sting,
> Like Circes change me to a loathsome swine,
> So I may live for ever in thy sight.
>   Into heaven joyes none can profoundly see,
>   Except that first they meditate on thee.

In much the same manner as Nashe has done in this poem for a humorous effect, the Gothic romancers have distorted and subverted the typical metaphor of courtly love; instead of exploiting metaphorically the fact that intense love is terrible and painful, they emphasize the fact that terror and pain can be erotic and generically involved in romance. The Gothic writers assert not only

that terror is strangely involved in love but that eroticism is an attribute of terror itself. Every satanic or Byronic hero, of course, derives his interest from this "strange but true" merging of positive and negative emotions. The very erotic and ambivalent description of Melmoth's "approach" to his victims is worth noting in this regard: "'I have heard,' said one of the company, 'that a delicious music precedes the approach of this person when his destined victim—the being whom he is permitted to tempt or to torture—is about to appear or approach him,'" (*Melmoth,* p. 12). In the hero of Gothic literature, and Melmoth is a prime example, the central paradox of feminine sexuality is tapped in order to produce one of the most successful heroic types of fiction.

The confused derivation of love is further stressed in the novel when Melmoth says of love that "passion must always be united with suffering" and the Indian maid goes further and asserts that she loves him because he has "taught" her "the joy of grief" and granted her "delicious tears," (*Melmoth,* pp. 221, 279). It is obvious that any attempt to justify these paradoxical attitudes toward love and eroticism by an appeal to psychological reality would reveal facts of the uncharted realms of the subconscious. The effective exploitation of the passionate attraction of horror or the involvement of horror and distinction in "fondness" and eroticism is either flagrant sensationalism or an important and disturbing discovery of psychological truth.

In other words, if an examination of these paradoxes of Gothic fiction does reveal anything strange and new about the mind, then they are successfully executing the basic function of paradox, the creation of mystery through the destruction of commonly held opinion, the demonstration of the ineptness or inadequacy of existing abstractions by showing that oppositions based on these abstractions may not be opposite in fact. If love is terrible and fear is pleasant then there must be something amiss with the words themselves or the way we feel about them. If the paradoxes mentioned above are real paradoxes,—that is, if they only appear to be contradictions when verbalized and are actually not contradictory in fact—then they are rather successful attacks on rationalism and logic because they are rather successful attacks on language. If the results of these attacks are no longer disturbing we should not therefore depreciate them, for, as W. V. Quine suggests, powerful antinomies have a way of dissipating into "tamer" veridical or falsidical paradoxes, given a sufficient length of time. He notes, in this regard, that "there was a time when the doctrine that the earth revolves around the sun was called the Copernican paradox even by the men who accepted it."[9]

The Gothic writers' attack on conventional ways of thinking and their questioning of rational attitudes through an appeal to the truth of the emotions is typical of the romantic period. Their work merges with the powerful content of subsequent romanticism through their use of paradox, in another way also. The Romantics typically sought a unity of experience, a resolution of opposing attitudes, a satisfying union through intensity of emotion, intensity of aesthetic involvement, and through their characteristic use of striking but appropriate metaphor. In "A Defense of Poetry" Shelley describes, in just these terms, the function of aesthetic involvement: "Poetry turns all things to loveliness: it exalts the beauty of that which is most beautiful, and it adds beauty to that which is most deformed; it marries exultation and horror, grief and pleasure, eternity and change; it subdues to union under its light yoke all irreconcilable things."[10] The Gothic novel, especially **Melmoth the Wanderer,** effects a union of opposing emotions or sentiments through the paradoxical but valid juxtaposition and mingling of incongruous emotions.

In the Gothicists, as in the Romantics, oxymoron of this type is most often involved with aesthetics. We get this effect strongly in the Indian Maid's response to nature:

> When the rains descended in torrents, the ruins of the pogoda afforded her a shelter; and she sat listening to the rushing of the mighty waters, and the murmers of the troubled deep, till her soul took its colour from the sombrous and magnificent imagery around her, and she believed herself precipitated to earth with the deluge—borne downward, like a leaf, by a cataract—engulphed in the depths of the ocean—rising again to light on the swell of enormous billows, as if she were heaved on the back of a whale—deafened with the roar—giddy with the rush—till terror and delight embraced in that fearful exercise of imagination.
>
> (*Melmoth,* p. 215)

Thus for the Gothicists the intense "exercise of the imagination" can produce a response in contemplation where "terror and delight" can "embrace." Within Maturin's discussion of the temptation of the Walburgs is a passage which reflects an important artistic and metaphysical goal of the romantics, the presentation of terrible beauty or the beauty in horror: "So he lay, as Ines approached his bed, in a kind of corse-like beauty, to which the light of the moon gave an effect that would have rendered the figure worthy the pencil of a Murillo, a Rosa, or any of those painters, who inspired by the genius of suffering, delight in representing the most exquisite of human forms in the extremity of human agony," (*Melmoth,* p. 322). In these passages it is evident that the aesthetic goal of the Gothicists and the romantics—the sublime—is in essence a paradox, an oxymoron which requires a sufficiently intense response to experience to entail a merger of emotions—or, at least, juxtaposition of symbols—which are traditionally considered to be in opposition if not mutually exclusive.

Occasionally in most Gothic tales, and often in Maturin's novel, the union effected by paradox and oxymoron is at a much higher and less sensational level than in the treatment of love and terror or horror and enjoyment, and in addition to comments on aesthetics, interesting comments on traditional ethics sometimes result. These disrupting comments on ethics are antinomies which place in question some basic beliefs about psychology and motivation which are the foundations of ethical theory. In places they attack Plato's ethical fallacy that each man will seek his own good. Stanton, one of the victims of Melmoth, admits that his "incessant and indefatigable" pursuit of Melmoth is the "master passion" but also "the master torment of his life," (*Melmoth,* p. 144). The Spaniard describes his motivation in similar terms: "I went no longer shrinking from, and depreciating *their worst,* but defying almost desiring it, in the terrible and indefinite curiosity of despair," (*Melmoth,* p. 125). The confused and paradoxical nature of motivation is emphasized also in the Spaniard's description: "This man was criminal, and crime gave him a kind of heroic immunity in my eyes. Premature knowledge in life is always to be purchased by guilt. He knew more than I did,—he was my all in this desperate attempt. I dreaded him as a demon, yet I invoked him as a god," (*Melmoth,* p. 152). A denial of the strict distinction made between pain and pleasure, a distinction necessary for many formal ethical systems, is suggested also by these paradoxes. Immalee acknowledges after introduction to her "demon-lover," Melmoth, that, "Formerly I wept for pleasure—but there is a pain sweeter than pleasure, that I never felt till I beheld *him,*" (*Melmoth,* p. 221). In this way theories of motivation, and consequently formal ethics, are disrupted by the paradoxical handling of language in this novel and in many Gothic tales.

Maturin, in his discussion of the Indian maid's introduction to religion, makes an ethical judgment on traditional religion and in so doing captures the paradoxical quality of historical religion more strikingly than I have encountered elsewhere: "Such was the picture that presented itself to the strained, incredulous eyes of Immalee, those mingled features of magnificence and horror,—of joy and suffering—of crushed flowers and mangled bodies—of magnificence calling on torture for its triumph,—and the steam of blood and the incence of the rose, inhaled at once by the triumphant nostrils of an incarnate demon, who rode amid the wreck of nature and the spoils of the heart!" (*Melmoth,* p. 225). Here we have finely and frankly conceived the union within religion of the power of beauty and the power of violence and terror.

In Maturin's description of the Indian we find an attempt to express an emotional and ethical union, which is even more strongly sought by the romantics, the union of passion and purity of earthly and ideal love, "as she spoke, there was a light in her eye,—a glow on her brow,—an expansive and irradiated sublimity around her figure,—that made it appear like the rare and glorious vision of the personified union of passion and purity,—as if those eternal rivals had agreed to reconcile their claims, to meet on the confines of their respective dominions, and had selected Isidora [Immalee or the Indian maid] as the temple in which their league might be hallowed, and their union consummated—and never were the opposite divinities so deliciously lodged. They forgot their ancient feuds, and agreed to dwell there forever," (*Melmoth*, p. 280).

Thus we see that many of the central conventions of Gothic fiction—the enjoyment of fear, terrible love or love terror, beauty in terror or the sublime, the Gothic hero, the savage women and nuns, incest and some of the recurrent attitudes toward religion—can be grouped and understood as paradox. Paradox, of course, is a natural result in a search for more and more intense and emotional effects. But much of the paradox of the Gothic novels, especially that of Maturin's masterpiece, does not derive from or terminate with sensationalism. Where the paradoxes are valid and exploit and reflect a truth of the mind, they execute two rather profound functions: one, a function which might be called scientific and the second, a function which might be called metaphysical. These paradoxes in one sense explore and reveal the subconscious in the important areas of sex and fear; in another sense they seek to unify experience by showing that any rational, logical attempt to analyze and distinguish the realities of experience and emotion cannot succeed fully. The Gothicists, in places at their very best, as the romantics at their best, seek to unify the world through a resolution of the opposites and disparities which exist in our attitudes towards experience. The Gothic novel—over and above its "persistent" popularity in popular forms of entertainment—involves a great, if confused, step forward in psychology, aesthetic theory, and our total approach to understanding ourselves—a step which could probably only have taken place violently in an uninhibited sensational literature such as this.

Notes

1. Aristotle, *De Sophisticus Elenchis* in vol. I of *The Complete Works of Aristotle: Translated into English,* edited by W. P. Ross, (London, 1937), paragraph 65a.

2. W. V. Quine, "Paradox," *Scientific American,* 206 (April, 1962), 96.

3. Quine, p. 84.

4. Quine, p. 88.

5. Lowry Nelson, "Night Thoughts on the Gothic Novel," *Yale Review,* LII (1956), 247.

6. Charles Robert Maturin, *Melmoth the Wanderer,* introduction by William Axton, (Lincoln, Nebraska, 1961), p. VII.

7. Nelson, p. 237.

8. (London, 1957) p. 156.

9. Quine, p. 89.

10. Percy Bysshe Shelley, "A Defense of Poetry" in vol. 7 of *The Complete Works of Percy Bysshe Shelley,* edited by Roger Ingpen and Walter E. Peck, (New York, 1930), p. 137.

Veronica M. S. Kennedy (essay date April 1969)

SOURCE: Kennedy, Veronica M. S. "Myth and the Gothic Dream: C. R. Maturin's *Melmoth the Wanderer.*" *Pacific Coast Philology* 4 (April 1969): 41-7.

[*In the following essay, Kennedy discusses the mythological aspects of Maturin's novel.*]

Melmoth the Wanderer, that macabre and haunting masterpiece of C. R. Maturin, the Dublin clergyman, had its origin, so he tells us, in a passage of one of his own sermons:

> The hint of this Romance (or Tale) was taken from a passage in one of my sermons . . . the passage is this.
>
> "At this moment is there one of us present, however we may have departed from the Lord, disobeyed his will and disregarded his word—is there one of us who would, at this moment, accept all that man could bestow, or earth afford, to resign the hope of his salvation?—No, there is not one,—not such a fool on earth, were the enemy of mankind to traverse it with the offer!"

On this passage Maturin built the vast mythic structure of his immense, interwoven novel, using elements from diverse sources, and uniting them by the force of his strange genius into a whole that staggers the mind of the reader by its uncanny closeness to the ugly dreams and nightmares that haunt the minds of unquiet sleepers. The very form of the novel, with its "Chinese Box" structure, mirrors the illogicality and shifting emphasis of the dream. Yet it is part of Maturin's triumph that the novel is clear and even orderly when one reviews it after the first breathless reading.

The elements used in the composition of *Melmoth the Wanderer* are mythical and symbolic. Maturin, who was as well-versed in the rich folk-lore of Ireland as in contemporary terror fiction and romantic poetry, made much use of traditional material in his novel. Thus, Melmoth the Wanderer himself includes touches of Zeus the Thunderer, Prometheus, the Satan of *Paradise Lost* and the Devil of folktale, of the German Faust of tradition as well as of the Faustus of Marlowe and the Faust of Goethe, of the Wandering Jew, of the Biblical and the Byronic Cain, of the other Byronic heroes—Lara,

Manfred, and the Giaour—of Mephistopheles, of Vathek, of Ruthven, of the *Bonhomme Misèr* of French folklore, of Celtic wizards, druids and demons, of the amorous and evil Genii of the *Arabian Nights,* of Don Juan and the Demon Lovers of ballad tradition as well as of the hero-villains of such "Gothick" writers as Anne Radcliffe and M. G. Lewis. Similarly, Immalee-Isadora is at once the Noble Savage of Rousseau, Eve before the Fall, Goethe's Gretchen, Melmoth's Good Angel, the Great Mother goddess in her bridal aspect, and Ideal Beauty. The Moncada brothers, Juan and Alonzo, have touches of the Archetypal Twin Gods—for example, Set and Osiris—one of whom must die. Donna Clara, in her anxiety to curb and thwart Isadora, shows traces of the traditional jealousy of the old for the young and beautiful woman; although she is Isadora's mother, she is much like the wicked stepmother or sister of myth or fairy-tale. Mythologically speaking, she is the Terrible Mother, like, for example, Kali. The themes of parricide and fratricide (albeit involuntary) echo the primeval dramas of the gods of many men: of Saturn and Cronos, and Loki and Baldur, to name but two myths. The symbols of the Night Journey and the crawling down dark passages echo the Orphic myths of death and rebirth, and there, is, overwhelmingly, the simple, archetypal contrast of darkness and light. These myths and symbols are the more effective for being set against highly realistic backgrounds. For instance, the opening chapters, describing the home of old Melmoth the Miser, and his death agony, are, though they deal with strange events and persons, extremely realistic in description; even in the inset stories there is a wealth of accurate description and historical detail that etches them sharply on the reader's mind.

Melmoth the Wanderer is a creature composed of conflicting elements. He is at once Faust and Mephistopheles, the seeker after forbidden knowledge and the tempter. An old clergyman describes him to Elinor Mortimer as the companion of Dr. Dee and "Albert Alasco", and says:

> ". . . Melmoth was irrevocably attached to the study of that art which is held in just abomination by all 'who name the name of Christ'."

At the very end, Melmoth warns John Melmoth and Moncada not to approach his death-chamber:

> ". . . Remember your lives will be the forfeit of your desperate curiosity. For the same stake I risked more than life—and lost it!—"

He speaks of himself as the devil's "agent", and he has this to say of his master:

> ". . . Enemy of mankind! . . . Alas! how absurdly is that title bestowed on the great angelic chief,—the morning star fallen from its sphere! What enemy has

man so deadly as himself? If he would ask on whom he should bestow that title aright, let him smite his bosom, and his heart will answer,—Bestow it here!"

Here, he seems to embody the favorite Romantic mythic hero, the Solitary who is self-sufficient to damn or to save. But he never succeeds in his principal quest; no one will exchange destinies with the Wanderer:

> "*. . . I have traversed the world in the search, and no one, to gain that world, would lose his own soul! . . .*"

In his destructive but insatiable search for knowledge at whatever cost, Melmoth is like Beckford's Promethean, but evil, Vathek, or Byron's Manfred; but he is closest to the figure of Faust, a powerful mythic figure of Renaissance as well as of Romantic literature. Melmoth, however, has in him many traces of other archetypal figures. He is the Demon Lover of the ballads and of *Kubla Khan,* and at times he almost approaches Don Juan, or that man who invented or perhaps lived his own myth, Casanova—himself, significantly enough, one who dabbled in Satanism and magic. The Wanderer even describes the end of Don Juan, when the devil carried him down to Hell. Don Juan, Faustus, Prometheus and the Wanderer all have spectacular and in some sense demoniac ends, appropriate to those who have dared to challenge the secret knowledge or the amorous prowess, the peculiarly divine powers of the gods. Melmoth tells John and Moncada what his particular fate in the afterworld may be:

> ". . . When a meteor blazes in the atmosphere—when a comet pursues its burning path towards the sun—look up, and perhaps you may think of the spirit condemned to guide the blazing and erratic orb. . . ."

Like innumerable beings and objects in ancient myth (the nymph Callisto and the ship Argo, for example) Melmoth the Wanderer will have a place in the physical heavens that will forever symbolize his earthly transgressions and character.

The Wanderer has magnetic, blazing eyes; Moncada says: "I had never beheld such eyes blazing in a mortal face." Further, we are told that "the burning intelligence of his eyes, . . . seemed like the fires of a volcano." Milton's Satan has extraordinarily brilliant eyes, and the eighteenth-century interest in Mesmer and Animal Magnetism influenced the bestowal of this trait on Gothic and Romantic hero-villains, as did the existence in real life of such bizarre creatures as Count Cagliostro. A fatal hypnotic power in the eyes is like that traditionally ascribed to the vampire; Polidori's Ruthven, who exerts a fatal fascination over beautiful young women, has this quality. Such burning eyes are attributes of many Gothic villains—Lewis's Ambrosio, Anne Radcliffe's Schedoni and Montoni, and Maturin's own Schemoli, for instance. The trait is preserved in such Victorian Gothic villains as Dickens' Bradley Headstone, and reaches, perhaps, its final nineteenth-century mythic embodiment in Bram Stoker's Dracula. Thence the mythic trait passed into that twentieth-century repository of popular myth, the film, reaching visual definition in the eerie virtuosity of the late Bela Lugosi. This suggests that Maturin indeed created a truly haunting mythic figure in his Wanderer, of the burning, tormented eyes, and the ". . . deep-toned voice, . . . like the toll of a strong but muffled bell."

Yet Melmoth is also the Wandering Jew, the mysterious figure who appeared so strangely in the chronicles of mediaeval Europe, and who, with such terrifying effect, symbolizes death or the death-wish in Chaucer's *Pardoner's Tale*. In the Wandering Jew we have a figure of myth and pseudo-history—more "real" to us than the Plague Maiden, less "real" perhaps than the mysterious "Master of Hungary" who preached the Shepherds' Crusade—who as a cursed, outcast wanderer exerts a mythic power over successive imaginations. Like Chaucer's strange shrouded old man, Melmoth the Wanderer looks for, yet doubts that he will find, death. He says: "Leave me, I must be alone for the few last hours of my mortal existence—if indeed they are to be the last." The horror of the undying life—of Tithonus and of the Struldbrugs—is one of the most potent and terrifying of mythic concepts.

Like Schiller's mysterious Armenian, and the witches and warlocks of medieval and later folklore, including such historical personages as Owen Glendower and Graeme of Claverhouse, Melmoth the Wanderer is invulnerable:

> ". . . I go accursed of every human heart, yet untouched by one human hand!"—as he retired slowly, the murmur of suppressed but instinctive and irrepressible horror and hatred burst from the group. He passed on, scowling at them like a lion on a pack of bayed hounds, and departed unmolested—unassayed—no weapon was drawn—no arm was lifted—the mark was on his brow—and those who could read it knew that all human power was alike forceless and needless,—and those who could not succumbed in passive horror. Every sword was in its sheath. "Leave him to God!"— was the universal exclamation.

Melmoth is like Cain and the Wandering Jew, branded with God's seal, invulnerable, but causing universal abhorrence. He bears the mark of God's anger but he has the invulnerability that was one of the temptations offered by Mephistopheles to Faust, and that has been the constant dream of those who sought to control supernatural and elemental forces by magic art. As Dr. Maud Bodkin has pointed out, wanderers—Melmoth, the Wandering Jew, Cain, the Ancient Mariner, the Flying Dutchman, Captain Ahab—are modern mythic figures who express that "haunting and inexpiable guilt which

may terrify the mind in dreams." The figure of the mythic, immortal wanderer is, as she says, most poignant:

> How should it fail to serve as a symbol, and to find echo in the emotional life of the individual whose consciousness of lonely frustrations and personal mortality wars with his impersonal vision of a vast inheritance and far reaching destiny?

As a lover, besides being, as Maturin himself says, a Zeus to Immalee's Semele, Melmoth is mocking and satiric. He tells Immalee of the follies and vices of the civilized world, not with any intention of warning her against them but to corrupt her innocent, Miranda-like delight in humanity. Indeed, in his role of lover Melmoth is especially repellent: "Beauty was a flower he looked on only to scorn, and touched only to wither." He makes the cynical remark to his victim that he is ". . . commissioned to trample and to bruise every flower in the natural and moral world—hyacinths, hearts, and bagatelles of that kind, . . ." He uses his hypnotic eyes to conquer Immalee and tells her:

> "I rivetted your eye—I transfixed your slender frame as with a flash of lightening—you fell fainting and withered under my burning glance."

Here he is the true Demon Lover; he is much like Hades when he took Persephone in the Vale of Enna.

He has other demoniac qualities. Melmoth says: "*I cannot weep.*" Traditionally one of the distinguishing marks of a demon in human form, of a witch, or of a warlock is an inability to weep, at any rate more than three tears, even under the most frightful torments. When the Wanderer rushes into Walberg's house it is like the visitation of a spirit: "A figure seemed to rush past . . . and enter the house like a shadow." So like is he to a demon or to the Angel of Death that Fra Jose expects him to appear in the cell of Isadora during a frightful storm, when, of course, devils were thought to ride the blast, herding the spirits of the damned in the Wild Hunt. But the Wanderer is a man, not a demon, in spite of his ability to pass through barriers, and to traverse rapidly immense distances. These special powers were offered to Faustus, and are part, as those who know the witch scenes in *Macbeth* always remember, of the powers traditionally attributed to witches and warlocks in that extensive mythology that grew out of and clustered round the cult of witchcraft. Melmoth's crime is that human one of rejecting salvation and his end is "the classic end of those who are possessed of the devil." Indeed, his end is impressively horrible. It is a variation of the fate of Ambrosio in *The Monk*, but Maturin handles it with an artistry that Lewis lacked. After a night of hideous sounds, quiet falls on the deserted house where Melmoth has returned to meet his fate. Young Melmoth and Alonzo Moncada, who have listened in horror to the onslaughts of the devil, go out on a cliff that overhangs the ocean:

> Through the furze that clothed this rock, almost to its summit, there was a kind of tract as if a person had dragged, or been dragged, his way through it—a down-trodden track, over which no footsteps but those of one impelled by force had ever passed. Melmoth and Moncada gained at last the summit of the rock. The ocean was beneath—the wide, waste, engulping ocean! On a crag beneath them, something hung as floating to the blast. Melmoth clambered down and caught it. It was the handkerchief which the Wanderer had worn about his neck the preceding night—that was the last trace of the Wanderer!

How much more effective is this disappearance of the Wanderer into the ocean, with only the traces of his last, terrible journey visible, than is the end of Ambrosio, whom the devil actually lifts up and dashes on to rocks—a scene that is fully described by Lewis. Maturin's implication is at once more horrible by far than Lewis's explicit narration and more truly mythical. The Wanderer is a Hero whose final end is left classically mysterious—like the end of Oedipus, for example—and also classically, ambiguously symbolic. As myth or symbol the sea is always ambivalent, equivocal, being at once birth and death. The end of the Wanderer, then, seems to hint at the possibility of a return and of a renewal of the cycle. Maturin's romance ends with the dream quality of agonizing repetition.

Maturin, like Blake's Milton, seems to have been "of the devil's party." In creating the powerful mythic figure of the Wanderer, he surrounded him with a group of lesser personages, most of whom are, to some extent, also symbolic, but he neglected to make the figure of Immalee-Isadora strong enough to provide a polarity of good in the romance as a whole. In depicting Immalee, Maturin used some interesting mythical touches. She lives innocent, wreathed in flowers, a gentle virgin goddess, worshipped by the young and the gentle, in what was once a temple to the terrible Kali herself. Maturin tells us that "her innocence made her fearless" and seems to be hinting at the medieval belief in the power of the virgin to tame the unicorn, an idea that might possibly have come to him by way of Milton's *Comus*. Yet Immalee innocently offers herself sexually to Melmoth. Here Maturin seems to suggest that she embodies the innocent sexuality of Milton's Eve before the Fall. Even after her corruption, when she bears the Wanderer's child and is dying as Isadora in the dungeons of the Inquisition, she loves the Wanderer with a constancy totally undeserved by him. Her last words are a cry that suggests Paradise will be wretched without him. Yet Maturin's symbol of Good in the Romance is too weak, so that, in spite of his use of the imagery of darkness and light to support the mythical implications of Immalee and the Wanderer, and in spite of the ultimate end of Melmoth, the emphasis of the work is thrown on to evil Darkness is made more striking than light; Maturin is indeed, as Lautréamont called him, "le Compère-des-Ténèbres."

As for the other, lesser personages of the novel, they, too, are mythic or symbolic. Their actions are often expressions of the subconscious desires of men. The parricide, for example, has actually realized the Oedipal dream of killing his father. Walberg's hatred of his father, though it develops only after famine has reduced the family almost to desperation, also reflects the Oedipus theme. Alonzo Moncada brings about the death of his brother; like many pairs of twin gods and demi-gods in many mythologies, they slay and are slain. Young Melmoth reembodies the Wanderer in youth, already interesting himself in the forbidden knowledge that would lead him to destruction. Thus, the powerful mythic motif of fatal curiosity—like that of Prometheus, Pandora, Psyche, Bluebeard's Wife—recurs, even though, for Young Melmoth, the catastrophe is averted. The close guardianship of Isadora by her mother suggests at once the theme of the jealousy of the older beauty for her young rival—that of Venus for Psyche, for example—and the ancient theme of the guarded princess. Like Danae or Rhea Sylvia or Rapunzel, Isadora must be reached in secret and with great difficulty. These few instances show that the romance is indeed a complicated texture of myth, symbol, and folklore.

Some other archetypal patterns also occur in the novel. The many night journeys and the passing through underground passages symbolize death and rebirth, and suggest the recurring imagery of nightmares. For Maturin's creatures, the night journey often ends in terror; their rebirths are births to new horror. The motif of love-in-death also occurs frequently throughout the romance. The loves of Immalee for the Wanderer, of Margaret and John Sandal, of Elinor Mortimer for John Sandal are all fully realized only in death. The guilty love of Moncada's parents results in the death of one of their sons and the exile—a life-in-death—of the other. The parricide's sister and her husband die in hideous circumstances because of their love. Even the miser's sublimation of his lusts into lust for gold is rewarded only by death. Death himself seems to be one of the persons of the novel.

Maturin uses the stock Romantic and Gothic motif of ruins with particularly striking effects. He draws from them the usual Romantic ideas: awe at their size, regret for vanished glory, presentiments that this age will soon decay and fall into ruins. But they also serve as "objects in a landscape," as objects that are terrifying in themselves. They have the visual and mythical menace of the Dark Tower and are part of the strange, almost animistic universe of Maturin, where passions are like the sea and clouds are like banner-bearing armies.

The imagery of the novel contributes largely to its symbolic and mythic meaning, as well as to the dream-like ambience of suffering and horror that surrounds the Wanderer. Much of the mythical potency of Maturin's writing lies in the imagery as well as in the events and personages of the romance. The roughest classification of Maturin's imagery reveals a definite scheme: images of death, beasts, the sea, storms, seafaring, shipwreck, supernatural beings, light, darkness, and physical suffering preponderate in the novel. References to "devouring," "rending," "overwhelming," "engulfing," abound in the images and tropes of the work. The effect of such a choice of imagery is obvious: it reinforces the impression of the Wanderer as a superhuman creature, almost one with the most powerful and destructive forces of nature, with the raging sea, with the fiercest beasts, and with the most cruel and destructive traits of man.

What, then, does Melmoth the Wanderer stand for? He symbolizes the longing of man for knowledge, for power, for longevity—the longing to surpass the ordinary powers and status of man. He unites in one figure the Sage, the Tempter, the Lover, and the Magus. He is the Dark Hero, but he is also a kind of superhuman being with Promethean qualities. He has some of the fatal interest of Lucifer, the charm of the damned and reckless soul, the fascination of the magnificently evil figure. He is truly the symbol of those larger aspirations of man that so often lead him to destruction, but might so easily lead him to glory. Appropriately, then, Melmoth is the center of a romance that partakes of the shifting menace and sometimes confused mythology of the world of dreams. In this ambivalent world one may be at once child and adult, innocent and guilty, pursued and pursuer. Maturin's mythical representative of humanity is presented in a dream world that is at once peculiarly characteristic of a certain period style—that of the Gothic romance—and at the same time is archetypal, therefore universal. Maturin's Gothic dream is thus a valid mythic presentation of the human predicament.

Dale Kramer (essay date 1973)

SOURCE: Kramer, Dale. "The Early Novels: *Fatal Revenge; or, the Family of Montorio* (1807)." In *Charles Robert Maturin,* pp. 26-38. New York: Twayne Publishers, 1973.

[*In the following essay, Kramer examines Gothic elements in Maturin's early fiction.*]

Maturin named his first novel **The Family of Montorio**; but, much to his irritation, his publisher imposed the more compelling title **Fatal Revenge,** by which the novel is generally known. Fully aware that the evangelical-minded Anglican church of Ireland would not smile on a clergyman's appealing for public favor as the author of a sensational novel, Maturin published the book under the pseudonym of Dennis Jasper Mur-

phy and at his own expense. Though the book has much effective language, it came too late after the novels it imitated to enjoy success. Nine years later, there were still forty copies unsold.[1]

Fatal Revenge is the most starkly Gothic in the joint traditions of Radcliffe and Lewis of any of Maturin's novels; **Melmoth the Wanderer** offers greater variety of mood. Lewis' influence is responsible for the detailed descriptions of revolting physical actions, machinations of witches, and conventual tombs in which drugged women are placed. Radcliffe furnishes the stronger formal influence; the denouement of **Fatal Revenge** reveals that most of the revolting details and all of the seemingly supernatural occurrences have been charades. Moreover, the management of the plot and the characters, especially the "frame" story and the mysterious, ultimately explained motivations of the monkish antagonist, are taken directly from *The Italian,* Radcliffe's finest novel. But, while no one can overlook the imitative qualities of Maturin's two Gothic novels—indeed, the imitative qualities of all of Maturin's works—the degree of their permanent interest relies not on what they borrow but on what they contribute. Maturin's originality in **Fatal Revenge** stems indirectly but inevitably from his interest in the nature of religious experience.

In the novel's preface, Maturin traces "*the fear arising from objects of invisible terror. . . . to a high and obvious source*" (italics Maturin's). Maturin may in part be defending himself against the irritation of the reader when he learns that the seemingly supernatural events of the story can be rationally explained. But, more pertinently, he is defending the plausibility of his characters' susceptibility to supernatural suggestions. Since the particular supernatural suggestion that the novel deals with is the obligation of two sons to murder their own father, the preface is essential to the rhetorical foundation of the novel. For example, one of the sons reflects late in his unwilling journey toward parricide that it is impious to contend with a spirit (the monk Schemoli) who can predict events accurately and who knows family secrets.

One of Maturin's best recent critics believes that Maturin's preface is simply a definition of the Gothic romance,[2] but the preface connotes broader matters. In most traditional Gothic romances, the heroes and heroines react straitlacedly in conventionally approved ways to unconventional situations. Horror arises from external threats, and little is learned about the characters' motivations—no more about the gentle Emily of *Udolpho* than about Lewis' Don Raymond or Lorenzo. In Maturin, on the other hand, the major characters react individually to unconventional situations. While the novel as a story remains absurd, the treatment of personality has elements of permanent interest.

Without being able to draw upon clinical psychology for confirmation of his insights, Maturin nevertheless attempts to define certain personality types susceptible to religious promptings capable of being perverted into areligious activity. Ippolito and Annibal, the brothers, are quite different psychological types: Ippolito customarily acts from impulse; Annibal, from conviction. They are in similar conditions, but Annibal is in the more critical and dangerous frame of mind. Impulse is more variable than conviction; Ippolito, therefore, has a built-in protection (his great agitations) from the horror of the deed he is made to contemplate: "Ippolito's emotions were vehement, [but] his mind was more disengaged than his brother's."

As an illustration of the classic form of the Radcliffean plot, it might be helpful to sketch the actions of the story. To do so distorts the effect of the novel even more than most summaries do. *Fatal Revenge* has such a complicated plot that Edith Birkhead says that many of the novel's readers "wander, bewildered, baffled, and distracted through labyrinthe mazes."[3] Although some of the hidden facts are revealed by obvious hints, the entire outline of events is made clear only by a long confessional letter late in the third volume, written by the monk Schemoli while under sentence of death. He has ingeniously plotted the death of his brother, the Count of Montorio. The following four paragraphs give the gist of that letter.

Schemoli's real name is Orazio Montorio, and as the elder brother he had held the title of count until his reported death some twenty years before the time of the novel's action. While a count, Orazio had married a reluctant Erminia di Amaldi. She was already secretly married to a cavalier, Verdoni; but she believed he had been killed by banditti and obeyed her worldly father's command to remain quiet about her child and to marry the wealthy Count Orazio. Shortly after the marriage, Verdoni, who had been held captive by the bandits, escaped and returned to find his wife remarried and the mother of Orazio's two sons. Deeply saddened, he planned to leave Italy forever; and Erminia, once she discovered Verdoni was still alive, intended to enter a convent after the birth of the child she was carrying.

In the meantime, though, she confessed her situation to Orazio's brother, an unfortunate choice for a confidant; for he was jealous of his brother's wealth and title, he had been a spurned lover of Erminia before she married Orazio, and he had an ambitious wife, Zenobia. (The scenes between Montorio and Zenobia are built upon the *Macbeth* motif of a vacillating husband and a ruthless wife.) The brother cleverly led Orazio to believe that his wife was unfaithful to him, a falsehood made easier to impart because Orazio had already felt that Erminia's lack of physical ardor meant that she did not love him. When Orazio saw Verdoni caressing a child

that he was told was Erminia's his impulsive and vindictive nature drove him to prompt and mad action. He dragged Verdoni along a secret passageway to his wife's chambers in the Castle of Muralto. Refusing to listen to an explanation from Erminia, he had Verdoni stabbed slowly to death before her eyes. Upon Verdoni's death, Erminia's "heart burst," and she too died.

Orazio dashed away, indifferent to his worldly condition, and took up residence on an abandoned island near Greece, where he lived "a strange kind of animal life." A murderer in his brother's employ pursued him there, but Orazio anticipated the assault on his life and destroyed the assassin. Orazio read letters to the murderer from the present Count Montorio which proved Erminia's and Verdoni's innocence and his own brother's culpability; and he also learned through the letters that his two sons were dead. He decided that fit revenge would be to have Montorio die, and, to be certain that Montorio's descendants will not benefit by his infamy, he must be killed by his own sons.

Upon thinking of this scheme, typical of unspeakable Gothic villainy, Orazio ceased to be mad and wandered in Asia Minor fifteen years, learning occult secrets and increasing his physical powers. He eventually assumed the garb of a monk. Having decided that superstition was his only aid, he studied the "human character in its fiercer and gloomier features," in order to see how superstition, by exercise of art and terror, might best impel the passions to extremes. Prepared then to wreak his terrible vengeance, he became confessor to the Montorio family, keeping his face hidden with his cowl. At this point in time, the novel proper opens in the first volume, with Orazio's machinations against the sons of the fraudulent Count Montorio.

The two sons, Annibal and Ippolito, are both interested in "dark pursuits" and in manifestations of the supernatural, and both are courageous in facing the physical danger into which their curiosity leads them. But the brothers differ sharply in their attitudes toward life and the nature of experience. Ippolito, the elder, has excellent qualities but is a libertine; he is a lover of heroic adventure and a credulous lover of the "marvellous"— the striking and brilliant effects that give to the senses evidence of supernatural forces at work in the immediate world. Since Orazio has acutely diagnosed each of his nephews to know how to persuade them to believe that their murder of their father is an inevitable act willed by spiritual forces, to attract Ippolito he manipulates disappearances and appearances, and he hires a coven of "witches" who perform rites in a vault below the streets of a bustling Naples. The younger brother, Annibal, is a moody and distrustful youth who Orazio-Schemoli believes would at once see through the fantastical contrivings he employs against Ippolito, but who would be susceptible to suggestion. With Annibal, then, Schemoli uses less sensational, more curiosity-provoking situations to make him believe that uneasy spirits still move on the earth. The story of Annibal's seduction to murder involves hidden staircases, a skeleton in a chest, a tomb (Orazio's) without a corpse, and a servant afraid to reveal to Annibal certain secrets of the house of Montorio.

The first three-quarters of the novel is taken up with the brothers' separate courses to parricide, and the reader is unaware of Schemoli's motivations. Ippolito lives in Naples; Annibal, with their parents at the Castle of Muralto; and they do not meet in the novel until shortly before they kill their father. Their tales are given in alternating chapters, initially in letters written by the brothers to each other, then by omniscient narration. The more complicated course, Ippolito's, is initiated by mysterious questions and commands of a stranger while Ippolito is getting out of cabs or while he is enjoying his dissipations, and by letters left in his rooms. (Ippolito does not know the stranger is his father's confessor Schemoli.) A conflict is set up between this stranger and a youth named Cyprian, who becomes Ippolito's servant and who attempts to keep Ippolito from his scenes of former dissipation by using *"female blandishments"* (italics are Maturin's). (The end of the novel reveals that Cyprian is a nun who fell in love with Ippolito by sight and left her convent in order to live near him. She eventually dies of the effects of suppressing her passion.)

Cyprian's influence, however, is ineffective; Ippolito shortly begins to have midnight assignations with the stranger. Having prepared Ippolito by telling him that he is doomed to commit a horrible crime, the stranger takes him to a subterranean chamber where his fate will supposedly be revealed to him after he has killed a strapped-down figure. Driven by the temptation that he will thereby be raised out of the ordinary nature of humanity, Ippolito "almost without consciousness" stabs the victim, who, when uncovered, resembles Ippolito's father, but is in fact only an ingeniously constructed dummy. Believing he has actually killed someone, and in horror at the evident thought that this murder somehow spiritually presages the death of his father, Ippolito flees Naples and wanders in the countryside. His reputation for dealing with shameful mysteries has preceded him, and he finds it difficult to locate lodgings and impossible to escape his thoughts.

When the stranger appears suddenly one day and asks, "Why do you linger here?" Ippolito pursues him and eventually descends a deep, winding staircase to one of the most elaborate systems of underground passageways in Gothic fiction. After stumbling on rags and human bones, he sees the stranger coming up to him through the "thick vapours of the vault." The stranger says that Ippolito will do the deed that he must do in three months. The stranger then moves off with his customary, incredible speed, and Ippolito follows in search of him through immensely long corridors. He eventually spies him and a monk carrying a figure in white; the stranger leaves, and the monk prepares to stab the figure in white. Ippolito frightens him off and takes the figure, an unconscious female, into the open air of a convent garden where she revives. He discovers that she is in love with his brother Annibal. Preparing to flee by boat with her, he is borne off by the river suddenly agitated by an earthquake, leaving her on the bank and presuming her to be killed by the turbulence. Ippolito is then arrested by the Inquisition. Another earthquake frees Ippolito from the prison, and he attempts to flee on a boat bound to Sicily; but, as the stranger had predicted, the ocean, in the form of a volcanic eruption that destroys the ship, throws him back on the shore. Only Ippolito of all those on the boat survives, and once on the shore he finds the stranger waiting for him. Worn down by strain and superstitious apprehension, Ippolito thereupon surrenders his will to the stranger.

All the while that Ippolito has been drawing out Schemoli's theatricalness and the accidents of nature, Annibal has been prying into the secrets of the Castle of Muralto. Annibal has learned that an old family servant, Michelo, knows some family secrets; and, when the servant tells him that he had been in the former Count's dark tomb and had felt a cold bony hand touch his face, Annibal eagerly decides to explore the matter. He first examines the shut-up apartments that had served as the bridal suite of Orazio, which the present Count had ordered closed forever. (A set of closed apartments, where a dark deed has occurred or where ghosts walk, is a standard setting in a Gothic novel.) On the first visit, Annibal falls in love with a portrait of the Countess Erminia, whom he feels is still alive.

On a second visit, Annibal hears a ghostly voice and sees an eye in a tapestry appear to look from side to side and finally to glare at a particular spot on a wall (a standard Radcliffean device). Struck with amazement and fear, Annibal tears off part of the wainscoting and descends a passage the wall had blocked off. He finds a plastered-over door; and, within a chamber behind the door, he finds a chest containing a skeleton, whose hand had been severed from the arm. He thinks it might be Count Orazio, killed on "that terrible night" that Michelo has vaguely alluded to. (The skeleton is actually that of Verdoni, of course.) Annibal thereupon decides to watch the tomb of Orazio, for there human agents may be at work, and they are less fearful than the evidently genuine ghost of the tapestry (who is, naturally, Schemoli, standing behind the tapestry and looking out through holes he had cut.) What happens at the tomb, however, is that Michelo disappears when Annibal leaves him briefly to pursue a pale, large figure; and, when they meet again, Michelo is in a "prophetic ecstasy," speaking of "woe" and of the necessity that the house of Montorio fall. He claims he is being controlled by someone not alive; the being had lain in Count Orazio's coffin, but what he said to Michelo is lost because Michelo dies just as he is about to relate this most crucial point.

Filippo, Michelo's nephew, tells Annibal of figures, one in monk's habit, that he has seen down a "secret" corridor, and the two decide to search the castle. They discover that the skeleton is no longer in the closed-off apartments, and Annibal is apprehended by the present Count Montorio and Schemoli, who lock him in a dusty room for several days, where a gloomy Schemoli visits him once a day. Ultimately, Schemoli concocts the confession that his was the skeleton Annibal had found, that his spirit has been imprisoned in the body of a man dead for two thousand years, and that he is forced to live on, conscious of the ways of the dead, until his murderer is killed. Annibal is proud of talking with spirits; and, Faust-like, he swears allegiance to Schemoli if Schemoli will tell him secrets of the dead. He nonetheless shrinks from Schemoli's revelation that he, Annibal, is the one chosen to avenge his, Schemoli's, murder; and that the one he must kill is his own father, whose guilty demeanor he had long suspected.

Dismayed by the results of his curiosity, and longing for normal happiness, Annibal escapes from Muralto with the aid of Filippo and goes to the countryside seeking peace and quiet. A religious procession with relics attracts him, and he sees a novitiate who resembles the portrait of the Countess Erminia. He saves her life when an earthquake causes a river to flood and learns that her name is Ildefonsa (supposedly of illegitimate birth, she is actually the daughter of Erminia and Verdoni, a fact not given until Schemoli's confession). The two communicate through notes dropped in flowers, and Ildefonsa eventually agrees to trust herself to his sense of honor and to flee with him at the first opportunity. Schemoli appears on the scene in the role of Catholic persecutor of reluctant novitiates, and he gives to Ildefonsa a drug that causes a deathlike state. At this point, Ippolito saves Ildefonsa from the monk's dagger and is separated from her by the agitation of the river. When Annibal and Ildefonsa are reunited, they reside with Filippo in the forest for some time. Trying to reach Puzzoli and safety, they are misled by their guide and waylaid. Filippo is killed, and Annibal and Ildefonsa taken captive and separated. Schemoli's prediction is fulfilled: the object of Annibal's love had been taken from him "at the moment of possession, and life had changed its complexion at the moment it was becoming bright with hope and joy." Like Ippolito only two days before, Annibal gives his will to Schemoli.

They go separately to Muralto, where Annibal finds Ildefonsa dying of poison administered by the countess, whose jealousy of Erminia had been reawakened by her husband's dressing Erminia's daughter in elaborate gowns in memory of his early love. On the night planned for the murder of the Count, the conscience-and-fear-wracked Count Montorio confesses to Schemoli that he had kept one fact from him. To make a partial reparation to his betrayed sister-in-law and his brother, he had taken their two sons and reared them as his own to inherit the title at his death, and he had propagated the false rumor that Orazio's sons had died. The agonized Schemoli tries to halt the brothers on their way to Montorio's chambers; but, stupefied, they do not notice his speechless contortions, and they walk by him to their "inevitable doom." Their "swords met in their father's body."

Deeply contrite, Schemoli confesses his deed and writes the account of his life given at the opening of this plot summary. He dies of a broken blood vessel just before his scheduled execution. His dying exultation is that "The last of the Montorios has not perished on a scaffold"—a vainglorious assertion of Gothic pride in noble villainy already used by Schedoni in Radcliffe's *The Italian* and used again by Maturin in **Bertram.** The brothers, broken in spirit and exiled, become army officers and successfully seek death at the siege of Barcelona in 1697.

As difficult as it may be to follow the paraphrase above, the entire plot of **Fatal Revenge** is vastly more complex and colorful than any summation could suggest. Not only does my paraphrase give in chronological order what the novel presents through a series of flashbacks, but there are several digressive stories, the most successful of which is the suspense-filled account of Filippo's escape from an assassin hired by the fraudulent Count Montorio, who is afraid that Filippo may know too much about the skeleton in the passageway. The pace and organization of this story lead us to suspect that Maturin's best genre may be the vignette, not the novel—a suspicion confirmed by the multiple stories that make up **Melmoth the Wanderer.**

In addition to illustrating the nature of a Gothic story, the paraphrase suggests other features of Gothic esthetics; most relevant are Schemoli's activities. He always moves with fantastic speed (Ippolito on a galloping horse cannot keep sight of him), and he enters the prison of the Inquisition to visit Ippolito in his cell. As his confession makes clear, he has no truly supernatural powers, only great physical endurance and the tricks he learned in Asia Minor—not to mention cleverness. But Maturin does not permit human limitations to restrict Schemoli's activities significantly. The necessity to keep the two temptations going simultaneously, often at a fever pitch, has Orazio dashing from Ildefonsa's convent to the areas of Ippolito's wandering, back to the convent to prepare for Ildefonsa's opiate-induced "death," and from there to entice Ippolito to enter the subterranean passageway, and finally, back again to the convent's underground cemetery to arrange for Ildefonsa's murder.

In the earlier part of the book, the simultaneous temptations of Annibal and Ippolito are somewhat more acceptable; but even here Orazio's efficiency precludes total plausibility. He is, at the same general span of time, accustomed each night to visit (1) Ippolito in Naples, (2) the imprisoned Annibal in Muralto, and (3) the tomb of Erminia, where he penitentially bleeds himself; and he also often visits at night the closed-off apartments that he had once shared with Erminia. Finally, there is no adequate explanation of how Schemoli managed to be at the precise point of the shoreline where Ippolito washed ashore after the eruption of an undersea volcano had destroyed the boat he was on.

Ernest Baker says that Orazio "embodies traits of the Wandering Jew from Godwin's *St. Leon* and Lewis' *Monk*"[4]; but, more essentially, Orazio conforms to the Radcliffean concept of a mere human villain whose supernatural appearance is deceptive. The inconsistencies and the incredible simultaneous actions, though they are more grossly employed in *Fatal Revenge* than is customary, are a natural result of the Gothicists' obsession with the immediate effect of a scene or atmosphere. The idea that readers might want a clear time scheme and plausible relationships among actions seldom occurred to Gothic novelists.

The love affairs in the novel also follow Gothic precedents in their basic conceptions. Cyprian, as a nun who flees her convent for love, comes from *The Monk*; and Ildefonsa's treatment as a novice at the hands of Schemoli and her Abbess is not only standard Gothic fare but anticipates Maturin's subsequently more virulent portrayals of the unnaturalness of conventual life. Annibal's falling in love with his half-sister is a tired bit of Gothicism that Maturin does not know what to do with; by the time Annibal learns of his relationship, he is more depressed by the thought of his guilt for murder than by the "horrors of *incest*."

As I have said, *Fatal Revenge* is a Radcliffean romance in that all of the seeming supernaturalness is explained in a rush toward the end of the novel by Schemoli's confessional letter. But there is one feature to the ending of *Fatal Revenge* that is unlike that of Radcliffe's *Mysteries of Udolpho* or *The Italian*. In *Udolpho,* the revelations toward the end of the novel of the real causes of mysterious circumstances have no effect upon the basic structural balance of the novel. Emily has throughout the novel been the main object of attention; she remains such during the revelations, which are fairly brief. In *The Italian,* Schedoni and Vivaldi had shared the primary interest, and both are actors in the scenes of revelation. In *Fatal Revenge,* on the other hand, the revelations cause a total *volte-face* of reader concern. Until the last quarter of the last volume, the main interest has been in the two brothers and in the self-delusive and perverse manner in which they individually allow themselves to be psychologically coerced into committing one of the greatest of social crimes. The progress of each may be redundant of the other's—for example, each regrets his thoughtless early interest in supernaturalism, each surrenders to Schemoli when a prediction comes true, each is helped or hindered by earthquakes miraculously local in effect; and Maturin may be obtrusive in marking out for the reader each of the several stages in the brothers' progress. But, during the individual stages, Maturin traces with insight and expository skill the feelings of the brothers as they attempt to learn whether they can escape from Schemoli's predictions that they will of necessity kill their own father. With the advent of the Radcliffean confession of Schemoli, the structure that has held together organically for some twelve hundred and fifty pages is thrust aside.

This violation of structural consistency has some potential for meaningful variety, but unfortunately such variety is not forthcoming. Orazio is a powerfully passionate figure, and he is an energetic schemer against the brothers; but as a repentant, magnificently suffering jealous husband and murderer, he is dull, prolix, and self-consciously posturing. By the time he reveals himself, we have already seen the complexity of the brothers' developing feelings; and, in comparison to those, Orazio's agonizings seem sudden and insufficiently prepared for. His erratic behavior and rumored cruelty when he had been Count are never explained; neither motivation nor natural malice is adduced to support his actions—only that he is "Italian." Later, in carrying out his scheme for revenge, he simply does what the occasion calls for in order to make the action more sensational. Like Ippolito, he is impulsive; but he never reflects in the least, whereas Ippolito withholds himself from any immediate commitment to the idea that he must do murder. Orazio's short-lived inner moral tensions have not the nearest degree of interest to those of the brothers, whose inclinations to the darker sides of experience are leavened by manliness, morality, and integrity. Part of the cause of the slackness of Orazio's characterization probably derives from Maturin's assumption that lovers of Gothicism would transfer to Orazio-Schemoli the fully motivated attributes of Ann Radcliffe's Schedoni. And, indeed, reading in sequence *The Italian* and *Fatal Revenge* makes Schemoli more impressive; but reading Radcliffe is no way to evaluate the skill of Maturin.

Most critics of Maturin have not evaluated *Fatal Revenge* as I have; indeed, some have found Schemoli's confession the most engrossing part of the entire three volumes.[5] Their preference is based on the force and vigor of Orazio's language, which Walter Scott illustrates with the following passage describing Orazio's state of mind during his flight following Erminia's death:

> My reason was not suspended, it was totally *changed*. I had become a kind of intellectual savage; a being, that with the malignity and depravation of inferior natures, still retains the reason of a man, and retains it only for his curse. Oh! that midnight darkness of the soul, in which it seeks for something whose loss has carried away every sense but one of utter and desolate privation; in which it traverses leagues in motion and worlds in thought, without consciousness of relief, yet with a dread of pausing. I had nothing to seek, nothing to recover; the whole world could not restore me an atom, could not shew me again a glimpse of what I had been or lost; yet I rushed on as if the next step would reach shelter and peace.

Another point concerning Orazio's story is made by Idman: "The progress of the violent action is admirably concentrated, and the rapidity and poignancy of the style is powerfully indicative of the anguish felt by the writer." But these are not qualities of Orazio's story alone. As I say above, Maturin writes well in short bursts, and Orazio's story is only one hundred and thirty-two pages long in the large-print, generously margined first edition. Other short sections, such as Ippolito pursuing Schemoli and saving Ildefonsa in the subterranean chapters, are equally "concentrated" and are even more relevant to Maturin's basic interest, the spirit of religion. The kind of passage admired by Scott is not found only in the concluding confession; for Ippolito, Annibal, even Montorio and Zenobia speak in comparably intense language, though perhaps not with the energy of Orazio in his despair. (One suspects, especially in light of *Melmoth the Wanderer,* that Maturin identifies more with the characters with the bleaker souls than with the comparatively more innocent characters. This self-identification may help to explain Maturin's neglecting to delineate Orazio's motivations more objectively.)

Maturin's language, while verbose and somewhat derivative in imagery, has an impetus and imaginative life. Indeed, it is ironic that the basic structural lesion in the novel develops partially from the effectiveness of the language. The linguistic quality of Ippolito's and Annibal's mental plights creates strong interest in the two young men, while a contradictory sympathy—for the cause of the brothers' miseries—is created by the novel's concluding emphasis upon Orazio-Schemoli. The disparate natures of the two sections—the finely traced motivations of Ippolito and Annibal, and the straightforward destructiveness of Orazio-Schemoli—are not absorbed into a uniform esthetic experience.

Despite the ill effect of the abrupt change in the center of interest, Maturin took considerable pains in planning the novel. With the possible exception of the laboriously historical *The Albigenses,* no other Maturin novel was so carefully contrived before its writing. The alternation of the early chapters between Annibal and Ippolito, though blatant and rather ridiculous in that Ippolito keeps scoffing Annibal's childishness when *he* has *serious* ghosts to contend with, provides a good example of Maturin's consciously structuring the novel. At the end of the first volume he quite skillfully pulls the two skeins together so that they begin to run simultaneously. Also, Maturin's delaying the appearance of Count Montorio and the monk Schemoli (in his "own" person) until after there have been three hundred and twenty pages of hints about their centrality to Annibal's and Ippolito's problems increases the suspense both about them and about the activities of Montorio's "sons." *Fatal Revenge,* like most Gothic novels that were written in imitation of Radcliffe, has many inconsistencies and several weakly explained mysteries; and there are innumerable indications within the text that the novel is an unrevised first draft. But despite all its flaws, bombast, and excessive sentimentality, it is an impressive first novel.

Notes

1. Penciled note on Maturin's letter to Longman's inquiring into the number of unsold stock; this information was furnished me by Dr. James C. Corson, owner of the letter.

2. Niilo Idman, *Charles Robert Maturin: His Life and Works* (London, 1923), p. 15.

3. Edith Birkhead, *The Tale of Terror: A Study of the Gothic Romance* (London, 1921), p. 82.

4. Ernest Baker, *The History of the English Novel* (London, 1929), V, 220.

5. [Sir Walter] Scott, *Quarterly Review* [3, no. 6 (May 1810):] 343; and Idman, p. 43.

Dale Kramer (essay date 1973)

SOURCE: Kramer, Dale. "And Yet Another Genre." In *Charles Robert Maturin,* pp. 127-40. New York: Twayne Publishers, 1973.

[*In the following essay, Kramer offers a close reading of Maturin's final novel,* The Albigenses, *paying particular attention to elements of religion and medieval history in the work.*]

The control found in *Melmoth* [*Melmoth the Wanderer*] is also present in *The Albigenses,* Maturin's last novel. But in this work, his command is part of the polish we can expect from a man who has been plying a craft for nearly twenty years rather than, as in *Melmoth,* the result of a cohesion of style and subject matter. This last fiction is a venture into a genre previously unattempted by Maturin, the historical novel. Maturin's friendship with Walter Scott has its direct literary result in *The Albigenses.* It is not certain that he knew that Scott was the author of the anonymously published stories by "the author of *Waverley*"; but Scott's authorship was widely suspected almost from the beginning of his career as a novelist. The imitation, in any event, is not flattery or a testimony of friendship so much as another desperate effort to benefit from a literary convention of current popularity. Scott had dominated the historical field ever since the publication in 1814 of *Waverley,* and the publication of each new novel further established the salability of fiction that used history.

Maturin's novel echoes the chivalry of Scott's *Ivanhoe, Old Mortality,* and *Quentin Durward,* as well as the morality of *The Monastery,* not to mention plot events and characters from these and other Scott novels. Chapter mottoes are taken from Byron's *Sardanapalus*; characters, dialogue, and scenes resemble Shakespeare's; and allusions to the *Don Quixote* of Cervantes abound. The extent and range of Maturin's debts to other writers substantiate a sense of stultification of creativity in *The Albigenses* that even the direct plagiarism of parts of Monçada's tale in *Melmoth* does not. The plagiarized material in *Melmoth* and the novel's Gothicism are consonant with each other and with Maturin's genuine personal interests; the borrowings in *The Albigenses* and its general historical bent are imposed upon each other by Maturin's choice of what for him is an unnatural mode. A knowledge of Maturin's personal condition at the time of writing supports the internal textual evidence that the novel was the work of a divided attention.

Maturin was still in perilous poverty, though *Melmoth* was reprinted in 1821; and by this time no hope of increased emolument from, or advancement in, the Anglican church could have remained. Most influential, however, of all the factors leading to the limitations of *The Albigenses,* was the state of Maturin's health.[1] He was failing rapidly as a result of an illness that is not specified in any record that I have seen. The seriousness of his situation is reflected in the frequent references, in the sermons being delivered during Lent of this year,[2] to the state of his health: "if health be spared"; "if life be spared"; "health long precarious, and now seriously impaired, compels me . . . to defer my task" of delivering the fifth sermon.[3] Harried also by financial problems, a sizable family, and parish duties, Maturin was forced to write *The Albigenses* in his spare time, usually by candlelight in his living room after his family had gone to bed.

Maturin intended this novel, according to the preface, to be the first book of a trilogy of "historical romances, illustrative of European feelings and manners in ancient times, in middle, and in modern." The "feudal ages" of *The Albigenses* appealed to him by "their splendid barbarism, . . . wild superstitions and dubious Christianity, their knightly gallantry and baronial oppression." An inauspicious feature of the preface is Maturin's admission that he has tried to please the critics in this novel. Cowed by previous unfavorable reception of his works, uncertain of the value of his own creative strengths, and encouraged only by his distant friend Walter Scott, it is little wonder that Maturin wrote in *The Albigenses* the least characteristic of all of his works of fiction.

I History and Fiction

The historical Albigenses were a Manichean sect that had flourished near the town of Albi in southern France. As Manicheans, they held that there are two opposing creative principles in the universe, good and evil; and that all physical things are evil. Since matter is evil, Christ could not have existed in human form. Moreover, since man lives in the physical world, freeing his spirit requires conscious effort and the denial of animal appetites. Marriage, as a relationship leading to a physical union and to the creation of more physical life, was strongly disapproved of. The eating of meat was forbidden; indeed, only fruit fallen from trees was fully acceptable as food. The popularity of the sect, despite its strict asceticism, is probably due to the Albigenses' division into the "perfect" (the leaders) and the "believers" (the followers). The lives of the "believers" were much less rigidly scrutinized; and thus the religious doctrines were more easily borne.

The beliefs of the Albigenses, who were a part of a larger southern European Manichean group, the Cathari (Greek *Catharoi,* "pure"), were obviously heretical in the eyes of the Catholic church. Nonetheless the Cathari movement grew with relatively little interference from Rome during the eleventh and twelfth centuries, partly because the movement seemed part of the religious, economic, and social revival of the era. But the rapid growth of the Cathari in the last half of the twelfth century, including its establishment of a system of bishops, caused apprehension among the Catholic hierarchy, which thereupon began to institutionalize the punishment of heretics which had previously been left to the occasional impatience of vigilante Catholic citizenry. Pope Innocent III (1198-1216) pressed for legitimate conversion; but, when his legate, Peter de Castelnau, was murdered in 1208, Innocent declared a crusade against the Albigenses.

Although the Albigenses were composed largely of poor people, they were not defenseless. The most powerful noble who succoured them (more out of tolerance or indifference toward religion than out of sympathy, as well as his resentment of the challenge to his authority within his own lands posed by the Pope's forces) was Count Raymond VI of Toulouse, who indeed was suspected to have been an accessory to the assassination of Peter de Castelnau. The principal leader of the papal forces was Simon de Montfort, who cruelly crushed the Albigenses and swept through the territories of Raymond. But Montfort died in the siege of Toulouse in 1218, and Raymond's territories were restored when the Pope learned of Montfort's inhumane methods. The Albigenses were not utterly destroyed, but the growth of the group was halted. The Cathari movement, as a whole, was not completely dispelled by the Inquisition that followed the crusade; and it survived into the fifteenth century.[4]

Maturin's treatment of the history essentially accords with what is known about the Albigenses, but we could not read *The Albigenses* as a substitute for a history of the period. Not only are there silent and pointless alterations, such as battle in which Simon de Montfort is killed taking place at Tarascon instead of Toulouse, and gross anachronisms, such as the reference to Montezuma (1480-1520 A.D.) in 1216; but Maturin alters the sequence of actual historical events in order to tighten the plot. For example, the wife of King Philip Augustus of France had been reconciled to her husband before 1216; but Maturin incorporates her flight from her husband into the novel to justify some of the action. Maturin usually notes his changes of history, but such admissions do not help the reader know the actual circumstances or the actual chain of events.

Maturin opens his novel in 1216, with the remark that "The crusade undertaken against the Albigenses in the reign of Philip Augustus, in the year 1208, had produced the most decisive results, and had terminated in the almost total extirpation of that people throughout the province of Languedoc." Count Raymond, who has gone to Rome to once more seek reconciliation with the Pope, has abandoned warlike preparation for the defense of a band of the remaining Albigenses, who are attempting to reach the temporarily safe kingdom of Arragon. The Albigenses' movement threatens the castle of the Lord of Courtenaye, who requests aid of Simon de Montfort. Much of the story deals with the efforts to possess the title of "champion of the church," officially held by de Montfort and sought by the Bishop of Toulouse and by Louis Dauphin of France. Of the two principal battles, both are won by the Albigeois forces. In the first, Raymond returns secretly from Rome in time to lay an ambush for the crusader knights who have arrogantly and foolishly left their men behind at the Courtenaye castle.

In this battle Simon de Montfort is seriously wounded, and a struggle for power ensues between the worldly and corrupt Bishop and the Dauphin. The struggle is climaxed but not resolved during the confrontation of

the three men during an impromptu council of war in the last volume during which Simon is goaded into a furious but futile attack on the Dauphin. A tenuous reconciliation is made by the three leaders just before their combined armies hasten to battle the beleaguered Albigenses before Raymond can come again to their support. In this battle, Simon de Montfort is killed; and the crusader forces are driven to taking refuge in the castle of Tarascon. The next morning, when Raymond takes the castle, he is assisted by an exotic development in the nonhistorical plot.

II ROMANCE AND CHIVALRY

The nonhistorical plot concerns the fortunes of two noble youths, Sir Paladour de la Croix Sanglante and Amirald, and the women they love, Isabelle of Courtenaye and Genevieve, the granddaughter of the Albigeois spiritual leader Pierre, respectively. Paladour and Amirald, who are brothers, are the sons of Count Raymond who were presumed killed in infancy during a raid on their father's castle. Neither knows his ancestry; nor, having been separated during the raid, does either know that his brother is alive. Amirald, who had been "abandoned" before the gates of Courtenaye Castle, had been reared and ill-used by the Lord of Courtenaye. Wounded during the first battle and tended to health by Genevieve in a secret cave among the mountains, Amirald eventually gives allegiance to the Albigeois cause. The elder brother Paladour has sworn a sacred oath during the burning of his ancestral home to kill the last enemy of his family, though he was so young that he does not remember his family's name and thus has to trust to fate that he will be able to discover the means for revenge. Dim remembrance of the oath and the garish surroundings during his swearing it have made Paladour melancholy and resigned. (He resembles the younger Montorio brother of *Fatal Revenge*; and, of course, the idea of children unaware of their true parents also appears in Maturin's first novel.) A sorceress, who in behavior and motives resembles Schemoli of *Fatal Revenge,* appears in an ominous situation in the early part of the novel and tells Paladour that she is destined to call for the fulfillment of his oath. But she will not identify his victim until the time to perform the deed has come.

The victim turns out to be his beloved Isabelle, niece of the Lord of Courtenaye and the daughter of the previous Lord who had destroyed Paladour's home and killed his mother. The sorceress has personal reason for attempting to exact revenge on the house of Courtenaye and for using the house of Raymond as her tool. The sorceress is Marie de Mortemar, once a beautiful and wealthy girl, whose possessions had been stolen by Raymond of Toulouse, the Bishop of Toulouse, and Isabelle's father. In addition to taking her wealth because she had been suspected of being a religious heretic, the three men had misused her person in such a way that she became insane; and, casting aside pride and religious pretension, she swore she would bear any future indignities necessary to gain revenge.

Marie waits until the wedding night of Paladour and Isabelle before she demands that Paladour redeem his pledge. Rather than kill his bride or live in dishonor at breaking his vow, Paladour attempts suicide; and, in the struggle to stop him, Isabelle receives a serious wound. Paladour rushes away, thinking Isabelle is dead. Marie, with uncharacteristic ruth, decides that Count Raymond's family has suffered sufficiently by his having lost the company and affection of his sons for twenty years. She secretly nurses Isabelle back to health and installs her as a page to Paladour, in which position she can watch over Paladour and guard against the effects of his gloominess. In the novel's last battle, Marie is captured by the Bishop's forces and is scheduled to be executed with all of the prisoner Albigenses before Count Raymond can free them.

By a stratagem (Marie is unaccountably left in an unlocked room next to the chapel), Marie poisons the communion bread; and, when the Bishop says high mass before the anticipated battle, the entire garrison is destroyed. Marie gloats over the Bishop's death agonies and then pitches herself out of the castle tower to her death. Paladour and Amirald are discovered to be Raymond's sons; Paladour and Isabelle are reunited; Amirald and Genevieve receive Pierre's blessing to marry. (Throughout the novel, Maturin pays little attention to the doctrines of the Albigenses, such as their ban on marriage; but it is hardly likely that as a churchman he could have been unaware of them.)

There are many other skeins in the plot, and plot incidents, that I have left out of this sketch for clarity. Among the extended events that I have omitted are Isabelle's abduction by the outlaw Adolfo, who falls in love with her and wants to marry her instead of ransoming her; Paladour's falling into the same outlaw's power and being put into a cell with a lycanthrope (a man who thinks he's a wolf), who helps Paladour free Isabelle during one of his brief periods of lucidity but whom Paladour is forced eventually to fight in self-defense; the machinations by the Lord of Courtenaye to destroy Paladour and Amirald in fear that they will learn that it was he who had murdered their mother; and a considerable amount of complicated intrigue by Marie de Mortemar that would collapse were she not coincidentally always in the right place, as when she stabs to death the outlaw Adolpho as he is about to kill Paladour.

The effect of the interwoven activities of the fictional characters in *The Albigenses* is less obfuscating, however, than the conflux of supernaturalism and emotion-alism in *Fatal Revenge.* The control given to the plot by the historical situation is beneficial, and even the implausible nonhistorical situation gains a measure of credence from the fictional characters being swept along by historical events in which they play minor directive roles.

III HISTORY AND CHIVALRY

As a historical novelist taking his lead from Walter Scott, Maturin is at best only partially successful. Unlike Scott's characters, especially those in the novels that portray the nearly contemporary history of the eighteenth century, Maturin's central nonhistorical characters express only vaguely the attitudes of the times or of the groups of which they form a part. Even Genevieve, as a member of the persecuted minority, says nothing to the point; indeed, she would seem to be no more heretical than the meekest parishioner in Maturin's own church. Moreover, with the exception of the contrast between the saintly pastor Pierre and the fanatical Albigeois leaders such as Mattathias, the warrior, and Boanerges, the preacher, there is little doctrinal distinction among the Albigenses; even the Catholics distinguish the Albigenses' despicableness only by noting that they are "heretics."[5]

In Scott, there is a layer of serious intellectual interchange, for the Scot rebel is wont to argue his position against a Scot or an Englishman reconciled to the Hanoverian claim; but Maturin's created characters reveal themselves to be without settled social and religious convictions when they are caught in a personal dilemma. Both Paladour and Amirald move from the Pope's forces to those of the Albigenses. Amirald's shift is carried out with some attention to motivation: he is torn between the simplicity of Genevieve's life and the grand world of chivalry. Likewise, Paladour's shift is not without psychological cause; but he seems basically unaware of the significance of his religious allegiance, though such matters were of course important in the world of chivalry. Wishing only to find death because he thinks he has killed his wife, but beseeched by the sorceress not to raise his lance against Raymond, he joins Raymond's army. But even Amirald's change is not made smoothly; in one chapter he swears total fealty to his liege the Dauphin even though the Dauphin will not renounce his intention to make the captive Genevieve his mistress. Amirald in effect thereby countenances the dishonor of his beloved and thus makes clear his sense of the comparative force of feudal and romantic obligations. But in the next chapter Amirald—who in the meantime has rescued Genevieve from a Catholic mob—joins the Albigeois forces and tells them of the crusaders' strategy of attack and thus breaks the solemn vows of feudal allegiance to the Dauphin which he had just renewed.

Maturin seems to have diagnosed Scott's popularity as based on the portrayal of chivalrous action, whether the scene be the Middle Ages or the Border Country of the eighteenth century. There are certainly generic similarities between Ivanhoe and the brothers Paladour and Amirald, despite the intensified artificiality of Paladour and Amirald. All three abide by an elaborate code of manners that could not be perfectly followed by a mortal being. But Maturin's talents fail him in making a context for his heroes; the details of Ivanhoe's bearing and actions, and his sense of identity with a moral code as well as with a courtly etiquette, create a degree of verisimilitude that Amirald and Paladour fall short of.

The effect of Maturin's portrayal of chivalry is doubly unfortunate because it coincides with his natural propensity, previously seen especially in *The Milesian Chief,* to create superheroes, whose reality is inevitably falsified by their flowery diction and pompous sentiments. *The Milesian Chief* survives, if in a limited sense, because the female foil has a complex life that modifies the moral perfection and ideal qualities of Connal O'Morven. But in *The Albigenses,* Genevieve and especially Isabelle contribute to the artificiality of characterization. Paladour in particular, but Amirald nearly as starchly, makes his way through life abiding by innumerable conventions of the most flaccid sentimental-historical fiction. He accepts a challenge to be Isabelle's champion in a joust with the powerful Simon de Montfort "with blushing and deferential awe to the fair being for whom he was perilling fame and life." When asked by Isabelle, "Who watches [is awake] at this late hour?," Paladour answers, "It is your beauty's servant and everwakeful meditator." When de Montfort blames himself because the crusader knights without their supporting men face certain death in the Albigenses' ambush, Paladour puts aside his enmity to express his feudal loyalty: "'Now foul befall the tongue that reproaches thee in an hour like this, noble de Montfort!' said the generous Paladour; 'for surely it was the noble heat of a true valour that lighted the flame that must consume us this day.'"

Isabelle, like Paladour, is beyond the reader's imaginative identification. Unlike Genevieve, who, because she is a fugitive heretic, is threatened with rape by one character after another, Isabelle experiences only one encounter with the coarseness of feudal life, and that vaguely, with the outlaw chief. He is suitably chastened by her reaction: "His inflamed eyes menaced more than scorn, and he seemed advancing to fulfil their threat. . . . At this moment, a slight but determined movement of the lady Isabelle (who half-started from her seat), her compressed lips, and the fixed and fearful bending of her eye on the walls of her prison [evidently portending suicide], made the bold outlaw shrink before her." When Adolpho proposes marriage to Isabelle in defiance of the difference in their social rank, he is again cowed by her sense of the outrage he is committing by merely thinking that they could make an equal union: "Isabelle sprang on her feet—both hands were compressed on her left bosom, as if *expecting* her heart would burst, and her eyes inflamed and dilated seemed starting from their sockets. . . . The outlaw, with all his atrocious boldness, was daunted at the sight: he rushed from her apartment, cursing the very pride to which he crouched."

The historical characters fare much better. Probably because only ruthless men with a strong streak of ego could stand above the prejudices of the era and remain visible through the dimming effect of seven centuries, and because evil is more engrossing in narrative than virtue, the Bishop of Toulouse affords an opportunity for powerful characterization that calls forth Maturin's finest powers. His personality dominates any event in which he takes part, especially during the confrontation between him and the Dauphin, and then during the confrontation of the ill Simon de Montfort facing the Bishop and the Dauphin, who have intuitively put aside their mutual loathing in order to meet Simon's challenge. Even though Maturin's portrayal of the Bishop as incredibly successful in battle (he kills an enemy with each swing of his sword during the ambush) is as false as the similar portrayal of Paladour and Amirald, the analysis of him as a clear-sighted man who works upon the susceptible, illiterate knights and feudal leaders in order to fulfill his own ambitions is well done. In a similar manner, Simon is a sound portrait of a physically powerful, mentally limited man who has gained eminence by his martial ability and by his cruelty but who can be goaded by a clever man such as the Bishop into an attack upon his future sovereign. The Dauphin is a libertine of the same cut as the Pretender in Thackeray's *Henry Esmond,* although, as is perhaps fitting for a rougher age, the Dauphin is willing to rape if efforts at seduction fail.

One of the more attractive features of *The Albigenses* is the honesty with which it handles social conditions during the era it presents. In few instances does Maturin palliate the crudity and violence of life during the thirteenth century. He is only slightly reticent about the rape and infamous treatment of Marie de Mortemar, the threats to Genevieve, and the licentious and drunken conduct of the knights. The great amount of interest shown in chastity and in lewd living is no doubt partly an effort by Maturin to appeal to his readers as much as a desire to be historically truthful. But such honesty still compensates for the preponderance of chivalric artificiality of manners when Isabelle and Paladour are present.

IV THE GOTHIC ELEMENT

Despite Maturin's desperate and conscientious efforts to write a historical and chivalric novel, he could not entirely put aside his *métier,* the fantastic. Nor could he avoid the expansive and introspective painting of the concrete that creates an aura of the supernatural and mysterious. But battle and history do not lend themselves readily to Maturin's brand of Gothic treatment. *The Albigenses* is not a historical Gothic novel, in the manner of either Clara Reeve's *Old English Baron* or Thomas Leland's *Longsword, Earl of Salisbury* (1762), but a novel in which history and Gothicism conflict with each other. The effectiveness of the one genre (a quasi-factual account of man's condition at a given point in time) works against that of the other (an imaginative heightening of fears of the unknown in life).

Marie de Mortemar poses as a sorceress; the Lord of Courtenaye keeps a retinue of witches; there is a night of ghost tales at Courtenaye Castle; and an aghast Genevieve sees the supposedly dead Isabelle standing near her bier (Isabelle's "burial" being part of Marie de Mortemar's plan to install her as Paladour's page). The sense of horror is partially dispelled by attempts at humor; a sequence during which Paladour is supposedly being put through a fearful test by Marie and the witches is presented only indirectly, through two foppish and superstitious knights who hide under the coverlets of their beds when they hear a scream that pierces the floors of the castle. As is usual with Maturin, the most effective Gothic bits are evocations of states of mind beyond the comfort of conscience. The Lord of Courtenaye, who wishes to serve the devil, uses language that on one occasion approaches that of *Fatal Revenge* in trying to convince Marie de Mortemar to introduce him to Satan: "I tell thee, it [the sight of Satan] is the unquenchable thirst of my spirit. The spirit that works within me needs a mightier one to strive with for mastery or subjection. Let me behold, if thou hast such power, my vassal or my chief. I would behold at once the entrance to that lower world and its dark and potent ruler, such as thou hast painted him!" In a similar vein, the description of Genevieve's reaction to the sight of the "dead" Isabelle in her shroud: "The hair of her flesh stood up—every pore tingled with distinct vitality—her eyes became, to her own perception, glazed, though she retained the full power of vision; the next moment they were dilated beyond her power of closing them; the figure appeared expanding in dimensions and advancing on her. . . . The air became tremulous with a purple light."

A small amount of the Gothicism in the novel shows Maturin simply whetting the reader's curiosity. One instance of this sort of thing is the blood on Paladour's armor the morning after his first, nocturnal encounter with Marie. She has posed as a mysterious "lady of the lake" who ferries him alone across a lake one gloomy night. During the trip, she tells him that she knows of his oath and has come to claim its fulfillment. The cause of the blood is never explained.

The absence of genuine or sustained supernaturalism does not prevent Maturin from decorating the novel with effective Gothic trappings. The description of the outlaw Adolpho's castle on an island is in the best Radcliffean manner, with secret passageways and with thundering waves crashing on the island's base far below the ramparts. Most striking, though, is the lycanthrope, one of the most garish products of Maturin's flamboyant imagination, and one of the earliest appearances in English fiction of the werewolf. The lycanthrope is strikingly presented, bearing in his hand food snatched from "the grave" and attacking Paladour in his sleep. Still, the frightening deportment of the man-wolf is quite different from the horrors in *Fatal Revenge,* whose mysteries are not explained until the novel's end. Maturin seems almost eager to rationalize and intellectualize the existence of the "fiend" in Adolpho's dungeon rather than attempt to sustain interest in the inexplicability of evil.

V THE RELIGION OF TOLERANCE

The Albigenses, not free of slanted scenes, contains some sharp if humorous criticisms of the medieval sale of indulgences; but in its entirety it presents a balanced view of religious faiths. Compared to *Melmoth, The Albigenses* is tolerant of Catholicism. But, of course, it needs to be remembered that Maturin, as an Anglican, could have claimed as part of his own religious tradition the Catholic church of the thirteenth century. He could well have seen the beliefs of the Albigenses as contrary to his own articles of faith, even though, as I have observed, he does not stress the doctrines of the Albigenses; he only vaguely refers to the Albigenses as precursors of English Puritans "centuries later."

Maturin generally favors neither Catholicism nor Albigenseanism; rather, he isolates individual adherents of either creed for praise or criticism. Pierre, the blind leader of the Albigenses, is kind and gentle-mannered; indeed, his influence on the Albigenses has been intentionally curtailed by the militaristic Mattathias and Boanerges. On the Catholic side, the Monk of Montcalm, the mediator sent by the Pope to try to curb the Bishop's intolerance and ambition, is concerned for the spiritual health of the Albigenses and tries to convert them by reason and prayer.

Maturin's criticism is leveled primarily at the fanatics of both sides of the dispute, such as Boanerges; the opportunists, such as the Bishop of Toulouse and Mephibosheth; and the psychological aberrants, such as the Abbot of Normoutier and Mattathias. Maturin opposes the cruel excesses and persecution and torture practiced by both of the groups. He satirizes both Catholicism's amorality, typified by the Bishop and the Abbot, and Albigensianism's hypocrisy and weakness of flesh, as seen most clearly in Mephibosheth's joining the monks at

Normoutier in a riotous "revel of misrule" and in his ultimately becoming converted to monastic Catholicism after eating sumptuous food from the Bishop's kitchen. Though Count Raymond is by no means a spokesman for Maturin, his vacillations indicate at least part of Maturin's view of the disputants: "—now indignantly opposing the superstitions and the domination of the Church of Rome,—now revolted by the enthusiasm and daring pretensions of the Albigeois:—such was Raymond of Toulouse."

It is pertinent that Maturin portrays the monks in the Abbot of Normoutier's establishment as little different from the Albigenses and no different from the laymen who are only nominal Catholics. The "revel of misrule" enjoyed during the abbot's absence primarily involves only gluttony, drinking, and high-jinks (until Mephibosheth destroys carvings of saints); in other words, the oppressed monks imitate their unworthy leader's way of life. Monks kidnap Genevieve as an offering for the Abbot of Normoutier, but so do knights, for the Dauphin; in a similar manner, outlaws kidnap Isabelle for their chieftain Adolpho. Maturin points out that the Cathari heresy gave cause for the establishment of the Inquisition, but *The Albigenses* contains no Catholic characters who would enjoy the role of an Inquisitor; and in this respect they are unlike the various clerics in *Melmoth* who would find in such a role the pleasure and the capstone of their careers.

Maturin's presentation, however, tends to favor the Albigenses, probably because the Albigenses are humble people while the Catholic crusaders are frequenters of courts and given to intrigue from habit as much as from a necessity for staying alive. Maturin pointedly draws a contrast between the mourning of an Albigensian mother for her son and that of the Countess de Montfort for her husband. Morally, the Albigensian's grief is higher; for she is concerned with her son's soul; but the Countess swears that the blood of "a thousand churls" will fall for every drop of her husband's, "and Christendom shall see [my] oath fulfilled." (Part of the effectiveness of this contrast, of course, relies on the sentimental concept of the moral superiority of the poor.) Moreover, while Maturin can praise the "fearless humanity" of Catholic monks who save Genevieve's life during a blizzard in the mountains, a rhetorically more powerful depiction of his concept of Catholicism is the Bishop of Toulouse's speech to Genevieve as he attempts to persuade her to become his mistress. The Bishop boasts that the Church of Rome enslaves men's minds—not merely bodies as did the old Roman Empire. He says that the Church sanctifies murder and rebellion and that it is beyond morality since it has the power to declare what is good and what is evil. That such views grossly distort all religions—not just that of the speaker—suggests a degree of blind loathing of Roman Catholicism on Maturin's part for which the Bishop's opportunism is not responsible. But this sort of scorn toward Catholicism is infrequent in *The Albigenses.*

Notes

1. Perhaps his health delayed the completion of *The Albigenses,* as it had *Melmoth.* The novel was originally scheduled for publication in the spring of 1822; see [Fannie E. Ratchford and William H. McCarthy Jr., eds., *The Correspondence of Sir Walter Scott and Charles Robert Maturin* (Austin, 1937)], p. 99. But no biographical data survives for this period of Maturin's life.

2. Published as *Five Sermons of the Errors of the Roman Catholic Church* (Dublin and London, 1824).

3. Maturin's last recorded duty was a baptism on August 8. He died on October 30, and was buried on November 2, 1824, in St. Peter's churchyard.

4. This history of the Albigenses is taken from Hoffman Nickerson, *The Inquisition: A Political and Military Study of its Establishment* (Boston, 1923); A. L. Maycock, *The Inquisition: From its Establishment to the Great Schism* (New York, 1927); "Cathari," *Encyclopedia Britannica* (Chicago, 1963), V, 71-72; and "Albigenses," *Encyclopedia Americana* (New York, 1964), I, 337-38. Because primary documents written by the Albigenses were destroyed by the order of the Inquisition established by Pope Innocent, the beliefs of the Cathari have to be conjectured from the statements of the victorious papal supporters.

5. On the other hand, two of the Catholics seem to be practicing Manicheans. The Lord of Courtenaye longs to see the Devil; he employs a number of witches and implores Marie de Mortemar to help him achieve his goal. The Bishop of Toulouse distinguishes between the powers of God and of Satan in a speech to Genevieve that I refer to later in the text. But whether Maturin uses this material ironically and humorously, or satirically, toward the Roman Catholic church is not clear; for he does not develop the matter beyond these scenes.

Claude Fierobe (essay date 1974)

SOURCE: Fierobe, Claude. "France in the Novels of Charles Robert Maturin." In *France-Ireland: Literary Relations,* edited by Patrick Rafroidi, Guy Fehlmann, and Maitiu Mac Conmara, pp. 119-31. Lille: Université de Lille III, 1974.

[*In the following essay, Fierobe examines the influence of French culture, politics, and society on Maturin's work.*]

Although only limited space is devoted to France in the novels of Maturin, it nevertheless plays an important rôle in many ways. Reference to it can be found first of all in the **Sermons,** those of 1819 and the **Five Sermons on the Errors of the Roman Catholic Church** of 1824, year of the author's death; also in two articles, one published in the *Quarterly Review* of April 1817 under the title **"The Tragic Drama, *The Apostate,* a tragedy in 5 Acts, R. L. Sheil",** the other on the subject of *Harrington and Ormond* by Mrs. Edgeworth, to be found in *The British Review and London Critical Journal* in which Maturin gives us a veritable history of the novel; finally in three of his own novels: **The Wild Irish Boy** (1808), **Women; Or, Pour et Contre** (1818), and **The Albigenses** (1824). It is to these novels that we shall limit our study with the exception of the last-named which must be left aside for the following reason: Maturin's deformation of the historical reality of the period he is writing about is so substantial and so typical of the author that the novel merits a detailed analysis that is outside the scope of this article. And yet, the conclusions we shall be led to draw from **The Wild Irish Boy** and **Women,** become clearer when seen against the background of Maturin's historical vision in The **Albigenses,** and in reference to his very explicit opinion of France that can be found in the 1819 **Sermons.**

The tide of events in France and Europe up to 1815 proved a matter of concern for every British subject. The ideas of the philosophers, the French Revolution and the Great Terror, the move towards imperialism and the ambitions and conquests of Napoleon, gave rise to divergent points of view in Britain. On the whole, however, the conflict with France under the Empire tended to give rise to a conservative outlook in Britain and Ireland. In the face of the French political situation, even the most liberal were convinced of the dangers of dictatorship arising from revolution and a brutal overthrow of the Establishment. In 1815 the English had good reason to feel self-satisfied: the war in Europe had strengthened their unity; resistance to revolutionary ideas and, later, to French imperialism, had in no way undermined the material power of the nation nor its prestige and politics. Such a state of affairs gave rise to an understandable pride for, having come out on top in a titanic combat, the English considered themselves better than their adversaries, better than the rest of Europe, believed themselves the chosen people of a Just God. Moral vanity and political satisfaction are complementary aspects of the same Conservatism. It is no wonder that the Anglican Church (still supported by the Tories) and Maturin with her shared these views.

Maturin was a minister of the Established Church and a Tory. If he clashed with his ecclesiastical superiors it was for doctrinal reasons (he had Calvinist tendencies), and not political ones. His attitude to France was the same as theirs: hostility towards French politics and ambitions, hostility also towards the French religion, Catholicism. Let us not forget that Maturin was an Anglican curate in Ireland, a country with a Catholic majority. His hostility towards French Catholicism was in fact part of a hostility towards Catholicism in general, a religion which he held responsible for all the troubles in Europe. For him, to attack France meant to attack a country of regicides and papists. His francophobia has also perhaps another explanation. His own family was most certainly of French origin, and he was always convinced that his Huguenot ancestors had been forced to flee to Ireland to escape the persecutions following the Revocation of the Edict of Nantes. His dislike of everything French perhaps has its roots, to a certain extent, in a personal grievance, a desire for revenge based on his belief that his family had been the victims of an injustice for which, let us repeat, France and Catholicism were responsible. In **The Wild Irish Boy** and **Women** Maturin takes as his target the French philosophers of the [eighteenth] century, and draws a picture of Paris at the fall of the Napoleonic Empire.

* * *

On several occasions Maturin directly attacks the philosophers of the Age of Enlightenment using his characters as a mouthpiece. In **The Wild Irish Boy** the hero, Ormsby Bethel, openly criticizes the choice of reading matter of his family who have just moved to Ireland:

> The whole of our library at home consisted of the works of the modern philosophers, and the French writers, who a few years before the revolution, had excited the thirst of outrage and innovation which could afterwards be only quenched by blood. When I wished for solid reading, I was presented with Godwin's *Political Justice,* Rousseau's *Contrat Social,* or Voltaire's *Dictionnaire Philosophique.* If I wished for lighter reading, I had only Voltaire's or the King of Prussia's bad verses against the immortality of the soul, or the insipid and infamous novels of Rousseau, Crebillon, or Diderot.[1]

Later, his young wife Athanasia Montolieu deplores the pernicious influence that these same authors had exerted on her:

> When I recollect myself, and so lately, the pupil of false sentiment and *all its works*; dying to be the heroine of a mad and wicked tale of a Rousseau, of a Goethe, of a Wollstonecraft . . .

(III, 300)

In **Women** the most sedate and reasonable character, Montgomery, who represents the voice of conscience for the hero, Charles de Courcy, speaks out against Mme du Deffand, Rousseau, d'Alembert, Diderot, Voltaire and Mme du Chatelet, for two reasons: firstly he considers their conduct immoral and their works harmful, secondly he hopes that Zaïra will spring to their defence and thus lose her prestige and glamour in Charles' eyes. We must point out here that Maturin's criticisms against France and the French are never really digressions, but an integrated part of the narrative and help to advance the plot. In fact, Montgomery's efforts are in vain since Zaïra shares his point of view and, indeed, it is through the mouth of the beautiful prima donna that the author puts forward his most damning attack:

> She spoke with honest, virtuous, English indignation (as Montgomery would have called it, had it been expressed by another) of the foreign authors, and especially of the French; speaking of them, her sentiments, her language, her very prejudices appeared English.[2]

«Honest, virtuous, English indignation»—here is the key-phrase which summarizes succinctly Maturin's view of France. The rock of British faith and virtue rears its head in the face of French immorality and atheism.[3] One of his favourite targets were the daring thinkers that made up the court of Frederic II at Potsdam, Voltaire especially, but also other Frenchmen—La Mettrie, Maupertuis, d'Argens. What were these people? The answer is supplied by Zaïra in a passionate outburst which voices all of Maturin's own resentment:

> She turned the whole force of her keen and polished severity against the philosophical assembly at Sans Souci, and exposed to just derision a number of men affecting to be the moral and intellectual legislators of Europe; and when they met, engaging in such low squabbles, such mean jealousies, such degrading and disgusting contentions (disgraceful to the dignity of a palace, and to the honour of literature), as must have exposed them to the ridicule of all Europe, and to the everlasting hatred of each other—Philanthropists, philosophers, reformers, all *Daniels come to judgment,* as they were, assembled to determine on the future destiny of mankind, and the regeneration of the world, they departed ridiculous, exasperated, and degraded, heaping shame on themselves by mutual hostility, and agreeing in but one thing, their *hatred to Christianity,* to which their opposition thus became an honour and a support.

(II, 84-5)

Until now his criticisms have remained quite vague, but Maturin does not lack precision when he attacks the teaching of the modern philosophers. He treats in turn what we might term the metaphysical domain, the moral domain and that of the workings of the mind. For him, the modern philosophy, with its overemphasis on Reason, is firstly a manifestation of pride and a revolt against God; secondly it is responsible for the destruction of values and a tool of moral decay; and finally it creates real confusion as far as the rôle of human reasoning is concerned.

* * *

The philosophers have taught the French to put everything to the test of Reason, even the most serious matters. «It is our privilege to reason on every part of life»

(I, 156) claims Ormsby's mother who swears by Diderot, Rousseau and Voltaire. In this she resembles the witty circle gathered by M. de Viosmenil in his villa where Zaïra is now resting, abandoned by de Courcy who has returned to Eva in Ireland:

> In France, nothing is more usual than the discussion of abstract questions on the most important subjects. The company, as they wandered through the gardens, spoke of the immortality of the soul, and the being of a God, with the perfect ease of continental latitudinarianism.

(III, 205)

This mania for logic is a formidable danger, perhaps the most formidable since it leads to the rejection of God who, at first the subject of a simple discussion, soon becomes an object of hatred. Cardonneau, the French friend of Zaïra, illustrates this point remarkably well. He discusses, with the intention of refuting, the immortality of the soul, and denounces the most important lesson of Christianity—that God is love. How can this be so, he asks, when hate and hostility are widespread, when the earth is ravaged by tempests, when one's fellow-humans prove a source of endless misery, when solitude makes a man his own worst enemy? Given all this, can one be blamed for believing that the world is not the creation of a God of love, but of an evil spirit playing with the suffering into which he plunges his unfortunate creatures? Such sacrilege upsets Zaïra, so Cardonneau, with the help of some vague historical considerations, goes on to prove the relativity of blasphemy and how little importance should really be attached to it. Maturin, then, is clearly telling us that logic (the logic of the French philosophers of the [eighteenth] century, of course) leads to atheism, and atheism to blasphemy.[4] According to him, the philosophers and their disciples are the most evident incarnation of the pride which sets up man against his God, the creature against his creator, and which finally denies all transcendental power. Already in this attitude, though without its nobility and dignity, we find glimmerings of the revolt that Melmoth, the greatest of Maturin's heroes, will define in these terms: «Mine was the great angelic sin, pride and intellectual glorying.»[5] The destiny of the wanderer will be that of every human being who, exalting mere Reason at the expense of the Divine, falls farther into sin and humiliation.

* * *

It is easy to understand that Maturin's condemnation of this human pride based on Reason goes together with a moral condemnation. Follow the teachings of the philosophers, he tells us, apply their principles and you will fall as low as Miss Percival. Having borne two children to the man Ormsby believes to be his father, Miss Percival, now separated from her lover, falls ill. Her weak state is conducive to real moral reform, but she lacks a guide, having only the philosophers who lead her yet farther astray. For them vice and virtue have no meaning, they are merely habits acquired not by a change of sentiments and principles but by a change of mode, rendered necessary by a natural progression towards the general good, produced by man and not by an all-powerful God:

> Here she learnt that to lament former depravity was foolish and unphilosophical where reformation was so easy, where physical necessity, controlling all the actions, rendered vice no longer more culpable than voluntary, and where the exclusion of future responsibility deprived the mind of all solicitude for the event, even should its progress terminate in renewed vice.
>
> (II, 93)

We can see then how Maturin considers the atheism of the philosophers to be responsible for the moral decay of his time. Obviously it is wrong of him to generalize in this way, but we must remember that this was not merely a personal opinion, but also that of the majority of British people traumatized by what was happening as a result of the teaching of the philosophers. Miss Percival owes her failure to having followed this philosophy. She will continue to get deeper in error: she will agree to go back to her old lover in Ireland, she will refuse to take account of the ties that bind her to her children and finally, on the death of her protector she will run away with the French valet Masseau and all the money she can lay her hands on, leaving a letter, suitably *philosophical* in its wording, to explain her conduct. In this letter she speaks of free will and of the need to promote the general good even at the expense of family ties; she goes on to explain that having it in her power to make a fellow human being happy, she is leaving with Masseau without her trapping herself in the odious and humiliating institution of marriage. Ormsby finds it hard to control his indignation at the philosophical style of the letter:

> I was used to this jargon: I understood it to be merely an apology for heads that cannot feel, a flimsy attempt to gloss over determined depravity by sophistry, to erect vice into a science and a system, and teach rampant and glaring corruption to assume the steady step, and talk the connected and consequential language of deliberate rectitude; like the day of deification in Paris, which offered for the object of worship a *harlot* in the costume of a goddess.
>
> (II, 91-2)

Thus Miss Percival illustrates the degradation into which disciples of the philosophers can easily fall. Athanasia, on the other hand, though on the point of following her example, pulls herself together in time. Her reading of Goethe, Mrs. Wollstonecraft and Rousseau had already poisoned her sensible but delicate mind and, at one point, seduced by their praise of feeling, she was on the brink of sacrificing her real feelings, of making imaginary duties real and real ones imaginary. But the voice of common sense and a loyalty to real values, helped to a certain degree by her passionate love for her husband, make themselves heard. The ensuing moral victory is summarized in one significant sentence: «I have banished all my French books». (III, 303). The illusion of superficial feeling is succeeded by a strong desire to do her duty; the act of banishing her French books is accompanied by a return to the straight and narrow. Once again the corruptive force of the French is countered by British integrity.

* * *

The enlightened philosophy, which puts man before God and plays havoc with traditional moral values, also leads to complete confusion as far as the role of reason is concerned, and in particular its relationship with feeling. According to tradition and common sense, reason is used when making a deliberate choice after a careful weighing up of the situation, whereas feeling and instinct come into play when emotion or urgency leave no time for deliberation:

> But the modern philosophy, like Molière's physician has «changed all that now». We are to adopt feeling as our guide in the greater movements of life; and we are to reason on the most minute events, and the most abrupt emergencies
>
> (*Wild Irish Boy,* I, 15-16)

Maturin goes on to illustrate this point by mocking the philosophers and, at the same time, hitting out at their desire of the general good:

> In the choice of a companion for life, in the choice of a mode of subsistence, nay in the noice of life and death itself, we are to abandon ourselves to an impulse, we are to consult a momentary feeling which, according to their account is also the result of the mean and mechanical causes . . . While he who assists the sufferers in a burning house is to pause and reason on the steps of the ladder, whether the life he preserves be of more consequence than that he neglects, whether he ought to throw back into the flames the infant he has just snatched, and inquire whether there be any possessor of an enlightened mind in the same danger, whose preservation from it would contribute to the «general good».
>
> (I, 16)

The height of Maturin's francophobia is reached in his description of Masseau, the French valet. Like Cardonneau in **Women,** Masseau is not only himself corrupt but also a corrupting influence, thought of the two he is the lesser evil since he has neither Cardonneau's culture and intelligence, nor his powers of persuasion. Ormsby's first impression of him is: «With the communicativeness he united much of the superficial knowledge of a Frenchman» (I, 133). They begin to discuss the philosophy of Newton and the Marchioness of Chatelet's criticism of his ideas. As far as Ormsby is concerned, it is like talking to a brick wall, for Masseau refuses to admit that Newton is worth reading in the original and dogmatically insists on the superiority of the French intellect:

> Ah non, Monsieur, Newton was a very weak writer, he said some good things but depend on it, he never would have been noticed but for the Marchioness du Chatelet.
>
> (I, 133)

A discussion on literature ends in the same way. For Masseau the only worthwhile British writers are those who translate French works: is it not significant that the poet-laureate, Colley Cibber, had chosen to translate Corneille's *Le Cid*? Masseau is grudgingly forced to recognize that Milton does have some talent, though he stresses the fact that he owes his polishing of «his native barbarism» (1, 136) to his trip to Paris. Moreover «what could be expected from a man who hated kings and wore latchets in his shoes»? (1, 136) Ormsby points out that Milton's honest nature made him hostile to the affectation that could be found at the Court of Charles II, to which Masseau replies with what is in his eyes an irrefutable argument: «It was the only civilized court England ever saw . . . the manners were perfectly French». (1, 136) Faced with such a character one cannot help but understand Ormsby's judgement: «I now found that France and the world were synonymous in the language of a Frenchman» (1, 133). Masseau in obviously a caricature of the typical Frenchman as Maturin imagined him, but a caricature merely exaggerates features, it does not invent them, and the valet's conceit was believed by the author to be characteristic of the French in general.

Maturin's hostility towards France as seen through his description of imaginary characters such as Miss Percival and Masseau, is in fact a deep dislike, for religious and moral reasons, of the French philosophers and of what they had done to France.

* * *

In fact Maturin does not limit himself to descriptions of individual situations and attacks on Voltaire and Rousseau. In **Women** he gives us a wider picture—that of French society at the fall of the Napoleonic Empire. It is through Mme St Maur's letters to Zaïra that we get a glimpse of France in 1814, more especially the reactions of the Parisian aristocracy to the arrival of the allies. Mme St Maur, the best friend and confidante of Zaïra, is a likeable character despite her French rationality. Maturin says of her:

> Madame St Maur's answer contained that mixture of frivolity, worldliness, clear sense, and strong affection which really formed her character.
>
> (II, 148-9)

That she has her good points as well as her bad we can attribute to Maturin's objectivity—he does not want to be accused of giving a deformed picture of Paris. Hence the amusing mixture of lighthearted chat and political considerations that we find in her letters:

> Amid all this we have one consolation,—justice, ample justice, is about to be done to the beauty of Parisian ankles; the petticoats are growing shorter every day, and provided they do, no matter how long the political faces are. Do you know they say milord Wellington has actually crossed the Pyrenees,—the Pyrenees?—my God, but that is impossible!
>
> (I, 227)

Be that as it may, Mme St Maur has too much national pride to doubt for an instant that the conquerors will in turn be conquered by Paris which, in the eyes of a Frenchwoman, is still the centre of the world.[6] Her main concern, as far as the political situation is concerned, is to find out which way the wind is blowing and place herself on the winning side. Her support of the Empire changes to an aversion for Bonaparte as soon as Paris is invaded by the allies: «She began her letter a Buonapartiste, and ends an absolute ultra» (II, 163). The diverse changes in the French political regime and the ease with which the French adapt themselves to these changes, do not fail to astound Maturin, as they do the majority of the British people who cling to their principles of loyalty and stability.

* * *

The entrance of the allies into the French capital is an event of importance which Maturin describes first from Dublin then from Paris. In Dublin rejoicing is widespread, and the author seems to share the general feeling. He insists first of all on how remarkable an event it is—anyone predicting such a thing two years ago would have been considered insane. This time it is real, and not just something invented by some minister: «The allies were in Paris repaying the friendly visits they had received from Buonaparte at Vienna, Berlin and Moscow» (II, 166). Maturin acclaims the official press, scorning the news-sheets of the opposition, especially *The Dublin Evening Post* which, three days before the allied entry into Paris had proclaimed: «Defeat and Distraction of the Allies» (II, 168). The reaction of most Dubliners is a feeling of what Maturin calls «loyal rational joy» (II, 169), a sense of relief in the face of a long-awaited victory. The most impartial and true to life description of the events of this period can be found in the following lines:

> The general sentiment was certainly that of joy. The appalling supernatural greatness of Buonaparte had terrified, even those who wished him well, and men seemed relieved, as from the spell of an enchanter.
>
> (II, 169)

Whatever the historical importance of the fall of Napoleon Maturin is mainly concerned with showing how it affects his heroes. Thus Zaïra agrees to sing in public the anthem composed by Pucitta: «Esulta Britannia, di Wellington madre», and it is on this occasion that her affair with de Courcy, who has come with hundreds of others to applaud her, comes out into the open.

* * *

From Dublin we move to Paris, and the descriptions of the two capitals resemble each other in that both are seen from a double point of view: historical and romanesque. Once again Paris is portrayed as the metropolis of Europe, this time with the arrival of the allies to justify the description, since everyone who matters seems to be there. Two things stand out for the reader; firstly the incredible accumulation of wealth—works of art both ancient and modern, riches brought from Herculaneum, Thebes, Alexandria, Milan, Moscow, Berlin and Vienna:

> All the riches of that dreadful harvest, that had been reaped in blood from one end of the earth to the other were accumulated there.

(III, 17)

Secondly the arrival of all the important figures of Europe—emperors, kings, heroes—, bringing together the finest examples of genius, patriotism, power and military worth. The implication of Maturin's description is clear: if the French capital is rich and beautiful, it is to the ruins of Europe, plundered by her armies that she owes this wealth. As for the exalted qualities of the allied statesmen, these merely serve to diminish France and the French by comparison. While a critical observer of the events of his time, the author does not forget that he is a novelist, and his description also helps to further the plot. Charles de Courcy, who has followed Zaïra to Paris, suddenly finds himself plunged into an atmosphere which is completely new to him: «Charles believed himself breathing empyreal air; he felt the military mania in all its first intoxicating inspiration». (III, 18) And the young man, aware of having been completely wrapped up in his own problems until then, begins to despise himself for having wasted his time between Zaïra's boudoir and the house of Eva Wentworth: «Europe had been won and lost, and he had not struck a blow for her safety, or her ruin!» (III, 19) The fall of the Napoleonic Empire, therefore, plays at least some part in de Courcy's detachment from Zaïra. Once again it is France, already the cause of so many evils, that pushes him towards his second infidelity. Moreover the young woman he falls in love with (Eulalie de Touranges) is herself French; she is pretty, admittedly, but being French is also, by definition, frivolous, cold-hearted and lacking in intelligence.

* * *

From this we can see the extent of Maturin's interest in France despite his criticism of French institutions, of the ambitions of the French leaders, of the perversity of French authors and of the superficiality of the French people in general. We might point out here that Maturin learnt the French language in 1817,[7] partly as a means of earning money through translations, but mainly to assuage his thirst for reading. It is worth noting that he owes a great deal to French authors—we find echoes of *La Nouvelle Héloïse* in *The Wild Irish Boy* for example, and Mme de Staël's *Corinne* served as a model for *Women.* Thus not only does Maturin use France as a background for his novels, but the latter are also deeply influenced by the works of French writers.

Maturin's portrait of France in *The Albigenses* confirms what we have already noted in *Women* and *The Wild Irish Boy.* The conflict between the Catharists and the Crusaders is merely a pretext for praising resistance to Papism. The Catholic leaders, Simon de Montfort and the Bishop of Toulouse are odious; the heretics on the other hand, lacking in malice and prejudice, have an admirable faith. The target of Maturin's criticism here is not France but French Catholicism, and it is in this question of religion that we find the real reason of his francophobia. The French people, made up of Catholics, that is fanatics, and of philosophers, therefore atheists, not only succumb to corruption but also help to spread it. France, Maturin writes in his «Sermon preached on the death of Lord Nelson» is a country which prides itself on setting up «the standard of depravity to the rest of Europe».[8] In this long sermon Maturin the preacher goes all out to condemn France and the French: the clergy half-heartedly serve a God in whom they have no faith, the nobility, lacking in all force and dignity, are only concerned with material things, the philosophers teach that «the contempt of the Lord is the beginning of wisdom» (p. 56).

From this we can see that there is no dividing line between Maturin's novels and his religious works. If his sermons provide us with the theory, if they are a treatise on ethics, his novels supply practical illustrations of that theory. The condemnation of France to be found in *The Wild Irish Boy* and *Women* is, without doubt, a condemnation on religious and moral grounds which a precise description of the political situation merely serves to heighten.

Notes

1. C. R. Maturin: *The Wild Irish Boy,* London, Longman, Hurst, Rees and Orme, 1808, 3 vols., III, 300.

2. C. R. Maturin: *Women; Or, Pour et Contre,* London, Longman, Hurst, Rees and Orme; Edinburgh, Constable, 1818, 3 vols., II, 83-4.

3. Despite his Irish patriotism and his hostility towards the Union of 1800, Maturin praised Britain on several occasions, sometimes in an extravagant way.

4. Philosopher, atheist and blasphemer are synonyms for him. We find for example in *Women*: "Cardonneau talking the whole time like an atheist, or in his own phrase *en philosophe*" and later: "His toothache had ceased and Cardonneau was able to talk blasphemy as well as ever" (III, 176-7).

5. C. R. Maturin: *Melmoth the Wanderer*, Lincoln, University of Nebraska Press, 1963, p. 380.

6. Paris "the metropolis of Europe" (*Women*, I, 228), becomes "the metropolis of the world" (II, 162).

7. "I (. . .) have latterly made myself master of French", Letter to Walter Scott, March 27th, 1817. F. E. Ratchford and W. H. Mc Carthy, Jr., eds.: *The Correspondence of Sir Walter Scott and Charles Robert Maturin,* University of Texas Press, 1937, p. 71.

8. C. R. Maturin: *Sermons,* Edinburgh, Constable; London, Hurst, Robinson and C° 1819, p. 54.

David Eggenschwiler (essay date June 1975)

SOURCE: Eggenschwiler, David. "*Melmoth the Wanderer*: Gothic on Gothic." *Genre* 8, no. 2 (June 1975): 165-81.

[*In the following essay, Eggenschwiler argues that Maturin's works are superior to those of other Gothic writers of his era, particularly in their stylistic sophistication, their intellectual coherence, and their psychological depth. In this respect, according to Eggenschwiler, Maturin stands squarely on the threshold between the Gothic and Romantic forms.*]

Melmoth the Wanderer is often called the greatest Gothic romance of the Romantic period, yet there has been little systematic attempt to justify its high praise. Anyone who has travelled with the Wanderer from Ireland to India, from dungeons to an island paradise, knows one reason for its popularity: it is almost an anthology of Gothic fiction. Charles Robert Maturin, an Anglican curate who admittedly wrote to supplement his small income, knew how to mine his predecessors for the sadistic monks, cynical villain-heroes, and persecuted heroines who had been popular for several decades; and, in doing so, he produced a usefully representative work for students of literary history. But obviously representativeness is not literary value; so one must look further for signs of *Melmoth* [*Melmoth the Wanderer*]'s greatness.

Defenders of the Gothic romance in general usually stress the psychological and moral complexity of the genre, showing that it explored relationships between love and hate, good and evil, fascination and repulsion that had not been so extensively treated before the late eighteenth century.[1] And surely Maturin describes these emotional paradoxes as dramatically as any writer of his time. But even on these grounds *Melmoth* and its predecessors have been considered only poor relatives of other Romantic works. Robert D. Hume has made the distinction clearly: "Romantic writing reconciles the discordant elements it faces, resolving their apparent contradictions imaginatively in the creation of a higher order. Gothic writing, the product of serious fancy, has no such answers and can only leave the 'opposites' contradictory and paradoxical. In its highest forms romantic writing claims the existence of higher answers where Gothic can find only unresolvable moral and emotional ambiguity."[2] In this view, the Gothic is at its best a rudimentary Romanticism with a sense of problems and complexities but without the imaginative coherence to understand these problems thoroughly and resolve them. It has psychological insights, challenges to rationalistic platitudes, intuitive rumblings from the unconscious, but no means to unite its fragments; as its authors warble their unnatural woodnotes wild, we are to find something lacking—reason in its most exalted mood, the Secondary Imagination, the hammer of Los—some faculty that could make harmonious thunderings out of all that interesting crash and rattle.

Yet it is precisely on this question that Maturin surpasses those terror romances (most notably *The Italian* and *The Monk*) that were his sources for many incidents, characters, and settings. Maturin wrote not only a more inclusive and psychologically acute Gothic romance than did these predecessors, but he also wrote a more complete one, for he seems to have understood better than his sources the ethical, philosophical, and psychological significances of the Gothic form. Writing at the end of the movement, he pointedly examined man's fascination with terror and the supernatural, thereby using his Gothic romance to evaluate its own imaginative form and forcing the reader to examine his own attractions to it. Briefly, he described many ways in which man compulsively pursues unnatural experiences, and he implied an ethical and religious norm of the natural that was commonplace in late eighteenth-century literature. In fact, his ideal of nature culminated in the soft primitivist's idyll of a tropical island, an appropriate symbol from the Age of Sensibility.[3] Then, however, he used a brilliant and solidly Romantic reversal. He showed that the ideal of nature was not fully human, that man's desire for the unnatural was a symptom of his spirituality, and that man's demonic drives were closely related to his striving for salvation. But he did not merely conclude that good is much like evil and love much like hate; he did not overturn the structure of his romance to play with moral ambiguities and unresolved paradoxes. With extensive help from Goethe, he formed a complex and coherent image of man that gave his Gothic horrors a fuller context and more explicit meaning. Working with the literary tools of Sensibility, he made a work that approached the center of Romanticism.

* * *

Maturin begins his ethical and psychological study in the frame story with old Melmoth, the dying miser who spends his last hours worrying that his servants will burn his candles wastefully, that his nephew and heir will steal his wine, and that a clergyman will charge him for the last rites. A conventional humours character, the old man has made country frugality an obsession. Instead of enjoying the fruits of a fertile land, he has turned them into useless counters in his rage to possess. Although the obsession may have begun in a rational motive of thrift, it has become irrational, a psychological monstrosity that is its own end and that destroys the wealth it pretends to conserve. His macabre estate is both literal evidence of the natural world he has perverted and a symbolic reflection of his arid, self-destroying mind:

> As Melmoth leaned against the window, whose dismantled frame, and pieced and shattered panes, shook with every gust of wind, his eye encountered nothing but that most cheerless of all prospects, a miser's garden,—walls broken down, grass-grown walks whose grass was not even green, dwarfish, doddered, leafless trees, and a luxuriant crop of nettles and weeds rearing their unlovely heads where there had once been flowers, all waving and bending in capricious and unsightly forms, as the wind sighed over them. It was the verdure of the church-yard, the garden of death.[4]

This first variation of the Gothic, symbolized by the deathly garden, the wasted Eden, is built on two main ethical traits, extremity and isolation. The extreme pursuit of a single object, even though the object may be worthy, sins against a sane, Aristotelian moderation and destroys a natural equilibrium within man and within the natural world he inhabits. This single-minded pursuit also breaks man's connections with other men and with nature; it destroys fellow-feeling and isolates him in the symbolic prisons, madhouses, and monastic cells that fill the romance. Old Melmoth must be withdrawn and suspicious of all people, and his wariness of his nephew suggests the first of several broken family ties in the book.

In itself, this account of miserliness is so obviously within the moral tradition of humours-comedy that it only implies the Gothic of the tales it introduces, but it is soon closely associated with that horror. The old man has another obsession besides wealth: he is fascinated by his ancestor, the Wanderer, a figure of demonic power who has roamed the world for two centuries. In a locked room with bricked-up windows (another image of isolation) old Melmoth keeps the Wanderer's portrait and a seventeenth-century manuscript he secretly studies. Since he also keeps his hoarded wine in this room, there is an implied relationship between the two obsessions, but his fascination with the Wanderer goes far beyond such ethical concerns as avarice. Lacking a sensible motive, it is a purely irrational interest in the forbidden and spiritually unnatural, and it is so strong that it seems partly responsible for summoning the Wanderer, whose shocking appearance helps to kill the old man. The obsession is then passed on to the old man's nephew, who decides not to return to college but to remain at the estate because "curiosity or something that perhaps deserves a better name, the wild and awful pursuit of an indefinite object, had taken strong hold of his mind" (16). This awful pursuit causes the following tales to be read or told, and since young Melmoth's position as audience of the tales is much like that of the reader of the romance, he helps to implicate the reader in an unnatural fascination similar to his own and to that of the other characters.

Stanton, the author of the old manuscript, is most completely dominated by such a fascination. While travelling in Spain in 1676, he first meets the Wanderer among Moorish and Roman ruins, in a violent storm, after seeing two lovers who have just been consumed by lightning. He is told of the Wanderer's appearance years before when, in the midst of a wedding feast attended by that mysterious Englishman, a priest is struck dead upon sensing the presence of the "evil power," the bride dies in her lover's arms, and the bridegroom goes mad. By the conventional use of the moldering, scarcely legible manuscript, Maturin presents these macabre fragments without comment or continuity; the broken text creates suspense, shock, and the strange "indefinite object" that lures young Melmoth and the reader to look further into this mystery. The crumbling manuscript with its well-timed hiatuses is stock-in-trade with Gothic writers, a bit of familiar machinery, but that, too, is much to the point. Maturin not only creates suspense, he calls attention to it and to the effect it has on young Melmoth's "inflamed curiosity," and he implies that this growing curiosity resembles the obsession that causes Stanton to spend the rest of his life searching for the Wanderer. What the fictional reader of the manuscript and the actual reader of Maturin's romance experience, Stanton carries to a self-lacerating extreme.

When the manuscript resumes after a few illegible pages, Stanton has returned to England, but his soul is "devoured" by one passion, the desire to look again on his inhuman countryman, the "constant subject of his contemplation." He admits to himself that he does not know what he would do if he found the Wanderer; he has no clear and conscious motive, such as the traditional Faustian longing for power or knowledge. He knows only that he has experienced something so unearthly and enthralling that he can no longer be content with his natural surroundings. Alone and palely loitering in London, he looks, as we do, for the strange creature to reappear. In order to find temporary relief he attends public amusements where Maturin further entwines this spiritual disease with moral and esthetic ones. There we find the "splendid, ostentatious, and obtrusive vices" of a legendary Restoration society. These excesses of spectacle and affectation are at the opposite extreme from old Melmoth's miserliness, but they, too, violate moderation and balance. They, too, sin against nature, and they are appropriately symbolized by a transvestite, "the Adonis of the day," who is exhibited in the park by a woman of fashion. It is also appropriate that these social excesses are described mainly in relation to the theatre, where rakes adore women as goddesses and assail them as prostitutes, critics savagely await their literary prey, and, above all, the happy souls of the gallery wait to be thrilled by "the ghost of Alamanzor's mother in her dripping shroud, or that of Laius" and by the "Spanish and Moorish subjects" that Howard, Settle, and Dryden use in their plays (32-33). Maturin's condescension to the simple tastes of the gallery is ironic, because his romance also conjures up such graveyard spectacles and most of it is set in mysterious, Catholic Spain. When the Wanderer suddenly appears to Stanton in the audience, the last strain is entwined, and the theatrical symbol is completed. The popular theatre is artificial and serves what Wordsworth criticized as the "degrading thirst after outrageous stimulation" in the audiences of his day; thus it becomes a useful image for social, religious, and esthetic desires to subvert nature. It will again be metaphorically related to desires for still more bizarre experience, and it becomes a symbolic reflection of Maturin's Gothicism, itself.

Because of Stanton's continuous pursuit of the Wanderer, a scheming relative is able to imprison him in a madhouse, where the themes developed in London are intensified. The extremes of Restoration society are represented by maniacal sectarians: a mad puritan, a mad loyalist, and a schizophrenic preacher-blasphemer. But more interesting than this familiar historical caricature, which Scott had already drawn in *Old Mortality,* is Stanton's development. After long isolation in his cell (which may be symbolic as well as literal), he finds that his revulsion at the other inmates begins to become interest: "The twitter of the sparrows, the pattering of rain, or the moan of the wind, sounds that he used to sit up in his bed to catch with delight, as reminding him of nature, were now unheeded. He began at times to listen with sullen and horrible pleasure to the cries of his miserable companions" (41). When the Wanderer appears, he tells Stanton that this fascination will increase:

> The time will come, when, from the want of occupation, the listless and horrible vacancy of yours hours, you will feel as anxious to hear those shrieks, as you were at first terrified to hear them,—when you will watch for the ravings of your next neighbor, as you would for a scene on the stage. All humanity will be extinguished in you. The ravings of these wretches will become at once your sport and your torture. You will watch for the sounds, to mock them with the grimaces and bellowings of a fiend.

(42)

The Restoration play has become the theatrical hysteria of bedlam; we have progressed from young John Melmoth's mental idleness to Stanton's "vacancy," a form of lethargy and perverse imaginative hunger that has gone far beyond the eighteenth-century's "spleen" and begins to suggest Baudelaire's *ennui.* Although Stanton is finally freed from this literal madhouse, he is not freed from his obsession, his passion and torment, which he admits is a form of madness.

After finishing the manuscript, John Melmoth rescues a shipwrecked Spaniard named Monçada, who tells him the remaining tales of the book. Monçada's own story begins with the unnatural act of parental betrayal. Because he was conceived before his parents were married, his mother decides that he will be a monk; to expiate her crime she offers him as a sacrifice, trying to buy her salvation by denying her natural ties. (Similar denials occur in two later tales: in the "Tale of Guzman's Family" a father is so maddened by poverty and starvation that he tries to kill his wife and children; in the "Lovers' Tale" a woman falsely denies her son's legitimacy to keep him from making a financially imprudent marriage.) From this perverted motherhood the tale moves to the perverted metaphorical fatherhood of the Church. The monks, particularly the spiritual Director of the family and the Superior of the monastery, are wildly jealous of their power and try to break Monçada's resistance by threats and torture. With the Inquisition in the background as the epitome of this lust for righteousness and power, the Spanish society thwarts the ends of nature it is intended to serve: in its familial, religious, and political institutions it sacrifices humanity for man's excessive longings.

But, once again, there are many acts and experiences that do not have even these rational motives, and again they originate in what Monçada calls the boredom and dreariness of monastic life (72). By now, however, they are not merely the pursuit of the unnatural, but the performance of it in elaborate acts of sadism. Of many instances, the most obviously gratuitous and perverse is the torture of a beautiful young novice:

> A naked human being, covered with blood, and uttering screams of rage and torture, flashed by me; four monks pursued him—they had lights. I had shut the door at

the end of the gallery—I felt they must return and pass me—I was still on my knees, and trembling from head to foot. The victim reached the door, found it shut, and rallied. I turned, and saw a groupe worthy of Murillo. A more perfect human form never existed than that of this unfortunate youth. He stood in an attitude of despair—he was streaming with blood. The monks, with their lights, their scourges, and their dark habits, seemed like a groupe of demons who had made prey of a wandering angel,—the groupe resembled the infernal furies pursuing a mad Orestes. And, indeed, no ancient sculptor ever designed a figure more exquisite and perfect than that they had so barbarously mangled.

(83)

The references to Murillo and the sculpture are pointed: the monks have artificially arranged the scene for erotically sadistic experience. It recalls Monçada's comments about his own persecution: "Whether I was mad or not, they cared very little; to enroll a son of the first house of Spain among their converts, or to imprison him as a madman, or to exorcise him as a demoniac, was all the same to them. There was a *coup de théâtre* to be exhibited, and providing they played first parts, they cared little about the catastrophe" (72). The theatrics of bedlam have become fatal.

Even Monçada, who has been imprisoned and tortured by the Church, feels overwhelmingly elated as he watches the procession of the Inquisition: "nothing was ever more imposing, or more magnificent. The habits of the ecclesiastics, the glare of the torches struggling with the dying twilight, and seeming to say to heaven, We have a sun though yours is set. . . . It was a sight to convert all hearts, and I exulted I was a Catholic" (194). This magnificence soon turns violent as the crowd seizes a parricidal monk and kills him with extremely horrible and minutely described cruelty. Even now Monçada finds himself engrossed in this spectacle ("It is a fact, Sir, that while witnessing this horrible execution, I felt all the effects vulgarly ascribed to fascination" [196]), and he vicariously participates in this "drama of terror." Like many Gothic writers who followed the *via media* of Anglicanism, Maturin both condemned and was intrigued by the unnatural violence and rituals of such conventional, fictional Catholicism. It is the subject of over one-third of the book and an effective analogy of Maturin's own Gothicism.

As Monçada flees from the Inquisition he stumbles upon a bizarre underground chambre, where an aged Jew who has been punished for seeking forbidden knowledge has him translate a manuscript containing the last three tales of the book. The two shorter tales do not extend much the themes already developed, but the long "Tale of the Indians," which is often called the finest section of the entire work, clarifies, elaborates, and finally transforms those themes.

Until this point in the romance the moral and psychological norm of nature has been vague or implicit. At times, Maturin has commented that the cruelty and obsession he has described violate nature (e.g., 40, 97, 101), but he has used the term only in a loose, popular sense to imply moderation, sanity, practical self-interest, compassion, toleration, sensibleness, and an easy enjoyment of physical nature—that is, the qualities that had become familiarly associated with the term through nearly a century of deistic usage. Now, Maturin makes his concept more explicit through some conventional cultural primitivism. On a lush and peaceful island off the coast of India lives Immalee—child of nature, softly noble savage, moral ideal. Shipwrecked as an infant, the maiden has blossomed alone on this island paradise, where she is worshipped as a white goddess by the natives of the area. Naive, intuitive, spontaneous, compassionate, joyful, beautiful, unself-conscious, she is a cliché of innocence. Having grown in sun and shower, she seems a personified part of the natural world that ministers to her and that she loves in tranquil joy. When the Wanderer appears and tells her of the ways of civilized men, she is shocked and puzzled by the horrors he cynically describes: the self-destroying worshippers of Juggernaut, the European wars from greed and boredom, the righteous hostility of religious sects. And she is elated when he describes an ideal Christianity of family love, toleration, and devotion—a rather broad-church religion of natural goodness and, of course, the antithesis of the Catholicism described in the preceding tale. In her innocence she is hardly a character at all, rather a moral personification that can turn a cute and sentimental phrase; she is a curio from the Age of Sensibility, but her initial flatness will prove useful in the full context of the romance.

Under the influence of the demonic Melmoth, Immalee begins to develop into a woman of feeling; she learns the pleasures of melancholy. Never having known fear, guilt, or the awareness of death, she is tutored in the ways of the world and finds the pains of consciousness enjoyable: "I begin to comprehend what he said—to think, then, is to suffer—and a world of thought must be a world of pain! But how delicious are these tears! Formerly I wept for pleasure—but there is a pain sweeter than pleasure, that I never felt till I beheld *him*" (221). Fallen from Innocence into Experience and suffering from Melmoth's frequent desertions, she loses her completely natural existence:

> Now she stood as if deserted even by nature, whose child she was; the rock was her resting place, and the ocean seemed the bed where she purposed to rest; she had no shells on her bosom, no roses in her hair—her character seemed to have changed with her feelings; she no longer loved all that is beautiful in nature; she seemed, by an anticipation of her destiny, to make alliance with all that is awful and ominous. She had begun to love the rocks and the ocean, the thunder of the

wave, and the sterility of the sand,—awful objects, the incessant recurrence of whose very sound seems intended to remind us of grief and of eternity.

(239)

Having lost her love of the beautiful, Immalee has acquired a taste for the sublime, a Gothic staple to which Maturin gives a solidly orthodox interpretation: vastness, powerfulness, and a suggestion of the eternal. Such feelings are still more unnatural in her relations with Melmoth, especially in her attraction to his power and in her increasing submissiveness, which Maturin describes as an "irresistably humiliating" impulse. This masochistic desire disturbingly recalls the neighboring Indians who throw themselves under the wheels of Juggernaut. Although she remains loving and morally pure, she has begun to show some of the psychological traits of Stanton and Monçada. Yet, with its beginnings of consciousness, love, and a vague religious sense, Immalee's fall from soft primitivism into the cult of feeling is not entirely unfortunate.

After a three-year break in the narrative, Immalee has been rescued from the island and returned to her family in Madrid, where she is given her Christian name of Isadora. The change from her Indian name signifies a new process of her transformation, one paralleling her development as Immalee but occurring in a new context and at a higher level of spiritual significance. As she developed from Innocence into the painful consciousness of Experience, so now, as Isadora, she passes through an increasingly Gothic Experience to achieve a higher spiritual Innocence, which is very different from the natural state in which she began on the island.[5]

In Madrid she first appears as an ideally pure Christian maiden. Her humility contrasts with her mother's dogmatic self-righteousness, her simple faith with the Catholic Church's ritualism, and her charity with the vengefulness of the Inquisition. But her separateness and her sorrow over Melmoth, who compassionately deserted her on the island, suggest that her state is precarious. When Melmoth reappears and begins to visit her at night, she passes into what Maturin calls both a "visionary existence" and a "fatal delusion" (273). Although she remains emphatically pure and devout, she becomes more possessed by her love for the cursed Wanderer; she even desperately claims that she will go with him to the infernal kingdom he mockingly describes as his own. Commenting on her religious naivety, Maturin states that "Isadora had not yet learned that theology of the skies, whose text is, 'Let us go into the house of mourning'" (274); but she is about to enter that house and learn that theology.

Retaining her Christian faith, she insists that Melmoth wed her, but she reluctantly agrees to elope with him into what turns out to be an unholy union. Following

him into a ruined monastery, where a prior once read forbidden books and where banditti now hide, she acquiesces in what she rightly fears is a murder, and she is married to Melmoth by a dead hermit. After this Gothic climax, she suffers in her secret marriage and pregnancy, estranged from her family and the confessional. Again Maturin reminds us that "grief and pain are very eloquent interpreters between us and eternity" (389), and, sensing her approaching death, Isadora speaks increasingly of Christ and immortality. To complete her pain, she must see her protective brother stabbed by Melmoth, she must be imprisoned and tortured by the Inquisition, and she must even welcome her suffering baby's death in the dungeon. And to complete her spiritual transformation through this pain, she turns more completely to God and eternity. When Melmoth appears in her cell to offer her escape at the cost of her soul, she refuses him and tells her priest, "'Oh that I had loved none but God—how profound would have been my peace—how glorious my departure'" (405). Yet this love of God has been reached through her terrible, indestructable love for Melmoth, and as the priest assures her of a place in paradise, she fittingly cries, "'Will he be there!'"

Immalee-Isadora's development from white goddess of nature to holy penitent of Christianity is thoroughly achieved through plot and characterization, but it is also underscored by a surprisingly extensive set of parallels to *Faust, Part I.* It has often been noted that Maturin was much influenced by Goethe, but there has been no attempt to explain why he borrowed to an extent that goes beyond influence and becomes systematic allusion. In creating the character of the Wanderer he used broadly traditional conceptions of Faust and Mephistopheles, which he combined into one figure; but in creating Immalee-Isadora he pointedly used the Gretchen tragedy, which Goethe had first published in the 1808 version of *Faust.* Like Immalee, Gretchen is simple, open, and pure, and Goethe's commentators have often considered her a part of nature.[6] But she, too, falls in love with a cursed, inconstant man, thereby losing her peacefulness but gaining a religious insight of which she was not previously capable.[7]

There is, however, an important difference between the two patterns, one that distinguishes the moral tragedy from the Gothic romance. According to her sincere religious beliefs, Gretchen's love for Faust causes her to sin, and she suffers most from guilt. In contrast, Maturin keeps his heroine morally pure, insisting on her chastity, marrying her to Melmoth, largely exonerating her in her brother's death, and making the Inquisition responsible for her child's death. This melodramatic purity prevents Isadora from achieving Gretchen's morally tragic stature, and it shifts the emphasis almost entirely to her involvement with the supernatural. Whereas Gretchen remains ignorant of Faust's magical powers,

Isadora has "visionary experiences" with Melmoth and a "wandering image of preternatural power" when she thinks of him. Although she is extraordinarily naive, she knows that he is no mere mortal, and she responds with fascination as well as fear to his demonic qualities. Whereas Gretchen's love leads her into fornication and infanticide, Isadora's leads her to the ruined monastery and the dead hermit. Ultimately, though, both journeys end in a heightened awareness of God.[8] Through his parallels with *Faust,* then, Maturin reinforces his theme of religious awakening; through his departures from *Faust,* he reinforces his emphasis on Gothic longings as the means to that awakening.

This final tale, the climactic and most complex section of the book, puts the rest of the tales into a larger perspective. In the others, Maturin used natural affection, goodness, and sanity as the norm by which he judged his characters' obsessions with Gothic experience. In this tale, he explores the norm of nature and, despite its great value, finds it inadequate to assess man's spiritual worth. Immalee-Isadora's devotion to the cursed Wanderer, her appreciation of sorrow and the sublimely awful, her dream-like ecstasy, and her supernatural wedding are all unnatural, but they are all signs that she is infinitely greater than the natural creatures among whom she originally lived on the island, and they are also processes of the fortunate fall by which she comes more consciously to God and salvation. Thus, we are forced to revaluate young John Melmoth's wild curiosity, Stanton's obsessive pursuit of the Wanderer, Monçada's fascination with the splendor and violence of the Inquisition, even the compulsive immorality, gratuitous sadism, and—eventually—the readers' own interest in these Gothic tales. Although these interests and obsessions range from the imprudent to the monstrously evil, they, too, are signs that man is a spiritual being who cannot live entirely in the natural world. In this, Maturin examines the genre of the Gothic romance, itself, and associates it with the ambiguities of Faustian striving.

But Maturin does not stop at this impasse, confronted by the ambivalent qualities of man's unnatural desires. After all, his heroine is not a raving monk with a whip, and her love for Melmoth is not the blood-lust of the Inquisition. All spiritual desires are not of equal worth. Maturin establishes the point most clearly in his opposition of Immalee-Isadora and Melmoth. By the end of the tale, she has a spiritual strength and stature almost as great as the Wanderer's, but opposite his. Her spiritual experiences are all associated with self-sacrifice and a love that even Melmoth defines as feeling that "our existence is so absorbed in his, that we have lost all consciousness but of his presence—all sympathy but of his enjoyments—all sense of suffering but when he suffers—*to be* only because *he is*—and to have no other use of being but to devote it to him, while our humiliation increases in proportion to our devotedness" (279).

She develops such self-denying love for the Wanderer and ends by recognizing God as its proper object: "Oh that I had loved none but God" (405). In contrast, Melmoth's power is inseparable from his self-assertion. Having begun with a proud longing for forbidden knowledge and power, he has become arrogant, cynical, and murderous, finding his only rest from self-absorption in his inconstant love for the woman he marries and finally tries to damn. Having sold his soul for an extra one-hundred-fifty years of life, he spends most of that time in the petty search for a person sufficiently desperate to take his place. She progresses from love to active faith, he from egoism to defiance.

In these relationships between nature and the human spirit, and between faith and defiance, Maturin has gone far beyond the Age of Sensibility and the unresolved contradictions that Professor Hume attributed to the Gothic romance. Maturin is of the Romantic tradition and anticipates Kierkegaard and Dostoevsky, two great religious Romantics who explored more fully the faith and despair of those who venture beyond the limits of nature. The mention of these later writers, however, should warn us not to overstate the case. While Maturin found man's natural and social qualities to be only parts of his whole self, he still considered them very important parts. Isadora does not become an existentially religious heroine; she retains her natural affections and her sense of human ties until her death. Her spiritual growth completes her natural self; it places it in its eternal context, but it does not destroy it.

This religious position is appropriate to the Anglican curate who once described himself to Sir Walter Scott as a "high Calvinist."[9] His sermons that were published one year before *Melmoth* give explicit theological statement of the themes I have pointed out in his romance.[10] On the one hand, in such pieces as the "Charity Sermon Preached for the Parish of Coolock," he stresses the importance of benevolence, compassion, and responsibility to others; and he repeatedly rails against vice, the desire for power, and ceremonial excesses (including monasticism and the worship of Juggernaut, which he describes in *Melmoth*). On the other hand, he repeatedly warns his parishioners that goodness, peace, and wisdom cannot come primarily through natural means: the belief "that the powers of unassisted nature are available advocates with the Deity" is presumptuous and worthless; peace can be found only "at the foot of the cross . . . in the sacrifice of all earthly cares, and the submission of all earthly feelings" and divine truth is "a discovery of that which was totally unknown,—of that which we could never have otherwise known" (*Sermons,* 431, 330, 215). While his Calvinism is "high," with an Anglican concern for communal worship and good works, it is assuredly Calvinism, calling on man to renounce his "utterly fallen" nature and to become a "new Creation" (*Sermons,* 222-223). This mixed theological position, which Maturin claimed made him unpopular with his church, underlies *Melmoth,* which was also unpopular with the Anglican orthodoxy. This position helps to show why in the romance he valued the norm of nature, the *via media* of Anglicanism, but why he also valued the Gothic extravagances that can lead man not only to the demonic but also to the foot of the cross, to "that which we could never have otherwise known."

As Maturin explores man's fascination with Gothic experiences, he also explores the popularity, danger, and value of the literary genre. Using characters who are enchanted readers of, listeners to, and spectators at, the bizarre theatricals, he shows that the Gothic quest is accompanied by a quest for the Gothic; and he expands his psychological and religious themes into a corresponding esthetic one. In this, too, he resembles his great Romantic contemporaries, who also made their art its own subject and a reflection of the human spirit. In *Melmoth* he develops the esthetic theme obliquely and metaphorically, but in one of his sermons he is explicit about the value of the romance:

> Where is the being who does not feel that restless consciousness of immortality within him that forbids him to sit down to the banquet of life while the sword of destruction impends over him? Man bears witness to the feeling in every stage of existence. The very first sounds of childhood are tales of another life—foolishly are they called tales of superstition; for, however disguised by the vulgarity of narration, and the distortion of fiction, they tell him of those whom he is hastening from the threshold of life to join, the inhabitants of the invisible world, with whom he must soon be, and be for ever.
>
> (*Sermons,* 358)[11]

The restless consciousness, the insufficiency of life's banquet, the tales of the invisible world—these are central themes in *Melmoth,* where they help to unify that Gothic anthology and to resolve the moral and psychological contradictions that it, like its predecessors in the form, reveals.

Notes

1. See, for example, Devendra P. Varma, *The Gothic Flame* (London, 1957), Chapter 8; Lowry Nelson Jr., "Night Thoughts on the Gothic Novel," [*Yale Review*], LII (1963), 236-57; Leven Dawson, "*Melmoth the Wanderer*: Paradox and the Gothic Novel," [*Studies in English Literature*], VIII (1968), 621-32.

2. "Gothic Versus Romantic: A Revaluation of the Gothic Novel," *PMLA,* LXXXIV (1969), 290.

3. In using this term throughout, I am relying on Northrop Frye's well-known essay, "Towards Defining an Age of Sensibility," *ELH,* XXIII (1956),

144-52, especially his discussions of emotional states and the relation of the soul to nature.

4. Charles Robert Maturin, *Melmoth the Wanderer* (Lincoln, Nebraska, 1961), p. 19. This edition is used throughout this essay with page references incorporated into the text.

5. Because her two names signify two importantly different periods in her life, I shall preserve useful, if confusing, distinctions by calling her "Immalee" when referring only to her life on the island, "Isadora" when referring only to her life in Madrid, and the unfortunately awkward "Immalee-Isadora" when referring to her entire life.

6. Typical is Alexander Gillies' comment in *Goethe's Faust* (Oxford, 1957), pp. 64-65: "Gretchen thus symbolizes for [Faust] . . . the orderliness and fullness of the universe. She is a part of nature. All her actions in her everyday life reflect naturalness and purity."

7. The two cases are elaborately similar in details: Gretchen also worries about getting married, finds no help from family or priest, helps to cause her interfering brother to be stabbed, is imprisoned, loses her newborn child, refuses her lover's offer of escape, turns passionately to God, is pronounced saved, and is last heard calling out for her lover.

8. Maturin creates another, fainter parallel in the "Lovers' Tale." Elinor Mortimer, whose lover has rejected her on their intended wedding day, also achieves a more intense religious awareness through suffering: "'Oh, my God!' she continued, 'you who have clothed my heart with such burning energies—you who have given it a power of loving so intense, so devoted, so concentrated—you have not given it in vain;—no, in some happier world, or perhaps even in this, when this "tyranny is overpast," you will fill my heart with an image worthier than him whom I once believed your image on earth. . . . [The stars'] glorious light burns for remote and happier worlds; and the beam of religion that glows so feebly to eyes almost blind with earthly tears, may be rekindled when a broken heart has been my passport to a place of rest'" (371).

9. *The Correspondence of Sir Walter Scott and Charles Robert Maturin* [, F. E. Ratchford and W. H. McCarthy Jr., eds.] (Austin, 1937), p. 10.

10. *Sermons* (London, 1819). Although most of the sermons are undated, the arrangement of the dated ones suggests that those I cite were delivered in 1817 and 1818.

11. In his first Gothic romance, *Fatal Revenge; or, The Family of Montorio* (London, 1807), Maturin

is much simpler in his portrayal of Gothic long-ings. Fascination with the supernatural causes two young Venetians to be manipulated by a vengeful trickster and illusionist, who terrifies them, drives them nearly mad, and makes them kill their appar-ent father. Although the young men end up sadder and wiser, they do not approach Isadora's conver-sion, and the narrator can point a pat moral: "they who desired the knowledge of things concealed from man, found their pursuit accompanied by guilt, and terminated by misery and punishment" (III, 493). Yet, in his prefatory defense of the Gothic romance, Maturin praises the "passion of supernatural fear" in a way that anticipates his later, fuller insights: "I must trace this passion to a high and obvious source. . . . It is the aspiration of a spirit; 'it is the passion of immortals,' that dread and desire of their final habitation" (I, v).

Jack Null (essay date spring 1977)

SOURCE: Null, Jack. "Structure and Theme in *Melmoth the Wanderer.*" *Papers on Language and Litera-ture* 13, no. 2 (spring 1977): 136-47.

[*In the following essay, Null argues that* Melmoth the Wanderer*'s fragmented and disjointed plot is a deliber-ate reflection of the central character's troubled psyche, rather than a structural failure of the work.*]

Although most critics feel obligated at least to remark upon the intricate structure of C. R. Maturin's **Melmoth the Wanderer,** no one has examined this structure closely. (A sentence or two usually serves to acknowl-edge the unusual organization and to conclude sum-marily with a brief judgment of its effectiveness and a vague allusion to its symmetry of design.[1]) Maturin's structure is not symmetrical; rather, it is composed of beginnings and fragments. Except for Stanton's frag-mented and inconclusive manuscript (tale no. 1), the first tale to end is of Guzman's family (no. 4); and to reach this ending, one must read 332 out of a total 412 pages. Unless one assumes that this eccentric structure is mere carelessness, a gigantic but beautiful freak, a new explanation of the structure is necessary. An ex-amination of the chronological cross-references and of the complex structure reveals the novel to be an em-bodiment of a way of perceiving the truth of human ex-perience. Attention to Maturin's structural experimenta-tion, to his manipulation of time and juxtaposition of tales as a construct for a specific psychological state, will alter the judgment that he was little more than a purveyor of popular Gothic sensationalism and that **Melmoth** [**Melmoth the Wanderer**] is little more than a Gothic pot-boiler. Some Gothic trappings and tradi-tional Gothic motifs appear in **Melmoth,** to be sure; but

Maturin has infused these motifs with a psychological intensity not inherent in the borrowed elements them-selves. Maturin achieves this intensity by fragmenting the structure to reflect organically the disorientation caused by the characters' loss of values. The disjunc-tion of the chronology and the fragmentation of the plot into tales reflect a world in great upheaval, a world be-come madhouse in which the characters search, aim-lessly and unsuccessfully, for selfhood, sanity, salva-tion.

The key to the chronology of Melmoth's adventures is found in the two concluding chapters, particularly in the short, surrealistic "Wanderer's Dream" sequence. In this passage and in Melmoth's speeches immediately preceding it, the exact terms of his pact with the devil and the timespan of 150 years allotted him to tempt others are clarified for the first time in the novel. The historical present of the beginning of the novel is the autumn of 1816 (5); the storm bringing young John Melmoth and Moncada together breaks on the night of 19 October (52), and "the narrative of the Spaniard had occupied many days" (406). One may assume therefore that Melmoth's allotted span expired near the end of 1816 or the beginning of 1817. If Melmoth made the pact 150 years earlier, he negotiated it in 1666-67. Per-haps Maturin intended the pact to coincide with other cataclysmic events of this *annus mirabilis.*

Confusing the exact date of the pact, however, is Mel-moth's statement to his namesake: "'Melmoth, you be-hold your ancestor—the being on whose portrait is in-scribed the date of a century and a half, is before you'" (407). If the portrait and its date of 1646 are supposed to commemorate the pact, then the specific reference both to a century and a half and to the hand in the dream pointing to the number 150 (410) is off by twenty years. It is difficult to believe that the devil would so capriciously overlook twenty years when striking bar-gains; it is difficult to believe that the man whose soul hung in the balance would not remember to the second when such a pact had been made and when it would ex-pire. But it is equally hard to ignore the date on that portrait which is referred to specifically so many times throughout the novel.

The remaining major references to Melmoth's career support either date; his appearances to various intended victims occur well after 1646 or 1666. One of his first visitations seems to have been at the ill-fated nuptials in the house of Don Pedro de Cardoza, resulting in the deaths of the priest Father Olavida and the bride Donna Ines and in the subsequent madness of the groom (24-29). Since this story is incomplete, one cannot date it definitively; but because the tale is told to Stanton on "the night of the 17th August 1677" (22) and since "none had gathered round [the tables in the Cardoza hall] for many years" (24), one may assume that this visit to the Cardozas is one of Melmoth's first after making the pact.

In "The Wanderer's Dream" Maturin presents what he probably considers the proper chronological order of Melmoth's temptings: "Suddenly a groupe of figures appeared, ascending as he fell. He grasped at them successively;—first Stanton—then Walberg—Elinor Mortimer—Isidora—Monçada—all passed him . . ." (410). This order is substantiated by internal chronology and cross-references. If Melmoth's life is reconstructed from internal dating, the result would be something like this. Melmoth is born near the end of the sixteenth century; he travels in England as a young man (1620s?) and later (after trouble in England, 1620s-30s?) in Holland and Poland with the clergyman from the "Tale of the Lovers." "Some years later" he dies in Germany (perhaps 1646 but more probably 1666), attended by this same clergyman, and soon thereafter (1666-67?) appears at the Cardoza wedding in Valencia and probably at the Lodge, where he leaves his portrait. Ten years later (1677) he appears to Stanton in Valencia (when two lovers are struck by lightning) and, later that year, in London. In 1680 he is with Immalee on her Indian isle but leaves her in 1680 or 1681 to tempt Stanton in the madhouse. Maturin's listing suggests that Walberg and Elinor's temptations follow next (1681-82?). Stanton is freed from the madhouse and seeks Melmoth (for four years?) on the Continent, then in England, and finally in Ireland, where he leaves his manuscript.[2] In 1683 Melmoth is in Madrid renewing his acquaintance with Immalee-Isidora; in late 1683 or sometime in 1684 he warns her father with the "Tale of the Lovers." In 1684-85 he tempts Isidora in the prison of the Inquisition. Then comes a hiatus of a century in his wanderings, during which the only definite information given is that sometime between 1692 and 1739 he dealt with Adonijah.[3] Moncada's adventures occur in 1798-99. The Wanderer comes home to Ireland in 1816 to be present at the death of Old Melmoth, at the shipwreck, and, finally, to keep his appointment with the devil.

It is clear, therefore, that Maturin does have a definite and consistent chronology in mind, which suggests careful planning. The result of that planning should also be apparent in the unusually fragmented and asymmetrical structure. And the structural importance of Stanton's manuscript becomes apparent because, disjointed as its shards may be, it adumbrates all the themes for the remaining tales; these tales in turn function as reflections of and variations on Stanton's tale. In short, Maturin builds thematic parallels, announced first in abbreviated fashion and then gaining emphasis and power by non-chronological repetition of the motifs.

The motifs Maturin chooses are, on the most superficial level, those of traditional Gothicism: the collapse of the family unit as bulwark of social order, for example, and the concomitant motif of religious persecution are found throughout the Gothic tradition. But the Walpole-Radcliffe-Lewis tradition usually explores the first motif only within an aristocratic context and focuses specifically on the incest motif. The religious persecution motif is uniformly seen by the traditionalists as a Catholic problem. Maturin's treatment of these motifs is more realistic, more varied, and for that reason, more universal than that of his predecessors. Indeed, Maturin anticipated comparison of his revival of these motifs with the more superficial treatment of them by the Radcliffe school in the preface to **Melmoth**:

> The "Spaniard's Tale" has been censured by a friend to whom I read it, as containing to [*sic*] much attempt at the revivification of the horrors of Radcliffe-Romance, of the persecutions of convents, and the terrors of the Inquisition.
>
> I defended myself, by trying to point out to my friend, that I had made the misery of conventual life depend less on the startling adventures one meets with in romances, than on that irritating series of petty torments which constitutes the misery of life in general. . . .
>
> [3]

Moreover, Maturin uses these motifs to make a statement, less sensational and more profound than that of the earlier Gothicists, about the role of suffering in salvation, both of oneself and of others. To embody what are essentially religious, as opposed to merely supernatural concepts, Maturin supplied examples beyond the traditional structure of intertwined plot and subplot. The result of this proliferation revivifies the old motifs and infuses them with a thematic intensity they had lost by 1820.

Each tale explores the motif of the disintegration of the family unit. Stanton is betrayed into the madhouse by his nearest relative, a cousin who covets his fortune. All the other sufferers are similarly betrayed by members of their families, those who should be closest to them. Moncada is committed to the convent as a result of his mother's vow. Within the "Tale of the Spaniard" the parricide who betrays Moncada's escape has, of course, killed his father and watched his sister and her lover starve to death. Adonijah the Jew has somehow betrayed his wife and child and caused their deaths. Isidora is betrayed by her father, mother, brother, and finally, her husband Melmoth. The Walbergs are tricked into their sufferings by the false promises of Ines Walberg's brother Guzman, and Walberg's sufferings are such that he looks upon the deaths of his parents as a blessing and contemplates killing his children. Mrs. Sandal lies to her son and thus forces a series of catastrophic events within her family in the hope of regaining control of the Mortimer fortune. Even Melmoth "was never known to appear [at the Lodge] but on the approaching death of one of the family, nor even then, unless when the evil passions or habits of the individual had cast a shade of gloomy and fearful interest over their dying hour" (20). And young John Melmoth has suffered from the strict and miserly treatment of his uncle, Old Melmoth. With the possible exception of Adonijah's experiences, about which very little is known, these families are all estranged. The ties that bind have frazzled and been replaced by chains of greed, sadism, revenge, and perverted religious doctrines.

That the topic of religious persecution is explored in so many variations should not be surprising, for Maturin states in his preface, "the hint of this Romance (or Tale) was taken from a passage in one of my Sermons . . ." (3); that is to say, the novel from its inception was seen primarily as a religious statement. In the madhouse Stanton sees the result of religious dissension in the interminable harangues between the puritanical weaver and the loyalist tailor. The mad ravings of these two Protestants, here reduced to their proper sphere of insanity, awaken the maniacal woman whose family was killed in the great fire of London. In a truly moving scene, the argument of the mad partisans gives way to the suffering of the woman as she relives the horror of watching her children burn. Her agony, the agony of the innocent, is the inevitable result of perverted religion as represented by the weaver and the tailor; and this agony, Maturin makes clear, transcends all matters of doctrine: "It was remarkable, that when this sufferer began to rave, all the others became silent. The cry of nature hushed every other cry,—she was the only patient in the house who was not mad from politics, religion, ebriety, or some perverted passion; and terrifying as the out-break of her frenzy always was, Stanton used to await it as a kind of relief from the dissonant, melancholy, and ludicrous ravings of the others" (40).

From this suffering that results from Protestant hating Protestant, Maturin turns immediately to the "Tale of the Spaniard" in which Catholic actively persecutes Catholic. The convent where Moncada is incarcerated is as much a madhouse filled with mad partisans as is that where Stanton suffered. In the convent all kinds of persecution and suffering result from the torturing of religion into strict doctrinal lines. Again, the innocent suffer most: not just Moncada and his family, all of whom suffer from the machinations of the Director, but also the young monk who is beaten and finally dies for comforting Fra Paolo (82), and the parricide's sister who enters the convent to be near her beloved and starves to death. Strict doctrinal lines force followers to external conformity but overlook the essence of religion, which must spring from the individual heart. So the dying monk who fakes the "miracle" of the fountain and the tree tells Moncada: "'The repetition of religious duties, without the feeling or spirit of religion, produces an incurable callosity of heart. There are not more irreligious

people to be found on earth than those who are occupied always in its *externals*'" (86). Juan echoes this sentiment in his letter to Moncada: "Must there not be something very wrong in the religion which thus substitutes external severities for internal amendment?" (100).

Central to the debate of external conformity and internal repentance is a theme that develops an effective corollary to the primary theme of Maturin's sermon. The central theme, of course, is that no one's sufferings are so great that he would willingly exchange them for surcease at the expense of his eternal soul. The corollary theme, developed in a number of variations in Moncada's tale, states that no one's suffering can atone for the sins of another. The parricide believes the opposite: "'Mine is the best theology,—the theology of utter hostility to all beings whose sufferings may mitigate mine. In this flattering theory, your crimes become my virtues—I need not any of my own. . . . I need not repent, I need not believe; if you suffer, I am saved,—that is enough for me. . . . I have literally worked out *my* salvation by *your* fear and trembling'" (174). One's own sufferings alone do not insure salvation, as Melmoth tells Moncada in the Inquisition prison (180), but neither will active promotion of the suffering of others. Moncada editorializes from the dungeon of the convent: "Alas! how false is that religion which makes our aggravating the sufferings of others our mediator with that God who willeth all men to be saved . . . if men were taught to look to the *one great Sacrifice,* would they be so ready to believe that their own, or those of others, could ever be accepted as a commutation for it?" (114). But Moncada himself lacks true religious tolerance, as is apparent when he hides in the home of the Jews; the prejudice Moncada demonstrates against the Jews (191) is proof that he has not yet learned the tolerance common to all religions.

"The Tale of the Indian" expands the theme of religion to its widest dimensions. In a passage reminiscent of Swift's practice in *Gulliver's Travels* or of the eighteenth-century device of the Oriental philosopher, the innocent Immalee is initiated into the world of contending religions by Melmoth. She is forced to reject each of the religions that she sees through his telescope and hears him describe, because each is built upon pain, torture, and superficial piety. But the Christians, Melmoth tells Immalee, "'know that God cannot be acceptably worshipped but by pure hearts and crimeless hands; and though their religion gives every hope to the penitent guilty, it flatters none with *false promises of external devotion supplying the homage of the heart*'" (228, my italics). To this, Immalee exclaims, "'Christ shall be my God, and I will be a Christian!'" (228). This significant climax occurs almost exactly in the center of the book. The structure of the first half of the novel is thus a progressive widening of the subject of religious bigotry in opposition to religious tolerance. From Stanton's experience of the bigotry between two Protestant sects, Maturin turns to Moncada's experience of bigotry among Catholics and finally views all religions with Immalee as tainted with the same hatreds. Immalee's embracing of Christianity is the keystone of the novel, because it indicates that this is the one religion that in theory rejects such hatred and violence.

From this wide religious vista, Maturin begins narrowing his thematic pattern again. After Immalee has announced her conversion to Christianity, Melmoth reveals to her that not even this most idealistic of religions is free from hatred and distortion. "'[A]ll agree that the language of the book [the Bible] is, "Love one another," while they all translate that language, "Hate one another"'" (236). And shortly thereafter Immalee is found and transported back to Spain, where with her family she learns that Melmoth is right. Her mother Donna Clara denies Immalee-Isidora's belief in universal love and indicates the basis of her own Catholicism: "'It is in vain I tell her that true religion consists in hearing mass—in going to confession—in performing penance—in observing the fasts and vigils—in undergoing mortification and abstinence—in believing all that the holy church teaches—and hating, detesting, abhorring, and execrating . . .'" (255). Isidora's sufferings at the hands of her family and Father Jose are unlike those of Moncada, although external circumstances are similar; Isidora is not a Catholic but a primitive Christian of no sect whatever. Thus the second half of the "Tale of the Indian" presents yet another variation on the theme of religious bigotry and persecution.

"The Tale of Guzman's Family" treats the persecution of Protestants by the Catholics, who reduce them to starvation and poverty. And "The Tale of the Lovers" shows one type of dissenter, Mrs. Sandal, turning against and hating another type, represented by Elinor Mortimer, in hopes of gaining material wealth for her son. The tale of Elinor Mortimer and John Sandal returns to England to deal with the same religious upheavals that Stanton viewed in the madhouse.

Although the novel has not yet ended—twenty pages are given to Isidora and seven to Melmoth's appearance at the Lodge and his death—the structural balance of the book is apparent. The novel consists of a series of religious persecutions that result directly from a perverted insistence on outward orthodoxy at the expense of the universal love that should exist in the hearts of all believers. From the madness of Puritan turning against Anglican as seen by Stanton, Maturin explores similar forms of madness in the persecutions of Catholics by Catholics, Protestants by Catholics, and one sect of dissenter by another. At the center of this series of persecutions stands a denunciation of all religions based on any doctrine except universal love: Immalee converts to Christianity because it is so founded.

Maturin concentrates his main action in two timespans: 1660-86, which may include the pact and certainly includes the tales of Stanton, Walberg, the Mortimers, Immalee-Isidora; and 1799-1816, which includes the adventures of Moncada and the final appearances and end of Melmoth. In these periods, Maturin finds similar conditions of political turbulence, bigotry, and the uncertainty of events on a grand scale; in both Maturin sees a turning-away from the doctrine of universal love in favor of schisms that threaten to splinter and damn the characters. But beneath the placid existence of humble lives lurk the real evils that enable Melmoth to tempt his intended victims: the monotony of any routine and the boredom resulting from it. Accepting the doctrine of universal love is not sufficient alone; it must be lived and practiced daily. Any doctrine runs the risk of sinking into mere abstraction, and boredom and monotony are the inevitable result. Again, Stanton's manuscript announces this theme in some detail, and the other tales develop variations upon it. In tempting Stanton, Melmoth paints a future life so vacant that insanity would be preferable: "'The time will come, when, from the want of occupation, the listless and horrible vacancy of your hours, you will feel as anxious to hear those shrieks, as you were at first terrified to hear them. . . . All humanity will be extinguished in you. . . . Then comes the dreadful doubt of one's own sanity, the terrible announcer that *that* doubt will soon become fear, and *that* fear certainty. Perhaps (still more dreadful) the *fear* will at last become a *hope* . . . you will wish to become one of them. . . . You will try, and the very effort will be an invocation to the demon of insanity to come and take full possession of you from that moment for ever'" (42-43).

To Moncada, the height of suffering is not physical torture but monotony, the endless ennui of incarceration which blurs the distinction between convent and madhouse, life and death. When Moncada first enters the convent, he decides to remain aloof, preferring the solitude of superiority to the company of the monks; but when the monks begin their own psychological tactic of avoiding him, he is reduced to desiring their curses as preferable to his position of outcast: "I assure you, with truth, that so horrible was this amputation from life to me, that I have walked hours in the cloister and the passages, to place myself in the way of the monks, who, I knew, as they passed, would bestow on me some malediction or reproachful epither. Even this was better than the withering silence which surrounded me" (119). The confessions Moncada hears from various monks who resort to evil deeds either to escape the boredom of hopeless routine or to find perverse pleasure in forcing others to share in their monotonous existence further amplify the theme. And Moncada's fear of "the long and lingering death of inanity" (179) not only provides Melmoth access to him in the Inquisition but also perverts Moncada's nobility to the level of the parricide in his attempt to win his own safety at the expense of another.

Immalee's isolation, her boredom with her lonely existence, and her unspoken yearning for human company make possible Melmoth's first appearance to her; but her isolation, because it has made her ignorant, is not accompanied by despair, and thus she is not yet a potential victim, as suggested by her failure to hear the mysterious music accompanying Melmoth. The enforced monotony of her respectable life as Isidora paves the way for Melmoth's reappearance. In a prayer to the statue of the Virgin, Isidora asks for surcease of memory and feeling, "'since life requires only duties that no feeling suggests, and apathy that no reflection disturbs'" (261); the statue responds only with a smile intimating "the profound and pulseless apathy of inaccessible elevation" (261). From this "pulseless apathy" (a phrase repeated in Elinor Mortimer's story), Isidora turns to nature for relief, but even nature in her walled garden has been reduced to the same level, "the stiff and stern monotony of the parterre, where even the productions of nature held their place as if under the constraint of duty, forced the conviction of its unnatural regularity on her eye and soul . . ." (273). A primitive free spirit, she lives in what she calls her "'Christian prison'" (278), from which only Melmoth can extricate her. When her father's letter announces the arranged marriage with Montilla, she does not fight the decision; and her acquiescence is justified (by Maturin as much as by the narrator Moncada) by an appeal to the truth of experience: "Romances have been written and read, whose interest arose from the noble and impossible defiance of the heroine to all powers human and superhuman alike. But neither the writers or readers seem ever to have taken into account the thousand external causes that operate on human agency with a force, if not more powerful, far more effective than the grand internal motive which makes so grand a figure in romance, and so rare and trivial a one in common life" (285).

Two tales are told to Isidora's father with the intent of awakening him from complacence to the dangers of his daughter's situation. In the first, the Walbergs suffer the physical torture of hunger, but it is the psychological effects of the hunger which Maturin emphasizes—the unrelieved monotony that reduces man to an apathy worse than pain or fear of death. "There is a withering monotony in the diary of misery,—'one day telleth another'" (319); and this "habitual misery" (328) soon reduces Walberg's father to "perfect apathy" and carries Walberg beyond insanity to the "stupefaction of despair" (331). In the second tale, Elinor Mortimer, after feeling the joy of John Sandal's love, is abandoned at the altar; when she goes to live with her Puritan aunt in Yorkshire, Elinor experiences a "motionless existence"

for the first time. "She rose at a fixed hour,—at a fixed hour she prayed,—at a fixed hour received the godly friends who visited her, and whose existence was as monotonous and apathetic as her own,—at a fixed hour she dined,—and at a fixed hour she prayed again, and then retired,—yet she prayed without unction, and fed without appetite, and retired to rest without the least inclination to sleep. Her life was mere mechanism, but the machine was so well wound up, that it appeared to have some quiet consciousness and sullen satisfaction in its movements" (363). Returning to Mortimer Castle to live with John and Margaret, Elinor must "undergo the torture of complacent and fraternal affection from the man she loved"—a torture of "cool and pulseless tranquillity" (368). After her cousins' marriage she retires again to Yorkshire to live "if possible, more secluded, and her habits [become] more monotonous"; she is reduced to a "fearful state of stupefaction and despair" (374). Margaret's death and his mother's confession destroy John's sanity: his eyes look at Elinor "in glassy and unmeaning complacency," and on his lips sits the "smile of vacancy" (377). His is the life of "pulseless apathy," but it is Elinor who is brought to despair by it for the purposes of Melmoth's temptation. The two tales have little effect on Isidora's father because his is a "mind not at all habituated to visionary impressions." Again, the monotony of habit triumphs. "There is no breaking through the inveterate habitudes of a thorough-paced mercantile mind, 'though one rose from the dead'" (384). Don Francisco ignores the warning and abandons Isidora to her fate.

The real enemy of man, then, is not an external force like physical torture, although this may wear a man down; nor is it a supernatural force like Satan or his ally the Wanderer. Monotonous and unquestioned habits of thought and the state of psychological despair brought on by such vacant habit produce apathy and an insensitivity of the heart which are indeed "pulseless." Melmoth thus quite correctly describes to Don Francisco the true enemy of mankind: "'What enemy has man so deadly as himself? If he would ask on whom he should bestow that title aright, let him smite his bosom, and his heart will answer,—Bestow it here!'" (334).

Melmoth the Wanderer, with its comparison of the late seventeenth and the early nineteenth century, stands not simply as an entertaining Gothic novel—indeed, its Gothic elements are very slight—but more as a plea for religious tolerance and, even more importantly, as a warning against the life of empty routine and listlessness. The latter theme places Maturin alongside his fellow Romantics, who also warn of the dangers of withdrawing and isolating the self from society and who urge a life of active resistance against social ills. Maturin's is a vision in which selfhood—encompassing the sense of present identity as well as the more orthodox concept of the soul—is hammered out on the anvil of suffering. He sees that suffering, that testing and proving, is greatest when external society fails the internal self. Then values fragment, and man can fall prey to his worst enemy, the apathy within the self, unless he can reforge the pieces of his broken world in the fires of love.

Notes

1. William Scholten suggests the tales comprising the novel are totally discrete but refuses to fault Maturin for the structure (*Charles Robert Maturin, the Terror Novelist* [Amsterdam, 1933], p. 91). Douglas Grant agrees at least in part when he comments on the structure as being "a casual arrangement, which saves Maturin from exposing his weakness in the handling of plot" ("Introduction," *Melmoth the Wanderer* [London, 1968], p. x). Edith Birkhead and Devendra Varma both dismiss the structure with an inaccurate metaphor: Birkhead describes the structure as "a series of tales, strung together in a complicated fashion" (*The Tale of Terror: A Study of the Gothic Romance* [New York, 1921; rpt. 1963], p. 86); Varma echoes this phrase ("a series of tales, intricately strung together") but also speaks of the "disconnected narratives" (*The Gothic Flame* [London, 1957], pp. 163-64). The metaphor of stringing tales together, like beads on a string, mistakenly suggests that the structure of *Melmoth* is similar to the structure of *The Canterbury Tales* and ignores Maturin's encapsulation of tales within tales. William E. Axton is more helpful when he speaks of the structure as "a system of interpolated tales nested one within another like the boxes of a child's toy" ("Introduction," *Melmoth the Wanderer* [Lincoln, Nebr., 1961], p. xv. Subsequent references to *Melmoth* are taken from this edition and appear in the text). This analogy is misleading, however, because it suggests structural symmetry, such as the concentric circles of consciousness M. A. Goldberg finds in *Frankenstein* ("Moral and Myth in Mrs. Shelley's *Frankenstein*," *Keats-Shelley Journal* 8 [1959]: 27-38). Moreover, the analogy of the Chinese boxes does not account for the strange positioning of Stanton's tale, which is structurally separate from the succeeding encapsulation of tales.

2. One example of Maturin's inconsistent dating, surprising because it occurs within the span of a few pages, is in the Stanton manuscript. As mentioned above, Stanton's first glimpse of Melmoth is dated specifically "the night of 17th August 1677." The manuscript, after a convenient hiatus of "a few blotted and illegible pages, became more distinct," and John Melmoth reads on to discover Stanton in London "about the year 1677, . . . his mind still full of his mysterious countryman" (29-30). That Stanton could see Melmoth in Spain in the middle of August and still make it back to London within the year is quite plausible. But the events within this London episode contradict the dating here. Stanton goes to the theater and there sees "the object of his *search for four years,*—the Englishman whom he had met in the plains of Valentia" (32, my italics). The four-year search is specifically repeated on the next page when Stanton encounters Melmoth outside the theater.

The date 1677 plus four years of searching would suggest that the proper date here is 1681. This latter date is contradicted, however, by further evidence that indicates 1677 is the accurate date for the London meeting, despite the double reference to the four-year lapse. Stanton is committed to the madhouse "some years after" Melmoth's prophecy (34). Then an indeterminate amount of time passes between his incarceration and Melmoth's visit; sufficient time must pass to bring Stanton to a state of general despair. If one allows a minimum in each instance—two years before incarceration (to account for the plural of "some years after") and six months after—he would be dating Melmoth's appearance around 1684. But cross-reference dating from the "Tale of the Indian" suggests that 1684 is too late for the temptation of Stanton. When Immalee first sees Melmoth on her isle, he is dressed in "the fashion of the year 1680" (215). He visits her three times in the space of ten days, and then stays away for some time (228). He returns and then absents himself again "to torture and to tempt in the mad-house where the Englishman Stanton was tossing on his straw" (229). Three years later, Immalee, now transformed to Isidora, meets Melmoth on a street in Madrid, and Maturin specifically dates the meeting as 1683 (251). Thus one must conclude that Stanton's four-year search for Melmoth is erroneous or perhaps should follow rather than precede the madhouse scenes, that he saw the Wanderer first in Spain in 1676 (21) or 1677 (22), that he saw him at the London theater shortly thereafter in 1677-78, that he was incarcerated in 1679-80 and was visited the third time by Melmoth in 1680-81.

3. The few pages devoted to Adonijah seem to be an attempt to bridge the chronological gap between the bulk of the adventures that occur in the last third of the seventeenth century and Old Melmoth's discovery of the truth about his ancestor around 1756 (13). Adonijah is 107 years old when Moncada meets him in 1799, so that his lifespan covers in a fragmentary fashion the missing part of the eighteenth century. Adonijah alludes to facts in his life suggesting that, in his zeal "'to see, yea, and to consort with, yea, and to deal with, the evil one in his strength'" (206), Melmoth has been the

cause of the deaths of his wife and child. He retired to his secret apartment to write a manuscript detailing Melmoth's temptations that might serve as a warning to others; he has worked on this manuscript for sixty years, having begun it then around 1739. Occupying the apartment with him are the skeletons of his wife and child; but he has two additional skeletons of Melmoth's victims, one of which seems to be Immalee-Isidora's and the other an unknown. He never explains how he came to possess these.

Mark M. Hennelly, Jr. (essay date autumn 1981)

SOURCE: Hennelly, Mark M., Jr. "*Melmoth the Wanderer* and Gothic Existentialism." *Studies in English Literature, 1500-1900* 21, no. 4 (autumn 1981): 665-79.

[*In the following essay, Hennelly argues that Maturin's preoccupation with themes of alienation and absurdity in* Melmoth the Wanderer *prefigures the existentialist concerns of such later writers as Fyodor Dostoevsky and Franz Kafka.*]

Charles Maturin's **Melmoth the Wanderer** (1820) focuses primarily on a man who sells his soul to Satan for one hundred and fifty added years of life, but also incudes such delicious examples of Romantic agony as cannibalism between lovers, blood-selling for grocery money, patricide, sororicide, a child fathered by the satanic Wanderer upon an emblem of spotless purity, and even talk of copulation with the Virgin Mary. It is little wonder, then, that William Axton dubs the work the "finest flowering . . . the last and greatest expression of" the Gothic novel.[1] Indeed, this convoluted series of tales, within tales, within tales, dramatizes all the critically acclaimed ingredients of the Gothic recipe: the aesthetic catharsis of terror and horror from an intimately involved reader, the psychological probing of the divided self, and the philosophical revelation of secret gnostic mysteries. But that which makes **Melmoth** [*Melmoth the Wanderer*] a most fertile watershed of Gothicism, that which links this literary curiosity with the firm tradition of later fiction like *Notes From Underground, The Trial,* and *Lord Jim,* and that which finally establishes it as a touchstone for future investigations of the Gothic legacy is its strong basis in existential thought. And this notion, which also helps thematically to unify all the varied interpolated tales, is at odds with the usual appraisal of Gothicism as a literary dead end. Robert D. Hume, for example, insists that "Gothic writing . . . has been on the decline, for evil is explained away sociologically today."[2] Consequently, after briefly relating **Melmoth**'s classic Gothicism to general existential concerns, I would like to analyze its preoccupation with five particular but overlapping existential themes: absurdity, isolation, failure of communication, loss of freedom, and the lack of responsible commitment.[3]

Reflecting on the earliest critical approach to Gothicism, which, like Ann Radcliffe's, stressed its affective purgation, Hume writes that "Inducing a powerful emotional response in the reader (rather than a moral or intellectual one) was the prime object of these novelists" (p. 284); and although the present essay maintains that Gothicism introduces, whether intentionally or not, significant moral and intellectual themes, certainly it is still true that an emotional catharsis from an intimately involved, almost captured audience is a primary goal and a presupposition for the effectual handling of complex ideational issues. Moreover, this catharsis provides an existential function. In **Melmoth,** the parricide tells Monçada (and Maturin characteristically underscores the statement's significance) that "*Emotions are my events*"; and thus he "was enabled to daunt a feeble mind by the narration of horrors, and to amaze an ignorant one with a display of crimes" (p. 158).[4] And all the many acts of reading, narrating, and performing before an audience in the novel create a *Doppelgänger* relationship between Maturin's own readers and the fictional audiences who are first terrified and then taught, almost as if the emotions must be purified and drained before the mind can be properly instructed and then provoked or committed to a responsible course of existential action. The Wanderer himself evolves from a demon who "*cannot weep*" to an authentic human being whose last request is for a "glass of water" (p. 408). In fact, as we will hear, reading **Melmoth** is a kind of nightmare trauma in which the reader discovers several conflicting sides of himself, victims and victimizers both. As Monçada realizes when he is mesmerized by a crowd tearing the parricide to pieces, "The drama of terror has the irresistible power of converting its audience into its victims" (p. 197), suggesting again that before the reader can become truly and existentially human, he must first accept the animal or emotional side of himself. In fact, the first tale within a tale, Stanton's manuscript, itself quite literally symbolizes the reader's frustration in making out the novel's absurdist meaning on the one hand, and yet his parallel difficulty in escaping identification with that very meaning on the other. Thus, although "The conclusion of this extraordinary manuscript was in such a state that, in fifteen mouldy and crumbling pages, [young] Melmoth could hardly make out that number of lines," still "He could but just make out what tended rather to excite than assuage that feverish thirst of curiosity which was consuming his inmost soul" (p. 44). Such an ambivalence serves implicitly to link Melmoth with Stanton's "master-passion," the "master-torment of his life" (p. 44)—the self-committed pursuit of the Wanderer—and thus finally with the double-edged monomania of the overreaching Wanderer himself. As the father of Immalee (later called *Isadora*), Don Francisco Aliaga, replies upon hearing the Wanderer's narration: "'That was exactly my case,' said Aliaga, wholly unsuspicious of the tendency of this tale" (p. 382). Finally, and in the existential vein of self-conscious black humor, Maturin is not above having fun with the morbid difficulties and fascinations of reader involvement with his novel's "passages so devious and intricate" (p. 204), both subterranean and literary. Thus, Immalee's mother, the pedantic Donna Clara, comically interjects after writing a letter often as obtuse as the text itself, "I will but add a few particulars to arouse your dormant faculties, which may be wrapt in lethargic obliviousness by the anodyne of my somniferous epistolation" (p. 290).

For the sake of brevity and avoidance of Donna Clara's own verbosity, we need only to outline the psychological and gnostic themes of Gothicism, both of which also reinforce an existential reading. Preferring to call the Gothic novel the "Romantic Novel," Robert Kiely pertinently writes: "The dualism of man's nature—of his taste, his impulses, his ambitions—the deep division in his very way of perceiving reality, seemed an inevitable adjunct to the first romantic stirrings of the young genre."[5] And we have already intimated this psychological theme of the Gothic divided-self, the numinous arena of existential self-consciousness, in discussing the relationships between the reader, young Melmoth, Stanton, and the Wanderer. Even their identical names serve to link the two Melmoths and thus to warn the younger, the reader-identification figure, lest he too fall fate to the soul-searching *Angst* of his overreaching ancestor, that unknown yet intimate existential "other." The Wanderer makes his ironic role as Everyman or double for even the saintliest Christian, clear to Don Francisco: "You yourself, Senhor, who, of course, as an orthodox and inveterate Catholic, must abhor the enemy of mankind, have often acted as his agent, and yet would be somewhat offended at being mistaken for him" (p. 333). As is usual in Gothic atmospherics, this divided self is ultimately projected upon a phenomenological world divided both spiritually and metaphysically. Stanton, in fact, views a psychomachia, theomachia, and cosmomachia all at once during a terrible storm: "All . . . was forgot in contemplating the glorious and awful scenery before him,—light struggling with darkness,—and darkness menacing a light still more terrible, and announcing its menace in the blue and livid mass of cloud that hovered like a destroying angel in the air, its arrows aimed, but their direction awfully indefinite" (pp. 22-23).

The most recent approach to Gothicism is reflected in G. R. Thompson's "Introduction" to *The Gothic Imagination: Essays in Dark Romanticism*: "What the essays persistently suggest is that the kind of high Gothic represented by *Melmoth,* or *Moby Dick,* or *Heart of Darkness* is the embodiment of the demonic-quest romance, in which a lonely, self-divided hero embarks on insane pursuit of the Absolute."[6] This *gnostic* theme, which I have treated elsewhere in connection with *Dracula,*[7]

dramatizes a Faustian quest to extend the boundaries of consciousness and often, in effect, to deny or escape the existential nature of reality. The Wanderer's "posthumous and preternatural existence" illustrates such overreaching the limits of mortality: "Mine was the great angelic sin—pride and intellectual glorying! It was the first mortal sin—a glorious aspiration after forbidden knowledge!" (pp. 380-81). But finally in Immalee's case, and perhaps in that of the involved and committed reader, the analogous "initiation" is a humanizing, not dehumanizing, "painful pilgrimage" (p. 277) through existential experience to the goal of a life-affirming gnosis: "she turned on him a glance that seemed at once to thank and reproach him for her painful initiation into the mysteries of a new existence. She had, indeed, tasted of the tree of knowledge, and her eyes were opened, but its fruit was bitter to her taste, and her looks conveyed a kind of mild and melancholy gratitude, that would have wrung the heart for giving its first lesson of pain to the heart of a being so beautiful, so gentle, and so innocent" (p. 236).

To be sure, previous criticism has linked Gothicism generally with existentialism. Thompson, for instance, concludes that "In a Romantic context then, Gothic literature may be seen as expressive of an existential terror generated by a schism between a triumphantly secularized philosophy of evolving good and an abiding obsession with the Medieval conception of guilt-laden, sin-ridden man" (pp. 5-6). Virginia M. Hyde suggestively associates traditional Gothic machinery with the existential imagery of Kafka;[8] and as his title implies, Hume in another essay on the Gothic links "Exuberant Gloom, Existential Agony, and Heroic Despair: Three Varieties of Negative Romanticism."[9] More particularly, Douglas Grant correctly insists that "We are always aware in *Melmoth the Wanderer* that if it belongs to the Gothic novel of the past—to the world of Ann Radcliffe and 'Monk' Lewis [footnote deleted]—it anticipates the psychological, metaphysical novel of the future. Dostoevsky and Kafka are low on the horizon, in the ascendant."[10] And David Eggenschweiler seconds the motion: "Maturin is of the Romantic tradition and anticipates Kierkegaard and Dostoevsky, two great religious Romantics who explored more fully the faith and despair of those who venture beyond the limits of nature."[11] Finally, Robert E. Lougy carries the implication of a modern, absurdist relevance one step further, feeling that if we try to dismiss the "abnormal imagination in *Melmoth* . . . we are reminded, as Maturin wants us to be, of the normal world in which we live, a world in which autos-da-fé, wars, Dachau and Auschwitz do exist, a world presided over by normal kings, queens, politicians, and generals. And we are perhaps forced to reconsider our definitions of madness."[12] Still, as far as I know, no previous study has devoted itself to locating specific existential themes in a single Gothic work, **Melmoth** or any other, for the sole purpose of seeing Gothicism as a prefiguration of modern existentialism.

But before discussing these specific themes, we should indicate the general kind of existential tone that **Melmoth** provides as it almost obsessively repeats the word "existence" again and again on its pages. There are as many forms of existentialism as there are existentialists; but as Walter Kaufmann has suggested, all of them seem to revolt against any authority—Church, State, Society—that places a synthetic, abstract system between the individual and real life experience.[13] Maturin regards such a life-denying barrier as "so imposing, peremptory, and *habitual*—it seemed so little a thing of local contrivance and temporary display,—so much like the established language of an absolute and long-fixed system, that obedience to it seemed inevitable" (p. 169). And though he certainly rails against Church, State, and Society, his underlying act of defiance is against the literary Romance for its extravagant delusions and departures from what his first paragraph introduces as "the very threads of our existence" (p. 5). Thus Maturin's Preface announces that "the misery of conventional life depends less on the startling adventures one meets with in romances, than on the irritating series of petty torments which constitutes the misery of life in general" (p. 3). And even though many readers would maintain that **Melmoth**'s own adventures are more "startling" than those usually comprising romances, the author insists that he titillates with no "romance-horrors . . . but [that] truth sometimes gives full and dreadful compensation, in presenting facts instead of images" (p. 168). Indeed, Maturin repeatedly disparages "the mere reader of romance" (p. 285), writing instead for that reader who is willing, or at least available, to risk what in another context he terms a "kind of transfer, this substitutional suffering" (p. 173) which best defines the bare facts of reader involvement in his arresting and disturbing fictional experience.

More particularly, as we've heard Douglas Grant suggest, **Melmoth**'s brand of existentialism prefigures the suffering and stagnation later appearing in Dostoevsky and the alienation and metaphysical frustration classically located in Kafka as both writers finally point toward that grand, common, existential dilemma: given such a horrifying universe, is heroism possible? Like Dostoevsky, Maturin can honestly indict Life as: "Oh complicated and mysterious horror!" (p. 400); for he addresses pitiful man as a dehumanized undergrounder, or an "insect perched on a wheel of this vast machine [who] imagined you were able to arrest its progress, while its rotation was hurrying on to crush you to atoms" (p. 170). Like Kafka, who also sees man as an insect, Maturin finds no ultimate meaning in an unpredictable life without absolutes, one appearing to be ruled at times by an "image of power, dark, isolated,

impenetrable" (p. 22), at times by "monstrous figures . . . frowning in their shapeless and gigantic hideousness" (p. 213). This real life "night-mare of the heart" (p. 207) spawns an outsider Everyman like Monçada who proclaims "I was the outcast of the whole earth, and I wept with equal bitterness and depression at the hopeless vastness of the desert I had to traverse" (p. 193). And again, the identifying reader, jolted out of armchair-romance *frissons*, can well echo Monçada's cry at witnessing the crowd dismembering the parricide: "I actually for a moment believed myself the object of their cruelty" (p. 197). No wonder that the dying monk whispers: "For sixty years I have cursed my existence" (p. 85), and that even that grand rebel, the Wanderer, is himself reduced to "the very image of hoary decrepid debility" (p. 410). Only by sharing specific existential themes, however, can we discover whether Maturin implicitly provides any heroic, or at least humanistic relief to such unrelieved, existential suffering and frustration.

The first existential theme, the absurdity of what Adonijah's underground manuscript calls this "insane and morbid existence" (p. 229), defines the nature of the reality pervading both the external and internal worlds of **Melmoth** and thus serves to interconnect all the other existential concerns in the novel. Leven M. Dawson labels this central ambience a sense of Romantic "paradox"[14]; while Veronica M. S. Kennedy relates it to myth: "the shifting menace and sometimes confused mythology of the world of dreams."[15] It is much closer, however, to the sense of relativism, meaninglessness, and even nihilism which torments the existentialist, but which he must finally accept as true—what Maturin, on his last page and after the Wanderer's final, agonizing damnation, describes as the "overwhelming mass of conviction that falls on the mind, that annihilates idiom and peculiarities, and crushes out truth from the heart" (p. 412). This brand of "ontological insecurity," to use R. D. Laing's term,[16] is clearly evident when Monçada awakens in the Inquisition cell after his near escape from the monastery and silently pleads "Where am I?" while plagued by "that dreary mixture of truth and delirium, of the real and the visionary, of the conscious and unconscious parts of existence" (p. 169). Given this absurdist universe, which the Wanderer details to Immalee, it is little wonder that she concludes: "I begin to comprehend what he said—to think, then, is to suffer—and a world of thought must be a world of pain!" (p. 221). In the catacombs under the monastery with the parricide, Monçada similarly "tried to *forbear to think*" (p. 157, Maturin's italics). For some characters, like Immalee, dream and reality, the numinous and phenomenological, have consequently become absurdly intermixed: "in the life that I now lead, dreams have become realities, and realities seem only like dreams" (p. 256). For others, as detailed in Stanton's "*album of a madhouse*" (p. 36, Maturin's italics), a clear consciousness of the differences between madness and sanity is paradoxically the worst madness of all. Thus the Wanderer taunts Stanton during his false imprisonment in the madhouse, which becomes a microcosm of the absurd universe and a macrocosm of the "incarcerated mind" itself:

> You will wish to become one of them [the insane], to escape the agony of consciousness . . . you will say, "Doubtless those wretches have some consolation, but I have none; my sanity is my greatest curse in this abode of horrors. . . . *I know I can never escape,* and the preservation of my faculties is only an aggravation of my sufferings. I have all their miseries,—I have none of their consolations. They laugh,—I hear them; would I could laugh like them." You will try, and the very effort will be an invocation to the demon of insanity to come and take full possession of you from that moment for ever.
>
> (p. 43, Maturin's italics)

Consequently, Immalee, fallen from delusory innocence into the existential world of damning self-consciousness, finds the wish-fulfillments of her Edenic island replaced by the fear-fulfillments of the civilized nightmare: "My life formerly was all anticipation,—now it is all retrospection. *The life of the happy is all hopes,—that of the unfortunate all memory*" (p. 264, Maturin's italics). Or as the Wanderer, more like Hamlet, describes the phenomenological condition of humanity: "Immortal Heaven! what is man? A being with the ignorance, but not the instinct of the feeblest animals!" a being whose formalistic charades, like wedding ceremonies, mock the essential nature of man: "What ideot [sic] trumpery, what May-Queen foolery is this?" (p. 395). And of course, just as the madhouse and vanity fair are images of existential absurdity, so too is monastic religion another one of the "many deliberate mockeries of God" (p. 85). As Monçada puts it, "All Spain is but one great monastery,—I must be a prisoner every step that I take" (p. 143). Such a religion boasts a hydra-headed God who willy-nilly seems to replace divine providence with demonic persecution: "'there are two Gods,' said Isadora sighing, 'the God of smiles and happiness, and the God of groans and blood'" (p. 291). And in "the world that thinks," different Gods have different worshippers; however, as the Wanderer tells Immalee, "there is one point in which they all agree—that of making their religion a torment;—the religion of some prompting them to torture themselves, and the religion of some prompting them to torture others" (p. 223). Given such cosmic cruelty or at worst indifference, personified in the parricide's "*rictus Sardonicus*" (p. 145), the Wanderer ultimately develops neither the tragic nor the comic mask, but rather the mocking persona of the black humorist, who can defy, and hence bring meaning to metaphysical absurdity by a deflating, sardonic sneer: "A mirth which is not gaiety is often the mask which hides the convulsed and distorted features of agony—and laughter,

which never yet was the expression of rapture, has often been the only intelligible language of madness and misery" (p. 270). His final problem, though, is that the Wanderer, this "demon of . . . superhuman misanthropy" (p. 233), most tragically mocks himself and his own feeble efforts to hide from the existential absurdity of natural, human feelings. Only by accepting and even celebrating this absurdity can essence and existence become one undivided unity for him.

This indifferent, absurd universe often provokes withdrawal or the second existential theme, isolation, which is not only a concern of the existentialists, but also a major preoccupation of most post-Romantic disciplines which explore the individual self and its subjective relationship to the world that impinges upon it. Robert Kiely, for example, in discussing the "Romanticism" of **Melmoth,** reports that "For all but a very few characters, life is a struggle out of isolation into oblivion"[17]; and Hume finds persecution of the alienated self to be at the very core of the work: "The imaginative center of the novel is the misery of sadistic nihilism."[18] As Monçada's description of his estrangement in the monastery suggests, however, isolation in **Melmoth** transcends the run-of-the-mill terrors of the Gothic torture chamber, like the underground charnel house where Ambrosio persecutes Antonia in *The Monk,* with its clanking chains, decomposing corpses, and hideous shrieks. Rather it captures the inner horror of a solitary confinement whose inferno of guilt and self-consciousness consumes the spirit, leaving physical deterioration only a pale imitation of the psychological: "In some circumstances, where the whole world is against us, we begin to take its part against ourselves, to avoid the withering sensation of being alone on our own side. Such was my appearance, too, my flushed and haggard look, my torn dress, my unequal gait, my constant internal muttering, and my complete isolation from the habits of the house, that it was no wonder that I should justify, by my exterior, all of horrible and awful that might be supposed passing in my mind" (p. 123). Even his fellow monks realize that Monçada "has been in a state of *alienation* for some time, he is giving an account to God for it,—we shall never hear a word about it" (p. 102, Maturin's italics).

In fact, the Inquisition, like Kafka's *Trial,* becomes an emblem of that sometime indifferent, sometime hostile universe which divides man against himself, intelligence against instinct, and also isolates each human being from every other human being and thus from the humanizing balm of sympathy. The Superior even hesitates to name Monçada's crime; and this produces even more existential *Angst*: "It is certain, that when we are conscious of guilt, we always suspect that a greater degree of it will be ascribed to us by others. Their consciences avenge the palliations of our own, by the most horrible exaggerations" (p. 104). Consequently, testifies

Monçada, "the power of the Inquisition, like that of death, separates you, by its single touch, from all mortal relations. . . . I was an isolated being, . . . the involuntary murderer of my brother, the only being on earth who loved me, or whom I could love or profit by,—that being who seemed to flash across my brief *human* existence, to illuminate and to blast" (p. 192, Maturin's italics). As Monçada finally understands, however, the Inquisition's subtle tortures are not only the embodiments of cosmic malevolence, but are also externalizations of the sado-masochism which, it seems, each creature must savor if he is at all to rationalize away his state of existential victimization and to discover a method in all that metaphysical madness. Thus, after being plagued by apparent demons, Monçada "slept the entire night, and the whole convent was delivered from the harassings of the infernal spirit. Alas! none haunted it, but that spirit which the natural *malignity of solitude* raises within the circle of every heart, and forces us, from the terrible economy of misery, to feed on the vitals of others, that we may spare our own" (pp. 127-28, Maturin's italics). And yet Monçada's isolation is finally relieved when he dares, existentially, to escape it, then involves himself in saving young Melmoth from drowning, and finally reaches out to Melmoth, in turn, for humanizing help. The Wanderer's self-imposed, satanic isolation, on the other hand, is never relieved, although it is temporarily abated, but then heightened, by what T. S. Eliot calls the "awful daring of a moment's surrender" with Immalee. As he tells her with typical Sartrean nausea, though, the lonely crowd in the city can finally be just as repulsive, estranging, and dehumanizing as the solitary confinement of the isolated self. If lonely self-consciousness circumscribes one's own personal hell, hell too is other people:

> The more civilized crowd together into a space which their own respiration, and the exhalation of their bodies, renders pestilential, and which gives a celerity inconceivable to the circulation of disease and mortality. Four thousand of them will live together in a space smaller than the last and lightest colonnade of your young banyan-tree, in order, doubtless, to increase the effects of foetid air, artificial heat, unnatural habits, and impractical exercise. The results of these judicious precautions is just what may be guessed. The most trifling complaint becomes immediately infectious, and, during the ravages of the pestilence, which this habit generates, ten thousand lives a-day are the customary sacrifice to the habit of living in cities.

(p. 231)

Consequently, in this existential universe where there is no exit, love does not usually provide the needed release from the universal *Angst*; rather it frustratingly highlights the failure of real communication, which is the third existential theme. As the parricide mockingly puts it, "clap me two lovers in a dungeon, without food, light, or hope, and I will be damned (that I am already, by the bye) if they do not grow sick of each other within

the first twelve hours" (p. 164). In a more serious vein, Monçada describes "*feeling that despair of incommunication* which is perhaps the severest curse that can be inflicted on those who are compelled to be together, and compelled by the same necessity that imposes their uncongenial union, not even to communicate their fears to each other" (p. 153, again the thematic italics are Maturin's). The unknowability of the other is archetypically personified in Maturin's repeated epithet for the Wanderer, "the stranger," which Camus would later convert into a byword for the alienated alter-ego.[19] Consequently, speech in the existential world relies on a forked tongue of "wild and fierce irony" (p. 180) which, again in the awful daring of a moment's surrender, can be self-revelatory and thereby transcend the false security of I-It autonomy with the terribly human vulnerability if I-Thou honesty such as Elinor's in "The Lover's Tale." Or, as Monçada's notes from underground beneath the monastery reveal with frightening candor, communication's very process of disillusionment can be far more brutal in its verbalizing of existential horror, than in its shrouding of it with silence: "The very thirst of my body seemed to vanish in this fiery thirst of the soul for communication, where all communication was unutterable, impossible, hopeless. Perhaps the condemned spirits will feel thus at their final sentence, when they know all that is to be suffered and dare not disclose to each other that horrible truth which is no longer a secret, but which the profound silence of their despair would seem to make one. The secret of silence is the only secret. Words are only a blasphemy against the taciturn and invisible God, whose presence enshrouds us in our last extremity" (p. 151). In fact, religion, especially Catholicism, becomes an emblem of institutionalized babel; for "where service was performed in an unknown tongue, the devotion of the people was always observed to be much increased thereby" (p. 35). At its most destructive and hypocritical moment, monastic religion, "whose whole life is artificial and perverted" (p. 75), preaches an unnatural self-division which separates man from himself and from his ability to communicate through interpersonal love. That Grand Inquisitor, the monastic Superior, for instance, believes that always "Love was a thing . . . connected with sin, even though consecrated by the name of a sacrament" and that "love in a convent" is an unspeakable blasphemy (p. 161). Such sentiments reveal that the gospel of his religion is actually "self-love" (p. 65), misnamed by the Walberg's priest as "the conquest of grace over the rebellion of nature" (p. 318).

Society similarly thwarts honest communication by its own art's conquest "over the rebellion of nature." Thus Immalee's spontaneous and innocent affection is hard pressed by the self-denying obligations of the toilette which cloy and mask one's true, existential nature: "The duties of the bath had been performed, but with a parade of soaps, perfumes, and, above all, attendants, who though of her own sex, gave Isadora [Immalee] an unspeakable degree of disgust at the operation. The sponges and odours sickened her unsophisticated senses, and the presence of another human being seemed to close up every pore" (p. 262). The Wanderer, of course, rightly lampoons such sanitizing affectation and pretense; and as Dale Kramer among others has noticed, he communicates with the Indian maiden to escape, at least temporarily, his disgust in intermingling with society's role-playing. In Kramer's words, "The attraction of Immalee for him is the possibility that her innocence might assuage the bitterness of contemplating his destiny."[20] Indeed, though again temporarily, his communication with Immalee serves to rejoin his perversely-divided self: "In the logic of the schools he was well-versed, but in the logic of the heart and of nature, he was 'ignorance itself.' It is said, that the 'awless lion' crouches before 'a maid in the pride of her purity'" (p. 219). Finally, however, Maturin drives home his most powerful and positive point, albeit a fleeting point, about existential communication in "The Lover's Tale" of Elinor Mortimer and John Sandal. After the moneyed, self-centered interests of society, personified in John's mother, have already destroyed their chance for a true marriage of mind and body, one in which "there was more eloquence in their silence than in many words" (p. 357), Elinor at last and at least is able to nurse John, now a helpless imbecile. Hers becomes an existential vigil of silent frustration while "she dreams of that smile which burst on her soul like the morning sun over a landscape in spring, and sees that smile of vacancy which tries to convey satisfaction, but cannot give it the language of expression" (p. 377). Ultimately, it is true communication, however, which recalls their love for one eternal moment and consequently undercuts the more usual failure of lasting communication illustrated in the Wanderer's separation from Immalee: "His [John's] lips are open, but long unaccustomed to utter human sounds, the effort is made with difficulty—and again that effort is repeated and fails—his strength is exhausted—his eyes close—his last gentle sigh is breathed on the bosom of faith and love—and Elinor soon after said to those who surrounded her bed, that she died happy, since he knew her once more!" (p. 381).

Both the absence of interpersonal communication and the I-It nature of sado-masochistic relationships help to program the fourth existential theme, the loss of freedom, which Maturin most often underscores with the metaphors of Sisyphus—mechanism and monotony: "The moment life is put beyond the reach of your will, and placed under the influence of mechanical operations, it becomes, to thinking beings, a torment unsupportable" (p. 85). And the Wanderer informs Immalee that sexuality usually increases rather than abates such torment since "the monotony of perpetual fruition" finds "no parallel even in the monotony of suffering" (p. 233). The dying monk's words to Monçada, ostensibly

reflecting the repressive nature of monasticism, most dramatically indict this universal lack of existential freedom: "I am a clock that has struck the same minutes and hours for sixty years. Is it not time for the machine to long for its winding up? The monotony of my existence would make a transition, even to pain, desirable" (p. 85).[21] Once again, Elinor's ability to feel, and especially to love, ensures her partial liberation from such general apathy and paralysis: "Her life was mere mechanism, but the machine was so well wound up, that it appeared to have some quiet consciousness and sullen satisfaction in its movements" (p. 363). In fact, it is that accursed, existential blessing of "consciousness" which finally provokes in her enough self-knowledge to accept freely her pain rather than to opt self-deludingly for capricious escapism: "as if we did not carry our own hearts with us wherever we go, and might not therefore be sure that an innate and eroding ulcer might be our companion from Pole to Equator" (p. 367).

I have implied that social and religious role-playing and overreaching monomania all strangle personal freedom and authenticity in the novel. Even young Melmoth artfully conceals his "real motive" for tarrying at his deceased uncle's mansion because a self-restricting, "wild and awful pursuit of an indefinite object, had taken strong hold of his mind" (p. 16). Besides these fatalisms, however, the other major emblem of existential determinism in the novel is simple poverty, especially when it both literally and metaphorically starves the Walbergs in "The Tale of Guzman's Family." Thus the father screams "My son sells his blood to a surgeon, to save us from perishing! My daughter trembles and screams on the verge of prostitution, to procure us a meal!" (p. 325); and both drastic alternatives reflect that a starved body personifies a starved mind, which itself inhibits free deliberation. But significantly, both also reflect the paradox that self-denial and self-sacrifice are the real measures of self-fulfillment in an existential universe where there is "an unequal division of the means of existence" (p. 232). The mother, Ines Walberg, best exemplifies the self-redemptive vision which accepts a world of limited freedom and frustrating vicissitudes and thus neatly defines Maturin's own existential gospel: she is "a woman whom the experience of misfortune has taught to look to the future with an anxious eye, and that eye, with ominous accuracy, had seldom failed to detect a speck of evil in the brightest beam of sunshine that had ever trembled on her chequered existence" (p. 312). In the topsy-turvy world of existentialism, then, it is not the discoverers of some good in the universe who survive, as much as it is the guardians against such self-restricting delusion who freely choose not to be blinded by the mere appearance of cosmic benevolence or divine providence.

Finally, if a character asserts his own unified integrity in the face of universal absurdity, if he is willing to deny his isolation and expose his human vulnerability, if he makes the blind leap of faith and communicates with another, and if he admits the limited scope of his freedom but still tries freely to carve out his selfhood within that scope, then he can transcend the pervasive lack of commitment, which is the fifth and last premise of **Melmoth**'s existential metaphysic. His involved existence becomes a defining hallmark of his essence. As Michael G. Cooke explains in his recent existential reading of romanticism, *The Romantic Will,* "What emerges in romanticism is the metaphysics of action, a constant engagement—at once practical and symbolic—upon a radical problem of being."[22] For the identifying reader, the major question after finishing **Melmoth,** however, is determining its final existential tone—is it one of humanistic commitment (Cooke's "constant engagement") to the problematic nature of existence, or one of nihilistic regression and escape from solving the other four metaphysical problems? All the existential sufferers whom the Wanderer tempts say no to him and yes to the pain of their existence. And yet defying romance conventions, the Wanderer's final separation from Immalee and coercion into hell hardly leave the reader with a sense of self-righteous approval or even purgation. Maturin tells us that his last shrieks could have been either those "of supplication, or the yell of blasphemy" (p. 411). Wish-fulfilling, Monçada and Melmoth "hoped inwardly they might be the former" (p. 411); while the self-identifying reader probably hopes they might be the latter, that is, the inalienable commitment of defiance against an alien universe. Even the committed Elinor at one point nearly despairs, like the Wanderer, and feels:

> Far better the dull and dusky winter's day, whose gloom, if it never abates, never increases—(and to which we lift up an eye of listlessness, in which there is no apprehension of future and added terrors), to the glorious fierceness of the summer's day, whose sun sets amid purple and gold,—while, panting under its parting beams, we see the clouds collecting in the darkening East, and view the armies of heaven on their march, whose thunders are about to break our rest, and whose lightnings may crumble us to ashes.

(p. 363)

And yet just as the Wanderer commits himself, however problematically, to Immalee's spark of life, so too Elinor rejects the monotony of a death-in-life "in which there is no apprehension of future and added terrors," and commits herself to "the glorious fierceness" of life's pain. Immalee, too, finally participates in the same kind of existential agony during her brief commitment to the glorious fierceness of the Wanderer's satanic existence. As Monçada's brother, Juan, suggests about his commitment to the parricide: "Such is the instrument with which I must work.—It is horrible, but necessary. I have read, that from the most venomous reptiles and plants, have been extracted the most sanative medi-cines. I will squeeze the juice, and trample on the weed" (p. 139). In conclusion, then, the novel seems to delight fiendishly in the ambiguity between heroic and horrific readings; and so it makes little difference whether both the parricide and the Wanderer are destructive, nay self-destructive, since ultimately the existential universe is always destructive and thus demands a fortunate fall to this kind of experience. As Stein famously tells Marlowe in *Lord Jim,* one of the later inheritors of **Melmoth**'s existentialism, "The way is to the destructive element submit yourself" (ch. 20). Maturin's own existential apocalypse finally rejoices in "that defiance of danger which danger itself excites. And we love to encounter it as a physical enemy, to bid it 'do its worst,' and feel that its worst will perhaps be ultimately its best for us" (p. 23).

Notes

1. William Axton, "Introduction" to Charles Maturin's *Melmoth the Wanderer* (Lincoln: Univ. of Nebraska Press, 1961), p. xii.

2. Robert D. Hume, "Gothic versus Romantic: A Revaluation of the Gothic Novel," *PMLA* 84 (March 1969):290.

3. For a further explanation of these five themes, see my "American Nightmare: The Underworld in Film," *Journal of Popular Film* 6 (1978):240-61.

4. All quotations from *Melmoth* are taken from the Univ. of Nebraska Press edition cited in note 1; page references will be included in the text. For two recent general evaluations of reader involvement in *Melmoth,* see Coral Ann Howells, *Love, Mystery and Misery: Feeling in Gothic Fiction* (London: Athlone Press, 1978), pp. 131-58, and David Punter, *The Literature of Terror: A History of Gothic Fiction from 1765 to the Present Day* (London and New York: Longman, 1980), pp. 130-59, passim.

5. Robert Kiely, *The Romantic Novel in English* (Cambridge, Mass.: Harvard Univ. Press, 1972), p. 17.

6. *The Gothic Imagination: Essays in Dark Romanticism,* ed. G. R. Thompson (Pullman, Wash.: Washington State Univ. Press, 1974), p. 2.

7. Mark M. Hennelly, Jr., "Dracula: The Gnostic Quest and Victorian Wasteland," [*English Literature in Transition*] 20 (1977): 13-26.

8. Virginia M. Hyde, "From the 'Last Judgement' to Kafka's World: A Study in Gothic Iconography" in *The Gothic Imagination* cited in note 6, pp. 128-49.

9. Robert D. Hume, "Exuberant Gloom, Existential Agony, and Heroic Despair," in *The Gothic Imagination,* pp. 109-27.

10. "Introduction" to Charles Maturin's *Melmoth the Wanderer,* ed. Douglas Grant (London: Oxford Univ. Press, 1968), p. xi.

11. David Eggenschweiler, "*Melmoth the Wanderer*: Gothic on Gothic," *Genre* 8 (June 1975):178.

12. Robert E. Lougy, *Charles Robert Maturin* (Lewisburg, Penn.: Bucknell Univ. Press, 1975), p. 74.

13. See *Existentialism from Dostoevsky to Sartre,* ed. and intro. Walter Kaufmann (Cleveland and New York: Meridian Books, 1956), p. 12.

14. Leven M. Dawson, "*Melmoth the Wanderer*: Paradox and the Gothic Novel," [*Studies in English Literature, 1500-1900*] 8 (Autumn 1968):621-32.

15. Veronica M. S. Kennedy, "Myth and the Gothic Dream: C. R. Maturin's *Melmoth the Wanderer,*" [*Pacific Coast Philology*] 4 (April 1969):47.

16. R. D. Laing, *The Divided Self* (Baltimore: Penguin, 1965), pp. 39-54.

17. Kiely, p. 201.

18. In *The Gothic Imagination,* pp. 125-26.

19. For a relevant account of the existential "stranger" in the nineteenth-century urban novel, see Philip Fisher, "City Matters: City Minds" in *The Worlds of Victorian Fiction,* ed. Jerome H. Buckley (Cambridge, Mass.: Harvard Univ. Press, 1975), pp. 381 ff.

20. Dale Kramer, *Charles Robert Maturin* (New York: Twayne, 1973), p. 116.

21. Kiely also comments on the "dull routines of living death" in the novel, p. 192. See also Jack Null's relevant remarks in "Structure and Theme in *Melmoth the Wanderer,*" [*Papers on Language and Literature*] 13 (Winter 1977): 136-47, esp. pp. 145-47.

22. Michael G. Cooke, *The Romantic Will* (New Haven: Yale Univ. Press, 1976), p. xii.

Diane D'Amico (essay date 1984)

SOURCE: D'Amico, Diane. "Feeling and Conception of Character in the Novels of Charles Robert Maturin." *Massachusetts Studies in English* 9, no. 3 (1984): 42-54.

[*In the following essay, D'Amico examines questions of identity in Maturin's novels. D'Amico asserts that Maturin's characters possess a psychological depth unusual in Gothic fiction.*]

Literary history has placed Charles Robert Maturin in the company of Horace Walpole, Ann Radcliffe, and Matthew Gregory Lewis as one of those whose works helped establish the potential of the English Gothic novel. ***Melmoth the Wanderer,*** the fifth of his six novels, is considered a culmination of that genre of mystery and the supernatural. By combining the qualities of a Faustus and a Mephistopheles, Maturin created a haunting and haunted figure, a hero-villain suitable for conducting the reader through the novel's maze-like structure of tales, a labyrinth that ultimately leads into the dark places of the human soul. The compelling quality of this dark vision has made ***Melmoth*** [***Melmoth the Wanderer***] Maturin's most famous novel; however, all six of his works depict such a journey inward. Whether he relied upon the conventions of the Gothic tale for basic narrative structure or employed the forms of the historical romance, his heroes wander in a fallen world where man-made prisons and cages and natural storms and chasms mirror their own guilty state. In ***The Fatal Revenge,*** Maturin's first novel, Ippolito's defense before the Spanish Inquisition might well serve as an epigraph for all six novels:

> There is no human being fully known to another; it is only by partial ignorance, that mutual esteem is preserved. To the wife of his bosom, to the friend of his soul, to his own consciousness and recollection, a man will not dare to reveal every thought that visits his mind; there are some which he almost hopes are concealed from the Deity.[1]

Maturin develops this theme of guilt, guilt which separates man not only from others but from his own inner self, through the delineation of complementary pairs of characters. At times a pair of brothers serves to suggest one identity fragmented; other times this divisiveness within is manifested in the protagonist's simultaneous attraction to two women who seem to represent opposing worlds. It should be stressed that there is a distinct difference between Maturin's heroes and their female counterparts: his male characters are figures of guilt (the lost soul seeking some bit of paradise, or, in more secular terms, the fragmented self seeking wholeness); his heroines, although often tormented with guilt, are nonetheless essentially pure of heart and often function as symbols of hope for the male hero lost in his own darkness.

The major events of three of Maturin's novels—***The Fatal Revenge, The Milesian Chief,*** and ***The Albigenses***—revolve around a pair of brothers, each pair modeled on the pattern of opposites linked in one identity. In Jungian terms, they represent the self and its shadow.[2] At times one brother functions as the shadow by representing the less developed, often suppressed, qualities of the other's personality. At other times, the shadow character embodies some hidden evil that lies within a man's very human nature. Both types (the shadow as representative of what is simply unknown, and the shadow as unrecognized evil) are most clearly portrayed in *The Fatal Revenge.*

When introduced, Ippolito and Annibal Montorio are set before us as contrasting personalities united by a dark persuasion:

> Annibal was timid, gloomy, and mistrustful, as Ippolito was bold, open, and credulous; both partook equally of that attachment of dark pursuits which characterized the family, of that inflexibility of sombrous resolution, with which they adhered to a visionary pursuit, however irregularly conceived.
>
> (I, 31)

Throughout the novel's complicated structure of dream-like twisting and turning, passion governs the decisions of Ippolito, as reason rules those of Annibal. In this manner, each functions as the other's dark form, for each represents what is lacking in the consciousness of the other. However, as these brothers involve themselves in "dark pursuits," neither the intensity of passion nor the caution of reason is adequate protection against the shadow in its demonic form, the mysterious monk Schemoli. As soon as each brother actually comes to believe in Schemoli's reality, that he is neither an hallucination nor an imposter but an actual revenant with supernatural powers, all hope is lost. Their belief that this ghostly figure is more powerful than either of them does, in fact, make him so. Schemoli is then able to lead both passion and reason "to the same point" (III, 284); each brother becomes convinced that he is fated to murder their father. Appropriately, Ippolito consents "to guilt in a convulsion of passion" and Annibal "from a conviction of reason" (III, 476).

Midway through the novel, Ippolito's dream effectively serves to prefigure the total self-destructiveness of this crime while at the same time indicating a second significant pairing of characters:

> Ippolito found himself in a vaulted passage, lit by a few sepulchral lamps: Annibal was beside him, and the stranger [Schemoli] bearing a torch, and in the habit of a funereal mourner, stalked before them. . . . The stranger, waving them to follow entered an apartment hung with the insignia of death. . . . In the centre of the room, stood a bier, covered with a pall: the stranger withdrew it, and pointed to Annibal and Ippolito, the corpse of their father beneath. Ippolito, retaining his natural impetuosity in sleep, snatched the torch from the stranger, and held it over the countenance of the dead. . . . As he still gazed, the body extended one hand to him, and another to Annibal, seized on both, and drawing them under the pall, lapt them in total darkness.
>
> (II, 357-58)

In these vaults of death, which are so suggestive of the hidden places of the soul, there seems to be a sinister connection between Schemoli, who leads the young men to "total darkness," and the father figure, the ultimate source of that darkness. Maturin, in conventional Gothic fashion, leaves the details of this connection a mystery until the final pages of the novel. Then, through the device of Schemoli's rather long confessional letter, Maturin reveals that Schemoli and Count Montorio are brothers, and that Montorio's sins are indeed responsible for the final darkness which envelops the entire family.

Although the narrative line of this novel is rather complicated, making plot summary somewhat awkward, it is important to trace at least the basic outline; for it indicates how the two sets of brothers (Ippolito and Annibal, Count Montorio and Schemoli) are employed by Maturin to represent the fragmented self and the impossibilities of integration once the shadow-side has grown too powerful. Schemoli's real name is Orazio Montorio, a man once capable of great love, although possessive in nature. His younger brother, simply referred to as Montorio, was envious of the elder's position and played upon Orazio's potentially jealous nature, taking weakness and transforming it into sin. Through trickery and deceit, the younger brother convinces Orazio that his wife is an adultress. Ultimately, this leads to her death, and when Orazio later discovers that she was actually innocent, that he has in effect murdered his only source of love and light, he goes into exile. Grief-stricken and tormented by guilt, he becomes, in his own words, "a demon in soul" (III, 404). Consequently, when he returns to the world of society, it is only for the evil purpose of vengeance. The dark side of human nature is now in complete control as he plots to destroy his brother by manipulating Ippolito and Annibal.

If we see Montorio and Orazio as representing one self, then in a very real sense Montorio creates the demonic Schemoli; for by succumbing to his own envy and greed, passions belonging to his shadow-side, he releases the evil within himself which then takes shape in Schemoli. Released from any restraint, this darker side is able to destroy the entire family, to envelop the entire self in darkness.

In *The Milesian Chief,* Maturin again depicts a divided family, the O'Morvens. However, instead of the Gothic conventions of subterranean passages and ghostly figures, man's divided soul is now represented by a particular time and place: eighteenth-century Ireland, a rebellious land under British rule. The two major male characters, Connal and Desmond O'Morven, in both their mixed heritage and political persuasion, symbolize two seemingly irreconcilable aspects of one identity. Their father is the son of a proud Irish chieftain; their mother, the sister of the powerful British Lord Montclare. When the novel begins, Connal, who has chosen to live with his Irish grandfather, is preparing to lead an uprising against the British. Desmond, on the other hand, has readily accepted a commission in the British army, which Montclare was able to arrange.

As with Ippolito and Annibal, this contrast between the two brothers is established in the beginning and maintained throughout: Connal is an "oak" unwilling to bend, full of gloomy pride, while Desmond is the "flower" full of spirit and softness, easily swayed by emotion.[3] In several dramatic scenes, Connal functions as the disciplined mind, and Desmond, the impetuous heart. For example, when Gabriella, a minor female character, offers herself to Connal as his mistress, although he finds her attractive, he immediately returns her to her grandmother's protection. Desmond, however, when next she turns to him, readily accepts, thus abandoning both honor and duty. Later when overcome with guilt, he easily succumbs to despair. Just as he is about to commit suicide, Connal fortuitously appears by his side and is able to convince his younger brother to do his duty and return to his regiment (II, 208).

Although this particular episode seems to indicate that the heart (Desmond) is totally dependent for survival upon the mind (Connal), a closer examination of the conflict within that mind makes it apparent that Desmond does function as a very necessary part of the self; for Connal cannot deny the inclinations of his heart and be at peace. Although the proud Connal accepts his role as Irish leader, he is not completely committed to the cause. As he immerses himself in revolutionary plans, he comes to believe that his people are not yet ready for independence. His own followers lack a sense of honor and self-discipline, the very qualities he himself possesses. This dilemma, combined with the intermingling of the two brothers in several dramatic scenes, suggests that we can see Desmond as Connal's shadow in that he represents Connal's weaker, less developed qualities, acting out what Connal may feel but not express. And Connal serves as Desmond's dark form in that he functions as his younger brother's unconscious side, the urgings of Desmond's at times unrecognized conscience.

As the novel develops, each brother begins to recognize his shadow-side (in part due to the love of a noble woman); however, in a fallen world, the peace which comes from this integration of conscious self with its shadow cannot last long. When Desmond's impetuous heart is tamed by his love for Ines, he can live with her only if he removes himself from the embattled world, and of course, this escape is short-lived. The fallen world enters in the shape of the evil monk Morosini, and the lovers' paradise is destroyed. In Connal's case, as he begins to assimilate Desmond's qualities into his consciousness, guided by his love for Armida, he becomes less of the Milesian Chief, the rebel leader. He is actually able to convince his men not to rebel against the British; however, the evil Wandesford betrays him, forcing him to fight in self-defense.

In this novel, Morosini and Wandesford embody the shadow in its blackest and most destructive form, as Schemoli did in *The Fatal Revenge.* Although these individual characters can be defeated, the evil forces they set in motion cannot be so easily restrained. Connal may be able to defeat Wandesford in a duel, but he cannot escape from the charge of treason. Found guilty, he is condemned to death. And in keeping with the bond between the two brothers, just as Connal is about to be shot, Desmond rushes onto the field to kneel by his side; thus both fall together. Although this scene is a bit melodramatic, it is thematically appropriate.

In *The Albigenses* (Maturin's attempt at a historical romance in the style of Sir Walter Scott), as in *The Milesian Chief,* a particular time and factual event suggest the conflicting elements of a divided world. As the title suggests, this novel is set in thirteenth-century Europe during the second crusade against the Manichean sect known as the Albigenses. However, Maturin's historical depiction is neither accurate nor consistent. There are anachronisms and a rearrangement of events to suit plot; however, the several Gothic devices (curses and dark castles, prophecies of specter bridegrooms and the howls of werewolves) are not successfully reconciled with or integrated into the historical drama. In fact, at times the novel does seem pieced together from two separate tales. Yet if we view the setting as primarily metaphoric, we can recognize that the two forms, historical novel and Gothic tale, do complement each other thematically.[4] The depiction of a crusade in which each side claiming to possess the whole of spiritual truth is willing to kill the other, and the Gothic conventions which serve to indicate the darkness within man's soul, point to the same theme—man's guilty, fragmented state.

That this theme interests Maturin more than the examination of a certain historical event is further evidenced in his use of the brother motif. Again two brothers are contrasted: the pensive, melancholy crusader Paladour and the younger, more enthusiastic Amirald who will, upon falling in love with an Albigensian peasant girl, side with her cause. This time the initial division between the brothers occurs when they are infants. When the story begins, neither knows of the other's existence, although during their first meeting, Paladour's response to Amirald's tale of his youth clearly indicates to the reader a yet unrecognized relationship: "One would think that we were both enchained, from our cradle, in one link of suffering—but thine hath been twined in flowers and mine forged in iron."[5] This bond of suffering is metaphorically suggested by the scar each bears on his shoulder. Furthermore, as with Connal and Desmond, their interdependence is evident at key points in the action when each comes to the other's aid. As the strong, disciplined one, Paladour protects Amirald in battle. As the more outwardly affectionate and impulsive one, Amirald provides Paladour with needed emotional strength. When the dark lady of the lake appears, whom Paladour believes haunts him, he grows so weak that he must turn to Amirald for support (I, 82).

As with Connal and Desmond, each brother is the other's shadow-self, but in this case Maturin provides a happy ending (perhaps due to a desire to please a reading public). The shadow in its demonic form, which seemed to be taking shape in the Gothic figures of specters and werewolves and in certain historical characters such as the Bishop of Toulouse, fades quickly, and each brother is then free to marry the woman he loves. Paladour, no longer believing himself fated to murder his bride on his wedding night, is able to marry the Catholic Lady of Courtenaye; Amirald and the Albigensian peasant girl Genevieve, overcoming all obstacles of class and religion, also marry. In the final pages of the novel, all conflicts seem resolved through the guiding power of woman's love: "The difference of birth and creed was never known to disturb the affection that subsisted between the high-born Lady of Courtenaye and the humble bride of Amirald" (IV, 275).

In *The Milesian Chief,* Maturin comments that love is "everything to a woman, only part to a man" (II, 179). In *The Albigenses,* he makes a further distinction between the sexes: Genevieve is a "mixture of strength and purity that is never to be found but in woman" (I, 142); Isebelle embodies "the union of brilliant and lively intelligence with perfect purity which is to be found in the human face scarce ever—in those of men never" (II, 212). When we look closely at the role of women in Maturin's novels, we find that his heroines are embodiments of love, serving as spiritual guides for their self-divided, therefore corruptible, male counterparts. In *The Fatal Revenge,* despite the fact that Rosalia runs away from her convent to serve as Ippolito's page (she disguises herself as a young boy to do so), she remains uncorrupted by the decadence around her. As a model of a more disciplined way, she attempts to direct this man, whom she loves rather desperately, away from spiritual self-destruction. Indeed, at one point she cries out to him that she is his "soul" and he must save her (I, 241).

In Maturin's novels, women can enter the world of experience and yet remain pure; men cannot. If on occasion one of his major female characters should not appear as a guide to wholeness and higher meaning, but as a temptress leading to destruction, Maturin makes it clear that it is only in the male character's mind that she appears as such. For example, in *Women,* when Charles rejects Zaira, believing she has led him into a life of false values, Maturin indicates that Charles is merely seeing "crimes in her conduct, to hide his sense of his own."[6] His perception of Zaira as a fallen woman points to his guilt, not hers. She still possesses "simplicity of character, sweetness of temper, and genuine humility" (III, 106). In fact, although Maturin sometimes pairs his female characters (Ines/Armida, Eva/Zaira) so as to suggest contrasting types of fair maiden and worldly woman, it is not to point to a weakness or potential for evil within either female character, but rather to indicate the conflicts and divisions within the male. Therefore, when analyzing these female pairs, rather than seeing them as shadows of each other, it is more accurate to see them as images of the anima, projections of the male unconscious in her varying forms of angel and fallen angel.[7]

In the three novels discussed so far, we saw how Maturin used the brother motif to depict man's divided self. In the three novels remaining, *The Wild Irish Boy, Women, Melmoth the Wanderer,* he uses two mother-daughter pairs and a slight variation (one woman in two contrasting environments) to depict the hero's need to find and join with the anima in her role as saintly guide if he is to reconcile the conflicts within the prisons and cages of his own mind.

In *The Wild Irish Boy,* an awkwardly constructed tale and perhaps Maturin's poorest work, there is at least a consistent use of the mother-daughter device in developing Bethel's character. Ormsby Bethel, a young and impressionable man, is at first hopelessly infatuated with Lady Montrevor, a woman he sees as "no less than archangel ruined." Her daughter Athanasia is shy and retiring, and in Bethel's mind, hardly worthy of notice. However, after various trials and tribulations, one of which is finding himself somewhat unexpectedly married to Athanasia, he recognizes that this sweet domestic creature is a suitable partner for him. He concludes that "Lady Montrevor was framed to be admired . . . Athanasia to be loved."[8] It is important to note that it is through Bethel's eyes that Lady Montrevor appears only fashioned to be admired. At the end of the novel, her first and only true love returns from her past, and they marry.

Women provides a much fuller and more satisfactory development of this theme of the hero's wavering emotions. Again there is the impressionable and sentimental young man, and again there are a mother and daughter for him to love: Zaira, the sophisticated actress who was raised by a lecherous father and abused by an ambitious husband; and Eva, a quiet, pious and very innocent young girl who was raised by a strict Methodist family. Eva was taken from Zaira at birth; therefore, neither knows they are mother and daughter until it is too late to prevent the painful consequences of being loved by the same man, a man who continually vacillates between the two worlds they inhabit. It is this inability to choose which ultimately destroys him and, as a consequence, Eva and Zaira as well. Either choice fully made would have offered hope, for both women are capable of "benevolence," and both sincerely love.[9]

When we turn to *Melmoth,* Maturin's finest achievement, we find that in her two names, one woman represents the two worlds of innocence and experience. When she is the island maiden in the world of nature, knowing only tranquillity, she is called Immalee; when she is returned to the world of society, the world of suffering, she is called Isidora. However, like Maturin's other heroines, the change of environment and name does not change her inner purity. Although she is forced to enter the world of deception, she is not corrupted by it. Most striking is the fact that even when she agrees to give her "heart and hand" to Melmoth, the hero-villain who has sold his soul to the devil, she appears actually transformed into a higher type by the sincerity of her love:

> As she spoke, there was a light in her eye,—a glow on her brow,—an expansive and irradiated sublimity around her figure,—that made it appear like the rare and glorious vision of the personified union of passion and purity.[10]

It is this power to reconcile opposites that so touches the heart of the Wanderer: "This union in the same slight and tender form of those eternal competitors, energy and fragility, beauty and death, made every human pulse in Melmoth's frame beat with a throbbing unknown before" (287). She is Melmoth's hope, the anima leading the way to peace and harmony. Despite what the world of society wishes the beautiful Isidora to be, she remains Melmoth's Immalee: "I am *truth.* I am Immalee when I speak to you Melmoth,—though to all others in this country, which they call Christian, I am Isidora" (267, Maturin's emphasis). Melmoth need only believe in Immalee and her unselfish and constant love, love unshaken by suffering, to be free from the devil's bargain, for it is not Satan's offer which has doomed the wanderer as much as it is his own refusal to believe in the goodness of mankind. He can perceive only the malignity and hostility of human nature and nothing more—the shadow in its blackest form.

Among Maturin's six novels, *Melmoth the Wanderer* is the one which dwells most unremittingly upon man's propensity for evil. Despite Maturin's preface which suggests that this romance will show us "the enemy of mankind" in the character of Melmoth, the tales within tales which follow show us more of our own willingness to assume this role. After all, it is not Melmoth who actually causes the horrifying events of the various narratives. He makes his demonic offer only to "the ear of guilt and suffering," guilt and suffering brought on by others (407). He appears at the deathbed of his relatives only if their own "evil passions . . . cast a shade of gloomy and fearful interest over their dying hour" (20). In fact, at times Melmoth sounds more like a preacher reminding us of our failings than a possessed man tempting us to spiritual destruction:

> I tell you, whenever you indulged one brutal passion, one sordid desire, one impure imagination—whenever you uttered one word that wrung the heart, or embittered the spirit of your fellow-creature—whenever you made that hour pass in pain to whose flight you might have lent wings of down—whenever you have seen the tear, which your hand might have wiped away, fall uncaught, or forced it from an eye which would have smiled on you in light had you permitted it—whenever you have done this, you have been ten times more an agent of the enemy of man than all the wretches whom terror, enfeebled nerves, or visionary credulity, has forced into the confession of an incredible compact with the author of evil . . . Enemy of mankind! . . . Alas! how absurdly is that title bestowed on the great angelic chief,—the morning star fallen from its sphere! What enemy has man so deadly as himself? If he would ask on whom he should bestow that title aright, let him smite his bosom, and his heart will answer, Bestow it here!

> (334)

By using Melmoth as an embodiment and spokesman for the dark side of human nature, Maturin reminds his readers that each man casts his own shadow. Each man must recognize, as does Stanton when in the horrors of the madhouse, that he knows Melmoth, that he has always known him (41). With this interpretation in mind, we can see that it is particularly appropriate that the tales be framed as they are, for the events in the opening scenes strongly suggest a type of original sin. The young John Melmoth, bearing both the same first and last name as the mysterious wanderer, inherits the task of dealing with the tattered manuscript, an emblem of his family's sinful past. The young man is warned to destroy the manuscript without first reading it. However, following the inclinations of his own curiosity (his own desire for increased knowledge), he reads. Thus, he willingly participates in the series of dark tales which follow.

Maturin underscores this theme of inherited sin by depicting weak and ineffective parents whose children suffer as a consequence. Such ignoble figures can be found in all Maturin's novels, and in *Melmoth,* there are two particularly striking examples.[11] Softened by Immalee's love, Melmoth actually tries to save her from his own dark power. Anonymously, he warns her father that the wanderer intends to seduce his daughter's heart and soul. Don Francisco only momentarily contemplates hurrying home to protect her. When the opportunity arises for him to make yet another business transaction, he quickly dismisses all thought of parental duty and remains away from home. Consequently, his greed can be seen to play a part in Immalee's death. In the case of Alonzo, in the "The Tale of the Spaniard," the child suffers because his parents directly place the burden of their own guilt, the cast of their own shadows, upon him. Because he was conceived before his parents married, his mother promises him to the Church as expiation for her sins. He is forced into a life of monastic denial, a life Maturin saw as leading only to the twisting of natural and healthy instincts: "The virtues of nature are always deemed vices in the convent" (182).

In this repressive world, even a parricide is accepted and given a position of power: as a type of executioner, he persecutes and torments those within the monastery walls who break its rules. He willingly accepts his role, believing in his twisted theology, that if another suffers he will be saved: "But your guilt is my exculpation, your sufferings are my triumph. I need not repent, I need not believe; if you suffer, I am saved,—that is enough for me" (174). From Maturin's perspective, the world of the Catholic Church, either by forcing an individual to repress his dark-side or by encouraging him to transfer it to another, only augments his shadow's power. As an individual wanders in the dark recesses of the self, the authorities of Church and parent not only fail to provide a light but may indeed obscure what light there is.

This returns us to Maturin's portrayal of the loving woman as a source of hope. For Maturin, only when the individual finds a suitable partner, only when "domestic felicity" is achieved, does the soul leave behind the hell within to find its own bit of paradise.[12] As indicated earlier, such "felicity" requires that the woman fulfill a very extraordinary role—she must be an embodiment of both purity and passion, reconciling in herself all opposing qualities; she must be the anima in her form as psychopomp coming to show the way.[13] However, since a woman is not such an anima, but a separate distinct person with her own shadow and animus,[14] it is not surprising that when domestic happiness does appear in these novels, as in the case of Paladour and Amirald, or Bethel, it seems contrived and imposed from without. The sinister warnings of Melmoth and the dark dreams of Ippolito have far more verisimilitude. Clearly, Maturin's strength was in depicting the self fragmented and searching for wholeness, not in actually finding it.

In Sir Walter Scott's review of Maturin's first novel, **The Fatal Revenge,** he praises the originality of characterization as an achievement that helps compensate for Maturin's dependence upon the work of others:

> He has indeed regulated his incidents upon those of others. . . . But his feelings and conception of character are his own, and from these we judge of his powers. In truth we rose from his strange chaotic novel romance as from a confused and feverish dream, unrefreshed and unamused, yet strongly impressed by many of the ideas which had been so vaguely and wildly presented to our imagination.[15]

When we apply the terms of shadow and anima to this conception of character, some of this vague and wild presentation of ideas becomes clearer. Despite the reliance upon melodrama and exaggerated posturings, co-incidence and contrived endings, Maturin's depiction of human nature has the haunting quality of some dark truth. His paired characters, both male and female, point to the fragmented nature of the human soul and the need for each individual to journey inward, seeking communion with his other self. In a fallen world, no man is born without a shadow, and to deny its existence leads only to increasing its power.

Notes

1. Charles Robert Maturin, *The Fatal Revenge; or, The Family of Montorio* (1807; rpt; New York: Arno Press, 1974), II, 487. Subsequent references to *Fatal Revenge* will be cited in the text by volume and page number.

2. In several of his works, Carl Jung discusses the role of the shadow. See for example, *The Structure and Dynamics of the Psyche,* Bollingen Series XX (New York, 1960), VIII, 208 for Jung's explanation of his choice of the word "shadow": "Even the term 'inferior part of the personality' is inadequate and misleading, whereas 'shadow' presumes nothing that would rigidly fix its content. The man 'without a shadow' is statistically the commonest human type, one who imagines he actually is only what he cares to know about himself." In *Two Essays on Analytical Psychology,* Bollingen XX (New York, 1953), VII, 29, Jung points out the potential for evil which lies within the realm of the shadow: "And indeed it is a frightening thought that man also has a shadow-side to him, consisting not just of little weaknesses and foibles, but of positively demonic dynamism. . . . Having a dark suspicion of these grim possibilities, man turns a blind eye to the shadow-side of human nature. Blindly he strives against the salutary dogma of original sin, which is yet so prodigiously true."

3. Charles Robert Maturin, *The Milesian Chief* (London: Clarke, 1812), I, 94; III, 173. Subsequent references to *Milesian Chief* will be cited in the text by volume and page number.

4. I am indebted to Charlene Bunnell's master's thesis "The Gothic: Its Worlds and Visions" (Western Illinois University, 1982) for a clearer understanding of the Gothic novel and its characteristics. Especially relevant to an understanding of Maturin is her contention that coexistent worlds of light and dark (known and unknown) form a key element in the Gothic structure. Maturin's repeated use of shadow characters indicates that such a duality exists in all his novels whether Gothic or historical. Perhaps this is why he seems most appropriately identified as a Gothic writer, despite the fact that only two of his six novels (*The Fatal Revenge* and *Melmoth*) are obviously of that genre.

5. Charles Robert Maturin, *The Albigenses* (1824; rpt. New York: Arno Press, 1974), I, 180. Subsequent references to *Albigenses* will be cited in the text by volume and page number.

6. ———, *Women; or, Pour et Contre* (London: Longman, Hurst, Rees, Orme, & Brown, 1818), III, 106. Subsequent references will be cited in the text by volume and page number.

7. See Carl G. Jung, *Two Essays,* 187: "No man is so entirely masculine that he has nothing feminine in him. . . . A man counts it a virtue to repress his feminine traits as much as possible. . . . The repression of feminine traits and inclinations naturally causes these contrasexual demands to accumulate in the unconscious. No less naturally, the imago of woman (the soul-image) becomes a receptacle for these demands, which is why a man, in his love-choice, is strongly tempted to win the woman who best corresponds to his own unconscious femininity—a woman, in short, who can unhesitatingly receive the projection of his soul." See also Jung, *The Archetypes and The Collective Unconscious,* Bollingen Series XX (New York, 1959), IX, 199: "The anima is bipolar and can therefore appear positive one moment and negative the next, now young, now old; now mother, now maiden; now a good fairy, now a witch; now a saint, now a whore."

8. Charles Robert Maturin, *The Wild Irish Boy* (New York: Sargent, 1808), II, 223.

9. Maturin's description of Eva and Zaira responding to the news of Napoleon's defeat makes it quite clear that these two women are similarly benevolent (II, 180).

10. Charles Robert Maturin, *Melmoth the Wanderer* (1820; rpt. Lincoln, Nebraska: Nebraska University Press, 1961), p. 280. Subsequent references will be cited in the text by page number.

11. As mentioned earlier, in the *The Fatal Revenge,* Orazio ultimately destroys his own sons through his desire for vengeance. In *The Milesian Chief,* the father is weak and ineffective, thus allowing himself to become dependent upon his family's worst enemy. This then leads to the separation of the brothers and their final destruction. In *The Wild Irish Boy,* we see Bethel's family in turmoil and decay also. Bethel's supposed father is a decadent libertine whose strongest emotion in regard to his son is envy of his youth and health. In *Women,* Charles is an orphan. Through a father's neglect, Zaira is made easy prey for an unscrupulous suitor, and Eva has a guardian who sees her only as a figure to reflect and embody his own religious zeal. Although *The Albigenses* does have a happy ending for the children, such an ending occurs in part because their father Count Raymond takes back the dark burden he placed upon Paladour: "On me, be thy curse, my son! . . . mine be thy guilt of that vow that I madly bound on thy soul whilst yet a child!" (IV, 239).

12. Niilo Idman, *Charles Robert Maturin: His Life and Works* (Helsingfors: Helsingfors Centraltryckeri, 1923), 10. Idman quotes one of Maturin's sermons in which he calls domestic felicity "the best, the only that deserves the name, the sole flower that has been borne unwithered from paradise."

13. Carl G. Jung, *Psychology and Alchemy,* Bollingen Series, XX (New York, 1953), XII, 58.

14. Although Maturin does characterize women as rather amazing creatures, it is important to stress that he does portray their emotional and psychological conflicts with depth and sensitivity. Zaira, Armida, Lady Montrevor, and Isidora are all complex characters, not merely narrative devices.

15. Sir Walter Scott, "Article III: *The Fatal Revenge,*" *Quarterly Review* (May 1810), 347.

Kathleen Fowler (essay date winter 1986)

SOURCE: Fowler, Kathleen. "Hieroglyphics in Fire: *Melmoth the Wanderer.*" *Studies in Romanticism* 25, no. 4 (winter 1986): 521-39.

[*In the following essay, Fowler examines* Melmoth the Wanderer*'s powerful religious themes.*]

> Oh that my words were now written! / Oh that they were printed in a book! / That they were graven with an iron pen and lead / in the rock for ever!
>
> (Job 19:23-24)

> I would that the ocean were my ink, and the rock my page, and mine arm, even mine, the pen that should write thereon letters that should last like those on the written mountains for ever and ever . . .
>
> (*Melmoth the Wanderer* 277)

> Mortals, write your lines with the chisel, I write my hieroglyphics in fire!
>
> (*Melmoth* [*Melmoth the Wanderer*] 277)

Most critics of Charles Robert Maturin's **Melmoth the Wanderer** (1820) find the work disturbing, but compelling. It is a book, all agree, that can be overlooked—or violently attacked—but, once read, not easily forgotten. That the novel unsettles readers is easy to explain. Its structure is exceedingly involuted and seemingly erratic. The language of a long series of narrators is irritatingly consistent. The author leans heavily on Gothic machinery: ghosts, enchanted islands, the Inquisition, ancient manuscripts, etc. Plot contrivances daunt even the Gothic devotee, while Melmoth's failure to find even one person willing to sell his soul amuses the more cynical critic.

Nonetheless, the novel *does* move its readers powerfully, a fact not so simple to explain. In part the novel's power inheres in the urgency of Maturin's religious message. Maturin's preface explains that the novel grew from a passage in one of his own sermons in which he had asked:

> At this moment is there one of us present, however we may have departed from the Lord, disobeyed his will, and disregarded his word—is there one of us who would, at this moment, accept all that man could bestow, or earth afford, to resign the hope of his salvation?—No, there is not one—not such a fool on earth, were the enemy of mankind to traverse it with the offer![1]

Old Melmoth notes in his will that the first tale of Melmoth, Stanton's manuscript, was to be found "among some papers of no value, such as manuscript sermons, and pamphlets on the improvement of Ireland, and such stuff" (21). We, of course, must attend respectfully to anything which is dismissed by old Melmoth's perverted sense of values Maturin is signaling us from the outset that the Gothic elements of his novel are deliberately implicated not only in the religious theme but also in social commentary, and that each is meant to be explored in the context of the others. Indeed, Maturin's keen and thoughtful social criticism qualifies and pulls against his religious theme; it enriches the text greatly and engages the reader's interest.

However, while the religious and social dimensions of *Melmoth the Wanderer* unquestionably give the work meaning and validity, the chief source of the novel's power, the chief reason it continues to move its readers, lies in the sensitive and imaginative artistry by which Maturin compels us to consider and explore these themes. *Melmoth the Wanderer* has an artistic integrity shaped and enforced by unusual literary techniques which I will examine in this article. The novel is not formed in the conventional manner, nor yet unformed; it is, I suggest, intentionally de-formed. The reader must herself wrest its integrity from apparent chaos; Maturin thereby generates a tension which, as I will try to show, serves his essential artistic and thematic purposes. By viewing the novel from the perspective of a religious work, as Maturin claimed it was, we find that many of its apparent flaws—the "miraculous" rescues, the failure of Melmoth's mission, even the bizarre novel structure—are, in fact, essential and meaningful elements of the novel. These disconcerting features actually contribute to its striking artistic unity while they support Maturin's most important thesis: that with faith,

man *can*, despite sore temptation, triumph over suffering to stand humbly before the majesty and mystery of a "taciturn" and invisible, but puissant God.

I shall return to the issue of the novel's deliberate and unconventional structural and linguistic dislocations, but—for the moment—I should like to consider the formal devices, most of them already well documented, which Maturin employs to unify the novel in fairly conventional and familiar ways. Foremost among them, of course, is the complex and fascinating figure of the Wanderer himself. A splendid Gothic hero-villain—descended from Faust, Mephistopheles, Milton's Satan, Cain, and the Wandering Jew, among others[2]—Melmoth undeniably dominates the work, despite his late entrance and widely spaced appearances. The novel is further unified by a pattern of concrete and figurative—and usually Biblical—imagery (fire, storm, shipwreck, animals, etc.).[3] This imagery is employed in a remarkable variety of contexts and is carried from narrator to narrator. (It even appears in the speech of the Catholic narrators, despite Maturin's insistence that they are not permitted to read the Bible.)

Recurrent themes, too, give the novel a sense of depth and texture. There are repeated allusions to painters and a number of pictorially presented scenes; and there are other motifs, such as the recurrent theme of madness and unfortunate love.[4] Finally, there is the unblinking observation and delineation of pervasive and ingenious human cruelty. This theme has received most critical attention and has been perhaps best analyzed by William Axton.[5] All the chief characters undergo suffering—suffering executed by "oppressive institutions" and motivated by "social or religious sadism,"[6] but, significantly, invariably permitted by God. Melmoth himself asserts that the sufferings which the characters undergo are permitted by a chastening God: "When Thy Hand . . . is upon them . . . only to convey the wanderer back to the cage."[7] The suffering is *not* engineered by Melmoth—his function is to tempt the sufferers, not to torment them—but solely by man himself. Melmoth repeatedly throws the responsibility back at us: "'Enemy of mankind!' . . . 'Alas! how absurdly is that title bestowed on the great angelic chief,—the morning star fallen from its sphere! What enemy has man so deadly as himself?'" (436).

In a central chapter of the novel, Maturin synthesizes and concentrates this theme by means of a stylistic technique as exciting as it is unusual. Melmoth gives Immalee a lecture on the evils of mankind which could serve as a powerful synopsis of the entire novel. While Maturin, in a footnote, disowns the sentiments of this "agent of the enemy of mankind," Robert Kiely feels that the "Swiftian lucidity and energy"[8] of the passage belie Maturin's disclaimer. I concur, and find that the text itself supports Kiely's insight. Virtually every evil which Melmoth describes in this one chapter is acted out in the experience of one of Maturin's characters. Don Aliaga is the plundering and corrupting merchant with a conscience "that could not endure the extinction of a light in [his] sleeping apartment." Fra Jose, connoisseur of fine foods and wines, and troubled by nightmares which are the "abortive births of repletion and indigestion" (339), is the man who "by unnatural diet and outrageous stimulation, [has] happily succeeded in corrupting infirmity into disease." The Walbergs' plight exemplifies "misery by the side of opulence" as well as the "years . . . wasted" and "property consumed" as "law triumphs." The evils and pettiness of wars are encapsulated in the bloody and battle-torn history of the Mortimers, who—like Melmoth's hypothetical "patriots"—are fiercely proud of their family's exploits. Even such an unlikely detail as the sea-fight finds its specific counterpart in the history of John Sandal. Melmoth tells Immalee:

> "So strong is this habit of aggravating misery under artificial circumstances, that it has been known, when in a sea-fight a vessel has blown up . . . the people of that world have plunged into the water to save at the risk of their own lives, the lives of those with whom they were grappling amid fire and blood a moment before, and whom, though they would sacrifice to their passions, their pride refused to sacrifice to the elements."

(304)[9]

Later in the work we are told that John Sandal

> when . . . the Dutch Admiral's ship blew up, amid the crater of the explosion . . . plunged into the sea, to save the half-drowning, half-burning wretches who clung to the fragments that scorched them, or sunk in the boiling waves . . . "he plunged amid the burning wave to save the lives of the men he had conquered."

(460-61)

Just as he would build his sermon around a Biblical quotation, the preacher Maturin uses Melmoth's cryptic speech as the text for his novel, allowing it to radiate outward from its central position into and throughout the larger work. This radiating technique is not only the mark of a conscious and skillful artist, but also another reminder that the social commentary is embedded in the religious framework of the novel.

Unifying devices notwithstanding, the novel's multiplicity of stories and unusual narrative structure do mightily vex and bewilder the reader. The narratives are related, one within the other, in an intricate structure usually described as nesting boxes, but which is, in fact, greatly unbalanced and asymmetrical. The novel moves steadily into the interior of a labyrinth. The reader expects that ultimately he will be led out again. Instead, he is abandoned somewhere within the maze seemingly without a map, or even a thread. Thus, instead of the expected closure, the tales are left disturbingly incomplete; the remainder of Monçada's story, for instance, is told in one sentence, after hundreds of pages of details. Elaborations are promised but never materialize. There are hints of many other tales which could be told, but which are not. There are any number of unanswered questions and unexplained contradictions which hang fire as the novel precipitates, with Melmoth, to its sudden close.

The narratives are not only left without closure; they are internally incomplete as well. This is partly the result of the perishability of the documents in which they are preserved. "The relics of art are for ever decaying . . ." says one of Maturin's narrators (30). Stanton's manuscript is mangled, obscured, marred by agitation, incomplete, illegible at points—altogether unsatisfactory. It raises more questions than it can answer—a standard Gothic technique for starting a novel; but, as noted above, Maturin violates the expectations raised from this familiar device by never supplying answers. Maturin, in fact, continues to exploit the damaged narrative device throughout the novel. Juan's letters to Monçada, for example, are often "unintelligible" and "defaced." More puzzling still, Adonijah cannot "supply the deficiency" from his own manuscript.

Oddest of all, there are lacunae in the spoken record. In describing the treatment which he had received before the Bishop's visit, Monçada (or the author) leaves gaps in his own narrative,

> "Under pretense that there was no part of my person which was not under the influence of the demon, *** *** This was not enough. I was deluged almost to suffocations with aspersions of holy water. Then followed, & c., *** *** The result was . . ."

(165)

and he resumes his tale. Later, when John Melmoth, speaking for the frustrated reader, interrupts Monçada to demand an answer, he is instantly rebuked:

> "Have patience with me, Senhor," said Monçada, who did not like interruption; "have patience and you will find we are all beads strung on the same string. Why should we jar against each other? our union is indissoluble." He proceeded with the story . . .

(298)

Young Melmoth is forced to be patient, and so are we, but the expected answers still are not forthcoming—only more questions.

Adonijah's manuscript offers a hint of how we are to interpret the novel. Adonijah's narrative, as Leigh Ehlers points out,[10] has been written in Spanish and then transcribed into Greek characters (356).[11] Consequently, it appears to be little better than hieroglyphics—alien and even impenetrable. To force this manuscript to yield up its secrets, the reader must possess *both* languages. With this key, the surface unintelligibility disintegrates. I believe that the equivalent clue to Maturin's larger puzzle is provided by his fundamental source, the Bible, that Book which even Melmoth concedes "contains nothing but what is good" (307). To possess **Melmoth the Wanderer,** then, the reader must possess not only its text but also its Biblical subtext. Throughout the novel, Maturin draws richly and creatively from the Bible as a whole, but it is *Job,* the tale of the archetypal sufferer undergoing temptation, which is the most significant subtext to this collection of narratives about suffering and temptation. Rather than maintaining the original structure of Job, Maturin takes the timeless classic and shatters it to produce a version which, in its very distortion and obscurity, reflects his fragmented and time-bound world. We do not see the world whole in the novel, nor even in representative "slices"; we can see it only in scattered pieces, nor can we even locate all the fragments.

Where the Book of Job tells a single tale about a single sufferer, Maturin makes the story of Job relevant to all of us by depicting a host of Jobs. These figures—from all ranks of society and with a variety of religious beliefs and cultural backgrounds—all endure intense misery yet maintain their faith even when near despair. Like the saints' stories popular in the Middle Ages, Maturin's tales attempt to demonstrate that piety, conscientiousness, and courage are attainable by human figures as well as by divine. On the other hand, Maturin forces us to recognize that the cruelty, immorality, and social injustice which Job laments in his world continue unabated in our own. Job's so-called friends, who serve as advisors and tormentors, have been fragmented into dozens of unsympathetic or hostile figures in the novel—sadistic monks, the self-serving Fra Jose, the complacent Margaret, the rigid, narrow-minded Puritan aunt of Elinor, and so forth. These people, like Job's friends, surround the sufferers only to accentuate and exacerbate their misery; they never ease or even explain it. When the sufferers resist the final temptation to renounce God—the "unutterable condition" which Melmoth offers each in their extremity—they are (like Job) granted new happiness, or at least peace. Maturin thus holds out the hope that Job's eventual reward for constancy is available to everyone.

Dale Kramer suggests, in an off-hand comparison, a similarity between Melmoth the Wanderer and Job's Satan:

> . . . like the devil in the Book of Job, Melmoth has only limited freedom. He cannot himself torture his intended victims, though he can help to ensnare them in the Inquisition by hinting to authorities that the victim is having converse with Satan or his agent (himself).[12]

I think that the connection between Melmoth and the Satan is highly significant and I would like to explore more fully the extent and the implications of this relationship. Like Job's Satan, Melmoth spends his time "going to and fro in the earth and . . . walking up and down in it" (Job 1:7, 2:2). Like Job's Satan, he apparently, despite his description as the "agent of the Enemy of Mankind," works under orders and in the service of God. The divine constraints which bind Melmoth are repeatedly hinted at in the novel. A judge of the Inquisition, baffled by Melmoth's undetected and apparently unrestrainable visits to Monçada in the prison, defends the Inquisition's helplessness by claiming that Melmoth's "power (through the reluctant *permission* of God and St. Dominic . . .) had been suffered to range even through the walls of the holy office" (231). One of the gossiping Spaniards described Melmoth's victims as "the being[s] whom he is *permitted* to tempt or to torture" (327). Inez "had heard in her early youth, before she quitted Spain, of a being *permitted* to wander through it, with power to tempt men under the pressure of extreme calamity" (237; emphasis mine).

It is only the righteous who are tempted by Melmoth to blaspheme and to renounce God. Melmoth, then, is apparently constrained to tempt only the Jobs of later generations, those rare servants of God who can each be described as "a perfect and an upright man, one that feareth God and escheweth evil" (Job 1:8). Balzac's wry suggestion notwithstanding, it is not that Melmoth is remarkably stupid in selecting his targets. Dona Inez, Fra Jose, the parricide—all would make easy victims for Melmoth, but they have already bargained away their souls. Note Melmoth's contemptuous dismissal of Don Aliaga as a potential victim for Satan: "'You!—oh, there's metal more attractive! Satan himself, however depraved, has a better taste than to crunch such a withered scrap of orthodoxy as you between his iron teeth'" (443). Melmoth's task is to seek out those who, like Job, have maintained their integrity in prosperity and then to test their steadfastness in the face of adversity. Like Job's Satan, Melmoth fails to part his victims from God not because he is weak, but because they are strong.

Like the figure of Job and the story of Job, the narrative voice of the Book of Job has been divided among many speakers in **Melmoth.** In the Biblical work there appears to be only one narrator.[13] He reports in prose Job's history and God's agreement with the Satan, then (in poetry) the exchanges of Job and his friends and finally the encounter between God and Job. The third person point of view is maintained consistently, although, within their speeches, the characters use the first person. In **Melmoth,** there is no such narrative consistency. True, we have Maturin's equivalents of prologue—the narration surrounding John Melmoth's visit to his dying uncle—and epilogue, where Melmoth appears to

Monçada and young Melmoth and then dramatically vanishes. But within this framework there is a series of narrators, and to identify and evaluate each of them becomes, as the novel progresses, increasingly difficult.

By the impersonal narrator we are at first given some characterization of Biddy Branigan and the housekeeper, and from them, in turn, some of Stanton. We know nothing about the credibility of the Spanish "hostess" who tells Stanton the story of Father Olavida. We know Monçada's origins, family history, and personal history in great detail, but the evidence comes entirely from Monçada himself. The impersonal narrator has already become silent, and within Monçada's long story the credentials and histories of the narrator become more and more uncertain. We know about the parricide only through Monçada's observations and through what he tells Monçada, either deliberately or while talking in his sleep. We learn, also through Monçada, about Adonijah, who gives Monçada a very brief sketch of his life and a number of other hints which are never elaborated.

Although he calls it "my writing," we cannot, in fact, be sure of the authorship of Adonijah's manuscript. If Adonijah wrote it, why can he not help with the missing pieces? Furthermore, how does he or would he know what occurred on an isolated island where the only two "human" actors are Immalee and Melmoth? Did Immalee tell him before she died? Why would she? Who is Adonijah to Immalee? He never even appears within the manuscript which Monçada copies. Did Melmoth tell him? This, at least, is remotely possible since Melmoth *does* tell two such tales to Don Aliaga.

We know still less about the next narrator, the "stranger at the inn." This narrator is described simply as having an air which invited Don Aliaga's trust and as "being only a writer and a man of no importance in public or private life" (439). He says of his tale: "I have witnessed part myself, and the remainder is established on a basis as strong as human evidence can make it." (399). How he became a witness to this history is unclear unless he, himself, is the "good" priest or perhaps the youngest son of Walberg. We simply do not know, and either theory—priest or son—must confront certain incontrovertibly contradictory information.

As to the second half of the stranger's claim, the entire novel serves to erode our confidence in the strength of "human evidence." If our information about the narrators' credentials is scanty and questionable, the reliability of their testimony is even more dubious. All of it (except that in Stanton's manuscript) is reported *by memory* through Monçada. (This includes the entire contents of Adonijah's long manuscript, which Monçada has transcribed but apparently has not brought with him.) Furthermore, the extremity to which Monçada and the others have been brought renders their memo-

ries and their interpretations distinctly suspect. Robert Kiely, examining the psychological course along which Maturin has each of his narrators progress, concludes:

> By means of first person narratives, Maturin attempts to explore the minds of his victimized characters, tracing their course from a state of physical sensation, to a keen but highly subjective observation of detail, to an increasingly distorted sense of external reality, and finally to a point of inventiveness which recreates an imaginary world more distinct and affective than the world of objective reality.[14]

This psychological disintegration is accompanied by, and demonstrated in, the frequent dreams and visions in the work which, as Judson Monroe notes, further baffle both character and reader.

> Within the formally realistic context . . . Maturin attempts to make the experience of reading *Melmoth* as nearly approximate the experience of an actual vision or dream as it is possible to do in a work of fiction, thus giving *Melmoth* a psychological validity along with the illusion of verisimilitude. He does this primarily by weaving his tales together so that, soon, neither they nor the reader can distinguish between what is really happening to them and what is merely a function of their imagination.[15]

I think Monroe is right when he asserts that all the characters (except Don Aliaga), "come to realize, as Immalee does of her life, that 'dreams have become realities, and realities seem only like dreams.'"

That the information we are given is illusory is evidenced by the very language of the novel. Everything is refracted not only by the imperfect perception of human witnesses but by their highly subjective expression— "perhaps," "it appeared," "it seemed," "it would seem," "I thought," "I felt," "I remember feeling." Claude Fierobe, analyzing such language in passages like the one in which Monçada sees the figure of Melmoth above the fire at the Inquisition, demonstrates convincingly that we cannot be sure here, or indeed at any point in the novel, what actually does occur.[16] This can be most clearly illustrated by a close examination of what can be deduced about the character and actions of the novel's mysterious central figure.

The picture of Melmoth which we draw from the various characters in the novel is forever shifting, reforming, dissolving again. We are given much apparently false, useless, or at least irrelevant data. Why, for example, does Melmoth appear at the deathbed of family members, and how does this connect with his "mysterious errand"? Again and again *we* must do the sorting through the endlessly proliferating misinformation, speculation, and—maybe—truth.

Melmoth plays a major role only in the tale of Immalee, where his erratic and conflicting behavior and his heavily ironic speeches merely intensify and complicate the mystery surrounding him. He appears also as the final narrator within Monçada's account of Adonijah's manuscript, but again without telling us anything concerning his history, activities, or motivations. What we do learn in this section about Melmoth is filtered through Elinor's friend, the minister, who is introduced within this already multiply embedded narrative and about whom, once again, we know very little. Melmoth's silence at this point is curious. Still more curious and provocative is his final "testimony," when he appears to Monçada and young Melmoth.

Critics repeatedly claim that Melmoth finally reveals his history explicitly. Certainly he claims that he is going to: "I-I-of whom you speak, am here—Who can tell so well of Melmoth the Wanderer as himself . . ." (536). But he reneges, telling his listeners: "The secret of my destiny rests with myself" (537). In an extraordinary speech, he then proceeds to report to them *only* what "fear has invented, and credulity believed of me [to] be true . . ." (536). Note the repeated qualifiers in this passage which make the speech a masterpiece of evasion: ". . . *if* my crimes have exceeded those of mortality . . . *if* I have put forth my hand, and eaten of the fruit of the interdicted tree . . . *It has been reported* of me. . . . *It has been said* that . . . *If* this be true . . ." (537-38; my emphasis). Ultimately this speech serves only to undermine completely the certainty of anything which we believe we may have concluded from the preceding tales.

The fate of the Wanderer is a vexed issue. We are given in the penultimate chapter, through his dream, a graphic and searing vision of damnation. Melmoth sees the clock of eternity strike and feels himself plunging into an ocean of fire while the souls of those he has tempted—last of all Immalee—ascend, ignoring his appeals for help. The vision ends in intense horror: "he fell—he sunk—he blazed—he shrieked!" (529). Critics generally read this passage as confirming Melmoth's final damnation, since it is conjoined with the subsequent evidence that someone, presumably Melmoth, has been dragged and cast into the sea. However, Monroe's general warning regarding the deceptive use of dreams in this novel applies to the Wanderer's dream too. Melmoth's final dream is not unlike the dream of execution at the stake which Monçada had in the prisons of the Inquisition, the dream which culminates in "we burned and burned" (236). Monçada's dream comes from terrors wrought to a psychotic pitch. It does not prove prophetic, nor is there evidence that Melmoth's dream will prove more so. I suspect that Maturin returns to the dream technique at the end of the novel in order to keep open the question of Melmoth's final destiny.

Embedded in the novel are two symbols which offer some further insight into Maturin's purpose in this work. Of Melmoth's likeness, there are two intact, evidently accurate representations: the portrait which young Melmoth finds in his uncle's closet and the miniature portrait which the Spaniard carries. There is nothing mysterious about the existence of the former; it is a natural possession of the sort often found on an old family estate. The portrait is remarkable, however, for its appalling eyes—eyes "such as one feels they wish they had never seen, and feels they can never forget" (17-18). When young Melmoth has finished reading Stanton's manuscript, the portrait seems about to speak to him, but, as this sensation passes, young Melmoth impulsively executes his uncle's wishes. He "tore, cut and hacked it in every direction, and eagerly watched the fragments that burned like tinder in the turf-fire which had been lit in his room" (60). Then, after he falls asleep, Melmoth appears either in a dream or in a vision and whispers: "'You have burned me then; but those are flames I can survive.—I am alive,—I am beside you'" (60).

The second portrait is puzzling altogether. Monçada wears it suspended on a ribbon "close to the heart." The narrator reports: "It was painted in a coarse and unartistlike style, but so faithfully that the pencil appeared rather held by the mind then by the fingers" (72). Still, we are never told who drew the picture or why, how Monçada came by it, or why he carries it as a "terrible treasure" (71). Nor are we told why he suddenly crushes it and destroys it utterly.

The only "valid" portraits of Melmoth, then—the only "tangible" evidence of his existence and the only chance we have for studying his figure in some detail—are broken and burnt beyond restoration. Of course, their destruction foreshadows the presumed fate of the Wanderer—dashed on the rocks and plunged into an ocean of fire. But they serve an even more important function. The true portraits are replaced by a collection of narratives which are *not* "faithful" to the original and which are themselves splintered and fragmented, perhaps beyond reconstruction. Consequently, we cannot see Melmoth "with our eyes"; we can only "hear of him with the hearing of our ears" (Job 42:5). We are as unsatisfied and uncertain about Melmoth under these circumstances as Job was about God before he encountered Him in the whirlwind. The torn and crushed portraits become fit emblems for the entire novel, which might itself be described as a portrait "one feels they wish they had never seen, and feels they can never forget."

The characters, then, and the events, the outcome, and even the Wanderer are all ultimately unknowable. But the most important unknowable in this novel is God himself. All of Job's doubts are swept aside by God's appearance in the whirlwind. The questions which Job has raised, of course, remain unanswered, but Job is now certain, at least, of the existence of God. The world of Maturin, fallen much further than Job's world, does not permit such visible manifestations of God. God has receded beyond the reach of the human eye.

Critics have interpreted the conspicuous silence of God in this novel as evidence that Maturin is portraying a universe without a God or at the mercy of a malevolent deity. Mark Hennelly, for example, in a recent article on *Melmoth* defines the work as existential, depicting a "horrifying universe" guided by either "cosmic cruelty" or "at worst indifference." He concludes that "Maturin finds no ultimate meaning in an unpredictable life without absolutes."[17] The novel can indeed be read in this way, and it certainly does explore the five themes which Hennelly identifies as existential: "absurdity, isolation, failure of communication, loss of freedom, and the lack of responsible commitment."[18] But each of these five themes is counterpoised within the novel by examples of profound courage, steadfast love, self-sacrifice, unflinching faith, and intense commitment—themes hardly prominent in modern existential works. I would therefore argue that *Melmoth* exhibits the ancient angst of the tormented believer found in the Book of Job rather than any prefiguring of the modern existentialism of Kierkegaard.

Maturin, while not flatly asserting God's existence and His involvement in the affairs of mankind, provides evidence everywhere of God's power and command, and His active if invisible presence in the world. We see the reflection of God much as we see Melmoth, in the fragments of Maturin's broken mirror, and the image is likewise distorted and incomplete.

Immalee tells Melmoth:

> "The presages . . . that visit me, are such as never visited mortality in vain. I have always believed that as we approach the invisible world, its voice becomes more audible to us and grief and pain are very eloquent interpreters between us and eternity—quite distinct from all corporeal suffering, even from all mental terror, is that deep and unutterable impression which is alike incommunicable and ineffaceable—it is as if heaven spoke to us alone, and told us to keep its secret, or divulge it on the condition of never being believed."
>
> (511)

In Maturin's work, God's communication with mortals is conducted privately through such means as the presages which visit Immalee. Young Melmoth, as listener, and we, as readers, are not privy to this communication or even fully convinced of its reality. Immalee, like Eliphaz, must build her faith on visions of the night, and we, like Job before his own vision, must doubt and wonder concerning them.

Almost all of the characters, hypocritically or sincerely, ignorantly or thoughtfully, posit a God who is overseeing their fates. The most persuasive testimony is that which is apparently extorted from Melmoth. When Immalee discovers the Christian Church through Melmoth's telescope, Melmoth speaks with startling fervor of its merits and beauties. "Perhaps . . . [says the narrator] another cause might have operated on this prophet of curses and made him utter a blessing where he meant malediction" (296), adding that Melmoth was "[p]erhaps constrained by a higher power . . ." (297). Later, Melmoth's testimony becomes more explicit. When forced by Immalee to state his religious beliefs, he declares:

> *"I believe in a God."* . . . "you have heard of those who believe and tremble,—such is he who speaks to you!" . . . "I believe it all—I know it all," . . . "Infidel and scoffer as I may appear to you, there is no martyr of the Christian church, who in other times blazed for his God that has borne or exhibited a more resplendent illustration of his faith, than I shall bear one day—and for ever."
>
> (389-90)

This passage, and others like it in the novel, echo of course the speeches of Ahasuerus in Percy Shelley's *Queen Mab*. Shelley, however, maintains that Ahasuerus himself is only an invention of weak believers—"a wondrous phantom, from the dreams / Of human error's dense and purblind faith."[19] Shelley imaginatively conjures up Ahasuerus as a mouthpiece to expose the cruel paradoxes at the heart of Christian beliefs. Like Shelley, Maturin excoriates those who perpetrate violence in the name of Christianity. But Maturin accepts the reality—perhaps even the inevitability—of such paradoxes, and refuses to allow us as readers either to dismiss them or to condemn God—or deny Him—because man is flawed.

Perhaps Maturin has not asserted God's reality or revealed God's secrets because he felt with Immalee that heaven's secrets could not be told. Thus, instead of a direct answer to the question of why Melmoth defends Christianity, we are told: "into this we dare not inquire, nor will it ever be fully known till the day when all secrets must be disclosed" (296). The key word in this passage is "dare," since presumptuous curiosity is the central sin of the novel. In his deliberate avoidance of a direct appearance or even assurance of God, Maturin keeps such an accusation from falling upon himself, while directing it against us as curious and frustrated readers.

Claude Fierobe finds Maturin's religion orthodox, but permeated by a grim belief in a vengeful God: "C'est un Dieu severe, voire terrible, qui depense la justice retributive."[20] However, even retributive justice should logically be balanced by rewards to the worthy faithful. If we accept Melmoth's testimony that God permits the sufferings, we might reasonably expect that the ultimate release from suffering which every major character ultimately experiences comes likewise through divine agency. Certainly the rescues of the various sufferers are remarkable, in fact—miraculous. for example, the prison of the Inquisition burns down immediately after Monçada has been sentenced to the stake, and *just after* he has finally and absolutely repulsed Melmoth; as if this were not enough, Monçada then becomes the sole survivor of a shipwreck off the Irish coast. Guzman's will is discovered, and *all* the Walberg children survive unharmed; the family suddenly becomes "wealthy" *and* "happy" (433). John's sanity is restored, and Elinor can die "happy, since he knew her once more!" (501). Immalee, it is true, dies with her daughter in the prisons of the Inquisition, but she clearly dies to salvation. Her very name suggests one who is "immolated," a sacrificial victim. The product of a "savage" and isolated childhood on an island "paradise," Immalee can find no home in this fallen world. Death for her, is the only recourse. Her dying words: "'Paradise!' . . . *'Will he be there!'*" (533) suggest that her salvation may be lonely, but the words are also a final demonstration of her virtue.[21] Against all reason, she still loves the wretched Melmoth. Like Job she can truly say that she has not "rejoiced at the destruction of him that hated me / or lifted up myself when evil found him; / neither have I suffered my mouth to sin / by wishing a curse to his soul" (Job 31: 29-30).

The novel's fortunate "accidents" accumulate in such number that they could be (and have been) attacked as feeble authorial contrivances. Perhaps, however—to use Maturin's perpetual perhaps—they are not the work of a *deus ex machina,* but rather the work of a real and living God—a *deus in persona,* as it were—rewarding these sufferers as He rewarded Job when the trial was over and the test was passed.

The actively intervening hand of God seems most clearly demonstrated in the encounter of Monçada with Adonijah the Jew. This latter figure is nearly as extraordinary as Melmoth himself. Like Melmoth he has been given lengthened life as a result of his quest for secret knowledge, although Adonijah characterizes it as a penalty. If Melmoth is in part a re-creation of the Wandering Jew, Adonijah—I propose—is Maturin's revitalization and transmutation of the Elijah legend. (Certainly the similarity of the names is unmistakable.) Adonijah, like Elijah, is the prophet who tarries to bear witness. Adonijah declares to Monçada that he is transmitting to him the duty of reporting the history of Melmoth, but Monçada shrinks from the charge.

> "To bear about that horrible secret inurned in my heart, was that not enough? but to be compelled to scatter its ashes abroad, and to rake into the dust of others for the same purpose of unhallowed exposure, revolted me beyond feeling and utterance."
>
> (270)

Soon, however, Monçada, like Adonijah, is captivated. When he relays the tale to young Melmoth, Monçada is under the same sense of compulsion as that which had confined Adonijah sixty years in his vault. Indeed, when we first see the Spaniard, he is exclaiming in evident agony: "God! Why did the Jonah survive, and the mariners perish?" (71). Another sole survivor of a shipwreck, Monçada repeatedly refers to himself as Jonah, the unwillingly driven prophet.

The transferral to Monçada of Adonijah's burden of prophecy is effected by the most striking miracle of the book. Adonijah addresses the young man who has come to him for protection:

> "Thou saidst thou wert beset by a power that tempted thee to renounce the Most High . . . and that thou didst declare, that were the fires kindled around thee, thou wouldst spit at the tempter, and trample on the offer . . ."
>
> (268-69)

When Monçada answers passionately "'I did—and I would—So help me God in mine extremity'" (269), Adonijah tells him his own history and his oath:

> "Then vowed I a vow unto the God of Israel, who had delivered me from their thraldom, that none but he who could read these characters should ever transcribe them. Moreover, I prayed, and said, O Lord God of Israel! . . . Grant, that a Nazarene escaped from their hands and fleeing unto us, even as a bird chased from her nest, may put to shame the weapons of the mighty, and laugh them to scorn. Grant also, Lord God of Jacob, that he may be exposed to the snare of the enemy, even as those of whom I have written, and that he may spit at it with his mouth and spurn at it with his feet, and trample on the ensnarer, even as they have trampled; and then shall my soul, even mine, have peace at the last. Thus I prayed—and my prayer was heard, for behold thou art here."
>
> (270)

Adonijah's complex prayer, then, is heard and answered—fulfilled indeed in every minute particular. Adonijah believes that this is the work of God, and I think Maturin means for us to believe it also.

As we sort through and try out various arrangements for Maturin's fragments—Melmoth's mysterious mission, his constrained testimony, the wonderful existence of Adonijah, the fulfillment of his prayer, the reprieve of the sufferers—our sense of plausibility fails. Our "willing suspension of disbelief," to use Coleridge's term, can only be stretched so far. Then it snaps. This, I believe, was precisely Maturin's intent. Maturin, in fact, asks us to relinquish this tacit agreement that however absurd the initial premises, subsequent explanations should be logical and credible. Instead Maturin asks for faith. To accept and believe, as Job does, in a

God who reveals himself directly "out of the whirl-wind" is, after all, no difficult matter. Not to believe after such an appearance would in fact be madness. Maturin, the minister of God, asks us to do the more difficult thing—to believe in a God whose image we can see only in glimpses "through a glass darkly," and through a splintered glass at that.

Instead of direct revelation, Maturin allows "grief and pain" to serve as "eloquent interpreters between us and eternity." He offers us the evidence of those who suffer, endure, prevail, and, finally, regain happiness, or at least peace, and asks us to draw from their histories the recognition of the "incommunicable" workings and purposes of God. Ultimately, Maturin does not attempt to answer the question of why suffering exists, any more than does the Book of Job. Instead, he speaks through the narrator of Immalee's tale to assert simply that there *is* an answer. "We shall be told why we suffered and for what: but a bright and blessed luster shall follow the storm and all shall yet be light" (323). Elsewhere, the same narrator says:

> Revelation assures us there is a period coming, when all petitions suited to our state shall be granted, and when "tears shall be wiped from all eyes." In revelation, then, let us trust—in anything but our own hearts.
>
> (357)

The unity of anguish, uncertainty, awe, and faith concentrated in the last sentence epitomizes the mixture of agonized doubt and strong faith which underlies the entire novel. Maturin constantly reminds us that faith is meaningless unless it is exerted against powerful doubt. Unexamined faith is ultimately either the hypocritical lip service of Dona Inez or the unfeeling and unthinking mechanical devotions of Elinor's aunt. To strengthen our faith and to help us examine it, Maturin refers us here, as elsewhere, back to revelation—back to the Bible. Ultimately *Melmoth* draws its power from Maturin's own doubt and faith in the Biblical Word of God, and his imaginative grappling with the Book of Job, the Biblical work in which that faith and doubt are expressed most powerfully and most succinctly.

In *Melmoth the Wanderer,* Maturin has shivered the text of Job—as Monçada and young Melmoth shiver Melmoth's portraits—and then challenged us to restore it. Maturin, in effect, asks us to create the novel with him, or even, perhaps for him. Apparently taking his cue in part from the fragmentary, illusory, contradictory, and syncretic nature of the oral tradition which surrounds such legendary figures as the Wandering Jew and Faust,[22] as well as other sources for his main character, Maturin uses careful artistic control to present a story which is out of control. We cannot reconstruct a coherent novel for Maturin unless we are willing to create imaginatively pieces which will fit the holes left by the missing shards, and unless we bond all of the pieces together with a faith in God which can re-unify the world and the novel.

By his repeated examination of the nature of knowledge and by his stance of reverent humility before the unknowable—both underscored by stylistic devices and by the tentative language of the writing—Maturin resolves and reconciles the doubt of this world and the faith in God which are the two "languages" in which this work has been written. The novel is informed, at every stylistic level, by Maturin's belief that the "deep truth is imageless," that certainty is unattainable in this middle earth, and that imagination, hope and faith must bridge the terrible gaps which have opened between the fragments of the fallen world. If we choose in our reading of this novel to reject the presence or the implications of Maturin's faith, *Melmoth* becomes indeed, as has been proposed, an early portrayal of a horrifying absurdist universe. In this case, however, the novel is damaged by structural weaknesses, creaking machinery, and the dubious premise that Melmoth could not find a willing victim. If, on the other hand, we are willing to acknowledge Maturin's faith as well as his doubt and to accept his theme of faith, then such "weaknesses" emerge as appropriate and even essential devices. The faith which underlies this novel is itself deeply troubled and is being tested and tempered just as Melmoth's victims are tested and tempered. But the testing itself, and the reader's own struggle for vision and certainty which it compels, interact to yield ultimately a brilliant modern rendering of the Book of Job. *Melmoth the Wanderer* is a theodicy quite as horrifying as any modern work in its presentation of man's inhumanity, yet it holds out the consolation that there *is* ultimately divine justice and that there *are* answers—even though they remain beyond the reach of our limited mortal vision.

Notes

1. Maturin's claim, here, of course, is qualified in interesting ways in the novel itself, as should become apparent in the course of this paper.

2. All of these sources—and more—have been pointed out by critics too numerous even to note here.

3. The best study of Maturin's patterns of imagery is Claude Fierobe, *Charles Robert Maturin (1780-1824), L'Homme et L'Oeuvre* (Paris: Editions Universitaires, 1974).

4. See Fierobe and Robert Kiely, *The Romantic Novel in England* (Cambridge, MA: Harvard UP, 1972).

5. William Axton, "Introduction," *Melmoth the Wanderer,* by Charles Robert Maturin (Lincoln: U of Nebraska P, 1961).

6. Axton xv.

7. Charles Robert Maturin, *Melmoth the Wanderer: A Tale,* ed. Douglas Grant (London: Oxford UP, 1968) 519. All page references are to this edition, hereafter cited in the text.

8. Kiely 190.

9. The entire speech can be found in Chapter XVII, 297-311; the battle citation is on page 310.

10. See "The 'Incommunicable Condition' of Melmoth," *Research Studies (Washington State University)* 49, 3 (Sept. 1981).

11. Leigh A. Ehlers anticipates many of my observations concerning the structure, manuscripts, and narrators of the novel, but, as will become obvious, we reach quite different conclusions concerning the use to which Maturin puts such devices.

12. Dale Kramer, *Charles Robert Maturin* (New York: Twayne, 1973) 97.

13. Biblical scholarship has shown that this is not accurate, but I am treating the Book of Job *only* as it would have been read and interpreted by Maturin.

14. Kiely 193.

15. Judson Taylor Monroe, *Tragedy in the Novels of the Reverend Charles Robert Maturin* (N.Y.: Arno, 1980) 195-96.

16. See Fierobe.

17. Mark Hennelly, "*Melmoth the Wanderer* and Gothic Existentialism," in *Studies in English Literature, 1500-1900* 21, 4 (Autumn 1981): 670.

18. Hennelly 665-66.

19. "Queen Mab," Part VII, lines 64-65, in *Shelley's Poetry and Prose,* ed. Donald H. Reiman and Sharon B. Powers (N.Y.: Norton, 1977) 53.

20. Claude Fierobe, "Les Derniers Feux 'Gothiques' En Angleterre," *Dix-huitieme siecle* 14 (1982): 391-406.

21. I should note that some critics have read this ambiguous line as exhibiting Immalee's dread that Melmoth might be there.

22. Behind Melmoth probably also stand the Rosicrucians like William Godwin's St. Leon or Percy Shelley's St. Irvyne. St. Leon's escape from the Inquisition to the reluctant protection of the terrified Jew is clearly a direct source for Monçada's encounter with the panic-stricken Solomon.

G. St. John Stott (essay date June 1987)

SOURCE: Stott, G. St. John. "The Structure of *Melmoth the Wanderer." Études Irlandaises* n.s. 12, no. 1 (June 1987): 41-52.

[*In the following essay, Stott analyzes Maturin's narrative technique in* Melmoth the Wanderer. *Contrary to critics who view the novel as disorganized and confusing, Stott argues that the work has a carefully conceived structure, through which Maturin gradually reveals the troubled psyche of the protagonist.*]

Melmoth the Wanderer (1820), the fifth novel of the Irish clergyman Charles Robert Maturin, is praised in the standard histories as a great gothic novel; indeed, as "Maturin's masterpiece."[1] The phrase has a certain nicety, for by it the critics have meant not so much Maturin's masterpiece, his undisputed chef-d'œuvre, his legacy to world literature, as Maturin's best work, a masterpiece for him, and in its way a powerful and insightful work,[2] but something not truly great. Such reservations are quite understandable when they follow from the grammatical flaws and errors of fact in the novel; but less so when they follow—as they usually do—from a feeling that its structure is irredeemably flawed. The novel, it will be remembered, is made up of a series of interrelated tales. In the family home in county Wicklow John Melmoth finds a strange manuscript among his uncle's papers and from this he learns the story of the Englishman Stanton (Stanton's Tale). Shortly thereafter the Spaniard Alonzo Monçada, the sole survivor of a shipwreck off the nearby coast, tells Melmoth his own story (the Tale of the Spaniard) as well as those he has learned when hiding from the Holy Office (the Tale of the Indians, the Tale of Guzman's Family and the Lovers' Tale). As Monçada tells the last two tales as part of that of the Indians, their action is at four removes from reality (see Figure 1)—and this has consistently been found to be intolerable. The first edition's review in the *Quarterly* saw in the interpolated tales "a clumsy confusion which disgraces the artist and puzzles the observer"; Alathea Hayter, in her introduction to the Penguin edition, called it a device which distances narrator from reader, and "chills the latter's interest and belief"; and most of those who have written in the century and a half between have thought of the tales as a testimony to Maturin's incompetence. Thus the placing of tale within tale has been called undisciplined (by Edward Wagenknecht), deficient (E. B. Murray), incoherent (Wilbur R. Cross), tortuously involved (Ernest Baker), and execrably bad (George Saintsbury).[3]

Such vehemence is hard to understand. No one could really be confused either by the tales themselves (as Edith Birkhead has noted: "Each separate story is perfectly clear and easy to follow")[4]; or by their interrelationships. Further, those relationships could only be thought to have been clumsily constructed if it were supposed that Maturin intended some pattern or effect other than that which he created. There is no reason to suppose that he did. Critics have talked as though the tales were supposed to be contained one within another like a nest of Chinese boxes or a Russian matrioska doll, but common sense tells us that Maturin would not have produced the pattern of interpolations he did had he been really trying for the Chinese boxes effect. If we allow him a minimum of intelligence or skill we must presume that he would not have produced a frame tale containing two others, the second of these containing a third, and it containing two further tales, if he were trying to set tale within tale, each one framed by the one that had gone before.

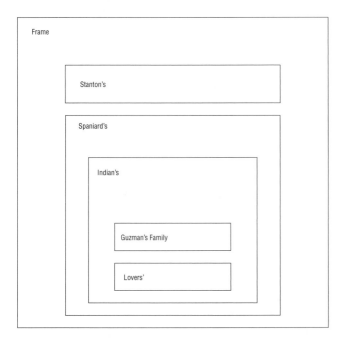

Figure 1: The Tales in Melmoth the Wanderer.

No small part of the critics' frustration with the tales has followed from the assumption that they are the novel's building blocks—and it must be admitted that were that so the novel's structure would indeed be chaotic. However, it is not so. Maturin builds the novel around a gradual revelation of his protagonist's identity and nature, and this revelation is organized independently of the novel's volumes, chapters, and tales. The Wanderer hardly changes during the course of the novel (his tenderness for Immalee is perhaps an exceptional example of character development), but our conception of him changes considerably. It is soon clear that he both visits and tempts individuals touched by monomania or despair, but the questions as to why he does this, and who (or what) he is, are left tantalizingly open throughout the work. Maturin gives us clues as to what the Wanderer is and what he is about, but no sooner do we seem to know the Wanderer's secret than Maturin forces us to think again by giving fresh evidence suggesting different conclusions. He draws us into a riddle, a riddle which is complicated by a fresh set of clues each time that the answer, the "truth" about Melmoth the Wan-

derer (hereafter Melmoth tout court) seems to be within our grasp. Rather than being a weakness, the structure of Maturin's novel is a source of its strength, and a reason to take it seriously.

The first clues are given shortly after Maturin has described John Melmoth's arrival at the Melmoth family seat. After having an interview with his dying uncle and listening to the gossip of the servants, John begins to entertain the possibility that a seventeenth century ancestor—John Melmoth the Traveller—is still alive in 1816, and that he has been seen by members of the household. This ancestor, he learns, was "never heard to speak, seen to partake of food, or enter any dwelling but that of his family"; further, "he was never known to appear but on the approaching death of one of the family" (p. 65). At this point it is too early in the novel to know whether Maturin will really deal in the supernatural or merely, like Ann Radcliffe, pretend to do so, only to explain away everything that seemed mysterious; but it is clear that the Wanderer is supposed to be taken for a haunt (either real or a product of the household's superstition)—a family spirit come to warn old Melmoth of his death. The most famous kind of this sort of spirit, the banshee, T. Crofton Croker was to report in 1824, "is peculiarly attached to ancient houses or families, and announces the approaching dissolution of any of the members by mournful lamentations."[5] Melmoth is obviously not meant to be thought to be precisely a banshee, for he is silent and male (the banshee was the *baen-sith,* the woman of fairyland); but he certainly seems meant to be thought to be something like one.

Maturin goes out of his way in these first few pages to convince us that we are beginning a ghost story. He takes time to detail Irish folk techniques of fortune telling and averting the evil eye; he specifies that old Melmoth was neither superstitious nor interested in the superstitions of others, and then goes on to detail what those superstitions might be: he informs us that John Melmoth the Traveller was supposed to have shared the interest of the seventeenth century in magic, astrology, and witchcraft, and in making this point gives examples of that century's credulity. In short, he introduces us into a world in which it would be credible that young Melmoth's uncle was being haunted by an ancestor's ghost. But then, in Stanton's Tale, he makes the first of a series of changes of tack. We learn that the Wanderer does not restrict his visits to members of his own family, or even to Ireland; and we arrive at a new understanding of his nature.

Stanton, an Englishman apparently unrelated to the Anglo-Irish Melmoths, sees the Wanderer in Spain, and some time later in London; and then becomes obsessed with the idea of seeing Melmoth again. His wish is granted. Confined by a brother in an insane asylum,

Stanton discontinues his religious exercises and sinks into spiritual despair—and Melmoth reappears and visits him. Maturin has already hinted that there is something demonic about the Wanderer: those whom he visits in Spain dabble in the black arts, and fear him as they do the devil. When Melmoth appears in Stanton's cell to offer freedom at an unmentionable price⁶ it is clear that he is no family spirit but something evil walking the earth. It is even possible, or so it seems, to give that evil a name. Demons will not come, Mephistophilis tells Marlowe's Faustus, unless their victim "use such means / Whereby he is in danger to be damned" (11. 295-96 in the 1604 text of *Dr. Faustus*). Melmoth, who gives Stanton a similar grim warning (only those are lost in the "lowest abyss," he tells the Englishman, "are sure to be visited by me" [p. 87]), and who appears in the asylum only when Stanton has put his soul at risk, cannot help but seem a latter-day Mephistophilis when we see him in Stanton's cell.

Stanton, needless to say, plays a Faustus to the Wanderer's Mephistophilis; but he is not the only Faustian figure in the tale. Father Olavida, whose encounter with Melmoth proves fatal, had sought the power of discerning evil; so had the monk who interrupts Olavida's funeral with a revelation of the father's pride; and most of the characters of the section seek knowledge or pleasure with a single minded intensity reminiscent of that of the Doctor of Wittenburg. Thus the asylum's insane had *obsessively* pursued "politics, religion, ebriety, or some perverted passion" (p. 97). They, like Stanton, had lost all capacity for normal enjoyment (just as, as Maturin had earlier observed, the lust for power of the Moorish architects of Granada had led to their loss of every other appetite [p. 69]) in short, they populate a Faustian world in which the coming of a Mephistophilis seems an inevitability.

By the time that all this becomes clear, Maturin breaks off Stanton's tale and offers in the resumed frame tale a new interpretation of the Wanderer. He describes how young Melmoth, after dreaming of his ancestor, started and sprung from his bed to find it broad daylight. "He looked round,—there was no human being in the room but himself. He felt a slight pain in the wrist of his right arm. He looked at it, it was black and blue, as from the recent gripe of a strong hand" (p. 106). Such a bruise forces a reinterpretation of the Wanderer. Although there were folk superstitions current in nineteenth-century Ireland that "spirits" could pinch and bruise, the doctrine of the church was that the spirits of the dead were totally immaterial. The New Testament had suggested this: "a spirit hath not flesh and bones," the resurrected Christ is reported to have instructed his apostles (Luke 24: 39, KJV); and the question had in theory been settled by Aquinas's teaching that there was no matter in a spirit's form. The last theologian to argue against this had been Augustine Calmet, writing

in the mid-eighteenth century. As a result, by 1820 the most normal interpretation of the incident in the novel would be that John Melmoth had not dreamed of the Wanderer, but had been visited by him; and that the Wanderer's "gripe" was that of a man somehow still alive.

With this new image of the Wanderer, Maturin leaves behind the gothicism and diabolism, the nightmare landscapes and supernatural evil of Stanton's tale. There are no mysteries for the next two hundred pages except those invented by foolish imaginations, and there is no evil except for that of (regrettably) ordinary men and women. This portion of the Tale of the Spaniard provides a grim commentary on the discovery that the Wanderer is in some sense human. In theory, if Melmoth is but a man any man could do his work. In the convent of the Ex-Jesuits, we discover, at least one does. It is a fellow religious who tempts Monçada to blaspheme in order to obtain his freedom. "Listen,-listen to me, and be happy. Renounce your vows, place yourself under my protection, and you shall have no cause to complain of the exchange. Rise from your bed, trample on the crucifix which you will find at the foot of it, and spit on the image of the Virgin that lies beside it . . ." (p. 220). Melmoth does not appear in the convent. Such is the "exhaustless malignity" of human nature—or at least that of the monks (p. 215)⁷—he is not needed.

The Wanderer is a man: so much seems clear. But he is obviously no ordinary man. Able to appear and disappear at will he has free access to any part of his family home or Stanton's asylum. During the storm which wrecks Monçada off the Wicklow coast he is unaffected by the raging elements. We want to know why, and how; and who the Wanderer really is: but until Monçada is imprisoned by the Inquisition Maturin offers no answer. Then, however, in the cells of the Holy Office, Monçada is visited by Melmoth, and the answers to our questions seem obvious. Once again we think we know what the Wanderer is. Monçada had never, he tells John Melmoth, "beheld such eyes blazing in a mortal face," as when the Wanderer visited him in his cell; "in the darkness of my prison," he remembers, "I help up my hand to shield myself from their preternatural glare" (p. 311). Neither had he heard before such anecdotes as Melmoth told. The Wanderer reminisced in 1799, with a "minute fidelity somewhat *alarming*" (p. 313, Maturin's italics), of the Restoration court in England, the death of the Duchesse d'Orleans in France, and the private history of Louis XIII. Since Melmoth did not look old enough to have been an eye witness to these events; indeed, since common sense suggested that no one alive at the end of the eighteenth century could have been an eye witness of events occurring a century and a half before (Louis reigned 1610-43), it is understandable that Monçada was alarmed and confused. We might share this alarm (or at least enjoy the drama of the situation), but we do not share the confusion. The brilliant eyes and fascinating conversation of the Wanderer are taken from M. G. Lewis's description of Ahasuerus, the Wandering Jew: "his eyes large, black, and sparkling" (inspiring a "secret awe, not to say horror" in their beholder), and his words thoroughly disquieting. "He named people who had ceased to exist for centuries, and yet with whom he appeared to have been personally acquainted. I could not mention a country, however distant, which he had not visited."[8] The parallel is unmistakable. Melmoth's prolonged existence, his terrifying gaze, his encyclopaedic knowledge gained through his transcendence of the normal limits of space and time, all make him somehow "like" the Wandering Jew.

This is no casual borrowing on Maturin's part. The image of the Wandering Jew informs the account he gives of Monçada's escape from prison. Ahasuerus was supposed to have refused to carry Christ's cross, and to have been punished with the fate of wandering the earth until Christ's return. The pages in question treat the continued stubbornness of the Jews in refusing to acknowledge the cross of Christ; the blasphemy of the parricide monk in *carrying* the cross, by supporting the banner of St Dominic (an inversion of the case of Ahasuerus); and the existence of a real Wandering Jew, Adonijah—"his existence prolonged beyond the bounds of nature" (p. 361). Such variations on a single theme give this part of the novel an impressive unity, and serve to confirm us in our feeling that this time we are right about Melmoth's characterization.

Sure as we might be, with the first hundred and fifty-three pages of the Tale of the Indians Maturin challenges our preconceptions once again. When Melmoth tempts Immalee on her Indian Island, it is a repetition of the events in Eden. Melmoth's role is made clear by such phrases as "arch deceiver" (p. 377), "fiendish acrimony" (p. 401), "diabolical heartlessness" (pp. 417-18), "Satanic smile" (p. 388), and "sensations like his master's when he visited Paradise" (p. 380). That of Immalee is no less clear. "Pain she had never felt—of death she had no idea," we learn on her first introduction to us (p. 375); "*thought should be a god*," she cries out when first shown the world outside her island home (p. 386, Maturin's italics)—and under Melmoth's tutelage she dramatically moves from innocence to experience.

Melmoth is satanic in these pages, but there is no danger of anyone confusing him (as Father Olavida did in Stanton's Tale) with Satan himself. He is the servant of Satan, just as Abraham was the servant of God. Abraham looked forward to "a better country, that is a heavenly" (Hebrews 11: 16); Melmoth, to "the wealth, the population, the magnificence" of his infernal inheritance (p. 460). Abraham argues with God to save the life of Lot (Genesis 18: 22-32); Melmoth, somewhat more truculently, for the life of Immalee. "This hour is mine, not thine," he insists (p. 424). He exaggerates, of course. He does not know when it is his master's time, and when not, as we soon see. In Stanton's Tale the Wanderer's visits had been preceded by a mysterious "celestial" music (Maturin could have got the idea from either folklore or the terror novel),[9] something that we assume is under his own control. But this assumption is shown to be false when he asks Isidora (as Immalee is called when she is brought to Spain), "in a choked and indistinct voice, if she had ever heard any music precede his visits to her, any sound in the air. 'Never,' was the answer.—'You are sure?'—'Perfectly sure'" (p. 515). There is no way of telling from this exchange whether there was music which Isidora could not hear, or no music at all; whether Melmoth induced the music or some other person or power did; or even whether it was for good or ill that Isidora heard nothing. But one thing is certain. If the Wanderer does not know whether or not Isidora heard any music, then he is not in control of the situation. He does not know when his victims really risk damnation, or when they are indeed likely to consider accepting his offer as a way of escape from their trials.

To go with this new view of Melmoth as a servant of Satan there is an explicit supernaturalism in these pages which tellingly confirms the Wanderer's new status as just one witness among many to Satan's power. We are presented with the ghost of a murdered servant, who watches Isidora through the window of the ruined priory where she is to marry Melmoth, only to disappear with "a faint and wailing cry" (p. 516); and the vivified body of a dead hermit, who (which?) performs the ceremony. These are unique manifestations in the novel thus far of the operation of demonic forces outside of Melmoth himself. The Wanderer's status is inevitably diminished thereby.

This view of Melmoth goes without explicit challenge for a while; but once the Wanderer forces himself upon Don Francisco Aliaga (Isidora's father) in order to warn him of the danger she is in, we have to think again. Melmoth insists that the number of those who are servants of Satan is large—that is includes every Christian who fails in his duty as well as those who confess to "an incredible compact with the author of evil" (p. 569)—and such a numeration serves to reclassify the Wanderer as a sinful human being rather than as a minister of evil. This view of the Wanderer is confirmed late in the Lovers' Tale (the one tale told by Melmoth himself) when we learn how he took upon himself what he has already called (p. 417) his "miserable destiny." Maturin probably drew upon William Godwin's *St Leon: A Tale of the Sixteenth Century* (1799) for the details, for he had already borrowed from this novel the idea of an escape from the Inquisition with Marrano's assistance. In Godwin's work St Leon is persuaded by a mysterious stranger to accept occult gifts—among them the power of living forever—that he might realize the potential of his genius. Melmoth is offered the same temptation. He keeps the company of a notorious Elizabethan magus, Dr John Dee, who was astrologer to Elisabeth I and geographical advisor to her court,[10] and Dee offers him what he cannot refuse: "posthumous and preternatural existence" and the chance to enjoy the "knowledge and power of the future world" (pp. 648, 646). Like Godwin's unfortunate hero, Melmoth accepts the offer, and binds himself to his temptor's terms. He dies, and then returns to life.[11]

Melmoth's revenance is supposed to have occurred in 1666 (that is, 150 years before the events of the frame tale [pp. 698, 41]). Dee, however, died in 1608. If Maturin knew this—and possibly he did, for his reference to Melmoth's intellectual vessel" as one "too great for the narrow seas in which it was coasting" and longing "to set out on a voyage of discovery (p. 646) suggests a more than casual familiarity with the astrologer's life—then he was probably hinting that Melmoth became a revenant at the instigation of another such.[12] But be that as it may, it is clear that, because of Dee, Melmoth becomes a revenant at the cost of his own soul. We cannot help, therefore, but see him now as Faustus, the scholar desperate for knowledge (the time when we could see him as Mephistophilis is clearly long past), with Dee and his companion Albert Alasco as the Valdes and Cornelius of his tragedy. There is no compact with the devil (as we have seen, Melmoth dismisses such pacts as incredible), but Melmoth's "pride and intellectual glorying" (p. 647) leads him to foreswear all hope of salvation.

Once alerted to this image of Melmoth as Faustus, we cannot miss the significance of Maturin's use of the Faust legend (drawing this time, however, on Goethe rather than Marlowe) as he brings the Tale of the Indians to its close. Melmoth brings Isidora to a miserable child-birth, prison cell, and death (just as Faust did *his* mistress), and as she dies she acts out a death scene that is obviously based on that of Margaret (Gretchen) in the first part of *Faust*. For just as we have in Goethe's work, "Stimme von oben: 'Ist gerettet!'" followed by "Stimme von innen, verhallend: 'Heinrich! Heinrich!'" (11. 4611-12), so we have in *Melmoth the Wanderer* Isidora reconciling herself to the church: "'My daughter,' said the priest, while the tears rolled fast down his cheeks—'my daughter, you are passing into bliss—the conflict was fierce and short, but the victory is sure—harps are tuned to a new song, even a song of welcome, and wreaths of palm are waving for you in paradise!' 'Paradise!' uttered Isidora, with her last breath—'*Will he be there*!'" (p. 691, Maturin's italics). As Isidora's cry works upon us, we know that if Isidora is a Margaret we were correct in thinking the Wanderer a Faustus or Faust.

In the last section of the frame tale, which follows the conclusion of the Tale of Indians (and with it the Tale of the Spaniard), echoes of *Dr Faustus* and *The Monk* suggest that the Wanderer is in the end destroyed like Marlowe's hero and Lewis's proud Ambrosio. However, Maturin also takes pains to suggest that the Wanderer's end might be otherwise. As he talks with young Melmoth and Monçada, the Wanderer compares himself with Adam. "If I have put forth my hand and eaten of the fruit of the inderdicted tree," he reflects (the conditional probably being Maturin's attempt to avoid ever admitting the nature of Melmoth's sin), "am I not driven from the presence of God and the region of paradise, and sent to wander amid worlds of barrenness and curse for ever and ever?" (p. 696). It is natural that he should feel shut out from grace and make a grim application of the Biblical story, but it should be noted that Melmoth offers a particularly despairing view of Adam's fall. The Christian Adam was redeemed—and the final force of this comparison has to be that there is hope for Melmoth's soul, just as there was to be hope for that of Goethe's Faust.

I am not, I should insist, under the illusion that all that *Melmoth* [*Melmoth the Wanderer*] offers us is the gradual revelation of the Wanderer's character. The novel's hold upon us comes as much, if not more from its insight into "the complexity, and often the paradoxicality, of extreme terror and despair,"[13] than from any sophistication in its revelation of character. Nor am I offering a source study. Hayter is right to see such studies proving little except that Maturin, "a well-read man, had not blocked off his imagination from the images and situations floating in European literary tradition."[14] Nevertheless, the way in which Maturin uses his sources is of interest—and the discovery of Melmoth's identity is handled with considerable sophistication. First, Melmoth's victims encounter him in ways that cannot help but lead us to think of him as the Wandering Jew, or Faust, or Mephistophilis, but no one encounter conjures up more than one image. Each image of the Wanderer is suggested by self-consistent clues. Second, successive partial characterizations of the Wanderer absorb the evidence for those which have gone before.

Rumor and speculation—for example, Biddy Brannigan's assertion that Melmoth restricted his visits to members of his own family—has to be discounted in the light of solid evidence about the Wanderer; but evidence itself, that is, what Melmoth is actually seen to do or heard to say, can be incorporated within each new interpretation. This successive rereading of the evidence in the light of each new interpretation unifies the novel and reinforces the credibility of each image of the Wanderer in its turn. Thus although seeing Melmoth's Mephistophilian qualities prevents our viewing him as no more than a family spirit, or haunt, it does not invalidate the evidence of the first part of the novel that he comes at times of death and despair. Neither do subsequent interpretations of the Wanderer affect our realization that Melmoth approaches his prospective victims much as Marlowe's Mephistophilis approached his—for all that our simple identification of Melmoth with Mephistophilis soon has to be abandoned. With each set of clues, in short, we are not simply presented with a new image, but also with the need to make an extra-textual assimilation to it of whatever composite image of Melmoth we have already formed. In Proustian terms, the series "describes its curve."[15]

The successive images are not arrived at, it should be noted, one to a tale. To be sure Melmoth seems to be little more than a ghost in the first section of the frame tale, and to be Mephistophilis in that of Stanton; but he is man rather than spirit in the second section of the frame tale *and* the first half of Monçada's narrative, while in the second half of the Spaniard's Tale he is modelled on Ahasuerus, the Wandering Jew. Again, while he is Satan's servant for most of the Tale of the Indians, and the Tale of Guzman's Family, where he seems to Guzman "the evil one, or some devoted agent of his in human form" (p. 557), we see him instead as Faust (or Faustus) in the Lovers' Tale, the ending of the Tale of the Indians, and the final section of the frame. The interpolated tales, to repeat a point made earlier, are not the blocks from which the novel was built. Instead, they are means to reinforce Maturin's dark vision of the world. Since the idea for the novel lay in Maturin's sermon meditation that no price could tempt anyone "to resign the hope of his salvation," even if the "enemy of mankind" were to canvas the world with the offer (p. 37: Maturin's Preface), some repetition was inevitable. Several temptations would have to have been repulsed before the novel could be seen as successfully making such a point. But Maturin could have had this repetition within a single narrative or (what he would no doubt have offered in his sermon, and what he might have first thought of) a series of independent tales as exempla for his theme.[16] Interpolation gave aesthetic as well as theological force to the work. By opting for multiple narrators and tales unfolding within tales rather than a simple, chronologically ordered narrative (or series of narratives), Maturin was able to heighten the effect of the Wanderer's appearances. Just as images seen in two mirrors set to face one another seem to be infinitely multiplied, so the violence, evil, and despair in *Melmoth* seem multiplied and intensified by their juxtaposition in the interpolated tales.

The technique was not a new one, and Maturin could have learned it from the first part of Charles Brockden Brown's *Arthur Mervyn: or Memoirs of the Year 1793* (1799), in which the unfolding of narrative within narrative serves, as R. W. B. Lewis has noted, to expand the works's "dark and violent cosmos."[17] However, Maturin uses the technique with far more skill than Brown.

Melmoth's interpolated tales become a labyrinth in which we wander, disoriented by the different patterns of human evil, and in which, no matter what path we take, we cannot avoid encountering the Wanderer himself. We look for an escape from evil, but all we find is the way offered by the Wanderer's blasphemy; a cure worse than the disease.[18] (Of course, since no one accepts Melmoth's offer, the novel offers some grounds for optimism. However, in fact the novel works to intensify the shadows rather than the light of its novel.)

No one within the novel, of course (except perhaps John Melmoth, if he is not too stupefied by what he has heard and seen), has anything but a partial picture of the Wanderer. All who encounter Melmoth see some aspect of him, not the whole; and for them he *is* what they see. But clearly Melmoth is more than any one character perceives; indeed, he is more than even what we perceive. "The secret of my destiny rests with myself," Melmoth announces (p. 696), and it would be just to say that to some extent the secret of his character also remains hidden. We have come close to knowing this secret in the course of the novel, but one hesitates to conclude that by the final page we have grasped it fully. Maturin was no doubt aware of this (hence his care to allow for a sequel),[19] but he was probably untroubled by the incompleteness of his readers' understandings. Rejecting the assurances of "Common Sense" philosophy that the world was knowable, he had written a novel in which—because he had chosen to rely on partial, fallible narrators—certainty is impossible. Possibly he had done this under the influence of Berkeley, for like the philosopher, Maturin had gone to Trinity College, Dublin, and there he would have known Berkeley's biographer, Joseph Stock,—a Fellow at Trinity before becoming Bishop of Killala in 1798. Maturin was no idealist, yet Berkeley's famous dictum, *esse is percipi* could well have suggested to him the idea of creating in Melmoth not a figure to be understood and interpreted by an omniscient narrator, but one whose nature is illuminated by the differing experiences of those whom he visits, and the readers' changing perceptions of the evidence.[20] The skill with which Maturin does this should not blind us to his carelessness in matters of style, and occasional historical detail; but it is considerable—and it is a sufficient rebuttal to those who would see nothing of merit in the novel's structure. When we take Maturin's insight into the psychology of violence and despair into consideration, *Melmoth the Wanderer,* clearly enough Maturin's masterpiece, comes very close to being a masterpiece indeed.

Notes

1. Thus Oliver Elton, *A Survey of English Literature 1780-1830,* 2 vols. (New York: Macmillan, 1924), 1: 219; Samuel C. Chew, in *A Literary History of*

England, ed. Albert C. Baugh (New York: Apple-ton-Century-Crofts, 1967), p. 1196.

2. See for example David Punter, *The Literature of Terror: A History of Gothic Fiction from 1765 to the Present Day* (London: Longman, 1980), p. 145; Carol Ann Howells, *Love, Mystery and Misery: Feeling in Gothic Fiction* (London: Athlone Press, 1975), p. 131; *Melmoth the Wanderer,* ed. Alathea Hayter (Harmondsworth: Penguin, 1977), p. 19. References to the text of *Melmoth* are to Hayter's edition and are given parenthetically in my text.

3. *Quarterly Review,* 24 (1821), 303; Hayter, p. 25; *Cavalcade of the English Novel from Elizabeth to George VI* (New York: Henry Holt, 1943), p. 124; *Ann Radcliffe* (New York: Twayne, 1972), p. 72; *The Development of the English Novel* (London: Macmillan, 1920), p. 159; "The Novel of Sentiment and the Gothic Romance," in *The History of the English Novel,* 10 vols. (London: Witherby, 1929), 5: 221; Introduction to *Tales of Mystery* (New York: Macmillan, 1891), p. XXIV. Claude Fierobe is exceptional in his enthusiasm: *Charles Robert Maturin (1780-1824): L'Homme et l'œuvre* (Paris: Éditions Universitaires, 1974), p. 607, though Judith Wilt, *Ghosts of the Gothic* (Princeton, N.J.: Princeton University Press, 1980), pp. 50-51, comes close to a positive assessment, and W. F. Axton has some grudging words of praise in the Introduction to his edition (Lincoln: University of Nebraska Press, 1966).

4. *The Tale of Terror* (1921; rpt New York, Russel, 1963), p. 85.

5. *Researches into the South of Ireland, Illustrative of the Scenery, Architectural Remains, and the Manners and Superstitions of the Peasantry* (London: John Murray, 1824), p. 91.

6. Maturin never gave explicit details of Melmoth's offer lest he be accused of treating the subject of Satanism, a complaint made about him in the past; however he gives broad hints with what are almost Melmoth's last remarks: "No one has ever exchanged destinies with Melmoth the Wanderer. *I have traversed the world in the search, and no one to gain that world, would lose his own soul!"* (p. 697, Maturin's italics).

7. The extent of the novel's demonstration of this is attributable to Maturin's anti-Catholicism; but the theme of human malignity follows from Maturin's new image of the Wanderer. There is a clear link between Melmoth's "obvious insensibility to the distress and terror around him" and the parricide's reflections on *"amateurs in suffering . . .* who have travelled into countries where horrible ex-ecutions were to be daily witnessed, for the sake of that excitement which the sight of suffering never fails to give" (pp. 113, 285; Maturin's italics).

8. *The Monk: A Romance,* ed. Howard Anderson (London: Oxford University Press, 1973), pp. 168, 169.

9. For example, in Ann Radcliffe, *The Mysteries of Udolpho* (1794), ed. Bonamy Dobrée (London: Oxford University Press, 1966), p. 71.

10. Frances A. Yates, *The Occult Philosophy in the Elizabethan Age* (London: Routledge & Kegan Paul, 1979), p. 87; Dee was notorious for his necromancy even in Maturin's day: see Peter J. Finch, *John Dee: An Elizabethan Magus* (London: Routledge & Kegan Paul, 1965), p. 15.

11. The details are borrowed from John Wilson Polidori's *The Vampyre* (1819): in *Three Gothic Novels,* ed. E. F. Bleiler (New York: Dover, 1966), p. 276 (cf. *Melmoth,* p. 647), but the borrowing merely establishes the Wanderer's revenance as part of a Faustian bargain, not that he is a vampire.

12. If this were so, then Melmoth would have been the second to accept such a bargain; it could be argued that that would be putting too great a strain on the novel's ostensible moral that *no one* would "resign the hope of his salvation," no matter what the offer.

13. Punter, p. 145. In *Melmoth,* H. P. Lovecraft wrote, "the Gothic tale climbed to altitudes of sheer spiritual fright"—*Supernatural Horror in Literature,* ed. E. F. Beilar (New York: Dover, 1973), p. 32.

14. Hayter, p. 16; for a discussion of *Melmoth's* sources see Willem Scholten, *Charles Robert Maturin: The Terror Novelist* (Amsterdam: H. J. Paris, 1933), and Niilo Idman, *Charles Robert Maturin: His Life and Works* (Helsinki: Helsingfors Central Tryckeri, 1923).

15. "As each successive revelation of character is made," Edmund Wilson has written of Proust, "we see perfectly that the previous descriptions of the character fit equally well our new conception, yet we have never forseen the surprise. Behind the series of aspects, we are aware of the personality as a complete and unmistakable creation; the series, as Proust says, describes its curve": *Axel's Castle: A Study in the Imaginative Literature of 1870-1930* (New York: Scribner's, 1931), p. 150.

16. Maturin first titled his work in progress "Tales," and this has suggested to some critics (e.g. Hayter, p. 25) that he did not have a single narrative in mind at first.

17. *The American Adam* (Chicago: University of Chicago Press, 1955), p. 96.

18. Fierobe, p. 607; cf. Wilt, pp. 51-2. For repetition as a key element in horror, see Bruce F. Kawin, *Telling It Again and Again: Repetition in Literature and Film* (Ithaca: Cornell University Press, 1972), p. 65; for dislocation as an aesthetic device, see C. N. Manlove, *Modern Fantasy: Five Studies* (Cambridge: Cambridge University Press, 1975), p. 6.

19. Monçada "announced his intention of disclosing . . . the fates of the other victims" of the Wanderer, and of detailing "the circumstances of the residence in the house of the Jew, his escape from it, and the reasons for his subsequent arrival in Ireland" (p. 692); Melmoth wondered if what he anticipated would be his last few hours of life would indeed be his last (p. 700).

20. Berkeley had remorselessly insisted in the first of his dialogues between Hylas and Philonous that the same object could be seen differently by different observers according to their perspective and faculties: *The Principles of Human Knowledge With Other Writings,* ed. G. J. Wamock (Glasgow: Fontana, 1962), pp. 158-73, 188-89; for *esse* is *percipi,* see p. 66.

Daniel P. Watkins (essay date autumn 1989)

SOURCE: Watkins, Daniel P. "'Tenants of a Blasted World': Historical Imagination in Charles Maturin's *Bertram.*" *Keats-Shelley Review,* no. 4 (autumn 1989): 61-80.

[*In the following essay, Watkins examines elements of Romanticism in* Bertram.]

Despite the fact that literary historians have always acknowledged the place of Charles Maturin's **Bertram** in Romantic literary history as 'a document of the taste of the Byronic period',[1] very few serious attempts have been made to explain and elaborate its critical importance to Romanticism. The few discussions of the play to appear during this century have been brief and usually descriptive rather than interpretative and critical. Bertrand Evans has situated it within a tradition of Gothic drama dating from the eighteenth century, cataloguing its themes, plots, character types and so on, and paying particular attention to what have been called its Byronic elements in order to assert that Byronism itself is part of Gothic tradition.[2] Joseph W. Donohue, Jr., follows Evans's approach of placing **Bertram** in Gothic tradition, but goes further than Evans in describing the development of Bertram as a character type. As Donohue states, 'the predisposition of the age was such that, as the agonies of the villain became more obvious and more detailed, greater sympathy was elicited for him. So by degrees the villain turned a hero who, through circumstances beyond his control, had become possessed by some evil force which drew him on to sin and despair, a force against which his conscience struggled valiantly but ineffectually.'[3] Dale Kramer also acknowledges the importance of Evans's work, but departs from its explanation of Bertram as merely a type, arguing instead that the hero of the play has a psychological complexity that distinguishes him 'from his ancestors in the Gothic drama'.[4] While these and a few other commentaries have helped to keep alive our awareness of the play's existence,[5] they have done little more than this because they rely primarily on plot summary, description of literary tradition, and character sketch as an expository strategy, leaving critical and conceptual matters relevant to the drama unconsidered. Thus **Bertram** remains little more than a literary curiosity, an example of a work that was tremendously popular in its day but that seems to possess no real literary merit or intellectual substance.

Even if critical investigations of **Bertram** have been lacking in our own day, at least one contemporary of Maturin saw the importance of the work and produced a serious and sustained commentary upon it that gives us a clue to its profound significance for Romantic studies. In *Biographia Literaria,* Coleridge gives an entire chapter of vilification to Maturin's drama because, in his view, it was an extreme example of certain British literary sensibilities—'bloated style', 'strained thoughts', 'figurative metaphysics', and 'horrific incidents, and mysterious villains'—that had travelled to Germany, been reformulated in dramatic form, and then returned to England, to the embarrassment and detriment of all that was good and proper in British culture. The works in this tradition, Coleridge pronounced, were 'the mere cramps of weakness, and orgasms of a sickly imagination on the part of the author, and the lowest provocation of torpid feeling on that of the readers'.[6]

The problem with such works as **Bertram,** for Coleridge, was not that they were bad literature (which seems to be our reason for marginalizing the drama) but rather that they were dangerous literature, a literature reflective of a commitment to

> godless nature, as the sole ground and efficient cause not only of all things, events, and appearances, but likewise of all our thoughts, sensations, impulses, and actions. Obedience to nature is the only virtue: the gratification of the passions and appetites her only dictate: each individual's self-will the sole organ through which nature utters her commands . . .[7]

Such 'materialism', Coleridge feared,

> may influence the characters and actions of individuals, and even of communities, to a degree that almost does

away the distinction between men and devils, and will make the page of the future historian resemble the narration of a madman's dreams.[8]

In *Bertram,* Coleridge found a perfect and, in his view, particularly ugly example of such madness, for it was a play that combined 'robbery, adultery, murder, and cowardly assassination'[9] into a general, misanthropic portrayal of human experience. It displayed 'confusion and subversion of the natural order of things,' threatening all 'law, reason, and religion'. It was, in short, a 'Jacobinical drama',[10] without 'moral sense',[11] providing 'melancholy proof of the depravation of the public mind. The shocking spirit of jacobinism seemed [in *Bertram*] no longer confined to politics.'[12]

The importance of Coleridge's denunciation of the play resides not so much in his personal moral outrage— though this in itself is interesting—as in his correct recognition of a literature entangled in quite specific historical crises. The moral stance that Coleridge takes is deeply situated in a vision of history as stable, ordered, and hierarchical, and the thrust of his moral argument is on behalf of this historical vision. The 'satanic hatred of Imogine's Lord' that he condemns, as well as his condemnation of Maturin's failure to bring his characters before 'the just vengeance of the law',[13] for instance, are condemnations of a literary imagination capable of displacing lords from the centre of social life; such an imagination subverts human order and purpose (as Coleridge would define them) and thus must be described as mad. Coleridge's large and serious critical effort in discussing *Bertram,* in short, is nothing less than an effort to define the proper bounds of historical and social order, and to ward off all serious threats (such as *Bertram*) to that order.

In the following pages, I want to offer a close analysis of certain issues and ideas in *Bertram* under the assumption that Coleridge was correct in arguing that the play's importance extends beyond literary history into social history, and beyond character portrayal into ideology. This is not to say, however, that I wish to endorse Coleridge's plea for a return to a pre-industrial, pre-Jacobinical, Burkean past of chivalry and aristocratic rule, or that I believe the play represents a species of madness. Rather, I want to provide an analysis that unfolds in historical terms the ideological forces behind Coleridge's denunciations of the play, his desire to retreat to a past, (imagined) edenical world, and his blunt accusation that literary imaginings of the demise of that world are simply mad. Such an analysis assumes that the popular excitement and moral revulsion inspired by *Bertram* arise from the play's distillation and articulation of powerful, contradictory historical forces. The many shocks, desires, fears, social relations, and structures of authority presented in the drama are inscriptions of the Romantic historical moment, both of

the immediate post-Waterloo situation and of the larger historical crisis involving the transition of British society from feudalism to capitalism. It is this historical imagination that gives the drama its particular power and claim to our critical attention.

The central historical feature of the drama is derivative, borrowing a stock plot device that had become commonplace to the Gothic imagination in the eighteenth and nineteenth centuries—namely, the use of cross-class marriage as a basis for psychological tension and unrest.[14] In this case, Imogine, a woman 'of humble birth' (1.5.),[15] marries Saint Aldobrand, a wealthy, bold, and powerful lord, against her will to save her destitute father:

> . . . What could I do but wed—
> Hast seen the sinking fortunes of thy house—
> Hast felt the gripe of bitter shameful want—
> Hast seen a father on the cold cold earth,
> Hast read his eye of silent agony,
> That asked relief, but would not look reproach
> Upon his child unkind—
> I would have wed disease, deformity.
>
> (1.5.)

This detail, more than Bertram's Byronic character, provides the key to the dramatic action. As a plot device, it explains Imogine's loneliness and even Bertram's alienation, and also provides stimulus for the various atrocities in the play that were so popular in its staging. Married against her will to someone she does not love, Imogine is emotionally weakened to the point of violating at a fundamental level the authority represented by her aristocratic husband (i.e., she succumbs to Bertram's advances), thus making possible everything that follows in the way of psychological turmoil, physical violence, and extreme passion.

But the detail is more than a plot device. It takes on broad historical significance when it is viewed as a sign of weakening aristocratic authority. Imogine's marriage to Saint Aldobrand is presented in such a way that it constitutes not so much an extension of aristocratic power, or show of aristocratic generosity, or even just another aristocratic action; rather, the violent and unjust conduct surrounding the marriage (the poverty of Imogine's father is held over her to force her hand, and even then she is drugged or hypnotized to ensure that the wedding ceremony goes off without incident) is one sign that aristocracy, however personally generous and admirable Saint Aldobrand may be, needs desperately to rejuvenate itself, and hence looks to outside human resources (Imogine) for energy and meaning. From the perspective of social class, the marriage stands at the centre of the drama as a sign of social instability, representing a fracture in the structure of aristocratic social relations, a small break from tradition that, through the course of the play, becomes a rupture, multiplying into violence and deceit, and promoting the decay of aristocracy. Traditional character concerns—the relative goodness of Aldobrand, the amoral actions of Bertram, and the extreme emotionalism of Imogine—are, from this point of view, less significant than the social effect of the marriage, which is to satisfy the immediate desires and needs of aristocracy while alienating others (in this case, Bertram and Imogine), so that the world becomes divided, throwing individuals out of the main flow of social life. The result is loss of integrity, personal regard, and social responsibility.[16] The seed of corruption and social deterioration is planted from the very beginning in the marriage of Imogine and Saint Aldobrand, and the actions of Bertram and Imogine are merely its fruits.[17]

One ideological consequence of the cross-class marriage is the privatization of human experience, the socially-enforced reliance of individuals on their own personal (and ever-narrowing) resources, a reliance that perpetuates and intensifies the divisions between individuals and their social worlds. Both Imogine and (for reasons not entirely identical with Imogine's) Bertram exemplify the loss of public life and the concomitant construction of private values that express both human need and human failure. Imogine, who for much of the play remains, at least superficially, within public life as daughter, wife, and mother, finds completeness in none of her roles, preferring the privacy of her room to the company of people in Saint Aldobrand's castle; treasuring the secretly-kept picture of Bertram over the flesh of her husband; and, ultimately, following the secret passion of a meeting with Bertram to the peril of domestic stability with her husband and child.

More telling here than the eventual liaison with Bertram is the fact that for all of her previous married life, and through almost the entire play, she never crosses the lines of social acceptability, carrying out her domestic and public role as though she were happy. As she tells her servant:

> Mark me, Clotilda,
> And mark me well, I am no desperate wretch
> Who borrows an excuse from shameful passion
> To make its shame more vile—
> I am a wretched, but a spotless wife,
> I've been a daughter but too dutiful.
>
> (1.5.)

Such a statement is remarkable for at least two reasons. First, it confesses a hollow, pointless individual existence, whose sole function is to support a domestic and class situation that offers little in return that can meet Imogine's real needs. Her own spotlessness in such a situation reflects the vileness and smothering authority of the class that brought her into its ranks against her will. Every compassionate gesture of her husband thus necessarily becomes 'a blow on th' heart' (1.5.), for it is also a gesture of domination, a show of compassion for a thing possessed. Even her child's love is a sign of her oppression, for she has given birth under conditions of alienation rather than of freedom. Second, that Imogine, a woman of rank, confesses such serious and sad realities to Clotilda, a servant, suggests that power and class relations in her world are such that aristocracy silences oppositional, or even questioning, voices from within its own ranks. The bond of confidence between Imogine and Clotilda, a woman socially beneath her, discloses this rigid aristocratic structure of authority and at the same time exposes the hard, unhappy conditions of sacrifice and alienation that such authority produces.

While not class-determined in the same way as Imogine's situation, Bertram's experiences that lead to his status as outlaw are equally entangled with the machinations of an anxious and uncertain aristocracy, and his character in this respect is the Romantic 'masculine' equivalent of Imogine's. Bertram is from the aristocracy and in his youth had been a favourite of his sovereign but, for reasons never made entirely clear, he is turned into 'an exiled outcast, houseless, nameless, abject' (1.5.). Two (apparently inconsistent) explanations of Bertram's change in fortune—one given implicitly in Imogine's confession to Clotilda, the other stated explicitly by Saint Aldobrand—are provided in the drama, and both bespeak anxiety and instability among the aristocracy. Imogine's account is extremely enigmatic, stating only that the once noble Bertram abruptly became an enemy of the sovereign. The only possible explanation for this change of fortune, based on textual evidence, is that Bertram's sovereign opposed his union with the lower-class Imogine. As Imogine describes Bertram's situation:

> [G]lory blazed
> Around his path—yet did he smile on her [Imogine]—
> Oh then, what visions were that blessed one's!
> His sovereign's frown came next.
>
> (1.5.)

The implication here is that the ruling class is absolute in its authority over *all* individuals, even those within its own ranks, obliging them to follow the dictates not of their own conscience and emotions but rather of the class that they serve. To view the situation in this way is to recognize that class authority does not reduce to individual authority—even if the individual is from the ruling class—but rather possesses a life and identity of its own that assigns and defines individual possibilities and limitations. In this respect, Bertram's situation is qualitatively no different from Imogine's: both are denied the freedom to choose an independent life based on their own needs and desires, and both are assigned a fate by the ruling class that is radically inconsistent with those needs and desires.[18]

At least on the surface, Saint Aldobrand's account departs widely from Imogine's, offering a loyalist explanation that uncritically accepts the authority and integrity of the state and casts Bertram as an absolute villain who opposes the state. In a condescending, patriotic, and self-aggrandizing lecture to Imogine, Saint Aldobrand explains:

> Thou knowest the banished Bertram—his mad ambition
> Strove with the crown itself for sovereignty—
> The craven monarch was his subject's slave—
> In that dread hour my country's guard I stood,
> From the state's vitals tore the coiled serpent,
> First hung him writhing up to public scorn,
> Then flung him forth to ruin.
>
> (4.2.)

Imogine does not contest this account of the past nor, on the other hand, does she ask Saint Aldobrand to recall for her the cause for Bertram's 'mad ambition' that led to his alleged treasonous actions, thus leaving open the possibility that her own confession to Clotilda is accurate, only emphasizing an earlier (and more immediately personal) phase of the history. To raise the possibility of compatibility between the two accounts of Bertram's exile is not to excuse what is clearly a weakness in Maturin's handling of plot and motivation, but to stress that the various accounts of Bertram's past are not *necessarily* mutually exclusive and to argue that, in either case, the political and ideological point remains the same on both accounts: under aristocracy, authority ultimately resides at the level of class rather than at the level of the individual, and any challenge to this reality is punishable by absolute exclusion from the main flow of human social life. Interpretations of the past, though they emphasize different details, unfold within an identical context of class authority.

One additional question bears consideration with respect to Bertram's past and those who have had a role in it. If Bertram is punished with exile for his affection for a lower-class woman, then why is Saint Aldobrand, who marries Imogine, exempt from the scorn of his sovereign? The answer to this question, once again, lies in the fact that actions in the drama are not depicted as being individually chosen, but rather as class determined. In Bertram's case, love for Imogine entailed defying his sovereign and following his own personal course of action. It is in this sense that Saint Aldobrand's remark that Bertram 'strove with the crown' is accurate; Bertram did not necessarily desire—and Saint Aldobrand does not suggest this—to become the new sovereign, but rather, as Imogine's remarks to Clotilda suggest, to make his own decisions about his personal life. Saint Aldobrand, on the other hand, does not move against, but with, the grain of aristocracy in marrying Imogine; that is, the marriage is not portrayed in terms of mutual affection, but rather in terms of Saint Aldo-

brand's conquest over Imogine and her destitute family. Likewise, his regard for her, as noted above, derives not from love but from possession. In short, as Maturin handles it, Saint Aldobrand's marriage to Imogine, unlike Bertram's love for this same woman, is a class rather than an individual action, calculated to invigorate rather than disrupt the prevailing structures of authority. That it ultimately has the reverse effect is one sign of the destabilized context within which it has taken place.

The drama, however, is not simply the story of social decay, but also of an emergent social class. Bertram's defiance and exile contain within them the seeds of an anti-aristocratic ethos even while Bertram himself retains his leadership position and posture of nobility among a group of banditti. Moreover, this anti-aristocratic ethos is clearly more powerful than the aristocratic claim to authority presented in the drama. Both of these facts (stock features of the Byronic hero) certainly were as critical to the play's immediate popularity as the stock of Gothic machinery that Maturin and Drury Lane hauled before the public for twenty-one consecutive nights, for they articulate, however melodramatically and subliminally, the triumphant bourgeois defiance of aristocracy.

The inchoate bourgeois ethos attached to Bertram's character is visible most immediately in his individualism. On one level, of course, the individualism described in the drama is not bourgeois at all but rather, like the individualism presented in Byron's Manfred, a last extreme assertion of aristocratic authority in the face of a changing world. But behind this aristocratic assertion stand the assumption of the autonomy of the individual subject and the strong sense of self-identity that became culturally prevalent with the rise of capitalism. Rejecting absolutely the institutional expression of feudal and aristocratic codes and values (for instance, Catholic religion[19]) Bertram in exile actively subverts the world from which he has been thrown, engaging, like Byron's Corsair, in a career of invasion and robbery of the aristocracy. Giving form and definition to his defiant personality are such sentimental traits as absolute devotion to and love for Imogine (just as the Corsair idealizes Medora), personal physical strength, and a moody disregard for what others think of him, regardless of the social status they carry with them. These, combined with his refusal even to submit to the punishment that has been allotted to him (he takes his own life instead), mark him as a personal identity rather than as a social figure—and this provides one context for Coleridge's condemnation of the play. In Bertram, what matters are not codes and systems of belief passed down by tradition, nor even the continuing thread of lineage itself (compare, for instance, Aldobrand's dying remark, 'Oh save my boy' (4.2.) to Bertram's unflinching defiance of all socially-sanctioned values), but rather the determination of life and value by one's own personal needs, desires, and experiences. Such a spirit of individualism does not die with Bertram's suicide at the end of the play, but rather lives as the very spirit of the dramatic action and of the culture that made the drama tremendously popular.

Related to Bertram's individualism—and to his suicide—is another feature telling the instability and ultimate demise of aristocracy, namely Maturin's handling of forms of punishment. What is sought by the society against which Bertram has sinned, and specifically by the military and religious authorities controlling this world, are Bertram's public confession of guilt and plea for mercy, followed by public execution. Such a course of events, while doing nothing to bring Saint Aldobrand back from the dead, or Imogine from madness, would effectively demonstrate the stability and continuing authority of the social order by casting Bertram's actions as an aberration from a social standard of propriety, and by publicly demonstrating the sanctity and justness of society. The actual course of events, however, has the reverse effect of throwing into relief the weakening of society and the changing nature of human pain and understanding of crime. When asked why he has murdered Saint Aldobrand, Bertram provides a simple, cold, and painfully narrow answer: 'He wronged me, and I slew him' (5.1.). This is followed immediately by Bertram's warning that public punishment cannot touch him for his crime, for his pain is immune to social judgment:

> Be most ingenious in your cruelty—
> Let rack and pincer do their full work on me—
> 'Twill rouse me from that dread unnatural sleep,
> In which my soul hath dreamt its dreams of agony—
> This is my prayer, ye'll not refuse it to me.
>
> (5.1.)

At the end of the same scene, when the Prior encourages him to pray for mercy, Bertram makes a similar remark: 'Give me your racks and tortures, spare me words' (5.1.). One major point here, of course, is clear even at the level of plot, namely that Bertram's crime and pain are so deeply personal that they cannot be publicly defined and dealt with. The ideological dimensions of his comments, however, are more complex. The utter privatization of value and judgment implicit in his explanation of his conduct is staggering, rendering powerless the world of the Prior and of the military. As Bertram himself knows, he can be executed but not conquered (5.1.), and this means that the example of his conduct permanently defies authority, leaving the horror of his deeds to echo through a hollow world.[20]

The shattering significance of Bertram's actions and comments is suggested by numerous passing comments and details in the later scenes that tend to describe individual situations in a language of social or public life, so that individual fates are made to appear as the fate of aristocratic social order itself. The Prior, for instance, intimates that the violence and powerful, awe-inspiring criminality of Bertram reverberate through the social order. His sense—or fear—that Bertram's deeds carry more than personal meaning is seen not only in his desperate, failed attempts to convince Bertram to accept the mercy—and hence judgment—of the church and state, but also in his several remarks identifying the immediate tragedy with the larger structure of social life. In response to Bertram's comment that

> I deemed that when I struck the final blow
> Mankind expired, and we were left alone,
> The corse and I were left alone together,
> The only tenants of a blasted world.
>
> (5.1.)

the Prior commands the knights attending the prisoner to 'Advance, and seize him, ere his voice of blasphemy / Shall pile the roof in ruins o'er our heads' (5.1.). In an earlier moment, too, he remarks of Saint Aldobrand that 'his halls are desolate—the lonely walls / Echo my single tread' (5.1.). Clotilda's sad comment that, after murdering Saint Aldobrand, Bertrand 'sat in dread society, / The corse and murderer . . . there together' (5.1.) bears testimony that the necessary vocabulary for describing the ugly situation is social rather than personal, and it is a vocabulary that echoes Bertram's own tendency to see social decay and death around him. Within such a context, where murder echoes through the 'halls', 'society' and the 'world', even the Prior's final, short, and chilling descriptions about Imogine's fatal struggle with madness (''Tis past', 5.3.) and about Bertram's suicide ('He dies, he dies', 5.3.) become a description too of the larger social order. The lord of the castle, Lord Aldobrand, is dead; Imogine and her child are dead, the former from madness and the latter presumably by his mother's hand; and Bertram, a once glorious noble youth, is dead by his own hand; the military is unable to prevent any of this, and the Prior is unable to rationalize or explain it in terms of any existing codes and values.

Bertram's internalization and privatization of pain to the point where social judgment is impossible is complemented interestingly by the portrayal of Imogine's madness. Maturin's decision to cast the heroine into madness while giving the hero the more socially-respectable conduct of defiance, noble speeches, and suicide is a sign of the patriarchal ideology governing the handling of gender relations in the drama, and as such it provides an important insight into yet another dimension of social conflict that is borne and acted out by individuals. Imogine's madness in the final act carries to an extreme the withdrawal and isolation that she had been identified with early on. Caught from the beginning between the pull of her own heart and the oppressive demands of a patriarchal society and family, she is, as a woman, powerless to act. At various moments, she is subject to a lover, a husband, a father, a monk—all men who make claims on her and assume responsibility for giving her an identity, so that, even more than Bertram, she never has a real home other than the nebulous and precarious dream world of her own mind. As she is pushed and pulled through the world of the drama, she finds ever fewer resources in society or within herself to draw on.

To cite only one example of her marginalization, at a moment of extreme crisis, when she is torn between her passion for Bertram and her sense of obligation to her husband, Imogine confesses her anguish to the Prior:

> Last night, oh! last night told a dreadful secret—
> The moon went down, its sinking ray shut out
> The parting form of one beloved too well.—
> With nought that lov'd me, and with nought to love
> I stood upon the desart earth alone—
> I stood and wondered at my desolation—
> And in that deep and utter agony,
> Though then, than ever most unfit to die,
> I fell upon my knees, and prayed for death.
>
>   (3.2.)

Her need and her plea to the Prior are for human compassion and spiritual solace, for a support, in other words, which will provide her with an enabling basis for her personality and identity. The response she gets from the Prior, however, is entirely deaf to these, insisting instead that all she needs to remember are her responsibilities to a situation and role she has not chosen:

> Art thou a wife and mother, and canst speak
> Of life rejected by the desperate passion—
> These bursting tears, wrung hands, and burning words
> Are these the signs of penitence or passion?
> Thou comest to me, for to my ear alone
> May the deep secret of thy heart be told,
> And fancy riot in the luscious poison—
> Fond of the misery we paint so well,
> Proud of the sacrifice of broken hearts,
> We pour on heaven's dread ear, what man's would
>   shrink from—
> Yea, make a merit of the impious insult,
> And wrest the function of mine holy office
> To the foul ministry of earthly passion.

The human ugliness of this speech is staggering, surpassed only by the Prior's subsequent condemnations of Imogine ('Thou art a wretch'; 'I do pronounce unto thy soul—despair,' 5.1.). While he is respectful of, and deferential towards, Bertram, a criminal who never displays the slightest regard for religious belief, the Prior refuses Imogine any possibility of integrity or even identity outside the narrow social roles that have been allotted to her, and when her own needs take her away from these roles he simply discards her as a blot on society. To put the matter somewhat differently, and much

more bluntly, the Prior's handling of Imogine suggests that, under patriarchy (whether aristocratic or bourgeois), a woman who needs compassion and personal support amid social and individual turmoil is worse than a man who commits murder.

The effect of the Prior's accusing response, of course, is to drive Imogine further into her own mind, rather than drawing her into the world of social exchange, and to pave the way for her eventual mad wanderings in the forest. While at this moment in the drama the Prior pleads with 'all-pitying Heaven' to 'release her from this misery' (5.3.) of madness, Imogine is utterly lost, voicing pain and horror that expose an opposite side of social deterioration from what Bertram's conduct discloses. When the Prior approaches the mad Imogine, for instance, and takes hold of her, she shrilly responds, 'Oh, spare the torture—and I will confess' (5.3.). This statement reverses Bertram's desire for physical torture as a way of awakening his soul from unnatural sleep, and in doing so again suggests the distance between masculine and feminine life in the world of the drama. That is, Bertram's mind, like that of Milton's Satan and Byron's Manfred, is its own place, enclosing a will and spirit that are perdurable, active and set, stone-like, against all social sensibility. Imogine's inner world, on the other hand, is entirely hollow and passive, her withdrawal into a subjective realm of desire grounded upon nothing more than dreams that have been shaped and defined by one sort or another of masculine authority. The passive longing of the soul is all that is allowed to her. Fear of physical torture, then, naturally paralyzes her, for her inner world has long been tortured by its very meagreness and narrowness, and only her flesh remains relatively free of pain. On this view, her situation throughout is more serious, more desperate, than Bertram's, though it appears less valorous by being defined against the bold, active resistance of Bertram to his world.

The point here of course is that any argument about Bertram's portrayal of an inchoate bourgeois ethos of individual autonomy must be clarified along gender lines, for the autonomy of the individual subject under capitalism, no less than the social situatedness of individuals under capitalism, is discriminatory. Imogine's position as an aristocrat and her display of subjectivity are not the same as Bertram's nobility and individuality, for both display her apparent inferiority to her masculine counterpart. The historical transformation of individual and social reality from aristocratic to bourgeois cultural formations, even while destroying the ideological centre of an entire way of life, retains certain hierarchies of value (in this instance, patriarchy) that enable the bourgeoisie to secure and extend its authority and identity. Imogine's character perfectly demonstrates this point, as it not only exemplifies—in madness and murder—aristocracy shrinking out of control, but also the emotionalism and absolute personal loyalty to the strong individual male that are demanded of women under bourgeois patriarchal social relations.

One major feature of the drama that serves as an institutional focus of the conflicts sketched thus far is religion, discussed briefly above in terms of Bertram's defiance and Imogine's madness. From the beginning, the monks and the Prior display an odd combination of integrity, fear, coldness, deceit, warmth, and overwhelming confusion. The Prior is unable to condemn Bertram absolutely, even after Bertram's worst crimes have been made known (see 5.1.), although, as mentioned above, he readily condemns the pitiful Imogine. And throughout the play, the various religious figures, who seem consistently to wish for peace and goodness, speak of their anxiety and fear over actual and imagined events. Perhaps the clearest indicator of the large social significance of their various comments and attitudes is the opening scene of the drama, which first describes several monks facing a severe storm, followed by a description of the wreck of Bertram's ship and the monks' desperate concern for the victims. As the storm rages, and before they are aware that a ship has capsized, the monks repeatedly express their fear and terror of the great storm besieging their convent, a storm so great, the first monk remarks, that 'relic, and rosary, and crucifix, / Did rock and quiver in the bickering glare' (1.1.). The immediate cause for such comments, of course, is the public demand for Gothic horror, and Maturin's eagerness to satisfy that demand. But narrow stage and public considerations notwithstanding, these opening scenes suggest fear and anxiety at the very centre of the feudal world, articulating doubts about even the continued existence of religious authority and credibility. When Bertram's ship is spotted in the storm, religious strength and faith erode even further, as the Prior first boldly commits himself to praying for the ship's members, refusing to leave the dangerous storm for the safety of the convent, and then collapses into the arms of his monks, who carry him away.

The distinction between this collective frenzy and Bertram's response to the storm is striking. Amid the monks' horror and fear that the ravings of nature are a sign of the impending doom of humanity, Bertram, silently and alone, carves his own private way to survival. And in the subsequent scenes of the drama, the sheer courage and will associated with this act never diminish, and the monks and Prior never recover their collective self-esteem, failing even to see Bertram to an execution that would display the continued authority of church and state. The religious figures, and especially the Prior, seek to follow a course of action geared to reflect and perpetuate aristocratic value, and yet at every turn they defile aristocracy and display powerlessness and awe in the face of Bertram's defiant will. Religion, however much it tries, cannot put the social order back together again once it has been invaded and disrupted by Bertram, whose mind repeatedly overwhelms all efforts to establish the controlling reality of feudal religion and social estate.

Two final, related matters need to be mentioned briefly that might clarify the apparently conflicting, or divergent, perspectives on the inchoate bourgeois individualism that I have thus far been tracking: the separation that Bertram claims and seems to demonstrate between his body and his mind, and his suicide. It is clear throughout the drama that Bertram cares very little about the direction that his life might take, or even about whether he lives or dies. As one monk explains after watching Bertram save himself from the storm: '. . . there was one did battle with the storm, / With careless, desperate force; full many times / His life was won and lost, as though he recked not' (1.3.). Once brought before the monks, too, he asks them to 'plunge me in the waves from which ye snatched me' (1.3.). This same disregard for his own life is seen again later when, as discussed above, he asks his captors to torture him ('Let rack and pincer do their full work on me'). This is not to say that Bertram lacks self-identity or self-worth. Rather, public struggle has come to be seen as pointless or impossible and the individual thus retreats into the recesses of his own inner world to establish a rigorous, defensive, and self-willed private system of values, one that is ostensibly independent of and resistant to the sordid public world of social life. At this level, the level of what Eli Zaretsky (writing in a different context) calls 'predetermined inner life',[21] Bertram is confident and strong, as is seen not only in the awe with which everyone from Imogine to the Prior approaches him (despite his clearly dissipated physical appearance), but also in his suicide. While Bertram's suicide is perhaps most immediately a sign of despair and inevitable doom, at the same time it indicates the possibility of preventing the triumph (through trial and execution) of aristocratic authority; thus suicide becomes a statement of the enduring defiance of Bertram's individual spirit. As he remarks in the final lines of the drama, 'I died no felon death— / A warrior's weapon freed a warrior's soul' (5.3). While this marks his personal demise, it also marks the final triumph of the individual against society, and emphatically and terribly displays the assumption of absolute division between individual and society that is at the core of bourgeois ideology. As Maturin handles it, in other words, suicide is not merely a private act: it carries far-reaching social significance, pointing at once to the death of nobility and to the triumph of individual will.

While Coleridge's commentary on **Bertram** does not follow the specific line of argument I have offered here, its anger and anxiety can be traced to many of the issues I have elaborated. Coleridge knew that **Bertram,** and other works of the period like it (including, he feared, his own *Rime of the Ancient Mariner,* which he spent years trying to contain within a Christian interpretative framework[22]) were products of a changing social world, and as such a threat to conservative, Christian social order. It was in this respect that **Bertram** was a 'jacobinical drama', contributing to 'the confusion and subversion of the natural order of things'.[23] The natural order for Coleridge in 1817, as I noted at the outset, did not include the disruptive, changing, historical force of post-revolutionary Europe, but the (ostensibly) fixed and stable social relations found in aristocratic rule and a strong Church supporting—and supported by—the state. On this view, the demise of aristocracy depicted in **Bertram** was also a depiction of demonic forces that threatened to destroy all life, making humanity into 'tenants of a blasted world', into people, that is, who lacked purpose, direction, or hope. Whether or not Coleridge was correct about the absolute demise of culture signalled by **Bertram** and its counterparts on the public stage, he was certainly right in recognizing that the content of the drama, and its amazing popular reception, were both a product and sign of marked social change during the period. For this reason, the energy behind his argument, and the areas of the play to which that energy was directed, should remind us of the great importance of **Bertram** as a cultural artifact, and of the importance generally of Romantic drama to an understanding of Romanticism in its historical definition.

Notes

1. Ian Jack, *English Literature 1815-1832* (Oxford, 1963), p. 181.

2. Bertrand Evans, *Gothic Drama from Walpole to Shelley* (Berkeley and Los Angeles, 1947), pp. 192-99. Note his remark, for instance, that 'mere failure to relate *Bertram* to that large share of the eighteenth century represented by the Gothic tradition would perhaps not in itself be a grave matter. But this failure illustrates a general misconception which is important. To misjudge the relation of *Bertram* to the Gothic tradition is to misjudge the relation of the Byronic in general to that tradition' (p. 199).

3. Joseph W. Donohue, Jr., *Dramatic Character in the English Romantic Age* (Princeton, 1970), pp. 88-89.

4. Dale Kramer, *Charles Robert Maturin* (New York, 1973), p. 69.

5. See, for instance, Willem Scholten, *Charles Robert Maturin: The Terror-Novelist* (Amsterdam, 1933), pp. 30-42, which offers a summary of the play's plot, a consideration of Maturin's borrowing from Schiller, Scott, and others, and a discussion of pre-production revisions of the drama that were urged upon Maturin. See also Robert E.

Lougy's brief comments on Maturin's revisions and upon the extreme popularity of the drama, in *Charles Robert Maturin* (Lewisburg and London, 1975), pp. 44-49.

6. Samuel Taylor Coleridge, *Biographia Literaria,* edited by James Engell and W. Jackson Bate, 2 vols (Princeton, New Jersey, 1983), II, 211.

7. Coleridge, *Biographia Literaria,* II, 213.

8. Coleridge, *Biographia Literaria,* II, 214.

9. Coleridge, *Biographia Literaria,* II, 233.

10. Coleridge, *Biographia Literaria,* II, 221.

11. Coleridge, *Biographia Literaria,* II, 225.

12. Coleridge, *Biographia Literaria,* II, 229.

13. Coleridge, *Biographia Literaria,* II, 227, 229.

14. To cite only two examples, note the Hesperus-Olivia marriage in Thomas Lovell Beddoes's *The Brides' Tragedy* and the Elvira-Conde de las Cisternas marriage in Matthew Lewis's *The Monk.* For a discussion of class issues in these works, see Daniel P. Watkins, 'Thomas Lovell Beddoes's *The Brides' Tragedy* and the Situation of Romantic Drama', [*Studies in English Literature, 1500-1900*] (forthcoming), and 'Social Hierarchy in Matthew Lewis's *The Monk*' [*Studies in English Literature, 1500-1900*], 18 (1986), 115-24.

15. Quotations from *Bertram* are taken from Natascha Wurzbach, ed., *British Theatre: Eighteenth-Century English Drama. Specimens of English 18th and Early 19th Century Drama* (Frankfurt, 1968), volume 19. Act and scene numbers are cited in the text (line numbers are not given in this edition).

16. To say this of course is not to deny the importance of individuals, but to insist upon their absolute importance within the context of social life.

17. It should be noted that one main difference between Maturin's handling of cross-class marriage in the Gothic imagination of 1816, and Matthew Lewis's handling of it in *The Monk* in 1795, is that Lewis condemns it, resolving social tensions by recreating an aristocratic and stable world, which excludes all other classes from the realm of real social authority. Maturin, on the other hand, does not seek any sort of resolution, allowing his play to end on a note of utter violence and social religious confusion. For a discussion of this matter in Lewis, see Watkins, 'Social Hierarchy in Matthew Lewis's *The Monk*'.

18. Maturin's handling of this issue of class authority anticipates Byron's treatment of it in *Werner,*

where Byron's aristocratic hero possesses little individual identity and autonomy. For a discussion of the connections between social class and individual identity in Byron, see Daniel P. Watkins, 'Byron and the Poetics of Revolution' [*The Keats-Shelley Review*], 34 (1985), 95-130.

19. To cite only one example of Bertram's defiant attitude toward religion, note the Prior's attempt to convince him to seek mercy after Saint Aldobrand has been murdered:

BERTRAM.

> Why art thou [the Prior] here?—There
> 　was an hovering angel
> Just lighting on my heart—and thou hast
> 　scared it—

PRIOR.

> Yea, rather with my prayers I'll woo it
> 　back,
> In very pity of thy soul I come
> To weep upon that heart I cannot soften—
>
> 　　　　　　　　　(*A long pause.*)
> Oh! thou art on the verge of awful death—
> Think of the moment, when the veiling
> 　scarf
> That binds thine eyes, shall shut out earth
> 　for ever—
> When in thy dizzy ear, hurtless the groan
> Of those who see the smiting hand up-
> 　reared,
> Thou canst but feel—that moment comes
> 　apace—
>
> 　　　　　　　　　(*Bertram smiles.*)
> But terrors move in thee a horrid joy,
> And thou art hardened by habitual danger
> Beyond the sense of aught but pride in
> 　death.
>
> 　　　　　　　　(*Bertram turns away.*)

20. My general thinking about the significance of punishment in the drama has been influenced by Michel Foucault's *Discipline and Punish: The Birth of the Prison,* translated by Alan Sheridan (New York, 1979), though certainly my interpretative comments are not derived from Foucault. These have been influenced by (amongst others) Eli Zaretsky's argument about the historical formation of subjectivity and Antonio Gramsci's comments on the social functions of law. See Zaretsky's *Capitalism, the Family, and Personal Life* (New York, 1976), and Gramsci's *Selections from the Prison Notebooks,* edited and translated by Quintin Hoare and Geoffrey Nowell Smith (New York, 1971), especially pp. 195-96 and pp. 246-53.

21. Zaretsky, *Capitalism, the Family, and Personal Life,* p. 40.

22. For an excellent discussion of the interpretative and reception history of the "Rime," see Jerome J. McGann, 'The Meaning of The Ancient Mariner', *Critical Inquiry,* 8 (1981), 35-67.

23. Coleridge, *Biographia Literaria,* II, 221.

Joseph W. Lew (essay date summer 1994)

SOURCE: Lew, Joseph W. "'Unprepared for Sudden Transformations': Identity and Politics in *Melmoth the Wanderer.*" *Studies in the Novel* 26, no. 2 (summer 1994): 173-95.

[*In the following essay, Lew examines Maturin's use of both Gothic and Romantic motifs in* Melmoth the Wanderer.]

> The choice of your new name must be your own—you must, for the future, either adopt the name you have heard, or another . . . *That of parricide.*[1]

Maturin's **Melmoth the Wanderer** (1820) continually presents characters with more than one identity: Immalee is also Isidora and Antonio, Manasseh. Conversely, the name "John Melmoth" brings together two apparently opposed characters: the rather non-descript young man of the opening sequence, and the dreadful Wanderer himself. At the same time, the structural similarities among the novel's embedded tales suggests strange affinities among characters as diverse as Monçada, Guzman, and Elinor Mortimer—a strategy resembling that which Owenson uses to critique colonialism in *The Wild Irish Girl; Woman, or Ida of Athens*; and *The Missionary.*

This comparison may seem arbitrary until one notes just how often Maturin attempted to jump upon literary bandwagons, particularly Sydney Owenson's. After producing a Gothic novel, **The Fatal Revenge, or the Family of the Montorio** in 1807, he imitated Owenson's immensely popular *Wild Irish Girl* (1805) with **The Wild Irish Boy** (1808); after the success of Porter's *The Scottish Chiefs,* he wrote **The Milesian Chief** (1812). In **Melmoth the Wanderer** (1820), he combined the Gothic and Byronic modes with yet another imitation of Owenson—the second half of Maturin's novel resembles, in many ways, Owenson's spectacularly successful *The Missionary* (1811).

Owenson's heroines share a certain cosmopolitanism, an ability to adjust to different milieu while maintaining a strong sense of a core self. Luxima, for example, compromises upon externals because of her love for Hilarion; as she dies, however, she reveals that she has always been a Hindu at heart. It was immediately recognized that Owenson's heroines were idealized versions of the author; the triumphs of her female protagonists even in death surely owe something to the unprecedented success of their creator. Autobiography enters equally into *Melmoth the Wanderer*; as Lougy notes, Guzman's wife is a portrait of Maturin's, and the pervading darkness of this novel, especially of the "Tale of Guzman's Family," can be linked to Maturin's financial extremities after 1816.[2]

Autobiography enters *Melmoth* [*Melmoth the Wanderer*] on the political level as well. *Melmoth the Wanderer,* particularly in its analyses of questions of identity and its persistent glorification of personal integrity, springs directly from Maturin's own compromised position as an Anglo-Irish curate out of political favor. In the guise of its Spanish Gothic and exotic East Indian settings, *Melmoth* explores problems of cultural and personal identity and assimilation—a problem particularly acute for the English in Ireland during Maturin's lifetime, but also becoming increasingly important in Great Britain's colonial holdings.

This paper examines the political implications of Maturin's most famous work. As he is not very well-known and did not write a memoir, I shall begin with a summary sketch of his life. From there, I proceed to examine the novel itself. As *Melmoth*'s structural peculiarities prevent the ease of exposition which more straightforwardly chronological narratives allow, I have tried to organize this paper thematically. I discuss the importance of the narrative's violent wrenchings of chronology, recreating within the reader the same divisiveness the narrative depicts in its major characters. These wrenchings then find a structural analogue in the generic disturbances which occur among and even within the novel's embedded tales. On yet another level, they occur again in blatant distortions of history. I concentrate upon the "Tale of the Indians," hoping to show that its various components, such as the themes of confinement and flight, the historyless heroine, the mingling of education and seduction, and the links between commerce and empire work with and against the Tale's outer frame in a way that is both a critique and subversive of that critique.

Charles Robert Maturin, one of six children, was born in Dublin in 1782. He attended Trinity College, Dublin, was ordained an Anglican minister at twenty-one, and married. In 1806, he was appointed curate at St. Peter's, Dublin; in 1807 and 1808, he published *The Fatal Revenge, or the Family of the Montorio* and *The Wild Irish Boy* at his own expense. In 1809, for reasons that remain obscure, his father was disgraced, losing his position at the Post Office; Charles, who relied upon his father for financial support, never truly recovered from this unexpected setback. Nor was he ever promoted to a more lucrative living than the £90 a year of St. Peter's; Lougy believes this is due both to the pro-Irish sentiments in the novels and to the taboo subject matters of the novels and plays. Although Maturin took pupils, the additional income could still not support the lifestyle to which he was accustomed. Worse, the success of his 1816 play, *Bertram* (with Edmund Kean in the title role), encouraged him to further extravagance. By 1818, he was deeply in debt.

By the time Maturin began working on *Melmoth,* he was aware that his particular brand of literary work contrasted strongly with his religious profession. In the Preface to *Melmoth,* he justifies moonlighting: "I cannot again appear before the public in so unseemly a character as that of a writer of romances, without regretting the necessity that compels me to it. Did my profession furnish me with the means of subsistence, I should hold myself culpable indeed in having recourse to any other, but—am I allowed the choice?" (p. 6). In one sense, this Preface mystifies: by 1820, writing novels had become legitimated as a way of supporting one's family; a woman as respectable as Fanny Burney could publish her last two novels by subscription for precisely this reason. The Preface's earlier reference to "Radcliffe-Romance" also misleads. *Melmoth* belongs to the male tradition of Gothic, which includes Walpole's *Castle of Otranto* and Lewis's *The Monk.*

Maturin's choice of mentors and of subject could only jeopardize his clerical career. His imitations of the politically suspect Owenson could taint him in a post-Union Ireland that was, if anything, more repressive even than Great Britain. Freethinkers who appear in the fictions could be assumed to be mouthpieces for their author. And perhaps most damningly, in the virulently homophobic atmosphere of the early nineteenth century, Maturin, in a scene reminiscent of the Rosario/Matilda imbroglio in *The Monk,* flirts with the topic of homosexual passion—unconvincingly resolving the hero's dilemma by revealing that the "man" the hero is in love with is actually a woman—but does not realize this "her"self! Beckford's long exile in Europe and the homosexual rumours Louis Crompton believes central to Byron's permanent exile from England should alert us to the compromising qualities of Maturin's work which manages to place itself, according to the mores of the time, both sexually and politically "beyond the pale."[3]

These facts are crucial to an understanding of this long and difficult novel, filled as it is with autobiographical figures: the young John Melmoth, who quits Trinity College, Dublin (Maturin's alma mater) in order to attend a dying rich uncle; Immalee, who spends most of her life isolated from all humans, and the end of it (as Isidora) misunderstood and persecuted; Solomon and Rebekah, who live in ultra-Catholic post-expulsion Spain as closet Jews; Guzman, condemned helplessly to watch his family starve; and The Wanderer himself, separated from others because of his terrible knowledge. Like early nineteenth-century historical romances such as *The Missionary,* **Melmoth the Wanderer** was written and appeared in a period of renewed censorship: the infamous "Six Acts" which were passed in 1819 outdid the 1790's suspension of Habeas Corpus in the oppressive tools they made available to Liverpool's government. **Melmoth,** then, becomes political allegory. It is literally about Civil War England, Spain under the Inquisition, and life on an Indian island, but also about contemporary Ireland.

Like *Frankenstein,* **Melmoth the Wanderer** is a layered narrative; structurally, it resembles a series of Russian dolls, each containing a smaller one inside. With the exception of the frame concerning young John Melmoth and the tale of Stanton, the other embedded tales (The Lover's Tale, The Tales of the Spaniard, of Guzman's Family) all concern dysphoric romances.[4] Elision, the dichotomy of the islanded Eastern heroine and her surprisingly mobile European suitor, the corrosive effects upon human relationships of money gained in the East Indian trade, and the education of the Oriental woman which is also a seduction, mingle in complex and at times deceptive ways in one of the longest sustained narratives of the novel: "The Tale of the Indians."

In a way strikingly analogous to the "Theme and Variations" form so popular in the classical style in music of the time, Maturin repeats the same structure in each of the stories he relates. In each, a hero or heroine (Stanton, Monçada, Immalee/Isidora, Guzman, Elinor Mortimer) falls into the depths of misery (always associated with poverty and with either madness or Inquisitorial imprisonment). While the hero or heroine experiences the dark night of the soul, The Wanderer appears, offering exemption from temporal sufferings. What the sufferer must exchange for this is unspeakable, and can only be revealed within the confessional. The manuscript records of these transactions is often faulty; Maturin signals this textual "problem" through the use of an asterisk.[5]

An Oriental setting or Oriental commerce has unexpected but highly conventional (in the structuralist sense of the term) effects upon eighteenth- and early nineteenth-century narratives. **Melmoth the Wanderer** clearly demonstrates how familiar these techniques were by 1820. The very subtitle, "The Tale of the Indians," splits the novel into two almost precisely equal halves.[6] The first half, set solely in Europe, deals primarily with European characters; the second begins off the coast of India and ends in Spain. Narrative conventions or expectations set up in the first half weaken or are violated in the second, as if the strength of Orientalist motifs and structural devices overpowers the practice of the first half. In order to fully understand how automati-

cally Maturin seems to have applied these conventions to the Orientalist part of his narrative, I must begin at the beginning.

Like most Gothic fictions, whether of the Walpole or Radcliffe school, **Melmoth** begins realistically. In fact, had one not read the Preface (dated 31 August 1820), one would initially have no clue that this was to be a "Radcliffe-Romance." Invariably, Gothic novels had begun in a more or less distant past, often the Middle Ages or Renaissance.[7] Where they began closer to the present, as in Radcliffe's *The Italian* or in *Frankenstein,* they were sure to be set in a Catholic, Southern European country. Maturin's opening narration breaks these rules. Its first phrase, "In the autumn of 1816" (incidentally only months after the "conception" of *Frankenstein*), sets it in a past so recent (to 1820) as to be almost present. This same sentence places it in England's back yard, Ireland, and introduces us to John Melmoth, the apparent hero of the novel. He does share a name with the title, and that same first sentence shows him leaving Trinity College, Dublin, for a journey "to attend [his] dying uncle." His schoolname indicates that he is a member of the Protestant Ascendancy, the politically dominant Anglo-Irish minority. That miserly uncle's household, including the conventionally generous and faithful housekeeper as well as an old sybil, recalls the Waverley Novels; actually, Maturin capitalizes upon the early nineteenth-century interest in Ireland and contributes to the polemics of novels about Ireland, as he had quite shamelessly once before.[8] Far from being super-human, John Melmoth travels "in the mail" (p. 7)—a coach that carried both passengers and mail. Only gradually do the sybil's hints of supernatural manifestations causing the uncle's illness gain force. Young John enters a forbidden closet, where his eyes are "rivetted" by the portrait of an ancestor, designated "Jno. Melmoth, anno 1646" (pp. 17-18); a short time later, he sees the living original of the portrait at his uncle's bedside.

After the uncle's death, John Melmoth reads a manuscript mentioned in the will, which was left in that closet, and which contains the first of the embedded narratives (that of Stanton). Later, during a storm, he falls into the sea and is saved by Monçada, the only survivor of a ship that has just foundered. Monçada narrates how he was forced into taking monastic vows, involuntarily caused the death of his brother in attempting to escape from the monastery in Madrid, was imprisoned by the Inquisition, and was tempted by "The Wanderer" in its dungeons. He escapes during a fire which destroys the building, eventually finding shelter in the underground library-cell of Adonijah who, like Ahasuerus (the Wandering Jew) but also Melmoth the Wanderer, outlives the allotted human lifespan; unlike them, Adonijah remains in one spot, having vowed to transcribe the history of Melmoth's ecumenical temptations. Adonijah is a philosopher in the older sense of the word, which still included the sciences (Keats' "natural philosophy") and medicine. In this womb lie images of life and death: medical implements such as the forceps, but also four skeletons: those of Adonijah's wife and son, Immalee, and a nameless fourth. The narrative which Monçada reads and transcribes (which he re-tells to John Melmoth, and which we read), is also simultaneously told to him by the skeleton itself. Adonijah says:

> "Behold, there are those near thee, who, though they have no longer a tongue, speak to thee with that eloquence which is stronger than all the eloquence of living tongues. Behold, there are those around thee, whose mute and motionless arms of bone plead to thee as no arms of flesh ever pleaded. Behold, there are those who, being speechless, yet speak—who, being dead, are yet alive—who, though in the abyss of eternity, are yet around thee, and call on thee, as with a mortal voice. Hear them!—take the pen in thine hand, and write." I took the pen in my hand, but could not write a line. Adonijah, in a transport of ecstasy, snatching a skeleton from its receptacle, placed it before me. "Tell him thy story thyself, peradventure he will believe thee, and record it." And supporting the skeleton with one hand, he pointed with the other, as bleached and bony as that of the dead, to the manuscript that lay before me.

(p. 271)

After a brief transition, Monçada plunges into the "Tale of the Indians" (p. 272). Yet at this point, as if at the very word "Indian," certain changes appear in the novel's structure; or rather, certain absences make themselves known.

First, and most obviously, the novel has, until this point, relied heavily upon the Gothic convention of manuscripts fortuitously discovered—a convention that dates back to Walpole's founding of the genre in *The Castle of Otranto* (1764). All of Melmoth's narratives, with the exceptions of the framing one of John Melmoth and that of Monçada (who verbally conveys his story to John Melmoth), are to be found in old, faulty manuscripts, "discoloured, obliterated, and mutilated beyond any that had ever before exercised the patience of a reader . . . Melmoth could make out only a sentence here and there" (p. 28). Sometimes, the emotion of the writer produces illegibility (an odd twist, during the annus mirabilis of the Second Generation Romantics, of the topos of inexpressibility), as, for example, in the letters which Monçada's brother smuggles into his monastery. At others, Maturin resorts to the convention of the manuscript destroyed by chance or time, a convention familiar to readers at least since Mackenzie's *The Man of Feeling* (1771): "The stranger, slowly turning round, and disclosing a countenance which—(Here the manuscript was illegible for a few lines), said in English—(A long hiatus followed here, and the next

passage that was legible, though it proved to be a continuation of the narrative, was but a fragment)" (p. 31). As in this passage, Maturin often indicates a flaw in the manuscript by an asterisk (*) centered between unconnected lines. Yet, in the Gothic, the utterly familiarized device of the novel's supposed facticity[9] becomes the mark of its fictionality; Maturin refuses to allow the reader long to forget the corrupted nature of the narrative s/he reads. But in the "Tale of the Indians" and its two pendant narratives "The Tale of Guzman's Family" and the "Tale of the Lovers"[10]—in other words, through more than two hundred fifty pages of the text—Maturin rarely refers to the manuscript nature of the text. The familiar asterisks indeed appear, but by this point the reader has seen so many, substituting for such regular structural points in the many structurally identical narratives, that they cease to signify because they provide less information.

Point of view changes oddly and inexplicably in the "Indians" section. So far, the novel has fluctuated at least explicably, if not logically, between limited third person and first person points of view. We begin quite close to John Melmoth's consciousness, although not inside it: John Melmoth always remains "he." We see other characters (the sybil, the housekeeper, old Melmoth) from John's point of view. John reads Stanton's manuscript; we, however, are provided with an edited version—Stanton is referred to in the third person, and the chronology of his movements is imprecise, as in an editorial reconstruction, but also formulaic: "Stanton, about the year 1676, was in Spain" (p. 28); "About the year 1677, Stanton was in London" (p. 39). Monçada recites his narrative in the first person, although again an editor intervenes, coyly deleting the precise year of the fire which destroyed the buildings of the Inquisition: "'It was on the night of the 29th November 17—'" (p. 240).[11] Monçada recites what he has read and transcribed to John Melmoth, only very occasionally drawing attention to himself as editor and third-person narrator.

The "Tale of the Indians" also refuses to conform to our notions of the logic of narration. We are led to believe that, as with Stanton's manuscript, the protagonist of the tale (Immalee/Isidora) has herself written the manuscript. We are as close to her consciousness as we were to the previous third-person narrators (John Melmoth and Stanton); we move inside it far enough to know her feelings at every moment.[12] We may wonder how she has learned so much about the feelings of her mother and father (especially in concern to the tales about and by The Wanderer which Don Aliaga hears), Fra Jose, or even her Inquisitors. In previous tales, Maturin had gone out of his way to provide admittedly farfetched explanations for his narrators' knowledge: Stanton happens upon an old woman who tells him a story about The Wanderer, and Monçada receives incredibly long epistles narrating the recent history of his parents, the unscrupulous Director, and his brother Juan, which Monçada equally incredibly swallows. The pattern of these revelations as well as the structure of each preceding tale (all of the protagonists—Stanton, Monçada, Guzman, Elinor Mortimer, and implicitly Adonijah—escape from their temptations alive, although not unscathed) encourage the first-time reader to expect an at least moderately euphoric ending to the story of the most virtuous, beautiful, and engaging of them all, Immalee/Isidora.[13] Yet the "Tale of the Indians" thwarts these expectations; Isidora dies in the dungeons of the Inquisition only a dozen pages before the end of the novel. She has not written down her story. We have no idea how Adonijah came about it. It is truly as if her skeleton had recited it for Monçada.

Until this point, Maturin has painstakingly allowed us to participate in his successive protagonists' journeys. I have already noted how realistically he has portrayed the discomforts of John Melmoth's journey from Dublin in the opening pages of the novel. Throughout the first half of the novel, we can easily trace both the land and the sea journeys of the successive protagonists. Maturin even provides a geographic link between the writer of the manuscript John Melmoth reads (Stanton), and his later live informant and transcriber of manuscripts (Monçada). Stanton "travels abroad shortly after the [English] Reformation," winding up in Spain "about the year 1676" (p. 28). While in Spain (where the bulk of the novel will be set[14]), Stanton first hears about another Englishman (The Wanderer), then encounters him.

Immalee's story will take her into smaller and smaller spaces, into increasingly claustrophobic confinement. Like Haidée, Immalee is islanded; like Gulbeyaz, she lives in a serail[15]; like Clarissa, she is immured. Melmoth's supernatural powers, however, fulfill the ultimate male fantasies of flight, for the Wanderer is subject to none of these confinements. In his natural life, he had (obscurely, it is true) exceeded the boundaries set to human knowledge; in "The Lover's Tale," we learn that he somehow lives beyond his death. In light or even because of these transgressions, mortal confines have become meaningless to him. He enters and exits madhouses, the cells of the Inquisition, and Aliaga's garden at will; he encounters hostile crowds who have no power to harm him; he can even pass from one side of the world to the other instantaneously. In Maturin's lifetime, technological improvements in sailing vessels had dramatically decreased the time required for a man to journey from London (or Madrid) to Calcutta (near the river Hoogly?); with growing English influence in the Near East and Mehmet Ali's modernization of Egypt, the Englishman could elide the circuit of Africa by crossing the Arabian Peninsula. While other narratives (such as Lawrence's *Empire of the Nairs*) elided the ocean journey, one had always to assume its existence, to account for the necessary lapse of time in the chronology of the tale. In *Melmoth the Wanderer,* elision strictly applies only to protagonists—a literary technique becomes reified, transformed into "actual" practice.

We do not finally meet Immalee until the middle of the novel; by that time, we have heard a great deal about Melmoth. Even though he makes only brief appearances, and those only at climactic moments of the various protagonists' lives, he has dominated the novel to which (like Émile, Telemachus, or Don Juan) he gives his name. We learn very little about how or why he has been cursed, but the clichés which spring to mind (to sell one's soul, to make a deal with the devil) all suggest a contract or trade; the devil, in other words, engages in commerce unscrupulously; as I shall show, The Wanderer is an able student of his master, easily outwitting the most prosperous businessman in the novel. In a strange parody of the growth of the British Empire in India, Immalee's island presence will be an unforeseen by-product of East Indian trade. Maturin hints, in fact, that The Wanderer may be released from his curse only if he finds someone who will "trade" places with him: in this hope, Melmoth quite literally haunts prisons and madhouses. The Wanderer's failure with Walberg, Monçada, and others leads him to hope that the isolated Immalee will be easier prey.

Immalee/Isidora's segregation from eligible males is, if anything, even more extreme than other heroines of Romantic narratives. From the age of three until just before her "entrance into the world," she lives on an otherwise uninhabited island. Maturin places it for us rather precisely: "'There is an island in the Indian sea, not many leagues from the mouth of the Hoogly . . .'" (p. 272). The formulaic opening hovers uneasily between banal facticity and the beginning of a fairy tale. Maturin's Indian island recapitulates the by-now conventional pun on "utopia": this island is a good place, a terrestrial paradise where even Melmoth may for a moment forget his fate, but also a no-place. The Wanderer begins his fiendish career only after the English Civil War. While the Hoogly itself was then still uncharted by Europeans, the entire area *near* the Hoogly River had been crossed and recrossed by European and especially English merchant vessels. The Portuguese had established a fort on the Hoogly at the beginning of the sixteenth century; Fitch was the first Englishman to visit the Hoogly, in 1584; the East India Company built a "factory," or fortified trading place there in 1651. Maturin simultaneously justifies and draws attention to this problem by the lengths he goes in order to evade it:

> from the peculiarity of its situation and internal circumstances, [the island] long remained unknown to Europeans, and unvisited by the natives of the contiguous islands, except on remarkable occasions. It is sur-

rounded by shallows that render the approach of any vessel of weight impracticable, and fortified by rocks that threatened danger to the slight canoes of the natives.

(p. 272)

The only "natives" Immalee sees are those who come to pay tribute to her as the kindly supplanter of the savage Kali, who had, according to legend, previously established her very first temple on this same island. The only European she encounters is the dreadful Melmoth the Wanderer.

Immalee finds it difficult to learn to reconcile the behavior of the nominal Christians (mere "Catholics," she calls them) with the "purity" of that religion and of her own youthful impulses. Maturin engages with a tradition of polemical characterization whose roots, in English literature, go back at least as far as Chaucer. Donald Howard argues that, in creating Criseide, Chaucer wished to explore just how far a "natural religion" (to use the eighteenth-century term) can lead a basically "good" person in the direction of Christianity.[16] Immalee, whose command of the Spanish language has been reduced to the barest catechism with which she greets The Wanderer ("God made me"), responds immediately, and in a way both rational and emotional, to Christianity. She rejects the spiritual and physical excess of the cults of Kali, of "Mohammed," and of the Hindus in favor of the simplicity and the good will of the Christian missionaries she sees from afar on her island. Yet the reader cannot help wondering precisely how much she responds to the 'self-evident' truth of Christianity, and how much she responds to the altered tone of The Wanderer, who is compelled (by a higher power) to speak only the truth of Revealed Christianity. In this initial rift, one may situate the later pessimism, the sense of disappointment felt by the informed reader who has uncovered Immalee's 'bastard conception': the overwhelming sense that Maturin's refusal to make Immalee truly an ingenue is both an artistic flaw in the novel, and an unearned method of gaining sympathy.

Turn-of-the-century writers ascribed great importance to the religious and moral education of "daughters" (to use the kinship classification favored by Fenelon, Wollstonecraft, and others). Especially after the execution of Louis XVI in 1793 and the burgeoning of the "atheistical" Cult of Reason, both male and female writers emphasized the crucial role of women (defined as mothers) in the continuance and preservation of the English Constitution. By the time Maturin had begun writing **Melmoth the Wanderer,** however, the war against France had been won, Napoleon had been twice deposed, the East India Company had irrevocably established an Empire in India, and Great Britain had tasted power over Egypt. Thus, with possessions in Canada, the West Indies, the Cape Colony, the penal colonies of Australia

as well as its predominant position in India, the British Empire had already become one upon which the sun never set. As J. C. D. Clark argues, this shift in domestic polemic was typical of the period immediately following Napoleon's defeat; with the final victory over the atheists and the Papists, the links among female education, religion, and patriotism grew more tenuous.[17]

Maturin's earlier imitations of regional and Gothic novels indicate important strains of his Romanticism; with the "Tale of the Indians," he parallels Shelley's strategy in *Prometheus Unbound* (1819) of expanding moral and political issues into cosmic proportions. Among such Romantic narratives, the Third Act reunion of Prometheus (Greek for a quality, "Forethought") and Asia (an entire landmass) provides the only possible euphoric ending to the basic plot of "Alastor." Like Shelley, Maturin postulates a redemptive marriage between a specifically Indian Orient (Immalee of the island off the Hoogly) and an Anglo-Irish Occident (Melmoth); yet what Shelley had analyzed politically as the cycle of "tyranny," Maturin explores eschatologically as the war between Good and Evil. Shelley's plots are heavily spiced with Manichaean dualism: in the prologue to *The Revolt of Islam,* an Eagle (evil, patriarchy) and a Serpent (good, what Brown calls "lawless love"[18]) battle for supremacy; in *Prometheus Unbound,* breaking the tyrannous circle directly ushers in the millennium. Maturin's plot, however, is unabashedly Christian, flavored by the polemics of the long war against France, and suspicious of any Other defined in religious terms. In order to understand Maturin's very mixed achievement, we will need to examine the two principle education scenes in the "Tale of the Indians" and to understand traditional Christian concepts of the nature of good and evil.

The cultural-political genealogy of Maturin's "corruption/seduction" metaphor predates him by several centuries. As far as they themselves were concerned, the English tended largely to see more danger to the mother country than to the peripheries. But the British were quite quick to point out the devastating effects upon "noble savages" of contact with other Europeans. In his unpublished study of the Elizabethan and Jacobean discourse on massacres, Christopher Highley quotes early seventeenth-century English texts which sympathize with the American Indians against their Spanish oppressors. By the end of the eighteenth century, Cook's discovery of the island-paradise of the Polynesian islands, the growth of the Tahitian cult in London, and the astoundingly rapid physical, moral, and social disintegration of the Tahitians made some writers, at least, face the possibility that English influence could be as dangerous as that of the Spanish. This cultural-imperialist discourse of seduction dovetailed quite neatly with already-existing Christian discourse on the natures of Good and of Evil. Augustinian theology (never entirely rejected by the Established Church) viewed Evil as a negative quality, as the absence of Good—in contrast with the Manichaeans, for whom both Good and Evil had the characteristics of substances. Rousseau's teachings, especially, helped to secularize the Augustinian concept; for Rousseau, all humans were born "good" only to be corrupted by Culture (Civilization). As is well known, Wordsworth gave this concept its ultimate English verse apotheosis with the Child-Philosopher of the "Intimations" ode.

The Wanderer's goal is, quite plainly, to "seduce" Immalee, body and soul. To her surprise, he speaks the language which she remembers from "the world of voices" (p. 284). Yet, "her language, from want of practice, had become so limited, that she was delighted to hear its most unmeaning sounds uttered by human lips" (p. 282). She does not even have a word for fishes, referring only to "those who grow in the waters," in her very ignorance condemning the periphrases of poetic diction (e.g., "the finny tribe"). One of his first tasks is teaching her words of her half-learned native tongue (we do not yet know what this is): "suffering, guilt, and care." The concepts are as foreign to her as the words: only "with much difficulty she was made to comprehend the meaning of these words" (p. 285). This process seems to reverse that of other Romantic narratives (such as *The Missionary* and the Haidée episode of *Don Juan*); in reality, it becomes the major clue to the deceptiveness of Immalee's status as Oriental, and part of the pattern of questions concerning identity which inform the novel. Immalee is a *white* goddess" (p. 279), protected by an "impregnable innocence" (p. 286) reminiscent of the island itself and of the Inquisitorial dungeons. The Wanderer strives to give the variety of "shade" to her whiteness—not an addition, but as a "corruption" of her unsullied good (p. 297).

When The Wanderer (who throughout this section is called merely "the stranger," in a manner similar to Owenson's "english [sic] traveller") sojourns on the island, even he experiences its "no-place" and "good-place" qualities. For the very first time, we see him smile (p. 286); he looks on Immalee with "compassion" (p. 284); repeatedly, we hear of a "lingering humanity trembl[ing] around his heart" (p. 287), or of his "compunction" (p. 288) towards his intended victim. With repeated visits, his "attitude" towards her changes; he "ceased to regard her as his victim," and "seemed to enjoy the few lucid intervals of his insane and morbid existence" (p. 298). Yet these "intervals" themselves can only be "islands" for him: the narrative hints that The Wanderer's visits to the island *cause* him to tempt Stanton.

The Wanderer's island vacations produce another break in the narrative—abruptly, we return to the narrative frame (the first, and one of the very few times within this Tale and its pendants). "Hold!" shouts John Melmoth on hearing Stanton's name. Monçada stops momentarily, or "holds," while the reader is left dangling, with nothing to "hold"; we are brutally reminded of the narrative distance between ourselves and Immalee. By this time, the identity between the text which Monçada had described and the one we read has obscured the process of transmission; in one sentence, Maturin brutally recapitulates the entire series of frames we have traversed: Monçada "proceeded with the story of the unhappy Indian, as recorded in the parchments of Adonijah, which he had been compelled to copy, and of which he was anxious to impress every line and letter on his listener, to substantiate his own extraordinary story" (pp. 298-99). The alienation effect is doubled and redoubled. Maturin reminds us, not merely of the narrated, but of the translated qualities of the narrative. Perhaps more importantly, the pleasure we derive from identification with the heroine is lessened by Monçada's appropriation of her story for its use-value for Monçada. Maturin seizes the chance to justify his future practical abandonment of the conventional reminders of "formal realism," tersely informing us that Monçada "did not like interruption" (p. 298).

We next see Immalee in Spain. The account of her ocean journey, typically, is elided from the narrative proper; much later, her transmutation is retrospectively related in a few sentences. Immalee's *rite de passage,* her journey by sea to her new identity as Isidora, the wealthiest heiress of Madrid, should take her from islanded obscurity to social triumph. Instead, it moves her only into ever more confined areas. Implicitly, we are asked to question the distinctions between Western and 'Oriental' methods of secluding women. Don Aliaga's Madrid residence is as inaccessible as Antony Harlowe's moated house. Isidora's room overlooks a garden; house and garden are both surrounded by a high wall—the opposite of Antony Harlowe's moat, this wall performs precisely the same function, and is also based upon merchant capital. Only servants and Donna Clara Aliaga's spiritual advisor, Fra Jose, pass freely in and out. The text repeatedly draws attention to Isidora's astonishment over the ease with which her suitor flouts the wall and the servants' vigilance. Shortly before her elopement, she "sat at her casement, pale but resolute, and trusting in the extraordinary promise of Melmoth, that by whatever means he was enabled to visit her, by those she would be enabled to effect her escape, in spite of her well-guarded mansion, and vigilant household" (p. 385). Like Clarissa, she is hurried by her lover through a garden, yet, despite the excitement of her situation, and "amid all the novelty of her feelings and situation, [Isidora] could not avoid testifying her surprise at the facility with which they passed through the well-secured garden gate" (p. 385). Melmoth, like his literary precursor Lovelace, self-consciously echoes the words and the deeds of his "master," the Satan of *Para-*

dise Lost. He, too, hesitates before ultimately destroying terrestrial gardens. (In fact, he goes one-up on Satan, for he spoils both the natural garden of the Indian island for Immalee, and the cultivated and cultured garden behind Aliaga's walls.) After a mock-marriage performed by the revitalized corpse of a hermit-priest in a ruined monastery and the murder of her brother by her demon-lover, Isidora eventually winds up in a yet more confined space. Aliaga's garden wall doubles over upon itself, as it were, forming the masonry of her cell in the dungeons of the Inquisition.

Immalee has reached marriageable age (she is near the same age as Clarissa, Sophia Western, Miss Milner, or almost any pre-Victorian heroine) when we first see her. She is thus ready to "enter the world": like other heroines, she is physiologically ready for the marriage market; yet she is also quite literally about to enter the world. Less than three years after we first meet her on the island, she is in Madrid, trying to learn the codes of the "world" she was born to, but not brought up in. More even than *Tom Jones,* we have a double perspective on Immalee's story. On a first reading, we experience it with her, we take her at her word. As with *Tom Jones,* later readings (when we know the "secret" of her past) change our view of her island life. Fielding's narrator, in his very third-person omniscience, suggests a God-like stance from which the knowledgeable reader may see the whole story and rejoice in its artistry, even calling attention to the naturalness of Partridge and Jenny Jones (alias Mrs. Waters) not meeting at the Inn at Upton. The "Tale of the Indians," which imitates *Tom Jones* in withholding necessary information (while hinting that The Wanderer possesses it), refuses to resolve into a unified vision. Fielding's novel suggests the visual metaphor of the panorama, the scene from above; Maturin's novel, however, suggests the blurred effect produced by the superposition of two quite similar, but not precisely identical photographic plates. In Spain, Immalee is renamed, in the senses both of being given a new name (for her, or for the naive reader) and in having an old name, Isidora, given to her again. She can identify neither name with the "truth" of her experience, as accepting one name entails abrogating the other and the experience it represents. No ultimate synthesis is possible. Although I begin by discussing the two phases of her life separately, neither the first, nor the second, nor any synthesis of these apparent contraries can reproduce the privileged, Fieldingesque point-of-view on the "true."

At this point, we learn that Immalee/Isidora has begun her life's journey in Spain, like Monçada, Stanton, Guzman's wife, and The Wanderer himself. With the exception of Monçada (whose story, unlike the other protagonists', is not closed), all are drawn irresistibly back to Spain, the magnetic pole of the novel. Monçada and Isidora, who escape from Spain by the symbolically feminine sea, suffer shipwreck. Both are the sole survivors of their respective ships. Isidora, cast ashore as a three-year-old on an uninhabited island-paradise near the mouth of the Hoogly, undergoes a sea change, to become the Immalee of the tale's opening.

At first glance, Spain seems a more appropriate symbolic pole vis-á-vis India than does England. The Treaty of Tordesillas (1494) assigned all newly discovered territory in the Eastern Hemisphere (with the exception of the Philippines) to Portugal. Neither in the late seventeenth century (when the Tale is set), nor in the period 1816-20 (the interval between the opening of the novel and its actual publication) did Spain have any *fortified* trading-posts near India, whereas France, the Netherlands, Portugal, and England had, or were establishing, empires there.

However, Spain too suffers from the Oriental taint, from the threat of the Orient corrupting it from within. Spain itself had become an Islamic colony as early as 711; the last Moorish stronghold at Granada fell only in the spring of 1492 (slightly preceding, even enabling, Columbus' first voyage). Spain's fierce Catholicism, its McCarthy-like hunt for heretics and for religious apostates derives in part from the centuries-long reconquista. Spain's Catholicism mimetically doubles, and even helped to produce England's own fierce Protestantism. Not coincidentally, for centuries, the only formidable dangers to England's political existence came from Catholic countries: first from Spain, then from France. Spain's intense effort to repress its Moorish past and its Moorish heritage, The Inquisition, allegorically suggests the repression of civil liberties during the struggles against Revolutionary France, finding echoes in the Suppression of Habeas Corpus, the Sedition Acts, and Pitt's spy-system.

Yet strategically placed Spaniards like Don Aliaga (Isidora's father) also had their chances at practicing the odd combination of Oriental despotism and Oriental trade. For two generations (1580-1640), Spain ruled Portugal and its Empire. Aliaga's relative's Eastern ventures were most probably initiated during this period of Spanish hegemony over the Portuguese empire—the Portuguese, after all, had early established a monopoly over the maritime "carrying trade" in the Indian Ocean.[19] But by the period in which the "Tale of the Indians" is set, Portugal had lost this monopoly, accepting the rights of the English to trade in India in 1654—coincidentally, a good approximate date for Immalee's birth. But after 1674, even the Dutch no longer posed a threat to the British in India; only the French could successfully carry on trade without kowtowing to the British—until they too lost their territory in India in 1759-1761. And in Maturin's own lifetime (1782-1824), the British East India Company successfully infiltrated the India trade of other European countries: "In the 1770's and 1780's,

Copenhagen, Ostend, and Lisbon became the centres of an Indian trade which was for the most part British in all but name."[20] The "relative . . . settled in the East Indies" from whom Aliaga receives "an offer of partnership" probably operated with British cooperation. Quite obviously, Isidora's own tragedy grows out of her experiences as Immalee, and of her marginal religious status in Spain, a status which resembles that of the Moriscos and the Mozarabs. Yet her brother's death, and ultimately the death of her child and her own death, are brought about by the commercial habits of her own father.

Immalee's history—how she got to the island, why she remembers that God made her—remains mysterious long after we have encountered her in her true "character" of Isidora. Her past remains a cypher until after her elopement with Melmoth. When Melmoth himself finally reveals that past to Don Aliaga and to the reader, the only acts left to Isidora are to give birth and to die. For Don Aliaga, this history is a twice-told tale, unlike the tales of Guzman's family or of the Mortimers, which he hears for the first time. Paradoxically, Aliaga's interest in it stems precisely from the fact that he has heard it before: the stranger's very knowledge suggests a secret kinship with or a power over Don Aliaga that captures his attention. In its brevity and in its structural position in "The Tale of The Indians," the stranger's narration resembles the retrospective account of Clarissa provided by Anna Howe:

> A certain Spanish merchant . . . had embarked for [the East Indies] with his wife and son, leaving behind him an infant daughter in Spain . . . Our Spanish merchant entertained ideas of settling in the East Indies, and sent over for his young daughter with her nurse, who embarked for the East Indies with the first opportunity, which was then very rare . . . The nurse and infant were supposed to have perished in a storm . . . in which the crew and passengers perished. It was said that the nurse and child alone escaped; that by some extraordinary chance they arrived at this isle, where the nurse died from fatigue and want of nourishment, and the child survived, and grew up a wild and beautiful daugter of nature, feeding on fruits . . . It was said that some vessel in distress arrived at the isle,—that the captain . . . undertook . . . to conduct her to her . . . family, who were then residing in the city of Benares . . . I have since heard," said the stranger, "that the family has returned to Spain.

> (pp. 502-03; Maturin's ellipses)

With this retrospective summation, so similar to flashbacks to a heroine's earlier life in earlier novels, many things fall into place. We learn how Isidora came to the island off the Hoogly, and from whom she learned that "God made me."

Most importantly, we learn that the end of her life uncannily recapitulates its beginnings. Evidently, the dead nurse was not merely a caretaker. Rather, she was Isidora's wet-nurse, sustaining her very life when her parents and older brother left for the East Indies, perhaps even teaching her how to survive after the shipwreck. According to contemporary beliefs, Isidora may also imbibe some of the nurse's "spirit"; if she does, the emotional, intellectual, and moral difference between Isidora and her biological mother is thus "explained."[21] Moreover, we understand that Aliaga's massive household does not merely conform to the standards of the wealthy Spanish nobility, but also (and perhaps more directly) reproduces the lifestyle to which Aliaga had grown accustomed in the East. Don Fernando's attempts to out-noble and out-honor the hereditary aristocracy also become more than the mere posturings of a parvenu. Like James Harlowe Jr., his arrogance in part derives from his self-consciousness of the impact of his Oriental wealth upon the home country; however, his excesses also arise from his childhood in the Orient, where economic and military superiority was reinforced by racial prejudice at an early age.

The Wanderer himself warns Aliaga to "lose not a moment to save [his] daughter" (p. 503). Yet Aliaga, like the other protagonists in the tale, is more comfortable as a reader and consumer of manuscripts than as a man of action. He receives letters from a mercantile correspondent and from his intended son-in-law, Montilla, and returns to his comfortable rut:

> "It is almost incredible, that after this warning, enforced as it was by the perfect acquaintance which the stranger displayed of Aliaga's former life and family circumstances, it should not have had the effect of making him hurry homewards immediately, particularly as it seems he thought it of sufficient importance to make it the subject of correspondence with his wife . . . After reading [the letters from his correspondent and from Montilla], Aliaga's mind began to flow in its usual channel. There is no breaking through the inveterate habitudes of a thorough-paced mercantile mind, 'though one rose from the dead.'"

> (pp. 504-05)

Theorists of the epistle such as Janet Altman discuss the letter's role in the dynamics of absence and presence.[22] The letter stands for, or signifies, the absent writer; the text substitutes for the *sujet parlante*. Donna Clara (Aliaga's wife) and her spiritual advisor Fra Jose receive this letter only hours before Isidora elopes with Melmoth; in the course of their sitting "up over [the letter] nearly the whole of the night," they ask, "'Did either hear some strange noise in the house?'"—the noise of Isidora's departure (p. 381).[23] In other words, Aliaga's paper substitute for his absent self arrives precisely at the critical moment. Unlike the delegated word/name of the despot, which only achieves effect with its alienation from the despot, Aliaga's letter is totally ineffectual. While it is by no means clear what Aliaga could have done to prevent the elopement, his letter-substitute contributes to the catastrophe. For Donna Clara and Fra Jose become more and more "perplexed" during their "intense" perusals of the letter; their inability to decipher the letter's warnings causes them to fail to investigate the audible sound of Isidora's departure.

The two names of the protagonist of the "Tale of the Indians" reflect her dual culture: Immalee of the eastern isle, Isidora of Spain. Born in a society and to a religion which Maturin depicts as most regimented and artificial (in our negative, post-Enlightenment sense of the word), she grows up entirely isolated from all society. A late version of the Noble Savage, she unites the best of the conventional attitudes of the Western (European), Eastern, and Savage (American) worlds. An ideal woman, she combines a stereotypically Hindu capacity to submit unquestioningly with the active, inquiring mind supposedly confined to northwestern Europe. She half-rememberingly, half-instinctually is drawn to Christianity, but her island/ingenue habits of thinking make the rigidities and the sophisms of Spanish Catholicism incomprehensible to her.

Even her Spanish name takes on some of the qualities of this duality. She is named after the great seventh-century archbishop, encyclopedist and theologian, Isidore of Seville. Yet her name, and also that of her patron saint, suggests another, more equivocal meaning. Isidora is also the "gift of Isis;" her name links her to a pre-Christian, Eastern (Egyptian) religious tradition. Its ambiguity of cultural reference recalls the resurgence of interest in the cult of Isis during the late eighteenth and early nineteenth centuries.[24] By the 1790's, comparatists and freethinkers were drawing upon similarities between the Isis-Osiris-Horus mythology and the Gospels in order to bolster their cases for a natural religion akin to revealed Christianity, going even so far as to create false etymologies linking the names of the Egyptian triumvirate to that of Jesus.

Isidora/Immalee's names also link her to other doubly-named characters in the "Tale of the Spaniard:" the comic-pathetic household of Don Fernan di Nunez, alias Solomon the Jew. Upon escaping from the Inquisition during the fire, Monçada runs through the streets of Seville. "Without perceiving it," he finds himself in a dark, apparently subterranean passage (p. 245); he bursts through a door and stumbles upon a mysterious, obsolete, and semi-chthonic ritual which he views through a large, heavy curtain which seems to have no purpose except the narrative one of hiding him. As he watches, the thematics of Immalee/Isidora's identity are played out in reverse before his eyes. Fernan reveals to his son Antonio that Antonio is "really" a Jew named Manassehben-Solomon; their servant Maria is "really" named Rebekah. Isidora learns that she is "really" a Spanish Catholic, and that she must "forget" both her island (autochthonous) way of life and of thinking; So-

lomon seems to have chosen his son's name with this very dynamic in mind, for he uses his son's Hebrew name, Manasseh (literally, causing to forget), as a talisman to make "Antonio" forget his Catholic upbringing.

Like Immalee/Isidora, Antonio/Manasseh shares in a double nature and possesses dual names. Like her too, he faces an unexpected "choice" among religions. But in many ways, he is Immalee's opposite. Immalee, who has almost forgotten her mother tongue, regains a living, although inadequate mother. She comes to relearn the "true" revealed religion, leaving behind her natural worship, or ameliorating what has been corrupted in Christianity by incorporating the best and purest of her naïve religious practices. She also leaves behind her ahistorical, fairy-tale island in order to enter the exciting, yet tragic world of historical process. She moves from East to West. Antonio also faces an incredibly painful choice: between his mother tongue and the religion in which he was raised, and the "hebrew" language and faith of his father, a dilemma all the more painful because of the absence of a (presumedly dead) biological mother. Hence Antonio must figuratively again bury his mother by abandoning his living mother tongue in favor of what Maturin sees as a mummified hebrew. He must deny his Christian upbringing and the realm of historical development in order to accept a revealed but outmoded religion which manifests itself in fossilized and obsolete religious practices—such as the ritual sacrifice of a cock which Monçada unwittingly witnesses, an episode which seems to derive from anti-Semitic lore and Maturin's own imagination. Antonio must move from West to East, losing by every facet of the process.

Solomon and Rebekah use Christian names as protective disguises. As Moriscos, they "pass" as Christians, but because of their lineage, their true religious convictions are always suspected by the Inquisition. Solomon is marked, as was Cain and his fictional descendant, The Wanderer. He is genetically distinct: his "physiognomy had something peculiar in it, even to the eye of a Spaniard, from the clustering darkness of his eye-brows, his prominent nose, and a certain lustre in the balls of his eyes" (p. 246). His face is a visible sign of his Oriental blood: indeed, his "Hebrew" features are iconographically identical to those of Turks. Solomon protects himself through a Christian exterior, choosing stereotypically Spanish Catholic names for members of his household to use in the larger world; he reveals his 'true' names only to a chosen few. As in 'primitive' thought, names hold power for him; the novel makes clear, however, that this power of the 'true' name is quite real: a single reference to "Father Abraham" signals to the officers of the Inquisition that "Fernan" is "really" a "relapsed" Jew. His public name and his public persona are merely a "technical formality" (p. 257), in the senses both of following prescribed customs and of being without practical meaning.

Neither Immalee/Isidora nor Antonio/Manasseh (at least in the brief scene in which we see him) can quite so easily separate their lived experiences into a "technical formality" of the public self, and a "true" personal core opposed to that public self. Antonio/Manasseh disappears from the novel. But Isidora/Immalee's two names refer to two irreconcilable identities that are equally hers—Isidora cannot "forget" Immalee, nor can she succeed in repressing her "natural" childhood, adolescence, or religion. Even the manuscripts Monçada first transcribes and then orates to John Melmoth share the dual natures of Immalee/Isidora and Antonio/Manasseh. Like a body inhabited by a soul, they are a form which "contains" meaning through "*the Spanish language* written in *the Greek characters*" (p. 270). We hear the narratives they "contain" in English, through Monçada's translation of them for John Melmoth's benefit, and John Melmoth becomes yet another book, one in which Monçada is "anxious to impress every line and letter" (p. 299); implicitly, John Melmoth also becomes Monçada's publisher, causing that same text to be "impressed" as the book we read.[25]

While Maturin's thematic use of double names may strike late twentieth-century readers as a "natural" (iconic) signification for humans torn between two cultures, this device, like so many others I have examined, derives from another discursive field. Peter Laslett shows that, throughout the seventeenth century (in which **Melmoth** is largely set), there was practical and legal confusion over the proper naming of bastards in parish baptismal registries: it was common to give bastard children of unwed mothers[26] the family names of either or both of their biological parents (if the father was known). Both names are often listed, joined by the word "alias" (Latin, "other"—and note the echo of this term in Isidora's family name, "Aliaga"); there seems to have been no preference for which name occurred first. Like the Morisco Antonio/Manasseh or the Indo-European Immalee/Isidora, the bastard (in patrilineal Great Britain) fits into neither its paternal nor maternal families. As Shakespeare's characterization of Edmund in *Lear* suggests, the bastard could be associated to the monstrous: s/he is illegitimate, the product of a literally unhallowed coupling. Having no established place within an increasingly bourgeois society, bastards came more and more to be perceived as threats. Isidora as a cultural "bastard" is submitted to the same unrelenting Inquisitorial scrutiny as the Moriscos and the Mozarabs; this dynamic foreshadows the fate of her child.

Throughout this discussion, I have assumed that the West (England) perceived itself as a rational, masculine principle, that it increasingly posited the East as its Other, personifying it as feminine, intuitive, in need of moral and scientific education, and that it projected the ideal relationship between England and the Orient in the form of a courtship plot leading to a patriarchal marriage with a dual sexual standard. In order further to test this hypothesis, I would like here to attempt an alternate analysis of this plot. For three hundred and fifty pages, Maturin exposes us to the purely evil machinations of The Wanderer. The logic of the narrative, as well as the cultural weight of *Clarissa* (upon whose Lovelace and Clarissa the characters of The Wanderer and Immalee are partially based) drives Maturin to produce an embodiment of "pure" good in Immalee. The two "marry" (p. 394), and Immalee bears a child. Synthesis? Throughout the eighteenth and nineteenth centuries, many English men and women—and Europeans in general—would have liked to have believed so. Already in 1808, Schlegel saw the possibility of redemption and renewal in the cross-fertilization of Western rationalism and scientism with Oriental poetry and religion. But Said convincingly argues that the West largely appropriated what it found useful in the "Orient."[27]

The situation of real-life "syntheses" resembling Immalee's or Haidée's "fair seed of hope" sheds light on this question. The daughter of Governor Crook of Fort St. David by an Indian woman married four Englishmen, including William Watts, Governor of Fort William. Their child, Amelia, married Charles Jenkinson, the first Earl of Liverpool. Their son Robert Bank Jenkinson, the second Earl, served as Prime Minister of England from 1818 to 1827. Not surprisingly, however, such success stories were as rare as that of Dick Whittington, who rose from being an apprentice to Lord Mayor of London. The children of English men and Indian women were predominantly illegitimate; they were not covered by either Hindu or Muslim law, nor were they British subjects; by 1822, such Anglo-Indians outnumbered Europeans in Calcutta by a margin of five to one.[28] By 1782, some Britishers objected against sending Anglo-Indians to England for education, claiming it would lead to the degeneration of the English.[29] In 1780, Innes Munro had warned: "It was by this means that the Spanish and Portuguese got so much of the dusky hue in their countenances having kept an unrestrained intercourse with their colonies till they were reduced to their present despicable state."[30] Even by 1780, the lines of racial prejudice had hardened. No one yet seriously suggested that Englishmen in India should not produce "coloured" babies—in fact, it was generally accepted that the pay scale for the majority of the East India Company's servants made marriage to an English-speaking woman economically impossible. Even in 1796, after a series of reforms, subalterns of fourteen or fifteen years' standing made only ninety-five rupees a month—roughly ninety-five pounds sterling a year.[31] Thus, although eyes were turned the other way in India, cries of racial corruption, of degeneration, of sullying the pure white of the English complexion were raised at the possibility of Anglo-Indians migrating in large numbers to England. The Augustinian concept of sin and the traditional iconographic associations between darkness and evil combined to produce an early 'biological' excuse for racism.

While this problem is quite apparent for the bastard fetus of Juan and Haidée, it is by no means so clear for the child of Immalee/Isidora and Melmoth. Yet, although Immalee is "really" a pure-blooded, old-Christian Spaniard, she has become partly Orientalized by the contamination of contiguity and the lack of what Elizabeth Inchbald, in the famous last phrase of *A Simple Story,* called "A PROPER EDUCATION." Neither her parents nor the Inquisition ever believes her totally free from the taint of heresy developed during her island life and "freethinking." Moreover, she has gone through a wedding ceremony of sorts.

Of sorts. The hermit who performed the wedding, who joined Immalee and The Wanderer together, was already dead before the ceremony. The text suggests that his body had been raised by the unhallowed arts of The Wanderer, and that the ceremony was therefore invalid.

Because of this, Immalee's child's legal status is anomalous. English and Spanish Civil Law would not have considered Immalee's marriage valid; however, according to Ecclesiastical Law (valid in Catholic Spain, retained in England after the Reformation), the child was considered legitimate as long as at least one of the parties believed the wedding a valid one. Thus, even among the anomalous category of bastards, Immalee's child possesses a marginal and contradictory position: the child is a bastard in the eyes of the state, yet legitimate in the eyes of God.

Far from being any sort of "synthesis," the child of Immalee and The Wanderer becomes a battleground between them: in its unborn state, it resembles the Everyman of medieval drama or the soul fought over by the forces of Good and Evil in medieval psychomachia. Immalee wishes it to be Christian; The Wanderer hopes to raise it to trade places with him and thus to give him peace. Having won her battle for the child's soul, Immalee/Isidora has persuaded Fra Jose to baptize the child. Yet the child, more than Immalee herself, can not be categorized. Immalee can only ask, "*Can* this be the child of a demon?" (p. 527). The answer, of course, is both yes and no. Throughout the "Tale of the Indians," we wonder what the plural in the title means, from where another, or other, or even "real" Indians will come. By the middle or end, if we have not forgotten the title completely, we wonder whether it means anything at all. We only encounter Immalee, and at the very end, her bastard child. No more than Frankenstein's creature can this breathing contradiction be

named. Born in the dungeons of the Inquisition, Immalee's hapless, unnameable infant cannot survive. It dies violently, strangled "unnaturally" by its own father. Like the murder of Elizabeth Lavenza, this crime occurs offstage; we only hear of it, and see the corpse with the "black mark" of Cain, of The Wanderer, around its neck—a mark which occurs over and over again in a work published two years previously: *Frankenstein.*[32]

Notes

1. Charles Maturin, *Melmoth the Wanderer* (London: Oxford Univ. Press, 1968), p. 246. All references are to this edition.

2. Robert E. Lougy, *Charles Robert Maturin* (Lewisburg: Bucknell Univ. Press, 1975).

3. Louis Crompton, *Byron and Greek Love: Homophobia in Eighteenth-Century England* (Berkeley: Univ. of California Press, 1985).

4. Even the "Tale of the Spaniard" glances upon this in the patricide's account of the lovers he imprisoned in an underground vault.

5. In discussing any particular narrative, I will refer to the characters by name. When referring to the structure of these narratives, I will follow Propp's example, but substituting the term "protagonist" for his "hero." I find the structure "hero/heroine" too bulky; to subsume Elinor and Immalee into the masculine noun "hero" would repeat the type of appropriation which these narratives thematize.

6. The Oxford edition is 542 pages long; the subtitle occurs on page 272.

7. Walpole's *Otranto*—twelfth-century Italy; Reeve's *Old English Baron*—fifteenth-century England; Radcliffe's *Udolpho,* late sixteenth-century France and Italy.

8. The two most popular and respected novelists in the years 1800-1814 set several novels in Ireland. Maria Edgeworth's *Castle Rackrent* (1800) is often credited with being the first regional novel (W. B. Coley, Marilyn Butler, etc.); she later wrote other novels on the themes of abuses in Ireland: *The Absentee* (1812) and *Ormond* (1817). Sidney Owenson, by far the most popular novelist of the day, took exception to Edgeworth's depiction of the Irish.

9. For discussions on the role of this device of realism in the early novel, see Ian Watt, *The Rise of the Novel* (Berkeley and Los Angeles: Univ. of California Press, 1964); and Lennard Davis, *Factual Fictions* (New York: Columbia Univ. Press, 1983).

10. Both are related to Don Aliaga, Immalee/Isidora's father, as he journeys to Madrid after a long ab-

sence. The former is related by a stranger who hopes to publish manuscripts relating to the Wanderer's exploits (thus structurally filling a place identical to Stanton, Monçada, the Wanderer himself, and Maturin), but is found dead the very next morning. The latter is related by Melmoth, in a futile attempt to save his intended victim-bride from himself.

11. Unless this is a slip on Maturin's part, Monçada seems to have experienced the same preservative effects of copying the manuscript as Adonijah himself. Monçada is described as a man "about thirty" (p. 70) when John Melmoth sees him in the autumn or winter of 1816. Even if the fire had occurred as late as 1799, Monçada would actually be at least a decade older than that.

12. At this point, the ironic perspective we have on Immalee's story does not preclude the possibility of a slightly edited first-person narrative. Any retrospective account implies the doubling of the "I" and the creation of distance: Dante the writer reflecting upon Dante the pilgrim.

13. S. L. Varnado, *Haunted Presence* (Tuscaloosa: Univ. of Alabama Press, 1987), does not refer to the "Tale of the Indians." While the repetition of plot structure does eventually grate on the reader, one must recognize that creating the expectation of the protagonist's survival is essential to the dramatic effect of Immalee/Isidora's death at the very end of the novel.

14. Significant portions of Stanton's tale and the "Tale of the Indians," as well as the entirety of the "Tale of the Spaniard," "The Lover's Tale," and the "Tale of Guzman's Family" take place in Spain, where the threat of the Inquisition is conveniently present.

15. Note the structural resemblance of Aliaga's house to a serail, complete with duenna and "eunuch."

16. Donald Howard, *Chaucer* (New York: Dutton, 1987).

17. J. C. D. Clark, *English Society: 1688-1832* (Cambridge: Cambridge Univ. Press, 1985).

18. Nathaniel Brown, *Sexuality and Feminism in Shelley* (Cambridge, MA: Harvard Univ. Press, 1979).

19. England's series of Navigation Acts (which eventually increased tension with her colonies on the Atlantic seaboard of North America) perhaps stem from the Portuguese example in the Indian Ocean. Because of their immense naval superiority, the Portuguese were able to force Arab and Indian merchants trading by sea to use Portuguese ships. Portuguese merchants thus became the middlemen, creating profits for themselves at the expense of both Arabs and Indians. First Holland, then England supplanted the Portuguese in this monopoly.

20. Holden Forster, *John Company at Work* (Cambridge: Harvard Univ. Press, 1951), p. 110.

21. For a detailed account of late eighteenth- and early nineteenth-century myths about breastfeeding, see Barbara Gelpi, *Shelley's Goddess: Maternity, Language, Subjectivity* (New York: Oxford Univ. Press, 1992), especially Chapter 2, "Her Destined Sphere," pp. 35-79.

22. Janet Altman, *Epistolarity* (Columbus: Ohio State Univ. Press, 1982).

23. Thanks to Maturin's contortions of chronology throughout the "Tale of the Indians," we read about the elopement and the letter long before we learn about Melmoth's chronologically previous warning to Aliaga.

24. Jurgis Baltrusaitis, *La Quête d'Isis* (Paris: Flammarion, 1985).

25. John Melmoth is the only one who has access to all of the embedded tales, as well as to his own. Because of his privileged status as witness of old Melmoth's death, as descendant of The Wanderer, as inheritor of Stanton's manuscript, and as addressee of Monçada's narratives, the knowledge he possesses is precisely the novel as we read it.

26. I restrict my discussion to unwed mothers because legally all children of married women "belonged" to her husband, whether or not he was the biological father.

27. Edward Said, *Orientalism* (New York: Pantheon, 1978).

28. Suresh Chandra Ghosh, *The Social Condition of the British Community in Bengal, 1757-1800* (Leiden: E. J. Brill, 1970), pp. 89-90.

29. *Original Papers Relative to the Establishment of a Society in Bengal,* ed. J. Cooper (London: n. p., 1784), pp. 29-30.

30. Capt. Innes Munro, *A Narrative of the Military Operations on the Coromandel Coast against the Combined Forces of the French, Dutch, and Hyder Ally Cawn, 1780-1784,* (London: n. p., 1789), p. 51.

31. Ghosh, *The Social Condition*, p. 67.

32. Joseph W. Lew, "The Deceptive Other: Mary Shelley's Critique of Orientalism in *Frankenstein*," *Studies in Romanticism* 30 (1991): 255-83.

Gráinne Elmore (essay date 1996)

SOURCE: Elmore, Gráinne. "Nightmares Transplanted." In *The Classical World and the Mediterranean,* edited by Giuseppe Serpillo and Donatella Badin, pp. 379-85. Cagliari, Italy: Tema, 1996.

[*In the following essay, Elmore discusses religious imagery and themes in Maturin's oeuvre.*]

Charles Robert Maturin's reputation is as a Gothic writer. He is famous only for two works, *Melmoth the Wanderer* (1820) and the earlier *Bertram; or, the Castle of St. Aldobrand* which was staged in Drury Lane in 1816 in preference to Coleridge's *Zapolya.* But Maturin was not simply a Gothic writer, he was the author of several types of fiction from the novel of manners to the historical romance. Many of his novels like *The Milesian Chief* and *Women; or, Pour et Contre* deserve to be rediscovered for their power and insight. Others, like *The Wild Irish Boy* deserve only to be left in obscurity. But all of his work demands to be reassessed and I hope that the following paper will prove that Maturin is as important to Anglo-Irish literature as he has been to Gothic.

Maturin's first novel, which he published himself in 1807 under the pseudonym of Dennis Jasper Murphy, was *Fatal Revenge; or, the family of Montorio.* It opens:

> About the year 1690, the family of Montorio, one of the most distinguished in Italy, occupied the hereditary seat, in the vicinity of Naples. To the tale of the strange fortunes of this family it may be necessary to affix a sketch of its character.
>
> It was marked by wild and uncommon features, such as rarely occur in those of more temperate climates. But in a country, like the seat of these adventures, where climate and scenery have almost as much effect on the human mind, as habit and education, the wonder dissolves, and the most striking exhibition of moral phenomena present only the reflected consequences of the natural.

By the time Maturin came to publish his *Five Sermons on The Errors of the Roman Catholic Church* shortly before his death in 1824, his views had not changed but become more extreme. Here is a section from the fifth sermon:

> Look to Spain—to Portugal—to Italy—what a picture do they present? A clergy without learning—a nobility without education . . . a country without a national character save that of indolence, beggary, sensuality, and superstition—a country that unites the widest extremes of mental and moral degradation, and combines all the refinements of vice with the simplicity of the profoundest ignorance—where the libertine rushes reeking from the brothel to the confessional . . .

The negative picture Maturin paints in both instances is not restricted to the Italians; his descriptions of the Spanish, the French and, to a large extent, the Irish, are conspicuously similar. Those from Catholic countries are repeatedly and uniformly described as, "superstitious," "weak," "hypocritical," "mistrustful" and "vicious."

Like his predecessors in Gothic fiction, Maturin set each of his Gothic works in the Mediterranean: Italy, Spain and southern France. Horace Walpole, whose novel *The Castle of Otranto,* published in 1764, was the first Gothic Romance, introduced a genre that tapped the public's appetite for the medieval, the supernatural and the unknown. More particularly, it served as an outlet for and verification of many English readers' prejudices against the waning power of Catholicism in a more rational Protestant Europe.

In Maturin's Gothic creations, as in those of Walpole, Radcliffe and Lewis before him, evil monks, nuns and priests abound. We find many examples of typical Gothic props such as empty coffins, secret doorways, subterranean passageways and glimpses of mysterious, silent rituals in hidden chambers, all set against the backdrop of the ruined, gloomy castle. A particularly popular theme in Gothic fiction was the Inquisition, used to highlight the unnatural, secretive life of monks and the terror and cruelty they inflicted on their victims. Maturin was particularly attracted to this theme but he treated it quite differently from other writers. He used it as a vehicle to show extreme religious persecution rather than merely torture, the depravity of religious and what he regarded as the "unnatural" way of life in the monastery or convent. In the Preface to *Melmoth the Wanderer,* which is not so much a novel as a series of tales within tales, Maturin explains himself:

> The "Spaniard's Tale" has been censured by a friend to whom I read it, as containing too much attempt at the revivification of the horrors of the Radcliffe—Romance, of the persecutions of convents, and the terrors of the Inquisition.
>
> I defended myself, by trying to point out to my friend, that I had made the misery of conventual life depend less on the startling adventures one meets with in romances, than on that irritating series of petty torments which constitutes the misery of life in general, and which, amid the tideless stagnation of monastic existence, solitude gives its inmates leisure to invent, and power combined with malignity, the full disposition to practise. I trust this defence will operate more on the conviction of the Reader than it did on that of my friend.

Maturin's manipulation of his subject matter and especially his attacks on monastic life, while they adhere to Gothic convention, are much more savage and sustained than other writers of the genre. These often ferocious attacks are aimed at showing the failings and the weaknesses of Catholicism which Maturin saw as a system of "forced hypocris," "artificial humiliation," "vice" and "sterility" and he writes in the "Spaniard's Tale" that

> In catholic countries . . . religion is the national drama; the priests are the principal performers, the populace the audience; and whether the piece concludes with a "Don Giovanni" plunging in flames, or the beatification of a saint, the applause and the enjoyment is the same.

In the "Spaniard's Tale" Maturin speaks through Alonzo, the Spaniard of the title who has been forced into a monastery by his parents and their scheming "director," or family priest. Alonzo is the illegitimate son of a nobleman, Moncada, and his lover who is from a lower class than he. Although they were married as soon as Alonzo was born, he has been offered to the Church as penance for his parents' sin. Despite his appeals and protests Alonzo is placed in a Madrid monastery and so begins a life of mental torture and despair at the hands of the other monks.

> I hated the monastic life. Inflict pain on man, and his energies are roused—condemn him to insanity, and he slumbers like animals that have been found inclosed (*sic*) in wood and stone, torpid and content; but condemn him at once to pain and insanity, as they do in convents, and you unite the sufferings of hell and of annihilation.

And he goes on later in the tale,

> Alas! . . . how are monks employed in the hour of reflection? It is an hour when they swallow their meal, they banquet on the little scandal of the convent. They ask, "Who was late at prayers? Who is to undergo penance?" This serves them for conversation: and the details of their miserable life supply no other subject for that mixture of exhaustless malignity and curiosity, which are the inseparable twins of monastic birth.

In another tale, "Tale of the Indians," Maturin actually uses Melmoth himself to be his mouthpiece. In the tale, Melmoth is describing the ways of the world and the distinctions between the different religions to Immalee, a young girl who has grown up in solitude on a desert island in the Indian Ocean. She represents innocence, a kind of Eve-like figure before the Fall. Melmoth/Maturin presents the true spirit of Christianity i.e. Anglicanism in the following way;

> . . . their religion enjoins them to be mild, benevolent and tolerant; and neither to reject those who have not attained its purer light . . . and though their religion gives every hope to the penitent guilty, it flatters none with false promises of external devotion supplying the homage of the heart; or artificial and picturesque religion standing in the place of . . . single devotion to God.

This speech is double-edged, for while Maturin promotes Anglicanism, he does so at the expense of Catholicism, drawing unfavourable parallels to the Catholic Church and its "artificial and picturesque religion."

But the question still remains, why was Maturin so obsessively critical of the Catholic Church? The answer does not lie simply in either Gothic convention or the wishes of a clergyman to argue certain theological points in the pages of his novels: the attacks are far too caustic. The answer lies in Maturin himself, his roots, his religion and his position in early 19th century Ireland.

Charles Robert Maturin was born in Dublin on September the 25th 1780 and later went on to become a Church of Ireland minister on leaving Trinity College in 1803, following the family tradition of clergymen. The first in this long line of ministers was Gabriel Maturin, originally a French Huguenot pastor. Gabriel came to Ireland as a result of the revocation of the Edict of Nantes in 1685, a decree that effectively put an end to religious freedom in France. Gabriel Maturin, being Huguenot and therefore a heretic, fled to Ireland. It is indeed ironic that, having escaped from a country of religious intolerance himself, he came to settle in another where he could benefit from his religion at the expense of others, namely the Catholic majority.

Nothing concrete is known of the Maturins before the appearance of Gabriel in Ireland, however Charles Maturin often told a story of how Gabriel was found as a child in the middle of a busy Parisian street called Rue des Mathurines. According to Charles, his ancestor was found and adopted by a "lady of rank" who gave him the name of the street where he was found and set about bringing him up as a strict Catholic. In time Gabriel converted to Protestantism and because of this was incarcerated in the Bastille for twenty-six years. After his release he was finally reunited with his wife and two sons who had escaped to Ireland via Holland and so came to settle in Dublin. It is noticeable that no dates were proffered by Charles to support this account of his family history. Consequently this story has often been dismissed by scholars as just that: mere fantasy on Charles' part, created out of his yearning for romance.

Although it may not be immediately apparent, there are many features about the story that might point to Maturin's lack of self-identity and his obsessive persecution complex. It is also hard to define whether Charles Maturin coloured his Huguenot ancestor with some of his own theological prejudices or whether the writer himself was impressed with Gabriel's dramatic suffering for his faith. For it is essential to have a full understanding of the religious aspect of Maturin's work to make a complete evaluation of the man and his work.

At the time Maturin was writing—the first quarter of the 19th century—religion played an important but divisive role in every country in Europe and especially in Ireland. Maturin was obviously aware of such religious tension in his own country and this in part explain his attraction to certain themes within Gothic fiction, namely the emphasis on religious persecution which brought with it themes of mental and physical torture. Maturin's bigotry as well as his often melancholy nature may also help explain his attraction to the genre. The theme of the Inquisition may at first seem archaic but we must remember that a revival of the Inquisition took place in 1814, when Maturin was still a relatively young man. Religious tension was also very much present in Maturin's own life since his personal views on Protestant doctrine differed considerably from those which he was obliged to hold as a Church of Ireland minister. He even went as far as to describe himself to Walter Scott (with whom he corresponded until his death in 1824) as a "high Calvinist." This difference as well as his literary aspirations ensured that Charles never attained promotion, despite his considerable popularity and flair for oratory, obvious in his sermons.

His choice of profession and his lack of advancement as a clergyman meant that Maturin lived in relative poverty all his life and although he enjoyed writing at first (he financed the publication of *Fatal Revenge* and *The Milesian Chief* himself) this pastime soon grew into a necessity in order to increase his paltry income and his father as well as his own ever-growing family. Charles Maturin increasingly came to attribute his poverty and lack of opportunity to unknown persecutors whom he felt were foiling his every attempt to lift himself out of abject poverty. Perhaps Charles felt persecuted for his religious opinions in much the same way that Gabriel Maturin had. But these feelings of persecution and fated poverty not only found expression in the many letters Maturin wrote to Scott, they also manifested themselves in some of the most powerful tales that the author composed.

The "Tale of Guzman's Family" from *Melmoth the Wanderer* provides us with one of the best examples of Maturin's talent for describing the very depths of human misery and despair significantly through the very themes of religious persecution and poverty. The tale begins with the description of Guzman, an old Spanish merchant and a miser. As he is nearing death and is a bachelor, he decides to make provision for his sole beneficiary, his estranged sister Ines. This estrangement has existed since Ines married a Protestant musician and left Spain after no support, either financial or emotional, seemed to be forthcoming from her brother or her fellow countrymen and women. The couple, having travelled to Germany in the hope of better circumstances find that they are always accompanied by poverty. The now repentant and softened brother sends word to Ines and her family to come back to Spain to be provided for and she gladly arrives with her husband Walberg and their four children, hoping to be joined by Walberg's elderly parents who are also travelling from Germany to share in their new fortune.

Guzman's confessor takes care of the family's needs and is always noticeably referred to as "the good priest," implying that he is very much the exception to the rule. Yet even this one "good" priest eventually comes under attack for his typical Catholic "monastic apathy" and "sanctified stoicism," criticisms which bear witness to Maturin's often savage bigotry. Like Charles Maturin's Huguenot ancestor, the family continue to reject suggestions of conversion to Catholicism, even though their situation in Spain (rather like Gabriel's situation in Ireland) is extremely delicate; they are presented as strangers who neither speak the language nor profess the faith of the country. Tragedy strikes when the Walberg family discovers that on his death, all Guzman's fortune goes to the Church, leaving them in an impossible position masterminded by evil priests who, using "undue influence, imposition and terror" have extracted another will from the dying merchant, depriving the heretic family of everything. This grave disappointment heralds Walberg's decline into near insanity and the acute misery of the once close family who now fully feel the force of the Spaniard's coldness, mistrust and rejection as they try unsuccessfully to find the means of survival.

Maturin describes in gruesome detail the dehumanizing effects of poverty and want on the family. We are told of Walberg's relief when his aged mother dies and later how he wrestles scraps of food from his father, consumed as he is with hunger. And it is not only Walberg who is driven to desperation; his son Everhard sells his blood and Julia, his eldest daughter, attempts prostitution in order to provide a meal for the family. Everhard narrowly escapes bleeding to death and Julia cannot bring herself to sell her body and chooses instead to die of starvation. It is noticeable that Melmoth's presence is much less prominent in the "Tale of Guzman's Family" than in any of the other tales, even though the purpose of each is to depict Melmoth's evil temptation of unfortunates. In fact the full horror of this tale comes not through Walberg's terror of Melmoth but through the desperation and futility of absolute poverty that eventually destroys any vestige of humanity, making suicide, self-mutilation or prostitution the only options. This tale is written in a highly-charged style, full of nightmarish images which give a personal feel to the story and reflects Maturin's deep-rooted fear of poverty.

There are many instances in Maturin's own experience to justify such a fear. He fought against poverty all his life and when he did manage to make a small profit through the sale of *Bertram* and *Melmoth* the money was quickly spent on extravagances, debts and the upkeep of his family. In "Tale of Guzman's Family" we see Walberg's deep resentment grow towards his father for being an extra burden on the already impoverished household and a parallel may be found in the author's own life experience. Maturin's father William broke the line of Maturin clergymen and worked for the government until his dismissal in 1809 on unfair charges of fraud. Having rejected the relative financial security of the church for secular life, William Maturin was now ruined and became another dependant on the struggling Charles who was forced to give up his house and with it his only other livelihood—preparation of students for Trinity College. Soon after, Charles was left with yet another huge debt when a relative for whom he stood security became bankrupt, leaving Charles to pay all. Plagued by financial strife and enjoying little success either in the church or through his literary career, one can begin to understand Maturin's persecution complex.

However, this sense of persecution did not only stem from money problems for, if we look more closely at Maturin and his situation in the Ireland of the 1800's, other reasons appear. After all, Maturin was a Protestant minister living and preaching in a predominantly Catholic and underprivileged country and this fact alone would be enough to cause him feelings of insecurity.

Furthermore, though the Protestant upper classes held the power in Ireland, Maturin could not, even as a Church of Ireland minister, claim these privileges. He did not belong to the Ascendancy since his ancestors came not from England but from France. Maturin therefore could be regarded as a minority member on four counts. Firstly, he was a Protestant in a country with a Catholic majority but he was not of the true Protestant Ascendancy class. Then, although he was an Anglican minister his leanings were towards Calvinism. Lastly, his growing reputation as a writer of romances further disadvantaged him within the church and almost lost him his curacy after the success of **Bertram** in 1816. Thus Maturin was an outsider on all counts, even as a Protestant: an alien in many respects like the Walberg family of his creation. For these reasons, the sense of threat and ultimate persecution was hardly a strange emotion to Maturin.

It is logical to conclude therefore that Maturin's deep-rooted feelings of threat, persecution and insecurity are given substance through his creativity, in his novels and plays. His fears and prejudices are found in the many voices contained in his work through which Maturin projects his own personal anxieties. Maturin was a complicated man; his personality harboured many inconsistencies, not least his feelings for his own country and people. He believed that Ireland could not become or indeed remain independent without the help of England or France yet he despised the Act of Union, which he saw as advantageous for England but insulting and disastrous for Ireland. He advocated religious freedom and prayed for an end to bitterness yet wrote in the fourth sermon from *Five Sermons on The Errors of the Roman Catholic Church* (1824) that

> . . . if the tears of the Roman Catholics could extinguish a single furnace that they lit for Protestants in

former times, we should have felt more indebted to them, than for weeping over us because we returned thanks to God for our deliverance from the greatest peril that ever threatened Europe . . . Now the Roman Catholics represent themselves uniformly as an oppressed and persecuted people; and it might occur to a man of plain understanding to ask—what language would the Roman Catholics hold if they obtained all they demand, if such be their language in a state of oppression, privation, and persecution?

Later in the sermon he introduces the burning question of Catholic Emancipation but he sidesteps the issue completely;

> Roman Catholics of Ireland hear me! Ye call on the rulers of the land for emancipation—*emancipate yourselves* from the yoke that has pressed on your intellects and your consciences for centuries,—a yoke that neither you nor your fathers were able to bear—a yoke that centuries ago has been shaken off by countries less civilized, as well as by the most civilized countries in Europe, England and Scotland . . . You are a high-feeling, a high-fated people. Wherefore are ye not a happy, and a free one?—because you do not *dare to think*. For centuries you have been deluded, benighted, and misled . . . Europe has wept for your blindness, bigotry, and infatuation . . . In your struggles for what you call political freedom, remember that spiritual freedom is far above it, and that freedom every man can bestow on himself.

I leave you with a few words from the Preface to Maturin's third novel, **The Milesian Chief** set in Ireland against the backdrop of the 1798 rebellion. The author is justifying his choice of setting for the novel but the following words give us an important insight into 19th century Ireland through Maturin's eyes:

> . . . I have chosen my own country for the scene because I believe it the only country on earth, where from the strange existing opposition of religion, politics, and manners, the extremes of refinement and barbarism are united, and the most wild and incredible situations of romantic story are hourly passing before modern eyes.

Heinz Kosok (essay date 1996)

SOURCE: Kosok, Heinz. "Charles Robert Maturin and Colonialism." In *Literary Inter-Relations: Ireland, Egypt, and the Far East,* edited by Mary Massoud, pp. 228-34. Gerrards Cross, England: Colin Smythe, 1996.

[In the following essay, Kosok examines representations of British colonialism and Irish nationalism in Maturin's oeuvre.]

Melmoth the Wanderer contains, in the 'Tale of the Indians', one of the fiercest attacks on colonialism anywhere to be found in nineteenth century literature. From his vantage point on an island in the Indian Ocean, Melmoth watches the ships passing by, convinced that 'every one bore its freight of woe and crime':

> There came on the European vessels full of the passions and crimes of another world—of its sateless cupidity, remorseless cruelty, its intelligence, all awake and ministrant in the cause of its evil passions, and its very refinement operating as a stimulant to more inventive indulgence, and more systematized vice. He saw them approach to traffic for 'gold, silver and the souls of men' (a quotation from *Revelation* 18)—to grasp, with breathless rapacity, the gems and precious produce of those luxuriant climates, and deny the inhabitants the rice that supported their inoffensive existence;—to discharge the load of their crimes, their lust and their avarice, and after ravaging the land, and plundering the natives, depart, leaving behind them famine, despair, and execration; and bearing with them back to Europe, blasted constitutions, inflamed passions, ulcerated hearts, and consciences that could not endure the extinction of a light in their sleeping apartment.
>
> (p. 300)

This passage sounds like an echo of Swift (whom Maturin's grandfather had succeeded as Dean of St. Patrick's). In *Gulliver's Travels,* Swift had written:

> . . . A Crew of Pyrates are driven by a storm they know not whither; at length a Boy discovers Land from the Top-mast; they go on Shore to rob and plunder; they see an harmless People, are entertained with Kindness, they give the Country a new Name, they take formal Possession of it for the King, they set up a rotten Plank or a Stone for a Memorial, they murder two or three Dozen of the Natives, bring away a Couple more by Force for a Sample, return home, and get their Pardon. Here commences a new Dominion acquired with a Title by *Divine Right*. Ships are sent with the first Opportunity; the Natives driven out or destroyed, their Princes tortured to discover their Gold; a free Licence given to all Acts of Inhumanity and Lust; the Earth reeking with the Blood of its Inhabitants: And this execrable Crew of Butchers employed in so pious an Expedition, is a *modern Colony* sent to convert and civilize an idolatrous and barbarous People.
>
> (pp. 289-290)

Just as Swift follows this ferocious attack on the false humanitarian excuses for colonial exploitation with Gulliver's ironic declaration that such a description 'doth by no means affect the *British* Nation, who may be an example to the whole World for their Wisdom, Care, and Justice in planting Colonies', so Maturin adds an authorial footnote to say that 'the sentiments ascribed to the stranger are diametrically opposite to mine, and that I have purposely put them into the mouth of an agent of the enemy of mankind'. Such a disavowal, understandable in view of Maturin's life-long struggle to derive recognition and financial security from a British reading public, cannot hide the fact that Maturin was highly critical of colonialism in general and of British

colonialism in Ireland in particular, although critics (with the exception of Fierobe, pp. 457-474, and Piper/Jeffares) have paid little if any attention to this aspect of his work.

Melmoth the Wanderer is perhaps not the best place to discover Maturin's attitude towards the Irish colonial situation, because the novel takes the reader on a complicated journey around the world, but even here one finds numerous authorial asides and footnote references to Ireland, 'a country that no one knows, and which the natives are particularly reluctant to dwell in from various causes' (p. 326). Moreover the introductory chapters, perhaps the best passages that Maturin ever wrote, are precisely observed descriptions of Irish scenery and social conditions, and the situation of the decaying Big House and its inhabitants is clearly referred back to the colonial past of the country. The first Melmoth to settle in Ireland was an officer in the army of Cromwell 'who obtained a grant of lands, the confiscated property of an Irish family attached to the royal cause' (p. 26), and his family's involvement in guilt of this kind seems to lie at the heart of the present barrenness of their possessions. It is significant that the question of guilt, the overriding concern of the novel as a whole, is here introduced in the form of responsibility for an act of colonial dispossession.

If the references to the specific situation of Ireland in *Melmoth the Wanderer* are hidden under the exotic products of Maturin's fertile imagination, and have usually been overlooked by literary critics, they are much more obvious in two earlier novels, *The Wild Irish Boy* and *The Milesian Chief.* In *The Wild Irish Boy* Maturin was perhaps too preoccupied with his attempt to capitalize on the success of Sydney Owenson's *The Wild Irish Girl* to give continuous attention to the conditions in Ireland. In his Preface he admits with disarming frankness:

> This novel from its title purports to give some account of a country little known. I lament I have not had time to say more of it; my heart was full of it, but I was compelled by the laws of this mode of composition to consult the pleasure of my readers, not my own.
>
> (I, p. x)

Nevertheless he introduces an 'old Milesian', the hero's uncle who resides in a castle in the west of Ireland and is roused by the anti-Irish sentiments of the hero's father to a 'flood of declamation':

> It was full of strong and peculiar phrases, many of them harsh to an English ear, and foreign to the idiom of the language; he was evidently thinking in Irish, though he spoke in English. He concluded by saying, 'Is it for those who have desolated the country, and razed every mark of power or of resistance from the face of it, to demand where is the proof of power, or of

resistance, and after beating down with the savageness of conquerors, the monuments of our strength and greatness, to ask with the insolence of conquerors, what monuments of strength and greatness are left to us?'

(I, p. 193)

It is significant that these anti-colonial sentiments are by no means limited to the perspective of one particular character but that they are endorsed, as the context makes perfectly clear, both by the narrator and by the author. This is confirmed when Lord Roschamp is shown as proudly and boastfully recounting at some length how he has maltreated a group of Irish peasants (II, pp. 210-212); such colonialist behaviour at its worst is implicitly condemned by the status of Lord Roschamp as the villain of the novel.

The Milesian Chief on the individual level is the story of a great passion doomed to failure, on the political level it is the story of an insurrection equally doomed to failure; the two levels are closely interwoven and subjected to constant interaction. The rebellion led by Conal O'Morven, the 'Milesian chief' of the title, is from the start a hopeless enterprise, as Conal realises at an early stage: 'I found . . . that it was impossible for Ireland to subsist as an independent country; impossible for her to exist without dependence on the continental powers, or (!) a connection with England.' (III, p. 52). This is underlined by the authorial narrator, who compares the rising to 'Emmet's insurrection, the isolated and hopeless attempt of a single enthusiast' (II, p. 143), and it is finally confirmed by the disastrous ending when Conal's rebel troops, routed from their mountain fortress, have to retreat to an island off the west coast and are practically exterminated there by superior government forces. Nevertheless, the author's sympathies are evidently on the side of the rebels. Not only does he allow his heroine to fall in love with Conal and to follow him without complaint through the degradations of his final defeat; he also makes Colonel Wandesford, the commanding officer of the regular troops, the villain of the novel, whose despicable behaviour on the private level foreshadows his cowardly and treacherous conduct in the field. It is due to his actions that the rebels finally turn into a 'ferocious band, mutinous to their leader, hostile to government, and formidable to the country' (IV, p. 47)—a savage indictment of the harsh measures of colonial repression. Most of all, Maturin installs Conal, the leader of the insurrection, a gentleman of superhuman strength, impeccable manners, incredible moral fortitude and a sense of justice that puts the English officers to shame, as the title hero of his novel.

But *The Milesian Chief* is not only a pessimistic analysis of an insurrection against the colonial status of Ireland, and insurrection that is shown to be both justified and without hope of success. It is also a presentation of a pre-British and even pre-Christian culture, exemplified by the old harper and the ruined tower as remnants of the feudal glories of the past, the 'relics of high antiquity, pillars, crosses, and cromlechs, the memorials of an age in which the cross was yet unknown' (I, p. 178), and in particular the numerous references to the traditions of Irish poetry and music. All this, it is implied, has been destroyed by a colonial power of which the villain Wandesford is the fitting representative.

That Maturin's personal experience of a colonialist situation in pre- and post-Union Ireland should be reflected in those of his novels that have a contemporary Irish setting is perhaps less surprising than the fact that it also surfaces in one of his plays, although, observing the conventions of the tragedy of his time, this play is as far removed in setting, theme and characters from the contemporary scene as it is possible to imagine. *Fredolfo* (produced in 1819) was his third drama, following after the sensational success of **Bertram** and the dismal failure of **Manuel** on the London stage. Despite a strong cast, including MacReady, Young and Charles Kemble, it closed after only one performance at Covent Garden, thus adding another cause for Maturin's bitter disappointment with the vagaries of the English literary and theatrical scene. It would, of course, be tempting to attribute the play's failure to its anti-colonialist stance, but it is more likely that its bewildering structure, its chaotic plotting and its far-fetched sentiments which, as one critic has put it, 'make reading the play an exercise in tolerance' (Kramer, p. 78), combined to produce the actors' lack of enthusiasm and the audience's hilarity. In the present context, the play cannot claim attention for its literary qualities but for the surprising fact that Maturin, in a play destined for the English stage, created a colonial situation that came as closely to a representation of Ireland as audience expectation, censorship and the generic demands for the contemporary tragedy allowed.

Fredolfo is set in fourteenth-century Switzerland, occupied by Austrian troops; the Prologue refers to

> . . . the spot where despotism fell and fate and freedom wing'd the shaft of Tell!

Wallenberg, the play's villain, is not only the personification of evil on an individual level, but at the same time the commanding officer of the occupation forces, while Fredolfo, a Swiss nobleman driven back to his mountain fortress, is not only the heroine's father and the victim of Wallenberg's persecution, but also the leader of native resistance, and Adelmar, who in his love for Urilda comes closest to the role of the traditional hero, is also a native freedom fighter who has spent several years in exile. The play is deeply pessimistic about the outcome of the struggle for national independence: Wallenberg neither respects the sanctuary of a church nor the basic rules of chivalry; when Adelmar surrenders his sword, he immediately stabs him with it, thus implicitly obliterating all hope for a successful rising. That Maturin himself was fully aware of the Irish parallels, becomes clear from the dedication to the Duke of Leinster 'because to the scattered nobility of a deserted Country, *you* set the *rare* and illustrious example of a resident Irish Nobleman'. In view of such references to Ireland that recur throughout Maturin's works, the patriotic sentiments of the prologue appear as highly ironic:

> Britons! o'er such a scene the muse to-night
> Rises rejoicing on her plumes of light,
> Proudly assured to every bosom here
> The soil of liberty is doubly dear!

It would, of course, be a gross over-simplification to see Maturin as a profound political thinker and an uncompromising Irish nationalist. He was clearly opposed, in a very general sense, to the Act of Union and participated in the patriotic sentiments he found in the early works of Sydney Owenson. However, he was much more interested in the evocation of individual passion and suffering than in any kind of political analysis. Moreover, he himself was the member of what one can only call a colonialist institution, the Church of Ireland. His attitude to the Catholic Church, evinced in his published sermons 'on the errors of the Roman Catholic Church', but even more so in his violent and vilifying descriptions of Catholic practices throughout his works, especially in *Melmoth the Wanderer,* take on the form of what one might call religious colonialism.

In this as in other respects Maturin suffered from the basic conflict that overshadows the works of nearly all nineteenth century writers from Ireland: the conflict between a personal Irish perspective and the necessity to write for an English reading public. Less hopeful than Maria Edgeworth and Mrs. Hall of effecting a change in the English attitude to Ireland, he nevertheless found it unavoidable to construct in his works an implied English reader with certain generic, thematic, psychological and political expectations. His choice of literary genres is indicative of such an attitude. The dominant literary form of the period was the Gothic novel; consequently Maturin attempted to adapt his personal interests, especially in *Montorio* [*The Family of Montorio*] and *Melmoth the Wanderer,* to the conventions of the Gothic novel as to setting, atmosphere, plot, characters, and standard motifs. When *The Wild Irish Girl* became a great success in England, he tried to copy it in *The Wild Irish Boy,* although his mode of composition was disastrously opposed to the rigid discipline demanded by the epistolary form. In *The Albigenses* he sought to imitate the model set by Scott; and when he realised that the literary scene in England was turning towards a more realistic type of fiction, he followed it in *Women.*

In his tragedies, he copied, and exaggerated, all the worst fashions of the blank-verse tragedy of the 'legitimate' theatres. The greatest individual influence on his work was probably that of Byron, but he lacked the Augustan discipline that enabled Byron to write *Don Juan* and *Sardanapalus* as well as *Cain* and *Manfred.* In all this, Maturin can be seen as a victim of what one might call literary colonialism, an experience that was, of course, common to numerous writers from the New Literatures in English who did not find a reading public in their own countries and therefore had to undergo various (and often degrading) intertextual compromises with the expectations of the only reading public that could guarantee their existence as writers, the reading public of Britain.

The case of Maturin provides an instructive example of the fact that this kind of literary colonialism does not necessarily end with the author's death. The posthumous reputation of Maturin as a writer depends almost exclusively on *Melmoth the Wanderer.* This novel was reissued in various editions in 1892, 1965, 1966, 1968, 1977 and 1989, and it was accorded the high honour of being included both in the World's Classics and the Penguin series. The standard argument for such an evaluation is, of course, that it is the 'best' of his works, but one might well argue that it is the best from an *English* point of view, because it conforms to certain generic conventions of English literature, especially those of the Gothic novel. On the other hand, the novel that deviated most clearly from the accepted patterns of English literature, and that in its subject matter even dared to treat of a rebellion against English dominance in Ireland, *The Milesian Chief,* remained practically inaccessible for more than one and a half centuries and had to be rescued from total oblivion by an American reprint series in 1979, although James Clarence Mangan in 1849 had declared it to be 'the grandest of all Maturin's productions'. The question of 'literary colonialism' is, of course, a very general one, and it does not lend itself to polemics, least of all to anti-British polemics, but it is precisely in such cases as that of Maturin that one can discuss it in historical perspective.

Works Cited

Anon. ('By the Author of *Montorio*' = Charles Robert Maturin), *The Wild Irish Boy,* 3 vols. (London: Longman, 1808; repr. New York: Garland, 1979).

Anon. ('By the Author of *Montorio* and *The Wild Irish Boy*' = Charles Robert Maturin), *The Milesian Chief: A Romance,* 4 vols. (London: Colburn, 1812; repr. New York: Garland, 1979).

Fierobe, Claude. *Charles Robert Maturin (1780-1824): L'homme et L'oeuvre* (Université de Lille: Editions Universitaire, 1974).

Kosok, Heinz. 'Charles Robert Maturin: *Melmoth the Wanderer*', in Paul Goetsch, Heinz Kosok and Kurt Otten (eds.), *Der englische Roman im 19. Jahrhundert: Interpretationen* (Berlin: Schmidt, 1973), pp. 56-75.

Kramer, Dale. *Charles Robert Maturin,* Twayne's English Authors Series (New York: Twayne, 1973).

Lougy, Robert E. *Charles Robert Maturin,* Irish Writers Series (Lewisburg: Bucknell U.P., 1975).

Mangan, James Clarence. 'Sketches and Reminiscences of Irish Writers: No. I.—Maturin', *The Irishman,* 24 March 1849.

Maturin, C. R. *Melmoth the Wanderer: A Tale,* ed. by Douglas Grant, Oxford English Novels (London, 1968).

Maturin, C. R. *Fredolfo: A Tragedy in Five Acts* (London: Constable, 1819).

Maturin, C. R. *Five Sermons, on the Errors of the Roman Catholic Church: Preached in St. Peter's Church, Dublin* (Dublin: Carry, 1824, 2nd ed. 1826).

Moynahan, Julian. 'The Politics of Anglo-Irish Gothic: Maturin, Le Fanu and "The Return of the Repressed"', in: Heinz Kosok (ed.), *Studies in Anglo-Irish Literature* (Bonn: Bouvier, 1982), pp. 43-53.

Piper, H. W., and A. Norman Jeffares, 'Maturin the Innovator', *Huntington Library Quarterly,* XXI (1958), pp. 261-284.

Scholten, Willem. *Charles Robert Maturin: The Terror-Novelist* (Amsterdam: Paris, 1933).

Swift, Jonathan. *Gulliver's Travels and Selected Writings in Prose & Verse,* ed. John Hayward (London: Nonesuch, New York: Random House, 1934 etc.).

Jacqueline Pearson (essay date winter 1997)

SOURCE: Pearson, Jacqueline. "Masculinizing the Novel: Women Writers and Intertextuality in Charles Robert Maturin's *The Wild Irish Boy*." *Studies in Romanticism* 36, no. 4 (winter 1997): 635-50.

[*In the following essay, Pearson discusses the influence of female novelists on Maturin's* The Wild Irish Boy. *Pearson argues that the novel represents Maturin's attempt to "masculinize" the Gothic genre.*]

Charles Robert Maturin is in a curious position within the literary canon. His Gothic blockbuster **Melmoth the Wanderer** (1820) has provoked much critical comment, while his other fiction is almost ignored. His second novel, **The Wild Irish Boy** (1808), seems a particular embarrassment to commentators, who find it narratively clumsy, "careless," full of "digressions," and showing "grossness of characterisation."[1] Moreover Maturin, especially in this novel, has been charged with "plagiarism,"[2] although no critic so far has looked in detail at

the nature and purposes of this borrowing. In this paper I shall consider Maturin's allusiveness, and suggest that to accuse him of plagiarism is to misunderstand his intertextual practices and those of his age. I shall read this allusiveness as part of a politico-cultural enterprise of masculinizing the novel, and argue that **The Wild Irish Boy** cannot be fully understood except in the context of its purposeful borrowing from, resistance to, and remaking of, female-authored models. To do so I shall examine Maturin's attitude to female literary authority in general, and his use of some texts by women.

One of the most important recent developments in the study of the literature of the late 18th and early 19th centuries is a recognition of the prominence of women as both producers and consumers of literature.[3] Both of these roles are important in Maturin's novels, where female characters are explicitly judged by their reading and female writers are implicitly criticized and corrected. The cultural prominence of women writers and readers caused not only comment but also anxiety in some contemporary male writers. Keats worked to render his work in some respects unreadable to women,[4] and Byron associated female readers with what he saw as a stultifying growth of prudery in the reading public, and defended himself against this by using a range of mocking, sexually suggestive images for women writers (Maria Edgeworth has "a *pencil* under her petticoat," Joanna Baillie has "*testicles*"[5]).

At the turn of the century the novel especially was dominated by women writers, and tended to be stereotypically gendered as feminine, as opposed to "masculine" discourses like history and politics. Women writers' ingenuity in feminizing the genres that excluded them has been well sketched,[6] but the converse, the tactics used by male novelists in the struggle against female hegemony of their form, is less familiar. Matthew Lewis and William Beckford, for instance, both wrote fiction under female pseudonyms mocking the novel of sensibility and its female practitioners,[7] and Lewis' later novel, *The Monk* (1796), uses the Gothic work of Ann Radcliffe but imposes upon this framework a specifically masculine sensibility and authority through its tough sexual explicitness, its centering on male characters, and its unRadcliffean refusal to explain the supernatural in rational, social terms or to reinstate a female-centered domestic ideology.

Sir Walter Scott is a central figure in the male writer's reappropriation of the novel.[8] Although his most influential precursors in historical and national fiction were female—Maria Edgeworth, Sydney Owenson Morgan, the Porter sisters—Scott opens his novel-writing career with emphatically masculine images for the novelist ("a . . . knight with his white shield").[9] The preface of *Waverley* (1814) constitutes "an elaborate suppression of prior"—and largely female—"narrative models."[10] Scott distances himself from female novelists and their work in quite specific terms: *Waverley,* we are told, has no sentimental heroine, no "castle" like that of *Udolpho* (33). He admires Edgeworth and acknowledges her influence, but this, and praise of other examples of "female . . . genius" (493) are relegated to a "postscript" (491). *Waverley* is thus framed by references to the practices of women writers and readers: specifically rejected in the preface, they can be safely reconsidered when the novel has completed its assertion of masculine authority. Lewis, Scott and others attempt to reestablish masculine authority over the novel by acknowledging their female precursors but also mocking them, marginalizing them, or regendering their structures and images.

Maturin, whose career as a novelist began in 1807, was keenly aware of women's dominance of fiction. As a Gothic novelist (**The Fatal Revenge; or, the Family of Montorio** [1807]; **Melmoth the Wanderer**) he was treading in the footsteps of Ann Radcliffe; as a writer of Irish "national tales" (**The Milesian Chief** [1812]) he was working in a mode dominated by Maria Edgeworth and Sydney Owenson Morgan; as a novelist of society life (**The Wild Irish Boy** [1808]; **Women; or, Pour et Contre** [1818]) he was aware of the example of Edgeworth and probably, although this is not explicitly signposted, of Frances Burney. As a male writer in a literary world dominated by powerful and popular female writers he must have felt an anxiety of influence in a particularly gendered way. This battle with individual women writers and with female dominance of the novel form can be seen especially in his earlier fiction: later, although he continues to make reference to women writers, he is less profoundly influenced by them and thus less anxious about them, his literary allegiances being directed toward the masculinized novel of Scott. While his first novel, **The Fatal Revenge,** is strongly influenced by Ann Radcliffe in its use of the explained supernatural and even in the name of the Gothic villain (Kramer 26), **Melmoth the Wanderer** has largely abandoned the model of Radcliffe in favor of that of Lewis, and the novel's ending instead imitates that of *The Monk,* and is wholly unlike any Radcliffean conclusion. His final novel, **The Albigenses** (1824), strongly influenced by Scott and his enterprise of controlling the female discourse of romance through the male discourses of history, uses masculine models and intertexts, making multiple allusions to Shakespeare, Wordsworth, Byron and *Don Quixote* rather than to the female models of his earlier fiction.

Maturin is throughout his career a highly allusive writer whose novels contain detailed discussions of and quotations from other literary texts. Books, libraries and reading play important roles in all the novels. Allusions are sometimes explicit, sometimes implicit, and can stop the action in ways that show clear purpose behind apparent clumsiness. Thus at the beginning of **Women,** the hero Charles de Courcy hears a woman in a carriage scream and pursues it to Dublin; when he arrives, he hears a bell, and "a striking passage in [Thomas] Clarkson's *Account of the Abolition of the Slave-Trade* rushed on his memory,"[11] a passage in which the bells of Bristol sound an "awful challenge" to the reformer who dares threaten their livelihood. This allusion interrupts a thrillingly Gothic chase to no obvious purpose, although it is helpful in establishing de Courcy's idealistic if naive character. Maturin also, though, draws attention away from the model of Charlotte Smith or Ann Radcliffe invoked in the opening sequence in favor of establishing the preeminence of a male author, and of coopting the authority of high-status moral and political discourses for his own fiction, using it defensively against the ghosts of female Gothic.

Maturin makes many references to women writers. Most important of his intertexts are, I shall demonstrate, Ann Radcliffe, Madame de Staël, and fellow Irish writers Maria Edgeworth and Sydney Owenson Morgan, but he uses a wide range of other allusions too. In **Melmoth the Wanderer,** Aphra Behn's play *The Roundheads* appears in the repertoire of the royalist tailor in Bedlam (I: 75-76), and Joanna Baillie is praised as "the first dramatic poet of the age" although a passage is simultaneously criticized for its "absurdity" (II: 220). Other allusions to the writing of women tend to attract similarly negative associations: Juan de Monçada, forced against his will to be a monk, quotes Madame de Genlis on the "corruption" (I: 185) of the monastic life, the parricide quotes Madame de Sevigné (II: 70) as he watches his sister and her lover starve to death, and in "The Lovers' Tale" Anne Mortimer is reading the letters of Lady Russell (III: 223) when visited by John Sandall, whom she accuses of "heartless treachery" (III: 225). In such examples women writers become symbolically associated with insanity, political instability, parricide, incest, treachery, corruption, and family breakdown, and in particular with images of imprisonment—Stanton in the madhouse, Monçada in the monastery, the monk and his lover walled up to starve, Maturin trapped in a web of female intertexts. This heavily negative imaging of women writers is, though, unusual, to be found only in a late novel highly indebted to masculine precedents. Elsewhere Maturin's use of female-authored intertexts tends to be more ambivalent.

Women demonstrates this nervous awareness of the achievements of women writers. For instance, de Courcy refers to Hannah More's *Coelebs in Search of a Wife* in an attempt to ingratiate himself with the evangelicals, but this use of female literary authority comically backfires when it becomes clear that these "rigid Calvinists" regard even the religious More as "'little better than she should be'" (I: 69). De Courcy also uses Elizabeth Montagu's Shakespeare criticism in an attempt to persuade his French friends of the richness of English literature (III: 43), though again his citation of female literary authority is not strikingly effective, and its failure images the gradual breakdown of his relationship with the brilliant well-read Zaira. In these two instances, female predecessors are apparently praised, yet this praise only partially masks mockery of them or a sense of the futility of their achievement.

Women is a densely allusive novel, its two contrasting heroines largely defined through their different reading practices. The hero shares the forename of the protagonist of *Coelebs,* but while More's didactic fiction insists on the power of a female-centered domesticity to contain and satisfy male desire, Maturin rewrites this comedy of the home as a tragedy in which the hero can neither wholeheartedly choose nor entirely reject domesticity. Indeed, for so allusive a novel, we might be surprised by the infrequency of its references to women writers. This constitutes a purposeful strategy for subordinating the temporary, local domination of women in Anglophone culture of 1818 to a longer-term universal literary history self-evidently in Maturin's eyes dominated by men, and to which even the most gifted female characters must submit.

If Hannah More is one ghost haunting *Women,* another is Germaine de Staël's influential novel *Corinne* (orig. 1807). Like de Staël, and like Sydney Owenson Morgan who will be discussed later, Maturin was concerned with female genius and how the female artist, like Zaira Dalmatiani in *Women* and Armida Fitzalban in *The Milesian Chief,* could function within gender ideologies which increasingly confined women to domestic life. De Staël and Morgan used these themes to justify their own practices as women writers. Morgan does this quite simply by presenting her heroines Glorvina and Ida of Athens as superwomen capable of combining individual genius with domestic and social duties. De Staël is more pessimistic, showing the brilliant artist Corinne destroyed by the demands of a British ideology of female passivity, silence, and "domestic duties."[12] Lord Neville loves Corinne but marries her more conventional English half-sister Lucille (a name Hannah More appropriated for the ideal domestic heroine of *Coelebs in Search of a Wife*). Corinne dies of a "broken . . . heart" (388), but not before Neville has become discontented with his duller wife. Their "domestic life" will be "exemplary," but only because the dying Corinne teaches Lucille "to resemble" (383) her. The narrator ironically leaves open the question of whether after loving Corinne Neville can be content with "common life" (389). Corinne wins a posthumous moral victory, educating Neville's daughter and imprinting her personality even upon his wife.

While Morgan and de Staël use the dilemma of female genius to defend their own involvement in the arts, Maturin, struggling against powerful female foremothers,

is more ambiguous. His portraits of brilliant artistic women—especially of the actress Zaira—are respectful and sympathetic, but none of his women of genius wins even Corinne's qualified victory. The conclusion of *Women* inverts that of *Corinne,* for Zaira the woman of genius survives, while the domestic woman Eva and their inconsistent lover Charles de Courcy die. The result of this, though, is only to deprive Zaira of Corinne's moral victory, for she is afflicted with "inexhaustible" grief (III: 408) and guilt at having caused the death of Eva, who is, it transpires, her own long-lost daughter. While Corinne suggests a genuine alternative to a stifling ideology of domesticity, Zaira, Eva and De Courcy are destroyed by their failure to adhere to domestic ideology; and while de Staël's novel ends with ironic suggestions that Neville may never be happy confined to "common life," Maturin's ends with a lamentation of the "unhappy futility of genius," especially female genius. Maturin's battle with his female predecessor takes the form of appropriations, reversals, and a denial of even qualified victory to female genius, which also functions as a denial of the victory over his text of Corinne's creator.

Maturin's treatment of women writers in general, and his use of specific female-authored intertexts, then, can be seen as part of an anxious enterprise to reassert his own masculine control over a woman-dominated form. This anxiety can be seen embodied in Maturin's persistent use of the image of transvestism or other forms of gender-reversal. In *The Fatal Revenge* and *The Albigenses* heroines adopt the Shakespearean disguise of pages to men they love, and in the parricide's tale in *Melmoth the Wanderer* his unknown sister adopts the Lewisian disguise of a monk. Most peculiarly of all, in *The Milesian Chief* Ines, supposed to be Endymion, is not consciously engaged in disguise, but is actually "unconscious of her sex,"[13] not knowing that she is a woman, or indeed what being a woman means. This tortured transvestite image, with its association with homosexuality, incest and madness, may image Maturin's discomfort in his own transvestite role, as a male author adopting the forms of female-dominated fiction.

The Wild Irish Boy is Maturin's most densely allusive novel, and the one in which a grasp of his use of female-authored intertexts is most important. A number of otherwise puzzling features can be better understood if we see Maturin engaged in a struggle to unsettle the hegemony of women writers over the form he is using. The novel's widely criticized narrative structure, for instance, becomes comprehensible as an attempt to unsettle female control over the text. The novel begins as a series of letters between Elmaide St. Clair and her female correspondents: as a female-authored text offered exclusively to female readers. Elmaide loves the hero Ormsby Bethel, although he is ignorant of her existence. When he is ill and depressed, she tries to cheer him by urging him in an unsigned note, "written in a female hand,"[14] to write his own life story. He complies, and the novel passes from a female text aimed at female readers to a male text addressed to a female reader, which imperceptibly passes into a male first-person narrative offered to a more general reading public. Female authority over the text is, in other words, gradually unsettled, male control gradually assumed, a control maintained despite included female narratives like Lady Montrevor's or Athanasia's. In an act of "breakdown" characteristic of the "Romantic novel,"[15] Elmaide disappears altogether from the novel, an extreme strategy for controlling and mastering the voice of the female writer. We hear no more of her until virtually the end, when we learn she has "died for love" (III: 388). This device is not the clumsy failure which it has been called but a subversion of a female-dominated form and an attempt to control and suppress the power of the woman writer. Only when Elmaide, original writer and commissioner of the novel, is safely out of the way can Maturin afford the lavish praise he gives to other women writers.

Even the title of this novel is, of course, allusive, recognizing and masculinizing one of the novel's main intertexts, Sydney Owenson Morgan's *The Wild Irish Girl* (1806), a novel which he also later used to structure the plot of his Irish novel *The Milesian Chief* (1812) (Kramer 44). Most critics have seen *The Wild Irish Boy* as an "opportunistic imitation" of Morgan, an attempt to "capitalize" on her success which was "improper," dishonest, and ultimately "damaging" to his reputation,[16] but Maturin's use of his female-authored intertexts is more significant and productive than this suggests. Indeed his title is somewhat misleading, for "*The Wild Irish Girl* and *The Wild Irish Boy* have much less in common than is generally believed" (Bleiler I: v). *The Wild Irish Boy* contains some brief discussion of Irish issues, and its protagonist speaks against the Act of Union of 1801, but it is in no real sense an Irish novel, unlike *The Wild Irish Girl* which is fundamentally concerned with English readings of Ireland and the Irish. Indeed, apart from the title, Maturin's only direct reference to Morgan's novel is Lady Montrevor's adoption of a masquerade-costume of "'*Glorvina in the Wild Irish Girl*'" (III: 356). Female literary creativity is trivialized, so that Lady Morgan becomes not a powerful predecessor on political and national themes, but only a dress-designer.

Despite this explicit trivialization of Morgan's novel, Maturin is nonetheless implicitly dependent upon it. Both novels, for instance, share an "erotic situation which involves near-incest," with both parent and child involved with the same lover (Bleiler I: vi). In Morgan's novel both Horatio and his father desire Glorvina, and Horatio interrupts his father's wedding to her at the altar. Maturin tones down the high romance of Morgan's plot to show Bethel manipulated into marrying

Athanasia, the daughter of Lady Montrevor with whom he is infatuated, but gradually coming to love his wife. Maturin is thus more wholehearted in his support of an ideology of domesticity than Morgan can be, and he uses her plot structures not, as she does, to demonstrate that traditional domesticity is only part of the life of a gifted woman, but to identify happiness and virtue with (female) domestication in a fairly unproblematic way.

Moreover, by converting the woman loved by both son and father into a man loving both mother and daughter, Maturin performs a gender reversal which is only one of many in *The Wild Irish Boy,* in which intertextual gender reversals become prominent. Lady Montrevor, for instance, constantly appropriates for herself the cachet of male literary characters like King Lear (II: 34; III: 63), Falstaff (III: 62), Voltaire's Candide (II: 339), Cassius (II: 63), Comus (III: 15), Prospero (II: 230) and Satan in *Paradise Lost* (II: 43; III: 323). If Lady Montrevor is culturally immasculated, Bethel is feminized, compared with Desdemona (II: 73), "the sorceress in 'Thalaba'" (III: 288), "Beatrice in the Monk" (III: 321) and Pope's Eloisa (II: 284). Possibly in a world where the major characters identify across gender boundaries, Maturin's anxieties about his own transgression of these boundaries are somewhat alleviated; in a world whose hero is like Desdemona and Eloisa, Maturin's own resemblance to Lady Morgan is less troubling.

There is one other key area in *The Wild Irish Boy* where Maturin engages with and revises Morgan's text. In both novels, female reading becomes a vital issue. Morgan's Glorvina is well-read, especially on Irish topics and in poetry in a range of languages. Her lover Horatio aids her sentimental education by giving her books, including "'*La Nouvelle Heloise*' de Rousseau . . . the '*Paul et Virginie,*' of St Pierre; the *Werter* of Goethe . . . and the *Atila* of Chateaubriand" (140).[17] She also has a "collection of *poesies choisies*" (151), and the "*Breviare du Sentiment,*" a gift from another male admirer (160). This library, with its emphasis on sentiment and eroticism, constitutes the antithesis of the reading usually recommended for young women in the period: *Julie, ou La Nouvelle Héloise* and *Werther* were considered especially dangerous because both seemed to validate individual desires as opposed to social or moral duties. While most prescriptive treatments of female reading seek to repress sexual knowledge and desire, Horatio seeks instead to foster Glorvina's sensibility and sexuality and construct her as a suitable partner. It is very notable that all this reading without exception is in French or German rather than English. Horatio appreciates the "morality" of English novels, but does not think they appeal to the "imagination" or the "heart" (140), and he seeks to foster these qualities in Glorvina by French and German reading. The prominence of these texts also has a political purpose, unsettling the hegemony of English culture over Glorvina and by implication over the Ireland which she embodies. For Morgan, political transformation can best take place through the achievement of individual desires, and the union of Horatio and Glorvina allegorizes a reconciliation between England and Ireland. Morgan at this early stage of her career shows a buoyant optimism in the power of individual relations to resolve political conflicts, in the ability of gifted women to combine domesticity with individual genius, and in female power to achieve reconciliation, both her own power as an author and the cultural and erotic power of her heroine Glorvina.

Maturin is less optimistic about the power for change of individual benevolence, about Anglo-Irish relations, and about female cultural authority. Indeed to some extent he can be seen in resistance to Morgan's project to transform into romance, and thus to feminize, the historical and ethnographical texts that underpin *The Wild Irish Girl.* His argument with Lady Morgan's novel focuses especially on this issue of women's reading, which is celebrated in *The Wild Irish Girl* as facilitating national and personal union. In **The Wild Irish Boy,** women's reading is almost always dangerous. The frame character, Elmaide St. Clair, derives her surname not from *The Wild Irish Girl,* but from the excessively romantic hero of Morgan's earlier novel *St Clair* (1803). This novel shows the shared reading of Rousseau and Goethe not as underpinning a healthy union of individuals and nations but as encouraging transgressive sexual impulses so intense they can produce only a tragic conclusion. Maturin's appropriation of the name St Clair not only enacts a further sexual reversal by transforming a male to a female character, but also, by embedding suggestions of the anti-romance plot of *St Clair* into the romance-celebrating plot of *The Wild Irish Girl,* works implicitly to convict Morgan of inconsistency, self-contradiction and lack of logic. Maturin's Elmaide, like St Clair's beloved Olivia, dies of unrequited love because she has developed a self-destructive false sensibility from her reading of "romance" (I: 74): *Werther* is specifically mentioned (I: 33). The feminized literary form which in *The Wild Irish Girl* facilitates maturity and union in **The Wild Irish Boy** proves literally fatal.

This episode is recapitulated in other included stories in **The Wild Irish Boy** which repeatedly reinforce the dangers of women's reading. A minor character, Mary, falls in love with the hero over the books he gives her (II: 189). In particular she causes her own misery by reading plays, which "represent the passions," especially love, in "exaggerated language" (II: 182), and are thus "dangerous, dangerous indulgences" (II: 184). Another female misreader, Miss Percival, is criticized for her reading of French literature and "the works of the modern philosophers" (I: 263), including "Godwin's Political Justice" (I: 201), which demonstrates her corrupt nature. Female reading of female-authored texts seems

particularly dangerous: Miss Percival's promiscuity seems authorized by her reading of "Mrs. Wollstonecraft's Rights of Woman" (I: 263), and the key text that develops Mary's dangerously acute sensibility is the story of Bertha in "Miss Baillie's . . . tragedy of 'Ethwald'" (II: 183).

Athanasia Montolieu,[18] whom the hero marries although he is infatuated with her mother Lady Montrevor, and whom he gradually comes to love, is also defined through her misreading. Before their marriage, Ormsby finds her reading "Rousseau's Heloïse" and feels "dread and disgust" (I: 262) at this sign of a lack of principle and of a taste for domesticity. Athanasia, indeed, has "formed her ideas exclusively on the French writers" (II: 321-22), including Rousseau, Madame de Genlis, and de Staël's *Delphine,* a novel whose "false sensibility" (III: 105) is attacked and which provides the name of the novel's villainess, Delphina Orberry. This unwise reading has entangled Athanasia in a dangerous flirtation: she has become "'the pupil of false sentiment, dying to be the heroine of a mad and wicked tale of a Rousseau, of a Goethe, of a Wollstonecraft'" (III: 300). The books she has read have taught her "that to yield to sentiment was . . . a virtue" (III: 378), and that no heroine can be happy with a husband. She even spends a night when her husband has been yearning for "domestic happiness" occupied "in novel reading" (III: 219-20).

Athanasia's conversion to "domestic" values (III: 296) is most tellingly indicated by her gradual abandonment of French literature for English, and of books by women for books by men. Rousseau's *Julie* is replaced by McKenzie's critical revision of it, *Julia de Roubigné,* and Madame de Staël by Scott's *The Lay of the Last Minstrel* (III: 297, 295). Her decisive commitment to domestic life is sealed by the revelation that she has "*banished all [her] French books*" (III: 303). In *The Wild Irish Girl* the heroine's reading affirms the health of individual desire and its power to effect political change. **The Wild Irish Boy** might be said to parody Morgan by showing what happens if individuals simply act on their own desires. Maturin uses the trope of female reading more conventionally and repressively, associating French and German reading in particular with "false sensibility," outlaw sexuality, revolution, and the endangering of domestic ideology. Where Morgan's Glorvina can use such reading freely, Maturin's masculinizing of the novel insists on the advantages of male censorship, and the dangers of female-centered literary romance and the work of female writers.

The major intertext in **The Wild Irish Boy** is not, however, despite the titles, *The Wild Irish Girl,* but another novel by an Anglo-Irish woman writer whom Maturin praises elsewhere,[19] Maria Edgeworth's *Belinda* (1801). In an extreme intertextual manoeuver, Maturin coopts real writers Southey, Thomas Moore, and Thomas Surr as minor characters (III: 153, 158-59, 163-68) who function as (exclusively male) embodiments of literary culture: Surr is even described as "the most distinguished novelist of the day" (III: 163). In a period when female participation in the arts, especially the novel, was so notable, this male dominance seems somewhat curious, a strategy of masculinization rather than an objective verdict. Still, Maturin presents all three highly critically as artists: Southey has "imagination" but is not "purified by taste" (III: 153), Moore has trivialized his gift into "brilliant levity" (III: 158), Surr has sacrificed a substantial talent to the popular taste for "the garbage of fashionable anecdote" (III: 164). This leaves the door open for direct and lavish praise of a female genius, Maria Edgeworth, for having succeeded where Surr failed in combining "a faithful representation of life, with . . . a forcible inculcation of good principles" (III: 166). Maturin recuperates literature for its male practitioners, but also criticizes the failings of some of his male contemporaries and appropriates some of the power and popularity of a distinguished female predecessor. He thus both identifies himself with, and shows himself in resistance to, a female tradition in the novel.

The Wild Irish Boy includes a number of other direct references to *Belinda*: Athanasia's governess reads it (I: 236), Lady Montrevor quotes Harriet Freke (II: 232), and Lady Castle-Wycomb is compared to the "matchmaking Mrs. Steinhope (*sic*) in Belinda" (II: 306). Interestingly, though, if Edgeworth as writer is praised, all her female readers here are morally suspect. Bethel's male friend Bellamy can authoritatively praise *Belinda*, but the "vitious taste of our fashionable novel-readers" (III: 164), and especially female novel-readers, can misuse even this ideal female-authored work. It is very apparent that what they see in *Belinda* is not its highly moral heroine or its praise of domestic ideology, but only its heroine's comic antagonists, the vain and worldly Mrs. Stanhope or the disturbingly disruptive feminist Harriet Freke. Even the best, most moral of female authors can be misread by the vicious tastes of female readers, an implication which undercuts Maturin's generous praise of Edgeworth's work.

Belinda haunts a number of Maturin novels. In *Melmoth the Wanderer,* phosphorescent paintings are used to create apparently supernatural terrors to torment the reluctant monk Alonzo de Monçada, as Harriet Freke had terrorized the black servant Juba, and in both *The Milesian Chief* (IV: 157) and in *Women* (I: 263; III: 207), female characters use the *sortes Virgilianae* in a way suggested by *Belinda*.[20] In addition, *Women* is structurally based on *Belinda*. In both, a young, idealistic but flawed hero is torn between a brilliant, experienced older woman (Lady Delacour in *Belinda,* Zaira in *Women*) and a young, naive woman of mysterious parentage (Virginia St Pierre in *Belinda,* Eva in *Women,* who is actually Zaira's daughter).[21]

Maturin's most obvious revision of *Belinda* in *Women* is a masculinizing one. In *Belinda,* Clarence Hervey achieves a happy ending because ultimately he chooses neither Lady Delacour nor Virginia, but the eponymous heroine, who combines and perfects their qualities of both sound understanding and strong feeling. Belinda represents a female authority working for moral and domestic values: she even succeeds in reconciling Lord and Lady Delacour by reawakening Lady Delacour's maternal feelings. While Maturin's revisions of *The Wild Irish Girl* depended on his scepticism about Morgan's proposition that female genius can be combined with female domesticity, his revisions of *Belinda* show him agreeing with Edgeworth on the crucial importance of domestic ideology, but very much less confident than she is about the possibility of achieving this idealized domesticity through female moral authority. In *Women* his masculinization of the novel depends on erasing this female moral authority: no character in his novel fulfills a similar role to that of Belinda. Zaira's cultural and moral authority does not reclaim her lover but is increasingly resented by him, until he leaves her as he had previously left Eva. Female moral authority cannot control male desire, but in its absence, there is nothing to prevent the tragic conclusion.

In *The Wild Irish Boy,* the *Belinda* pattern of flawed hero divided between older and younger heroines persists, though Ormsby Bethel is more deeply flawed than Clarence Hervey, and the younger heroine is fragmented into Elmaide St Clair, Mary, and Athanasia, all of whom more closely resemble the weak, misreading Virginia than the rational and moral Belinda. Other ingredients from *Belinda* are apparent: Bethel is manipulated into gambling by Lady Montrevor's enemy Delphine Orberry, as Belinda's fiance Mr Vincent is by Lady Delacour's enemy Mrs. Luttridge; Jewish moneylenders play significant roles in both; both books contain a specifically Wollstonecraftian anti-heroine (Harriet Freke in *Belinda,* Miss Percival in *The Wild Irish Boy*); a masquerade plays a crucial part in both.

The most detailed use of *Belinda,* however, lies in the characterization of Lady Montrevor, who is closely based on Edgeworth's popular Lady Delacour—so closely indeed that it seems that Maturin is experimenting by placing the same character in a darker and more disturbing context as a means of challenging what perhaps seemed to him Edgeworth's over-optimism, even complacency, about the power of domestic ideology. Both women are unhappily married, but remain faithful despite indulging in platonic flirtation. Both are brilliant society-women, creating self-images that are apparently "vain, volatile, dazzling" ([*The Wild Irish Boy*] II: 48), but are really façades hiding secret sorrow. Both are intelligent and well-read and speak in a highly allusive idiom, and are especially associated with a potentially dangerous self-displaying form of theatricality.[22] Both relate their stories in inset texts, had thwarted relationships with men they really loved before marriage, take drugs to relieve their suffering, and have daughters but show little maternal feeling towards them.

Both Lady Montrevor and Lady Delacour are centers of Gothic conventions within predominantly domestic novels, "disrupting" their forms and assumptions.[23] Both come to believe themselves the victims of a haunting: Lady Delacour's is a malicious stratagem of Harriet Freke's, Lady Montrevor's proof that her first love, long supposed dead, is alive and watching over her. Both believe these ghosts prove that death is imminent. Lady Delacour sometimes suggests a Radcliffean heroine, with her "Mysterious Boudoir" (*Belinda,* ch. x), her cache of secret letters in a locked casket, and her conclusion, ultimately finding a role within a transformed domesticity. Lady Montrevor is more reminiscent of the Gothic of Lewis' *The Monk,* a text which is several times referred to. The episode in which, disguised as St. Veronica, she is almost raped by a monk, is particularly Lewisian. The ending of **The Wild Irish Boy** is more uncomfortable than that of *Belinda* partly because Lady Delacour as Radcliffean heroine has a well-marked literary trajectory toward a happy, domestic ending; Lady Montrevor as a more Lewisian heroine is less easily incorporated into the happy ending and indeed adds an ironic note of interrogation to an ending that seems to draw attention to its fictionality by sheer exaggeration.

Domestic ideology finally triumphs in **The Wild Irish Boy,** as in *Belinda,* with Ormsby reunited with Athanasia and his child, and the widowed Lady Montrevor beginning again with her first love. As in the revision of *Belinda* in **Women,** Maturin's most obvious excision is the eponymous heroine. In Edgeworth's novel the happy ending is enabled by the moral and domestic authority of Belinda. Even the Delacour marriage is recuperable, and Lord Delacour, who has killed an alleged lover of his wife in a duel, can be converted into a loving husband by the redomestication of his wife through Belinda's moral authority. Maturin lacks this confidence in female moral authority and in the power of a female-centered domesticity to reconstruct the erring male. No female power can recuperate or domesticate Lord Montrevor, and only his death (ironically in the effort to preserve the appearance of domesticity and prevent his daughter's elopement with a bigamist) can free Lady Montrevor for a happy life within a reconstructed family. Such moral authority as exists tends, indeed, to be masculine, though it is fragmented into a number of minor characters, like the idealized clergyman Mr Corbett (who plays a part reminiscent of Dr X-in *Belinda*), and Bethel's friend Hammond.

Finally the happy ending is possible because Lady Montrevor's first love, believed dead, is actually alive, and has intervened secretly in her life and that of Bethel,

now revealed as his son. While in *Belinda* the return from the dead of a patriarch, the father of Virginia, is a relatively minor incident, in **The Wild Irish Boy** the return of the father enables every aspect of the happy ending; it displaces Bethel's potentially incestuous attachment to his surrogate mother Lady Montrevor, banishes the ghosts of the past, facilitates the victory of "domestic" happiness (III: 181, 207, etc.), and frames both Bethel's achievement of literal fatherhood and Maturin's achievement of masculine authority over the text. In *Belinda* the patriarch returned from the dead is a doubtful authority-figure, prone to depression and even madness, and the novel's final scene is female-dominated and stage-managed by a resurrected matriarch, Lady Delacour returned from her deathbed and reconstructed as domestic wife and mother. Maturin masculinizes the novel by emphasizing the power, rationality, and virtue of its last father-figure and minimizing the importance of female moral authority within the family, emphasizing instead its dependence on male vision and desire and the self-destructiveness of evil both male and female.

The Wild Irish Boy demonstrates both explicitly and implicitly Maturin's admiration for Maria Edgeworth and especially for *Belinda,* but he criticizes her original rather than simply duplicating it. Indeed, that he appreciates Edgeworth but also feels the need to assert his own power by mocking her work and turning it against its author is apparent from one small but significant act of appropriation. One of the most counter-domestic of many corrupt female characters in **The Wild Irish Boy** is Miss Percival, who has taken the work and example of Mary Wollstonecraft literally and borne two illegitimate children, and who after the death of her lover robs him and elopes with his French valet, finally dying in misery. This woman is, it transpires, the mother of Ormsby Bethel. Interestingly, Maturin needs to reconstruct Bethel's paternity, so that he is revealed not as the son of the selfish rake he supposed his father but of his more sentimental and caring brother, but he sees no need, as any woman writer would have done, to revise his maternity. This marks in general terms a male resistance to the ideologies of maternity and gynocentric domesticity in *Belinda,* but the debt to Edgeworth's novel is marked quite specifically by giving this adulterous mother the surname of the character who in *Belinda* symbolizes the moral power of domesticity and motherhood, Lady Anne Percival. While Maturin uses *Belinda,* and claims admiration for the novel, he also profoundly alters it to remove its two most powerful embodiments of female authority, Belinda herself, who is simply erased, and the perfect wife, mother and homemaker Lady Anne Percival, who is transformed into his promiscuous homebreaker.

Maturin's novels can, then, usefully be understood as an attempt to appropriate and masculinize the work of influential female predecessors, Ann Radcliffe, Madame de Staël, Sydney Owenson Morgan and Maria Edgeworth. This project should not be seen as misogynist. His novels create compassionate and convincing female portraits, and he admires a number of women writers, though his attitude reveals ambivalence: he needs to assert his creative power over them, but he cannot offer too destructive a critique, since he is visibly their pupil, and to destroy them is to destroy himself.

His strategies for masculinization take a range of characteristic forms. He draws critical attention to female writing, often subliminally associating it with a range of negative qualities—madness, betrayal, imprisonment, parricide—while overtly praising certain women writers. He may displace female central characters by male—a wild Irish girl becomes a wild Irish boy. As in *The Milesian Chief* or *Women,* he may transpose the domestic comedy of his female models into tragedies of male egotism, converting a stereotypically female form into a male one; or, as in *The Wild Irish Boy,* delay the averting of tragedy to the last moment. He draws attention to issues of gender by introducing transvestite characters and regendering literary allusions. In particular he resists the myths of female genius and of gynocentric domesticity which were so empowering to women writers of the period. To some extent he affirms an ideology of domesticity by showing, in all his novels, the disastrous effects of its absence, but he emphasizes not female success in achieving it (as in *Belinda*), but either the success of the male or, more often, the failure of both sexes to establish and maintain it. *The Wild Irish Boy* and *Women,* his revisions of *Belinda,* function by erasing the title character and the moral authority Edgeworth's novel allows her, and resist as sentimental fantasy the images of a healthy society as a sequence of female-centered domesticities which underpin *Belinda.* Like Lewis and Scott, Maturin provides evidence of the position of a male writer within a female-dominated genre, and this can be followed nowhere more clearly than in that key text of competing gendered literacies, *The Wild Irish Boy.*

Notes

1. Robert E. Lougy, *Charles Robert Maturin* (Lewisburg: Bucknell UP, 1975) 24; Dale Kramer, *Charles Robert Maturin* (New York: Twayne, 1973) 38, 40.

2. "A Note on Charles Robert Maturin" in *Melmoth the Wanderer* (London, 1892) I: lv.

3. E.g., Anne K. Mellor, *Romanticism and Gender* (New York: Routledge, 1993), esp. 7.

4. Margaret Homans, "Keats Reading Women, Women Reading Keats" (*Studies in Romanticism* 29 [1990]: 341-70).

5. Leslie A. Marchand, ed., *Byron's Letters and Journals* (Cambridge: Belknap P of Harvard UP, 1973-1981) 6: 106, 237; 7: 202 217; 5: 203.

6. Gary Kelly, *Women, Writing and Revolution 1790-1827* (Oxford: Clarendon, 1993).

7. Lewis' "The Effusions of Sensibility" reprinted in *The Life and Correspondence of M. G. Lewis* (London, 1839) vol. 2: Beckford's *Modern Novel Writing* (1796) and *Azemia* (1797).

8. Ina Ferris, *The Achievement of Literary Authority: Gender, History, and the Waverley Novels* (Ithaca: Cornell UP, 1991).

9. *Waverley* 33. References are to Andrew Hook, ed. (Harmondsworth: Penguin, 1985).

10. Nicola J. Watson, *Revolution and the Form of the British Novel, 1790-1825* (Oxford: Oxford UP, 1994) 126.

11. *Women, or Pour et Contre* (Edinburgh, 1818) I: 13; further references to this edition appear in the text.

12. Madame de Staël, *Corinne; or, Italy* (orig. 1807); translated by Isabel Hill (London, 1833), e.g. 220.

13. *The Milesian Chief* (New York: Garland, 1979) II: 107; subsequent references to this edition appear in the text.

14. *The Wild Irish Boy* (New York: Arno, 1977) I: 74; subsequent references to this edition appear in the text.

15. Robert Kiely, *The Romantic Novel in England* (Cambridge: Harvard UP, 1972) 1.

16. Watson 116; E. F. Bleiler, Introduction to *The Wild Irish Boy* I: v.

17. References to *The Wild Irish Girl* are to Brigid Brophy, ed. (London: Pandora, 1986).

18. The surname recalls the novelist Madame de Montolieu, author of the popular French novel *Caroline de Lichtfeld* (1786), and hence constitutes a further appropriation, and criticism, of female literary authority.

19. E.g., in *Women* III: 54.

20. *Belinda,* chapter XIII. References to *Belinda* are to Eiléan Ní Chuilleanáin, ed. (London: Everyman, 1993).

21. A number of verbal links connect these two characters—for Eva, "Reading became her only resource" (III: 141), and for Virginia, "Reading . . . was now almost her only pleasure" (359).

22. Heather Macfadyen, "Lady Delacour's Library: Maria Edgeworth's *Belinda* and Fashionable Reading" (*Nineteenth-Century Literature* 48 [1993]: 423-39).

23. Teresa Michals, "Commerce and Character in Maria Edgeworth" (*Nineteenth-Century Literature* 49 [1994]: 17).

Judith Wilt (essay date 2002)

SOURCE: Wilt, Judith. "'All about the Heart': The Material-Theology of Maturin's *Melmoth the Wanderer.*" In *The Fountain Light: Studies in Romanticism and Religion: In Honor of John L. Mahoney,* edited by J. Robert Barth, pp. 256-73. New York: Fordham University Press, 2002.

[*In the following essay, Wilt examines the theological ramifications of* Melmoth the Wanderer.]

Byron's *Manfred* and Southey's *Thalaba the Destroyer* have blasphemous potency; Shelley's *Prometheus Unbound* and Blake's *The Marriage of Heaven and Hell* reach through and past the domain of the divine. Coleridge's "The Ancient Mariner" tells us of the spiritually unutterable, in terms so banal we must attend closely in order to unutter them. So does Blake's "The Tyger." And Mary Shelley's *Frankenstein.* But none of these masterworks displays its unutterance with more relish and reach and blasphemy, more enigmatic and desperate force, than Charles Maturin's **Melmoth the Wanderer** (1820), whose devilish protagonist, archpriest and Irishman, cavalier rebel and savage savant, bears in his body the "incommunicable condition" incapable of exchange, or change—the human condition.[1]

At once the God-licensed tempter of Job, the aristocrat self-licensed tempter of Richardson's eponymous heroine Clarissa, and the eloquent but outbargained rogue of a dozen romances and folktales from the Wandering Jew to *Paradise Lost,* Melmoth is a privileged voyeur of the human heart. The Irish peasant Biddy, half-sibyl, half-impostor, tells us early in the narrative frame that "it's all *here*; it's all *about the heart*" (13). To each of the hearts in extremity he visits, he offers what appears to be extrication from the prison of mortality, and each time he is rejected for the simplest of reasons. The "condition" he makes, the condition he visibly is in, this mortal immortal, is torment. The condition cannot be relieved because it is everywhere. It cannot be "communicated" because you already have it. The Christian spin on this, as T. S. Eliot would later put it in "Little Gidding," goes: "We only live, or else suspire / Consumed by either fire or fire."[2] But "consumed" is inexact. We cannot bargain for immortality because that too we already have.

Charles Robert Maturin was an incoherent mix of passions and actions, a theologian and a dandy, a family man and misanthrope, a formidably well-educated elitist and at once a hater and a craver of popular approval. He was a member of the Anglo-Irish Ascendancy and also an Irish patriot, an ambitious artist vowed to clerical poverty and obedience. He wrote melodramas that blazed with incest and malice and violence. But his fables rode on a realist's assessment not just of the petty sins of people but of the paradoxical and systematic capture by institutional violence of human property—"real," national, intellectual and moral, while the humans, bewildered, erupted in rage or sank into torpor.

Like his Gothic-writing forebears, Horace Walpole and Ann Radcliffe, he transferred to precincts Mediterranean and historical his overpowering sense that the "castle" of human culture had somehow fallen into the hands of tyrants. Like his contemporary and would-be patron Walter Scott,[3] he wrote his usurped and now "British" home into his texts from his own equivocal position as Anglo-Irish. Missteps in Irish inheritance is a powerful motif in his novels **The Wild Irish Boy, The Milesian Chief,** and **Women Pour et Contre**; inheritance deflected, alienated, bankrupted, corrupted: in **The Milesian Chief** a former heir lives as his own land's steward. **Melmoth the Wanderer** opens as an Anglo-Irish inheritance passes from uncle to nephew while the landless natives watch their opportunity to continue to haunt the process.

But unlike Scott or Radcliffe (let alone Shelley or Byron), Maturin was an Anglican clergyman: his preface argues that the novel is actually an extension of a thought in one of his Sermons.[4] For him all these issues of inheritance have a theological grounding as well as an historico-cultural aspect, one that hovers between gnostic elevation and Christian incarnation. The question, what are we heir to and how can we express our claim to it? becomes, what is the "incommunicable condition"? and (how) is it assuaged, or at least expressed, however incommunicably, in the Mysteries of original sin, atonement, and, especially, "faith." Descendent of Huguenots, ancestor of Oscar Wilde, Maturin throve addictively on paradox, and pursued both the theology and the "theater" of faith and good works beyond Reformation or Counter-Reformation solutions, into the incommunicable abyss. Here all actions, all passions, all desires, lead only to torment, including the desire-not-to-desire; all theories of suffering, from philosophers and theologians alike, founder on the same pointless "why?": the answer simply reports and redoubles the condition. Each man kills the thing he loves, dies of the desire he deplores.[5]

The "secret" Melmoth carries is in fact understood by the reader, in its orthodox vesture, its hapless "point," the moment it surfaces as a secret: the price of relief from mortality is immortal damnation. The heterodox core of the secret, however, is not a point but a fullness, a brilliant pleroma, a space of limitless depth and silence: "the secret of silence is the only secret. Words are a blasphemy against that taciturn and invisible God, whose presence enshrouds us in our last extremity," says the novel's most verbose and important theologian narrator (195), the Catholic Alonzo de Monçada. "What a difference," says a narrator within his narration, "between *words without meaning* and that *meaning without words* which the sublime phenomena of nature . . . convey to those who have 'ears to hear'" (321). Words are the business of the post-lapsarian sublime: words spun from the material of the body: tongue, lips, ears to hear, eyes to read. Words are the body's meanings, the "material-theological," the human condition. But the body and its words are also the gateway to the pleroma, the edge of the "only" secret, the dark material foundation which Christian incarnationalism stubbornly weds to the realm of light. At this gateway one must resist the temptation to ask, or answer, what, or why.

Consider this exchange between the Master of the Inquisition and one of the novel's tersest theologians, who has just revealed the unconscious presumption of one of the city's best beloved and well-doing clerics:

> He sought the secret of discovering the presence or agency of the evil power.
>
> Do you possess that secret?
>
> My master forbids me to disclose it.
>
> If your master were Jesus Christ, he would not forbid you. . . .
>
> 'I am not sure of that.'
>
> You believe, then, it requires strength of mind to keep these abominable secrets?
>
> No, I rather imagine strength of body.
>
> (38)

The orthodox Anglican Maturin abominates orthodox Catholic Inquisitions, of course: the satire here is clear. Yet at another level this exchange, fathoms deep in the novel's Chinese boxes of buried narrative, represents a genuine passion to know, not the strength of the mind but strength itself, harbored unequivocally in the body.

It's true that the final wry comment acknowledges the Inquisitor's capacity to pry the Illuminated's secret out of the body's harbor, as he shortly does. But like "incommunicable condition," "strength of body" seems to float free of its sentence into that meaning without words which is the novel's paradoxical object of worship and curiosity. Strength *is* the body's, the body is the silence that grounds its words, and strength reclaims its own in the "enshrouding" presence of the divine. For though the tortured Illuminatus "uttered the following remarkable confession," what follows on the page is that blank space starred with asterisks which, under the tropes of "discoloured, obliterated and mutilated"

(28) and above all "illegible" (39), unutters the secret every time. Unuttered, the secret origin of the felt and suffering "separateness" of humankind; unuttered the secret dynamic of the suffering reintegration, at-onement; ineffably unuttered the secret suffering action whose divine word is "faith," human word is "love."

* * *

In the design of the novel the moral action repeats a cycle of resurrection and reburial, disclosing and unuttering, while the plot travels from Ireland through England to Spain and India, and circles back through Spain and England to Ireland. It travels also from theologies of faith to ontologies of love to a narratology still withholding its secret in the grammatical conditional. Melmoth himself can provide only a blizzard of "ifs" in his last prophecy of his end (537-538), and the frame narrator's grammar breaks down over the task of reporting it: footmarks on the turf to the edge of the Irish seacoast look "as if a person had dragged, or been dragged, his way through it" (542). In the frame story, an Anglo-Irish landlord, childless possessor of confiscated Irish estates gifted by Cromwell, lies dying, dreading the loss of the material comforts which his miserliness has already denied him. He dreads even more the visit of the elder brother of that confiscating ancestor, mysteriously unaged after 150 years, who represents in the historico-cultural register (take your pick) the intellectual counterpart of that ancestral religio-imperial avidity, and/or its avenging opposite.

"John Melmoth the Traveler" (26), student of ancient knowledges and connoisseur of suffering, is rumored a steady attendant at the deathbeds of guilty self-tormenters, but this is the dull routine of his "service" to his rumored diabolical master. The spice in the routine is presence, enabling presence, at the moment when the innocent, the not yet human, the always already human persons, first suffer the knowledge of their excruciating "condition." His true target is not the old miser but the new heir, his namesake and great-great-nephew John Melmoth, the timid and dependent university student, to whom he offers *himself* and his story as the fruit of the tree of knowledge.

Old Melmoth, it turns out, has by instinct hoarded, along with his wine and his rents, a blazing-eyed portrait of the Traveler and a disintegrating manuscript left about him by one of his obsessed targets from the seventeenth century, an English Restoration intellectual and dandy named Stanton, who first saw Melmoth convulsed in laughter as the shattering storm which both men had witnessed struck dead by lightning two innocent young lovers. The Traveler's countenance was—"here the manuscript was illegible"—and he told Stanton—"a long hiatus followed here" (31). And the relationship that followed, "the master passion . . . and master-torment of his life" (59), is set in motion as a fiery current flowing irresistibly between two poles, "the human condition" and "the Power" (31). This is the elemental force which the speaker of Shelley's "Mont Blanc" feels coming down the Arve, and Byron's Manfred went up the mountain to draw forth, the unnamable energy, mysteriously ordering, which dwells unfathomably behind all things.

Stanton's story provides the pattern for all the tales of the novel. From his eminence of philosophical reflection, intellectual mastery, and material freedom, he is reversed by human greed and institutional violence to incarcerated immobility, filth, and madness. This heart's extremity is Melmoth's cue; he appears, and delivers the incommunicable revelation of man's real condition. Stanton's "rejection" of the exchange of the human's condition for any other condition turns the screw of the master-torment a little tighter, makes the human more viscerally itself. The circumstances by which Stanton was freed from that particular extremity are irrelevant and hence unnarrated in the manuscript which he wrote as part of his obsessive pursuit of the bargainer he rejected. Tracing the Traveler to his Irish family home years before, he cast the text, with its pulsations of revelation and illegibility, into the house, as a shipwrecked captain commits his log in a bottle to the ocean (59), communicating his condition, but through a glass, darkly.

Two things besides the general pattern are important about this first tale. The first is a certain sardonic evenhandedness in the tales' depiction of religious madness. In the English madhouse Stanton hears a Puritan weaver repeat compulsively for hours the "points" of his Doctrine, and a Cavalier tailor monotonously recount the forms and costs of the garments he has made for the mighty. Much longer stays in Spain for other tales will license much more detailed descriptions of the iniquities of Counter-Reformation Catholicism so necessary to the nineteenth-century British imagination. But a brief visit to India will incriminate Hindu and Muslim cultural institutional religious practice as well. Indeed, *Melmoth* [*Melmoth the Wanderer*] provides an interesting example of a process which Marilyn Butler has described, where radical thinkers using new knowledges of eastern religions contended with orthodox Christian thinkers for the "sacred" ground of the figures of Satan, and of that ambiguously animating/destroying "fire" which he represented.[6]

The second element of importance in this tale is its location of the formal meeting of Melmoth and Stanton, who are the poles of the current between Power and the human condition, in a Restoration theater, one moreover showing plays that are a jumble of classical themes and contemporary costume, exotic characters and locales and English political intrigue, artificial emotion and real violence, even rapes (40). The educated Stanton deplores this jumbled communication until his gaze wanders from the spectacle to encounter the eyes of his long-sought interlocutor, when his "heart palpitates with violence" and his body reels in "nameless and deadly sickness" (43). The face of another spectator disrupts the safe boundaries of the theatrical; the stage overflows the boxes and vice-versa. In Counter-Reformation Spain "(the Catholic) religion is our national drama" (105); in Reformed England (Protestant) drama (and increasingly, as Ian Watt suggested long ago, the novel[7]) is the national religion.

The critical impulse that frames such comments, however, dies into the awe of fact, and "drama . . . nation . . . religion" also floats free of its sentence to join "strength of body" and "incommunicable condition" as the material-theological basis of the novel. For the vertiginous bilocation between spectator and spectacle, intrinsic to the human condition as Melmoth's instant presence to all his targets is to the nature of the Power, is fundamental to the theology of suffering, and so is the body's strength to admit and endure this vertiginous doubleness and the heart's capacity to circulate it.

The secular exploration of material-theological suffering begins when a powerful storm wrecks a vessel on the coast of young Melmoth's Irish property. Rushing down with a crowd of villagers equally powerless to help, he is pulled nearly in two by an irresistible attraction *both* to the tormented cry of the drowning men repeating the shrieks of wind and wave ("his senses reeled under the shock, and for a moment he echoed the storm with yells of actual insanity" [64]), *and* to the racking laugh of the unmoved spectator on the rock above him, which identifies the spectator as the Traveler described in the manuscript he has just read. Breaking out of his paralysis toward the stronger desire, he climbs after the Traveler, but falls into the sea to become one with the sufferers. Gripped by a fellow drowning man, he is carried to shore with him, where the two are found "locked in each other's hold, but stiff and senseless" (70).

The young boy would wish to credit himself and his fellow would-be rescuers with the received simplicities about the virtuous dynamic of suffering and empathy: "How much good there is in man . . . when it is called forth by the sufferings of his fellows!" (65). But the narrator cautions that the compound the young boy called "good" had in it elements of curiosity, pride of physical strength, and comparative consciousness of safety, not to mention the darker incitement to revel in the experience of the Absolute Worst, and the equivocal pleasure of storytelling to come. The young boy also tries to credit his rescuer directly, but Alonzo de Monçada, tempered in torture and as it turns out once targeted for temptation by the Traveler himself, reports impartially that he saved his own life, and that of young

Melmoth, out of "instinct," that is the strength of the body, or, to use another more "polite" dialect, as he says, "the influence of my better genius" (71).

This linking of one body's suffering/strength with another body's life follows the line of Enlightenment empiricist thinking on association and sympathy. But as Steven Bruhm points out in his learned and provocative *Gothic Bodies: The Politics of Pain in Romantic Fiction,* there can be very dangerous surges and overloads in the currents of "sympathy." Tracing the arguments for the physiological basis of social sympathy and the pain/terror foundation of Burkean aesthetics, Bruhm shows how the "I know how you feel" experience of pain that shapes a community of sympathetic bodies can become a competitive and finally substitutional anti-ethic claiming "This hurts me more than it hurts you."[8] Here the empathetic spectator may even link with the torturer, co-opting, sympathetically, the virtuous space of the victim, the living space of the Other, erasing his interiority and even claiming his body, the strength of his body, as the spectator or torturer's own prosthesis. Such is the politics of the patriarchal male; such may be the politics of the revolutionary state, or the counter-revolutionary church. Such, closer to the bone, is the politics of the God of Abraham and Isaac, the God of the sacrifice of Christ.

It is no accident that the bulk of **Melmoth the Wanderer,** 460 of its 540 pages in the Oxford Edition, is narrated by the Spanish Catholic, Monçada, who has suffered in his (strength of) body an amount of experience equal in range, and nearly in pages, to what he has seen, read, and written of the sufferings of the Other—Jew, Puritan, and Catholic, male and female—and who has remained true to the faith of his culture. He has not turned aside from his suffering either to atheism or to conversion: he has never "exchanged" his condition (as Englishmen of the Reformation had done). Eagerly solicited by young Melmoth, the thirty-year-old Monçada first recounts his own history of familial and "Jesuitical" and Inquisitorial persecution in "The Tale of the Spaniard," climaxing with an encounter with the Traveler. He then reports, from a manuscript written in Greek (but in Hebrew characters) by a steadfastly unconverted Jewish scholar, which he translated into English, "The Tale of the Indian." The "Indian" is a young girl named Isadora, born in Spain but shipwrecked on an island off India, where as "Immalee," she begins her heart's true history with the same kind of encounter.

Maturin makes his two central targets Spanish and Catholic, partly as a bow to the general English national sense of having properly "left behind" a whole series of "ancient" tyrannies. More deeply, he wants to evoke in properly ambiguous Gothic style the premodern ferocity of the religious current flowing between the unutterable Divine Power and the incommu-

nicable human condition, mediated and modernized by the Anglican *via media,* but also, of course, obscured and miniaturized by it. Further, while Alonzo and Immalee are in some respects both gendered humanly female to Melmoth's, the Power's, masculine pole, Maturin also needs Alonzo's specifically masculine body through which to stage the drama of faith in/as suffering—which generates narrative—as he needs Immalee's feminine sexuality to stage a similar drama for love in/as suffering—which generates, as we shall see, a more carnal product.

These two tales are related in another interesting way to two classics of eighteenth-century literature. They echo, translate, even plagiarize, the Gothico-Puritan drama of incarceration, temptation, torture, and no-exit extremity of Samuel Richardson's *Clarissa* (1748) and of the convent-captivity novel it inspired, Diderot's *La Religieuse* (1760), published in English as *Memoirs of a Nun* in 1796. Enthralled by Richardson's story of an independent-minded daughter undergoing a series of imprisonments designed as trials of her duty, virtue, character, and, finally, strength of body, the great French philosophe began a hoax tale of a daughter forced by family into convent life, in which she experiences the suffering of assault, seduction, maddening persuasions toward conversion, and equally maddening routine. Like Clarissa, Marie Suzanne in her intelligent self-awareness tries to discover the tiniest fragments of private space in her community of duty. She too makes a leap from intolerable duty into the fiery imprisonment of a seducer devil's phantom freedom.

Diderot, an outsider to the vexations of religious desire, was mainly interested in the exposure of institutional violence and the classic porno-sublime of the suffering and death of a beautiful woman: he solves, or rather abandons, the problem of the no-exit with a last-minute rescue of his heroine. Richardson, on the other hand, no stranger to the critique of institutions, or to the porno-sublime, *is* aflame with religious desire, and feels the no-exit dilemma with excruciating precision, forcing his characters into that exhausted extremity where the "enshrouding presence" of God finally awards them—the shroud.

The heroine of *Clarissa* accepts the incommunicable condition as a triumphant exit, and continues, rather as Melmoth does, in a postmortal narration that promises (threatens!) never to end. But the novel's antagonist, the trial-giver and tempter Lovelace, does not accept it; instead he sets out to claim her dead heart, still speaking its suffering, as though he could still wring from it that acknowledgment of himself that would keep them both immortal. In "The Tale of the Spaniard," Maturin, like Diderot, reworks this material into a convent captivity, transposing the tempter's passion-pursuit for the reluctant cleric into the masculine, homoerotic register.

In "The Tale of the Indian" he returns to the structure of *Clarissa,* allowing the heroine this time *both* roles, displaying in the (hetero)sexual register the woman's flight but also the woman's enigmatic refusal to stop pursuing the heart's (Melmoth's heart, her idea of Melmoth's heart, her own heart's) extremity.

Mario Praz was the first to document fully the "plagiarisms" from Diderot's convent captivity tale in Maturin's "The Tale of the Spaniard," where Alonzo de Monçada is forced into monastic life to "buy" his parents indemnity from the illegitimacy that was their sexual sin.[9] Like his female counterpart in *Memoirs of a Nun,* Monçada suffered the mind-numbing monotony of the vocationless and workless conventual life, the spite lurking behind the theatrical competition in the performance of religious duties, the licensed same-sex overtures from the next "cell," the scene where freedom would mean trampling one's mother's body—all transposed from the bourgeois setting of Jansenist France to the convent of "ex-Jesuits" still impudently functioning in eighteenth-century Madrid despite the suppression of the order in 1767. But the most significant aspects of the tale are Maturin's own: the blasphemous playing at demonic possession and sacred miracle, the hinting at obscene Marian rites, the exquisitely appropriate entombment with the parricide monk who feasts on the cannibal moments of the human family in extremis—above all, the wrestling with an ethic of suffering and theology of atonement that a Christian can neither manage nor leave alone.

The theology is delivered early and insistently, in earnest debates between Monçada and other clerics, and both upholds and radically qualifies the standard accounts that legitimize human suffering with divine sanction. There was indeed *"one great Sacrifice"* (147) between the Father and the Son, but it remains, and should remain, Monçada argues, incommunicable and unduplicatable. Whatever its nature, the Sacrifice must be regarded as a deeply ambiguous index to the proper ethical relationship between human and human, or human and divine, and it certainly gives no warrant to any person or institution to deal in sacrifice, or to buy, or buy off, suffering, or to essay in one's inconceivable ignorance to move the levers of justice.

Faith, we come to understand, actually lives in the utter darkness of the meaning-without-words of that Sacrifice which figures the gap between the Power and the Human. But Faith maintains that great Sacrifice was One—we can't repeat it or take anything from it or give anything to it. We can't restage it in the body of the putatively erring or damned Other; we can only marvel at the damnable pleasure we take in his or her pain. We can't even restage it in our own body, where we experience the pain of our pleasures.

Faith, and theology as well, rather holds the mystery of the one great Sacrifice apart, if only by a hair's breadth, from the mystery of the human body's mysterious cleaving to its own suffering as the vessel of its consciousness. Burke revived the Greek conception that suffering produces wisdom in the bodily registering of pain and terror as "the strongest sensation." Theologian Albert W. J. Harper comments this way on the complex dynamic of suffering and consciousness: "Conscious suffering suffers from at least a twofold conflict: the mind is desirous of bringing its suffering to an end and conquering it by coming upon a reason for its suffering, but the pride of consciousness also wants to make the most of the conscious state it feels it possesses in what has been described as the 'loquaciousness' of suffering."[10] Consciousness teeters between the desired "loquaciousness" of suffering and that "shattering" of language and identity which Elaine Scarry has noted is the true goal of the torturer, despite his putative quest for the words that would answer his questions.[11]

"You will be surprised to hear these sentiments from a Catholic," the Spaniard Monçada tells the Anglo-Irish Melmoth—Maturin here simultaneously reiterating the Reformers' claim that the whole mediating edifice of "theology" itself is a "Catholic" barrier to the true communication between God and man, while demonstrating that the communication does occur, in spite of theology. A similar intention governs his characterization of the man who guides Monçada out of his persecuting convent, and into the hands of the Inquisition. The "parricide monk" is an "amateur" of spectacles of suffering (207). By taking a hand in Monçada's life, planning a rescue by Monçada's brother which will actually bring Alonzo to cause Juan's death, the monk is restaging in the daylight the kin-murder that he insists made him the impenetrable and aridly skeptical "man" he is, trying to exorcise in this substitutional manner the memory of the patricide that visits him nightly.

The parricide monk is doing this in cynical, and reverse, homage to the "theology" that makes promiscuously available to the "pride of consciousness," and blasphemously "substitutional" (224) for both pride and politics, the dynamic of the *one great Sacrifice.* The consequence, for the monk, is grimly logical: having adopted "the best theology" (225), that is, the substitute of every other suffering body for his own in a version of the Hobbesian war of each against all, he ventures out of the audience one day into the spectacle, a procession of high ecclesiastics, where his crime makes him the natural substitute for a superstitious crowd looking for a scapegoat for its own suffering, and his body is torn apart by them all until his loquaciousness shatters in formless cries and disappears.

Alonzo de Monçada is a careful religious thinker; the parricide monk is a keen theologian. But the subtlest theologian of them all is of course Melmoth the Traveler. In his brief appearance in "The Tale of the Spaniard," as a member and secret manipulator of the Inquisition, he makes only one contribution to the novel's theology of suffering, but it is a key one: "There is no error more absurd, and yet more rooted in the heart of man, than the belief that his suffering will promote his spiritual safety" (233). At first glance we would not be surprised to hear the person rumored to be the devil's agent begin his argument this way: detach man from this root, and "suffering" becomes merely a commodity, available for substitution, circulation, or, in the words of the devil's bargain, "exchange." Yet Melmoth's real role in the scheme of the things, as with every literary evocation of the devil, "the spirit that always wills the bad but always works the good," is to expose to scorn that very calculus of "spiritual safety"—without, however, uprooting the intimacy of the human heart and its suffering, the virtual equation of consciousness, wisdom, and suffering. Monçada may flee the Inquisition, as he swam from the wrecked ship to the coast of Ireland, by the instinctive strength of his body rather than from virtue, but he does not seek safety of any kind, nor does he seek, dangerously, to know the end (the fullness, or the goal) of the strength of his body.

This, we may speculate, was Melmoth's own original sin. The men to whom he offers "exchange of destinies" have refused the exchange but they cannot forget what they have glimpsed in him, the loquacity of *his* suffering. Each of them at some level still covets this loquacity, as they pursue him, the supremely narratable being. Stanton and Monçada remain alive after their meeting with Melmoth because they and their object *hold* one another in written and spoken narrative, narratives that always reach a space of blotted ink, unreadable words, lost pages, which testify to the incommunicable.

What is this but a classic metaphor for theology itself, a tense and paradoxical picturing of the science of the nature of God's Creation, where both poles of the current, both the Power and the human condition, are gendered male. The paradigm that grounds this one, however, the paradigm for strength of body spun into personal consciousness, is surely birth: the paradigm is sexuality, classically gendered as "woman." Melmoth's own hyperloquacious consciousness, we discover, can be exposed, and perhaps even redeemed, only in a narrative that admits (relocates him in) its origin in his body, a narrative whose agent is a woman.

The woman was born Isadora to a Spanish merchant family but was shipwrecked onto a prelapsarian Isle near India as a toddler, and worshipped as the goddess Immalee by native visitants to the Isle. She is a different story altogether for Melmoth the Traveler. The men he visits are targets because they are ripe with suffering; they are his duty, for he is, he says, assigned to conduct them to the logic of the last choice—the death

of consciousness or the hyperconsciousness of the damned. But Immalee, her consciousness diffused throughout the natural streams and fruits and lights and leaves which feed and clothe and stimulate her as she grows like a plant on the Isle, seems to be a personal choice, not an assignment. Maturin creates Melmoth as a devil's disciple, but the line between Master and Servant is more blurred in this fable than in any of the other tales. Insofar as he is Satan to her Eve he has in a manner broken from his "service" to his dark master; he has gone back to the springs of creation to be *himself* the one to pull apart the poles of Divine and Human and make the lightning crackle between them. More deeply, he has gone to her out of desire, not just to give her the bitter inheritance of separation, suffering, consciousness and the last choice, but also to give himself the same gift again, to reenter, through her innocent interlocutories and her infinitely alluring strength of bodily and spiritual endurance, that dynamic, round upon round, of pain and loquacious consciousness which is the condition of the human.

The first exchanges in the Isle are thus straight out of *Paradise Lost*. Melmoth's Satan engages Immalee's Eve in three quests—for knowledge not just of what is good but of what is; for "thought," which separates thinker from objects of thought, and, more dangerously, thought-objects of sense perception from thought-objects of imagination; and for language, the capacity to "talk thoughts" (287) and even "write thoughts" (318), which creates that artificial world which is most paradoxically the most human world. But their later exchanges on the Isle and in Madrid take "thought" in the direction of intersubjective (hetero)sexual passion. Looking upon the facts of natural and human life that Melmoth discloses, Immalee reasons, "To think, then, is to suffer" (288). But as she comes to recognize that lightning may strike from inside as well as outside, that the worm may fly in to devour the rosebud but the rose may also already be "sick" of a desire to fly from its stem, she learns to feel, and then to court, that "secret sentiment" (319) which the prudent would "banish" or "crush" (319), but the seeker or traveler would clasp and define herself by, Love.[12] The Love which thought forbids is the supreme teacher of suffering: the "mysterious terror which always trembles at the bottom of the hearts of those who dare to love" (321) stubbornly holds open the beating, bleeding muscle of the heart that thought would prudently close.

In all the exchanges between Melmoth and Immalee, whether on the Isle, or after she is rescued to resume the life of Isadora in Madrid, the woman, the human, grips this terror as her portion. And slowly, seeking as well as fighting the magnetic force of her terror/desire, Melmoth is drawn to re-experience human passion, human self-contradiction, human despair. He marshals against this force his weapons of "spoken thought" and perhaps even "written thought," blasting her alternately with fiery satire and icy disdain, but to no real avail. In the foreground of "The Tale of the Indian" we seem to read *her* story, as she moves through the "stages" of love (362-364), from active desire through the permanent paradox of absence or presence as "equally unsupportable," to that "profound and perilous absorption of the soul when it is determined to penetrate the mysteries" (365). In the background of this narrative, however, we follow the story of Melmoth's *own* increasing absorption: in the mystery of her insistent attachment; in the command which lies beneath her constant plaint, "will he be there?" (287, 323, 533); above all in the tell-tale and utterly material sound and sight and feel of the mighty muscle of her heart, beating "like a wave against a rock" (353), throbbing "almost visibly in the white and palpitating bosom" (365), moving eerily "in his hand . . . like a bird with a string tied round its leg" (376).

In the foreground, we focus on Melmoth's blasphemous challenge to Immalee to wed him, in spite of her family, in the teeth of reason, and in the dead of night—with Death as the celebrant (394) and a voyage to hell as their wedding trip (355). In the background, however, we see his return to her, after every failure or reversal, after his every attempt to wither her by abandonment. Struggling with compassion (285), with a Hamlet-like tendency to "blunted purpose" (288), tempted by the cool "breeze" of her purity (309), both relieved and horrified by his success in driving her through the stages of the passion of love, Melmoth comes back again and again, and finally gets what he ought not to want—not an "exchange" of destinies in the abstraction of eternity but a mortal and profoundly carnal union, a mutual absorption in desire which produces incontrovertible evidence of the material-theological. Melmoth's encounters with Monçada and young Melmoth generate stories: his encounter with Immalee generates a child. Beneath the trinity of theology, the trinity of (hetero)sexuality.

This infant is a curious and profound glitch in the story of Melmoth as scripted by the myth of the devil's bargain. Behind this parabola of self-extension we see Maturin invoke the trinitarian theology of divine incarnation/extension, along with its Miltonic shadow trinity of Satan, Sin, and Death. But its formal premise is emphatically human and embodied. With the birth of his child, Melmoth is back in the original human bargain for immortality, where the corporeal and spiritual self continues in a trajectory of (hetero)sexuality, family, race, even nation, while the core of personhood, figured in the beating heart, casts its desire, its motion, its meanings without words, into the secret of silence, toward the taciturn and invisible God. From that perspective, when Melmoth looks upon his daughter, he looks upon his end, and so does Maturin's own narrative.

As Maturin's nest of stories unfolds toward its end, the narrative scatters into illegibilities and into multiple genres—the dream, the vision, the melodramatic scene. And theologies grow less readable too. Immalee is imprisoned with her child by the Inquisition as a way of entrapping the devilish figure who is usurping its Power: "if there be human elements in him, if there be anything mortal clinging to his heart, we shall wind round the roots of it and extract it" (524). This might have made an interesting ending, but Maturin bypasses it: Melmoth visits Immalee and his child, and departs, still untrapped. On the night of his visit, the night before mother and infant were to be separated, the infant died, with a black mark around its throat. But whether the mark of mortality is code for the original incommunicable human condition, or from the murdering hand of Immalee's "maternal despair" (530), or from the hand of an enraged father snatching back the sign of his renewed bargain with his own humanity, the narrative will not say.

Immalee's heart "breaks" after the death of her infant, but as her bodily death approaches, that mighty muscle still beats its command to love. For though she has, like all of Melmoth's targets, refused to "exchange" her redeemable mortal immortality for his unregenerate preternatural immortality, she is hoping to meet more than her God in that secret silence. Though at one level she plunges into the grave to escape the pursuing Melmoth, she also seeks him, accepting her deathbed confessor's promise of heaven only on a condition, the human condition of love-desire: "'Paradise!' uttered Isadora, with her last breath, '*will he be there!*'" (533).

The orthodox theology of Maturin's intention, properly immaterial, provides a final sequence on the Irish coast in which Melmoth returns to the frame story, to his original home, stricken in age but still frozen in preternatural Gothic outlawry, dreaming, and then apparently experiencing, a fall into hell. But the command of Immalee, italicized as an exclamation, not a question, to constitute a Paradise with the bodily "thereness" of her lover-tutor, beats like a wave against the rock of his self-narrated picture of flaming damnation. *Either* picture is a plausible context for the final moment of the novel, where "an overwhelming mass of conviction . . . falls upon the mind . . . and crushes out the truth from the heart" (542). It is a truth that can be "exchanged" only in "looks of silent and unutterable horror" between the two men, Monçada and young Melmoth, who are heirs to the communicable properties of their now-dead families, and to the incommunicable condition, always already communicated, of the human.

Notes

1. Charles Maturin, *Melmoth the Wanderer,* ed. Douglas Grant (London, 1968) 237. Maturin's novel

directly quotes *Thalaba* and records its debt to the supernatural poetry of Byron and Coleridge in submerged language. The novel also refers directly to its Gothic inquisition-narrative forebear, Ann Radcliffe's *The Italian,* and has sly indirect fun with Matthew Gregory Lewis's *The Monk.*

2. *The Complete Poems and Plays, 1909-1950* (New York, 1971) 144.

3. Douglas Grant, the Oxford Edition's editor, tells us there that Scott tried to interest Lady Anne Jane Hatton, the Marchioness of Abercorn, in the financial plight of the Maturin family (543); Maturin hopefully dedicated the novel to her.

4. One of the best modern treatments of the novel takes Maturin's rather tendentious claim seriously, broadly arguing that the novel in both theme and structure is a reflection on the text of the book of Job: "Maturin has shivered the text of Job . . . and then challenged us to restore it." Kathleen Fowler, "Hieroglyphics in Fire: *Melmoth the Wanderer,*" *Studies in Romanticism* 25 (1986): 538.

5. As Carlo Testa points out, the pact-with-the-devil analysis of desire common before Goethe, which held that desire should and can be transferred from irregular object A to theologically sound point B, was being challenged by the time of Blake and Maturin: now the devil is a device for asking more broadly, "what is desire itself?" And all answers simply continue the problematization of the question. *Desire and the Devil: Demonic Contracts in French and European Literature* (New York, 1991) 15-16.

6. "Romantic Manichaeism: Shelley's 'On the Devil, and Devils' and Byron's Mythological Dramas," *The Sun Is God: Painting, Literature and Mythology in the Nineteenth Century,* ed. J. B. Bullen (Oxford, 1989). Butler's essay does not consider *Melmoth,* but traces the fascination of poets and political philosophers with Zoroastrianism, "the thinking radical's form of religion," whose stylized worship of the sun and fire reinforces the primacy of flux and contrariety in being (15).

7. See *The Rise of the Novel: Studies in DeFoe, Richardson and Fielding* (Berkeley [1957], 1967) 74-85. Michael McKeon has more recently complicated and challenged Watt's argument that a slowly secularizing English Protestantism generated in the eighteenth century a personal individualism fundamental both to the rise of the middle class and to the formal realism it preferred for its fiction: McKeon explores earlier genres of prose narrative, including the movement from medieval hagiography to Renaissance spiritual biography, to locate the origins of realism. *The Origins of the English Novel, 1600-1740* (Baltimore, 1987) 91-96.

8. *Gothic Bodies: The Politics of Pain in Romantic Fiction* (Philadelphia, 1994) 15, 114.

9. Praz retells this story in *The Romantic Agony* (London, 1933) 177. Roving learnedly and eclectically among English and Continental writing both canonical and non-canonical, Praz in this book made the first twentieth-century argument for the importance of *Melmoth;* see esp. chs. 2, "The Metamorphoses of Satan," and 3, "The Shadow of the Divine Marquis [De Sade]."

10. *The Theodicy of Suffering* (San Francisco, 1990) 39.

11. *The Body in Pain: The Making and Unmaking of the World* (New York, 1985), see Introduction, esp. 3-11. Scarry's moving and broadly influential study introduced this dynamic between pain's agency in making the suffering body express the face of its "aliveness" or "sentience," and pain's capacity (especially in the hands of political torturers) to shatter the linguistic and pre-linguistic "voice" which is the body's personal extension of itself toward being, ultimately toward the Divine Power. In her reading, the Old and New Testaments record the distribution of voice, with its inevitable quality of embodiedness, as the current that flows between the human and the Divine, providing a new theology where the moral distance between man and God remains, but "no longer depends on a discrepancy in embodiedness" (184).

12. Maturin brings Melmoth to Immalee as a virtual embodiment of Blake's lament in *Songs of Experience,* "O Rose, thou art sick, / The Invisible worm / That flies in the night / In the howling storm / Has found out thy bed / Of crimson joy, / And his dark secret love / does thy life destroy." On the Isle, Immalee has seen the worm destroy the flower, but argues to Melmoth that no horror attends this, for "the worm was not the native of the flower; its own leaves could never have hurt it." But he responds with an invitation to enter the human world of "forbidden passion," where the hurt is invisible, internal, self-generated, where one leaf on a stem may be poison to the next leaf (285-286).

Works Cited

Bruhm, Steven. *Gothic Bodies: The Politics of Pain in Romantic Fiction.* Philadelphia: University of Pennsylvania Press, 1994.

Butler, Marilyn. "Romantic Manichaeism: Shelley's 'On the Devil, and Devils' and Byron's Mythological Dramas." *The Sun Is God: Painting, Literature and Mythology in the Nineteenth Century.* Ed. J. B. Bullen. Oxford: Clarendon Press, 1989.

Eliot. T. S. "Little Gidding," *T. S. Eliot: The Complete Poems and Plays.* New York: Harcourt, Brace & World, 1971.

Fowler, Kathleen. "Hieroglyphics in Fire: *Melmoth the Wanderer.*" *Studies in Romanticism* 25 (1986): 521-539.

Harper, Albert W. J. *The Theodicy of Suffering.* San Francisco: Mellen Research University Press, 1990.

Maturin, Charles Robert. *Melmoth the Wanderer.* Ed. Douglas Grant. London: Oxford University Press, 1968.

McKeon, Michael. *The Origins of the English Novel, 1600-1740.* Baltimore: The Johns Hopkins University Press, 1987.

Praz, Mario. *The Romantic Agony.* London: Oxford University Press, 1933.

Scarry, Elaine. *The Body in Pain: The Making and Unmaking of the World.* New York: Oxford University Press, 1985.

Testa, Carlo. *Desire and the Devil: Demonic Contracts in French and European Literature.* New York: Peter Lang, 1991.

Watt, Ian. *The Rise of the Novel: Studies in DeFoe, Richardson and Fielding.* 1957. Berkeley: University of California Press, 1967.

FURTHER READING

Biographies

Idman, Niilo. *Charles Robert Maturin, His Life and Works.* London: Constable & Co., 1923, 326 p.

Offers a comprehensive overview of Maturin's literary career.

Kramer, Dale. *Charles Robert Maturin.* New York: Twayne Publishers, 1973, 166 p.

Provides a brief but insightful analysis of Maturin's life and career.

Criticism

Berns, Ute. "The Romantic Crisis of Expression: Laughter in Maturin's *Melmoth the Wanderer* and Beyond." In *A History of English Laughter: Laughter from Beowulf to Beckett and Beyond,* edited by Manfred Pfister, pp. 83-98. Amsterdam: Rodopi, 2002.

Examines the role of laughter in *Melmoth the Wanderer,* analyzing it within the framework of the Gothic and Romantic genres.

Dansky, Richard. "The Wanderer and the Scribbler: Maturin, Scott, and *Melmoth the Wanderer.*" *Studies in Weird Fiction* 21 (summer 1997): 2-10.

Examines *Melmoth the Wanderer* in relation to the fiction of Sir Walter Scott.

Ehlers, Leigh. "The 'Incommunicable Condition' of Melmoth." *Research Studies* 49, no. 3 (September 1981): 171-82.

Analyzes the Gothic aspects of *Melmoth the Wanderer.*

Haslam, Richard. "*Melmoth* (OW): Gothic Modes in *The Picture of Dorian Gray.*" *Irish Studies Review* 12, no. 3 (December 2004): 303-14.

Examines the influence of *Melmoth the Wanderer* on Oscar Wilde's *The Picture of Dorian Gray.*

Kosok, Heinz. "The Colonial Experience in the Works of Charles Robert Maturin." *Anglia* 117, no. 3 (1999): 353-67.

Discusses Maturin's treatment of British colonialism in his novels and plays.

Kullmann, Thomas. "Nature and Psychology in *Melmoth the Wanderer* and *Wuthering Heights.*" In *Exhibited by Candlelight: Sources and Developments in the Gothic Tradition,* edited by Valeria Tinkler Villani, Peter Davidson, and Jane Stevenson, pp. 99-106. Amsterdam: Rodopi, 1995.

Compares the Gothic elements in *Melmoth the Wanderer* and Emily Brontë's *Wuthering Heights,* paying particular attention to their depictions of nature and the human psyche.

Lanone, Catherine. "Verging on the Gothic: Melmoth's Journey to France." In *European Gothic: A Spirited Exchange, 1760-1960,* edited by Avril Horner, pp. 71-83. Manchester: Manchester University Press, 2002.

Examines the influence of *Melmoth the Wanderer* on the works of Honoré de Balzac and Charles Baudelaire.

Lougy, Robert E. *Charles Robert Maturin.* Lewisburg, Penn.: Bucknell University Press, 1975, 89 p.

Offers a brief critical survey of Maturin's work.

Miller, Robin Feuer. "The Metaphysical Novel and the Evocation of Anxiety: *Melmoth the Wanderer* and *The Brothers Karamazov,* a Case Study; In Honor of Rufus Mathewson, 1918-1978." In *Russianness: Studies on a Nation's Identity,* edited by Robert L. Belknap, pp. 94-112. Ann Arbor, Mich.: Ardis, 1990.

Examines themes of good and evil in *Melmoth the Wanderer* and Fyodor Dostoevsky's *The Brothers Karamazov.*

Monroe, Judson Taylor. *Tragedy in the Novels of the Reverend Charles Robert Maturin.* New York: Arno Press, 1972, 217 p.

>   Examines elements of tragedy and Gothic horror in Maturin's fiction.

Moynahan, Julian. "The Politics of Anglo-Irish Gothic: Maturin, Le Fanu and 'The Return of the Repressed.'" In *Studies in Anglo-Irish Literature,* edited by Heinz Kosok, pp. 43-53. Bonn: Bouvier, 1982.

>   Compares Gothic motifs in the writings of Maturin and Joseph Sheridan Le Fanu.

Nikolopoulou, Anastasia. "Medievalism and Historicity in the English Gothic Melodrama: Maturin's *Bertram; or the Castle of St. Aldobrand.*" *Poetica* 39-40 (1994): 139-53.

>   Examines aspects of melodrama and medieval history in *Bertram.*

Oost, Regina B. "'Servility and Command': Authorship in *Melmoth the Wanderer.*" *Papers on Language and Literature* 31, no. 3 (summer 1995): 291-312.

>   Examines Maturin's use of multiple storytellers in *Melmoth the Wanderer.*

Scholten, Willem. *Charles Robert Maturin: The Terror Novelist.* Amsterdam: H. J. Paris, 1933, 197 p.

>   Explores aspects of Gothic horror in Maturin's oeuvre.

Smith, Amy Elizabeth. "Experimentation and 'Horrid Curiosity' in Maturin's *Melmoth the Wanderer.*" *English Studies* 74, no. 6 (December 1993): 524-35.

>   Analyzes the influence of Denis Diderot's *La Religieuse* on *Melmoth the Wanderer.*

Tilby, Michael. "From Gothic Terror to Romantic Spleen: A Further Source for Baudelaire's 'L'Horloge'?" *Studi Francesi* 47, no. 3 (September-December 2003): 631-36.

>   Examines the impact of *Melmoth the Wanderer* on Charles Baudelaire's poem "L'Horloge."

Additional coverage of Maturin's life and career is contained in the following sources published by Thomson Gale: *British Writers Supplement,* **Vol. 8;** *Dictionary of Literary Biography,* **Vol. 178;** *Gothic Literature: A Gale Critical Companion,* **Ed. 3;** *Literary Movements for Students,* **Vol. 1;** *Literature Resource Center;* *Nineteenth-Century Literature Criticism,* **Vol. 6;** *Reference Guide to English Literature,* **Ed. 2;** *St. James Guide to Horror, Ghost & Gothic Writers;* **and** *Supernatural Fiction Writers.*

Elizabeth Palmer Peabody
1804-1894

American prose writer and editor.

INTRODUCTION

Peabody was a groundbreaking American educator, philosopher, author, linguist, and scholar. She played a central role in the vital cultural and political debates of her era and was a friend and peer of such notable nineteenth-century American writers and thinkers as Ralph Waldo Emerson, Nathaniel Hawthorne, Theodore Parker, William Ellery Channing, and Margaret Fuller. Her greatest passion lay in educational reform. A pioneer of early childhood education, Peabody established the first English-speaking kindergarten in the United States, founded on the educational principles of German educator Friedrich Froebel. She devoted her entire career to the principle of developing the innate spirituality and individual talents of children. Peabody published a number of important books, essays, book reviews, and history texts over the course of her career. Her influential works on education include the book *Record of a School* (1835) and her contributions to a monthly periodical she founded and edited, *Kindergarten Messenger,* which appeared from 1873-77. Her *Reminiscences of Rev. Wm. Ellery Channing, D.D.* (1880) and *Last Evening with Allston, and Other Papers* (1886) still stand as important records of the intellectual life of nineteenth-century America. Peabody served as editor of such Transcendental journals as the *Dial* and *Aesthetic Papers,* and she was probably also the first woman publisher in the United States. A passionate reformer throughout her life, Peabody was involved at various periods in abolitionism, the struggle for Native American rights, and the woman suffrage movement.

BIOGRAPHICAL INFORMATION

Born in Billerica, Massachusetts, on May 16, 1804, Peabody was raised in Salem, the eldest of seven children. Her father, Nathaniel Peabody, was a former instructor at Phillips Academy in Andover, and he instilled in Elizabeth a life-long passion for scholarship, teaching her Latin when she was still a young girl. Peabody's mother, Elizabeth (Palmer) Peabody, arguably exerted a more powerful influence over the young girl's education, introducing her to seminal works in the fields of philosophy, history, and literature. Educated by pri-

vate tutors, Peabody eventually mastered ten languages, and by her late teens she had obtained her first teaching position. Over the next several years she taught in Salem, worked as a private tutor in Maine, and founded her own school in Brookline, Massachusetts. While in Brookline she taught the daughter of renowned Unitarian minister William Ellery Channing, with whom she soon developed a friendship based on long discussions of philosophy and literature. Peabody's first book, *First Lessons in Grammar on the Plan of Pestalozzi, By a Teacher in Boston* (1830), was published anonymously.

After the closure of her school in 1832, Peabody struggled to earn a living, relying on private tutoring and textbook writing for her income. Her fortunes changed in 1834, when Amos Bronson Alcott invited her to help form the Temple School, an experimental learning institution based on Platonic principles. Peabody's account of her experiences with Alcott, *Record of a School,* came out in 1835, and Alcott's own chronicle, *Conversations with Children on the Gospels* followed in 1836-37. While both works established Alcott as one of the most original thinkers in New England intellectual circles, their candid discussions of religion and sexuality also stirred up controversy. Peabody herself felt uncomfortable with Alcott's forthrightness on certain issues, but she remained loyal to his educational style, and in 1837 she published "Mr. Alcott's Book and School," an article defending his methods. Through Alcott, Peabody also made the acquaintance of other Transcendentalist thinkers. She became a founding member of the Transcendentalist Club in 1837.

Peabody's association with Alcott proved damaging to her own career prospects, however, and after declining enrollment forced the closure of the Temple School, she lived in Salem with her family for several years, unable to secure employment. In 1840 Peabody opened a bookstore in Boston, which quickly became a meeting place for New England intellectuals. Peabody soon began to publish a range of political and intellectual writings, including abolitionist essays and reformist tracts, as well as children's books and the lone issue of the Transcendentalist journal *Aesthetic Papers,* which included Henry David Thoreau's controversial essay "Civil Disobedience." As Peabody's philosophical ideas evolved, she came to believe that the only means by which society could realize the ideals of Plato and Christ was through the education of its children. She developed these ideas more fully in a pair of important essays, "Plan of the West Roxbury Community" and "A Glimpse of Christ's Idea of Society," both of which appeared in the journal *Dial* in 1841.

After closing her bookstore in 1850, Peabody spent ten years teaching, working for the abolitionist cause, and writing and lecturing on the subject of education. In 1860 she opened the first English-speaking kindergarten in the United States. Three years later she coauthored *Moral Culture of Infancy, and Kindergarten Guide, with Music for the Plays* (1863) with her sister, Mary Peabody Mann. (Biographies of Peabody frequently include substantial discussion of her sisters Mary Peabody Mann, an author married to educator Horace Mann; and Sophia Peabody Hawthorne, an artist married to Nathaniel Hawthorne.) Peabody worked to refine her teaching methods over the next decade, visiting Europe in 1867 to observe the kindergarten system firsthand. In 1873 Peabody founded the *Kindergarten Messenger,* a teaching journal. During these years she continued to publish essays on literature and other subjects in such magazines as the *Atlantic Monthly* and *Harper's.*

In the 1880s Peabody returned to Concord, where she joined the teaching staff at Alcott's School of Philosophy. She continued to travel and lecture throughout the decade, and in her late eighties she became involved in the cause of Piute Indian Leader Sarah Winnemucca, assisting her in her efforts to establish proper schools on her Nevada reservation. Peabody died in Jamaica Plain, now part of Boston, on January 3, 1894.

MAJOR WORKS

Peabody remains best known for her writings on the subject of education. Her first major work, *Record of a School,* chronicles the pedagogical experiments of Amos Bronson Alcott during the brief life span of his Temple School in Boston. The work is derived from Peabody's detailed notes on Alcott's classroom discussions with his students and offers insight into the application of Transcendentalist ideas in the teaching of young children. Peabody's records from this period also formed the basis for Alcott's *Conversations with Children on the Gospels.*

Peabody also wrote a number of shorter prose works of lasting merit. In 1841 she published two influential essays in the *Dial,* "Plan of the West Roxbury Community" and "A Glimpse of Christ's Idea of Society," in which she expressed her conviction that the key to establishing a truly moral society lay in early childhood education. In these writings Peabody described her vision of an ideal society based on Christian principles, in which virtues such as cooperation and social equality took precedence over capitalist principles of competition. She also published an important review of Nathaniel Hawthorne's *Twice-Told Tales* in *The New Yorker* in 1838, in which she described the influence of Wordsworthian Romanticism on American writers of her era.

Late in her career Peabody published a number of seminal works on kindergarten education which include outlines of her guiding principles, analyses of childhood language development, and teaching exercises. *Guide to the Kindergarten and Intermediate Class and Moral Culture of Infancy, with Songs and Music* (1877), a revised version of *Moral Culture of Infancy, and Kindergarten Guide, with Music for the Plays,* is considered one of the most important American contributions made to the literature of this subject. Peabody's *Reminiscences of Rev. Wm. Ellery Channing, D.D.* provides a glimpse into the intellect of the Unitarian minister, both through his letters and through Peabody's own valuable commentary. The voluminous *Letters of Elizabeth Palmer Peabody, American Renaissance Woman,* published in 1984, provides a complex portrayal of her intellectual development, her numerous personal relationships with other Transcendentalist thinkers, and the refinement of her educational philosophy.

CRITICAL RECEPTION

Most critics agree that Peabody is one of the most important figures of American Transcendentalism, although in her lifetime her significance remained partially obscured by the fame of her peers. One of the first thorough assessments of her career appeared in 1902, when George Willis Cooke's essay "Elizabeth Palmer Peabody" was published in *An Historical and Biographical Introduction to Accompany* The Dial. In the 1940s and 1950s, writers began to examine Peabody's position in the development of Transcendental philosophy and practices. Josephine Roberts was among the first to recognize Peabody's role in the establishment of Alcott's Temple School, while John Wilson explored Peabody's efforts to integrate Transcendentalist ideas with methods of early childhood education. Scholars like Bruce Ronda began to evaluate the evolution of Peabody's teaching philosophy in greater detail in the 1970s, paying particular attention to her thoughts concerning childhood morality and creativity. Other scholars, notably Philip Gura and James Perrin Warren, have analyzed Peabody's theories of linguistics, while Arlin Turner, Scott Harshbarger, and John L. Idol, Jr. have investigated the importance of her writings on Hawthorne. Ronda also edited *Letters of Elizabeth Palmer Peabody, American Renaissance Woman*, an important addition to Peabody's body of work. A number of valuable biographies of Peabody have also appeared since the mid-twentieth century, including Louisa Hall Tharp's *The Peabody Sisters of Salem*, published in 1950; Gladys Brooks's *Three Wise Virgins*, which appeared in 1957; and Megan Marshall's *The Peabody Sisters*, published in 2005.

PRINCIPAL WORKS

First Lessons in Grammar on the Plan of Pestalozzi, by a Teacher in Boston [anonymous] (prose) 1830

Self-Education; or, The Means and Art of Moral Progress [anonymous translator; from *Du perfectionnement morale, ou de l'éducation de soi-même*, by Joseph Marie de Gérando] (prose) 1830

First Steps to the Study of History, Being Part First of a Key to History (prose) 1832

Visitor of the Poor [anonymous translator; from *Le visiteur du pauvre*, by Joseph Marie de Gérando] (prose) 1832

Key to History, Part II: The Hebrews (prose) 1833

Key to History, Part III: The Greeks (prose) 1833

Record of a School: Exemplifying the General Principles of Spiritual Culture [anonymous] (prose) 1835; revised edition, 1836; revised as *Record of Mr. Alcott's School, Exemplifying the Principles and Methods of Moral Culture,* 1874

Theory of Teaching, with a Few Practical Illustrations, by a Teacher (letters) 1841

The True Messiah; or, The Old and New Testaments, Examined According to the Principles of the Language of Nature [anonymous translator; from *Le vrai messie,* by Guillaume Caspar Lencroy Oegger] (prose) 1842

*Significance of the Alphabet [editor] (prose) 1846

First Nursery Reading Book, Intended to Teach the Alphabet, by Means of English Words, Whose Analysis Shall Give the True Sounds That Were Originally, and Even Now Are Generally, Attached to the Characters in All Languages (prose) 1849

Crimes of the House of Austria against Mankind. Collected from Accredited History [editor] (prose) 1850; also published as *Crimes of the House of Austria against Mankind. Proved by Extracts from the Histories of Coxe, Schiller, Robertson, Grattan, and Sismondi, with Mrs. M. L. Putnam's History of the Constitution of Hungary, and Its Relations with Austria,* 1852

The Polish-American System of Chronology, Reproduced with Some Modifications, from General Bem's Franco-Polish Method (prose) 1850

Chronological History of the United States Arranged with Plates on Bem's Principle (prose) 1856

Report and New Prospectus of Kindergarten (prose) 1862

Moral Culture of Infancy, and Kindergarten Guide, with Music for the Plays [with Mrs. Horace Mann] (prose) 1863; revised edition, 1869; revised as *Guide to the Kindergarten and Intermediate Class and Moral Culture of Infancy, with Songs and Music,* 1877

†The Identification of the Artisan and Artist: The Proper Object of American Education. Illustrated by a Lecture of Cardinal Wiseman on the Relation of the Arts of Design with the Arts of Production. Addressed to American Workingmen and Educators, with an Essay on Froebel's Reform of Primary Education, by Elizabeth P. Peabody (prose) 1869

Lectures on the Nursery and Kindergarten, no. 1: The Education of the Kindergartner (prose) 1874

Lectures on the Nursery and Kindergarten, no. 2: The Nursery (prose) 1875

After Kindergarten—What?: A Primer of Reading and Writing for the Intermediate Class and Primary Schools Generally [with Mary Mann] (prose) 1878

Reminiscences of Rev. Wm. Ellery Channing, D.D. (prose) 1880

Last Evening with Allston, and Other Papers (prose) 1886

Lectures in the Training Schools for Kindergartners (prose) 1886; also published as *Education in the Home, the Kindergarten, and the Primary School* 1887

Letters to Kindergartners (prose) 1886

Letters of Elizabeth Palmer Peabody, American Renaissance Woman (letters) 1984

*This book, by Charles Kraitsir, was ghostwritten by Peabody.

†This pamphlet consists of Peabody's essay "A Plea for Froebel's Kindergarten as the First Grade of Primary Education," and an 1852 lecture by Cardinal Nicholas Wiseman.

CRITICISM

William Ellery Channing (letter date 11 March 1831)

SOURCE: Channing, William Ellery. Letter from *Reminiscences of Rev. Wm. Ellery Channing, D.D.*, by Elizabeth Palmer Peabody, pp. 321-23. Boston: Roberts Brothers, 1880.

[*In the following excerpt from a letter to Peabody, written March 11, 1831, Channing encourages her to express her views honestly and without restraint, while at the same time cautioning her against adopting an overly pessimistic view of society.*]

St. Croix, March 11, 1831.

My Dear Miss Peabody,—I have just received your letter of February 1. I thank you for it. Painful as the disclosures are, I wish to receive them. I fear, however, for you. I fear that your mind is acting too exclusively and intensely on a few subjects. I trust, too, that your deep impressions of the guilt of a part of our community are to be ascribed, in a measure, to your position, your recent solitude, and your recent disappointments in what you thought tried virtue.

My own inquiries have led me to somewhat different results. That as deep depravity exists now as in the worst times I doubt not; but that there is a deeper and wider action of pure and noble principles I also incline to believe; and I suspect that vice will never run to greater excess than when it is an exception, or when it resists and triumphs over the prevalent sentiment of the community on the side of virtue. Still there is a terrible strength of moral evil in the world, and this I would see and feel as I have not yet felt. Only let me not despair; let me never forget that the Infinite Power is on the side of truth and holiness; that there is an infinite fountain of moral energy and disinterested love. I would feel that what we call the deepest vice is yet superficial compared with the principle of virtue and spiritual growth within us. I care not how faithfully and terribly human passions and crimes are portrayed to me; I want no deception,—I can bear the worst. But I desire to hear no language of despondency, not a moment's doubt of the triumph of virtue.

One of the great ends of peculiar guilt is to call forth peculiar virtue. You have seen this in your suffering friends. I wish it might be seen still more in the increased energy with which we, who are horror-struck by crime, strive to subdue it even in its victims as well as to prevent its spread. Let us, however, fulfil this part of our duty calmly, and feel that we are resisting vice, not only by acts of direct opposition, but still more, perhaps, by a consistent, steady testimony to virtue in our common life. Who ever knew the depth of human crime like Jesus? But *within* him was a power of goodness which he felt was to prevail over evil; and the existence of that power in any degree in ourselves is a pledge and prediction of the same result. Do not let me hear of your "nature fainting," etc. Tell me, however, your real feelings; this I do not mean to interdict. You can hardly gratify or serve me more than by setting before me society just as it is, and nothing which I write must check the freedom of your communications.

I am glad you are writing, not merely because this will keep you out of harm, or give an innocent direction to your mind, but because you have thoughts worthy to be communicated; and because your own mind will work itself into clearer views by the effort of communication. You want, however, a counsellor and friend. You are apt to prejudice the truth by placing it in unhappy connections. For example, in your remarks on the first chapters of Genesis you threw a doubtfulness over some great truths by supposing them to be taught, or veiled, in the narrative which has nothing to do with them. I saw then one of your intellectual dangers. You are led astray by slight connections and analogies, and are apt to see in past or present facts what other eyes cannot discover. I have thought, too, that your interpretations of life are not always to be trusted, and that you are in danger of substituting your own structures for reality. I would not trouble you with these remarks, did I not think that you have still a gifted eye, which looks far into the hidden wisdom of God.

Elizabeth Palmer Peabody (letter date 7 August 1836)

SOURCE: Peabody, Elizabeth Palmer. Letter from *Letters of Elizabeth Palmer Peabody: American Renaissance Woman*, edited by Bruce A. Ronda, pp. 180-81. Middletown, Conn.: Wesleyan University Press, 1984.

[*In the following letter to Amos Bronson Alcott, written August 7, 1836, Peabody expresses reservations concerning the publication of Alcott's* Conversations with Children on the Gospels. *The letter reveals the contrast between Alcott's radical pedagogical theories and Peabody's more rigorous, and traditional, approach to early education.*]

August 7th 1836

Dear Sir:

The very day after my letter to you I received a communication from a friend; by which I learn that much more extensive than either you or I were aware of is the discussion of such subjects as it is known were discussed in connection with the birth of Christ censured even by friends of your system and of yourself, and that something of an impression was gratuitously taken up that I left the School on that account—an impression for which I can in no ways account, except it was thought I ought to leave it. For I have been *very wary* what I said about it—generally leading off from the subject when it was mentioned, but turning attention upon your purity of association being so much like that of children. For I always wanted the plan to succeed in this particular of it especially, so sure I am that it is impossible to keep children ignorant and that it is better to lead their imaginations than to leave them to be directed by idle curiosity. And yet I do not think I should ever have ventured so far myself. And a great many questions I thought were quite superfluous, and what was to be gained by them was not worth the risk of having them repeated and misunderstood abroad. A great deal is repeated, I find, and many persons, liking the school in every other respect, think it is decisive against putting female children to it especially.

I have told you this in the spirit of friendship, and hope you will not despise it. I am conscious of the effect of a few week's freedom from the excitement of being a part of the School, or taking down that exaggerated feeling which made every detail of it seem so very important to the great course of Spiritual Culture; and I never was under half the illusion in this respect that you were.

But with respect to the Record: whatever may be said of the wisdom of pursuing your plan as you have hitherto done in the schoolroom, where you always command the spirits of those around you (only subject to the risk of having your mere words repeated or misinterpreted) I feel more and more that these questionable parts ought not to go into the printed book, at least that they must be entirely disconnected with *me*.

In the first place, in all these conversations where I have spoken, I should like to have that part of the conversation omitted, so that it may be felt that I was entirely passive. And I would go a little farther: there is a remark of Josiah Quincy's about the formation of the body out of "*the naughtiness of other people*" which is very remarkable. Please to correct that in my record. But if you wish to retain it, you can add a note in the margin saying: "the Recorder omitted Josiah's answer in this place, which was & c. & c."—putting Josiah's answer in your note.

There are many places where this might be done, and thus the whole responsibility rest upon you. I should like, too, to have the remarks I made on the Circumcision omitted. I do not wish to appear as an interlocutor in that conversation either. Besides this, I must desire you to put a preface of your own before mine, and express in it, in so many words, that on you rests all the responsibility of introducing the subjects, and that your Recorder did not entirely sympathize or agree with you with respect to the course taken, adding (for I have not the slightest objection), that this disagreement or want of sympathy often prevented your views from being done full justice to, as she herself freely acknowledges. In this matter yourself also is concerned.

Why did prophets and apostles veil this subject in fables and emblems if there was not a reason for avoiding physiological inquiries & c? This is worth thinking of. However, you as a man can say anything; but I am a woman, and have feelings that I dare not distrust, however little I can *understand them* or give an account of them.

Yours, etc.
E. P. Peabody

William Ellery Channing (letter date December 1836)

SOURCE: Channing, William Ellery. Letter from *Reminiscences of Rev. Wm. Ellery Channing, D.D.,* by Elizabeth Palmer Peabody, pp. 386-89. Boston: Roberts Brothers, 1880.

[*In the following excerpt from a letter to Peabody, written December 1836, Channing compares Peabody's worldview to his own. Channing argues that Peabody's emotional responses to events fail to recognize the inherent goodness in life and that her tendency to see suffering in the world derives from a fundamental misunderstanding of God's will.*]

Boston, December, 1836.

My Dear Miss Peabody,—I almost reproach myself for not having written you immediately on receiving your last; and nothing would have prevented it if I could have hoped that a word of mine would do you good. But I was suffering from an indisposition which took from me my usual energy; and a work of some importance weighed on my mind and impelled me to efforts in another direction, which however have resulted in little.

I did not feel that I misunderstood you; but, as far as I could comprehend your case, I believed that relief must come chiefly from *within,* not from without. I know what sickness of heart is; but not such as yours; for I have less tenderness of nature, and have leaned less on those around me; have lived perhaps too much in *thought,* too little in the *affections.* I am not then the person to speak best to your suffering nature; I have not felt and conquered all your trials. Still, we have all one heart, and all have a key to others' anguish, and may sometimes soothe by a tone of sympathy, where we can do little good by a word of wisdom.

In reading your letter, I felt immediately that we viewed life from very different positions. Your remarks about the Sullivan family show how exclusively you look on things with the eyes of affection. I see no perplexity where you see "desolation,"—that terrible word, to me perhaps the most ominous in the vocabulary of woe! To me, such people are the very people to die. That such a family has *lived* makes me thankful to God; for I see in them the glory and immortal destiny of human nature: they throw their own light over their race. And I rejoice too in their death; for how natural is it that the heavenly should ascend to the heavenly, and what a link do such form between the present and the future worlds! As to the surviving relatives, they suffer deeply; but what a mysterious union is there of hope and joy with the deepest sufferings of truly virtuous friendship! Unhappily friendship is seldom virtuous enough. It seldom clings to the divine in its objects as it should do. It clings more to the personal, outward, temporary; and it is fit that such friendship should be purified by suffering. Among the chief goods which God gives us is the living image within us of a virtuous friend translated to a better world. I can never cease to thank God for having known such a friend, and for having the treasure of his spiritual presence in my memory. You seem to be impressed with nothing in life more than with the tortures of wounded affection, and speak of tenderness of heart as "punished." The fault in such cases is in the affections. They are, to use your own language, "*passions* which form no part of God's nature." The true affection is that which rests primarily on the *divine,* the universal, the disinterested, the unbounded, in our fellow-creatures. The affections of nature are low, until enlightened and sanctified by some glimpse of the Godlike and the eternal in their objects. It is this infusion of the moral principle into all our affections which makes them worthy of us; and we find in it a healing, strengthening, sustaining power in severest suffering. In most people, the balance is on the side of the *feeling,* not of the heavenly principle. Hence so much suffering! Hence it is good that friends are taken. This dispensation brings out to us the spiritual in them, and purifies our love for them, and blends with it an all-conquering faith. Such affection is the perfection of beauty; and accordingly I believe that suffering, instead of extinguishing the beauty of the soul, lends it new grace. The beauty which has most touched my heart in life has not been that which has shone out radiantly in youth and prosperity, but that which has revealed itself unconsciously, with a mild, dewy light, in sore trial.

These remarks are enough to show our different modes of vision. . . .

You think that life *may* be determined by "something in the Divine mind, of which there is no germ or signature in the human breast." I am accustomed to believe that God has revealed to us, in the *moral* nature, the ultimate, the end, the supreme good, the great interpretation of the universe. It seems to me one of the intuitions of the moral nature that there is nothing *greater* than rectitude, disinterestedness, pure love, truth, and wisdom. If there be, it must be harmonious with these. I believe, however, that we know the best from the beginning, and this it is which constitutes the unity of our eternal being. With this conviction, I have no fear that my affections are to become instruments of torture.

Amos Bronson Alcott (journal date 24 December 1865)

SOURCE: Alcott, Amos Bronson. Journal entry from *The Journals of Bronson Alcott,* edited by Odell Shepard, p. 376. Boston: Little, Brown and Company, 1938.

[*In the following journal entry, written December 24, 1865, Alcott describes his affection for his long-time friend and colleague.*]

December 24

E. P. Peabody spends the day with me. Still the same sympathetic, serviceable, and knowing woman whom I have met from the first. The good purposes that she has furthered and brought to consummation during the last thirty years, who shall find out and properly celebrate? I think her one of the most generous souls that I have known, and a part of the life of New England.

Amos Bronson Alcott (letter date 24 May 1874)

SOURCE: Alcott, Amos Bronson. Letter from *The Letters of A. Bronson Alcott,* edited by Richard L. Herrnstadt, p. 638. Ames: Iowa State University Press, 1969.

[*In the following letter to Peabody, written May 24, 1874, Alcott praises her work in Kindergarten education.*]

Concord May 24th 1874.

Dear Miss Peabody,

I had a kind note from Misses Garland and Weston, as from yourself, inviting me to attend the closing exercises of their Kindergarten Class, last Thursday. The rainstorm prevented my going to Boston as I intended on that day. Nor did I see Mr. Emerson or Ellen, and Louisa is staying in Boston.

But you are sure of showing intelligent people in all ranks and relations of life, the fitness and beauty of Froebel's plans for educating the little ones into the pleasurable use of their hearts, hands and heads—combining play with instruction.

If patience and persistency are to have their perfect rewards surely that satisfaction shall be yours.

I have read your **"Glimpses of Psychology,"** and esteem them divinations of the true method and spirit of touching the soul of childhood to its finest issues. When parents and the community generally, shall conceive the child to have had a divine as a human parentage, and that its life begins before its advent into bodily organs, we may hope to have something deserving the name of spiritual and intellectual education.

I always refer in memory to the attempt which we made almost forty years ago at showing how this theory might be practically worked out on children coming to us under the best advantages then permitted by the state of education in Boston. And I think it was a charming success.

I was glad to learn your high appreciation of 'Maurice.'

Will you thank Misses Garland and Weston for their kind remembrance.

> Your friend,
> A. Bronson Alcott

Amos Bronson Alcott (letter date 7 July 1879)

SOURCE: Alcott, Amos Bronson. Letter from *The Letters of A. Bronson Alcott,* edited by Richard L. Herrnstadt, p. 771. Ames: Iowa State University Press, 1969.

[*In the following letter to Dr. William Fairfield Warren, president of Boston University, written July 7, 1879, Alcott offers a brief analysis of Peabody's views on Transcendentalism.*]

> Concord July 7th 1879.

Dear Sir,

I should have mailed the Book sooner to your address.[1] But Miss Elizabeth Peabody was so desirous of reading it on my account of its contents and the youth of its author, that I allowed her to take it for a few days. She now returns it, with saying that she intends writing to Mr. Gunsaulus her views of the book. She thinks Transcendentalism tends to Pantheism as the author implies, but questions the accuracy of his criticisms of the writers named by him. But she is much interested in him, and will doubtless write him a characteristic letter of her views, particularly of Dr. Channings religious opinions.

I mention this to show you the agreement of a thoughtful woman, and one who shared deeply in the transcendental movement, as in the Unitarian, and is a critical observer of the times.

I shall be happy to learn your views of the Book, from your Orthodox standpoint.

> Very truly
> Yours,
> A. Bronson Alcott

Note

1. See Letters 79-50 and 79-52.

George Willis Cooke (essay date 1902)

SOURCE: Cooke, George Willis. "Elizabeth Palmer Peabody." In *An Historical and Biographical Introduction to Accompany* The Dial. Vol. 1, pp. 140-57. New York: Russell & Russell, 1961.

[*In the following essay, originally published in 1902, Cooke evaluates Peabody's long career as an educator and author.*]

Not less as a contributor to *The Dial* than as one of its publishers does Elizabeth Palmer Peabody deserve recognition. To the second number of the second volume she contributed an article entitled **"A Glimpse of Christ's Idea of Society."** This paper was first sent as a letter to Harriet Martineau, at the request of George Ripley. It was followed in the third number by an account of the **"Plan of the West Roxbury Community."** These articles were the result of her intimate acquaintance with Dr. Channing, as well as with George Ripley. In her *Reminiscences of Dr. Channing* she showed how fully he was in sympathy with Ripley in his Brook Farm experiment. She said that Channing "agreed with Ripley in the important proposition that it was entirely impossible to live under our civilization without being an involuntary party to great social wrong all the time. Division of labor, he said, was good for the acquisition of national wealth, but sacrificed the individuals composing the nation. He therefore looked upon Ripley's plans with interest and favor, although he had a thousand doubts about its immediate success. The year before, when Jonathan Phillips [one of the most active supporters of Dr. Channing in his charity and church work] was living at the Tremont House, there had been a meeting in his parlor, playfully named the Club of Jacobins, which was frequented by George Ripley, John S. Dwight, Theodore Parker, and other critics of the times, who talked of social reforms; and these meetings greatly interested Dr. Channing. . . . He was most interested in the enterprise as an illustration of the practicability of uniting manual labor with intellectual pursuits. He wanted our agricultural population to see that the land could get cultivated, and that in the best manner, while neither themselves nor their children were made beasts of burden; that leisure could be redeemed for intellectual pursuits and the arts that adorn life; and through a levelling-up process, the distinction of classes disappear by the universalizing of good manners."

Miss Peabody's intimate association with Dr. Channing at this period brought her into sympathy with Mr. Ripley and his efforts for the reformation of society. She did not become a member of the Brook Farm community, probably restrained therefrom because Dr. Channing could not give it his full sympathy, and because she was greatly influenced by Emerson's individualism, as opposed to the idea of association. However, her communications to *The Dial* indicate the fullness of her appreciation of the effort being made by Ripley and his associates. The restraining influences that kept her from connecting herself with Brook Farm may be seen in the other paper she contributed to *The Dial,* and which appeared in the last number under the title **"Fourierism."** It was written at the time when Brook Farm was introducing the theories of Fourier. The article is a general report of the substance of what was said concerning the teachings of Fourier at a convention held in Boston during the last days of 1843 and the first of 1844. At that time members of the several communities then existing in New England and New York met to discuss the problems of association, with the result that Fourierism was adopted at Brook Farm, owing to the zealous efforts of Albert Brisbane and William Henry Channing. Miss Peabody did not accept the teachings of Fourier without qualification, and she expressed doubts as to their results when put into practice at Brook Farm. Her articles on **"Christ's Idea of Society"** and on **"Fourierism"** were reprinted in her *Last Evening with Allston, and Other Papers,* published in 1886.

Elizabeth Palmer Peabody was born in Billerica, Mass., May 16, 1804, the daughter of Nathaniel Peabody, a physician for many years in Salem and Boston. Her mother was a very capable and efficient teacher, one of the earliest and most successful of the women who took up that profession. They were teaching in Andover, Mass., he as the principal of the boys' school there, and she of that for girls, when they became acquainted, and were soon after married. They removed to Billerica, a few miles distant, in order that he might study medicine with a prominent physician there; and she opened a boarding-school with thirty pupils. Here Elizabeth was born; but in 1805 the family removed to Cambridge for one year, in order that Mr. Peabody might complete his medical education. Then they settled in Lynn, he as a physician, and she to her work as a teacher, being for some time at the head of an academy. In 1808 they removed to Salem, which was their home for many years.

Mrs. Peabody was a highly educated woman for her day, and she was a teacher for eighteen years. She was thoughtful, original, and capable, inventing her own methods, and using them with rare skill. She was influenced by the ideas of women then dominant, and by the social theory that they must be retiring and subordinate; but she had a high ideal for women and of their mission as teachers. She thought that women should not be taught in too robust and independent a manner, but she was remarkably broad-minded for her time. Writing of her own methods as a teacher, Miss Peabody said that "they were implicitly suggested by my mother, who followed her motherly instinct with her own children. She always seemed to me an entirely different and generally opposite influence to that of all others with whom I came in contact. My mother's idea of education was predominantly moral—to fill my mind with images of kind, heroic, and thoroughly high-principled people, which her fine instinct picked out of society around us, as well as from history and literature. Every kind of hollow pretension was her supreme abhorrence; all moral affectation and religious cant she saw through; and the nervous weakness of self-indulgent fine ladies she thoroughly despised. But she was not censorious of individuals nor wanting in tenderness, and referred their faults so invariably to bad education or no education that when I entered on this vocation myself—a vocation for which she educated me, considering it the highest and the proper activity of every American woman who loved her country—moral education became to my mind the essence of all education, and I never thought of any intellectual acquisition nor of any artistic power except as subservient to moral and social ends."

It was the aim of Mrs. Peabody to make her pupils familiar with history as affording motives for moral action, and with the best literature as giving the mind intellectual and spiritual incentives. Her range of subjects was somewhat narrow, but her method was novel, and it was effective. It made her pupils familiar with all the great English writers, and it gave them the capacity of enjoying and appreciating them. Such was the training received by Elizabeth Peabody, and it admirably fitted her for her work as teacher, lecturer, and author. Her father taught her Latin in an old-fashioned but effective manner; and at a later time she was instructed in German and French by those native to these languages. Her education was quite unusually thorough and wide of range for the early part of the nineteenth century.

At the age of sixteen Elizabeth Peabody became a teacher. In 1820 the family moved to Lancaster, Mass., and there she taught for two years, some of her pupils of both sexes being older than herself. The medical practice of her father proving not to be what it had been represented, he removed to Boston. Elizabeth opened a school in Mount Vernon street, and after two years she went to Gardiner, Maine, where she was the tutor in a wealthy family of English Unitarians. In 1825 she took up the work of teaching in Brookline, and was in intimate intercourse with Dr. Channing, acting as his amanuensis, reading to him from French and German books, and making record of his conversations and his sermons, which she afterwards published in her *Reminiscences [Reminiscences of Dr. Channing.*] In 1826 Dr. Channing put his daughter Mary under Miss Peabody's care in a school gathered for her by Eliza Lee Cabot, who became the wife of Dr. Charles Follen, the German exile and scholar, and the intimate friend of Channing. In this school she continued for seven years, and it was highly successful. Interest in the methods pursued by Amos Bronson Alcott in his famous Temple School led Miss Peabody to volunteer her services as his assistant on the opening of the school in September, 1834. In his diary Alcott wrote of her as one "whose reputation, both as regards original and acquired ability, is high,—she unites intellectual and practical qualities of no common order." The school was placed in her charge in the afternoons, when she taught Latin and geography; and she also recorded Mr. Alcott's conversations with his pupils in the mornings. In June, 1835, was published the first volume of these conversations under the title of *Record of a School.* Early in 1837 appeared two volumes of *Conversations with Children on the Gospels,* from the reports of Miss Peabody, though a few of the conversations were recorded by her sister, Sophia Peabody, who became the wife of Hawthorne. The result of the publication of these volumes was the closing of the Temple School, most of the pupils being withdrawn because of the criticisms to which it was subjected in the newspapers and elsewhere. In later years, the *Record of a School* was twice reprinted, on each occasion receiving revision in order to give it fidelity to Miss Peabody's growing educational theories.

During these years of teaching Miss Peabody was at work as an author, chiefly along educational lines. She published an *Introduction to Grammar [First Lessons in Grammar*], *First Steps to History, Key to the History of the Hebrews, Keys to Grecian History,* and other works, mostly text-books. She also translated De Gérando's *Visitor to the Poor.* After leaving the Temple School she went to live in Salem with her parents, but she continued her educational work with adults, already begun in Boston. This consisted of conversations with women on historical and educational subjects, the first course being held in Boston in 1833, and another in 1836. Two other courses were given, in 1844 and 1845. For about twenty years she devoted much of her time to this work of teaching women history and literature by means of what she called "conferences," which were partly devoted to lectures by her, partly to the reading of essays by members of the class, and partly to conversation on the topic of the day. As she began these conferences in 1833, she preceded Margaret Fuller in the holding of conversations, who did not begin hers until November, 1839, and then under Miss Peabody's auspices. As the pioneer in this kind of educational work, which has led up to the women's clubs of the present day, it is interesting to have Miss Peabody's own account of her methods, which she gave in an article prepared for *Barnard's Journal of Education.*

"My classes met me twice a week, and took the shape of Historical Conferences. For instance, I will describe one of the several I had in three different cities. The term was six months, admitting of fifty sessions. I proposed to take up ancient history before the eighth century, when there was no pretence anywhere of a historical record of events, and little biography of persons except in the old Hebrew Scriptures, but history was to be guessed out by researches among ancient monuments. The text-books I used were Heeren's *Researches in Ancient India, Persia, Babylon, Egypt, Ethiopia, Phœnicia, and Ancient Greece*; Layard's *Nineveh*, Landseer's *Cylinders of Babylon,* Karl Otfried Müller's *History of the Dorians* and his work on the *Etruscans.* There were enough ladies in the class for each to take a separate country, concerning which she read as much as she could at home between the sessions. We met at ten o'clock, and each lady put into my hands a few questions that she had written to guide me in bringing out from her what proved a lecture to the rest, who in turn all lectured to her, and thus was brought before us all that was going on in these several civilizations, more or less isolated from each other. My part was to put in the Hebrew life at the time, and help to compare these contemporaneous developments of humanity so far as the antiquities accessible serve to elucidate it. The plan proved a great success, and our sessions were sometimes prolonged for four hours, so interesting were the conversations. The ladies made their recitations in answer to the questions either viva voce or by abstracts, or read extracts from books. Müller's *Etruscans* being in German, the accomplished lady who took it made a free translation of the whole of it. The next year another conference took up the eight centuries immediately preceding Christ. Our text-books were Herodotus, Thucydides, Xenophon, Livy, and Plutarch. We proceeded contemporaneously with the divisions of Sardanapalus's empire, the Israelites and Jews, Persia, Greece, and Rome, sometimes taking a century, sometimes half or quarter of a century, sometimes a decade, and after the recitation or abstract, to aid which I wrote and printed my *Keys to Grecian History,* that consist only of questions, we would converse; and I read to them K. O. Müller's 'History of Greek Literature,' some of August Schlegel's lectures on the 'Greek theatre,' Mitchell's *Introduction to Aristophanes,* Xenophon's *Memorabilia of Socrates,* and Plato's *Eutyphron, Apol-*

ogy of Socrates, Crito and *Phædo*; and I think we took some extra sessions to read translations of the Greek tragedies. There were some of the Hebrew students, brothers and friends of my scholars, who came to me sub rosa while this conference was going on, and asked my advice as to their historical reading, who followed out this course and read the tragedies, and I advised them to read the Greek historians and Livy in the originals. There was at that time no professor of history in any college in the United States."

The conferences of 1844 were devoted to the eighteenth century, and to the causes that led to the French Revolution. So late as 1866 Miss Peabody returned to this work of historical instruction, though more distinctly in the form of lectures. In that year she read a historical paper in the parlor of Mrs. Josiah Quincy, and those present were so much interested by it that they besought her to give them a course of historical lectures, which resulted in her preparing twenty lectures on the great civilizations of antiquity. She said of these lectures that they were very imperfect as literary productions, but they deeply interested those who heard them, and they were frequently repeated in the parlors of her friends, in several cities.

In 1839 Miss Peabody again removed to Boston, this time to open a book-store at 13 West Street, then at the south end of the city. She kept periodicals for sale, as well as foreign books, and, at the suggestion and with the assistance of Washington Allston, painter's materials. This book-store was the first one in Boston where foreign books, especially French and German, were kept on sale and could be ordered. One side of it was occupied by her father, who sold homeopathic medicines, then as much an innovation as the reading of foreign books. Miss Peabody was not only a book-seller, but she was also a publisher. The first book she issued from the press was Dr. Channing's work on *Emancipation,* which he put into her hands in order to encourage her in this enterprise. Although he gave her the copyright, yet she so far relinquished it as to permit the various anti-slavery societies throughout the country to bring out cheap editions, with the result that she did not sell the edition of one thousand copies she had printed. She brought out other books, but the competition of the other book-sellers made it impossible for her to succeed. Concerning this experience she wrote: "About 1840 I came to Boston and opened the business of importing and publishing foreign books, a thing not then attempted by any one. I had also a foreign library of new French and German books; and then I came into contact with the world as never before. The Ripleys were starting Brook Farm, and they were friends of ours. Theodore Parker was beginning his career, and all these things were discussed in my book-store by Boston lawyers and Cambridge professors. Those were very living years for me. Being so much occupied as I was

at this time I was obliged to deny myself to my friends, except on Wednesday evenings; and I may be said to have set the fashion in Boston of having regular reception evenings. The book-publishers combined against me, and though my friend Dr. Channing gave me his *Emancipation,* and Hawthorne his *Grandfather's Chair,* yet I could not fight them all successfully, and finally relinquished business."

For several years Miss Peabody's book-store was a notable centre of intellectual and reformatory interest. There every question of the day was discussed, and there all the new books were subjected to faithful criticism. Brook Farm was carefully considered there for many months before it became a fact, and it was talked over by Ripley, Parker, Brownson, Dwight, Warren Burton, Samuel Robbins, Adin Ballou, and others, in that friendly place of meeting. These men agreed in being discontented with society as it then existed, and they were united in wishing for a humaner and juster form of social organization. In this little book-store they debated all features of the problems thus presented, stating their differences with charity and good-will, and yet inciting each other to make the effort to secure a better form of social existence. In the same place all phases of theological opinion found expression, especially those that were in any way individualistic or in harmony with the social reforms of the day. The come-outers of all kinds were sure to find each other in this place, and to find there fit audience for their theories. It is related of W. H. Channing, by his biographer, that he had come, in the winter of 1841-42, to doubt in regard to all forms of church organization. He went into Miss Peabody's book-store, and a discussion arose on the miracles, during which he said that Jesus mistook the impulse of beneficence for the power to set aside natural laws. To this some one present, perhaps Miss Peabody herself, replied that such a theory made Christ insane, denied free-will, and made God incapable of spiritual activity. Channing did not reply, but went away, secluded himself for some weeks, and then came forth a most pronounced Christian believer. On the next Sunday he gave a most eloquent vindication of his new and radiant faith. Col. T. W. Higginson says the Brook Farm people were often to be met in Miss Peabody's "atom of a shop." "There I made acquaintance," he continues, "with Cousin and Jouffroy, with Constant's *De la Religion* and Leroux' *De l'Humanité,* the relics of the French eclecticism, then beginning to fade, but still taught in colleges. There, too, were Schubert's *Geschichte der Seele* and many of the German balladists, who were beginning to enthrall me. There was Miss Peabody herself, desultory, dreamy, but insatiable in her love for knowledge and for helping others to it. James Freeman Clarke said of her that she was always engaged in supplying some want that had first to be created; it might be Dr. Kraitsir's lectures on language, or General Bem's historical chart. She always preached the need, but never accomplished the supply until she advocated the Kindergarten; there she caught up with her mission and came to identify herself with its history."

The period from 1850 to 1860 Miss Peabody devoted to the advancement of the study of history in the schools of the country. In connection therewith she published several historical works, a number of them text-books. As the result of her acquaintance with several natives of Poland, exiled from that country because of their love of liberty, she published, in 1850, her book on *The Crimes of the House of Austria against Mankind,* into which she compressed with burning indignation a complete record of autocratic despotism on the part of the royal family of Austria. Among her Polish friends was one by the name of Podbielski, who brought to this country a system of historical charts, which had been invented and used in his country. It was introduced into France, in 1832-40, by General Bem, who had successfully given it a place in the schools of that country. Miss Peabody revised and extended this chart, explained it to Longfellow, George B. Emerson, Dr. Barnas Sears, and others. She published this work, as revised by her, in New York, in 1852, as **Bem's Polish-American System of Chronology.** It afforded a mnemonic aid to memory, as well as giving a systematic outline of the chief events of history. In 1856 she published a history of the United States for schools arranged on this plan. Rowland G. Hazard's *Essay on Language, and other Papers,* was edited and published by her in 1857. Hazard was a native and a resident of Rhode Island, who had become an intimate friend of Dr. Channing by means of their common philosophical studies. Through Channing Miss Peabody became acquainted with him, with the result that she brought his volume to the attention of the public. In 1859 she published a translation of De Gérando's **Self-Education,** and a biographical sketch of William Wesselhoeft, one of the earliest Boston homeopathic physicians.

Miss Peabody was always an enthusiast, and she undertook nothing to which she did not give the most devoted service. Her enthusiasm for Bem's chronological system was great and lasting, as were all her other educational affections. In 1871 Count Zaba brought to this country a revised form of it, or one of similar import, and it made a great impression in Boston, Cambridge, Chicago, Canada, and elsewhere. "If I were twenty-five years younger," she wrote of this method of teaching history, "I would renew the effort I made in 1850 and the years after, to universalize this method by carrying it over the State myself, which was interrupted by the Civil War when it was in the full tide of successful experiment, and still hope, before I die, to set it a-going by enlisting some one as enthusiastic and persevering as myself to do it." This enthusiastic coadjutor did not

appear, and Bem's *System of Chronology* is now as dead and forgotten as possible, her zeal for it not serving to keep it before the public.

Miss Peabody was a born teacher, and with a real genius for imparting instruction. From her childhood to extreme old age she was constantly engaged in this profession, often changing her methods of activity, but never getting away for any length of time from the one passion of her life, that of educating mankind. Whatever was the immediate subject of her interest her enthusiasm for it was of the most intense nature, and she could not think or talk of anything else. Emerson once said of her enthusiasms, "Miss Peabody always keeps a whole stud of Phœnixes on hand." Her next enthusiasm was for the Kindergarten, and it proved to be fortunate and successful. It was the one passion of her life that the public came to approve and to accept. Her whole previous career as a teacher had prepared her for this work, and she took it up in a true apostolic spirit, believing it the one means by which mankind was to be redeemed from its social, intellectual, and spiritual defects.

It may be said of Miss Peabody that she followed as a teacher the spirit and intent of transcendentalism. She attempted to draw out from her pupils that which was in them, not to give them something from without, but to open their own inward lives, to produce in them the results of self-development. "My secret is," she wrote, "that I never undertake to manage my pupils. I have no power of commanding. I never do command children, but am very respectful and courteous to them, and throw myself on their mercy, as it were, by telling them of the obligation I am under to their parents and to God to help them educate themselves. I take great pains not to reprove or exhort them before each other, but only in tête-à-tête or by writing a note to them. The relation has no antagonism in it, but is altogether sympathetic. Another principle of my discipline was to avoid exciting a spirit of rivalry, and to have no emulation. I had no marks of merit, no going up or down in classes, and required the whole recitation from each scholar, which at first would seem the longest way, but proved in the end the shortest, because it was so absolutely thorough, and it almost precluded the necessity of repetition and review. In short, I lived with my scholars as Froebel says we should always do with our children. They were always writing to me as to a confessor, in after life, to get my moral and spiritual advice." This was so near to the idea and method of Froebel that she most readily took up his theory when she came to know of it. It was first brought to her attention by the wife of Carl Schurz, who was then a resident of Watertown, Wisconsin. In that city had settled, in 1855, a German by the name of Carl Siburg, whose wife had been a pupil of Froebel, and was an expert in the theory and practice of the Kindergarten. To her the Schurzes had sent their daughter, and Mrs. Schurz described to Miss Peabody the methods and results of her education. At once Miss Peabody was impressed with the beauty and the utility of this system, and sought in all directions for aids in comprehending it, securing one of Froebel's minor works as her guide. In 1860 she opened in Boston a school for little children on the basis of what she supposed was Froebel's system. This school became popular, and it was copied elsewhere. "In the course of the next ten years some innocent because ignorant, inadequate attempts were made at Kindergartens," she wrote in later years; "but without such study into the practical details of the method as to do any justice to Froebel's idea; and on the whole the premature attempt was unfortunate. The most noted one was my own in Boston; but I must do myself the justice to say that I discovered its radical deficiency by seeing that the results promised by Froebel, as the result of his method, did not accrue, but consequences that he deprecated, and which its financial success and the delight of the children and their parents in the pretty play-school did not beguile me into overlooking."

In 1867 Miss Peabody, after seven years of Kindergarten teaching in the imperfect manner she then knew, took the money she had secured from her lecturing under the auspices of Mrs. Quincy and went to Europe to study the system at first hand. "An hour in the Hamburg Kindergarten opened my eyes," she said afterwards. Having devoted a year to mastering Froebel's system she returned to Boston with the intention of raising money enough to bring to that city an expert Kindergartner. On her return she found that Mrs. Kriege and her daughter had opened a Kindergarten and a training-school in Boston the year before under the auspices of Mrs. Horace Mann. When they left the city to return to Germany, four years later, they were succeeded by two of their pupils, Miss Garland and Miss Weston. Marie Boelte opened a Kindergarten in New York soon after, and as Mrs. Kraus-Boelte she trained Miss Blow of St. Louis, and other expert Kindergartners. It will be seen, therefore, that the efforts of Miss Peabody led directly to most of the chief Kindergarten labors in this country. All the writers on the history of education have recognized her important services in this direction. For instance, George H. Martin, in his *Evolution of the Massachusetts Public School System,* says of her work: "The apostle of the Kindergarten movement in Massachusetts was Miss Peabody, and to her efforts with tongue and pen is due whatever success the movement has had." In his *History of Education in the United States,* Richard G. Boone justly says: "What Baroness Marenholtz-Bœlow did for Europe, Miss Peabody has done for America. She was the earliest, as she has been one of the most persistent, advocates of its merits. Hers was the first literature on the subject—hers a pioneer labor."

In May, 1873, Miss Peabody began the publication in Boston of *The Kindergarten Messenger,* a monthly magazine of twenty-four pages, which she continued to the end of 1874. Then her Kindergarten contributions appeared for one year in the *Journal of Education,* but that arrangement not proving satisfactory, the *Messenger* was resumed with the first of 1875. It had a limited circulation, but Miss Peabody gave to it devoted service, and made it a valuable means of extending the Kindergarten method. In 1876, the expense and labor proving too great for individual effort, the magazine was surrendered to W. N. Hailman, who edited and published in Milwaukee *The New Education.* The work on *Moral Culture of Infancy and Kindergarten Guide,* which Miss Peabody had published in 1863, in connection with her sister, Mrs. Mary Mann, she repudiated after her return from Europe "as an ignorant and abortive attempt." She rewrote it, and in this revised form it became a means of bringing Froebel's method into wide recognition.

After 1868 Miss Peabody's life was largely devoted to the work of the Kindergarten, principally in lecturing and by means of her writings. In 1870 she gave an address in Chicago before the Society of Superintendents and Principals on **"The Genuine Kindergarten versus Ignorant Attempts at it"**; and she repeated it before the Wisconsin Teachers' Convention, as well as in Milwaukee, Cleveland, and other cities. Soon after returning from Germany she organized in Boston the Kindergarten Association, which proved a valuable ally to her labors. For many years she gave courses of lectures to Kindergartners, and these were repeated in several of the leading cities of the country. She also organized the National Froebel Union. In 1886 she published *Letters to Kindergartners,* and in 1893 *Lectures in Training Schools for Kindergartners.* The Report of the Commissioner of Education for 1870 contained one of the first official recognitions of the Kindergarten in this country, being a paper by Miss Peabody on **"The Necessity of Kindergarten Culture in our Systems of Public Instruction."** In the same year she published a pamphlet *Plea for Froebel's Kindergarten as the First Grade of Primary Art Education.* In Barnard's *Kindergarten and Culture Papers* appeared articles from her pen on **"The Development of the Kindergarten in the United States," "Froebel's Principles and Methods in the Nursery,"** as well as other essays.

During the early years of her advocacy of the Kindergarten Miss Peabody lived for a time in Cambridge. Then she removed to Concord, where she was deeply interested in the sessions of the School of Philosophy, to which she gave several addresses. Afterwards she was again a resident of Boston, and then she went to Jamaica Plain, one of the rural suburbs of the city, where she died January 3, 1894. She planned to write her autobiography, but the failure of her eyesight made this task impossible of accomplishment. Much of the story of her early life was told in her *Reminiscences of Dr. Channing,* which she published in 1877, a book that is most instructive for the whole early period of the transcendental movement. She was able to edit her lectures to Kindergartners during her last years, and to bring together a number of her early writings, first printed in *The Dial* and the *Æsthetic Papers,* under the title of *Last Evening with Allston, and other Papers,* which was published in 1886.

The last enthusiasm of Miss Peabody was for the Indians, in whose behalf she devoted much effort with tongue and pen. She became the special champion of the interests of Sarah Winnemucca, by some strange perversion of knowledge called "Princess," by whom she was cheated and defrauded until she was rescued by her friends from the clutches of one who had grossly imposed upon her sympathies and her generosity. If in this instance deceived, Miss Peabody saw the real needs of the Indians and wisely advocated their cause. She desired for them an education that would fit them for an industrial and moral life.

With the transcendental movement from first to last Miss Peabody was familiar, being a most important part of it herself. She was intimate with Emerson, Margaret Fuller, who gave her first course of conversations in her West Street rooms, Theodore Parker, George Ripley, Alcott, Thoreau, James Freeman Clarke, and all the others of that noble company. She was attracted by Mazzini, Frederic Maurice, and the other leaders of liberal thought in Europe. She never tired of talking of these men or of commending their teachings to others. Always poor, always dependent upon her own exertions, she did more for others than for herself, and never failed to champion any cause that commended itself to her enthusiastic and heroic nature. Mrs. Ednah D. Cheney, who knew her long and well, has truly said of her: "She was a thorough transcendentalist, and worked with Emerson and Alcott and Parker in all that great movement. Her powers of conversation were large, although she was sometimes led by her enthusiasm for the causes or the people she loved into larger discourse than suited the occasion or the audience. These philanthropic interests turned her attention from literature, in which I think she might have taken a much higher position if she had been more swayed by personal and intellectual ambition." Mrs. Caroline H. Dall also justly estimated her merits and her defects when she wrote: "A woman of remarkable accumulations of learning, and as remarkable a breadth of sympathy. Her own great powers did not accomplish all they ought, because it was impossible for her to apply them systematically."

A beautiful tribute to the memory of Miss Peabody, who "literally gave herself to the cause" of the Kindergarten, was the establishment in the West End of Bos-

ton, in April, 1896, of the Elizabeth Peabody House, a settlement for Kindergartners in one of the poorer districts of the city. For its maintenance was organized an Association of her friends and others interested in the teaching of the children of the slums. There her life of philanthropy, lofty thought, and childlike transparency is continued in her spirit of devotion to the good of others.

Josephine E. Roberts (essay date September 1942)

SOURCE: Roberts, Josephine E. "Elizabeth Peabody and the Temple School." *New England Quarterly* 15, no. 3 (September 1942): 497-508.

[*In the following essay, Roberts examines Peabody's crucial role in supporting Amos Bronson Alcott's Temple School in the 1830s. Roberts describes Peabody's initial involvement in the experiment, as well as her steadfast efforts to chronicle, and defend, Alcott's educational practices.*]

Alcott's famous educational experiment in Boston of the eighteen-thirties owes more to Elizabeth Peabody than any printed material on that subject suggests.[1] The books which merely mention Miss Peabody as Mr. Alcott's assistant err in understatement.

When Amos Bronson Alcott, after an educational sojourn in Philadelphia, returned to Boston in the summer of 1834 with some rather surprising letters written by his pupils under ten years of age, he was enthusiastic about starting a school in Boston. But there were obstacles in the way until his undaunted and equally enthusiastic friend and admirer, Elizabeth Peabody, removed them. In the first place, so many schools were already well established in Boston that a new undertaking might be hazardous. Besides, Mr. Alcott did not know the right people to approach. But Miss Peabody stuffed the children's journals into her ever-present bag and set out to "gather" a school for him, because, she wrote, "Alcott is a man destined, it appears to me, to make an era in society, and I believe he will."[2] Almost at once Elizabeth, by means of Alcott's journals and her own enthusiasm, "engaged" four children. Then Mrs. Alcott pointed out another difficulty in the way. But let Elizabeth Peabody herself tell the story in a letter to her sister Mary, then in Cuba:

> On Saturday Mr. Alcott came and brought me the journals of his scholars and their letters to him—they are all under ten years of age! He stayed and talked like an embodiment of intellectual light—and yet calm, solemn, and simple as ever. I told him I wanted him to make an effort for a school here—and he said he wished to—but he thought he could not do it without a modification of his plan. He must have a school at different

hours from other schools and for a shorter session—two hours and a half—say. I told him there would be a difficulty in this.—[A caller interrupted at this point] When he went away, I told Mr. Alcott I would inquire about the children in town and see whether there was not a chance for him. When he went away, I took up the journals etc.—and was *amazed* beyond measure at the composition. I read some of them to Mr. Rice[3] and he immediately engaged William. After dinner I went down to Mrs. Gustavus Tuckerman and she engaged three. I called at Mrs. Bliss's but she was not at home. I then went to [?] Mary's to make one or two more inquiries and found Mrs. Alcott at home alone. We talked over the prospect. She thought it would never succeed without more book learning and that Mr. Alcott could never put his mind to that—He needed an assistant and yet it was out of the question to find an assistant who was competent and that he could afford to pay. I told her I would be his assistant—that is, I would teach two hours and a half a day for a year in his school for such compensation as he could afford to pay. When she found I was really in earnest, she was in *a rapture* and Mr. A. too when he came in. I told him I would only engage until your return—on these terms. They both said the terms were altogether too little, but it is not a partnership and he could give me no more possibly—with 30 scholars—as his expenses would be great. However, he said if there could be anything more given, he would, for in justice I should have full half the income. I told him it was not with me a plan for life but only a temporary scheme.[4]

Elizabeth's offer was not, of course, pure philanthropy. In February of that year she wrote, "I am so poor." She had been barely able to pay her bills from the proceeds of her Historical School, her Reading Party, and her savings, and expected to go home in May "pennyless and prospectless" except for what she might get from her articles in the *Christian Examiner.* "If Mr. Emerson should offer me a place in his school, I would take it for $300,"[5] she said. So the plan for assisting Alcott came as "a light for the next winter" and made her "feel very happy."[6] In addition to the other activities just mentioned, she was at the time teaching seven hours a day in private homes.

Nor was her interest wholly a pecuniary one. She earnestly desired closer association with the man whose mind at the moment she most admired. She spent an entire day reading his Philadelphia journal and pronounced it "a beautiful philosophic treatise."[7] She believed wholeheartedly that Alcott had "a beautiful and very great mind."[8]

There followed numerous calls back and forth between Alcott and Miss Peabody to discuss ways and means for the school. "In the latter part of the evening Mr. and Mrs. Alcott came and we talked about houses, etc.,"[9] Elizabeth wrote to her sister in July. A night or so later she called on the Alcotts and then added, "That house next Trinity Church has been put in repair and the plan seems to be that somebody take it and take Mr. Alcott and his school to board."

In August she "met Mr. Alcott and went and looked at a room in the Temple for a schoolroom."[10] By September they had the room in shape for the beginning of school. "Here I was interrupted by Mr. Alcott and went up to Parkers and thence to the schoolroom. That table all repaired of mine is put before the Gothic window in the schoolroom and opposite is another table of this shape ⌣ where Mr. Alcott is to sit."[11] Other details follow, but the same items are described more fully in a letter written two weeks later after the school had opened and the finishing touches had been added.

> I will tell you now a little about the schoolroom. It is about 60 feet *solid* with the upper part of the Gothic window to light it and two of those little holes thus

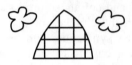

> which gives an uncrossed light. Just before the window stands our long table at which I sit. Opposite the window is the appearance of a door the same shape as the window, and Mr. Alcott is going to have a piece of furniture including closets, library shelves, and blackboard there—with a bust on top. Before that stands a table in the form of a half moon round which he can take a class. The corner at his right hand is occupied by the stove which stands out so far as to afford room for a shelf behind it on which are two fine geraniums now and which is to be filled with flowers. There is my green sofa near the stove. The desks for the children are to look toward the wall and to go all round the room except at this corner. In the two corners next the street are high pedestals with a fine Socrates on one and as fine Plato on the other. Opposite each other on the sides of the room (each side has a door in the middle) between the doors and the front wall are two pictures which Mr. Rice lent us—quite large landscapes—one an ancient temple and festival and the other some fine mountains. Opposite the stove is my picture of Dr. Channing. And a bas relief of Christ is to be put up on the left hand of the pieces of furniture I mentioned. There is a carpet on the floor, and they sit in very pretty chairs.

> When school begins they take their chairs and sit in a large semicircle before Mr. Alcott and he talks to them, reads to them, hears them read and spell and define words. These exercises take up all the time until recess.

> After recess I take them and give them Latin lessons, Arithmetic and Geography lessons. Thus you see I am not obliged to go there until eleven o'clock, but at present I prefer to go because it is very entertaining to me to hear Mr. Alcott talk.[12]

Elizabeth's account differs from printed sources, which have given the impression that, after the school was well under way, Elizabeth Peabody went and offered her services. Here certainly it is evident that Elizabeth not only helped find and furnish the place but also secured the first scholars and herself provided the book learning necessary for the school's success. Mr. Alcott's own appreciative words about his assistant suggest, also, that her help was given in the initial stages of the school. "Her [Elizabeth Peabody's] proposition to aid me comes from the deep interest she feels in human culture and her friendly desire to establish me in the city."[13]

Elizabeth's account of the first days is somewhat enlightening.

> Eighteen scholars came, eight girls and ten boys— Willy Rice, S. G. Williams, J. Sewall, H. Higginson, three Gustavus Tuckermans, George Kuhn, Robert Rogers, August Shurtleff, Helen Shurtleff, Luisa Peabody, Susan Wainwright, Lucy Channing, Mary Rogers, Sarah Barret, Emma Savage, Pamela Colman—a lovely set of children. The three Tuckermans will be the hardest to manage. They are just like Jane. At ten o'clock Mr. A. made them sit round in a semicircle and read them a very simple story and asked them what they came to school for and talked till nearly twelve without any of us finding out what time it was. Among other things he wanted to know if they thought punishment was necessary and each one said yes—separately. They all said too that they preferred to be punished when they did wrong. The little Tuckermans demurred, however, in this a little. I then tried them in Arithmetic. At two I came home—Sept. 23—Went to school and found four new scholars—Lemuel Sh[], John Davis, two little Colmans. We had a very good time.[14]

As time went on, Elizabeth added to her own teaching load in the Temple School. In addition to the three subjects mentioned, she speaks often of the literature which she read to her "dear little class":

> With my class at the Temple I read on Tuesday and Friday afternoons all the rest of the Homeric hymns and some extracts from the hymn to Venus and now we are prepared for the Iliad. On Wednesday I began the Faery Queen, and Mary Ruth Channing joined us, and Caroline Sturgis will join us next Wednesday. You never saw a deeper interest. It was really delightful.[15]

When the temperature in December went down to zero and they had "a dreadful time to keep the children warm"—only two came to school that day—Elizabeth lightened her reading a little by giving the tots Peter Bell and the Ancient Mariner instead of Homer and "you have no idea with what breathless interest"[16] they listened! Another time she took the Alcott pupils to a nearby room to see Greenough's "Soul of a Child," which was on exhibition. The children were "deeply interested," in this work of art, which Elizabeth called "a dream of heaven."[17] She had many pleasant talks with the scholars from time to time.

Meanwhile, what about remuneration? In the early days Elizabeth wrote, "I intend to give my services to Mr. Alcott this quarter. The next quarter I shall ask $100.

But he cannot afford to give much."[18] By December the agreement had been changed slightly, adding Mary as a possible substitute assistant after her return from Cuba.

> After school I had a talk with Mr. Alcott, and you or I can have a hundred dollars a quarter for assisting him *half the school hours*. This should be you when you return and then you will have 400 dollars secured which will pay for your board and clothes, and the school I intend to keep, in which you will assist, will pay mine and leave something—I hope—to put into *the bank* to take care of us when we are too old to work. I shall not take $100 a quarter at present however - - -

> Mr. Alcott came in the evening and we talked over matters and things. I have secured—as far as there is earthly security—a situation for you in his school with $400 a year. I hope I shall be able to get a school and then we can live here together. If I cannot you must try your luck in Salem and leave this place to me—that is all that I can say.[19]

Elizabeth was at this time very eager to start a school of her own. "I shall do infinitely better than I have ever yet done with a *new* school, I know. I have got some excellent ideas from Mr. Alcott."[20] But this plan never materialized. Perhaps the opening of a girls' school by Dr. and Elizabeth Follen was the reason, because Elizabeth said when she heard of it, "I think this is our death blow, my dear Mary, and fear there is no hope for you but a Salem school and for me but to continue Mr. Alcott's assistant and live alone."[21] At any rate Mary did begin teaching in Salem in April, 1835.

Although Elizabeth's enthusiasm for Alcott's teaching lasted for a good while, her criticism was not long in beginning. In the early days of October she wrote, "Would that I could convey to you his instructions! They are full of life and liberty."[22] After listening to many of Alcott's Socratic conversations, she told her sister approvingly, "Mr. Alcott's sole purpose in the mental way during the first two months seemed to be to bring out clearly in the children's consciousness the perception of their spiritual existence, as being the most real and permanent."[23] While advising Mary to teach her Cuban pupils printing, she wrote, "Mr. Alcott requires a great deal of this from his children and it gives them very quiet habits. *Self command* is a great feature of his school."[24] But later she became critical. "Mr. Alcott's teaching is superlative, but he seems to me to require *too much* in the way of self control. It is unnatural."[25] Nevertheless she still practised his methods with her Sunday school pupils and wrote proudly to her sister, concerning an allegory which one of Alcott's pupils made, "This is the way our children talk; *they create*."[26]

Mr. Alcott's method of conversing with the children is too well known to bear repetition. If to us these seem to have been startlingly precocious youngsters who could follow his Orphic philosophy, at least Elizabeth Peabody believed enough in the method to devote many hours, often far into the night, to writing a record of the school,[27] which Mr. Emerson later noted in his journal as "very good." He expressed his approval also to Elizabeth, who wrote to her sister, "I have had a delightful letter from R. Waldo Emerson who says my *Record* [*Record of a School*] is the only book of facts he ever read which was as enchaining [*sic*] as one of Miss Edgeworth's fictions, and many pleasant things besides."[28] This journal was begun in January, 1835, and continued for three months.

To her, then, we owe what we know about this adventure in new education. Through her *Record* we can see that, four years before the "Divinity School Address," certain of Emerson's views were being practised in Alcott's teaching: the immanence of God in nature, the benevolence of God, the reliance of man upon God. Not that Alcott necessarily anticipated Emerson's ideas, or that he necessarily learned them from Emerson: transcendentalism was a germ in the air; everyone had it. Once Elizabeth sent Mary a small book which contained "the beautiful theory of such a practice as Mr. Alcott has long since attempted."[29] Emerson put into memorable words these precepts of transcendentalism while Alcott put them into action—or as near action as transcendentalism ever came. Certainly each one was interested in the work of the other. "Waldo E. and his wife came down to listen to one of Mr. Alcott's conversations with the children. It was not one of the brightest but was very interesting."[30] And Alcott read the manuscript of Emerson's *Nature* in September, 1836.

So far as payment is concerned, there is no record that Elizabeth ever received any. By December she must have been hard pressed for funds, because she asked and received Alcott's permission to teach all morning on Mondays, Wednesdays, and Fridays and be free the other days. Her reason apparently was to have time to prepare for her "Historical Lessons," which she gave to a group of young ladies in the afternoons of the remaining days. At this time she was still being paid to read to little Ann Rice in the evenings. She was also assiduously seeking pupils for her sister Mary, who was expected soon from Cuba. It is fairly apparent that Elizabeth needed cash. And no one could live on less than she.

By March 15, 1835, Elizabeth was living with the Alcotts. Were a room and board, then, Alcott's method of redeeming his promise? One can only surmise.

At first Elizabeth was pleased with the arrangement. "It was really delightful to find ourselves in a small family by ourselves," even though Mr. Alcott had "not yet brought that book case. He promised to this afternoon, but I have no faith in him."[31] As time went on, Elizabeth became more and more disillusioned about her idol with the "very great mind." Idols should be kept aloft, secure in their sanctuary niches, not seen in their sinister and sceptical moods at the dinner table. Not even "the nice-handled knives and forks" made up for the host's manners. The very first meal at 26 Front Street was uncomfortable. When Elizabeth stated that she had no desire to live for two centuries. Alcott accused her of "a suicidal sentiment" and then went on to abuse all doctors because of the harm they did. When she tried to defend the physicians, Alcott told her that she did not know how to observe. By the end of the meal Elizabeth had decided to be silent henceforth on subjects that might lead to disagreement but had put down Alcott as one who lacked humility and a sober estimate of his place among his fellows. She herself was "exceedingly trustful of the Future" and believed that "the soul of the race is inexhaustible."[32] Mrs. Alcott also irritated her. Although Elizabeth enjoyed the rare privilege of a room of her own at the Alcotts, she felt frequently that she was being treated shabbily. Of Mrs. Alcott Elizabeth once said that it would "be more comfortable to live on the top of a whirlwind than to live with her."[33] Even though her host had written her a sonnet of appreciation and her hostess had named the latest Alcott baby (Beth, in 1835) for her, Elizabeth found a namesake and a sonnet poor substitutes for civility and a salary.

After Elizabeth went into quarters of her own, the feeling toward Mr. Alcott grew even less cordial. She disapproved of too much reflection of the part of the children, of too much publicity, and of the embodiment of evil in concrete forms. She thought that his method of education was negative and told him flatly that a year of open-minded observation of his methods had convinced her of the rightness of her own! Not, she said, that she expected her opinion would make any difference to him, for she supposed no one would ever be able to influence him![34] A conversation which she once had with him made her think less of him and of herself, but it gave her a "grumpy satisfaction" of feeling herself better than she formerly believed! Elizabeth was at the time succeeding quite well with a school of her own in Boston.

And then, ironically enough, Alcott, quite unintentionally, made Boston so uncomfortable for the Peabody sisters that they had to retire to their home nest in Salem. Elizabeth had to give up her successful school; and Mary and Sophia, their hopes of living in Boston. Mary had been teaching in Salem during most of the time since her return from Cuba, but during one period of unknown length she had substituted for Elizabeth at the Alcott school while Elizabeth was caring for a sick friend in Lowell, Massachusetts. Sophia also had made records of the school "conversations" during a part of 1836. Mary was always hoping for the chance to teach in Boston, but Elizabeth's school was not large enough to support two. Elizabeth kept wishing for Mary's company and for the chance to bring her family into the city. The invalid artist Sophia, of course, longed for the art treasures there. Then suddenly Alcott's publication of *Conversations on the Gospels,* made up of discussions held with his Temple School babes, brought an irate Boston down upon the heads of all who had been associated with the school; for in these conversations, Mr. Alcott had dared to define birth as "a spiritual act and fact prior to embodiment." And that was heresy to a prudish generation.

Inasmuch as the Peabody sisters were fellow sufferers, one might suppose that they would be among the first to point fingers of blame at Mr. Alcott. Instead, they rallied to the victim's defense. Sophia, though she has been called a prude,[35] declared that "the community have not yet arrived at a state pure enough to comprehend the essence of things."[36] Mary Peabody thought the conversations "true and beautiful." "His genius is certainly to teach," she said. "If he had been cultivated on all sides, he would undoubtedly have been as popular as he is remarkable in that vocation."[37] Although Elizabeth had at first objected[38] to the publication of the *Conversations,* she too now felt "the absurdity of the kind of fault-finding there has been,"[39] and defended the work as Platonic doctrine, Wordsworthian philosophy, and "certainly . . . the doctrine of Christianity."[40]

So it appears that, in spite of vicissitudes in the professional collaboration of these two transcendentalists, Elizabeth Peabody was the first promoter, the chief recorder, and the last defender of Alcott's Temple School.

Notes

1. The following account is based largely on Elizabeth Peabody's manuscript, "Cuba Journal," made up of letters directed to Mary Peabody during the year 1834 and part of 1835, privately owned by Mr. Horace Mann, Southwest Harbor, Maine.

2. "Cuba Journal" [undated entry].

3. Unidentified, with whom Elizabeth was then staying and whose children she was teaching.

4. "Cuba Journal" [undated entry].

5. "Cuba Journal," February 8, 1834.

6. "Cuba Journal" [undated entry, above].

7. "Cuba Journal," September [1834].

8. "Cuba Journal," July 31 [1834].

9. "Cuba Journal," July 31 [1834].

10. "Cuba Journal," August [1834].

11. "Cuba Journal," September 14 [1834].

12. "Cuba Journal," September 21 [1834].

13. F. B. Sanborn and William T. Harris, *A. Bronson Alcott, His Life and Philosophy* (Boston, 1893), I, 177, quoting from Alcott's journal of September 22 [1834].

14. "Cuba Journal," September 22 and 23 [1834].

15. "Cuba Journal," December 16 [1834].

16. "Cuba Journal," December 16 [1834].

17. "Cuba Journal," November 21 [1834].

18. "Cuba Journal," October 25 [1834].

19. "Cuba Journal," December 26 [1834].

20. "Cuba Journal" [undated entry].

21. "Cuba Journal," January 5 [1835].

22. "Cuba Journal," October 14 [1834].

23. "Cuba Journal," December 29 [1834].

24. "Cuba Journal," October 25 [1834].

25. "Cuba Journal" [undated entry, 1835].

26. "Cuba Journal," February 25 [1835].

27. Elizabeth Palmer Peabody, *Record of a School* (Boston, 1835 and later editions).

28. Elizabeth Palmer Peabody to Mary Peabody, August 8, 1835, private collection of Mr. Horace Mann.

29. "Cuba Journal," January 23, 1835.

30. "Cuba Journal" [undated entry].

31. "Cuba Journal" [week before Easter, 1835].

32. "Cuba Journal," April 11, 1835.

33. "Cuba Journal" [November, 1835].

34. Sanborn and Harris, I, 189-190, letter of Elizabeth Palmer Peabody to Alcott, October 8, 1835.

35. Randall Stewart, in his edition of the *American Notebooks of Nathaniel Hawthorne* [(1932)], accuses Sophia, later Mrs. Hawthorne, of "prudishness or false delicacy" because in her editing of her husband's journals, "Passages relating to sex were revised or omitted," Introduction XV.

36. Sanborn and Harris, I, 224.

37. Mary Peabody to Horace Mann [1837], Library of the Massachusetts Historical Society, Boston.

38. In a letter to Sophia Peabody dated September 12, 1836, formerly in the possession of the late Mr. W. T. H. Howe, Cincinnati, Ohio, Alcott says he supposes that Elizabeth is "abject." But "tell her"

he says, "nothing definite will be done regarding the 'Record of Conversations' till I hear from her."

39. Sanborn and Harris, I, 224.

40. Sanborn and Harris, I, 199.

John B. Wilson (essay date June 1956)

SOURCE: Wilson, John B. "A Transcendental Minority Report." *New England Quarterly* 29, no. 2 (June 1956): 147-58.

[*In the following essay, Wilson examines Peabody's ambivalent attitude toward Transcendentalism. According to Wilson, Peabody devoted much of her career to reconciling the individualism of Transcendental philosophy with the fundamentally social nature of culture and education.*]

"The danger that besets our Transcendentalists is that they sometimes mistake their individualities for the Transcendent," Dr. William Ellery Channing once remarked to his former secretary, Miss Elizabeth Peabody.[1]

Biographer and associate of Dr. Channing, called the spiritual father of transcendentalism in New England, and herself a member of the "Hedge Club," Miss Peabody constantly sought a corrective for this ultra-egoism and misguided individualism that had prompted the wildest vagaries of thought and conduct in the lunatic fringe of the movement. She objected severely to the "transcendental wild oats" which Louisa Alcott reproved with gentle satire and which Emerson good-naturedly mocked in his essay "New England Reformers." Such "Ego-theism" had caused Bronson Alcott to declare himself an educational philosopher superior to all others, including Dr. Channing, Christ, and Pestalozzi.[2] It had evoked from Margaret Fuller the statement that she had met all people in America worth knowing and had found no other intellect in any way equal to her own.[3] And it had inspired some ridiculous fads and excesses in dress, diet, education, and social reform at the transcendental colonies, Brook Farm and Fruitlands, and at the solitary retreat of Henry Thoreau on Walden Pond.

Miss Peabody had protested against Margaret Fuller's "too conscious attempt at individual self-culture versus the culture which is alike in all men," and she commented that had Dr. Hedge remained in Boston he might have introduced transcendentalism in such a way that it would not have become identified with the extreme individualism invariably associated with it.[4]

When Emerson was preparing his "Divinity School Address" of 1838 for the press, after having presented it before the faculty and student body in Cambridge, Miss Peabody saw the original manuscript. Therein she read a passage, omitted in the delivery, which, she observed, might have "saved many a weak brother and sister transcendentalist from going into the extremes of egotheism which has discredited a true principle." Despite her urging, Emerson refused to insert in the published address the statement she referred to. As she recalled years later, it was phrased about as follows: "Too soon one shall have the puppyism of a pretension of looking down on all human culture, setting up every little self magnified."[5]

In an article, **"Ego-theism, the Atheism of Today,"** contributed to the *Religious Magazine,* Miss Peabody attacked the philosophy of Hegel and the cult of Fourier. These were the extreme forms of individualism that had led the transcendentalists astray from the true ideal, she maintained.[6]

From Kant's declaration that man can never know God, but can only know his own "idea" of God, Hegel went on to deny the existence of a transcendent deity. German thought had therefore degenerated into "egotheistic atheism," Miss Peabody charged. The corrective for such a heresy was the very Platonic-Puritan basis on which the doctrines of Kant and Hegel had been superimposed, the Platonic teachings of divine immanence and mystic union and the Puritan emphasis on a transcendent, personalized deity, "The Father of our Lord Jesus Christ."[7]

A second deplorable tendency of transcendentalism, influenced by the French socialist Fourier, was its readiness to confuse *new* organization with reform, she declared. "New organization," Fourier's plan, was egotheistic because it was the result of one man's hasty generalization. Upon what Miss Peabody called a *non sequitur,* Fourier wished to build a new morality, a new religion, and new human relationships, abolishing the traditional ties of family and state. *Reform,* on the other hand, "is the making of outward arrangements conform more thoroughly with the principles of humanity acknowledged in the abstract by all human conscience in all ages."[8]

In one of her lectures before a normal-school class, Miss Peabody emphatically stated that in its old age transcendentalism had developed "into a new kind of bigotry . . . which shuts up its votaries in a dungeon from the light of Universal Experience."

> If he is not self-intoxicated, every man soon learns that his window does not command the whole horizon . . . that we are all free to look out of each others' windows, some being higher up in the tower of common humanity than our own, commanding wider views. . . .[9]

As much as any other transcendentalist, Miss Peabody had "looked out of other windows." Furthermore, she had consistently upheld the authority of tradition and had grasped the meaning of historical continuity. Emerson could reprimand Alcott for attempting to present Christ to the children of the Temple School as the ultimate example of Spirit incarnated: "I say, no, let us postpone everything historical to the dignity and grandeur of the present hour. . . . Come, forsake the historical, and let us go to the Most High."[10] But Elizabeth Peabody insisted always that "Truth is to be found in both directions, for it is in God, for whom 'a thousand years are as one day,' and who speaks in the past, present, and future, the same essential truth."[11]

Accordingly, in the ideals, character, and achievements of Boston's "Renaissance Man," the artist Washington Allston, Miss Peabody found a synthesis of past and present, Hebraic and Hellenic. In her *Last Evening with Allston,* a report of an interview with the old artist shortly before his death in 1843, Miss Peabody confessed that it was his life and philosophy that did more than anything else to mold her own aesthetic creed. She felt that Allston, better than any other living man, had made the great traditions of the past his inspiration for splendid creative activity, and that he had harmoniously fused, in his life and his works, the Greek and the Hebrew heritages.

Allston was "profoundly religious," Miss Peabody wrote; "and with him, as with Michael Angelo, *salvation* was the ultimate art of humanity." But unlike Michael Angelo, "Allston sought the expression of the infinite form of human character to the last, without laying aside the fine arts, but rather by their instrumentality."[12] His was, therefore, the symmetrical Hellenic personality, "in which no faculty had been left to grow rank, but all were cultivated harmoniously and faithfully,"[13] and at the same time he exemplified the Hebraic "holy life, flowing on the one hand from a deep sensibility to religion . . . ; and on the other from a severe and uncompromising self-restraint as to every questionable indulgence."[14] His idea of the Good and his concept of the Beautiful verified the sentence of Milton, "He who would make a true poet must be in himself an heroic poem."[15]

What Elizabeth Peabody learned from Dr. Channing, Emerson, Washington Allston, and from her omnivorous readings in theology, history, and philosophy she made peculiarly her own. It was precisely this eclectic combination of modified individualism, the aesthetic ideal, and a positive philosophy of history that enabled her to effect a reconciliation between transcendentalism and humanism and to integrate all her interests around a dynamic concept of culture that combined the best features of both Hebraism and Hellenism.

Thus, Miss Peabody was never tempted to sacrifice physical or rational to "spiritual" development, as was Bronson Alcott; and she was not inclined to submerge the past in the present and to pronounce the intuition of the moment always superior to the wisdom of the ages, as Emerson and Thoreau often did. Her progressive theories of education never led to a skeptical attitude toward the teaching process, as with Alcott. Recognizing the moral element to be paramount, she did not allow it to nullify the aesthetic, as did Theodore Parker and George Ripley. She preserved the golden mean between Thoreau's withdrawal from society at Walden and George Ripley's attempt to reorganize society at Brook Farm, and she avoided the selfish self-culture advocated by Margaret Fuller as well as Parker's "canine appetite for knowledge," always continuing her various philanthropies and her attempts to diffuse culture and improve educational systems. Perhaps of all members of the "Hedge Club," only Miss Peabody achieved a working synthesis of what seem to some critics to be irreconcilable elements in transcendentalism—past and present, society and solitude, moral and aesthetic, education of self and education of others.

An example of Miss Peabody's ability to apply Coleridge's principle of "the reconciliation of opposites" is found in a letter which she wrote to Horace Mann in 1838. Therein she combined literature, philosophy, religion, and pedagogy to produce the humanistic formula, the mean between pessimism and optimism:

> The fall of the angels from Heaven into Hell is but an image of the fall of the Powers of the Inward nature of man from the peacefulness and happiness of Innocence into the fiery misery of Evil—a process which must take place before any outward evil action can be done. Satan in the heavenly state was Self-respect, that sentiment which governs all other powers. . . . The host that followed Satan is all the powers of the mind. Each evil Angel being but a good power wrongly bent and still half glorious with its spiritual origin. The armies of Satan and of Michael (whose very name means Likeness of God) in their encounter represent the struggle of the good and evil of our natures. . . .[16]

Thus, man is neither wholly good nor wholly bad. The humanistic credo, *homo rationis capax,* was Miss Peabody's yardstick for measuring human nature. She was convinced, moreover, that good would triumph eventually, for a "recovering principle has been at work in the world since the fall," which indeed might be regarded as a "fortunate fall," as Milton argued in *Paradise Lost.*

She continued to develop this historical-allegorical thesis until, in 1854, she stated it in the form of an essay, published in 1881 in the St. Louis *Journal of Speculative Philosophy* and included in her collection, *Last Evening with Allston and Other Essays,* as **"Primeval Man."**

Her thesis in this essay represents a sharp break with the primary tenet of transcendentalism, that intuition is the best mode, perhaps the only method, of discovering absolute truth:

As a spirit of Reason, communing fully with his kind in love, and comprehending Nature by intuition, I submit that the "Image of God" is not *material,* and must be sought and found not by physiological but by historical research.[17]

Her method of searching history, language, and literature for spiritual truths had been learned from a study of Herder's *Spirit of Hebrew Poetry,* which she used in Marsh's 1833 translation as a textbook in her "conversation classes" for the ladies of Boston and Salem. In a series of articles published in the *Christian Examiner* for 1834 she gave a detailed analysis of her procedure. It consisted of comparing Hebrew scripture and Greek mythology as a means of discovering "basic" allegorical truths and of assigning a symbolic character to identical word roots in cognate languages. By such methods of inquiry Miss Peabody arrived at the concept of an Adam that named everything about him, his earliest communications with his fellows being the result of his speech instinct acted upon by natural environment.[18]

To substantiate her thesis, Miss Peabody did considerable research on earthly paradises, the Eden of the Hebrews, the lost Atlantis, the Persian Kingdom of Ormuzd, the long reign of gods on earth related in Chinese and Indian legendaries. All these stories to her became symbols of a great general truth, "that the race began as one social organism," that "man did appear on earth, not only in physical and in intellectual power, but *morally free* to good and evil, primevally the lawgiver."[19]

Having accepted the doctrine of historical primitivism, Miss Peabody was ready to embrace its corollary, sentimental primitivism, that wherever found in a natural state, unspoiled by civilization, man was morally free and instinctively good. Hence, she could lay aside all her other tasks to assist Sarah Winnemucca, princess of the Piute tribe, to raise funds for the "first school taught by an Indian," which the Princess had begun in a log hut built by her fellow tribesmen in Nevada. Of this enterprise Miss Peabody wrote in the Boston *Transcript*:

> The distinguishing characteristic of this New Departure is that, instead of being, as usual, a passive reception of civilizing influences proffered by white men who look down upon the Indian as a spiritual, moral, and intellectual inferior, it is a spontaneous movement, made by the Indian himself, *from himself,* in full consciousness of free agency, for the education that is to civilize him.[20]

Miss Peabody's "whole stud of Phoenixes," of which Emerson spoke admiringly,[21] were all attempts to aid man in regaining this primitive state of excellence from which he had lapsed. One of the most successful of these projects was the "atom of a bookshop" on West Street, where her father sold homeopathic remedies and where she acted as hostess to half the intelligentsia of Boston. J. F. Clarke later recalled that two German,

four French, and the best English periodicals, literary and scientific, were in stock there.[22] There Thomas Wentworth Higginson made his first acquaintance with the German transcendentalists and the French eclectics.[23] There Margaret Fuller held her conversations for the ladies of Boston. A supplementary venture, the Peabody press, issued editions of Hawthorne's tales for children and Dr. Channing's *Emancipation.* In April, 1842, Miss Peabody's name appeared as publisher of the *Dial,* and in May, 1849, the first and only number of *Aesthetic Papers* was edited and published by Elizabeth Peabody.

Despite her great variety of projects designed to disseminate culture and elevate man, Miss Peabody will be remembered primarily as the founder of the kindergarten system in America. She had been assistant to the Emerson brothers in a "finishing-school" for young ladies, and the associate of Bronson Alcott in his progressive "Temple School" in Boston. She stoutly championed the efforts of her brother-in-law, Horace Mann, to establish universal, free, public education in Massachusetts, and she did yeoman service in founding the first normal schools in that state.

Yet her essays in *Aesthetic Papers* indicate that, as late as 1849, she had not discovered her ideal system of education. She confessed that her experiments up to that time had been apprentice efforts and journey work. American education lacked spiritual idealism, she charged.[24] It fell short of the classical Greek pedagogy in developing sound and graceful bodies.[25] It failed to utilize music as a means of leading the soul of childhood to worship its divinity.[26] It neglected artistic exercises in painting and modeling[27] and entirely overlooked the important "science" of philology, wherein word analyses reveal "the universe in its symbolic character."[28]

It was not until 1859 that Miss Peabody found an existing system of education that embodied her spiritual and aesthetic ideals. Visiting in the home of Carl Schurz in Jamaica Plain, she was impressed by the unusual development of the six-year-old child of the family and learned that he had been a pupil in Froebel's kindergarten in Germany. Soon afterwards she obtained a copy of Froebel's *Education of Man* in the French version of Countess von Bulow and opened a kindergarten of her own in Boston. On her journey to Europe, observation of infant-schools established by Froebel in Hamburg, Dresden, and elsewhere convinced her that the German educator had devised a teaching technique based on aesthetic principles. Froebel had "worked out a series of artistical exercises, which aim to educate—that is, *draw forth*—the powers of children from a more profound depth than ordinary education respects," she later wrote.[29]

But the aesthetic nature is not all of the soul, she observed. Froebel had provided also for the social and moral natures. Rousseau's plan had developed individual idiosyncrasies, but Froebel's system made the child a normal social and moral being.[30] Unlike Pestalozzi, who began education with "object-instruction" for developing the "understanding," Froebel first addressed the "spiritual nature," she concluded triumphantly.[31]

Characteristically, even though she spent much time promoting the kindergarten movement in the United States, Miss Peabody did not isolate this project from her other activities. Instead she related the new interest to her transcendental philosophy and her broad program of culture.

The creative activity that led to artistic production in Froebel's kindergarten, Miss Peabody wrote, was "the special desideratum of an age which is so keen and energetic that it hurries our young men into pursuits in their amusements which take on the character of gambling; and hence gambling in business, gambling in politics, where even human beings, instead of being regarded as brothers to be kept, are used as dice, to be recklessly thrown in our game."[32]

Recognizing a social problem, she could fuse education, industry, and art into a new solution:

> The only preventive or cure for this passion of gambling is industry, and the only industry that is attractive is artistic; and why should not all industry become artistic, now that the great cosmic forces are suborned, by our advancing civilization, as the legitimate slaves of men, to do all the hard work for men?[33]

In this connection she referred to her publication of 1869, ***The Artist and Artisan Identified, The Proper Object of American Education.*** This pamphlet had contained Cardinal Nicholas Wiseman's lecture of 1852 before an industrial group of Manchester on "The Relation of the Arts of Design with the Arts of Production," to which Miss Peabody had added an essay entitled **"A Plea for Froebel's Kindergarten as the Primary Art School."** Peabody recognized that to encourage the American workingman to exercise individual initiative would enable him to consider himself a creator and transform him from a mere automaton into a man. Furthermore, like Wiseman and his master, John Ruskin, she denounced art for mere ornament's sake and urged a union of use and beauty, as in nature:

> High art excludes the fantastic, and is always simple,—because it is useful, like nature. The identification of artist with artisan will restore it, because the necessities of execution control design when artist and artisan are one. The modern artist is apt to design with no regard to use or nature.[34]

Art, philology, history, theology, and pedagogy were therefore elements of a new synthesis, through which Miss Peabody sought to furnish a corrective for transcendental doctrines and dogmas dangerously overstressed by other members of the "Hedge Club"—namely, sole reliance on intuition, a deification of the individual, and a disregard of historical continuity.

Though the transcendentalists often disagreed as to means, they usually agreed as to ends. Men and women are placed on earth to grow and gain their destined perfection, whether through activity, the exercise of intuition, or the searching of symbols, Margaret Fuller wrote.[35] Activity was Theodore Parker's solution, artistic activity Miss Peabody's. Exercise of intuition was more in favor with Thoreau, Emerson, and Alcott than with Hedge, Ripley, and Parker. Margaret Fuller and Elizabeth Peabody were seekers for symbols in their colloquies on Greek mythology, Peabody and Alcott in their "conversations" on the figurative meanings of words.

Yet Parker's ideal of human character was also Peabody's, Fuller's, Emerson's, and Ripley's—"the stature of the perfect man in Christ."[36] All would have agreed with him that "the influence of real Christianity is to disenthrall man; to restore him to his nature, until he obeys Conscience, Reason, and Religion, and is made free by that obedience."[37] This is Christian humanism, a fusion of the Hebraic and the Hellenic, in the sense that their well-rounded man, their "natural" man, was also a moral man. This identification did not exactly result in "the interest in man apart from theological determinations" that Symonds stated as the *sine qua non* of humanism,[38] but it was a man-centered philosophy of religion designed to elevate the human race here as well as save it hereafter.

Notes

1. Elizabeth Peabody, *Reminiscences of the Rev. William Ellery Channing, D.D.* (Boston, 1880), 356.

2. Odell Shepard, editor, *The Journals of Bronson Alcott* (Boston, 1938), 129.

3. Ralph Waldo Emerson, *et al., Memoirs of Margaret Fuller Ossoli* (Boston, 1852), I, 234.

4. *Reminiscences of Channing,* 365.

5. *Reminiscences of Channing,* 65. Emerson furnished his own corrective occasionally: "Because our education is defective, because we are superficial and ill-read, we are forced to make the most of the position of ignorance. Hence, America is a vast know-nothing party, and we disparage books, and cry up intuition. With a few clever men we have made a reputable thing of that, and denouncing libraries and severe culture, and magnifying

the mother-wit of bright boys from the country colleges, we have even come so far as to deceive everybody, except ourselves, into an admiration of un-learning and inspiration, forsooth." *The Journals of Ralph Waldo Emerson,* edited by Edward Waldo Emerson and Waldo Emerson Forbes (Boston, 1904-1914), IX, 89.

6. *Last Evening with Allston and Other Essays* (Boston, 1886), 245.

7. *Last Evening with Allston,* 247.

8. *Last Evening with Allston,* 248.

9. *Lectures in the Training Schools* (Boston, 1886), 25-26.

10. [Emerson,] *Journals,* V, 231.

11. *Reminiscences of Channing,* 144.

12. *Last Evening with Allston,* 5.

13. *Last Evening with Allston,* 1.

14. *Last Evening with Allston,* 26.

15. *Last Evening with Allston,* 6.

16. Quoted by Miss Queenie Bilbo in an unpublished Ph.D. dissertation, "Elizabeth Palmer Peabody" (New York University, 1932), 189. The excerpt is from Miss Peabody's unpublished correspondence.

17. *Last Evening with Allston,* 153.

18. "The Spirit of Hebrew Scripture," *Christian Examiner,* XVI (May, 1834), 174-202. In this article Miss Peabody quotes Herder's argument that in the northern languages words were absolute counters or echoes from external nature, unmodified by the influence of mind; but Oriental languages were the exact opposite—subjective rather than objective. In his *Ueber den Ursprung der Sprache* (1772), Herder had attacked literal interpretations of the Genesis account of speech origin. Language, he held, was the inevitable result of a union between nature and man's reflective powers. Although Herder is generally credited with the "Bow-Wow" or onomatopoetic theory of language origin, his Kantian insistence on innate powers influenced Max Müller and later theorists, who postulated a speech instinct, the "Ding-Dong" theory.

19. *Last Evening with Allston,* 155-157. The italics are Miss Peabody's.

20. "Preface," *Sarah Winnemucca's Practical Solution of the Indian Problem* (Cambridge, Mass., 1886). The italics are Miss Peabody's.

21. George Willis Cooke, *An Historical and Biographical Introduction to the Dial, As Reprinted in Numbers for the Rowfant Club* (Cleveland, 1902), I, 151.

22. Edward Everett Hale, editor, *Autobiography, Diary, and Correspondence of James Freeman Clarke* (Boston, 1891), 144.

23. *Cheerful Yesterdays* (Boston, 1898), 86.

24. "The Dorian Measure with a Modern Application," *Aesthetic Papers* (1849), 96.

25. *Aesthetic Papers,* 101.

26. *Aesthetic Papers,* 103.

27. *Aesthetic Papers,* 104.

28. *Aesthetic Papers,* 107.

29. Mary Mann and Elizabeth Peabody, *Moral Culture of Infancy, and Kindergarten Guide* (New York, 1869), 35.

30. *Lectures in the Training Schools,* 79.

31. *Lectures in the Training Schools,* 80.

32. *Lectures in the Training Schools,* 78.

33. *Lectures in the Training Schools,* 78.

34. Elizabeth Peabody, *The Artist and Artisan Identified—The Proper Object of American Education* (Boston, 1869), 43.

35. A. B. Fuller, editor, *Woman in the Nineteenth Century* (Boston, 1855), 19-20.

36. "A Lesson for the Day," *Dial,* I (October, 1840), 196.

37. "A Lesson for the Day," 207.

38. John A. Symonds, *Renaissance in Italy: The Revival of Learning* (London, 1902), 26.

Arlin Turner (essay date 1975)

SOURCE: Turner, Arlin. "Elizabeth Palmer Peabody Reviews *Twice-Told Tales.*" *Nathaniel Hawthorne Journal,* edited by C. E. Frazer Clark, Jr., pp. 75-84. Englewood, Colo.: Microcard Editions Books, 1975.

[*In the following essay, an introduction to Peabody's review of Nathaniel Hawthorne's* Twice-Told Tales, *Turner examines Peabody's appreciation for Hawthorne's stories.*]

In April, 1838, Sophia Peabody received at Salem a parcel of New York magazines from her cousin George Palmer Putnam. In one of them, she wrote her sister Elizabeth on April 17, "is your review of Mr. Hawthorne."[1] Her reference was to an unsigned review of

Twice-Told Tales, some 3,500 words in length, published in the *New-Yorker* for March 24 (V, 1-2). This review, which seems to have escaped notice, is printed below.

Elizabeth Peabody was spending the spring and summer with her brother Nathaniel and his family at West Newton. During her absence, packets of letters were exchanged between her and the Peabody household, with letters between her and Hawthorne sometimes included. Sophia commented further on Elizabeth's review: "It is beautiful. I like it all but the expression, 'sweet story-teller, with the flowery name, whose caged melodies' & c. It sounds too much like 'the rose baptized in dew.'" Elizabeth would recognize, she assumed, the phrase quoted from the beginning of a review of *Twice-Told Tales* in the *American Monthly Magazine* for March (n.s. V, 281-283), presumably by Charles Fenno Hoffman: "A rose bathed and baptized in dew—a star in its first gentle emergence above the horizon—all types of the soul of Nathaniel Hawthorne; every vein of which (if we may so speak) is filled and instinct with beauty."

In the year between the publication of *Twice-Told Tales,* March 6, 1837, and the appearance of Hoffman's review, no review of consequence had been published except that by Henry Wadsworth Longfellow in the *North American Review* for July (XLV, 59-73). The *Salem Gazette* of March 14 had published a note to introduce a reprinting of one of the tales, "Fancy's Show Box," and the *Knickerbocker Magazine* for April (IX, 422-425) had included slight comment, along with several quotations. The reviews by Hoffman and Elizabeth Peabody were both published in the same month, March, 1838, and both in magazines edited by Park Benjamin, who thus continued the effort he had exerted over several years to win recognition for Hawthorne's work.[2]

Elizabeth Peabody's review, published a year later than the book and in its length and its nature suggesting less a review than an evaluative essay, testifies that both the reviewer and the editor valued the work highly and wanted to give it greater acclaim than it had received. The review was but one of many efforts Miss Peabody made to encourage and assist Hawthorne to the high literary achievement she had become certain was possible for him. Before *Twice-Told Tales* was published, she had learned that he was the author of stories she admired in magazines and annuals, but only in November, 1837, did she meet him. By early 1838 she and her sisters Mary and Sophia were unabashedly devoted to the handsome, retiring young author. Within a few months Elizabeth Peabody was busy trying to secure for Hawthorne employment that would support him and leave time for his writing, and to find publishers for what he would write. His appointment as inspector in the Boston custom house in January, 1839, was in part in response to her efforts, and she herself published in 1841 three children's books from his pen.[3]

This review of *Twice-Told Tales* reveals Miss Peabody's judgment of Hawthorne's writings at the beginning of their acquaintance. (It is in fact the only criticism of his works she published until after his death.) She obviously had the contents of the volume well in mind. Inaccuracies in some of the short quotations from the tales suggest that she knew them so well as to risk quoting from memory. All of the contents but three receive comment, and all are praised, though not equally. She demands work of the highest order. "The Gray Champion" and other stories of American history please her greatly, but on second thought, "we cannot spare him from the higher paths, to confine him to this patriotic one." "The Prophetic Pictures" is "a masterpiece in its way," but "First-rate genius should leave the odd and peculiar, and especially the fantastic and horrible, to the inferior talent." Such tales would be to "Sunday at Home," "Sights from a Steeple," and "Little Annie's Ramble" as the effects of Byron are to Wordsworth's poetry.

In stating that to her mind "Sunday at Home" is worth a thousand sermons and that "The Gentle Boy" is "worth a thousand homilies on fanaticism in all its forms, contrasted with the divinity of the natural sentiments, and the institutions growing therefrom," Elizabeth Peabody might have been thinking of Emerson as a reader of Hawthorne's tales. Less than three months after her review appeared, she took Emerson the sketch "Footprints on the Sea-Shore" to read and had him reply "that there was no inside to it. Alcott and he together would make a man."[4] When she visited Emerson at Concord a year later, she brought him a volume of *Twice-Told Tales* to replace her own copy, which she had left with him earlier and now found he had not read. "He is in a good mood to do so," she wrote on June 23, 1839, "and I intend to bring him to his knees in a day or two, so that he will read the book, and all that Hawthorne has written."[5] Her review may be read as a Transcendentalist evaluation of this book and Transcendentalist guidance for works to be written. She quotes from Emerson's poem "The Rhodora." Emersonian phrases and turns of thought abound: "know thyself"; "the eye of Reason"; "the faculty of fancy is below the imagination"; "every man's mind is the centre of the whole universe—the *primum mobile*—itself at rest, which wheels all phenomena, in lesser or greater circles, around it"; "the poetic storyteller . . . will draw his materials from the wells of nature and involve the sanctities of religion in all his works"; "the ideal beauty may be seen clearest and felt most profoundly in the common incidents of actual life"; "the true story-teller . . . sits at the fountain-head of national character, and he must never stoop below the highest aim, but for ever seek the primal secret—for ever strive to speak the word which is answered by nothing less than a creation"; "the track of his footsteps will be hallowed, and every thing become sacred which he has touched.—

Then, and not till then, we shall have a country; for then, and not till then, there will be a national character."

A long letter Elizabeth Peabody wrote Hawthorne's sister Elizabeth at about the time she was writing her review for the *New-Yorker* reflects no less certainty as to Hawthorne's genius and no less firmness in outlining the course he must follow: ". . . there is good reason for believing that he is one of Nature's ordained priests, who is consecrated to her higher biddings. . . . I feel sure that this brother of yours has been gifted and kept so choice in her secret places by Nature thus far, that he may do a great thing for his country." The men of affairs to whom Hawthorne may turn for patronage "live in too gross a region of selfishness to appreciate the ambrosial moral *aura* which floats around our ARIEL,—the breath that he *respires*. I, too, would have him help govern this great people; but I would have him go to the *fountains* of greatness and power,—the unsoiled souls,—and weave for them his 'golden web,' . . .—it may be the *web of destiny* for this country. In every country *some one man* has done what has saved it. It was one Homer that made Greece, one Numa that made Rome, and one Wordsworth that has created the Poetry of Reflection."[6]

In her review in the *New-Yorker* Elizabeth Peabody found Hawthorne to be Wordsworthian, and said so with emphasis; without naming Emerson, she proved him Emersonian, as if she were demonstrating that he measured up to the criteria of the essays "Nature" and "The American Scholar"; she had published a review of these two works a month earlier.[7] With the *Twice-Told Tales* as evidence, she had a prediction to make of its author: Genius "wells up at the top of the hill; and in this instance descends in many streams—. . . may it preserve the sweetness and purity of its fountains, far up in the solitudes of nature! We can wish nothing better for Mr. Hawthorne or for ourselves. He will then take his place amongst his contemporaries, as the greatest artist of his line; for not one of our writers indicates so great a variety of the elements of genius."

Notes

1. This letter is in the Berg Collection, New York Public Library. It has been made available to me, along with other letters in the Berg Collection mentioned below, by the curator, Mrs. Lola L. Szladits.

2. For a survey of the tales and sketches by Hawthorne that Benjamin published initially, the others that he reprinted, and his criticism of Hawthorne's writings, see my article "Park Benjamin on the Author and the Illustrator of 'The Gentle Boy,'" pp. 85-91 of this volume.

3. Letters exchanged among Elizabeth, Mary, and Sophia Peabody, Nathaniel, Elizabeth, and Mary

Hawthorne are in the Berg Collection. Selections appear in Julian Hawthorne, *Nathaniel Hawthorne and His Wife* (Boston: J. R. Osgood, 1885), and in Rose Hawthorne Lathrop, *Memories of Hawthorne* (Boston: Houghton, Mifflin, 1897). See three important articles by Norman Holmes Pearson: "Elizabeth Peabody on Hawthorne," *Essex Institute Historical Collections,* XCIV (July, 1958), 256-276; "A Good Thing for Hawthorne," *Essex Institute Historical Collections,* C (Oct., 1964), 300-305; and *Hawthorne's Two Engagements* (Northampton, Mass., 1963). See also Louise Hall Tharp, *The Peabody Sisters of Salem* (Boston: Little, Brown, 1950), pp. 113-132.

4. Ralph Waldo Emerson, *The Journals and Miscellaneous Notebooks, VII, 1838-1842,* ed. A. W. Plumstead and Harrison Hayford (Cambridge, Mass.: Belknap Press of Harvard University Press, 1969), p. 21, June 6, 1838.

5. Rose Hawthorne Lathrop, *Memories of Hawthorne,* p. 29.

6. Julian Hawthorne, *Nathaniel Hawthorne and His Wife,* I, 165-167.

7. In the *Democratic Review,* I (Feb., 1838), 319-329. A letter of Hawthorne's to Louis O'Sullivan, editor of the *Democratic Review,* April 19, 1838, calls this review unworthy of Miss Peabody, "particularly poor," but recommends another essay of hers, which appeared in the *Democratic Review,* III (Nov., 1838), 253-268, under the title "Claims of the Beautiful Arts." (Professor Norman Holmes Pearson has kindly made available to me this letter and others, in the texts he has prepared for the edition of Hawthorne letters.) William Ellery Channing wrote Elizabeth Peabody a similar judgment, saying that this review "would be a bad model for a book which seeks general circulation." See her *Reminiscences of Rev. Wm. Ellery Channing, D.D.* (Boston: Roberts Brothers, 1877), p. 393.

Bruce A. Ronda (essay date second quarter 1977)

SOURCE: Ronda, Bruce A. "Elizabeth Palmer Peabody's Views of the Child." *ESQ: A Journal of the American Renaissance* 23, no. 2 (second quarter 1977): 106-13.

[In the following essay, Ronda evaluates the evolution of Peabody's educational philosophy over the course of her career. Ronda pays particular attention to Peabody's efforts to nurture morality and self-esteem in young children.]

Elizabeth Palmer Peabody's activities as an educator, writer, publisher, and intimate of Transcendentalists and reformers spanned more than sixty years. Despite the length and variety of her career, much of the scholarship about her has examined only specific events, particularly her involvement in Bronson Alcott's Temple School.[1] This essay explores Peabody's work as teacher and educational theorist from her first classroom experiences in the 1820's to her championship of Friedrich Froebel's methods in the late 1880's, focusing throughout on her views of the nature of the child and on the educational methods that grew from them.

Perhaps the most striking feature of Peabody's approach to the child was her method of synthesizing current philosophies to create a position which, while not logically consistent, was practical and moderate. One of the major schools of thought on human nature and education was, of course, the Unitarian, which Peabody absorbed first through her on childhood education and second through her long contact with William Ellery Channing. Peabody also read Locke, who believed that ideas are combinations of sense impressions and that children need to have their senses trained and kept sharp. The ideas and behavior of children depend on their being nurtured by wise, moral teachers in a stimulating environment. Peabody's mentor Channing agreed but added that children are themselves living organisms, predisposed to doing right and having what Peabody called a "yet unfallen nature." This implication that the child has inclinations and wisdom prior to sense data Locke generally would have denied. But Channing and Peabody held both to the primacy of sense data and to the existence of inherent moral principles.

In her work with Bronson Alcott, Peabody witnessed a teacher who pushed to an extreme his view of the child as spiritually precocious and intuitively wise. While agreeing with Alcott, Peabody insisted on emphasizing the education of the senses. She also rejected Alcott's ahistorical approach, believing that children need to be aware of the larger worlds of society and the past.

These various views—the child as blank slate needing sensory training, the child as inherently leaning toward the good, the child as unfallen, wise, and knowing, the child as socially and historically ignorant—all came together in Peabody's work as champion of Friedrich Froebel's kindergarten and as trainer of kindergarten teachers. While her synthesis was not logically coherent, it gave her a flexible and balanced view of the child which avoided both extremes of Lockean sensationalism and Alcottian child-worship and maintained that the child was both body to be trained and spirit possessing divine insight.

Elizabeth Peabody began her career as an educator in 1820 at the age of sixteen when she opened a school in Lancaster, Massachusetts.[2] Three years later she became governess to the children of a family in Maine. There she wrote a series of letters on teaching to her sister Mary, which were collected and published in 1841 as *Theory of Teaching.*[3]

Peabody's letters show how thoroughly she had absorbed Locke's perspectives on human nature and education. In "Some Thoughts Concerning Education," Locke argued that the child imitates adult models and rapidly absorbs sense impressions. Peabody followed suit: "In the child, we find immense physical and intellectual activity, extreme quickness of the senses, and susceptibility to impressions. . . ."[4] Locke also proposed that education "be suited to the Child's Capacity and Apprehension," that the child not be weighed down with rules and theories it cannot understand. This too Peabody echoed. Anticipating Bronson Alcott's characteristic method of instruction, the conversation, Peabody wrote that "children should be encouraged to speak naturally and freely of all they see, think, and feel. Thus their conversation will be what it should be, the perfect reflection of all objects, colored by the individual soul."[5]

This comment seriously qualified Peabody's standing as a Lockean. Locke concluded the essay by observing that his subject was a gentleman's son whom he "considered only as white Paper, or Wax, to be moulded and fashioned as one pleases . . ." (p. 325). But for Peabody, the child's individual soul affected what the senses received. When in 1825 she returned from Maine and became William Ellery Channing's secretary, he quickly confirmed her beliefs that children possess intuitive notions of good and evil, incline toward the good, and are instinctively aware of the reality of the spiritual life.[6]

Peabody believed from her own experience that children have an instinctive religious consciousness well before their exposure to organized religion or moral education. In a lecture to kindergarten teachers near the end of her life, she recalled that once as a child she had been asked by a visitor the question, who made you?

> I remember my pleased surprise at the question, that I feel had never been addressed to my consciousness before. At once a Face arose in my imagination,—only a Face and head,—close to me, and looking upon me with the most benignant smile, in which the kindness rather predominated over the intelligence; but it looked at me as if meaning, "Yes, I made you, as you know very well." . . . Though it was the first time I thought God and had given the name "God" to the thought, it seemed not new to me. I had felt God before.[7]

Subsequently, the young Elizabeth read Scottish common sense philosophers, whose work was so influential in early nineteenth century New England. These writers taught that environment and adult guidance were crucial for childhood education. While some in this school, particularly Thomas Reid, believed that there are innate moral principles and a potential for doing good in man, the Scots and their American Unitarian disciples agreed that without moral and religious education the child may turn to selfishness, thwarting the possibilities for a truly moral life.[8]

When Peabody became Channing's secretary, she was delighted to have him agree with her childhood perception that children instinctively know God and wish to do the good. As she recalled in her *Reminiscences of Dr. Channing,* Channing encouraged her to believe "that generosity is a stronger characteristic of childhood than selfishness; that selfishness, in fact, is only the abnormal reaction of innocent self-defense" against parental cruelty, capriciousness, or lack of skill in child-rearing. Channing's manner with children reflected his respect for their intuitions, and Peabody wanted to model her teaching style after his. She wrote of him in 1825, "he treats children with the greatest consideration, and evidently enjoys their conversation, and studies it to see what it indicates of the yet unfallen nature."[9]

While she was still Channing's secretary, Peabody opened a school in Brookline. To supplement her earnings, she took to lecturing and writing. From 1827 to the early 1830's, she gave lectures and readings to groups of women on historical and cultural subjects, and in the early '30's she published three history textbooks (Tharp, pp. 87-88).

At this point in her teaching career, Peabody mixed three perspectives on the child. From Locke, she had learned that the child is a sensate and highly imitative creature. Like the common sense philosophers, she felt that proper environment and adult guidance are required for moral education and a moral life, although she believed that the child had more than mere potential for knowing and doing good. And from her own childhood memories and from Channing, she learned that, while wise guidance is required, the child does possess an intuitive awareness of morality.

To these characteristics of her viewpoint should be added one more—wide reading of and love for history and social criticism. In her lecture series in the late 1820's, she read to her audiences passages from Harriet Martineau's work dealing with the English industrial revolution and social change (Tharp, pp. 87-89). Throughout her life, Peabody advocated an educational system that helped children understand the ways in which the past shaped the present.

With these inconsistent views in comfortable balance, Elizabeth Peabody encountered the next and most famous stage in her work as a teacher. She became Bronson Alcott's assistant at Temple School in Boston. When Alcott came to Boston in 1834 with plans to open a school, Peabody was considering starting one of her own and had even collected some students. Nevertheless she contributed these as well as time and energy to Alcott's project, working diligently to find a suitable site for the school and gathering and borrowing furnishings for it (Tharp, p. 93).

Temple School opened in September 1834 with Alcott as master and Peabody as assistant. Believing as she did in the existence of innate principles in the child, Peabody was impressed with Alcott's desire to explore the child's mind and help him recognize his essential spiritual nature. As she confided in her journal, Alcott worked "to bring out clearly in the children's consciousness, the perception of their spiritual existence, as being the most real and permanent." Alcott urged his pupils to be introspective, and the method he chose for that end was the journal, the purpose of which Peabody interpreted in this way: ". . . the effect of the external world—upon the internal life is made more obvious to their own perceptions—by putting down in a permanent form the pictures which run [?] through their own minds, and the thoughts and feelings they excite."[10]

Increasingly in 1835 and 1836, Peabody began to indicate in letters and elsewhere that she was not in complete sympathy with Bronson Alcott. One issue was the training of the child's senses, particularly through play and physical education. In his early years as a schoolmaster in Connecticut, Alcott had encouraged his pupils to play organized games on a regular basis. But by the time he opened Temple School, he was convinced of the primacy of spirit and spiritual education, and he simply allowed his students a few minutes of unsupervised play on the Boston Common every day. In the face of Alcott's insistent spiritualizing of the child, Peabody's Lockean training reasserted itself, and she argued for a direct connection between sense data and the "higher faculties." In her account of Alcott's teaching at Temple, *Record of a School,* which in its first (1835) edition is generally enthusiastic, Peabody slipped in this comment: "The understanding process can be helped a good deal, and it must be done by directing the attention to details, by directing the *senses,* for (although this is a fact that teachers do not generally advert to), the education of the senses in children is naturally *behind* that of the higher faculties of the soul."[11] Far from agreeing with Alcott's approach of shutting out sensory impressions through a heavy reliance on introspection, or at best interpreting sense data only allegorically, Peabody was proposing a more dynamic relation of sense perception and moral truth.

A second source of Peabody's growing discontent with Alcott was her suspicion that for all his desire to allow children to discover truths within themselves, he was guilty of manipulating discussions so that children would see and articulate his point. Once, she related in her *Record* [*Record of a School*], Alcott led his students into a discussion of capital punishment. He impressed on the children the loftiness of "the law of love" over "the law of strict justice." Most children, she noted, seemed to agree that mercy is better than severity. Yet, she added in a footnote, she suspected that Alcott had "unconsciously led them into his own views; by contradistinguishing mercy and justice." Capital punishment was a question requiring practical understanding and knowledge of social circumstances, Peabody thought, "not spontaneous reason, but reflective understanding." There were limits to untutored insight and dangers in over-guiding the discussion (pp. 151-158).

By the time of the publication of *Conversations with Children on the Gospels* in 1836 and 1837, for which she and her sister Sophia were the recorders, Peabody felt even more strongly that Alcott was not allowing spiritual truth simply to emerge from the children's own conversations, but was forcing them toward his own insights. On one occasion, Alcott conversed with his pupils on the story of the marriage feast at Cana. The children seemed thoroughly confused at the miracle of water turning into wine, so Alcott talked about miracles in general. These outward actions are shadows, emblems of spiritual glory, he taught. What do water, wine, marriage, symbolize, he asked? No one knew.

> Did you ever hear the word Chastity? That word represents something more than purity, for it implies self-restraint. This story may represent deep love, as one of you said at the beginning of the conversation; and when deep love is restrained by principles, it is chastity.

Here Peabody interrupted Alcott's monologue and charged:

> I think you have led the children into an allegorical interpretation of this passage, when their minds did not tend toward it. In no conversation has it been so difficult to keep them to the subject, nor have you suggested so much. I cannot help being gratified at this myself, because I do not believe the Evangelist had any idea of setting forth any thing but the kind sanction of Jesus to the innocent festivities which celebrate marriage.[12]

On another occasion in the *Conversations,* in discussing the stories of Jesus healing the sick and demon-possessed, Alcott apparently gave the impression that the sick were responsible for their condition. In a lengthy exchange, Peabody asserted with increasing frustration that Jesus and the gospel writers specifically denied that sickness is necessarily a result of sin. Alcott blandly maintained that "whatever was the fact with the individuals," the important matter was that the children's "minds . . . be possessed with the Ideas at first. And you see that they seem to apprehend these as if by a spiritual instinct. They can recur to Mark and Luke and the historical view hereafter" (II, 144).

Alcott's casual attitude toward "the historical view" was a third source of irritation to Peabody. She saw in his method a focus that was too exclusively on the child itself in its present circumstances. Alcott viewed the child as the human being most in touch with divine truth, the rest of life being spoiled by adult experience. Thus he had no sense, at least at this time, of the power of cultural and social inheritance, or of the influence of the child's surroundings on his spiritual insight. After one particularly distressing argument at the Alcotts' house, where Peabody was boarding in the spring of 1836, she confided in her journal this attack on Alcott's denigration of the past and absorption in his own thoughts.

> There seems to be a little envy at work where there is no more than gracious appreciation of what institutions and the Past have done for mankind. . . .
>
> But I am quite sure that he has planted himself on dangerous ground—far from his own humility and self-estimation—without a desire of having the key that unlocks all wisdom—in his own metaphysical system—he subjects everything to the test of his talismanic words—and as they answer to him in his predisposed ear—they take their places—nor does he do anything more—at the utmost of his liberality—than to *endure* the suggestion of a contrary view. It seems no part of his plan—to search the thought and views of other minds—in any faith that they will *help his own.* He only seems to look in books for what agrees with his own thoughts,—and he rather avoids than seeks any communication with persons who differ from himself.[13]

Finally, Peabody disapproved of the way in which Alcott demanded constant introspection from his students, encouraging them to reflect deeply on their feelings and motives, while at the same time requiring the group to discipline itself and develop a common conscience. She thought it an abusive public parading of children's half-formed and private feelings. As she wrote in her **"Explanatory Preface"** to the second edition of ***Record*** (1836):

> The instinctive delicacy with which children veil their deepest thoughts of love and tenderness for relatives, and their reasonable self-gradulations should not be violated, I think, in order to gain knowledge, or for any imagined benefit to others. . . . And Mr. Alcott, I believe, agrees with me in this, notwithstanding that he practically goes sometimes upon the very verge of the rights of reserve.[14]

Peabody preferred to address individuals in the classroom and thought "private conscience in the young" the best means of enforcing good behavior. Rather than seeking group consensus, Peabody wanted to "establish a separate understanding with each particular scholar, and act the part of a religious friend with each" (***Record,*** pp. xiv-xvi).

By the time she left Temple School in August 1836, Peabody had come to disagree with Alcott on these several important points: sense education, the conduct of discussions, historical education, privacy, and discipline. During the summer of 1836, a final conflict arose. Peabody realized that Alcott now possessed all the records which she and her sister Sophia had kept of the conversations with Temple students on the gospels. Peabody wrote to Alcott, asking that he reconsider publication or at least write explanatory prefaces and relegate questionable material to footnotes and appendices. She was concerned that these accounts, particularly of the discussions of birth which took place in mixed company, might threaten her and her sister's reputations.

> Why did Prophets and apostles veil this subject in fables and emblems if there was not a reason for avoiding physiological inquires & c? This is worth thinking of. However you as a man can say anything; but I am a woman, and have feelings that I dare not distrust, however little I can understand them, or give an account of them.[15]

In December 1836 the first volume of *Conversations* appeared. The book was promptly labelled "obscene" and Alcott was called a public disgrace and a threat to the social order (Shepard, pp. 193-195).

Elizabeth Peabody had meanwhile moved to Salem, and it might be imagined that she breathed a sigh of relief that she had escaped from Temple School in time. If she did so, it was in private, for in early 1837 she published a defense of Alcott, **"Mr. Alcott's Book and School,"** in the *Register and Observer.* In this article, Peabody muted her criticisms of Alcott, and wrote, "Were his the common mode of dogmatic instruction, I, for one, would not put my children under the guidance of his mind."[16] Conversing with children, respecting the integrity of their own intuitive morality—on these matters Peabody and Alcott had always agreed.

Peabody had moved some distance from Alcott's techniques and goals well before her August letter and departure from the school. She had always looked upon her position at Temple as temporary and probably felt she had learned all she could from a man whose personality and teaching manner she often found offensive. Her flexible position allowed her to walk between the extremes of sensationalism and Alcott's worship of the precocious child; she was able to agree with him on nurturing the moral insight of the young without falling into his errors of ahistorical thinking and the denial of the physical.

After her departure from Temple School, Peabody was anything but idle. Manager of West Street Bookstore in Boston, publisher, member of Hedge's Club, she was an active member of reform and Transcendentalist circles. She actively maintained her interest in education but confessed in 1849 that she still had not formulated any satisfactory theory about it. American education could do much more: helping children develop

sound and graceful bodies, utilizing music, painting, and sculpture, even using philology to establish the symbolic character of words.[17]

In 1859 Peabody visited Carl and Margarethe Schurz and met their remarkable six-year-old, who had been a pupil in Friedrich Froebel's kindergarten in Germany. Margarethe was an enthusiastic supporter of Froebel's methods, and had herself operated a German-speaking kindergarten in Wisconsin in 1856. She easily conveyed her enthusiasm to Peabody, who opened a kindergarten in Boston in 1860, travelled to Europe in 1867 to study German kindergartens firsthand, and devoted much of the rest of her life to training kindergarten teachers and popularizing the idea in America.[18]

In 1888, six years before she died, Peabody collected and published her talks to young women training to be kindergarten teachers as **Lectures in the Training Schools for Kindergartners.** From these lectures and from other sources, it is clear that the appeal of Froebel's educational system for Peabody was the way in which it held together the various views of the child that she herself had espoused throughout her life.

Froebel affirmed the importance of play and physical training. "It was Froebel's wisdom," she wrote, "instead of repressing, to accept this natural activity of childhood, as a hint of Divine Providence, and to utilize its spontaneous play for education."[19] All knowledge and self-awareness comes first through the body. To the new-born, the center of his attention is his body, not, as Alcott claimed, his memories of a divine state recently left behind.[20]

At the same time, Froebel did not contradict Peabody's belief in inherent moral and spiritual principles which exist in the child independent of sense data. The impulses which the sense organs receive are simply the means for establishing the child's awareness of self. "True education," she told her audiences, "shall lead out the imprisoned spirit, growingly conscious of individuality, by means of the symbolism of the prison house itself, which is that correlation of necessary forces we call the material universe" (*Lectures* [*Lectures in the Training Schools for Kindergartners*], p. 93). Froebel's system made room for a child that was both primarily sensate and instinctively moral. This combination was a new version of Channing's teachings, Peabody said, and she delighted in comparisons between the two. Froebel simply put into more scientific language what Channing said "in more poetic Christian phrase" when he named the child as "the original man" (*Reminiscences,* pp. 92-93).

Peabody recognized elements of Unitarian educational theory and Scottish common sense philosophy in Froebel's method. She agreed with Froebel that the child has potential for evil as well as good. The universe is moral, she wrote, but evil will result if the child does not adopt "the laws of order, by which God creates the universe." What is required is something "outside the child's conscious individuality," namely *"the human providence of education"* (**Lectures,** p. 14).

As she looked back on her career, and particularly on her encounter with Bronson Alcott, Elizabeth Peabody realized that Alcott was not wrong in encouraging self-expression. It was his methods of introspection, journalizing, and the collective conscience that seemed so inappropriate for children. Froebel provided in his kindergarten what seemed to Peabody far healthier and more applicable means of achieving self-expression: body movement, painting, drawing, sculpture. As Peabody observed, "Froebel . . . instead of beginning with thinking, begins by *doing something,* to be thought about,—thus preventing that abstract introversion which Dr. Channing thought the questionable thing in Mr. Alcott's method" (**Lectures,** p. 78). "Artistic production," she wrote in her **"Preface"** to the third edition of her **Record** (1874), was a better method of education than "self-inspection."[21]

One may be tempted to dismiss Elizabeth Peabody as an eccentric dilettante holding together a variety of philosophical positions on the nature of the child, the contradictions of which a keener mind would have seen and confronted. But Peabody was not a philosopher; she was in all things a teacher. She sought ways of imagining the child's essential self and methods that would address and educate that self. She sought a position that would allow for physical and moral education, for honoring the child's inherent moral awareness, and for teaching as if the child might still lapse into evil. She wanted to encourage self-expression and at the same time teach the child of a society and a history that was beyond the self. In a time before Freud revealed the psychological dramas and traumas of childhood, before genetics taught of biological inheritance, and before a public diversity of moral systems challenged Christian preeminence, Elizabeth Peabody was able to conceive of and teach, through her inconsistent and illogical views, a whole child, an organic unity.

Notes

1. Josephine E. Roberts, "Elizabeth Peabody and Temple School," *New England Quarterly,* 15 (1942), 497-508; Louise Hall Tharp, *The Peabody Sisters of Salem* (Boston: Little, Brown, 1949), pp. 87-113; Ruth M. Baylor, *Elizabeth Palmer Peabody, Kindergarten Pioneer* (Philadelphia: Univ. of Pennsylvania Press, 1965). In "A Transcendental Minority Report," *New England Quarterly,* 29 (1956), 147-158, John B. Wilson seriously considers Peabody's career, comparing her views to those of her Transcendental and reform associates.

2. "Elizabeth Palmer Peabody," *DAB* [Dictionary of American Biography (1928-)].

3. [Elizabeth Palmer Peabody,] *Theory of Teaching, with a few practical illustrations, by a Teacher* (Boston: E. P. Peabody, 1841).

4. John Locke, *The Educational Writings of John Locke,* ed. James Axtell (Cambridge: Cambridge Univ. Press, 1968), pp. 171-172; Peabody, *Theory of Teaching,* p. 53.

5. Locke, p. 181; Peabody, *Theory of Teaching,* p. 125.

6. Elizabeth Palmer Peabody, *Reminiscences of Rev. William Ellery Channing, D.D.* (Boston: Roberts Brothers, 1880), pp. 74-75, 123, 127-128.

7. Elizabeth Palmer Peabody, *Lectures in the Training Schools for Kindergartners* (Boston: D. C. Heath, 1888), pp. 70-71.

8. See Daniel Walker Howe, *The Unitarian Conscience* (Cambridge, Mass.: Harvard Univ. Press, 1970), pp. 30, 52.

9. Peabody, *Reminiscences,* p. 160.

10. Elizabeth Palmer Peabody, MS. journal, December 29, 1834, Henry W. and Albert A. Berg Collection, New York Public Library, Astor, Lenox, and Tilden Foundations. I am grateful to the library for permission to quote from the Peabody manuscripts in the Berg Collection.

11. *Record of a School Exemplifying the Principles and Methods of Moral Culture* (Boston: James Munroe, 1835), pp. 34-35.

12. *Conversations with Children on the Gospels* (Boston: James Munroe, 1836-1837), II, 17.

13. Peabody, MS. journal, April 11-April 15, 1836, Berg Collection, New York Public Library.

14. Peabody, *Record of a School Exemplifying the General Principles of Spiritual Culture, with an Explanatory Preface, and Other Revisions* (Boston: Russell, Shattuck, and Co., 1836), p. viii.

15. Peabody, quoted in Odell Shepard, *Pedlar's Progress: the Life of Bronson Alcott* (Boston: Little, Brown, 1937), p. 189.

16. Peabody, quoted in Tharp, p. 111.

17. Elizabeth Palmer Peabody, "The Dorian Measure," originally published in *Aesthetic Papers* (1849), reprinted in *Last Evening with Allston, and Other Papers* (Boston: D. Lathrop and Co., 1886), pp. 122, 124, 127-128.

18. Wilson, 156; Baylor, pp. 18, 35-36, 51.

19. Elizabeth Palmer Peabody, "A Plea for Froebel's Kindergarten," in *Last Evening with Allston*, pp. 334-335.

20. Peabody, *Lectures*, pp. 30, 58.

21. Peabody, "Preface," *Record of Mr. Alcott's School. Exemplifying the Principles and Methods of Moral Education* (3rd ed., rev., Boston: Roberts Brothers, 1874), p. 4.

Philip F. Gura (essay date third quarter 1977)

SOURCE: Gura, Philip F. "Elizabeth Palmer Peabody and the Philosophy of Language." *ESQ: A Journal of the American Renaissance* 23, no. 3 (third quarter 1977): 154-63.

[*In the following essay, Gura examines the diverse influences behind Peabody's linguistic theories.*]

Octavius Brooks Frothingham's *Transcendentalism in New England* remains, even after one hundred years, one of the most perceptive discussions of the Transcendentalist movement. Writing forty years after Emerson's *Nature* had shattered the still-youthful Unitarian synthesis, Frothingham noted how in New England "the ideas entertained by foreign thinkers blossomed out in every form of social life." New England furnished "the only plot of ground on the planet where Transcendental philosophy had a chance to show what it was and what it proposed," and the distinctive element of American Transcendentalism was just this *pragmatism.* "The test of a truth," Frothingham concluded, is its "availability," and in the New World "the thinker was called on to justify himself on the spot by building an engine, and setting something in motion."[1]

He was speaking of such famous enterprises as Brook Farm and Henry Thoreau's sojourn at Walden Pond, but his words apply equally well to Elizabeth Palmer Peabody's role in the discussion among Transcendentalists in the 1830's and '40's of the philosophy of language, a subject which has humanistic implications increasingly difficult for our generation to comprehend. The Transcendentalists' concern with this topic had its roots in the controversy over biblical exegesis which surfaced when the Unitarians openly challenged the Trinitarian reading of Scripture, and their interest spread after the dual streams of German idealism and Swedenborgian correspondence laid the foundation for an understanding of language significantly different from one based on Lockean empiricism. Hans Aarsleff, in *The Study of Language in England, 1780-1860,* touches the heart of the matter when he explains that, in the nineteenth century, language study, even when called philology, was not merely "a matter of knowing the forms, syntax,

phonology, historical relationships and other aspects" of particular tongues. The questions were of larger significance. "What, for instance, was the origin of thought? Did the mind have a material basis? Did mankind have a single origin? Was the first language given by revelation or had man invented it in the process of time?"[2] If we understand that the scholars involved in this study considered their work an attempt to answer such questions and to apply the answers *practically* to such spheres as theology, education, and literature, their dedication to what in retrospect seems like inane, or at best, antiquarian wordplay begins to come into meaningful focus. Among the American Transcendentalists involved in this re-examination of language, Peabody was the première purveyor of language theory, both in its theoretical and practical aspects.[3]

I

John B. Wilson recently concluded that Peabody learned her methods of "searching history, language, and literature for spiritual truths" from a study of J. G. Herder's *The Spirit of Hebrew Poetry,* which she used as a textbook in her "conversation classes" for ladies of Boston and which she reviewed for the *Christian Examiner* in 1834. This review, which establishes the tone for much of her later theorizing, deserves close scrutiny, especially because it illustrates that the origin of the concern over the philosophy of language can be traced to the problem of establishing the authenticity of Scriptural texts, one aim of Herder's book (Wilson, p. 234). Peabody begins in a manner typical of her Unitarian upbringing, stressing that the words of the Old Testament were the product of men who were "limited in their power of taking in what was so freely poured upon them by their partaking in the spirit and character of the age in which they lived." This notion of language was expressed by many Unitarians schooled in Locke's *Essay Concerning Human Understanding,* who saw words as merely the arbitrary creations of men for the purpose of communication among themselves. But Peabody, already showing signs of her reading in Idealistic philosophy, discusses the *poetry* of the Scriptures, what she describes as the "expression of abstract and spiritual truths by sensible objects, by the forms, colors, sounds, changes, [and] combinations of external nature." This poetic language existed because "the human mind in its original principles, and the natural creation, in its simplicity," were but different images "of the same creator, who linked them for the reciprocal development of their mutual treasures."[4]

Primitive languages thus were "naturally poetic," but, as a society "ramified" and people talked by imitation and custom and not from their primitive experiences, a thousand arbitrary and accidental associations "connected themselves with words and deadened the impressions" they would naturally make on people. Suggesting a theory of the development of the forms of language similar to that advanced in 1836 by Rowland Gibson Hazard (whose works Peabody later published), she saw language as moving to a level of "analytical" (today we would call it *technical*) expression where words no longer were pictures of the natural world but were merely social conventions. This language was commonly known as *prose,* and, while it provided a more precise expression of the differences among things, it sacrificed the "force, impressiveness, and exciting power" of poetry. The most poetic expression of all thought, then, existed in the early stages of the human mind, *but* (and this was critical for those engaged in philological study) since poetry had formed the basis for the first language, "it must always exist as a part of all [subsequent] languages." Proceeding from this premise, Herder then explained the primitive poetical radicals of the Hebrew language and pointed out that the true genius of the Hebrew tongue was displayed in its "formation and derivation of words from the original roots, and of those original roots from external and internal nature."[5]

Peabody coupled her study of Herder with what she knew of Greek mythology and discovered "the basic allegorical truths between the poetry of both cultures, which allowed her to assign a symbolic character to identical root words" in the languages. This enterprise led to a vision of primitive man as an original poet who named everything around him through the interaction of his speech instinct and the natural environment; that is, it proved that originally there was a reason (explained by the common origin of all things in the Oversoul) why such a word meant such a thing. For Peabody, the chief lesson of Herder's volume was the suggestion that, if one went back far enough in his study of language, he could not only locate the original roots of a tongue but ascertain how these roots *themselves* were derived from "external and internal nature." This theory—here is the linch-pin of the meaning of language for Transcendentalists—implied that there was a universality to the oldest roots of languages which, if properly understood, revealed what Peabody's friend Bronson Alcott called a "Universal Grammar." This grammar, in addition to providing a key to the more economic assimilation of the various modern tongues, also demonstrated the common origin of all men's thoughts in nature's reflection of the Oversoul. And if all language was derived from a common source—the interaction of the Reason with Nature—it declared a brotherhood of man far more inclusive than any defined by the arbitrary claimers of American *political* democracy (Wilson, *passim*).

What Peabody and others were seeking in the 1830's and '40's was a theory of language which refuted the empiricists' claims that all words were arbitrary signs which had no final relation to the things they named.

This search was part of their general revolt against Lockean epistemology, but it soon involved them with reform in other areas. Peabody's early essay on Herder epitomizes this concern with a *natural language,* the parts of which were intimately connected to the objects of the exterior world, and for convenience this sense of a transcendent correspondence between words and things can be termed a belief in a "language of nature" which returned men to a more primitive, that is, *vital* relationship to the world they inhabited.

One result of Peabody's continuing interest in a theory of language compatible with Idealistic philosophy was her sponsorship and publication of the works of theorists whose ideas interested her, most prominently the Rhode Island industrialist Rowland Gibson Hazard and the Hungarian philologist and schoolmaster Charles Kraitsir. Both men advanced theories similar to the one Peabody had groped towards in her essay on Herder; and, while ultimately Kraitsir is the more influential, together they suggest how and why a theory of a language of nature could make a difference in spheres of practical activity.

II

In 1836 Hazard anonymously published *Language: Its Connexion with the Present Condition and Future Prospects of Man.* Peabody, then serving as what might be called private secretary to William Ellery Channing, transcribing his sermons for the press, was so taken by the book that she promptly read it aloud to the Unitarian divine. In a reminiscence, she recalled that Channing immediately "recognized a rare metaphysical genius in its author," and that the following summer he wrote her from Newport that he had discovered the identity of the author, met him, and thought that he would be "a star in the intellectual firmament by-and-by."[6]

The attraction this home-spun philosopher had for Peabody and Channing (Hazard admitted to writing his booklet "in fragments on steamboats, at hotels, and during such hours as could be spared" from his business dealings) resided in his articulation of an epistemology remarkably similar to that being introduced into America by such thinkers as Coleridge and Victor Cousin. Hazard's biographer had astutely recognized this as early as the 1880's, when he mentioned that the distinctions in language which Hazard described were not wholly unlike "the distinctions made by Kant and afterwards in a modified way by Coleridge" between the functions of the Reason and the Understanding. Hazard had concluded that behind every word man uttered there was a primitive non-verbal stage when all he had was an "ideal" or "primitive" perception of the thing in his mind. "Primitive perceptions" were the feelings men had *before* they possessed the proper word or sign to fit their ideas expressly, the *cause* of the effect we call language. In Hazard's words, they consisted in one's "impression of things, and all the images, sensations and emotions of the mind which are independent of words, and which having a separate and prior existence, induce us to resort to language when we would impart them."[7]

But just as Herder had revealed that people no longer understood the poetry of Scripture, Hazard, too, saw men as having strayed from this "language of ideality" (as he termed it) which best expressed their primitive perceptions (Durfee, p. 63). Men now resorted to a "language of narration" which expressed their basic thoughts without any high degree of connotation or the need for the "imaginative or reasoning power," or to a "language of abstraction" which was used in contemporary logical discourse, for example, in barren theological treatises. These forms did no justice to the innate linguistic capabilities of men, and Hazard called for a return to a language which allowed men to discover "the relations among their perceptions" without being first obliged to express them abstractly and to rediscover the language of poetry where "instead of the immediate connection between words and ideals, the associations between the ideals themselves are made use of" (Hazard, pp. 12-14).

Hazard's implication throughout was that, while the languages of narration and abstraction were needed for *persuasion,* the language of ideality was necessary for *conviction.* Poetic discourse had to be used in religious discussions, especially to show that "the power of perceiving truth in the form of ideals" (as opposed to dry abstractions) was the principle necessary to nurture a faith. He posited a gradual unfolding of human nature until men realized through these primitive perceptions the religious truths by which they had to live. To his mind there was a direct relationship between the language of ideality and man's attempt to comprehend the divinity of divinity: through the language of poetry man came to understand how his "finite spirit" blended with "the infinite" so that men always were holding "communion" with omniscience. The poet, the highest example of man using language, became, like Emerson's model, a "liberating god" (Hazard, pp. 88, 135).

Peabody was enough taken by such ideas to publish a large selection of Hazard's essays in 1857, long after she had been introduced to more sophisticated theories of language. What appealed to her was Hazard's sense that there existed a language which addressed itself "to all, and which may be understood by all," one which (like Hebrew poetry) tapped deep roots within racial memories and spoke of the bond of all men. In his intuitive moments, man felt the conviction inherent in a language which demonstrated that "God, through the medium of His works, holds communion with the soul, shadows out the mysterious relations which exist between visible and invisible, the finite and infinite." This sentiment dovetailed perfectly with the New England Idealists' sense of a Reason, the promptings of which could be felt in moments of pure transcendence. And more importantly, as Harold Durfee has shown, it was a sentiment which linked Hazard, as well as such Transcendentalists as Peabody and Theodore Parker, to such important theologians as Horace Bushnell, who also advanced the premise that the most profound religious truths could be offered symbolically, that is, through the language of ideality.[8]

III

Another of Peabody's important essays on the subject of language is her review of the "Preliminary Dissertation on Language" prefixed to Bushnell's *God in Christ* (1849), one of his most important theological formulations. This review-essay first appeared in her own magazine, the short-lived but significant single issue of *Aesthetic Papers* which she published after the demise of *The Dial* (which in its last two years also appeared under her imprint), and she used the appearance of Bushnell's work to attract more notice to her important discovery, the work of the Hungarian emigré Charles Kraitsir.[9]

Trained as a doctor, Kraitsir was swept up in the revolutionary activity in Poland in 1830 and forced to emigrate to France and England. By 1833 he came to America and in Maryland established an academy on the model of the European *gymnasium.* His pedagogical gifts, especially in language, attracted wide notice, and in 1840 he was named Professor of Modern Languages at the University of Virginia. But the growing furor over slavery rekindled his libertarian feelings; he removed to the Boston area and, in 1844, began a successful series of lectures based on his unusual philological theories. By 1845 Peabody, still living a penurious existence despite the intellectual success of her bookstore and publishing ventures, became a teaching assistant in the academy he started in Boston.[10]

Peabody was interested in Kraitsir's claim for a theory of language which would unlock foreign tongues and make language study easier. From the copious notes she made of his public lectures, she published his *The Significance of the Alphabet* (1846), a pamphlet which—despite Kraitsir's (and several reviewers') claims that it was an aid in the instruction of foreign languages—proved one of the most remarkable philosophical documents of the period. Presented with an opportunity to review Bushnell's book on a similar subject, she took the time to compare it closely to Kraitsir's.[11]

Bushnell, Peabody said, understood that his topic—God in Christ—could not be broached without "falling upon language itself" and considering its nature in a more profound way than had yet been done. Moreover, he realized that men were "linguistic, as truly, as naturally, as they are locomotive or intellectual" and therefore he saw the *a priori* reason to believe that language was *not* arbitrary nor accidental, but sprang *from nature,* to which it had a vital connection. Thus, the Hartford theologian was close to saying that men named things through a pre-established law connecting the mind and the natural world (**"Language,"** pp. 215-216).

But Bushnell did not perceive that "the same laws of imagination determined the elements of single words to their subjects, so that every word which is not an imitation of nature, like *hum, buzz, boom,* is, as it were, a poem; in short, that there is some natural and inevitable reason why every word should be what it is." Viewing the seeming confusion of the various tongues, Bushnell retreated to the empiricists' position that language was "the creature of convention" and did not see that "within the multitudes of languages, and beneath the confusion of tongues, there must be something of a universal character, which gives meaning to the articulations of sound." In short, what he missed was the philological speculation of Kraitsir, who had shown (at least to Peabody's satisfaction) that the key to the study of languages lay not in their sounds—which *did* vary greatly for the same object in different tongues—but in the very *articulations* of sound (**"Language,"** p. 215).

What Kraitsir had discovered after years of study in the modern languages was that a unity derived from certain *organic* principles underpinned speech. "All men," he declared, "however diverse they might become by conflicting passions and interests, have yet *the same reason* and *the same organs of speech,*" and the underlying unity of all languages is based on a *physiological* premise: man could produce only a limited number of sounds through his vocal organs. The relationship between a man's consciousness (his Reason) and his organs of speech *was* language. Speech, concluded Kraitsir, was but "the explosion of reason," and it had to explode in one of three ways: from the throat in *gutturality,* from the lips in *labiality,* or from the teeth in *dentality.* Let me quote his explanation at length:

> Languages therefore have a certain unity. Differing superficially more or less, they begin to resemble each other, as soon as the observer goes beneath the surface; and they unite at the centre into three fundamental articulations, symbolizing the three organs of speech by which they are severally made, and correlative to three obvious categories of nature, cause, living and moving effect, dead or dormant effect. . . . There are three classes of sounds, in consequence of the harmony between our organs and the several categories, into which nature is divided in our conception. On examining languages we find the general fact that the causal is not expressed without the guttural; what is living and moving not without labials and linguals; what is dead or dormant not without dentals.

Kraitsir thus posited an amazing correspondence between the worlds of matter and spirit; for articulated sounds, the way air filtered through the throat, lips, and teeth, were a function of how man's Reason comprehended a stimulus in relation to the three great organic categories of existence: birth, life, and death. The modifications of voice made by men who in speaking brought "the external universe into relation with the spirit within themselves" was *the* constant underlying all languages.[12]

Kraitsir conceived of the purpose of his speculations as chiefly *educational,* revolutionizing the teaching of foreign languages. He was concerned with the perversion of spoken English and the fact that words "as pronounced" no longer "symbolized ideas" as they had when they first exploded from man's Reason. One had to *read* the words to discern any difference between *know* and *no,* or to see any "*angle in knee,* any *ken in knowledge,* and *keenness in knife,* any *getting into things* by *gnawing.*" People tended to drop gutturals from their speech but, luckily for those trying to ascertain the roots of different languages, kept them in their writing. Taking the Latin language for his key, Kraitsir believed that if men, in learning it, took care not to soften their gutturals and to pronounce their diphthongs as diphthongs, all other languages could be more easily assimilated. Men would learn that languages of the same family "told tales on one another" and that "the same raw material lay at the bottom of the great variety of tongues" (*Significance,* p. 25).

Peabody easily transferred the implications of Kraitsir's "glossology," as he named his science, from the *educational* to the *theological.* She praised Bushnell's suggestions that there was "a *logos* in the forms of things" by which they were prepared to serve as "types or images of what is inmost in our souls" and that "the outer world which envelops our being" was itself a "language" of sorts. But, she noted, he missed the point that language represented not only *external* nature but "the ideas of man and the operations of his mind." In short, Kraitsir provided scientific, philological proof of Emerson's premises in *Nature,* that words were signs of natural facts, natural facts signs of spiritual facts, and all nature the symbol of spirit. An awareness of the true form of language with its "direct reference to organic sounds" revealed the "original poetry of the unworn human mind" and thus verified Herder's and Hazard's sense of the keen power and truth of the primitive language of ideality (**"Language,"** pp. 215-218).

Peabody closed her assessment by quoting from a letter Kraitsir had received from one who had attended his lectures on the structure of the universal language.

> The identity of roots presented by him affects the imagination with a sense of the closest fraternity, and revealed to my mind with new force the words of an elo-

quent advocate for the study of language who, on dwelling upon the sympathies it stirred up, exclaimed with the prophet, "Have we not all one father? Hath not one God created us?"

Peabody saw Kraitsir's theories, then, not only as revolutionizing the teaching of foreign languages but as making men aware of their common brotherhood under God. And the men who saw this most clearly had learned the true relation of the articulations of sound to the Reason as man encountered the things of this world through that faculty and attempted to describe his sights to another. Language was perceived not only as a tool of communication, but as itself a veritable revelation (**"Language,"** p. 224).

Mary Lowell Putnam, a proper Bostonian who in 1849 reviewed Kraitsir's work for the *North American Review* under the bland running title of "The Pronunciation of the Latin Language," put the matter even more succinctly. She identified the genius of Kraitsir as residing in his understanding that language offered a profound insight into man's *spiritual* relationship to nature. Kraitsir demonstrated that "in the childhood of man, when nature mirrored herself in his thought, and thought passed unconsciously into instinctive speech, what is now called metaphor was then natural language."[13] This was precisely the understanding to which the artist Henry Thoreau would come when he transformed the philologist's theories for his own literary and teleological purposes. That, however, is another story.

IV

Thus Elizabeth Peabody became particularly enamored of certain philological theories which presented evidence that originally man used what we call a language of nature, a vocabulary which derived its force from a symbiotic relationship between man's highest faculty, his Reason, and the natural world. She initially was attracted to the ideas of men like Hazard and Kraitsir because they provided a theoretical foundation for a renewed understanding of the metaphors in which Christian (and *all*) history was written. Hazard and eventually Bushnell came to believe that religious truths could be expressed only through the rhetorical forms of symbol or paradox, that is, *in a poetic mode,* and Peabody saw in their theories the injection of faith and ideality necessary to keep Unitarianism a viable faith in the nineteenth century. Further, Kraitsir's painstaking etymological studies (in 1852 he published his massive *Glossology: Being a Treatise on the Nature of Language and the Language of Nature*) provided what many thought a *scientific* proof of the universality of the symbols men made and used. Peabody's wholehearted espousal of his concepts is more evidence of the Transcendentalists' insatiable desire to perceive, or provide, a philosophical unity to a world which by 1840 seemed badly fragmented.

But one other aspect of Peabody's interest in philology remains: the eminently practical activity of the use of language theory in the educational experiments she and Bronson Alcott performed at the latter's Temple School in the 1830's. Noticing Peabody's pedagogical gifts, Alcott had enlisted her to teach Latin for two hours a day to the young Brahmins enrolled in his classroom, but she was so taken by the master and his methods that she began spending all day in the school and took the lengthy notes which she published in 1835 as *The Record of a School, Exemplifying the Principles and Methods of Moral Culture.* According to Odell Shepard, the most important exercise of the day in the Temple School "was the defining of words, in which Alcott lost no opportunity to draw (some would say drag) in a moral, spiritual or philosophical lesson." The **"Explanatory Preface"** Peabody contributed to the 1836 edition clarified how these lessons were carried out.[14]

The novelty of Alcott's school, she explained, arose from the "psychology" (that is, that Idealistic epistemology) on which he based his philosophy of education. He believed that the contemplation of spirit was "the first principle of Human Culture and the foundation of self-education." Rather than paying undue attention to the outside world, children should examine their spiritual depths and *then* look outwardly at the material presence. Nature was only to be made use of as "imagery to express the inward life we experience." The vocabulary lessons which began each day were designed to teach children to handle words in just this "spiritual" way, to make them speak of "the outward as the sign of the inward" principles which they intuitively understood but were in danger of forgetting as they matured into the materialistic nineteenth-century world (*Record,* pp. iv-v).

Alcott's lessons in language were admitted "to be the most valuable," Peabody reported, and many were struck with the "advantages, necessarily to be derived from the habit of inquiring into the history of words from their material origin, and throughout the spiritual application of them, which the imagination makes." She attested to Alcott's ability to make his students aware that words were the keys to understanding the *deeper* language which suffused nature and illuminated man's spirit—a language, in Sampson Reed's phrase, not of words but of things.[15]

Illustrating again how all these applications of language theory were interwoven, she mentioned that Alcott believed that the "contemplation of Spirit in God" was "necessarily wrapt up in a study of language." His description of Jesus (taken from his *Conversations with Children on the Gospels*) virtually portrayed the Christ as a poet whose success in enlisting people for his cause for over eighteen hundred years was accounted for by his genius for language. Christ influenced people because of his concern with the "living word" which rose spontaneously from His soul and clothed itself "in the simplest, yet most commanding forms." As expressed in the Gospel parables, Christ's ideas became "like the beautiful yet majestic nature" whose images He "wove so skillfully into his own diction," and the best way to understand His message was to parse and spell His words with primitive imagination.[16]

Alcott's lessons on the Gospels, then, took the form of reading the biblical lesson for the day and asking the children for their "associations with words, their impressions of events, the action of their Imagination, and the conclusions of their Reason upon them." Here is an example using the word "type."

> One boy said [it was] a metal letter which is used to stamp signs upon paper. What is a word or type the sign of? said Mr. Alcott. They severally said, of a thought, of an idea, of a feeling; of an object; of an action; of a quality. Language, Mr. Alcott said, is typical of whatever goes on within us, or is shaped out of us. What is the body the type of? Of a mind. What is the earth a type of? Of God; mind; heaven; were the several answers.

Some people "think and say," he continued, "that the outward and natural things are all because they do not know what they are typical of." But he could show them that *all* outward things "proceeded out of those spiritual realities, of which they are types." This is a far cry from John Locke's position on the nature of the real world and how man came to describe it (***Record,*** pp. xi, 75).

What Peabody and Alcott together sought in their teaching was to ascertain those primitive forms of words which related men to the natural facts whence they then could mount to the spiritual realm. They desired to assemble (in Alcott's words) "a spelling book containing the roots of language and nothing more," and both lamented that no "Universal Grammar" had yet been discovered so that all languages might be taught with equal facility and with an eye towards the spiritual and moral meanings of their vocabularies. Hints towards this "Universal Grammar," Peabody continued, anticipating Kraitsir, came from the Latin language, in which the articulation of sound was regarded as a "material" and where air was an element which was "hewn and carved into harmonious and beautiful forms *to give outness* to the movements and modifications of their thoughts" (***Record,*** pp. xxix, xxxv). In studying the Latin language, one discovered "an architecture of sound" and "theme syllables" which defined "in forms as with a graver's tool" every shade of meaning. Moreover, both Alcott and Peabody always stressed that the attainment of any practical facility in languages—of understanding their architectural tectonics—was but the preliminary to a moral understanding of the word, especially in its Christian form.

Despite such high-minded principles, the Temple School was soon forced to close because its preceptor sinned against the twin Boston taboos of race and sex. Parents were irate to discover that in his conversations on the Gospels Alcott was drawing out his students on the intricacies of the Immaculate Conception, and the last children were withdrawn when he admitted two Black youngsters to the school. But while it was in operation, the Temple School proved itself an educational enterprise of critical importance to the Transcendentalists' belief that the leading-out of a pre-existent spirit was the main occupation of those educating the nation's youth. The practical success of the venture is attested to by a wonderful line recorded in Peabody's journal: "I never knew I had a mind till I came to this school," remarked one enthusiastic student. The evidence suggests that the reason for such sentiment lay in the imaginative stress placed on language at that Masonic Temple on Tremont Street while Alcott and Peabody were teaching there (***Record,*** p. 69).

I hope this essay has suggested, first of all, the sheer *complexity* of language study as it was discussed among the Transcendentalists, and, secondly, that Elizabeth Palmer Peabody was one of those most concerned with the meaning of language for her generation. With her, language theory was more than an obsession; it was a matter of epistemological integrity. She knew that, if one rejected Lockean empiricism for German Idealism, he must rethink his attitudes towards the origin and function of language. The philosophers of language to whom Peabody was drawn were those who explained man's symbols in ways which suggested the inextricable tie between the natural and moral worlds. Language was *anything but* arbitrary for men like Hazard and Kraitsir, Reed and Oegger. There was a veritable *Reason* to it, and man had best heed it if he wanted to comprehend his transcendent nature. For the Transcendentalists the word was, indeed, with God, but in a way which reflected their readings among nineteenth-century language theories more than a belief in the infallibility of scriptural revelation.

Notes

1. *Transcendentalism in New England* (New York: Putnam's, 1876), pp. 105-106.

2. Princeton: Princeton Univ. Press, 1967, p. 4.

3. Biographical information on Peabody is available in Ruth M. Baylor's *Elizabeth Palmer Peabody: Kindergarten Pioneer* (Philadelphia: Univ. of Pennsylvania, 1965), which contains an important bibliography of her writings as well as a list of books published under her imprint. Louise Hall Tharp's *The Peabody Sisters of Salem* (Boston: Little, Brown, and Co., 1950) lacks scholarly apparatus but draws the parameters of Peabody's life

well. The only essay that suggests Peabody's association with language theorists is John B. Wilson's "Grimm's Law and the Brahmins," *New England Quarterly,* 38 (1965), 234-238.

4. Elizabeth Peabody, "Spirit of Hebrew Poetry," *Christian Examiner,* 60 (May 1834), 174, 175.

5. "Spirit of Hebrew Poetry," pp. 175-176.

6. [Rowland Gibson Hazard], *Language: Its Connexion with the Present Condition and Future Prospects of Man by a Heteroscian* (Providence: Marshall and Brown, 1836); reprinted in Rowland G. Hazard, *Essays on Language and Other Papers,* ed. Elizabeth Peabody (Boston: Peabody, 1857), and Rowland G. Hazard, *Essays on Language and Other Essays and Addresses,* ed. Caroline Hazard (Boston: Houghton Mifflin, 1889). The best modern essay on Hazard is Harold A. Durfee's "Language and Religion: Horace Bushnell and Rowland G. Hazard," *American Quarterly,* 5 (1953), 57-70. Biographical information is available in William Gammell, *The Life and Services of the Honorable Rowland Gibson Hazard* (Providence: Reid, 1888). The Channing anecdote is found in Elizabeth Peabody, *Reminiscences of Reverend William Ellery Channing* (Boston: Roberts, 1880), pp. 185-186. It is worth noting that Peabody also translated and published a selection from a work of the French Swedenborgian, Guillaume Oegger: *The True Messiah; or the Old and New Testaments examined according to the principles of the language of Nature* (Boston: Peabody, 1842).

7. Gammel, p. 18; Hazard, pp. 11-12.

8. Hazard, p. 131. Durfee's article is provocative throughout, and I am indebted to it for many of my initial formulations about the role of language in religious discourse.

9. Horace Bushnell, *God in Christ: Three Lectures Delivered at New Haven, Cambridge, and Andover, with a Preliminary Dissertation on Language* (Hartford: Brown and Parsons, 1849). For a sense of how important Bushnell thought the "Dissertation," see Mary B. Cheney, *Life and Letters of Horace Bushnell* (New York: Harper's, 1880), pp. 90 and 192. On Bushnell and language, see Frederick Kirscenmann, "Horace Bushnell: Cells or Crustacea," in Jerald Brauer, ed., *Reinterpretation in American Church History* (Chicago: Univ. of Chicago Press, 1968). Elizabeth Peabody, "Language," *Aesthetic Papers* (Boston: Peabody, 1849). Her essay on the "Dorian Measure" in the same issue also is pertinent here.

10. Biographical information on Kraitsir is slight. A scarce pamphlet, *Karoly Kraitsir* (n.p., n.d.) was left to the Harvard College Library in 1863 by Charles Sumner. More readily available is the summary of that source in Michael West, "Charles Kraitsir's Influence on Thoreau's Theory of Language," [*Emerson Society Quarterly*], 19 (1973), 262-274. West is the most profound student of Thoreau's knowledge of nineteenth-century philology; see his "Scatology and Eschatology: The Heroic Dimensions of Thoreau's Wordplay," *PMLA,* 89 (1974), 1043-1064.

11. Tharp, pp. 213-214. Kraitsir, *The Significance of the Alphabet* (Boston: Peabody, 1846).

12. Kraitsir, *Significance,* pp. 3-4; Kraitsir, *Glossology: Being a Treatise on the Nature of Language and the Language of Nature* (New York: Norton, 1852, 1854 ed.), p. 114.

13. [Mary Lowell Putnam], "Review of Kraitsir's *Significance,*" *North American Review,* 67, Nos. 142-143 (January and April 1849), 167.

14. For Peabody's role in the Temple School, see Tharp, *passim,* and Odell Shepard, *Pedlar's Progress: The Life of Bronson Alcott* (Boston: Little, Brown, 1937), pp. 112-219. Quotation here is from Shepard, p. 168. Elizabeth Peabody, *The Record of a School, Exemplifying the Principles and Methods of Moral Culture* (Boston: Munroe, 1836).

15. *Record,* p. vi. The presence of Sampson Reed is implicit behind much of this essay. His *Observations on the Growth of the Mind* (Boston: Hilliard and Metcalf, 1836) greatly influenced both Alcott and Emerson. See, for example, Clarence P. Hotson, "Sampson Reed, A Teacher of Emerson," *New England Quarterly,* 2 (1929), 249-277; and the section on him in Kenneth W. Cameron's *Emerson the Essayist* (Raleigh, N.C.: Thistle Press, 1945).

16. Peabody, *Record,* p. x; Bronson Alcott, *Conversations with Children on the Gospels,* (Boston: Munroe, 1836-37), I, xxxiv.

Bruce A. Ronda (essay date 1984)

SOURCE: Ronda, Bruce A. Introduction to *Letters of Elizabeth Palmer Peabody: American Renaissance Woman,* edited by Bruce A. Ronda, pp. 1-46. Middletown, Conn.: Wesleyan University Press, 1984.

[*In the following essay, Ronda provides an overview of Peabody's principal intellectual and moral beliefs.*]

Elizabeth Palmer Peabody's career demonstrates, especially in the formative 1830s, [the] intense struggle between the need to cultivate the self and the ideology of domesticity. She insisted on a career, on private space, and emerged as an unforgettable individual, but she did not challenge the domestic, nurturing, service-oriented identity of women. While she enthusiastically accepted the intuitionism of her ante-bellum Romantic colleagues, and made frequent use of notions of dynamic organicism, she funneled those insights into the distinctive reforms of the post-Civil War period which emphasized social service and middle-class ideals rather than the primacy of the self. Because she lived so long (1804-1894) and was involved in reform on both sides of the Civil War, Peabody became an important link between two phases of nineteenth-century social and intellectual life. In more than one sense, she served as a mediator, explaining, interpreting, amending the thought of her prewar colleagues for postwar Americans who, like their parents before them, were caught up in rapid and unpredictable social change. . . .

In the early 1840s, Elizabeth Peabody wrote to Orestes Brownson about his publishing her essays on the Hebrew Scriptures. She described herself as one raised "in the bosom of Unitarianism" and as having gained those "principles of philosophizing" characteristic of Transcendentalism in the decade of the 1830s.[1] This shift, to an elaboration and refinement of the Unitarian heritage, was simultaneously personal and intellectual, affecting Peabody's self-image and her status as a single professional woman, as well as affecting her thought and expression.

Like other young adults in her time, and ours, Peabody was absorbing information and theory at an amazing rate. Her March 1823 letter to her sister Sophia demonstrates all the traits of a precocious young person proud of new learning. Her emotional maturity, however, lagged behind. In the early 1830s, Peabody experienced a series of personal crises for which she was quite unprepared: the New Bedford incident of the winter of 1830, in which she tried to intervene on behalf of some of her pupils and ended up alienating several of her supporters because of her intrusiveness; the triangle with Horace Mann and her sister Mary, who later married Mann; her sometimes deeply bitter arguments with Mary over issues of discretion and propriety. Elizabeth Peabody was groping toward recognition of levels of living beyond the mental. These crisis moments may well have combined with a growing realization on her part that her life was not going to conform to the accepted pattern of courtship and marriage prescribed for young women. A torrent of strong feeling, clearly evident in the letters of the early 1830s, gave her personality more distinctiveness and set her off from the more reserved wives and daughters in her circle. On the other hand, she never plunged through to the conviction of her brother-in-law Nathaniel Hawthorne or that of Her-

man Melville that will and rationality are in the service of that which is more fundamental, one's passions and psychic inclinations. . . .

Peabody's validation of her feelings and her willingness to push at the limits of the liberal outlook made her favorably inclined toward the educational reforms of Amos Bronson Alcott. In 1834 she agreed to serve as Alcott's assistant at Temple School, a private academy held at the Masonic Temple on Tremont Street in Boston. She also began boarding with the Alcotts. At first, as her letters and journal entries indicate, she was in full agreement with the reformer. Alcott's desire to bring out the "spiritual existence" of children echoed the educational philosophy of her mother: "it seems to me that the self-activity of the mind was cultivated by my mother's method in her school . . . Not so much was poured in—more was brought out"—and of Channing.[2] Because she had already come to believe in the existence of innate knowledge in children, Peabody had no trouble approving of Alcott's desire to explore the child's mind, highlighting its essentially spiritual character, primarily through the techniques of conversation and of journal-keeping. Alcott worked "to bring out clearly in the children's consciousness, the perception of their spiritual existence, as being the most real and permanent."[3] Under his guidance, Peabody moved closer to the central Romantic view of the child as morally and spiritually advanced, as a lucid transmitter of divine wisdom. This was certainly Alcott's view at Temple, and while Peabody had growing reservations about his pedagogy, especially the sometimes painful introspection which the pupils' assignment of keeping journals involved, she did agree that children were more in touch with the organic essence of all life than adults were. Another Romantic principle was that of the creative force of the imagination, to which Alcott gave a standard formulation. Peabody recorded this exchange of teacher with pupils at Temple: "Can you understand this definition: imagination is the power that represents, re-presents spirit? Yes. Imagination represents spirit, soul, mind, the outward world, and God. . . . What is imagination? Imagination is the power whereby you picture out thoughts that never were realized in the world."[4] Influenced by her work at Temple, Peabody could give a similar definition: "It is the concentration of profound feeling, reason, of the perception of outward nature into one act of the mind, that prepares the soul for vigorous effort in all the various departments of its activity."[5]

The aspect of her work at Temple that particularly shaped her understanding of the imagination was an investigation of children's speech. She began her 1834 review of Herder's *The Spirit of Hebrew Poetry* in good rationalist fashion, but then moved in a distinctly Transcendental direction. Beyond the historicity of the Biblical texts lay their poetry, "the expression of abstract and spiritual truths by sensible objects, by the forms, colors, sounds, changes, and combinations of external nature."[6] The imagination, she implied, invested those inner and eternal truths with imagery drawn from the outer world. But the full creative power of the imagination remained limited for her, since the human mind and the natural order were reflections of the same divine originator, a point Archdeacon Paley would not disown.[7]

By late 1836, Peabody had stepped into another debate that served to separate Christian Unitarians from their radical dissenters. In her November 23 letter to Mary, she described the controversy about miracles between Andrews Norton and George Ripley, and demonstrated a vigorous and accurate grasp of the intellectual issues at stake. She also recognized the social dimension of the conflict, noting Andrews Norton's denunciation of the Transcendental movement as appealing to women. That she was present at a meeting of the *Christian Examiner*'s editorial board speaks of the enlarged opportunities for discussion of important issues open to her. And, in the last years of the decade, Peabody herself became a kind of mentor for the emerging talents of Jones Very and Nathaniel Hawthorne.

Thus, by the close of the 1830s, Peabody had become fully engaged with the Transcendental phase of Romanticism. She had felt personally the need for recognizing and honoring intense emotion as a valid source of insight, connecting that recognition to the Romantic doctrine of Reason. She saw in the child a model of moral and spiritual wholeness. She saw imagination as the crucial creative act of the mind. She developed, in Susan Conrad's words, a "romantic strategy of investigating history . . . for the spiritual truths it might reveal."[8] Although her historical awareness led her to advocate restraint of the more ecstatic flights of her peers, as in the case of Jones Very, history could be for her nonetheless a means to regenerate human culture, certainly a central Romantic desire.

Elizabeth Peabody did not, however, fully conform to the Romantic ethos and aesthetic. She shaped a distinctive version of the Transcendental code, combining Romantic impulses, a concern with history, a commitment to her vocation of teaching, and consciousness of her gender and status as a woman. She discovered in the kindergarten movement the perfect vehicle for what became her conservative idealism. Kindergarten reform became all the more relevant in a postwar reform world anxious to define the role of the reformer in ambitious terms.

Already in the 1830s Peabody had begun to distance herself from some of the more wide-eyed Transcendentalists. While her enthusiasm for Alcott's goals at Temple School remained strong, she began to doubt his method. She wondered, for example, whether some physical stimulation was not crucial in early education, besides the education of the mind and encouragement of the moral life. She worried that Alcott manipulated his students' discussions, rather than allowing genuine expression. She was annoyed that he had so little sense of historical and cultural particularities and seemed to subsume all experience under grand and sweeping generalizations.[9]

The rift between Peabody and Alcott was a complex affair made up of theoretical and pedagogical issues, seasoned with personal and emotional clashes. Peabody felt increasingly vulnerable as a single woman boarding with the Alcotts, where her privacy, especially of her mail, seemed to be threatened. She connected her own sense of defenselessness in the face of possibly hostile public opinion toward Temple School with Alcott's probing and revealing of his young students' feelings. There were certain insights and intimations in a child's inner life that were better left unexplored and unexpressed, she thought: "the instinctive delicacy with which children veil their deepest thoughts of love and tenderness for relatives, and their reasonable self-gratulations should not be violated . . . in order to gain knowledge."[10] When Alcott was preparing to publish his *Conversations with Children on the Gospels,* Peabody wrote to implore him to suppress some passages: "Why did Prophets and apostles veil this subject in fables and emblems if there was not a reason for avoiding physiological inquiries & c? This is worth thinking of. However you as a man can say anything, but I am a woman, and have feelings that I dare not distrust, however little I can understand them, or give an account of them."[11] Peabody's fears that her association with Alcott would unsettle her own professional status, which had already been shaken in the controversy over her New Bedford students, were not unfounded. After publication of the first volume of *Conversations* in December 1836, she could not find work in Boston and had to rejoin her family in Salem.

The poet Jones Very provided another opportunity for Peabody's tempering of the Romantic afflatus. As her letters to Emerson indicate, Very believed he was the embodiment of the Second Coming; he had announced his mission one day when he was alone with her. She had an almost desperate desire to calm him, derived apparently in part from disagreement with such a messianic possibility, from her awareness of the impropriety of his presence, and perhaps out of fear of his sudden frenzy.[12]

Peabody provided the fullest prewar expression of her versions of idealism, reform, and religion in her 1858 essay **"Egotheism, the Atheism of Today,"** in two essays on Brook Farm, and in **"The Dorian Measure,"** an essay in her *Aesthetic Papers.* In **"A Glimpse of**

Christ's Idea of Society," she argued that Jesus encouraged His followers to see the kingdom of God and the Church as identical, and proclaimed that the kingdom would not come until Christ's influence is spread to all corners of the earth. This gradual, organic unfolding of the kingdom may come about in various ways, she noted. Even the apparently secular revolutionary movements are part of the transformation of society. The great danger in such movements is that the individual is lost sight of, and she offered in contrast the example of Jesus, who combined self-sacrificial love of others with a perfect sense of his own personhood. Self and society together must unfold organically. "The final cause of human society is the unfolding of the individual man into every form of perfection, without let or hindrance, according to the inward nature of each." Education provides, of course, the principal aid to such unfolding.[13]

In **"Egotheism,"** Peabody outlined the consequences of failing to maintain this self-society balance. People caught up in their inner, subjective versions of reality "deify their own conceptions; that is, they say that their conception of God is all that men can ever know of God. In short faith commits suicide . . . and the next step to this is necessarily EGOTHEISM . . . not recognizing that there is, beyond our conception, inconceivable Power, Wisdom, and Love—of the immanence of whose substantial being within us our best conception is but a transient form . . . we find this 'latest form of infidelity', as the understanding has rather blindly denominated it . . . for man proves but a melancholy God."[14] Although she names no names, one can feel her criticism of Alcott, Very, and, in an ambiguous fashion, of Emerson as well.

In **"The Dorian Measure,"** Peabody gave further shape to her views. She identified, in early Greek culture, a love of moderation and balance. The Dorian view of the state was not simply that it was a negative influence, as modern society and her Transcendental colleagues saw it, but that it was a means of collective identity, making each citizen "a living member of the body of the state." The Dorian educational system, featuring music, dance, and gymnastics, led to individual cultivation and group participation. She hoped that by adopting some of the Greek practices in a Christian context, we would ensure that the United States would be a truly Christian nation. We were already divinely sanctioned: "Never before the birth of our political constitution, which was not made by men, but grew up from the instincts of Christian men who had brooked no control of their relations with God, was there any nation on earth, within which the life eternal could unfold its proportions."[15] The notion of America's providential history was widely held both during the Revolutionary period and well into the nineteenth century. Peabody recalled that Channing's Unitarianism seemed to her a direct consequence of the Puritan migration, and both part of the inevitable march of God's history:

> The moral character of the Unitarian movement did not originate with Dr. Channing, of course; but was the logical evolution of the Pilgrim emigration,—for that was a mighty deed, and lifted the first doers of it from the ground of the Calvinist speculations, from which doubtless they started, into that superiority to scholastic abstractions which Robinson evinced, when he said that more light was to break out from the written word than Luther or Calvin had seen; and which Roger Williams practically demonstrated, even before the first pilgrims were dead, by founding the first community in Christendom—if not on earth—that separated Church and State. . . . The American and French revolutions were further exertions of human power to realize the freedom and dignity of man, and had helped to give a new method of religious as well as political thinking.[16]

Although the organic metaphor was part of the Romantic critique against mechanistic philosophy and elitist politics, Peabody used the metaphor to express her more conservative social thinking. Society-as-organism was a harmonious-sounding concept, but one increasingly out of phase with social changes. Labor leaders, including Orestes Brownson and Thomas Skidmore, rejected the organic version of society as a ploy to maintain feudal distinctions of inferior and superior. Unitarian elites embraced the metaphor, but found, as in the cases of such disturbers of the peace as Abner Kneeland and Bronson Alcott, that maintenance of that harmony required the law or public opinion to silence dissent, or, as in the case of the return of fugitive slaves, the presence of military force. Class, ethnic, racial, and geographical divisions developed rapidly in the 1840s and 50s, making Peabody's vision of a harmonious Christian society ever more untenable.[17]

The conservative implications of her organicism for the condition of women and families are apparent in **"The Philosophy of History in the Education of Republican Men and Women,"** which appeared in the February 1855 issue of *The Una*. Peabody claimed that a knowledge of history would deepen women's understanding of the dynamics of the family, which, not surprisingly, she saw as an organism and a microcosm of the larger organism that is society. The oppression of women and children, and particularly the practice of polygamy, was widespread in the Asian world and could be seen among Mormons, she charged. American women should know the past in order to prevent such tyranny from upsetting the living organism of the family.[18] If Mormons and Asians represented the sexual free-for-all, the polymorphously perverse, end of the spectrum, then stark individualism, or egotheism, represented the other. That end of the spectrum, she appeared to believe, was occupied by people like Caroline Dall. In her books and lectures, Dall argued that women were discriminated against economically, legally, and educationally, and required fair treatment as citizens, not as wives and mothers. "We have not laid a secure foundation for any statement on this subject, unless we have made it clear that 'woman's rights' are identical with 'human rights'; that no father, brother, or husband can have all the privileges ordained for him of God, till mother and sister and wife are set free to secure them according to instinctive individual bias."[19] To Peabody, this insistence on individual rights violated the organic and family-centered definition of woman. Dall's willingness to make such statements publicly, insistently, and sensationally prompted Peabody's sharp response. Horace Mann had a far more satisfactory view of women's role, she felt: "He thinks a woman is doing a *higher* & nobler & finer duty when she is educating her own children than when she is addressing public audiences; when her left hand does not know what her right hand is doing—and in this I recognize a high ideal of woman—The *inward* scope is the *highest* scope of human action."[20]

VI

In the post-Civil War period, Elizabeth Peabody was taken up in many causes: freedman's education, Indian rights, memorials for dead writers. The list of friends and correspondents she had acquired by the end of her life is impressive:

> Wordsworth, De Geranda [o], Carlyle, Mazzini, Kossuth and his sister, Harriet Martineau, Mary Somerville, Mary Howitt, Fredrika Bremer, F. W. Maurice . . . Wilberforce, William W. Story, Robert Browning, Sir Edwin Arnold, William Henry Channing, Tom Hughes, Canon Farrar, Dean Stanley . . . William Ellery Channing, Ralph Waldo Emerson, Washington Allston, Margaret Fuller, Lucretia Mott, Lydia Maria Child, Wm. Lloyd Garrison, Catherine Sedgwick, Fanny Kemble, Charles Sumner, Agassiz, E. P. Whipple, Theodore Parker, Whittier, Charlotte Cushman, Henry James, Harriet Beecher Stowe, Bronson Alcott, Thoreau, Longfellow, Dr. Holmes, and many others.[21]

But the kindergarten movement was clearly her great postwar cause and the one that linked her most securely with her prewar endeavors.

In 1859, Peabody met the daughter of Carl and Margarethe Schurz. Margarethe had operated a German-speaking kindergarten in Wisconsin in 1856, following the methods of German educational reformer Friedrich Froebel, and Agathe had been in her mother's class. Peabody was charmed and impressed by the girl.

> It was her remarkable behavior that so impressed E. P. that she remarked to Mrs. Schurz, "that little girl of yours is a miracle, so childlike and unconscious, and yet so wise and able, attracting and ruling the children, who seem nothing short of enchanted."
>
> Said Mrs. Schurz, "No miracle, but only brought up in a kindergarten."

"A kindergarten?" asked Miss Peabody. "What is that?"

"A garden whose plants are human. Did you never hear of Froebel?" asked Mrs. Schurz.[22]

Margarethe Meyer Schurz (1833-1876) began her kindergarten with her own children as pupils. In his *Mother Play* and other volumes, Froebel described the need for sense-training, using colors, shapes, and textures. To this, he counseled, should be added music and cooperative games. Pervading his pedagogy was a sense of the unity of God, humanity, and nature, on which early childhood education should be based and which kindergarten teachers should seek to stimulate in children. Froebel pursued his reforms in the period of intense nationalism following the Napoleonic wars. Patriotic Germans were stimulated by the idealist philosophies of Fichte, Schelling, and Hegel. The Hegelian dialectic influenced Froebel's educational theories dramatically: the eternal law in all things is manifested in nature and in the spirit, and comes together in the eternal Unity, which is God. All things are destined "to unfold their essence . . . to reveal God in their external and transient being . . . education consists in leading man, as a thinking, intelligent being, growing into self-consciousness, to a pure and unsullied, conscious and free representation of the inner law of Divine Unity, and in teaching him ways and means thereto."[23]

In 1848 Froebel traveled to Hamburg to give a course on the kindergarten. Hamburg was the home of Heinrich Christian Meyer, a liberal manufacturer, whose oldest daughter, Berthe, helped arrange Froebel's visit, and whose children all attended the educator's lectures. Berthe, with her fiancé, Johannes Ronge, moved to England after the failure of the 1848 Revolution. Margarethe went with her sister and met the German exile Carl Schurz there in 1851. The following year they were married and emigrated to the United States. Eventually settling in Wisconsin, Schurz was swept into abolitionist politics, and in this domestic void Margarethe determined to recall and re-create the liberal educational ideas of Froebel for her children.

Stimulated by her contact with the Schurzes, Elizabeth Peabody established a kindergarten, the first English-speaking one in America, on Pinckney Street in Boston in 1860. By 1861 there were thirty pupils, two assistants, a French teacher, and a teacher of gymnastics, in addition to Elizabeth and her sister Mary, who joined her after the death of her husband, Horace Mann, in 1859. By 1867, however, Peabody was dissatisfied with the results of her work and journeyed to Europe to learn about kindergartens firsthand. Upon her return fifteen months later, she plunged vigorously into the movement that dominated her life for the next quarter-century—kindergartens along genuinely Froebelian lines.[24] The kindergarten movement caught up all the threads of

Peabody's life and career: her mother's influence, her early work as teacher and tutor, the seminal effect of Channing and his Unitarianism, the Romantic and Transcendentalist revolt, her acceptance within those dissident circles, her passion for history, and her conservative idealism.

The focus on the education of young children was virtually a leitmotif for Peabody. It grew out of her mother's tutelage and developed in the spacious quarters of Temple School. The Romantic celebration of the child, as in Wordsworth's "Intimations" ode, lifted up the young as those closest to virtue and divinity, and meshed with the heightened attention paid to children throughout the nineteenth century. As Carl Degler has written, children were beginning to be seen as different from adults, as occupying a period of life worthy of recognition, care, even extension. "Simply because children were being seen for the first time as special, the family's reason for being, its justification as it were, was increasingly related to the proper rearing of children."[25]

Such rearing, many nineteenth-century people agreed, was women's special task. In the two previous centuries, fathers were the central parental figures, or else, as the child-rearing literature advised, parents divided the tasks of nurture. But in the early nineteenth century, women alone were emerging as the primary care-givers, at a time when industrial and institutional changes were altering many of the premodern functions of the family. Women now concentrated their efforts on their children, and to that end a considerable advice literature became available. Literature for children flourished throughout the century, accentuating the interest in and concern for the young.[26]

The kindergarten movement represented the taking up of this domestic concern for children to the national level, making it a national reform. The manner in which Elizabeth Peabody, as leader of the nationalization of early-childhood education, carried out this reform was consistent with the tendencies of her thought from the prewar years. The Froebelian kindergarten would be based on the organic metaphor, on "mother love," on systemization and rationalization, and on the development of public-minded citizens.

The uses to which Peabody put the notion of organicism were seen in her essay on Brook Farm and in **"The Dorian Measure."** The kindergarten pupil should be encouraged to grow organically, both physically, through play, and spiritually, through music and art. Indeed, said Peabody, Froebel saw the two dimensions as one: "True education shall lead out the imprisoned spirit, growingly conscious of individuality, by means of the symbolism of the prison house itself, which is that correlation of necessary forces we call the material universe."[27] . . .

There are impressive continuities in Elizabeth Peabody's vocational and intellectual life which link her early and late years. Vocationally, of course, teaching provided the major continuity, as did her interest in history, her work as a mentor and encourager of others, and her efforts as chronicler of her age and her contemporaries. Self, society, and cosmos as living and interwoven organisms, reflecting divine origin and divine aspiration, unfolding according to universal law, constituted the most crucial belief that spanned her many years.

There were, to be sure, differences between the young and the older Peabody. In her late twenties, she was concerned to carve out and defend her professional status at the same time as she allowed herself to experience deep feeling and to recognize her intuition as a legitimate source of truth. By the late 1860s, she had achieved her status as an intellectual woman, and was increasingly channeling her emotional life through the sluices of middle-class reform activity.

But the continuities seem more impressive. Despite her personal eccentricities and her associations with known radicals like Parker and crackpots like Jones Very, Elizabeth Peabody did not, as William Lloyd Garrison and Margaret Fuller did, see American culture as fundamentally flawed; rather, she accepted the ruling conventions, seeking to liberalize and humanize society within those conventions.

Ironically, much as Peabody fit impressively into the organic and systematic nature of reform in post-Civil War America, by the end of her life the theories of childhood education were changing again, and made her outlook appear old-fashioned. Susan Blow, her disciple and an ardent Froebelian, began to encounter individuals who ridiculed the emphasis on unfolding the divine essence and who preferred to rely on data from psychology and physiology in designing curricula. By 1905 Blow was giving courses at Columbia Teachers College in conjunction with Patty Smith Hill, a defender of the new scientific, secular approach that came to inform the Progressive education movement.[28]

Thus, the conventional division of intellectual and reform life at the time of the Civil War may not explain the richness and continuity of a person like Elizabeth Peabody. It was not until near the end of the nineteenth century that the steady assault of secular and scientific thinking and the preoccupation with the ambiguities of urban and industrial life began seriously to wash away the religious foundations of a considerable number of thoughtful Americans. In the new century, Americans began to return to private pleasures and to lose their zeal for public service. Simultaneously, modernism began to champion the artist-hero alienated from a stifling bourgeois society.

What has often prevented historians in the past from treating Elizabeth Palmer Peabody as a serious figure in social and intellectual history is that her concerns centered on children and on women, both single and married, rather than on politics or economics. Even more, she has evaded our understanding because she was not an alienated self. We find Thoreau, Emerson, and the early Brownson, certainly Melville, Poe, Dickinson, and Fuller more appealing and contemporary because they assaulted and threatened their culture; they assumed a kind of lonely Romantic splendor on the edge of society. It was not so for Peabody. She was a profound optimist. She cared about neither status nor possessions, but was passionately involved in causes, believing that change was possible, indeed inevitable. Her sister Sophia once paid her this tribute: "As I sit and look on these mountains, so grand and flowing and the illimitable aerial blue, beyond and over, I seem to realize with peculiar force that bountiful, fathomless heart of Elizabeth, forever disappointed, but forever believing; sorely rebuffed, yet never bitter; robbed day by day, yet giving again, from endless store; more sweet, more tender, more serene, as the hours pass over her, though they may drop gall instead of flowers upon this unguarded heart."[29] Our post-Freudian, nuclear age is deeply aware and perhaps paralyzed by an awareness of forces within and without that terrify and oppress us. We feel a kinship with Margaret Fuller when she confessed, "I have no belief in beautiful lives; we were born to be mutilated: Life is basically unjust."[30] And we may likewise feel that Peabody was naïve in her boundless enthusiasms, in her cosmic optimism. We feel a great gulf between ourselves and a person who could say:

> I cannot understand unhappy people. . . . Those people who say that life is not worth living, find it so because they do not go to work to make it worth living. Why does sadness overpower them? Is it so much harder for them than for others to see sin and suffering? What right have they to add their weight to the world's burdens? Is it a sign of intellect to be cowardly? And do these people not dream that the spiritual power which makes an intellectual condition impossible is vastly superior to any power that the intellect alone can attain?[31]

Or is it possible, on the one hand, to acknowledge the insights of Augustine, Pascal, and Kierkegaard concerning the deviousness of the heart, the life of the demonic that is part of the human condition, and yet, on the other hand, acknowledge Elizabeth Peabody's resilient core of faith, which sustained her?

Although obviously Peabody was at times not at all loving, she believed in the dynamic, reconciling power of love. This belief allowed her to enter vicariously into the lives of the people whose causes she espoused. As Sarah Clarke recalled:

> While most mortals instinctively take care of number one, she alone totally neglected that important numeral,

and spent all her life, all her strength, her marvellous enthusiasm, her generous fiery ardor in the cause of others. She was no longer herself Elizabeth Peabody, she was a company of exiled Poles, of destitute Germans, banished Frenchmen, expatriated Italians or Hungarians, all of whom must be helped, must be put on their feet, must be made known to those able and willing to help them.[32]

Although Peabody stressed self-sacrifice throughout her life, and Sarah Clarke illustrated the way in which she threw herself into the lives and causes of others, these impulses sprang neither from ego-diffusion nor weak will nor "self-annihilation," as she would put it, but, rather, from a self-assurance that allowed her to expand herself sympathetically into the lives of others. She had as a young woman experienced, through the intervention of Channing, a reorientation of self, a conversion she herself described as a "rebirth."

In thinking of the moral orientation toward life that her letters reveal, it might be useful to compare Peabody with that strong woman of the same period Margaret Fuller. Both were intellectuals, both reform-minded, and both caused raised eyebrows because of their unorthodox behavior and appearance. Despite the distress, amusement, or anger they caused their community, both also conformed to the ideals of nineteenth-century middle-class womanhood. Fuller agreed with the notion that women are incomplete without men, and felt herself fulfilled only when she took Ossoli as lover and husband. Peabody was particularly concerned about sexual fidelity and propriety, although she herself remained celibate and single. For Fuller, however, liberation was always self-awareness, which led to a progressively greater sense of alienation from American culture, such that personal fulfillment could be achieved only through exile. For Peabody, liberation was achieved only by an awareness of a moral, guided universe, powered by the dynamic and personal force of love and by an understanding that true maturity is achieved by seeing that same universal power operating within the self and others.

Like many other women of the nineteenth century, Elizabeth Peabody worked to confer on women the same privileges and duties that men enjoyed. For her specifically it was enhanced educational opportunities, but through her example, she doubtless encouraged others to study history, read widely, engage in reforms, and agitate for social change. Building on the efforts of the Revolutionary and immediate post-Revolutionary generations of women, which included Peabody's mother, nineteenth-century women worked steadily to enhance their role in society while simultaneously linking with each other both formally and informally in supportive ways. But to think of women like Peabody and Fuller or Peabody and Caroline Dall as engaged in similar work of women's social and cultural advancement invites doubt as to the depth of their similarity.

Gerda Lerner has suggested that a distinction be made between efforts for women's rights, which involve access to society's privileges and opportunities equal to that of men, and efforts for women's emancipation, which imply, in her words, "a radical transformation of existing institutions, values, and theories."[33] Both efforts qualify, in Lerner's eyes, as "feminist," although the first is reformist and the second is the more challenging and advanced, the more radical, position. Catherine Beecher, champion of women's education and of domesticity, qualifies as a feminist in the first category; Elizabeth Cady Stanton is clearly an emancipationist. Assigning both the descriptive term "feminist" may stretch the word more than is warranted, but Lerner's intent is clear, and helps locate Elizabeth Peabody in the cultural geography of the nineteenth century. In her own rigorous education and in the equally rigorous classes and discussions she conducted for women, in her desire to be fully a part of the Transcendentalist movement, including running a bookstore and helping issue the *Dial,* in her tireless reforming, Peabody was a living demand for equal access to at least some of society's institutions. She was, in Lerner's terms, a champion of women's rights. Comparing her with Margaret Fuller, who had a vision of the human intellect as androgynous and who felt stifled by the narrowness and conventionality of American society, or with Caroline Dall, whose willingness to mention female menses in a public lecture violated even Peabody's sense of decorum, is instructive. In her acceptance of some of society's deepest cultural assumptions—the sanctity of the family, the nurturing role of women, the unique connection of women to children's education—Elizabeth Peabody was, despite all her fears to the contrary, a decorous and tactful nineteenth-century woman.

Notes

1. Peabody to Brownson, [ca. 1840] (MS. InND).

2. Elizabeth Peabody, "Female Education in Massachusetts: Reminiscences of Subjects and Methods of Teaching," quoted in Conrad [*Perish the Thought: Intellectual Women in Romantic America, 1830-1860* (New York: Oxford University Press, 1976)], p. 203.

3. Peabody, MS Journal, 29 December 1834 (MS: NN-B).

4. Elizabeth Peabody, *Record of a School: Exemplifying the General Principles of Spiritual Culture* (Boston: James Munroe, 1835), p. 166. For a discussion of Alcott's philosophy of education, see Bruce A. Ronda, "Genesis and Genealogy: Bronson Alcott's Changing Views of the Child," *The New England Historical and Genealogical Register* 135 (October 1981): 259-73.

5. Peabody, *Record of a School*, 3rd ed., quoted in Conrad, p. 205.

6. Peabody, "The Spirit of Hebrew Poetry," 175.

7. See Philip Gura, "Elizabeth Peabody and the Philosophy of Language," *ESQ* (1977): 155.

8. Conrad, p. 216.

9. [Bruce A.] Ronda, "[Elizabeth] Peabody's Changing Views [of the Child]," [*ESQ* (1977):] 108-110.

10. Elizabeth Peabody, *Record of a School,* 2nd ed. (Boston: Russell, Shattuck, 1836), viii.

11. Peabody to Bronson Alcott, 7 August 1836 (MS, copy, MH), in Bronson Alcott's MS "Memoir 1878."

12. Peabody to Emerson, 20 October 1838, 3 December 1838 (MS, MSaE).

13. Elizabeth Peabody, "A Glimpse of Christ's Idea of Society," *Dial* 2 (1841): 226.

14. Elizabeth Peabody, "Egotheism, the Atheism of Today" (1858), reprinted in *Last Evening with Allston and Other Papers* (Boston: D. Lothrop, 1886), p. 245.

15. Elizabeth Peabody, "The Dorian Measure," in *Aesthetic Papers* (Boston: E. P. Peabody, 1849), p. 99.

16. [Elizabeth] Peabody, *Reminiscences [of the Reverend William E. Channing* (Boston: Roberts Brothers, 1880)], pp. 27-28. For discussions of the providential view of American history, see Sacvan Bercovich, *The Puritan Origins of the American Self* (New Haven: Yale University Press, 1975), [David] Levin, *History as Romantic Art* [(Stanford: Stanford University Press, 1959)], pp. 24-40; and Ernest Lee Tuveson, *Redeemer Nation* (Chicago: University of Chicago Press, 1968).

17. Daniel Howe provides a brief but cogent description of the Unitarian view of society as organism, which appears to lie behind Peabody's social thought, in *The Unitarian Conscience* [(Cambridge: Harvard University Press, 1970)], pp. 125-31.

18. Peabody, quoted in Conrad, pp. 214-16.

19. Caroline Dall, quoted in [Carl] Degler [*At Odds: Women and the Family in America from the Revolution to the Present* (New York: Oxford University Press, 1980)], p. 343.

20. Peabody to Caroline Dall, 21 February 1859 (MS, MHi).

21. Maria S. Porter, "Elizabeth Palmer Peabody," *The Bostonian* 3 (January 1896): 341.

22. Peabody, "Origin and Growth of the Kindergarten" (1882), quoted in Agnes Snyder, *Dauntless Women in Childhood Education, 1856-1931*

(Washington, D.C.: Association for Childhood Education International, 1972), p. 31.

23. Friedrich Froebel, *The Education of Man,* quoted in Snyder, p. 24. Biographical details and lengthy discussions of Froebel's philosophy of education may be found in *Kindergarten and Child Culture Papers: Papers on Froebel's Kindergarten . . . Republished from the American Journal of Education,* rev. ed. (Syracuse: C. W. Bardeen, 1890), pp. 17-48, 69-124, 181-89.

24. Snyder, pp. 48-56.

25. Degler, p. 66. See also Bernard Wishy, *The Child and the Republic* (Philadelphia: University of Pennsylvania Press, 1968), chs. 3, 5.

26. [Barbara] Epstein [*The Politics of Domesticity: Women, Evangelism, and Temperance in Nineteenth Century America* (Middletown: Wesleyan University Press, 1981)], pp. 21-22; Degler, pp. 68-69, 75.

27. [Elizabeth] Peabody, *Lectures* [*Lectures in the Training Schools for Kindergartners*] (Boston: D. C. Heath, 1888)], p. 93.

28. Snyder, pp. 70-79.

29. Sophia Hawthorne to Mrs. Elizabeth Peabody, 29 September-10 October 1850 (MS, NN-B).

30. Fuller, quoted in Barbara Welter, "Mystical Feminist," in *Dimity Convictions* (Athens: Ohio University Press, 1976), p. 174.

31. Springfield (Mass.) *Kindergarten News* 4 (February 1894): 45.

32. Sarah Clarke, "This comes saluting the friends of Elizabeth Peabody—" (MS, MB).

33. Gerda Lerner, contribution to symposium "Politics and Culture in Women's History: A Symposium," *Feminist Studies* 6, #1 (Spring 1980): 50-51.

Abbreviations

InND: Indiana, University of Notre Dame

MB: Boston Public Library

MH: Harvard University, Houghton Library

MHi: Massachusetts Historical Society; Mann, Clarke, Andrew, Peabody Papers

MS: manuscript in the author's hand

MSaE: Essex Institute, James Duncan Phillips Library; Peabody Papers

MS copy: manuscript in another hand

NN-B: New York Public Library; Henry W. and Albert A. Berg Collection

Scott Harshbarger (essay date summer 1990)

SOURCE: Harshbarger, Scott. "Transatlantic Transcendentalism: The Wordsworth-Peabody-Hawthorne Connection." *Wordsworth Circle* 21, no. 3 (summer 1990): 123-26.

[*In the following essay, Harshbarger offers a close reading of Peabody's 1838 review of Nathaniel Hawthorne's* Twice-Told Tales. *Harshbarger asserts that Peabody's review, along with her correspondence with William Wordsworth during the same period, demonstrates the profound influence of Wordsworth's poetic sensibility on American Transcendental writing.*]

Annabel Newton's *Wordsworth in Early American Criticism* [(1928; rpt. 1978)] is the only full published treatment of Wordsworth's influence on American writers. With few exceptions—Leon Howard ("Wordsworth in America," [*Modern Language Notes*] [1953], 359-65) and Robert F. Gleckner ("Coleridge and Wordsworth Together in America," [*The Wordsworth Circle*], XV [1984], 17-19)—she is correct in her assessment that "America, on the whole, either neglected him altogether or regarded him with an aspect of indifference until 1824" (p. 189). After 1824, however, Wordsworth's reputation in America dramatically grew, so that in 1851 the *North American Review* could boast that "No country contains a larger number of intelligent admirers of Wordsworth's genius than our own" (LXXIII (1851), 494; qtd in Newton, p. 188). According to William Charvat, "The major figure of the period was Wordsworth, and his influence on American thought was penetrating. It was his work that vitalized American moralism into a dynamic and creative force. It was he who gave American idealism a philosophy to work with. Without him, American transcendentalism might have reached only a few minds capable of philosophic subtlety, for he prepared a common-sense and practical nation for the vision of Coleridge and Emerson. Indeed, it appears to me that many Americans understood no more of transcendentalism than they found in Wordsworth." (*The Origins of American Critical Thought: 1810-1835* [(1936; rpt. 1968)], p. 71). Lawrence Buell, following Charvat, emphasizes Wordsworth's conservative appeal: the Unitarian-Whig orthodoxy favored "a conservative sort of Romanticism first espoused by the Boston literary establishment during the 1820s and 1830s. . . . Wordsworth's inspiring didacticism and Scott's regional historicizing, almost never vulgar and always seemingly on the side of common decency, civic responsibility, and tolerance, appealed to their moralistic, patriotic, progressivist but not populist case of mind" (*New England Literary Culture* [(1986)] p. 44).

As the work of a few modern critics suggest, one such conservative sensibility belonged to Nathaniel Hawthorne. According to Richard Harter Fogle, Hawthorne "quoted freely from Wordsworth's poems in his account of the 1855 visit [to the Lake District] in the English Notebooks, and shows remarkable acquaintance with Wordsworth elsewhere in the Notebooks, citing his poems most appositely in connection with things and places" ("Nathaniel Hawthorne and the Great English Romantic Poets," [*Keats-Shelley Journal* 21-22 (1972-73):] 233). Roberta Weldon finds the footprints of Wordsworth's Leech Gatherer in Hawthorne's "The Old Apple-Dealer" (*Nathaniel Hawthorne Journal* [1977]) while, on a more ideological plane, Jonathan Arac uses Wordsworth in "The Politics of The Scarlet Letter" to support his argument that Hawthorne is a political quietist (*Ideology and Classic American Literature* [1986], p. 255).

But it is an unsigned review appearing in the *New-Yorker* in 1838, and not generally available to Hawthorne scholars until 1974, that best suggests the extent of Wordsworth's influence on Hawthorne and his critical milieu. Beginning with this general observation, "The Story without an End, of which all true stories are but episodes, is told by Nature herself," the reviewer conjectures that Hawthorne's is "the wisdom which comes from knowing some few hearts well. . . . There is throughout the volume a kindliness and even heartiness of human sympathy—a healthy equilibrium of spirits, and above all, a humor, so exquisitely combined of airy wit and the 'sad, sweet music of humanity,' that it contradicts the notion of misanthropical or whimsical seclusion" (**"Elizabeth Peabody Reviews Twice-told Tales,"** ed. with intro. by Arlin Turner, *Nathaniel Hawthorne Journal* [1974] pp. 78-79). Having sweetened Wordsworth to characterize Hawthorne's work, the reviewer moves on to speculate about the latter's character:

> We will venture our reputation for sagacity on the assertion that he is frank and communicative in his character, winning thereby the experience of whatsoever hearts come in his path, to subject it to his Wordsworthian philosophy.
>
> *Wordsworthian philosophy* we say, and with consideration; not that we would imply that he has taken it from Wordsworth. We mean to speak of the kind of philosophy, which cannot be learnt except in the same school of Nature where Wordsworth studied, and by the same pure light. We mean that he illustrates the principle defended by Wordsworth in his prose writings, as well as manifested by him in his metrical compositions, viz: that the ideal beauty may be seen clearest and felt most profoundly in the common incidents of actual life, if we will but "purge our visual ray with euphrasie and rue." Mr. Hawthorne seems to have been born to this faith. His stories, generally speaking, have no dramatic pretension. Their single incident is the window through which he looks 'into the mind of man— / [His] haunt, and the main region of [his] song.'
>
> (79)

Combining an allusion to *Hart-Leap Well*—"The moving accident is not my trade; to freeze the blood I have no ready arts"—with a quote from the "prospectus," this writer displays more than a passing acquaintance with the work of Wordsworth. If, as Arlin Turner remarks, it "may be read as a Transcendentalist evaluation of this book and Transcendentalist guidance for works to be written" (77), the reviewer's "Transcendentalism" seems to owe more to Wordsworth than Emerson or Thoreau.

More light is shed on this circumstance, and on the Hawthorne-Wordsworth connection, once we realize that the reviewer of *Twice-Told Tales* for the *New-Yorker* was not only a friend and neighbor of Hawthorne, but had been carrying on a lively correspondence with William Wordsworth since 1825. An important figure of the Transcendentalist Movement, Elizabeth Peabody founded the West Street Book Shop and publishing house, where met Boston's intellectuals and reformers, and where she published the Transcendentalist *Dial* from 1842-1843, and the *Aesthetic Papers* in 1949, the latter featuring the first publication of Thoreau's "Resistance to Civil Government" as well as Peabody's own essays on aesthetics, language, and history (*Dictionary of Literary Biography* [1979]). As a future pioneer of the Kindergarten movement in America, and a teacher since age sixteen, Peabody focuses in her first letter to Wordsworth (December 9, 1825), on education: "When very young, & during the whole period of youth, I was dissatisfied with the manner in which the old communicated with the young—feeling especially that the system pursued in schools—the whole theory of education may perhaps be denominated mechanical—and that the soul was neglected . . . the education I received was wanting in power to connect together the heart and the intellect" (**"Elizabeth Palmer Peabody to William Wordsworth: Eight Letters, 1825-1845,"** ed. Margaret Neussendorfer *Studies in the American Renaissance* [1824], p. 183). Introduced to Wordsworth by W. E. Channing, Peabody found the poet's interest in children, and in "connecting the intellect with the heart" congenial and inspiring. Never shy to make suggestions, Peabody writes that inasmuch as "poetry is the best means by which to develop the nobler part of their nature . . . the expression of one's thought who goes forth to Nature—'with a heart / That watches & receives,'" Wordsworth might consider writing "a volume for children." In this way "perhaps a new & deeper tone [might be] given to the art of education" (p. 184).

Wordsworth, whose letters to Peabody have yet to be recovered, is quoted as replying "if I am to serve the very young by my writings, it must be by benefiting at the same time, those who are old enough to be their parents" (p. 187). This "key" in hand, Peabody progressively explores in the rest of the letters her understanding of Wordsworthian philosophy: "I understand your idea—the divine idea of poetry—to be this: that nature and providence if viewed in a certain light are poetical altogether, and produce happiness; and that this light is the emanation of the unsophisticated, constantly regenerating mind" (p. 188). It is his emphasis on the power of the innocent mind which makes Wordsworth "the poet not of the English nation—but of the English language" (p. 189). For although "there is a vast difference in the circumstances" of English and American society, the "weight of custom" which Wordsworth sees as the chief enemy of the spirit has its New England counterpart in the "paper mills and saw mills and other machines that deform our Yankee streamlets." It is, therefore, to "the deep stream of romance [which] still flows calm & untouched beneath all that meets the eye" that Wordsworth's poetry speaks and inspires. Peabody's hope is that poetry might mould great souls "which would do in the republic of letters, in the empire of lofty sciences, what they did fifty years since in politics. And it is necessary that this more interior revolution should take place, to give life to—or even to perpetuate those forms of freedom which Washington and his friends left to us." For this reason, she writes, "you can never know what a deep and even wide enthusiasm your poetry has awakened here;" indeed, in her countrymen's "hour of suffering . . . they say, go to Wordsworth & the Bible" (p. 190). Perhaps a measure of Wordsworth's impact on American readers, this letter records Wordsworth's transformation from a possible writer of children's books into national saviour.

Six years later, Peabody's fervor has not abated. On the contrary, she opens her letter of September 7th, 1835, with a declaration that she is "one of your disciples" (p. 193). Peabody writes to tell Wordsworth that she has incorporated his poetry into her curriculum, having read Peter Bell "to a class of little girls—about half a dozen—under twelve years of age" (p. 193). Praising the "last songs that have waked up anew the hearts of all your foster children," she then thanks him "in the first place for all you have sung of women": "You have done all that Milton left undone." The disciple then closes with this paean: "how truly may your disciples put in your claim as the Columbus of Poetry on whom a New World has opened with its mines & solitudes.—I would even say more—as the Messiah of the reign of the Saints—a true Christian prophet" (p. 194).

Having characterized Wordsworth as a kind of New World Messiah in her previous letter, Peabody, around the time when she was probably writing her review for the *New-Yorker,* sends Wordsworth, along with three works by Emerson,

> this little volume of Tales—as you will agree that the popular story tellers are the ballad makers of the nations; and I should like to show you—what I think is best in this line. The author is a very retired young man though for some years the inhabitant of a city—but his early & his college years were passed in the country—

His daily teacher have been woods & rills—
The silence that is in the starry sky
The sleep that is among the lonely hills—

he has not encountered that current which sweeps everything into publicity & common stock—even before it has quite become itself. You may not be able to see all this in his book—however, I know that he looks upon literary life as a moral enterprise—for which he is willing to sacrifice present interests if need be. The 'Gray Champion,' the 'Maypole of Merry Mount' and 'The Great Carbuncle' will give you an idea of the materials of romance that we have here, but perhaps the 'Sunday at home,' 'Little Annie's Ramble' and the 'Vision of the Fountain' will prove a vein of his mind in which you will sympathize more. If some of the other tales evince a morbid direction of the fancy—yet I think they are redeemed by the glimpses of the inner nature which he gives us in the Reflection with which he closes each.

(February 1838, pp. 197-198)

It is significant that Peabody should select 'Little Annie's Ramble' as one of the tales with which Wordsworth might sympathize, since it was one of the most popular of the volume, and one from which she quotes at length in her review. To excerpt her excerpt: "As the pure breath of children revives the life of aged men, so is our moral nature revived by their free and simple thoughts, their native feeling, their airy mirth for little cause or none, their grief soon roused and soon allayed. Their influence on us is at least reciprocal with ours on them. When our infancy is almost forgotten, and our boyhoods long departed, though it seems but as yesterday;—when life settles darkly down upon us, and we doubt whether to call ourselves young and more, then it is good to steal away from the society of bearded men, and even of gentle woman, and spend an hour or two with children," (p. 80). The echoes of the "Intimations Ode" here are a revealing indication of Peabody's sense of Hawthorne's Wordsworthian philosophy.

Framing her recommendation of Hawthorne's tales are statements which argue a poetic link between the English and American writers: "I have been led to feel more vividly than even before, that our government has truly quite another foundation than a paper constitution of mere human device,—that it grew from living roots—and that in fact the revolution was only a change of form—& of quite outward form—leaving the heart of society unscathed and unchanged" (p. 197). "The "heart" which American and English society share, despite a revolution and "a paper constitution," has not skipped a beat. It is to and for this common heart that Wordsworth and Hawthorne, as balladeer and storyteller of a common nation, speak: "Am I right in supposing you care for our American authors?—You will understand still better perhaps what may be hoped from us—by knowing how extensively and powerfully your own and Mr. Coleridge's works are acting upon us. It is only twelve years—since your works were republished—and you have seen the new beautiful edition in one volume—published last year.—I was still more glad to see another edition in one volume—in fine print—at the low price of $1.25 cents.—It proved the demand among the mass of our people—And made me feel that you were among the ballad makers," (p. 199).

A year later, Peabody's letter to Wordsworth is taken up almost exclusively with promoting the work of her future brother-in-law, whose works Wordsworth apparently never would receive: "I am especially desirous that you should read Hawthorne's Tales for a year more of constant reading of them makes me value them still more highly. He writes constantly and scatters his leaves through our journals & newspapers—wherever he can get them published without expense or trouble. . . . How happy I should be if I could get for him a word of Wordsworth's—I would make it a text for hundred homilies—and he would listen as to holy writ—for he would acknowledge this authority" (p. 201). To what extent Hawthorns would regard Wordsworth's approval as holy writ is open to conjecture; Hawthorne never did say much directly about the poet whose rise to fame in America paralleled his own. Of course the main evidence is to be found in the remainder of Hawthorne's work, which, although influenced to an extent by Wordsworth directly, owes most of its Wordsworthian qualities to the American artistic and critical milieu shaped by responses to the British poet's writings. Nevertheless, the last word on this connection should go to Elizabeth Peabody, who, acquainted with both parties, gives an account of Hawthorne's relationship to Wordsworth true in spirit, if not in letter: "At present he has an office in our Custom House—which is an immense change from his life of absolute seclusion. He seems to be greatly amused with the people with whom it brings him in contact & thinks it may be for the advantage of his mind & art bye and bye—when he has left it.—He will not write while engaged in this business.—When I asked him what he did—he said he was from sunrise to sunset quarreling with sea captains & owners—about measuring out their cargoes of salt & coal & potatoes—according to the laws—and then he went home to his room and read Wordsworth. What an alternation!" (p. 202).

Susan H. Irons (essay date 1992)

SOURCE: Irons, Susan H. "Channing's Influence on Peabody: Self-Culture and the Danger of Egoism." In *Studies in the American Renaissance,* edited by Joel Myerson, pp. 121-35. Charlottesville: University Press of Virginia, 1992.

[*In the following essay, Irons examines the complex relationship between Peabody and her mentor, William Ellery Channing.*]

In a lifetime that spanned the nineteenth century, Elizabeth Palmer Peabody cultivated many of the major and minor thinkers of her time. An inventory would be long and impressive. However, throughout her life, one relationship remained central—that to William Ellery Channing. At a very formative period in Peabody's life, the relationship was intense and intimate, thus shaping her perspectives and philosophy in ways that continued to be factors well after Channing's death in 1842 when Peabody was thirty-eight. He was her first and most powerful mentor. And in her seventy-sixth year, she wrote a long and eulogistic reminiscence of Channing, a gesture which speaks to his enduring importance in her life, since she never prepared her own memoirs for publication.[1]

Scholars have not sufficiently examined the complexity, impact, and implications of Peabody's relationship to Channing, which was rooted in strong shared religious beliefs and a commitment to the process of self-culture. Channing's concerns over the potential absorption in the self resulting from a concept of self-culture which ignored the necessity of Jesus Christ's mediation proved his most critical legacy to Peabody. His early recognition of self-culture's danger of "egotheism" profoundly affected the development of Peabody's concepts of self-culture and through that her concept of vocation and response to Transcendentalism.

Factors in Peabody's emotional and psychological development combined to cause her to seek a strong mentor such as Channing. First, her family situation provided a maternal role model whose strong influence Peabody continued to acknowledge throughout her life.[2] Bruce Ronda describes Mrs. Peabody as a model for her daughter of "both strength of character and maternal self-sacrificial spirit," while her father was unassertive, a "largely silent figure in this story, a disappointment to his wife and possibly to himself."[3] Channing was twenty-four years older than Peabody, a gentle and intelligent family-oriented Unitarian minister who had the potential to fulfill the role of substitute father for the young Peabody.

Other circumstances and events conspired to make Channing an object of Peabody's adolescent hero worship. In her *Reminiscences of Dr. Wm. Ellery Channing, D.D.,* she recollects that one Sunday when she was eight or nine, her mother heard that Channing was going to be the guest minister at Salem's Second Church. "I must go," she said, "and take Elizabeth, because it takes genius to reach children" (p. 13). While visiting in Boston in 1817, she heard him preach again, and there the thirteen-year-old Peabody met Channing personally for the first time, an event much anticipated, when he came to pay a clerical visit to her hosts (*Rem* [*Reminiscences of Dr. Wm. Ellery Channing, D.D.*], p. 36). Channing's sister later reported his memory of the visit: "'I have had a genuine pleasure and surprise today; a child ran into my arms and poured out her whole heart in utter confidence of my sympathy!'" (*Rem,* p. 38). When again in Boston in 1820, in an effusive letter to her friend Maria Chase, Peabody records her impressions of hearing the "celebrated and justly admired preacher" (*Letters* [*Letters of Elizabeth Palmer Peabody*], p. 52). She perceives that he has "that irresistible and almost unrivaled power over the minds of almost every audience that he has addressed" (*Letters,* p. 53), and she herself wishes to see "this wonderful man in every situation possible" (*Letters,* p. 54). After hearing one of Channing's famous sermons in May 1822,[4] Peabody enthusiastically wrote to her mother, "If there is anything sublime on earth, it is the sight of a good and pious man, at a moment of deepest agitation, resting calmly upon the goodness of God" (*Letters,* p. 57). She insists that she will always remember the "calm beauty of holiness that dwelt upon his countenance as he said things" (*Letters,* p. 57). Around this same time,[5] Peabody again spoke personally with Channing. In *Reminiscences,* she remembers feeling that he understood and approved her principles of education, and that she "felt consecrated by the impressiveness with which he gave me his blessing and a God-speed" (p. 42). Her increasing acquaintance with Channing gave her "pleasurable excitement" (*Rem,* p. 92). His impressions on the young Peabody were strong, elevating him in her estimation to a level of uncritical adoration and idealization. Her published letters of this period do not reveal comparable feelings about any other figure. In her mind, Channing had already assumed a position of great importance.

Peabody was soon in frequent and intimate contact with Channing and his family. When she and her sister Mary opened a school in Brookline in 1826, Channing enrolled his daughter Mary as one of their pupils. His conviction that "the close relation of parents to the teachers of their children" was "the most sacred of obligations to society" (*Rem,* p. 279) would inevitably lead him into close communication with his child's teacher, and Peabody would certainly have been receptive to increased contact with a person she so highly revered. Charles Foster observes that this situation gave them a reason for "long conferences" on the principles of education which "soon expanded into discussions of theology, philosophy, and literature in which Channing as Unitarian-Transcendental Socrates confronted Miss Peabody with the fundamental issues of their mutually liberal faith."[6] Thus, from 1826 to 1832 Peabody was in the "habit of spending my evenings at Dr. Channing's whenever he was in his city home" (*Rem,* p. 67), and she corresponded with him whenever he was out of town. Their evenings revolved around Channing's reading aloud to Peabody while she copied his sermons or Peabody reading aloud to him; and always there were the long discussions.[7]

Opportunities were exactly what the aspiring and eager intellectual young woman was seeking. Her schooling ended when she left her mother's school and began her teaching career, and for a woman in her position at this time, there were no options for continuing her formal education. Anne C. Rose hypothesizes that if Peabody had been a man, she "undoubtedly would have been a minister—and a good one."[8] While such an option was closed, the rigorous course of reading and studying which she pursued with the leading Unitarian of the day furnished her with an education comparable to and possibly surpassing that of any divinity school student. Moreover, that she was able to satisfy her intellectual and theological scholarly ambitions through her relationship with Channing probably contributed to her failure to take a more insistent or zealous stand on women's rights issues. She was able to remain within woman's sphere as a teacher while at the same time engaging in a satisfying intellectual and educational endeavor. Without a relationship such as this one, Peabody might have experienced frustrations which would have fueled an earlier involvement in questions of women's educational opportunities.

Examination of the religious and theological issues which formed the core of Peabody and Channing's relationship is especially interesting in light of Nina Baym's assertion that Peabody was not a Transcendentalist but followed the movement from "the perspective of an unyielding Evangelical Unitarianism."[9] Was Channing's strong influence a factor in formulating Unitarian beliefs so resolute that Peabody continued to return to them throughout her life? Their theological discussions were anchored in their mutual Unitarianism. Channing opposed Calvinist doctrine, and, as Ronda summarizes, "Found himself the spiritual head of the liberal revolt against religious orthodoxy in the early nineteenth century" (*Letters,* p. 52*n*). Peabody describes herself as raised "in the bosom of Unitarianism" (quoted in *Letters,* p. 18) and "something of a Unitarian doctrinaire" as a result of her extensive reading and studying of ecclesiastical history, Biblical criticism, and other theological material (*Rem,* p. 40). In *Reminiscences,* Peabody uses the notes she took during their conversations to recreate some of their religious discussions which were prompted by their reading and consideration of contemporary ecclesiastical controversies. Both Channing and Peabody entertained the new ideas of Ralph Waldo Emerson and the other Transcendentalists and endeavored to see them as evolutions of their own beliefs. However, early on Channing raised questions of caution which Peabody later came to echo. He told Peabody that "the danger that besets our Transcendentalists is that they sometimes mistake their individualities for the Transcendent." He goes on to explain that "what is common to men and revealed by Jesus transcends every single individuality, and is the spiritual object and food of all individuals" (*Rem,* p. 365). Many of Emerson's followers do not recognize this and "fall into a kind of ego-theism, of which a true understanding of Jesus Christ is the only cure, as I more and more believe"

(*Rem*, p. 365). In an 1841 letter to Peabody reprinted in both *Reminiscences* and in the *Memoir of William Ellery Channing,* Channing shares his concerns with her: "I do fear a tendency, in the present movement, to loosen the tie which binds the soul to the great Friend and Deliverer [Jesus Christ]."[10] Peabody also eventually embraces Channing's same concerns. Her 1858 essay, **"Egotheism, the Atheism of To-day,"** employs Channing's original term in a Christian indictment of the over-glorification of the individual in Transcendentalism. Using Baym's criteria, if Peabody insists upon the "mediating necessity for Christ," then she is not a Transcendentalist. The central religious belief of Christ's necessity, which she affirmed in her years with Channing, though challenged at times, remained one of the foundations of her religious beliefs.

While their religious quest was at the core of their relationship, the blueprint for living and translating beliefs into action was self-culture. As evidenced by her self-imposed regimen of reading and studying, Peabody was already practicing a form of self-culture before her relationship with Channing. In an 1823 letter to her younger sister Sophia, the nineteen-year-old Peabody outlines an impressive plan of theological study for Sophia for "the cultivation of your intellect, your taste, and your heart" (*Letters,* p. 59), urging her to tackle it with "effort and industry" (*Letters,* p. 64). Peabody's efforts toward self-culture prodded her to search for a mentor, a great mind to help her in the cultivation of her own mind and soul, and she found such a person in Channing, himself awash in the ideas of self-culture. David Robinson points out Channing's "repeated insistence that the soul could grow—that it was a living thing not unlike a plant or animal, and that, like a plant, with careful culture it could be nurtured to develop a certain potentiality of its nature."[11] As recorded in *Reminiscences,* their discussions could read as a practicum in self-culture with their emphasis on religion, intellect, morality, social relations, and aesthetics, for Peabody quotes Channing as saying, "'Self-education is the only education and we should look upon ourselves as one among our pupils with a certain impersonality'" (*Rem*, p. 135). Together they translated Baron Marie De Gerando's *Self-Education: Or the Means and Art of Moral Progress,* and Peabody published the translation under her name in 1830 (*Letters,* p. 94). Channing's sermon, *Self-Culture,* published in 1838, articulates and formalizes the principles of self-culture which Peabody and Channing had been practicing for years, proclaiming that he who "does what he can to unfold all his powers and capacities, especially his nobler ones, so as to become a well proportioned, vigorous, excellent, happy being, practises self-culture."[12]

While embracing the ideas of self-culture, Peabody and Channing did not want self-culture to become egoism. The synthesis of their religious beliefs with the concepts of self-culture spawned concerns over an extreme individualism. They confronted the tension between their conviction of the centrality of Jesus Christ and the glorification of the self inherent in self-culture. They had to develop perspectives which would prevent self-culture from becoming too egocentric and from focusing on the individual to the exclusion of God, society, and duty. The system of self-culture which Channing articulates in *Self-Culture* anticipates an overemphasis on the self by stressing the moral and religious components of self-culture. He makes clear that the moral element is to be cultivated "above all others, for on its culture the right development of all others depends." He goes on to stress that the most important part of self-culture is to overcome the self-seeking and to exalt the disinterested, or "to enthrone the sense of duty within us."[13] His emphasis on morality and duty heavily reinforced the values Peabody had absorbed from her mother. Both Channing and Peabody extended self-culture to social culture, with the concept of social culture implying a person's moral responsibility to facilitate the self-culture of others and through changing minds and therefore lives, to change society. Such a belief served to validate their respective major career choices, the ministry and education. Both professions involved facilitating the self-culture of others and therefore a contribution to the improvement of society.

These tenets of self-culture offer a lens through which to view Peabody's widely varying activities and vocations. For Peabody, teaching, writing, publishing, editing, and providing access to important works in her bookshop and lending library were all efforts to promote self-culture. References to her intentions are numerous. For example, in an 1836 letter discussing a proposed education journal, Peabody describes an intended article on **"Moral Poetry of England in Education"** whose purpose would be "showing young persons how they may make these authors assist them in the Science of Selfknowledge" (*Letters,* p. 188). In the prospectus to *Aesthetic Papers,* Peabody expresses her intent to use the aesthetic plane to reconcile "antagonistic views of Philosophy, of Individual and of Social Culture, which prevail among the various divisions of the Church, and of the Scientific and Literary world." She hopes that bringing them together will produce a "white radiance of love and wisdom" from the "union of the many-colored rays, that shall cultivate an harmonious intellectual and moral life in our country."[14] In the bookshop and Foreign Lending Library which she owned and ran in the 1840s, Peabody stocked a wide range of foreign literature and philosophy. Madeleine Stern points out that the shop was the "principal means for the dissemination of foreign literature" in Boston at the time.[15] An 1840 copy of *Catalogue of the Foreign Library* indicates about three hundred French, German, British, and Italian works and translations as well as works by locals Emerson, Nathaniel Hawthorne, Bronson Alcott, and Channing (Channing had the most titles of any author, nine). Not only did Peabody promote the self-culture of others through the literary works she sold, but she made the shop available as an intellectual meeting place. Margaret Fuller held some of her famous Conversations there, and several Brook Farm planning meetings were held there.

The profession of teaching placed an extra demand upon Peabody to attend her own self-culture as well as to facilitate that of others. As she herself articulates it, "In my vocation as teacher, it was of paramount importance that my intellectual and moral philosophy should be true, or I might do infinite mischief to the children committed to my care for development and education" (***Rem,*** pp. 119-20). Her dedication to education as a consecrated profession for women began with her mother's influence. Mrs. Peabody taught her daughter that "educating children morally and spiritually as well as intellectually" was "the most sacred of the duties of the children of the Pilgrims who founded the Republic to bless all the *nations* of the earth" (***Rem,*** p. 40). Channing reinforced and intensified Peabody's sense of moral duty and high calling, instilling in her the sense of teaching as a religious calling and conveying to her that the "ministration of Christianity to the development of individual character" was "as much the business of every-day life and the school as of the pulpit" (***Rem,*** p. 135). Under Channing's influence, her clerical ambitions, if present, were sublimated into a religious zeal in the sacredness of her responsibilities as a teacher. For Peabody, the elevation of teaching to the level of preaching empowered women's sphere. Through a vocation sanctioned for women, she was told she could be as effectual and as influential as a minister: "*You* in your school-room, can live Christ's life, and preach Christ more effectually, perhaps, than the minster in his pulpit!" (***Rem,*** p. 126). Peabody had no need to question the limits of women's roles when she felt herself ordained a high priestess of education.

As Peabody gained intellectual, moral, and professional maturity in the 1830s, she maintained her ties with Channing while also establishing significant relationships to other figures. She continued in frequent company with Channing, discussing her thoughts, projects, and new friends with him. His reflections and cautions concerning her activities in this decade influenced her self-evaluation and ongoing development. She also cultivated new connections, primary among which were her association with Bronson Alcott and the first few years of her friendship with Emerson. In these relationships, Channing's example and his early warnings about the potential egoism of extreme individualism were factors in Peabody's assessment of their ideas.

For example, Channing raised questions which Peabody eventually came to second about the intense self-analysis of Alcott's methods during Peabody's years at

the Temple School (1832-36). Channing's views of Alcott's methods were based upon visits to the school, conversations with Peabody and Alcott, and Peabody's ***Record of a School.*** In a letter dated 24 August 1835, Channing comments upon the first edition of Peabody's ***Record of a School*** which he has just read. Suggesting difficulties which they have discussed before, Channing expresses his concerns that the "free development of the spiritual nature may be impeded by too much analysis of it. The soul is somewhat jealous of being watched, and it is no small part of wisdom to know when to leave it to its impulses, and when to restrain it." He goes on to point out that the "strong passion of the young for the outward is an indication of Nature to be respected" (***Rem,*** p. 357). Channing probably objected to Alcott's method because of its extreme focus upon the individual, a method he might see as promoting egoism in children. In the same letter, Channing is critical of Peabody's chapter on "General Principles." Peabody must have considered Channing's concerns and suggestions, for in the second edition of the book in 1836, she left out this chapter and wrote a new preface.

Peabody's new preface in the second edition reflects Channing's concerns, for the stance of her essay anticipates criticisms of Alcott's approach and refutes them by attempting to place his method of self-analysis within a broader moral context. The obvious strain of this tack is evidence of Peabody's own growing skepticism of Alcott's methods of encouraging intense abstract introspection in the children. The full title of the book is ***Record of a School Exemplifying the General Principles of Spiritual Culture,*** and Peabody does discuss the educational principles of the school in terms of spiritual culture and self-culture or "human culture." She also moves quickly to draw a relationship between human culture and social responsibility: "To contemplate Spirit in our selves, and in our fellow men, is obviously the only means of understanding social duty, and quickening within ourselves a wise Humanity." She finds that "Contemplation of Spirit is the first principle of Human Culture; the foundation of Self-education." Peabody explains that Alcott applies this principle to early education to lead the "young mind to self-education."[16] It is the contemplation of God, she assures the reader, which is "constantly checking any narrowing effect of egotism, or self complacency, which it [the method] may be supposed to engender."[17] Channing found this component of Alcott's curriculum insufficient to counteract the dangers of egoism; Peabody would later arrive at similar conclusions.

The real tour de force which Peabody performs to reconcile Alcott's methods to herself and to doubts such as Channing's is to attempt a re-definition of self analysis:

> Some objections have been made, however, to the questionings upon consciousness, of which specimens are given in the lessons on Self-Analysis,—It is said that

their general tendency must be to produce egotism.—
This might be, if in self-analysis, a perfect standard
was not always kept before the mind, by constant reference to Jesus Christ, as the "truth of our nature;" . . .
WE have found the general influence of the lessons on
Self-Analysis, to be humbling to the self-conceited and
vain—though they have also encouraged and raised up
the depressed and timid, in one or two instances. The
objection seems to me to have arisen from taking the
word self in too limited signification. The spirit within,
is what is meant by self considered as an object of
philosophical investigation. I think myself, that the lessons would more appropriately have been styled, analysis of human nature, than self-analysis. . . .[18]

Peabody's anxiety over accusations of egoism is obvious. In "Elizabeth Palmer Peabody's View of the
Child," Ronda surmises that by the time she left the
Temple School in August 1836, Peabody also differed
with Alcott on points of "sense education, the conduct
of discussions, historical education, privacy and discipline."[19] Much later, in 1871 when a third edition of
Record of a School, retitled **Mr. Alcott's School,** was
being prepared, Peabody insisted to Alcott and to the
publisher that she be allowed to include a new preface
and an appendix to discuss how her philosophy of education had evolved since the second edition. The publisher refused, much to Peabody's dismay, and her distress is chronicled in her letters to Alcott at this time
which seek his help in securing the modifications.[20] The
very brief preface which she is finally allowed only
hints at the changes in her educational philosophy and
method.

It was soon after the close of the Temple School and
her distancing from Alcott that Peabody came into more
frequent contact with Ralph Waldo Emerson. As Peabody became more enamored of and immersed in the
new ideas as articulated by Emerson, she began to establish her intellectual independence from Channing;
however, his pervasive influence continued, and she
persisted in seeking his approval. As a wise mentor,
Channing encouraged Peabody in her explorations,
while at the same time not hesitating to issue warnings
and cautions and to question some of her thoughts. Peabody records in **Rem** that between 1836 and 1840 she
was in "more constant and close relation" with Emerson's mind than with Channing's; however, she wrote
to Channing frequently from Emerson's home (p. 367).
In retrospect, Peabody felt that her "long apprentice-
ship" with Channing "enabled me to receive a peculiar
blessing" from Emerson, and that Emerson's "doctrine
of Thought made me completely understand Dr. Channing's doctrine of Love" (**Rem,** p. 367). Peabody probably saw her association with Emerson and his ideas as
an evolutionary step in her own development and self-
culture. It was important for Peabody to feel that she
had Dr. Channing's approval, and she reports that he

"rejoiced" in Emerson's personal influence on her as
Emerson helped to correct her "morbid moral sensibility" (**Rem,** p. 366).

However, Peabody came to experience tensions between
the ideas of Channing and Emerson. With the delivery
of Emerson's Divinity School Address, questions arose
over his ideas about the role of Jesus Christ in self-
culture. Peabody insisted that Emerson had been misunderstood and that he still continued to place Christ in a
central role as example. Knowing Emerson to be
grounded in the same beliefs as she and Channing, Peabody refused to perceive the subtle changes taking place
in his ideas. It was upsetting to her to hear that Channing himself raised questions about the extreme individualism which he discerned in the Divinity School
Address and in other works by Emerson. She queried
Channing whether she had really understood all that she
had learned from him if he questioned Emerson's ideas.
She confronted Channing, and **Rem** contains a long account from notes taken at the time of her conversation
with him on this topic. Peabody insisted that Emerson
omitted one originally intended passage in his address
which would have "saved many a weak brother and sister Transcendentalist from going into the extreme of
ego-theism, which has discredited a true principle"
(**Rem,** p. 373). She reports that he left out a "warning
against making the new truth a fanaticism" (**Rem,**
p. 373), against the "puppyism" which would be "pres-
ently developed because every *step* of *human culture*
was immediately exaggerated in its last word—& so
made false—by *human vanity patronising* it—" (**Letters,**
p. 386). Peabody accepted Emerson's excuse that he
left it out because his speech was running too long, and
she refused to see it as an indicator of a new direction
in his thoughts.

Even as Peabody persisted in affirming the points which
she and Emerson had in common, an important fundamental difference was developing. Emerson and Peabody initially shared Unitarian ideas toward Christ and
self-culture. In *Apostle of Culture,* David Robinson observes that Emerson's journals and sermons in his earlier years reflect a reverence for Christ, expressed in his
own terms, which coincides with that of Channing.[21] He
portrays Christ as a moral ideal, and his "idea that Christ
embodies the potential perfection of each individual
makes this position indistinguishable from that of Channing or Ware,"[22] and thus also Peabody. But as early as
1830, Robinson points to a journal entry which he believes shows the beginnings of a major change: "'For
there is no being in the Universe whose integrity is so
precious to you as that of your soul.'" Robinson interprets these words, within the context of the journal entry, as an early sign of a "necessary choice between a
method of self-culture guided by the authority of historical Christianity as embodied in Jesus, and a self-
culture not only aimed at the self, but directed by the

self—the self, it must be remembered, which is acting universally, or as one with God."[23] Robinson observes that, by 1835, Emerson had completely rejected the exclusive authority of Jesus, though he still continued to profess a respect for him.[24] His elimination of Christ from the ideology of self-culture left his doctrine of self-culture extremely vulnerable to the egoism which Channing and Peabody feared. Within his system there was no figure to check or balance the self-absorption in and glorification of the individual. There was no effort to establish a responsibility to other men or to society. This evolution contributed to the secularization of Emerson's theory of self-culture, while Peabody's theory remained that of Channing. In a long developing conflict in Unitarian thought over "the radical individuality of the potentially divine soul against the authority of the example of Christ,"[25] Emerson was taking one direction, while Channing and Peabody chose another. In observing that Channing never took the step which Emerson did, Robinson insists that Channing "clung much more firmly to a Christ-centered religion, never going as far as Emerson did in labelling Jesus' claim to divinity a poetic effusion."[26] But no matter how Peabody saw herself within the context of her own time, no matter what ideas she may have been trying on, she came down firmly in Channing's camp.

While both Peabody and Channing supported the spirit of the new movement, as the ideas of Transcendentalism grew and coalesced, so did their concerns about egoism. Peabody was privy to and influenced by Channing's concerns. In his disappointment in the *Dial,* Channing lamented to Peabody that Henry Hedge had not been the one to introduce Transcendentalism, for he might have prevented its identification with "the extreme Individualism which is now perhaps indelibly associated with it in America," for Hedge believes in "the Christian Church as a visible body in the midst of society" (*Rem,* p. 371). Both Channing and Peabody fundamentally believed that the strong theological component of their ideology of self-culture held at bay the threat of egoism and allowed them to interpret self-culture as having a component of social responsibility and progress as well as of personal growth.

Peabody's increasing concern over the threats of egoism engendered by Transcendental ideas are evident in her writing from the 1840s. From this decade her works all display the strong stamp of Christianity, the rhetoric of self-culture, and an underlying assumption of the importance of self-culture. Most often through these ideals of Christianity and the moral example of Christ, Peabody criticizes extreme individualism and egoism. In **"A Glimpse of Christ's Idea of Society,"** a response to the ideas of Brook Farm, published in the *Dial* in 1841, Peabody asserts that the self and society must grow together in order to achieve Jesus Christ's idea of human society. She deplores the errors which have led

men "to neglect social organization wholly, or regard it as indifferent" and "to treat of an isolated cultivation of the soul, as if it could be continuously independent of all extraneous influence."[27] In Peabody's cosmology, as humans work toward the perfection of Jesus, they begin "to love and assist each other."[28] In turn, it is the responsibility of the society to assist its members in developing themselves.[29] One can surmise that she envisioned the communal emphasis of Brook Farm as an antidote to the threat of self-absorption and egoism of Transcendentalism and hoped to see the venture establish a careful balance between self and society.

In her essay, **"The Dorian Measure,"** first published in *Aesthetic Papers* in 1849, Peabody further develops her concept of the mutual roles of the state and the individual. She holds up the early Dorian society and its ideas about collective identity and education as a model for Christian societies. Once again, while the "unfolding of each of its members into the harmonious exercises of his power" is important, so is the progress of the society.[30] And in this case, Peabody's goal was to insure that the United States become a Christian society and not a nation of egoists.

In her efforts to formulate a perspective which carefully balances the development of the individual and the development of an appropriate government, Peabody applies her concepts of the mutuality of personal and social culture and her strong Christian principle to a national vision. The central query of this essay is: "Can Christ govern mankind as completely as Apollo governed the Dorians?"[31] To achieve such a millennium, Peabody insists that America's political forms must be inspired by the Christian religion, and that through public education the government should teach a Christian system of culture. Such a vision is reminiscent of Channing's hearty endorsement of public education as a means of facilitating self-culture when he called public schools "the chief hope of our country."[32] Peabody's view of public education as a source of self-culture is evident in her arguments for the inclusion of gymnastics, music, dance, drawing, more foreign languages, and philology in a normal curriculum. In a manifesto which emphasizes Christianity and moral, intellectual, and aesthetic education for men and women, Peabody pleads for the strengthening of the institution of public education. Meanwhile, individuals who endeavor to cultivate their natures "enter spiritually into the legislature of their country" and "help redeem its heart to progress."[33] Such a collective national vision refuses to allow an individual to become locked into an egocentric view but insists that the individual recognize the interdependence of individual and government.

Peabody's 1858 essay **"Egotheism, The Atheism of To-Day"** is her most full-blown indictment of the egoism springing from Transcendentalism. The essay distills Peabody's distress over both the Transcendental-ists' rejection of the moral role of Christ and glorification of the individual. Seventeen or eighteen years after Channing first employed the term "ego-theism" to describe those Transcendentalists who "sometimes mistake their individualities for the Tran-scendent" (*Rem,* p. 365), Peabody wields the term to encapsulate the same concerns and arguments which Channing had articulated. She is clear-sighted and sear-ing in her perceptions and articulations of the spiritual state of those she describes:

> But when faith stagnates in the mere affirmation of the spiritual, men deify their own conceptions; i.e. they say that their conception of God is all that men can ever know of God. In short, faith commits suicide, as Cato did, at the summit of the moral life, and the next step to this is necessarily EGOTHEISM, which denies other self-consciousness to God than our own subjective con-sciousness;—not recognizing that there is, beyond our conception, inconceivable Power, Wisdom, and Love,—of the immanence of whose substantial being within us our best conception is but a transient form. Thus Egotheism, in the last analysis, is Atheism; and we find this "latest form of infidelity," as the under-standing has rather blindly denominated it,—though not without a degree of religious instinct,—in the sci-ence, philosophy, and politics of the age,—at once glo-rifying and saddening its poetry;—for man proves but a melancholy God.[34]

Peabody displays a socially conservative, strongly Uni-tarian view in her sermonlike pronouncements against egotheism. She deplores the Egotheist who "sees that nothing man says or does is so great as himself, the sayer and doer."[35] The only hope she holds out for any egotheist is a turn to the faith of Jesus Christ and to the principles of Christianity. Her rhetoric and her admon-ishments place her firmly within Channing's evangeli-cal Unitarianism and at odds with the later ideas of many of the Transcendentalists.

Biographical data gleaned from *Rem,* from Peabody's letters, and from Channing's letters to Peabody con-cerning the last years of Channing's life further con-firms the reciprocity and intensity of their lengthy per-sonal and intellectual relationship. Peabody copied hundreds of Channing's sermons, preparing them for publication. Upon a few occasions, Channing assisted Peabody financially, giving her a sermon to publish for profit or sending small amounts of money when she was in dire financial straits. Channing gave Peabody emotional support, advice, and personal criticism. While their relationship continued strong and vital to each of them, it is possible to speculate that a natural tension grew between them during Channing's last years when Peabody was exploring and studying new perspectives and ideas, the kind of tension which results when a stu-dent endeavors to differentiate herself from a mentor, or when a young adult separates and establishes her indi-

viduality from a parent. However, in retrospect, Pea-body clearly insists upon the magnanimity of Chan-ning's intellect, which made him ever open to considering new ideas and to giving his blessings to her explorations. In the conclusion of *Rem,* she recounts her last conversation with Channing. In the spring of 1842, she went to tell him good-by before he left on his summer journey. As Peabody left him, Channing "kindly took both my hands in his and said: 'Well, will you write to me this summer, and make me partner of your new thoughts?'" Peabody responded, "'I do not know, Sir . . . I have hardly learned how to clothe them with words.'" Channing's reply speaks to the claim they felt upon each other through the years of their relationship: "'But if you learn anything from this young friend of yours, or from any other source, don't you think *I* have the *first* right to it?'" (*Rem,* p. 449). Peabody never wrote to Channing that summer, an act which seems uncharacteristic of the pattern of their past frequent communication. In October, she received word of his death. Why she did not write to Channing that summer and why she makes a point of documenting the fact is open to speculation.

But she did subsequently communicate with Channing. Sixteen years after his death, in a letter dated 4 July 1858, Peabody discusses three separate incidents of communications from Channing through a spiritual me-dium. The contents of the communications concerned theological and philosophical ideas which Peabody claimed were in complete harmony with her own. In one incident, she even says that his view "was in accor-dance with those I had thought of—and even main-tained in an unpublished written essay of mine" (*Letters,* p. 287). She was once again able to experience accord between their thoughts and ideas, a closure which Chan-ning's death had denied her.

Channing's influence on Peabody was seminal. Through the mutuality of their relationship, Peabody formulated the religious and moral convictions which remained the foundations of her life. With Channing, the leading Unitarian of his day, Peabody questioned, studied, and strengthened her Evangelical Unitarian beliefs, particu-larly the notion that Jesus Christ was a mediating ne-cessity in one's life. Caught in the spirit of their histori-cal place and moment, Channing and Peabody were swept up in the doctrine of self-culture, of "unfolding" their powers and their capacities. Channing early planted in Peabody concerns and cautions about the po-tential egoism of self-culture which grew through the years. The nature and strength of their religious beliefs combined with the concept of self-culture to produce a doctrine of self-culture which guarded against the ex-treme individualism or over glorification of the self. Channing's *Self-Culture* articulates and formalizes the tenets of this ideology as practiced by Peabody and him. It insisted upon the moral role of Christ in self-culture which would prevent one from over focusing on self, and it emphasized moral responsibility and duty, elements which forced a person to turn outwards as well as inwards.

Peabody's own ideas on self-culture preserved Christ's role and also insisted on a balance between self-culture and social culture. Individuals had a responsibility not only to cultivate themselves but also to facilitate the self-culture of others and through them to improve society. Society, in turn, had a responsibility to facilitate the culture of its individual members. This balance prevented egoism and became Peabody's vocational rationale. Neither Peabody nor Channing could tolerate extreme individualism, when "self-respect" becomes "self-worship";[36] and this antipathy, as best expressed in Peabody's **"Egotheism, The Atheism of Today,"** separates them from some of the Transcendentalists on important issues. Among the many riches of Channing's legacy to Peabody, a crucial one is the abhorrence of the Egotheist whom the Devil offers "material, moral, and spiritual power, on condition of the soul's 'falling down and worshipping ME.'"[37]

Notes

1. *Reminiscences of Rev. Wm. Ellery Channing, D.D.* (Boston: Roberts Brothers) was published in 1880, the centennial year of Channing's birth. It is a long, loosely organized reminiscence based upon letters and Peabody's copious notes from their conversations. This book is hereafter cited as *Rem* in the text.

2. See especially "Female Education in Massachusetts" in *Barnard's American Journal of Education,* 30 (July 1880): 584-87, for a letter from Peabody discussing her mother's own education and her influence on her daughter.

3. *Letters of Elizabeth Palmer Peabody: American Renaissance Woman,* ed. Bruce A. Ronda (Middletown, Conn.: Wesleyan University Press, 1984), p. 15. Hereafter cited as *Letters* in the text.

4. Channing's farewell sermon to his Federal Street congregation in Boston delivered before leaving for a European tour, 26 May 1822.

5. There is some confusion about the date. In *Reminiscences,* Peabody dates this conversation as taking place the spring before he left for Europe in August 1821. However, Channing left for Europe in May 1822.

6. Charles H. Foster, "Elizabeth Palmer Peabody," in *Notable American Women,* ed. Edward T. James, 3 vols. (Cambridge: Harvard University Press, 1971), 3:32.

7. See Ann Douglas' *The Feminization of American Culture* (New York: Alfred A. Knopf, 1977) for a close study of the relationship between ministers and women during this period.

8. Anne C. Rose, *Transcendentalism as a Social Movement, 1830-1850* (New Haven: Yale University Press, 1981), p. 53.

9. Nina Baym, "The Ann Sisters: Elizabeth Peabody's Millennial Historicism," *American Literary History,* 3 (Spring 1991): 27.

10. *Reminiscences,* p. 432, and William Henry Channing, *Memoir of William Ellery Channing,* 3 vols. (Boston: William Crosby and H. P. Nichols, 1848), 2:449.

11. David Robinson, "The Legacy of Channing: Culture as a Religious Category in New England Thought," *Harvard Theological Review,* 74 (April 1981): 223.

12. Channing, *Self-Culture,* in *William Ellery Channing: Selected Writings,* ed. David Robinson (New York: Paulist Press, 1985), p. 228.

13. Channing, *Self-Culture,* p. 229.

14. Peabody, "Prospectus," in *Aesthetic Papers* (Boston: E. P. Peabody, 1849), p. iii.

15. Madeleine B. Stern, "Elizabeth Peabody's Foreign Library (1840)," *Books and Book People in 19th Century America* (New York: R. R. Bowker, 1978), p. 121.

16. Peabody, *Record of a School Exemplifying the General Principles of Spiritual Culture,* 2d ed. (Boston: Russell, Shatruck, 1836), p. iii.

17. *Record of a School,* p. v.

18. *Record of a School,* p. vii.

19. Ronda, "Elizabeth Palmer Peabody's View of the Child," *ESQ: A Journal of the American Renaissance,* 23 (2d Quarter 1977): 110.

20. See Peabody's letters to Alcott dated 29 July 1871, 22 August 1871, and 30 August 1871.

21. David Robinson, *Apostle of Culture: Emerson as Preacher and Lecturer* (Philadelphia: University of Pennsylvania Press, 1982), p. 56.

22. Robinson, *Apostle of Culture,* p. 57.

23. Robinson, *Apostle of Culture,* p. 58.

24. Robinson, *Apostle of Culture,* p. 59.

25. Robinson, *Apostle of Culture,* p. 24.

26. Robinson, in *William Ellery Channing: Selected Writings,* p. 31.

27. Peabody, "A Glimpse of Christ's Ideal of Society," *Dial,* 3 (October 1841): 217 (also reprinted

as "Brook Farm Interpretation of Christ's Idea of Society" in *Last Evening with Allston, and Other Papers* [(Boston: D. Lothrop, 1886)], pp. 181-201).

28. "A Glimpse of Christ's Ideal of Society," 218.

29. "A Glimpse of Christ's Ideal of Society," 226.

30. Peabody, "The Dorian Measure, with a Modern Application"; reprinted in *Last Evening with Allston, and Other Papers,* p. 104.

31. "The Dorian Measure," p. 116.

32. Channing, *Self-Culture,* p. 255.

33. "The Dorian Measure," p. 134.

34. Peabody, "Egotheism, The Atheism of Today," *Monthly Religious Magazine,* 21 (March 1859): 165-74; reprinted in *Last Evening with Allston, and Other Papers,* p. 245.

35. "Egotheism, The Atheism of Today," p. 252.

36. "Egotheism, The Atheism of Today," p. 250.

37. "Egotheism, The Atheism of Today," p. 252.

Diane Brown Jones (essay date 1992)

SOURCE: Jones, Diane Brown. "Elizabeth Palmer Peabody's Transcendental Manifesto." In *Studies in the American Renaissance,* edited by Joel Myerson, pp. 195-207. Charlottesville: University Press of Virginia, 1992.

[*In the following essay, Jones evaluates Peabody's exploration of Transcendentalist ideas in her writings.*]

In her 1984 bibliographic review of Elizabeth Palmer Peabody, Margaret Neussendorfer comments that Peabody's "writings have, in general, been overlooked in favor of her activities and her relations with more widely known contemporaries."[1] Bruce Ronda's selected edition of Peabody's letters, also published in 1984, helps re-inforce this narrow focus of Peabody scholarship by producing a virtual catalogue of the Transcendentalists and their activities.[2] Because of Peabody's wide ranging contacts, scholars have studied her for what she reveals about the others. Yet neither Neussendorfer's observation nor the easy availability of an edition of Peabody's letters has generated any proliferation of new Peabody scholarship which shifts focus from her associations to her texts.

The very nature of Peabody's writing directs the reader to some other individual. Although not a person to suppress her opinions, when Peabody did write, she often did so to elucidate the thoughts of others. As Joel My-

erson recalls, Theodore Parker described Peabody's role in the Transcendental Club "to be the '*Boswell*' of the day."[3] Surveying the Peabody material listed in *First Printings of American Authors,* one discovers quickly that the textbooks, memoirs, and translations shift attention away from Peabody herself. Her histories are of the Hebrews and the Greeks; her educational writings include Pestalozzi's plan for *First Lessons in Grammar* and General Bem's principle for a *Chronological History of the United States*; her memorials are of Madame Susanne Kossuth Meszlenyi and Dr. William Wesselhoeft; her writings on behalf of American Indians include **"Sarah Winnemucca's Practical Solutions of the Indian Problem"**; her *Last Evening* is with Washington Allston; her *Record* [*Record of a School*] is of Bronson Alcott's school; and her *Reminiscences* are of William Ellery Channing.[4]

In her shorter works Peabody often maintained a similar perspective, acting as critical intermediary between some other text and the reading public. In a review of Emerson's *Nature,* Peabody defines the role of critics to be "priests of literature." Critics, she explains, are a necessary "intermediate class" because the genius' "most precious sayings are naked, if not invisible to the eyes of the conventional." Therefore, "criticism," according to Peabody, "in its worthiest meaning, is not, as is too often supposed, fault-finding, but interpretation of the oracles of genius."[5] On another occasion, in one of her many lectures, Peabody described herself as from her childhood belonging "by nature rather to the reflective than perceptive class."[6] Generally, Peabody observed this distinction by maintaining the reflective pose of the literary priest rather than the perceptive role of the literary prophet.

Perhaps another reason why Peabody's writings have been passed over relates to her prose style. Myerson describes it as "a manful attempt to match the abstractness of the subjects upon which she usually wrote."[7] Her contemporaries were not as generous. Ralph Waldo Emerson and Margaret Fuller both complained that her style was difficult. Emerson faulted her use of the superlative; Fuller criticized her "impossibility of being clear and accurate in a brief space."[8] Even Peabody herself was sensitive to her failure to find language adequate for her ideas (*L* [*Letters of Elizabeth Palmer Peabody*], p. 264).

Despite the tendency to turn critical emphasis away from Peabody's texts, reason enough exists to examine Peabody's writings for what they offer of her own Transcendental views. The very activities for which she is noted emphasize her importance in the Transcendentalist circle and outweigh interest in her just because of the people she knew. George Willis Cooke aptly describes Peabody as "a thorough transcendentalist." John Wilson concludes that "Perhaps of all members of the

'Hedge Club,' only Miss Peabody achieved a working synthesis of what seem to some critics to be irreconcilable elements in transcendentalism—past and present, society and solitude, moral and aesthetic, education of self and education of others." Her own busy efforts reflected specific Transcendentalist concerns and yielded distinctive results which distinguish her among her peers. Philip Gura states that "Among the American Transcendentalists involved in . . . [the] re-examination of language, Peabody was the premier purveyor of language theory, both in its theoretical and practical aspects." Wilson asserts that compared to Peabody's efforts to learn and to teach history other Transcendentalist ventures into history and historiography were dilettantish. And, according to Madeleine Stern, Peabody's little book store at 13 West Street, Boston, was "the principal means for the dissemination of foreign literature" of its time.[9]

Peabody's writings also record certain curiosities and controversies which should make them compelling pieces for study. For example, Peabody, like George Ripley, angered Andrews Norton by boldly pursuing a line of thought alien to Unitarian belief. In 1834, Peabody contributed a series of six articles on the Hebrew Scriptures for the *Christian Examiner*; however, Norton suspended the series after running only three installments (*L,* p. 248).[10] Anne Rose argues that Norton took this action because he was "disturbed by her doctrine" and adds further, "For just that reason, the 'Spirit of the Hebrew Scriptures' is interesting to us."[11]

Another Peabody text, **"A Vision,"** has borne a rather paradoxical invisibility in the limited consideration of Peabody's writing.[12] The present discussion seeks to bring this text back into view. Although Neussendorfer describes **"A Vision"** as "peculiarly Transcendentalist,"[13] no extended discussions of it have appeared to place it either in the context of Peabody's works or the literature of the Transcendentalist period generally. However, **"A Vision"** is an important essay on both counts. First, it is one of the rare documents which expresses a moment of inspiration so crucial to the Transcendentalists, made more rare because it is the voice of a woman. Second, in the scope of Peabody's writings, it represents one of the few occasions when Peabody casts off her typical stance as literary priest to assume the voice of literary prophet. As such, **"A Vision"** conveys the truths which crystallized for her at the height of her Transcendentalist years and which continued to undergird her various activities throughout the remainder of her life.

However peculiar **"A Vision"** may be, the text is a particularly Transcendentalist literary text, for it bears those three "main tendencies in Transcendentalist writing" which Lawrence Buell identifies: "impulses to prophesy, to create nature anew for oneself, and to speak in the first person singular."[14] Another significant characteristic of **"A Vision"** which marks it as a Transcendentalist text is that it has as its source and reflects in its culmination an inspirational experience.[15]

Surprisingly, despite the primacy Transcendentalists gave to the inspirational moment, instances of such mystical experiences are rarely recorded. Buell lists Bronson Alcott, Brownson, Emerson, Henry David Thoreau, and Fuller, but not Peabody, as having recorded them.[16] However, **"A Vision"** begins as a moment's "transfiguration from within" to arrive at a Truth of which the essay is an expression. But just as Buell describes the difficulty of authenticating a true inspiration from its moment to its literary manifestation,[17] so too is it difficult to conclude confidently that Peabody, or any of her contemporaries, actually experienced moments of divine inspiration. Peabody admitted to having "divinations," but she was grateful that her mentor Channing did not label her as "being visionary" because of them.[18] She worked to improve her knowledge of language in order, as she explained, to "get weaponed to contend with the great Silence adequately and win from her the expression of what God has graciously pleased to say to *me* individually" (*L,* p. 264).

Peabody attached much importance to inspiration and distinguished carefully between inspiration and hallucination. In 1838, writing to Emerson about the insanity of Jones Very, she made a clear distinction "between trusting the Soul & giving up one's mind to . . . *individual illuminations*" (*L,* p. 209). She expressed her deep concern that people were equating Very's hallucinations with Transcendentalism "which," she added, "shows how very entirely they do *not* apprehend *the ground* of a *real belief* in Inspiration" (*L,* p. 209). Peabody concluded: "What a frightful shallowness of thought in the community—that sees no difference between the evidence of the most manifest insanity & the Ideas of Reason" (*L,* pp. 209-10).

Peabody's "belief in the power of intuition to apprehend truth directly" (*L,* p. 274) clearly included an inclination to mystical experience. Thomas Wentworth Higginson's description of her as "dreamy" (*L,* p. 233) is reinforced by her own recollection of meditative experiences scattered throughout her writings. Peabody recalled that in her childhood her "first conception of God . . . embodied itself spontaneously in a genial human face."[19] This experience became an early lesson in the difficulty of using language to capture a vision. She called the vision "A man," and was promptly corrected for not knowing that God made her. From the ensuing conversation with her mother, Peabody was left "with another image of God in my mind, conveying not half so much of the truth as did that kind Face, close up to mine, and seeming to be so wholly occupied with His creature."[20] As a young adult, Peabody continued to have mystical experiences. Peabody recounts one such occurrence to Dorothea Dix in 1827:

> I do not know why it was—but my mind instantly ran over the past with the thought of "how little has my manner represented what was passing within" and all seemed to concentrate into one agonizing sensation which before I was aware exhibited itself in that language which before is understood by all human hearts altho' there are no articulate sounds.—It is actually the fact that it took me more than a week to recover from that *one* unregulated movement of Memory.
>
> (*L,* p. 75)

In an 1830 letter to Sarah Russell Sullivan, Peabody confessed to a contemplative nature: "I intended," she wrote, "to close my day by writing to you—but I fell into a reverie in the latter part of the evening, which ran away with the rest of my time" (*L,* p. 92). In another letter, Peabody mentioned "*day* dreams" which she compared favorably with dreams of sleep (*L,* p. 116). Perhaps her day dreams were the meditations she made reference to elsewhere (*L,* pp. 131, 140). Peabody implied in a letter to Horace Mann that meditations were a natural part of her intellectual growth. In that same letter, Peabody added, "thoughts and processes of feelings are *events* with me" (*L,* p. 140).

By the 1850s, Peabody's belief in intuitive inspiration expanded to include spiritualism. As Ronda explains, Peabody's "conviction that humanity is essentially spiritual rather than material" made spiritualism an obvious leap (*L,* p. 274). She participated in seances and hoped to introduce her niece Una (Nathaniel Hawthorne's daughter) to spiritualism (*L,* p. 274). In the 1880s, Peabody continued to defend spiritualism and recalled conversing through a medium with the Reverend Channing.[21]

Buell's omission of Peabody's essay in his "hasty census"[22] perhaps results from the difficulty of authenticating a true mystical experience in a woman who may merely have been lost in thought. His omission may also be a continuation of the skepticism originally held regarding the essay specifically and Peabody's merits generally. **"A Vision"** first appeared as the lead article in the March 1843 issue of the *Pioneer,* edited by James Russell Lowell. That issue turned out to be the final number of that three-issue periodical. Sculley Bradley notes that Russell's co-editor, Robert Carter, was actually the working editor for both the February and March issues of the *Pioneer* while Lowell was recuperating from eye surgery. Bradley goes on to say that after a promising first issue under Lowell, the Carter issues of February and March declined in quality. Although Bradley cites several difficulties with Carter's editorship generally, several concerns were raised about **"A Vision"** specifically. Lowell wrote to Carter requesting an opportunity to review Peabody's article before it went

to press.[23] Ten days later Lowell's sister, Mary Lowell Putnam, expressed strong reservations about **"A Vision"** to her brother:

> I hear that the first article in the next number is to be a *Vision* by E. P. Peabody. Now, with all my regard for Miss Peabody, I cannot think that her abilities qualify her to write a leading article for *any* periodical. Her name alone would be an injury to any work to which she should be a contributor—& her vision should be something very *transcendent* indeed to enable it to make head against this prejudice.[24]

Bradley concludes that desperate times sought desperate measures: "If Carter sent it [Peabody's essay] to Lowell, as requested, its appearance as the leading article suggests that the desperate young editor had nothing else on hand to substitute for Miss Peabody's incoherent fantasies."[25] Myerson offers a different conclusion, suggesting that "Lowell . . . thought her piece very good," while acknowledging that Lowell's "sister's views were shared by many people."[26] It is interesting to note that in September 1842, not too many months before Peabody's essay appeared, Lowell described an inspirational moment of his own in which he "clearly felt the spirit of God" and which enabled him to speak "with the calmness and clearness of a prophet."[27] Indeed he may have liked Peabody's essay for its nearness to his own experience.

Whether or not Lowell or anyone else liked **"A Vision,"** for Peabody the essay was an important statement. She wrote to Mary Moody Emerson about the significance of **"A Vision"**: "that 'Vision' which you have . . . seriously, in my religious experience, cast forth to seek the individual visible church, to which I belong" (*L,* pp. 265-66). Furthermore, when Peabody gathered essays for her collection *Last Evening with Allston, and Other Papers,* she included **"A Vision"** among those essays which were selected because they were "suggestive and heart awakening."[28]

In the opening of **"A Vision,"** "a gleam of light" marks Peabody's passage from studious pose to an inspirational experience (p. 62). At the onset of the inspiration, Peabody focuses on a pamphlet which "contains a new definition of life" (p. 62), but which she fails to identify further. Typically, one would expect her to proceed with an analysis of the pamphlet; however, on this occasion, she proceeds with her own vision. Her transition from reflection to inspiration is consistent with Emerson's belief that one can prepare for and nurture inspirational moments: "the oracle comes," Emerson asserts, "because we had previously laid siege to the shrine."[29] This is precisely what happens to Peabody. As she explains in the concluding paragraph, she suddenly receives a Truth of which she already had an inkling of awareness: "It was doubtless because I was all along dimly sensible of the deep and mysterious fact that I have last related" (p. 72). Her gleam of light, as sparked by the pamphlet, enlightens her on "the mysterious *death in life* which so extensively characterizes modern genius." And, she notes, "suddenly I found myself taken off my feet" (p. 62).

The vision includes both visual and aural impressions. Peabody remarks, "I did not pretend to ask about probabilities; I did not question my perceptions; I saw, and believed my senses." Temporal realities were also suspended: "'one day'" seemed "'as a thousand years, and a thousand years as one day'" (p. 63). And, as measured by clock or calendar, "no interval of time" expired (p. 72).

When Peabody itemizes the components of her vision, she acknowledges that the medium of language is insufficient to contain it, because much of its "significance" was in its "simultaneousness" (p. 63). Through this concession, Peabody relates what Buell describes as the Transcendentalists' difficulty in communicating an inspirational experience. As he notes, in communicating such a moment, re-creation outweighs analysis. Even if analytical language is applied to the experience, it cannot be sustained very long.[30] Peabody's own recognition of this difficulty is evident in her study of language and her championing of Charles Kraitsir. She confesses to Mary Moody Emerson her own hesitation to textualize thought:

> I have not an understanding sufficiently practiced—a logical expression equal to the height of my thought. I have had an instinct of this from the first and when occasionally I have ventured out of that magic circle of Silence which seems to be an Eternity enclosing absolute truth, I find clouds arise, and myself lose the vision. . . . We have lost the key to language, that great instrument by means of which the finite mind is to compensate itself, for its being fixed to a point in space and compelled to the limitations of the succession we call time. We use words that are no longer symbols but counters—Our logomacy does not coincide with the eternal logos, and yet we are so constituted that words affect us according to their nature in some degree, and talking about one thing while we are thinking about another, and inextricable confusions arise!

(*L*, p. 264)

These comments on language, which come after the composition of **"A Vision,"** reflect Peabody's continued concern with finding language equivalent to her thought. For Peabody, Gura concludes, "language theory was more than an obsession; it was a matter of epistemological integrity."[31]

Although Peabody herself recognizes the difficulty of matching language with the moment, the application of words to vision does not render the essay "incoherent" as Bradley claims.[32] Certainly it is dense, replete with images from ancient civilizations, recounted in mythology, history, and art. Yet the vision is also ordered, conveying simultaneous experience through a sequential progression which coincides with her enlightenment.

One thematic question unifies the essay: "Where are the living fountains" of genius (p. 68)? Peabody poses this question after she experiences the failures of either art or society to sustain genius. She recounts her vision of the Orient wherein she views Chinese theocracy, Brahmin castes, and Chaldean power. But she also sees there "enslaved *men* . . . bound in the iron chains of necessity," and sages "lost . . . in the ecstasy of contemplation" (p. 64), sapping the "elasticity of life . . . from their mighty political structures." Her perception of the Orient is that despite its "traces of an energy and reach of intelligence so marvellous, . . . life was ever departed or departing." Leaving the "magnificent, but melancholy, East," Peabody looks on "beautiful Greece." Although exhilarated by "the heroism of its early days" (p. 65), she discovers that "the men out of whose creative genius arose the beautiful forms of Grecian art and policy were hovering around them, phantom-like, with a painful expression of exhaustion, as if they were dying away into them." Prompted by this disturbing sight, Peabody enters into a conversation with "a voice" which tells her that a creative work is "rendered permanent in beauty by the presence of the soul absorbed in it" (p. 66). She protests, "But Expression—Beauty . . . is not life; it is only the aspect of life." Since beauty lacks the fountain of life, another voice, Socrates, suggests for her consideration "Man is the quarry for man." Before her appear "the political fabrics of Greece and Rome," more complete than recorded by Herodotus or other historians of those ancient times (p. 67). But still man within his own institutions is not the fountain of life. Peabody declares "mournfully": "Man not only forsakes his life . . . when he pours himself into perishable material, builds himself into stone, moulds himself into marble, spreads himself upon canvas; he does himself no better justice when his quarry is man. The forms of society are more perishable than the works of plastic art." Then Peabody "leaving the works, enter[s] . . . into the *mind of man*," where the first voice offers to show her "the life that may not die" (p. 68). But the offer is a test, her own Edenic temptation, to become herself "divine" by abandoning "the gloomy precincts of being" called "matter" and becoming "wholly the living soul" (pp. 68-69). After all, the voice asks, "what makes God God, but that He forever casts out of himself Material and Form"? Peabody responds to her companion voice: "Imprison me not in my own memory and imagination. Rather than that, I would range chaos itself, free of the material wherewith to express an ever-renewing affirmation of the life which underlies both myself and it" (p. 69). After two more solicitations by the voice to enter the land of thought, Peabody declares, "I would seek for the living souls that have passed into chaos, and left only the expression of life in the land of Thought" (p. 70). What ensues is the regression of the world, a de-Genesis experience. Society, policy, and art give way to "the solid earth, which stood forth fresh in the primeval vegetation" (pp. 70-71). Then the earth begins to recede into its germination: "The ocean and the sky rushed together, and there was no more light." Peabody is in "dark Chaos," yet she feels "invigorate[d] . . . with a new faith in Being" (p. 71). She comes to understand that in the apparent chaos exists the living fountain. This enlightenment is the climax of the experience:

> Thou art my master . . . O dark Chaos, and I am thy child. . . . There is no life that satisfieth me, but that which underlieth thee,—into whose great bosom have passed the Powers that pitched the tents of Beauty on the fields of Time. It is for the spirit with whose bright footsteps these are fair that I would struggle with all the powers of darkness. I may not live by the dead, nor have I life within myself—
>
>   (pp. 71-72)

Suddenly Chaos is transformed. She finds herself "in a Personal Presence" who says to her: "'I am the way, the truth, and the life; whosoever cometh unto Me, I will in no wise cast out.' For 'I was in the beginning with God, and was God, and without Me was not any thing made that is made'" (p. 72). Peabody arrives at a Truth which stands as the source for all her activity. She discovers Christ to be the fountain of life.

Peabody's vision of Christ at the center of all life, proper originator of all thought and action, asserted itself in every aspect of her work. Her writings about self, history, society, education, and art remained Christ-centered. In 1838, she was amused to report to Horace Mann that they both were going back to primitive times in their imaginations (*L,* p. 191). While he sought "to prove that all things began in Chaos and still in Chaos are," it was her "object to prove that all things began in a Paradasiacal [*sic*] harmony, from which man has strayed, but to which he must return" (*L,* p. 191). Peabody's method for leading mankind back to paradise was, as Susan Conrad points out, a familiar Transcendentalist position, that is, to re-see Jesus as a man and to try to recapture an understanding of the individual who had been lost in traditional historical approaches to Christ. As the "supreme individual who respected other individuals," his life should stand as the active paradigm for human society. Peabody conceived of Christ's "inclusive social vision" as "an organic interpretation of society. Individual development and social harmony should exist simultaneously, thus ensuring both continuity and growth."[33] The impact of this perspective affected Peabody's attitudes and activities as she sought to recapture that paradisiacal harmony mankind had lost.

In the conclusion of **"A Vision"** Peabody stated that "the world of Thought, which had declared itself . . .

Heaven . . . was indeed Hell" (p. 72). Despite her own vast learning, Peabody believed that all "intellectual acquisition" was "subservient to moral and social ends."[34] The great danger of elevating thought itself to divine importance was the resulting condition of egotheism. In **"Egotheism, the Atheism of To-day"** Peabody defined egotheism as failing to recognize that beyond individual conception exists "inconceivable Power, Wisdom, and Love,—of the immanence of whose substantial being within us our best conception is but a transient form."[35] She was heavily influenced by Channing in this belief,[36] but she did not hesitate to make the battle her own. Peabody persistently argued against the egotheistic extremes of some Transcendentalists. In the headnote to a Peabody letter to Caroline Dall, Ronda emphasizes Peabody's concern that both Dall and Margaret Fuller (deceased by the time of the writing) suffered from egocentrism (*L,* p. 302). Peabody comforts even as she criticizes Dall by assuring her that "the more there is to crucify—*the great[er] the power acquired by the sacrifice*—'He scourgeth whom he would bring to glory'—If like great Margaret *your Me* is '*mountainous*'—it may become for you the Pisgah on which you shall mount to see the promised land" (*L,* p. 302). In her *Reminiscences* Peabody suggested that Frederic Henry Hedge "might have introduced Transcendentalism in such a way that it would not have become identified with . . . extreme Individualism."[37] She also recalled an unsuccessful effort she made to have Emerson reinsert a portion of his Divinity School Address which had been omitted in the public reading into the printed text. He refused what Peabody saw as a way to prevent "many a weak brother and sister Transcendentalist from . . . *ego-theism*."[38] Peabody explained her philosophical guard against egotheism with the metaphor of windows:

> God makes man separately an eye, and if he would see into the Infinite Oversoul, he must look with it out of his own window. But this is only the way to begin to search for truth. If he is not self-intoxicated, every man soon learns that his window does not command the whole horizon, that God not only has given a window to him, but to every other man; . . . it is with *all* the sons of man that "wisdom dwells," and they must intercommunicate with mutual reverence if they would know her well.[39]

"All the sons" who look out individual windows span all time. A second tenet of Peabody's Transcendentalism was her agreement with Channing's view that "Truth is to be found in both directions, for it is in God, for whom 'a thousand years are as one day,' and who speaks in the past, present, and future, the same essential truth."[40] Margaret Fuller commented during one of her conversations "that she did not like a mind always looking back"; Peabody responded that "there was a great deal of consolation in it. Memory was prophecy. She didn't like such a mind, but since she happened to have it she wanted support for it."[41] She believed in the past as a valuable source of instruction, sometimes somber lessons indeed, for present generations: *"when the moral causes at work for the deterioration of men come to predominate over the causes at work for their improvement, so that the new individuals born into society have not a fair chance for virtue, it is the part of Infinite Mercy and Justice to exterminate the race entirely."*[42] Consequently Peabody "defended history as the most moral and most enlightening of all studies because it reveals 'Man's foibles and God's providence . . . God's disposition of events, every one of which is a *word* proceeding out of his mouth.'"[43] Peabody articulated this idea as an experience in **"A Vision"**: "I looked around upon the Past, which I understood at once, in the new 'light which lighteth every man that cometh into the world': '*Thou went in the world,* and the world knew thee not. But as many as receive, to them givest thou Power to become the Sons of God!'" (p. 72).

The limits Peabody perceived in each civilization, oriental and occidental, as she rejected each, reflected her belief in what may be learned through historical study. Yet this view did not diminish but affirmed the individual's obligation to experience a personal relationship with God. Peabody saw the necessity of both: "With the religion of history must always be combined the religion of experience, in order to a true apprehension of God."[44] The individual act of faith, receiving Christ, must accompany any historical lesson.

The link between receiving Christ and knowing history was an intimate bond. Peabody believed in "history as affording motives for moral action."[45] Chiefly Peabody's action remained oriented, not in effusive literary outpourings, or in communal living, but in education. Even in the classroom Peabody's perspective remained Christ-centered. Peabody stated that "moral education became" in her opinion "the essence of all education."[46] For Peabody, education was no less than the salvation of man. She agreed with the sentiments expressed by an "eloquent" but unidentified speaker: "for *education* is the highest function of humanity in earth and heaven, cementing the links of the chain of love which binds us all to one another and to God."[47]

This high purpose which Peabody perceived in education was also expressed in her aesthetic. In the introduction to *Aesthetic Papers* she asserted that "All art, in its origin, is national and religious. The feeling expressed is of far greater importance than the vehicle in which it is conveyed."[48] **"A Vision"** presents this didactic argument in its portrayal of the high cost of art created for its own sake: "The Elysium of Art is but the sport of my childhood, the gymnastics of my youthful strength. I have created it, and, vampire-like, it doth destroy me" (p. 71). Clearly, then, Peabody viewed art, as she viewed history and education, as the tool for the larger purpose of bringing man, individually and in his societies, closer to God.

Thus, **"A Vision"** was Peabody's personal literary expression of the Transcendentalist inspiration which provided a foundation for the "whole stud of Phoenixes" that Emerson claimed she kept "on hand."[49] Peabody once said that the imagination "prepares the soul for vigorous effort, in all the various departments of its activity."[50] This short imaginative text contained the major themes of her active life. **"A Vision"** speaks to the lessons of the past to which the present must be educated. It grounds art in its religious impulse. It confronts the failure of language to recreate spiritual truth. And, **"A Vision"** maintains the delicate balance a Transcendentalist had to maintain so not to fall from disinterested love "into the abyss of Egotheism."[51] **"A Vision"** is, as much as any text Peabody composed, her own Transcendental Manifesto.[52]

Notes

1. Margaret Neussendorfer, "Elizabeth Palmer Peabody," in *The Transcendentalists: A Review of Research and Criticism,* ed. Joel Myerson (New York: Modern Language Association, 1984), p. 233.

2. *Letters of Elizabeth Palmer Peabody: American Renaissance Woman,* ed. Bruce A. Ronda (Middletown: Wesleyan University Press, 1984); hereafter cited as *L* in the text.

3. Joel Myerson, *The New England Transcendentalists and the* Dial (Rutherford, N.J.: Fairleigh Dickinson University Press, 1980), p. 196.

4. Joel Myerson, "Elizabeth Palmer Peabody 1804-1894," in *First Printings of American Authors,* ed. Matthew J. Bruccoli et al., 5 vols. (Detroit: Gale, 1977-87), 3:279-84.

5. "Nature—A Prose Poem," *United States Magazine, and Democratic Review,* 1 (February 1838): 319-20.

6. *Lectures in the Training Schools for Kindergartners* (Boston: D. C. Heath, 1886), p. 71.

7. Myerson, *New England Transcendentalists,* p. 196.

8. Emerson to Peabody, 3 December 1836, *The Journals and Miscellaneous Notebooks of Ralph Waldo Emerson,* ed. William H. Gilman, Ralph H. Orth, et al., 16 vols. (Cambridge: Harvard University Press, 1960-82), 5:262, quoted in Myerson, *New England Transcendentalists,* p. 196; Fuller to Emerson, 18 April 1842, *The Letters of Margaret Fuller,* ed. Robert N. Hudspeth, 5 vols. to date (Ithaca: Cornell University Press, 1983-) 3:60, quoted in New *England Transcendentalists,* p. 196.

9. George Willis Cooke, *An Historical and Biographical Introduction to Accompany the* Dial, 2

vols. (Cleveland: Rowfant Club, 1902), 1:157; John B. Wilson, "A Transcendental Minority Report," *New England Quarterly,* 29 (June 1956): 152; Philip F. Gura, "Elizabeth Palmer Peabody and the Philosophy of Language," *ESQ: A Journal of the American Renaissance,* 23 (3d Quarter 1977): 154; John B. Wilson, "Elizabeth Peabody and Other Transcendentalists on History and Historians," *Historian,* 30 (November 1967): 83; Madeleine B. Stern, "Elizabeth Peabody's Foreign Library (1840)," *American Transcendental Quarterly,* no. 20 (Fall 1973): supplement, 5, rpt. in her *Books and Book People in 19th-Century America* (New York: R. R. Bowker, 1978), p. 121.

10. "Spirit of the Hebrew Scriptures," *Christian Examiner,* 16 (May, July 1834): 174-202, 305-20; 17 (September 1834): 78-92. Peabody asked Orestes Brownson to complete the series in *Brownson's Quarterly Review.* Noting in her letter to Brownson that the series was actually written in 1826, she rather proudly observed: "Had not Mr Norton cut off untimely my little series which consisted of six numbers, it would have . . . recorded quite a little historical fact, there in the bosom of Unitarianism, an unlearned girl, with only the help of those principles of philosophizing she gathered from the perusal of Coleridge's friends, & . . . relying simply on her own poetical apprehension, as a principle of exegesis, should have seen just what is here expressed, concerning the *socialism* of true Religion & the divinity of Christ" (*L,* p. 248).

11. Anne C. Rose, *Transcendentalism as a Social Movement, 1830-1850* (New Haven: Yale University Press, 1981), p. 54.

12. "A Vision," *Pioneer,* 1 (March 1843): 97-100, reprinted in her *Last Evening with Allston, and Other Papers* (Boston: D. Lothrop, 1886), pp. 62-72. All subsequent references are to the 1886 edition and are cited parenthetically in the text.

13. Neussendorfer, "Elizabeth Peabody," p. 236.

14. Lawrence Buell, *Literary Transcendentalism: Style and Vision in the American Renaissance* (Ithaca: Cornell University Press, 1973), p. 20.

15. Buell, *Literary Transcendentalism,* p. 55. The second chapter of this book ("Transcendentalist Literary Method: Inspiration versus Craftsmanship") examines closely the Transcendentalists' descriptions of the moment of inspiration. Buell recalls the comments of Emerson, Alcott, Brownson, and Jones Very to support his overall conclusion that "All Transcendentalist attempts to describe how art is to be created, and the impact which it should make upon its audience, begin and end with the idea of inspiration" (p. 55). Buell goes on to define *inspiration* not as "a great idea for a poem or story, so much as the experience of that Truth or Reality of which the finished work was to be the expression" (p. 59). Further, he explains, the experience, the "true mystical experience, that is, is a transfiguration from within and not a message or thunderbolt from without" (p. 59).

16. Buell, *Literary Transcendentalism,* pp. 59-60. Theodore Parker counted the individual "Happy" whose inspirational moments numbered "ten . . . in a year, yes, in a lifetime." Parker described these moments as "the seed-time of life" when "in the deep silence of the soul; when the man turns inward to God, light, comfort, peace dawn on him. . . . Resolution comes over him with its vigorous wing; truth is clear as noon; the soul in faith rushes to its God. The mystery is at an end" (*The Centenary Edition of the Works of Theodore Parker,* 15 vols. [(Boston: American Unitarian Association, 1907-12)], vol. 1, *A Discourse of Matters Pertaining to Religion* (1907), ed. Thomas Wentworth Higginson, pp. 204-205.

17. Buell, *Literary Transcendentalism,* p. 62.

18. *Reminiscences of Rev. Wm. Ellery Channing, D.D.* (Boston: Roberts Brothers, 1880), p. 81.

19. Peabody, *Reminiscences,* p. 123.

20. Peabody, *Lectures,* pp. 70-71.

21. Jane Marsh Parker, "Elizabeth Peabody: A Reminiscence," *Outlook,* 49 (February 1894): 215.

22. Buell, *Literary Transcendentalism,* p. 60.

23. Sculley Bradley, *The Pioneer: A Literary Magazine* (New York: Scholars' Facsimiles & Reprints, 1947), pp. xviii-xxii.

24. Quoted in Sculley Bradley, "Lowell, Emerson, and the *Pioneer,*" *American Literature,* 19 (November 1947): 237.

25. Bradley, "Lowell," 238.

26. Myerson, *New England Transcendentalists,* p. 279 *n*19.

27. Lowell to G. B. Loring, 20 September 1842, *Letters of James Russell Lowell,* ed. Charles Eliot Norton, 2 vols. (New York: Harpers, 1894), 1:69, quoted in Cooke, *Introduction,* 2:95.

28. Peabody, *Last Evening,* Dedication.

29. *The Complete Works of Ralph Waldo Emerson,* ed. Edward Waldo Emerson, 12 vols. (Boston: Houghton Mifflin, 1903-1904), 2:331, quoted in Buell, *Literary Transcendentalism,* p. 63.

30. Buell, *Literary Transcendentalism,* p. 45.

31. Gura, "Elizabeth Peabody," 162.

32. Bradley, "Lowell," 238.

33. Susan Phinney Conrad, *Perish the Thought: Intellectual Women in Romantic America, 1830-1860* (New York: Oxford University Press, 1976), p. 211.

34. Quoted in Cooke, *Introduction,* 1:143.

35. "Egotheism, the Atheism of To-Day" (1858), rpt. in *Last Evening,* p. 245.

36. John B. Wilson, "Activities of the New England Transcendentalists in the Dissemination of Culture" (Ph.D. dissertation, University of North Carolina, 1941), p. 316.

37. Peabody, *Reminiscences,* p. 371.

38. Peabody, *Reminiscences,* p. 373.

39. Peabody, *Lectures,* p. 26.

40. Peabody, *Reminiscences,* p. 144.

41. Caroline H. Dall, *Margaret and Her Friends* (Boston: Roberts Brothers, 1895), p. 152.

42. Peabody, "Spirit of the Hebrew Scriptures," 17:87.

43. Quoted in Wilson, "Elizabeth Peabody," 85.

44. Peabody, "Nature," 321.

45. Cooke, *Introduction,* 1:143.

46. Quoted in Cooke, *Introduction,* 1:143.

47. Peabody, *Lectures,* p. 87.

48. "The Word 'Aesthetic,'" *Aesthetic Papers,* ed. Peabody (Gainesville, Fla.: Scholars' Facsimiles & Reprints, 1957 [1849]), p. 3.

49. Quoted in Cooke, *Introduction,* 1:151.

50. *Record of a School: Exemplifying the General Principles of Spiritual Culture,* 2d ed. (Boston: Russell and Shattuck, 1836), p. xlii.

51. Peabody, "Egotheism," p. 247.

52. This article was written before the appearance of Nina Baym's "The Ann Sisters: Elizabeth Peabody's Millennial Historicism," *American Literary History,* 3 (Spring 1991): 27-45. Baym redresses the lack of Peabody criticism with her insightful reading of important Peabody texts.

James Perrin Warren (essay date 1999)

SOURCE: Warren, James Perrin. "Fuller, Peabody, and the Mother Tongue." In *Culture of Eloquence: Oratory and Reform in Antebellum America,* pp. 85-114. University Park: Pennsylvania State University Press, 1999.

[*In the following essay, Warren discusses the impact of Peabody's writings on nineteenth-century theories of language and education.*]

Elizabeth Peabody occupies a privileged position in the study of language theories and in the application of linguistic theories to education. The second edition of **Record of a School** (1836), with her **"Explanatory Preface,"** suggests the connection between language and educational reform, as does the entire book. Peabody translated Guillaume Oegger's *True Messiah* [**The True Messiah**] for Emerson and published it in 1842. She published (and ghostwrote) Charles Kraitsir's *Significance of the Alphabet* in 1846. She published the articles **"Language"** and **"The Dorian Measure"** in the first issue of her abortive journal, *Aesthetic Papers* (1849). During the heyday of the New England Renaissance, then, Elizabeth Peabody was central to the development and dissemination of current language theories. Most important, she applied her interest in language to the education of children, especially in developing the kindergarten in America.[1]

Peabody connects language and cultural reform from the early stages of her long career. In the **"Explanatory Preface"** to the **Record of a School,** for example, Peabody notes that the "lessons on language, given in the **Record,** have generally been admitted to be most valuable" (vi) and that "spelling and defining words are the most prominent intellectual exercises of the school" (xxviii).[2] Bronson Alcott's emphasis on language in the Temple School develops "spiritual culture" through a characteristic dualism. As Peabody notes in the preface, Alcott's Socratic method leads the students from outward, material things to inward, spiritual realities (vi, xxii). The dualism extends to the type of language that is thus developed, for the scholars "should be led to nature for the picturesque and for poetry, not for the purpose of scientific analysis and deduction. They should look upon its synthesis as sacred" (xxiii). Peabody's view of "spiritual culture" as bound to an aesthetic "synthesis" of nature through language strongly recalls the central arguments of Emerson's *Nature,* which Peabody would eventually review in the February 1838 issue of *U. S. Magazine and Democratic Review.*[3]

Alcott's application of transcendental language theory to the education of children leads his scholars to the Language of Nature, and he employs the outer matter-inner spirit dualism so consistently that it becomes a predictable piety in the conversations of the Temple School. In addition, his version of Socratic method is, as Peabody notes, "very autocratic" (21). While purporting to show the freely developing spirits of children engaged in mind-expanding, contemplative conversations, Peabody's **Record** delivers an image of Alcott as a repressive interlocutor, obsessed with discipline. In the conversation on the word *sign,* for example, Alcott leads his scholars, predictably enough, toward the correspondence theory of language and meaning:

The word *sign,* gave rise to the following questions and answers. What is a sign? A token. What is a token?

Any thing that shows something else. What is the body a sign of? The mind. What is the mind a sign of? Heaven. What is Heaven? Heaven is the sign of goodness, and earth of Heaven. What is goodness a sign of? Happiness. What is happiness a sign of? Goodness. What is goodness a sign of? said Mr. Alcott again. Eternity. What is eternity the sign of? They all said they did not know. Mr. Alcott said that eternity was the sign of God's lifetime, or of God; and that there we must stop—we could go no farther. They all acknowledged it. Mr. Alcott then quoted these lines of poetry:

"Significant is all that meets the sense,
  One Mighty alphabet for infant minds."

What is significant? said he. The answer was, all that meets the eyes! What does it all signify? Something beyond the senses. Mr. Alcott made this last answer himself.

(***Record*** 50)

Peabody's disapproval of Alcott's ideas and methods is only tacit here, even though the dialogue between the tautological scholar and the insistent Alcott is humorous. A year later, however, she is rebelling against the "common conscience" Alcott promotes through the conversations on the Gospels.[4] By the time she writes **"A Plea for Froebel's Kindergarten"** (1869), Peabody has clearly outgrown Alcott's restrictive reductions.[5]

In the interim between the ***Record*** and her wholesale conversion to Froebel's ideas of kindergarten, Peabody develops versions of transcendental language theory that parallel those of Emerson and Thoreau. Before 1835, for instance, she translates Guillaume Oegger's *True Messiah* for Emerson, who records several pages in *Journal B*.[6] In a previous chapter I suggested that Emerson was interested in Oegger as much for his language as for his ideas, since *The True Messiah* offers the same dualism between spirit and matter that Emerson found in Boehme and Swedenborg. Oegger is interesting in connection with Peabody, however, because the translated subtitle of *The True Messiah* emphasizes the Language of Nature as a means of reading the Old and New Testaments. Oegger fits within the tradition of linguistic mysticism that seeks "a perfect language, a language which cannot have been lost but in the lapse of ages, and of which the traces may be found, when Philosophy will direct her researches to that point."[7] Peabody's first recorded work in language theory thus recapitulates the theory Emerson is elaborating in the journals, lectures, and essays of the 1830s. In her 1838 review of *Nature,* Peabody views Emerson himself as a figure of eloquence, exemplifying the authority and power of the poet-orator, and her only complaint is that "our poet grows silent with wonder and worship" instead of expanding upon how "the relation between mind and matter stands in the will of God." For Peabody, language does not involve the accidental or random, just as "there is *no accident in the world.*" Words

and things are equivalent, and the "true and perfect mind" of the poet perceives their relation to "the will of God."[8]

In the 1840s, however, as Peabody deepens her commitment to the study of language by working with Charles Kraitsir, her ideas move much closer to those of Thoreau. For Thoreau, as for Fuller and the later Emerson, language is subject to severe limitations, and Peabody sees this point most sharply in relation to her own expression. In a letter to Mary Moody Emerson, Peabody remarks that "when occasionally I have ventured out of that magic circle of Silence which seems to be an Eternity enclosing absolute truth, I find clouds arise, and myself lose the vision." She then gives a theoretical explanation for the inadequacies of language: "Since I knew Dr. Kraitsir I have seen a little into the reason why we puzzle ourselves so much and perpetually lose the truths which the great God gives us whereby to live. We have lost the key to language, that great instrument by means of which the finite mind is to compensate itself, for its being fixed to a point in space and compelled to the limitations of the succession we call time. We use words that are no longer symbols but counters."[9] In Kraitsir's theory of the Language of Nature, the "key to language" is the relationship of sound to meaning, a relationship that languages of convention have adulterated. Peabody's letter registers the power of "the great Silence" opposing her, as well as the divided state of current languages, which combine vestiges of the original Language of Nature with latter-day languages of convention. In recognizing a double limitation upon the correspondence between thoughts and words, she sounds remarkably like Thoreau.

Charles Kraitsir's importance to Peabody becomes abundantly clear in *The Significance of the Alphabet,* which Peabody edited and published in 1846.[10] The opening paragraph of the book echoes Peabody's letter to Mary Moody Emerson:

> Language is the image of the human mind, the net result of human culture: if it is Babel, it is because men have abandoned themselves to chance, and lost sight of the principles by which language was constructed. But these principles are inherent in their nature, and men cannot lose their nature. All men, however diverse they may become by conflicting passions and interests, have yet the same reason, and the same organs of speech. All men, however distant in place, are yet plunged into a material universe, which makes impressions of an analogous character, upon great masses.

(3)

Although language is represented as caught between its original principles and its modern, Babel-like avatars, the paragraph begins and ends with the image of language as a unified, diverse "net result of human culture" that reveals "the same reason, and the same organs of speech." The parallel structure implies a parallel between the mind and speech, suggesting that the Language of Nature can renew the human mind and human culture.

Kraitsir and Peabody develop these connections by focusing on the reform of language-teaching in America, particularly the teaching of Latin and English. Despite the composite, apparently chaotic nature of English, the two theorists adamantly assert the unity of language and thought. Peabody and Kraitsir make three assumptions about language: first, that the basic units of sound are also basic units of meaning; second, that the essential language of humankind is an "organic formation," an Adamic Language of Nature; third, that the apparent Babel of modern languages veils an essential unity of "human thought and feeling," although the unity accommodates the diversity of cultures and languages (*Significance* [*Significance of the Alphabet*] 19-20).

Kraitsir's version of transcendental language theory provides Peabody with a coherent set of assumptions about the central role that language plays in developing human culture. The significance of *Significance* is, finally, that it expresses Peabody's abstract vision of a Language of Nature at the same time that it applies that vision to the practical problems of education in America. The book combines Peabody's two abiding concerns—language and education. This is why the theoretical statements lead so easily to the "vast importance" of studying language: "There is no subject connected with the mind or destiny of man, upon which a profound insight into philology will not throw a broad light" (20). Peabody characteristically combines abstract theory with practical application, although she never appears tempted to deliver public lectures as a means of combining them. Instead, print remains Peabody's medium of choice and the elementary classroom is her abiding point of application. For instance, the glossological table of germs in *The Significance of the Alphabet* (12) becomes the basis for Peabody's *First Nursery Reading Book* (1849).[11] As late as 1863, in *Moral Culture of Infancy, and Kindergarten Guide,* Peabody describes the use of the *First Nursery Reading Book* in a kindergarten and cites Kraitsir as the philological authority for her methods of teaching reading.[12] Kraitsir's influence on Peabody's development of the kindergarten movement is fundamental, although her response to Kraitsir resembles her earlier reaction to Alcott's theories and methods. In applying Kraitsir's theories to the kindergarten, Peabody elaborates and modifies the basic assumptions announced in *The Significance of the Alphabet.*

The processes of modification and elaboration are equally important in Peabody's essays of the 1840s, before she focuses her abundant energies on the kindergarten movement. In the volume of her failed periodical, *Aesthetic Papers,* for example, Peabody employs the language of philology to discuss topics that she explores under the titles **"The Word 'Aesthetic'"** (1-4), **"The Dorian Measure, with a Modern Application"** (64-110), and **"Language"** (214-24). In all three essays her aim is to open new territories of cultural reform, applying the insights of philology to cross boundaries of cultural discourse.

Peabody announces and enacts the strategy of crossing discursive boundaries in her introductory essay, **"The Word 'Aesthetic.'"** By opposing the restricted definition of the word, Peabody argues for a new sense of criticism: "The 'aesthetic element,' then, is in our view neither a theory of the beautiful, nor a philosophy of art, but a component and indivisible part in all human creations which are not mere works of necessity; in other words, which are based on idea, as distinguished from appetite" (1). Peabody's aesthetic position lies on the boundaries between the individual and the universal, between the artist and the critic. She resolves these two dualisms by applying the first to the second: art tends, in history, to move from the universal and unconscious expression of national and religious ideals toward the individual artist's expression of his own spirit; criticism, on the other hand, moves from mere reactions of individual taste toward more universally applicable standards. As she succinctly phrases it, "The progress of criticism is the reverse of that of art" (4). Peabody's goal is to create a dynamic, progressive relationship between the poles of her various dualisms. Her discursive strategy crosses boundaries by creating a temporal dialectic: the discussion of a single word and its several definitions becomes a compressed history of art and criticism, ending with a projected future of purified, spiritualized individuality.

In the long second article, the Dorian measure figures the harmony of Dorian civilization, which meets Peabody's demands for the term *aesthetic.* She therefore represents the political, religious, and cultural elements of the Dorians' world as ideally measured: education, in one telling sentence, "was called by the Dorians, *learning music*" (84). Peabody employs the Dorians as an idealized image of aesthetic civilization, so her central question becomes one of correspondence: "But the question for us is, whether, on the new platform upon which Christendom finds itself, now that the spiritual future has descended as it were into human life, there may not be found a harmony corresponding to the Dorian measure;—whether there may not be a social organization which does as much justice to the Christian religion and philosophy, as the Dorian state did to Apollo" (86). The question is for the most part rhetorical, but the second half of the essay outlines the "social organization" that will, according to Peabody, bring nineteenth-century American culture into perfect correspondence with her historical model.

The aspect of culture that Peabody sees as most promising is, not surprisingly, education, "a subject of greater importance than government" for the Dorians (87). Her rhetoric approaches the apocalyptic tone of the jeremiad when she concludes that "a true spirit of culture must do for the national heart what the ever-incoming grace of God does for the individual soul" (98). Peabody's idealism becomes the means of measuring nineteenth-century American culture, and her method for filling in what American culture lacks is to propose "*a system of education* correspondent to our large privileges" (99). The system of education Peabody envisions is hardly systematic or comprehensive. Instead, the Dorian correspondence allows her to make some intriguing proposals about early childhood education. She argues, for example, for physical exercise, dance, and musical training, as well as the traditional training in drawing and geometry (100-106). But her most radical proposals concern reading and writing, which should be taught "in such a manner as to make our own language the 'open Sesame' to all speech" (106).

As she nears the end of her essay, Peabody names glossology as the "true philological art" that will "make the native tongue appreciated in all its deep significance, and prepare the mind for such a comparison of our own with other tongues, as shall immensely facilitate their acquisition" (106). She claims, moreover, that "philology should be studied as the most important of sciences, not only for the sake of knowing the works of art and science that the various languages contain, but because words themselves are growths of nature and works of art, capable of giving the highest delight as such; and because their analysis and history reveal the universe in its symbolic character" (107). Peabody emphasizes the "true study of language" (108) as the key to her projected system of education because language embodies the aesthetic: language crosses all boundaries, since every aspect of culture is bound within words, and a fully renewed culture will therefore find its ultimate measure in language.

Given the structure of Peabody's argument in **"The Dorian Measure,"** we can view her essay **"Language"** (214-24) as a focused elaboration of her statement that philology is the "most important of sciences." In **"The Dorian Measure"** Peabody places Charles Kraitsir's theories within the context of cultural arguments; in **"Language"** she views those theories within the context of "the fact of language, and its want of effectiveness" (214).

Peabody's method of treating the dual nature of language once again depends upon a temporal dialectic, powered by her progressivist vision of the future. She structures the essay by placing Horace Bushnell's "Preliminary Dissertation on Language" in opposition to Kraitsir's *Significance of the Alphabet*.[13] While she approves of Bushnell's observations in several cases, Peabody complains that he does not recognize the necessary connection between sound and sense; hence he defends the arbitrary, conventional origin of language and meaning, focusing on the diversity of languages as evidence.[14] Peabody cites *Significance* in order to argue for the universal character of language (216), pronouncing Kraitsir's most important discovery to be "that words are to be considered, not merely or chiefly by their effect on the ear, but *in the process of their formation by the organs of speech*" (220). The dynamic, expressive origin of language becomes the temporal ideal toward which all language-users should strive, and because it is dynamic Peabody sees the proposed origin as natural and essential.

These conclusions lead Peabody to consider how humankind can recapture the Adamic origin of language. Since *Significance* contains the truth about language, she proposes "a sequel of some practical elementary books which may make it possible to apply its principles for the purpose of transforming the present system of language-teaching in schools. It is said the author is superintending the preparation of some. A whole series is necessary, from the *a b c* book to a manual of the Sanscrit" (221). Peabody's disingenuous promotion of her collaboration with Kraitsir represents glossology as a transforming power, a force that will operate on every intellectual level to educate Americans in the Language of Nature.

Peabody's most significant elaboration of Kraitsir's theories appears in the ways in which she translates and expands upon Herder's *The Spirit of Hebrew Poetry* in **"Language"** (221-23). Although she owned a copy of James Marsh's translation as early as 1833, when she used it as a text in a Boston conversation class, Peabody alters Marsh's translation in several important ways.[15] In introducing Herder, Peabody quotes Marsh's translation exactly, but she inserts an italicized addition of her own: "One of the interlocutors asks,—after having granted, with respect to the Hebrew, the symbolism of the radical sounds, or the utterance of the feeling that was prompted, while the object itself was present to the senses; *the sound of the feelings in the very intuition of their causes*:—But how is it with the derivations from these radical terms?" (221) Peabody's insertion emphasizes the intuitive and emotional aspects of sound symbolism because they are closest, she believes, to the "prophecy that binds the world's history into a rounded whole" (***Letters*** [**Letters of Elizabeth Palmer Peabody**] 267).

Peabody's theoretical emphasis on the intuitive and emotional aspects of language and her practical emphasis on childhood education function within the culturally accepted versions of the feminine that we know as domestic ideology. As [Sarah Josepha] Hale's *Lectures*

[(Boston: Whipple and Damrell, 1839)] and Fuller's conversation classes show, domestic ideology distributes and controls power by gendering discursive and cultural space. Peabody knowingly employs the domestic idiom in her translation of Herder: "The root of the mother-word will stand in the centre, and around her the grove of her children. By influence of taste, diligence, sound sense, and the judicious comparison of different dialects, lexicons will be brought to distinguish what is essential from what is accidental in the signification of words, and to trace the gradual process of transition" (222). The compound "mother-word" and the phrase "her children" are Peabody's substitutions for Marsh's more abstract "primitive word" and "its offspring" (Marsh 1:35). Peabody uses the maternal image to represent the "essential" signification of words, while "her children" are the derivations from that central root. By blending horticultural and domestic metaphors, Peabody implies that language is essential and natural, both in form and in meaning. The figuration also gives a nurturing sense of order to the "growth" of language, controlling the emotional and intuitive origins of meaning.

The conjunction of domestic ideology and organic metaphor is most important in Peabody's ideas concerning kindergarten. She introduces the *Kindergarten Guide,* for instance, by asking the question of definition— "Kindergarten—What Is It?"—and her answer strongly echoes the strategies of *Aesthetic Papers*: "*Kindergarten* means a garden of children, and Froebel, the inventor of it, or rather, as he would prefer to express it, *the discoverer of the method of Nature,* meant to symbolize by the name the spirit and plan of treatment. How does the gardener treat his plants? He studies their individual natures, and puts them into such circumstances of soil and atmosphere as enable them to grow, flower, and bring forth fruit,—also to renew their manifestation year after year" (10). Peabody employs the method of Fuller's Boston conversations: examining the word *kindergarten,* she creates an essentialist etymology that applies the organic metaphor of gardening to the problem of educating children. The extended analogy argues for a nurturing approach to education, one that allows the individual child to "grow" in the same way a plant does, although it also allows the gardener/teacher to "prune" redundant growths (11). Peabody's figural strategy naturalizes both language in general and the language of domesticity, for one mother-word reveals the "essential" approach to educating children.

The kindergarten movement becomes, for Peabody, the means of unifying her concerns with language, cultural reform, and education. Circumspect and conservative, Peabody never addresses the public sphere of eloquence by delivering lectures or making orations. So, for instance, in the 1869 essay **"A Plea for Froebel's Kindergarten,"** she confines her plea within the boundaries of domestic ideology. In discussing the training of kindergarten teachers, Peabody begins with grand abstractions encompassing "outward nature" and "human nature," but she uses the "universal motherly instinct" as a means of limiting and controlling the abstractions, bringing them within the grasp of "any fairly cultivated, genial-hearted young woman, of average intellect."[16]

Peabody's conservative strategy entails the continued use of Kraitsir's theory of language in her kindergarten work. As editor and chief writer of the *Kindergarten Messenger,* Peabody asserts that "command of language is the intellectual benefit of the Kindergarten, a benefit that can hardly be too much appreciated."[17] In an essay titled **"Command of Language to Be Gained in Kindergarten,"** Peabody applies Kraitsir's glossological schema to the dynamic, domestic relationship of teacher and child:

> Imagination is baffled in endeavoring to conceive how human communication began; we see how it begins *now* with every individual, by the help of the mother, and those who supply the mother's place. The articulate words are defined to the child by gestures, and expression of face, and modulation of tones; and the play of the organs of speech may be analyzed into symbolization of the moving or dead phenomena, by motions of lips and tongue against the palate and the teeth, while the inward and causal is expressed by the motions of the throat modifying the breath as it comes up from the centre of life and the source of energy.[18]

Peabody's description of the "play of the organs of speech" follows Kraitsir's three-part division of articulatory phonetics/semantics: labial sounds evoke the living phenomena of the outer world; dental sounds signify the dead phenomena of the outer world; guttural sounds express the inner causes of all phenomena (*Glossology* [(New York: George Putnam, 1952)] 161). As in the 1869 "Plea," however, Peabody mixes the abstract terms of language theory with a more limited, accessible vocabulary. The imagery of "gestures," "expression of face," and "modulation of tones" suggests the importance of nonverbal—one is tempted to say "preverbal"—communication. Moreover, she cautions her readers to give the children "not scientific process— but the result of science," and she promotes the kindergarten teacher as a model of "elegance of expression" (**"Command"** 8). Thus the kindergarten teacher becomes a domestic, feminized figure of eloquence.

If, as Nina Baym has persuasively argued, Peabody is important for "the gendering of millenialism," she is no less so for the gendering of nineteenth-century ideas of language and cultural reform.[19] Peabody interprets the Language of Nature within antebellum domestic ideology, but, at the same time, she employs it to create figures of empowered female speakers. Peabody is clearly less radical in her ideas and less artful in her expression than Margaret Fuller, but her version of a mother-tongue is both radical and artful in its implications for the culture at large. By creating a gendered theory of language and providing a specific cultural space for its application, Peabody's own mother-tongue speaks eloquently across the most fundamental boundary dividing word and deed.

Notes

1. Three biographies of Peabody exist: Ruth M. Baylor, *Elizabeth Palmer Peabody: Kindergarten Pioneer* (Philadelphia: University of Pennsylvania Press, 1965); Gladys Brooks, *Three Wise Virgins* (New York: E. P. Dutton, 1957), 83-153; and Louise Hall Tharp, *The Peabody Sisters of Salem* (Boston: Little, Brown, 1950). Baylor includes a useful bibliography of Peabody's publications, 191-207. The most significant account of Peabody is Philip Gura's "Elizabeth Palmer Peabody and the Philosophy of Language," *ESQ* 23 (1977): 154-63. Gura summarizes the influences on Peabody and places her synthesis of language theories within the framework of Unitarian theology.

2. All quotations are from *Record of a School: Exemplifying the General Principles of Spiritual Culture,* 2d ed. (Boston: Russell, Shattuck, 1836).

3. My source for this last piece of information is Hudspeth's note in [Margaret] Fuller, *Letters [of Margaret Fuller* ed. Robert Hudspeth, 6 vols. (Ithaca, N. Y.: Cornell University Press, 1983-94)] 1:329n.

4. The phrase is opposed to the "private conscience," which Peabody favors (*Record* xiv). The issue of conscience is of course directly related to Alcott's methods of discipline; see Richard Brodhead, "Sparing the Rod: Discipline and Fiction in Antebellum America," *Representations* 21 (1988): 67-96. Peabody's sharpest disagreement with Alcott came as a result of his book *Conversations with Children on the Gospels* (Boston: James Munroe, 1836-37). The two-volume work is available in a reprint edition (New York: Arno Press, 1972). Peabody's "Recorder's Preface" to the first volume registers her disagreement (iv), as does the "Recorder's Remark" in the second volume (17). See also Peabody's 7 August 1836 letter to Alcott in *Letters of Elizabeth Palmer Peabody,* ed. Bruce A. Ronda (Middletown: Wesleyan University Press, 1984), 180-83.

5. Originally published as "A Plea for Froebel's Kindergarten as the First Grade of Primary Education," in *The Identification of the Artisan and Artist* (Boston: Adams, Lee & Shepard, 1869), 42-48, the essay appears in Elizabeth Peabody, *Last Evening with Allston, and Other Papers* (Boston: D. Lothrop, 1886), 331-42. In the essay, Peabody clearly shows her willingness to include such "outer" elements as blocks, sticks, curved wires, and drawings in her curriculum.

6. [*The Journals and Miscellaneous Notebooks of Ralph Waldo Emerson* (1960-82)] 5:66-70 prints the pages of Peabody's manuscript translation that Emerson transcribed into *Journal B,* and Emerson discusses Oegger in several other passages in the journal. Peabody eventually published the translation, *The True Messiah; or The Old and New Testaments, examined according to the Principles of the Language of Nature* (Boston: Peabody, 1842). [Kenneth Walter] Cameron publishes several pertinent passages in *Emerson the Essayist* (Raleigh, N.C.: Thistle Press, 1945), 2:83-99.

7. Oegger, quoted in Cameron, *Emerson the Essayist* 2:84.

8. *United States Magazine and Democratic Review* 1 (February 1838): 323, 320.

9. Peabody, *Letters* 264. Peabody concludes the paragraph by saying that she hopes Kraitsir will teach her enough philology and mathematics so that she "may possibly get weaponed to contend with the great Silence adequately" (264).

10. In her essay "Language," published in *Aesthetic Papers* (1849), Peabody gives "the history of the book": "It was merely the enlargement by Dr. Kraitsir of some notes taken by a hearer of one or two lectures of a series which he delivered in Boston to an audience of about a score of persons" (223). The "hearer" is, of course, Peabody herself, who in this instance performs the duties of recorder in much the same way she did for Alcott and Fuller.

11. The *Nursery* version of Kraitsir's table of germs gives concrete, bodily names for the classes of sounds. So, for instance, labials are called "lip letters," gutturals "throat letters," and "lingual dentals" "tongue and throat letters" (*Nursery* 12). The back cover of *Aesthetic Papers,* also published in 1849, advertises the *First Nursery Reading Book, The Significance of the Alphabet,* and the *Lexeology of English,* which will later become Kraitsir's *Glossology.*

12. *Kindergarten Guide* (Boston: T. O. H. P. Burnham, 1863), 75-97. The book is a collaboration between Peabody and her sister, Mary Peabody Mann. The description of the reading lesson occurs in Peabody's introductory essay, "Kindergarten—What Is It?" 18-21. The essay originally appeared in *Atlantic Monthly* 10 (November 1862), 586-93; the lead article in the volume is, by the way, Thoreau's lecture-essay "Wild Apples."

13. Horace Bushnell, *God in Christ. Three Discourses, Delivered at New Haven, Cambridge, and Andover, with a Preliminary Dissertation on Language* (Hartford: Brown & Parsons, 1849). Peabody lists 1837 as the publication date for *Significance,* which is five years before the date of my copy.

14. *Aesthetic Papers* 214-19; cf. *God in Christ,* 14-24, in which Bushnell argues against the "modern ethnologists" who seek a unified origin of language and, in parallel fashion, a unified origin of humankind; Bushnell's version of the origin is to give an "experiment" of two strangers "thrown together" without any language—the two proceed "arbitrarily, or, at least, by causes so occult or remote that we must regard them as arbitrary" (19-20) to name objects and develop a language corresponding to "the Logos in the outward world, answering to the logos or internal reason of the parties" (21). See [Philip] Gura, *Wisdom of Words* [(Middletown, Conn.: Wesleyan University Press, 1981)], 15-71, for commentaries on Bushnell and Unitarian theories of language.

15. In a letter of April 1833 to Maria Chase, Peabody proposes to use Herder in a series of conversations with Salem ladies, "on the plan of my Boston class." *The Spirit of Hebrew Poetry* is, she says, "an exquisite book" (*Letters* 107). She reviews the book in *Christian Examiner,* 60 (May 1834): 174-75. In September 1846, Peabody sends a copy of Marsh's translation to Phoebe Gage, calling it "a favorite book of mine" and claiming that Herder's poetic criticism develops "*truth,* on the perception of which is conditioned the apprehension of the more Universal Truth—the prophecy that binds the world's history into a rounded whole" (*Letters* 276). James Marsh, whose translation was published in two volumes (Burlington: Edward Smith, 1833), was responsible for publishing the American edition of Coleridge's *Aids to Reflection.* See Gura, *Wisdom of Words,* 39-51, for a discussion of Marsh.

16. The essay appears in *Last Evening with Allston, and Other Papers,* 340; rpt. edition (New York: AMS Press, 1975).

17. "Language in Children," *Kindergarten Messenger* (June 1875), 129.

18. *Kindergarten Messenger* (November 1873), 8.

19. "The Ann Sisters: Elizabeth Peabody's Millennial Historicism," [*American Literary History*] 3 (Spring 1991), 32. The entire article (27-45) is of signal importance to students of Peabody, and it is of equal importance to those concerned with the revaluation of nineteenth-century American literature. Baym argues that we should read Peabody in her own right, on her own terms, and her essay is intended to distinguish Peabody from other (male) writers such as Emerson. From my reading of Peabody's work, I would suggest that she is no more independent of Emerson or Thoreau than they are of her.

FURTHER READING

Biographies

Baylor, Ruth M. *Elizabeth Palmer Peabody: Kindergarten Pioneer.* Philadelphia: University of Pennsylvania Press, 1965, 228 p.
    Examines Peabody's career as an educator.

Brooks, Gladys. *Three Wise Virgins.* New York: Dutton, 1957, 244 p.
    Assesses Peabody's career alongside those of Dorothea Dix and Catharine Maria Sedgwick.

Edwards, June. *Women in American Education, 1820-1955: The Female Force and Educational Reform.* Westport, Conn.: Greenwood Press, 2002, 154 p.
    Evaluates Peabody's role in the educational reform movement of the nineteenth century.

Fenner, Mildred Sandison. *Pioneer American Educators.* Port Washington, N.Y.: Kennikat Press, 1944, 158 p.
    Provides an overview of Peabody's career as an educator.

Marshall, Megan. *The Peabody Sisters: Three Women Who Ignited American Romanticism.* Boston: Houghton Mifflin, 2005, 602 p.
    Examines Peabody's role in the Transcendentalist movement, as well as her efforts on behalf of educational reform.

Neussendorfer, Margaret. "Elizabeth Palmer Peabody." In *The Transcendentalists: A Review of Research and Criticism,* edited by Joel Myerson, pp. 233-41. New York: Modern Language Association of America, 1984.
    Provides a brief evaluation of Peabody's career.

Tharp, Louisa Hall. *The Peabody Sisters of Salem.* Boston: Little, Brown and Co., 1950, 372 p.
    Offers a detailed examination of Peabody's life and career.

Criticism

Baym, Nina. "The Ann Sisters: Elizabeth Peabody's Millennial Historicism." *American Literary History* 3, no. 1 (spring 1991): 27-45.
    Analyzes Peabody's writings on social reform, evaluating her ideas within the context of Transcendentalism.

Deese, Helen R. "A New England Women's Network: Elizabeth Palmer Peabody, Caroline Healey Dall, and Delia S. Bacon." *Legacy* 8, no. 2 (fall 1992): 77-91.

    Explores the correspondence between the three prominent women.

Idol, John L., Jr. "Elizabeth Palmer Peabody: A Tireless Hawthorne Booster." In *Hawthorne and Women: Engendering and Expanding the Hawthorne Tradition,* edited by John L. Idol, Jr. and Melinda M. Ponder, pp. 36-44. Amherst: University of Massachusetts Press, 1999.

    Analyzes Peabody's reviews of Hawthorne's work.

Myerson, Joel. *Transcendentalism: A Reader.* Oxford: Oxford University Press, 2000, 712 p.

    Includes an overview of Peabody's life and works.

Ronda, Bruce A. *Elizabeth Palmer Peabody: A Reformer on Her Own Terms.* Cambridge: Harvard University Press, 1999, 391 p.

    Offers a comprehensive analysis of Peabody's career as an author and educator.

————. "Scandal and Seductive Language: Elizabeth Peabody Reads *Clarissa.*" *ESQ: A Journal of the American Renaissance* 44, no. 4 (fourth quarter 1998): 301-23.

    Examines the influence of Samuel Richardson's novel on Peabody's literary sensibility.

Stern, Madeleine B. "Elizabeth Peabody's Foreign Library (1840)." *American Transcendental Quarterly,* no. 20 (1973): 5-12.

    Provides some insight into Peabody's personal library.

Wilson, John B. "Elizabeth Palmer Peabody and Other Transcendentalists on History and Historians." *Historian* 30 (November 1967): 72-86.

    Explores Peabody's views on history.

————. "Grimm's Law and the Brahmins." *New England Quarterly* 38, no. 2 (June 1965): 234-39.

    Examines Peabody's theories concerning language and linguistics.

Additional coverage of Peabody's life and career is contained in the following sources published by Thomson Gale: *Dictionary of Literary Biography,* **Vols. 1, 223; and** *Literature Resource Center.*

Vanity Fair: A Novel without a Hero

William Makepeace Thackeray

(Also wrote under the pseudonyms Charles J. Yellowplush, Ikey Solomons, Michael Angelo Titmarsh, and George Savage Fitzboodle) English novelist, short story and sketch writer, essayist, and poet.

The following entry presents criticism of Thackeray's novel *Vanity Fair: A Novel without a Hero* (1848). For additional discussion of the novel, see *NCLC*, Volume 14; for criticism devoted to *The History of Henry Esmond, Esq., a Colonel in the Service of Her Majesty Q. Anne, Written by Himself* (1852), see *NCLC*, Volume 22; for criticism devoted to *The Luck of Barry Lyndon* (1844), see *NCLC*, Volume 43; for information on Thackeray's complete career, see *NCLC*, Volume 5.

INTRODUCTION

Thackeray's *Vanity Fair: A Novel without a Hero* represents a milestone in the development of fictional realism in England. Published in its entirety in 1848, after appearing serially in nineteen monthly parts in 1847-48, the novel chronicles the fortunes of diverse members of London society in the first half of the nineteenth century. Epic in scope, the novel seeks to recreate, through detailed depictions of its characters, the culture and attitudes of the early Victorian age in a prose style that is discursive and sardonic, yet also sympathetic and highly evocative. The title *Vanity Fair,* taken from John Bunyan's *Pilgrim's Progress* (1678), refers to the foolishness and futility of human ambition, particularly as it relates to issues of social class and material gain. Although *Vanity Fair* contains some of the most memorable characters in Victorian literature—in particular the shrewd and charismatic Becky Sharp, described by critic Harold Bloom as coming "closer to being Falstaff's daughter than any other female character in British fiction"—the heart of the book resides in the narrative voice. Ironic, astute, and versatile, Thackeray's narrator effortlessly takes on numerous points of view throughout the novel, at times recounting events from an omniscient perspective, at other times adopting the guise of an ordinary person, one with the same preoccupations and concerns as the book's characters. Unlike most early Victorian authors, Thackeray eschewed conventional plot devices in favor of a character-driven ap-

proach to the novel form, in a style reminiscent of eighteenth-century novelist Henry Fielding. The novel is widely regarded to be Thackeray's masterpiece and is as original and ambitious as any novel from the Victorian era, earning comparisons to George Eliot's *Middlemarch* (1871-72) and Charles Dickens's *Bleak House* (1851-52).

PLOT AND MAJOR CHARACTERS

If there is a plot in *Vanity Fair,* it is loosely defined, emerging more through the lives of Thackeray's characters than through an overarching sense of story. The novel opens with a metaphor that presents the various characters as puppets being prepared for a performance at a country fair. Following this brief preface, Thackeray transports the reader to Chiswick Mall, a prominent school for girls outside of London, during the period of the Napoleonic wars. Here the author introduces two of the work's central characters: Amelia Sedley, the daughter of a prosperous London merchant, and Becky Sharp, the orphaned child of French bohemian artists. As Thackeray describes the class distinctions between the two friends, he also depicts the differences in their temperaments. While Amelia is kind-hearted and docile—representing, in Thackeray's era, the ideal woman—Becky is strong-willed and irreverent, determined to overcome the disadvantages of her origins. Although the narrative frequently shifts its focus to other characters, the tension between these opposing personae remains constant throughout the work.

As the novel unfolds, Becky's social machinations bring her into contact with a range of people, from Amelia's fatuous brother Joseph, whom she nearly marries, to the wealthy and jaded dowager Lady Crawley. When Becky contrives a secret marriage to Lady Crawley's uncouth nephew, Rawdon Crawley, the old woman's fondness for Becky turns sour, and the newlyweds are cut off from the Crawley fortune. Undeterred, Becky persists with her social schemes, charming generals and other prominent personages in her efforts to lead an affluent life, largely through unscrupulous business deals, over-extended credit, and outright theft.

Amelia's life, meanwhile, takes an unexpected turn when her father's investments fail—a result of Napoleon's unexpected resurgence on the Continent—and her family plunges into poverty. In spite of her sudden change of fortune, Amelia retains the love of her long-time paramour, the superficial and egotistical army officer George Osborne, and the couple is married over the objections of George's father. Their marriage proves short-lived, however: George is killed at the battle of Waterloo, and Amelia is plunged into a state of despairing self-pity, which only worsens at the birth of her son, George. Ill-equipped to raise her child properly, Amelia leaves him in the care of Osborne's estranged father. Her sense of misfortune is exacerbated by the meteoric rise of her friend Becky, who has gradually elevated herself into the elite circles of the upper class. Osborne's friend William Dobbin, whose sincerity and strong moral code are unique among the novel's many characters, and whose loyalty to George always superseded his secret love for his friend's wife, tries to convince Amelia to marry him. Amelia refuses, however, in large part because of his disparaging attitude toward Becky Sharp.

Becky suffers her own reversal when she becomes involved in a scandalous affair with the dissipated Lord Steyne. Rawdon promptly leaves her, taking custody of their son, and Becky is forced to flee England for an extended period. Toward the end of the novel Becky seduces Joseph, while also playing a suspicious role in

his unexpected death. Amelia finally recognizes the duplicity of Becky's nature and agrees to marry William. They settle into a respectable middle-class life, while Becky, now wealthy, continues to circulate in high society. The novel ends with a refrain of Thackeray's original conceit: the narrator announces the conclusion of the play, and the puppets are closed once again in their box.

MAJOR THEMES

The novel's title serves as an appropriate summation of Thackeray's central theme. Whereas John Bunyan's Vanity Fair represented worldly temptation—the carnival of material pleasure designed by Satan to steer Christians off of the path of virtue—Thackeray presents Vanity Fair as the inescapable human condition, a place in which people have no choice but to try to enact fulfilling lives, even as they recognize the futility of their endeavors. In this sense, Thackeray's Vanity Fair signifies a wide-ranging, generally cynical view of humanity. None of his characters are immune from his trenchant satire, and the motivations for their actions are always transparent.

Underlying this theme is the more fundamental issue of character. Thackeray's subtitle, *A Novel without a Hero,* openly admits that none of *Vanity Fair*'s main characters will elicit much sympathy from the reader, and indeed they all seem either unwilling to be, or incapable of being, sincere or honest. Thackeray's characters are either brazenly duplicitous and prevaricating, like Becky Sharp; pretentious, like George Osborne; loutish and self-absorbed, like Rawdon Crawley; cowardly and delusional, like Joseph Sedley; or insipid and weak-willed, like Lady Crawley's maid, Briggs. Even such generous and kind-hearted characters as William Dobbin and Amelia Sedley are marred by weakness, rigidity, and overall drabness. Ultimately, a tightly woven fabric of deceit comes to represent the nature of reality itself.

At the center of this constellation of personalities stands the narrator himself. By turns omniscient and myopic, he adopts numerous guises throughout the work, weaving in and out of the characters' lives as both an observer of and a participant in the society they inhabit. Because he adopts numerous, often contradictory points of view, the narrator in many ways embodies the same inconsistency, pretense, and guile as the work's protagonists, thus revealing himself to be as flawed as anyone else in the novel. The theme Thackeray conveys in this way may be that human beings are governed by self-interest: that they carry themselves through society—backbiting, gossiping, and continually judging each other—in pursuit of selfish ends. The author's own illustrations for the book further demonstrate this point; the novel's frontispiece portrays a jester gazing into a cracked mirror, symbolizing at once his vanity and his lack of integrity or wholeness.

Another important theme of the novel revolves around the question of class. The primary targets of Thackeray's ridicule are the social ambition and posturing he found inherent in middle-class values. For Thackeray—himself an unrepentant member of the upper class—the aspirations of one class to emulate another represented the most brazen form of hypocrisy.

CRITICAL RECEPTION

A work as variegated and complex as *Vanity Fair* inevitably elicits a broad range of responses. Early critical reactions to the novel were mixed. A number of prominent authors expressed high praise for the novel, notably Charlotte Brontë, who called the work a "Herculean feat" and its author a "Titan" among Victorian writers. Other contemporary reviewers, however, objected to the work on moral grounds. Robert Bell took exception to the "vicious and odious" qualities of the main characters, while reviewer Harriet Martineau was so dismayed by the work's pervasive cynicism that she refused to finish reading it. In spite of the furor sparked by the book's supposed amorality and ruthlessness, however, most critics agreed that the novel represented a landmark work of realistic fiction. Thackeray himself regarded *Vanity Fair* as a response to the sentimentality of Charles Dickens and an effort to expose the materialism and hypocrisy of his day.

Beginning in the twentieth century, critical interpretations began to steer away from moral consideration of the novel, focusing instead on Thackeray's stylistic innovations. In the 1920s Percy Lubbock embraced the novel's unique form as impressionistic and "panoramic," arguing that the work was held together by virtue of Thackeray's incisive characterizations rather than through coherence of story. In 1954 John A. Lester, Jr. published an article entitled "Thackeray's Narrative Technique," one of the first substantial analyses of form in *Vanity Fair*. Other critics began to recognize the possible strategies behind the work's structural imbalances, arguing that the lack of a clearly developed plot allowed the novel's themes to serve as the framework of the story. Writing in the 1950s, Geoffrey Tillotson examined the unifying powers of the narrator himself, extolling the versatility and verbal adroitness of the novel's point of view. In more recent years critics have returned to the moral considerations that preoccupied Thackeray's contemporaries. Some scholars, notably John Peck, have argued that the work betrays Thacker-

ay's own questionable attitudes toward the middle class, while other writers have identified racist elements in Thackeray's portrait of colonial culture. In the 1990s a range of specialized interpretations of the novel emerged, addressing such issues as Thackeray's depictions of female sexuality, his interpretation of history in the Napoleonic era, and his attitudes toward the place of religion in society.

PRINCIPAL WORKS

The Yellowplush Correspondence [as Charles J. Yellowplush] (sketches) 1838

Catherine: A Story [as Ikey Solomons] (novella) 1839-40; published in journal *Fraser's Magazine*

The Paris Sketch Book. 2 vols. [as Mr. Titmarsh] (sketches) 1840

A Shabby Genteel Story [anonymous] (novella) 1840; published in journal *Fraser's Magazine*

The Second Funeral of Napoleon, in Three Letters to Miss Smith of London; and The Chronicle of the Drum [as M. A. Titmarsh] (prose and poetry) 1841

The Irish Sketch Book [as M. A. Titmarsh] (sketches) 1843

The Luck of Barry Lyndon [as Fitz-Boodle] (novel) 1844; revised as *The Memoirs of Barry Lyndon, Esq.* 1856

The Book of Snobs (sketches) 1848

The Great Hoggarty Diamond (novel) 1848; also published as *The History of Samuel Titmarsh and the Great Hoggarty Diamond*, 1849

Vanity Fair: A Novel without a Hero (novel) 1848

The History of Pendennis: His Fortunes and Misfortunes, His Friends and His Greatest Enemy. 2 vols. (novel) 1850

The History of Henry Esmond, Esq., a Colonel in the Service of Her Majesty Q. Anne, Written by Himself (novel) 1852

The English Humourists of the Eighteenth Century: A Series of Lectures Delivered in England, Scotland, and the United States of America (essays) 1853

The Newcomes: Memoirs of a Most Respectable Family (novel) 1855

Miscellanies: Prose and Verse. 4 vols. (essays, sketches, short stories, and poetry) 1855-57

The Virginians: A Tale of the Last Century (novel) 1859

The Four Georges: Sketches of Manners, Morals, Court and Town Life (sketches) 1860

Lovel the Widower (novel) 1860

The Adventures of Philip on His Way through the World; Shewing Who Robbed Him, Who Helped Him, and Who Passed Him By (novel) 1862

The Roundabout Papers (essays) 1863

Denis Duval (unfinished novel) 1864

The Complete Works of William Makepeace Thackeray.
30 vols. (novels, short stories, sketches, poetry, essays, and letters) 1904

The Letters and Private Papers of William Makepeace Thackeray. 4 vols. (letters and journals) 1945-46

*Originally published serially in 1841 in the journal *Fraser's Magazine.*

CRITICISM

Dublin University Magazine (review date October 1848)

SOURCE: "Contemporary Writers—Mr. Thackeray." *Dublin University Magazine* 32, no. 190 (October 1848): 444-59.

[*In the following review, the anonymous reviewer praises the insight and humor with which Thackeray depicts* Vanity Fair's *central characters.*]

[T]he work whose title [*Vanity Fair*] stands at the head of this paper, beyond all question, establishes the reputation of Mr. Thackeray as a writer of fiction, upon a basis far too secure to be ever hereafter disturbed by the fickle breath of popular applause. In *Vanity Fair* he has given to the world a work which will endure as long as the joys and sorrows, the passions and the emotions, of the human heart, have power to charm the minds of men. . . .

Vanity Fair proposes to be pen-and-pencil sketches of English society; and we think the taste of the public mind is altogether in favour of sketches, properly so called. The work before us consists of a series of very brilliant ones—with a description of the effect which the combinations of fate or fortune produces upon each of the *dramatis personæ,* rather than any deep analysis of the passions or feelings of the human heart. Many extraneous circumstances have possibly combined to lead Mr. Thackeray into this peculiar style of writing, in which he has certainly attained a rare excellence. The foibles and the weaknesses of mankind, rather than their deeper vices or virtues, are the subjects of the story. . . .

It seems to us beyond all question, that *Vanity Fair* has been written month by month, as occasion required, or as the printers called for it, for the pages abound with minute deviations from the original conceptions of the author. Thus the author occasionally sketches a character, and losing sight, as the story progresses, of the outline which he had originally drawn, throws in other ingredients which have the effect of materially altering

the character he intended to paint. Several instances of this occur; but let the portrait of Rawdon Crawley serve as a specimen of what we mean. He sets out with describing this gambling, racing, tandem-driving guardsman—this heavy dragoon "with small brains and strong desires"—to be about as thorough and worthless a profligate as it is possible to conceive. He tells us of his fleecing greenhorns at play, swindling tradesmen, and committing all the vices common to such distinguished members of society. He says that the only honest act in his very wicked and depraved life, was his marriage with the little governess—he makes him not only connive at her flirtation with the superannuated General Tufto, but actually shows him on the general's staff, and living in his quarters; and then, utterly oblivious of the character he had intended to draw, towards the conclusion he develops in him some of the finest and most beautiful qualities in our nature—such as his affection for the child, and his lofty and soldier-like bearing in regard of the amorous advances to the green-eyed Rebecca of the profligate peer. These faults, incidental to the serial mode of writing, are, however, after all, but trivial; and, upon the whole, we have seldom read a story which has given us greater pleasure than *Vanity Fair.* Our interest has never for a moment been allowed to flag; and although there occasionally occur some pages of "filling-up," which are in nowise necessary to the progress of the tale, they but serve as settings for the brighter and more sparkling gems with which it abounds. In point of style Mr. Thackeray is behind none of his contemporaries. There is neither affectation nor mannerism to be found in his pages; and as a writer of the pure, good, honest Saxon school, he is, beyond all question, unrivalled; he is vigorous, and at the same time agreeable—commonly terse, and always humorous; but there is no straining after effect, no attempt at fine writing. The details of his story are woven together with careless ease, and the incidents narrated in the most off-hand and pleasant manner possible.

The great characteristic of Mr. Thackeray's style is the species of quaint and quiet humour with which, by one little touch, he opens the secret doors of the heart. His personages are so real, and described with so much graphic power, that our interest is strongly excited, and never allowed to drop. We used actually to long for the appearance of each successive number, with an ardour only to be equalled by that excited by his great contemporary, Dickens; and upon looking over *Vanity Fair,* now that its numbers have been collected, we are in nowise surprised at the pleasure we then felt; for, to the true lover of fiction, there has scarcely ever been served up a dish of more exquisitely-seasoned food.

The knowledge which the author of *Vanity Fair* seems to possess of the fair sex is tolerably extensive; but it is a species of knowledge which in our opinion rather goes to prove that it is with the less amiable portion of it he has, for the most part, associated; he has certainly more power in delineating the foibles and the weaknesses of woman's heart, than in displaying the attractive charms of her better nature. Lady Jane is amiable, so is the poor little Amelia; but they are only milk-and-water heroines after all: there is nothing noble about them—there is nothing of the generosity and self-devotion so inherent in the nature of a true woman. . . .

If *Vanity Fair* be a novel without a hero, it most assuredly is not without a heroine. Her character is well worthy an attentive study. It is an accurate portrait of a clever adventuress, thoroughly devoid of any principle, and, in our opinion, not in the least overdrawn. The daughter of a clever, drunken, careless, profligate artist, slight in person, pale in features, with an intellectual head and attractive eyes, brought up in the society of his reckless and dissipated companions—familiar, from her childhood, with every variety of difficulty and embarrassment, as well as the shifts and contrivances by which they might be evaded—having considerable experience in duns, and an eye not inapt for the recognition of a bailiff, Miss Sharp proves an admirable helpmate for the heavy dragoon, with whose creditors she effects a compromise—whose future fortunes she directs with an able and experienced hand. She is also a clever intriguante, extracting, with admirable skill, from the elderly gentlemen, with whom she carries on flirtations, a precarious means of livelihood; "doing" tradesmen; getting something out of every person with whom she comes into contact; setting up a mansion in the most fashionable part of London, and teaching the world how to live upon nothing a-year; obtaining, in despite of the formidable difficulties of low birth and want of money, ingress into the most fashionable of London society; snubbing countesses, receiving dukes and personages of royal lineage at her *petits soupers*—the portrait of Rebecca is, indeed, drawn with a piquancy and power quite charming and irresistible. . . .

We have dwelt at such length upon what we consider the excellence of this work, that there is no chance of our incurring the censure of ill nature, if we now point to what, it must be admitted, are its defects. Among all the characters which rise before us when we have closed the book, there is not, with the exception of William Dobbin, one thoroughly good or honest man. In the mingled elements of their nature, that of evil is too largely blended. We sincerely hope we may never discover that the real *Vanity Fair,* of which this work professes to reflect the image, is so entirely peopled with knaves and fools. In short, we have a better opinion of human nature than Mr. Thackeray. Our experience is possibly shorter, and far more limited; and frail and imperfect as is the heart of man, we cannot help thinking that it is not so thoroughly imbued with selfishness, so steeped with vanity, and so degraded by vice, as it has been represented to us. We should be sorry to coincide

in the view of that high authority, whose worldly experience would lead us to believe every one a rogue until we find him out to be honest. Such a philosophy is naturally repugnant and distasteful to us. With all its faults and all its foibles, we have a kindly feeling for poor human nature; and we would be sorry to strip ourselves of the delusion, if one it be, that we have been gifted with more high and generous impulses, with loftier feelings, and honester hearts, than is represented by this great satirist. But, then, it may be said, his work is meant to deal only with our foibles, and to exhibit our vices. True, and therefore the contemplation of the dark side of the picture is the more distasteful. The tone of Mr. Thackeray's mind is essentially sarcastic; he is too prone to indulge his inclination of representing men or things in a satirical point of view, and, like Lord Byron, whenever a genial or sunshiny trait of our better nature is exhibited, it is spoiled with a dash of sarcasm, which mars its beauty, and prevents us from enjoying the full pleasure of its effect. Even in the less equivocal characters which figure upon its pages, some fatuity, selfishness, or vanity arises, to break the spell. We should like to ask Mr. Thackeray if he believes that in the real *Vanity Fair* no good man, or no virtuous woman exists, who is not, at the same time, silly and selfish, for such, we fear, is the inevitable impression this book is calculated to convey?

We are by no means disposed to cavil or to find fault with the author that he has not visited, with more severity, upon the head of Rebecca, the consequences of her moral transgressions,—that he has omitted to visit upon her that amount of retributive justice which, had the subject been handled by one of the common-place writers of the day, would assuredly have been the result. In the ultimate disposition of her destiny, he has exhibited a knowledge of the world far too intimate and far too fine, to err in following so ordinary a track. Alas! too little do we know what lies beneath the mask of many of those whom we see fulfilling, with a zeal apparently so fervent, the ordinary duties of life, and affecting the semblance of a rigid adherence to the rules of virtue and religion. We fear Mr. Thackeray is not astray on this point, and that hypocrisy is one of the commonest vices in *Vanity Fair.*

Notwithstanding, however, the defects to which we have adverted, and which we think, regarding the work in an artistic point of view, are its only blemish, *Vanity Fair* bears upon its pages the indelible impress of a genius so original and so striking, that it must at once lift the author into a high position among the writers of his age and country. But we think the genius and the power displayed in this work are capable of still higher flights; and if he have only the inclination, we see no reason why an exalted place among the standard writers of England should not yet be occupied by the author of *Vanity Fair.*

United States Magazine, and Democratic Review
(review date October 1848)

SOURCE: Review of *Vanity Fair*, by William Makepeace Thackeray. *United States Magazine, and Democratic Review* n.s. 23, no. 124 (October 1848): 377-79.

[*In the following excerpt, the anonymous reviewer discusses the realism of Thackeray's character portrayals.*]

Vanity Fair is the embodiment of the Maxims of La
Rochefoucault. Every thought, every action is traced to
one spring—the intensely egotistical instinct of human
nature.

Mr. Thackeray has been already before the public under
the pseudonym of M. A. Titmarsh. We owe to his pen
many humorous sketches: **"Jeames' Diary,"** the **"Snob
Papers,"** and several other productions have been acknowledged by him. And although he now appears in a
different and more important character, we must welcome him as an old friend, not as a new acquaintance.
He is not yet forty years old, but has seen life under
many faces. Since he left Cambridge, he has been a
painter, an editor, an occasional contributor, and finally
a regular man of letters. He has travelled, resided in
foreign countries, mixed with all orders of society both
at home and abroad, being himself well connected; in
short he has enjoyed and improved every opportunity of
knowing man; and now, mark the conclusion he has
reached—the old, dreary conclusion: "all is vanity!"

For Vanity Fair is the world, and through its booths and
busy places of pleasure and sorrow, the author leads the
reader with Sentiment on one arm and Satire on the
other. Would we could say that Vanity Fair is only the
world which Mr. Thackeray has frequented; but we fear
that, after all, every world out of Utopia is but a Vanity
Fair.

There is no hero to this novel; probably because the
male characters, being true copies from Nature, are all
below the epic proportions of novel-heroes. What personage is there, in this picture of every day life, that
would at all realize the conceptions of the least romantic of fair readers? Not Dobbin, certainly; though kind,
warm-hearted, generous and a soldier, he is not intellectual enough; and, worse than all, he lisps, and he is not
handsome. Not Rawdon Crawley, the "heavy dragoon;"
he is too heavy by far; a novel hero would be ashamed
of the constant luck at cards of Rawdon Crawley: no
novel hero ought to live by his wits; if poor, he should
meet, in the Xth chapter, some rich old gentleman in
want of an heir. Nor will George Osborne do; true, he
rides well, dances well, fences well, spars well, and
looks very well; but he is frivolous, vain, and intensely
selfish. He is a worldling, even in his boyish days; a

fair character throughout for *Vanity Fair,* but no hero;
we have no sympathy for him; although he marries
poor, sweet Amelia, and thereby gets disinherited, we
despise him because he repents of his generosity; the
only redeeming trait about him is, that he gets killed in
the middle of the book. The other personages are either
too low, or insignificant, or too old, or too mean; in
fact, every actor in the cast has some defect that un-
qualifies him for the part of a hero—precisely as in real
life.

But we have two heroines; sweet, kind, tender Amelia
is certainly one; soft, yielding creature, she seems out
of place in *Vanity Fair*; yet we do meet once in a while
such exceptions. But the other is our favorite; Rebecca
Sharp, clever, keen, pliant little "Becky" What though
she is heartless, selfish, designing, intriguing; we love
her because she is talented, energetic—and successful.
The adventures of these two women of opposite disposition are the woof and web of the story; all the rest is
only nap, but a nap of most excellent quality. We will
try to draw out the separate threads, and coil them up
into as small a space as possible, advising our readers
to buy the cloth itself, if they wish to know more.

Amelia, wealthy John Sedley's daughter, and Rebecca,
whose father was a poor, dissipated artist, meet together
at school; "Becky," who pays for her tuition by her services, contrives to win the friendship of her sweet companion, and on the day that the latter leaves school,
manages to exchange her present position for that of a
governess in the family of Sir Pitt Crawley. She enjoys
a short respite, however, in a visit to her wealthy friend;
and then she makes a desperate attempt at Joseph Sedley, Amelia's brother, a rich East Indiaman. She fails—
never mind, reader, this is her first attempt, she will do
better bye-and-bye. After drawing largely upon the
bounty of her fair friend, she enters the family of Sir
Pitt Crawley; and here she makes a fair trial of her talents; she subdues the avaricious old baronet, both his
sons, Pitt a hypocrite and Rawdon a profligate; Lady
Crawley, her daughters, Sir Pitt's brother, the parson, a
swearing, fighting, drinking clergyman, the parson's
wife, a meddling intriguer, all yield to the ascendancy
of her pliant, yet energetic genius. But she brings all
her fascinations to bear upon Rawdon, who, though a
younger brother, expects a large fortune from his aunt,
Miss Crawley. The latter, a whig, a free thinker, and a
humorist, visits Sir Pitt, and Becky fails not to subju-
gate her likewise; so that the spinster insists upon taking the favorite to London. There Becky exerts her genius to such good purpose that the aged maiden dotes
on her, and that when Sir Pitt, who cannot bear her absence, comes to tell her that he has lost his wife, and
proposes to make her Lady Crawley, she is obliged to
confess that she is married, being already wedded in secret to his son Rawdon. Did I not say that she would do
better bye-and-bye?

But Becky's condition is not much improved by this connection; true, she is Mrs. Captain Crawley; but the aunt revokes her will, Sir Pitt declines giving assistance to his son, and Becky Sharp is obliged to turn *sharper* in order to live. We next follow the young couple to Brighton, where they meet, among other persons, George Osborne and his wife, Amelia. George has been shamed by his friend Dobbin into marrying her in spite of her father's bankruptcy, thereby incurring the curse of his own father, and—what is worse in his eyes—getting disinherited. Here Rebecca appears to great advantage, making love to Osborne out of pure deviltry, devising ways and means for raising money and for not paying any bills, and urging her accomplished husband in a career of profitable gambling.

He of Elba happening to escape, our characters are transported to Belgium, where Becky defrays expenses by her fascinations, makes her husband aid-de-camp to Lord Tufto, who is in love with her, becomes the cynosure of all eyes, and artfully contrives to amass quite a sum of money, for fear that Rawdon might get killed at Waterloo—but he does not, although he distinguishes himself.

Here the story becomes dilatory, diffuse, and it loses much of its interest. After all, there is more sense than people are generally willing to allow, in making heroes and heroines marry at the conclusion of a drama or a novel. Laugh as we may at Aristotle and the classic school, some *unity* is absolutely necessary to make a plot interesting; and human ingenuity has yet devised no plan more successful for preserving the unity of action, than to keep a marriage in reserve for a catastrophe.

During a lapse of years, it is somewhat tiresome to trace how Sir Pitt dies, leaving the baronetcy to Sir Pitt junior, who also inherits the fortune of his maiden aunt, Rawdon being cut off with £100; how George Osborne gets killed at Waterloo, and how his widow, sweet Amelia, finds, in due time, some consolation in the birth of George O., junior; how fat Joseph Sedley goes to India, leaving a small annuity to support his bankrupt father and family; how kind, warm-hearted Dobbin also betakes himself to the East Indies, after performing certain acts of generosity seldom witnessed in *Vanity Fair*; and how Rebecca and her husband, after shining and gambling at various places on the continent, finally return to England, Becky having artfully compromised his debts there, at a trifle on the pound.

With the return of Becky to London, the story becomes once more lively and interesting. By dint of skill, impudence, perseverance and intrigue, our heroine achieves a wonderful standing. She subjugates the Marquis of Steyne, a new and very interesting character, makes a free use of his cash and of his influence, moves in the first circles, is smiled upon by royalty, and completely succeeds in obtaining the great aim of her life, and asserting for herself that rank in society which she conceives is due to a woman of her talents. She has a son whom she hates, and sends to school under the wing of the marquess; and she intrigues to obtain a government appointment for her husband; but just as the latter's name is about to be gazetted, just as "Becky" has gathered a nice private purse, her edifice of fortune is demolished at one blow. Poor Becky, she is like a spider in a well regulated household; she weaves a web most industriously, only to see it swept off by an evil genius. Lord Steyne, who has no idea—the old rake—of dealing out cash and influence forever without return, gets Rawdon arrested on a small debt, and leaving the latter to mope at a spunging house, visits his wife most assiduously. But as the guilty pair are enjoying their opportunity, they are surprised by the sudden appearance of Rawdon, who has been liberated by Lady Pitt Crawley. A grand scene ensues; Rawdon, the vulgar wretch, knocks the marquis down, strips Becky of her jewelry, and scatters her private purse to the winds. No duel follows, however; the matter is hushed up, Rawdon is sent to govern a distant island, where he dies after a few years, and Becky is left to shift for herself on about £300 a year. After a few efforts to rise superior to her fate, she almost gives up, and becomes a perfect vagabond, travels from city to city in rather disreputable company, and finally takes to small gambling, rouge, and cognac.

Meanwhile Amelia's life has been quiet, sedate and obscure. She lives in poverty with her broken down parents, and her only consolation is her George, so like—too like we think—his father. But a better day is coming; her mother dies, her son is taken care of by his wealthy grandfather, and Joseph, fat, rich Joseph, her brother, returns from India, with lank, lisping Dobbin, who has been twelve or fifteen years in love with Amelia. Fat Joseph unties the strings of his fat purse and makes Amelia keep house for him. That is not all; her old father dies, leaving her—a little more leisure; and old Osborne likewise makes his final exit, leaving her considerable property. Who happier now than sweet Amelia, with her dear boy and plenty of means? One day, our happy party, including Dobbin, take into their heads to travel, and Pumpernickel, in Germany, being recommended for fat Joseph's damaged liver, they establish themselves there, and begin to enjoy life.

Thither also the novelist leads "Becky," to bring about his catastrophe. She re-asserts her old dominion over Amelia and her corpulent brother, and although Dobbin opposes her, brings about his marriage with her old friend. For her own part, she captivates her former admirer. Joseph, so completely, that although they do not marry, she extorts all his property and kills him—with kindness probably—in a wonderfully short time. Fortified with wealth, she returns to England, where she silences envy, leads the fashion, and begins to entertain some esteem for her neglected son, who, through a series of providential demises, has succeeded to the title of his uncle.

Such is the bare outline of a story told with the most marvellous richness of lively detail, elegant phrase, and humorous situation. Once in a while, while reading this work, we had occasion to ejaculate mentally, "Boz come again—no more, no more of that." But aside from the occasional influence of school and prevailing taste, Mr. Thackeray is original; so much so, that it is with diffidence that we venture a hint that "Becky" may possibly have been suggested by a character in Sue's "Mathilde," whose name we forget. But Sue's characters are abstractions or chimeras, while Thackeray's are of human flesh and blood. Our author is too cynical to indulge in the melting mood; yet, in perusing *Vanity Fair,* the reader will occasionally experience that delightful involuntary thrill which the pathos of Sterne and Dickens so often produces.

H. K. (essay date February 1864)

SOURCE: H. K. "On Thackeray." *Macmillan's Magazine* 9, no. 52 (February 1864): 356-63.

[*In the following essay, the author examines the character of Becky Sharp, asserting that she is among the most memorable protagonists in English literature.*]

Vanity Fair took the world by surprise. Its appearance was a kind of era in the lives of men whose ages were at that time within four or five years of twenty; and, for aught we know, in the lives of men older and wiser.

One's most intimate and dearest friends before this era were probably Hamlet, Don Quixote, Robinson Crusoe, My Uncle Toby, or, probably, for tastes vary, Mr. Tom Jones, or Mr. Peregrine Pickle. Latterly, also, we had got to love Mr. Pickwick, the Brothers Cheeryble, and dear old Tom Pinch; and were conceiving an affectionate admiration of Eddard Cuttle, mariner; but when these wonderful yellow numbers were handed eagerly from hand to hand, to be borrowed, read, re-read, and discussed, it became evident that the circle of our acquaintance had been suddenly and singularly enlarged; that we were becoming acquainted with people—strange people, indeed!—who forced themselves on our notice, and engaged our attention, to a degree which none of our former acquaintances had ever succeeded in doing.

These wonderful new people, too, were so amazingly common-place. They were like ourselves in detail. There was nothing whatever about them except that we could not get them out of our heads; that we discussed their proceedings as we would those of the real people our neighbours; that we were amused with their foolishness, and intensely angry at some of their proceedings. Any fool could have written about such people as these: there was nothing worthy of notice in the book at all, except that it had taken entire possession of us, and of the world. Through the exquisite perfection of the art, the art itself was not only ignored, but indignantly denied.

How melancholy it is to look back at the long line of our sweethearts, loved so dearly for a time, then neglected, then cast off, and only remembered by their names, and by a dull regretful wonder at *that* having been so dear to us at any time. Were we ever so silly as to have wept over the death of Virginia, our first lady-love, when she was shipwrecked in the Mauritius? and how soon after were we furiously indignant at the treatment of Rosamund by her papa about the purple jar and the new shoes? Then it was that impertinent *espiègle* little thing, Julia Mannering; then Flora M'Ivor, and, then by a natural reaction from such overstrained sentimentalism, Evelina Burney. And so we went on from one imaginary young lady to another, until we became so *blasé,* so used to the storms of the great passion, that we could love no more, at least, not in the old degree. We understood women. We had been through too much: when at last that queer old-fashioned, dear little body, Jane Eyre, married Fairfax Rochester, we merely said that the girl was a fool, and lit our cigar. We could love no more.

Fools that we were! we were just on the eve of a crisis in our lives, of the greatest passion of all (for an unworthy object certainly)—a passion different from, and more profound than, all which had gone before. At the time that these yellow numbers began to appear, we made acquaintance with one, Miss Rebecca Sharp, and from the moment she threw her "dixonary" out of the window, we loved as we had never loved before. We were fully alive to that young lady's faults; indeed she did not take any vast trouble to conceal them; but in spite of this she simply gave a whisk of her yellow hair, and an ogle with her green eyes, took us by the nose, and led us whithersoever she would.

And did ever woman lead man such a dance as she led us? Never, since Petronius wrote the first novel eighteen hundred years ago. There was one Ulysses, and there is one Becky Sharp, the woman of many experiences and many counsels, the most of them far from satisfactory. There is no killing or shelving her; she always rises to the occasion, save once, and that one time is the only time on which she was really guilty. Then she is prostrated for a period, and shows you accidentally what you were hardly inclined to believe, that she had some sort of a heart.

Is there anything like the rise, the fall, and the rise of this woman, in literature? It is hard to say where. Many other characters in prose fiction, and often, though far less often, in poetry, grow and develop; but we know of none which enlarges and decreases again, like that of Becky Sharp—which alters in quantity and degree, but never in quality, by the breadth of a hair. False, clever, shifty, and passionately fond of admiration in her father's studio, she carries those qualities and no others with her, using them in greater or less degree, according to her opportunities, through her life. One finds her sipping gin and water in her father's studio, and imitating Miss Pinkerton; one finds her entertaining a select audience of Lord Steyne and Lord Southdown, with a wonderful imitation of the Dowager Lady Southdown; and one finds her at last with the plate of sausages and the brandy bottle, entertaining two German students with an imitation of Jos. Sedley, in the later and not so prosperous times when she lived at Numero Kattervang doose. But it is Becky Sharp still. Her mind, her tact, her power, enlarge according to her circumstances, but her character never develops; the pupils of her green cat's-eyes may expand and contract according to the light, but they are cat's-eyes still. Becky Sharp was crystallized and made perfect by her drunken disreputable father and mother in early years; and whether you find her among drunken art-students, talking *their* slang, or among the dwellers in the gardens of the west, where the golden apples grow, talking *their* slang—whether she does battle with a footman or a marquis—she is still the same dexterous, unprincipled, brilliant, and thoroughly worthless Becky Sharp of old. Any apprentice can make a more or less successful attempt to *develop* a character by circumstances; to make it "grow under his hand," as the slang goes. It required the hand of an almost perfect master to draw a character which politely declined to develop on any terms whatever. A sort of Lot's wife of a character, who, though changed into a pillar of salt, persisted in looking back to Sodom, and, what is more, succeeded in the end in getting back there—if not to the old place itself, at least to the most fashionable quarter of Zoar.

Yes, Rebecca Sharp, although she pitched one overboard for the next man she came across, although she debauched one's moral sense, and played the deuce with one's property, still holds the first place among one's ideal lady-loves. . . .

How we devoured with amazed admiration this new view of life, *Vanity Fair.* How we wondered what kind of man it was who had written these wonderful words—who had poured out a flood of such strange experiences? To a raw boy of eighteen, we can remember that William Makepeace Thackeray was an awful and mysterious personage—a man whose very clothes would have been interesting, even if he himself had not been inside them.

D. H. Stewart (essay date December 1963)

SOURCE: Stewart, D. H. "*Vanity Fair*: Life in the Void." *College English* 25, no. 3 (December 1963): 209-14.

[*In the following essay, Stewart examines the underlying morality of Thackeray's artistic vision.*]

I

Placed in the company of *Madame Bovary* or *Anna Karenina*, *Vanity Fair* appears to lack the art of the first and the profundity of the second. Such comparisons are, however, invidious; they indicate an unwillingness to treat *Vanity Fair* on its own terms. Whatever greatness it has derives not from those features which it shares with other novels but from its unique vision. Uniqueness, after all, is what makes a "classic."

To be sure, *Vanity Fair* is flawed. Every classic is. I believe that the reason why critics today hold it in such low esteem has less to do with its alleged technical incompetence and psychological ineptness than with its failure to supply the resonance or "numina" that we are taught to expect from a novel. By "numen" I do not mean the "in-dwelling spirit" of a literary work (this is the territory of critical spiritualists); rather I mean the noetic activity which transforms the particulars of a novel (indeed, of any work of art) into motifs which are felt to be mysteriously universal because they appear frequently throughout Western literature.

Vanity Fair suffers in our century because it is empirical, not "mythic." It has hardly ever been mistaken for an allegory—in any sense of that much misused term. Things may not be what they seem in *Vanity Fair,* but neither do they set off Bunyanesque or Jungian echoes in our heads; instead, things stand for nothing. Things remain things—an inauspicious sign indeed during a period when we tend to forgive a novelist as hasty, clumsy and at times monotonous as, for example, Dostoevsky if only he arouses a numinous response so that we can speak of his "archetypal" quality, his "mythic dimension."

Vanity Fair wants two things to give it this added resonance: it wants a conjuration of nature and a foreshadowing of future change. Urbanite that he was, Thackeray seems totally uninterested in external nature. Without condescending to snobbery, we may endorse Arthur Quiller-Couch's complaint that Thackeray had never coursed a hare. Some trees were cut once at Queen's Crawley, and there was a little hunting from time to time, but we always watch from inside a manor or a carriage. All one need remember are the hunting scenes in Tolstoy to see how slight Thackeray's concern is. In *Vanity Fair* the years go by without seasons; the sun almost never shines, but there is no rain or snow either. Even the distinction between daylight and dark is insignificant, except insofar as night enables ladies to exhibit their jewels to best advantage in the light of elegant candelabra. The reason for this is obvious: *Vanity Fair* happens indoors—let the men march to Quatre Bras and soak themselves in a cloudburst before Waterloo; we stay snug in Brussels.

Vanity Fair is, of course, a puppet theater, as Thackeray constantly reminds us, an indoor show with paper palms and synthetic grass. It is also a bourgeois world busily burying nature beneath housing projects (St. Adelaide Villas, Anna-Maria Road, West) and ash-heaps. This is why instances when Thackeray attempts to implicate natural law are so rare: once he does it ironically when Lord Steyne accused Becky of fibbing after she pretended to be preparing food for him and not primping before her mirror. Caught, she retorts plaintively,

> "Is it a crime to try and look my best when *you* come here?" . . . and she rubbed her cheek with her handkerchief as if to show there was no rouge at all, only genuine blushes and modesty in her case. About this who can tell? I know there is some rouge that won't come off on a pocket-handkerchief; and some so good that even tears will not disturb it.
>
> (Chap. 48)

These are perhaps the saddest and most pessimistic lines in *Vanity Fair.* That nature (the very physics of rouge) should conspire in such duplicity sounds a near tragic note, more painful than that awful pulsation of tainted blood which runs in the Gaunts and Bareacres— "the dark mark of fate and doom"—which justifies the shocking "stain"-homonym. Most of the time, however, nature abandons men to the synthetic, hot-house world that the bourgeoisie built.

Unlike *Anna Karenina* and like *Madame Bovary,* though for a different reason, *Vanity Fair* lacks a sense of the future. In *Anna Karenina* the moral erosion of the aristocracy together with the rumble of railway trucks leaves no doubt about a coming cataclysm. *Madame Bovary,* on the other hand, is sterile: oriented toward form and structure rather than content, it elucidates an infinite present which echoes neither backward nor forward in time. In *Vanity Fair,* it is as if all of Thackeray's considerable energy were exhausted on the evocation of "now" and "here" as products of "was" and "whence." So absorbed and triumphant is Thackeray in the empirical and moral experience which he calls into being, so thoroughly immersed in social reality as a product of history, that he neglects even to ask the question, What next? Exhaustion everywhere saps the novel's fiber. We see how "was" becomes "is," and we see "is" in all its glorious detail and variety, but there is no

impulse to show that "what is" *must* produce "what shall be." His habit of looking back perhaps deprived Thackeray of the faculty for prediction. Whatever the reasons, the future he implies is little more than endless replications of the present. There is no alternative, no way out.

II

Yet Thackeray suggests ethical issues which more than compensate for his deficiencies. We can think of *Vanity Fair* in the same way that we think about an epic or drama, as a created universe with its own unique infinity. Hegel labelled this the "bad infinity," which is satisfactory aesthetically but defective when contemplated outside the particular work. Just as we can speak of a "bad infinity," if we consider the work metaphysically, so we can speak of what might be called its "bad gospel," if we consider it ethically. Some complete and absolute system of moral values operates within a novel as clearly as its cosmology and system of ideas. While we live in a fictional world, we know not only *that* things exist and *where* they exist; we also know *what they are worth,* hence we can ascribe values as well as definitions.

Although all infinities and gospels in literature are "bad," some are better than others. Complexity, comprehensiveness, and originality all come into play. Hardy's philosophy is not regarded very highly, yet his projection of it in the Wessex novels is sufficiently complex, comprehensive, and original so that he retains the respect and admiration of many. His infinite universe lives and breathes while H. G. Wells's scarcely gasps, although the latter's philosophy probably makes better sense. Too often we must "think" Wells's books instead of "living" them.

Vanity Fair challenges us not by its infinity but by its gospel. The world is a bald *fact*; interest and diversity appear only through the multitude of ethical, human responses to it. What Thackeray saw clearly were the ethical implications of bourgeois reality, which have been examined systematically and made central recently in our thinking largely by Marxists and existentialists. Thackeray, it seems, was either indifferent to or unaware of both the social theory and the systematic philosophical inquiry of his time. All he had was a comfortable, if not comforting, emulsion of eighteenth-century thought which enable him to hold in his head all at once Swift, Fielding, and Goldsmith. I suspect that if the claim that Thackeray had an eighteenth-century mind means anything, it means that the mind most like his was Bernard Mandeville's with its strange combination of savagery and sentiment. Perhaps a firmer commitment to consistent ideas might have saved Thackeray from the flaccid resolution of dilemmas that impairs much of his later work, but in *Vanity Fair* his commitment is not merely sufficient but prophetically right. It is as if he knew beforehand what Simone de Beauvoir testified to:

> I remember having felt a great calm in reading Hegel in the impersonal setting of the Bibliothèque Nationale, in August 1940. But when I found myself again in the street, in my life, outside the system, under a real sky, the system was no longer any use to me: it was, under the pretext of the infinite, the consolations of death which it had offered me; and I still wanted to live in the midst of living men.

What does this mean for *Vanity Fair*? It means first that the moral center of the book is not a principle that can be formulated; it is precisely the evolving situation in which conventional moral principles are repeatedly reversed and inverted so that one never reaches a resolution. Having read *Vanity Fair,* how is one "edified" or "instructed?" Toward what course is one moved? Unanswerable questions, I think; for Thackeray never challenges with ideas. There is no metaphysical concern. Above and beyond particulars, there is only an emptiness—abhorrent alike to the Christian and the pagan idealists of our own time. Things, they insist, must mean *something*.

In order that our aesthetic and moral responses will coincide, Thackeray contrives vicarious experiences for us that contradict each other. On one page we discover that Becky never blushes, and a few pages later she does; Dobbin never fibs, Thackeray tells us several times, yet Dobbin does fib more than once. How are we to understand these contradictions? Either we nourish an exasperation which, if prolonged, sours into antagonism and leads to the accusation that Thackeray sometimes forgets and sometimes prevaricates; or we say: why of course, people and our knowledge of them are in the large sense wholly untrustworthy, and we are perhaps startled that Thackeray not only sees this but renders it by continuously subverting our convictions about everything. He makes our certainties equal to the margin of our errors.

Thackeray lies, cheats, dissembles, suppresses information. All right, let him. He gives us a world that reflects honestly the real world—which certainly deceives us quite as often, quite as blatantly. A better wisdom than that which condemns his contradictions would express gratitude to Thackeray for making it difficult after reading *Vanity Fair* to deceive oneself into believing he was ever quite undeceived. We are hoaxed and defrauded again and again by the showman in his belled cap, yet we assume he believes in truth and strives to reveal it to us, so we listen intently, accept the reality before us, keep faith, but can never finally close our ears to the intolerable clack and squeak of the marionettes. A wretched, bitter, futile game indeed.

Thus the emptiness, the void is borne in upon us; and it is given still greater weight by the consciousness of death in *Vanity Fair* which is nearly continuous. So many people die, but die so naturally, that one sometimes forgets how close Thackeray stands to the grave. Consider, for example, the memorable opening of the novel's eighteenth installment (Chap. 61):

> . . . As you ascend the staircase of your house from the drawing towards the bedroom floors, you may have remarked a little arch in the wall right before you, which at once gives light to the stair, which leads from the second story to the third (where the nursery and servants' chambers commonly are) and serves for another purpose of utility, of which the undertaker's men can give you a notion. They rest the coffins upon that arch, or pass them through it so as not to disturb in any unseemly manner the cold tenant slumbering within the black ark.
>
> That second-floor arch in a London house, looking up and down the well of the staircase, and commanding the main thoroughfare by which the inhabitants are passing; by which Cook lurks down before daylight to scour her pots and pans in the kitchen; by which young Master stealthily ascends, having left his boots in the hall, and let himself in after dawn from a jolly night at the Club; down which Miss comes rustling in fresh ribbons and spreading muslins, brilliant and beautiful, and prepared for conquest and the ball; or Master Tommy slides, preferring the banisters for a mode of conveyance, and disdaining danger and the stair; down which the mother is fondly carried smiling in her strong husband's arms, as he steps steadily step by step, and followed by the monthly nurse, on the day when the medical man has pronounced that the charming patient may go downstairs; up which John lurks to bed yawning, with a sputtering tallow candle, and to gather up before sunrise the boots which are awaiting him in the passages;—that stair, up or down which babies are carried, old people are helped, guests are marshalled to the ball, the parson walks to the christening, the doctor to the sick-room, and the undertaker's men to the upper floor—what a memento of Life, Death, and Vanity it is—that arch and stair—if you choose to consider it, and sit on the landing, looking up and down the well! The doctor will come up to us too for the last time there, my friend in motley. The nurse will look in at the curtains, and you take no notice—and then she will fling open the windows for a little, and let in the air. Then they will pull down all the front blinds of the house and live in the back rooms-then they will send for the lawyer and other men in black, etc. . . .

Life transformed into a miniature, jejune novel! Yet the trace of whimsy that colors it makes everything sinister. Sit on the landing! Look up and down the well! And then if we *do* "choose to consider it," what we come out with is little more than the grim "etc.," which, I suggest, is the morality of the void. It is hardly a sentimental, Victorian *memento mori*.

The second thing that the existential rather than metaphysical orientation means for *Vanity Fair* is that everything is rooted in and defined by its history. Existentialists celebrate an acute consciousness of looking backward from the vehicle of time that hurls them into an unknown future. Thackeray's vision is similar but restricted, for his "reminiscential method" generally minimizes our sense of the future. The striking digression on the demise of stage coaches, at the end of the novel's seventh chapter, could serve as an epigraph here because it hints at Thackeray's constant fascination with genealogy and exhibits both his "science of names," which is so often historical as well as satiric, and his endless references to greying hair and the dyes that remedy it, to facial lines too cunning even for the rouge pot. The very stone rusts on the faces of buildings in *Vanity Fair.* Antique portraits glower from every wall; the first Queen Elizabeth is our contemporary; boys and girls live half choked by old dust. Clocks and watches tick across the novel, but they tell no time. Instead, they are status symbols or valuta for bribes. Thus the novel's ethic is felt to be defined by a past in which everything has already happened, good and evil; and nothing can be done to keep everything from happening over again.

This, I think, is one quality of the experience we get from *Vanity Fair.* As if to spite our meaningless vision of the dumbshow of history, Thackeray willed into existence a miraculous, crooked mirror which first warps the crazy contortions of reality into a seemingly coherent and objective picture and then retards time so that for once we can see things and the values attached to them in slow motion. To put it another way, he thrusts us into a world where everything is relative and fluctuating; then he supplies a rubber yardstick and says, "Measure!" One difference between *Vanity Fair* and the fictional world of Camus is that in Camus the word "measure" is interrogative, not imperative. I think it is this imperative that accounts for *Vanity Fair*'s peculiar urgency: hope remains even if faith has vanished, but of course it is this faithless hope that keeps the puppet-theater open.

The existential tendency means a third thing in *Vanity Fair.* It means that Thackeray's infamous "ambivalence" becomes essential to the book's power. We can explain it as the product of unresolved dilemmas brought from Thackeray's private life into his works; or we can explain it as an accurate reflection of the essential ambivalence in nineteenth-century bourgeois society. These are good explanations, as far as they go; but one may press further and say that Thackeray has dramatized, prophetically, the disintegration of *all* fixed value systems and the substitution for them of both money and, more important, power—power derived from individual willed expedience. Becky is the Napoleonic paradigm, harbinger of the modern return to barbarity in which any nonentity with sufficient reserves of energy and instinctive cunning can will himself onto any throne and there dictate whatever system of values, whatever justice he may choose. If not a queen herself,

she could be consort to every ruling brigand in the modern world. Becky conspires with the world to define good and evil just as I do. When she wins, her definitions prevail; when I win, mine do.

There is, it seems to me, something terrible in our plodding, skeptical, tearful Thackeray that few have seen and fewer accepted. It is not his "irresolution" but this, that Becky *would* have been good with £5000 per year; that is, she could, with £5000, have built round herself a society in which *she* defined value. By simply excluding competitive moralities, she would have defined the one applying in her world. We have witnessed so many coteries, so many whole nations which have contrived to exist for a decade, or a century, or an age, yet whose values are patently illusory and false. Our own may be one, for all we know. But falseness is irrelevant. The fact is, they exist; they live; they rule. This is the terror. With wide-eyed bewilderment, Thackeray meditated upon a world in which a dozen mistaken moralities plunged like wild horses in a corral containing hysterical children whose one conviction was that safety lay in being astride. But which horse? From which could a sturdy rider subdue the rest? Thackeray did not know. Perhaps he did not need to since, of course, brute violence had not yet driven off his saving compassion. We have not yet reached Sartre's world when he portrays the dedicated partisan burned and disembowelled by uniformed maniacs in a cellar and then asks, Where are your values now, kind friend, when you are alone, betrayed, convinced of defeat, Godless and dying in agony? Not this far; yet the moral vacuum which produces such things is everywhere felt.

Where are right and justice in *Vanity Fair*? In fatuous Amelia? the spooney Dobbin? shrewd Becky? Or is there even some criterion in Thackeray's mind as there was in Flaubert's when he scorned his heroine and her world from the viewpoint of the *intelligentsia*? I believe not, for even if we were willing to assert that a spirit of compassion animates the book, we should immediately declare it is too diffident to be efficacious, especially when we compare it with Tolstoy's providential compassion which bestows dignity even upon pets and gamebirds. In Thackeray every value is somewhere negated. All that one is left with is the excruciating *Geworfenheit* of man (the being thrown) into the stream of time.

This is why the truest gesture Thackeray ever made was slamming the lid shut on his puppets at the end—to the dismay and aggravation of most critics. Mr. J. Y. T. Greig's outcry imitates many:

> Here is the most infuriating paradox of all. . . . He can put men and women on their legs and endow them with vitality; and this, after all, is the one essential gift of the novelist. . . . And Thackeray was so perverse

that he did not seem to value what the gods in their magnanimity had bestowed on him. The miracle of creation once performed, he would set about spoiling it. He had little reverence for his own creations; he would treat them either as a manufactured article, or when the fancy took him, as a moral emblem.

(*Thackeray, A Reconsideration,* OUP., 1950, p. 112.)

But this is the whole point, the origin of our dread in *Vanity Fair.* Thackeray *willed* these living, three-dimensional human beings into existence, breathed life into them, compelled our eyes to believe in their reality as surely as we believe in our own. But then the inevitable and infallible Thackerayan grimace, and bang! the box goes shut. Our pretty follies must end—including our art. Surely the author who will calumniate Empire and Church, impugn even that Supreme Power to whom Amelia prayed, mock men and men's works and men's mores—such an author will mock men's art too. The inflated value placed on art by Flaubert and Yeats is little more than a desperate modern prejudice, however comforting. What Thackeray seems to ask is this: who are we, for all our talent and energy, to presume that either our creations or we ourselves are of much worth? We may be men; but we are also, sadly, only instruments—sometimes highly specialized, as for example when we are artists. And the show, after all, is an old one.

Vanity Fair is a great book because, for one thing, it disciplines and chastens not only the pride of the reader but the pride of the artist as well. It is not a very romantic book and for this reason perhaps difficult for twentieth-century readers, as *Rasselas* is. For Thackeray, the past existed independently of his mind and deserved his reverence for its achievements and lessons. He had an obligation of honesty toward the past which shows up in the fidelity of his representations and the moment-by-moment justice of his judgments. For the romantic, the past exists in and for himself and deserves his affection for the thrill or escape it seems to provide. His obligation is to elaborate and communicate this subjective thrill. This was not Thackeray's way. If it is true that he shares with other great writers the distinction of being god-like, then Thackeray is unique in being a god with a troubled conscience. In *Vanity Fair,* he dramatized the absurdity of creation as well as being. It is a gospel with terrible relevance.

Ann Y. Wilkinson (essay date September 1965)

SOURCE: Wilkinson, Ann Y. "The Tomeavesian Way of Knowing the World: Technique and Meaning in *Vanity Fair.*" *ELH* 32, no. 3 (September 1965): 370-87.

[*In the following essay, Wilkinson analyzes Thackeray's use of gossip as a narrative technique. Wilkinson asserts that the pervasive cynicism in* Vanity Fair, *embodied in the attitudes of its narrator and principal characters, reflects Thackeray's view that human behavior is fundamentally inconsistent and unreliable.*]

> And here, haply a great man coming up, Tom Eaves's hat would drop off his head, and he would rush forward with a bow and a grin, which showed that he knew the world too—in the Tomeavesian way, that is.[1]

The "Tomeavesian way of knowing the world" in *Vanity Fair* needs definition, an exercise which promises more than diversion, for upon an understanding of it depends the justification and explanation of many problems, critical and moral, which have plagued and annoyed readers of the novel since its publication. The phrase calls into question the problem of technique in the novel—point of view, structure, tone, texture—and, since technique is ultimately always a way of seeing, organizing the shapeless mass of experience, mental and "actual," the Tomeavesian way of knowing the world, and thus organizing it, calls into question also the meaning and morality of *Vanity Fair.* One may point out here, for more discussion later, that it is important to emphasize the two distinct types of experience just mentioned, mental and "actual," because the total "experience" of the book, for the reader, includes *the process of organizing the world by the narrator,* as this process goes on before our eyes, as well as the more ordinary materials of fiction, the "scenes" and "panorama" that make up the story itself. Really to be involved in the novel, for the reader, is not to be "bounced" into the world of Regency London, as E. M. Forster has it,[2] because in fact we get relatively little of that sort of experience at first hand here, but rather it means being enticed into the labyrinth of the narrator's memory and of his mental processes by the thread of Becky's story, and then trying to find the man-eating Becky at the center of the maze. She escapes us finally; the thread is snapped, and she is cut off from us, in all her undoubted vitality, forever, while we are left stranded in the narrator's mind. What we are left with is not an understanding of the characters of Becky, Amelia, and the rest, but a way of seeing the world—all that is implied in the "Tomeavesian way."

To begin the definition: Thackeray is speaking in the passage quoted of that way of knowing the world which consists in knowing the secrets, especially the discreditable ones, of great men, and in "giving them credit"—in the financial sense when necessary, but in the moral (or immoral) and social sense always—on the basis of this secret knowledge. That this secret knowledge exists and is recognized in the novel is of course the basis for the charge of cynicism against Thackeray, but the cynicism goes deeper even than this, so deep that ultimately its usefulness in guiding the attitude of the reader is lost because its own sources are confused. That is, this secret knowledge not only exists, and not only forms the basis of social credit, so that though Virtue is worth exactly nothing a year in Vanity Fair a poor man, like a great one, can live very well on nothing a year if only he can get credit, literally, for living a grand enough discreditable life; in addition to this, which is cynical enough, another twist in the maze brings home to us the astonishing and dismaying fact that this "secret knowledge" need not be knowledge, and therefore believable, at all, any more than the virtuous façade is believable. The fact is that it does not matter in the least whether one is guilty or not (the presence of guilt ensuring credit) so long as *Rumor* has it that one is guilty. This is cynicism twice compounded, and worse confounded, for what, with this kind of ethic operating in the Fair, are we to make of the appeal for our sympathy when Rawdon Crawley asserts that if Becky wasn't guilty, she was as good as guilty—which is worse? Truth recedes behind Rumor in Vanity Fair until its very existence is not believed in, or, worse, not valued so much as the rumor. Even if the truth asserted the vice of the person involved, this knowledge would remain valueless unless Rumor were added; credit exists only in so far as Rumor of viciousness exists. It is not only that Virtue is worth nothing a year in the world of the Fair, but that Truth unrumored, whether of virtue or vice, is worth nothing. Everyone and his credit exist only in so far as there is gossip about him.

This brings us to another obvious sense of "credit" which is pertinent here: if Thackeray speaks of Tom's cynical way of knowing the world, he clearly lays himself open to that same charge, for Tom, in rushing off to bow and scrape before the great man, terminates a conversation in which Thackeray the narrator has picked up most of his information about Gaunt House and its goings on, and thus his way of knowing the world is not so direct as Tom's here, but is reliant upon second hand evidence and, worse, Rumor. If Tom—and people like Raggles—give credit for the rumor which their own eavesdropping seems to confirm, Thackeray for the most part credits Rumor without confirmation, for he looks in on notoriously few scenes, but reports innumerable conversations with a whole corps and network of Tom Eaveses.

The problem I wish to lay out is this: to say that Thackeray is a gossip is a commonplace, but to examine that commonplace is to enter into the complexities of technique and vision in the novel: what does the technique of gossip require or make necessary in the matter of point of view, scene versus panorama, to use Percy Lubbock's terms,[3] structure, character of the narrator *vis à vis* his friends and enemies in the novel, the novelist's—and the narrator's—concern for Truth as opposed to a good story? Finally, this questioning of technique requires the questioning of the nature of Truth itself in the world of the Fair, and *the value of this truth* if it is

ever reached. The crucial and far-reaching issues of the book lie beyond the surface of the style, which is variously cynical, snickering, urbane, sneering, pococurantist, sympathetic or sentimental, but always glossy enough to keep us effectively out of the world it describes; it, like the figure of the narrator, becomes a barrier which keeps us looking over at scenes in a middle and far distance where we cannot see what "really" is going on, and whose "reality" therefore, for us, is in the second-hand and third-or fourth-hand reports we get through the narrator of what is happening.

The experience of reading such a novel makes us accomplices of the gossiping narrator rather than privileged observers shifted into the most advantageous position for seeing the all that is there, if not yet the all that is not there. Our unspoken trust in the writer is based on the assumption that he will, indeed, let us see all that is there, not trying to trick us in some violation of the convention of fiction. If he "sees" little and reports a great deal, how are we to know what is going on at all if we cannot assume his integrity in reporting at least what he sees, hears, and knows? Yet in the relatively few "scenes" there are we do not always feel that the author is in control; indeed, suspicion is bound to arise that if he *is* in control he is not entirely truthful. The quality of our participation in the world of *Vanity Fair,* in so far as "scenes" bring it to life, is that of accomplices to a master eavesdropper, as opposed, say, to the direct, dramatic participation in the world of Dickens' novels, or the reflective, philosophically grounded participation in the world of George Eliot's novels. Fielding, Thackeray's teacher in the novel, makes us spectators, but not accomplices. We see what he sees when he is looking at the scene, and we hear him discourse about it; if he is keeping information from us, he never tells us that he doesn't know what is going on, so that we can trust what he *does* tell us. With Thackeray, however, we find not so much that we are being kept in deliberate suspense but that he himself does not know quite what has happened.

That we are eavesdroppers more than spectators in the world of Vanity Fair means: a) that the events going forward are insignificant, mattering little to the course of the world whether they are known or not; or b) that *we* are insignificant, not meant to know what goes on in this world; or c) that if the events *are* significant, and we too are important, these events still are no business of ours and we have no right to be there. In any case there is no continuity of responsibility or sympathy, in reader as in author, except what little, very little, is suggested by our desire to look in on the behind-the-scenes affairs of possibly discreditable people. In all of these alternatives the technique of gossip appears to denigrate and diminish the issues the fictional world presents to us, and to damage the values of fiction as well. And we can even measure the degree of denigration, as we get the eavesdroppers' reports at further and further removes.

I suggest that instead of accepting any of these alternatives and their consequences we must look at the technique of gossip itself as significant to the meaning of the novel, rather than as a troublesome hindrance to the progress of the story; as, moreover, accounting reasonably for many of the inconsistencies, moral and technical, which have been noted in the novel; as, finally, offering by its very nature a new kind of dramatic and even epistemological experience to the reader.

Thackeray's point of view in the novel is usually called omniscient. Professor Tillotson says that it is the point of view of the historian whose tale "is given out unmistakably as history, as merely a further piece of the history everybody is already familiar with." And he points out that in *The Newcomes* the narrator does liken himself to an historian reconstructing the past—but an historian with a creative license.[4] The narrator of *The Newcomes* explains:

> . . . so, in the present volumes, where dialogues are written down, which the reporter could by no possibility have heard, and where motives are detected which the persons actuated by them certainly never confided to the writer, the public must once for all be warned that the author's individual fancy very likely supplies much of the narrative; and that he forms it as best he may, out of stray papers, conversations reported to him, and his knowledge, right or wrong, of the characters of the persons engaged. And, as is the case with the most orthodox histories, the writer's own guesses or conjectures are printed in exactly the same type as the most ascertained patent facts. I fancy, for my part, that the speeches attributed to Clive, the Colonel, and the rest, are as authentic as the orations in Sallust or Livy, and only implore the truth-loving public to believe that incidents here told, and which passed very probably without witnesses, were either confided to me subsequently as compiler of this biography, or are of such a nature that they must have happened from what we know happened after. . . . You tell your tales as you can, and state the facts as you think they must have been. . . . Blunders there must be in the best of these narratives, and more asserted than they can possibly know or vouch for.
>
> (Ch. XXIV)

This position is perfectly legitimate, for it is not Thackeray, ostensibly, who is telling the tale, but Pen, who is reconstructing as best he may the "history" of the Newcomes. And fiction masquerading as history is nothing new or objectionable. But this same "historian" closes his "history" with this total betrayal to the truth of even made-up history:

> But for you, dear friend, it is as you like. You may settle your fable-land in your own fashion. Anything you like happens in fable-land. Wicked folks die apropos . . .—annoying folks are got out of the way; the poor are rewarded—the upstarts are set down in fable-land. . . .

"Anything you like" does not happen in history, though it may in fableland. But we have read the entire novel with the assumption that Pen knows either what happened or what "must have happened from what we know happened after. . . ." Now it seems that nothing at all happened after, except what *we* supply in fancy, and therefore perhaps nothing at all happened at all. In any case, even if Pen had been historian to the end, the situation is different in *Vanity Fair,* where we have a nameless voice, but one not speaking as an historian, as Professor Tillotson would have it, but as a gossip, a teller of a good tale that happened some time ago. If he were really posing as an historian, he could by no means drop all the veils he does, and have his pen refuse to tell, or even ask the reader, "Who knows . . . ?" Apparently, sometimes he knows and sometimes he doesn't, but we have no way of knowing when this historian is being capricious and when he is being incompetent. Thus the claiming of the role of historian for Thackeray the novelist does him no service, for he must be a most amateurish and temperamental, not to say unethical, historian who would play with the truth of his story as this one does.

Neither does Professor Tillotson's assertion that the narrator is concerned above all with truth do him a service: "The 'person writing,' whose presence is felt everywhere in the novels, is a person interested in being truthful—that is the first thing, and almost the last, to say about his authorial character."[5] Again, Thackeray himself offers an assertion of his truthfulness: "I ask you to believe that this person writing strives to tell the truth. If there is not that, there is nothing," he says in his Preface to *Pendennis* [*The History of Pendennis*], and in *Vanity Fair* he solemnly asserts that "the moralist . . . is bound to speak the truth as far as [he] knows it . . . and a deal of disagreeable matter must come out in the course of such an undertaking" (Ch. VIII). But assertion is not demonstration by any means, and, moreover, he is untruthful even in making this assertion, for on every page he stops to talk with Brown and Jones and Hob and Nob and Tom Eaves, and takes away from these little gossips the material of his story, without further confirmation or apology. And if he were really interested in being truthful above all, he wouldn't, one repeats, drop the veil so often or, as in the "discovery" scene, profess complete ignorance of the guilt or innocence of what he nevertheless feels free to term a "corrupt heart." Either he has prejudged Becky and found her corrupt without evidence, in which case he is hardly truthful, even in intention, or he knows that she is guilty, in which case he also fails of truthfulness to the reader.

Nor can the narrator be called "omniscient" in other aspects. The omniscient pose allows a narrator free access into all minds and all places. He has, in a manner of speaking, 360 degrees of vision and complete mobility, with the added strength of being able to move the reader with him as he shifts positions. But this narrator of *Vanity Fair* often cannot see into minds and often cannot move from place to place.

In fact, the narrator of *Vanity Fair* is not historian, nor a lover of truth, nor in any real sense omniscient, though it is part of his pose to like to seem so at times. He is, simply, a gossip who is telling a story he has gleaned largely through gossiping with other eavesdroppers, who report the scene to him perhaps even at third or fourth hand, since they too, like the narrator, are to be supposed gossiping all the time. Moreover, a gossip, in this like an historian, is telling a story everyone is more or less familiar with, but, unlike an historian, is allowed all the vagaries and capriciousnesses, even the prejudgments, he likes to have in the telling. And he is not above all interested in the truth, but in the telling of a good story, with as much suggestiveness as he can put in without entirely ruining his own reputation.

In this process of suggestive relation of a story which he is putting together from a whole network of gossiping acquaintance, what happens is that reality is refracted and removed even further—that is, further from the reader than the narrator himself—with the result that perhaps the only reality we finally know in *Vanity Fair* is what little inheres in a bit of gossip. And it is not only we who are limited to this kind of reality, but, we soon see, the characters in the novel itself, whose actions in the Fair are all based on Rumor. Becky is named corrupt first in an "awful kitchen inquisition," and apparently the narrator needs no other information. After all, whether in "reality" she is or is not guilty, the fact is that if she had not the reputation of possible guilt she would not make her way in *Vanity Fair*. Pragmatically speaking, she does not exist for the people in the Fair unless a Rumor exists of her guilt, actual or potential; so, whether it is real or not, it is yet effectively the moving force in Becky's career. In this queer dissociation and transformation, actual, substantial reality becomes insubstantial, unreal, uneffective, while what is in actuality unreal and insubstantial becomes a moving force and therefore a reality. In what way, then, do Becky, Lord Steyne, and Amelia exist? And do they exist in the same way? And how are we, the readers, to know them, and to judge the vision which creates them? These are crucial questions for the novel, and we cannot answer them if we assume that Thackeray and his narrator are always the same person.

With the traditional assumption that writer and narrator are identical, we have no choice but to see Thackeray as incompetent, dishonest, or at least dismayingly two-sided in his personality,[6] an artist who can create a scene, let us look in on it, and then beg off when a crucial question of the nature of a character is urgently raised. Where does this leave us, the readers, if this is the case? Guilty for looking in on something that is none of our affair and that we can't ever know the truth of? Implicated as being as malicious as the world of *Vanity Fair* for assuming even the subject of Becky's possible guilt to be adultery? More likely, it would leave us simply angry and dismayed at Thackeray's own confusions and evasions. For he has wanted here to have things two ways: Becky is to be implicated by Thackeray's own gossip (and ours), just as if it were the world and not the observer of the world who is gossiping, and at the same time Thackeray is to appear generous and openminded by leaving the whole question not only unanswered, but unanswerable.

Moreover, if Tom Eaves is to be sniggered at for social hypocrisy, for rushing forward with a bow and a grin at the approach of a great man, what are we to think of Thackeray, who has gotten the most enjoyment out of Becky, who has used her to show up the pretensions and vices of the social world, who has put into her mouth sympathetically the crucial remark that "I could be a good woman too on 5,000 pounds a year,"[7] who has shown her parodying society and taking a fool for what she can get—and then turns on her and warns the reader against this monster who curls her tail around the slime of corpses? What has been Becky's crime if not the presumption of an outsider to get into society, especially since she cannot understand what else she should or could do, given her superior talents and brains? What is her punishment but the leaguing of Thackeray with the society which has thus been assaulted by this upstart and the necessary chastisement of the intruder by the insiders? To say she is punished because she is a bad woman, as Thackeray, by main force, makes her, is mistaken, because, on the evidence of our own eyes, and with Thackeray's own sudden relinquishment of control, we do not in fact know if Becky is guilty or not. To punish her for being "just as good as guilty" as Rawdon does and Thackeray does, is surely to be more vicious than to give her credit for being guilty even if she is not, as Raggles does.

And as Tom Eaves would sacrifice anything he owns to dine with Becky, so does Thackeray sacrifice control of his novel to dine with Becky. He is forced to insist that Amelia, uninteresting as her life is and her mind is, is better and more entertaining for the reader than that vicious Becky. Because, however, this is in fact not so, Thackeray again gets "credit" for thinking the right things while in fact he is enjoying Becky's antics in the social world, and enjoying her skill and wit in having the *haut monde* to dine with her on nothing a year.

This will not do, though it has been the assumption of most readers of the novel. It simply destroys the work, except as a flawed and often dismaying work of genius. Even G. Armour Craig's most useful and valid observations on the style of **Vanity Fair** only palliate this situation without justifying it. Of the evasive account of the marriage of Becky and Rawdon he says:

> The concealment of the circumstances of the marriage may appeal to the lazy, and satisfy the benevolent, and it may give the sarcastic something to work on too. But its most important effect is that the narration here, clustered about with confidential comments and dismissive questions, sets before us a way of knowing the world. It is a way so inferential, so dependent upon unfinished implications, that it comes close to the character of a gossip. And a good gossip, while its unfinished sentences and its discreet and indiscreet omissions may keep us from the exhilaration of indignation or rhapsody, can suggest values and insights superior to the vocabulary of the purveyor or the listener.[8]

This is true and, so far as a narrative technique goes, as legitimate as Pen's pose as an historian. We assume in this case that the gossip knows what has happened and how, but wants to retail it in this typically gossipy, eye-winking way. It is when he *doesn't know,* yet *must* know, as in the discovery scene, that the technique of gossip as adopted by Thackeray himself utterly breaks down. Our confidence is gone. He doesn't know at all what has happened, yet has judged her. This makes him vicious or stupid, or both, and leaves us at sea for the rest of the novel. It is true that the sobering comment by the narrator that this Bankruptcy is the end of Becky's schemes puts the matter in its proper perspective, as Professor Craig points out: the terms of financial enterprise used to describe the moral collapse suggest the "terrible irresolution of a society in which market values and moral values are discontinuous and separate."[9] This is an enlightening observation, but it should go one step further: the terrible thing is not that the market values and moral values are discontinuous and separate (that is horrible enough, but it is an intermediate position): what is so appalling is that they are in fact identical in a new way. Ideally, a man's social worth should mirror his moral stature; then in a materialistic society, the two values separate and have no continuity or connection; then, as a further step in disintegration, moral value is simply equivalent to financial value; it is quantitatively measured and can be described in financial terms, as it is here. Becky is bankrupted. She has lost credit. What kind of credit? Does she lose credit literally, financially, (from Raggles) because her moral credit is gone? No, because she would not have gotten credit from Raggles if she *had* moral credit to begin with. Does she lose moral credit because her financial credit suddenly collapsed? No, because so far as the world of the novel goes, she is not generally thought to have had any to begin with, and so far as we go, we simply cannot tell what has happened. Here, at the crux of the novel, the narrator's moral vision is entirely confused. If that narrator is Thackeray himself, then the validity of the entire work can be held in question, undercut by this collapse in technique.

But let us suppose that it is not Thackeray who is the narrator here. Suppose it is a gossip created just for the purpose? From this point of view, the idea that the circumstantial style suggests an "inferential" way of knowing the world makes complete sense and adds a new dimension to the technique of the novel. For Thackeray the man may know the world inferentially, but Thackeray the novelist must know at least what he wants to put into a scene. If he fails here, he fails utterly, as in the discovery scene just mentioned. But if what Thackeray the novelist wants to put into the scene is the difficulty of a created onlooker—and the reader placed there with him, or listening to him—has in inferring the truth and reality of a scene, then he has succeeded perfectly. The gossip cannot know anything; even what he sees with his own eyes is subject to the secret knowledge of other eavesdroppers whose own point of view must add an immediate distortion. The very business of a gossip is to thread his way through a mass of entangled circumstances, knowing (though not necessarily caring) that it is impossible to know everything about any character, any action, any motive; knowing moreover that circumstances may be contradictory though coexistant, and that the reality which lies behind these circumstances eludes the grasp of the onlooker and is anyway not essential to a good story, which functions better by means of a little detail with a lot of suggestion. Further, the true gossip, for all his petty malices and talkiness and meddlesomeness, yet does not commit the ultimate presumption of the omniscient novelist: he doesn't presume to know everything; in fact, he begs off from the really crucial issue of motivation and morality, though his opinion may well be that Becky is "corrupt," whether she is innocent or not.

Technically, this device works just as well as that of historian to fulfill what was apparently one of Thackeray's consistent intentions in his fiction: to remove the reader from actual participation in the "scenes" of his work, perhaps because he felt safer that way, perhaps because the scene-making talent is not preeminently his. To this end he does here what he does also in other novels: sets his novel in a past which is unarguable but over which he can reminisce, making use of "half-scenes," "interjections," bits of dialogue to support dramatically what he has been saying reflectively, and so on.[10] In fact, the device of the gossip works best of all, in this respect, because here we must listen, for the most part, to a narrator who stands between us and a clear view of the scene, but also to his reportage of what other gossips have told him. Because this is so eminently true for much of the novel, we come almost to feel that the whole thing exists essentially in the narrator's mind, insofar as we have to rely on its vagaries and memories and all its other movements for our point of view. And even when he is reporting other gossips, it is mainly for the purpose of *suggesting* how a character is known in the world of the Fair, rather than in fact for the purpose of offering any real difference in judgment. The narrator in these reportings of other "points of view" *seems* to be gathering up all manner of information so as to come at the reality of the situation. But this is not so. In this he is unlike George Eliot, who, though no gossip, is just as concerned with the problems of how her characters structure reality and, omniscient as she is, must still not structure reality as any one of them does, but accumulate it by entering each separate point of view as an element making up a total reality. Rather, the effect of these reportings of the eponymous Tom Eaves (and all the Browns, Joneses and Smiths who meet in the clubs and streets of the city)[11] is that of suggesting a multiplicity of points of view, and the effect of this, in turn, is to suggest that the truth is simply not known by any single observer, including the narrator. In practice, however, the narrator essentially only reports the gossip of people who support *his* point of view. But the theoretical multiplicity of points of view and judgments of character and action allows for the credibility of the technique of redoubling—necessary in any case with the parallel lines of the two stories and the inevitably slow advancement of the linear movements because of the shortness of the monthly number.

This redoubling is frequently attended by a shift in the attitude of the narrator: from the cavalier, even cynical, witty, urbane tone of the man of the world who does not suffer fools gladly, to the sentimental, duty-conscious, home-loving, emotional tone of the domestic creature who does suffer fools gladly—since Amelia, judged by the urbane Thackeray, could only be called a fool, and not a very interesting one at that. This shift in tone, however it may correspond to a personality split in Thackeray himself (though I think we do not pay enough attention to his statements elsewhere as to the silliness of Amelia and her view of the world),[12] is still not justifiable in terms of the artistic integrity of the novel if we assume that Thackeray himself is the narrator. But if we assume that the narrator is a created *persona,* a gossip, then the tone shift is possible and even appropriate to the narrative position. Thackeray himself need not be held to blame for these shifts in tone (even though he may have felt them himself) because he has provided a suitable vehicle artistically for them. And he need not be held to blame for lapses in information at crucial times; the *persona* can ask with perfect blamelessness, "Is she guilty?" because though he tells the story as if he knew "all about it," this is the nature of a gossip, and when he fails to know, we know that he is just another figure in the world of the Fair, and must therefore be as remote as anyone else from the real inner motivations of the characters in his story. No one knows the truth about people in the Fair, and no one cares, because with the values that rule the Fair Rumor is worth more than truth, as being evidence of social importance.

If this is so, the novel becomes a kind of existential document, in the way that "My Last Duchess" is. It is an experience[13] which takes place in the reading of the novel, with the reader involved in half-truths, malice, and sentiment, and left just as frustrated as the *persona* is in his inept attempts to get at what is really happening. This would not be to say that Thackeray as novelist has no moral vision, no judgments to make, any more than Browning has no moral judgments of the Duke. But these will not be expected of the *persona,* the gossip, who notoriously shifts his grounds and changes his mind as more or less of the total picture is available to him, and indeed as the vagaries of his own personality seem to lead him. It is not to be expected of this character any more than it is to be expected of Browning's Duke that he is in a position to deliver the moral judgments of Browning himself. In this sense, the whole of the novel is a monologue, much of it the direct reminiscence, asides, conjectures, or descriptions of the *persona,* the rest of it taking place with the monologue suspended and the *persona* standing by (but still hovering about the scene, threatening to break in with tidbits and asides even then, and certainly thrusting into the scene his normative adjectives) with the reader, watching a scene which will either support his gossip or will give him evidence for new gossip. The idea that the narration is a kind of dramatic monologue may be supported, ironically, by the otherwise maddening and damaging imagery of the puppeteer and his puppets, for the *persona*-narrator can fancy himself such a showman—it is his justification for telling "a good story" that he imagines himself to be in control of, though manifestly he is not; but Thackeray cannot use this image without destroying the validity of his work completely, and in any case it is not borne out by the vitality and complexity of the world of his novel.

The problem we are faced with in this view of the narrative technique of *Vanity Fair,* is one of judgment: how shall we have this world and the people in it? Can we assume that the righteousness and the malice, the pious judgments and the "betrayal" of Becky by the narrator, have nothing to do with Thackeray himself? If this is a dramatic monologue, is it true here, as Professor Langbaum has its connection with the poetic dramatic monologue of the nineteenth century, that "judgment is largely psychologized and historicized," so that in judging of the characters, and more, of the narrator's inconsistent account of them, we "adopt a man's point of view and the point of view of his age in order to judge him—which makes the judgment relative, limited in applicability to the particular conditions of the case"? If this is true, does it follow also that the kind of monologue-novel which is *Vanity Fair* is, by reason of its relativity of judgment, "an appropriate form for an empiricist and relativist age, an age which has come to consider value as an evolving thing dependent upon the changing individual and social requirements of the historical process," an age in which "judgment can never be final," requiring always to be "checked against fact, which comes before judgment and remains always more certain"?[14] The answer, I think, is that this explanation helps us to understand the existence of the *persona* in the first place. Thackeray's own views are not relative and empiricist, but those of the age largely were, in practice if not in protestation. His own traditional judgments do not fit the intuitively realized world of his novel, and because they do not he cannot himself function in that world, but must create the kind of narrator in whom inconsistency and bafflement and relativism will not seem to be hypocrisy or simply a flawed understanding of the world. The narrator's way of seeing the world contains all of these inconsistencies, and this, we come to see, is not because Thackeray is two-faced or bungling, but because, as we know on the evidence of our own eyes, the "facts" themselves in this world are never certain. Not only is judgment here always relative, but the more disturbing point is that it is almost impossible in this world to check judgment against fact, because the facts are removed and refracted. What we judge, ultimately, is not Becky or Amelia so much as it is the narrator himself, and here, if our judgment is "psychologized and historicized," we must judge him against the "facts" of this world, which are precisely this, that no facts are clearly discernible. It is perhaps for this reason that so much argument outside the novel is possible as to the judgments made of the characters inside the novel.

I am not trying to say that Thackeray has no moral vision, or that his moral vision does not enter the novel. I think it *does* enter, but I am fairly sure it does not *control* the world of the novel. Yet there are times certainly when the judgments of the *persona* must be those of Thackeray. One is tempted to believe that these coincidences can be recognized by the presence of judiciousness, tolerance, or "pococurantism," as one of Thackeray's contemporaries qualified his style.[15] Becky probably *could* be a good woman on 5,000 pounds a year, since she is good-tempered, not miserly (she hoards, it is true, but in the saving spirit, not the miserly, thinking of possible bad times to come, as well she might in her position), tolerant and intelligent (she does not tolerate fools, but she has not time or inclination for active jealousy or ill-will). It is true that she would not miss a half-crown's worth of soup any more than Lady Jane does. And if she gave it out of the obligations of her position (if she had it) instead of out of Christian charity, the result would be the same, and she would certainly be pragmatically as good as any other character in the Fair, and would undoubtedly be so viewed by the people in the Fair. On the other hand, Becky is not and

never has been, so far as we have known her in the novel, such a foul monster as the final judgment would have her appear. In the case of the first judgment, reason and the logic of the novel supports its claim; in the case of the second, nothing in the novel supports such a violent and emotional rejection.

Similarly, nothing in the world of *Vanity Fair* allows for the emotional indulgences of the narrator in describing Amelia, good but uninteresting. Uninteresting good people are less tolerable than amusing wicked people, as in Jonsonian comedy. For all its detachment and "cynicism," the portrait of Miss Crawley is done much more lovingly, in reality, than is the portrait of Amelia. The subject gave zest to Thackeray, and he loves her for it. So, though he judges her as she lies terror-stricken and without her wig, she is still one of his people, one of those who make the Fair so interesting—and so judgeable. The issues surrounding Becky and Miss Crawley are always taken into account and judged, though not always unambiguously, by the characters themselves as well as by narrator and reader. But the issues around Amelia—innumerable social, psychological and economic ones—are never judged of by her or by her narrator, and are therefore all but inaccessible to the reader.

One would like to think that the clear judgments of the social and moral realities surrounding Becky belong to Thackeray, and that the emotionalism of her rejection and of the descriptions of Amelia's character and life do not. It is impossible, no doubt, to draw this conclusion, but this destructive and aimless oscillation resulting from the discontinuity between his bases for judgment and his view of a world in which these bases are irrelevant are made part of the character of the narrator, the gossip, who is present on the streets and in the houses of the world he describes and who, we can see for ourselves, does not himself know how to judge of reality, much less of morality.

This view of the narrative techniques of *Vanity Fair,* I think, offers solutions to otherwise irreducible inconsistencies. As creator of his fictional world, Thackeray cannot *not* know what is going on in it, as if it had a life of its own entirely. A "Who knows . . . ?" question is possible in general cases, when the question is simply thrown out to be reflected upon in a general way, the particular case representing a whole class of similar situations. But when the development of his own characters and of the movement of the novel depends upon the outcome of a particular situation in which these particular persons are involved, Thackeray cannot shrug his shoulder and plead ignorance. It simply doesn't hold. We know he knows, or else he is simply a bungler who hasn't thought out anything at all. This is possible, but it makes a poor tale of the whole achievement. On the other hand, since Rumor with Painted

Tongues is a controlling image in the consciousness of the narrator, and since we see him getting information from Tom Eaves, who gets it from namesakes all over the fair, we have in this view of the narrator as *persona* a good basis for redeeming Thackeray from the imputation of bungling or of bad faith—and are able as well to account for the inconsistencies which run fault-like through the novel. He may with believability not know the ultimate motivations and outcomes of a particular situation. In fact, since we are there with him eavesdropping, we know he doesn't know any more than we do, and thus the whole problem of the novel comes home to us: the ultimate unknowability of the truth in crucial (or uncrucial) human situations, and the depravity of Society willing to credit or discredit individuals simply on the basis of rumor, with the idea that rumor has more reality in the Fair than some unknown reality, so that one can go upon it in doing business.

The very technique of gossip, then, with its attendant redoublings, asides, and inconsistencies, implies much of the form of the novel, and contains an important part of its statement as to the chances for the survival of truth in Vanity Fair. The novelist's responsibilities to his audience in this view, as well as to his art, are not shrugged off. He has shown us here not only a faithful description of the Fair, but has also suggested to us the more important idea that even this description is laid open to the probability of one-sidedness or partial truth. For all his sententiousness, it becomes clear that the truth is not self-evident and there to be acted upon by all who live in the Fair and judge of those who live in the Fair. It is in fact many removes way, behind all the gossip and rumor, and is perhaps ultimately inaccessible.

The process of reading this novel involves a constant questioning in the reader's mind, despite the apparent "safeness" of these scenes removed from our immediate view, as to what in fact happened and why. A good deal of reconstructive energy and imagination are required of the reader in a way that is not necessarily implied for the narrator, who is after only telling a story. The aesthetics of this novel require, then, that the reader be aroused to the responsibility of himself asking the moral questions and focusing on the issues that surround each character. In this way this work of art fulfills Coleridge's description of a work of art that it changes the quality of the imagination: as we become aware of the barriers to our perception of the facts here, we become aware that we need a new way of assessing motivations. Our reading then becomes an action, in the sense that it is active participation in the moral chaos of this fictional world. In fact, then, the novelist's responsibility is fulfilled not by way of the pronouncements of the narrator, but by way of arousing in the reader a moral energy and a moral questioning that may be far more beneficial than a mere pronouncement of rights and wrongs on the part of either the narrator or the author. That, because of the discontinuity between Thackeray's norms and the operative forces of the world he saw, no clear answers and judgments are possible—this is perhaps the most important lesson we have to infer from this Tomeavesian way of seeing the world.

Notes

1. William Makepeace Thackeray, *Vanity Fair* (New York, 1925), Ch. XLVII. Because of the numerous and accessible editions of Thackeray's works, I have cited passages by Chapter only, rather than by page, so that the reader may use whichever edition he has by him. Subsequent citations to the novels will be in the text itself.

2. E. M. Forster, *Aspects of the Novel* (New York, 1927), pp. 119-120.

3. Percy Lubbock, *The Craft of Fiction* (New York, 1931), pp. 59-76, and *passim.*

4. Geoffrey Tillotson, *Thackeray the Novelist* (Cambridge, 1954), p. 75.

5. *Ibid.,* p. 115.

6. Gordon N. Ray, in *The Buried Life, A Study of the Relation Between Thackeray's Fiction and His Personal History* (London, 1952), sees the source of Thackeray's discrepancies between his creation of character and his estimate of them in the writer's life itself, emanating especially from his desire for a home circle denied by the illness of his wife. See Ch. 3, pp. 30-47, for the discussion of *Vanity Fair* in these terms.

7. Thackeray himself rather blurs the issue, but not so much as to preclude his sympathizing with Becky here altogether: when George Henry Lewes wrote, in an otherwise favorable criticism of Thackeray's work, of this "detestable passage" in *Vanity Fair* which implies that "honesty is only the virtue of abundance!" Thackeray wrote back that he didn't mean to imply that at all, but that we should "look humbly and leniently upon the faults of [/] less fortunate brethren" because there was no doubt in his mind that Becky would have been respectable with 5000 a year. This is rather different from being a "good woman," as Becky will have it, but it does nevertheless point up the moral ambiguity in the values of the world of the novel, the more so since there is an admixture here of a rather sentimental and irrelevant piety. The interchange can be found in *The Letters of William Makepeace Thackeray,* ed. Gordon N. Ray (Cambridge, Mass., 1946), II, 353-354.

8. G. Armour Craig, "On the Style of *Vanity Fair,*" *Style in Prose Fiction,* ed. Harold C. Martin (New York, 1959), p. 96.

9. *Ibid.,* pp. 102-103.

10. For a detailed cataloguing of these technical devices, see John A. Lester, "Thackeray's Narrative Technique," *PMLA,* LXIX (1954), 392-409.

11. Tillotson, *op. cit.,* quotes statistics from the *Thackeray Dictionary* as to how many of these figures populate the worlds of his novels: 18 Browns, and one Browne; 27 Joneses and a character figuring at "the Wells" as "Jonesini"; and 22 Smiths. Professor Tillotson sees them as connecting links between novels, and representatives of the same social class, the "same individual plumply allegorical" (p. 111).

12. See, for example, *The Letters,* II, 309, in which Thackeray writes to Mrs. Carmichael-Smyth: "Of course you are right about Vanity Fair and Amelia being selfish—it is mentioned in this very number. My object is not to make a perfect character or anything like it." Amelia is to suffer and achieve real humility, he says, and this will be possible because she has the quality of "LOVE." In fact, however, this redemption never really occurs, and this is probably because of the doubleness in Thackeray's vision, the simultaneity of critical judgment and of uncritical sympathy, which makes the creation of a *persona*-narrator necessary.

13. Professor Tillotson takes exception to Percy Lubbock's assertion that Thackeray's "intrusions" into his story too violently wrench the reader out of the experience of "living into" the story, and I think quite properly, but he offers instead the idea that what the reader "lives into" is the musing and judgment of Thackeray the historian and critic over his characters (*op. cit.,* pp. 90-91).

14. Robert Langbaum, *The Poetry of Experience, The Dramatic Monologue in Modern Literary Tradition* (New York, 1963), p. 107.

15. David Masson, *British Novelists and Their Styles* (Boston, 1892), p. 250. This "pococurantism" is a "profoundly reasoned" one, and is moreover, Masson qualified, a "skeptical acquiescence in the world as it is," or, to use Thackeray's own words in describing the mind of Pendennis, "'a belief, qualified with scorn, in all things extant.'"

Maurice L. McCullen, Jr. (essay date November 1969)

SOURCE: McCullen, Maurice L., Jr. "Sentimentality in Thackeray's *Vanity Fair.*" *Cithara* 9, no. 1 (November 1969): 56-66.

[*In the following essay, McCullen examines aspects of sentimentality in* Vanity Fair *through a close analysis of three pivotal scenes.*]

That "dash of Sterne" which Thomas Carlyle found in Thackeray[1] has not gone unnoticed by later critics of Thackeray's fiction. It is generally assumed that Thackeray possessed a sentimental streak which occasionally spilled over into his writing.[2] In addition to these assumptions, one can find perceptive if impressionistic epithets, e.g., Thackeray as "a big, fierce, weeping, hungry man," or as "the sentimental cynic,"[3] and an occasional blunt assertion, e.g., "He is a sentimentalist and a cynic. . . ."[4] There is, however, almost no discussion of the extent of Thackeray's sentimentality, its nature and its quality.[5] Whereas Thackeray the realist has received adequate critical attention from his day to our own, Thackeray the sentimentalist has been too often acknowledged and then quickly passed by.

An analysis of the sentimental content of **Vanity Fair** is not only overdue, but is particularly in order at the present time.[6] Thus, in the discussion below I will analyze three scenes from the novel to reveal the nature and extent of the sentimentality to be found in them. By focusing attention on complete scenes one can see what may be called a "method" of sentimental presentation. The evidence indicates that Thackeray drifted into lapses of sentimentality almost by accident. He began characteristically with a legitimate emotion, but as his imagination fed upon the scene in which his character is to embody the emotion (in **Vanity Fair** it is Amelia), the scene tended to dissolve into sentimentality. Each of the three scenes considered below drifts into sentimentality in essentially the same ways; analysis of the drift reveals characteristics common to passages of Thackerayan sentimentality.

Chapter 26 opens with a dinner-party in the hotel rooms of George and Amelia Osborne. After dinner Amelia wishes to visit her parents for the first time since her marriage. George will not go with her (he goes alone to the opera) and she goes off sadly, accompanied only by George's supercilious valet. The dinner is a prelude which can be quickly dispensed with. For present purposes note only the use of two qualifying adjectives: "timid" and "little." Amelia, who is twice called "timid," puts on her "little bonnet," and drops George a "little curtsey." As she walks sadly down the great staircase and into a hired carriage, her "littleness" is implied.

She arrives "before the little garden gate" a "weeping, trembling, young bride." Thackeray dutifully pokes fun at the emotional meeting between mother and daughter ("when don't ladies weep?"), but closes with the injunction to "respect Amelia and her mamma whispering and whimpering and laughing and crying in the parlour and the twilight."[7]

The next paragraph in the scene must be quoted in full.

> There were but nine days past since Amelia had left that little cottage and home—and yet how far off the

time seemed since she had bidden it farewell. What a gulf lay between her and that past life. She could look back to it from her present standing place, and contemplate, almost as another being, the young unmarried girl absorbed in her love, having no eyes but for one special object, receiving parental affection if not ungratefully, at least indifferently, and as if it were her due—her whole heart and thoughts bent on the accomplishment of one desire. The review of those days, so lately gone yet so far away, touched her with shame; and the aspect of the kind parents filled her with tender remorse. Was the prize gained—the heaven of life—and the winner still doubtful and unsatisfied? As his hero and heroine pass the matrimonial barrier, the novelist generally drops the curtain, as if the drama were over then; the doubts and struggles of life ended: as if, once landed in the marriage country, all were green and pleasant there: and wife and husband had nothing to do but to link each other's arms together, and wander gently downwards towards old age in happy and perfect fruition. But our little Amelia was just on the bank of her new country, and was already looking anxiously back towards the sad friendly figures waving farewell to her across the stream, from the other distant shore.

(250)

One long sentence in the paragraph has received critical notice. It is the sentence which contains Thackeray's strictures on the romance novelists' handling of marriage ("As his hero and heroine pass the matrimonial barrier, the novelist. . . ."). Miss Blodgett cites it as evidence of Thackeray's realistic intentions.[8] I agree, but the significance of the passage depends just as much upon the comment which encrusts this protestation of realistic method; and that comment does not tend toward realism, it pulls in the opposite direction. Whatever the author's intentions, the paragraph is really beginning to drift toward the sentimental. "Our little Amelia" has returned to "that little cottage and home, to her loving parents, to. . . ." Her timid, anxious littleness is again stressed and at the same time the irrevocable sadness of her situation is insisted upon. The gulf image which begins and ends the paragraph reinforces this view of Amelia, and offers the best indicator of the drift that is taking place in the scene. The word "gulf" is used in the common sense of wide separation in the second sentence of the paragraph. In the last sentence of the paragraph the word is not used, but is imaginatively implied. Moreover Amelia's sad little anxious figure is placed on one side of the gulf ("her new country") opposite a symbolic group ("sad friendly figures waving farewell") representing her old life from which she is forever cut off.

The next two paragraphs drift further toward complete sentimentality. While her mother gets the tea things ready, Amelia walks upstairs and finds herself, "she scarce knew how, in the little room which she had occupied before her marriage." She even finds herself in her own chair, and sinks "back in its arms as if it were an old friend" to pine and sigh. The author sighs with

her: "Already to be looking sadly and vaguely back: always to be pining for something which, when obtained, brought doubt and sadness rather than pleasure: here was the lot of our poor little creature, and harmless lost wanderer in the great struggling crowd of Vanity Fair" (251).

A snowball effect is evident here; language and mood are building to a climax. But another paragraph intervenes before the crucial paragraph in the scene. In it there seems to be a last attempt at balance, for amid the telling of Amelia's thoughts as she sits in her little chair, and the author's comments upon those thoughts, is the description of Amelia's mood as "selfish brooding." The balance has tipped too far, however, and the next paragraph, which I quote in full, stamps the scene with finality.

> She looked at the little white bed, which had been hers a few days before, and thought she would like to sleep in it that night, and wake, as formerly, with her mother smiling over her in the morning. Then she thought with terror of the great funereal damask pavilion in the vast and dingy state bedroom at the grand hotel in Cavendish Square. Dear little white bed! How many a long night had she wept on its pillow! How she had despaired and hoped to die there; and now were not all her wishes accomplished, and the lover of whom she had despaired her own for ever? Kind mother! How patiently and tenderly she had watched round that bed! She went and knelt down by the bedside; and there this wounded and timorous, but gentle and loving soul, sought for consolation, where as yet, it must be owned, our little girl had but seldom looked for it. Love had been her faith hitherto; and the sad, bleeding, disappointed heart began to feel the want of another consoler.

(251)

The writing in this paragraph is florid and strained. Counterfeit words and phrases which abound in the scene multiply and reach a crescendo. Again we find that loaded and over-used word "little," a word which for Thackeray at least triggers an emotional response. It invests the scene with a heavy atmosphere of idealized childhood which, because of the constant diminution of everything associated with Amelia, takes on an unreal, doll-house quality. The picture is one of innocent, vulnerable childhood shielded from harm by the protective umbrella of mother love, smiling down from above. It is a cradle scene, complete with easy psychological equivalents for the modern reader. This personal, rather foetal, position of security is contrasted to—what? Not evil certainly, but to the "funereal" impersonality of the hotel, to that world without mother, which holds "terror" for Amelia. The security symbol, Amelia's "little white bed," is apostrophized with renewed intensity, with a far keener sense of loss than any expressed thus far. The reader is invited to imagine the many nights Amelia has "wept on its pillow." Suddenly the protec-

An illustration of Amelia Osborne being helped into her carriage.

tive mother image returns. Fake urgency and confused imagery testify to the high emotional content of the writing. Thackeray sees the cradle scene, but in the cradle now is a physically mature young woman. The retention of the kind mother, patient and tender, is at this point a mistake, the pathos spurious and false.

And there is more. Amelia is now moved actively within the image. She performs the action toward which the entire scene moves. She goes to her dear little bed, kneels, and prays. Thackeray the realist is nowhere in sight, and the emotion flows out of control: "wounded and timorous, but gentle and loving," "our little girl" with her "sad, bleeding, disappointed heart" asks her maker for consolation. The curtain is drawn on her prayers—and on this scene—by the fierce question: "Have we a right to repeat or to overhear her prayers? These, brother, are secrets, and out of the domain of Vanity Fair. . . ."

The cumulative effect of the repeated images, words, and phrases reeks of sentimentality. Thackeray has

moved with the practiced skill of a writer of melodrama from the drab hotel, through the little gate, into the little house, up the steps and into the little room to position Amelia on her knees before her bed in prayer. And for what? Amelia's unhappy position in marriage has been made dramatically clear in the first section of the chapter. True, only the author knows at this point how low Amelia's fortunes will fall. Still, such reinforcement seems unnecessary, especially when it is so aggressively emotional in its appeal.

Another example of overt sentimentality in the novel occurs when George Osborne receives advance news of his marching orders (chap. xxix). This scene is shorter and somewhat smoother. It is seen primarily through George's eyes, although there is someone peeking over George's shoulder to add comment. Here the blacks and whites of melodrama are clearly marked: George the black (gambler, woman-chaser, bad husband) prepares to take leave of Amelia the white (loving, dutiful, good wife). In the scene's climax such rhetoric as "this little timid heart" which becomes "the little heart" which moreover "nestles," creates again by diminution the image of vulnerable innocence. It is not left to the imagery this time to suggest that such innocence is abused, we have George—"selfish, brutal, and black with crime! Heart-stained, and shame-stricken, he stood at the bed's foot, and looked at the sleeping girl. How dared he— who was he, to pray for one so spotless! God bless her! God bless her!" (280).

In addition to the straining and the shrillness, there is a good deal of sentimental triteness as well. The emotional pitch of the scene culminates in the last two paragraphs of the chapter (280-281), and there is again a bid for a sentimental response from the reader. These paragraphs are loaded with words which by themselves carry an emotional content: *timid, pale, soft, gentle, fair, poor,* etc. In context, these words are heavily sentimental: "the poor child," "little soft hand," "sweet pale face," "gentle pale face," "two fair arms" which close "tenderly" around George's neck. Despite the truth in Miss Blodgett's idea that "[the author-narrator] self-consciously refuses to protract, or even to present, emotionally pregnant scenes of parting and return," this scene of parting is protracted. It is also very sentimental. Lending itself as it does to Thackeray's basic technique of contrast (Becky and honest Rawdon must also say their good-byes), the farewells are carried over to the next chapter—and the sentimentality with them.

These scenes prove that there are soft spots in the hard realistic surface of *Vanity Fair.* Again and again Thackeray appears to have been surprised by his own narrative and swept into sentimentality. Although such soft spots cannot be explained away, they have been accounted for and analyzed. Interpreting the biographical information to account for Thackeray's over-reaction to the peril in which worldly circumstances can place an innocent young woman, a prominent Thackerayan expresses his belief that Thackeray identified Amelia with Isabella Shawe Thackeray.[9] A textual analysis of Thackeray's over-reaction to the perils of goodly innocence defines the qualities which characterize that over-reaction in **The Newcomes**: there are three: "They are (a) the delivery of commonplaces, either genial or sorrowful, by the author, (b) the use of stereotyped words and word groupings that by their very nature have sentimental connotations, and finally (c) the deliberate evocation of the pathetic image."[10] Each of these qualities may be found in Chapter 50 of **Vanity Fair**.

In this chapter, "the high point of the novel for many Victorian readers,"[11] Amelia is forced by her economic situation to send young George to his purple-faced Philistine of a grandfather. She at first tries to increase "the small pittance upon which "the little family" lives, but her painted screens do not sell and her application for private students is in vain. Thackeray's comment again stresses the idea of abused innocence: "Poor simple lady, tender and weak—how are you to battle with the struggling, violent world?" (476). Stereotypes of the blatant and excessive variety already noted above are also present in this authorial commonplace. Other stereotypes will be readily observable below. As for the deliberate evocation of the pathetic image, nearly the whole of the chapter could be entered into evidence, for again a complete scene is underway.[12]

The dominant image implied in the early part of the scene, before little George's transference to Russell Square, is of something shrinking and hunted which grows increasingly wild and anguished as the chances of escape fade.

> She starts up of a night and peeps into his room stealthily, to see that he is sleeping and not stolen away. She sleeps but little now. A constant thought and terror is haunting her. How she weeps and prays in the long silent nights—how she tries to hide from herself the thought which will return to her, that she ought to part with the boy, that she is the only barrier between him and prosperity. She can't, she can't! Not now, at least. Some other day. Oh! it is too hard to think of and to bear.
>
> (476-477)

Amelia's struggle to keep her son is likened by Thackeray to a combat, a siege which Amelia is losing:

> One truth after another was marshalling itself silently against her, and keeping its ground. Poverty and misery for all, want and degradation for her parents, injustice to the boy—one by one the outworks of the little citadel were taken, in which the poor soul passionately guarded her only love and treasure.
>
> (477)

Amelia battles nobly, against great odds; indeed, against the whole of Vanity Fair, but with her father's admission that the annuity from Jos is mortgaged she can battle no longer. "O my God! my God! have mercy upon me, and give me strength to bear this trial" (478).

> Still the father did not know what that explanation meant, and the burst of anguish with which the poor girl left him. It was that she was conquered. The sentence was passed. The child must go from her—to others—to forget her. Her heart and her treasure—her joy, hope, love, worship—her God, almost! She must give him up; and then—and then she would go to George i.e., die: and they would watch over the child, and wait for him until he came to them in Heaven.
>
> She put on her bonnet, scarcely knowing what she did. . . .
>
> (478)

The scene crests with Amelia's reading of the story of Samuel to her son:

> And then, in her sweet simple way, George's mother made commentaries to the boy upon this affecting story. How Hannah, though she loved her son so much, yet gave him up because of her vow. And how she must always have thought of him as she sat at home, far away, making the little coat: and Samuel, she was sure, never forgot his mother: and how happy she must have been as the time came . . . when she should see her boy. . . . This little sermon she spoke with a gentle solemn voice, and dry eyes, until she came to the account of their meeting—then the discourse broke off suddenly, the tender heart overflowed, and taking the boy to her breast, she rocked him in her arms, and wept silently over him in a sainted agony of tears.
>
> (478-479)

Mr. Osborne, of course, is delighted to take his grandson, and soon the widow is left alone. George comes to see her often, "but he is not her little boy any more." When George does not come, the widow walks the long walk into London and sits across the street from the Osborne house where

> It is so pleasant and cool. She can look up and see the drawing-room windows illuminated, and, at about nine o'clock, the chamber in the upper story where Georgy sleeps. She knows—He has told her. She prays there as the light goes out, prays with an humble humble heart, and walks home shrinking and silent. She is very tired when she comes home. Perhaps she will sleep the better for that long weary walk; and she may dream about Georgy.
>
> (483)

The scene and the chapter end in the next paragraph. Amelia has followed George and his aunt to church:

> There she sat in a place whence she could see the head of the boy under his father's tombstone. Many hundred fresh children's voices rose up there and sang hymns to

the Father Beneficent; and little George's soul thrilled with delight at the burst of glorious psalmody. His mother could not see him for a while, through the mist that dimmed her eyes.

(483)

This scene is surely "an emotionally pregnant scene of parting" of the type which Miss Blodgett does not find in the novel. Shrinking, hunted innocence attempting unsuccessfully to defend its little citadel from the world—a stirring picture surely, which grows dark with frantic desperation as we read. Once again innocent Amelia is driven to the wall, her senses deadened, her reason all but destroyed: "She put on her bonnet, scarcely knowing what she did. . . ." In critical and crushing situations Amelia becomes numb and robot-like.

As the scene wears on, Thackeray becomes precious and coy. We read: "It is so pleasant and cool" across from the Osborne house, as though Amelia goes there in a mood other than anguished. Again, "Perhaps she will sleep the better for that long weary walk. . . ." Understatements like these have the effect of increasing, not reducing, sentimentality—and such is the intention. Tritenesses like "a sainted agony of tears" and "She prays there as the light goes out, prays with an humble humble heart, and walks home shrinking and silent" may appear to be merely further examples of stereotypes; however, one should note the heavy cloud of religiosity which hangs over this scene. Amelia is repeatedly found praying; she is seen to be saintlike. The author dwells upon her grief until the reiteration rings false. Not that her prayers and despair ring false in themselves. It is rather the truthfulness of the author who dwells with such seeming enjoyment on her grief that is questionable. What else can be made of the picture in which the weeping mother watches young Georgy (who himself is experiencing an emotional experience, albeit of a far different order) sitting beneath his father's tombstone?

Again, as we have seen in each example, "The chief source of sentimentality in Thackeray is the author's use of himself as commenting Chorus. This position—at the heart of the novel—makes for sermonizing that is unavoidably of a sentimental turn."[13]

At least one general characteristic of Thackeray's sentimentality has thus far gone largely unnoticed: it is repetition. Repetition of words such as "little," or "gentle," or "tender," or the use of these adjectives combined with nouns like "heart" or "soul," is a clear sign that a bid for an emotional response is in progress. These are key words in the sentimental rhetoric of the novel, and they are employed over and over. Repetition of a different order—indicating turbulent or confused emotions—is also present in most of Thackeray's sentimental scenes, e.g., "God bless her! God bless her!," "She can't, she can't!", "an humble, humble heart."[14]

It should be evident that Thackeray's sentimentality is a result of "clusters" of characteristics. In addition to the repetition of stereotyped words and phrases that call up a pathetic image, which then as a rule receives some authorial comment, it is noteworthy that the backdrops of these sentimental scenes are often religious. This religiosity can be seen above in the analogies to sainthood, the images of praying—in or out of church, the allusions to prayer, and the confessional quality which Thackeray assigns to private grief. The private grief itself tends to focus upon an inanimate object such as a little crib, a little coat, or a little bed. These talismens (which are always emptied or lost—or about to be emptied or lost) are then invoked and addressed as evidence, seemingly, of genuinely heightened emotion. The sanctity which Thackeray sees in private grief is insisted upon; it is called into play by concrete objects always associated with a character's past.[15]

Thus, in summary, whereas there can be no serious quarrel with the prevailing viewpoint that Thackeray's intentions—and his practice—were basically realistic, the ambiguity of tone noted by writers from his own day to ours is hardly to be quarreled with either. This ambiguity of tone, it seems clear, was a result of the sentimentality which in its turn was rooted in Thackeray's temperament. Certain innocent characters in certain threatening situations triggered a flood of emotion in this writer, causing him to bid rather aggressively for an emotional response from his readers. Thackeray would become increasingly mellow, it is true, but the nature and the extent of that mellowing—and the method by which it is transmitted to his writing—can be clearly seen his treatment of Amelia in *Vanity Fair*.

Notes

1. *Correspondence of Thomas Carlyle and Ralph Waldo Emerson* (Boston 1883), 11, 262.

2. For a review of scholarship on this matter see *Victorian Fiction: A Guide to Research,* ed. Lionel Stevenson (Cambridge, Mass., 1964) pp. 164-174. Thackeray's sentimentality is largely assumed in recent histories of the novel. Edward Wagenknecht's assertion is quoted above (note 4). See his *Cavalcade of the English Novel* (New York, 1953), p. 283. Walter Allen in *The English Novel* (New York, 1954), p. 203, affirms that "Thackeray's satire is suspended in favor of his sentimentality" where the "good woman is concerned." Lionel Stevenson is less candid, calling Thackeray's treatment of Amelia "ambiguous" and the emotional effect of the story "uncomfortable." *The English Novel: A Panorama* (Cambridge, Mass., 1960), p. 265. The critical cry "ambiguous" is not a recent thing, going back as it does at least to Trollope's study of Thackeray. It remains a critical approach to tone in the novels. See note 6 below.

3. The first epithet is found in Carlyle's letter to Emerson quoted above. The second is taken from the title of Lambert Ennis' *Thackeray, The Sentimental Cynic* (Evanston, 1950). Ennis' point of view is implied in his title.

4. Wagenknecht, p. 283.

5. The exception is Russell Fraser's "Sentimentality in Thackeray's *The Newcomes*," *NCF* [*Nineteenth-Century Fiction*], III (December, 1949), 187-196. I am much indebted to this fine article. In a subsequent study of *Vanity Fair* (*NCF*, 1957), Fraser does not mention the sentimentality in the novel.

6. Clarification of seeming critical disagreement by a demonstration of the evidence is certainly in order. For example, Arnold Kettle finds the treatment of Amelia ambiguous because of Thackeray's changing attitude toward her. *An Introduction to the English Novel* (New York, 1960) I, 165-166. Kathleen Tillotson in her *Novels of the Eighteen-Forties* (Oxford, 1961), p. 246, recognizes some slight ambiguity of tone, but believes that Thackeray's judgment of Amelia is "firm." On the other hand, Dorothy Van Ghent simply assumes that Thackeray is sentimental. *The English Novel: Form and Function* (New York, 1953), p. 142. A recent article confuses the matter still further. In her defense of the "author-narrator" Harriet Blodgett makes the following statements apropos of the narrator's realism: The author-narrator "objects to the excesses and falsifications of romantic sentimentalism." He "self-consciously refuses to protract, or even to present, emotionally pregnant scenes of parting and return." In her summary Miss Blodgett observes: "The creators of sentimental novels or romance heroines may aggrandize emotional displays; the realist's intentions, as all his rhetoric makes evident, are otherwise." "Necessary Presence: The Rhetoric of the Narrator in *Vanity Fair*," *NCF*, XXII (December, 1967) pp. 220, 222. In this interesting paper, the sentimental cynic is too much absent. As I shall show, whatever Thackeray's intentions, he was in fact demonstrable sentimental in this novel. I question several of John Loofbourow's conclusions for similar reasons. In his *Thackeray: And the Form of Fiction* (Princeton, N. J., 1964), Loofbourow finds that in Ch. 50 (which I analyze below) patterns of conflicting ironies or satires add up to "fashionable parody" and that "Amelia's compulsive fantasies . . . anticipating religious ironies in the novel's final love scene, discredit the Victorian image of romantic maternity" (pp. 84-88). It is difficult to see Chapter 50 of the novel as "fashionable parody." It is even more difficult to see Amelia in this chapter as discrediting "the Victorian image of romantic maternity." Satire must

have an object, and Amelia is hardly the object of satire in this chapter; irony is present in the chapter, as Loofbourow correctly asserts, but irony is not the dominant tone. The dominant tone is sentimental.

7. *Vanity Fair*, ed. Geoffrey and Kathleen Tillotson (Boston, 1963), p. 249. All citations are taken from this edition.

8. p. 220.

9. Gordon N. Ray, *The Buried Life* (Cambridge, Mass., 1952), Ch. 3.

10. Fraser, pp. 191-192.

11. Ray, *Thackeray: The Uses of Adversity* (London, 1955), p. 502, n. 25.

12. While I refer to this chapter as a complete scene in the interests of conformity, it is actually a hybrid of the variety that John A. Lester has isolated as a main type of "semi-scene" and called "The Intermittent Scene." "Thackeray's Narrative Technique," *PMLA*, LXIX (June, 1954), 392-409.

13. Fraser, 187.

14. This rhetorical figure is first commented upon, so far as I know, by J. Y. T. Grieg. He finds it to be symptomatic of unresolved conflict in Thackeray's mind, and he would limit it to adjectival repetition. *Thackeray, A Reconsideration* (London, 1950), p. 109.

15. Thackeray's penchant for looking back into the past, his "reminiscential manner" in Grieg's phrase, has received so much critical comment that Grieg assumes it as a critical commonplace (Ch. 16). It is noteworthy that this manner tends to be objectified in terms of physical objects whose *importance* lies in the past.

D. J. Dooley (essay date autumn 1971)

SOURCE: Dooley, D. J. "Thackeray's Use of *Vanity Fair*." *Studies in English Literature, 1500-1900* 11, no. 4 (autumn 1971): 701-13.

[*In the following essay, Dooley discusses the various meanings of "vanity" explored in* Vanity Fair. *Dooley also examines the diverse influences behind Thackeray's moral vision, paying particular attention to the writings of St. Augustine and John Bunyan.*]

Some years ago, Joseph E. Baker pointed out that ***Vanity Fair*** was enriched by being set in a very old moral tradition. But his statement "The novel elaborates a conception Thackeray found in Bunyan . . ." needs to be qualified; nor is the moral tradition as homogeneous as he makes it appear to be. *Vanity* has different senses in Ecclesiastes, Augustine, and Bunyan; and "Vanity Fair" does not mean exactly the same thing for Thackeray as it did for Bunyan. Thackeray explores the operations of many kinds of vanity—excessive love of self, the values of the fashionable world, inordinate ambition, the pursuit of such apparently legitimate goals as a happy marriage and a stable family relationship; some of these involve subjective moral evil, but some do not. Thackeray was sometimes the censorious moralist, but generally he attributed far more importance to earthly things than did Bunyan or the author of Ecclesiastes. When he jumped out of bed and ran around the room shouting "Vanity Fair!" he had found an excellent organizing concept for his masterpiece, but it would be fallacious to assume that he had also found a clear and unambiguous moral perspective.

In an article entitled "'Vanity Fair' and the Celestial City," Joseph E. Baker pointed out a few years ago that Thackeray's first novel was both given coherence and enriched by being set in a very old moral tradition.[1] Thackeray took his title from Bunyan, but Bunyan was hardly original in describing a Pilgrim and a Celestial City, and in showing the need for man to pass through a Worldly City in order to reach the Celestial one. Baker found such conceptions clearly expressed in the opening words of John Healey's translation of Augustine's *City of God,* published in 1610:

> That most glorious society and celestial city of God's faithful, which is partly seated in the course of these declining times wherein "he that liveth by faith," is a pilgrim amongst the wicked; and partly in that solid estate of eternity, which as yet the other parts do patiently expect . . . have I undertaken to defend in this work.[2]

Even Augustine, Baker observed, was a link in a chain, for Plato's *Republic* describes the realm or *civitas* of absolute Beauty, Truth, and Goodness, a realm in which the life of the world participates to some degree. In his article, therefore, Baker showed that by his references to Bunyan, Thackeray summoned up a long tradition of ethical discourse and gave his novel complex moral harmonies. Yet in a brief discussion he could hardly have been expected to explore all of the meanings given to "vanity" and "Vanity Fair" by Thackeray, the sometimes quite different meanings given to the same terms by Bunyan, and the variety of meanings found in the long tradition going back to St. Augustine, Plato, and the Bible. In brief, Baker made the tradition seem much simpler than it actually is, and he also ignored some of the complexities in Thackeray's use of it. When Thackeray jumped out of bed and ran three times round the room shouting "Vanity Fair! Vanity Fair! Vanity Fair!" he had found the right title and the right means of organizing his masterpiece, but he had not found a clear and unambiguous moral perspective.

Even Baker's statement "The novel elaborates a conception Thackeray found in Bunyan . . ."[3] offers certain difficulties. What was Bunyan's conception? Thackeray, Baker writes, shows a worldly world in which vanities are bought and sold; Bunyan's description of Vanity Fair summarizes the material of the novel:

> Therefore at this fair are all such merchandise sold as houses, lands, trades, places, honors, preferments, titles, countries, kingdoms, lusts, pleasures, and delights, of all sorts, as whores, bawds, wives, husbands, children, masters, servants, lives, blood, bodies, souls, silver, gold, pearls, precious stones, and what not.
>
> And, moreover, at this fair there are at all times to be seen jugglings, cheats, games, plays, fools, apes, knaves, and rogues, and that of every kind. Here are to be seen, too, and that for nothing, thefts, murders, adulteries, false swearers, and that of a blood-red colour.[4]

Every word of this, Baker aptly comments, suggests a great scene from Thackeray. But he also declares that *"The City of God* and **Vanity Fair** may be read as the philosophical generalization and the concrete illustration of the vanity of worldly desires,"[5] which would lead one to assume that Bunyan and Augustine are saying the same thing and that Bunyan's long list of merchandise includes the very temptations against which Augustine would like to warn his fellow mortals. However, in *The City of God* (Bk. XXII, Ch. 24), Augustine rapturously praises the rich endowments of humanity— the blessing of fecundity, the arts which minister not merely to the bare necessities of life but to its enjoyment, the perfection of human skill in painting, pottery, sculpture, and even cookery. His conclusion therefore is that, though human life is predominantly miserable, it contains many kinds of glories and wonders. Bunyan's thought is very different:

> . . . the name of that town is Vanity; and at the town there is a fair kept, called Vanity Fair; it is kept all the year long; it beareth the name of Vanity Fair, because the town where it is kept is lighter than vanity; and also because all that is there sold, or that cometh hither, is vanity. As is the saying of the wise, "all that cometh is vanity."[6]

Baker has conjured up not one but two views of human existence, and it will not take us long to decide whether Thackeray inclines towards the more tolerant position of Augustine or the more rigorous position of Bunyan.[7]

Bunyan's conception, of course, can be traced to the Old Testament:

> All nations before him are as nothing, and they are counted to him less than nothing, and vanity.
>
> (Is. 40:17)
>
> Vanity of vanities, saith the preacher, vanity of vanities; all is vanity.
>
> (Eccles. 1:2)

I have seen the works that are done under the sun; and, behold, all is vanity and vexation of spirit.

(Eccles. 1:4)

Annotating Ecclesiastes, M. Leahy says that *vanity* means a breath or vapor, so that "vanity of vanities" is the Hebrew way of saying "the merest breath."[8] When Bunyan writes that the town in which the Fair is held is lighter than vanity, it is clear that he is using the word in its biblical sense: the chief thing about Vanity Fair is the insubstantiality or emptiness of what it has to offer. According to Louis F. Hartman, the writer of Ecclesiastes possesses a materialistic and pessimistic outlook on life which arises from his gloomy notions of life after death. Though his advice to us is to make nothing transitory our final goal but instead to fulfill the duties which God has given us, he does not in any way review the disappointments of this life from the perspective of a blessed hereafter.[9] Bunyan, in contrast, emphasizes the blessed hereafter; all things, even the ties of marriage and blood, are worthless in comparison to it. As Louis L. Martz shows, the beginning of Bunyan's story strongly establishes that the way of the Christian is entirely different from the way of the world:

> Is it heroic to flee, as Christian does, from the city that he thinks is doomed to destruction, leaving his wife and four small children there; and worse than that— stopping up his ears with his fingers to avoid their appealing cries? Bunyan deliberately presents the scene in a way that will shock our sensibilities. He knows that Christian's actions will seem "brainsick," ridiculous, and frantic to the average man; Christian's neighbours say exactly that. Thus, with his sure, quick hand, Bunyan dramatically sets forth at once his main point: the way of a Christian is not the way of the world: It is utterly opposite to the judgments of this world and to all worldly considerations.[10]

It is not surprising, then, that Bunyan makes "houses, lands, trades, places, honors"—earthly necessities as well as earthly vanities—count as nothing.[11]

When Thackeray concludes his novel with the melancholy question "Ah! *Vanitas Vanitatum!* which of us is happy in this world? Which of us has his desire? or, having it, is satisfied?" he is expressing a sentiment perfectly in harmony with Ecclesiastes. Whether or not he is implying that heaven perfects what earth leaves unsatisfactory, he is undoubtedly showing how foolish we are to put our hopes in ephemeral things. When Glorvina O'Dowd is pursuing Dobbin, who in his turn is pining for Amelia, Thackeray observes, "So these two were each exemplifying the Vanity of this life, and each longing for what he or she could not get."[12] Even if Dobbin eventually gets his desire, the other part of the precept applies: he is allowed to marry Amelia only after he has realized that she is not worth his devotion. Baker states that excessive love of self is the root of the

trouble in Thackeray's world: "to him, as to St. Augustine, this is what motivates the earthly city."[13] Because Thackeray in the well-known letter to his mother described all the people in the book as odious except Dobbin, Baker feels justified in accusing even Amelia of selfishness. (Thackeray also excepts Briggs a few sentences farther on: "Dobbin and poor Briggs are the only 2 people with real humility as yet." From a letter to Mrs. Carmichael-Smyth, 2 July 1847, in *Letters* [*Letters and Private Papers of William Makepeace Thackeray* (Cambridge, 1945-46)], ed. G. N. Ray, II, 309.) Yet when Thackeray tells how Amelia gratefully picked up the crumbs dropped now and then by her rich father-in-law, he puts stress on her humility and altruism: "it was, I say, her nature to sacrifice herself and to fling all that she had at the feet of the beloved object" (57:552). In the passage from which this quotation is taken—it occurs as late as Chapter 57, when Thackeray is beginning to modify his picture of Amelia—Thackeray expresses the utmost admiration for poor women like her who are secret martyrs and victims; he also makes Fortune, rather than Amelia's own limitations, responsible for her misery. Similarly we might question whether Dobbin's troubles are of his own making; any imputation of selfishness to *him* can only be facetious: "If Captain Dobbin expected to get any personal comfort and satisfaction from having one more view of Amelia before the regiment marched away, his selfishness was punished just as such odious egotism deserved to be" (30:289). If even these two worthy people are examples of the vanity of life, the kind of vanity which Thackeray is talking about in his peroration is not a result of the corruption of the human will; it must be caused by an irremediable defect in the human condition. All of us, no matter how well intentioned, make the wrong choices; we are all victims of a tragic irony. In Hardy's terms, "In the ill-judged execution of the well-judged plan of things the call seldom produces the comer, the man to love rarely coincides with the hour for loving."[14] Hardy puts the blame on some "purblind doomsters" or on the "President of the Immortals"; Thackeray, without assigning responsibility for our melancholy condition, simply lays it down as a general rule. He might have got from Bunyan the idea that the pleasures of this world are light, airy, and fleeting, but was he following Bunyan when he anticipated Hardy?

Baker is of course right in stressing the importance of self-love in *Vanity Fair*. When Jos Sedley is introduced to us, we are told that "He was as vain as a girl; and perhaps his extreme shyness was one of the results of his extreme vanity" (3:29). His self-centeredness explains his neglect of his needy parents; it produces such pathetic scenes as that in Chapter 59 when old Mr. Sedley is up and dressed in his best suit by six o'clock in the morning to welcome his son home, but Jos lingers among the "splendid tailors' shops in the High Street of Southampton. . . ." That "young whiskered prig"

George Osborne is similarly, if more elaborately, portrayed. Though Thackeray forebears entering into minute particulars about the love scene between him and Amelia, he emphasizes that it is almost impossible for George to think of anyone but himself:

> This prostration and sweet unrepining obedience exquisitely touched and flattered George Osborne. He saw a slave before him in that simple yielding creature, and his soul within him thrilled secretly somehow at the knowledge of his power. He would be generous-minded, Sultan as he was, and raise up this kneeling Esther and make a queen of her. . . .
>
> (20:187)

Part of the satire of these two is directed at their vain attempts to be something which they cannot possibly be. Later in life, Jos would give you to understand that he and Brummell had been the leading bucks of the day. When he furnishes himself, at Southampton, with a crimson waistcoat, a rich blue satin stock, and a gold pin, Thackeray slyly observes that his "former shyness and blundering blushing timidity had given way to a more candid and courageous self-assertion of his worth" (59:570). George is much more of a spark or a gay blade, but Rawdon gives a horse-laugh when his name is mentioned in Chapter 14: aspiring to sophistication, he has become a butt and a joke. The ironic note is struck most clearly when Becky is flirting with him in Brussels: "So Mr. Osborne, having a firm conviction in his own mind that he was a woman-killer and destined to conquer, did not run counter to his fate, but yielded himself up to it quite complacently" (29:275). As Thackeray reminds us on numerous occasions, his is the high-and-mighty style of the fool; he even curses the people who keep him in luxury as "money-grubbing vulgarians." On the whole he seems to deserve Becky's harsh epitaph for him, spoken years after his death: "that selfish humbug, that low-bred cockney-dandy, that padded booby, who had neither wit, nor manners, nor heart . . ." (67:658). Yet the chapter entitled "A Quarrel about an Heiress" establishes that he has nerve and courage; his good qualities are unfortunately vitiated by his personal vanity and his vain, empty outlook on life.

When Becky criticizes George for selfishness and heartlessness, it is certainly a case of the pot calling the kettle black. Her type of vanity, however, is different from his; she has risen above her humble beginnings, she declares, because she has brains and the rest of the world are fools. Apparently, then, Thackeray wishes to anatomize more obvious and less obvious forms of vanity. In Becky's case vain ambition is especially emphasized; she is clear-sighted about everything except the uselessness of her social aspirations. Since she rises so high and falls so dramatically, she is the prime example of the uselessness of such ambitions. They fit into Bunyan's categories—"places, honors, preferments, titles"—

but in *Pilgrim's Progress* there is no elaborate study of how vanity operates in ambitious people such as is to be found in another work which Thackeray presumably knew, Johnson's *Vanity of Human Wishes.*[15] The way in which Becky's imagination fashions hopelessly immoderate ambitions is exactly described in Walter Jackson Bate's synopsis of this poem:

> its general subject is the enormous clutter of fitful desires and rival ambitions, of fears, projections, envy and self-expectation that human feelings create in their confused impulse to assert themselves and find satisfaction. To this is added the unwelcome discovery, which we naturally try to resist, that even to attain our wishes brings languor or indifference afterward, while at the same time we are inspiring envy and hostility in others, and moving into the decay that seems so rapid and remorseless to a conscious being.[16]

In his poem, Johnson deals particularly with "scenes of pompous woes." Thackeray on the other hand is mainly concerned with people below the top rungs on the ladder of society but extremely conscious of the social hierarchy: vain standards go with vain ambitions. Rawdon says of George that "He'd go to the deuce to be seen with a lord," and we are told of Jos that "The presence of a lord fascinated him and he could think of nothing else" (14:136, 62:597). These two merely exaggerate the deference to people in high places which almost everyone in the novel takes for granted. As Baker says, "Social *mores* are distinguished from any true standards of value; and they are worlds apart."[17] The central character of *Pilgrim's Progress* is a plain man who will not cultivate My Lord Luxurious and Sir Having Greedy; he will have nothing to do with the fashionable world—with all that "Vanity Fair" now connotes. Still Bunyan's Vanity Fair is not motivated solely or principally by social emulation or display, and Johnson's satire of Britain's "modish tribe" seems a more likely source for Thackeray.

The indictment of fashionable values and those who live by them is forceful and comprehensive in *Vanity Fair.* Lionel Stevenson writes that, if Thackeray called his book a novel without a hero, he could have called it with equal truth a novel without a villain.[18] But we are given enough information about the misdeeds of a number of characters to be able to make very strong cases against them. To return to Becky, we are told in the second chapter that at school she was never known to have done a good action in behalf of anybody. As her parting from Amelia at the end of Chapter 6 shows, she is a consummate hypocrite: "one person was in earnest and the other a perfect performer. . . ." After she has left the Sedley home, Blenkinsop the housekeeper is brought in to inform us that she was caught reading Mrs. Sedley's letters and was always snooping in drawers. At the end of Chapter 8, Thackeray puts her in a class of faithless, hopeless, and charityless people whom he wants us to have at with might and main. She is the epitome of cold calculation; when Rawdon leaves for the battle of Waterloo, he rode away "with something like a prayer on his lips for the woman he was leaving," but Becky "wisely determined not to give way to unavailing sentimentality on her husband's departure," calmly begins estimating how well off she will be if he is killed (30:286-287). Her behavior towards her son brings an outburst of indignation from Thackeray: "O, thou poor lonely benighted boy: Mother is the name for God in the lips and hearts of little children; and here was one who was worshipping a stone!" (37:369) Whether or not her unfortunate upbringing warped her personality, Thackeray makes it plain that she could have followed the way of duty and responsibility but did not choose to do so. No matter what Amelia's failings, when she and Becky meet and kiss after years of separation, Thackeray contrasts them in black-and-white terms: "Ah, poor wretch, when was your lip pressed before by such pure kisses?" (65:636) His view of Becky as a hardened little reprobate persists to the very end; it is supported by Jos's quivering plea to Dobbin—"You don't know what a terrible woman she is" (67:614)—and by the insurance arrangements from which she profits so handsomely. Though this is not the whole of her story, the moralist must condemn her perverted values, as he does those of Lord Steyne and old Osborne, to take two other examples.

"Good society can never go wrong," declares Mr. Osborne. Thackeray sets down the abominable principle with relish, and proceeds to show its ironic consequences. The irony is particularly heavy regarding the marriage arrangements: when George Osborne is informed that he must break with Amelia, it is not to a suitable substitute that he is ordered to transfer his affections but to a "black Princess," a "Hottentot Venus," and, when his sister Maria makes a perfect Vanity Fair alliance with Frederick Augustus Bullock, Thackeray sarcastically observes that she would have taken "gouty, old, bald-headed, bottle-nosed Bullock Senior" if he had been available. A main strand in the plot is the operation of retributive justice upon people like Mr. Osborne, who have paid too much attention to empty social considerations and too little to duty and charity. But Thackeray also emphasizes the widespread harm which vanity causes: servants suffer for the sins of their masters, children for the vanity of their parents:

> O, Vanity Fair—Vanity Fair! This might have been, but for you, a cheery lass: Peter Butt and Rose a happy man and wife, in a snug farm, with a hearty family, and an honest portion of pleasures, cares, hopes, and struggles:—but a title and a coach and four are toys more precious than happiness in Vanity Fair: and if Harry the Eighth or Bluebeard were alive now, and wanted a tenth wife, do you suppose he could not get the prettiest girl that shall be presented this season?
>
> (9:83)

In placing so much emphasis on the distorted values of the fashionable world, Thackeray is taking one or two items from Bunyan's long list and giving them considerably more prominence than Bunyan does. It is also noteworthy that he shows how these values militate against happiness in this world; his stress is not on the celestical city but the earthly one.

Following Bunyan, Thackeray describes Vanity Fair in the prologue "Before the Curtain" as a very noisy place, full of bustle, and crowded with bullies, bucks, knaves, policemen, quacks, and yokels. There is nothing to suggest that it is the meeting place only of the fashionable world, even though Thackeray is going to concentrate on that sphere of society. As in Bunyan, it is a place of distracting activity. But Thackeray looks at it with different eyes from Bunyan's; though he declares that melancholy is uppermost in the mind of the sagacious observer of the scene, he puts in a word for mirthfulness. He himself is always in danger of being distracted from his moralizing. He is thorough in his attack on vanity, but he cannot adopt a consistent attitude to it. After describing Becky in the second chapter as a young misanthropist, not in the least kind or placable, he introduces her to a shy bachelor in the third chapter and invites us to admire the dexterity with which she handled him: "If Miss Rebecca can get the better of *him,* and at her first entrance into life, she is a young person of no ordinary cleverness" (3:29). From the very beginning, therefore, Thackeray was doing two slightly contradictory things: censuring unprincipled pícaros and admiring the ingenuity with which they kept themselves afoot in Vanity Fair, attacking the values of fashionable society and displaying its fascination. Bunyan and Hardy, in different ways, view the world as a trap; for Bunyan it is a trap which man must avoid on his way to heaven, for Hardy it is a trap which he cannot avoid because the gods use the temptation of happiness to lead him into it. Thackeray takes both these views at different times; but he also emphasizes, as St. Augustine did, the delights and pleasures of the world. The roast-beef passage is often cited as an example of his tolerance; as a conscious moralist, he cannot regard earthly pleasures as fully satisfactory, but he will not follow Bunyan and put them sternly aside:

> It is all vanity to be sure: but who will not own to liking a little of it? I should like to know what well-constituted mind, merely because it is transitory, dislikes roast beef? That is a vanity; but may every man who reads this, have a wholesome portion of it through life, I beg: aye, though my readers were five hundred thousand. Sit down, gentlemen, and fall to, with a good hearty appetite; the fat, the lean, the gravy, the horse-radish as you like it—don't spare it. Another glass of wine, Jones, my boy—a little bit of the Sunday side. Yet, let us eat our fill of the vain thing, and be thankful

therefore. And let us make the best of Becky's aristocratic pleasures likewise—for these too, like all other mortal delights, were but transitory.

(51:485)

The earthly pleasures symbolized by a roast of beef may be vain in certain senses, but they are not negligible; they are transitory, but they are still real.

To summarize, Thackeray sometimes uses *vanity* with the biblical meaning of light as air; it suggests the insubstantiality of earthly things, presumably (as Baker says) in comparison with any true standard of value. Again, though it would be much too cynical to see inordinate love of self as the motivating force for every character in the novel, Thackeray puts plenty of emphasis on this unbiblical sense of *vanity*. He also stresses the vanity of ambition; it is vain in one way because it reflects excessive love of self and an inflated opinion of one's own merits, and in another way because the goals it seeks are not worth striving for. Even ambitions which are not the product of excessive self-love, which in fact seem entirely reasonable and lawful, are still vain, for human affairs are governed by a sad irony: none of us, having his desire, is satisfied. When we turn to the term "Vanity Fair," we find Thackeray employing it somewhat in the sense given by the *O.E.D.*: "a place or scene where all is frivolity and empty show; the world or a section of it as a scene of idle amusement and unsubstantial display." But basically this is Bunyan's concept, and Thackeray's is slightly different: he concentrates on the fashionable section of society, and he does not always find the display insubstantial and the amusement idle. Whereas Bunyan's Vanity Fair is the work of Satan, Thackeray's is of a type to justify Geoffrey and Kathleen Tillotson's observation that "The Fair is not at fault but its occupants."[19]

As the Tillotsons also say, "All told, Thackeray the moralist is not to be summed up in a word."[20] Chesterson takes away from **Vanity Fair** an impression of the author's "avuncular indulgence," Gordon N. Ray, of his resigned and reasonably cheerful melancholy, but Lionel Stevenson considers that the emotional effect of the novel is uncomfortable, since readers are given a sense of involvement yet are left undecided where their sympathy ought to reside. This effect, he thinks, proceeds from Thackeray's complicated personal relationship with his material.[21] The ambiguities and irresolutions are as much attributable to the intellectual and moral *données* as they are to the author's emotional involvement with his story. Thackeray does not invoke one clear and unambiguous moral tradition such as Baker describes—or as Shaw describes somewhat differently in the Preface to *Three Plays for Puritans*:

> Vanity of vanities, all is vanity! moans the Preacher, when life has at last taught him that Nature will not dance to his moralist-made tunes. Thackeray, scores of

centuries later, was still baying the moon in the same terms. Out, out, brief candle! cries Shakespear, in his tragedy of the modern literary man as murderer and witch consulter. Surely the time is past for patience with writers who, having to choose between giving up life in despair and discarding the trumpery moral kitchen scales in which they try to weigh the universe, superstitiously stick to the scales, and spend the rest of the lives they pretend to despise in breaking men's spirits.[22]

Thackeray could follow Bunyan in describing the distracting activity of Vanity Fair and the worthlessness of the goods laid out in its booths, and he could follow Johnson in describing the vanity of human wishes, and he could follow Ecclesiastes in saying that man's life is full of frustration and disappointment, but he could not stick to the scales provided by any one of them. Ray calls his irony all-pervasive;[23] with his ability to look at a question from many sides, he was not likely to overlook the vanity of that excessive moral scrupulousness which sees nothing good under the sun.

Notes

1. Joseph E. Baker, "'Vanity Fair' and the Celestial City," *Nineteenth-Century Fiction,* X (1955-1956), 89-98.

2. Baker, p. 92.

3. Baker, p. 97.

4. Baker, p. 90.

5. Baker, p. 93.

6. John Bunyan, *Pilgrim's Progress,* with an introduction by Louis L. Martz, Rinehart Editions (New York, 1949), p. 91.

7. This is not to say that Thackeray was directly influenced by Augustine or even read him—only that he did not follow Bunyan's conception strictly and that a more tolerant and liberal version of the tradition than Bunyan's did exist.

8. M. Leahy, *A Catholic Commentary on Holy Scripture* (London, 1953), p. 491. In his *Dictionary of the Bible* (Edinburgh, 1902) James Hastings gives *vanity* the objective sense of emptiness, worthlessness, uselessness, deceit, and illusion. *The Interpreter's Dictionary of the Bible* (New York, 1963) says that the word has a variety of meanings deriving from physical concepts of insubstantiality, but never connoting the subjective attitude of false pride which it usually has in modern English.

9. Louis F. Hartman, C.S.S.R., *Encyclopedic Dictionary of the Bible* (New York, 1963).

10. Martz, introduction to *Pilgrim's Progress,* p. viii.

11. To the suggestion of insubstantiality, Bunyan adds that of evil: his Fair was set up by Beelzebub and

his colleagues. In the second part of *Pilgrim's Progress,* the town in which the Fair is located seems much improved, so that Christiana and her family settle down for a long stay in it instead of hurrying on their journey.

12. *Vanity Fair,* ed. Geoffrey and Kathleen Tillotson, Riverside Editions (Boston, 1963), Ch. 43, p. 423. Subsequent references will be to chapter and page of this edition.

13. Baker, p. 92.

14. Thomas Hardy, *Tess of the D'Urbervilles* (London, 1965), p. 50.

15. "All times their scenes of pompous woes afford," wrote Johnson. In a poem entitled *Vanitas Vanitatum*—apparently written long after *Vanity Fair,* since it first appeared in the *Cornhill Magazine* in July 1860, but still interesting for the light it throws on the author's approach to his subject— Thackeray saw history as a chronicle of Fate's surprises, "Of thrones upset and sceptres broken. . . ." He found material for a hundred sermons in an album containing the autographs of kings, princes, poets, marshals, and other men of note, and when adjured to stop railing "against the great and wise" by his hypothetical reader, replied that the pages of history showed him one example after another of "how Wealth aside was thrust" and "Princes footed in the dust . . ." (*The Oxford Thackeray*) VII, 96-98.

16. Walter Jackson Bate, *The Achievement of Samuel Johnson* (New York, 1961), p. 18.

17. Baker, p. 98.

18. Lionel Stevenson, *The English Novel: A Panorama* (Cambridge, Mass., 1960), p. 267.

19. Introduction to *Vanity Fair,* xiii.

20. Introduction to *Vanity Fair,* xiii.

21. G. K. Chesterton, *The Victorian Age in Literature* (London, 1948), p. 79; Gordon N. Ray, *Thackeray: The Uses of Adversity* (London, 1955), p. 425; *The English Novel,* p. 266.

22. George Bernard Shaw, *Prefaces* (London, 1934), p. 716.

23. *Thackeray: The Uses of Adversity,* p. 404.

John A. Sutherland (essay date 1971)

SOURCE: Sutherland, John A. "The Handling of Time in *Vanity Fair.*" *Anglia* 89, no. 3 (1971): 349-56.

[*In the following essay, Sutherland examines inconsistencies in* Vanity Fair's *chronology.*]

Vanity Fair was written serially, under pressure and, for the most part, with imperfect preparation. It was the longest work Thackeray had hitherto attempted and had multiple plots twisted together over an ambitiously long time span. With this in mind it is less surprising that there should be errors of internal chronology in the work than that there are not so many as to ruin it altogether. It would be small-minded to seize on these for the sake of catching Thackeray out but there is some value in tracing through such discrepancies how the novelist, in the course of the novel, developed a practice of connecting his narrative in time which was to serve him for the rest of his fiction writing career.

The first thing one notices in considering the chronology of *Vanity Fair* is how disproportionate its overall arrangement is. Of its 600-odd pages 300 are concerned with the two years before Waterloo the other 300 with the twenty-five years after it; the first half of the novel is compact the second sprawling. For convenience the pre-Waterloo period can be sub-divided into two more segments, those of the unmarried and the honeymoon careers of the heroines or in terms of dates Summer 1813-Winter 1814, Spring 1815-Summer 1815. In the first of these Thackeray's identification of events against calendar time is meticulous and exact. In the second it is still close but such punctiliousness is clearly beginning to embarrass him. In the third of the novel's eras, Waterloo onwards, there emerges a studied vagueness about dating which suggests that the novelist has gauged his readership's indifference to chronological precision and is taking full artistic advantage of it.

The novel begins with promising exactitude:

> While the present century was in its teens, and on one sunshiny morning in June . . .
>
> (p. 11)[1]

In the following fifty pages we learn that Rebecca is to stay a fortnight with the Sedleys, that she is nineteen years old and Amelia seventeen, that Jos is twelve years older than she is, that George is twenty-three and Dobbin five years his senior, that the year coyly given as the "teens" of the century must be 1813 and that the "sunshiny morning in June" is the 15th. Thackeray's chronometer is heard clearly in these early well-planned pages. There are, however, significant gaps after Becky goes to take up her position as governess at Queen's Crawley in July 1813. We learn that she quickly ingratiates herself with the boorish baronet and his household. She herself tells Amelia this in her second letter (her first is begun the day of her arrival) which opens "I have not written to my beloved Amelia for these many weeks past . . ." (p. 98). This is undated but juxtaposed with a snooping letter from Mrs. Bute Crawley dated "December—". The position and contents of these letters make it clear that they belong to December 1813, shortly after Becky has settled in. In this same December letter Becky reports the annual visit of "the great rich Miss Crawley" with whom, we gather, the new governess soon becomes a favourite. There follow two intervening chapters which cover, with great generality, "fifteen or eighteen months" (p. 113) during which Amelia languishes for a heartless George. Then we have chapter fourteen which opens:

> About this time there drove up to an exceedingly snug and well appointed house in Park Lane, a travelling chariot with a lozenge on the panels.
>
> (p. 127)

The carriage contains Becky and a sick Miss Crawley "returning from Hants". Arrived in London Becky promptly ousts Miss Briggs as companion while that less designing spinster is enjoying her "Christmas revels in the elegant home of my firm friends, the Reverend Lionel Delamere and his amiable lady" (p. 129). This action is obviously intended to be consecutive with the December 1813 visit which Becky described in her letter. But, in a sense, it cannot be. For hard on Miss Crawley's cure a few weeks after, Becky secretly marries and elopes with Rawdon and this is demonstrably sometime around February 1815. What Thackeray has done is coolly to remove a year out of Becky's life, for her as for the whole "Arcadian" set 1814 simply does not happen—they go direct to 1815. The reasons are fairly clear, the passive Amelia may mark time for a year and a half doing nothing but pine for the man of her dreams, active Becky may not. It touches on a problem which Thackeray faces throughout *Vanity Fair* namely that Becky does so much more with her time that in any truly parallel treatment she would monopolise the narrative. The solution, as here, is to black out by one means or another sections of the adventuress-heroine's life so that her sprints only serve to keep her abreast of Amelia's tedious marathon[2]. But it is only in these carefully chronicled early pages that such narrative syncopation can, by reference to his own time references, be proved against Thackeray.

The section between the heroines' marriages and Waterloo, May to mid-June 1815, is the most complicated and tight-knit in the novel, chronologically speaking. So much happens in the way of making new marital relationships and breaking old family ones that Thackeray barely manages to get his characters to Brussels in time for the battle. And his habit of moving backwards and forwards rather than in a straight line of narrative produces something very like a tangle when the action must be synchronised with a close timetable. This is easiest shown by a summary of the events of May 1815. We enter the month with this comment:

> Some ten days after the above ceremony, three young men of our acquaintance were enjoying that beautiful

prospect of bow windows on the one side and blue sea on the other, which Brighton affords to the traveller.

> (p. 208)

The three young men are Jos, George and Rawdon; the "ceremony" is George's wedding which took place "at the end of April" (p. 205)—the 25th as we later learn[3]. This, then, gives us a date of about May 4 for the above scene. The young men walk along to meet the London coach which delivers Dobbin returning as an unsuccessful envoy to George's father. The narrative loops back for a chapter to follow this episode centring on Dobbin's announcement to old Osborne that George "married Miss Sedley five days ago" (p. 221) which, if we are pedantic enough to calculate, means that the interview takes place in the last days of April. The day after this Mr. Osborne writes a dismissive letter to his son which is given to Dobbin to hand over. When this is opened we discover that it is dated "May 7" (p. 231), at least a week in the future. Chapter twenty-five brings us up to Dobbin's arrival again, his gloomy tidings and the dinner that night at the Ship Inn. But in describing the woes of Amelia we go back once more to "the night before Dobbin came" (p. 234) when, we are told, "scarce a week was past" since the wedding which, give or take a couple of days, is the most accurate time correlation we have from Thackeray in this section. The Osbornes leave Brighton for London the day after Dobbin's arrival and that same evening Amelia goes to visit her mother in Fulham, an occasion for nostalgic retrospection:

> There were but nine days past since Amelia had left that little cottage and home—and yet how far off the time seemed since she had bidden it farewell.
>
> (p. 250)

If we are to believe the "ten days" reference of a day earlier it should indeed seem far off.

The fact is that it irks Thackeray to work in such close confines and, worse than this, it makes him seem clumsy, careless and arrogant about details. Clearly he felt so himself for in chapter twenty-five he offers this apology:

> Our history is destined in this chapter to go backwards and forwards in a very irresolute manner seemingly, and having conducted our story to to-morrow presently, we shall immediately again have occasion to step back to yesterday, so that the whole of the tale may get a hearing.
>
> (p. 234)

It is not, in context, a suave aside but a self-conscious acknowledgement of the inartistic congestion which telling the story according to a close schedule has involved him in. And it is at about this stage of the novel that Thackeray seems to have realized that this cramping narrative scale and scrupulous notation of time did not suit a novelist of his expansive inclinations. For after Waterloo (which is done in straight sequence following Gleig's account[4]) the narrative is relaxed and extended to the dimensions which we normally consider characteristic of Thackeray's mature fiction.

The tone and scope of the novel's new larger-scale organization is given when after the victory we are told that the Crawleys stay "some two or three years" at Paris "of which we can afford to give but a very brief history" (p. 351). Two years has been the sum of the whole history up to this point. As striking as the larger perspective, however, is the vagueness—"some two or three years". Thackeray ceases to be the exact chronicler and becomes the great novelist. The importance of what happens at this middle stage of the novel is not always appreciated. Praise like the following is, strictly speaking, appropriate only to the second half of the novel or, to put it another way, the novel as it is enlarged by its second half:

> *Vanity Fair* is his first novel on a big scale, and it is a great novel because its big space is scrupulously occupied. For all its immensity, it works under a statute of limitation. There is no fat on its mammoth frame.[5]

Had Thackeray died half-way through *Vanity Fair* as he did half-way through *Denis Duval* few would have foreseen a novel deserving this description. Lengthy perhaps, but not big.

The epic size and magnificent ease of the novel as it continues seem intimately connected with a disdain for chronological precision. From Waterloo to the end of the work only a few firm dates are given: little Rawdon's birth on March 26, 1816, old Sir Pitt's death on September 14, 1822, Dobbin's return to England in Spring 1827, the summer holiday at Pumpernickel in 1830. These are the few reference points which we have in trying to draw up a calendar for the post-1815 action. Consequently it is, for example, impossible to put a date to the crop of deaths which occur as the years go by and most of the important scenes can only be placed approximately. But there are practical advantages for Thackeray. Imprecision and the fact that much larger tracts of time are covered mean that he does not have to calculate which day, month or even year it is as he goes "backwards and forwards" in his story—hence there is no more of that clumsiness which mars the seventh number. The larger scale and vaguer time reference also mean that Thackeray can perpetrate anachronisms without disconcerting the reader or embarrassing himself and this becomes a useful assistance in achieving the effects he desires.

In order to show this it is again necessary to follow a maze of contradictory dates, but ones which do not stand out from the narrative as indiscreetly as those ear-

lier. For example we can only deduce as a probability that Becky and Rawdon return to England in late 1817. When Rawdon breaks open his wife's escritoire the night he surprises her alone with Steyne he finds that "she has kept money concealed from me these ten years" (p. 537) which confirms the impression that Becky's years of triumph in society are 1825-27. But if this is the case how does one explain landlord Raggles' woeful complaints after the crash?

> "Har you a goin' to pay me? You've lived in this 'ouse four year. You've 'ad my substance: my plate and linning. You ho me a milk and butter bill of two 'undred pound, you must 'ave noo laid heggs for your homlets, and cream for your spanil dog."
>
> (p. 528)

Now it is made clear to the reader in chapter thirty-seven that the Crawleys take up residence with Raggles immediately on their return from the continent so that by the best reckoning we can make they must have lived in his "'ouse" seven or eight years. So whereas Thackeray wants to maximize the London period in order to stress the extent of Becky's treachery to Rawdon we see that he also wants to minimize it to make her debts credible (it would be incredible that she could have lived on "nothing a year" for eight years, even with creditors as trusting as Raggles). In the structurally loose and chronologically vague organization of the latter part of the novel double dealing of this kind can pass unnoticed. This chronological ambiguity also makes believable lecherous Lord Steyne's withholding some eight years before making a serious attempt on Becky's virtue[6]. Answering from impressions rather than calculation most readers would, I think, say that Steyne's connection with the Crawleys lasts some two or three years rather than the best part of a decade.

The fact that all the events are on a sliding time scale means that characters can age or be preserved according to the demands of the immediate scene. Little Rawdon, for example, is described as "about eight years old" (p. 431) when he eavesdrops on his mother singing to Steyne and has his ears boxed. But this is set in the period of old Sir Pitt's death when the boy should, in fact, be six (one remembers, incidentally, how censorious the narrator is of Becky when she forgets the age of her son). Clearly Thackeray had a sturdy eight year old in mind for this scene and so advanced Rawdon to that age. Rawdon's father is subject to the same alterations. Shortly after the above episode we are told that he "was now five-and-forty years of age" (p. 473) which, at a generous estimate, means that the "young dragoon" who won Becky at Queen's Crawley was thirty-five years old. But, of course, he was not. Thackeray has for the nonce made Rawdon middle aged in order to convey an effect of time passed. So also with *his* father. When old Sir Pitt is visited by his newly married son and heir he confides that "I'm not very fur from fowr-score—he, he". And this was the man who told Becky in proposing six or seven years before "I'm good for twenty years" (p. 142) and who is shown in an illustration to the second number as hale man apparently in his fifties.

In this second half of the novel Thackeray has learned and is applying the lesson that imprecision about dates allows him to organise his material to its most powerful effect and to range at will over impressively long stretches of narrative history. It means that he can survey a whole period, such as Amelia's unhappy years at Fulham, without the irksome necessity of having to synchronise events with each other or place them in order. It also means that he can, without strain or artifice, concentrate or expatiate as he wants; the three years between Dobbin's return from India and the continental expedition are digested into less than fifty pages, the subsequent few months at Pumpernickel stretched to nearly seventy. There is a price which has to paid for this freedom. Thackeray's indefiniteness about chronology encourages the reader to be lazy and unalert in this second half of the novel. A notorious example of this effect are the nonsensically transposed paragraphs in chapter fifty-nine which went uncorrected, and apparently unnoticed, for a century[7]. But, on the whole, the gain in narrative liberty and ease outweighs the loss in definition. The large hazy expanses of the second half of the novel suit Thackeray's genius better than the clear but smaller scale of the first.

One knows that in many ways Thackeray was a careless novelist, and self-confessedly so. The careful chronology of the early chapters was probably born of a good intention which in his "idleness" (Trollope's word) he could not sustain over a year and a half. One knows too that serial publication was not always good for Thackeray, encouraging him to improvise rather than construct. But in this case these disintegrative influences seem to have been benign. The suspension of a close imposed time-table on the action, which occurs about chapter thirty-six of *Vanity Fair,* accompanies a release of creative vision in which the characteristic Thackerayan grandeur and ease of narrative could fully develop.

Notes

1. Page references are to *Vanity Fair,* eds. Geoffrey and Kathleen Tillotson (London, 1963).

2. The other outstanding examples are Becky's social career in postwar London and her years of exile on the continent both of which are blurred to make them seem shorter than they historically are.

3. In chapter thirty-eight.

4. See the Tillotsons' introduction to *Vanity Fair,* p. xxix.

5. *Ibid.,* p. v.

6. See chapter thirty-seven where Steyne is shown as being among the company in the first scene at 201 Curzon St.

7. See Gordon N. Ray, *Thackeray: The Uses of Adversity* (London, 1955), pp. 495-6.

Robin Ann Sheets (essay date fall 1975)

SOURCE: Sheets, Robin Ann. "Art and Artistry in *Vanity Fair.*" *ELH* 42, no. 3 (fall 1975): 420-32.

[*In the following essay, Sheets argues that art plays a central role in* Vanity Fair, *both as a symbol of truth and as a vehicle for deception.*]

The world of Vanity Fair abounds with plays and paintings. The houses are crammed with portraits, most of which contain an image of what never was—Lady Bareacres as the Dancing Nymph of Canova and Joseph Sedley as the triumphant tiger-hunting potentate. In this society of opera and allegorical waterworks, the characters can be grouped according to their attitudes toward art, with Becky, Dobbin, and the narrator representing the three most important positions. For Becky and most members of her audience, art is an exercise in deceit; for Dobbin, art is a source of beauty with divine sanction; and for the narrator, who is wrestling with the problems of writing a novel, art is, or at least should be, a means of conveying historical and moral truth. The conflicting theories suggest that art itself is the subject of *Vanity Fair,* and their resolution provides new insight into the evolution of Thackeray's own ideas about the nature of narrative fiction.

I

Throughout his life Thackeray questioned the meaning and purpose of art, not only in his magazine reviews of contemporary writers and painters, but also in his novels and short stories. An excruciatingly self-conscious novelist, he often incorporates stringent criticism of himself and other artists into his fiction. He fills his works with artists, who are often deceitful, and artifacts, which are often dangerous.

In his early stories Thackeray shows the perils of reading such popular forms of fiction as the Gothic novel, the Newgate novel, and the silver-fork novel. In *A Shabby Genteel Story* (1840), Caroline's seduction is attributed to her reading of fairy tales and Gothic novels, while Fitch's madness has been precipitated by his study of *Lalla Rookh* and *Don Quixote.* **The Yellowplush Correspondence** (1837-38) indicates that Charles's corruption has been partially caused by his involvement with fashionable fiction, just as *The Memoirs of Barry Lyndon* (1844), Thackeray's first novel, shows that Lyndon's fatal delusions have been encouraged by reading historical romances.

Moreover, the stories which precede *Vanity Fair* also suggest that if works of art are suspect, the men who produce them are even more so. Charles Yellowplush, Major Gahagan, and Barry Lyndon pride themselves on their talents as writers, yet the works they have created are primarily attempts at self-exoneration. Unreliable narrators and incorrigible liars, they use their writing abilities to falsify the histories of their lives. Some of the artists in other stories are more amiable. The painters Andrea Fitch and Michael Angelo Titmarsh are relatively harmless, but they are ridiculed for their eccentric and irrational commitment to the world of imagination.

Using satire and parody, Thackeray began his writing career with attacks on the outworn conventions of certain forms of fiction. But as he learned how easily writers could make lords of livery boys and swains of swindlers, it seems likely that his attacks on individual writers led him to question the integrity of their artistic medium. Implicit in these early works are Thackeray's doubts, not simply about the honesty of the writer, but also about the deceitfulness of art and the emptiness of language. It is in this context that Becky's role as an artist becomes crucial.

Becky Sharp *is* an artist, as she herself says. George Osborne praises her drawing ability, Mrs. Bute Crawley compliments her on her dancing, Miss Crawley admires her adroitly written letters, Lord Steyne's wife acclaims her talent at the piano, and Pitt extolls her success at the art of cooking. Literally and metaphorically, Becky is the child of art. She is the daughter of a drawing master and a French opera singer, and it is by art that she makes her way in Vanity Fair. She begins life as an actress, performing the part of an ingénue at school and doing caricatures of the schoolmistress for her father's friends at night. A "perfect performer"[1] who delights in mimicry, Becky amuses others by her imitations of Joseph, Miss Briggs, and Lady Jane. An accomplished musician, she sings her way from the parlor of Mrs. Bute's country home to the drawing room of Steyne's mansion and finally to the royal chambers of the Prince of Peterwaradin. Her achievements rival those of the age's best actresses; indeed, Rawdon swears that she is "*better* than any play he ever saw" (337, my emphasis). Becky triumphs at Lord Steyne's ball by acting two charades—Clytemnestra and Nightingale—with the "air of a consummate comedian" (498). After her catastrophe and the resulting scandal which forces her to leave England, she roams Europe as a singer and actress. She is, as the narrator tells us, like a spider: she stands at the center of Vanity Fair weaving a black web of artifice (432).

Around Becky are swarms of other artists. The professional artists are either disreputable—like her father and his bohemian friends—or deceitful—like the fortune-hunting drawing master, Mr. Smee. The amateur artists also cluster around Becky and imitate her duplicity. The self-centered George Osborne is an actor and, like Becky, a good mime. Having performed roles in garrison theatrical entertainments, he is a great lover of the drama—and of actresses. In his life, and in General Tufto's, the theater is a sign of corruption. George and Amelia's son inherits his father's love for actresses; he too has an instinctive interest in Becky Sharp. Little George visits all the playhouses to learn the names of all the players. Skillful at the art of manipulating people, he is a good actor on and off the stage, and a dauntless mime. Moreover, there are also many would-be artists in *Vanity Fair*—characters like Mr. Pitt Crawley and Mrs. Bute Crawley, who are repeatedly called artful not because they pretend to aesthetic sensibilities or talents, but because they scheme. Their only art is that of misrepresentation; their only end is money.

Supporting their entire world of fine art is its great patron, Lord Steyne. Lord Steyne purchases Becky's art, just as he had once purchased her father's paintings. He encourages her singing and her dancing, and provides the financial and social security necessary for her charades. The most enthusiastic of her admirers, he is the only person in high society who understands that Becky's art is counterfeit. He is delighted with her skill at deceiving people; he even admires the frauds she perpetrates on him. After he discovers how she has tricked him out of a thousand pounds, he exclaims in ecstasy, "What a splendid actress and manager! . . . She is unsurpassable in lies" (506). Thus for Lord Steyne and the world he represents, the artist becomes dissembler and manipulator. In the vocabulary of the novel, to be artful is to be dishonest, and artifice indicates fraud or pretension.

II

When Rebecca plays the piano, she lures men to her side: during the early phase of her adventures, Rawdon pursues her with notes inserted in her music, and years later Steyne hovers near the keyboard whenever she performs. But Amelia's musical talents are so meager that she cannot even attract the attention of her fiancé. From all accounts, Becky writes witty and well-constructed letters, while Amelia's abound in cliché and error. When scandal forces Becky to leave England, she manages to fend for herself, however disreputably. When Amelia faces financial ruin, she is helpless. She tries her hand at painting, but her pastoral scenes are such "feeble works of art" (476) that she cannot sell them anywhere. As often as Becky is called artful, Amelia is called artless; the word refers to both her innocence and her ineptitude.

However, while Amelia is at Pumpernickel she learns to develop her artistic capabilities. In this fairy tale town where art is the silly sustenance of life, Amelia immerses herself in music. Becky's voice is ruined, but Amelia's singing is constantly improving under the tutelage of the renowned Madame Strumpff. Furthermore, Amelia is still doing sketches which are more warmly received now than in former days. Not only does Amelia become a "goodnatured little artist" herself (598), she also learns to respond to the great operas of Mozart and Beethoven, which represent to her "a new world of love and beauty" (600). Although Amelia fears that it is wicked to take such pleasure in the tender parts of *Don Juan*, Dobbin tells her that the beauty of art is a blessing for which we should all thank Heaven.

Indeed it is Dobbin who introduces Amelia to the joys of art. An artist himself, Dobbin plays the flute in his room and regularly attends concerts and plays. During the visit to Pumpernickel, Dobbin teaches Amelia to improve her own skills and to develop her sensitivity to other artists. He also helps her to see the reflection of her own creator in the order and beauty of great music. Although Dobbin is an ardent admirer of music and drama, he remains unimpressed by Becky's performances. As the narrator says, "He was so honest, that her arts and cajoleries did not affect him, and he shrank from her with instinctive repulsion" (231). By rejecting Becky and her belief that art is a means of deceiving people, Dobbin brings another concept of art into the novel, one which had intrigued Thackeray for some time.

Dobbin echoes some of the ideas about art which Thackeray had expressed earlier in his career when he regularly reviewed gallery exhibitions. In many of the essays which he published from 1839 to 1844, Thackeray suggests that the man who learns to appreciate art will also learn to lift his eyes to heaven. For example, in **"Caricatures and Lithography in Paris,"** he says that God created "that fair and beautiful world of art" as an alternative to the crass and materialistic world of Victorian England.[2] After praising Charles Eastlake in **"A Pictorial Rhapsody,"** Thackeray concludes that a work of art, like a work of nature, should "fill the mind with an inexpressible content and gratitude towards the Maker who had created such beautiful things for our use."[3] Thackeray's admiration for Eastlake sounds sincere: he must have been very much attracted by the belief that the artist could provide man with a vision of a higher reality created and sustained by God. But although Thackeray was drawn to the idea, he could never give it his unqualified assent. Even in these early essays, such theories of art are undercut, first by the presence of the sardonic editor Oliver Yorke, and secondly by the character of the *persona*—that eccentric and indigent would-be painter who is prone to drink while he writes, Michael Angelo Titmarsh. Thus it is difficult to define Thackeray's final attitude toward his subject: what he respects at one moment, he ridicules at another.

The situation in *Vanity Fair* is equally complex. There is no reason to think that Thackeray disagreed with Dobbin's praise of the great composers. There are, however, several factors which prevent Dobbin's concept of art from dominating the novel. First of all, Dobbin instructs Amelia about art while they are spending a holiday in the phantasmal spa of Pumpernickel, and the very frivolity of the town threatens the dignity which Dobbin attributes to art. Everything in Pumpernickel is insubstantial, even its monarchs. The reigning Duke is referred to as "His Transparency" and the Princess of Humbourg-Schlippenschloppen, in whose honor the festivities occur, seems not to exist and sends a proxy to her own wedding. The town itself is full of grotesque artifacts: the statue of Victor Aurelius XIV surrounded by water nymphs, the groaning leaden Tritons in the garden fountains, the licentious pavilion painted with the story of Bacchus and Ariadne. The army consists of a magnificent band of marching musicians, while the political parties, the Strumpff and the Lederlung party, exist to quarrel about the merits of the town's two most famous singers. "There are festivals and entertainments going continually on . . ." (610), and the theater is world-renowned. There are no serious problems in Pumpernickel: the most violent conflict occurs when the Duke breaks a bassoon over the head of a musical director who was conducting too slowly.

Pumpernickel certainly is not Paradise, but it does offer an interlude, an escape from the vicious atmosphere of Vanity Fair. Pumpernickel is so different from London that its values and customs cannot be easily transported across the sea. Although Becky and Amelia seem to have reversed their positions on the subject of art, there is no reason to assume that the pattern of change will continue after the characters return home. Amelia is *happier* with her drawings now, but they are probably still unmarketable in London. Becky's voice may be cracked, but she has other arts which will help her to survive as she connives to regain a place in English society.

Furthermore, Dobbin's theory of art is not only undermined by the setting in which he expounds it, it is also limited in its application. Dobbin's respect for art is based primarily on his love for music, which is a nonrepresentational art. Whenever Dobbin stops listening to music and begins to rely on language, he loses some of his innocence. Dobbin is described as an artful diplomat who speaks eloquently in his friends' behalf. The narrator, for example, believes that Dobbin makes judicious use of "the guileless arts" (573) when he twists the truth in order to assist Amelia. But although the Major is an honorable man, when he operates in Victorian society, he too uses language to deceive people and manipulate their desires. A more admirable artist than Becky Sharp, Dobbin is nonetheless an "artful rogue" (635) who distorts reality for the sake of a dream which he himself has created. Although Dobbin would argue that the end justifies the means, his artfulness remains a skillful misrepresentation of reality to suit his own purposes.

III

The narrator remains the most important artist in the novel, and the most perplexed. Dobbin's theory of art is no help to him, and Becky's is a distinct hindrance. With his novel, the narrator intends to provide the reader with accurate knowledge of historical facts and enough understanding of moral laws to guide him in his daily life. The narrator of *Vanity Fair* seems to speak for Thackeray himself, for as Charles Mauskopf has shown, Thackeray often wrote as if he accepted his readers' demands for social realism and moral signification. Surveying the articles and reviews that Thackeray published before 1848, Mauskopf argues that "Thackeray's basic conception of the novel which emerges from this large body of criticism was that it should be an historical record of the manners of a particular time, encompassing all levels of society in an objective and consistent method of treatment, and should, at the same time, attempt to inculcate a moral upon the minds of its readers."[4] Although Mauskopf's analysis of selected magazine articles is sound, it is still necessary to compare the prescriptions contained in Thackeray's relatively conventional literary criticism with his own achievement in his highly ironic fiction. In *Vanity Fair* the narrator seems unable to achieve the goals which Thackeray had defined for the nineteenth century novelist. His theory of fiction is difficult to apply, and in the end it is Becky's concept of art that threatens to dominate the novel.

The narrator and Becky are aligned in many ways. Thackeray has drawn the two artists in the same pose, that of puppeteer.[5] He has also put Becky's letters side by side with the narrator's story. The narrator tells us that Becky's verbal accounts are misleading and incomplete, but who is to tell us that his are not? The narrator attempts to record a series of events exactly as they happened and to extract therefrom a universally applicable moral. If, however, he fails to tell the truth and apply the moral, then he raises the possibility that his art is as false as Becky's and that he is, as he himself implies in the preface, a quack.

By the end of *Vanity Fair* the narrator has told us a good deal about his own life and, more importantly, about the circumstances which surrounded his writing of the novel. He is a befuddled middle-aged spectator trying to piece together his own recollections and the hearsay of others. He met Amelia Sedley and Joseph when they were in Germany. He says, "It was on this very tour that I, the present writer of a history of which every word is true, had the pleasure to see them first, and to make their acquaintance" (602). Later, in Pumpernickel, he caught sight of Amelia at the opera and overheard the story of Becky Sharp at a dinner party given by Lord Tapeworm. Intrigued, he began to investigate their lives. He believes that the work which has resulted represents a "little world of history" (14), yet he concedes that it originated in the fairy tale town of Pumpernickel. History and fantasy are ironically fused and the illusory atmosphere of Pumpernickel qualifies the narrator's claims for historical authenticity.

Nonetheless, throughout the novel the narrator argues that he has conducted a historical search into the materials of his story. To verify his results, he refers us to the documents which he himself examined: the East India Register giving an account of Joseph Sedley's career; the Road Books describing Lord Steyne's country homes; the map showing the location of Pumpernickel; and innumerable newspapers—newspapers which tell contradictory stories about battles, parties, and people.

In the interests of his "veracious history" (455), the narrator talked to the servants at Miss Pinkerton's about Becky's relationship with Mr. Crisp; he spoke with Dobbin about George and Amelia's wedding; he consulted Amelia's physician, Dr. Pestler, about Amelia's problems raising little George; he questioned the ubiquitous lackey Tom Eaves about the Steyne family. The narrator insists that he has done this in order to record Amelia's memoirs as accurately as possible and that as a result of his commitment to historical truth, he has been forced to sacrifice many literary niceties.

Yet despite all this, he has not been able to get the facts straight. He does not know what part Miss Wirt played in Jane Osborne's abortive affair with Mr. Smee; he cannot give certain details about Becky's adventures in Paris; he cannot ascertain what Lord Steyne's plans were for disposing of Becky in Rome. He is unable to unravel the mystery of Mr. Crisp and concludes the incident by asking, "But who can tell you the real truth of the matter?" (24). He cannot define Becky's relationship to Lord Steyne with precision; at the end of the discovery scene, he asks, "What *had* happened? Was she guilty or not? She said not; but who could tell what was truth which came from those lips; or if that corrupt heart was in this case pure?" (517).

Within the world of Vanity Fair, the answer to this question becomes irrelevant because the appearance of guilt—or of credit, for that matter—is equivalent to the actuality. After Becky has disappeared from England, the narrator remarks, "Was she guilty or not? We all know how charitable the world is, and how the verdict of Vanity Fair goes when there is a doubt" (538). Society is made up of people like Tom Eaves and Tape-worm. Full of verdicts founded on rumor and supposition, it is represented by its newspapers which purvey different and often contradictory accounts of the same event. The would-be historian lives in a world where neither personal testimonies nor public documents can provide objective evidence. He becomes a writer who cannot tell us what events really happened, whose stance varies from "I have heard" to "I suspect" to "I doubt" to "I do not know" and who leaves us with the question. "What, after all, *did* happen?"

The narrator suffers a similar embarrassment in his role as moralist. The novelist frequently adopts the preacher's stance and style in order to defend himself from the charge of writing "from mere mercenary motives" (81). He promises that as a moralist he will speak the truth as far as he knows it and that he will comment on the story in order to demonstrate the wickedness and folly of Vanity Fair. With the homiletic tone of an Old Testament prophet, he reasserts his pledge to moral truth throughout the novel. He defends the just causes of little boys, extols the virtues of motherhood, demonstrates the ultimate worthlessness of money, explains the transitory nature of worldly possessions, and emphasizes the power of death.

The narrator is even aware of his own personal deficiencies. His habitual willingness to confess his sins seems to indicate humility and self-knowledge, but it also serves to cast doubts on his own values. It is one thing for him to say that he, like George and Dobbin, is attracted by the follies of love; it is quite another for him to admit that he would be as hypocritical as the Crawley family if he had a wealthy old aunt and that he would go to Lord Steyne's party if he had an invitation.

Unable to maintain his pose as a preacher, the narrator steps down from the pulpit and into the world while his visions of eternity vanish with a whiff of roast beef. A man of experience, the narrator himself is a part of the Fair. He tells his readers to mistrust themselves and everyone else, to flatter and pander to men of wealth, and to condone evil. On one hand, he condemns the utter worthlessness of material possessions; on the other, he suggests that if Becky had had a bit more money—say 5,000 pounds a year—she very likely would have been an honest woman.

As a preacher the narrator claims allegiance to absolute values; as a man of the world he sees that moral and economic values are arbitrarily assigned. Speaking from the pulpit, he tries to define irrefutable laws of human conduct; coming into the Fair, he confronts a society based on situation ethics. The narrator asks men to act in accordance with God's judgment, but he consigns them to a community where they will be judged by one another. He has a strong, even stern, sense of morality,

but he describes a world where goodness and evil are hard to distinguish.

In searching for a moral code, the narrator finds only the unstable ethics of knaves and fools instead of the absolute truth he desires. While commenting on the way friends fight over money, the narrator explains the law that governs his society: "Everybody does it. Everybody is right, I suppose, and the world is a rogue" (170). Readily accepting as normative the fluctuating and hypocritical assessment of what "everybody" else does, the narrator often excuses the behavior of his characters because he believes that he and his readers would probably behave in the same way given the same circumstances. Thus he approves of Becky's scheming to succeed in the marriage market because he thinks that other orphans would do the same thing, and he tolerates Joseph's stupidity because he claims that men have been stupid since the time of Solomon.

The world of Vanity Fair is a rogue. Its citizens change their moral minds according to the situation at hand, their only consistent principle being that of self-interest. Caught in this society, the narrator is unable to maintain a consistent moral position. Throughout the novel, he is in favor of truth, beauty, and goodness, and opposed to folly, vice, and crime. But he varies the definitions of these abstract ethical terms, and he has a difficult time applying them to himself and to the characters of his novel. His moral code becomes as relative and as subjective as that of Vanity Fair.

Surely the narrator's pose of historian-moralist is as ironic as his pose of omniscient novelist. The narrator repeatedly claims that he is the novelist "who knows everything" (318), but even this phrase is suspect because it identifies him with Tom Eaves, Wenham, and Tapeworm—characters who also claim to know everything but who are in fact no more than obsequious and inconsistent gossip-mongers.[6] When he relays obscure information and when he prepares to enter the minds of his characters, the narrator asserts his role as an omniscient novelist. Yet within the very same chapters he proves himself ignorant of external events and the characters' psychology. Just as he fails to explain the mystery of Becky Sharp's life, so does he fail to fathom her consciousness. His pose becomes ludicrous, and in Thackeray's fictive world, the convention of the omniscient novelist becomes impossible. It seems to me that the role of the novelist as historian and moralist collapses in a similar manner, and that implicit in this failure is Thackeray's statement not only about the impossibility of the omniscient narrator convention, but also about the limitations of narrative fiction.

The novelist as historian-moralist *is* a sham. Art—the novel as the narrator defines it—*is* false. Confronted with the unknowability of truth, man is unable to record events exactly as they happen. His own prejudices obscure his interpretation of reality and make the abstraction and application of an absolute moral principle impossible. The artist dedicated to realism is the most unreliable, just as the characters skilled in mimicry are the most insincere. The novelist who pretends to relay the events of a story exactly as they occur and to extract from them a meaningful and consistent moral is perpetrating fraud.

The reason that mimetic art is deceitful in *Vanity Fair* is centered in the emptiness of its language. In an excellent essay, Henri Talon says, "But when everybody lies, mutual communication becomes a parody. In Vanity Fair, apart from objects of daily use, nothing has its fitting name and disorder prevails. The characters are the counterfeiters of language, and language is between them like an insulator, not a conductor."[7] For the people of Vanity Fair, the words "credit" and "guilt" need not correspond to an objectively existing thing or act. Words have their own meaning and value apart from an external objective reality; the sign is as good as or even better than the thing signified. When words do not correspond to some objective, communally held body of meanings, but become arbitrary and subjective tokens, then literary art ceases to function as a mimetic structuring of extra-literary reality.

If art can no longer fulfill this function, then it must acquire another, and the direction in which Thackeray turned his fiction may best be understood by analyzing his two drawings of the novelist character. When the novel appeared in monthly numbers, Thackeray drew the author as a clown preaching to the rogues and wenches of the Fair. In the title page for the finished novel—presumably the last illustration Thackeray executed for *Vanity Fair*—he drew the author in a completely different pose. No longer actively engaged in the world of Vanity Fair as a preacher, he muses over his reflection in a cracked mirror. What he sees there—the shattered image of himself—is perhaps his most startling perception of himself in the pages of the novel. Just as the discontinuous and fragmented face of the clown looks back from the mirror, so do the several faces of the narrator brood over the world of the novel: now as omniscient novelist, now as struggling historian, now as moralizing preacher. Readers of *Vanity Fair* have understandably attempted to re-integrate Thackeray's broken image of the novelist into a coherent and reliable consciousness. But in *Vanity Fair,* the face of Thackeray's artist, like the Victorian self and Humpty-Dumpty, cannot be put back together again. The novelist can no longer be a historian or a preacher lecturing to his fellow citizens. He is a lonely man who sees himself in his novels, and he must therefore develop a subjective narrative technique that must therefore develop a subjective narrative technique that will acknowledge his imperfection and alienation.

For Thackeray, it was impossible to create an all-knowing narrator who could stand safely beyond the story, secure with an infallible knowledge of history and an unshakeable sense of moral values. In his later fiction, Thackeray employs a number of different narrators, all of whom are limited by either personal quirk or circumstance. But despite his rejection of omniscience, he was never able to entirely resolve the problems which had emerged from *Vanity Fair.* Although Thackeray knew that the individual could not attain a fixed point of view outside himself, he also believed that the individual who was lost inside his own mind had laid himself open to many errors. Morally and epistemologically, Thackeray found the subjective point of view dangerous, as dangerous for the later narrators as it had been for Charles Yellowplush and Barry Lyndon.

Henry Esmond, painter, playwright, and poet, has the information necessary to write the history of his life, but he lacks candor and insight into the consequences of his acts. By means of his autobiography, Esmond attempts to set himself right, with the public and with his own conscience. Batchelor, the tragicomic narrator of *Lovel the Widower* (1860) and would-be novelist, finds that his fears and fantasies constantly intrude into the story he is trying to tell. As a recorder of external events he is an utter failure: unable to keep his eye on the action, he digresses on his own digressions. In this work, as in *The History of Henry Esmond,* the narrator's flaws are a major source of irony and his dilemma as an artist is an essential part of the subject.

The narrators of the Pendennis novels, *Pendennis* [*The History of Pendennis*] (1848-50), *The Newcomes* (1853-55), and *Philip* [*The Adventures of Philip on His Way Through the World*] (1861-62), are generally more reliable, but they are sometimes in doubt about the facts of their stories and often unsure about the moral implications. However, they recognize that they are not gods, but rather men who must accept the deficiencies of intellect and will. For them, there is no such thing as epistemological or ethical certainty. Less egocentric than Esmond and Batchelor, they confess their own weaknesses and plead for tolerance and forgiveness for all. As these narrators relate the histories of their close friends, they rely on sincerity and sympathy rather than knowledge and judgment to earn the reader's respect. The Pendennis novels are not Thackeray's best, but their narrators, who remain as kind and gentle men despite their various faults, represent Thackeray's attempt to deal effectively with the limitations of the individual perspective.

As a novel about art, *Vanity Fair* provided the stimulus for such later experiments with narrative technique. From this great novel, Thackeray learned that the function of the artist is neither to transcribe history nor propound morality. Having seen himself in the cracked mirror of his fictive world, Thackeray's narrator was forced to adopt a different stance.

Notes

1. *Vanity Fair: A Novel Without a Hero,* edd. Geoffrey and Kathleen Tillotson (Boston: Houghton Mifflin, 1963), p. 66. Subsequent references to this edition will be incorporated into the text.

2. "Caricatures and Lithography in Paris," in *The Paris Sketch Book* (London: John Macrone, 1840); reprinted in *The Works of William Makepeace Thackeray,* ed. Anne Ritchie, 13 vols. (London: Smith, Elder & Co., 1899-1900), V, 146.

3. "A Pictorial Rhapsody," *Fraser's,* 21 (June 1840); reprinted in *Works,* XIII, 328.

4. Charles Mauskopf, "Thackeray's Concept of the Novel: A Study of Conflict," [*Philological Quarterly*] 50 (1971), 239.

5. This is one of the incidental drawings not reproduced in the Tillotson edition. See *Works,* I, 15.

6. For a good analysis of the gossip-mongers, see Ann Y. Wilkinson, "The Tomeavesian Way of Knowing the World: Technique and Meaning in *Vanity Fair,*" *ELH,* 32 (1965), 370-87.

7. Henri-A. Talon, "Thackeray's *Vanity Fair* Revisited: Fiction as Truth," in *Of Books and Humankind,* ed. John Butt (London: Routledge, 1964), 139.

Bruce K. Martin (essay date 1975)

SOURCE: Martin, Bruce K. "*Vanity Fair*: Narrative Ambivalence and Comic Form." *Tennessee Studies in Literature* 20 (1975): 37-49.

[*In the following essay, Martin examines the question of Becky Sharp's guilt in her affair with Lord Steyne. In Martin's view, Thackeray's treatment of Becky's humiliation is noncommittal and reflects his underlying ambivalence toward all his characters.*]

Much critical discussion on **Vanity Fair** has concerned Thackeray's powers of creating characters. Not surprisingly, Becky Sharp has been singled out as his consummate triumph of characterization. Interestingly, though, there has been little agreement over Becky's behavior toward her husband and Lord Steyne culminating in her fall from grace in Chapter 55. While tacitly assuming Becky to be guilty of something, more critics disagree sharply on what she is guilty of and on Thackeray's rationale for the degree of guilt assigned to her.[1] This diversity of critical interpretation suggests the complexity of Thackeray's presentation of the crisis and the need for further examination of it.

The present essay will argue that Thackeray is ultimately noncommittal about Becky's guilt and that his inconclusiveness serves a definite structural objective. He judges Becky's guilt as "not proved," in accord with the novel's complex design. The possibility of her being guilty of something very serious adds to the mounting pressure for punishment of Becky after the Waterloo chapters, while the continuing possibility of her innocence and the harsh aftermath of her discovery by Rawdon create pity for Becky in her banishment and permit her to resume her initial role as rogue heroine. Thackeray's indefiniteness at this stage reinforces the complexity of action and character demanded by the comedy of the novel.

I

Perhaps the most striking aspect of Becky's crisis is the extent to which Thackeray raises, without resolving, the question of her guilt. No critic who claims that Becky is innocent of adulterous sex with Steyne has demonstrated her innocence. The narrator's questions following the catastrophe—"What *had* happened? Was she guilty or not?" (517)[2]—presumably refer not to the altercation between Becky, Steyne, and Rawdon upon his return home—this Thackeray has given in objective detail—but to what occurred between Lord Steyne and Becky before her husband's return. Steyne's informing Becky of Rawdon's appointment the night before the ball in no way dispels the possibility of a tryst after the party once Rawdon has been detained. Presumably Steyne's ardor for Becky is at its height at the party,[3] while the news of Rawdon's appointment plus his removal by Moss might make Becky more ready to comply.

At the same time, while Steyne may be wise to many of Becky's tricks, she is his equal in trickery. That she would risk much before cementing a permanent bargain seems doubtful. Steyne's immediate suspicion of a trap suggests that she has not made such a bargain by the time Rawdon returns, for it would be a strange and amusing trap were the wife already to have given in to her suitor before the husband's discovery. Steyne's protestation of Becky's guilt seems directed more toward the supposed scheme between husband ("the bully," Steyne calls him) and wife to blackmail him, than toward her sexual activity. Furthermore her resistance to pressure from Steyne long after Rawdon's arrest may signify that she never intends sex with the Marquis. Obviously Steyne expects it, but her awareness of the impracticality of ever giving him the ultimate prize surely remains. Her regrets the next day after Rawdon discovers them—"Good heavens! was ever such ill luck as mine? . . . to be so near and to lose all. Is it all too late?" (529)—refer to some further concession which she had hoped to win, presumably with the promise of sex. Whether Becky intended to fulfill that promise remains an open question.

Thackeray's ambiguity regarding Becky and the sex issue can be related to his treatment of the entire crisis
and to the novel's overall structure. More to the immediate point, however, is his apparent desire to shift the
question of her guilt from sexual fidelity to general loyalty of motive. After establishing sex as the lure used
by Becky, Thackeray deftly turns the issue away from
sex to the broader issue of vanity. His refusal to confirm Becky as an adulteress reflects not simply a prudish aversion to explicit sex in his novel,[4] but also the
recognition that his audience might become preoccupied with the sexual question and lose sight of the wider
social and moral issues surrounding *Vanity Fair*. But in
so shifting his novel's emphasis Thackeray moved only
from one ultimately unanswered question to another,
since by the end of the novel the reader feels even more
uncertain of Becky's fidelity of motive than of her
sexual fidelity to Rawdon. All the evidence in Becky's
favor Thackeray manages to qualify but not to refute
entirely. Her claims of innocence to Pitt in Chapter
55—the references to Rawdon's poverty and the appointment she had secured for him—are undercut by
her exaggerations of her affection for her husband and
by her obviously fake appeal to Pitt's ego. In the same
scene her blaming Steyne for the detention of Rawdon
appears questionable in view of her earlier falsely blaming Rawdon to Steyne for misspending money the Marquis had given her (Chapter 48). Her claim to Rawdon
in Chapter 52—"I have your interests to attend to, as
you can't attend to them yourself" (505)—similarly
seems dubious in its context, where Thackeray describes
how Rawdon, Jr., and Briggs were gotten out of the
house through collusion between Steyne and Becky.

The most substantial fact in Becky's favor is the appointment which she secures for Rawdon. As early as
Chapter 48 we see her telling Steyne to get her and
Rawdon "a place." Yet even this is subject to the hardly
very favorable interpretation that she may have an ulterior motive in pursuing a colonial appointment for her
husband. While Becky can eliminate Rawdon temporarily as an obstacle to her progress with Steyne, any
more profitable bargain demands more permanent removal. Though no such motive is indicated by Thackeray, it seems as plausible as the notion that Becky,
with her acquired taste for London social life, would
very readily accompany her dull husband to a colonial
outpost. Thus the appointment, though benefiting Rawdon financially, might work to his ultimate disadvantage.

Especially when combined with other evidences of her
disregard for Rawdon, an ulterior motive on Becky's
part appears to explain her seeking the appointment for
him. The most damning indication of her desire for
freedom from Rawdon is, of course, the money given
her by Amelia which she hides in the desk. In addition,
Becky increasingly mistreats Rawdon, causing him to
fear her independence and to tighten his watch on her.
Her disloyalty is further suggested by Steyne's sudden
willingness to befriend Pitt, whom he previously has
snubbed, and by Steyne's secret purchase of diamonds
and other gifts for Becky. Such things reinforce the impression of Becky as a totally selfish schemer, who confides her real intentions to no one.

In light of thoughtful scrutiny, though, these "proofs" of
Becky's disloyalty appear inconclusive. The financial
independence she gains from Rawdon by hiding money
may be the means of protecting both of them from his
irresponsible spending or from his many creditors. And,
given Rawdon's increasing bent toward policing Becky,
his detention at Moss's may be expedient if Becky is to
receive concessions from Steyne conducive to both her
and Rawdon's further security. Though she may be using sex only as a false lure for Steyne, Rawdon would
hardly countenance her pursuing their common benefit
in this way, for Steyne, unlike George Osborne, is dangerous game. Becky's neglect of Rawdon may signify
only the intensity of her pursuit of the Marquis, and her
exclusion of Rawdon from that pursuit may indicate
merely her recognition of Rawdon's dull-wittedness.
Thus it can be argued that Rawdon's desperate resistance to her more shrewd, if less honorable, design on
Steyne forces her to resort to Wenham and Moss as a
way of keeping her husband quiet.

The opinions of other characters concerning Becky's
treatment of Rawdon reflect both the general unreliability which Thackeray attributes to the society of the
novel and the biases of particular commentators. The
satire of *Vanity Fair* aims, among other things, at fashionable society's propensity toward gossip. Such satire
is reinforced in Chapter 47, at the height of Becky's
overtures to Steyne and shortly before her fall, by
Thackeray's introduction of Tom Eaves as a representative of the curious, obsequious, and untrustworthy gossips who regard Mrs. Crawley as a dangerous upstart.
They supply the basis for the suspicions of the Becky-
Steyne relationship felt by Pitt, who himself, despite his
awareness of Steyne's black reputation, is not above
patronizing the wealthy Marquis. And Thackeray attributes Lady Jane's dislike for Becky largely to jealousy over Pitt. Even Macmurdo, the most objective and
disinterested of Becky's critics, relies on the countless
rumors of the social and military sets, both bent on destroying Becky from a selfish desire to preserve caste,
and admits, "She may be innocent after all. . . . Steyne
has been a hundred times alone with her in the house
before" (524). If Wenham's weak excuses for Steyne
and Becky arouse Macmurdo's suspicion, that suspicion
depends partly on the same scandalmongers characterized by Thackeray as most unreliable. At the close of
the crisis section of the novel, Thackeray again undermines the guilt pronounced against Becky by a society
disposed, for reasons of vanity, to believe the worst of

her: "Was she guilty or not? We all know how chari-table the world is, and how the verdict of Vanity Fair goes when there is a doubt" (538). And Rawdon him-self unwittingly echoes this judgment when he says, "If she's not guilty, Pitt, she's as bad as guilty" (537), for like Vanity Fair he equates appearance with fact.

Hence the reader cannot be certain either of Becky's in-nocence or of her guilt. Thackeray tells us that she may or may not be guilty. At the same time we see that de-spite the paucity of evidence society will find her guilty. The ambiguity of the narrator's final verdict, plus the power of rumor in Vanity Fair, suggests that Becky need not be guilty for punishment to fall. But whether guilty or not, she merits Rawdon's anger, for there is no question but that he has been deceived and, for what-ever reasons, cruelly treated by her. Yet the shallowness suggested by the most favorable interpretation of Becky's behavior is lost on a society bent upon the most unfavorable interpretation. Becky thus stands con-victed of the wrong charge.

II

The key to the inconclusive treatment of Becky's guilt, as well as the mixed feelings aroused in the reader by her crisis, can be found partly in the structuring of events before her downfall. Becky's whole experience with Steyne represents the final step of a progression beginning with her departure from Miss Pinkerton's academy, where Thackeray sets up the comic paradigm to be repeated, with important variations, until she de-parts from Curzon Street, at the end of Chapter 55. In the context of Miss Pinkerton's pompous farewells to her pupils, Becky's greetings in French and her refusal of the hand so condescendingly offered her appear most appropriate humiliations for the vain school-mistress. Becky climaxes her jibes at the expense of "the Semira-mis of Hammersmith, the friend of Doctor Johnson, the correspondent of Mrs. Chapone herself," by throwing the revered dictionary out the coach window. In the first chapter Thackeray indicates Becky's position as a so-cial outsider, her consequent reliance upon her wit, and her ability to expose and exploit fraud. Becky is thus cast as the nemesis of vanity, determined and able to survive in Vanity Fair by preying on the conceit of oth-ers.

Her subsequent adventures represent attempts, with varying success, to improve her position against a soci-ety at best indifferent to her welfare. Her predicament as a penniless orphan becomes the rationale for her bra-zen pursuit of Jos Sedley, whose comically disastrous "courtship" constitutes the first phase of action involv-ing Becky. Miss Sharp's near-conquest of fat Jos con-stitutes an attack not only on the vain young Sedley, but also on the would-be gentility of the merchant class to which his family belongs. Jos's heavy drinking repre-

sents a necessary "accident" in the plot. As with the need for keeping Rawdon Crawley away from his aunt,[5] Thackeray could not allow Becky to triumph here, for he intended her to move elsewhere in search of secu-rity. So brilliant is his handling of Becky and so amus-ing the predicament of the drunken Jos that the reader detects no authorial manipulation. Rather, the entire episode reinforces the picture of Becky as keenly alert to the vanity of others and able to exploit their egoism.

Each of the later phases of her experience corresponds to the first. Becky moves from the London merchant class to the old landed aristocracy, but again we see her preying on the vanity of those she meets by turning their comic weaknesses against them. In attacking the Crawleys, she continues to seek a secure marriage. Our amusement stems from her clever advances upon Sir Pitt, Pitt, Jr., and Miss Crawley, each of whom displays a particular brand of vanity: old Pitt in his boorishness; Pitt, Jr., in his pious worldliness and personal vanity; and Miss Matilda in her paradoxical combination of radical political views and tyrannical personal behavior. Moreover Becky's victims expose each other's vanities; Pitt implicitly uses his father's greed to subdue the old man while Miss Crawley's wealth inspires an unable characteristic amiability among her relatives. And most impor-tant, Thackeray here casts Mrs. Bute Crawley as an an-tagonist to Becky and an indirect victim of Miss Sharp's comic strategy. Mrs. Bute's indignation at the upstart Becky's advance is depicted as sordid greed hiding be-hind concern for class and respectability.[6] Becky ap-pears much more knowing about herself and others, for in telling Amelia, "Revenge may be wicked, but it's natural . . . I'm no angel" (19), she acknowledges the impurity of her motives. Because she establishes herself among people with equally impure motives but without her clear-sightedness, her humiliations of her victims delight the reader.[7]

The second phase of the Becky plot ends, of course, with the disclosure to Miss Crawley of her marriage (Chapter 15). Here again Thackeray introduces an "ac-cident," the death of Lady Crawley, to force Becky to show her hand and precipitate a failure, and thus shift her story to its next phase. After marriage Becky's ob-jective continues to be security, or more particularly cash, and this she seeks from two sources, Miss Craw-ley and George Osborne. The possibility of securing funds from Miss Crawley is virtually terminated at the end of Chapter 25, while the assault on Osborne's capi-tal ends abruptly with the third "accident" of the novel, his death at Waterloo. As Becky next exploits family connections, Thackeray again makes her actions laugh-able by providing her not only with vain victims, but also a comic antagonist, the amusing Countess South-down, whose spirited opposition to Becky reflects reli-gious hypocrisy.[8] The final phase of Becky's activities before her downfall is her relationship with Steyne, which, though beginning in Chapter 37, does not take precedence over her relationship with the Crawleys until Chapter 47. Even here Becky's success remains partly tolerable through the presence of snobbish adversaries, headed by the haughty Lady Bareacres.

As suggested earlier, Thackeray alters the basically comic pattern in Becky's adventures to retain the reader's interest and to conform to the broader structure of the novel. One most obvious alteration is the social shift, whereby Becky moves from the merchant class of the Sedleys to the old gentry, represented by the Crawleys, and finally into the upper echelon of London society. But in moving Becky up the social scale Thackeray committed himself to a pattern which carried with it the danger of tiring the reader; he could not afford too many steps in Becky's progress into upper society. Given the need to extend his novel twenty full numbers, he at some time in the writing of *Vanity Fair* must have sensed the inadequacy of the social structure as the basis for plotting.[9] Despite its appropriateness for social satire and picaresque variety, Thackeray utilized this pattern for only two-thirds of the novel, ultimately subordinating it to a more complex structure.

Of crucial relevance to such complexity are the moral implications of Becky's social rise. Her exploitation of the socially vain people she meets can only temporarily offset the fact that she herself, for whatever motives, is on the social ladder and infected by the climbing disease. But for most of the novel Thackeray, like Becky, chooses to ignore the implications of her climb.[10] Not until her episode with Steyne does Thackeray explicitly show that Becky herself is subject to the social vanity on which she has so readily capitalized. Up to this point the reader has observed Becky pursuing, in succession, marriage, money, and "credit." With the advent of Steyne, however, Thackeray makes it clear that she is operating in a quite different sphere, with a presumably different objective. The narrator assumes a different tone in the initial description of Steyne from that employed in first describing Sir Pitt:

> The candles lighted up Lord Steyne's shining bald head, which was fringed with red hair. He had thick bushy eyebrows, with little twinkling blood shot eyes, surrounded by a thousand wrinkles. His jaw was underhung, and when he laughed, two white buck-teeth protruded themselves and glistened savagely in the midst of the grin. He had been dining with royal personages, and wore his garter and ribbon. A short man was his lordship, broad-chested, and two-legged, but proud of the fineness of his foot and ankle, and always caressing his garter-knee.
>
> (366)

Compared with the earlier picture of Sir Pitt—"a man in drab breeches and gaiters, with a dirty old coat, a foul old neckcloth lashed round his bristly neck, a shin-

ing bald head, a leering red face, a pair of twinkling grey eyes and a mouth perpetually on the grin" (68)—the description of Steyne is notably grim. The ensuing dialogue between Becky and Steyne, who joke in mock-pastoral terms about Becky's "moral shepherd's dog," lacks the lightness of tone with which old Pitt's rascality is treated. Similarly the lengthy history of Steyne's family given in Chapter 47 differs in both content and tone from the amusing sketch of the Crawleys in Chapter 11. The taint of hereditary illness, the mystery of imprisoned relatives, and Steyne's ruthlessness toward his wife inspire a profound revulsion wholly unrelieved by the comic elements dominating Thackeray's treatment of the Crawleys.

This change in Thackeray's treatment of Becky's would-be lovers corresponds to a change in Becky's objectives in pursuing them, or at least to Thackeray's belated acknowledgment of her total motives. Thus the hypocrisy of her social ascent becomes apparent in her pursuit of Steyne, who represents to her more than simply wealth. Not until she is about to be presented at court do we learn that "to be, and to be thought, a respectable woman, was Becky's aim in life . . ." (460). Her appearance at court is a watershed in the development of her snobbery, a point after which she can no longer function principally as a punitive comic agent. In shifting from the Crawleys to Steyne, Becky has come to regard herself not merely as shrewdly opportunistic, but as inherently more deserving than others. She comes to equate social position with virtue, something she has never done before, and to believe in social respectability as an end and not simply the means to a material end. Hence her reaction to being presented to George IV, whom Thackeray castigates elsewhere as a "contemptible imposter"[11]: "This may be said, that in all London there was no more loyal heart than Becky's after this interview. The name of her king was always on her lips, and he was proclaimed by her to be the most charming of men" (463). Becky comes not only to profit by the social system but to believe in it. Her change from economic to social values marks her as deserving the humiliation she earlier had meted out to others.

Accompanying Becky's shift of values after the Waterloo chapters is a shift to a more innocent class of victims, whom she injures more seriously than she did George Osborne or Lady Southdown. In working for "credit" instead of cash, she begins to trample on honest, simple people. This new class of victims includes the landlords, milliners, and nurses cheated by Becky as she leaves Paris. Upon returning to England she and Rawdon continue to bleed merchants of their hard-earned funds. The most sustained portrait of an innocent victim is that of Raggles, the ex-butler to Miss Crawley, who rents Becky and Rawdon the house in Curzon Street and supplies their food; "a good man; good and happy" (359) is Thackeray's description of

Raggles, whose loyalty to the family of his former mistress results in imprisonment for him and poverty for his family. Unlike Briggs, another well-meaning victim of Becky's thoughtless financial schemes, Raggles is no foolish sentimentalist but simply an honest tradesman who mistakenly attributes honesty to Miss Crawley's family. After Becky's downfall the cry of honest Raggles, "I little thought one of that family was a goin' to ruing me—yes, ruing me" (528), underscores the indiscriminateness of Becky's later victimizings.

Perhaps the most pathetic victims of her increased ruthlessness in the second half of the novel are her son and husband. By giving Becky a son shortly after Waterloo, Thackeray set up another cause of pressure for the downfall she later suffers, as her mistreatment of Rawdon, Jr., further disqualifies her for the tolerance sustained so long by the punitive comedy in which she is the central agent. Equally important here, as several critics have noted,[12] is the growth of responsibility undergone by Rawdon, whose new-found maturity centers on a concern for the boy, in marked contrast to Becky's neglect. And nowhere is Thackeray's strategy in placing his chapters more evident than in his placement of the chapters devoted to Amelia after Waterloo and before Becky's downfall, in which Amelia's devotion to George, Jr., despite hardship forms a sharp and damning contrast to Becky's mistreatment of her son amid prosperity. Through direct portrayal of little Rawdon's distasteful treatment by his mother, and through more oblique indications—references to the elder Rawdon's affection for the boy or Amelia's sacrifices for Georgy—Thackeray, in virtually every chapter between Rawdon's birth and his final separation from his mother, presents Becky's failure as a mother as the least tolerable of her mounting offenses.

III

Through these cumulative pressures—Becky's acquired snobbery, her growing tendency to inflict pain on undeserving victims, and her increasingly apparent shortcomings as a wife and mother—Thackeray causes the reader to demand some type of punishment. But, while the developing crisis with Steyne at first appears to be such a punishment, Thackeray's ambivalent treatment of Becky's behavior toward Steyne renders her punishment less than comic. Despite the ironic appropriateness of her being turned out by the society she has duped for so long, Vanity Fair's escape without punishment creates some pity for Becky.

The partial injustice of her punishment becomes apparent in Chapter 64, where Thackeray shows Becky wandering through Europe, hounded by rumors of her past. Instead of describing her vices on the Continent, he concentrates on the mistreatment of Becky by people with mixed motives: on Wenham's slandering her to Pitt, on the desire of fashionable society to have her deported, and on the rumors which foil her attempts to establish herself in Europe. Significantly Thackeray climaxes this persecution with Becky's meeting Steyne, who threatens her life. To the reader Becky is partly redeemed by her helplessness at his hands. Given the sharp fall she has suffered and her precarious relationship with a society indisposed, for reasons of vanity, to allow her even a modicum of security, the independence Thackeray grants her in the end appears an appropriate affront to the citizens of Vanity Fair, while the prohibition against her re-entering high society sufficiently punishes her for her earlier errors of egoism.

The justness of Becky's final position is suggested also by her actions during the crisis between Amelia and Dobbin. Dobbin's outcry against the sentimental Amelia's unqualified reacceptance of Becky works in both his favor and Becky's. On the one hand, since his initial appearance Dobbin has seemed as alert as Becky to the vanity of others, yet totally lacking in the ambition which drives Becky up the social ladder. Further the reader can see that despite Dobbin's reliance upon undependable rumor, Becky is certainly not what she claims; her protest to Amelia of devotion to Rawdon, Jr., for example, confirms Dobbin's distrust as well founded. In view of his many years of patient devotion, his objections to Becky's quick readmittance into Amelia's favor seems reasonable, while Amelia's seeming indifference to his ultimatum appears unreasonable. At the same time, despite Becky's roguery in dealing with Amelia, her misadventures after leaving Rawdon have marked her as deserving the minimal security Amelia would offer. Thackeray conveniently resolves the reader's conflict of sympathies at this point by having Becky intervene in Dobbin's behalf. Her intervention seems to assure his winning the long-sought Amelia, but, more important, it suggests the element of fair play in Becky's character and further qualifies her for the limited success she achieves in the end.

The conclusion of the novel finds Becky with friends, but also with enemies, financially secure, but only on the fringe of polite society. Thackeray defines this final situation as the degree of success to which her keenness of wit and mistreatment by vain society, as well as her moral limitations, entitle her. Lest the reader become overly sympathetic with Becky after her heroic defense of Dobbin, Thackeray inserts the briefly described episode involving the death of Jos Sedley, to remind us that Becky continues to be "no angel."

The ambivalent treatment of this final Sedley episode[13] preserves the balance inherent in the "unheroic" view of life sustained throughout the novel and in the comic form in which Thackeray chose to embody that view. The same principle operates in his treatment of Becky's crisis, with which this discussion has been chiefly concerned, for there he avoided creating too much or too little sympathy for Becky. The crisis represents a pivotal point in the novel, where the pattern of punitive comedy gives way temporarily to humiliation for Becky herself, before returning to the view of Becky as certainly no worse than those whose egos she has offended. Had Thackeray pronounced her guilty of disloyalty to Rawdon, the novel might have moved out of the comic sphere; at any rate, it might have seemed unnecessary to continue the novel beyond Becky's punishment. To pronounce her innocent, on the other hand, would detract sharply from the carefully developed demand for punishment of some sort and also would remove the novel from comedy by creating largely unalloyed pity for Becky.

To be sure, the completed novel hardly resulted solely from adherence to a formal type or from the author's non-heroic perspective. Of the many extrinsic factors governing its composition, the demands of serialization especially helped dictate the shape and size of *Vanity Fair.* That some looseness resulted cannot be denied. Clearly, though, Thackeray's ambivalent treatment of Becky at key points in the novel, and particularly his noncommittal attitude toward her activities immediately before her crisis, helped minimize unavoidable looseness by keeping the novel from what, in terms of serialization, would be a premature conclusion. The narrative ambivalence surrounding Becky's fall permits a combination of both types of comedy—that in which Becky is punisher and that in which she is punished—while allowing, indeed requiring, the novel to extend beyond the crisis with Steyne. Narrative ambivalence thus helps sustain both the comedy and the unity of *Vanity Fair.*

Notes

1. For example, Kathleen Tillotson, *Novels of the Eighteen-Forties* (London: Oxford Univ. Press, 1956), 250, implies Becky's responsibility for Rawdon's arrest, but skirts the question of her ultimate objective: whether in consorting with Steyne she envisioned an adulterous relationship which would give her independence from Rawdon or, as she claims, she acted principally in Rawdon's interest to secure him the appointment. On the other hand, F. E. L. Priestley, "Introduction" to *Vanity Fair* (New York: Odyssey, n.d.), xvi, asserts that Becky's claim of innocence "at least means that she had not yet rendered to Steyne the services as mistress for which he had paid so extravagantly, and obviously in advance." Without indicating why we are to assume that Steyne and Becky have not consummated their relationship earlier in the day or even after the charade party of the night before, Priestley, by his phrase "at least," raises without resolving the important questions of whether Becky may not be innocent of

more than adultery and why Thackeray permits her to retain even this much innocence. A view somewhat different from Priestley's is taken by Frank Chandler, *The Literature of Roguery* (Boston: Houghton, 1907), II, 465, who maintains that "Becky's mendacity is indeed so unusual that the reader does not know whether to believe her protestations of innocence at the critical moment." But where Chandler attributes the reader's uncertainty over the crisis of Becky's cleverness, Andrew Von Hendy, "Misunderstandings About Becky's Characterization in *Vanity Fair,*" *Nineteenth-Century Fiction* 18 (1964-65), 283, sees the questions posed by the narrator at the close of Chapter 53 as reflections of Becky's own moral confusion. Assuming that Becky had contemplated adultery all along, he concludes that "Her moral bankruptcy, rather like Bulstrode's, prevents her from being honest even with herself." Finally, G. Armour Craig, "On the Style of *Vanity Fair,*" in *Style in Prose: English Institute Essays, 1958,* ed. Harold C. Martin (New York: Columbia Univ. Press, 1959), 104, after allowing that Becky is guilty of preparing for adultery, insists that Thackeray's final questioning of her guilt reflects his inability or unwillingness to face squarely the implications of her behavior. "Thackeray will not—he can not—support us as we revolt from such a spectacle," Craig concludes.

2. William Makepeace Thackeray, *Vanity Fair,* ed. Geoffrey and Kathleen Tillotson (Boston: Houghton, 1963). Chapter and page citations refer to this edition and will be included in the text.

3. Von Hendy, 281-83.

4. He probably felt such an aversion, though. See Walter Houghton, *The Victorian Frame of Mind* (New Haven: Yale Univ. Press, 1957), 357, 419. Gordon N. Ray, *Thackeray: The Age of Wisdom, 1847-1863* (London: Oxford Univ. Press, 1958), 123-26, tells of Thackeray's early protests against Victorian prudery and his recourse to innuendo in his later works, but notes that as the editor of *Cornhill* "Thackeray displayed a caution that he would himself have been the first to ridicule earlier in his career" (301).

5. In Chapter 16 Thackeray's self-conscious narrator recognizes the demands of serial publication and the need for deferring certain things until the structurally appropriate time when he explains why, as Becky tried to soften the shock of her marriage, he chose to keep Rawdon away from his aunt: "If Rawdon Crawley had been then and there present, instead of being at the club nervously drinking claret, the pair might have gone on their knees before the old spinster, avowed all and been forgiven in a twinkling. But that good chance was

denied to the young couple, doubtless in order that this story might be written, in which numbers of their wonderful adventures are narrated—adventures which could never have occurred to him if they had been housed and sheltered under the comfortable uninteresting forgiveness of Miss Crawley" (153).

6. Thus there is more than coincidence in the fact that Mrs. Bute was educated at Miss Pinkerton's and that mutual admiration between former student and teacher has persisted.

7. As John Dodds has observed in "Introduction" to *Vanity Fair* (New York: Holt, 1955), xvi: "Were it not that she employs her wits against people even less admirable than herself we might be shocked by our absence of moral qualms about her. As it is, there is a kind of wild justice in her breezy assault upon the citadels of the stupid and the mighty."

8. The Countess's worldliness is illustrated in Chapter 33, where she, Lady Emily, and Pitt discuss the best means of approaching Miss Crawley. Pitt, fearing that the religious assault proposed by Emily will lose them his aunt's £70,000, insists upon the importance of proceeding cautiously, and Lady Southdown readily defers to his materialistic arguments. Thackeray wryly notes: "Lady Southdown, we say, for the sake of the invalid's health, or for the sake of her soul's ultimate welfare, or for the sake of her money, agreed to temporise" (324).

9. Concerning the bearing of serial publication on *Vanity Fair,* see Tillotson, *Novels of the Eighteen-Forties,* 25-47, 239-42; and Edgar F. Harden, "The Discipline and Significance of Form in *Vanity Fair,*" *PMLA* 82 (1967), 530-41.

10. While Becky's refusal of the marriage offer by Glauber, old Pitt's physician (Chapter 11), hints at her capacity for snobbishness—"as if I was born, indeed, to be a country surgeon's wife!" she writes Amelia (98)—her share of this fundamental characteristic of the society she invades remains largely latent until much later in the novel.

11. *The Letters of William Makepeace Thackeray,* ed. Gordon N. Ray (Cambridge, Mass.: Harvard Univ. Press, 1945), III, 570. His essay on George IV in *The Four Georges* [(1860)] offers an even stronger condemnation.

12. For example, Tillotson, *Novels of the Eighteen-Forties,* 248-49, or Priestley, xxxii-xxxiii.

13. See Von Hendy, "Misunderstandings About Becky's Characterization in *Vanity Fair,*" 281-82.

Jay W. Margulies (essay date March 1977)

SOURCE: Margulies, Jay W. "*Vanity Fair*: No Prizes Worth Winning." *Research Studies* 45, no. 1 (March 1977): 1-13.

[*In the following essay, Margulies analyzes the sense of disappointment that underlies the aspirations of* Vanity Fair's *central characters.*]

Vanity Fair is a complex narrative about the inevitability of failure. People have aspirations and dreams which they either don't realize or do only to find them unsatisfactory. We watch young, hopeful people become middle-aged and discover, as is said of Dobbin, "The more he thought of this long passage of his life, the more clearly he saw his deception" (ch. 67).[1] Insight, however, does not lead to freedom; life is a game of chance in which all players lose. Dobbin, Amelia, Becky, George, Mr. Osborne, all act in ways that subvert their apparent goals and thus can achieve only the most transitory gratifications. This dynamic is illustrated clearly in the description of parsimonious Sir Pitt Crawley's efforts to save money:

> He had a taste for law, which cost him many thousands yearly; and being a great deal too clever to be robbed, as he said, by any single agent, allowed his affairs to be mismanaged by a dozen, whom he all equally mistrusted. He was such a sharp landlord, that he could hardly find any but bankrupt tenants. . . . For want of proper precautions, his coal mines filled with water: . . . and . . . he lost more horses than any man in the country, from under-feeding and buying cheap.
>
> (ch. 9)

The best moments in the novel are those when a character recognizes his failure; in particular, sees the inability of his love-object to reciprocate his affection: such moments as Mr. Osborne in his study after George's marriage and Rawdon's return from the spunging-house. Consider also Dobbin's speech acknowledging the speciousness of his dream, in contrast to his reunion with Amelia one chapter later.

> You are not worthy of the love which I have devoted to you. I knew all along that the prize I had set my life on was not worth the winning; that I was a fool, with fond fancies, too, bartering away my all of truth and ardour against your little feeble remnant of love.
>
> (ch. 66)

This statement is clear, pointed to the degree of pain; the reunion, however, is as murky as the rain surrounding the figures, the lady hidden in the old cloak, the sentiment barely concealed in the narrator's distancing humor:

> She . . . was kissing one of his hands with all her might; whilst the other, *I suppose,* was engaged in holding her to his heart (which her head just about reached)

and *in preventing her from tumbling down.* She was *murmuring something about*—forgive—dear William—dear, dear, dearest friend—kiss, kiss, kiss, *and so forth*—and in fact went on under the cloak *in an absurd manner.*

(ch. 67; emphasis mine)

The recognition scenes have a key element in common: they all show one person's attempt to sever the emotional bonds felt for another who has proved unworthy of love and trust. They are highly charged; the happier scenes are much less so. These latter are anticlimactic, undercut by the author who refuses to yield to his own fondness for sentiment or to allow the reader to indulge this emotion. But although Thackeray's views on adult relationships are quite negative, he avoids a modern sense of despair. For despite his acute awareness of human pain, he has an interest and delight in human activity, in roguery, in power, that modifies his intellectual and moral premises. The novel shows the failures of activity, but it also reveals Thackeray's deep-rooted sense of the necessity for man, unheroic and with limited power, to recognize illusion and to accept responsibility for his own fate.

The novel centers around the movement of Becky Sharp and Amelia Sedley from adolescence to middle age. Amelia is cast as the conventional heroine[2] whose goal is to be established in a satisfactory marriage. She believes that love is the only important aspect of human relations. We see her as friend, daughter, betrothed, as wife and mother; in all these roles she appears inadequate. Unable to trust her own capacity to give or to share, she cannot establish connections based on mutual need and affection. She lavishes her love on George and Georgy, persons incapable of returning it. And she uses others to protect her from being, in the narrator's words, "on the wing" (ch. 12); "receiving parental affection if not ungratefully, at least indifferently, and as if it were her due." She cannot understand why her ambitions do not produce the expected happiness; and to counter a nonspecific feeling of "shame" (ch. 26), she sees herself as a tragic victim, doomed because "of the crime she had long ago been guilty—the crime of loving wrongly, too violently, against reason" (ch. 18).

Many readers of *Vanity Fair* have been critical of Thackeray's portrayal of Amelia. The criticisms are twofold. First, that she is a weak, simple, passive person and therefore too inadequate a heroine, unfit to carry much of the weight of the novel; and, second, that Thackeray's attitude toward her is sentimental. Mark Spilka writes that Thackeray "asks us to take it on faith that his heroine is dear, sweet, simple, gentle, and kind. . . . Amelia Sedley . . . is never vividly 'present' in her given role." Spilka criticizes the author because "his lavish praises of Amelia . . . are only part of a more general attempt to shield her from close scrutiny.

The result is a dramatic fraud, sustained, oppressive, and for the most part unrelieved."[3] Even one of Thackeray's most sympathetic readers, Gordon N. Ray, complains that although she "was particularly dear to her creator, . . . the handicap of Amelia's passivity is in the end insurmountable; she does nothing, she merely endures or enjoys as circumstances dictate."[4] Such criticism, however, is misdirected. It is inaccurate to claim that Thackeray attempts "to shield her from close scrutiny." He is under no illusions about her flaws; indeed, as A. E. Dyson says, "At a very deep level Thackeray was critical of" her.[5] The narrator tells us and shows us that she is "cold," "kind," "hopeless," and "selfish" (ch. 43). And it is clear that Thackeray, as he himself said, chose not to make her "a higher order of woman."[6]

The author does admire Amelia, but this admiration is not sentimental. He likes her partly because of her passivity, because she is uncomfortable in Vanity Fair. But he also finds the power she gains precisely because of her weakness compelling.

> Almost all men who came near her loved her; though no doubt they would be at a loss to tell you why. She was not brilliant, nor witty, nor wise overmuch, nor extraordinarily handsome. . . . I think it was her weakness which was her principal charm:—a kind of sweet submission and softness, which seemed to appeal to each man she met for his sympathy and protection.
>
> (ch. 38)

> I know few things more affecting than that timorous debasement and self-humiliation of a woman. How she owns that it is she and not the man who is guilty. . . . It is those who injure women who get the most kindness from them—they are born timid and tyrants, and maltreat those who are humblest before them.
>
> (ch. 50)

This paradox, explicitly stated, fascinates Thackeray. And if he fails to condemn fully its debasing features, he nevertheless thoroughly exposes them. Critics who fail to see the "truth" of the exposure, who, because they are immune to her "charm," are infuriated by Amelia, inevitably use Thackeray's observations of her timidity and tyranny to attack him.

Amelia's activities revolve around two courtships. The first suitor, George Osborne, is an unworthy hero. Although encouraged by his father and friends, including Dobbin, to consider himself a talented and superior person, he is never shown doing anything to merit this reputation. Rawdon Crawley understands him, and treats him as a "mark." Becky calls him "Cupid," "[flattering] him about his good looks, . . . [and watching] over him kindly at *écarté* (ch. 25). Watching him lose, needless to say. We see George as the dupe of men with titles, and gentlemen who despise "City fellows" (ch. 14). The narrator sums him up as "the hero among . . . third-rate men" (ch. 21).

While everyone favors the match, George is apathetic, telling Dobbin that although Amelia is "faultless . . . there's no fun in winning a thing unless you play for it" (ch. 13). When he finds the marriage fiercely opposed by his father, he becomes enthusiastic, because he sees himself making "a tremendous sacrifice in marrying this young creature," and because he sees her as "a slave before him . . . and his soul within him thrilled secretly somehow at the knowledge of his power" (ch. 20). Like Amelia, George believes that marriage is the endpoint of activity. He envisions himself, the rake reformed, as the country gentleman. (This fantasy occurs before Mr. Sedley's bankruptcy.) "He was a little wild: how many young men are; and don't girls like a rake better than a milksop? He hadn't sown his wild oats as yet, but he would soon: . . . and his allowance, with Amelia's settlement, would enable them to take a snug place in the country somewhere, in a good sporting neighbourhood; and he would hunt a little, and farm a little; and they would be very happy" (ch. 13). Implied here is George's failure as a rake, and the limited scope of his activities. He is a milksop, a "little" man who in the future will try to sow his wild oats.

It is a mistake to think that Amelia is blind to George's flaws. True, we are told again and again that she believes him gallant and brilliant. However, we also learn of the "misgivings and fears which she dared not acknowledge to herself, though she was always secretly brooding over them."

> Her heart tried to persist in asserting that George Osborne was worthy and faithful to her, though she knew otherwise. . . . How many suspicions of selfishness and indifference had she encountered and obstinately overcome. . . . She did not dare to own that the man she loved was her inferior; or to feel that she had given her heart away too soon. . . .
>
> So imprisoned and tortured was this gentle little heart.
>
> (ch. 18)

Such undercurrents are a major feature of the anxiety she feels after marriage. She cultivates her sense of her own inadequacy, of her own inferiority. She decides that she is "not worthy of him," and condemns herself for being "very wicked and selfish" because she was unable to refuse him (ch. 25).

Shortly after her return to London following her honeymoon trip, Amelia recognizes that her marriage is unsatisfying; the section is one of the most important in the novel. Alone she visits her parents; George has "business"—he attends the theatre—and therefore cannot accompany her. She goes up to her former bedroom.

> Here was the . . . harmless lost wanderer in the great struggling crowds of Vanity Fair.

Here she sate, and recalled to herself fondly that image of George to which she had knelt before marriage. Did she own to herself how different the real man was from that superb young hero whom she had worshipped? . . .

> She looked at the little white bed, which had been hers a few days before, and thought she would like to sleep in it that night, and wake, as formerly, with her mother smiling over her in the morning. Then she thought with terror of the great funereal damask pavilion in the vast and dingy state bed-room, which was awaiting her at the grand hotel in Cavendish Square. Dear little white bed! How she had despaired and hoped to die there; and now were not all her wishes accomplished, and the lover of whom she had despaired her own for ever?
>
> (ch. 26)

The contrast is between past and future, between "the little white bed" and "the great funereal damask pavilion." The thought of her marriage bed terrifies her. Marriage with George is both a spiritual death and a sexual emptiness. The pedestal of purity onto which George has placed her is a barrier against and protection from active sexual involvement. As a rake and husband, George is inadequate; rather than asserting his power, he leaves his wife alone. "They were only a week married, and here was George already suffering ennui, and eager for others' society! She trembled for the future" (ch. 25). Amelia creates her own image of the woman dying from a sexual wounding, a symbolic rape victim: "She was wrapped in a white morning dress, . . . her large eyes fixed and without light, . . . holding [a] sash against her bosom, from which the heavy net of crimson dropped like a large stain of blood." George, however, is packing to leave her: "the great game of war was going to be played, and he one of the players" (ch. 30).

Despite the fact that Thackeray has established an unheroic heroine, the structure of her story is the same as in most other nineteenth-century English novels where a young woman is the central character; the problem on a formal level is how to remove George as husband and substitute a more adequate figure. George dies in battle at Waterloo. Enter Dobbin as suitor; and his courtship guides the remaining Amelia sections of the novel.

But Amelia is not willing to be courted. She cannot abandon the illusion on which she had established all her expectations. Her private wish for a permanent separation from George (actually, for his death, because his departure, with Becky, for example, would seem then to be an intolerable rejection of her) and for a return to "the little white bed" has been granted. No longer is she faced with an active reminder of what she believes to be her failure. She surrounds herself with false memories, a picture of George, and Georgy; these act as her protectors and enslavers. She does not have to give her love to another adult; "this child was her being" (ch.

35).[7] George, her "angel" and "saint in heaven," has been elevated by her into a superego figure, both jealous and protective. Their child is and becomes living confirmation of the truth of her memories: "The elder George returned in him somehow, only improved. . . . The widow's heart thrilled as she held him to it" (ch. 38).

Dobbin's role in the first courtship is a curious one. His action is both noble and perverse: "But for him [the marriage] never would have taken place" (ch. 20). His "George, she's dying" (ch. 18), is an eloquent plea; but it doesn't ring true. Perhaps because of her tears and perpetual suffering, Amelia is the most resilient character in the novel. Dobbin even admits that she *might* have recovered the shock of losing" George, and questions his own motives in advancing the marriage. "Why was it? Because he loved her so much that he could not bear to see her unhappy: or because his own sufferings of suspense were so unendurable that he was glad to crush them at once—as we hasten a funeral after a death, or, when a separation from those we love is imminent, cannot rest until the parting be over" (ch. 24).[8]

Clearly an oedipal pattern has been established among Dobbin, George, and Amelia. Dobbin's feeling "as if he was a criminal after seeing her" directly precedes his bringing about a reunion of the lovers (ch. 18). Their marriage day is one of pain for him: "Never since he was a boy had he felt so miserable and so lonely. He longed with a heart-sick yearning for the first few days to be over, that he might see her again" (ch. 22). Dobbin excludes himself as a sexual force in this triangle, and adopts the role of voyeur, "[loitering] about, . . . [and watching] the lights vanish from George's sitting-room windows, and shine out in the bedroom close at hand" (ch. 27).

These aspects of Dobbin's behavior indicate the neurotic nature of his love for Amelia. His modesty, his generosity, his promotion of her marriage to George are not quite the virtues they appear to be. His selflessness is the way whereby he gratifies his psychosexual needs. After George's death and the birth of Georgy, Dobbin sees "with a fatal perspicuity" that he is still unloved by Amelia, and exiles himself to India (ch. 35). There he learns that she plans to marry the Reverend Mr. Binney. His "years of constancy and devotion" (ch. 59) are being requited by Amelia's betrayal of him. This perception, of Amelia once again being attached to another man, allows Dobbin to take action, to return to his pursuit of the unattainable woman.

When Dobbin returns to England, he begins to dominate the action, assuming the role of social harmonizer. Although Amelia has rejected the clergyman, Dobbin is still unable to win her, and again accepts his limited relationship with her: "I will not change, dear Amelia. . . . I ask for no more than your love. I think I would not have it otherwise. Only let me stay near you, and see you often" (ch. 59). Dobbin's love is an end rather than a means; it traps him. Even when he realizes that he has been worshipping falsely and achieves a convincing therapeutic recovery from his paralyzing fixation, Dobbin understands that no glories await him. The future holds only "duty. . . . When I am old, and broke, I will go on half-pay, and my sisters shall scold me. I have 'geliebt and gelebet.' . . . I am done." He accepts responsibility for his "deception." And even sees that winning Amelia would not have brought happiness: "Suppose I had won her, should I not have been disenchanted the day after my victory?" (ch. 67).

Amelia, too, can finally acknowledge that she has been deluded; she can accept the fact of George's unworthiness. But she is unable to love Dobbin until he is unable to love her. When she finally writes to him, she does so largely because Becky's friends fill her "with intolerable terror and aversion" (ch. 67). And because the behavior patterns of a lifetime are strong, Dobbin cannot abandon Amelia. Once more he rescues her. But at the end we learn he has transferred his love to a new object, his daughter, who becomes the new taboo female.

Thus far I have mainly discussed *Vanity Fair* as a marriage novel centering around Amelia. Thackeray's main themes are also developed in the action dominated by Becky Sharp. Unscrupulous, energetic, and unwilling to accept a permanent role as governess, she uses her brains and beauty in an attempt to rise to a leading place among the powerful and prestigious. But she cannot continue her success. For every action she takes to improve her position, she takes one which ultimately destroys her victory. She is more ambiguous in her interests than we might imagine. She treats everything as means and nothing as an end, for she can never be long satisfied. When she thinks she has a goal, she is being self-deceptive. As Barbara Hardy has written, "Some of Thackeray's most interesting revelations about Becky are her limitations, her inefficiencies and her failures, though it must be said that her capacity to put up with failure, to adapt and survive, is of course also an important part of the complex portraiture."[9] This "capacity to put up with failure," which so impresses us, results in large part from the fact that the goal Becky fails to attain is only an illusory one.

She sees marriage as an escape "from the prison in which she found herself" (ch. 2). Her first attempt ends in failure when Jos does not propose; but she then wins Rawdon Crawley. Rather than regretting her misfortune when she learns that had she waited she might have been Sir Pitt Crawley's wife, "she wisely turned her whole attention towards the future." In the midst of "doubt and mystery," she determines to act without delay (ch. 15). In this particular instance she leaves Miss Crawley's house. Her marriage to Rawdon is the central action that causes his disinheritance (as Amelia's to George causes his); but Becky's subsequent deeds prevent a reconciliation with the aunt. Had she stayed, for example, "the pair might have gone down on their knees before the old spinster, avowed all, and had been forgiven in a twinkling" (ch. 16).

But Becky's greatest social blunder is her open hostility to her son. She is fully consistent in this, although it is quite clear she knows the importance to her success of feigning love. Her malignant indifference to children never changes, and her actions toward them limit the duration of the sympathy she can establish with the other women in the novel. Lady Jane is horrified at Becky's behavior; this horror finally gives her enough strength to stand up against her sister-in-law. "She never loved her dear little boy, who used to fly here and tell me of her cruelty to him. . . . Her soul is black. . . . I tremble when I touch her. I keep my children out of her sight." Lady Jane forces her husband to "choose, sir, between her and me" (ch. 55). Becky is "pleased" by this attack, because she believes it is motivated by jealousy; but she is wrong. She provokes Lady Jane's hostility by the coldness of her own behavior toward young Rawdon. This antagonism is far more important than Pitt's attentiveness to her.[10]

In contrast, Rawdon's best quality is his ability both to give and receive love. He is the only one in the novel to show normal adult sexual feelings. His love for Becky is strong, healthy, and physical: "He had never been so happy, as, during the past few months, his wife had made him. All former delights . . . were quite insipid when compared to the lawful matrimonial pleasures which of late he had enjoyed" (ch. 30). Becky, however, comes close to emasculating him. Because he is willing to be "her upper servant and *maître d'hôtel*," she begins to grow contemptuous of him. "He was Colonel Crawley no more. He was Mrs. Crawley's husband" (ch. 37).

Rawdon also shows a deeply rooted affection for his son. His "best and honestest feelings" come out in his "paternal" love (ch. 52). The two establish an adult/child friendship. The descriptions of young Rawdon watching his father shave every morning and of the two playing games and going out together are a refreshing contrast to the possessiveness or indifference other parents in *Vanity Fair* show toward their children. But Rawdon has to see his son "in private," for he is afraid of Becky; the relationship "increase[s] her scorn for him." She causes him to be "ashamed of this paternal softness" (ch. 37). Becky ceases to be his sexual companion, and the son cannot completely compensate for this loss. Rawdon is not consciously aware of the real cause of his estrangement from his wife. For just as her

hostility to the father/son relationship causes "her contempt for her husband [to grow] greater every day," so too does it foster a change in his feelings, separating him from Becky "more than he knew or acknowledged to himself" (ch. 52).

Becky has an inflated sense of her own power to manipulate people. Certainly, with men like Jos Sedley and George Osborne she can be cutting and cruel, and then use her charms to attract them to her again. When she finds herself able to control a person, she loses all respect for him; but she overreaches herself. Her letter to Rawdon at the spunging-house, if not designed to entice the "suspicions" it does, is very foolish. ("Everybody with *foison* of compliments and pretty speeches—plaguing poor me, who longed to be rid of them, and was thinking *every moment of the time* of *mon pauvre prisonnier*" [ch. 53].) The final scene between Rawdon and Becky results in the return of his power, and, consequently, in her defeat. She has physically imprisoned him—whether by agreeing to have him arrested, or by allowing him to remain there, the difference is unimportant—and she has psychologically imprisoned him, having "beat and cowed [him] into laziness and submission" (ch. 45). But when she feels the force of his anger, she begins to respond: "She stood there trembling before him. She admired her husband, strong, brave, and victorious." For the first time Becky is sexually excited: the language is that of a rape. "'Come here,' he said.—She came up at once. 'Take off those things.' She began, trembling, . . . quivering and looking up at him. . . . 'Come up stairs,' Rawdon said to his wife. 'Don't kill me, Rawdon,' she said" (ch. 53). Throughout the novel Becky seeks social manifestations of power, money, and prestige, all of which prove unsatisfactory. The only thing that finally can gratify her is what must produce the destruction of her conscious intentions.

Becky's actual behavior makes overwhelmingly clear that the critics who accept David Cecil's view that she is incapable of murder are wrong.[11] Her good nature and her respect for Dobbin do not mean that she relates to people as people rather than as objects to be used. Her "good" acts, such as helping Dobbin win Amelia and singing for Lady Steyne, occur when she is able to show her superiority. After Amelia's verbal attack on her in Brussels, we are told: "Rebecca was of a good-natured and obliging disposition; and she liked Amelia rather than otherwise. Even her hard words, reproachful as they were, were complimentary—the groans of a person stinging under defeat" (ch. 31). Just as she can accept abuse from those envious of her, so too can she provide help. She enjoys being able to show Amelia that she is a "fool," and calling her a "silly, heartless, ungrateful little creature" just before showing her George's letter (ch. 67). And her action aiding the union of Dobbin and Amelia, it is interesting to note, leads to

Amelia's removal from Germany and permits her to reign over Jos.

In moral and psychological terms Becky and Dobbin are the most powerful figures in *Vanity Fair*; and they are opposite yet complementary personalities. Both act independent of family pressures (for all the talk of them Dobbin's sisters rarely appear, and his parents never do). Both assume they are unlovable and unloved, and their lives reveal the different ways they compensate for this assumption. Becky uses others; Dobbin invites them to use him. Becky, who "never had been a girl" (ch. 2), wants a parent, a man of integrity whom she cannot control; Dobbin wants a child, a passive figure who needs his protection. Hence, open antagonism from this man could not be disregarded. The aid she provides for him at the end of the novel can be seen as a response to his attack on her as "not a fit companion for Mrs. Os-borne and her son" (ch. 66), or a bribe permitting her to murder Jos with psychological impunity. That Becky never kills anyone before Jos merely indicates that she never felt as desperate before.

The absence of adult relationships and the loneliness of the individual seem to me to be the most salient features of *Vanity Fair.* No two people are able to achieve intimacy, which Erik Erikson describes as "the capacity to commit [themselves] to concrete affiliations and part-nerships and to develop the ethical strength to abide by such commitments."[12] Rarely even do Thackeray's illus-trations show two people touching or looking at each other; there seems to be a frozen space between them. But the novel is not about a world of contemporary alienation, the individual doomed by an inability to make actions meaningful to anyone other than himself. Thackeray is a critic of "nineteenth-century bourgeois society,"[13] but he is ultimately an affirmative writer. He attacks a social system that emphasizes the attaining of money and power rather than the sharing of affection. However, he affirms the family structure in a way that Lawrence, Woolf, or even Butler is unable to do. By showing us the failures of his characters, he, the author, the narrator, addressing himself to the reader, implies the possibility of overcoming the limits of Vanity. Like young Rawdon, who never suffers the narrator's criti-cism (ironic or otherwise), so too the reader has the po-tential for a more rewarding life than the novel's major actors.

Thackeray achieves these effects by creating a narrator who befriends the reader and who maintains a distance from the world and inhabitants of Vanity Fair. Both nar-rator and reader are in and out of that world. The narra-tor keeps jarring the reader with the information that he is creating a fiction, a story about a place devoid of na-ture and sunshine, beauty and art. The reader puts his trust in the narrator's integrity and deep sense of com-passion and justice. (It would be difficult to argue that

anyone in Vanity Fair deserves a better fate than he re-ceives—or a worse one.) The narrator presents himself as a fallible man not afraid to expose his own illusions, and not afraid to play with them either. The mirror into which he peers to see himself and his creations is cracked; he is both jester and preacher. He plays with the reader's trust and subjects him to contradictions, qualifications, equivocations. Paradoxically, the more he makes the reader aware of his limitations, the more the reader trusts him.[14]

The narrator warns constantly that knowledge is am-biguous, that truth is not constant but is dependent on perspective, that even words are not circumscribed by their dictionary definition. "The truth is, when we say of a gentleman that he lives elegantly on nothing a-year, we use the word 'nothing' to signify . . . that we don't know how the gentleman in question defrays the ex-penses of his establishment" (ch. 36). Thus, only in its specific context can we infer the meaning of a word. Thackeray's criticism of life in Vanity Fair is produced in part, as Geoffrey Tillotson observes, from "a score of critical epithets that recur constantly—'little,' 'great,' 'poor' (often with 'little'), 'dingy,' 'old,' 'dismal,' 'simpering,' 'darling,' 'sacred.'"[15] But these words are often used ironically and ambiguously. They are as de-liberately imprecise as more obvious examples.

> [Miss Sharp] made a respectful, *virgin-like* curtsey to the gentleman.
>
> (ch. 3)

> The boy was the image of his father, as his *fond* mother thought.
>
> (ch. 50; emphasis mine)

Thackeray's information is revealed to the reader with-out certainty. "Perhaps" frequently begins a clause that is seemingly intended to explain something. The rhe-torical question mark ends the same sort of sentence. Rumors are a constant source of information about char-acters. In such a world can honesty be unambiguous?

> Walpole Crawley . . . was impeached for peculation, as were a great number of other honest gentlemen of those days.
>
> (ch. 7)

> Briggs saw [Becky take the lace and brocade from Sir Pitt's house], asked no questions, told no stories; but I believe quite sympathized with her on this matter, and so would many another honest woman.
>
> (ch. 48)

Almost everyone is called "honest" in this novel. And, who knows? In a world where virtue is vice undiscov-ered or washed away by a visit to the king, perhaps they all are.

The epithet Thackeray uses most is "old." It becomes a refrain, an enforcement of the premise that in *Vanity Fair* the future yields decline and growth is part of a process of losing life-illusions, of movement toward death. Heavy stress is placed on the aging of the young and on the dying of the old. Both Amelia and Becky are first seen as "the young ladies": they lose their youth very early. The former is a widow and mother at nineteen; the latter, making her way in society, "forgot the time when she ever *was* young" (ch. 41). The narrator delights in noticing gray hairs starting on people's heads. "'What matters it,' [Amelia] asked, 'for an old woman like me?'" (ch. 46). Dobbin, whose "head has grizzled," is "too old to listen to the banter of the assistant-surgeon and the slang of the youngsters," although his commander, "old O'Dowd, . . . laughed quite easily" (ch. 43). He is a "love-smitten and middle-aged gentleman" (ch. 57) who vows that Amelia, wearing an evening dress during their stay in Germany, "did not look five-and-twenty" (ch. 63). The narrator calls her "a young woman," but cannot drop the matter there: "Ladies, she is but thirty still, and we choose to call her a young woman even at that age" (ch. 57). When Becky has no audience her face relaxes: it is "haggard, weary, terrible" (ch. 52).

The parents of the major figures are old when they first appear. Mr. Osborne, often called "the old gentleman," or "old Osborne," is the "pitiless old enemy" of Mr. Sedley whom he calls "the old pauper, the old coalman, the old bankrupt" (ch. 56). Such persons cannot grow old; the change time brings is forgiveness of their children and death.

While the people in *Vanity Fair* decline, the society that forms a background for their activities remains a constant. Time has no effect on it. The social and political upheavals on the continent, the rise and fall of Bonaparte, English colonialism, the struggles for reform: these lose almost all significance as determinants of human aspirations and behavior. Dobbin evaluates this pattern precisely when he returns from India, and goes to "his old haunt at the Slaughters'."

> Long years had passed since he saw it last. . . . Many a passion and feeling of his youth had grown grey in that interval. There, however, stood the old waiter at the door in the same greasy black suit, with the same double chin and flaccid face, with the same huge bunch of seals at his fob, rattling his money in his pockets as before, and receiving the Major as if he had gone away only a week ago. . . . The faithful waiter, . . . with whom ten years were but as yesterday, led the way up to Dobbin's old room, where stood the great moreen bed, and the shabby carpet, a thought more dingy, and all the old black furniture covered with faded chintz, just as the Major recollected them in his youth. . . .
>
> "You ain't got young," John said, calmly surveying his friend of former days.

Dobbin laughed. "Ten years and a fever don't make a man young, John," he said. "It is you that are always young:—No, you are always old."

The waiter, flabby and in mourning clothes, and the room, with its "shabby" and "black" accouterments, represent the society. They wait to collect the debts of even its dead citizens: "Fine young fellow [Captain Osborne]. . . . He owes me three pounds at this minute. Look here, I have it in my book" (ch. 58). As its inhabitants grow old and their illusions die, the society itself remains "always old," but "a thought more dingy." For the people of Vanity Fair only filial and parental love remains to provide happiness. But that is limited because children grow up and abandon their sources of nourishment. And what is left for the parent whose baby "drank in her life" (ch. 36)? For the readers, what hope remains? Are we encouraged to think of ourselves as puppets, prisoners, or children, shut up in a womb-like box? Or are we outside that box, outside that world: "on the wing"?

Notes

1. All quotations from *Vanity Fair* are from the Riverside Edition (Boston: Houghton Mifflin, 1963), edited by Geoffrey and Kathleen Tillotson, based on the Cheap edition of 1853. References will be cited in the text by chapter.

2. See A. E. Dyson, "*Vanity Fair*: An Irony against Heroes," *Critical Quarterly,* 6 (1964), 11.

3. Mark Spilka, "A Note on Thackeray's Amelia," *Nineteenth-Century Fiction,* 10 (1955), 202, 207.

4. Gordon N. Ray, *Thackeray: The Uses of Adversity (1811-1846)* (New York: McGraw-Hill, 1955), p. 424.

5. Dyson, p. 17; See Myron Taube, "The Character of Amelia in the Meaning of *Vanity Fair,*" *Victorian Newsletter,* 18 (Fall, 1960), 1-7, for a survey of criticism on Amelia.

6. *The Letters and Private Papers of William Makepeace Thackeray,* ed. Gordon N. Ray, 4 vols. (Cambridge: Harvard University Press, 1945-1946), II, p. 424.

7. Myron Taube has a somewhat different interpretation of these actions in "The George-Amelia-Dobbin Triangle in the Structure of *Vanity Fair,*" *Victorian Newsletter,* 29 (Spring, 1966), 9-18.

8. Thackeray uses this image of the marriage as a funeral in two chapters to describe Dobbin's emotions. The language both times is nearly identical. In chapter 20 we read: "Was he anxious himself, I wonder, to have it over?—as people, when death has occurred, like to press forward the funeral, or when a parting is resolved upon, hasten it."

9. Barbara Hardy, *The Exposure of Luxury: Thackeray's Radical Themes* (Pittsburgh: University of Pittsburgh Press, 1972), p. 28.

10. Hardy, p. 32, also believes that Becky "is not fully sensitive to Lady Jane's moral disgust, which proceeds not only from jealousy but from her maternal disapproval of Becky's hypocrisy and harshness about little Rawdon."

11. Lord David Cecil, *Victorian Novelists* (1935; rpt. Chicago: University of Chicago Press, 1958), p. 91; Walter Allen, *The English Novel* (New York: Dutton, 1954), pp. 204-205; and Dyson, p. 18. J. Y. T. Greig, *Thackeray: A Reconsideration* (London: Oxford University Press, 1950), pp. 111-112, discusses other actions by Becky he finds inconsistent with his understanding of her personality. Andrew Von Hendy, "Misunderstandings about Becky's Characterization in *Vanity Fair*," *Nineteenth-Century Fiction*, 18 (1963), 279-283, reviews this subject.

12. Erik Erikson, *Childhood and Society*, 2d rev. ed. (New York: Norton, 1963), p. 263.

13. David H. Stewart, "*Vanity Fair*: Life in the Void," *College English*, 25 (1963), 213. Although I disagree with his conclusion, Stewart's analysis of the novel has been especially helpful to me.

14. This sentence owes much to one by Juliet McMaster, *Thackeray: The Major Novels* (Manchester: Manchester University Press, 1971), p. 27, that I especially admire: "Paradoxically, his very exposure of his story as fiction made his readers the more ready to think of it almost as fact, for they had been invited to participate with the author in the whole process of creation."

15. Geoffrey Tillotson, *Thackeray the Novelist* (Cambridge: Cambridge University Press, 1954), pp. 91-92.

Bruce Redwine (essay date autumn 1977)

SOURCE: Redwine, Bruce. "The Uses of *Memento Mori* in *Vanity Fair*." *Studies in English Literature, 1500-1900* 17, no. 4 (autumn 1977): 657-72.

[*In the following essay, Redwine analyzes symbols of death in* Vanity Fair.]

In Chapter 19 of **Vanity Fair,** after Mrs. Bute's nursing methods have terrorized Miss Crawley into believing that she is on her deathbed, Thackeray digresses from the main body of his narrative:

> Recollection of the best ordained banquets will scarcely cheer sick epicures. Reminiscences of the most becoming dresses and brilliant ball-triumphs will go very little way to console faded beauties. Perhaps statesmen, at a particular period of existence, are not much gratified at thinking over the most triumphant divisions; and the success or the pleasure of yesterday become of very small account when a certain (albeit uncertain) morrow is in view, about which all of us must some day or other be speculating.[1]

Although Thackeray avoids a direct reference to death in this passage, we can certainly sense death's presence: it palls the memory of banquets, ball-triumphs, and diplomatic successes. The previous scene has been a parody of a death-bed scene; here, the allusion to death serves as a *memento mori.* Accordingly, the reference to banquets and epicures recalls the classical function of a skeleton at a Roman banquet—a function which has become associated with the Horatian *carpe diem,* the command to enjoy transient pleasures. Thackeray, however, inverts the classical tradition of the *memento mori* and turns what was formerly a hedonistic injunction into a moral one. He follows the Christian tradition and suggests that the reader consider the insignificance of worldly pleasures in view of human mortality. To be sure, he says that he will not "cajole the public into a sermon" (19:180), and his self-deprecating amiability prevents this passage from becoming one. He wears the motley of the fool: "O brother wearers of motley! Are there not moments when one grows sick of grinning and tumbling, and the jingling of cap and bells? This, dear friends and companions, is my amiable object—to walk with you through the *Fair,* to examine the shops and the shows *there*; and that we should all come home after the *flare,* and the noise, and the gaiety, and be perfectly miserable in private" (19:180-181, italics added). We can even hear the "jingling of cap and bells" in the jingling of the rhymes "Fair," "there," and "flare." But such humor only subdues the dominant tone of melancholy and remorse; it does not prevent us from leaving the passage with a sense of uneasiness. Disquietude, if not absolute misery, is the primary object of Thackeray's use of *memento mori.*

Recent criticism has begun to focus upon some of the varieties of *memento mori* in **Vanity Fair.** U. C. Knoepflmacher has noted that the numerous death scenes in the novel "stem from Thackeray's desire to remind the reader that death, the end of life, is the only true vanquisher of vanity,"[2] and Barbara Hardy has broadened the concept of *memento mori* to include a "domestic flaw or discord" in the feasts of the novel.[3] Juliet McMaster, going even further, has emphasized how the reader gains a "new sympathy" for a dying character by being forced "to contemplate his own death."[4] All of these observations are illuminating. There is, however, a more extensive and systematic use of *memento mori* which usually involves either a sudden shift from comedy to pathos or a manipulation of the reader's expectations. We shall examine this usage in terms of three categories: (1) deathbed conversions, (2) emblems and imagery, and (3) Thackeray's subversion of the traditional happy ending.

It is a tautological truism that death itself is the ultimate reminder of mortality. Nevertheless, an effective use of *memento mori* requires something more than the simple presentation of death. Assuming that we too are susceptible to the same vanities enumerated in *Vanity Fair,* the appearance of death must in some way make us want to change our values. Not surprisingly, all the death scenes, with the exception of Dobbin's near fatal illness, involve some kind of conversion. These conversions can take the form of an ordeal of fear which results in a heightened sense of awareness or an act of repentance. In either case, they imply the belated rejection of vanity and emphasize the total inadequacy of worldly values to prepare us for death. A deathbed conversion, then, presupposes the disparity between worldly and moral values; and the greater the disparity, the greater the shock we receive from the conversion. Conversely, where such a disparity does not exist, death presents no surprises. When Dobbin calmly bequeaths his few possessions and asks to be buried with a chain of Amelia's hair (57:554), we are not shocked. His behavior fulfills our expectations of his character, and we are more aware of Dobbin's strength and unselfishness than we are of death itself.

All other characters in *Vanity Fair,* however, experience either fear or remorse when confronting death, and their deathbed conversions are true examples of *memento mori.* Miss Crawley and Sir Pitt undergo their conversions through ordeals of fear. The terror of death humbles and humanizes these characters, and we in turn find our attitudes being changed from contempt to a sympathy based upon the recognition of human mortality.[5] This change of attitude is evident even in our response to the essentially comic scene to which I alluded at the beginning of this essay: the vain and pampered Miss Crawley is not sick, but Mrs. Bute's excessive attentions make her believe she is on the verge of dying. In part, we are amused by the scene because it justifies our antipathy for her character and placates our desire for poetic justice: the haughty Miss Crawley no longer enjoys being pampered for her money; she is now being pampered to "death." The "dreadful terrors of death" (19:180) she now experiences will eventually cause her to reject the mercenary solicitude of Mrs. Bute and Becky ("'I won't be starved and choked with poison. They all want to kill me'" [25:246]). Though her fears are laughable, we can no longer regard Miss Crawley simply as a comic figure. Her fears of death are those of any human being. Comedy has turned into pathos. As Miss Crawley slowly fades away, she appears like a reminder of death—a pathetic, "lonely old woman" on whom death, that "dark curtain was almost ready to descend" (25:246).

Sir Pitt's invalidism after his stroke introduces a similar shift from comedy to pathos. Like Miss Crawley, Sir Pitt enjoyed power. He shocked his heirs with his unorthodox behavior, and it is amusing to watch how "he laughed at his sons, and at the world" (39:389). But after his stroke and soon before his death, he is lowered to a position of abject dependency. He becomes a speechless invalid, "a whimpering old idiot put in and out of bed and cleaned and fed like a baby" (40:395). Since Sir Pitt is speechless, we cannot definitely know if he undergoes a conversion like Miss Crawley's. Yet his very muteness suggests a new awareness which is too terrible to be verbalized: he too spends his last days in terror and cries and sobs. The fact that he uses "the very chair which Miss Crawley had . . . at Brighton" (40:395) during her conversion seems to complete the parallel.

Whereas Miss Crawley and Sir Pitt experience fear when confronting death, Mr. Sedley, Mr. Osborne, and George Osborne all experience remorse. Thackeray clearly wishes the reader to regard these conversions as belated but sincere acts of repentance. To allay the reader's suspicion of their sincerity and to prevent us from questioning whether they are motivated by fear of punishment, Thackeray mutes the drama of these conversions. He relies on understatement and simplicity of expression as ways to suggest sincere remorse. When Mr. Sedley is on his deathbed, we learn that he and Amelia have been finally reconciled. An effusive reconciliation would have probably struck us as superficial and sentimental. But Thackeray avoids this trap by using understatement; he tersely describes the act as a "tacit reconciliation" (61:586). He further conveys the sincerity of Mr. Sedley's "confession" by reducing it to the simple statement: "'O, Emmy, I've been thinking we were very unkind and unjust to you'" (61:586).

Similarly, Thackeray subdues Mr. Osborne's conversion to the point of literal muteness. Before he dies, Mr. Osborne has a "fit" (61:590) and loses his power of speech. As in Sir Pitt's case, we cannot ascertain the extent of his conversion, but Thackeray hints at it: "What was it that poor old man had tried once or twice in vain to say? I hope it was that he wanted to see Amelia, and be reconciled before he left the world to the dear and faithful wife of his son: it was most likely that; for his will showed that the hatred which he had so long cherished had gone out of his heart" (61:591). It would have been difficult to believe the confession of a man of such an adamant will as Mr. Osborne's. But his muteness, his pathetic and futile struggle to express remorse, suggests a transformation in his character which cannot be verbalized, only implied. Understatement helps make a difficult truth credible.

George Osborne's conversion in the face of impending death is perhaps the best example of Thackeray's use of understatement as a means to convey sincerity. George dies about halfway through the novel, but Thackeray deliberately withholds until much later Dobbin's recollection of the incident:

> William was too much hurt or ashamed to ask to fathom that disgraceful mystery [George's infatuation for Becky], although once, and evidently with remorse on his mind, George had alluded to it. It was on the morning of Waterloo as the young men stood together in front of their line, surveying the black masses of Frenchmen who crowned the opposite heights, and as the rain was coming down, "I have been mixing in a foolish intrigue with a woman," George said. "I am glad we were marched away. If I drop, I hope Emmy will never know of that business. I wish to God it had never been begun!"

(66:640)

This is George's only sympathetic moment in the novel. The approach of death is represented by formations of French troops; and before this sight, George expresses sincere remorse for the first time.

Again, we may question the sincerity of this conversion. But just as Thackeray understates Mr. Sedley's and Mr. Osborne's conversions, so he underplays George's. Like those two conversions, George's is not dramatically presented but given an inconspicuous location in the novel. We do not learn of it until near the end; and when we do, we seem to stumble upon it by chance. Dobbin casually introduces the recollection as an afterthought. The confession itself is subdued: simple, concise, and without excuses. What is more, Thackeray complicates Dobbin's recollection through setting. It is the carnival season in Germany, and Thackeray describes the bar-room where Dobbin sits as a place of diverse and riotous activity: "Emmy had passed blushing through the room anon, where all sorts of people were collected; Tyrolese glove-sellers and Danubian linen-merchants, with their packs; students recruiting themselves with butterbrods and meat; idlers, playing cards or dominoes, on the sloppy, beery tables; tumblers refreshing during the cessation of their performances;—in a word, all the *fumum* and *strepitus* of a German inn in fair time" (66:639). The "fair time" atmosphere should make us suspicious of this setting, especially when we take Horace's "fumum" and "strepitus" in their original context, namely, as a part of a warning to avoid the "smoke" and "din" of Rome.[6] Amid this tumultuous setting, Dobbin sits alone. He has just overheard the drunken conversation of two German students who are conniving friends of Becky's. He recalls Becky's schemes and his suspicions that George was infatuated with her. It is only then that he finally reveals George's words.

This scene contrasts the tumult of the external world with the loneliness of private experience. We saw this same contrast earlier when Thackeray compared life to a fair and asserted that his "amiable object" was to make us "perfectly miserable in private." Lonely though such experiences may be, they still represent a truer kind of existence than that of the noisy crowd. Dobbin's reflections upon the past contribute to his loneliness; and in a sense, the recollection of George's conversion at Waterloo is Dobbin's personal *memento mori*. That is, by keeping his promise not to reveal George's infatuation for Becky, Dobbin prevented an early marriage to Amelia and doomed himself to loneliness. This may seem to undercut the value of George's speech, but it actually works in furtherance of an essential truth. Dobbin and Amelia cannot be happy together, and Thackeray never intended that they should be.[7]

Thus, Dobbin's recollection of George's conversion brings death into the fair and invites the comparison between two modes of existence. In the first, men are not deceived; the exigency of the moment heightens their self-awareness. Death, embodied in "black masses of Frenchmen," has a palpable presence which gives a sense of urgency and authenticity to Dobbin's recollection. In the second, men are self-deluded and unaware of the instability of their existence. The bar-room setting with its "smoke" and "din" suggests an obscure and unsubstantial kind of reality where time, slackened by schemes, passes slowly. Dobbin's life need not be authenticated by such a comparison, but the comparison suggests that George had a rare insight before he died. Against this bar-room backdrop of "mawkish draught[s]" (66:640) and schemes, George's conversion seems refreshing and convincing.

Initially, George's death at Waterloo is surprising, but it is not so shocking that we are disturbed and changed. As Kathleen Tillotson notes, Thackeray's terse description of George dead on the battlefield represents "Death, sudden, august, and mysterious."[8] When we first learned of his death, George still appeared vain and foppish, and his death did not alter our antipathy for his character. But at this late point, he seems to have died with a flash of awareness, and we must change our low regard for him. Thackeray has not only broken a character's stereotype, but he has also delayed the impact of death and remorse upon the reader. He has played upon our expectations. The shock of suddenly realizing that our perceptions were not entirely correct partially recreates that shock of sudden awareness which George experienced when he confronted death. Perhaps for this reason, George's conversion lingers on in the reader's imagination in a disturbing fashion.

* * *

Emblematic descriptions represent another form of *memento mori*. The two that we shall consider are the descriptions of Steyne and the portals of Steyne's family house. These descriptions are closely related to the imagery of the novel. In particular, Thackeray weaves the emblems associated with Steyne into a larger fabric of recurring images. We shall discuss the descriptions of Steyne and his family portals by way of introduction to the imagery.

We first meet Steyne in Chapter 37 during a party at Becky's house. The topic of conversation concerns finding a suitable female companion for Becky, and it results in some levity and witty humor regarding Becky's "*moral* shepherd's dog" (37:365)—that is, her female companion. The narrator, however, calls the custom of beautiful women being accompanied by homely companions "as jolly a reminder as that of the Death's-head which figured in the repasts of Egyptian *bon-vivants*" (37:364-365). Shortly after this comment, Steyne is described for the first time as he stands near Becky. Becky's description appears first and emphasizes her resplendent beauty: "There was a score of candles sparkling round the mantelpiece, in all sorts of quaint sconces, of gilt and bronze and porcelain. They lighted up Rebecca's figure to admiration, as she sate on a sofa covered with a pattern of gaudy flowers. She was in a pink dress, that looked as fresh as a rose; her dazzling white arms and shoulders were half covered with a thin hazy scarf through which they sparkled . . ." (37:365). Then Thackeray's sketch and description of Steyne immediately follow: "The candles lighted up Lord Steyne's shining bald head, which was fringed with red hair. He had thick bushy eyebrows, with little twinkling bloodshot eyes, surrounded by a thousand wrinkles. His jaw was underhung, and when he laughed, two white buck-teeth protruded themselves and glistened savagely in the midst of the grin" (37:366). From both its ghastly sketch and description, Steyne's face seems to be in a state of decomposition. A "bald head . . . fringed with red hair" and a "thousand wrinkles" suggest decay. Also, he is described in a manner which evokes the image of a grinning skull. His bald head shines; and when he laughs, his jaw juts out and exposes white protruding teeth. Steyne's face appears like a death's-head.

The development of Steyne's emblematic description illustrates what Geoffrey Tillotson calls a "delayed image" or "the method of delaying the completion of what is to be said of a thing."[9] Hence, the description of Steyne's face completes the image of the "Death's-head which figured in the repasts of Egyptian *bon-vivants*." Thackeray's simile of an Egyptian death's-head appeared a page before Steyne's description, and the comparison was made in reference to the role of ugly companions. Shortly after this simile, we have the companion-piece descriptions of Becky and Steyne appearing like a diptych in the narrative. These two descriptions contrast with one another in the same way that Thackeray contrasted a beautiful woman with a death's-head. Although Miss Briggs will become Becky's official female companion, Steyne later be-

comes her court sponsor and surreptitious admirer and companion. Tillotson explains that the function of the "delayed image" is "to keep us on the watch, expectancy improving our sense of the continuity."[10] In this example, "expectancy" results in the unexpected reification of an image.

Of course, the emblematic description of Steyne's face appears in the middle of a comic setting; and for this reason, the full impact of its unpleasantness seems diminished. We are initially distracted by the witty comedy of the scene, the amoral banter which plays on Becky's search for a "*moral* shepherd's dog." But Steyne uses his wit as an elegant distraction from his ungentlemanly intentions. He develops the pastoral conceit which turns Becky into a "lambkin" and Rawdon into a "Shepherd" (37:366). The witticism appears amusing, but the references to Rawdon have a vicious undertone. He calls Rawdon a "debauched Corydon"; and when Rawdon fleeces Southdown at cards, he says "'he's pastorally occupied too: he's shearing a Southdown'" (37:366-367). Steyne's humor is malicious; but to his own displeasure, he finds that it cuts both ways. For Becky reminds him of the rumor that he won his marquisate at cards.

Such humor is witty, vicious, and amoral. It is, in fact, the same kind of humor that Thackeray saw in Congreve's plays. In his lecture on Congreve, Thackeray refers to Congreve's theater as a "temple of Pagan delights," and he defines Congreve's comedy in the very terms of the *carpe diem* tenet: "We have had in Congreve a humorous observer of another school, to whom the world seems to have no moral at all, and whose ghastly doctrine seems to be that we should eat, drink, and be merry when we can, and go to the deuce (if there be a deuce) when the time comes."[11] Steyne's and Becky's amoral wit could easily fit into one of Congreve's plays.[12] However, for Thackeray, Congreve's hedonistic comedy is indeed a "ghastly doctrine," and he cannot discuss it without ultimately bringing in the *memento mori* motif. Hence, he compares Congreve's comedy to a pagan feast; and at the end of the comparison, he imagines the revelry being disrupted by a "chaunt": "What is that dirge which *will* disturb us? The lights of the festival burn dim—the cheeks turn pale—the voice quavers—and the cup drops on the floor. Who's there? Death and Fate are at the gate, and they *will* come in."[13] Steyne's appearance in this comic setting is not so melodramatic, but it does "disturb us." We are subtly reminded that behind this comic façade there is a core of physical and moral decay.

It would be an exaggeration to say that Steyne's characterization ever truly appalls us. Rather we see in his portrayal a certain fascination with grandeur and death. As Gordon N. Ray notes, Thackeray "communicates to the reader his own fascination with the details of genealogy, family history, and heraldry; he makes us share his conviction that if Lord Steyne is a 'worn-out old man,' he is also a 'great prince.'"[14] But Steyne is also doomed, and it is not coincidental that Thackeray's image of "Death and Fate . . . at the gate" is also an image associated with the "great prince." Steyne's family suffers from hereditary insanity, and Thackeray emblazons this impending doom onto the portals of Gaunt House: "The dark mark of fate and doom was on the threshold,—the tall old threshold surmounted by coronets and carved heraldry." And further: "So there was splendour and wealth, but no great happiness perchance behind the tall carved portals of Gaunt House with its smoky coronets and ciphers" (47:457). Portals provided Thackeray with the perfect image for dealing with splendor and doom. Materially, they were imposing monuments of family wealth and position and stood as entrances to the highest levels of society; but figuratively, they represented the negation of the material world and symbolized the passage to death.

At first glance, a fascination with grandeur and death may seem incompatible with the moral function of *memento mori*. After all, our awakening as Christians assumes that an awareness of mortality should cause us to reject worldly splendor and seek spiritual values; and to be unduly attracted to the august and morbid defeats that purpose. Thackeray, however, frequently plays upon the reader's fascination in order to lead him ultimately to a moral position. In his use of imagery dealing with portals, gates, and arches, Thackeray builds up awe in the reader's mind only to undermine it through admonitory emblems and anticlimax.

Chapter 51 marks the high point of Becky's rise in society, and it opens with Becky gaining access to the "august portals" (51:484) of London society. The chapter depicts a party at Steyne's house; and during the party, Becky performs in two charades and sings. Her performance dazzles her aristocratic audience, and she scores a "triumph" (51:498). In a number of ways, Thackeray seems to pattern Becky's success on the classical model of a Roman triumph. The scene occurs within the glitter and pageantry of a ball-room where "she saw fortune, fame, fashion before her" (51:498). Her triumph is processional: she dances about the room, and the company encircles and applauds her. She crushes her enemies: "she *écraséd* all rival charmers" (51:499). And her booty takes the form of all the riches her admirers would have laid at her feet: "She might have had pearls melted into her champagne if she liked—another Cleopatra; and the potentate of Peterwaradin would have given half the brilliants off his jacket for a kind glance from those dazzling eyes" (51:499). All of these aspects of Becky's triumph were traditional parts of a Roman triumph, and the parallel Thackeray draws is awe-inspiring. Finally, there is a strong implication that those "august portals" which we saw at the beginning of the chapter are triumphal arches. They stand as monuments of worldly success.

The Roman triumph, however, had another tradition. As the imperator led his triumphal procession, a slave whispered admonitions which were either intended to avert evil influences or to remind him of his mortal condition. Tertullian maintained the latter; but in a curious example of early Christian apologetics, he argued for *carpe diem*. That is, the reminder of mortality increased the imperator's delight:

> Even in the triumph, as he rides in that most exalted chariot, he is reminded that he is a man. It is whispered to him from behind: "Look behind thee; remember thou art a man." ["Respice post te! Hominem te memento!"] That he is in such a blaze of glory that the reminder of his mortal state is necessary for him—makes it the more delightful to him. He would be less, if he were at that moment called a god, because it would not be true. He is greater, who is called to look back, lest he think himself a god.[15]

Thackeray was aware of this tradition; and in one of his late essays, he compares himself to just such a slave who also whispers Tertullian's warning:

> I wished him not to be elated by too much prosperity; I warned him against assuming heroic imperatorial airs, and cocking his laurels too jauntily over his ear. I was his conscience, and stood on the splash-board of his triumph-car, whispering, '*Hominem memento te.*' As we rolled along the way, and passed the weathercocks on the temples, I saluted the symbol of the goddess Fortune with a reverend awe. 'We have done our little endeavour,' I said, bowing my head, 'and mortals can do no more. But we might have fought bravely, and *not* won.'[16]

Thackeray's interpretation of Tertullian's quotation is the opposite of its original intention.[17] He interprets Tertullian according to the orthodox classical tradition which, as H. A. J. Munro explains, sought "to appease" the power of "dreaded Nemesis."[18] Hence, Thackeray's is not an exhortation to intensify the enjoyment of glory, rather to temper exultation, to remind one of human mortality and the vagaries of fortune.

As we look awestruck upon Becky's rise and triumph, Thackeray also acts as our conscience and whispers warnings in our ears. Soon after we approach those "august portals," we hear a somber and resonant voice, like that of the ecclesiast, comment upon the impermanence of London's fashionable districts: "Ah, ladies!—ask Reverend Mr. Thurifer if Belgravia is not a sounding brass, and Tyburnia a tinkling cymbal. These are vanities. Even these will pass away" (51:484). But suddenly the authorial voice shifts to a tone of self-mockery and bathos: "It is all vanity to be sure: but who will not own to liking a little of it? I should like to know what well-constituted mind, merely because it is transitory, dislikes roast-beef. . . . And let us make the best of Becky's aristocratic pleasures likewise—for these too, like all other mortal delights, were but transitory" (51:485). Is this contradictory and an argument for *carpe diem*? Perhaps not. The comic tone softens the moralizing voice of the preacher and allows the warning to slip into our consciousness like a whisper.

There are other warnings in the chapter, some none too subtle. The first and third parts of the Agamemnon charade present straightforward depictions of luxurious sensuality and death. In the first part, an aga is executed in his harem; and in the third, we watch Clytemnestra's murder of Agamemnon. The second part of the charade describes a scene which is less straightforward and may even be puzzling: "It is sunrise on the desert, and the Turks turn their heads eastward and bow to the sand. As there are no dromedaries at hand, the band facetiously plays the 'The Camels are Coming.' An enormous Egyptian head figures in the scene. It is a musical one,—and, to the surprise of the oriental travellers, sings a comic song, composed by Mr. Wagg. . . . 'Last two syllables' roars the head" (51:493). The last two syllables are "memnon," and the charade is intended to allude to the Colossi of Memnon which stand in Egypt. They were reputed to sing each morning at dawn.

Egyptian monuments were favorite nineteenth century mementoes of death and vanity; and in a comic and unobtrusive manner, this Egyptian memento develops themes begun earlier. Thackeray's "enormous Egyptian head" continues the Egyptian death's-head motif begun with Steyne. And by subtly directing our attention to Egyptian ruins, it makes those "august portals" appearing at the beginning of the chapter appear less monumental. Like Egyptian monuments, triumphal arches also become ruins. Our fascination with the august has begun to be eroded, but the final levelling does not occur until later in the novel.

Chapter 61 deals with the deaths of Mr. Sedley and Mr. Osborne, and it begins indirectly with a commentary upon the significance of a "little arch" and recess found in "most houses" (61:584). The arch is located immediately opposite the staircase of the second floor, and one of its functions is to facilitate the passage of a coffin from the bedroom to the main floors. The arch is in one of the most frequently used parts of the house; yet no one, from servants to owners, pays much attention to it. It is this conspicuous yet unnoticed aspect of the arch which fascinates Thackeray:

> —that stair, up or down which babies are carried, old people are helped, guests are marshalled to the ball, the parson walks to the christening, the doctor to the sick room, and the undertaker's men to the upper floor— what a memento of Life, Death, and Vanity it is—that arch and stair—if you choose to consider it, and sit on the landing, looking up the well! The doctor will come

up to us too for the last time there, my friend in motley. . . . Your comedy and mine will have been played then, and we shall be removed, O how far, from the trumpets, and the shouting, and the posture-making.

(61:584-585)

For Thackeray, the arch serves as a subtle "memento of Life, Death, and Vanity." He holds up this *memento mori* for the reader's consideration; but he does not treat it in a vein of high seriousness, rather one of comedy. And like the unrecognized significance of the "arch and stair," it is a comedy based upon perceiving the true importance of common appearances. It is the realization that "However much you may be mourned, your widow will like to have her weeds neatly made" (61:585). In part, the memento of the arch functions to lower vanity to a level of morbid comedy.

However, more comprehensively, "how far" indeed is this "little arch" from the grand arches and portals which we have seen until now. From the beginning of the novel, death has been depicted in august terms. Thackeray used the euphemism of the closing of the "great filligree iron gates" (1:14) to describe Miss Jemima's eventual death, and the sermon delivered at Sir Pitt's funeral referred to death as that "gloomy and mysterious portal" (41:408). Then there were those "tall carved portals of Gaunt House" emblazoned with the "dark mark of fate and doom" (47:457). The steady development of these images suggests a plan intended to increase our fascination with grandeur and death. But now Thackeray has suddenly dropped the trap-door and left us with an anticlimactic "little arch." The sense of monumental grandeur has been stripped away. Death, amid commonplace objects and the events of everyday life, appears before us. Thackeray has succeeded, in Juliet McMaster's words, "in evoking the remote through the familiar, and making the word flesh."[19] An effective use of anticlimax has shocked us into a new awareness of death which is both immediate and personal.

* * *

The traditional ending for a comedy is, of course, a marriage. Dobbin's marriage to Amelia comes near the end of the novel; and although the ceremony itself is not described, Dobbin's reunion with Amelia on the quay at Ostend serves as a kind of wedding ceremony and marks the real high point of their new relationship. Never again will they appear so tearfully happy. The scene itself is quite stylized, and it effectively structures our responses and expectations. The day is "rainy and gusty" (67:659), and Dobbin's ship struggles through a storm to reach the port where Amelia waits for him. Dobbin wears the same old cloak he had at Waterloo, the same cloak which had "*manchen Sturm erlebt*"— that is, weathered many a storm (66:649, 67:659). In his construction of the scene, Thackeray reworks the classical trope of life as a tempest; and he makes marriage the haven, the place of refuge. To make sure that we do not miss this trope, he finalizes their reunion with, "The vessel is in port. He has got the prize he has been trying for all his life" (67:660). We are certainly suspicious of the value of Dobbin's "prize," and Thackeray's sarcasm toward Amelia's sentimentality undercuts our enjoyment of the scene: "She was murmuring something about—forgive—dear William—dear, dear, dearest friend—kiss, kiss, kiss, and so forth—and in fact went on under the cloak in an absurd manner" (67:660). But on the whole, the scene's classical framework reinforces our sympathies for Dobbin and makes us want to believe that he has successfully weathered the tempestuous seas of life and attained happiness. So, Thackeray encourages us to desire the traditional comic resolution of a happy marriage, but we are later forced to correct our expectations.

Tugging at our sympathies are some black and disquieting premonitions. For the scene's classical trope is countered by a number of portentous images which have been developing throughout the novel. Rain occurs infrequently in the novel; but when it does, it is usually associated with marriages and deaths. It rained when George married Amelia (22:205-208), and it is raining now during Dobbin's and Amelia's reunion. It also rained on the days when George was killed at Waterloo (66:640) and when Mrs. Sedley was buried (57:553). Thackeray pointedly emphasizes the connection between marriages and deaths at Mrs. Sedley's funeral: "They buried Amelia's mother at the church-yard at Brompton; upon just such a rainy, dark day, as Amelia recollected when first she had been there to marry George" (57:553). Marriages in *Vanity Fair* can suddenly reverse their polarity and become institutions of unhappiness, and the rain at George's and Amelia's wedding accurately presaged such a reversal. Soon after her marriage, Amelia looked sadly upon her marriage bed and saw it as an "enormous funereal bed" (26:248).

Furthermore, for Amelia's first marriage, Thackeray uses a water-haven trope which is similar to the one used for her reunion with Dobbin. Again the imagery describes marriage as a "prize" and port ("haven"), but the trope for her first marriage has negative associations: "Was the prize gained—the heaven of life—and the winner still doubtful and unsatisfied. . . . But our little Amelia was just on the bank of her new country, and was already looking anxiously back towards the sad friendly figures waving farewell to her across the stream, from the other distant shore."[20] What we see here in the imagery dealing with ports and marriages is the same kind of double aspect that we saw with portals and death. Unifying these two images, there is a kind of pun, a *figura etymologica*, working on the Latin *portus* and *porta*; both words have the common root denoting "a passage." Just as portals can be either images of grandeur or death, so ports can be images of marital happiness or dissatisfaction.

Thus, the scene of Dobbin's and Amelia's reunion at Ostend functions as a kind of *memento mori*. The scene presages Dobbin's eventual dissatisfaction with his own marriage, and it warns us of the vanity of loving foolishly. This is clearly Thackeray's intent; for he writes in one of his letters, "the impression at present is that he [Dobbin] is a fool for his pains that he has married a silly little thing and in fact has found out his error rather a sweet and tender one however, *quia multum amavit* I want to leave everybody dissatisfied and unhappy at the end of the story—we ought all to be with our own and all other stories."[21] But in a sense, Dobbin's "error" is also our error, and the scene not only makes us dissatisfied but also instructs us by playing upon our sympathies and expectations. We want to see Dobbin bring his trials to a happy resolution, and the way the scene is structured around a port-marriage trope initially seems to support these hopes. But such hopes, like Dobbin's love for Amelia, are also foolish. The desire for the comic resolution of marital bliss cannot fit into Thackeray's view of life in *Vanity Fair*. We too must be dissatisfied at the end of the novel. So, the imagery and tone forebode unhappiness, and we check the "error" of our own expectations.

In the presentation of Dobbin's and Amelia's reunion scene, Thackeray has followed his own dictum that he will not sermonize. The reunion scene is a reminder of the ultimate emptiness of happiness; and rather than preach to us, he manipulates our responses and lures us into seeing our own errors. Similarly, in the development of portal imagery, he exploits our fascination for grandeur and death in order to shock us into a new awareness of death. Miss Crawley's and George's deathbed conversions are also reminders of mortality, but they are presented in a comic and/or delayed manner which plays upon our antipathies for these characters. The full impact of these and other examples of *memento mori* has been delayed by a comic or unobtrusive presentation. We are amused or puzzled by these reminders, but they are difficult to forget and seem to leave us with a growing sense of uneasiness. Thackeray appears to have accomplished his "amiable object." He has led us through a fair and pointed out its gaiety and amusements. But just beyond the gaiety and frivolity there seems to be a persistent nothingness which makes us "perfectly miserable in private."[22]

Notes

1. *Vanity Fair*, eds. Geoffrey and Kathleen Tillotson (Boston, 1963), 19:180. Hereafter references will appear in text and will include both chapter and page numbers.

2. *Laughter and Despair: Readings in Ten Novels of the Victorian Era* (Berkeley, 1971), p. 82.

3. *The Exposure of Luxury: Radical Themes in Thackeray* (London, 1972), p. 125.

4. *Thackeray: The Major Novels* (Manchester, 1971), p. 8.

5. See McMaster, pp. 20-21. In discussing Miss Crawley's deathbed scene, McMaster notes that Thackeray "creates understanding and sympathy" by appealing to the reader's "awareness of the incongruous proximity of death in Vanity Fair [sic]."

6. "Abandon cloying luxury and the pile that towers to the lofty clouds! Cease to wonder at the smoke, the riches, and the din of wealthy Rome!" (*Horace: The Odes and Epodes,* trans. C. E. Bennett [(Cambridge, 1968)], *Odes,* 3.29).

7. Henry George Liddell recalled the following exchange between Thackeray and Liddell's own wife: "At this time *Vanity Fair* was coming out in monthly parts in its well-known yellow paper covers. He [Thackeray] used to talk about it, and what he should do with the persons. Mrs. Liddell one day said. 'Oh, Mr. Thackeray, you must let Dobbin marry Amelia.' 'Well,' he replied, 'he shall; and when he has got her, he will not find her worth having'" (*The Letters and Private Papers of William Makepeace Thackeray,* ed. Gordon N. Ray [(London, 1945)], II, 641-642, n. 21).

8. "*Vanity Fair,*" in *Thackeray: A Collection of Critical Essays,* ed. Alexander Welsh (Englewood Cliffs, N. J., 1968), p. 85. Tillotson refers to the famous description at the end of the ninth number where George suddenly appears "lying on his face, dead, with a bullet through his heart" (32:315).

9. *Thackeray the Novelist* (Cambridge, 1954), pp. 32, 34.

10. G. Tillotson, p. 34.

11. *The English Humourists of the Eighteenth Century,* ed. George Saintsbury (London, 1908), XIV, 514, 524.

12. See Hardy, p. 125, n. 2. Hardy compares Steyne's and Becky's wit to Congreve's, but she stresses the lack of love in their wit.

13. *The English Humourists,* p. 515.

14. *Thackeray: The Uses of Adversity, 1811-1846* (London, 1955), p. 416.

15. *Apology,* trans. T. R. Glover (London, 1931), pp. 156-157, sec. 33.

16. "On Some Late Great Victories," in *Roundabout Papers,* ed. George Saintsbury (London, 1908), XX, 395.

17. Thackeray's secondary source for the Roman triumph was apparently William Smith's *A Dictionary of Greek and Roman Antiquities* (1842; rpt. London, 1882), pp. 1163-1167. Note the almost identical word usage in the Thackeray and Smith accounts:

Thackeray: "In ancient times Pliny (*apud* Smith) relates it was the custom of the Imperator 'to paint his whole body a bright red;' and, also, on ascending the Hill, to have some of the hostile chiefs led aside 'to the adjoining prison, and put to death'" (p. 396).

Smith: ". . . in ancient times, his [the imperator's] body was painted bright red. (Plin. *H. N.* [*Historia naturalis*] xxiii.36.). . . . Just as the pomp was ascending the Capitoline hill some of the hostile chiefs were led aside into the adjoining prison and put to death" (p. 1166).

The dictionary quotes, with citation, Tertullian's "Respice post te! Hominem memento te!" ("Hominem memento te!" is a variant word order for "Hominem te memento"; see *Tertulliani Quae Supersunt Omnia,* ed. Franciscus Oehler [(Leipzig, 1853)], I, 239). But the dictionary does not relate Tertullian's interpretation of the command. Thackeray was either unaware of Tertullian's interpretation or chose to ignore it.

18. *Criticisms and Elucidations of Catullus* (Cambridge, 1878), pp. 75-78.

19. McMaster, p. 7.

20. See p. 250, n. 6 of this edition of *Vanity Fair.* The editors gloss "heaven" as a probable error for "haven."

21. *Letters,* II, 423.

22. I wish to acknowledge my indebtedness to the helpful criticisms and suggestions of Professors Hugh Witemeyer and U. C. Knoepflmacher.

Richard C. Stevenson (essay date 1977)

SOURCE: Stevenson, Richard C. "The Problem of Judging Becky Sharp: Scene and Narrative Commentary in *Vanity Fair.*" *Victorians Institute Journal,* no. 6 (1977): 1-8.

[*In the following essay, Stevenson examines Thackeray's ambivalence toward the character of Becky Sharp.*]

The question of how to judge Becky Sharp is one that is raised repeatedly in the later part of *Vanity Fair*: "Who knows but Rebecca was right in her speculations"[1] says the narrator after Becky's famous consideration of what she could be on five thousand a year; "'How cool that woman is,' said one . . . 'What an honest and good-natured soul she is,' said another. 'What an artful little minx,' said a third. They were all right very likely" (488), sums up the narrator; "Was she guilty or not? We all know how charitable the world is, and how the verdict of Vanity Fair goes when there is a doubt" (538), and so on. When one views the "authorial presence," in Juliet McMaster's words, not as "the artist himself, but [as] a humanly fallible narrator,"[2] this relativistic narrative stance anticipates twentieth-century literary impressionism. Thackeray's narration suggests, as Ann Wilkinson has put it, "that the truth is simply not known by any single observer, including the narrator,"[3] or, in the words of G. A. Craig, Thackeray "could not be cleared without being untruthful, and he could not be truthful without being obscure."[4]

This view of Thackeray's "obscurity" is one that is congenial to modern taste,[5] and it surely has laid to rest the old attacks against Thackeray on the simplistic basis of the author as narrator. But there is also danger implicit in this position if it is taken too far—the danger of imposing a twentieth-century outlook on a work that remains essentially Victorian. Thackeray was undoubtedly moving in a modern direction with the equivocating narrator of *Vanity Fair,* but at the same time he developed an extensive symbolical groundwork for moral judgments, a groundwork that is manifested in his use of scenic detail. Thackeray's use of scene allowed him an important means of expressing authorial attitudes that may complement, clarify, or, at critical points, modify that effect of his narrator's ramblings.[6] What Thackeray sometimes provides, then, is a kind of narrative counterpoint that builds a tension between the cumulative effects of scenic detail—what we are "shown"—and the effects of the narrative commentary—what we are "told." This tension is very much to his purposes and it accounts, I think, for much of the peculiar power we find in the narration of *Vanity Fair.* If we were to stop with either the narrator's stated ambivalence about Becky *or* a resounding moral judgment based on the "facts"—like Lady Jane's pronouncement on her as "'a wicked woman—a heartless mother, a false wife'" (531)—we would be missing much. Rather, the text provides us with a "double" yet coherent way of viewing Becky: on the one hand we are given a firm basis on which to judge her severely, and on the other we are encouraged to see the limitations of that judgment and to feel a guarded admiration for the way in which she comports herself in *Vanity Fair.* No one would dispute, for example, that Becky is a "heartless mother"; the outgrown shirt which she carries about in her work box for public display acts as a convenient scenic device to sum up her true maternal instincts. But we must also join the narrator in his obvious admiration

for the artful way in which she uses the pretense of motherly affection to manipulate sentimental dunces like Jos and Amelia.

A central example of Thackeray's brilliant "double" method of handling Becky is found in the famous ending of Chapter 53—Rawdon's discovery of his wife's *tete-à-tete* with Lord Steyne—and Thackeray's preparation for it in the preceding chapters. The great opportunity to prepare for the discovery scene, as Percy Lubbock has noted, is the depiction "of Becky's triumph in the face of the world"[7] at the Gaunt House festivities which take place on the preceding evening. But Lubbock points to this section in order to illustrate his well-known contention that Thackeray usually botches any attempt to give a "dramatic display of a constituted scene"[8]: he "let the opportunity slip. There was a chance of a straight, unhampered view of the whole meaning of his matter; nothing was needed but to allow the scene to show itself, fairly and squarely. All its force would have been lent to the disaster that follows." Instead, Lubbock claims, "the triumphal evening passes in a confused haze that leaves that situation exactly where it was before."[9] The only "rift in the haze . . . is a single glimpse of Steyne, applauding Becky's triumph."[10]

I would argue the point in precisely the opposite fashion. Thackeray, in his own rather than in a Jamesian fashion, brilliantly highlights his three principals in this episode in a use of scene that is highly dramatic and that specifically prepares for the discovery to follow in Chapter 53. The clearest example of the scene "showing itself, fairly and squarely," is the terse depiction of the charade in which Becky performs as Clytemnestra, Rawdon as Agamemnon, and Steyne, in the passage to which Lubbock refers, as overlord of the performance and most vocal member of the audience:

> The king of men (it is Colonel Crawley, who, indeed, has no notion about the sack of Ilium or the conquest of Cassandra), the anax andron is asleep in his chamber at Argos. A lamp casts the broad shadow of the sleeping warrior flickering on the wall—the sword and shield of Troy glitter in its light. The band plays the awful music of Don Juan, before the statue enters. . . .

> Clytemnestra glides swiftly into the room like an apparition—her arms are bare and white,—her tawny hair floats down her shoulders,—her face is deadly pale,—and her eyes are lighted up with a smile so ghastly, that people quake as they look at her.

> A tremor ran through the room. "Good God!" somebody said, "it's Mrs. Rawdon Crawley."

> Scornfully she snatches the dagger out of Aegisthus's hand, and advances to the bed. You see it shining over her head in the glimmer of the lamp, and—and the lamp goes out, with a groan, and all is dark.

> The darkness and the scene frightened people. Rebecca performed the part so well, and with such ghastly truth, that the spectators were all dumb, until, with a burst,

all the lamps of the hall blazed out again, when everybody began to shout applause. "Brava! brava!" old Steyne's strident voice was heard roaring over all the rest. "Bye—, she'd do it too," he said between his teeth.

(493-494)

At this point the relations between Becky, Rawdon and Steyne are shown with extraordinary clarity: Becky, performing for Steyne, is fully ready to sacrifice Rawdon to her ambition; Rawdon, described a few pages later as "scared at these triumphs . . . [which] seemed to separate his wife farther than ever from him somehow" (499), vaguely senses betrayal—he refuses to come forward with Becky to acknowledge the applause—but is not yet ready to see what is quite evident to others; and Steyne, "roaring over all the rest," compliments himself for the brilliance of his protegee's performance, on and off stage, and prepares to reward her willingness to play Clytemnestra to his Aegisthus with an introduction to George IV. And, of course, Rawdon's appointment as governor of Coventry Island—a sure appointment with yellow fever and death—is also in the works.

Becky's role in a later charade, in which she embodies "the innocence of theatrical youth" (497) and is repeatedly embraced by Lord Southdown posing as her "Mamma,"[11] provides another commentary on her actual role in society, and again, "Lord Steyne's voice of applause was loudest of all" (498). There are a number of other strategic ways in which Thackeray prepares for the end of Chapter 53—the scene between Rawdon and Lady Jane, for example, in which he tries to express how his warm relations with her and little Rawdon have altered his view of the world and brought about an ill-defined desire for a different way of life: "'I—I'd like to change somehow. You see I want—I want—to be—.' He did not finish the sentence, but she could interpret it" (514). The change that in fact takes place in the next paragraphs, as Chapter 53 comes to its end, is hardly what Rawdon could have had in mind. But the scene does provide him with his one majestic moment in the novel, a moment when the confusion and ambiguity which have clouded his vision are swept away by an instant of clear insight. And what is of particular interest for our purposes here is that the narrator's role in this discovery scene seems to be one of hedging that clarity, of restoring the issue of Becky's innocence or guilt to the realm of relativistic questioning: "What *had* happened? Was she guilty or not? She said not; but who could tell what was truth . . ." (517) and so on. It is at a moment like this in **Vanity Fair** that an awareness of Thackeray's contrapuntal uses of scene and narrative commentary are of critical importance. Here, I think, are found some primary clues to the novel's form and peculiar power.

A delicate set of tactics is at work as Rawdon is described returning home from the bailiff's to find Becky, as he describes it later to Pitt, "in diamonds and sitting with that villain alone" (521). The situation and the carefully engineered chain of events, including the charades of the previous evening, are all made to bear on this moment so as to contribute to the reader's response. But what is of special importance here is the almost obsessive attention paid to a specific set of scenic details—the finery that represents Becky's ascent in "the world." It is this collection of "vanities" that Thackeray uses, more than anything else, I think, to sum up Becky's moral state at the moment of discovery, thus providing a counterpoint to the narrator's equivocating commentary.

As Rawdon enters the room, his wife is described "in a brilliant full toilette, her arms and all her fingers sparkling with bracelets and rings; and the brilliants on her breast which Steyne had given her" (515). And as Rawdon's description to Pitt later emphasizes, it is this finery that provides the focus for his anger. When Becky melodramatically pleads with her husband, she clings to him with hands that are "all covered with serpents, and rings, and baubles. 'I am innocent'" (515). And, after he has struck Steyne and commanded Becky to throw down all her jewelry, there follows Rawdon's famous *coup de grâce* as he tears a final diamond ornament from Becky's gown and flings it in the lord's face, giving Steyne, in one of the novel's finest ironic lines, "the scar [he wore] to his dying day" (516). If this line is a mock heroic flourish, as Geoffrey Tillotson has suggested,[12] part of its effect is to remind us of Rawdon's slumbering Agamemnon—an Agamemnon who has finally thwarted tradition and his own obtuseness to awaken and dispatch the enemy. For one critical moment Rawdon attains heroic stature, "strong, brave, and victorious" (515) before his Clytemnestra's admiring eyes.[13]

Thackeray ends the chapter with a still life that epitomizes the total effect: we see Becky sitting alone, surrounded by still more emblems of her abortive career:

> The drawers were all opened and their contents scattered about,—dresses and feathers, scarfs and trinkets, a heap of tumbled vanities lying in a wreck. Her hair was falling over her shoulders; her gown was torn where Rawdon had wrenched the brilliants out of it. . . . She thought of her long past life, and all the dismal incidents of it. Ah, how dreary it seemed, how miserable, lonely and profitless! Should she take laudanum, and end it, too—have done with all hopes, schemes, debts, and triumphs? The French maid found her in this position—sitting in the midst of her miserable ruins with clasped hands and dry eyes. . . . "Mon Dieu, Madame, what has happened?" she asked.
>
> (516-517)[14]

This query is the one that is picked up and expanded in the chapter's last paragraph, as Thackeray's narrator plays with the question of what Gordon Ray and others have aptly called Becky's "technical virtue."[15] Thus, as the narrator *tells* us one thing—it is impossible to know precisely what had happened or was about to happen between Steyne and Rebecca—he *shows* us something else. The scenic detail, the tumbled heap of finery that surrounds Becky here, inevitably fixes our attention, not on the "technical question," but on her "essential guilt"[16]: she has sold out Rawdon just as she has sold herself for these emblems of material and social success. And it is Rawdon, looking back on these events later, who sums up the moral effect of the scene with as much precision as is necessary: "'If she's not guilty, Pitt, she's as bad as guilty; and I'll never see her again,—never'" (537).

Barbara Hardy has aptly referred to Becky as both "clever producer and actress,"[17] and this showmanship is nowhere clearer than in the scene in which Jos comes to visit her in room No. 92 of the Elephant Hotel in Pumpernickel, a scene which will serve as a final illustration of Thackeray's "double" narrative technique in *Vanity Fair.* Becky at this point is at the low point of her fortunes, living under circumstances that are in glaring contrast to the relative splendors of Curzon Street and, especially, of Gaunt House. As Jos approaches, he finds the seedy-looking student from across the hall "on his knees at No. 92, bawling through the keyhole supplications to the person within" to make what appears to be an assignation; Jos, though he overhears the exchange, "did not comprehend it, for the reason that he had never studied the language in which it was carried on" (631). Jos's lack of comprehension continues in a very important sense in the colloquy that follows between himself and Becky. The scene of the "queer little apartment" is briefly but pointedly described. There are various articles of clothing hanging about in disarray and Becky herself wears, "by way of morning robe," a soiled pink domino which, with its associations of mask and masquerade, is most appropriate to what ensues. The objects in the scene that are given special attention, however, are "a rouge pot, a brandy bottle, and a plate of broken meat" (631), all of which Becky conceals in the bed as she prepares the scene for her visitor's entry into the room. Once Jos is seated, Becky begins her performance at once as she rapidly moves the topic of conversation to her thwarted maternal instincts:

> "I had but one child, one darling, one hope, one joy, which I held to my heart with a mother's affection, which was my life, my prayer, my—my blessing; and they—they tore it from me—tore it from me"; and she put her hand to her heart with a passionate gesture of despair, burying her face for a moment on the bed.
>
> The brandy-bottle inside clinked up against the plate which held the cold sausage.
>
> (632-633)

The clink of bottle and plate here acts as the correlative of Becky's moral state, a case, once again, where

Thackeray's use of simple scenic detail sums up the desired effect with admirable precision.

At this moment Becky stands morally indicted, both as a "heartless mother" and as a charlatan, but the effect of the passage hardly stops there. At the same time that we are made to hear the false note we also hear the narrator's ironic summation of Becky's performance—"if ever there was a white-robed angel escaped from heaven to be subject to the infernal machinations and villany of fiends here below, that spotless being—that miserable, unsullied martyr—was present on the bed before Jos" (633).[18] Becky's "exhibition of so much grief" is quite adequate to enchant the civilian, who is no more capable of distinguishing between white robes and a soiled pink domino than he is of perceiving that Becky is sitting on a brandy bottle. By the balance of scenic detail and narrative commentary here, Thackeray joins our necessarily harsh moral judgment with an artistic judgment—our renewed admiration for Becky's sure sense of theater, her extraordinary ability to make the best of poor circumstances by capitalizing on the weakness and vanity of those, like Jos, who are not permitted the kind of vision that Thackeray fosters in his reader. The cumulative effect of this kind of contrapuntal narrative technique is to provide us with a dimension of life in *Vanity Fair* that is enormously rich and suggestive. Thackeray's creation of a style that at once "tells" *and* "shows" in large part accounts for the brilliant success of this Novel Without a Hero.

Notes

1. *Vanity Fair,* eds. Geoffrey and Kathleen Tillotson (Boston: Houghton Mifflin Co., 1963), p. 410. All subsequent references to *Vanity Fair* will be to this edition with page numbers indicated in parentheses.

2. *Thackeray: The Major Novels* (Toronto: University of Toronto Press, 1971), p. 5. See also Harriet Blodgett's commentary on the same theme in "Necessary Presence: The Rhetoric of the Narrator in *Vanity Fair,*" [*Nineteenth-Century Fiction*] 22 (1967), 211-223.

3. "The Tomeavesian Way of Knowing the World: Technique and Meaning in *Vanity Fair,*" *ELH,* 32 (1965), 381.

4. "On the Style of *Vanity Fair,*" *Style in Prose Fiction,* ed. Harold C. Martin, English Institute Essays (New York: Columbia University Press, 1959), p. 112.

5. There are, of course, dissenters to this view. For example, according to Russel A. Fraser in "Pernicious Casuistry: A Study of Character in *Vanity Fair,*" [*Nineteenth-Century Fiction*] 12 (1957), 138, Thackeray's ambivalence, his insistence on

having "it both ways, [is] to speak, not consciously, impartially, but uneasily, irresolutely, for two points or view, each opposed to the other. It is a flaw in Thackeray's handling of character. And the flaw persists." At the other extreme, see John E. Tilford's attempt to demonstrate that Thackeray's narrator presents a clear moral indictment of Becky in "The Degradation of Becky Sharp," [*South Atlantic Quarterly*] 58 (1959), 603-608: "Far from being fond of [Becky], Thackeray continually indicates his distaste for her" (605).

6. In this sense, in *Vanity Fair* may function in a manner similar to that of the illustrations. For an informative discussion of the role played by the illustrations in *Vanity Fair,* see Joan Stevens, "Thackeray's 'Vanity Fair,'" [*Review of English Literature*] 6 (1965), 19-38.

7. *The Craft of Fiction* (New York: Viking Press, 1957), p. 103.

8. Lubbock, p. 100.

9. Lubbock, pp. 103-104.

10. Lubbock, p. 105.

11. P. M. Plunkett notes that this "protective 'Mama,' whose absence Thackeray so often invokes to excuse [Becky's] misdemeanors in the novel, is somewhat cynically granted to her in the charade as the adjunct to her cardboard innocence." Plunkett also points out that the Agamemnon charade "provides Thackeray with one of his most powerful symbols" in "Thackeray's *Vanity Fair,* Chapter 51," *Explicator,* 23 (1964), Item 19. See also Stephen Butterfield, "The Charades of *Vanity Fair,*" [*Massachusetts Studies in English*] (Fall 1968), 94-95.

12. *Thackeray the Novelist* (New York: Cambridge University Press, 1954), p. 84.

13. As Barbara Hardy has noted in commenting upon this scene, Thackeray "has the kind of mind on which nothing is lost—brooch, ring, banknote, painted face, emotional and intellectual activity," *The Exposure of Luxury: Radical Themes in Thackeray* (Pittsburg: University of Pittsburg Press, 1972), p. 29.

14. This passage is a good example of the way in which Thackeray may blend narrative tactics within a short space. To use Lubbock's terms, the passage is scenic—we are "placed before a particular scene, an occasion, at a certain selected hour" (66); it contains panoramic narrative commentary—"vanities lying in a wreck"; and it is also scene that is "pictorally treated" (70), that is, it provides "the reflection of somebody's mind" (115)—in this case, Becky's: "Ah, how dreary it seemed, how miserable, lonely and profitless!"

15. *Thackeray: The Uses of Adversity, 1811-1846* (New York: McGraw-Hill 1955), note 14, p. 502. See also Kathleen Tillotson, *Novels of the Eighteen-Forties* (Oxford: Oxford University Press, 1954), pp. 247-248, and Barbara Hardy, *The Exposure of Luxury,* p. 31.

16. These two terms are Kathleen Tillotson's. Mrs. Tillotson notes that Rawdon acts as the basis for our judgment in this scene, which is certainly true, but I would argue that Thackeray's use of scene here considerably extends the basis for that judgment.

17. Hardy, p. 29.

18. Thackeray, of course, also treats Becky with narrative irony in precisely the opposite fashion—the outwardly condemnatory phrase: "All the world used her ill, said [Becky], and we may be pretty certain that persons whom all the world treats ill, deserve entirely the treatment they get" (19). Juliet McMaster, in commenting on this passage, illuminates another aspect of what I have been calling Thackeray's "double" way of presenting Becky: Mrs. McMaster notes that Thackeray's "complex irony . . . is frequently true to some extent in both senses. While he wants us to make no mistake about Becky's unscrupulous self-seeking, he uses his narrator to expose the pharisaical confidence of the puritan respectable classes in the just distribution of their own comforts and the miseries of others" (p. 10).

Michael Lund (essay date summer 1979)

SOURCE: Lund, Michael. "Beyond the Text of *Vanity Fair.*" *Studies in the Novel* 11, no. 2 (summer 1979): 147-61.

[*In the following essay, Lund examines the role of the reader in interpreting what happens in* Vanity Fair. *Lund argues that the reader, more than the author, bears the responsibility of bringing the novel's characters to full realization.*]

In his landmark study of the novel, *The Rhetoric of Fiction* (Chicago: Univ. of Chicago Press, 1961), Wayne Booth noted that while every novel contains an implied reader (the author's assumed audience), modern criticism has often "ignored, lamented, or denied" (p. 89) the reader's importance in the literary experience. Since 1970, however, a number of important works have attempted to fill this gap. Wolfgang Iser in *The Implied Reader: Patterns of Communication in Prose Fiction from Bunyan to Beckett* (Baltimore: The Johns Hopkins Univ. Press, 1974) explores the reader's active role, insisting that literature involves both a "prestructuring of the potential meaning by the text" and "the reader's actualization of this potential through the reading process" (p. xii). To talk of the text as a thing "out there," apart from any apprehension of it, then, is to falsify literary experience, as Walter Slatoff points out in his *With Respect to Readers* (Ithaca: Cornell Univ. Press, 1970): "one cannot escape the fact that literary works are experienced by individual living readers and that it is this experience which makes them valuable" (p. 21). To some critics, the reader's effort is perhaps even more significant than the text: David Bleich's "subjective criticism" suggests that "it is the reader who determines whether a piece of writing is literature,"[1] and Norman Holland's psychoanalytical approach asserts that "a reader responds to a literary work by using it to re-create his characteristic psychological processes."[2] The most succinct concept of the form of reader response underlying the following consideration of Thackeray's *Vanity Fair* (1847-48), however, comes from Stanley Fish, who seeks "an analysis not of formal features, but of the developing responses of the reader in relation to the words as they succeed one another in time."[3]

Walter Slatoff has outlined the particular area of such response that I wish here to pursue in detail, the "inevitable and valid imaginative filling in and fleshing out which we perform as we read" (p. 17). That is, though we frequently think and speak of a fictional character, for instance, as being "fully realized," it can never really be so—there would be no end to the detail that would have to be included to satisfy the literal meaning of the term. What actually happens when we read is that we are given by the text a great number of key facts and features from which we infer other necessary attributes and, thus, ultimately conceive of a complete person, "fully realized." Slatoff goes on:

> When an author gives a character a name, he indicates he is creating a person and intends him to be perceived as such; our very use of the word "character" implies that what we experience is a person.
>
> This sort of filling in or rounding out is very different from the loose speculation, daydreaming, or psychologizing about the lives and motives of fictional characters that so irritates anyone who believes that reading must at least be guided and limited by the text. The phenomenon I am talking about is as unavoidable (so long as we read as men and not machines) as our assumption when we hear a voice or see a body that it belongs to a whole person. That this phenomenon does occur, that we must in some respects move beyond the text, of course makes it very difficult to determine just what constitutes a valid reading. Ignoring such responses reduces the difficulty, but also reduces the value and relevance, of our work.
>
> (pp. 17-18)

To put it another way, I will try to show here how some fictional events deserve critical attention even though they do not actually occur in the text. I wish to demonstrate how it is the reader who "fully realizes" character—particularly Amelia Sedley—in *Vanity Fair.*

Though his first major work, *Vanity Fair* remains Thackeray's best known and most frequently analyzed novel. Much of the critical interest has centered around its form, especially its careful manipulation of the kinds of popular fiction—sentimental, historic, adventure, etc.—of his day.[4] The form of the reader's response to this particular text, then, would seem to deserve a similar attention. In fact, Wolfgang Iser has already selected it as a pivotal work in his history of the "implied reader," terming it an "outstanding example" of a transitional state in the novel's history, where "the author-reader relationship is as different from the eighteenth-century 'dialogue' as it is from the twentieth-century demand that the reader find for himself the key to a many-sided puzzle" (pp. 102-3). Professor Iser echoes a number of Thackeray scholars in pointing out that, despite *Vanity Fair*'s unabashedly obtrusive narrator, much work is still left to the reader's imagination if the novel's actions and statements are to be appreciated in full.[5]

One aspect of the novel to which the reader is particularly invited to contribute is its plot or causality, which is often left open to the reader's interpretation. Plot in *Vanity Fair* is primarily the histories of two women: one, the shrewdly competent Rebecca Sharp, consistently exploits the conventions of high society to rise within it; the other, the compassionate but vulnerable Amelia Sedley, is exploited by Rebecca and others in their campaigns to achieve social prominence. Because the character and adventures of Becky have been so thoroughly discussed by others,[6] I will offer here only a brief summary of the reader's response to her career before considering in more detail the story of Amelia.

In both Becky and Amelia's stories Thackeray elicits the reader's involvement in the novel's causality by the careful use of the omniscient narrator convention. Although Thackeray's authorial voice repeatedly explains the actions, for example, his very thoroughness frequently leads to confusion rather than understanding.[7] In one early summary of the plot, for instance, the narrator gives much information about a rumored note of proposal to the young Rebecca Sharp but no clear picture of events and their cause-and-effect relationships:

> Thus the world began for these two young ladies. For Amelia it was quite a new, fresh, brilliant world, with all the bloom upon it. It was not quite a new one for Rebecca—(indeed, if the truth must be told with respect to the Crisp affair, the tart-woman hinted to somebody, who took an affidavit of the fact to somebody else, that there was a great deal more than was made public regarding Mr. Crisp and Miss Sharp, that his letter was *in answer* to another letter). But who can tell

you the real truth of the matter? At all events, if Rebecca was not beginning the world, she was beginning it over again.[8]

The number of questions one might raise about this brief account suggests how such commentary, which at first appears to be helpful, only puzzles the reader. What did the Crisp letter actually say? In what ways did Becky solicit the letter? Who is this unidentified "tart-woman," or the equally unspecified "somebody" and "somebody else," and is any a reliable source? Is the narrator himself reliable in his parenthetical commentary, or does he really care about the "real" truth of this case? What exactly is he suggesting in his ironic use of the terms, "an affidavit of the fact"? *Is* Rebecca beginning or beginning again the world? Is this incident supposed to show that others are the cause of Rebecca's actions, or is it the other way around? Despite the wealth of commentary Thackeray provides, we will never know from the text. Although the reader is guided through a number of possibilities by the narrator, his expectation of unequivocal or easy answers is in the end defeated, and he is left on his own to select some final version of the history of events. As Jack P. Rawlins has pointed out, the novel in this method turns to its true subject—the reader himself—by frustrating his conventional expectations, calling attention to the inadequacies of certain modes of perception characteristic of the popular fiction reader of Thackeray's age, and our own.[9] Rawlins notes: "We read romantic novels with an easy moral absolutism and live according to a more pragmatic creed. By casting us as the characters of his novel, Thackeray asks us to account for the discrepancy" (p. 13).

While in some places too much explanation serves Thackeray's purpose of requiring his reader to fill in some aspects of Becky's story for himself, at other points the narrator's commentary is more pointed. The "famous little Becky Puppet," as Thackeray called her,[10] has consistently elicited admiration from the novel's readers for her artful successes in a world openly hostile to her. But, as Rawlins in particular has shown, each time we accede to Becky's morality by applauding her, the ever-present narrator reminds us that we have failed to judge properly the causes and effects of Becky's actions: "If we wish social success for her, we are discouraged by repeated reminders . . ." (p. 29). According to Stanley Fish, whose analysis of reader response I cited earlier as a guide for this study, this is the same kind of literary experience created by Satan's appearances in Milton's *Paradise Lost*:

> in the early books, Satan's false heroism draws from the reader a response [admiration] that is immediately challenged by the epic voice, who at the same time challenges the concept of heroism in which the response is rooted. Subsequently, Satan's apparent heroism is discredited by covert allusions to other heroes in

other epics, by his ignoble accommodation to the "family" he meets at the gates of Hell, by his later discoveries squatting at the ear of Eve in the form of a toad, and, most tellingly, by his own self-revelation in the extended soliloquy that opens Book IV.[11]

Similarly, in *Vanity Fair* the reader's repeated feeling of satisfaction at Rebecca's ability to ridicule the vanities of others in her climb toward acceptance in high society is gradually overcome by his growing awareness of the extent of her own unprincipled behavior: her eagerness to marry Joseph Sedley or Sir Pitt Crawley, her patronizing use of Rawdon and abuse of their son, her relationship with Lord Steyne, her later life on the Continent. Here again the novel's true subject becomes the reader, who is called upon to unravel carefully the fiction's causality, determining what character is responsible for which result. "What *had* happened? Was she guilty or not?" (p. 517), asks the narrator at one of the novel's most famous moments—Lord Steyne discovered alone with Rebecca by her husband Rawdon Crawley—and then, almost incredibly, does not answer. Here, and elsewhere in the novel, each reader must decide for himself; he must fill in, beyond the text of the omniscient but evasive narrator, the degree and nature of Becky's guilt, the extent of her culpability for the sufferings of others and of herself.

The reader's understanding of Becky, then, bound up in his developing responses to her continuing actions, becomes as important to the existence of a complete *Vanity Fair* as the actual presentation of those events in the text itself. Our relationship to Amelia, the other focal point in our response to the novel, has generally seemed less complex and, perhaps for that reason, has not been as thoroughly studied as our response to Rebecca's actions.[12] In this other major history of *Vanity Fair,* however, the reader also plays a vital role, actually helping to create the character and determine the fate of the central figure, Amelia Sedley.

Our earliest conception of Amelia's nature is a relatively simple one; we recognize her honest heart but regret her inability to understand, and thus protect herself from, those who are using her. We know from the start, for instance, that her love for George Osborne is pure, but idealized and sentimental: "He was her Europe; her emperor: her allied monarchs and august prince regent. He was her sun and moon . . ." (p. 112). Amelia, a "silly little thing" (p. 37) according to the narrator, is the innocent prey of individuals like George and institutions like Miss Pinkerton's which have formed her character. As long as she remains this passive victim, our sympathy for her continues to at least balance our exasperation at her weaknesses. When she abandons the passive role for an active one, our reaction to her subsequent fate is less sure. That moment occurs not in the text of *Vanity Fair* but outside it, in the reader's response, very near the middle point of his experience of the novel, at the end of the ninth number (of the twenty monthly parts in which the novel was originally published, from January, 1847, through July, 1848), at the end of chapter 32 (of 67). Joseph Sedley's invitation to his sister Amelia, to leave Brussels on the eve of Waterloo, is the occasion for a new relationship between reader and text, providing a fundamental impetus for the rest of our experience of *Vanity Fair.*

The transition in our conception of Amelia from passive victim to active participant in Vanity Fair is, in part, the product of one characteristic provided her by the text—her habit of refusing to admit to unpleasant facts in her world. Although she begins even before her marriage to receive hints that her husband is not "one of the most gallant and brilliant men in the empire" (p. 119), she simply ignores the evidence (for reasons with which, by the way, Thackeray is not altogether unsympathetic):

> And she had misgivings and fears which she dared not acknowledge to herself, though she was always secretly brooding over them.
>
> Her heart tried to persist in asserting that George Osborne was worthy and faithful to her, though she knew otherwise. . . . She did not dare to own that the man she loved was her inferior; or to feel that she had given her heart away too soon. Given once, the pure bashful maiden was too modest, too trustful, too weak, too much woman to recall it.
>
> (p. 169)

Thus, although she "knows" in some vague sense about George's true character, she manages not to think of it, to continue the illusion of his greatness at all conscious moments. When her father is ruined, Amelia fears that the real George might not honor their engagement and so simply refuses to think about that future: "She lived in her past life . . . the business of her life, was—to watch the corpse of Love" (p. 172). When Dobbin engineers George's return to Amelia, she rescues her picture of him as "'the greatest and best of men'" (p. 187), suppressing any latent suspicions she had held. But it is not long before she is again pressured by events to recognize George's shortcomings: "They were only a week married, and here was George already suffering ennui, and eager for others' society" (p. 233). Worse, of course, is the fact that George's flirtation with Becky is not unsuspected: "A dim uneasy sentiment about Rebecca filled her mind already [on their honeymoon in Brighton]; and although they kissed each other most tenderly at parting, yet we know what jealousy is; and Mrs. Amelia possessed that among other virtues of her sex" (p. 239).

Though the truth about George's relationship with Rebecca becomes clear to everyone, the text fails to make explicit the degree of Amelia's own knowledge.[13]

Does she really know, or is she continuing to make herself incapable of seeing?—a consistently evasive narrator refuses to say. Although he pointedly asks—"Did she own to herself how different the real man was from that superb young hero whom she had worshipped?" (p. 251)—Thackeray never presents any direct answer. The closest the text comes to showing Amelia's awareness is that the narrator suggests what she is *not* thinking. At the ball where George will later slip Rebecca a note proposing they run away together, Amelia witnesses at a distance her husband's attentions to her rival. Engaged in small talk with Dobbin (about man's impulse to gamble), Amelia "was thinking of something else. It was not the loss of the money [through George's gambling with Rawdon] that grieved her" (p. 278)—but further than such indirect statements the narrator will not go. At one point, though, the narrator explains his refusal to be more explicit in reporting Amelia's fears of losing George: "Have we a right to repeat or to overhear her prayers? These, brother, are secrets, and out of the domain of Vanity Fair, in which our story lies" (p. 251). As Rawlins observes, "Thackeray is explicit about the sides of life that do not fit into *Vanity Fair*; his famous veil is drawn over all scenes of honest emotion, grief, love, or religious faith . . ." (p. 26). Into such space thus deliberately left vacant by the narrator we readers step, here filling in Amelia's unspoken distress with our own sympathetic apprehension of it. Again, Thackeray turns his novel to its truest subject, the reader, who this time must construct a realm of experience and knowledge more fulfilling to human desires than Vanity Fair. Amelia's suffering consciousness—torn between recognizing the truth and refusing to accept it—must be realized in the reader's response if it is to exist at all.

If by this method of omission Thackeray encourages the reader to round out for himself Amelia's state of mind, serial publication accomplishes even more.[14] The last scene of the eighth number intensifies the dramatic portrayal of Amelia's consciousness, while still avoiding any explicit presentation of her thoughts. As George prepares to march with the British army against Napoleon in the morning, Amelia lies in bed, at times in a slight sleep, and then more wakeful. When George comes to her bed, Amelia's "fair arms closed tenderly round his neck as he stooped down. 'I am awake, George,' the poor child said, with a sob fit to break the little heart that nestled so closely by his own. She was awake, poor soul, and to what? At that moment a bugle from the Place of Arms began sounding clearly, and was taken up through the town; and amidst the drums of the infantry, and the shrill pipes of the Scotch, the whole city awoke" (pp. 280-81; number ends here). In August, 1847, the Victorian reader filled in for himself the "what" of Amelia's thoughts—and had no occasion for his version of Amelia's prospects, or other future events, to be contradicted or confirmed until September! In modern editions of the novel, of course, we but turn the page and let the text continue to inform us, but for Thackeray's original audience how much idle time in thirty days might be turned to rounding out beyond the text the terms of Amelia's despair? How many blank pages from *Tristram Shandy's* text would be needed to represent in a spatial framework the temporal nature of the actual reading experience? And when Number 9 does appear, Thackeray continues, and even intensifies, the reader's creation of the character of Amelia Sedley.

Thackeray's technique throughout Number 9 is to delay Amelia's confrontation with two dreadful truths: George's unfaithfulness and his death (the famous last sentence of the number is: "Darkness came down on the field and city: and Amelia was praying for George, who was lying on his face, dead, with a bullet through his heart" [p. 315]). How Amelia responds to these facts depends as much upon the reader as the text; as he proceeds through Number 9, the reader creates, by anticipating, Amelia's sorrow. Left behind in Brussels when the army advances toward the front, Amelia is apparently able at first to subdue or repress any fears about George's loyalty by concentrating on the danger he is in. When she is paid a visit by Rebecca, however, her secret dread threatens to rush to the front of her consciousness: "Rebecca's appearance struck Amelia with terror, and made her shrink back. It recalled her to the world and the remembrance of yesterday. In the overpowering fears about tomorrow she had forgotten Rebecca,—jealousy—everything except that her husband was gone and was in danger. Until this dauntless worldling came in and broke the spell, and lifted the latch, we too have forborne to enter into that sad chamber. How long had that poor girl been on her knees, what hours of speechless prayer and bitter prostration had she passed there!" (p. 297). Again, the narrator is evasive, demanding that the reader fill in for himself Amelia's "speechless" prayers: does she now desire deliverance from the truth, from her unfaithful husband, from potential widowhood, from her own illusions? Her behavior in this encounter with Rebecca reveals a mental tension very close to breakdown. She accuses her visitor: "'Are you come to fetch him from me?' she continued in a wilder tone. 'He was here, but he is gone now. There on that very sofa he sate. Don't touch it. We sate and talked there. I was on his knee, and my arms were round his neck, and we said, "Our Father"'" (p. 298). Amelia's account of her last moments with George is perhaps another product of a mind accustomed to reshaping reality, for the narrator's versions of that scene include no such details of a tender reconciliation (pp. 279-81, 290). As the scene with Becky continues, the reader recognizes that Amelia's thoughts are increasingly divorced from reality. A few moments after her outburst, "She had forgotten her anger, her jealousy, the very presence of her rival seemingly. For she walked silently and almost with a smile on her face, towards the bed, and began to smooth down George's pillow" (p. 299). When she is later found by Mrs. O'Dowd (the veteran campaigner, wife of the Major in George's regiment), Amelia is "almost crazy with grief" (p. 299) and later will seem in "hysteric insanity" (p. 309) as the cannon from Waterloo are heard in Brussels. This collapse of rational control increases the reader's participation in an approaching moment of dramatic choice for Amelia. From this unsettled state of mind she will eventually regain her composure by accepting as final certain assumptions about the nature of reality—and the reader will establish her new bent of consciousness before the text does.

Amelia's mind is made up when rumors that the French are about to invade the city inspire her brother Joseph to propose a retreat. With Amelia in this crucial scene are Mrs. O'Dowd, one of the few good characters in *Vanity Fair,* and Ensign Stubble, an idealistic youth who had been wounded and then returned to the city to be nursed by the two women:

> "I can't stand it any more, Emmy," [Joseph] said; "I won't stand it; and you must come with me. I have bought a horse for you—never mind at what price—and you must dress and come with me, and ride behind Isidor."
>
> "God forgive me, Mr. Sedley, but you are no better than a coward," Mrs. O'Dowd said, laying down the book.
>
> "I say come, Amelia," the civilian went on; "never mind what she says; why are we to stop here and be butchered by the Frenchmen?"
>
> "You forget the ——th, my boy," said the little Stubble, the wounded hero from his bed—"and—and you won't leave me, will you, Mrs. O'Dowd?"
>
> "No, my dear fellow," said she, going up and kissing the boy. "No harm shall come to you while *I* stand by. I don't budge till I get the word from Mick. A pretty figure I'd be, wouldn't I, stuck behind that chap on a pillion?"
>
> This image caused the young patient to burst out laughing in his bed, and even made Amelia smile. "I don't ask her," Jos shouted out—"I don't ask that—that Irishwoman, but you, Amelia; once for all, will you come?"
>
> "Without my husband, Joseph?" Amelia said, with a look of wonder, and gave her hand to the Major's wife.
>
> (pp. 313-14)

In this carefully orchestrated scene, a number of characters respond to Joseph's proposal before Amelia does. Accustomed as he is to filling in Amelia's state of mind at this point in her history, the reader too, I suggest, thinks of likely answers before she ultimately delivers her own response here. That is, the reader creates in himself the state of mind that the character Amelia will later exhibit in the text.

At the beginning of the scene, Jos's allusion to the great price paid for his means of escape adds an additional unsavory element to his already cowardly offer, making everyone—including the reader—expect immediate refusal from Amelia (regardless, by the way, of whatever logic might actually support retreat!). Mrs. O'Dowd, however, preempts a negative reply from Amelia, saying what, no doubt, Amelia and most readers are already thinking, that Mr. Sedley is acting like a coward at this time of his country's great need. Jos nevertheless repeats his offer, and this time "little Stubble," the "wounded hero," counters from his sickbed with an appeal to regimental loyalty and to woman's wartime role as nurse, encouraging again all of us who would not be thought cowards or traitors to anticipate a speedy denial from Amelia. But Mrs. O'Dowd substitutes her response for Amelia's a second time, presenting herself as a conspicuous example of the military wife's duty to await word from her husband before undertaking any action. Her momentary vision of herself accepting (a very fat) Joseph's proposal ("stuck behind that chap on a pillion") further ridicules that alternative, and the reader agrees to this assessment by thinking the same thoughts which lead to Amelia's "smile"—none of us would choose to appear in such a comic, humiliating pose. At Joseph's second repetition of his request, Amelia finally delivers her simple reply. After Jos's thrice-made cowardly offer, and the several heroic dismissals of it, Amelia's "Without my husband, Joseph?" becomes an eloquent final word indeed. But either at this point or sometime later in Amelia's history, the reader must realize that this action will dramatically affect the course of future events in *Vanity Fair*.

The sequence of exchanges and the gestures of the characters in this scene stimulate a chain of thought, which Amelia unconsciously follows, that makes her response not only a repudiation of Joseph's proposal but of any suspicion of George's loyalty to his marriage. That is, the replies which are substituted for hers encourage her to adopt a pose of noble heroism appropriate to them. The resulting unequivocalness of her own answer and her deliberate movement toward Mrs. O'Dowd equate George with the Major—honorable wives are remaining loyal to honorable husbands. Amelia's response would probably have been similar had she spoken immediately to Joseph's offer, but the context of the entire scene has elevated her stance to a nobility which spills over to the object of her loyalty, George Osborne. Amelia's refusal of her brother's offer thus becomes a proud assertion of her marriage's sanctity at a critical moment in her life—she denies the suspicions which have haunted her, declares her husband's innocence, and accepts a version of reality which will lead to considerable suffering in her future.

This proud state of mind, however, actually exists at this point primarily in the reader's mind as he antici-

pates and participates in Amelia's rhetorical declaration.[15] The narrator does not now chronicle the thought process that culminates in her simple statement; and no further picture of Amelia or her thoughts appears in Number 9 (except the momentary image, in the last sentence, of her praying while George lies dead on the battlefield). The starkly presented dramatic scene, however, with its artfully ordered dialogue, encourages the reader to take for Amelia a series of mental steps from confusion and doubt to heroic denial and conviction. When Amelia speaks at the end of this critical scene of the novel, her mind and the reader's are one. Thus, just as Rebecca's social triumphs elsewhere expose our complicity in the morality of *Vanity Fair* by eliciting our admiration, so Amelia's history here calls into play our weakness for sentimental and heroic attitudes.

Amelia's heroic pose of loyalty is intensified again in the reader's mind while he waits for the appearance of the next number of the novel; Amelia will, in effect, be frozen in this idealistic pose for a month. As she thus awaits word of George's fate—thinking of him as a loyal husband and hero—so does the reader wait for word of Amelia's destiny, thinking of her as a loyal wife and heroine. As she has ignored or repressed any knowledge of George's unfaithfulness while she waits, so too does the reader, though probably to a lesser degree. And Thackeray prolongs the reader's conception of a courageous Amelia who displays unlimited faith in her husband even more by again keeping her in the background of events until the last chapter of Number 10. The next reference to Amelia is, at this point in the reader's experience, a familiarly evasive one: the narrator wonders, "when Rebecca was flaunting at Paris, the gayest among the gay conquerors there . . . our Amelia, our dear wounded Amelia, ah! where was she?" (p. 327). When the narrator does finally give more than this kind of passing reference to Amelia or her situation, more than twelve months have passed in her life. Of what she has been thinking during that time we are as usual told little, though we may have thought much: "She has spent the first portion of that time [twelve months] in a sorrow so profound and pitiable, that we who have been watching and describing some of the emotions of that weak and tender heart, must draw back in the presence of the cruel grief under which it is bleeding" (p. 347). Once again her sorrow must be the reader's creation, existing between the lines of the text for many pages. We learn later that the birth of Amelia's son gives her life new meaning (the "child was her being" [p. 347]), but whatever understanding of her past and the child's father she has finally arrived at is clearer, more "fully realized," in the reader's mind than in the text.

The reader's conception of Amelia's state of mind created in the scene with Joseph and Mrs. O'Dowd, though, is eventually confirmed by the narrator and the novel's plot. In Number 11 we are told that Amelia's doting on Georgy is related to an exalted image she has retained of his father: "She talked constantly to him about this dead father, and spoke of her love for George to the innocent and wondering child; much more than she ever had done to George himself, or to any confidante of her youth" (p. 377). And when the Reverend Mr. Binney offers to become Georgy's stepfather, her response is exactly what the reader has predicted: she "said that she never, never could think of any but—but the husband whom she had lost. . . . [On] the days of marriage and widowhood, she kept her room entirely, consecrating them (and we do not know how many hours of solitary night-thought, her little boy sleeping in his crib by her bedside) to the memory of that departed friend" (p. 379). And finally (in Number 13) the narrator confirms precisely what the reader has already experienced: "All her husband's faults and foibles she had buried in the grave with him: she only remembered the lover, who had married her at all sacrifices; the noble husband so brave and beautiful, in whose arms she had hung on the morning when he had gone away to fight, and die gloriously for his king" (p. 445). During the six weeks or more of nervous collapse, when the doctors who attended her "feared for her life or for her brain" (p. 347), the noble stance she took defending her marriage to Joseph and the others had intensified to the point of unshakeable conviction she displays for so many years thereafter.

During her years of widowhood, in which Amelia worships her dead husband's memory, years described in the second half of *Vanity Fair,* the reader's original compassion for her as a helpless victim is lessened.[16] Although Dobbin has from the beginning represented a better man and a willing husband for her, it would be impossible to document the exact moment in Amelia's widowhood at which every reader would want her to drop the pose of noble loyalty to George Osborne he shared momentarily with her on the eve of Waterloo.[17] George's last appearance in the novel (before his death) had encouraged us to hope for his reform; gazing at the sleeping Amelia, her husband had thought: "Good God! how pure she was; how gentle, how tender, and how friendless! and he, how selfish, brutal, and black with crime! Heart-stained, and shame-stricken, he stood at the bed's foot . . ." (p. 280). But while this apparent or potential change of heart might warrant a temporary suspension of the reader's judgment, it is hardly sufficient to make us accept him automatically as the untainted hero Amelia later claims him to be. Wherever in the second half of the novel the reader retreats from Amelia's apparently unquestioning faith, it is not until *Vanity Fair*'s conclusion (Numbers 19-20) that Amelia herself openly abandons her illusions about George and is ready to recognize Dobbin's true worth. She accepts then the same moral Thackeray intends for his reader—that heroic stances are sometimes as vain and foolish as

cowardly ones, that our dismissal of Joseph's offer of retreat is in its own way as artificial and rhetorical as "Waterloo" Sedley's later military posturing.

Amelia's coming to see the world more realistically is, of course, a major element in the entire novel's action. In the last chapter of the book, Rebecca Crawley shows Amelia the love-letter written her by George and explains: "'He wrote that to me—wanted me to run away with him—gave it me under your nose, the day before he was shot—and served him right!'" (p. 658). The picture of history Amelia had enshrined in her heart is now at last abandoned; but what replaces it is, as usual, left up to the reader to determine:

> Who shall analyze [Amelia's] tears, and say whether they were sweet or bitter? Was she most grieved, because the idol of her life was tumbled down and shivered at her feet; or indignant that her love had been so despised; or glad because the barrier was removed which modesty had placed between her and a new, a real affection? "There is nothing to forbid me now," she thought. "I may love him [Dobbin] with all my heart now. Oh, I will, I will, if he will but let me, and forgive me." I believe it was this feeling rushed over all the others which agitated that gentle little bosom.
>
> (p. 658)

Amelia's education into the true character of men reaches at this point the fulfillment Thackeray foresaw much earlier in his composition of *Vanity Fair*; at work on Number 7 he wrote his mother about the futures of his characters: "Amelia's [humility] is to come, when her scoundrel of a husband is well dead with a ball in his odious bowels; when she has had sufferings, a child, and a religion."[18] Although she still tends to idealize those she loves, Amelia does in the end admit one far-reaching mistake in her life. The creative impulse for Amelia's fictional life, then, comes in large part from the reader who helped to create and sustain her idealistic vision as he read about George's courtship and marriage of Amelia. As Amelia's response to this series of events was withheld from him, the reader filled in the details of her thoughts and feelings from the few actions and statements she did make. The idealistic faith in her husband's character the reader assumes for her proves a major causal force in the novel's history.

The reader's role in the literary event of Thackeray's *Vanity Fair,* then, is considerable, particularly as he becomes involved in the novel's plot or causality. In his response to one of the novel's two main characters, Becky Sharp, the reader finds himself called upon to purify his understanding of causality in Vanity Fair, to resist the temptation to approve her unprincipled exploitation of the corrupt social system to which he pays a certain measure of allegiance in real life. In his response to the other major figure in the fiction, Amelia Sedley, the reader's compassion is succeeded by a recognition that she has, to some degree, created her own misfortune. By glorifying her husband's memory Amelia cuts herself off from a potentially fulfilling emotional life in the present. The frame of mind which dictated such a course of action, as well as the suffering which followed from it, was conceived by the reader as he witnessed a series of events culminating in Joseph Sedley's proposal of retreat from Brussels on the eve of Waterloo. The impetus for Amelia's subsequent history in **Vanity Fair** was the reader's creation, a rhetorically inspired, idealistic loyalty to an unworthy character.

While the text of **Vanity Fair** (and, of course, many other nineteenth-century novels) has been studied extensively, the form of the reader's developing response, "in relation to the words as they succeed one another in time" (in Fish's terms), has only recently begun to receive the critical attention it deserves. The careful use of the omniscient narrator convention (choosing sometimes *not* to tell) and of the temporal space between parts' publication has enabled Thackeray—and other Victorian novelists, I am sure—to engage the reader's creative ability in the filling in and rounding out of literary experience beyond the text.

Notes

1. *Readings and Feelings: An Introduction to Subjective Criticism* (Urbana: National Council of Teachers of English, 1975), pp. 20-21. This statement is italicized.

2. *Five Readers Reading* (New Haven: Yale Univ. Press, 1975), p. 40. This statement is italicized.

3. "Literature in the Reader: Affective Stylistics," in *Self-Consuming Artifacts: The Experience of Seventeenth-Century Literature,* by Stanley Fish (Berkeley: Univ. of California Press, 1972), p. 399. The essay originally appeared in *New Literary History,* 2 (Autumn 1970), 123-62.

4. Among the many helpful studies of form, see Edgar F. Harden, "The Discipline and Significance of Form in *Vanity Fair,*" *PMLA,* 82 (Dec. 1967), 530-42; John Loofbourow, *Thackeray and the Form of Fiction* (Princeton: Princeton Univ. Press, 1964); Juliet McMaster, *Thackeray: The Major Novels* (Toronto: Univ. of Toronto Press, 1971); Bernard J. Paris, "The Psychic Structure of *Vanity Fair,*" *Victorian Studies,* 10 (June 1967), 389-410; J. A. Sutherland, *Thackeray at Work* (London: The Athlone Press, 1974); Kathleen Tillotson, *Novels of the Eighteen-Forties* (London: Oxford Univ. Press, 1954).

5. Iser, *Implied Reader,* p. 106: "empty spaces [in the narrative] are bound to occur, spurring the reader's imagination to detect the assumption which might have motivated the narrator's attitude." See

also G. Armour Craig, "On the Style of *Vanity Fair,*" in *Twentieth Century Interpretations of Vanity Fair,* ed. M. G. Sundell (Englewood Cliffs, N.J.: Prentice-Hall, 1969), p. 72: "[Thackeray] could not be clear without being untruthful, and he could not be truthful without being obscure"; and Juliet McMaster, p. 9: "The reader has to be prepared to make his own independent judgment just as much in the passages of commentary as in the passages of direct scenic presentation, and frequently more so, because of the deceptive plausibility of the commentator's arguments."

6. For an excellent summary of critical approaches to Becky, see John Hagan, "*Vanity Fair*: Becky Brought to Book Again," *Studies in the Novel,* 7 (Winter 1975), 479-506.

7. Iser, *Implied Reader,* p. 118: "The reader is offered a host of different perspectives, and so is almost continually confronted with the problem of how to make them consistent." See also U. C. Knoepflmacher, *Laughter and Despair: Readings in Ten Novels of the Victorian Era* (Berkeley: Univ. of California Press, 1971), pp. 50-83, and McMaster, pp. 1-49.

8. William Makepeace Thackeray, *Vanity Fair,* ed. Geoffrey and Kathleen Tillotson (Boston: Houghton Mifflin Company, Riverside Edition, 1963), pp. 23-24. Subsequent references will be to this edition and will include pagination in the text. The Tillotsons' Introduction also provides helpful insight into the novel's composition.

9. *Thackeray's Novels: A Fiction That Is True* (Berkeley: Univ. of California Press, 1974), pp. 1-35; 234-36. See also Iser, *Implied Reader,* p. 119: "Thus, instead of society, the reader finds himself to be the object of criticism."

10. This description appears in "Before the Curtain," printed as a preface to the text, though Thackeray wrote it after the novel was completed. For a history of Becky's appeal, see John Hagan, who refutes all those who have suggested Becky deserves the admiration she inspires.

11. *Surprised by Sin: the Reader in Paradise Lost* (Berkeley: Univ. of California Press, 1971), p. 344. That Thackeray borrowed more than a title from Bunyan seems clear, particularly if Fish is correct in arguing that altering the reader's perspective is the narrative's primary goal in *The Pilgrim's Progress* (*Self-Consuming Artifacts,* pp. 224-64). Loofbourow, p. 26, notes this similarity between Milton and Thackeray: "One of the ironies of literature is that Becky's heroic adventures have been taken . . . seriously . . . it is the same response that once made Satan the hero of *Paradise Lost.*"

12. An example of the traditional dismissal of Amelia as uninteresting (or worse) is Dorothy Van Ghent, *The English Novel: Form and Function* (1953; rpt. New York: Harper & Row, 1967), p. 176, who says that "beside [Becky] there is room and meaning for Amelia only as a victim." A. E. Dyson, "*Vanity Fair*: An Irony Against Heroes," in *Twentieth Century Interpretations,* p. 87, however, argues that Amelia's "characterization is at least as subtle as Becky's," and Bernard J. Paris, p. 410, agrees: "Critics who regard Amelia and Dobbin as puppets have failed to appreciate the complexity of their characterization. . . ." Juliet McMaster, pp. 92-96, and Katharine M. Rogers, "A Defense of Thackeray's Amelia," *Texas Studies in Literature and Language,* 11 (1969), 1367-74, have furthered this recent revaluation of Amelia's role in the novel.

13. This omission has been noted, but not explored, by several critics. Dyson, p. 74, observes that "we are never shown Amelia's deepest moments of grief, though we know the torment they must be." In another context, Barbara Hardy, *The Exposure of Luxury: Radical Themes in Thackeray* (Pittsburgh: Univ. of Pittsburgh Press, 1972), p. 35, notes one place where Thackeray "leaves the narrative of [Amelia's] feelings incomplete."

14. Juliet McMaster is particularly insightful in her discussion of Thackeray's handling of serial publication, noting that the novel's "continuous fabric of existence goes on, over months or years, with its dramas and disappointments but without resolution, for the novel's characters as for its readers" (p. 24). She also points to "an existence of the characters outside the novel" (p. 25), the central concept I attempt to develop here. See also James M. Keech, "'. . . Make 'em Wait': Installment Suspense in Thackeray's *Vanity Fair,*" *The Serif,* 3 (1965), 9-12.

15. Barbara Hardy, pp. 24-25, has discussed another moment in the novel where the reader's and a character's minds share a single thought, when Rebecca admires Rawdon striking Lord Steyne in chapter 53.

16. Barbara Hardy, p. 57, sums up our relationship to Amelia: "We shall begin by loving her and feeling with her, in her friendship, love, grief, maternal affection, but we shall eventually learn the limitations of sensibility uncontrolled by reason: she will worship her unworthy husband, alive and dead, spoil her son, and make sentimental demands on Dobbin, her patient lover."

17. Fish, *Surprised by Sin,* p. 344, makes the same observation in regard to the reader's relationship to Satan in *Paradise Lost*: "At *some point* during this sequence of actions the reader becomes immune to the Satanic appeal because he has learned what it is, or to be more precise, what it is not. 'Some point,' however, will be a difficult point for each reader, depending on the extent to which he is committed to the false ideal Satan exemplifies."

18. *The Letters and Private Papers of William Makepeace Thackeray,* ed. Gordon N. Ray (London: Oxford Univ. Press, 1945), II, 309.

Henry N. Rogers (essay date fall 1982)

SOURCE: Rogers, Henry N. "*Vanity Fair* as Satiric Myth." *Publications of the Arkansas Philological Association* 8, no. 2 (fall 1982): 49-65.

[*In the following essay, Rogers examines the role of the narrator in* Vanity Fair, *and argues that Thackeray uses satire as a means of organizing the novel's diverse characters and themes.*]

Attempting to grasp the multiplicity of a lengthy Victorian novel, even a good one, is at times like trying to catch water with an open hand; something—a character, a subplot, a minor theme—keeps slipping through one's critical fingers. Upon sufficient provocation, however, one feels compelled to make the effort. The provocation for this essay is the fact that so much of Thackeray's *Vanity Fair* seems to "slip through" so many different approaches to it. Generally regarded as Thackeray's greatest work, it continues to present significant critical problems. The novel's unity, or lack of it, is a point of contention,[1] and the story's obtrusive narrator raises questions because of possible inconsistency or unreliability in commentary and attitude.[2] These and other major considerations indicate a more general difficulty in relating and reconciling various aspects of the work to their overall context. I find, however, that when its form is examined closely, *Vanity Fair* does in fact possess an underlying structure which coherently encompasses both the "Puppet Master" and the story he tells and is essential to the nature and meanings of each.

Such satiric elements as the "Puppet Master," his ironic wit, his satiric object—the vanity and hypocrisy of the "Fair" society—have all received much attention. Yet it must be realized that these are integral features of *Vanity Fair*'s underlying structure described by Northrop Frye in *Anatomy of Criticism* as the mythos—a generic plot which recurs throughout literature—of irony and satire. This "generic narrative" is characterized by the presence of romance forms which lack their traditional meanings, with irony arising from the discrepancy between form and implied content.[3] The mythos may range from satire or militant irony, in which relatively definite standards encounter the absurd, to pure irony where the author's attitude and the reader's appropriate perspective are unclear. The underlying structure of *Vanity Fair* is heavily ironic satire. Its form is dependent upon the narrator-satirist—the "show-man"—who creates a token fantasy the content of which is by implication absurd. He selects the materials of his story and comments upon its events and characters with wit and humor. The satiric frame, and the action and commentary within it, are therefore controlled by the satirist (ostensibly Thackeray himself, but the identification is unimportant here). That action is informed by the structural elements of satire and irony which, as narrative, are "best approached as a parody of romance."[4] The phrase is certainly descriptive of the two principal plots operative in *Vanity Fair*. Becky Sharp's parody-romance quest and the comic action involving Amelia and Dobbin both lack conventionally ideal meanings—they are "ironically displaced." Indeed, the entire work is marked by the parody of form which characterizes satire, and it is this consistency of satiric form encompassing narrator and narrative which proves to be significant.

A satiric frame of reference for *Vanity Fair* is rapidly set up. In the short preface "Before the Curtain," the author refers to himself as "the Manager of the Performance," who "is proud to think that his Puppets have given satisfaction to the very best company in this empire."[5] Thus the element of fantasy necessary to satire is suggested, and it is established within the narrative as the narrator assumes a relationship with his readers similar to that between Manager and patrons. As an omniscient story teller, he speaks directly to the audience as he guides it through "Vanity Fair": "And, as we bring our characters forward, I will ask leave, as a man and a brother, not only to introduce them, but occasionally to step down from the platform, and talk about them" (I, 81). Making his "history" a fantasy, the narrator suggests the absurdity of its content even as he separates himself and his readers from its action. This shift in perspective, a method conventional to ironic satire, provides author and audience an altered view of human existence.

The satiric framework functions consistently throughout the novel. The narrator keeps himself constantly in the forefront, emphasizing his separateness from the story's content and the ostensible reliability of his commentary. At the same time he carefully identifies his external position and the viewpoint it affords with that of "my kind reader," with whom, he suggests, he shares many thoughts and opinions. This mutual identification helps make acceptable to the reader the narrator's ideas and attitudes and, correspondingly, the novel's larger satiric perspective. That perspective, emerging from the interaction of narrative commentary and underlying structure, is a cynical and pessimistic vision in which all standards are finally inadequate and all individuals and societies are imperfect. The narrative frame is essential in enabling the satirist to extend meaning beyond "Vanity Fair," to validate its content in the context of the reader's own experience.

Although a token fantasy, the nature of the "Fair" which narrator and reader perceive is strongly realistic, so that the satiric undercutting of assumed norms and values in the novel tends to involve those of the reader. The novelist can thus appeal to the reader's personal experience for support of his observations. More than a naive moralist who praises virtue and attacks vice, he also distrusts and questions all idealized forms such as codes of morality. The reader is frequently asked to agree with opinions which see the work's characters and society, and by extension himself, as foolish, hypocritical, and vain. Hypocrisy and vanity characterize those who deplore Lord Steyne's immorality yet are eager to attend his prestigious entertainments. These qualities, so prevalent in the world of the "Fair," are not confined within it: "In a word everybody went to wait upon this great man—everybody who was asked: as you the reader (do not say nay) or I the writer hereof would go if we had an invitation" (II, 63).

The satiric frame, then, enables the satirist to turn to his reader, and hence to the context of human experience, for confirmation not merely of isolated statements, but of the inclusive content of *Vanity Fair.* The ultimate appeal is for affirmation of the work in its entirety and of its creator's melancholy and cynical view of humanity: "This, dear friends and companions, is my amiable object—to walk with you through the Fair, to examine the shops and shows there; and that we should all come home after the flare, and the noise, and the gayety, and be perfectly miserable in private" (I, 182). This perspective and the ironic meanings of the novel's various plots move *Vanity Fair* as a whole toward the point at which satire collapses and irony gains dominance— when, in Frye's words, satire's "content is too oppressively real to permit the maintaining of the fantastic or hypothetical tone."[6] The work remains satire primarily because the narrative framework keeps a discernible distance between satirist and audience and the story's action and maintains throughout an element of fantasy. The external structure insures a measure of "safety" for the reader; as Kathleen Tillotson notes, "It is needed merely as relief, from a spectacle that might otherwise be unbearably painful."[7] Therefore the reader can perceive and confirm the book's meanings in terms of his own experience, largely because he is separated and to a certain degree insulated from the content of that novel and the full impact of those meanings.

Thus the narrative framework greatly influences the interaction of interpretive commentary and underlying structure which makes the novel ironic satire focus upon all forms of romanticism—"the imposing of oversimplified ideals on experience."[8] The work's consistency and range are reflected by the narrator's rhetorical characteristics, for, as Frye points out, the romantic conception of "The beauty of perfect form, in art or elsewhere" is a traditional object of satiric attack.[9] As a consequence there is a "constant tendency to self-parody in satiric rhetoric which prevents even the process of writing itself from becoming an oversimplified convention or ideal."[10] The tendency is prominent in the rhetoric of *Vanity Fair,* for the "showman" keeps his role as author conspicuously in the forefront even as he exposes its limitations. Although he has many artistic possibilities open to him, his creation is finally "only a homely story" (I, 56). Such self-parody is also instrumental in maintaining the narrative's external structure, helping to distance narrator and reader from the action. It has thematic significance as well, for evidences of the writer's fallibility emphasize the universality of a principal theme, that of human inadequacy and imperfection. Since it is related to "puppets" as well as audience, the narrator's flawed nature helps to extend thematic implications to himself and his readers. Elements of self-parody disclose the satirist's consciousness of his deficiencies even as they implement his convincing and assured presentation of a particular point of view, one which in fact insists upon his own imperfection.

The narrator's state of mind is distinguished by compassion as well as a satiric sense of ridicule, however. An apparent contradiction, this combination of pity and ridicule is central to his attitude and to the work which embodies it. As Sister Corona Sharp has noted, both attributes show an awareness of the inadequacy of people to cope with circumstances.[11] Scorn and sympathy arise naturally from the cynical and ironic perspective which informs the novel's satire. Man is to be mocked or pitied, individually and collectively, in his foolishness, absurdity, and ineffectuality in the face of his existence. The satirist can view his characters, readers, and himself with amusement and compassion because of his pessimistic comprehension of the human predicament.

The satiric perspective of *Vanity Fair* is infused with irony, then, manifesting the fundamental cynicism of the narrator's attitude. Yet the point of moral reference necessary to satire is present. The novel, as satire, retains the forms of comedy and romance but lacks their traditional meanings. If ideal moral values are not ideally represented in the book, they are nonetheless implied by their absence from their conventional forms. And the novel's action suggests that standards and situations opposing the terrible inhumanity of "Vanity Fair," while themselves imperfect and of doubtful meaning, do have a certain amount of value. *Vanity Fair*'s dominant satire presents a world in which the stabilizing influence of conventions, including those of morality, is necessary, even as it reveals the absurdity and insuffi-

ciency in that world. The satirist's primary concern is that his work fully express and demonstrate the validity of this perspective, and so it is within the context of this inclusive satiric design that the novel's narrative actions must be considered.

Reflecting satire's tendency to contradict ideals of perfect artistic form, *Vanity Fair* contains two major fictions placed in conscious ironic juxtaposition, rather than a single unified action.[12] As the protagonist of a parody-romance plot, Becky Sharp functions as a romance hero instead of heroine, emerging from an obscure background to undertake adventures and pursue goals. Her aims appear conventional: social prestige, wealth, and marriage. She achieves them all during the course of her career, yet her role, her experience, and her entire quest lack traditional implications. As the narrator states, the world of "Vanity Fair is a very vain, wicked, foolish place, full of all sorts of humbugs and falsenesses and pretentions" (I, 80). Her success within its social order therefore suggests that Becky shares those qualities and modes of conduct which it rewards. Rather than advancing conventional romantic values against evil opposition, Becky meets a corrupt order on its own terms; her goal is not to change that order but to alter her position within it. Throughout this action, irony produced by the divergence of romance forms and realistic content reveals Becky's nature and that of the society in which she moves.

Rebecca's origin parodies that of a romance hero, the discovery of whose obscured identity often reveals royal blood. The daughter of an opera singer and a drunken painter, the concealment, not revelation, of her background is always essential to Becky's progress in society. That her indomitable courage and resolution are perverted by self-centeredness and a lack of humanity is evident: "'I'm no angel.' And to say the truth she certainly was not" (I, 18). She so disdains "womanly" qualities that her rare moments of feeling parody the romance hero's times of temptation and trial, since Becky regards her own infrequent instances of human emotion as weakness.[13]

In "Vanity Fair" a young woman's future is dependent upon her ability to make a successful marriage, so it follows that Becky's aim is matrimony. Her initial effort is her "campaign" to ensnare Amelia's brother, Jos, and, of course, his fortune. She fails here, but similar motives—love is irrelevant—inform her pursuit of Rawdon Crawley, a "quest" which ironically parallels the romance hero's traditional "major adventure." This comic subplot is displaced from its inception. As her tearful response to Sir Pitt's proposal indicates, Becky would have preferred to marry that reprehensible aristocrat, Rawdon's father and rival, because of his greater wealth and rank: "surely, surely we may respect the agonies of a young woman who has lost the opportunity of becoming a baronet's wife" (I, 149-150). If money and position are temporarily denied her by her marriage, however, it is nevertheless as Mrs. Rawdon Crawley that she later comes nearest to complete success.

The Crawley's day-to-day existence is a biting parody of a romance hero's progress through an unreal world: "No one in a romance . . . ever asks who pays for the hero's accommodation."[14] Becky and Rawdon move through cities and society with much the same absence of visible support. To do so, they cheat, swindle, and give every appearance of possessing the wealth and social stature which they lack. Through deceit and dishonesty, Becky forces her way upward in society and away from her husband. Practicing her arts upon Lord Steyne, she soon "moved among the very greatest circles of the London Fashion" (II, 94). Rawdon uncovers her treachery even as she and Steyne are celebrating its success.

Rawdon's discovery of her duplicity makes the marriage ironic for Becky, not its failure to contain traditional meanings. She has had no misconceptions about her husband or what the marriage would offer; her wedded life is not marred by the absence of human values because she never expected it to contain them. For Becky, then, the comic action is disrupted—and her larger romance quest thwarted—by her exposure and consequent loss of social position, not by the lack of human values which her selfishness never permits her to acknowledge.

Something quite different happens to Rawdon, however, which is extremely important for the novel's dominant satiric structure and tone. Crawley marries for the conventional reason—love—and finds traditional values of love and trust within his marriage. Yet he does so because he is deceived. Because Rawdon is necessary to her, Becky plays a part to win and keep him. Even as it serves his wife's selfish purposes, Rawdon's delusion turns him to human values which place him in opposition to Becky's quest and the "Fair" society. Through his transformation, he becomes an effective point of satiric reference, as he comes to embody those standards advocated by the novel. Rawdon's protest is neither articulate nor fully conscious, but his personal example provides a forceful if implicit commentary.

The action involving Crawley and Rebecca also provides a particular example of the functional unity of the novel's satiric perspective and its fictional structure. The subplot parodies with devastating force the idealized notion that virtue is rewarded and evil punished. It is Rawdon—who loses wife, beloved son, and eventually his life—and not Becky who suffers most. The ironic discrepancy between assumed moral concepts and the reality of Crawley's experience implies strongly the doubtful adequacy, even the relevance of such standards when confronted by the complexities of existence. As I have indicated, similar questions are inherent in the established satiric perspective. This relationship between the meanings of narrative action and point of view is specific and limited, but it nonetheless characterizes the satiric consistency of *Vanity Fair.*

Becky's progress after Rawdon discovers her treachery ironically parallels the ritual death and recognition scene, or exaltation, which a romance hero experiences. She is rejected by high society, for a time drops from view, and later rises again to prosperity and seeming respectability. The process involves no alteration of character, however, but the re-establishment of a reputation to cover her immorality. Her time in Bohemia reveals completely Mrs. Crawley as she has always been: "a woman without faith—or love—or character" (II, 231-2). And the crucial adventure, important though it is, is merely one among many others.

Becky finds her Bohemian period among the dregs of society far from disagreeable: "Becky took to this life, and took to it not unkindly" (II, 240). This substantiates an idea which has become increasingly evident—that the goals she has sought, largely obtained, and then lost have proven unsatisfactory: "Her success excited, elated, and then bored her" (II, 94). Thus Becky's fall is actually a loss of objectives she has discovered to be of little value, and the larger action of her career is finally the most ironic parody of conventional romance structure—the quest whose goals are not there.[15] Her aims are ultimately unimportant in themselves—it is the seeking itself which has meaning. Lacking essential humanity, she is, as Bernard Paris has noted, pure aggressive will.[16] Defined wholly by externals her identity consists entirely of the role through which that will functions, and it is exercised in the conflict which characterizes romance. As the ironic quest implies, therefore, Becky finds meaning only in the seeking itself, even as it defines her. She thus bears a strong ironic resemblance to the most naive of romance protagonists, a character who experiences interminable adventures without development or aging.[17]

Becky's character, then, is seen to be so closely identified with the nature of the ruling social order that its gradual disclosure is in essence a revelation of "Vanity Fair." Her movement through various social classes shows that the qualities displayed on the lower levels are those which, hypocritically masked, rule in the higher. The novelistic society progressively approaches the terrible world of extreme irony where life is presented "in terms of largely unrelieved bondage."[18] Scenes of obsession and imprisonment accumulate in the narrative with powerful impact, scenes whose actors tend to become figures of madness and misery. Old Sir Pitt's wife is without mind or will, and Sir Pitt himself is an unfeeling monster who ends a terrible figure—"a whimpering old idiot put in and out of bed and cleaned and fed like a baby" (I, 409). The greatest of aristocrats, Lord Steyne becomes almost inhuman, an ogre figure of immense cruelty and depravity who sadistically imprisons his wife and daughter and, haunted by the fear of madness, dies a "wornout wicked old man" (II, 244).

Thus "Vanity Fair" is a world with strong suggestions of the demonic in its savagery and oppression, a society so reflected in Rebecca's character that she becomes the embodiment of its essential nature. As her "romance" develops, she is an increasingly ironic figure, her qualities disclosed in such a manner that her malignancy seems almost infernal. The narrator likens her explicitly to such figures as the "siren with the imprisoning image of shrouding hair" and she who sits eternally among the rocks, "the femme fatale or malignant grinning female."[19] Becky is a "syren, singing and smiling, coaxing and cajoling," a monster whose "hideous tail" may be discerned below the water's surface "writhing and twirling, diabolically hideous and slimy, flapping amongst bones, or curling round corpses" (II, 231). Clearly Becky is a natural inhabitant of the terrible "Vanity Fair" world of madness and obsession, bondage and misery. Although her "quest" never ends, it is during her final adventure—her victimization of Jos Sedley—that Rebecca comes to fully epitomize the ruling order. This action draws together the stages of Becky's career, for Jos was her initial quarry. Helplessly neurotic, he now is easy prey for her. The force of society's immorality, vanity, and acquisitive will is centralized in Becky and unleashed upon Sedley. Jos is a pitiable, miserable prisoner whom she murders spiritually and physically: "The Solicitor . . . swore it was the blackest case that had ever come before him" (II, 284).

Rebecca's role in this action demonstrates dramatically those demonic qualities previously ascribed to her. These elements grow increasingly prominent, so that while the individuality and realism of her characterization are not lost, she becomes symbolic of the dreadful, immoral society of "Vanity Fair." Thus Becky's meaning for the novel as a whole can be more clearly perceived. Irony is often devastating in the action surrounding her, but the principle mythic form underlying *Vanity Fair* is satire, "which defines the enemy of society as a spirit within that society."[20] During the culminating action of her parody-romance quest, Rebecca in effect becomes the "source of all evil in a personal form"[21] found near the boundaries of irony—the source being that hostile spirit within society delineated by the narrative's dominant satire. Her role is therefore a powerful revelation and condemnation of the vanity and aggressive will which make the "Fair" a world suggestive of an inferno. That hellish society and its chief representative remain undefeated, and Becky's last fleeting appearance, once again in the guise of respectability, re-

iterates all their implications: "Emmy, her children, and the Colonel, coming to London some time back, found themselves suddenly before her at one of these fairs. She cast down her eyes demurely and smiled as they started away from her" (II, 285).

The parody-romance plot, then, functions consistently within the novel's informing satire. Its irony reveals both Rebecca and "Vanity Fair" in a manner which substantiates the narrator's moral commentary concerning them. It also contributes to the larger satiric design, for it implies in various ways—Rawdon's catastrophe and the enduring power of Becky and the ruling society—that those values confronting and judging Rebecca are themselves of doubtful validity. These standards are more closely called into question by the work's other principal plot, the comic action featuring Amelia and Dobbin. Hero and heroine possess many moral and humanitarian qualities, and their characters, values, and aims in life are largely antithetical to those of Mrs. Crawley. Despite their "goodness," however, their experiences end without the attainment of complete satisfaction even in their marriage. Both Amelia and Dobbin are self-deceived, and their obsessions cause them years of suffering. When the delusions are at last eliminated, their union still lacks much of its traditional significance. The comic structure, whose central figures and final resolution are in many respects conventional, is ironically displaced, and the implications are important.

The basic differences between Becky and Amelia are rapidly established and kept in focus as their histories unfold. Becky is aggressive will untempered by essential humanity; Amelia is all compliance and feeling. Becky is hypocritical, vain, and immoral, while Amelia's values are those advocated by the satiric commentator. She thus stands in opposition to the standards of Rebecca and her society, but her effectiveness in this role is largely nullified by her own shortcomings. If Becky is a parody of a comic and romance heroine. Amelia is a conventional one whose faults, and "virtues," are ironically exposed. Too frequently, in fact, Emmy's virtues are her faults. Her tender sensibilities are so extreme and unselective that they are often ludicrous. There are numerous occasions in the novel when "between her two customs of laughing and crying, Miss Sedley was greatly puzzled how to act" (I, 15). Undisciplined by intelligence or reason, the exercise of Amelia's feelings leads her blindly to marry George Osborne, worship their son, and contribute to her brother Jos' calamitous end. Her dullness and insipidity are also symptomatic of more serious flaws, for Mrs. Osborne lacks the insight, courage, and will to oppose the vanity she encounters. Finally, of course, Amelia too is vain and egotistical. In her love of Osborne, her treatment of Dobbin, even her late renewed friendship with Rebecca, Amelia is selfishly obsessed, wanting always to gratify her emotional needs.

Dobbin is closer to a conventional satiric norm in his role as comic protagonist, for he has the capacity to see the evils of society and the courage to reject and resist them. William discerns Becky's falsity almost instinctively, though he comments upon her primarily by the example of his own conduct. Dobbin's nature also emphasizes Amelia's shortcomings, for his active goodness and more reasoned affections contrast significantly with her passive "virtue." Dobbin therefore is characterized by qualities of feeling and intellect appropriate not only to comic hero and satiric exemplar but romance hero as well. His pursuit of Emmy is a quest, with her as the single goal which he seeks through years of suffering. But Dobbin too is self-deceived.

The initial obstacle to the Colonel's success is, of course, Amelia's marriage to George, which he himself foolishly promotes. Osborne's death does not improve the situation, however, because Amelia immediately resurrects him, without those flaws even she had begun to see, in the person of their son. This prolonged obsession with George continues to be the major obstruction to a larger comic resolution, for he remains Dobbin's principal rival even after his death. Emmy becomes the lonely, grieving widow, a role she finds congenial for "many long, silent, tearful, but happy years" (I, 389). She keeps Dobbin as a slave for too long, however, confronting her folly only after his love has been "flung down and shattered" beyond perfect repair.

Whatever Amelia's faults, Dobbin's own self-deception is ultimately responsible for his frustration and disappointment: "the Major was a spooney" (II, 258). Not until Amelia repays with scorn and cruelty his efforts to protect her and Jos from Becky does he confront the delusion which has misdirected the course of his life: "'No, you are not worthy of the love which I have devoted to you. I knew all along that the prize I had set my life on was not worth the winning; that I was a fool'" (II, 266). They are finally united, but the principal element of displacement in the comic resolution has already been established: "William had spent it all out. He loved her no more, he thought, as he had loved her. He never could again" (II, 275). The consequences of the conventional comic movement from illusion to reality are therefore not totally satisfactory for the couple. The loss of Emmy's obsession enables her to love Dobbin, yet it also brings the realistic knowledge of their situation. William endures years of longing and neglect because of his own delusion, yet its elimination makes complete fulfillment impossible for him. For both, the loss of illusion opens the way for marriage but also prevents their full contentment with that union. The comic resolution, while bringing a measure of joy and satisfaction, results in disappointment as well, and the ironic displacement strongly implies that perfect happiness is unattainable—a vain illusion—in a realistic world.

Consideration of the comic plot also reveals the underlying significance of the progressively developed relationship of Becky and Amelia. Her comic role has shown that Amelia's character is almost pure feeling, defined primarily by the human relationships which permit its expression, whereas Becky is an aggressive will defined by the external role through which that will functions. The extent of their dissimilarity makes powerfully ironic their most important resemblance—the selfishness and vanity which in different forms motivates them. As Bernard Paris points out, Amelia and Becky are in essence representatives respectively of complaint and aggressive neurotic approaches to existence.[22] Amelia's various faults, diverse as they are from Rebecca's, are clearly related to the qualities which the two women hold in common. This psychological relationship, in light of the otherwise wide divergence between them, emphatically suggests the universal pervasiveness and power of vanity, the novel's dominant theme.

The treatment of human vanity in *Vanity Fair* indicates the essential manner in which the narrator and his commentary interact with the content of his narrative, particularly its two main actions. In accordance with his announced intention, the "showman" speaks continually of vanity, pointing it out in all its forms and warning of its power and omnipresence. The establishment of a satiric perspective, with its element of fantasy and direct contact with the reader, suggests a separation from the story and the vanity to be exhibited there. The narrator labels fashionable society and its antecedents "Vanity Fair," where vanity is to be found in all its selfishness and diversity. Yet the boundaries of "Vanity Fair" are never specifically drawn. Certainly its realm is not confined to the loftiest elevations of society, for the lower classes are discovered to share its values even as they hypocritically criticize individuals and groups of superior social standing and wealth. Becky's progress through the spectrum of society, from the aristocracy to Bohemia, clearly discloses that self-centered vanity is itself classless. Only as individuals exhibit values and qualities antithetical to the "Fair" are they seen to be outside it. Amelia, Dobbin, Lady Jane—Rawdon, eventually—, and a few others are *not* inhabitants of "Vanity Fair" because of their morality and humanity—their social position and wealth are irrelevant. It appears to be bounded, then, not be external concerns, but by internal factors. The "Fair" extends to the lines delineated by the ascendency, within an individual or a group, of moral values and essential humanity. It is at this point that the vanity exemplified in "Vanity Fair"—excessive self-regard—is confined. As the Amelia-Dobbin plot indicates, however, vanity in its Biblical and more inclusive sense—the fallibility of all human desires—is universal. It is present even in those, like Emmy and William, outside the "Fair," even, as the narrator suggests, in those outside the novel—"do not say nay." The selfishness of "Vanity Fair" may be tempered by certain standards and qualities; the imperfection and delusion of man's wishes and their inevitable consequences are inescapable in the human condition. This in essence constitutes the statement of theme expressed through the interaction of narrative comment and underlying structure. The narrator's description and interpretation, as they add meaning and dimension to the action, are substantiated by that action. The final authorial remarks summarize succinctly the novel's consistent thematic treatment of human vanity: "Ah! Vanitas Vanitatum! Which of us is happy in this world? Which of us has his desire? Or, having it, is satisfied?" (II, 285).

The pessimism evident in the satirist's closing words is inherent in the novel's dominant mythos of satire and irony. The narrator's ironically satiric perspective, Becky's parody-romance quest, the displaced Dobbin-Amelia comic plot all function together to call into question the adequacy and validity of accepted moral standards and humane qualities within a world of realistic human experience. There are few conventional, and optimistic, implications to be derived from the novel's underlying structure. It does indicate that assumed codes of morality and behavior, while ultimately doubtful, are nonetheless preferable to the near-demonic inhumanity of Rebecca and "Vanity Fair." Religion is tenuously offered as a solution to the human predicament, but on the whole, the possible transcendence of earthly concerns through spirituality receives little more than cursory consideration.[23] The most affirmative structural element within **Vanity Fair** is the hint that a new and more ideal social order may be evolving with Lady Jane's family, which includes young Rawdon and the Dobbins. Such structural features are tentative and of comparatively small force within the novel's irony, but they are important to its dominant satire, indicating that conventions and ideals which are doubtful in themselves can yet have a certain value.

Thus **Vanity Fair,** informed by the mythos of satire and irony, is very ironic satire. Upon examination of his pervasive influence, the "showman" narrator emerges as a satiric commentator of consistency, reliability, and perception and a powerful cohesiveness of plot, characterization, and theme manifests itself. The external framework creates a satiric point of view from which the flaws of a ruling society can be exposed. Ironic elements within that viewpoint, however, imply that the standards against which the dominant order is measured are themselves of dubious validity. Such ideals of morality and behavior are called into question by the ironic plots and subplots in the narrative action. The ironic discrepancy between form and content in the parody-romance quest reveals the essentially inhuman, near-demonic nature of "Vanity Fair" and its principal representative, Becky Sharp. The displaced comic action involving Dobbin and Amelia, the progression of which

parallels Becky's adventures, dramatizes the universality of the vanity which rules absolutely in the "Fair." The histories of Becky, Amelia, and Dobbin, as well as those of Rawdon and others, indicate the tentative value of morality and "virtue" in the novelistic world, and, by implication, in the world of narrator and reader. Nevertheless, these strongly ironic narrative actions suggest that such standards do have some meaning. They are finally what separates society outside "Vanity Fair" from an inhuman order which is almost an inferno. The novel's controlling satiric perspective, marked by irony, cynicism, and compassion, recognizes the complexity of human experience, definitely ambiguous and probably absurd, as "bigger than any set of beliefs about it."[24] It is the element of fantasy and detachment which insulates the reader from the full ironic impact of the narrative action and maintains the dominant satire. With all its realism and depth of seriousness, **Vanity Fair** is not real life. When his purposes have been achieved and his meanings conveyed, the satirist can say: "Come, children, let us shut up the box and the puppets, for our play is played out" (II, 285).

Notes

1. Gordon N. Ray, *Thackeray: The Uses of Adversity* (New York: McGraw-Hill, 1955), p. 427.

2. Robin Sheets, "Art and Artistry in *Vanity Fair,*" *ELH,* (Fall, 1975), pp. 420-432.

3. Northrop Frye, *Anatomy of Criticism* (New York: Atheneum, 1968), p. 230.

4. Frye, p. 233.

5. William Makepeace Thackeray, *Vanity Fair: A Novel without a Hero,* "Edition deluxe" 2 vols. (New York, n. d.), Vol. I, p. 10. Further references to this work will be noted in the text by volume and page numbers within parentheses.

6. Frye, p. 224.

7. Kathleen Tillotson, "*Vanity Fair,*" in *Thackeray: A Collection of Critical Essays,* ed. Alexander Welsh (Englewood Cliffs, N. J.: Prentice-Hall, 1968), p. 84.

8. Frye, p. 231.

9. Frye, p. 233.

10. Frye, p. 234.

11. Sister M. Corona Sharp, "Sympathetic Mockery: A Study of the Narrator's Character in *Vanity Fair,*" *ELH,* (1962), p. 334.

12. Ray, p. 422.

13. John Hagan, "*Vanity Fair*: Becky Brought to Book Again," [*Studies in the Novel*] 7 (1975). pp. 479-506.

14. Frye, p. 223.

15. Frye, p. 239.

16. Ray, p. 424, and Bernard J. Paris, "The Psychic Structure of *Vanity Fair*," [*Victorian Studies*] (1967), p. 403.

17. Frye, p. 186.

18. Frye, p. 238.

19. Frye, p. 238.

20. Frye, p. 47.

21. Frye, p. 239.

22. Paris, pp. 389-410.

23. Hagan, pp. 479-506.

24. Frye, p. 229.

Joe K. Law (essay date September 1987)

SOURCE: Law, Joe K. "The Prima Donnas of *Vanity Fair*." *College Language Association Journal* 31, no. 1 (September 1987): 87-110.

[*In the following essay, Law discusses Thackeray's use of opera motifs in his depictions of Amelia Sedley and Becky Sharp.*]

"In the evening to the opera and fell asleep," William Makepeace Thackeray confessed in his diary on 18 November 1844.[1] That was not, however, his customary response to this art form. His letters and diaries, especially those of his earlier years, reveal a lively interest in the opera. On 21 May 1832, for example, he recorded in his diary his opinions of soprano Wilhelmine Schroeder-Devrient and Beethoven's *Fidelio*: "She acted & sung very nobly, but the opera nevertheless is dull" (**Letters** [**Letters and Private Papers of William Makepeace Thackeray**], I, 202). A few years later, in 1838, he praised Gluck's *Orfeo ed Euridice* by comparing it to "very fine Mozart, so exquisitely tender and simple and melodious" (**Letters,** I, 363). More than a decade later his enthusiasm for opera had not dimmed, for he wrote a friend, urging her to hear Meyerbeer's *Les Huguenots,* "really the finest thing in the world" (**Letters,** II, 557). The extent of Thackeray's operatic interest is perhaps best indicated in a comment by his daughter Anne:

> Magnificent envelopes, with unicorns and heraldic emblazonments, used to come very constantly, containing tickets and boxes for the opera. In those days we thought everybody had boxes for the opera as a matter of course. . . . My father always loved music and understood it too; he knew his opera tunes by heart.[2]

Thackeray seems also to have known a number of people prominent in London's operatic life. Among his acquaintances he numbered the composers Michael William Balfe, John Barnett, and Julius Benedict, the last of whom seems to have secured him an introduction to Jenny Lind.[3] Through Benjamin Lumley, a long-time friend and manager of Her Majesty's Theatre for a number of years, Thackeray may have met Henriette Sontag, whom he especially admired.[4] The English soprano Adelaide Kemble, who had studied with the great Giuditta Pasta and won acclaim in Italy as well as England before her early retirement upon her marriage, was a particularly close friend of Thackeray and his daughters.[5]

Thackeray's acquaintance with the musical life of London and his fondness for the popular operas of his day were to provide him with materials for his fiction. His novels are filled with musical allusions, and references to opera appear frequently among them. His operatic allusions typically provide moments of local illumination, often suggesting the character of minor personae or adding wry commentary on human nature.[6] In *Vanity Fair,* however, the operatic allusions take on a greater structural and thematic importance than in his other works. Like many novels of the age, *Vanity Fair* appeared serially in eighteen single monthly issues and a concluding double number. As the last issues appeared, Thackeray needed a device to recall and summarize the actions of the characters his readers had been following for nearly two years. With Amelia Sedley Osborne and Rebecca Sharp Crawley, he drew upon his knowledge of opera to create an operatic analogy to his novel, casting these two women as the rival prima donnas of his own work. In the last two issues (Chapters 61-67, or Numbers 18-20) Thackeray associated his two principal women with the opera and with well-known operatic heroines in ways that would provide ironic commentary on them while recalling the roles of each and foreshadowing the conclusion of the novel. Although the association of the two rival heroines with operatic heroines is most apparent in this final portion of the novel, it is actually the culmination of the pattern which Thackeray had established early in the novel and maintained throughout. Both Amelia and Becky had already been associated with actual singers of the early nineteenth century, and the character of each woman had already been revealed in her musical performances.

A list of her accomplishments introduces Amelia. To say that she could "sing like a lark, or a Mrs. Billington" is more than an historically appropriate pretty compliment.[7] Elizabeth Billington (1768-1818) was one of the most celebrated singers of her day, and some of her qualities as a singer seem analogous to qualities in Amelia's character. although Mrs. Billington's mastery of florid singing was complete, connoisseurs preferred her in simple, lyrical music. Charles Burney, who found her displays of bravura singing excessive, nevertheless wrote that "the natural tone of her voice is so exquisitely sweet . . . that nothing but envy or apathy can hear her without delight."[8] Another admirer wrote, "Her whole style of elocution may be described as sweet and persuasive rather than powerful and commanding. It naturally assumed the character of her mind and voice."[9] In her personal life, the character of her mind was not that usually associated with the popular image of the prima donna, for Mrs. Billington was noted for the sweetness of her temper and her generosity towards her rivals.[10]

A similar natural sweetness of voice and disposition inform Amelia's actions and her singing. She is introduced to the readers with the comparison to Mrs. Billington or a lark, and a part of that comparison reappears upon her introduction to William Dobbin. When he first sees her, she is descending the stairs to leave for Vauxhall, singing "like a lark" (p. 53). The impact of her singing is described with the same natural metaphor: "[T]he sweet fresh voice went right into the Captain's heart and nestled there" (p. 53). Later that evening Dobbin finds himself humming not the song he has just heard in Vauxhall but the song which Amelia had sung earlier (p. 57). Years later, when Dobbin finally declares his love for her, he recalls having heard her sing as she came down the stairs (p. 577).

Amelia's movingly natural song is poured out for the benefit of others, never for self-aggrandizement. When she learns that his father has disinherited him, she comforts her young husband by singing "Wapping Old Stairs." Thackeray calls particular attention to her performance of "that stanza . . . in which the heroine, after rebuking Tom for inattention, promises 'his trowsers to mend, and his grog too to make,' if he will be constant and kind, and not forsake her" (p. 237). Not only is the song an historically appropriate choice, but it also reflects accurately the situation of Amelia with her already inattentive husband. She intends no rebuke but attempts only to comfort by expressing her own love and loyalty. Nevertheless, the reader can recognize both the ironic appropriateness of the song and Amelia's naively romantic notions of poverty. Shortly after this incident, Amelia once again comforts with her songs. This time she puts aside her own apprehensions in order to cheer her parents. This she does in part by singing "all of her father's favourite old songs" (p. 252). Years later, after the death of her mother, singing is again a customary part of those things done for her father's benefit (p. 553).

The association of Amelia with a well-known singer and a corresponding musical characterization of her is paralleled in Thackeray's treatment of Becky Sharp, who is associated with several singers of the early nineteenth century. The first linking of Becky with an actual singer is implicit rather than explicit, but it is no less striking for that. When the newly married George Osbornes and Rawdon Crawleys arrive in Brussels in 1815 to await battle orders, the "miraculous Catalani was delighting all hearers" there (p. 265). Angelica Catalani (1780-1849) was, like Mrs. Billington, one of the most celebrated singers of her day. A beautiful woman, she was noted for her virtuosity, not her musicality. The composer Louis Spohr heard her in Naples in 1817 and, after a long catalog of her accomplishments, concluded, "What I missed most in her singing was soul. . . . We were never once moved, but we did have the pleasure always associated with the spectacle of the easy mastery of mechanical difficulties."[11] The financial aspects of Catalani's career also attracted a good deal of notice. Spohr's commentary indicates that he had paid seven times the regular price for his ticket to hear her. Such was often the case when Catalani sang. Together with husband Valabrégue, Catalani had also become an operatic manager, economizing on all elements of the production in order to pocket as much money as possible. There are a number of records of Valabrégue's comment that an opera company need consist of no more than his wife and four or five puppets.[12] Apparently audiences became tired of the puppet show and Catalani's soulless perfection, and from 1818 until her retirement in 1831 she toured Europe constantly, bearing the sobriquet "the trilling gypsy."[13] Perhaps the most telling summary of her achievements is the one attributed to Stendhal: "She had a throat of pure silver and a heart of pure stone."[14]

That summary applies equally to Becky Sharp, Catalani's counterpart in the novel. Although Catalani is present only momentarily in the comment that she delighted all hearers in Brussels, Becky is linked to her by implication. She, too, gives a brilliant performance in the Belgian opera house. She does not sing there, but all eyes are upon her as she dazzles General Tufto and George Osborne, wholly eclipses poor Amelia, and even silences Mrs. O'Dowd (pp. 270-73). Once the reader recognizes this kinship between Catalani and Becky, other similarities emerge as well. Becky's musical skills are considerable, and she uses them exclusively for financial gain. The first mention of her music (her refusal to teach piano at Miss Pinkham's school) makes it clear that she expects tangible benefits from her musical exertions: "I am here to speak French with the children, . . . not to teach them music, and save money for you. Give me money, and I will teach them" (p. 23). Her attitude never alters. Her singing of "Ah! bleak and barren was the moor" is an artful attempt to gain financial security by snaring Joseph Sedley (pp. 40-41); her thoughts of an opera box after a marriage to old Sir Pitt Crawley have to do with status, not music (p. 148); she skillfully varies her repertoire to ingratiate herself more profitably with her audience, singing sentimental English ballads for Joseph Sedley, who does not understand French (p. 40), French songs for Lord Steyne, who does understand them (p. 367), Handel and Haydn for the pious Crawleys (p. 409), and Mozart's sacred music for Lady Steyne (p. 474). Her marked attentions to professional singers bring rewards, for they "leave off their sore throats" to sing at her parties and give her free lessons (p. 488). When she scores a financial triumph over Steyne, Becky expresses that triumph by rattling off a brilliant voluntary on her piano (p. 467). Becky's mixing of music and finance connects her with Catalani, as does the brilliance of her solutions of mechanical difficulties, both musical and otherwise. The brief mention of Catalani may also foreshadow the conclusion of Becky's career, as retold in "A Vagabond Chapter." Like Catalani, Becky spends a number of years traveling about the Continent, concertizing with decreasing success.

Becky is also momentarily associated with several other singers. On one occasion, she hushes others at a party so that a singer can be heard. Becky's concern explicitly links her with professional singers, for she is "an artist herself, as she truly said" (p. 488). On this particular occasion the singer is Giuditta Pasta (1798-1865), who was particularly esteemed as a powerful actress. The kinship with Becky is at once evident, for she has already displayed considerable skills as both actress and singer. That combination of skills becomes even more evident in the charades episode which follows soon after the mention of Pasta (pp. 492-99). There, on the occasion of her greatest social triumph, Becky is compared favorably to three other popular singers of the middle and later 1820s: Catherine Stephens (1794-1882), Maria Caradori (1800-1865), and Giuseppina Ronzi de Begnis (1800-1853) (p. 498). In his annotations to *Vanity Fair,* J. I. M. Stewart points out that all three singers retired early (Stephens in 1835, Caradori in 1845, and Ronzi de Begnis soon after 1825) and suggests that "Becky's admires (for the moment) appear to be comparing her tactfully with professional ladies who discreetly got away from the stage."[15] While such a reading is plausible, it overlooks the fact that these three singers would still have been professionally active at the time of the incident recounted. Further, it seems still more appropriate to recall that these three singers were celebrated as much for their beauty as for their talents (Caradori and Ronsi de Begnia are cited as instances of stage beauty in Thackeray's *Cornhill* essay **"De juventute"**) and that all three assumed places of respect upon retiring from the stage, especially Stephens, who married the Earl of Essex in 1838.[16] These three singers seem to have attained the goals which Becky values, and the comparison becomes ironic in retrospect, for Becky's career steadily declines from the night these comparisons are made.

The charades episode also reinforces the musical presentation of Becky's duplicity. Her adroit changes of repertoire now become more pronounced changes of roles. Clytemnestra becomes the Nightingale and sings and dances "with all the innocence of theatrical youth" (p. 497). Becky's falseness shows through her brilliant performance, and her fall is appropriately accompanied by the same music. As Rawdon pauses in the street, he hears a snatch of her song and Steyne's harsh shouts of "Brava!" before he enters the house to find them alone together (p. 515). Throughout the novel, music has shown Becky's duplicity and greed just as it has shown Amelia's sweet and generous temper.

In the final chapters of the novel, Thackeray intensifies this musical characterization by creating a unified pattern of operatic allusions which recall the actions and character of each woman. Moreover, the pattern which emerges from these references reinforces the reader's judgment of the flaws in the character of each, thus clarifying the moral vision of the novel.

Thackeray begins with Amelia as he reunites the remaining characters in the European tour episode beginning in Chapter 62 ("Am Rhein"). Amelia's presence in the German opera house with Major Dobbin draws the attention of most of the men in Pumpernickel, and she experiences a kind of triumph that recalls Becky's more ostentatious triumph in the Belgian opera house years earlier. Amelia's presence apparently provides her first exposure to the music of Cimorosa, Mozart, and Beethoven. Their music reveals to her a "new world of love and beauty," and she responds to it because she has "the keenest and finest sensibility" (p. 600). By this point in the novel, however, the reader, while convinced of her sincerity, has become suspicious of Amelia's keen sensibility. The reader willing to linger momentarily over the operatic passages which most move Amelia will find that the action of these operas suggests parallels to the action and characters of *Vanity Fair,* often providing ironic commentary on the novel.

One work which Amelia particularly admires is Mozart's *Don Giovanni,* the plot of which revolves about rape, murder, deceit, and divine retribution. It is, however, the "tender parts" (especially Zerlina's arias "Batti, batti" and "Vedrai carino") which move her (p. 601). In an essay on this last portion of *Vanity Fair,* Robert T. Bledsoe has suggested that anyone knowing the opera and the novel "would expect Amelia's devotion to the memory of her asinine husband, a would-be Don Juan, to be associated with the devotion of the sad Elvira to Don Giovanni."[17] Because her response is to Zerlina's music, Bledsoe continues, "by implication she puts George Osborne in the ill-fitting shoes of . . . the rustic Masetto," a comparison that is nevertheless satirically appropriate because Osborne is "in a real sense a country bumpkin."[18] Bledsoe concludes that Thackeray "thus uses *Don Giovanni* to imply that Amelia is a bit dull. Perhaps that is narrative overkill (we never doubted either George Osborne's dullness or hers)."[19] A closer look at both the opera and the novel, however, suggests that the passage is considerably more complex and more successful than Bledsoe allows.

Bledsoe writes that Amelia does not identify herself with Elvira because he "of course, does not have enough insight to make such a comparison."[20] it is more accurate to say that she has enough insight not to make the comparison. The heroic Elvira—who follows the don from Burgos to Seville, intervenes to prevent his seduction of Zerlina, and constantly exhorts him to reform—has almost nothing in common with the passive Amelia. It is true that Elvira's love for the rake does not fail, but, unlike Amelia, she is very clearly aware of the kind of scoundrel she has married. These two women differ too greatly, then, to permit any real identification between them.

The parallels between Zerlina and Amelia, however, are much clearer. Neither has the heroic stature or the social status of Donna Elvira or Donna Anna, the other principal woman of the opera. Just as these two ladies overshadow Zerlina, Amelia is usually socially overwhelmed by the presence of other women, particularly her wealthy sisters-in-law and Becky. Neither Amelia nor Zerlina displays much feminine independence: Amelia clings in turn to George, to young George, and at last to Dobbin; Zerlina has her Masetto and addresses to him the two tender, pleading arias which Amelia so admires. Both women are essentially passive, relying on the actions of others to bring them out of their difficulties. Just as the timely intervention of the group of nobles twice saves Zerlina from the don's advances, so too the return of Jos and Dobbin rescues Amelia from her financial difficulties.

There is, however, a strength in this passivity which should not be overlooked. Zerlina may not be particularly active, but the two arias which she addresses to Masetto find her cajoling him into doing precisely what she wants. In "Batti, batti" she tells him that he may strike her if he wishes and she will continue to love him; as a result, he loses all suspicion of her behavior with the don. The other aria consoles him after he has been beaten by Don Giovanni, and its promise of comfort makes all other thoughts, including his renewed suspicions of the don, vanish. In her seeming passivity, then, Zerlina controls her present lover.

To put George Osborne into the position of this controlled lover yields only the most limited satirical return. If, however, he assumes the role of the don himself, the ironic parallels are much clearer. It is not only the role he fancies for himself, but it is also the role others in the novel assign to him. The impressionable young Ensigns Spooney and Stubble think Osborne "a regular Don Giovanni, by Jove," and their phrase is re-peated, as if for emphasis (p. 115). Although he is a poor Don Juan at best (that is clearly Becky Sharp's opinion of him), his good looks, swagger, and lordly manner are enough to allow him to bully his father and to impress the simple Amelia. His condescending attitude towards her also suggests the don's behavior towards the peasant Zerlina. At that, Osborne is a more suitable Don Giovanni than the pathetic Tapeworm, the Chargé d'Affaires in Pumpernickel, who, in spite of "looking as much as possible like Don Juan," is unable to attract Amelia's attention (p. 605).

Masetto does, however, seem to have a clear counterpart in the novel: Major William Dobbin. It is apparent early in the novel that he is the most appropriate choice for Amelia, but he has the disadvantage of being compared to the elegant Osborne. Osborne's looks and manner would seem to negate Bledsoe's judgment that George is "in a real sense a country bumpkin."[21] "Bumpkin" is, however, precisely the word which the elder Osborne applies to his son's friend Dobbin (p. 219). In addition to the awkwardness which inspired this epithet, Dobbin's faithfulness to Amelia, his seeming defeat at the hands of Osborne, and his willingness to be manipulated by Amelia also suggest similarities with the operatic rustic. Further, Amelia's treatment of him also recalls Zerlina's treatment of Masetto in the opera. Zerlina appears to be genuinely attracted to the don, all her attentions being diverted momentarily from Masetto by the don's powerfully glamorous appearance, but she again takes up the peasant once the nobleman's true character is revealed. In a similar manner, Amelia's attraction to George and her faithfulness to his memory are based on his superficial attractiveness and the conventions of romantic fiction. It may seem a harsh judgment of Amelia's behavior towards Dobbin to say that while she remains faithful to her heavily fictionalized memories of George she willfully manipulates the feelings of the man who repeatedly demonstrates his love for her, but it is a judgment Thackeray encourages: "She didn't wish to marry him, but she wished to keep him. She wished to give him nothing, but that he should give her all" (p. 647). Once she is finally aware of the relative worth of Osborne and Dobbin, she is eager to marry Dobbin. The fascination with Don Giovanni/ Osborne is over, and Masetto/Dobbin looks forward to the promised consolation of Zerlina/Amelia. The set of parallels among the operatic and novelistic characters is a fairly involved one, but it serves to recall the romantic entanglements of the novel, to place and evaluate characters in light of their operatic counterparts, and even to foreshadow the marriage at the conclusion of the novel.

There is one earlier reference to *Don Giovanni* which is not a part of the present pattern but which might profitably be considered in conjunction with it. Barbara Hardy has suggested that the psychological state of Don

Giovanni at his final supper—"sensual, reckless, flaunting, afraid, blasphemous"—corresponds to that of Lord Steyne.[22] She does not explore her equation of the two, but tracing the implication of the identification of lord and don does enrich the text. The reference occurs in the "third act" of the first charade, when the "band plays the awful music of 'Don Juan,' before the statue enters" (p. 494). Then, as the little orchestra plays the music which accompanies the agent of divine retribution in Mozart's opera, Becky enters as Clytemnestra and mimes the murder of Agamemnon, appropriately played by her own husband, Rawdon. Steyne's delighted shouts of "Brava!" can be heard above the rest, and with them he seems to approve the scene he is witnessing and to mock all the qualities implicit in the music. Those same hoarse, mocking shouts are heard again as Rawdon stands in the street before he surprises Steyne with Becky. Although Steyne is not dragged off to hell in the scene that follows, some of the details of this scene do recall the parallel scene in the opera: the interrupted supper, the punishment of the rake, and the intervention by an agent of the moral order which had been mocked on the previous night. Thackeray here introduces a portion of the opera, with its equally powerful music and subject matter, which is far removed from the customary sphere of activity in *Vanity Fair.* The figure of Steyne, who is genuinely dangerous in his defiance of the established order, approaches Mozart's libertine much more nearly than conceited dandies like Osborne or Tapeworm. This contrast helps place more clearly the limits of the central characters. For the most part, they are uninterested in the larger issues beyond their own small concerns. Like Amelia, they are concerned with only the "tender parts."

Amelia's admiration of Beethoven's *Fidelio* also seems to be based on the tender utterances of Leonore, as delivered by Wilhelmine Schroeder-Devrient. Leonore seems at first an unlikely choice for Amelia's admiration, since her heroism stands in such marked contrast to the victimization of Amelia or Zerlina. It is not her heroic action, however, which most moves Amelia; it is rather the self-sacrificing nobility of Leonore which draws her tears. The line "*Nichts, nichts, mein Florestan*" (at which Amelia "fairly lost herself") occurs at the climax of the dungeon rescue scene (p. 603). There, in response to her husband's exclamation, "*Meine Leonore, was hast du für mich getan!*" Leonore dismisses her own heroic actions with those words which so affect Amelia. As Bledsoe points out, Amelia is, in her own mind, a Leonore, the ideal constant wife and an exemplar of "heroically self-assertive self-abnegation."[23] For the reader who follows out this comparison, it is difficult not to see Amelia's identification as at least slightly ridiculous. Florestan is a political prisoner, the victim of a corrupt governor; George Osborne, however, has been repeatedly exposed as a shallow, conceited young man. The recollection that Amelia's devo-

tion has been lavished on so unworthy an object accords well with the amused tone with which Thackeray has presented Amelia's overly sentimental vision of life in the earlier portions of the novel. Bledsoe does not work out this parallel of Osborne and Florestan, but he does contrast Leonore's unselfish devotion to her husband with the selfish behavior of both Amelia and Becky, with their constant demands on others, calling their behavior typical of the "horribly transformed" conjugal emotions of the universe of *Vanity Fair.*[24]

If the reader is willing to linger a bit longer over this operatic allusion and speculate about its connection with the character of Dobbin (who is also present at the performance), still other dimensions emerge. It is worth noting that Dobbin himself seems much closer to the heroic ideal embodied in Leonore than does Amelia. In the opera, Leonore has disguised herself as a boy, taken the allegorical name Fidelio, and sought her missing husband all over Spain. Likewise Dobbin has demonstrated his fidelity by disguising his own feelings and traveling even more extensively in his attempts to aid Amelia. If one chooses, however, to see Dobbin in the place of Florestan (certainly he is more deserving of such devotion than George Osborne and has been unjustly treated), then the answer of Leonore (once more the distinctly unheroic Amelia) ironically becomes a statement of fact: she really has done nothing to relieve the sufferings of the man who loves her. No matter how a reader chooses to interpret this operatic reference, then, *Fidelio* emphasizes the shortcomings and foolishness of Amelia.

There is one other potential irony in this reference to the performance in Thackeray's naming of an actual nineteenth-century soprano. The choice seems an historically unavoidable one, for Schroeder-Devrient was the outstanding Leonore of the period. Thackeray had heard her sing the role in Weimar in 1830 and in London in 1832, on the latter occasions noting the nobility of her singing and acting (*Letters,* I, 202; III, 443). The praise of Schroeder-Devrient in both the diary entries and in this brief episode in *Vanity Fair* is undoubtedly genuine. An awareness of her achievement, however, need not preclude the knowledge that the singer was, in her private life, far from a model of heroic conjugal loyalty. Her first marriage ended in divorce on the grounds of her confessed adultery, and she subsequently had two more husbands and a number of lovers.[25] Her extramarital activities were an open secret, and she once complained of the way in which English "ladies stare at me and quiz my behavior."[26] Amelia, however, seems wholly unaware of any discrepancy between the woman on stage and the character she portrays, a bit of naiveté which accords well with her own lack of self-knowledge.

One other operatic performance is mentioned in Pumpernickel: the controversy stirred by the admirers of two fictitious sopranos, Mesdames Strumpff and Lederlung. Their partisans divide along national political lines, the two women becoming the "two flags of the French and the English party at Pumpernickel" (p. 611). The English narrator joins his fellow countrymen in favoring Strumpff. "The Lederlung was a prettyish little creature certainly and her voice (what there was of it) was very sweet," he concedes, but Madame Strumpff "was clearly the greater singer of the two, and had three more notes in her voice . . ." (p. 610). The narrator also provides a description of one of the English favorite's performances and begins to suggest a comparison to her rival in the same role:

> . . . Strumpff was not in her first youth and beauty, and certainly too stout; when she came on in the last scene of the "Sonnambula" for instance in her night-chemise with a lamp in her hand, and had to go out the window, and pass over the plank of the mill, it was all she could do to squeeze out of the window, and the plank used to bend and creak again under her weight—but how she poured out the finale of the opera! and with what a burst of feeling she rushed into Elvino's arms—almost fit to smother him! Whereas the little Lederlung—but a truce to this gossip. . . .
>
> (p. 611)

The opera mentioned here is Vincenzo Bellini's *La Sonnambula,* a work first performed in 1831.[27] Like the other operas Thackeray cites, the plot of this work has certain connections with the action of **Vanity Fair.** *La Sonnambula* concerns Amina, a simple village maiden who is to marry Elvino, her equally simple swain. Asleep, she walks into the chamber of the inn where the newly returned County Rodolpho is staying, lies down upon his couch (he discreetly leaves), and is discovered there by the villagers who have come to welcome the count. She protests her innocence, but Elvino spurns her. At the end of the second act, in the scene described by Thackeray, she proves her innocence when she sleepwalks across a treacherous bridge in the presence of the assembled villagers. Still sleeping, she sings a plaintive aria about her lost love ("*Ah! non credea mirarti*"); then, awakened by the villagers, she is reunited with Elvino and concludes the opera with a brilliant cabaletta ("*Ah! non giunge uman pensiero*").[28] The text of the final scene of *La Sonnambula* suggests some parallels between Bellini's heroine and Amelia. The sleeping Amina sings over a bouquet of withered flowers, lamenting that Elvino's love has withered as quickly as the violets that he gave her. Amelia, too, mourns a love which the reader recognizes as an unlasting love. As Amina awakens to a restored love, she sings of a union that will form a heaven of love on earth. This portion of the finale of the opera seems to foreshadow the conclusion of the novel: Amelia will be awakened from her false dream to be finally united with Dobbin.

In addition to this identification of Amelia with Amina, Thackeray also seems to encourage an identification of Amelia with Madame Strumpff. Not only is Strumpff the darling of the English contingent in Pumpernickel (as is Amelia), but Amelia also takes singing lessons from her, apparently to good effect (p. 612). This cluster of identifications prevents a facile and sentimental equation of operatic and novelistic heroines, for the figure of Strumpff intervenes. The musical exertions of Madame Strumpff may be enormously affecting, but the sight of the middle-aged, overweight soprano is amusing. It should remind the reader that Amelia, too, is a middle-aged lady, "a little stouter in figure" than before, still playing at being a romantic heroine (p. 565). No matter how genuine her emotions, there is something faintly ludicrous in the operatic exaggeration of her feelings. Thackeray's description of Amina's embrace of Elvino ("almost fit to smother him") is amusing, but it carries with it an unpleasant element of suffocation. That same combination reappears when the awakened Amelia finally rushes to embrace Dobbin: "Grow green again, tender little parasite, round the rugged oak to which you cling!" (p. 661). This identification of Amelia as a tender but suffocating parasite suggests that the forthcoming marriage of Amelia and Dobbin may not be entirely the heaven of love on earth that the opera promises.

The composite figure of Strumpff/Amina/Amelia is not the only one suggested in Thackeray's brief reference to *La Sonnambula*. The other may be described as Lederlung/Amina/Becky. Lederlung's favor with the French recalls Becky's ancestry and foreshadows her imminent reappearance with a momentarily assumed French accent. The narrator's abrupt dismissal of Lederlung ("but a truce to this gossip") is reminiscent of his refusal to speak of Becky's innocence or guilt with Lord Steyne, and it looks forward to a similar reluctance to speak directly of her subsequent career (pp. 517, 617-18). It is even more telling to consider Becky in the role of Amina. Here the word "role" is especially important. Throughout the novel, she has concentrated her energies towards appearing to be the innocent victim of others and, like Bellini's heroine, has often urged her innocence. When she is reunited with Joseph Sedley, Becky feigns a love as pure and as undying as Amina's love for Elvino (the painting of Jos substitutes for Amina's withered violets). Somehow, though, it is not a convincing performance. Although Strumpff/Amina/Amelia may not be a wholly satisfying romantic heroine and although Lederlung/Amina/Becky may command the admiration of some, the narrator finds the former somewhat more convincing.

The comparison of Becky with Lederlung is implicit in the text; after Becky reappears in the novel, Thackeray uses two other operatic allusions which link her explicitly to operatic roles. Perhaps the first thing that should be noted about these references is the distinction between Becky's and Amelia's connection with operatic heroines: Amelia goes to the opera as a spectator; Becky, however, is a performer. As in the initial portions of the novel, she is consciously playing the role of someone she is not, and she is performing for profit.

The first operatic performance with which she is linked occurs in "A Vagabond Chapter," where Thackeray recounts a disastrous performance of Boieldieu's *La Dame blanche* sung by a debutante called Madame Rebecque (the *nom de guerre* of Mrs. Rawdon Crawley) (p. 625). The principal female role in this opera (one cannot imagine Becky in any other) is that of Anna, an orphan who manages to restore a young heir to rightful possession of the family fortune. The plot to restore him is too complicated to summarize here, but it involves Anna's disguising herself as the statue of the legendary protector of the family and appearing in that form to the young man. At the end of the opera Anna marries him and is elevated to the status of a lady. Even this curtailed summary suggests some of the features of Becky's part in *Vanity Fair.* She, too, is an orphan; she plans to restore Rawdon to his aunt's favor and fortune; her performance at charades is worthy of Anna; at the end of the novel she is even calling herself Lady Crawley.

The other operatic character associated with Becky is Rosina in Rossini's *Il Barbiere di Siviglia.* The association of these two charming schemers is a natural one. Like Becky, Rosina is an apparently innocent, harmless orphan, but she is quick-witted and clever, determined to have her own way. Becky does not actually sing the role of Rosina on the stage, but in the final chapter of the novel, when she learns that Amelia has already written to Dobbin as she recommends, she performs a snatch of Rosina's music by way of comment: "Becky screamed with laughter—'*Un biglietto,*' she sang out with Rosina, '*eccolo qua!*'—the whole house echoed with her shrill singing" (p. 659). The line which she sings here occurs in the first act of Rossini's opera. There Rosina has already written a letter to her lover. When Figaro, her co-conspirator, suggests writing, she surprises him by producing the letter immediately. In *Vanity Fair* Becky appropriates Rosina's words, apparently approving Amelia's surprising show of spirit as just the sort of thing she would have done herself.

Once again the reader must consider the ironic differences between the operas and the novel in order to appreciate fully Thackeray's allusions. Both Anna and Rosina plot with noble (or at least admirable) ends in view; Becky's aims are selfish. There is no love here, only the seeking of wealth and position. Unlike the plots of her operatic counterparts, Becky's schemes never succeed. She fails in her attempt to reconcile her husband and his aunt, and her eagerness for position results only in her assumption of a title that is not justly hers. Even her concern for Amelia is mixed with mercenary designs. She does want to bring Dobbin and Amelia together, but she also wants Amelia out of the way so that she may prosper with Jos and the other men who surround her (pp. 650-51, 656-69).

There is one other curious feature of Becky's musical performances in the latter portion of the novel. Because of her early successes, it is rather surprising to learn that her performances are no longer so successful. Certainly it is clear that she has the requisite talent and training for a profitable career as a singer. Thackeray suggests, however, that Becky's subsequent musical failures are symptomatic of her moral failure. There is the suggestion, for example, that her fiasco in *La Dame blanche* resulted "partly from her incompetency, but chiefly from the ill-advised sympathy of some persons in the parquet (where the officers of the garrison had their admissions) . . ." (p. 625). The reader is not surprised by Becky's acquaintance with the officers, but this episode provides the first hint of her musical decline. A conversation which follows soon after provides more information about the cause of that decline. Fritz and Max, two German students, discuss some concerts that Becky has scheduled and canceled, and they conclude that her voice is gone. One recalls having heard her "trying out of her window a schrecklich English ballad, called 'De Rose upon de Balgony,'" the same song with which Becky had earlier won such acclaim at charades, and comments that her voice is indeed cracked. "Saufen and singen," comments Fritz sagely, "go not together" (p. 640). It is for such reasons that Becky's performances no longer succeed, and there is a simple justice in Thackeray's having Madame Rebecque hissed off the stage and reporting that this Rosina is shrill. This moral judgment, together with the similarities and distinctions among Anna, Rosina, and Becky, shapes the reader's response to Becky upon her final appearances.

In addition to these operatic reminiscences, Thackeray provides one other musical characterization of his rival heroines by presenting them as domestic singers for the last time in this final portion of the novel. Before sending the letter to recall Dobbin, Amelia expressed her despair musically. Finally aware of his worth and increasingly surrounded by Becky's disreputable associates, Amelia often turns to the piano to sing certain songs of which Major Dobbin was fond. Thackeray identifies only one of them: Weber's "Einsam bin ich nicht alleine." Not really operatic in scope, this song is part of the incidental music Weber provided for P. A. Wolff's *Preciosa,* a play in which a beautiful girl (actually a kidnapped aristocrat) brought up by gypsies falls in love with a nobleman, who leaves his home to follow her and to marry her. The song cited in the novel is the girl's expression of love for the absent noble, and Thackeray's comment as he introduces the title suggests its popularity (p. 652). Long forgotten, the song may be translated as follows: "I am lonely but not alone, for your beloved, precious image hovers about me, sweet and mild in the moonlight. Whatever I think, whatever I do, whether in joy, pleasure, or pain, wherever I wander, wherever I remain, I am always with you, my dear. Unattainable as the stars, shining bliss like their splendor, you are near, yet oh so far, and fill my entire soul."[29] The reader familiar with this song might find these words a moving indication of Amelia's new devotion to Dobbin, but Thackeray prevents so flattering a reading by framing her performance with descriptions of Amelia's behavior: "Emmy was not very happy after her heroic sacrifice. She was very *distraite,* nervous, silent, and ill to please. The family had never known her so peevish." After this song has been identified, Thackeray continues, ". . . as she warbled in the twilight in the drawing-room, she would break off in the midst of the song, and walk into her neighbouring apartment, and there, no doubt, take refuge in the miniature of her husband" (p. 652). This framing commentary increases the irony. That Weber's song is the Major's favorite suggests that the "beloved, precious image" of the song text is his, but Amelia's actions and the narrator's commentary recall that image of her dead husband which has so powerfully controlled her own life. As well as recalling her foolish devotion to George's memory, Amelia's peevish behavior also suggests a self-interest which has, unlike Becky's, become apparent only gradually throughout the novel.

Amelia's song at the piano, with its stage context of an orphan surrounded by strangers, recalls one of Becky's first appearances at the piano: her "Ah! bleak and barren was the moor," so artfully directed at Joseph Sedley. Should the reader be slow to make the connection, Thackeray provides a clue. As Amelia, "very tired and unwell," lies awake, she hears "Rebecca singing over to Jos the old songs of 1815" (p. 654). The musical performances have come full circle, and when the reader finds the two women at their old places at the piano, he can evaluate the character of the two singers more perceptively than at their first appearances.

This final bringing together of Becky and Amelia at the piano, together with the whole set of operatic heroines with whom both are associated, helps the reader to recall the action of the novel, to judge the two principal women of the novel, and even to foresee its resolution. In addition, the set of operatic allusions also enriches the reader's appreciation of the theme of the novel. Both Amelia and Becky are associated with the role of Amina, and the rivalry of the Amelia-like Strumpff and the Becky-like Lederlung in the same role suggests that Amelia and Becky should be evaluated as rival heroines of the novel. The evaluation that follows, particularly in the light of the balanced appropriate operatic references, indicates that each woman is found wanting. By comparing the operatic and novelistic heroines, one finds that Amelia's foolishness and selfishness are em-phasized by the comparison, as are Becky's deceit and greed. The genuine emotion of Amelia and the exhilarating brilliance of Becky do not prevent the reader from recognizing that both women stand condemned of vanity. This judgment is closely allied to the moral vision of the novel, and Thackeray's virtuosic handling of the multiple operatic allusions helps to make that vision clearer. Neither prima donna is wholly satisfying, and readers must, as in life, be content with a performance that falls short of the ideal.

Notes

1. *The Letters and Private Papers of William Makepeace Thackeray,* ed. Gordon N. Ray (Cambridge: Harvard Univ. Press, 1945-46), II, 157. Hereafter cited parenthetically as *Letters.*

2. Anne Thackeray Ritchie, *Chapters from Some Memoirs* (New York: Macmillan, 1894), pp. 69-70, 73. Among the operas Thackeray mentions in his papers are Bellini's *Il Pirata*; Rossini's *Il Barbiere di Siviglia, Le Comte Ory, Mosé,* and *Guillame Tell*; Mayr's *Medea*; Weber's *Der Freischütz*; Meyerbeer's *Robert le diable* and *Le Prophete*; Boieldieu's *Les Voitures versées*; Donizetti's *Lucia di Lammermoor, L'Elisir d'amore, La Fille du régiment*; and Mozart's *Die Zauberflöte.* His letters and diaries also indicate that Thackeray heard and admired the leading singers of his day, among them Marietta Alboni, Giulia Grisi, Gilbert-Louis Duprez, Adolphe Nourrit, Giovanni-Battista Rubini, Antonio Tamburini, Henriette Sontag, and Jenny Lind.

3. For Thackeray's acquaintance with these composers see Lionel Stevenson, *The Showman of Vanity Fair: The Life of William Makepeace Thackeray* (New York: Scribner's, 1947), p. 62, and *Letters,* II, 142, 621 and III, 409, 417. A rather surprising criticism of Jenny Lind appears in *Letters,* II, 510.

4. For his friendship with Lumley, see *Letters,* II, 165, 269, 666. In addition to the many references to Sontag in *Letters* (especially III, 379, on her death), see Eyre Crowe, *With Thackeray in America* (London: Cassell, 1893), pp. 24-25. Sontag also receives special attention in Thackeray's nostalgic 1860 *Cornhill* essay "De juventute," *Centenary Biographical Edition of the Works of William Makepeace Thackeray* (London, 1910-11; rpt. New York: A.M.S. Press, 1968), XX, 76.

5. As Mrs. John Sartoris, the singer appears frequently in Thackeray's papers. *Letters,* III, 392 n and 559-60 provide two amusing glimpses of her performances, but a much clearer estimate of her abilities may be found in Henry F. Chorley, *Thirty Years' Musical Recollections,* ed. Ernest Newman (New York: Alfred A. Knopf, 1926), pp. 137-38.

6. Although no volume by Thackeray is without mention of music, few commentators have gone beyond providing historical identifications. Geoffrey and Kathleen Tillotson and J. I. M. Stewart have provided extensive annotations to *Vanity Fair,* and Ronald C. McCail has identified a contemporary prototype of a musician and the source of a musical parody in *The Ravenswing* in "Thackeray, Sir George Smart, and Weber's 'Oberon,'" [*Review of English Studies*] 30 (1979), 423-31. John K. Mathison, "The German Sections of Vanity Fair," [*Nineteenth-Century Fiction*] 18 (1963), 235-46, and George J. Worth, "More on the German Sections of *Vanity Fair,*" [*Nineteenth-Century Fiction*] 19 (1965), 402-04, both discuss Thackeray's use of musical references to point up the moral and aesthetic standards of an entire society.

7. William Makepeace Thackeray, *Vanity Fair,* ed. Geoffrey and Kathleen Tilloston (Boston: Houghton Mifflin, 1963), p. 14. Subsequent references to this edition are cited parenthetically in the text.

8. *A General History of Music from the Earliest Ages to the Present Period* [1789], ed. Frank Mercer (1935; rpt. New York: Dover, 1957), II, 1021.

9. Quoted in George T. Ferris, *Great Singers: Faustina Bordoni to Henrietta Sontag* (London, 1879; rpt. Freeport, NY: Books for Libraries Press, 1972), p. 100.

10. See Ferris, pp. 91, 130-31.

11. Quoted in Henry Pleasants, *The Great Singers: From the Dawn of Opera to Our Own Time* (New York: Simon and Schuster, 1966), p. 117.

12. See, among others, Pleasants, p. 119; Ferris, p. 144.

13. Pleasants, p. 119.

14. Quoted in Marie Brown, ed., "Angelica Catalani," in Joan Sutherland, *The Art of the Prima Donna,* London Records, OSA 1214, 1961, p. 3. This phrase seems to be another version of Stendhal's comment "that God somehow forgot to place a heart within reasonable proximity of this divine larynx." See his *Life of Rossini,* trans. Richard N. Coe (Seattle: Univ. of Washington Press, 1970), p. 337.

15. J. I. M. Stewart, ed., *Vanity Fair,* by William Makepeace Thackeray (Harmondsworth: Penguin, 1968), p. 810.

16. Ibid.

17. Robert T. Bledsoe, "*Vanity Fair* and Singing," *Studies in the Novel,* 13 (1981), 56.

18. Ibid.

19. Ibid.

20. Ibid.

21. Ibid.

22. *The Exposure of Luxury: Radical Themes in Thackeray* (Pittsburgh: Univ. of Pittsburgh Press, 1972), p. 110.

23. Bledsoe, p. 57.

24. Ibid., p. 58.

25. Pleasants, p. 156.

26. Quoted in Arthur Loesser, *Men, Women and Pianos: A Social History* (New York: Simon and Schuster, 1954), p. 288.

27. In their editions of *Vanity Fair* the Tillotsons and Stewart comment that Thackeray has permitted an anachronism to slip into the text at this point, since the events in this chapter seem to them to take place before 1831. Thackeray's chronology is, however, rather indistinct here. Further, in a later chapter he refers to Becky's operatic debacle in *La Dame blanche* as having occurred in 1830 (p. 625), an event which certainly predates her arrival in Pumpernickel, perhaps by more than a year. Thackeray's chronology, then, may be more accurate than his editors allow.

28. Bledsoe discusses *La Sonnambula* in some detail. He too identifies Amelia and Dobbin with Amina and Elvino, and he also notes the similarities of Becky's and Amina's protestations of innocence. In discussing the finale of the opera, however, he brings in the text of the finale of the first act in addition to the text specified by Thackeray; moreover, he discusses only the concluding portion of Amina's final aria (the cabaletta "*Ah! non giunge*"), omitting the first part of it altogether.

29. The original German text is as follows:

> *Einsam bin ich nicht alleine, denn es schwebt ja süss und mild um mich her in Mondenscheine dein geliebtes, teures Bild. Was ich denke, was ich treibe, zwischen Freude, Lust und Schmerz, wo ich wandle, wo ich bleibe, ewig nur bei dir, mein Herz. Unerreichbar wie die Sterne, wonneblinkend wie ihr Glanz, bist du nah', doch ach! so ferne, fullest mir die Seele ganz.*
>
> (Leipzig: C. F. Peters, n.d.)

Charles J. Heglar (essay date March 1994)

SOURCE: Heglar, Charles J. "Rhoda Swartz in *Vanity Fair*: A Doll without Admirers." *College Language Association Journal* 37, no. 3 (March 1994): 336-47.

[*In the following essay, Heglar examines the role of Rhoda Swartz in* Vanity Fair. *According to Heglar,*

Thackeray uses Rhoda's identity as a wealthy Black woman to launch a subtle attack on the materialism and hypocrisy of the English middle class.]

While William Makepeace Thackeray's **Vanity Fair** has enjoyed a great deal of critical attention since its serialization in 1847-48, very little of it has been directed to the character Rhoda Swartz. "The impetuous and wooly headed, but generous and affectionate" mulatto appears in the first chapter, is mentioned in several others, plays a major part of Chapters Twenty and Twenty-one, and does not completely disappear until Chapter Sixty-one. Since she is not one of the five major characters, some lack of attention is justified, but an analysis of her role in the novel rewards the reader with heightened insights into other characters and into at least one of Thackeray's thematic concerns.

One of the few critics to briefly discuss Swartz is Jack P. Rawlins. In his study of Thackeray's fiction, Rawlins takes a political/biographical approach to Swartz. He uses her to illustrate his point that Thackeray's satire does not offer a positive alternative to what or who is satirized as negative or undesirable. Consequently, the reader cannot determine whether Swartz is a fit or unfit bride for George Osborne because both Georgia and his father are being criticized—the former for vanity, the latter for greed. Without a positive alternative, Rawlins contends, it is impossible to judge Thackeray's racial attitude from the episode.[1] This may be true for the one scene mentioned, but an analysis of Swartz that spans the novel offers a fuller response by revealing her function in the whole rather than in the part.

James Nesterby gives the novel and Thackeray's characterization of Swartz an even more political-biographical reading. Nesterby fully notes the critical neglect of the black characters in **Vanity Fair**.[2] Moreover, he concludes that the portrayal of Swartz and other black characters should alter the perception of Thackeray as an author: "In attacking a defenseless segment of England's population, however, Thackeray's commentary on black people alters his satire to racism."[3]

While Rawlins' reading is incomplete because he analyzes only one episode, Nesterby's analysis avoids the question of why Swartz appears in the novel. If Swartz and the other black characters are merely racist tumors on Thackeray's major work, the satire is seriously flawed. I contend that while Thackeray's portrayal of Swartz is obviously racist, the racist portrayal should be explored as a part of the overall design of the novel. Furthermore, even though Swartz invites political and cultural analysis, the initial focus should be on her role in the context of the novel.

Since Thackeray's novel is in many respects a satire of the English middle class, one must be wary of the tone. However, the author has been generous in his consistent use of clues to help us escape the problems of a too literal reading. One of the most obvious is the naming process. For instance, Becky is a "Sharp," shrewd character; Betsy Horrocks is a horror or a whore; Dobbin is a trusty work horse, and so forth. The name Swartz is also obvious; it is the German word for black, which constantly draws the reader's attention to her race.

Less obviously, it directs attention to Swartz's father, a German Jew.[4] Throughout the novel, Thackeray associates Jews with money, especially in the sense that they hold the debts of Englishmen. Examples abound. Dobbin and Rebecca and Rawdon Crawley use the services of "Hebrews" to bid against each other for the piano at the bankruptcy sale of the Sedleys' property (159). Before his marriage, Rawdon had been pursued by Moses and Levy for money he had borrowed from them (285). Lady Bareacres' wealth had been swallowed by her debts to "those inexorable Israelites" (471). Additionally, Rawdon is in the debtor's prison run by Mr. Moss, another Jew, as a part of Lord Steyne's plan to seduce his wife, Rebecca (510). Thus, Thackeray uses the name Swartz to convey both blackness and material wealth as dominant characteristics.

This view controls the reader's introduction to Swartz. She is presented as the "rich wooly haired mulatto from St. Kitts" (14) and the "impetuous and wooly headed" (15) Miss Swartz. Thackeray uses hair texture as an especially important element of her appearance as a black. Her wealth is pointed to in two ways. She pays double tuition as a pupil at Miss Pinkerton's school for girls, and in one of her few lines of dialogue she pleads with Amelia to write frequently regardless of the cost (15).

The first chapter is as close as Thackeray comes to giving Swartz any internal development. She is described as generous and affectionate, and there is a hint that she is not firmly in control of her emotions. Her affection for the departing Amelia has led her to hysteria, and the doctor has been called to sedate her. As a parlor border who pays double, Miss Pinkerton allows her this "luxury" (14). The extremity of her emotion leads the reader to compare her behavior with that of the other pupils. While many of them express their regret that Amelia is leaving, none of them is accused of "hysterical whoops." Swartz's reaction is clearly beyond the realms of decent emotional control, which is what the reader suspects she was sent to school to learn.

This type of comparison and contrast between characters is another of the frequently used strategies that give us clues to the meaning of the novel. Sometimes the characters initiate the comparison, sometimes the narrator, and sometimes the comparison is implicit and the reader initiates it. Frequently, this is done with the major characters, but there are a number of interesting comparisons of Swartz to other characters. These comparisons do a great deal to give depth to and to define Swartz. This is more important for her than for any other character of similar stature in the novel, because she has less direct dialogue—only two statements are directly attributable to her (15, 201)—little or no internal development, and usually is presented through the eyes of or spoken for by another character.

The narrator makes the first overt comparison when he explains that Amelia is the heroine of the story because she is more amiable than Rebecca. He clarifies this comparison by explaining that "she was the best natured of all, otherwise what on earth was to have prevented us from putting up Miss Swartz, or Miss Crump or Miss Hopkins, as heroine in her place?" (20). There is an element of irony here since the novel deals with representatives of the English middle class, and Swartz, a swarthy, wooly-headed West Indian, is alien to that representation. Since Miss Crump and Miss Hopkins do not appear in the novel, the narrator's list contains only one character for ironic, not serious, consideration.

The comparison of Amelia and Swartz is returned to and extended in Chapters 20 and 21. Many characters participate in pointing out the differences between the two: George, Amelia, Georgia's sisters and father, but not Swartz herself. George Osborne establishes the context for the comparisons when he describes to Amelia a new acquaintance with whom his sisters and father have become enamored. His description emphasizes her blackness and her material wealth. "Diamonds as big as pigeon's eggs" set off her dark complexion. Her hair is as curly as Sambo's—the Sedleys' black butler before their bankruptcy. George continues to exaggerate her appearance, suggesting that she wore a nose ring with feathers in her top knot (193). These last details give her the imagined look of a gaudy savage at court when she goes there to meet the king of England.

The narrator then catalogues her wealth: plantations in the West Indies, money in the funds, and a high rating on a major stockholders' list (193). There is an obvious, if implicit, contrast between the wealth of Swartz and the destitution of Amelia and her family. Just as obvious is the contrast between Amelia's English good looks and simplicity of dress and Swartz's attempt to cover her own looks with ostentatious display.

The narrator also points out that wealth is the major reason that Maria and Jane Osborne are so taken with Swartz, although they do not directly admit it. They find her "the frankest, kindest, most agreeable creature—wanting a little polish, but so good natured. The girls Christian-named each other at once" (194). It is telling that the sisters no longer call her Swartz with all of its connotations; they accept her as one of themselves; as George says later: "Jane and Maria have got to love her as a sister" (194). Of course, the greed and

the materialism of the Osborne sisters make this very appropriate—they would love Amelia if she had two hundred thousand pounds (195); in addition, they actively encourage George to propose to Swartz so that she will in fact become their sister, regardless of her lack of polish.

Unlike the other Osbornes, George is not so crass in his materialism. He wants to be a gentleman with a leisurely lifestyle and social recognition, but he does not concern himself with the money necessary for this because his wealthy father is so generous. He rejects Rebecca as a potential system-in-law because her status is too low. He rejects Swartz, in spite of her wealth and status, because she is too alien. He especially notes her wooly hair and dark skin, and he refers to her in uncivilized terms: "Belle Sauvage" (193) and "Hottentot Venus" (204). For George she is too black; as he explains to his father, who insists that George propose to her: "I don't like the colour, sir. Ask the black who sweeps opposite Fleet Market, sir" (204). The narrator would seem to agree; at one point he describes the ludicrously overdressed Swartz as "about as elegantly decorated as a she chimney sweep on Mayday" (199). George obviously cannot accept Swartz as a suitable marriage partner in English society. For a wife he prefers Amelia, whose appearance and pleasant personality are pointed out in numerous places.

When Swartz is physically present in the Osborne home, George is constantly contrasting her with Amelia:

> The contrast of her manners and appearance with those of the heiress, made the idea of a union with the latter ludicrous and odious. Carriage and opera boxes, thought he; fancy being seen in them by the side of such a mahogany charmer as that!
>
> (198)

George goes on to contrast the dresses of the two, their behavior, and their voices (199). Swartz even makes the mistake of sitting in Amelia's accustomed place and playing one of Amelia's favorite songs (201).

Like his daughters, Osborne Sr. has no problem accepting Swartz as his daughter. Her wealth allows him to progress rapidly from calling her Miss Swartz, to Miss Rhoda, to Rhoda (196). In this way, the father and daughters acknowledge that her wealth makes her one of them, not an alien. However, they are crass materialists and social climbers. Osborne Sr. offers 5,000 pounds to Swartz's chaperone if the marriage occurs and orders George to propose in spite of his engagement to Amelia and his aversion to Swartz (197). Just as Osborne Sr. accepts Swartz on a materialistic basis, so does he reject Amelia on the same grounds, her lack of money.

Once George elopes with Amelia, Osborne Sr. proposes himself; as he says: "[I]f Miss S. will have me, I'm her man. I ain't particular about a shade or so of tawny"

(220). Apparently, Swartz's guardians do not think very highly of the Osbornes; her chaperone fails to inform her of George's supposed interest (198), and her partisans reject Osborne Sr.'s proposal "scornfully" (412).

Throughout this interplay Swartz is usually spoken for or about, although the narrator does point out that she responds to the flattery of the Osbornes with "quite a tropical ardour" (199). The narrator also indicates that she feels some attraction to George, but this is the same narrator who sarcastically notes that "Love may be felt for any young lady endowed with such qualities as Miss Swartz possessed . . ." (196). No qualities are cited; this is clearly an ironic reference to her wealth. Swartz cannot spell and knows only a few songs and piano pieces.

Her character is completely vapid with the exception of her affection for Amelia. When she realizes that the book from which she has been playing may be Amelia's, she has another emotional outburst, which leads to her second, and last, lines of direct dialogue (201). When George realizes that she is Amelia's friend, he encourages her to visit Amelia, who needs friends since her family is now bankrupt and the Sedleys' friends from more prosperous days have largely deserted them. George's objection to Swartz is as a wife in English society, not as a friend or acquaintance; he was not above an affair with a quadroon when he was stationed in the West Indies. A part of his reputation as a lady's man includes "that beautiful quadroon girl, Miss Pye, at St. Vincent's" (115).

Amelia's feelings toward Swartz are not so obvious. She never refers to her as Rhoda; she always uses the highly connotative Swartz. When she is having problems with George before his eventual proposal and their elopement, she "couldn't bring her mind to tell Miss Swartz, the wooly-haired heiress from St. Kitts" (114). After she recognizes Swartz in George's description of his sisters' new friend—Amelia either recognizes Swartz from the age given or the fact that Swartz cannot spell (194)—she feels comfortable enough to tease George about leaving her for Swartz's wealth. "But the fact is, she was a great deal too happy to have fears or doubts or misgivings of any sort . . ." (195); apparently, she does not perceive Swartz as a rival, in obvious contrast to her feelings about the poor, but English, Rebecca.

After Swartz's marriage to a "sprig of Scottish nobilty," further placing her outside of Thackeray's English middle class and satirically identifying her with English stereotypes of Scottish money grubbing, she has found her place in Vanity Fair; she is no longer identified as Swartz—with one exception. After Amelia has been re-established in society by her brother's generosity and her son's inheritance of George's share of the Osborne

wealth, Maria, the more crass and materialistic of George's sisters, sees fit to visit Amelia after a lapse of fifteen years: "During Emmy's cares and poverty the other had never once thought about coming to see her; but now that she was decently prosperous in the world, her sister-in-law came to see her as a matter of course" (594).

The very next person to visit Amelia is Rhoda McMull:

> Our old friend Miss Swartz, and her husband came thundering over, . . . and was as impetuously fond of Amelia as ever. Swartz would have liked her always if she could have seen her. One must do her that justice. But, *que voulez vous?*—in this vast town one has not time to go and seek one's friends; if they drop out of the rank they disappear, and we march on without them. Who is ever missed in Vanity Fair?
>
> (594)

The narrator's sarcasm is tangible. By returning to Miss Swartz instead of the more correct Mrs. McMull, the narrator reminds the reader of her associations with money and blackness. In addition, the reader is subtly reminded of Rhoda's last scene as Miss Swartz, when George asked her to visit Amelia, whom Swartz declared was such a dear friend. In the same way the reader realizes that Swartz has neglected Amelia because of her poverty, just as Maria has done. Thus, the narrator exposes the insincerity of her friendship for Amelia—her one evident virtue. She is reduced to money and color; outer image in Thackeray's satire for once represents inner character: her blackness is both literal and figurative, in Western cultural terms. For most of those satirized in *Vanity Fair,* wealth or title can hide their inner character, but despite her wealth Swartz wears her moral deficits in plain view.

This analysis of Swartz's character is reinforced by Thackeray's use of a similar character for similar purposes in the 1861 to 1862 serialization of his novel *Philip* [*The Adventures of Philip on His Way through the World*]. As Gordon Ray, the Thackeray scholar, has pointed out, "[t]hough time has confirmed the judgement of Thackeray's contemporaries, that *Philip* must rank lowest among his long fictions, it contains many admirable things."[5] One of those things, at least for the purposes of clarifying the role of Swartz, is Greenville Woolcomb, another West Indian mulatto. As with Swartz, his name directs attention to his differences from the English middle class, but this time there is an interesting comment on his social acceptability; his hair was "so *very* black and curly, that I really almost think that in some of the Southern states of America he would be likely to meet with rudeness in a railway car." The narrator goes on to say sarcastically that in England his wealth makes him a man and a brother[6]—a slogan from the antislavery movement which would be heavily ridiculed later in the novel.

Like Swartz, Woolcomb is very rich, poorly educated (again spelling is a special target), and a dandyish, gaudy dresser. His name is also meant to point to a racial characteristic—kinky hair—that makes him non-English. He is given few lines of dialogue and almost no internal development, which in this case is partly due to an internal narrator, but not entirely, since the narrator, Arthur Pendennis, frequently claims to be omniscient.

Philip, the main character, and Woolcomb are rivals for the affection of Agnes Twysden, Philip's cousin. Initially Agnes is in love with Philip, who has a decent inheritance coming to him, but through the poor investments and dishonesty of his father, he loses it. Agnes and her family decide that Woolcomb and his wealth are preferable to Philip and poverty. The narrator makes the elements of the choice clear:

> [Woolcomb] . . . is very ignorant, though very cunning; very stingy, though very rich; very ill tempered, probably, if faces and eyes and mouths can tell truth: and as for Philip Firmin . . . he is a man; he is a gentleman; he has brains in his head, and a great honest heart of which he has offered to give the best feelings to his cousin.
>
> (17: 289)

This is very similar to the triangle formed by George, Amelia, and Swartz.

Once Agnes marries Woolcomb, Philip finds true love with Charlotte. In his occasional appearances, Woolcomb is strongly identified with the Twysdens, who are the most crassly materialistic characters in the novel, just as Swartz is identified with the Osbornes. Because of his wealth, Woolcomb is called the "Black Prince" just as George calls Swartz the "Black Princess." After his marriage, Woolcomb's inability to control his temper becomes widely known, for he frequently beats his wife. Like the hysterical Swartz, Woolcomb does not have the sophistication, the emotional control, to function properly in English society. However, Agnes is not to be pitied:

> [Woolcomb] . . . needed no skill, or artifice, or eloquence. He had none. But he showed her a purse, and three fine houses—and she came. . . . She knew quite as much about the world as papa and mama; and the lawyers did not look to her settlement more warily and cooly than she did herself.
>
> (18: 244)

Clearly, Woolcomb's marriage shows how low, at least in Thackeray's opinion, some elements of the English middle class would stoop for money.

In the final segment of the novel, Woolcomb runs for a Parliamentary seat being vacated by one of his wife's relatives. Although the voters despise him and although he does not have the ability to make a public speech—apparently his control of English is too poor—the voters feel compelled to vote for him for economic reasons. Campaigning for Woolcomb's rival, Philip, a journalist, uses articles and speeches to denounce Woolcomb, but his efforts are doomed by economic factors. In a last-gasp effort on election day, Philip has an effigy of Woolcomb run through the town on a wagon with a banner reading: "Vote for me! Am I not a man and a brudder [sic]?" (18: 286).

In the climactic scene of the election, Woolcomb smashes his head through a carriage door which reveals a will naming Philip as the heir to a fortune. The banner is taken off the wagon and draped over the scene of Woolcomb's public humiliation. All things considered, the scene is not only a mockery of abolitionists' slogans but also a mockery of the idea of blacks properly functioning in English society. Money alone allows them, in turn, to mock English society by their presence.

Both Swartz and Woolcomb function as intensifiers of Thackeray's theme that money is overvalued in Victorian society. Neither is given any merit as a person, and close inspection reveals that money alone is their measure. They gain entrance to society through wealth, and they judge others on this basis, but they are unable to function with any sophistication in proper society as Thackeray defines it. Once this function of the principal black characters is established, Thackeray's attitude toward other characters—such as Sambo or the blacks who serve George and Amelia before they depart for Europe or Mr. Quadroon, to whom Pitt Crawley sells a seat in Parliament for 1500 pounds a year—is clearer. These characters also denote money. Swartz and Woolcomb have the money to intrude. In a different way the servants represent the conspicuous display of the English middle class.

In many ways Swartz and Woolcomb are a means for Thackeray to intensify his satirical attack on the materialism of the English middle class. They lack manners and breeding; they also seem to be beyond the benefits of an education. However, many of the English characters, such as the elder Pitt Crawley and George Osborne Sr., are just as ignorant, ill-bred, and mannerless. By focusing a portion of his satire on complete aliens, Thackeray, perhaps, hoped to make his point clearer to his audience.

Thackeray could even subtly show the similarities between the black and white characters in tangible terms. After George has rejected his father's demand that he propose to Swartz and jilt Amelia, there is this description: "Mr. Osborne pulled frantically at the cord by which he was accustomed to summon the butler when he wanted wine—and almost black in the face, ordered that functionary to call a coach for Captain Osborne" (204).

Notes

1. Jack P. Rawlins, *Thackeray's Novels: A Fiction That Is True* (Berkeley: U of California P, 1974) 21-23.

2. James R. Nesterby, "Portraits of Blacks in Thackeray's *Vanity Fair*," *Journal of English* 8 (1980): 146-48.

3. Nesterby 126.

4. William Makepeace Thackeray, *Vanity Fair: A Novel Without a Hero*, ed. Kathleen Tillotson and Geoffrey Tillotson (Boston: Houghton, 1963) 194. Hereafter cited parenthetically in the text by page number(s) only.

5. Gordon N. Ray, *Thackeray, The Age of Wisdom, 1847-63*, Vol. 2 (New York: McGraw Hill, 1958) 388.

6. William Makepeace Thackeray, *The Adventures of Philip on His Way Through the World Showing Who Robbed Him, Who Helped Him, and Who Passed Him By*, Standard Library Edition, Vol. 17 (Boston: Houghton, 1889) 213. Hereafter cited parenthetically in the text by Volume number (17 or 18) and page number(s) only.

John Peck (essay date spring 1994)

SOURCE: Peck, John. "Middle-Class Life in *Vanity Fair*." *English* 43, no. 175 (spring 1994): 1-16.

[*In the following essay, Peck analyzes Thackeray's portrayal of class distinctions in* Vanity Fair.]

> This revolting reflex of society is literally true enough. But it does not shew us the whole truth. Are there not women, even in *Vanity Fair*, capable of nobler things than are here set down for them?
>
> (Robert Bell, *Fraser's Magazine*, 1848)[1]

Everywhere we turn in the early reviews of *Vanity Fair* we encounter this kind of criticism; the reviewers are enthusiastic but appreciation of the brilliance of Thackeray's performance is always qualified by reservations about his view of human nature.[2] Modern critics have, of course, moved beyond the moral quibbling evident in the early reviews. Essentially, criticism of the novel now follows one of three courses: there is appreciation of the complexity of its moral and social vision, or praise for Thackeray's handling of the narrative voice, or, and perhaps most persuasively, a sense of the disturbing darkness of his vision.

Barbara Hardy, identifying Thackeray as a radical social critic, takes the first approach, seeing the novelist as a wise and concerned social commentator.[3] All of

Gordon Ray's work on Thackeray, including his biography, was informed by just such a sense of the author's purpose and achievement.[4] The second approach, focusing on the narrative voice, is more concerned with Thackeray's ability to tease and disturb the reader by means of a voice that is so full of twists and turns that it allows us no comfort or security. A. E. Dyson's essay, 'An Irony Against Heroes',[5] sets the standard here, but the same principle underlies structuralist and deconstructive readings of Thackeray; the most sophisticated example is J. Hillis Miller's brilliant essay on **Henry Esmond [*The History of Henry Esmond, Esq.*]**[6] It is a way of looking at Thackeray in which irony is always a central consideration. The third approach to **Vanity Fair,** seen at its best in an essay by Robert E. Lougy,[7] focuses on the darkness of the novel, the frequent references to death, the sense that we live precarious existences in a world where death is ever-present. This idea also makes itself felt in feminist and psychoanalytic readings: for example, we might consider how Amelia, visiting her mother, looks at 'the little white bed, which had been hers a few days before' and contrasts it with 'the great funereal damask pavilion in the vast and dingy bedroom, which was awaiting her at the grand hotel in Cavendish Square'.[8] The approach of Lougy, and those working along similar lines, differs from the social approach of critics such as Barbara Hardy in that the emphasis is on disturbing currents beneath society rather than on a critique of manners and morals in society.

What links all three approaches, however, is that, directly or indirectly, they declare themselves as moving beyond the moralistic fault-finding that features in the early reviews. It is at this point one hesitates: were the early readers wrong? Were their moral reservations really so simplistic? Or could it be that, whatever deeper patterns exist in **Vanity Fair,** its *épater les bourgeois* characteristics might be what really matter? Hindsight has benefits, but it could be that we have lost a sense of what was central to **Vanity Fair**'s first readers, a sense of why the novel is so disturbing. Moreover, in distancing ourselves from this sense of shock, we might also have lost an awareness of the social and political relevance of the novel. **Vanity Fair** is obviously a multi-layered work, but I want to suggest that discussions of, say, Thackeray's irony surrender a sense of the impact the novel made in its time, an impact that was dominated by the issue of class.

There is no novel that thrusts us more quickly into a whole set of assumptions about class than **Vanity Fair.** By the end of the first scene we understand most of the niceties and pretensions of social gradation. The world of the school is a middle-class world, where characters are rebuked if their speech is not 'genteel' enough (p. 4), where a girl must cultivate those 'accomplishments which become her birth and station' (p. 5), where '*industry* and *obedience*' (p. 5) are prized virtues, but where money is, in the end, everything. Below, we see a world of servants, of tradesmen, and even the mixed-race Miss Swartz, who is only admitted to the school because she pays double. Above is another world, glimpsed through the 'high and mighty Miss Saltire (Lord Dexter's granddaughter)'. (p. 7) It is sometimes assumed that *Vanity Fair* is entirely about middle-class life. It is not: there are clear divisions between the aristocracy, the gentry, the middle class and all those who fall below.[9] But the world of the aristocracy, even of the gentry, is outside and beyond this school where even Miss Saltire is 'rather shabby' (p. 8); generally, there is something shabby about the school's whole environment of middle-class respectability.

To say that class is central in *Vanity Fair* is to say nothing new. What is less commonly noted, though, is the relentless nature of Thackeray's onslaught on the middle class. Some critics, indeed, suggest just the opposite; Robert Colby, for example, argues that the narrator positions himself 'as a solid member of the middle class'.[10] What I wish to suggest, however, is that Thackeray, who is indulgent to the aristocracy and gentry, regards the middle class as an almost alien race. Everyone is now familiar with the idea of an 'other' in Victorian thought, whether it be woman, the Irish, people of colour, or the working class,[11] but, in the case of Thackeray, even the middle class is perceived as a strange and threatening 'other'. We begin to see this with the middle-class merchant, Osborne. Described as a 'savage determined man' (p. 237), with a face that is usually 'livid with rage' (p. 257), there seems something animal-like about him, and indeed his fortune has been made importing animal skins from Russia. He is seen in an angry scene with his son:

> Whenever the lad assumed his haughty manner, it always created either great awe or great irritation in the parent. Old Osborne stood in secret terror of his son as a better gentleman than himself . . .
>
> (p. 258)

In confrontation, the father is reduced to spluttering incoherence; everything falls apart as he feels he is facing a gentleman. It is a penetrating representation of the drive, but also the limitations, of a middle-class businessman, yet, at the same time, Thackeray's patronising view of someone whom he considers less than civilised.

Initially something rather different seems to be conveyed in the presentation of Mr. Sedley, who, although a businessman, is 'kind to everybody with whom he dealt' (p. 206), but the novel offers some alarming hints about his cruelty. He is described as 'a coarse man, from the Stock Exchange, where they love all sorts of practical jokes' (p. 30), who has bred his daughter to marry George Osborne, and who has 'a feeling very much akin to contempt for his son. He said he was

vain, selfish, lazy and effeminate' (p. 61). Jos might well be all these things, but the strain in the relationship comes at precisely those points where the child fails to conform to the father's expectations, where the right kind of manly energy (or, in the case of daughter, the right degree of submissiveness) is not exhibited. Osborne and Sedley represent two faces of tyranny, the tyranny of the strong and the tyranny of the weak, for Sedley, especially when ruined, dominates his family just as much as Osborne. Like all middle-class men, they want their sons to be gentlemen, but are then torn between deference and contempt.

Contempt is, in fact, a central notion in the novel. When the bankrupt Sedley presents a servant with a half-guinea, the man pockets it 'with a mixture of wonder and contempt'. (p. 318) When, rather more noisily, George Osborne apes the manner of a man of standing, demanding an immediate interview with his father's solicitor,

> He did not see the sneer of contempt which passed all round the room, from the first clerk to the articled gents . . . as he sat there tapping his boot with his cane, and thinking what a parcel of miserable poor devils these were.
>
> (p. 323)

Such contempt, of one class for another, pervades the novel, including the fact that Thackeray looks down on the middle class with almost unrelieved disdain; for Thackeray, middle-class existence, entirely based around money, lacks culture, character, any kind of substance. Osborne, for example, sings the praises of life

> at our humble mansion in Russell Square. My daughters are plain, disinterested girls, but their hearts are in the right place . . . I'm a plain, simple, humble British merchant—an honest one, as my respected friends Hulker and Bullock will vouch . . .
>
> (p. 248)

It is a vain speech, but the only merit claimed is respectability. It would seem that Thackeray can only perceive middle-class life in these terms; his characteristic note is arrogant disdain, a belief that those below him on the social scale have no individuality, no intellectual life, no complexity.

But aren't all Thackeray's judgements just as jaundiced? Isn't he equally quick to condemn the aristocracy and the gentry, indeed everybody at every level of society? The fact is that he isn't, a point which starts to become evident if we consider something basic about our response to *Vanity Fair,* our impression of how Thackeray fills up the pages. Becky, obviously, makes the greatest impact. She wastes very little time on the middle class. She is grateful for a refuge in Amelia's house, having already decided that she aspires higher than the Reverend Mr. Crisp. (p. 16) Her first target is Jos Sedley, who, as an employee of the East India Company, has taken a sideways step out from, and yet up in, British society. She then raises her sights to the gentry, in the person of Rawdon Crawley (although she misses out on the landed gentry, represented by Rawdon's father, Sir Pitt). Finally, with Lord Steyne, she aspires to the aristocracy. What we are most likely to remember from the novel are Becky's forays into the higher levels of society, but this can distort a true picture of what happens page by page; in the first third of the novel, before the characters move to Brussels, there is just one sequence where Becky works for Sir Pitt and one sequence in the home of Miss Crawley. Most of the time, episodes are set in the middle-class homes of the Sedleys and the Osbornes. The same is true of the last third of the novel.

But what we remember are the eccentrics, rather than the dull round of middle-class life. Sir Pitt makes an impression because he is larger than life; we are less likely to take notice of his wife, Rose. An ironmonger's daughter, with 'no sort of character, nor talents, nor opinions, nor occupations, nor amusements' (p. 98), Rose is invisible in the same kind of way that Mrs. Sedley is invisible. She has entered into a business transaction, selling her heart 'to become Sir Pitt Crawley's wife. Mothers and daughters are making the same bargain every day in Vanity Fair'. (p. 176) The hint of sympathy here needs to be set against the underlying assumption that the middle-class wife has no character, no individuality. By contrast, the gentry—the entire Crawley family—may be eccentrics, but another way of putting it is that they are conceived of as individuals with character traits that are all their own. Consequently, Sir Pitt might be disreputable but eschews middle-class respectability. Similarly, the women of the family, Miss Crawley and Mrs. Bute Crawley, have their ridiculous side but also exhibit strength and resourcefulness that is absent in the middle-class women.

It is this derision of middle-class characters that, more than anything else, created disquiet in the early reviews. The point could be demonstrated across the board, but is most clearly seen in the response of John Forster. His review is sophisticated and enthusiastic: he relishes Thackeray's 'witty malice' and his 'accomplished and subtle' mind, and delights in Becky and Steyne, seeing that it is with 'characters where great natural talents and energy are combined with unredeemed depravity that the author puts forth his full powers'. He then, however, voices his reservation:

> Nor is it so much with respect to these exceptional characters that we feel inclined to complain of the taunting, cynical, sarcastic tone that too much pervades the work, as with respect to a preponderance of unredeemed selfishness in the more common-place as well as the leading characters, such as the Bullocks, Mrs.

Clapp, the Miss Dobbinses even, and Amelia's mother. We can relish the shrewd egoism of Miss Crawley; can admire, while we tremble at, the terrible intentness of Mrs. Bute Crawley . . . but we feel that the atmosphere of the work is overloaded with these exhalations of human folly and wickedness.[12]

The sequence of names is revealing: the Bullocks, the middle-class family of the future, are grabbed from insignificance to lead Forster's list. He then picks out other marginal middle-class characters, before altering his tone for the gentry figures. More than anything else, Forster seems to resent criticism of characters who might resemble himself. Most novelists at the time presented their audience with an ultimately flattering reflection of itself; Thackeray does not, and, consequently, irritates and unsettles his critics.

Timing is of importance here; *Vanity Fair* appeared in 1848, when a sense of being middle class was still in a process of formation. Indeed, novels were serving a vital role in creating a sense of middle-class identity and self-worth.[13] Defining middle-classness through fiction had, of course, been going on since the eighteenth century, but *Vanity Fair* appears at a significant juncture in a process of social change. Albeit reluctantly, Thackeray acknowledges a move away from a certain social formation, and searches for a new social dispensation to succeed that based upon property, rank and status.[14] It is a brilliant move to set the novel at the time of Waterloo, for this enables Thackeray both to comment on the developing democratic order of his own day and to show the coming into existence of this new social order. Behind the giddiness of Regency life, there is a sense of social change, of society re-drawing itself along new lines.

The point is most interestingly conveyed through the character of the young Pitt Crawley, who reorganises his life along what are, essentially, middle-class lines in order to revive the fortunes of a gentry family that has been in decline. He assumes the orderliness, the earnestness, and also the social ambition, of a middle-class man. As is so often the case in the novel, therefore, Thackeray is astute in his sense of a new order taking shape in society. But the fact that has to be returned to is that Thackeray's judgements are simultaneously suspect, because he cannot see any real depth of value in the middle-class mind. Rather than finding a new moral energy in middle-class experience, Thackeray castigates it as mediocre and selfish. Even in his picture of Dobbin, as we will see, there is an inability to avoid condescension, an inability to take the character seriously. Middle-class characters, and middle-class values, remain for Thackeray alien and vaguely threatening.

Vanity Fair therefore, to a quite extraordinary extent, insults its readers, who for the most part are likely to resemble those 'vulgar intellects' (p. 791) that have always dominated Amelia's life. Middle-class life is seen as dreadful. The Osborne daughters are typical: 'all their habits were pompous and orderly, and all their amusements intolerably dull and decorous'. (p. 132) Maria is engaged, 'but hers was a most respectable attachment'. (p. 138) Jos's much-repeated slight stories provide a kind of parody of the limited number of things that happen in the lives of these characters. Life is so dull that even the most trivial deviation from correctness becomes an anecdote:

> "Do you remember when you wrote to him to come on Twelfth Night, Emmy, and spelt twelfth without the f?"
>
> "That was years ago," said Amelia.
>
> "It seems like yesterday, don't it John?" said Mrs. Sedley.
>
> (p. 36)

The impression is of pathetically empty lives and nervous deference to correctness. The topic that is always returned to in this world is money, as in a surprisingly eloquent speech from George Osborne:

> "Ours is a ready-money society. We live among bankers and city big-wigs, and be hanged to them, and every man, as he talks to you, is jingling his guineas in his pocket . . . Curse the whole pack of money-grubbing vulgarians!"
>
> (p. 246)

Perhaps George's eloquence stems from the fact that the sentiments are really Thackeray's own.

Yet as much as Thackeray mocks such lives, he also offers a disquieting sense of claustrophobic containment. We have already seen the reference to Amelia's marriage-bed; the Sedleys' bed is 'a sort of tent, hung round with chintz of a rich and fantastic India pattern, and *double* with calico of a tender-rose colour; in the interior of which species of marquee was a feather-bed, on which were two pillows, on which were two round faces . . .'. (p. 36) The characters are surrounded by material goods, yet also enclosed and trapped by them. In a similar way, they are trapped in their homes, trapped in their families, trapped in their class. When characters, such as George Osborne, attempt to move beyond their circle they simply reveal their crassness. At the same time, there is always a sense of fragility, that middle-class wealth can disappear as quickly as it has appeared, leaving the characters in smaller homes, locked into an even narrower round.

Thackeray provides his most cutting commentary on such existences through his use of two outsiders, Jos Sedley and Mrs. O'Dowd (we could include Becky here, but Becky is a quite exceptional case whereas Jos and Mrs. O'Dowd are representative figures on the margins of British society). With Jos, a lack of social confidence, slavish devotion to material goods, excessive consumption, pomposity and deference are carried to a ridiculous extreme. But behind it all is a sense of an empty life, for 'he was as lonely here as in his jungle as Boggley Wallah'. (p. 27) Jos represents a gross, distorted reflection of middle-class aspirants. Mrs. O'Dowd is used in a similar way, but with the added complication there often is with Thackeray's Irish characters. Initially, with her boasting about her family and connections, we are likely to regard her as just a vulgar Irishwoman, but she really provides an ironic echo of the grovelling and social deference that is so central in the lives of Osborne and his children. In the end, Mrs. O'Dowd is actually superior to the middle-class characters, for she is grand and theatrical, energetic and resourceful, rather than mean and mediocre.

Thackeray's patrician disdain is most obvious in his presentation of middle-class wives who, although a different note is struck at the end of the novel, are seen as insignificant ciphers. There is sympathy for them, as victims of their husbands, but they are primarily seen as empty women who could not play any active role in the middle-class accumulation of wealth. Mrs. Sedley, in particular, is an invisible character, with an 'easy and uninquisitive' nature (p. 139), whose thoughts cannot extend beyond the home. Thackeray's heroines, especially Becky, are always formidable women, but in the case of his middle-class wives he imagines concubines for domestic tyrants. There is something chilling in Amelia's deference to George:

> crying over George's head, and kissing it humbly, as if he were her supreme chief and master, and as if she were quite a guilty and unworthy person needing every favour and grace from him.
>
> This prostration and sweet unrepining obedience exquisitely touched and flattered George Osborne. He saw a slave before him in that simple yielding faithful creature, and his soul within him thrilled secretly somehow at the knowledge of his power.
>
> (pp. 235-6)

It is an astute passage, especially in its understanding of the victim's sense of her own guilt, but the picture is only achieved by imagining the woman as a nonentity, who tolerates exploitation and abuse. That would be acceptable if all Thackeray's women were like this, but one of Thackeray's distinguishing traits as a novelist is his strong women; in the context of this novel, even leaving aside Becky, we can see the energy of the gentry wife, Mrs. Bute Crawley, who takes action, even if she misjudges her tactics, while her husband fritters away his time. Similarly, Lady Jane, Mr. Pitt Crawley's wife, who seems innocent, even naive, can show the qualities of her class in standing up to and resisting Becky, and resisting her husband: 'you must choose, sir, between her and me'. (p. 697)

What is always apparent, then, is Thackeray's patronising contempt for the middle class. Dobbin is mocked at school because his father is a grocer, but it is Thackeray, throughout the novel, who can never resist telling us that a character's father was a grocer; for example, Miss Grits, who marries the Reverend Binney, bringing with her five thousand pounds. (p. 741) It is as if he can never believe that the children of grocers might be as interesting as the children of the aristocracy or gentry.[15] James Crawley, who ruins his chance of inheriting Miss Crawley's fortune through smoking in her house (p. 432), is simply laughed at; the middle-class children are always sneered at. Thackeray's contempt invariably becomes most apparent at just those points where he attempts to be most sympathetic. For example, after the dazzle of 'How to Live Well on Nothing a Year', Thackeray moves to 'A Family in a Small Way', where he offers compassionate reflections on the vagaries of fortune, but then the carping begins: 'Had Mrs. Sedley been a woman of energy, she would have exerted it after her husband's ruin'. (p. 484) She is, however, a small-minded woman, who cannot rise above 'colloquies with the greengrocer about the penn'orth of turnips which Mr. Sedley loved'. (p. 485) Sedley, on the same page, is seen 'pompously' (p. 485) presenting his grandson as the child of Captain Osborne. We are left not with a sense of life's vagaries, but with an impression of the vulgarity and shortcomings of this couple.

Thackeray in **Vanity Fair,** as is true throughout his career, is the awkward outsider in the Victorian novel. Others, for example, Dickens, at this time in *Dombey and Son* and *David Copperfield,* were presenting the middle-class audience with a critical yet, in the end, flattering image of itself. Thackeray does not oblige. **Vanity Fair** is obviously a funny novel, but the source of the amusement is usually someone acting inappropriately for a person of their class. Only Becky has the panache to carry it off, to humiliate others rather than herself. The stance in the novel raises the familiar yet teasing question of Thackeray's politics. The view that is generally held is that Thackeray was a liberal, even a radical, who by the late 1850s had moved steadily to the right.[16] But what seems nearer the truth is that, fairly consistently throughout his career, he displays a familiar form of populism, resenting all those who possess money and power. There is, throughout **Vanity Fair,** the idea of an escape to a rural arcadia, such as the muddy yet happy life Becky's child enjoys in the French countryside when he is placed out at nurse. (p. 461) Informing Thackeray's populism is this longing for a traditional order; it is an impractical politics, lacking constructive ideas, motivated mainly by resentment, by a readiness to condemn those who seem to represent change, who undermine his sense of a more innocent order.

What complicates the picture, however, and complicates **Vanity Fair,** is his awareness that a fundamental change is taking place. He might have felt unhappy about it, but he could not ignore the fact that the initiative, not only economically but also politically and socially, was moving towards the middle class. There is a reluctant realisation that the middle-class position offers the only hope for the future. This is prepared for by a sense that permeates the novel of aristocratic decline; in addition, there is also a late and unexpected indication of a collapse of gentry power. The future of the aristocracy is conveyed in such details as the impoverished Bareacres family, the appearance of the brass plates of businesses in Gaunt Square, and the strain of madness in the Steyne family: the 'dark mark of fate and doom was on the threshold'. (p. 595) The position of the gentry seems less extreme: young Pitt has, after all, restored the family's fortunes, but then, less than ten pages from the end of the novel, Pitt loses his place in Parliament as a result of the 1832 Reform Act.

It does seem that the future lies with the middle class, and appropriately, the last third of the novel concentrates on Dobbin and Amelia. It is conventional to admire Thackeray's presentation of Amelia, the way in which he has made his sentimental heroine a selfish heroine, but it can be argued that she is simply another of Thackeray's small-minded middle-class women, presented with all his characteristic contempt.[17] He has to bring Amelia to the centre of the novel, but proves incapable of taking a middle-class heroine seriously. Exactly the same problem is evident in the portrayal of Dobbin:

> We all know a hundred whose coats are very well made, and a score who have excellent manners, and one or two happy things who are what they call, in the inner circles, and have shot into the very centre and bull's eye of the fashion; but of gentlemen how many? Let us take a little scrap of paper and each make out his list.
>
> My friend the major I write, without any doubt in mine. He had very long legs, a yellow face, and a slight lisp, which at first was rather ridiculous. But his thoughts were just, his brains were fairly good, his life was honest and pure, and his heart warm and humble.
>
> (p. 792)

A patrician voice encounters one of nature's gentlemen: the tone is extraordinarily condescending. The fact is that Thackeray cannot begin to comprehend a character such as Dobbin; he can only be commended on the basis of the way in which he combines upper-class gentlemanliness with a humble sense of his place. The problem with Amelia and Dobbin is that Thackeray requires them to carry the burden of a social and moral role, but is unable to give them the substance required. They remain members of an alien species, seen from a superior perspective, and evaluated in terms of how they compare to, and at times prove better than, their social superiors.

Thackeray's overt effort to point to the future through Amelia and Dobbin is, therefore, rather bungled. Yet the novel, none the less, offers a strong sense of a move towards a new order in society. By the end of *Vanity Fair,* most readers feel they have moved from Waterloo to a post-Reform Act world. This is more than a matter of chronology; a complex case about democratisation, about a shift towards middle-class values, is articulated in the second half of the novel. This sense of a change is not conveyed through subtle characterisation but through a mass of seemingly trivial details. This is entirely appropriate: *Vanity Fair* is, from the outset, a novel crammed full of precise details about the material and social world. In the second half of the novel we are offered an abundance of fresh images that combine to convey a sense of change. It starts when the characters return from the continent: at this point a different kind of detail begins to appear. There is less about what people spend their money on, and rather more about the ordinary, yet distinctively new, characteristics of middle-class life.

To begin with an example which should clarify what I am talking about, we hear a lot in the novel about the dull and pompous round of middle-class entertaining. As early as the aborted trip to Vauxhall, for example, Mr. and Mrs. Sedley have been to dine with Alderman Balls. But we have to wait a long time before we are offered a full guest-list for a middle-class dinner. Eventually, however, we encounter

> a party of dismal friends of Osborne's rank and age. Old Dr Gulp and his lady from Bloomsbury Square: old Mr Frowser the attorney, from Bedford Row, a very great man, and from his business, hand-in-glove with the 'nobs at the West End', old Colonel Livermore, of the Bombay Army, and Mrs Livermore from Upper Bedford Place: old Serjeant Toffy and Mrs Toffy; and sometimes old Sir Thomas Coffin and Lady Coffin, from Bedford Square.
>
> (p. 539)

Thackeray conveys the tedium of the occasion. He also reminds us that social aspiration is always a factor, for it is obviously felt to be a coup when a judge can be induced to attend. But, as much as the passage might be designed to operate at the expense of Osborne, other impressions are conveyed as well. The linking of the characters with streets in the Bloomsbury area of London acknowledges the coming into existence of a new middle-class locality, yet also points forward to other middle-class characters, such as the Bullocks, who make the move into more fashionable areas. Osborne's guests seem to be a generation of middle-class characters who have achieved status and respectability, but who, unlike the Bullocks, stop at this point. Yet they are far from insignificant people. All belong to a professional class, a class that would grow and grow in Victorian England.[18] They are middle class but interested in more

than money; they have opted for professions that reflect duty and social obligation. Thackeray sneers at such dull people, but at the same time there is a reluctant acknowledgement of a new, solid middle class. The precariousness of Sedley's existence seems a thing of the past; these are middle-class characters who have established secure roots in the social order.

There are other details in the novel that point to the rise of a new professional middle class. At the opening of *Vanity Fair,* the army is the only profession open to young middle-class men who are intent on bettering themselves. But as peace takes over from war, there is a growing sense of a professional class; indeed, young George is taught by a man who prepares his pupils for 'the Universities, the senate, and the learned professions'. (p. 715) We begin to encounter characters such as Wenham, 'the wit and lawyer' (p. 637), who acts on behalf of Steyne. Rawdon has, in the past, fought duels, but now the professional man Wenham negotiates a settlement. It is a shift towards a society where, as in the words of the newspaper report of Rawdon's job, 'We need not only men of acknowledged bravery, but men of administrative talents to superintend the affairs of our colonies'. (p. 699) We might begin to feel that Becky has been overtaken by events, that her kind of spectacular rise is no longer possible in a society where success is most likely for the diligent.

Middle-class confidence, too, is increasing. Even Jos develops 'a more candid and courageous self-assertion of his worth'. (p. 751) This is not entirely surprising, for he is presented at court; the narrator makes a disparaging comment, that Jos had 'worked himself up to believe that he was implicated in the maintenance of the public welfare' (p. 767), yet there is a sense in which this is true, for Jos, as a fairly senior colonial civil servant, is 'implicated'. The developing role of the civil service and the increasing importance of the empire in Victorian England was complemented by a growth in financial services. Banks could still collapse, indeed there was a banking crisis in 1847 and another ten years later, but in the latter stages of *Vanity Fair* we seem to have moved beyond the gambling of the Waterloo era, whether at the card table or on the stock exchange, towards secure banks, such as Hulker, Bullock and Co. and Stumpy and Rowdy's, with substantial reserves.[19] It is middle-class bankers, such as Fred Bullock, who now seem in the vanguard of society. But financial services extend beyond banks; in the giddy world of *Vanity Fair,* it represents quite a shift towards sobriety when the narrator moves to talking about the fact that no Insurance Office will take on Rawdon Crawley as a client, because of the climate on Coventry Island. (p. 706)[20] Everywhere the impression is of a more controlled society. The idea is even conveyed in a description of Pitt's study:

with the orderly Blue Books and letters, the neatly docketed bills and symmetrical pamphlets; the locked account-books, desks and dispatch boxes, the Bible, the *Quarterly Review,* and the *Court Guide,* which all stood as if on parade awaiting inspection of their chief.

(p. 678)

The military imagery that is so common in the novel is called upon again, but is now at the service of a middle-class vision of order.

Nowhere is this sense of a new social formation better conveyed than in the different light in which middle-class women are seen in the latter stages of the novel. Thackeray's contempt never disappears, indeed it becomes more barbed as he is forced to concede that Maria Bullock and her circle are no longer the wilting middle-class women that have appeared in the novel up to this point:

> Emmy found herself in the centre of a very genteel circle indeed; the members of which could not conceive that anybody belonging to it was not very lucky. There was scarce one of the ladies that hadn't a relation a peer, though the husband might be a drysalter in the City. Some of the ladies were very blue and well informed; reading Mrs Somerville, and frequenting the Royal Institution; others were severe and Evangelical, and held by Exeter Hall.

(pp. 781-2)

The tone is sarcastic, rather pathetically so, but behind the sarcasm we can see three remarkable points: these are self-confident middle-class women, taking a pride in their own rank and status; part of this pride can be attributed to their success in moving towards the centre of society, making the leap from trade to aristocratic connections; yet at the same time these are intelligent women, with a range of intellectual interests. These are women with minds and a justified sense of their own importance. No wonder Thackeray's tone is so unbalanced; he does everything he can to mount a case against Maria Bullock, dismissing her 'twopenny gentility' (p. 782) and mocking her 'scheming and managing' (p. 782) to attract accounts to her husband's bank, but she is likely to strike us as an active woman playing a role in the family business. The middle class remain people that Thackeray looks down on, but now that they are asserting themselves he sinks below contempt and is reduced to sniping abuse.

Yet it is this unbalanced animosity that gives the novel so much of its strength, for Thackeray's perverse and hostile stand represents a unique perspective on the redrawing of the lines in society. He sneers, and, as the novel goes on, sneers more and more, but at the same time reluctantly concedes the presence and importance of the middle class. There is, however, one final twist: he might resist the impulse, but by the end of the novel

Thackeray himself has begun to acquire something of a middle-class outlook. We see it in his revised attitude to Becky. Dobbin states the case against Becky, trying to persuade Amelia that she is dangerous. He then makes the same case to Jos: 'Be a man, Jos: break off this disreputable connection. Come home to your family'. (p. 874) Manliness, distancing oneself from anybody disreputable, and the family, are Dobbin's key points. Jos protests that Becky is innocent, and, indeed, it would be hard to say what she has done wrong, but she stands as a vivid illustration of transgression, the kind of social deviant that was required if the middle class was to be convinced of the soundness of its moral codes. What is more curious is that Thackeray now seems to share this view of Becky. The point is underlined in his final selection of a detail to illustrate her villainy: she is involved in an insurance fraud, making a claim on Jos's life. It is a strange reversal of Thackeray's earlier celebration of Becky's vitality when he starts judging her from the perspective of an insurance company.

Thackeray makes one final protest against middle-class values: his late hint that Dobbin finds his marriage a disappointment is a gesture against the period's increasing reverence for the family. But it seems only a token gesture against the drift in the novel towards the family, towards private life. Yet, perhaps this is not entirely the case. Thackeray had to finish his novel. He also had to cater for, and to some extent satisfy, his audience. The steps towards a middle-class compromise might be simply steps he could not avoid in concluding *Vanity Fair.* His venom towards Maria Bullock seems closer to his true self. And the subsequent novels also suggest that he could never come to terms with the middle-class world, that he never had any time for, or understanding of, middle-class people. They remain an inferior breed, admirable in so far as they emulate the manners of their social superiors, but always condemned for attempting to do so.

Notes

1. In *Thackeray: The Critical Heritage,* ed. G. Tillotson and D. Hawes, London, Routledge & Kegan Paul, 1968, p. 64.

2. A representative selection of reviews and other responses can be found in the Critical Heritage volume, ibid., pp. 51-87.

3. See Barbara Hardy, *The Exposure of Luxury: Radical Themes in Thackeray,* London, Peter Owen, 1972.

4. See, in particular, the second volume of the biography: Gordon Ray, *Thackeray: The Age of Wisdom: 1847-1863,* London, Oxford University Press, 1958.

5. Dyson's essay is reprinted in *Thackeray: 'Vanity Fair': A Casebook,* ed. Arthur Pollard, London, Macmillan, 1978, pp. 163-82.

6. '*Henry Esmond*: Repetition and Irony', in J. Hillis Miller, *Fiction and Repetition,* Oxford, Basil Blackwell, 1982, pp. 73-115.

7. Robert E. Lougy, 'Vision and Satire: The Warped Looking Glass in *Vanity Fair*', reprinted in *William Makepeace Thackeray's 'Vanity Fair': Modern Critical Interpretations,* New York, Chelsea House Publishers, 1987, pp. 57-82.

8. See, for example, Carol Hanbury MacKay, 'Controlling Death and Sex: Magnification v. The Rhetoric of Rules in Dickens and Thackeray', in *Sex and Death in Victorian Literature,* ed. Regina Barreca, London, Macmillan, 1990, pp. 120-39, and, on *Henry Esmond,* '*Adam Bede* and *Henry Esmond*: Homosocial Desire and the Historicity of the Female', in Eve Kosofsky Sedgwick, *Between Men: English Literature and Male Homosocial Desire,* New York, Columbia University Press, 1985, pp. 134-60, and Nina Auerbach, *Woman and the Demon: The Life of a Victorian Myth,* Cambridge, Harvard University Press, 1982, pp. 82-100; *Vanity Fair,* vol. xi. *The Oxford Thackeray,* London, Oxford University Press, 1908, p. 320. All subsequent references are to this edition.

9. Norman McCord, in *British History: 1815-1906,* Oxford, Oxford University Press, 1991, makes the point that there 'are serious problems in identifying a coherent middle-class within nineteenth-century society. This is at first sight surprising, for contemporaries had no doubt of the existence of a powerful, articulate, and coherent middle class'. (p. 98) His point is that there were a great many people who might be labelled middle class but who felt very little community of interest. It is, I suggest, the provisionality and uncertainty of the middle class position that Thackeray exploits in *Vanity Fair.*

10. Robert A. Colby, *Thackeray's Canvass of Humanity: An Author and His Public,* Columbus, Ohio State University Press, 1979, p. 246.

11. See, for example, Sheila Smith, *The Other Nation: The Poor in English Novels of the 1840s and 1850s,* Oxford, Clarendon Press, 1980; Mary Poovey, *Uneven Developments: The Ideological Work of Gender in Mid-Victorian England,* London, Virago, 1989; and Patrick Brantlinger, *Rule of Darkness: British Literature and Imperialism, 1830-1914,* Ithaca, Cornell University Press, 1988.

12. Reprinted in *Thackeray: The Critical Heritage,* op. cit., pp. 53-8.

13. A point frequently made, for example in Mary Eagleton and David Pierce, *Attitudes to Class in the English Novel,* London, Thames & Hudson, 1979: 'Characteristic of the Victorian middle class, as seen through the novel, is a consciousness of itself as a *new* middle class in a new kind of society and with the energy, power, and obligation to solve the problems of society'. (p. 33)

14. See David Musselwhite, 'Notes on a Journey to *Vanity Fair*', in *Partings Welded Together: Politics and Desire in the Nineteenth-Century English Novel,* London, Methuen, 1987, where he expands the idea that there is, in *Vanity Fair,* a need to constitute 'a mechanism of social reproduction and legitimacy in lieu of that formerly afforded by land and "connection"'. (p. 141)

15. The class issue continues to make itself felt in Victorian criticism, perhaps most interestingly in relation to the topic of this essay in Leslie Stephen's comment that Dickens 'was successful beyond any English novelist . . . in exactly hitting off the precise tone of thought and feeling which would find favour with the grocers'. From Stephen's Introduction to the 1878-9 edition of Thackeray's novels, reprinted in *Thackeray: The Critical Heritage,* op. cit., p. 362.

16. Dyson comments: 'In 1848 . . . Thackeray confessed himself a Republican but not a Chartist. He had no wish to be associated with the hated "levellers", yet his picture of society is remarkably in tune with theirs'. (*Thackeray: 'Vanity Fair': A Casebook,* op. cit., p. 173) Gordon Ray writes: 'Between 1848 and 1855 Thackeray had contrived to remain a "Whig and Quietist" in politics . . .' (*Thackeray: The Age of Wisdom,* op. cit., p. 250), but then as a result of the Crimean War, became more radical (pp. 251-3), although Ray also describes his position after 1855 as 'a moderate liberalism'. (p. 312) Then, however, according to Ray, he moved to 'actual conservatism' (p. 312), becoming 'reconciled to "the ornamental classes"'. (p. 312)

17. One of Amelia's admirers was Trollope: 'She is feminine all over, and British,—loving, true, thoroughly unselfish . . . I know no trait in Amelia which a man would be ashamed to find in his own daughter'. (*Thackeray,* London, Macmillan, 1879, p. 105).

18. 'The increasingly complex organization of society and the economy involved a growing need for specialists with distinctive qualifications. After 1850 there was a continuing crystallization of professions'. (Norman McCord, op. cit., p. 337.)

19. See McCord, op. cit., pp. 184-5, 326-9.

20. On the growth of insurance, see McCord, op. cit., p. 327; Asa Briggs, *Victorian Things,* London, Penguin, 1990, p. 40; and Keith Robbins,

Nineteenth-Century Britain, Oxford, Oxford University Press, 1989, p. 127.

J. Russell Perkin (essay date winter 1998)

SOURCE: Perkin, J. Russell. "The Implied Theology of *Vanity Fair.*" *Philological Quarterly* 77, no. 1 (winter 1998): 79-106.

[*In the following essay, Perkin examines Thackeray's treatment of Christian themes in* Vanity Fair.]

> My dearest Mammy. I must write you a line, and kiss my dearest old Mother, though we differ ever so much about the Old Testament.
>
> (Thackeray, *Letters* [*Letters and Private Papers of William Makepeace Thackeray*] 3:168)

1

In *The Imitation of Christ,* Thomas à Kempis declares "'Vanity of vanities, and all is vanity,' except to love God and serve Him alone."[1] *Vanity Fair* ends with the same words from Ecclesiastes: *Vanitas Vanitatum* (689).[2] However, Thackeray was no admirer of the *Imitatio Christi,* for he wrote to Jane Brookfield on Christmas Day, 1849:

> The scheme of that book carried out would make the world the most wretched useless dreary doting place of sojourn . . . a set of selfish beings crawling about avoiding one another, and howling a perpetual miserere.
>
> (*Letters* 2:616)

It may seem perverse to attempt to describe a theology of a novel as skeptical and worldly as *Vanity Fair,* and certainly Thackeray concerns himself much more with the vanity of existence than with the love of God. Twentieth-century readers are more likely to agree with Robyn Warhol that the narrator of *Vanity Fair*

> is only playing preacher, as he is playing historian, and as his characters are playing out the play. Readings of *Vanity Fair* informed by more recent literary theory have suggested that Thackeray's text expressed profound doubts about the ability of narrative fiction to do more than play. . . .[3]

Similarly, Barry Qualls does not treat *Vanity Fair* at length in his study of secular pilgrims in Victorian fiction, arguing that Thackeray does not provide a narrative of natural supernaturalism, but rather a parodic treatment of the secular world.[4] I would agree with Qualls's overall distinction between Thackeray on the one hand and Eliot, Brontë, and Dickens on the other. However, I will argue that there are in Thackeray's novel hints of a realm of existence beyond that of the world of vanity, and it is from those hints that the implied theology of the novel can be constructed; I will further suggest in conclusion that this implied theology is in some ways closer to an Augustinian orthodoxy than it is to the Broad Church position with which William Makepeace Thackeray the historical individual can be identified.[5]

Thackeray's religious beliefs can be inferred from his letters and journalism, though the evidence must be handled carefully, because it is somewhat ambiguous.[6] It is certain that he went through phases of skepticism, which have been documented by his biographer.[7] He struggled throughout his life with the powerful influence of his Evangelical mother, trying to distance himself from aspects of her creed and yet at the same time trying to show her that he did believe in what he considered to be the essential truth of Christianity. "My dearest Mammy," he begins one letter, "I must write you a line, and kiss my dearest old Mother, though we differ ever so much about the Old Testament" (*Letters* 3:168).

A quick survey of Thackeray's strongly expressed religious opinions may help to place him on the Victorian ecclesiastical map. He particularly disliked the Evangelical creed in which he was raised, and he rejected its belief in the historical accuracy of the Old Testament narratives. As his Christmas letter to Jane Brookfield already quoted suggests, he disliked any attempt to revive medieval devotional practices. On the other hand, he admired and respected Thomas Arnold, and greatly admired Stanley's *Life* of Arnold, which he reviewed favorably in the *Morning Chronicle* and which he recommends to anyone who wants to know "how great, and good, and noble" a country parson may be.[8] He was well aware, from his youthful visit to Weimar, of German biblical criticism, and he no doubt distressed his mother by writing from Weimar: "the doctrine here is not near so strict as in England—many of the dogmas by w[h]. we hold are here disregarded as allegories or parables—or I fear by most people as fictions altogether" (*Letters* 1:140). Thackeray thought that the authors of *Essays and Reviews,* reviled by some as the "*Septem contra Christum,*" were "good men" (Ray 2:367). He admired Francis Newman and Clough, "thinking men, who I daresay will begin to speak out before many years are over, and protest against Gothic Xtianity" (Ray 2:121). I think that S. S. Prawer sums up Thackeray's religious views fairly when he writes:

> No-one who scans Thackeray's letters and diaries can long remain in doubt that he retained Christian beliefs throughout his life which enabled him to remain, without difficulty, a member of the Church of England.[9]

The opinions that I have quoted tend to put Thackeray in the Broad Church camp, as does his emphasis on the ethical dimension of Christianity. The essence of his faith seems to have been a belief in the importance of "doing your duty," which duty was clearly set out, largely identified with the idea of being a gentleman, and sanctioned by the divine example of Jesus Christ. He expresses his reverence for Christ with a reticence akin to the reserve practised by the Tractarians. For example, he wrote to his mother:

> Why do I love the Saviour? (I love and adore the Blessed Character so much that I don't like to speak of it, and know myself to be such a rascal that I don't dare)—Because He is all Goodness Truth Purity—I dislike the Old Testament because it is the very contrary: because it contains no Gentleness no Humility no forgiveness. . . .
>
> (***Letters*** 2:206)

A similar statement occurs when he writes to Robert Bell to thank Bell for his review of *Vanity Fair*: "You have all of you taken my misanthropy to task—I wish I could myself: but take the world by a certain standard [*drawing of a large cross*] (you know what I mean) and who dares talk of having any virtue at all?"[10]

Thackeray rejected the notion of eternal punishment as barbaric, and in spite of his frequently expressed intolerance for those of other races and nationalities he regarded tolerance as an ideal.[11] In interpreting the Bible, Thackeray tended to demythologize, and his disputes with his mother over biblical interpretation suggest, as Prawer asserts, that his "revulsion against the Old Testament is bound up with attempts to free himself from the influence of his mother's overpowering personality."[12] The conflicts with his mother were particularly acute when they disagreed over the religious upbringing of Thackeray's two daughters, and his views are perhaps most clearly stated in the letters he wrote to the girls on this topic during the times when they lived with their grandmother. He wrote to Anne Thackeray: "To my mind Scripture only means a writing and Bible means a Book. It contains Divine Truths: and the history of a Divine Character: but imperfect but not containing a thousandth part of Him . . ." (***Letters*** 3:95-96). Eight years after Thackeray wrote this letter, Benjamin Jowett would scandalize Oxford and the Church of England by his contribution to *Essays and Reviews,* in which he declared that the first principle of biblical hermeneutics should be "Interpret the Scripture like any other book."[13] Thackeray's treatment of Jesus Christ as the embodiment of all human perfection is in accord with the image of Jesus emphasized in liberal Protestantism, and which was summed up in one of Matthew Arnold's more unfortunate phrases as the "sweet reasonableness" (translating St. Paul's *epieikeia*) of Jesus.[14]

The passages just quoted help to provide a context for another letter, this time the famous one which Thackeray wrote to his mother on July 2, 1847, on the appearance of the seventh monthly number of *Vanity Fair.* He claimed that he was not concerned "to make a perfect character or anything like it," a point his novel clearly signals to the reader in the subtitle of the volume edition, *A Novel Without a Hero.* "What I want," he continues in his letter, "is to make a set of people living without God in the world[15] (only that is a cant phrase) greedy pompous mean perfectly self-satisfied for the most part and at ease about their superior virtue" (***Letters*** 2:309). This statement has often been repeated by critics, for it is Thackeray's clearest statement of intention concerning his novel; however, what is not generally quoted is the conclusion to the paragraph in which the statement occurs, which, strikingly enough, is a prayer, "Save me, save me too O my God and Father, cleanse my heart and teach me my duty" (2:309). This fact should perhaps cause interpreters of the novel to take more seriously than they usually do the reference to "living in the world without God."[16]

A knowledge of Thackeray's religious opinions should alert the reader to possibilities of interpreting *Vanity Fair* that would otherwise be overlooked. It is also worth noting that at least some Victorians regarded Thackeray as a serious moralist who could be read in the context of Christian belief. The most famous example of such a Victorian admirer is Charlotte Brontë, who clearly views Thackeray as a latter-day prophet:

> There is a man in our own days whose words are not framed to tickle delicate ears: who, to my thinking, comes before the great ones of society, much as the son of Imlah came before the throned Kings of Judah and Israel; and who speaks truth as deep, with a power as prophet-like and as vital—a mien as dauntless and as daring. . . . I regard him as the first social regenerator of the day. . . .[17]

2

There has not been a great deal of discussion of religion in *Vanity Fair,* beyond the obvious recognition of the significance of the title. The dominant view among critics is that the novel has a religious dimension, but that it is not particularly important. A typical view is A. E. Dyson's, that "religious judgments are inescapably present, though not directly expressed," because Thackeray "has nothing of Bunyan's clear-cut doctrine to depend upon."[18] Barbara Hardy is more skeptical, suggesting that religion sits very lightly on Thackeray and that his novels are characterized by an absence of "embodied religious feeling."[19] In what follows, I will suggest that Thackeray's understanding of Christianity, although not dogmatic, was more clearly formulated than Dyson's comment suggests, and that the reserve which Hardy identifies does not necessarily indicate that Thackeray took Christianity lightly.

In examining the religious dimension of *Vanity Fair,* I am well aware that the novel is the most worldly of literary genres, and that Thackeray's novel is a particularly good example of a polyphonic or dialogic novel. Whether one defines the genre of the novel in terms of realism, focussing on the secular world of human society, or whether one follows Bakhtin's emphasis on dialogism, the genre is equally far from the ordering principles and the concern with the divine which characterize most theology. I also have in mind Bakhtin's specific comments about what he sees as the monologic conclusion to *Crime and Punishment*.[20] However, I will argue that Christian belief is one of the numerous languages of *Vanity Fair,* and that the pervasive title metaphor of Vanity Fair is one of a number of means by which Thackeray puts Christianity into the dialogical world of his novel. Before looking at his use of Ecclesiastes and Bunyan, I will elaborate on the notion of dialogism in *Vanity Fair.* In a pioneering discussion of dialogical form in the Victorian multiplot novel, Peter K. Garrett analyzes the instability of Thackeray's narrative voice. His discussion of "one of the world's most devious novels"[21] comes to the conclusion that, because of "the doubtful authority of the narrator as moral commentator,"

> every comment or interpretation which the narrator introduces can exert only conditional authority. His formulations raise but cannot resolve the novel's issues; they must be tested against the implications of the narrative as a whole.[22]

Bakhtin's poetics of the novel provide another valuable dimension for the analysis of *Vanity Fair,* in addition to the points which Garrett makes. For Bakhtin, the conflicting voices, or as he calls them "languages," in a novel represent competing world views, "each characterized by its own objects, meanings and values," grounded in specific social circumstances and embodied in particular stylistic features in the text.[23] Garrett's analysis can be extended by defining some of the voices in *Vanity Fair.* Thackeray's narrator, as is well known, is far from stable, and he embodies a number of different and sometimes incompatible attitudes. At different points in the novel his voice approximates to the voices of various characters, whether he is adopting the satirical tone and suspiciousness about people's motives which characterize Rebecca Sharp, or whether he is speaking in the voice of the bourgeois gentleman, like William Dobbin. One particularly distinct voice which Thackeray employs is that of the disillusioned cynical moralist, who in the manner of La Rochefoucauld sees every human action as the result of self-interest. Such analysis is characteristic of Matilda Crawley and of Lord Steyne, as well as of the narrator in his cynical voice. Thackeray thus links this skeptical attitude to a class whose ascendancy is coming to an end, but at the same time the attitude has a great deal of persuasive force in the novel (it is in fact closely related to the postmodern reading of *Vanity Fair*). If, as has been ar-

gued, *Vanity Fair* redefines gentlemanliness in middle-class terms, it also embodies a considerable degree of resistance to such a redefinition.

An example of the cynical voice occurs during the narrator's introduction of Rawdon Crawley, when Mr. Pitt Crawley is quoted as alluding to Rawdon's contempt not only for death, but for "what follows after death." The narrator then adds, in a manner which prevents the reader from identifying with Pitt Crawley's censure, "He was always thinking of his brother's soul or of the souls of those who differed with him in opinion—it is a sort of comfort which many of the serious give themselves" (98). Here virtue, or at least the appearance of it, is reduced to self-interest, as Thackeray astutely identifies one of the temptations of religious faith.

A second voice of Thackeray's narrator is more sentimental, indulging in the kind of ironically tinged nostalgia of which Thackeray is a master and which characterizes, for example, *The Roundabout Papers.* Here the social position can be characterized as more middle-class, for the references tend to be to bourgeois pleasures and experiences. This narrative voice can thus be identified with the aspect of the narrator who is a character on the same social level as William Dobbin, and who shares some of Dobbin's experiences. When employing the sentimental voice, the narrator often includes himself in the behavior he observes, and his tone tends to be the understanding irony of mature years, rather than the bitter cynicism of the more aristocratic voice. An example occurs in Chapter 6, "Vauxhall," where after disingenuously suggesting that he doesn't understand the language of the fashionable world, the narrator says ingratiatingly that "we must if you please preserve our middle course modestly amidst those scenes and personages with which we are most familiar" (52). The narrator twice refers to his own experience of visiting Vauxhall. Like Dobbin, he was not socially accomplished enough to avoid being on his own, and he remembers being alone at Vauxhall as "one of the most dismal sports ever entered into by a bachelor" (56). Like Joseph Sedley he also knows from personal experience the dreadful after-effects of drinking too much Vauxhall punch (58-59).

The voices I have just described may be termed worldly cynicism and worldly sentimentalism respectively; for the perspective of religious belief we must turn to a consideration of the intertexts of Ecclesiastes and *Pilgrim's Progress,* which are the sources of the title metaphor. The book of Ecclesiastes is an example of wisdom literature, but instead of the conservative advice which characterizes much of the wisdom tradition, it presents a more disillusioned, skeptical view of the world. The writer, who identifies himself as Qoheleth,[24] investigates a range of possible attitudes to life and comes to the conclusion that each of them has as its root vanity or emptiness. For Qoheleth, the repetitive cycles of nature and the fact of human mortality produce the same conclusion to each of his investigations: "This also is vanity and vexation of spirit." The only advice he can offer is that one should enjoy life as long as one is able to. There is no point to striving for virtue, zealously observing God's ordinances, nor is there any need for radical repentance, for

> All things come alike to all: there is one event to the righteous, and to the wicked; to the good and to the clean, and to the unclean; to him that sacrificeth, and to him that sacrificeth not; as is the good, so is the sinner; and he that sweareth, as he that feareth an oath.
>
> (Eccles. 9:2)

The appeal of this wisdom to a disillusioned Evangelical like Thackeray is obvious, and it in fact has affinities to the attitudes he embraced as a student under the influence of Edward FitzGerald (see Ray 1:131-32). Just as Qoheleth returns repeatedly to his refrain that all is vanity, so Thackeray's narrator constantly reiterates the title of the novel, referring to both the social world of the diegesis and the social world he shares with the narratee as "this Vanity Fair of ours" (213). As in Ecclesiastes, "vanity" becomes the negative principle which underlies all human activities, all different world views.

In a passage in Ecclesiastes (1:12-2:26) which one commentator has referred to as the "royal fiction" or "royal experiment,"[25] Qoheleth surveys the world from the perspective of King Solomon, and he comes to the same conclusion he reaches elsewhere, that "all is vanity and vexation of spirit" (1:14). Similarly, in *Vanity Fair* Becky is admitted to the society of the "best" people:

> Ah, my beloved readers and brethren, do not envy poor Becky prematurely—glory like this is said to be fugitive. It is currently reported that even in the very inmost circles, they are no happier than the poor wanderers outside the zone; and Becky, who penetrated into the very centre of fashion, and saw the great George IV. face to face, has owned since that there too was Vanity.
>
> (503)

The view that vanity is all-pervasive obviously has something in common with the cynical voice which I earlier attributed to both Miss Matilda Crawley and to the narrator. But Matilda Crawley is terrified of death, like a number of Thackeray's characters, whereas the narrator continually alludes to the common end of all humanity. Miss Crawley is thus exposed as a fair-weather cynic, while the narrator's awareness of mortality is one of the principal reasons for his disillusionment, as it is for Qoheleth. For example, the narrator describes a lady's companion as a *memento mori,* "as jolly a reminder as that of the Death's-head which figured in the repasts of Egyptian *bon-vivants,* a strange sardonic memorial of Vanity Fair" (376).

The references to mortality in *Vanity Fair* both reinforce the vanity theme I have just identified and more specifically serve to undermine social pretentions by drawing attention to the common end of all humanity, rich and poor, gentle and common. Death and madness overshadow high society throughout the novel, from the moment when Becky Sharp first enters Great Gaunt Street, with its hatchments and closed shutters, "in which gloomy locality death seems to reign perpetual" (67). Miss Crawley, the witty lady of fashion, becomes a hysterical invalid, and the narrator underlines the moral of her demise with an allusion to the celebrated poetic account of decline and death in the last chapter of Ecclesiastes: "The last scene of her dismal Vanity Fair comedy was fast approaching; the tawdry lamps were going out one by one; and the dark curtain was almost ready to descend" (257). The famous meditation on the arch in the staircase at the beginning of Chapter 61 reenacts the same biblical passage, brilliantly employing imagery of bourgeois Victorian family life in order to reinforce the point that mourning doesn't last very long, and those "who love the survivors the least" are those who are most passionately mourned (604). Such passages, as they accumulate, begin to take on a prophetic dimension, emphasizing the emptiness of social status in the face of death, and implying the need for more durable and genuine virtues than the values of *Vanity Fair.*

The narrator's sentimental voice also figures in the references to "vanity," for they do not all refer to mortality. Some of them take a more tolerant view of vanity, implying that it is merely ordinary human frailty, not without its lovable or humorous side. These passages counter the prophetic voice in the novel, and remind one that Thackeray was a humorist as well as a satirist and moralist. A good example is the opening to chapter 36, "How to Live Well on Nothing a-Year," with its references to the entertainment habits of the "Jenkinses in the Park," and which begins:

> I suppose there is no man in this Vanity Fair of ours so little observant as not to think sometimes about the worldly affairs of his acquaintances, or so extremely charitable as not to wonder how his neighbour Jones, or his neighbour Smith, can make both ends meet at the end of the year.
>
> (360)

The narrator details the kind of subterfuges the Jenkinses employ, with an amused detachment that comes from being someone who does not himself have to employ such measures. While he suggests that his "I" is here intended to personify the censoriousness of the world, "the Mrs. Grundy of each respected reader's private circle" (362), it is clear that the passage is more of an expression of curiosity and interest in the ways of the world than of genuine moral disapproval, for he then implicates himself in what goes on: "Many a glass of wine have we all of us drunk, I have very little doubt, hob-and-nobbing with the hospitable giver, and wondering how the deuce he paid for it" (362). Clearly this narrator is not too proud to dine with the Jenkinses; in fact, wondering how the meal was paid for only seems to add to the interest of the experience. Thus the recurring theme of *vanitas* is used with varying degrees of moral intensity throughout the novel, contributing to the dialogical quality which emerges as one analyzes it.

According to Northrop Frye, the Hebrew word *hebel,* whose core meaning is fog or mist, and which the Vulgate renders as *vanitas,* is a concept like "the *shunyata* or 'void' of Buddhist thought."[26] Peter Garrett suggests something similar when he implies that **Vanity Fair** is a representation of the postmodern condition:

> The final stress on common vanity may be seen as the conclusion of the novel's moral argument, but it can also be seen as a return to the basis of its logic. Its elaborate, restless play on patterns of difference and similarity, exaggerating oppositions in order to collapse them, never allowing the reader a single, stable perspective or standard, this method too rests on *vanitas,* or emptiness, the emptiness which underlies the production of meaning from sheer difference.
>
> (127)

This is a compelling statement, and it expresses a conclusion similar to that of W. David Shaw in his subtle analysis of **Vanity Fair** in *Victorians and Mystery.* Shaw sees Thackeray's text as characterized by double ironies which result in the collapse of moral norms, so that "moral language, like the moral masks of the performers, is empty of content."[27] It is certainly true that the moral language employed in the text and the world view that Thackeray characterizes as "Vanity Fair" are incommensurate. It is also true that the narrator expresses a variety of diverse positions through the course of the novel. However, it is up to the reader to decide whether the result of the incommensurability is that the various positions cancel each other out. My own contention, in spite of the eloquent voices I have just quoted, is that the ironies of **Vanity Fair** do not necessarily result in postmodern skepticism. In order to pursue this argument further, it is necessary to consider another of **Vanity Fair**'s intertexts.

Thackeray's title owes some of its resonance to the fact that it is a double allusion. If the concept of *vanitas* functions in Ecclesiastes to show the nothingness of any attempt to order existence, and can thus be assimilated to a poststructuralist idea of *différance,* Vanity-Fair in John Bunyan's *Pilgrim's Progress* (1678) has a more limited, specific function in a Christian allegory. Like Thomas à Kempis, Bunyan uses *vanitas* to mean life without God. Such a reading of Ecclesiastes was encouraged during the Reformation when the name Qo-

heleth was rendered, incorrectly, as "the Preacher" (*Prediger*) in the Reformers' references to the book.[28] *The Preacher* is the subtitle of Ecclesiastes in the King James Bible, as well as the translation of "Qoheleth."

It is interesting to note that the cover of Thackeray's original installment represents a preacher, albeit one wearing ass's ears like his auditors. In an ambiguous passage the narrator refers to both this illustration and the title:

> . . . my kind reader will please to remember that these histories in their gaudy yellow covers, have 'Vanity Fair' for a title and that Vanity Fair is a very vain, wicked, foolish place, full of all sorts of humbugs and falsenesses and pretentions. And while the moralist who is holding forth on the cover, (an accurate portrait of your humble servant) professes to wear neither gown nor bands, but only the very same long-eared livery, in which his congregation is arrayed: yet, look you, one is bound to speak the truth as far as one knows it, whether one mounts a cap and bells or a shovel-hat, and a deal of disagreeable matter must come out in the course of such an undertaking.
>
> (83)

When we remember the meaning that Bunyan gave to Vanity-Fair, then the "theological voice" in Thackeray's novel will begin to make itself heard. It is partly qualified by Thackeray's tone, as in the passage above, with its hint of parodic allusion to Sunday-school discourse in the phrase "a very vain, wicked, foolish place," and its reference to the "long-eared livery." The Christianity of the implied author is also concealed by the fact that the novel restricts itself to the world of Vanity Fair, so that to a large extent the theology that one finds in the novel is a negative theology, hinted at through the discourse of one who declares himself bound to "speak the truth as far as one knows it." This statement could refer either to the limitations of the speaker or to the unknowability of the truth.

While Thackeray's approach to theology is largely negative, some positive content is implied by Thackeray's allusions to *Pilgrim's Progress* and to the Bible.[29] For Bunyan, Vanity-Fair is the symbol of a godless world, a world moreover of competitive capitalism where everything is up for sale:

> Therefore at this Fair are all such merchandise sold, as houses, lands, trades, places, honours, preferments, titles, countries, kingdoms, lusts, pleasures, and delights of all sorts, as whores, bawds, wives, husbands, children, masters, servants, lives, blood, bodies, souls, silver, gold, pearls, precious stones, and what not.
>
> And moreover, at this Fair there is at all times to be seen jugglings, cheats, games, plays, fools, apes, knaves, and rogues, and that of all sorts.
>
> Here are to be seen too, and that for nothing, thefts, murders, adulteries, false-swearers, and that of a blood-red colour.[30]

There are many parallels between this passage and Thackeray's novel: *Vanity Fair* has thefts, false-swearers, adulteries (at least hinted at), and possibly a murder. We see the sale of property and honors; we see the commercialization of all human relationships in what George Osborne, speaking more than usually perceptively, characterizes as a "ready-money society" (204), and the imagery of the novel often echoes Bunyan's fairground references to jugglings and games.

However, Thackeray's novel only has one city, the world he constantly refers to as Vanity Fair, whereas in Bunyan's allegory "Vanity" is only a town on the way to the Celestial City, which is the goal the pilgrims have in sight from the beginning. Thackeray takes a small part of Bunyan's original conception and expands it to a vast extent, for he is writing a satirical novel, not an allegorical dream-vision.[31] As Jack Rawlins points out, there are generic reasons why "In *Vanity Fair,* everyone is in pursuit of *vanitas.*"[32] And as Robyn Warhol aptly remarks, "Of all the canonic English novels of the realist period, *Vanity Fair* is the one that makes the least pretense of presenting a slice of life: as 'Before the Curtain' makes clear, the novel is only a slice of a fair."[33] Thus Walter Allen is simply making a basic error of genre when he denigrates Thackeray as a novelist by saying that "No novelist of genius has given us an analysis of man in society based on so trivial a view of life."[34] It is precisely because it is a satirical novel that *Vanity Fair* is not a moral allegory; the Celestial City is not directly represented, and the satire is firmly anchored in the quotidian realities of the time and place of its setting.

But this does not mean that *Vanity Fair* is without a theological dimension. It alludes to the possibility of the existence of what Augustine called the city of God, although the nature of that city is left undefined. The implied theology of the novel is to this extent a liberal theology. Thackeray's understanding of Christianity in many ways resembles that of Matthew Arnold a generation later. Like Arnold, Thackeray focusses on "conduct," which, Arnold reiterates throughout *Literature and Dogma,* is three-fourths of human life.[35] Responding to an article in the *Guardian* on the meaning of Christmas, Arnold wrote in the Preface to the Popular Edition of *Literature and Dogma* (1883):

> How strange that on me should devolve the office of instructing the *Guardian* that 'the fundamental truth' for Christians is not the incarnation but the imitation of Christ! In insisting on 'the miracle of the Incarnation,' the *Guardian* insists on just that side of Christianity which is perishing. Christianity is immortal; it has eternal truth, inexhaustible value, a boundless future. But our popular religion at present conceives the birth, ministry, and death of Christ, as altogether steeped in prodigy, brimful of miracle;—*and miracles do not happen.*[36]

Like Arnold, Thackeray uses religious language to facilitate ethical judgments, but there is no sense in *Vanity Fair* of a God who acts in history. In fact, Thackeray's representation of the narrator as a stage manager or a puppet-master could be seen as a parody of a Calvinist deity. Thackeray does not use the analogy between God and the author of a novel to make serious theological points, as Catholic novelists of the twentieth century such as Muriel Spark or David Lodge have done; instead, these passages treat omniscience and authority in a comic manner that emphasizes the limitations of knowledge. They are also countered by other passages in which the narrator is a fallible character whose knowledge of what happened is imperfect. Thus, like many liberals who do not entirely reject Christianity, Thackeray takes advantage of the traditional implications of Bunyan's metaphor without committing himself to the theology it implies, in order to make a moral critique of his society.

Another of the means by which *Vanity Fair* implies a theology is in the theological overtones of language which also has a secular signification. If it were not for the pervasive use of the title metaphor and the references to Ecclesiastes and Bunyan, these nuances of language would be less striking, but in the structure Thackeray has created, they resonate significantly. One particularly resonant term is the word "world."

The Thackeray letter with which I began refers to characters living in the "world." This word occurs frequently in *Vanity Fair,* and, like almost everything else in the novel, it is not a simple term.[37] In Christian theology, *world* (Gr. *kosmos*) can refer simply to all of creation, to heaven and earth. Hence one of the best-known verses of Christian scripture, John 3:16, declares that "God so loved the world, that he gave his only begotten Son, that whosoever believeth in him should not perish, but have eternal life." But at the same time, and especially in John's gospel, being a Christian is opposed to being "of the world," as has been emphasized recurrently throughout the Christian tradition. Jesus declares "My kingdom is not of this world" (John 18:36), and throughout John's gospel Christ is figured as the light which comes into the world to save sinners.

"World" can mean the adult affairs of human society, so that a young person coming of age is said to make his or her way in the world, which is the basic subject matter of the *Bildungsroman.*[38] "World" more specifically can refer to "high or fashionable society" (*OED* "world," 18). In both of these uses, in a culture steeped in biblical language, there is often at least a hint of the religious contrast of "this world" with what the Nicene Creed calls the "world to come." Miss Crawley is a "worthy woman of the world" (140), or alternatively, "a godless woman of the world" (97); a "man of the world" is someone knowledgeable about and accepting of the social conventions of a given society, and the expression becomes even more morally ambiguous when applied to a woman, who was expected to be more attuned to a higher realm.[39] Immediately following the reference to Miss Crawley as a "worthy woman of the world" we are told that "Mr. Crawley sent over a choice parcel of tracts, to prepare her for the change from Vanity Fair and Park Lane for another world" (140).

When Becky and Amelia leave the finishing school at the beginning of the novel, the narrator echoes Milton: "The world is before the two young ladies" (9). This somewhat sententious observation, not without irony given the limited expectations implied by the schooling at Miss Pinkerton's Academy, obviously refers primarily to the social world, and to the experiences, especially of love, which await them. The Miltonic echo, and the ambiguity of the word "world," might also suggest that they are beginning a kind of parodic pilgrim's progress. Similarly, when Becky goes from London to Queen's Crawley, she "was accommodated with a back seat inside the carriage, which may be said to be carrying her into the wide world" (72). Victorian readers, schooled in *Pilgrim's Progress,* were sensitive to echoes of that book in the literature of their own time.[40] For example, Elizabeth Rigby's review of *Vanity Fair* in the *Quarterly Review,* which is better known for its comments on *Jane Eyre,* notes that Becky Sharp is a pilgrim, but unfortunately a pilgrim "travelling the wrong way."[41]

By the time we get to the end of the novel, Thackeray's ambiguous use of the word "world" has associated its use with a context of Christian moral and theological discourse. Thus when the narrator asks pointedly, wearing his preacher's robes, "Which of us is happy in this world?" (689), he could be reflecting on the vanity of the world from the point of view of the skeptical moralist of Ecclesiastes, as the Latin quotation—"*Vanitas vanitatum*"—preceding this question might imply; alternatively, he could be hinting at a Christian alternative to the world. If "this world" means everything that exists, the first sense I mentioned above, then its vanity can be seen as simply the endless cycles of change and repetition that characterize the world, and the novel's world-view can be seen as akin to the bleak view of life which is to be found in Ecclesiastes. The "progress" of Bunyan's title is a journey, a narrative of repentance and salvation, whereas a fair is a static location where the same "jugglings, cheats, games, plays, fools, apes, knaves, and rogues, and that of all sorts" have been witnessed for centuries.[42] On the other hand, *Vanity Fair* read as a Christian moral satire would condemn life without God by implying the existence of a realm other than the world ("that which is not world," in T. S. Eliot's phrase), the love of God opposed to vanity by Thomas à Kempis. The dialogical nature of the novel form means that sources such as Bunyan may be carni-

valized, and Ecclesiastes is at least as readily identified with skeptical disillusion and resignation as with Christian teaching; however, true dialogue works both ways, and Thackeray's use of terms such as "world" and "vanity," combined with the resonance of some of his biblical allusions, generates for the reader the possibility of a sphere completely separate from Vanity Fair. His greatest novel is woven out of many voices, one of which is clearly Christian. *Vanity Fair* is suspended between these two alternatives, holding them in dialogue, just as in specific passages the narrator presents the reader with different possibilities without choosing between them.

3

At several points in *Vanity Fair* the narrator draws attention to a gap in the text, something which is not narrated, leaving the reader to speculate about what is left unsaid.[43] These passages allow him to gesture beyond the limitations of the satirical world which circumscribes the novel, without actually departing from its generic norms by directly representing a world of grace. These passages could be seen as an example of a negative theology, invoking an absent God, or at least a God who is only seen by indirection. As W. David Shaw shows in *The Lucid Veil,* this negative approach is a common theme in Victorian theology, and it can be found in the self-consciously orthodox Tractarians, in their doctrine of reserve, as much as in more skeptically minded and intellectually daring theologians.[44]

One example of such a passage occurs after Amelia returns from her wedding-journey to Brighton. The narrator describes her visit to her mother and her old room and asks: "Have we a right to repeat or to overhear her prayers? These, brother, are secrets, and out of the domain of Vanity Fair, in which our story lies" (262). This passage acknowledges that there is a realm "out of the domain of Vanity Fair" which is a possible location for the implied norms of the satire, and the prayers suggest that that realm has a religious dimension. Prayer is more directly represented when Lady Jane prays for "that poor wayworn sinner" (533), her brother-in-law Rawdon. Lady Jane is the most unequivocally good character in the novel, and her influence produces the moral transformation of Rawdon, the most positive change which takes place in any character in *Vanity Fair.*

Another example of a recognition of the boundaries of the novel's world occurs in the following passage:

> Well, well—a carriage and three thousand a-year is not the summit of the reward nor the end of God's judgment of men. If quacks prosper as often as they go to the wall—if zanies succeed and knaves arrive at fortune, and, *vice versâ,* sharing ill luck and prosperity for all the world like the ablest and most honest amongst

us—I say, brother, the gifts and pleasures of Vanity Fair cannot be held of any great account, and that it is probable . . . but we are wandering out of the domain of the story.

(385)

The reference to "God's judgment" and the imagery of reversal links this passage to the parable of Dives and Lazarus, which will be discussed shortly. The boundaries of "the domain of the story" are useful to Thackeray in that he does not have to specify any specific alternative to the rising and falling movement which governs the world of Vanity Fair, while at the same time he is able to imply that there *is* such an alternative by relying on the traditional Christian remedies which for many of his readers would have come readily to mind.

One of the most extended passages of self-conscious narration in *Vanity Fair* occurs at the conclusion to Chapter 8. It is significant that it comes immediately after the long letter in which Becky takes over the role of narrator, introducing the reader to Queen's Crawley in a manner that reveals a lively satirical energy akin to that of the primary narrator. The narrator is at pains to distance himself from Becky's irreverent mockery of the Crawley family, and he claims the right to abuse villainy "in the strongest terms which politeness admits of," perhaps calling to mind Alexander Pope's chaplain who "never mentions Hell to Ears polite." If he did not abuse villains, the narrator concludes:

> you might fancy it was I who was sneering at the practice of devotion, which Miss Sharp finds so ridiculous; that it was I who laughed good-humouredly at the reeling old Silenus of a baronet—whereas the laughter comes from one who has no reverence except for prosperity and no eye for anything beyond success. Such people there are *living and flourishing in the world*— Faithless, Hopeless, Charityless—let us have at them, dear friends, with might and main. Some there are, and very successful too; mere quacks and fools: and it was to combat and expose such as those no doubt, that Laughter was made.

(84; emphasis added)

Here the phrase "living in the world" takes on the religious overtones I have already discussed as a result of being identified with the absence of the three Christian virtues. The passage implies a severe judgment on Becky, certainly a harsher one than many readers would see as one of the "implications of the narrative as a whole."[45] Thackeray here has his cake and eats it too: he has used the convenient mask of Becky's letter to provide a mocking portrait of the entire Crawley household, but now he stands back and makes moral distinctions which Becky is unable or unwilling to make. And yet on another level the novel's satire potentially extends to all of humanity, for it is orthodox Christian theology to claim that no human being has sufficient virtue to be justified on his or her own merits. Finally, before I take the passage quoted above too seriously, it is important to note, as Peter L. Shillingsburg has shown, that the end of Chapter 8 cannot be regarded as an example of the narrator speaking in a "trustworthy" voice, because it is in two ways double-voiced discourse. First, the narrator echoes the stage manager of Drury Lane greeting the audience: "I warn 'my kyind friends'"; in the next paragraph he links himself with the position of a black slave, echoing the abolitionist slogan, "Am I not a friend and brother?" (84).[46] I do not think that this ventriloquism negates the point I am making about the effect of the religious references, but it certainly qualifies them, ensuring that any conclusion is drawn by the reader and not the narrator.

Earlier I quoted an example of what I called the cynical voice in the novel, suggesting that eternal values are often alluded to for the worldly comfort of the religious person. But there is another voice to be considered in *Vanity Fair,* that of the moralist as Christian preacher, "having at" those living without faith, hope and charity "with might and main." This voice has often caused problems for readers. In his introduction to the Penguin edition of *Vanity Fair,* J. I. M. Stewart quotes the following address from the narrator to the reader: "Picture to yourself, oh fair young reader, a worldly, selfish, graceless, thankless, religionless old woman, writhing in pain and fear, and without her wig. Picture her to yourself, and ere you be old, learn to love and pray!" (141-42). Stewart's comment is "What, it is asked, could be said for such stuff?"[47] One thing that can be said is that the passage is a brief example of the preacher's voice, reflecting on the vanity of Miss Crawley's worldly values and drawing a moral conclusion. Such a passage would undoubtedly seem heavy-handed were it offered unequivocally as the moral of the entire work, or even as the last word on Matilda Crawley; however, as a voice within the work, expressing the possibility of a set of values that exists outside of Vanity Fair, it seems to me to have its place. The narrator here, in the manner of a preacher, addresses the reader directly and demands that the reader reevaluate her (or his) moral priorities. By having the statement addressed to a "fair young reader," Thackeray again introduces an element of parody, momentarily and absurdly—in the context of the entire novel—moving his narrative discourse into the world of Mrs. Sherwood and the Evangelical novel. But under this guise, wearing "the very same longeared livery" as his reader, the preacher has for a moment mounted his tub.

Another significant aspect of the religious subtext of *Vanity Fair* is Thackeray's use of the parable of Dives and Lazarus (Luke 16:19-31). This parable—found only in Luke's gospel—is unusual in including a named character and in depicting life beyond the grave; biblical

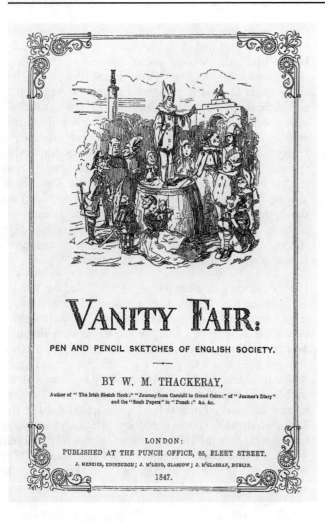

Cover of the 1847 first installment of Vanity Fair.

episodes of the Bible."[49] There are a number of allusions to the parable in his correspondence. Its relevance to *Vanity Fair* is obvious. It points to the vanity of riches, and the reversal of fortune of the two men can be paralleled in the worldly reversals of a number of Thackeray's characters. The representation of death and the testimony of the dead ties in with the novel's fondness for meditations on mortality. The parable is an important means of hinting at another realm, where a moral judgment will take place that will reverse the standards of *Vanity Fair.*

One allusion to Dives and Lazarus, which occurs in the course of an extended meditation on the subject of an auction of the goods of the late "Lord Dives," combines the vanity theme and the reference to the parable: "O Dives, who would ever have thought, as we sat round the broad table sparkling with plate and spotless linen, to have seen such a dish at the head of it as that roaring auctioneer?" (171). Here the judgment after death is a secular one, namely that the heir of the wealthy lord is rapidly dissipating his fortune and that his carefully accumulated property is being sold off. The use of the name Dives adds a hint of divine judgment, and the whole scene also is an example of the vanity theme. Compare the following passage from Ecclesiastes: "Then I looked on all the works that my hands had wrought, and on the labour that I had laboured to do: and, behold, all was vanity and vexation of spirit, and there was no profit under the sun" (Eccles. 2: 11).

In another passage Thackeray contrasts two imagined deathbed speeches, creating a fable which has echoes of the story of the Pharisee and the tax collector (Luke 18:9-14) and perhaps also that of the rich man and the poor widow (Luke 21:1-4). Thackeray's rich and self-satisfied man boasts, among other things, of having loaned his college friend Jack Lazarus fifty pounds. The poor man owns up to his sins and asks for forgiveness from the "Divine Mercy." The passage hints at a judgment beyond death, and brings in one of the more explicitly Christian statements by the narrator: "Which of these two speeches, think you, would be the best oration for your own funeral? old Sedley made the last; and in that humble frame of mind, and holding by the hand of his daughter, life and disappointment and vanity sank away from under him" (607). The parabolic formula "which of these" emphasizes the degree to which Thackeray is imitating the narrative devices of the gospels. The narrator's parable implies that everything is not vanity, but after that it is silent. We do not, as in Bunyan or in the parable in Luke's Gospel, follow Mr. Sedley into the world where vanity no longer exists; instead, the passage is followed immediately by a judgment in a very different register. Old Osborne tells George "Look at your poor grandfather, Sedley, and his failure. And yet he was a better man than I was, this day twenty years—a better man I should say, by ten

scholars have seen parallels with the literature of the Cynics in its critique of wealth and its use of reversal, as well as in the common satirical device of testimony from beyond the grave.[48] In the parable, Lazarus is a poor beggar who spends his time at the gate of a rich man's house (the Vulgate's *dives,* "rich man," led to the popular creation of the proper name of the rich man). When the two men die, Lazarus is carried by angels to the bosom of Abraham; Dives sees him from the torments of hell and asks for mercy and for his brothers to be warned of the fate in store for them. Abraham tells him that they have the prophets, to whom they should listen, and "If they hear not Moses and the prophets, neither will they be persuaded, though one rose from the dead" (Luke 16: 31).

The parable of Dives and Lazarus was a favorite biblical point of reference for Thackeray, probably because it is one of the more "novelistic" parables, with analogues in classical literature. As R. D. McMaster points out, Thackeray was fond of alluding to "the everyday and anecdotal, one might say secular and novelistic, thousand pound" (607). The reader who reacts negatively to the account of old Sedley's death, perhaps finding in it sentimentalism or falseness, is not only forced to consider as the other alternative the complacent speech of the well-to-do man, but will find himself or herself brought up short by the cross calculation of the senior Osborne, whose attitude is the result of excluding any possibility of sentimentality from one's calculation of value.

Thackeray's allusions to the parable of Lazarus and Dives serve to cast a critical shadow over the novel's preoccupation with the world of the upper bourgeoisie, and they add to the references to mortality in the novel the suggestion that at death human beings are judged by a set of values outside of those of Vanity Fair. The book of Ecclesiastes specifically suggests that the life of a rich man is one of vanity; this is the significance of the "royal experiment." Thus, to answer one of the questions readers of the novel like to debate, Becky would not have been good with £5,000 a year (see 422). She refuses to face the possibility of other values than those of Vanity Fair, just as, the narrator's revealing analogy tells us, Sir Pitt Crawley's children do not like to confront the *memento mori* which his body provides them with:

> It may, perhaps, have struck her that to have been honest and humble, to have done her duty, and to have marched straightforward on her way, would have brought her as near happiness as that path by which she was striving to attain it. But,—just as the children at Queen's Crawley went round the room, where the body of their father lay;—if ever Becky had these thoughts, she was accustomed to walk round them, and not look in.

> (423)

4

To this point, my main argument has been that *Vanity Fair* includes a Christian perspective, present in a series of allusions, in religiously inflected diction, and in a number of double-voiced passages. The consistent ironies of the novel, and the lack of positive content in its theology, are compatible with the doctrinal fuzziness of the Broad Church position, particularly with the extremely influential liberal restatement of Christianity to be found in Matthew Arnold's *Literature and Dogma* (1873), a work whose reception-history suggests that it straddles the divide between orthodoxy and apostasy. Once again, however, Thackeray's greatest novel resists definition. Certainly no one would term it a "Broad Church novel"; in conclusion I would like to suggest that *Vanity Fair,* through its invocation of some dominant motifs from the tradition of western Christianity, in fact exposes some of the weaknesses and difficulties inherent in the Broad Church position. In particular, Thackeray's novel resists the temptation of identifying

the secular ideal of gentlemanliness with the demands of the Christian gospel.[50] It was this identification, or confusion as one might more accurately term it, which led John Henry Newman to make his provocative statement that a lying, filthy Irish beggar-woman might be in a state of grace whereas a "good wise honest humble conscientious man earnestly trying to fulfil his duty" (to quote Thackeray's paraphrase of Newman's lecture; *Letters* 2:676) might not have the same prospect of heaven if his conduct was the result of natural virtue. Thackeray's reaction to this statement was predictably one of outrage (*Letters* 2:676), but his own novel raises some of the same doubts about the worth of the gentlemanly ideal.

In the introduction to his life of Thackeray, Gordon Ray argues that Thackeray's achievement as a Victorian moralist was to redefine "the gentlemanly ideal to fit a middle-class rather than an aristocratic context" (Ray 1:13). This is a useful starting point in an examination of Thackeray's fiction, but a careful reading of *Vanity Fair* soon reveals that the gentlemanly ideal is seriously flawed, and one possible alternative which is adumbrated is the ideal common to Thomas à Kempis and John Henry Newman.

Almost everywhere in Thackeray's novel, we see human goodness and gentlemanliness as weak and foolish, and vulnerable to selfishness and deceit. William Dobbin's chivalrous conduct is the result of a false idealization of his friend George, and an equally blinkered veneration of Amelia. He attributes to her qualities that she does not really possess, just as he thinks that a fashion plate with "an impossible doll's face simpering over it" (435) resembles her. And as John Sutherland points out, after marrying Amelia he devotes his life to doing nothing in particular, except working on "a book which he is unlikely to finish, and which few will want to read."[51] Lady Jane is far more of an actively good character, and her rescue of Rawdon is the most spontaneously charitable moment in the novel. The gentlemanly ideal simply does not amount to much, on the evidence *Vanity Fair* provides. It may well be that on a conscious level Thackeray regarded the Christian and the gentlemanly codes as congruous, whereas his novel, by representing the inadequacy of the latter, and the vanity of all human endeavour, suggests that the alternative of a Christian life is "difficult, exacting, and contrary at many points to natural instincts."[52]

Similarly, the novel makes clear, at the level of plot and frequently in the narrator's discourse, that human beings are all foolish and flawed, hence the subtitle, *A Novel Without a Hero*. The narrator as preacher, as Thackeray both depicts and describes him, wears "the very same long-eared livery, in which his congregation is arrayed" (83). This does not mean that there are not relative standards, by which Dobbin, for example, is superior to George and Becky, but it does mean that any human being is tainted with what Christian theology calls original sin. As Thackeray wrote to Bell, "take the world by a certain standard [*drawing of a large cross*] (you know what I mean) and who dares talk of having any virtue at all?"[53] Reticence and the decorum of the literary form he is working in prevent him from mentioning the divine alternative by name, but it is certainly implied in *Vanity Fair* by the title and the allusions I have discussed. The lack of definition or content for this ideal is another double-edged aspect of *Vanity Fair.* It is generally read as another sign of Thackeray's skepticism, but it is worth pointing out that the perfect man, the Rousseauistic Jesus of nineteenth-century liberalism, was often a projection of the culture's ideal of itself. This meant that Jesus sometimes resembled a public-school gentleman; in more sinister versions, the Jewishness of Jesus was denied, as the perfect man was defined through ethnocentric and sometimes racist assumptions.[54] Thackeray's hint that the workings of God are greater than human comprehension means that his novel does not fall into the sentimental mire of Victorian liberalism at its worst, which is perhaps another way of saying that ironists tend to be conservatives.

As a final approach to Thackeray's theological *aporia* in *Vanity Fair,* I want to return to the novel's preoccupation with the vanity of human life with particular reference to human mortality. The frequent reiteration of these themes points in two different directions, which may turn out to be but two sides of the same coin. They may be taken as evidence of the need for divine grace, or they may be seen as the reason for a skeptical attitude to life. The latter alternative is the one most critics of the novel have chosen to emphasize, but the evidence for the former is there too. I think Joseph Baker's Augustinian interpretation of *Vanity Fair* remains a valuable perspective, however inadequately it is documented from Thackeray's text. Baker does at least imply that he is aware of the dialogic nature of the novel, for he refers to Thackeray's prose as "ambivalent, or multivalent."[55] In expanding on this comment, I hope that I have reinvigorated a neglected and unpopular approach to *Vanity Fair.*

Vanity Fair does not reject Christianity; neither is it an affirmation of that faith. Thackeray's narrator at times might seem to be offering a sentimental moral to his story, but such sentimentality is always countered by what I have called the cynical voice, so that the reader is not given any final resting place. One of the best images for the novel as a whole is the opening to chapter 61, "In Which Two Lights Are Put Out." Human life is presented at all its stages, from youth to age, male and female, servant and master. The passage is finely observed and richly textured, but at the same time the whole pageant of human activity on the staircase of the house takes place under the sign of the "little arch"

(603) which both provides light to the stair and facilitates the easy removal of coffins from the house: "what a memento of Life, Death, and Vanity it is—that arch and stair" (604). As with the book of Ecclesiastes, so with *Vanity Fair* we can either regard vanity as the corrosive concept which undoes any human attempt to order existence and exposes the void that lies beneath all appearances, or we can view vanity as the condition of living in Vanity Fair, in a world without God, who provides the ordering principle beyond "the domain of Vanity Fair, in which our story lies" (262). It is up to the reader to decide whether the remedy recommended by Thomas à Kempis is applicable; the narrator remains almost ostentatiously noncommittal on the matter.[56]

Notes

1. *The Imitation of Christ,* trans. Leo Sherley-Price (Harmondsworth: Penguin, 1952), 27.

2. All quotations from *Vanity Fair* are from the edition edited by Peter Shillingsburg (New York: Norton, 1994), and will be identified by page numbers in the text. Unless otherwise noted, quotations from Thackeray's letters are from *The Letters and Private Papers of William Makepeace Thackeray,* ed. Gordon N. Ray, 4 vols. (Harvard U. Press, 1945-46).

3. *Gendered Interventions: Narrative Discourse in the Victorian Novel* (Rutgers U. Press, 1989), 99.

4. See *The Secular Pilgrims of Victorian Fiction: The Novel as Book of Life* (Cambridge U. Press, 1982), 6-7, 190-93.

5. Joseph E. Baker, "*Vanity Fair* and the Celestial City," *Nineteenth-Century Fiction* 10 (1955): 89-98, reads *Vanity Fair* from an Augustinian perspective, but does not devote much critical attention to the complexities of Thackeray's text.

6. I am grateful to Professor Peter Shillingsburg, editor of the *Thackeray Newsletter,* for permission to use material originally published in my article, "'Scripture only means a writing': Thackeray's Religious Opinions," *Thackeray Newsletter* 42 (Nov. 1995): 9-11. I have drawn on that discussion here in my summary of the evidence concerning Thackeray's religious beliefs.

7. Gordon N. Ray, *Thackeray,* 2 vols., vol. 1, *The Uses of Adversity 1811-1846* (Oxford U. Press, 1955), vol. 2, *The Age of Wisdom 1847-1863* (New York: McGraw-Hill, 1958), e.g., 1:131-32; 2:121-23. Subsequent references are given in the text.

8. *The Book of Snobs,* ed. John Sutherland (New York: St. Martin's Press, 1978), 218 n. 6, 51.

9. *Israel at Vanity Fair: Jews and Judaism in the Writings of W. M. Thackeray* (Leiden: Brill, 1992), 13.

10. I am here quoting from the more reliable text of this letter in Edgar F. Harden, ed., *The Letters and Private Papers of William Makepeace Thackeray: A Supplement to Gordon N. Ray, The Letters and Private Papers of William Makepeace Thackeray,* 2 vols. (New York and London: Garland, 1994), 1:228.

11. See, for example *Letters* 1:467.

12. Prawer, *Israel at Vanity Fair,* 341.

13. "On the Interpretation of Scripture," *Essays and Reviews* (1860; Westmead, England: Gregg, 1970), 377.

14. E.g., *Literature and Dogma,* in *Dissent and Dogma,* vol. 6 of *The Complete Prose Works of Matthew Arnold,* ed. R. H. Super (U. of Michigan Press, 1968), 219, 405-6.

15. This is an allusion to Ephesians 2:12, and, as Gordon Ray notes, the same biblical phrase forms the basis of a well-known passage in Newman's *Apologia* (see Thackeray, *Letters* 2:309 n. 80).

16. Jack P. Rawlins does quote this passage, and he comments on its intensity in *Thackeray's Novels: A Fiction That Is True* (U. of California Press, 1974), 31, but he doesn't believe that its sentiments are embodied in *Vanity Fair*: "We cannot seriously believe that behind Thackeray's curtain her [Amelia's] prayers are anything but vanity in a pious guise" (p. 32).

17. Preface, *Jane Eyre,* ed. Margaret Smith (Oxford U. Press, 1975), 4. Also relevant here are the comments on Thackeray's morality in the reviews of *Vanity Fair* by Robert Bell, *Fraser's Magazine* (Sept. 1848), rpt. Geoffrey Tillotson and Donald Hawes, eds., *Thackeray: The Critical Heritage* (London: Routledge, 1968), 62-67 and John Forster, *Examiner* 22 July 1848, rpt. Tillotson, 53-58. More comments by Charlotte Brontë can be found in her letters to W. S. Williams, rpt. Tillotson, 51-52.

18. "*Vanity Fair*: An Irony Against Heroes," *Critical Quarterly* 6 (1964): 14.

19. *The Exposure of Luxury: Radical Themes in Thackeray* (London: Peter Owen, 1972), 12.

20. M. M. Bakhtin, *Problems of Dostoevsky's Poetics,* ed. and trans. Caryl Emerson (U. of Minnesota Press, 1984), 39-40.

21. Dyson, "*Vanity Fair,*" 12.

22. *The Victorian Multiplot Novel: Studies in Dialogical Form* (Yale U. Press, 1980), 107, 109.

23. "Discourse in the Novel," *The Dialogical Imagination: Four Essays,* trans. Caryl Emerson and Michael Holquist (U. of Texas Press, 1981), 292.

24. It is not clear what this word means, or even whether or not it is a proper name. For a summary of scholarly conjecture on this topic, see James L. Crenshaw, "Ecclesiastes, Book of," *The Anchor Bible Dictionary,* ed. David Noel Freedman, et al., 6 vols. (New York: Doubleday, 1992), 2:271-72.

25. Crenshaw, "Ecclesiastes," 271, 273.

26. *The Great Code: The Bible and Literature* (Toronto: Academic Press, 1982), 123. The Jerusalem Bible translates the word "futility" and the New English Bible "emptiness." My own biblical quotations are of course from the King James Bible.

27. *Victorians and Mystery: Crises of Representation* (Cornell U. Press, 1990), 146.

28. Crenshaw, "Ecclesiastes," 271.

29. See C. Stephen Finley, "Bunyan Among the Victorians: Macaulay, Froude, Ruskin," *Literature and Theology* 3 (1989): 77-94 for an excellent discussion of the Victorian reception of Bunyan. Finley's analysis of J. A. Froude's view of Bunyan as the representative of a lost world of theological wholeness (pp. 78-79) accords with my sense of Thackeray's use of *Pilgrim's Progress.*

30. *The Pilgrim's Progress,* ed. Roger Sharrock (Harmondsworth: Penguin, 1965), 125.

31. For *Vanity Fair* as satire, see Mark H. Burch, "'The world is a looking-glass': *Vanity Fair* as Satire," *Genre* 15 (1982): 265-79.

32. Rawlins, *Thackeray's Novels,* 24. Rawlins sees *Vanity Fair* as an amalgam of several distinct genres, including satire.

33. Warhol, *Gendered Interventions,* 85.

34. Walter Allen, *The English Novel: A Short Critical History* (1954; Harmondsworth: Penguin, 1958), 176.

35. See, for example, *Literature and Dogma,* 173.

36. *Literature and Dogma,* 146.

37. The article on "world" in Karl Rahner and Herbert Vorgrimler, *Theological Dictionary,* trans. Richard Strachan (Freiburg: Herder, 1965), is the main source for my discussion of the theological significance this word.

38. The *OED* cites *Bleak House* under "world" 17a: "The world is before you; and it is most probable that as you enter it, so it will receive you."

39. The quotations from novels which illustrate the phrase "man of the world" in the *OED* make it clear that for Thackeray it would have more pejo-

rative implications than it does today: "This gentleman whom Mr. Jones now visited, was what they call a man of the world; that is to say, a man who directs his conduct in this world as one, who being fully persuaded there is no other, is resolved to make the most of this" (*Tom Jones*); "A true, fashionable, unprincipled man of the world" (Mme. D'Arblay, *Early Diary*).

40. Barry Qualls has studied these echoes, although he does not treat Thackeray at length in his study of secular pilgrims, arguing that for him there is no secular scripture or natural supernaturalism, merely parodic treatment of the world, with the echoes of the sacred language providing hints of the values implied by the older beliefs. See *Secular Pilgrims*, 6-7, 190-193.

41. Elizabeth Rigby, *Quarterly Review* (Dec. 1848), rpt. Tillotson, *Critical Heritage*, 81.

42. Bunyan, *Pilgrim's Progress*, 125.

43. Although his focus in reading *Vanity Fair* is very different from mine, Wolfgang Iser makes a similar point about the role of gaps or absences in the novel. He comments that "The reader is given only as much information as will keep him oriented and interested, but the narrator deliberately leaves open the inferences that are to be drawn from this information." *The Implied Reader: Patterns of Communication in Prose Fiction from Bunyan to Beckett* (Johns Hopkins U. Press, 1974), 106. I am grateful to Michael Lund for drawing my attention to this passage.

44. *The Lucid Veil: Poetic Truth in the Victorian Age* (London: Athlone, 1987).

45. Garrett, *Victorian Multiplot Novel*, 109.

46. These points are noted in Shillingsburg's edition of *Vanity Fair*; see also his useful discussion of them in "Reading the Boring Bits: The Crawley Genealogy," *Thackeray Newsletter* 38 (Nov. 1995): 5-10.

47. Introduction, *Vanity Fair: A Novel Without a Hero* (Harmondsworth: Penguin, 1968), 22.

48. Ronald F. Hock, "Lazarus and Dives," *The Anchor Bible Dictionary*, 267.

49. *Thackeray's Cultural Frame of Reference: Allusion in The Newcomes* (McGill-Queen's U. Press 1991), 5.

50. For a discussion of this aspect of Broad Church moral thinking, see A. O. J. Cockshut, *Anglican Attitudes: A Study of Victorian Religious Controversies,* (London: Collins, 1959), 64-65.

51. Introduction, *Vanity Fair: A Novel Without a Hero* (Oxford U. Press, 1983), xxix.

52. Cockshut, *Anglican Attitudes,* 64.

53. Harden, ed., *Letters,* 1: 228.

54. Among the many analyses of nineteenth-century liberal Protestant theology, Karl Barth's essay on Schleiermacher stands out. See "Schleiermacher," ch. 11 of *Protestant Theology in the Nineteenth Century: Its Background and History,* no trans. (London: SCM, 1972), 425-73. For discussions of ethnocentrism and racism in liberal theology, see Shmuel Almog, "The Racial Motif in Renan's Attitude to Jews and Judaism," *Antisemitism Through the Ages,* ed. Shmuel Almog, trans. Nathan H. Reisner (Oxford: Pergamon, 1988), 255-78; Alan T. Davies, "The Aryan Christ: A Motif in Christian Anti-Semitism," *Journal of Ecumenical Studies* 12 (1975): 569-79; Suzanne Heschel, "The Images of Judaism in Nineteenth-Century Christian New Testament Scholarship in Germany," *Jewish-Christian Encounters Over the Centuries: Symbiosis, Prejudice, Holocaust, Dialogue,* ed. Marvin Perry and Frederick Schweitzer (New York: Peter Lang, 1994), 215-40.

55. Baker, "*Vanity Fair* and the Celestial City," 95.

56. Research for this article was assisted by a Saint Mary's University Senate Research Grant. I would like to acknowledge the assistance of my father, Dr. J. R. C. Perkin, who gave me the benefit of his biblical scholarship when commenting on an early draft, and of the Revd. Dr. Paul Friesen, who pointed me in the right direction when I was beginning to investigate anti-Semitism and nineteenth-century theology. I was able to clarify several points as a result of the questions and discussion following my presentation of a version of the article to the Christianity and Literature Study Group at the ACCUTE conference, Memorial University, 1 June 1997.

Phyllis Susan Dee (essay date fall 1999)

SOURCE: Dee, Phyllis Susan. "Female Sexuality and Triangular Desire in *Vanity Fair* and *The Mill on the Floss.*" *Papers on Language and Literature* 35, no. 4 (fall 1999): 391-416.

[*In the following excerpt, Dee examines the question of Amelia Sedley's sexuality through an analysis of her relationships with George Osborne and William Dobbin.*]

In René Girard's structural paradigm of triangular desire, set forth in *Deceit, Desire, and the Novel*, female sexuality is an organizing theme. Girard's triangle is a metaphor for relations in which the mediator inspires the subject's desire for the object. Intense rivalry compounds the mediation as it augments the prestige of the idolized Other and strengthens the bond between mediator and subject, forcing the mediator to affirm his own right or desire of possession. The object of desire is, in effect, emptied of its concrete value and enclosed in an aura of metaphysical virtue. Reality is consumed by rivalry and, often, hatred (13-14, 83-85, 99). . . .

VANITY FAIR

Vanity Fair is a novel without a hero; happily, it has a heroine. Initially, the narrator equivocates: Amelia Sedley need not be described "as she is not a heroine" (5). When Becky Sharp is in disgrace, however, the narrator turns once again to Amelia, now a widow, living quietly in poverty: "So, never mind, whether she be a heroine or no," Amelia's gentle hand and ready smile are a consolation to her old father and a source of satisfaction to the narrator as well (648).

The narrator's ambivalence about heroic characters suggests that Amelia will be an imperfect heroine. In her analysis of female discursive strategies, Lisa Jadwin observes that "Amelia believes wholeheartedly in the totalizing myth of female inferiority" enforced by "submissive, self-abnegating behavior" (664). If gender is performative, however, as at least one feminist critic has claimed, Amelia's submissive, self-effacing behavior may conceal a more complex personality.[1] Girard's configuration of triangular desire eclipses the role of women, but in the course of the novel Amelia emerges from the shadow cast by the men who love, and hate, her.

The form of desire that Girard terms "triangular" is a hierarchical arrangement: Amelia is the object of desire in a triangle formed by herself, George Osborne, and Mr. Osborne. In the model, Mr. Osborne functions as the mediator of desire. A match between George and Amelia has long been assumed: Amelia "was bred from her childhood to think of nobody but him" (242), and George "has loved Amelia Sedley ever since they were children" (243). Thus, there appears to be a straight line between subject and object of desire. However, "the mediator is there, above the line, radiating toward both the subject and the object" (Girard 2). At present, the senior Osborne is glowering rather than radiating: he is angry over the impending ruin of Amelia's father, a stockbroker.

Although Osborne has ordered George to marry Amelia, he demands that his son terminate the relationship once her father's bankruptcy is confirmed. George, who has courted Amelia at the urging of his friend Dobbin, forming yet another triangle, responds to Osborne senior: "Who told me to love her? It was your doing. I might have chosen elsewhere . . . but I obeyed you" (227).

Osborne, who controls his son through the bonds of mediation and the careful doling out of allowance, is confident that his hold over George is secure. George, however, is the mediator of Dobbin's desire for Amelia and, as such, he asserts his superiority by moving closer to the object and openly declaring his passion and possession: "I'll marry her tomorrow," George declares. "I love her more every day, Dobbin" (228).

In obedience to his father, George discards Amelia. Dobbin, however, visits the neglected girl, whose anguish over the loss of her lover could represent an opportunity for this undeclared rival. According to Girard, the mediator shows his disciple the object and forbids him to obtain it (7). Not only is Dobbin forbidden to reveal his love for Amelia, he cannot desire what his mediator has devalued; so Dobbin comes away from Amelia's house "as if he [were] a criminal after seeing her" (195). If Dobbin feels like a criminal it is because he has betrayed his mediator through his undiminished love for an object George no longer desires. If Dobbin is to continue loving Amelia, George must re-invest her with value and desirability. George, however, is under the influence of his father's mediation as well.

In order not to let his idol topple, Dobbin must reunite George and Amelia, an action that will enhance George's prestige and Amelia's worth:

> Without knowing how, Captain Dobbin found himself the great promoter, arranger, and manager of the match between George Osborne and Amelia. But for him it never would have taken place . . . and having made up his mind completely that if Miss Sedley was balked of her husband she would die of the disappointment, he was determined to use all his best endeavors to keep her alive.
>
> (208)

Enjoying his role as mediator/idol, George is willing to be led by Dobbin.

When George weds Amelia, Osborne banishes and disinherits his son. As Osborne is no longer the mediator of desire, his devaluation of Amelia should count for nothing. However, it is virtually impossible to break the bonds of mediation, and George finds himself unable to desire Amelia without his father's mediation.

George finds a temporary mediator in Rawdon Crawley and is soon "carrying on a desperate flirtation with Mrs. Crawley" (314). At the Duchess's grand ball, George deposits Amelia on a bench: "While her appearance [is] an utter failure . . . Mrs. Rawdon Crawley's *debut* [is], on the contrary, very brilliant," and George's mind throbs with "triumph and excitement" as he plans to elope with his new love and abandon his old (318). George's admiration for Rawdon is genuine, as is always the case in triangular desire, and his passion for

Rawdon's wife is irresistible. George's capricious passions may seem outrageous: a newly wed husband about to abandon his bride for an accomplished flirt. The bonds of mediated desire, however, are only impulsive in that they rely on the whims of men. Caught in the hierarchy of desire, George must be both idol and idolater, husband and scamp.

* * *

There is an aggressive quality to Amelia's relations with men during her widowhood. Earlier in Amelia's life, only George and Dobbin were in love with her, and George not consistently. Now, every one of the men she encounters falls in love with her:

> Wherever she went she touched and charmed every one of the male sex, as invariably as she awakened the scorn and incredulity of her own sisterhood. I think it was her weakness which was her principle charm—a kind of sweet submission and softness, which seemed to appeal to each man she met for his sympathy and protection.
>
> (435)

What is this woman doing? She systematically presents an erotic "kind of sweet submission and softness" to men, but Amelia is "not brilliant, nor witty, nor wise overmuch, nor extraordinarily handsome" (435). In a social milieu where the subjugation of women is the norm, why is Amelia's representation of that role so provocative? This question is particularly vexing because Amelia's "soft submission" is not submission at all; she does not submit to any of these infatuated men.

Amelia's stimulating behavior falls into the category of coquetry. Girard has defined "coquetry" as a form of mediated sexual desire in which the beloved concurrently inflames and rejects the lover's desire. The coquette, who needs the desire of the lover in order to feel valued, does not merely feign indifference; she feels no desire. Were she to surrender herself, she could no longer regard herself as desirable. Thus, the coquette must continually provoke desire in a lover or lovers (Girard 105-06). Amelia, throughout her widowhood, has been explicit: she has no desire to marry. In fact, she has no desire at all. She is clearly indifferent to the desire her soft submission evokes in all of the men who come near her. Nonetheless, she continues to excite a passion that might otherwise alarm such a timid soul as Amelia, who does not regard herself as a siren.

As Girard explains, the lover's desire produces a second desire, which is fixed on the same object as the original desire (105). Amelia's desire is for herself, and it can only exist while she is the object of another's desire. Were her coquetry to cease, were she not to provoke desire, she could not regard herself as "precious," to use Girard's term. This affirmation of self-worth is essential to Amelia. As each man responds to her appeal for "sympathy and protection," Amelia moves closer to eradicating the memory of her honeymoon, when George precipitously withdrew his sympathy and protection, abandoning Amelia to "despair and remorse" (265).

* * *

In sexual desire, the beloved's desire is a desire for the self. The senior Osborne's desire is a narcissistic wish for self-affirmation through the prestige of his son:

> [George] should go into Parliament; he should cut a figure in the fashion and in the state. [Osborne's] blood boiled with honest British exultation as he saw the name of Osborne ennobled in the person of his son, and thought that he might be the progenitor of a glorious line of baronets.
>
> (220)

But his son thwarted that desire, first by marrying Amelia and then by dying. As Girard notes, "Only someone who prevents us from satisfying a desire which he himself has inspired in us is truly an object of hatred" (10-12). By his untimely death, George has prevented the senior Osborne from gratifying his ultimate desire. As the desiring subject hates the mediator who deprives him of his beloved object, Osborne hates his son for cheating him of the idealized son for whom he anticipated a distinguished career. Osborne is consumed with impotent rage.

Amelia, the passive object of desire in the triangular relations between Osborne and George, and between George and Dobbin, becomes the object of Osborne's stymied rage. He hates her: "It is she who has tumbled my hopes and all my pride down" (398). He punishes Amelia by refusing to acknowledge her as George's widow and, in effect, turning her out of his house.

Without Osborne's sanction, Amelia remains in a social and juridical limbo. For the Osbornes and polite society, she does not exist. Under the law, her claim to legitimacy is recognized; she and George were married in church. No law, however, compels Osborne to support or recognize the widow and her son Georgy. Amelia's status is that of a cast-off mistress, her future as secure as that of her broken and bankrupt father, who assumes responsibility for his unclaimed daughter.

As Sedgwick notes, all social institutions and bureaucracies are maintained by homosocial relations between men. The law that does not assist Amelia, the church that officiates at her wedding but has no further connection with her, and the military that welcomes her as George's wife are all examples of male-dominated institutionalized power relations that maintain and support gender inequality. It is not surprising, therefore, that only a man can rescue Amelia from social invisibility.

If Dobbin is responsible for Amelia's marriage to George, he is equally responsible for her rehabilitation. Shortly before Osborne's death, the old man agrees to a reconciliation. Dobbin and Georgy, two males, have mollified Osborne: "If she took your son away from you, she gave hers to you" (692). Amelia did not take George from his father, but she must make restitution for his loss.

For Dobbin, the triangular relation is still in force. His reverence for the memory of George continues to mediate his desire:

> Our honest friend had but one idea of a woman in his head . . . a gentle little woman in black . . . a soft young mother tending an infant and beckoning the Major up with a smile to look at him; a rosy-cheeked lass coming singing into the room in Russell Square, or hanging on George Osborne's arm, happy and loving.
>
> (489)

The images of Amelia as the youthful object of George's desire, as George's wife and then his widow, and as the mother of George's son haunt Dobbin's memory. If there is no unmediated Amelia, neither is there a position in Girard's model that does not strip the object of desire of an identity unmarked by masculine sexual desire: "object of desire" is never the subject position of authority or agency.

When Dobbin returns to England, his first impulse is to "take [Amelia] in his arms, and swear that he would never leave her. She must have *yielded*, she could not have but *obeyed* him" (662, italics mine). Dobbin has never applied the vocabulary of dominance-submission to his love for Amelia until now. Clearly, he is prepared to become the possessor of the object. (Does the object wish to be possessed?) According to Girard, when the distance between the subject and mediator is sufficient to eliminate any contact between the two, rivalry is nonexistent (9). Since distance is always a spiritual dimension in Girard's triangle, George's death represents the elimination of the rival but does not diminish the prestige of the mediator. Rather, as Dobbin's more aggressive language indicates, Amelia had become a real, accessible woman whom Dobbin can embrace, and command, in the absence of a forbidding rival.

Every female character who considers Amelia's feminine charms concludes that "she is but a lackadaisical creature, and . . . has no heart at all" (437). For Dobbin, however, Amelia's is the "image that filled our honest Major's mind by day and by night, and reigned over it always" (489). Girard finds that as the mediator draws nearer to the object of desire, passion becomes more intense and the object is emptied of its concrete value and invested with metaphysical virtue. The jealous rival becomes "less capable than ever of giving up the inaccessible object. . . . Other objects have no worth at all in the eyes of the envious person" (Girard 13-14, 85).

Dobbin's love for Amelia "remains fresh as a man's recollection of boyhood" (490). The narrator's comment is extremely acute. It is his youthful love for Amelia and her youthful image, as mediated by George, that compels Dobbin's imagination. Mediation does not recognize real distance or time and rarely encounters spontaneous desire. Only the rival's tenacity and despair are genuine.

Dobbin realizes he has invested Amelia with metaphysical virtues that she in fact does not possess. After fifteen years of devotion, he admits "I knew all along that the prize I had set my life on was not worth the winning" (763). Despite the erotics of Amelia's sweet submission, she has never aspired to greater wit or brilliance than she actually possesses. It is George and, in imitation of his idol, Dobbin himself who attribute to Amelia virtues she does not possess. If the prize was not worth the winning, who determined its value? If Dobbin has been "a fool, with fond fancies" (763), who has fueled these fancies? Not the little widow. Poor Amelia has a very limited repertoire of gender behaviors, which, admittedly, she exploits to the best of her ability. Her charms, however, are empirical rather than transcendent.

Critics have characterized Amelia as emasculating, "unworthy of the cult that Dobbin has built around her" (Herbert 93), and full of selfish vanity (Levine 140). However unworthy she may be, Amelia must be defended. Dobbin, who has carried Amelia's shawl since Vauxhall, is serving George as much as Amelia through his devotion, just as he was then.

If Dobbin loves the widow of his admired friend, Amelia is not compelled to love him in return. Had she overlooked or devalued that "beautiful and generous affection," or insulted that "constant and kind heart," her behavior would be indefensible (694). Had selfish vanity prevented her from feeling and expressing her gratitude to Dobbin, whose bounty "supported her in poverty" and who "gave her her husband and son," she would rival Becky Sharp's greedy vulgarity (694). Amelia, however, has been neither crass nor calculating.

It appears that Amelia has struggled not to love Dobbin better, but to love her freedom less. To enact sweet submission is one thing, to submit another: "A hundred times on the point of yielding, she [has] shrunk back from a sacrifice which she [feels is] too much for her" (760). The sacrifice she cannot make is not of her freedom per se, but of control over her own sexual destiny. She has not recovered from the earlier sexual rejection by her husband.

If Amelia is unworthy of Dobbin's adoration, which she is, the captain's slavish devotion robs her of any genuinely human characteristics. The dynamics of triangulation are expressed in terms that reify the object of desire much as Freud's vocabulary codifies female sexuality as passivity and lack rather than active, human desires ("Femininity" 359; *Three Essays* 61). In the mediation of desire, "the impulse toward the object is ultimately an impulse toward the mediator" (Girard 10). As the relation of subject to mediator intensifies, the object of desire remains passive, as does the woman in psychoanalytic theory, as do all women in relations of dominance-submission. In the relations between Osborne and George, and between George and Dobbin, Amelia is the passive receptor. Even Osborne's rage is directed at a passive Amelia.

At least since John Stuart Mill's 1869 *The Subjection of Women,* it has been a commonplace that women are required to marry despite their anticipated subjugation within marriage. Amelia is a perfect example. She has been bred to need a husband and to comply with the expectation of an institution that confines and silences women. Given the dictates of such a system, the preferred female is one who does not actively experience sexual desire but rather simply responds to the desire of others. Thus, Amelia represents the sexual norm. . . .

*   *   *

In defending any interpretive paradigm, it seems unwise to generalize about authorial intent. While Amelia is invariably the object of desire, I am reluctant to claim that Thackeray envisioned her as revising or resisting that role. Nonetheless, sufficient evidence in the text shows Amelia's evolution from submissive object of George's erratic desire to resistant object of Dobbin's marathon desire. In addition, Amelia's display of helplessness and submission is sexually provocative without sexual intent. I cannot claim, however, that Thackeray intended the young widow to be seen as a coquette.

Thackeray's version of triangular desire thwarts Amelia's desire for sexual autonomy and agency. Even when she chooses to preserve her sexual freedom (or freedom from the responsibility of sexuality), the young widow can only react to the actions of others. No matter how often Dobbin importunes her, she can only refuse him. She cannot dismiss or silence him; she cannot send him away. In a sense, she remains under siege. When Dobbin discovers that he is no longer under Amelia's thrall, he acts; he leaves. Amelia can only react to his departure. As a consequence of her inability to act, Amelia is perceived as parsimonious. There is a meanness in her refusal to share Dobbin's ennobling passion. While Dobbin is not diminished by his fruitless pursuit of the widow, Amelia is seen as quietly and selfishly emasculating.

In the economy of homosocial desire, an emasculating woman must be punished. Despite Girard's precept, Dobbin's metaphysical desire is suddenly replaced by disillusionment and he departs. Bereft of Dobbin's loving constancy, Amelia discovers the worth of her suitor. Although the lovers are reunited and wed, Amelia must pay for having assumed control of her sexual destiny, and her husband must be restored to his rightful place in masculine sexual hegemony, a place of power.

Now that Amelia has surrendered herself, she can no longer play the coquette, whose inability to desire fuels the desire of others. As Girard would have it, Amelia's pursuit of her fleeing lover has cost the heroine her sexual status as the desirable but unattainable woman of Dobbin's dreams. Thackeray goes even further; for Dobbin, Amelia has lost her value: "Although he never said a word to Amelia that was not kind and gentle," Dobbin has wed himself to an unremarkable woman he has ceased to love (784).

Dobbin's final act of the novel is to embrace not his wife but "his little Janey, of whom he is fonder than of anything in the world" (784). Critics, who have seen in this daughter a future temptress, an apprentice to Becky Sharp, have failed to observe that Janey will be yet another woman who does not deserve Dobbin's love (Dyer 218; Jadwin 679-80). In Thackeray's novel, woman as object of desire is unworthy of desire.

Note

1. See, for example, Judith Butler's *Gender Trouble,* 136.

Works Cited

Butler, Judith. *Gender Trouble: Feminism and the Subversion of Identity.* New York: Routledge, 1990.

Dyer, Gary R. "The 'Vanity Fair' of Nineteenth Century England: Commerce, Women, and the East in Ladies' Bazaar." *Nineteenth Century Literature* 46 (1991): 196-222.

Freud, Sigmund. "Femininity." 1932. *Freud on Women: A Reader.* Ed. Elisabeth Young-Bruehl. New York: Norton, 1990. 342-62

———. *Three Essays on the Theory of Sexuality.* 1905. Trans. James Strachey. New York: Basic, 1962.

Girard, René. *Deceit, Desire, and the Novel: Self and Other in Literature.* Trans. Yvonne Freccero. Baltimore: Johns Hopkins UP, 1965.

Herbert, Christopher. *Trollope and Comic Pleasure.* Chicago: U of Chicago P, 1987.

Jadwin, Lisa. "The Seductiveness of Female Duplicity in *Vanity Fair.*" *Studies in English Literature, 1500-1900* 32 (1992): 663-89.

Levine, George. *The Realistic Imagination: English Fiction from Frankenstein to Lady Chatterly.* Chicago: U of Chicago P, 1981.

Mill, John Stuart. *The Subjection of Women*. 1869. Arlington Heights, IL: Harlan, 1980.

Thackeray, William Makepeace. *Vanity Fair: A Novel Without a Hero*. 1847-48. New York: Random; Modern Library, n.d.

Mary Hammond (essay date autumn 2002)

SOURCE: Hammond, Mary. "Thackeray's Waterloo: History and War in *Vanity Fair*." *Literature and History* 3d series 11, no. 2 (autumn 2002): 19-38.

[*In the following essay, Hammond examines the relationship between* Vanity Fair's *historical context and Thackeray's attitude toward the social and moral issues of his day.*]

Ever since the appearance of the first instalment of William Makepeace Thackeray's **Vanity Fair** in January 1847, reviewers and critics have been troubled by the novel's confusing mixture of historical references. To what extent is it 'about' 1815, or the 1840s? Throughout the work the author foregrounds the relationship between history and its representation, but in so playful a fashion that he adds to, rather than solves, the problem. 'Our surprised story now finds itself for a moment among very famous events and personages, and hanging onto the skirts of history',[1] his narrator comments at the opening of Chapter XVIII as the narrative's chronology reaches Napoleon's escape from Elba. The playful placing of the 'surprised' story in 1815 here serves only to *dis*-place it; on one level the narrative becomes a sort of time-machine which, wandering arbitrarily and innocently between one period and another, is never actually rooted anywhere. But on another the adjective 'surprised' is rendered ironic by the long build-up to the battle provided by the illustrations and chapter headings that have so consistently referred to it. For the reader, the irony suggests that a story might—and frequently does—profess one motive while secretly enacting another, and that this particular story's profession of innocence of involvement in history had best be regarded with a certain amount of scepticism. The constant slippage in the novel between historical fact and narrative fancy, those 'little chapters' which 'seem to be nothing and yet affect all the rest of the history' (52), lies at the heart of the critical confusion and has frequently led to discussions of Thackeray's 'unreliability' as a storyteller. But is his narrative style evidence of nothing more than sloppy technique? Or should we try to read into the blending of periods some subtle commentary on his own?

Robert Bell, reviewing the novel for *Fraser's Magazine* in September 1848, recognised in it what he felt was both contemporaneity and universality, reading the history as allegory: 'The vices painted in this book lie about us as "thick as leaves in Vallambrosa". We tread amongst them every day of our lives . . . Alas! There will always be a *Vanity Fair* in this world, of which this crafty book will be recognised as the faithful image.'[2] A month previously, however, George Henry Lewes—clearly wanting to read the book as straightforwardly historical—had praised Thackeray's 'fine faculty for historical romance',[3] but taken him to task for what he saw as a lack of attention to historical accuracy which smacked of sheer carelessness:

> He becomes suddenly aware of the discrepancy between the costume of the period in which he has laid his scene and the costume in which he has depicted the characters in his pictorial illustrations. All he does on the discovery is to notify the fact in a note, and flippantly pretend that the real costume was too hideous for his purpose. He has been guilty, however, of the same confusion of periods throughout the work. Sometimes we are in the early part of the present century—at others we are palpably in 1848. Writing from month to month encourages such laches, but for the sake of such a reputation as Mr. Thackeray has now arrived at, it will be well that he should be more upon his guard.[4]

Earlier still, in 1848, Abraham Hayward had called the novel 'a plain old-fashioned love story' which draws on an earlier time when 'the war fever was at its height: Napoleon was regarded as an actual monster: [and] the belief that one Englishman could beat two Frenchmen, and ought to do it whenever he had an opportunity, was universal, (perhaps beneficially so, for "those can conquer who believe they can")'.[5] For Hayward, the pleasure of this text resides in what he sees as its invocation of a simpler, prouder, more youthfully confident Britain, a Britain with a passion and a purpose and a real monster to fight. For this reason, perhaps, Hayward chooses to overlook Thackeray's historical 'inaccuracies'; while noting that, in 1815 'tight integuments for the nether man were held indispensable . . . [and that] this fact . . . is forgotten in the woodcuts, Old Sedley, Mr Chopper, Rawdon Crawley & c. & c. being represented in trousers', he merely remarks on the fact as 'curious'.[6] The inconsistencies trouble Lewes far more. For him, Thackeray's handling of past and present, text and illustrations points to a 'cavalier impertinence of manner as if he were playing with his subject'.[7] Or, indeed, with his reader. For Lewes, this playful impertinence spoils the book, interrupting the necessary suspension of disbelief and trivialising a potentially serious subject.

Other critics have seen the interplay of relations between narrative and history in this novel as an exciting formal departure, or as evidence of contemporary social, political and economic anxieties. Charlotte Brontë famously saw in Thackeray's novel the mark of 'an intellect profounder and more unique than his contemporaries have yet recognised' and dubbed him 'the first social regenerator of the day'.[8] More recently, David Musselwhite has read the complex interplay between the concerns of the 1840s and the doubtful glories of a remembered past as autobiography. For him, Thackeray's own precarious financial, emotional and professional position is being enacted in the novel's timeframe:

> Thackeray postponed writing the Waterloo number twice and it is to be remarked how contorted the novel's time scheme becomes as Waterloo approaches . . . Caught between a doting mother and a child-bride, for months separated from his daughters and without a house, in desperate financial straits and yet ambitious to make his way in the world, Thackeray, too, came close to a breakdown. Came close, that is, to his Waterloo.[9]

As attractive as the metaphor might be and as correct as Musselwhite's central placing of the pivotal scene of Waterloo assuredly is, his reading here is not, in the end, all that helpful. It consigns to an individual authorial history the relationship between the novel's production context and its preoccupation with, and yet marginalization of, Waterloo. In this reading Thackeray becomes Napoleon, a man of plentiful ambition, motivation and talent, but one fatally lacking in (emotional) resources and support. The blurring of boundaries between national identities, victors and vanquished, and authors and texts certainly raises some interesting questions in the context of this 'Novel Without a Hero' which centres on the battle of Waterloo, and I will return to it. Somewhat uncharacteristically, though, Musselwhite glosses over it; while elsewhere he explores with real insight the part played by the social, political and economic conditions of the 1840s in the novel's collapsing of historical time, here he settles for the suggestion that the significance of Waterloo in the novel lies in what it can tell us about the author.

Joan Stevens has provided a rather more useful reading of the battle's significance in her seminal analysis of the contemporary context of the London skyline depicted in Thackeray's original frontispiece. According to Stevens, not only would readers have recognised the name of the author and associated him with the lively and insightful reviews in the *Morning Chronicle* and the irreverent articles and sketches of *Punch,* but 'everybody, almost, would know also the setting of the woodcut. Associated as it is with the title, *Vanity Fair,* it points to and identifies the world of the novel, locating it for contemporary readers as positively "here" and "now", in London, and in the 1840s'.[10] Stevens' argument hinges on her placing of the illustration (which depicts, among other things, statues of Nelson and the Duke of Wellington) in the context of contemporary public controversies around London's fondness for casting the nation's heroes in bronze. She is right to place it thus; *Punch* joined the controversy to an extent which

the majority of Londoners would have found it difficult (and Thackeray, as a regular *Punch* contributor, impossible) to ignore. Stevens somewhat underestimates the significance of this context, however, in assuming that because the running joke in Punch 'came to a climax in September 1846'[11] (i.e. when Thackeray was working on the first instalments of *Vanity Fair*), public interest in the controversy in particular and Waterloo in general were factors only in its initial stages. In fact, statue jokes—centred particular on Matthew Wyatt's 60-ton bronze Duke—continued several to an issue until the very end of 1847, to such an extent that *Punch* was finally forced to publish a public appeal to stem the flood:

> The Last Appeal. We beg our correspondents will send us no more jokes upon statues, such as 'statu quo', 'The Statue of Limitations', and the like enormities, which every leader of every newspaper now commits. Though we are Editors, we have our feelings as well as other men.[12]

What it is important to note here is that Thackeray's novel was surrounded, not just in its early stages but throughout most of its execution, by debates around the correct way to commemorate war heroes, in particular the 'Hero of Waterloo'. It might, then, be possible to suggest that Waterloo itself was a subject which, far from seeming historically distant to most of Thackeray's readers, may have occupied a conspicuous and important place in their sense of their own time. Seen in the light of this possibility, Thackeray's narrative and illustrations—so consistently drawing on Waterloo imagery—might provide more than a contextual clue for his readers or a setting for his story. The battle which Stevens rightly sees as 'the preoccupation, the hinge'[13] of the narrative might, in fact, serve a still more important if now somewhat arcane purpose in Thackeray's overall design.

It is my contention here that this is the case. I have found several recent critical approaches particularly helpful. Using Freud and Derrida to explicate the connection between memory/history and narrative, John Schad argues that the battle's narrative purpose as a kind of structuring absence is to highlight the cultural repression of the uncomfortable associations that the memory of Waterloo evoked after the Peterloo massacre of August 1819.[14] I want to build on this notion of a re-visioned, re-emergent history which reflects on the 1840s, though I will assume (or, more correctly *re*sume) a more contextual approach which will have a double focus. First I want to place *Vanity Fair* in the context both of its time and of other contemporary references to the Napoleonic Wars in the belief that this will help to illuminate Thackeray's own position within or against a particular, historically specific discourse of war writing. Second, I want to explore what the novel's relation to history might be able to suggest to us about the ways in which Britain may have re-imagined war and the past in this, a period of intense social and political unrest that would mark the end of a long period of relative peace. I will argue that the pivotal position occupied by the ever-present but narratively absent battle must be read against contemporary discursive practices which subtly integrated a revisioned memory of Waterloo with the vigorously imperialist but resolutely individual middle-class ambitions of the novel's present. Here I am indebted to John Peck's work on *Vanity Fair* as a critique of middle classness. Rather than seeing the Waterloo setting merely as a 'brilliant move' which 'enables Thackeray both to comment on the developing order of his own day and to show the coming into existence of this new social order',[15] though, I will suggest that it is a critique of the reshaping of the 'official' history of war which lies at the heart of Thackeray's satire of middle-class life.

How, then, did Charlotte Brontë come to see in the author of a book which, it is beginning to emerge, is 'about' the 1840s looking back on 1815, the 'first social regenerator of the day'? How can looking back on a nation's 'victorious past' energise—even rescue—the present?

The extent to which the 1840s were thought of as a 'present' in need of rescue and regeneration is indicated by the wistful tone of Hayward's enthusiastic review which saw in *Vanity Fair* a return to a glorious, romanticised British history. It is supported also by the types of novels that were achieving success at the time. Elizabeth Gaskell's *Mary Barton* (1848) enters the world of the working classes in order to show them as worthy, close-knit, clean and honourable. Gaskell was writing against prevailing middle-class wisdom which, formed through familiarity with the works of Chadwick, Mayhew and others, was accustomed to literary tours through the slums which combined horror, sympathy and a perverse kind of pleasure in approximately equal measures. Brave as it is, though, *Mary Barton* is only able to achieve narrative resolution by shipping the working classes off to a new life in a 'Little England' in Canada. Disraeli's *Coningsby* (1844) and *Sybil* (1845), both of which were reviewed by Thackeray for the *Morning Chronicle*,[16] also explicitly take as their theme the 'Condition of England' question, and answer it by placing hope in an aristocracy pure enough in blood to command instantaneous, instinctive loyalty, but rendered sympathetic by a sojourn amongst the poor whom it will ultimately lead to happiness. Disraeli's solution was not exactly new. As Thackeray put it:

> If we might venture to suppose that Disraeli had borrowed his ideas from anyone, we should say that the 'Hero Worship' of Mr. Carlyle had been carefully read by him. Young England, too, is pining, it appears, for the restoration of the heroic sentiment and the appearance of the heroic man.[17]

We know, then, that Thackeray was familiar both with the 'Condition of England' Question and with Carlyle's influential work of 1814, 'On Heroes, Hero-worship and the Heroic in History', and that, judging by this review, he probably viewed the idea of Hero-worship as social panacea with rather less enthusiasm than some of his contemporaries. In fact, as Robert P. Fletcher has shown, while Thackeray and Carlyle began an amicable acquaintanceship in the 1830s based on a shared 'understanding of the symbolic process—an understanding that led both to debunk worn-out icons'[18] by the 1840s their relationship was strained and at times quite vituperative. Thackeray was almost certainly addressing Carlyle's 'On Heroes' in his 1840 *Paris Sketch Book*,[19] but what we might also conjecture is that his 'Novel Without a Hero' was also intended in part as a form of reply to Carlylean philosophy. Fletcher has seen this possibility as evidence of Carlyle's 'search for the authority of history' while Thackeray, having grown 'more complacent about the proliferation of fictions and shams in Victorian society . . . surrenders . . . to the current rules of the game'.[20] However, this argument somewhat undermines Brontë's vision of Thackeray as a 'social regenerator'. The critical disagreement calls, I think, for a re-examination of the extent to which *Vanity Fair* engages—if at all—with contemporary problems and/or with contemporary debates about them.

The problems were many and varied. In Parliament, among the most widely debated issues were the repeal of the Corn Laws (1846) which marked the waning power of the landed gentry,[21] working-class conditions, the Chartist movement which threatened a rise in working class power, the Irish Question, the situation in Europe (and particularly France), and the passing of the Limited Enlistment Bill. This last revolutionised Britain's army, emphasising soldiering as a profession rather than a life sentence and going some way towards improving conditions in the ranks. *The Times* stressed both the extents to which these improvements mattered in Britain at the time, and the ways in which public opinion about war was changing:

> The interest which was felt in the improvement of the army question may be supposed to be nearly universal throughout the country . . . So long as war exists, or the chance of war, that is as long as human nature continues to be what it is, so long will it be necessary for a great country to keep on foot a standing army. To this idea, once most unpopular and once unconstitutional, Englishmen have at last reconciled themselves. They look upon it as an evil, but an indispensable evil . . . The mighty empire of India and the undeveloped treasure of Australia would be deemed worth retaining by men who despised the glories of Waterloo or grew pale at the bloodshed of Badajoz.[22]

Here the troubled present looks to history as a way of combining imperial (financial) and military goals in a manner which might appeal both to a dispossessed aristocracy and to a threatened bourgeoisie. Through the grimly businesslike tone the battle of Waterloo becomes a model for the protection of Britain's imperial interests. If one can't join in the traditional reverence for Waterloo, *The Times* seems to suggest, one must at least admire and support the army which cut its teeth there, the same army which now safeguards one's interests abroad.

The effect of foreign relations upon the finances of individual speculators is a constant source of anxiety throughout the nineteenth century, and with good reason. During the build-up to the battle of Waterloo itself, *The Times* had reported that news of the rebellion was first received in London through the *Moniteur* of 11 March, and that speculation about its genuineness was already, five days later, being reflected in the touchiness of the stock exchange:

> The Funds, in some degree [have] recovered their former depression. They are, however, still in a state of uncertain vacillation, liable to be easily influenced by slight rumours, but not yet likely to rise or sink very much until advice of more decisive operations is received.[23]

The army and the middle classes had frequently, therefore, been involved in a peculiarly ambivalent relationship: while good defence is imperative for an empire, wars—still conducted in this period largely by the aristocracy—can be bad for business. Some kind of screen through which imperialist manoeuvres might be read as grim necessities—such as *The Times* provides above—is therefore crucial. When patriotic appeal fails, money talks. What is most interesting in this period is how the two are often invoked together, and how often they are thought of as inseparable. Both Thackeray and Dickens use middle-class financial ruin as plot devices in serialised novels which appear in the mid-forties, just as financial anxiety and instability are at their height, and both make the most of the ironic opportunities thus presented. For Dickens, the public shame and social ruin associated with Paul Dombey's bankruptcy is out of all proportion to the 'crime' in a world that is filled with cheats in currency of every description, including patriotism:

> It was an innocently credulous and a much ill-used world. It was a world in which there was no other sort of bankruptcy whatever. There were no conspicuous people in it, trading far and wide on rotten banks of religion, patriotism, virtue, honour. There was no amount worth mentioning of mere paper in circulation, on which anybody lived pretty handsomely, promising to pay great sums of goodness with no effects. There were no shortcomings anywhere, in anything but money. The world was very angry indeed; and the people especially, who, in a worse world, might have been supposed to be bankrupt traders themselves in shows and pretences, were observed to be mightily indignant.[24]

For Thackeray's John Sedley, financial ruin is a direct result of international scheming to destroy Britain—his own downfall cannot be imagined separately from the larger threat to his country:

> I say that the escape of Boney from Elba was a damned imposition and a plot, Sir, in which half the powers of Europe were concerned, to bring the funds down, and to ruin this country. That's why I'm here, William. That's why my name's in the Gazette. Why, Sir?— because I trusted the Emperor of Russia and the Prince Regent.

> (201)

The relationships between winners and losers, nations and individuals and morality and profit are crucial to the works of both writers, and in **Vanity Fair,** despite (or perhaps because of) its Napoleonic setting, they say as much about the 1840s as 1815, as I will demonstrate. My point here, however, is that it is becoming possible to see how Britain's military past is being generally used in this period as a form of social cement. Working-class conditions, middle-class anxieties and foreign unrest loom large on the political agenda, and their address within the army is an appeal both to the agitators and to the ranks above them to unify in the memory of a glorious past and the promise of a fair, peaceful, but above all well-defended imperial future. This return to the past could, as Hayward put it, only be beneficial, for 'those can conquer who believe they can.'

The Wellington Statue controversy and the re-shuffling of the army were not the only Napoleonic issues in the public's eye at this time. A further indication of the high profile accorded to the Wars during this period is provided by the news of the proposed presentation of a medal to all British survivors of the Peninsular wars. Created on June 1, 1847 at the personal request of the Duke of Wellington, news of the medal prompted even the normally conservative *Illustrated London News* (which, incidentally, was firmly on the side of the Duke in the great statue debate) to exclaim:

> Forty-one years from the date of the first land battle— that of Maida, fought in 1806—and fifty-three from the first naval engagement—Howe's victory over the French fleet—comes the mark of honour to those engaged in them! What a weary heart-sickening interval! . . . What a contrast to the more generous policy of those we fought against! Napoleon distributed the Cross of the Legion of Honour almost on the field of battle . . . [Furthermore] every [British] man and officer engaged in the last conflict of the war [Waterloo] received a medal without exception [on 10 March, 1816], though some of the regiments and many of the officers saw service for the first time . . . As in many other things, it is not till public opinion was strongly expressed on the subject that the Duke and the Government have given way.[25]

While the *Illustrated London News* suggests in the same article that 'the spirit of the time has gone; we are in the midst of other days; and, though these triumphs are not forgotten, it is not underrating them to say they are less thought of than of yore', its emphasis on the strength of 'public opinion' indicates that the 'spirit of the time', far from being 'gone', was actually proving in some way important to uphold.

Five years earlier, enthusiasm for Napoleonic history and patriotism over the memory of Waterloo was certainly fresh for at least one contemporary middle-class tourist. In August-September 1841, an anonymous Scotsman took a trip through the battlefield, and a year later he published his impressions, a copy of which he respectfully presented to the Duke himself. These are worth quoting at length:

> I cannot describe my feelings, neither before, during, nor after this visit. I had longed, almost from the day of the battle, to visit that hallowed spot! Hallowed it must forever be in the hearts of all true Britons! I had desired to see the field on which the immortal Wellington had won the freedom and peace of Europe—I had longed to tread on the very earth where our gallant army, our Scots Greys and Forty-Second, and Life Guards conquered, and where so many of them died for their country. I had wished above everything to see the chateau of Hougoumont, the glorious defence of which had saved Europe; and which, I understood, remained in all its honourable dilapidation, just as it was left after the dreadful fray . . . Every stone, and tree, and house, as we approached, that bore the imprint of age, was to me an object of veneration and regard, as having seen all these scenes of surpassing interest . . . but here I must notice the strange sort of breathless haste with which we set out and proceeded along. I did not observe the fact, until I felt myself perfectly overcome, and was obliged to stop. This, I suppose, is quite natural, and I believe no Briton ever approaches the field in a perfectly cool and collected state. *A person feels as if he were pushing forward to fight the battle over again.*[26]

(emphasis mine)

This traveller with a compulsion to revisit and even repeat the past was not a lone fanatic. Thackeray himself refers to a sight-seeing tour through the battlefield, using it in *Vanity Fair* to suggest the levelling action of war on social pretensions as well as national allegiances, and the exposure of the inevitable reduction of both to self-interest:

> When the present writer went to survey with eagle glance the field of Waterloo, we asked the conductor of the diligence, a portly warlike-looking veteran, whether he had been at the battle. 'Pas si bete'—such an answer and sentiment as no Frenchman would own to—was his reply. But on the other hand, the postilion who drove us was a Viscount, a son of some bankrupt Imperial General, who accepted a pennyworth of beer on the road. The moral is surely a good one.

(272)

Here Thackeray subtly blends victors and vanquished in a theme that is to recur throughout the novel; his narrator professes to be solidly English, but surveys the battlefield with an 'eagle glance', that symbol of Imperial France. His comic linking of memory and its commodification, however, is not mere invention; the anonymous Scotsman indicates that battlefield tourists were numerous enough to sustain quite a lucrative business:

> And now let me say a word regarding the swindling and cheating that is carried on here, by everyone who can, by hook or by crook, lay their hands on a stranger. All the fine feelings in which a person would wish to indulge, are dispelled, by the swindlers who have congregated to this locality, to rob the unwary . . . Even our guide, John Pirson, partaking of the spirit of extortion which seems to pervade every person here, could not be satisfied. We had bought a sketch of the battle, by General Muffling, from him, and a cannon ball, also a veritable button, found on the field, with the Imperial Eagle, and inscribed 'Garde d'Honneur' . . . but still he . . . tried me more than once after all this, with pieces of bombshell and other trifles, which he carried in his pockets.[27]

There is no sense of irony here, not even a tacit awareness either of the absurdity of condoning the purchase of souvenirs at the same time as he condemns their sale, or of the significance of his choice of one souvenir over another. Obviously, though, for this particular traveller it is the mark of authenticity that matters: the sketch is signed, the button bears a legend. Waterloo is something fixable, finite (and under those terms, commodifiable); a shrine which all true Britons ought to visit and mark with an authenticated purchase, but only time has the right to erase. The irritation with which he reports on the exploitation of tourists is matched only by the near-reverence with which he reflects on the battle: 'Such mockery as this absolutely turns the dread seriousness with which the Field of Waterloo is viewed into ridicule—if that can possibly be done.'[28]

It is unlikely, of course, that such breathless awe was universal. But a certain amount of reverence and patriotism around the memory of the battle which crystallised in its commodification was quite widespread: five years later *Punch* bears out the extent to which Napoleonic history and memorabilia are still popular:

> Bonaparte Mania . . . Fifty pounds were asked or offered—we don't remember which—for the shell of the identical egg NAPOLEON was eating when a shell of another description fell into the egg-cup, and he exclaimed, 'Ha, ha! that is a good sign; the yolk is broken, and thus will we break the yoke of oppression'.[29]

A week later it comments with equal flippancy on the Peninsular Medal, carrying a cartoon which continues the theme of the material quantification of history in the shape of an 'Old Peninsular Man' greeting a prize pig with the words 'Hello! My boy, you've got your medal, I see.' The pig replies 'Yes! Yes! When do you get yours?' At which the veteran merely shakes his head.[30]

The creation of the medal at this particular moment is significant. Not only does it serve to indicate how much the wars of 30-40 years before were still (or back) in the public imagination, but it might suggest that they were being kept there for a purpose. We could read this several ways. The creation of the medal might be a reminder of former victories over an old enemy which would hearten a disillusioned Britain anxious about foreign affairs, particularly in France. It might be a means of maintaining the resurgent popularity of the Duke which had declined considerably during the 1820s and 1830s (particularly after Peterloo).[31] Or it might be an attempt to narrow the gap between officers and men in response to class pressures, part of what Eric Hobsbawm has described as a 'concentrated effort' on the part of the middle classes in this period 'to give themselves confidence and pride in their historic task' by reshaping 'the institutions of Britain in a manner suitable to industrial capitalism'.[32] Probably all these possibilities were in play. However we read it, though, the minor controversies over the medal and the Duke's statue, coupled with the major one over the radical changes to the army, meant that the worlds of 1815 and 1847-48 were in constant public dialogue throughout the composition and publication of *Vanity Fair,* and that discourses around Waterloo were therefore an integral part of the effort to understand, as well as to re-shape, the 1840s.

* * *

David Musselwhite has pointed out that as a journalist who covered the last great meeting of the Chartists and as the son of a woman living in Paris who sent him regular reports of the fighting, Thackeray was 'a peculiarly privileged witness of what was happening in England and France in 1848'.[33] But he was also, significantly, an experienced professional who was by no means new to the task of representing, pictorially and in words, the world of 1815 for an 1840s audience. In December 1840 he had been present when the body of Napoleon was brought with great pomp and solemnity from St. Helena to Paris to be re-buried at Les Invalides. He wrote up the occasion in *The Second Funeral of Napoleon,* calling it 'humbug' and 'French braggadocio' from beginning to end. He mocked the French official rhetoric that glorified the scars borne by its heroes, pointing out that 'it is a known fact that cannon-balls make wounds and not cicatrices'.[34] He mocked the Anglo-French spirit of co-operation when 'men get a character for patriotism in France merely by hating England'.[35] He mocked the absurd scenes of emotion amongst fake marble statues, pointing out that 'one may respect the dead without feeling awe-struck at the plumes of the hearse'.[36] When *The Times* objected to his flippancy and conceit, he replied in an article in *Fraser's:*

O you thundering old Times! Napoleon's funeral was a humbug, and your constant reader said so. The people engaged in it were humbugs, and this your Michael Angelo [one of Thackeray's many pen-names] hinted at. There may be irreverence in this, and the process of humbug-hunting may end rather awkwardly for some people. But surely there is no conceit. The shamming of modesty is the most pert conceit of all, the *precieuse* affectation of deference where you don't feel it, the sneaking acquiescence in lies.[37]

If there is evidence here of the ironic treatment of public hysteria over its heroes which was to achieve fruition in *Vanity Fair,* there is evidence also of the confidence of Thackeray's commentary on issues of Napoleonic history. He knew sham when he saw it; his commentary throughout *The Second Funeral* is informed as well as satirical. In fact, we know that he studied the Napoleonic Wars both while a student at Cambridge,[38] and later out of continuing personal interest.[39] We know also that when contemplating the writing of the Waterloo sequence in *Vanity Fair,* he wrote to a friend to request a copy of the newly-released *The Story of the Battle of Waterloo* by George Robert Gleig[40] and that he read it, since a reference to it appears in one of his footnotes to the first serialised edition.[41] Given his background knowledge, then, and the evidence that he did some fairly careful research, how do we explain the historical 'inaccuracies' and the mixing of periods which drew the notice of several contemporary critics and infuriated at least one of them?

Significantly, alongside *Vanity Fair* Thackeray was also writing 'Novels by Eminent Hands, or *Punch's* Prize Novelists,' a series of ten three-part parodies of some of the most successful novels of the day. Among these is 'Phil Fogarty—A Tale of the Fighting Onety-Oneth By Harry Rollicker' which, commencing on Saturday 7 August 1847, is a send-up of a then hugely popular Napoleonic tale written by Charles Lever. Thackeray's version not only plays on a familiar connection and turns the French into Irishmen (one of the major villains being one Marquis de Mahony), thereby collapsing a current issue into a historical narrative, but his illustrations faithfully represent them wearing breeches, that very garment which Hayward noticed was lacking from the illustrations in *Vanity Fair.* Phil Fogarty and his comrades, however, are depicted wearing trousers, a device that serves to foreground the comic collapsing of eras and enemies. These are clearly meant to be contemporary characters revisiting the past in imperial France as a way of combating the problems of the present in Ireland. In this piece, Fogarty and his retinue are simultaneously those ostensibly 'present' and those forever safely removed, for whom the war is one glorious, boyish, morale-boosting adventure. The stilted posturings of the French/Irish enemy officers, the false camaraderie and exaggerated bravery of the British, and the utter incredibility of the meetings between our hero and all the famous names of the day from Madame de Stael to Napoleon himself, turns **'Phil Fogarty'** into a farce explicitly about the glorification of past wars for the purposes of present expediency.[42]

The mixture in *Vanity Fair* is more subtle than this, but it utilises many of the same devices and even, at times, the same jokes. On meeting Becky and Rawdon's party in Brussels Mrs O'Dowd fancies she sees a likeness to her brother 'Molloy Malony' in the earl of Uxbridge (281) and shortly afterwards refers to Wellington's familial relations with the Malonies (282). For the contemporary reader this strengthens Thackeray's theme of an ironic mixing of heroes and villains, past and present. As John Peck has suggested, the fact that the irony either confused or irritated contemporary critics can be attributed to the specificity and originality of this critique: 'most novelists at the time presented their audience with an ultimately flattering reflection of itself; Thackeray does not.'[43] We must, I think, at least begin to suspect that Thackeray's 'cavalier impertinence with his subject' is as deliberate in the novel as it is in **'Phil Fogarty,'** and that it too centres on a subtle critique of discursive practices around the remembrance of war at times of national crisis.

* * *

For Richard Cobden, whose works were widely disseminated via parliamentary speeches, newspapers and pamphlets from the 1830s to the 1860s and with whose work it is therefore highly likely that Thackeray and a large part of his readership were familiar, peace is not merely the absence of war, but a complex preparation for it. While ultimately, as Daniel Pick has pointed out, Cobden 'recoils from' his own intimation that 'war might have become structural, built into the system, intrinsic to modernity,'[44] throughout his writings he is loud in his condemnation of the aristocracy's romanticization of war which leads to the 'erecting of monuments of warriors, the myriad memorials of battles in the names of bridges and streets' and is evidence of what he calls 'this bellicose national character.'[45] For Thackeray, however, the middle classes, not the aristocracy, are the real root of this bellicosity in the 1840s. While for Cobden 'war is never desired by 'the people', but only by politicians and military men whose ambition and cupidity are fired by prospects of advancement and profit,'[46] for Thackeray some at least of 'the people' are willing to share those prospects and imagine warfare in terms which will safeguard them. While lampooning the aristocracy in the characters of the Crawley family, bearers of one of the 'most respected of the names beginning in C, which the Court-Guide contained' whose current head is nonetheless taken by Becky for a servant (65-69), Thackeray's narrative rejects the 'genteel rose-water style' (50) of the popular courtly romance and concerns itself explicitly with pre-

serving a 'middle course modestly amidst those scenes and personages with which we are most familiar' (52). Thackeray is writing for, about, and against the middle classes of which he is a part and whose culpability in matters politic both domestic and foreign is, he suggests, profound. Writing against a background of middle-class displacement of the aristocracy in areas of social power, articulating a Cobdenite notion of peace as war-preparation, Thackeray goes beyond Cobden in his invocation of a new ruling class for whom the romanticization of war disguises motives which are, in essence, largely fiscal. 'Vanity Fair' as a concept sits at the crossroads between war and commerce; *Vanity Fair* as a novel articulates and illuminates this position by placing the battle centrally yet, as Patricia Marks puts it, resisting 'the rhetoric of romantic ideology' in favour of 'the language of commerce'.[47]

Thackeray explicitly posits an economic model of social relations. Almost all 'good' qualities in the novel are commodified; such heroism as there is resides in ultimate self-interest: 'if this is a novel without a hero, let us at least lay claim to a heroine. No man in the British army which has marched away, not the great duke himself, could be more cool or collected in the presence of doubts and difficulties than the indomitable little aide-de-camp's wife' (299) the narrator enthuses. His enthusiasm, however, is not for Becky's bravery but for her avarice; the remark comes in response to her calculating assessment of her financial position as Rawdon marches away to battle. Old Sedley too walks around wearing his wealth, 'rattling his seals like a true British merchant' (19), and laughs uproariously at Becky Sharp's attempts to snare his son, for 'he was a coarse man from the Stock Exchange where they love all sorts of practical jokes' (23). This particular joke backfires: Becky ends up with Jos and Old Sedley loses everything in the war. But the connection and the joke centre here on Becky and Sedley's recognition of one another. Just like the old man, just like the Napoleon she has so often been equated with, Becky is a speculator, staking all on the best prospect that presents itself.

She loses so consistently, of course, that a real tension arises between the expectations which the narrative raises around its clever, selfish, lively, perspicacious heroine and its constant denial of her reward. David Cecil has seen in this tension a flaw, a compromising of the novel's consistency:

> Becky, if she is to provide an ironical contrast to Amelia, ought to be treated with perfect justice. We should feel her, bad as she is, to possess some virtues denied to Amelia. And so she does, as her character was originally conceived. But Thackeray has not had the nerve to carry out his original conception. He seems to fear that he will make us like her so much that we forgive her faults. And thus, in order to restore a moral balance, he endows her with bad qualities foreign to her

nature. Fear, conscious or unconscious, of public opinion, has made him run a flaw through his most striking character, and in doing so destroy the consistency of his most brilliantly conceived book.[48]

But Becky has been designed, not just as an 'ironical contrast' to Amelia, but as a means of illuminating the hypocritical world of the other characters, the majority of whom share her faults but—significantly—seldom her failures. Only old Seldon and Napoleon fail as spectacularly—and fittingly, given their frequent linking with her in the text as the novel's other great speculators. The novel's narrative 'inconsistency' as described and criticised by David Cecil certainly flouts accepted novelistic conventions (balance, contrast, closure, particularly through socially beneficial marriage), but this inconsistency is integral to its design, for like its title it stands in a metonymic relation to the system it is designed to parody. Becky's 'flaw'—her consistent badness—is the necessary thorn in the reader's side, designed to prod to life and maintain an awareness of the king-pin of Thackeray's social critique. We are deliberately prevented from liking her wholeheartedly by the novel's perverse encouragement to like the characters—Miss Jemima, Rawdon, Little Rawdie—whom she will mis-use, but we are left nonetheless with a lingering sense of dissatisfaction and disappointment at the book's end. After all, Becky is our main protagonist and she did everything *right,* everything she could, everything the other characters do to succeed—and yet she fails. Conventional happy-ending narrative closure is permitted only to Dobbin and Amelia, those worthy but uninteresting characters whom even Thackeray felt deserved each other and whose emotional reunion is represented with a certain sense of tedium, if not of scorn: 'She was murmuring something about—forgive—dear William—dear dear, dearest friend—kiss, kiss, kiss, and so forth—and in fact went on under the cloak in an absurd manner' (683). Becky's thorough badness—the villainy in her heroism or, perhaps more precisely in the context of this satire on the worship of greed, the heroism in her villainy—renders impossible either a conventionally 'good' or a conventionally 'bad' ending for her. The final illustration shows her serving wares at a charity stall with the caption 'Virtue Rewarded. A booth in Vanity Fair'; she performs 'goodness', she is wealthy and calls herself Lady Crawley, but she has no position in society and she is snubbed both by Amelia her oldest friend, and by her own son (688-89). There is no moralising here; Becky is not being punished for being 'bad', because the novel refuses to allow us to celebrate uncomplicatedly the happiness of the characters who are 'good'. The terms are quite simply and effectively destabilized in order to carry out their author's satirical design, which centres firmly on a questioning of the self-protective middle-class conventions which determine their meaning.

The positing of morality and class as performance through the notion of deception is crucial here. *Vanity Fair* famously announces itself as a text about performance, from the moment of the author's introduction, which takes the form of an overture complete with rising curtain and a sketch of the players in clown's costume. It is precisely because she is the daughter of an artist accustomed to selling representation and an opera girl accustomed to performance that Becky is rejected by the Miss Pinkertons, the Lady Janes and the Miss Crawleys; the latter is actually ready to forgive Becky's financially-motivated elopement with Rawdon until she learns her ancestry (168). Becky's flattery and falsehoods are intolerable precisely because they are in danger of professionalizing—and therefore exposing to the world—the performances by which other women secure their futures. Intolerable, too, is her genuine Frenchness. Not the gentile Frenchness of the aristocracy, but the common, dangerous Frenchness which threatens middle England, 'enthroning Napoleon at home linguistically'[49] as Patricia Marks has expressed it, it both exposes the pretensions of Miss Pinkerton (who does not know the difference (7), and shocks Amelia (who does (10)). Becky is precisely the wrong mixture of performance and genuineness and self-interest. Her presence as failure in the novel draws overt attention to the absurd arbitrariness of the conventions which determine when the mixture is 'right': 'it was only from her French being so good, that you could know she was not a born woman of fashion' (289).

Not just a Napoleon invading society, Becky is the heart of that society's hypocrisy writ large in the language of commerce. After her greatest defeat, the revelation of her dalliance with Lord Steyne, Becky reflects that 'all her lies and her schemes, all her selfishness and her wiles, all her wit and genius had come to this bankruptcy' (535). The 'bankruptcy' referred to here is at once financial, social and moral. Money and social standing are inseparable as currency, but the characters depend above all upon the sustaining of performance as reality if they are not to go into liquidation. An example of this is Chapter XXXVI, 'How to Live Well on Nothing a Year' in which Becky and Rawdon 'are' wealthy until their performance of wealth is brought to an end by Rawdon's exposure of Becky's performances as both wife and mistress. In this text, 'commerce' depends for its value as much upon a codified belief system as upon hard currency.

Nowhere, though, is the deliberate exposure of the connection between self-interest and performance made more explicit than in the pivotal Waterloo scene that brings together nations and individuals in a mad scramble for profit masquerading as duty. Suvendrini Perera suggests that:

> this imperial history recalls not only the triumphs of the glorious past but, equally, imperial defeats: the

failed Napoleonic ambitions of the novel's present, as well as the competing imperial aspirations of 1848. The historical stage of *Vanity Fair* encompasses Plassey as well as Waterloo, Clive and the old campaigner Wellington . . . as well as various Bonapartes.[50]

The imperial sub-text of the battle of Waterloo certainly pervades this text, not only in the battle's ramifications for the aspirations of the characters (the ruin of Old Sedley, the death of George which enables the return to wealth of his son), but in the battle's constant appearance for contemporary readers coupled with Becky's fluctuating fortunes in her bid for social domination. Waterloo for her is an opportunity to make important social connections and a fast profit, nothing more nor less. The intimate connection between war and profit is made manifest in her. Chapter titles such as Chapter LIV, 'Sunday After the Battle' and Chapter XXVIII, 'In Which Amelia Invades the Low Countries' make the connection between war and social advancement explicit, permeating scenes both before and after the battle proper. Thackeray's initial vignettes continue to emphasise the link, depicting in one instance a clown bowing before Napoleon (Chapter XVIII, 177) and in another the figure of Becky dressed as Napoleon and gazing covetously at England (Chapter LXIV, 637), while the text equates her with Wellington (299). The relationship between Becky's casting as a villain by the illustrations and the other characters, and her casting as hero(ine) by the narrator de-stabilizes these terms as comprehensively as Thackeray has destablized notions of 'good' and 'bad'. The battle becomes a symbol for the material hopes of characters who are all both heroes *and* villains. Conventional notions of morality dissipate. National identity blurs. Individuals stand in for nations. The battle is the locus for the performance of imperial self-interest as national pride. Here, at last, is the Fairground itself.

The battle of Waterloo is also, however, implicit in the text as 'history', a site for imaginative re-visiting in times of national crisis. War represents value for money; one ticket provides unlimited re-entry. The incisive commentary on current issues that Thackeray's readers were likely to have recognised in **'Phil Fogarty'** is less overt, but it is there nonetheless. In an ironic aside which draws on the anxieties about imperialism and competition which abounded in the 1840s, the presence of the British becomes a boon for Belgian tradesmen: 'It was a blessing for a commerce-loving country to be overrun by such an army of customers; and to have such creditable warriors to feed' (272). Ironic, too, is the reference to the current fashion for the literal redrawing of this history, and for the displays of military strength which were familiar to all Londoners in the 1840s: 'As our painters are bent on military subjects just now, I throw out this as a good subject for the pencil, to illustrate the principal of an honest English war.

All looked as brilliant, and harmless as a Hyde Park review' (273). Wellington and Napoleon are linked in an image of nations united through faith in a hero, and this must surely have resonated for a contemporary audience with Carlylean philosophy and almost a decade of Wellingtonian political posturing: 'Everybody had such a perfect feeling of confidence in the leader (for the resolute faith which the Duke of Wellington had inspired in the whole English nation was as intense, as that more frantic enthusiasm with which at one time the French regarded Napoleon)' (273).

Thus, before the contemporary reader's eye, is the history of 1815 re-written from the 'present' of the 1840s. When Thackeray invites us to 'lay down the History-book, and to speculate upon what *might* have happened in the world, but for the fatal occurrence of what actually did take place (a most puzzling, amusing, ingenious, and profitable kind of meditation)' (277), he locks the reader into an uncomfortable semantic grip between documented 'fact' and 'profitable speculation'. There is the 'History-book' on one side, under pressure from its constant ironic undermining by Thackeray's own current—and unreliable—'history book' and his mock-authoritative tone. On the other is 'speculation', under pressure from its links with an unstable economy and its flavour in this text of individual self-interest. Nations are reduced to the level of greedy individuals, war rationale is exposed as mythical, Napoleon and Wellington, already linked on p. 273, appear as objects of veneration or hatred, as heroes or villains, only depending on one's point of view:

> The august jobbers assembled at Vienna, and carving out the kingdoms of Europe according to their wisdom, had such causes of quarrel among themselves as might have set the armies which had overcome Napoleon to fight against each other, but for the return of the object of unanimous hatred and fear.
>
> (277)

Above all, though, the importance of historical narrative is stressed:

> Could the Corsican but have waited in his prison until all these parties were by the ears, he might have returned and reigned unmolested. But what would have become of our story and all our friends, then? If all the drops in it were dried up, what would become of the sea?
>
> (277)

Here, Thackeray makes explicit the link between historical narrative and the individuals who not only comprise it, but actively make it what it is. The stress is on narrative (the 'sea', that which is fluid, ever-changing), not on fact. At this moment the reader is released from the grip of history book versus speculation by the realisation that they are actually one and the same. Like

Becky, they realise that history is conveniently malleable and recyclable and that makes it potentially profitable: 'Who can tell you the real truth of the matter? At all events if Rebecca was not beginning the world: she was beginning it over again' (15).

Waterloo, then, is in this text that which is re-remembered, re-written, and above all re- (and mis-) represented. It is significant that the only character who brags about his deeds during the battle and to whom the word 'Waterloo' is forever attached (573) is Jos Sedley, who spent most of it trying to get away and is in consequence the novel's most unreliable witness as well as its most eloquent authority on the subject. At a deeper level, of course, the novel itself is an unreliable witness. Filled with references to the battle, hinging and relying on it, knowing all about it, it is nonetheless never actually 'there' at all. When Thackeray ducks, the reader must duck also. The action upon which everything turns remains, therefore, absent, off-stage, a mere legend which is open to all sorts of interpretations, as many and varied as his readers. Ultimately, Thackeray makes his readers write the battle for themselves, inviting them to join in a 'speculation' which is both philosophical and also unavoidably commercial.

The collapsing of past and present, hero and coward/villain, fact and fantasy, commerce and war at both a formal and a thematic level leads on one hand to reader confusion over the mixture of genres, as we have seen. But it leads on the other to an enduring impression of the unreliability of historical narrative itself which it is difficult to discard. I believe that it is this unreliability which lies at the heart of the novel. Profoundly aware of the social and political issues of the day, unconvinced by Carlyle's 'Hero-Worship' and surrounded by absurd attempts to re-cast Waterloo as a model of straightforward morality and patriotism which might purify the present, Thackeray simply put them together. It was—as he very well knew through his work in *Punch*—precisely the juxtaposition of contemporary and Napoleonic references which lent the work both its comedy and its incisive social commentary.

In dubbing Thackeray 'the first social regenerator of the day', then, Charlotte Brontë was, perhaps, using contemporary jargon advisedly. She was pointing to Thackeray's well-timed critique of current practices of remembering the war. She was applauding the fact that he was one of the few writers of his day not only to understand the self-interested nature of middle-class anxiety, but to point out that 'cannon-balls make wounds, not cicatrices' and that it has always been so. Though the satire in his novel is subtle, complex and at times confusing, it is, as I have attempted to show, so deeply rooted in contemporary references and so inextricably bound up with war and history as fantasy, that it could be seen to suggest that Britain's future might more profitably be thought about in some other way than as an eternal 'pushing forward to fight the battle over again'.

Notes

1. William Makepeace Thackeray, *Vanity Fair: A Novel Without a Hero,* ed. Peter Shillingsburg (1847-48; London and New York, 1994), p. 177. All subsequent references are to this edition and appear parenthetically in the text.

2. Robert Bell, Review of *Vanity Fair, Fraser's Magazine* (September 1848), 321-22.

3. George Henry Lewes, Review of *Vanity Fair, Athenaeum* (12 August 1848), 796.

4. Lewes, Review, 794.

5. Abraham Hayward, Review of *Vanity Fair,* the *Edinburgh Review* (January 1848), 53.

6. Hayward, Review, 53.

7. Lewes, Review, 794.

8. Charlotte Brontë, Preface to Second Edition of *Jane Eyre* (1848, London, 1994), p. 6.

9. David Musselwhite, *Partings Welded Together: Politics and Desire in the Nineteenth-century English Novel* (London, 1987), pp. 118, 131.

10. Joan Stevens, '*Vanity Fair* and the London Skyline', *Costerus,* II (1974), 13.

11. *Ibid.,* 20.

12. *Punch,* vol. 13 (Saturday 20 November, 1847), 200.

13. Stevens, '*Vanity Fair* and the London Skyline', 37.

14. John Schad, 'Reading the Long Way Round: Thackeray's *Vanity Fair*', *Yearbook of English Studies,* 26 (1996), 25-33.

15. John Peck, 'Middle-Class Life in *Vanity Fair*', *English: The Journal of the English Association* (Spring 1994), 43:175, 1-16.

16. *Coningsby* on 13 May 1844, *Sybil* exactly a year later on 13 May 1845. See William Makepeace Thackeray, *Contributions to the Morning Chronicle,* Gordon Ray (ed.) (Urbana, 1955), pp. 40-48, 77.

17. W. M. Thackeray, Review of *Coningsby,* the *Morning Chronicle* (13 May 1844), *Contributions to the Morning Chronicle,* Gordon Ray (ed.), p. 42.

18. Robert P. Fletcher, '"The Foolishest of Existing Mortals": Thackeray, "Gurlyle", and the Character(s) of Fiction', *CLIO: A Journal of Lit-*

erature, History and the Philosophy of History, 24:2 (Winter 1995), 113.

19. Fletcher, "'The Foolishest of Existing Mortals'", 115.

20. *Ibid.,* 115.

21. Musselwhite, *Partings,* p. 139.

22. *The Times* (Saturday 22 May) 1847, p. 4.

23. *The Times* (Thursday 16 March) 1815, p. 3.

24. Charles Dickens, *Dombey and Son* (1844-46; London, 1970), pp. 908-9.

25. *The Illustrated London News* (Saturday 5 June) 1847.

26. Anonymous, *Notes Taken During a Month's Trip in August, 1841* (Glasgow, 1842), pp. 69-71.

27. *Notes Taken During a Month's Trip,* p. 76.

28. *Notes Taken During a Month's Trip,* p. 76.

29. *Punch,* vol. 13 (Saturday 18 September 1847), 103.

30. *Punch,* vol. 13 (Saturday 25 December, 1847), p. 253.

31. As John Schad has shown, the Peterloo massacre was 'indelibly written into the memory of Waterloo' due to the involvement of Waterloo veterans, some of whom not only carried out the massacre wearing their Waterloo medals, but were also, famously, both among the demonstration's organisers and, paradoxically, also among its victims ('Reading the Long Way Round', p. 26).

32. Eric Hobsbawm, *Industry and Empire* (Harmondsworth, 1968).

33. Musselwhite, *Partings,* p. 121.

34. W. M. Thackeray, *The Second Funeral of Napoleon* (1841), *The Works of William Makepeace Thackeray Vol. XXII* (London, 1885), p. 352.

35. Thackeray, *The Second Funeral of Napoleon,* p. 367.

36. Thackeray, *The Second Funeral of Napoleon,* p. 373.

37. W. M. Thackeray, 'On Men and Pictures', *Fraser's Magazine* (July 1841), *The Works of William Makepeace Thackeray Vol. XXV* (London, 1885), p. 203.

38. Ann Monsarrat, *An Uneasy Victorian: Thackeray the Man 1811-63* (London, 1980), p. 33.

39. Monsarrat, *An Uneasy Victorian,* p. 57.

40. W. M. Thackeray, Letter to John Murray (June 3, 1847), *The Letters and Private Papers of William Makepeace Thackeray Vol. II, 1841-1851,* collected and edited by Gordon N. Ray (Oxford, 1945), p. 294.

41. See Norton edition of *Vanity Fair,* p. 273.

42. *Punch,* vol. 13 (Saturday 7 August 1847), p. 57.

43. Peck, 'Middle-class Life', p. 6.

44. Daniel Pick, *War Machine: The Rationalization of Slaughter in the Modern Age* (New Haven and London, 1993), p. 27.

45. Quoted in Pick, *War Machine,* pp. 21-22.

46. Pick, *War Machine,* p. 23.

47. Patricia Marks, '*Mon Pauvre Prisonnier*: Becky Sharp and the Triumph of Napoleon', *Studies in the Novel,* 28:1 (Spring 1996), pp. 76; 80.

48. David Cecil, 'A Criticism of Life', W. M. Thackeray, *Vanity Fair,* Peter L. Shillingsburg, (ed.) (London, 1994), p. 820.

49. Marks, '*Mon Pauvre Prisonnier*', p. 80.

50. Suvendrini Perera, *Reaches of Empire: The English Novel from Edgeworth to Dickens* (New York, 1991), p. 101.

Agnieszka Setecka (essay date 2004)

SOURCE: Setecka, Agnieszka. "Courtly Love in the World 'without a Hero': W. M. Thackeray's *Vanity Fair.*" *Studia Anglica Posnaniensia* 40 (2004): 311-22.

[*In the following essay, Setecka examines Thackeray's treatment of themes of courtly love and adultery within the context of Victorian social mores.*]

The contemporary popular image of the Middle Ages, perpetrated by novels and films alike, is that of wars, crusades and the romance. The narratives of King Arthur and the Knights of the Round Table or of Tristan and Isolde, function in a number of versions or adaptations, as stories, films or operas. The still evident popularity of the romance might result from the fact that it is a source of certain ideals, or myths,[1] which contributed to the development of the Western culture. In his study of medieval culture Jaeger (1985) points to the concept of courtliness as an example of "a civilising force" (1985: 9), and claims that it is "in origin an instrument of the urge of civilising" (1985: 9). He claims that courtly literature blossomed in the second half of the 12th century as a result of new ideals of courtliness (1985: 14), but it also helped to propagate these ideals. Thus, the courtly romance had "a pedagogic function"; the genre "put forward an ideal model of the civilised warrior" and was "the single most powerful factor in transmitting ideas of courtesy from the courtier class in which they originated to the lay nobility" (Jaeger 1985: 14). The "civilised warrior", or a knight, of medieval romance was later transformed into a refined courtier of the renaissance and a gentleman of the 19th century, as Ossowska (2000), Gilmour (1981)[2] and Girouard (1981) indicated in their works. The knight was supposed to be loyal to his lord, pious and courageous. Significantly, he was also supposed to have a lady of his heart, to whom he might devote his services.[3]

The love that a knight would bestow on his lady could be described as courtly love, *amor courtois,* although many critics now express their misgivings about the term as a critical concept.[4] The debate that has been conducted for a long time on the subject does not so much provide a definition of courtly love, as points to complexity and elusiveness of the phenomenon. Indeed, there is no single definition that would be wholly satisfactory. As Bumke wrote,

> Courtly love could be unrequited love or it could culminate in sensual fulfilment. Love could be directed at a lady of high nobility or at a woman of more humble descent. If the chosen lady was married, courtly love was adulterous in nature. On the other hand, love for one's own wife could also be courtly, as could the love between two unmarried people. Courtly love frequently required lengthy service by the man, yet sometimes it was quickly consummated without service.
>
> (Bumke 2000: 361)

Even the work of Andreas Capellanus, the author of the late 12th-century treatise, *De Amore (The art of courtly love),*[5] does not much help to understand courtly love because, as numerous scholars pointed out, his perspective might have been ironic (Burnley 1998: 151; Bumke 2000: 362). However, it is not the aim of the following article to analyse different definitions of the phenomenon or to discuss its role in the medieval world. Rather, the main concern of this paper is to present the ways in which ideals associated with courtliness and courtly love survived in the 19th-century novel. Obviously, the altered social and political situation, as well as the dominance of realism in fiction, required a form different than romance and a new ideal of love and manners. Still, the romantic concepts persist, even if they are transformed, or "displaced", to borrow Frye's (1990) term,[6] in order to fit the form of realistic fiction and comply with Victorian morality.

The displacement of ideals presented in romances work in different ways in the Victorian novel. One possibility is the displacement in the direction of the moral, which Frye mentions in his essays. He defines it as an attempt to "make the desirable and the moral coincide" (Frye 1971: 156). Therefore, although "love and marriage are

not yet indissolubly linked" (Belsey 1994: 107) in medieval courtly literature, Victorian writers aligned passion with the institution of marriage in order to comply with the strict moral codes of the 19th century, as it could be seen in *Jane Eyre* by Charlotte Brontë. Adulterous love, the moral implications of which are often ignored in romances (Bumke 2000: 396), could hardly be glorified in 19th-century fiction. Rather, it was pushed to the margins, stigmatised and rendered unwholesome as it leads lovers to ruin, as it is exemplified by George Eliot's *Mill on the Floss.* William Makepeace Thackeray, whose *Vanity Fair* will be the subject of analysis in this paper, presents yet another attitude to the ideals of courtesy and courtly love: in *Vanity Fair* they are pushed down the pedestal to the level of imperfect characters, acquiring a comic, if not ironic, quality.

Whereas medieval courtly poets "described a fairy tale world with none of the political, economic, and social problems and conflicts that confronted noble society in real life" (Bumke 2000: 275),[7] the 19th-century narrator in *Vanity Fair* mockingly points to sober reality behind the appearances of honesty, nobility and love that his characters are determined to keep. He adopts the tone of irony, which, according to Hutcheon (2002), is a trope characteristic both for satire and parody. Hutcheon points out that whereas the object of satire is outside the text (human vice), parody is strictly textual (or, in fact, intertextual), because it refers to other texts or literary conventions. *Vanity Fair,* then, could be seen both as a satire (as it stigmatises human vice), and as a parody of heroic or courtly conventions, much in the tradition of Cervantes' *Don Quixote.* For parody to be effective and recognisable, the two texts must overlap: the old text is incorporated into the new one, in order to undermine the earlier conventions (Hutcheon 2002: 169). Indeed, on the surface, the world of *Vanity Fair* seems to be built on the ideals reaching back to the medieval period. However, the ironic attitude of the narrator not only reveals that the conventions of courtliness and courtly love are no longer valid in the 19th century, but also offers a critical comment on the conventions themselves.

The action of *Vanity Fair* is set at the beginning of the 19th century, in the period of Napoleonic wars. Although at that time Britain could boast a great degree of democracy, the novel seems to reconstruct the system of feudalism characteristic of medieval Europe.[8] The apparently more democratic relations are, in fact, only well masked feudal dependencies. The poor remain at the bottom of social hierarchy, their fate depending on the whims of their betters. Children internalise the rules of the system already at school, where the richest dandy, Cuff, became "the unquestioned king of the school" and he "ruled over his subjects and bullied them, with splendid superiority. This one blackened his shoes; that toasted his bread; others would fag out, and give him balls at cricket during whole summer afternoons" (Thackeray 1992: 50). Dobbin's attachment to George Osborne is also reminiscent of a relation between a liege lord and his vassal. Moreover, not only do birth and wealth, so crucial for an ideal courtier in medieval romance, remain the two most important factors contributing to success in society, but also the two main male characters, as soldiers, are descendants of medieval knights. As the narrator indicates, wars and the courage of knights has been the subject of literature: "Time out of mind strength and courage have always been the theme of bards and romances; and from the story of Troy down to to-day, poetry has always chosen a soldier for a hero" (Thackeray 1992: 400).

However, if the world of the romance reappears in *Vanity Fair,* it is in a displaced and less desirable form: the liege relations, much idealised in medieval courtly literature, are presented here in a more critical (ironic) light. The necessary attributes of a courtier in the shape of wealth and birth are not necessarily accompanied here by personal traits like beauty, nobility of character and courtly language. Sir Pitt, for example, this most desired man for any young girl to marry and a great statesman, is described as "a man who could not spell, and did not care to read; who had the habits and cunning of a boor; whose aim in life was pettifogging; who never had a taste, or emotions, or enjoyment, but what was sordid and foul: and yet he had rank, and honours, and power, somehow; and was a dignitary of the land, and a pillar of the state" (Thackeray 1992: 108). Similarly, when the narrator recounts the excitement of young men about going to the war, he adds: "I wonder is it because men are cowards at heart that they admire bravery so much, and place military valour do far beyond every other quality for reward and worship?" (Thackeray 1992: 400), thus checking a little the readers' admiration for the young soldiers. In any case, instead of concentrating on great deeds, as a romance writer might have done, the narrator claims not to be a "military novelist", and remarks that his "place is with the non-combatants" (Thackeray 1992: 388).

Significantly, there is a striking parallel between the configurations of characters in *Vanity Fair* and in some romances. In fact, the relationship between Amelia, George Osborne and William Dobbin brings to mind the two famous love triangles in literature: Guinevere—King Arthur—Lancelot, and Isolde—King Mark—Tristan. Becky, who apart from being married to Rawdon has a number of admirers, might also remind of a noble and beautiful lady of courtly literature, although in the novel she fulfils the role of a dangerous temptress. Still, neither are the Vanity Fairians created on a grand scale, nor do their feelings seem to have the passionate quality characteristic of courtly love. Moreover,

not a single character in the novel deserves the name of a courtly lover, and it is not only because the social reality has changed.[9]

George Osborne, for example, is a hero only in Amelia's eyes: she "loved, with all her heart, the young officer in His Majesty's service . . . she thought about him the very first moment on waking, and his was the very last name mentioned in her prayers. She never had seen a man so beautiful or so clever; such a figure on horseback, such dancer, such a hero in general" (Thackeray 1992: 146). Although she must have been dimly aware of George's unworthiness, Amelia "did not dare to own that the man she loves was her inferior; or to feel that she had given her heart away too soon. Given once, the pure bashful maiden was too modest, too tender, too trustful, too weak, too much a woman to recall it" (Thackeray 1992: 225). Even when she married him, and the spell was broken, she still obstinately refused to leave the world of romance she invented for herself; she did not want to "own to herself how different the real man was from that superb young hero whom she had worshipped" (Thackeray 1992: 345). Thus, Amelia constructs George in a romantic manner, and invests their love and their marriage with the romantic significance. It is only Rebecca who finally makes Amelia face the truth. And the truth is that, apart from his good looks, George is deprived of all the features of a noble knight. Not only is he not faithful to the woman of his heart, but also he is a "selfish humbug, that low-bred cockney dandy, that padded booby, who had neither wit, nor manners, nor heart" (Thackeray 1992: 941), to use Rebecca's words. Even George, although usually rather conceited, considers himself "selfish, brutal and black with crime" in comparison to Amelia (Thackeray 1992: 388). George's self-complacency and his selfishness make him an easy prey for the temptress Becky. Unlike Lancelot who "had only one heart, and it was no longer his; he had entrusted it to another [Guinevere] so that he could bestow it nowhere else" ("The Knight of the Cart", Chrétien de Troyes 1990: 185), George neglects Amelia to enjoy the company of other women within a week of their marriage. In fact, he is seduced[10] by Becky's "twinkling green eyes" (Thackeray 1992: 345), and thus fails the test of faithfulness and truthfulness.

Moreover, the relationship between George and Amelia reminds more of the medieval marriage policy than of courtly love celebrated by minstrels and romancers alike. Medievalists indicate that "marriage was primarily a political institution, and instrument of dynastic politics" (Bumke 2000: 380) and that "the conditions and contracts of marriage were negotiated between the families, at best between the groom and the father of the bride. Sometimes children were betrothed as infants" (Bumke 2000: 381). Similarly, George and Amelia "had been bred up by their parents for this very purpose [marriage], and their banns had, as it were, been ready in their respective families any time these ten years" (Thackeray 1992: 40); their marriage was arranged also for financial and dynastic reasons. In addition, instead of letting Amelia rule completely over his heart and fulfilling her every whim, as a courtly lover should, George enjoys his power over his wife: "He saw a slave before him in that simple, yielding, faithful creature, and his soul within him thrilled secretly somehow at the knowledge of his power. He would be generous-minded, Sultan as he was, and raise up this kneeling Esther and make a queen of her" (Thackeray 1992: 252). Thus, there is a contrast between Amelia's romantic vision of her marriage and the truth about her union with George, a contrast that corresponds to medieval construction of love in romances and the contemporary actuality.

Paradoxically, the profligate Rawdon proves to be a more faithful lover, and most devoted to his mistress and then wife Rebecca. Not unlike Sir Lancelot who "find[s] grief in no act suits [Guinevere], since her will is [his] pleasure" ("The Knight of the Cart", Chrétien de Troyes 1990: 242), Rawdon, this heavy dragoon, was completely under the sway of his wife:

> No one will say it is unmanly to be captivated by a woman, or, being captivated, to marry her; and the admiration, the delight, the passion, the wonder, the unbounded confidence, the frantic adoration with which, by degrees, this big warrior got to regard the little Rebecca, were feelings which the ladies at least will pronounce were not altogether discreditable to him. When she sang, every note thrilled in his dull soul and tingled through his huge frame. When she spoke, he bought all the force of his brains to listen and wonder. If she was jocular, he used to revolve her jokes in his mind, and explode over them half an hour afterwards in the street to the surprise of the groom in the Tilbury by his side, or the comrade riding with him in Rotten Row. Her words were oracles to him, her smallest actions marked by an infallible grace and wisdom.
>
> (Thackeray 1992: 200)

However, as the above quotation clearly indicates, for all his virtues and achievements in the "noble sciences" of "boxing, rat-hunting, the fives court, the four-in-hand driving" (Thackeray 1992: 117), Rawdon Crawley does not seem to be a character fit for a courtly lover. The narrator's use of irony depreciates his valour, and underlines his stupidity and his bad manners. The love talk, so celebrated by courtly poets,[11] is reduced here to Rawdon's misshapen sentences and his awkward complement: during the early days of his courtship he pays Rebecca the compliment of being "a neat little filly" (Thackeray 1992: 127) and his uncouth gallantries make him a ridiculous figure. Interestingly enough, however, his love for Rebecca improves him, he finds himself "converted into a very happy and submissive

married man. His former haunts knew him not" (Thackeray 1992: 219). Apparently, striving for improvement was characteristic of a courtly lover, as medieval romances indicate.[12]

George's vanity and unfaithfulness as well as Rawdon's stupidity would have precluded them from the ranks of courtly knights in a medieval romance. Dobbin, who is constructed as a man of sounder moral principles, and devoted to Amelia, would seem to be a much better candidate. However, although by far the most moral, he is not cut out for a hero or a courtly lover either. In the novel he occupies the position comparable to that of a vassal, who serves his liege lord and admires his wife. Like a romance hero he is loyal to George, and is ready to serve him. The fight that he picked up at school in defence of little George might be seen as a parody of the duels often featuring in romances. The narrator compares the combat to "the last charge of the Guard, . . . Ney's column breasting the hill of La Haye Sainte, bristling with ten thousand bayonets, and crowned with twenty eagles . . . the shout of the beef-eating British, as leaping down the hill they rushed to hug the enemy in the savage arms of battle" (Thackeray 1992: 55). In addition, Dobbin is hopelessly in love with Amelia but, like Tristan who brings Isolde to King Mark, he makes George marry her. Still, if he is a Tristan at all, than definitely on a less heroic level. Neither is he of noble origin, his father being only a grocer in the city, nor is he handsome and, as Becky indicates, "how could one love a man with feet of such size?" (Thackeray 1992: 384). In addition, even Amelia had to admit that she did not much care for him, as "[h]e lisped; he was very plain and homely-looking; and exceedingly awkward and ungainly" (Thackeray 1992: 315). Thus, Dobbin is an opposition of a perfect graceful courtier. He reminds rather of Sancho Pança than of a true idealised knight of romance.

Nevertheless, Dobbin's devotion to Amelia does carry traces of romantic passion, although on a more down-to-earth level. He fell in love with her at first sight, when she entered the room singing, and her "sweet fresh little voice went right into the Captain's heart, and nestled there" (Thackeray 1992: 60). He is ready to defend her honour, both before the laughing company of George's friends (Thackeray 1992: 150), and before his own sisters (Thackeray 1992: 230). He never betrays her and, in fact, is the only male character in the novel unaffected by Becky's charm: he was "so honest, that [Becky's] arts and cajoleries did not affect him, and he shrank from her with instinctive repulsion" (Thackeray 1992: 315). He serves Amelia, carrying her shawls when she goes to Vauxhall, or buying her a piano (a rather ridiculous love token); he idealises her and suffers from all the symptoms of love-sickness. As Burnley (1998) indicates, "[b]oth love-longing and idealisation . . .

flow from the essential inaccessibility of the beloved" in courtly literature. Inaccessibility could be achieved "by placing the lady in a socially elevated position by comparison with the lover" or "by ensuring that she is married" (1998: 170). Indeed, Amelia is inaccessible to Dobbin for both those reasons; even when George is killed she claims that he is her husband "here and in heaven" (Thackeray 1992: 820). Therefore, Dobbin can only admire her and love her without hope that his desires would ever be fulfilled: "And so William was at liberty to look and long, as the poor boy at school who has no money may sigh after the contents of the tart-woman's tray" (Thackeray 1992: 821).

However, although Dobbin "bore his fate, knowing it, and content to bear it" (Thackeray 1992: 487), he grew tired after fifteen years; his patience wears out and he suddenly realises that the object of his most passionate desire does not deserve his attentions: "No, you are not worthy of the love which I have devoted to you. I knew all along that the prize I had set my life on was not worth the winning; that I was a fool, with fond fancies, too, bartering away my all of truth and ardour against your little feeble remnant of love" (Thackeray 1992: 925). With such words Dobbin decides to withdraw from Amelia's service, and thus he "broke the chain by which she held him, and declared independence and superiority. He had placed himself at her feet so long that the poor little woman had been accustomed to trample upon him" (Thackeray 1992: 925). Thus, William does not stand the trials of love, which might be a comment on futility of courtly love.

Becky plays the role of a temptress in **Vanity Fair,** like Lady Bertilak in *Sir Gawain and the Green Knight,* or the ladies that Sir Lancelot meets on his way to save Guinevere from the wicked Meleagant ("The Knight of the Cart", Chrétien de Troyes 1990). She learns the art of seduction early in life and when she puts it to practice at Miss Pinkerton's school, where the Reverend Mr. Crisp falls in love with her "being shot dead by a glance of her eyes which was fired all the way across Chiswick Church from the school-pew to the reading desk" (Thackeray 1992: 14). Later she managed to seduce George, daring to "separate those whom God joined" (Thackeray 1992: 412), and even Lord Steyne, who presented her with jewels and money. If she fails with Joseph Sedley, it is not because of his superior moral attributes, but because he gets drunk and thus is unable to pursue his courtship. Still, for a time it appeared that she would conquer him. The scene when Joseph helps her to wind the silk she used for knitting a green purse seems to allude to another scene of seduction, taking place in *Sir Gawain and the Green Knight* where Lady Bertilak tempts Sir Gawain with the green girdle: "And before he had time to ask how, Mr. Joseph Sedley, of the East India's Company's service, was ac-

tually seated *tête-à-tête* with a young lady, looking at her with the most killing expression; his arms stretched out before her in an imploring attitude, and his hands bound in a web of green silk, which she was unwinding" (Thackeray 1992: 47). She reminds of Lady Bertilak for yet another reason: she is a charmer leading men into temptation: her son, Rawdon, sees in her a fairy out of this world: "When she left the room, an odour of rose, or some other magical fragrance, lingered about the nursery. She was an unearthly being in his eyes, superior to his father—to all the world; to be worshipped, and admired at a distance" (Thackeray 1992: 516). In a carriage the boy can only sit silently lost in admiration for his mother: "he gazed with all his eyes at the beautifully dressed princess opposite him" (Thackeray 1992: 516).

The ending of the novel, if not a tragic one, brings with it a complete disillusionment. Both Dobbin and Amelia have finally realised the vanity of their ideals about love. Amelia's eyes are finally opened to George's unworthiness, and so is Dobbin disillusioned about his beloved. Although he seems to have won what he strove for, the reader is not left with the impression that he "has his desire" or "having it, is satisfied" (Thackeray 1992: 951). However, Dobbin's (or Amelia's, for that matter) desire is unfulfilled not because his lady is still inaccessible, but because she is incapable of being what his fancy made of her. In other words, the perfect lady that he constructed in his mind is not possible. Such a conclusion to the novel ultimately undermines the ideal of courtly love.

The example of **Vanity Fair** shows that the ideals of courtliness and courtly love have survived in the Victorian novel, although they are transformed and adapted to the requirements of realistic fiction. The tone of irony that the narrator adopts suggests a critical attitude to the medieval ideals of courtliness and courtly love. Not only does it imply that the courtly values are no longer valid in the 19th century, but also that they might not have worked outside the romance in the Middle Ages. Vanity Fair does not present idealised figures, and the ideals glorified in the medieval romance are here pushed down the pedestal to the level of the ordinary. Although the characters, in their vanity, see themselves in heroic terms and profess to believe in certain values inherited from the chivalric age, the narrator mockingly points to their mediocrity.

Notes

1. In his classic text, *Love in the Western culture,* Rougemont (1956) claims that the story of Tristan provides with one of the most powerful myths in Western culture, the myth of passionate adulterous love.

2. Gilmour, in fact, claims that the Victorian middle class tended "to stress the gentleman's origins in the gentry rather than the aristocracy" (1981: 6). Still, "the gentry remained a club that was run by old fashioned rules" (1981: 6) and belonging to the group of gentlemen depended on possessing certain qualities that used to be characteristic of aristocracy. She writes that the idea of a gentleman was based on "the principle of exclusion . . . the possession of money . . . historic origins in military service and landed society" (1981: 9).

3. How important the lady was to a true knight might be seen in Cervantes' *Don Quixote*. Although knight errantry is there ridiculed, the novel nevertheless shows what were the necessary attributes of knights. When Don Quixote decides to turn a knight errant, he prepares his weapons and secures a horse. Then he needs nothing but a lady of heart: "And now, his armour being secured, his head-piece improved to a helmet, his horse and himself new-named, he perceived nothing but a lady, on whom he might bestow the empire of his heart; for he was sensible that a knight errant without a mistress was a tree without either fruit or leaves, and a body without a soul" (Cervantes 1993: 12).

4. Many critics stress the fact that the term courtly love "reflects modern critical assumptions more than medieval practice" (Kay 2000: 84), and is "essentially a modern invention . . . with little corroboration in medieval texts" (Ferrante 1980: 686). Burnley claims that the influential article by Paris in 1883, and in particular Lewis' essay, contributed to making the phrase "courtly love" "an unanalysable label for a sharply defined set of beliefs bout love in medieval literature rather that simply meaning that kind of love characteristic of courtly contexts" (Burnley 1998: 149).

5. Kay suggests that Andreas Capellanus' work might have been just a rhetorical exercise, in the tradition of Ovid: "This clever and ironic text humorously applies medieval techniques of intellectual codification and argument to the Ovidian erotic tradition, with such success that for a long time scholars accepted it as a serious treatise on love" (2000: 88). Similarly, Burnley indicates that his perspective is ironic (1998: 151), and Benson claims that "he was trying to be funny" (1984: 238).

6. Frye defines displacement as "the alteration of a mythical structure in the direction of greater plausibility and accommodation to ordinary experience" (1990: 148-149).

7. Bumke (2000: 330-335) indicates that in some romances the harsher aspects of reality could be seen between the lines. On the whole, however, courtly literature tends to idealise life at court, the beauty of the ladies, and the valour of the knights.

8. "Thackeray's was the last generation in which the aristocracy held its prestige, threatened already by the rise of industry . . . but still dominant socially and politically" (Humphreys 1988: 191).

9. The materials concerning courtly love very often stress the background of the court a necessary precondition for courtly love (for instance Bumke 2000: 361).

10. Dobbin compares Rebecca to a snake (Thackeray 1992: 378), and George's note urging Rebecca to elope with him is described as being "coiled like a snail among the flowers" of the bouquet (Thackeray 1992: 385). The snake (or the serpent) suggests temptation, like that of the first people in paradise.

11. A number of scholars indicate the importance of language and the art of conversation. Benson (1984), for example, writes that "the form of speech . . . is an essential part of any style of love. Courtly love, however, is especially dependent on the forms of speech, since not only is every lover a poet, but the main characteristics of the courtly lover—his courtesy, humility, and religion of love—are expressed in speech. To be adept at 'luf talk' is therefore the first requirement of the courtly lover" (1984: 243).

12. Andreas Capellanus (1960) indicates that love should improve a lover; it "can endow a man even of the humblest birth with nobility of character" and teaches nobility. Love can also make a man chaste as he would never think about another woman (1960: 31-32).[12]

References

PRIMARY SOURCES

de Cervantes Saavedra, Miguel

1993 *Don Quixote*. Hertfordshire: Wordsworth Classics.

Chrétien de Troyes

1990 *The complete romances of Chrétien de Troyes*. (Translation and introduction by David Staynes). Bloomington-Indianapolis: Indiana University Press.

Thackeray, William Makepeace

1992 *Vanity Fair*. Ware: Wordsworth Editions.

SECONDARY SOURCES

Andreas Capellanus

1960 *The art of courtly love*. (Introduction, translation and notes by John Jay Parry). New York: Columbia University Press.

Benson, Larry D.
1984 "Courtly love and chivalry in the later Middle Ages", in: R. Yeager (ed.), 237-257.

Belsey, Catherine
1994 *Desire. Love stories in Western culture.* Oxford-Cambridge, Mass.: Blackwell.

Bumke, Joachim
2000 *Courtly culture. Literature and society in the High Middle Ages.* Woodstock-New York: The Overlook Press.

Burnley, David
1998 *Courtliness and literature in Medieval England.* London-New York: Longman.

Cohen, William A.
1996 *Sex scandal. The private parts of Victorian fiction.* Durham-London: Duke University Press.

Ferrante, Joan M.
1980 "*Cortes' Amor* in Medieval texts", *Speculum* 55: 686-696.

Frye, Northrop
1971 *Anatomy of criticism. Four essays.* Princeton-New Jersey: Princeton University Press.
1990 *Words with power.* San Diego-New York-London: Harcourt Brace Jovanowich.

Gaunt, Simon and Sarah Kay (eds.)
1999 *The troubadours. An introduction.* Cambridge: Cambridge University Press.

Gilmour, Robin
1981 *The idea of the gentleman in the Victorian novel.* London-Boston-Sydney: George Allen and Unwin.

Girouard, Mark
1981 *The return to Camelot. Chivalry and the English gentleman.* New Haven-London: Yale University Press.

Głowiński, Michał (ed.)
2002 *Ironia* [*Irony*]. Gdańsk: Słowo/Obraz terytoria.

Humphreys, A. R.
1988 "Thackeray: Novelist of society", in: Joanne Shattock (ed.), 185-201.

Hutcheon, Linda
2002 "Ironia, satyra, parodia—o ironii w ujęciu pragmatycznym [Irony, satire, parody: A pragmatic approach to irony]", in: Michał Słowiński (ed.), 165-190.

Jaeger, C. Stephen
1985 *The origins of courtliness. Civilising trends and the formation of courtly ideals 939-1210.* Philadelphia: University of Pennsylvania Press.

Kay, Sarah
2000 "Courts, clerks and courtly love", in: Roberta L. Krueger (ed.), 81-96.

Krueger, Roberta L. (ed.)
2000 *The Cambridge companion to medieval romance.* Cambridge: Cambridge University Press.

Ossowska, Maria
2000 *Ethos rycerski i jego odmiany.* [*Knightly ethos and its varieties*]. Warszawa: Wydawnictwo Naukowe PWN.

Paterson, Linda
1999 "*Fin'amor* and the development of the courtly *canso*", in: Simon Gaunt and Sarah Kay (eds.), 28-46.

de Rougemont, Denis
1999 *Miłość a świat kultury zachodniej* [*Love in the Western culture*]. (Translated by Lesław Eustachiewicz). Warszawa: Instytut Wydawniczy Pax.

Shattock, Joanne (ed.)
1988 *Dickens and other Victorians.* Houndmills-Basingstoke-Hampshire-London: Macmillan Press.

Yeager, R. (ed.)
1984 *Fifteenth-century studies. Recent essays.* Hamden, Connecticut: Archon Books.

FURTHER READING

Criticism

Bloom, Harold. *William Makepeace Thackeray's* Vanity Fair. New York: Chelsea House, 1987, 162 p.
> Provides a range of critical perspectives on *Vanity Fair.*

Burch, Mark H. "'The World Is a Looking-Glass': *Vanity Fair* as Satire." *Genre* 15, no. 3 (fall 1982): 265-79.
> Examines the relationship between narrator and structure in *Vanity Fair.*

Dyson, A. E. "*Vanity Fair*: an Irony against Heroes." *Critical Quarterly* 6 (1964): 11-31.
> Examines Thackeray's use of irony and realism in *Vanity Fair.*

Hagan, John. "*Vanity Fair*: Becky Brought to Book Again." *Studies in the Novel* 7, no. 4 (winter 1975): 479-506.
> Evaluates Thackeray's attitude toward the character of Becky Sharp.

Harden, Edgar F. "The Fields of Mars in *Vanity Fair.*" *Tennessee Studies in Literature* 10 (1965): 123-32.
> Offers a close analysis of *Vanity Fair*'s major themes.

————. *Vanity Fair: A Novel without a Hero.* New York: Twayne Publishers, 1995, 127 p.

Provides a brief critical overview of *Vanity Fair.*

Jadwin, Lisa. "The Seductiveness of Female Duplicity in *Vanity Fair.*" *Studies in English Literature, 1500-1900* 32, no. 4 (autumn 1992): 663-87.

Argues that Thackeray's female protagonists, in particular Becky Sharp, exploit traits of submissiveness and docility in order to subvert traditional limitations on the role of women in society.

————. "Clytemnestra Rewarded: The Double Conclusion of *Vanity Fair.*" In *Famous Last Words: Changes in Gender and Narrative Closure,* edited by Alison Booth, pp. 35-61. Charlottesville: University Press of Virginia, 1993.

Examines the relationship between Thackeray's narrator and the character of Becky Sharp.

Johnson, E. D. H. "*Vanity Fair* and Amelia: Thackeray in the Perspective of the Eighteenth Century." *Modern Philology* 59, no. 2 (November 1961): 100-13.

Analyzes the moral significance of Amelia Sedley's character.

Lindner, Christoph. "Thackeray's Gourmand: Carnivals of Consumption in *Vanity Fair.*" *Modern Philology* 99, no. 4 (May 2002): 564-81.

Offers a Marxist interpretation of Thackeray's attitudes toward middle-class materialism.

MacPhail, Fiona. "Vanitas Vanitatum: The Conclusion of Thackeray's *Vanity Fair.*" In *Fins de romans: Aspects de la conclusion dans la litterature anglaise,* pp. 564-81. Caen: Presses Universitaires de Caen, 1993.

Offers an in-depth reading of *Vanity Fair*'s conclusion.

Milner, Ian. "Theme and Moral Vision in Thackeray's *Vanity Fair.*" *Philologica Pragensia* 13, no. 4 (1970): 177-85.

Discusses *Vanity Fair*'s moral ambiguity.

Musselwhite, David. "Notes on a Journey to Vanity Fair." *Literature and History* 7, no. 1 (spring 1981): 62-90.

Provides a close reading of *Vanity Fair*'s central themes.

Nesteby, James R. "Portraits of Blacks in Thackeray's *Vanity Fair.*" *Journal of English, Sana'a University* 8 (September 1980): 126-58.

Argues that *Vanity Fair*'s Black characters are little more than stereotypes and that Thackeray's undisguised racism undermines the power of his satire.

Norton, Sandy Morey. "The Ex-Collector of Boggley-Wollah: Colonialism in the Empire of *Vanity Fair.*" *Narrative* 1, no. 2 (May 1993): 124-37.

Examines representations of colonialism in *Vanity Fair.*

Paris, Bernard J. "The Psychic Structure of *Vanity Fair.*" *Victorian Studies,* no. 10 (1967): 389-410.

Offers a psychological analysis of the narrator in *Vanity Fair.*

Rader, Ralph W. "The Comparative Anatomy of Three Baggy Monsters: *Bleak House, Vanity Fair, Middlemarch.*" *Journal of Narrative Technique* 19, no. 1 (winter 1989): 49-69.

Offers an in-depth comparison of structural techniques in *Vanity Fair,* Charles Dickens's *Bleak House,* and George Eliot's *Middlemarch.*

Sharp, M. Corona. "Sympathetic Mockery: A Study of the Narrator's Character in *Vanity Fair.*" *ELH* 29, no. 3 (September 1962): 324-36.

Provides a close analysis of the narrative voice in *Vanity Fair.*

Stevens, Joan. "*Vanity Fair* and the London Skyline." *Costerus* 2 (1974): 13-41.

Examines Thackeray's depiction of London in *Vanity Fair.*

Sutherland, John A. "The Expanding Narrative of *Vanity Fair.*" *Journal of Narrative Technique* 3 (1974): 149-69.

Offers an in-depth examination of *Vanity Fair*'s structure.

Swanson, Roger M. "*Vanity Fair*: The Double Standard." In *The English Novel in the Nineteenth Century: Essays on the Literary Mediation of Human Values,* edited by George Goodin, pp. 126-44. Urbana: University of Illinois Press, 1972.

Explores Thackeray's treatment of moral issues in *Vanity Fair.*

Taube, Myron. "Contrast as a Principle of Structure in *Vanity Fair.*" *Nineteenth Century Literature* 18, no. 2 (September 1963): 119-35.

Discusses Thackeray's use of major themes as an organizing principle in *Vanity Fair.*

Thompson, Leslie M. "*Vanity Fair* and the Johnsonian Tradition of Fiction." *New Rambler* C7 (1969): 45-9.

Examines the influence of Henry Fielding and Samuel Johnson on *Vanity Fair.*

Vega Ritter, Max. "Manhood in *Vanity Fair.*" *Cahiers Victoriens et Edouardiens,* no. 38 (October 1993): 87-102.

>Examines the relationship between masculinity and sexuality in *Vanity Fair.*

———. "Women under Judgment in *Vanity Fair.*" *Cahiers Victoriens et Edouardiens,* no. 3 (1976): 7-23.

Discusses Thackeray's portrayals of female characters in *Vanity Fair.*

Wolff, Cynthia G. "Who Is the Narrator of *Vanity Fair* and Where Is He Standing?" *College Literature,* no. 1 (1974): 190-203.

>Examines the question of narrative point of view in *Vanity Fair.*

Additional coverage of Thackeray's life and career is contained in the following sources published by Thomson Gale: *British Writers,* **Vol. 5;** *British Writers: The Classics,* **Vol. 2;** *Concise Dictionary of British Literary Biography, 1832-1890;* *Dictionary of Literary Biography,* **Vols. 21, 55, 159, 163;** *DISCovering Authors;* *DISCovering Authors: British Edition;* *DISCovering Authors: Canadian Edition;* *DISCovering Authors Modules: Most-studied Authors* **and** *Novelists;* *DISCovering Authors 3.0;* *Literature Resource Center;* *Nineteenth-Century Literature Criticism,* **Vols. 5, 14, 22, 43;** *Novels for Students,* **Vol. 13;** *Reference Guide to English Literature,* **Ed. 2;** *Something About the Author,* **Vol. 23;** *Twayne's English Authors;* *World Literature and Its Times,* **Vol. 3; and** *World Literature Criticism,* **Ed. 6.**

How to Use This Index

The main references

> **Calvino, Italo**
> 1923-1985 .... CLC **5, 8, 11, 22, 33, 39,**
> **73; SSC 3, 48**

list all author entries in the following Thomson Gale Literary Criticism series:

AAL = *Asian American Literature*
BG = *The Beat Generation: A Gale Critical Companion*
BLC = *Black Literature Criticism*
BLCS = *Black Literature Criticism Supplement*
CLC = *Contemporary Literary Criticism*
CLR = *Children's Literature Review*
CMLC = *Classical and Medieval Literature Criticism*
DC = *Drama Criticism*
FL = *Feminism in Literature: A Gale Critical Companion*
GL = *Gothic Literature: A Gale Critical Companion*
HLC = *Hispanic Literature Criticism*
HLCS = *Hispanic Literature Criticism Supplement*
HR = *Harlem Renaissance: A Gale Critical Companion*
LC = *Literature Criticism from 1400 to 1800*
NCLC = *Nineteenth-Century Literature Criticism*
NNAL = *Native North American Literature*
PC = *Poetry Criticism*
SSC = *Short Story Criticism*
TCLC = *Twentieth-Century Literary Criticism*
WLC = *World Literature Criticism, 1500 to the Present*
WLCS = *World Literature Criticism Supplement*

The cross-references

> See also CA 85-88, 116; CANR 23, 61;
> DAM NOV; DLB 196; EW 13; MTCW 1, 2;
> RGSF 2; RGWL 2; SFW 4; SSFS 12

list all author entries in the following Thomson Gale biographical and literary sources:

AAYA = *Authors & Artists for Young Adults*
AFAW = *African American Writers*
AFW = *African Writers*
AITN = *Authors in the News*
AMW = *American Writers*
AMWR = *American Writers Retrospective Supplement*
AMWS = *American Writers Supplement*
ANW = *American Nature Writers*
AW = *Ancient Writers*
BEST = *Bestsellers*
BPFB = *Beacham's Encyclopedia of Popular Fiction: Biography and Resources*
BRW = *British Writers*
BRWS = *British Writers Supplement*
BW = *Black Writers*
BYA = *Beacham's Guide to Literature for Young Adults*
CA = *Contemporary Authors*
CAAS = *Contemporary Authors Autobiography Series*
CABS = *Contemporary Authors Bibliographical Series*
CAD = *Contemporary American Dramatists*
CANR = *Contemporary Authors New Revision Series*
CAP = *Contemporary Authors Permanent Series*
CBD = *Contemporary British Dramatists*
CCA = *Contemporary Canadian Authors*
CD = *Contemporary Dramatists*
CDALB = *Concise Dictionary of American Literary Biography*

CDALBS = *Concise Dictionary of American Literary Biography Supplement*
CDBLB = *Concise Dictionary of British Literary Biography*
CMW = *St. James Guide to Crime & Mystery Writers*
CN = *Contemporary Novelists*
CP = *Contemporary Poets*
CPW = *Contemporary Popular Writers*
CSW = *Contemporary Southern Writers*
CWD = *Contemporary Women Dramatists*
CWP = *Contemporary Women Poets*
CWRI = *St. James Guide to Children's Writers*
CWW = *Contemporary World Writers*
DA = *DISCovering Authors*
DA3 = *DISCovering Authors 3.0*
DAB = *DISCovering Authors: British Edition*
DAC = *DISCovering Authors: Canadian Edition*
DAM = *DISCovering Authors: Modules*
    DRAM: *Dramatists Module;* **MST:** *Most-studied Authors Module;*
    MULT: *Multicultural Authors Module;* **NOV:** *Novelists Module;*
    POET: *Poets Module;* **POP:** *Popular Fiction and Genre Authors Module*
DFS = *Drama for Students*
DLB = *Dictionary of Literary Biography*
DLBD = *Dictionary of Literary Biography Documentary Series*
DLBY = *Dictionary of Literary Biography Yearbook*
DNFS = *Literature of Developing Nations for Students*
EFS = *Epics for Students*
EXPN = *Exploring Novels*
EXPP = *Exploring Poetry*
EXPS = *Exploring Short Stories*
EW = *European Writers*
FANT = *St. James Guide to Fantasy Writers*
FW = *Feminist Writers*
GFL = *Guide to French Literature,* Beginnings to 1789, 1798 to the Present
GLL = *Gay and Lesbian Literature*
HGG = *St. James Guide to Horror, Ghost & Gothic Writers*
HW = *Hispanic Writers*
IDFW = *International Dictionary of Films and Filmmakers: Writers and Production Artists*
IDTP = *International Dictionary of Theatre: Playwrights*
LAIT = *Literature and Its Times*
LAW = *Latin American Writers*
JRDA = *Junior DISCovering Authors*
MAICYA = *Major Authors and Illustrators for Children and Young Adults*
MAICYAS = *Major Authors and Illustrators for Children and Young Adults Supplement*
MAWW = *Modern American Women Writers*
MJW = *Modern Japanese Writers*
MTCW = *Major 20th-Century Writers*
NCFS = *Nonfiction Classics for Students*
NFS = *Novels for Students*
PAB = *Poets: American and British*
PFS = *Poetry for Students*
RGAL = *Reference Guide to American Literature*
RGEL = *Reference Guide to English Literature*
RGSF = *Reference Guide to Short Fiction*
RGWL = *Reference Guide to World Literature*
RHW = *Twentieth-Century Romance and Historical Writers*
SAAS = *Something about the Author Autobiography Series*
SATA = *Something about the Author*
SFW = *St. James Guide to Science Fiction Writers*
SSFS = *Short Stories for Students*
TCWW = *Twentieth-Century Western Writers*
WLIT = *World Literature and Its Times*
WP = *World Poets*
YABC = *Yesterday's Authors of Books for Children*
YAW = *St. James Guide to Young Adult Writers*

Literary Criticism Series
Cumulative Author Index

Alexie, Sherman (Joseph, Jr.)
1966- .... **CLC 96, 154; NNAL; PC 53**
See also AAYA 28; BYA 15; CA 138;
CANR 65, 95, 133; CN 7; DA3; DAM
MULT; DLB 175, 206, 278; LATS 1:2;
MTCW 2; MTFW 2005; NFS 17; SSFS
18

al-Farabi 870(?)-950 .... **CMLC 58**
See also DLB 115

Alfau, Felipe 1902-1999 .... **CLC 66**
See also CA 137

Alfieri, Vittorio 1749-1803 .... **NCLC 101**
See also EW 4; RGWL 2, 3; WLIT 7

Alfonso X 1221-1284 .... **CMLC 78**

Alfred, Jean Gaston
See Ponge, Francis

Alger, Horatio, Jr. 1832-1899 .... **NCLC 8, 83**
See also CLR 87; DLB 42; LAIT 2; RGAL
4; SATA 16; TUS

Al-Ghazali, Muhammad ibn Muhammad
1058-1111 .... **CMLC 50**
See also DLB 115

Algren, Nelson 1909-1981 ..... **CLC 4, 10, 33;
SSC 33**
See also AMWS 9; BPFB 1; CA 13-16R;
103; CANR 20, 61; CDALB 1941-1968;
CN 1, 2; DLB 9; DLBY 1981, 1982,
2000; EWL 3; MAL 5; MTCW 1, 2;
MTFW 2005; RGAL 4; RGSF 2

**al-Hariri, al-Qasim ibn 'Ali Abu
Muhammad al-Basri**
1054-1122 .... **CMLC 63**
See also RGWL 3

Ali, Ahmed 1908-1998 .... **CLC 69**
See also CA 25-28R; CANR 15, 34; CN 1,
2, 3, 4, 5; EWL 3

Ali, Tariq 1943- .... **CLC 173**
See also CA 25-28R; CANR 10, 99

Alighieri, Dante
See Dante
See also WLIT 7

al-Kindi, Abu Yusuf Ya'qub ibn Ishaq c.
801-c. 873 .... **CMLC 80**

Allan, John B.
See Westlake, Donald E(dwin)

Allan, Sidney
See Hartmann, Sadakichi

Allan, Sydney
See Hartmann, Sadakichi

Allard, Janet .... **CLC 59**

Allen, Edward 1948- .... **CLC 59**

Allen, Fred 1894-1956 .... **TCLC 87**

Allen, Paula Gunn 1939- .... **CLC 84, 202;
NNAL**
See also AMWS 4; CA 112; 143; CANR
63, 130; CWP; DA3; DAM MULT; DLB
175; FW; MTCW 2; MTFW 2005; RGAL
4; TCWW 2

Allen, Roland
See Ayckbourn, Alan

Allen, Sarah A.
See Hopkins, Pauline Elizabeth

Allen, Sidney H.
See Hartmann, Sadakichi

Allen, Woody 1935- .... **CLC 16, 52, 195**
See also AAYA 10, 51; AMWS 15; CA 33-
36R; CANR 27, 38, 63, 128; DAM POP;
DLB 44; MTCW 1; SSFS 21

Allende, Isabel 1942- ... **CLC 39, 57, 97, 170;
HLC 1; SSC 65; WLCS**
See also AAYA 18; CA 125; 130; CANR
51, 74, 129; CDWLB 3; CLR 99; CWW
2; DA3; DAM MULT, NOV; DLB 145;
DNFS 1; EWL 3; FL 1:5; FW; HW 1, 2;
INT CA-130; LAIT 5; LAWS 1; LMFS 2;
MTCW 1, 2; MTFW 2005; NCFS 1; NFS
6, 18; RGSF 2; RGWL 3; SATA 163;
SSFS 11, 16; WLIT 1

Alleyn, Ellen
See Rossetti, Christina

Alleyne, Carla D. .... **CLC 65**

Allingham, Margery (Louise)
1904-1966 .... **CLC 19**
See also CA 5-8R; 25-28R; CANR 4, 58;
CMW 4; DLB 77; MSW; MTCW 1, 2

Allingham, William 1824-1889 ...... **NCLC 25**
See also DLB 35; RGEL 2

Allison, Dorothy E. 1949- .... **CLC 78, 153**
See also AAYA 53; CA 140; CANR 66, 107;
CN 7; CSW; DA3; FW; MTCW 2; MTFW
2005; NFS 11; RGAL 4

Alloula, Malek .... **CLC 65**

Allston, Washington 1779-1843 .... **NCLC 2**
See also DLB 1, 235

Almedingen, E. M. .... **CLC 12**
See Almedingen, Martha Edith von
See also SATA 3

Almedingen, Martha Edith von 1898-1971
See Almedingen, E. M.
See also CA 1-4R; CANR 1

Almodovar, Pedro 1949(?)- .... **CLC 114;
HLCS 1**
See also CA 133; CANR 72; HW 2

Almqvist, Carl Jonas Love
1793-1866 .... **NCLC 42**

**al-Mutanabbi, Ahmad ibn al-Husayn Abu
al-Tayyib al-Jufi al-Kindi**
915-965 .... **CMLC 66**
See Mutanabbi, Al-
See also RGWL 3

Alonso, Damaso 1898-1990 .... **CLC 14**
See also CA 110; 131; 130; CANR 72; DLB
108; EWL 3; HW 1, 2

Alov
See Gogol, Nikolai (Vasilyevich)

al'Sadaawi, Nawal
See El Saadawi, Nawal
See also FW

al-Shaykh, Hanan 1945- .... **CLC 218**
See also CA 135; CANR 111; WLIT 6

Al Siddik
See Rolfe, Frederick (William Serafino Aus-
tin Lewis Mary)
See also GLL 1; RGEL 2

Alta 1942- .... **CLC 19**
See also CA 57-60

Alter, Robert B(ernard) 1935- .... **CLC 34**
See also CA 49-52; CANR 1, 47, 100

Alther, Lisa 1944- .... **CLC 7, 41**
See also BPFB 1; CA 65-68; CAAS 30;
CANR 12, 30, 51; CN 4, 5, 6, 7; CSW;
GLL 2; MTCW 1

Althusser, L.
See Althusser, Louis

Althusser, Louis 1918-1990 .... **CLC 106**
See also CA 131; 132; CANR 102; DLB
242

Altman, Robert 1925- .... **CLC 16, 116**
See also CA 73-76; CANR 43

Alurista .... **HLCS 1; PC 34**
See Urista (Heredia), Alberto (Baltazar)
See also CA 45-48R; DLB 82; LLW

Alvarez, A(lfred) 1929- .... **CLC 5, 13**
See also CA 1-4R; CANR 3, 33, 63, 101,
134; CN 3, 4, 5, 6; CP 1, 2, 3, 4, 5, 6, 7;
DLB 14, 40; MTFW 2005

Alvarez, Alejandro Rodriguez 1903-1965
See Casona, Alejandro
See also CA 131; 93-96; HW 1

Alvarez, Julia 1950- .... **CLC 93; HLCS 1**
See also AAYA 25; AMWS 7; CA 147;
CANR 69, 101, 133; DA3; DLB 282;
LATS 1:2; LLW; MTCW 2; MTFW 2005;
NFS 5, 9; SATA 129; WLIT 1

Alvaro, Corrado 1896-1956 .... **TCLC 60**
See also CA 163; DLB 264; EWL 3

Amado, Jorge 1912-2001 ... **CLC 13, 40, 106;
HLC 1**
See also CA 77-80; 201; CANR 35, 74, 135;
CWW 2; DAM MULT, NOV; DLB 113,
307; EWL 3; HW 2; LAW; LAWS 1;
MTCW 1, 2; MTFW 2005; RGWL 2, 3;
TWA; WLIT 1

Ambler, Eric 1909-1998 .... **CLC 4, 6, 9**
See also BRWS 4; CA 9-12R; 171; CANR
7, 38, 74; CMW 4; CN 1, 2, 3, 4, 5, 6;
DLB 77; MSW; MTCW 1, 2; TEA

Ambrose, Stephen E(dward)
1936-2002 .... **CLC 145**
See also AAYA 44; CA 1-4R; 209; CANR
3, 43, 57, 83, 105; MTFW 2005; NCFS 2;
SATA 40, 138

Amichai, Yehuda 1924-2000 .. **CLC 9, 22, 57,
116; PC 38**
See also CA 85-88; 189; CANR 46, 60, 99,
132; CWW 2; EWL 3; MTCW 1, 2;
MTFW 2005; WLIT 6

Amichai, Yehudah
See Amichai, Yehuda

Amiel, Henri Frederic 1821-1881 .... **NCLC 4**
See also DLB 217

Amis, Kingsley (William)
1922-1995 ...... **CLC 1, 2, 3, 5, 8, 13, 40,
44, 129**
See also AITN 2; BPFB 1; BRWS 2; CA
9-12R; 150; CANR 8, 28, 54; CDBLB
1945-1960; CN 1, 2, 3, 4, 5, 6; CP 1, 2,
3, 4; DA; DA3; DAB; DAC; DAM MST,
NOV; DLB 15, 27, 100, 139; DLBY 1996;
EWL 3; HGG; INT CANR-8; MTCW 1,
2; MTFW 2005; RGEL 2; RGSF 2; SFW
4

Amis, Martin (Louis) 1949- .... **CLC 4, 9, 38,
62, 101, 213**
See also BEST 90:3; BRWS 4; CA 65-68;
CANR 8, 27, 54, 73, 95, 132; CN 5, 6, 7;
DA3; DLB 14, 194; EWL 3; INT CANR-
27; MTCW 2; MTFW 2005

Ammianus Marcellinus c. 330-c.
395 .... **CMLC 60**
See also AW 2; DLB 211

Ammons, A(rchie) R(andolph)
1926-2001 ...... **CLC 2, 3, 5, 8, 9, 25, 57,
108; PC 16**
See also AITN 1; AMWS 7; CA 9-12R;
193; CANR 6, 36, 51, 73, 107; CP 1, 2,
3, 4, 5, 6, 7; CSW; DAM POET; DLB 5,
165; EWL 3; MAL 5; MTCW 1, 2; PFS
19; RGAL 4; TCLE 1:1

Amo, Tauraatua i
See Adams, Henry (Brooks)

Amory, Thomas 1691(?)-1788 .... **LC 48**
See also DLB 39

Anand, Mulk Raj 1905-2004 ...... **CLC 23, 93**
See also CA 65-68; 231; CANR 32, 64; CN
1, 2, 3, 4, 5, 6, 7; DAM NOV; EWL 3;
MTCW 1, 2; MTFW 2005; RGSF 2

Anatol
See Schnitzler, Arthur

Anaximander c. 611B.C.-c.
546B.C. .... **CMLC 22**

Anaya, Rudolfo A(lfonso) 1937- ...... **CLC 23,
148; HLC 1**
See also AAYA 20; BYA 13; CA 45-48;
CAAS 4; CANR 1, 32, 51, 124; CN 4, 5,
6, 7; DAM MULT, NOV; DLB 82, 206,
278; HW 1; LAIT 4; LLW; MAL 5;
MTCW 1, 2; MTFW 2005; NFS 12;
RGAL 4; RGSF 2; TCWW 2; WLIT 1

Andersen, Hans Christian
1805-1875 .... **NCLC 7, 79; SSC 6, 56;
WLC**
See also AAYA 57; CLR 6; DA; DA3;
DAB; DAC; DAM MST, POP; EW 6;
MAICYA 1, 2; RGSF 2; RGWL 2, 3;
SATA 100; TWA; WCH; YABC 1

Arden, John 1930- .... **CLC 6, 13, 15**
See also BRWS 2; CA 13-16R; CAAS 4; CANR 31, 65, 67, 124; CBD; CD 5, 6; DAM DRAM; DFS 9; DLB 13, 245; EWL 3; MTCW 1

Arenas, Reinaldo 1943-1990 .. **CLC 41; HLC 1**
See also CA 124; 128; 133; CANR 73, 106; DAM MULT; DLB 145; EWL 3; GLL 2; HW 1; LAW; LAWS 1; MTCW 2; MTFW 2005; RGSF 2; RGWL 3; WLIT 1

Arendt, Hannah 1906-1975 .... **CLC 66, 98**
See also CA 17-20R; 61-64; CANR 26, 60; DLB 242; MTCW 1, 2

Aretino, Pietro 1492-1556 .... **LC 12**
See also RGWL 2, 3

Arghezi, Tudor .... **CLC 80**
See Theodorescu, Ion N.
See also CA 167; CDWLB 4; DLB 220; EWL 3

Arguedas, Jose Maria 1911-1969 .... **CLC 10, 18; HLCS 1; TCLC 147**
See also CA 89-92; CANR 73; DLB 113; EWL 3; HW 1; LAW; RGWL 2, 3; WLIT 1

Argueta, Manlio 1936- .... **CLC 31**
See also CA 131; CANR 73; CWW 2; DLB 145; EWL 3; HW 1; RGWL 3

Arias, Ron(ald Francis) 1941- .... **HLC 1**
See also CA 131; CANR 81, 136; DAM MULT; DLB 82; HW 1, 2; MTCW 2; MTFW 2005

Ariosto, Lodovico
See Ariosto, Ludovico
See also WLIT 7

Ariosto, Ludovico 1474-1533 ... **LC 6, 87; PC 42**
See Ariosto, Lodovico
See also EW 2; RGWL 2, 3

Aristides
See Epstein, Joseph

Aristophanes 450B.C.-385B.C. .... **CMLC 4, 51; DC 2; WLCS**
See also AW 1; CDWLB 1; DA; DA3; DAB; DAC; DAM DRAM, MST; DFS 10; DLB 176; LMFS 1; RGWL 2, 3; TWA

Aristotle 384B.C.-322B.C. .... **CMLC 31; WLCS**
See also AW 1; CDWLB 1; DA; DA3; DAB; DAC; DAM MST; DLB 176; RGWL 2, 3; TWA

Arlt, Roberto (Godofredo Christophersen) 1900-1942 .... **HLC 1; TCLC 29**
See also CA 123; 131; CANR 67; DAM MULT; DLB 305; EWL 3; HW 1, 2; IDTP; LAW

Armah, Ayi Kwei 1939- . **BLC 1; CLC 5, 33, 136**
See also AFW; BRWS 10; BW 1; CA 61-64; CANR 21, 64; CDWLB 3; CN 1, 2, 3, 4, 5, 6, 7; DAM MULT, POET; DLB 117; EWL 3; MTCW 1; WLIT 2

Armatrading, Joan 1950- .... **CLC 17**
See also CA 114; 186

Armitage, Frank
See Carpenter, John (Howard)

Armstrong, Jeannette (C.) 1948- .... **NNAL**
See also CA 149; CCA 1; CN 6, 7; DAC; SATA 102

Arnette, Robert
See Silverberg, Robert

Arnim, Achim von (Ludwig Joachim von Arnim) 1781-1831 .. **NCLC 5, 159; SSC 29**
See also DLB 90

Arnim, Bettina von 1785-1859 ...... **NCLC 38, 123**
See also DLB 90; RGWL 2, 3

Arnold, Matthew 1822-1888 ..... **NCLC 6, 29, 89, 126; PC 5; WLC**
See also BRW 5; CDBLB 1832-1890; DA; DAB; DAC; DAM MST, POET; DLB 32, 57; EXPP; PAB; PFS 2; TEA; WP

Arnold, Thomas 1795-1842 .... **NCLC 18**
See also DLB 55

Arnow, Harriette (Louisa) Simpson 1908-1986 .... **CLC 2, 7, 18**
See also BPFB 1; CA 9-12R; 118; CANR 14; CN 2, 3, 4; DLB 6; FW; MTCW 1, 2; RHW; SATA 42; SATA-Obit 47

Arouet, Francois-Marie
See Voltaire

Arp, Hans
See Arp, Jean

Arp, Jean 1887-1966 .... **CLC 5; TCLC 115**
See also CA 81-84; 25-28R; CANR 42, 77; EW 10

Arrabal
See Arrabal, Fernando

Arrabal (Teran), Fernando
See Arrabal, Fernando
See also CWW 2

Arrabal, Fernando 1932- ... **CLC 2, 9, 18, 58**
See Arrabal (Teran), Fernando
See also CA 9-12R; CANR 15; DLB 321; EWL 3; LMFS 2

Arreola, Juan Jose 1918-2001 .... **CLC 147; HLC 1; SSC 38**
See also CA 113; 131; 200; CANR 81; CWW 2; DAM MULT; DLB 113; DNFS 2; EWL 3; HW 1, 2; LAW; RGSF 2

Arrian c. 89(?)-c. 155(?) .... **CMLC 43**
See also DLB 176

Arrick, Fran .... **CLC 30**
See Gaberman, Judie Angell
See also BYA 6

Arrley, Richmond
See Delany, Samuel R(ay), Jr.

Artaud, Antonin (Marie Joseph) 1896-1948 .... **DC 14; TCLC 3, 36**
See also CA 104; 149; DA3; DAM DRAM; DFS 22; DLB 258, 321; EW 11; EWL 3; GFL 1789 to the Present; MTCW 2; MTFW 2005; RGWL 2, 3

Arthur, Ruth M(abel) 1905-1979 ..... **CLC 12**
See also CA 9-12R; 85-88; CANR 4; CWRI 5; SATA 7, 26

Artsybashev, Mikhail (Petrovich) 1878-1927 .... **TCLC 31**
See also CA 170; DLB 295

Arundel, Honor (Morfydd) 1919-1973 .... **CLC 17**
See also CA 21-22; 41-44R; CAP 2; CLR 35; CWRI 5; SATA 4; SATA-Obit 24

Arzner, Dorothy 1900-1979 .... **CLC 98**

Asch, Sholem 1880-1957 .... **TCLC 3**
See also CA 105; EWL 3; GLL 2

Ascham, Roger 1516(?)-1568 .... **LC 101**
See also DLB 236

Ash, Shalom
See Asch, Sholem

Ashbery, John (Lawrence) 1927- .. **CLC 2, 3, 4, 6, 9, 13, 15, 25, 41, 77, 125, 221; PC 26**
See Berry, Jonas
See also AMWS 3; CA 5-8R; CANR 9, 37, 66, 102, 132; CP 1, 2, 3, 4, 5, 6, 7; DA3; DAM POET; DLB 5, 165; DLBY 1981; EWL 3; INT CANR-9; MAL 5; MTCW 1, 2; MTFW 2005; PAB; PFS 11; RGAL 4; TCLE 1:1; WP

Ashdown, Clifford
See Freeman, R(ichard) Austin

Ashe, Gordon
See Creasey, John

Ashton-Warner, Sylvia (Constance) 1908-1984 .... **CLC 19**
See also CA 69-72; 112; CANR 29; CN 1, 2, 3; MTCW 1, 2

Asimov, Isaac 1920-1992 ..... **CLC 1, 3, 9, 19, 26, 76, 92**
See also AAYA 13; BEST 90:2; BPFB 1; BYA 4, 6, 7, 9; CA 1-4R; 137; CANR 2, 19, 36, 60, 125; CLR 12, 79; CMW 4; CN 1, 2, 3, 4, 5; CPW; DA3; DAM POP; DLB 8; DLBY 1992; INT CANR-19; JRDA; LAIT 5; LMFS 2; MAICYA 1, 2; MAL 5; MTCW 1, 2; MTFW 2005; RGAL 4; SATA 1, 26, 74; SCFW 1, 2; SFW 4; SSFS 17; TUS; YAW

Askew, Anne 1521(?)-1546 .... **LC 81**
See also DLB 136

Assis, Joaquim Maria Machado de
See Machado de Assis, Joaquim Maria

Astell, Mary 1666-1731 .... **LC 68**
See also DLB 252; FW

Astley, Thea (Beatrice May) 1925-2004 .... **CLC 41**
See also CA 65-68; 229; CANR 11, 43, 78; CN 1, 2, 3, 4, 5, 6, 7; DLB 289; EWL 3

Astley, William 1855-1911
See Warung, Price

Aston, James
See White, T(erence) H(anbury)

Asturias, Miguel Angel 1899-1974 .... **CLC 3, 8, 13; HLC 1**
See also CA 25-28; 49-52; CANR 32; CAP 2; CDWLB 3; DA3; DAM MULT, NOV; DLB 113, 290; EWL 3; HW 1; LAW; LMFS 2; MTCW 1, 2; RGWL 2, 3; WLIT 1

Atares, Carlos Saura
See Saura (Atares), Carlos

Athanasius c. 295-c. 373 .... **CMLC 48**

Atheling, William
See Pound, Ezra (Weston Loomis)

Atheling, William, Jr.
See Blish, James (Benjamin)

Atherton, Gertrude (Franklin Horn) 1857-1948 .... **TCLC 2**
See also CA 104; 155; DLB 9, 78, 186; HGG; RGAL 4; SUFW 1; TCWW 1, 2

Atherton, Lucius
See Masters, Edgar Lee

Atkins, Jack
See Harris, Mark

Atkinson, Kate 1951- .... **CLC 99**
See also CA 166; CANR 101; DLB 267

Attaway, William (Alexander) 1911-1986 .... **BLC 1; CLC 92**
See also BW 2, 3; CA 143; CANR 82; DAM MULT; DLB 76; MAL 5

Atticus
See Fleming, Ian (Lancaster); Wilson, (Thomas) Woodrow

Atwood, Margaret (Eleanor) 1939- ... **CLC 2, 3, 4, 8, 13, 15, 25, 44, 84, 135; PC 8; SSC 2, 46; WLC**
See also AAYA 12, 47; AMWS 13; BEST 89:2; BPFB 1; CA 49-52; CANR 3, 24, 33, 59, 95, 133; CN 2, 3, 4, 5, 6, 7; CP 1, 2, 3, 4, 5, 6, 7; CPW; CWP; DA; DA3; DAB; DAC; DAM MST, NOV, POET; DLB 53, 251; EWL 3; EXPN; FL 1:5; FW; GL 2; INT CANR-24; LAIT 5; MTCW 1, 2; MTFW 2005; NFS 4, 12, 13, 14, 19; PFS 7; RGSF 2; SATA 50; SSFS 3, 13; TCLE 1:1; TWA; WWE 1; YAW

Aubigny, Pierre d'
See Mencken, H(enry) L(ouis)

Aubin, Penelope 1685-1731(?) .... **LC 9**
See also DLB 39

Auchincloss, Louis (Stanton) 1917- .. **CLC 4, 6, 9, 18, 45; SSC 22**
See also AMWS 4; CA 1-4R; CANR 6, 29, 55, 87, 130; CN 1, 2, 3, 4, 5, 6, 7; DAM NOV; DLB 2, 244; DLBY 1980; EWL 3; INT CANR-29; MAL 5; MTCW 1; RGAL 4

Auden, W(ystan) H(ugh) 1907-1973 . **CLC 1, 2, 3, 4, 6, 9, 11, 14, 43, 123; PC 1; WLC**
See also AAYA 18; AMWS 2; BRW 7; BRWR 1; CA 9-12R; 45-48; CANR 5, 61, 105; CDBLB 1914-1945; CP 1, 2; DA; DA3; DAB; DAC; DAM DRAM, MST, POET; DLB 10, 20; EWL 3; EXPP; MAL 5; MTCW 1, 2; MTFW 2005; PAB; PFS 1, 3, 4, 10; TUS; WP

Audiberti, Jacques 1899-1965 .... **CLC 38**
See also CA 25-28R; DAM DRAM; DLB 321; EWL 3

Audubon, John James 1785-1851 . **NCLC 47**
See also ANW; DLB 248

Auel, Jean M(arie) 1936- .... **CLC 31, 107**
See also AAYA 7, 51; BEST 90:4; BPFB 1; CA 103; CANR 21, 64, 115; CPW; DA3; DAM POP; INT CANR-21; NFS 11; RHW; SATA 91

Auerbach, Erich 1892-1957 .... **TCLC 43**
See also CA 118; 155; EWL 3

Augier, Emile 1820-1889 .... **NCLC 31**
See also DLB 192; GFL 1789 to the Present

August, John
See De Voto, Bernard (Augustine)

Augustine, St. 354-430 .... **CMLC 6; WLCS**
See also DA; DA3; DAB; DAC; DAM MST; DLB 115; EW 1; RGWL 2, 3

Aunt Belinda
See Braddon, Mary Elizabeth

Aunt Weedy
See Alcott, Louisa May

Aurelius
See Bourne, Randolph S(illiman)

Aurelius, Marcus 121-180 .... **CMLC 45**
See Marcus Aurelius
See also RGWL 2, 3

Aurobindo, Sri
See Ghose, Aurabinda

Aurobindo Ghose
See Ghose, Aurabinda

Austen, Jane 1775-1817 ...... **NCLC 1, 13, 19, 33, 51, 81, 95, 119, 150; WLC**
See also AAYA 19; BRW 4; BRWC 1; BRWR 2; BYA 3; CDBLB 1789-1832; DA; DA3; DAB; DAC; DAM MST, NOV; DLB 116; EXPN; FL 1:2; GL 2; LAIT 2; LATS 1:1; LMFS 1; NFS 1, 14, 18, 20, 21; TEA; WLIT 3; WYAS 1

Auster, Paul 1947- .... **CLC 47, 131**
See also AMWS 12; CA 69-72; CANR 23, 52, 75, 129; CMW 4; CN 5, 6, 7; DA3; DLB 227; MAL 5; MTCW 2; MTFW 2005; SUFW 2; TCLE 1:1

Austin, Frank
See Faust, Frederick (Schiller)

Austin, Mary (Hunter) 1868-1934 . **TCLC 25**
See also ANW; CA 109; 178; DLB 9, 78, 206, 221, 275; FW; TCWW 1, 2

Averroes 1126-1198 .... **CMLC 7**
See also DLB 115

Avicenna 980-1037 .... **CMLC 16**
See also DLB 115

Avison, Margaret (Kirkland) 1918- .. **CLC 2, 4, 97**
See also CA 17-20R; CANR 134; CP 1, 2, 3, 4, 5, 6, 7; DAC; DAM POET; DLB 53; MTCW 1

Axton, David
See Koontz, Dean R.

Ayckbourn, Alan 1939- ...... **CLC 5, 8, 18, 33, 74; DC 13**
See also BRWS 5; CA 21-24R; CANR 31, 59, 118; CBD; CD 5, 6; DAB; DAM DRAM; DFS 7; DLB 13, 245; EWL 3; MTCW 1, 2; MTFW 2005

Aydy, Catherine
See Tennant, Emma (Christina)

Ayme, Marcel (Andre) 1902-1967 ... **CLC 11; SSC 41**
See also CA 89-92; CANR 67, 137; CLR 25; DLB 72; EW 12; EWL 3; GFL 1789 to the Present; RGSF 2; RGWL 2, 3; SATA 91

Ayrton, Michael 1921-1975 .... **CLC 7**
See also CA 5-8R; 61-64; CANR 9, 21

Aytmatov, Chingiz
See Aitmatov, Chingiz (Torekulovich)
See also EWL 3

Azorin .... **CLC 11**
See Martinez Ruiz, Jose
See also DLB 322; EW 9; EWL 3

Azuela, Mariano 1873-1952 .. **HLC 1; TCLC 3, 145**
See also CA 104; 131; CANR 81; DAM MULT; EWL 3; HW 1, 2; LAW; MTCW 1, 2; MTFW 2005

Ba, Mariama 1929-1981 .... **BLCS**
See also AFW; BW 2; CA 141; CANR 87; DNFS 2; WLIT 2

Baastad, Babbis Friis
See Friis-Baastad, Babbis Ellinor

Bab
See Gilbert, W(illiam) S(chwenck)

Babbis, Eleanor
See Friis-Baastad, Babbis Ellinor

Babel, Isaac
See Babel, Isaak (Emmanuilovich)
See also EW 11; SSFS 10

Babel, Isaak (Emmanuilovich) 1894-1941(?) . **SSC 16, 78; TCLC 2, 13, 171**
See Babel, Isaac
See also CA 104; 155; CANR 113; DLB 272; EWL 3; MTCW 2; MTFW 2005; RGSF 2; RGWL 2, 3; TWA

Babits, Mihaly 1883-1941 .... **TCLC 14**
See also CA 114; CDWLB 4; DLB 215; EWL 3

Babur 1483-1530 .... **LC 18**

Babylas 1898-1962
See Ghelderode, Michel de

Baca, Jimmy Santiago 1952- . **HLC 1; PC 41**
See also CA 131; CANR 81, 90, 146; CP 7; DAM MULT; DLB 122; HW 1, 2; LLW; MAL 5

Baca, Jose Santiago
See Baca, Jimmy Santiago

Bacchelli, Riccardo 1891-1985 .... **CLC 19**
See also CA 29-32R; 117; DLB 264; EWL 3

Bach, Richard (David) 1936- .... **CLC 14**
See also AITN 1; BEST 89:2; BPFB 1; BYA 5; CA 9-12R; CANR 18, 93; CPW; DAM NOV, POP; FANT; MTCW 1; SATA 13

Bache, Benjamin Franklin 1769-1798 .... **LC 74**
See also DLB 43

Bachelard, Gaston 1884-1962 ...... **TCLC 128**
See also CA 97-100; 89-92; DLB 296; GFL 1789 to the Present

Bachman, Richard
See King, Stephen

Bachmann, Ingeborg 1926-1973 .... **CLC 69**
See also CA 93-96; 45-48; CANR 69; DLB 85; EWL 3; RGWL 2, 3

Bacon, Francis 1561-1626 .... **LC 18, 32**
See also BRW 1; CDBLB Before 1660; DLB 151, 236, 252; RGEL 2; TEA

Bacon, Roger 1214(?)-1294 .... **CMLC 14**
See also DLB 115

Bacovia, George 1881-1957 .... **TCLC 24**
See Vasiliu, Gheorghe
See also CDWLB 4; DLB 220; EWL 3

Badanes, Jerome 1937-1995 .... **CLC 59**
See also CA 234

Bagehot, Walter 1826-1877 .... **NCLC 10**
See also DLB 55

Bagnold, Enid 1889-1981 .... **CLC 25**
See also BYA 2; CA 5-8R; 103; CANR 5, 40; CBD; CN 2; CWD; CWRI 5; DAM DRAM; DLB 13, 160, 191, 245; FW; MAICYA 1, 2; RGEL 2; SATA 1, 25

Bagritsky, Eduard .... **TCLC 60**
See Dzyubin, Eduard Georgievich

Bagrjana, Elisaveta
See Belcheva, Elisaveta Lyubomirova

Bagryana, Elisaveta .... **CLC 10**
See Belcheva, Elisaveta Lyubomirova
See also CA 178; CDWLB 4; DLB 147; EWL 3

Bailey, Paul 1937- .... **CLC 45**
See also CA 21-24R; CANR 16, 62, 124; CN 1, 2, 3, 4, 5, 6, 7; DLB 14, 271; GLL 2

Baillie, Joanna 1762-1851 ...... **NCLC 71, 151**
See also DLB 93; GL 2; RGEL 2

Bainbridge, Beryl (Margaret) 1934- . **CLC 4, 5, 8, 10, 14, 18, 22, 62, 130**
See also BRWS 6; CA 21-24R; CANR 24, 55, 75, 88, 128; CN 2, 3, 4, 5, 6, 7; DAM NOV; DLB 14, 231; EWL 3; MTCW 1, 2; MTFW 2005

Baker, Carlos (Heard) 1909-1987 .... **TCLC 119**
See also CA 5-8R; 122; CANR 3, 63; DLB 103

Baker, Elliott 1922- .... **CLC 8**
See also CA 45-48; CANR 2, 63; CN 1, 2, 3, 4, 5, 6, 7

Baker, Jean H. .... **TCLC 3, 10**
See Russell, George William

Baker, Nicholson 1957- .... **CLC 61, 165**
See also AMWS 13; CA 135; CANR 63, 120, 138; CN 6; CPW; DA3; DAM POP; DLB 227; MTFW 2005

Baker, Ray Stannard 1870-1946 .... **TCLC 47**
See also CA 118

Baker, Russell (Wayne) 1925- .... **CLC 31**
See also BEST 89:4; CA 57-60; CANR 11, 41, 59, 137; MTCW 1, 2; MTFW 2005

Bakhtin, M.
See Bakhtin, Mikhail Mikhailovich

Bakhtin, M. M.
See Bakhtin, Mikhail Mikhailovich

Bakhtin, Mikhail
See Bakhtin, Mikhail Mikhailovich

Bakhtin, Mikhail Mikhailovich 1895-1975 .... **CLC 83; TCLC 160**
See also CA 128; 113; DLB 242; EWL 3

Bakshi, Ralph 1938(?)- .... **CLC 26**
See also CA 112; 138; IDFW 3

Bakunin, Mikhail (Alexandrovich) 1814-1876 .... **NCLC 25, 58**
See also DLB 277

Baldwin, James (Arthur) 1924-1987 . **BLC 1; CLC 1, 2, 3, 4, 5, 8, 13, 15, 17, 42, 50, 67, 90, 127; DC 1; SSC 10, 33; WLC**
See also AAYA 4, 34; AFAW 1, 2; AMWR 2; AMWS 1; BPFB 1; BW 1; CA 1-4R; 124; CABS 1; CAD; CANR 3, 24; CDALB 1941-1968; CN 1, 2, 3, 4; CPW; DA; DA3; DAB; DAC; DAM MST, MULT, NOV, POP; DFS 11, 15; DLB 2, 7, 33, 249, 278; DLBY 1987; EWL 3;

EXPS; LAIT 5; MAL 5; MTCW 1, 2; MTFW 2005; NCFS 4; NFS 4; RGAL 4; RGSF 2; SATA 9; SATA-Obit 54; SSFS 2, 18; TUS

Baldwin, William c. 1515-1563 .... **LC 113**
See also DLB 132

Bale, John 1495-1563 .... **LC 62**
See also DLB 132; RGEL 2; TEA

Ball, Hugo 1886-1927 .... **TCLC 104**

Ballard, J(ames) G(raham) 1930- . **CLC 3, 6, 14, 36, 137; SSC 1, 53**
See also AAYA 3, 52; BRWS 5; CA 5-8R; CANR 15, 39, 65, 107, 133; CN 1, 2, 3, 4, 5, 6, 7; DA3; DAM NOV, POP; DLB 14, 207, 261, 319; EWL 3; HGG; MTCW 1, 2; MTFW 2005; NFS 8; RGEL 2; RGSF 2; SATA 93; SCFW 1, 2; SFW 4

Balmont, Konstantin (Dmitriyevich) 1867-1943 .... **TCLC 11**
See also CA 109; 155; DLB 295; EWL 3

Baltausis, Vincas 1847-1910
See Mikszath, Kalman

Balzac, Honore de 1799-1850 ... **NCLC 5, 35, 53, 153; SSC 5, 59; WLC**
See also DA; DA3; DAB; DAC; DAM MST, NOV; DLB 119; EW 5; GFL 1789 to the Present; LMFS 1; RGSF 2; RGWL 2, 3; SSFS 10; SUFW; TWA

Bambara, Toni Cade 1939-1995 .... **BLC 1; CLC 19, 88; SSC 35; TCLC 116; WLCS**
See also AAYA 5, 49; AFAW 2; AMWS 11; BW 2, 3; BYA 12, 14; CA 29-32R; 150; CANR 24, 49, 81; CDALBS; DA; DA3; DAC; DAM MST, MULT; DLB 38, 218; EXPS; MAL 5; MTCW 1, 2; MTFW 2005; RGAL 4; RGSF 2; SATA 112; SSFS 4, 7, 12, 21

Bamdad, A.
See Shamlu, Ahmad

Bamdad, Alef
See Shamlu, Ahmad

Banat, D. R.
See Bradbury, Ray (Douglas)

Bancroft, Laura
See Baum, L(yman) Frank

Banim, John 1798-1842 .... **NCLC 13**
See also DLB 116, 158, 159; RGEL 2

Banim, Michael 1796-1874 .... **NCLC 13**
See also DLB 158, 159

Banjo, The
See Paterson, A(ndrew) B(arton)

Banks, Iain
See Banks, Iain M(enzies)
See also BRWS 11

Banks, Iain M(enzies) 1954- .... **CLC 34**
See Banks, Iain
See also CA 123; 128; CANR 61, 106; DLB 194, 261; EWL 3; HGG; INT CA-128; MTFW 2005; SFW 4

Banks, Lynne Reid .... **CLC 23**
See Reid Banks, Lynne
See also AAYA 6; BYA 7; CLR 86; CN 4, 5, 6

Banks, Russell (Earl) 1940- .... **CLC 37, 72, 187; SSC 42**
See also AAYA 45; AMWS 5; CA 65-68; CAAS 15; CANR 19, 52, 73, 118; CN 4, 5, 6, 7; DLB 130, 278; EWL 3; MAL 5; MTCW 2; MTFW 2005; NFS 13

Banville, John 1945- .... **CLC 46, 118**
See also CA 117; 128; CANR 104; CN 4, 5, 6, 7; DLB 14, 271; INT CA-128

Banville, Theodore (Faullain) de 1832-1891 .... **NCLC 9**
See also DLB 217; GFL 1789 to the Present

Baraka, Amiri 1934- .... **BLC 1; CLC 1, 2, 3, 5, 10, 14, 33, 115, 213; DC 6; PC 4; WLCS**
See Jones, LeRoi
See also AAYA 63; AFAW 1, 2; AMWS 2; BW 2, 3; CA 21-24R; CABS 3; CAD; CANR 27, 38, 61, 133; CD 3, 5, 6; CDALB 1941-1968; CP 4, 5, 6, 7; CPW; DA; DA3; DAC; DAM MST, MULT, POET, POP; DFS 3, 11, 16; DLB 5, 7, 16, 38; DLBD 8; EWL 3; MAL 5; MTCW 1, 2; MTFW 2005; PFS 9; RGAL 4; TCLE 1:1; TUS; WP

Baratynsky, Evgenii Abramovich 1800-1844 .... **NCLC 103**
See also DLB 205

Barbauld, Anna Laetitia 1743-1825 .... **NCLC 50**
See also DLB 107, 109, 142, 158; RGEL 2

Barbellion, W. N. P. .... **TCLC 24**
See Cummings, Bruce F(rederick)

Barber, Benjamin R. 1939- .... **CLC 141**
See also CA 29-32R; CANR 12, 32, 64, 119

Barbera, Jack (Vincent) 1945- .... **CLC 44**
See also CA 110; CANR 45

Barbey d'Aurevilly, Jules-Amedee 1808-1889 .... **NCLC 1; SSC 17**
See also DLB 119; GFL 1789 to the Present

Barbour, John c. 1316-1395 .... **CMLC 33**
See also DLB 146

Barbusse, Henri 1873-1935 .... **TCLC 5**
See also CA 105; 154; DLB 65; EWL 3; RGWL 2, 3

Barclay, Alexander c. 1475-1552 .... **LC 109**
See also DLB 132

Barclay, Bill
See Moorcock, Michael (John)

Barclay, William Ewert
See Moorcock, Michael (John)

Barea, Arturo 1897-1957 .... **TCLC 14**
See also CA 111; 201

Barfoot, Joan 1946- .... **CLC 18**
See also CA 105; CANR 141

Barham, Richard Harris 1788-1845 .... **NCLC 77**
See also DLB 159

Baring, Maurice 1874-1945 .... **TCLC 8**
See also CA 105; 168; DLB 34; HGG

Baring-Gould, Sabine 1834-1924 ... **TCLC 88**
See also DLB 156, 190

Barker, Clive 1952- .... **CLC 52, 205; SSC 53**
See also AAYA 10, 54; BEST 90:3; BPFB 1; CA 121; 129; CANR 71, 111, 133; CPW; DA3; DAM POP; DLB 261; HGG; INT CA-129; MTCW 1, 2; MTFW 2005; SUFW 2

Barker, George Granville 1913-1991 .... **CLC 8, 48**
See also CA 9-12R; 135; CANR 7, 38; CP 1, 2, 3, 4; DAM POET; DLB 20; EWL 3; MTCW 1

Barker, Harley Granville
See Granville-Barker, Harley
See also DLB 10

Barker, Howard 1946- .... **CLC 37**
See also CA 102; CBD; CD 5, 6; DLB 13, 233

Barker, Jane 1652-1732 .... **LC 42, 82**
See also DLB 39, 131

Barker, Pat(ricia) 1943- ...... **CLC 32, 94, 146**
See also BRWS 4; CA 117; 122; CANR 50, 101; CN 6, 7; DLB 271; INT CA-122

Barlach, Ernst (Heinrich) 1870-1938 .... **TCLC 84**
See also CA 178; DLB 56, 118; EWL 3

Barlow, Joel 1754-1812 .... **NCLC 23**
See also AMWS 2; DLB 37; RGAL 4

Barnard, Mary (Ethel) 1909- .... **CLC 48**
See also CA 21-22; CAP 2; CP 1

Barnes, Djuna 1892-1982 .... **CLC 3, 4, 8, 11, 29, 127; SSC 3**
See Steptoe, Lydia
See also AMWS 3; CA 9-12R; 107; CAD; CANR 16, 55; CN 1, 2, 3; CWD; DLB 4, 9, 45; EWL 3; GLL 1; MAL 5; MTCW 1, 2; MTFW 2005; RGAL 4; TCLE 1:1; TUS

Barnes, Jim 1933- .... **NNAL**
See also CA 108; 175; CAAE 175; CAAS 28; DLB 175

Barnes, Julian (Patrick) 1946- . **CLC 42, 141**
See also BRWS 4; CA 102; CANR 19, 54, 115, 137; CN 4, 5, 6, 7; DAB; DLB 194; DLBY 1993; EWL 3; MTCW 2; MTFW 2005

Barnes, Peter 1931-2004 .... **CLC 5, 56**
See also CA 65-68; 230; CAAS 12; CANR 33, 34, 64, 113; CBD; CD 5, 6; DFS 6; DLB 13, 233; MTCW 1

Barnes, William 1801-1886 .... **NCLC 75**
See also DLB 32

Baroja (y Nessi), Pio 1872-1956 .... **HLC 1; TCLC 8**
See also CA 104; EW 9

Baron, David
See Pinter, Harold

Baron Corvo
See Rolfe, Frederick (William Serafino Austin Lewis Mary)

Barondess, Sue K(aufman) 1926-1977 .... **CLC 8**
See Kaufman, Sue
See also CA 1-4R; 69-72; CANR 1

Baron de Teive
See Pessoa, Fernando (Antonio Nogueira)

Baroness Von S.
See Zangwill, Israel

Barres, (Auguste-)Maurice 1862-1923 .... **TCLC 47**
See also CA 164; DLB 123; GFL 1789 to the Present

Barreto, Afonso Henrique de Lima
See Lima Barreto, Afonso Henrique de

Barrett, Andrea 1954- .... **CLC 150**
See also CA 156; CANR 92; CN 7

Barrett, Michele .... **CLC 65**

Barrett, (Roger) Syd 1946- .... **CLC 35**

Barrett, William (Christopher) 1913-1992 .... **CLC 27**
See also CA 13-16R; 139; CANR 11, 67; INT CANR-11

Barrett Browning, Elizabeth 1806-1861 ... **NCLC 1, 16, 61, 66; PC 6, 62; WLC**
See also AAYA 63; BRW 4; CDBLB 1832-1890; DA; DA3; DAB; DAC; DAM MST, POET; DLB 32, 199; EXPP; PAB; PFS 2, 16, 23; TEA; WLIT 4; WP

Barrie, J(ames) M(atthew) 1860-1937 .... **TCLC 2, 164**
See also BRWS 3; BYA 4, 5; CA 104; 136; CANR 77; CDBLB 1890-1914; CLR 16; CWRI 5; DA3; DAB; DAM DRAM; DFS 7; DLB 10, 141, 156; EWL 3; FANT; MAICYA 1, 2; MTCW 2; MTFW 2005; SATA 100; SUFW; WCH; WLIT 4; YABC 1

Barrington, Michael
See Moorcock, Michael (John)

Barrol, Grady
See Bograd, Larry

Barry, Mike
See Malzberg, Barry N(athaniel)

Barry, Philip 1896-1949 .... **TCLC 11**
See also CA 109; 199; DFS 9; DLB 7, 228; MAL 5; RGAL 4

Bart, Andre Schwarz
See Schwarz-Bart, Andre

Beresford, J(ohn) D(avys)
1873-1947 .... **TCLC 81**
See also CA 112; 155; DLB 162, 178, 197;
SFW 4; SUFW 1

Bergelson, David (Rafailovich)
1884-1952 .... **TCLC 81**
See Bergelson, Dovid
See also CA 220

Bergelson, Dovid
See Bergelson, David (Rafailovich)
See also EWL 3

Berger, Colonel
See Malraux, (Georges-)Andre

Berger, John (Peter) 1926- .... **CLC 2, 19**
See also BRWS 4; CA 81-84; CANR 51,
78, 117; CN 1, 2, 3, 4, 5, 6, 7; DLB 14,
207, 319

Berger, Melvin H. 1927- .... **CLC 12**
See also CA 5-8R; CANR 4, 142; CLR 32;
SAAS 2; SATA 5, 88, 158; SATA-Essay
124

Berger, Thomas (Louis) 1924- .. **CLC 3, 5, 8,
11, 18, 38**
See also BPFB 1; CA 1-4R; CANR 5, 28,
51, 128; CN 1, 2, 3, 4, 5, 6, 7; DAM
NOV; DLB 2; DLBY 1980; EWL 3;
FANT; INT CANR-28; MAL 5; MTCW
1, 2; MTFW 2005; RHW; TCLE 1:1;
TCWW 1, 2

Bergman, (Ernst) Ingmar 1918- ...... **CLC 16,
72, 210**
See also AAYA 61; CA 81-84; CANR 33,
70; CWW 2; DLB 257; MTCW 2; MTFW
2005

Bergson, Henri(-Louis) 1859-1941 . **TCLC 32**
See also CA 164; EW 8; EWL 3; GFL 1789
to the Present

Bergstein, Eleanor 1938- .... **CLC 4**
See also CA 53-56; CANR 5

Berkeley, George 1685-1753 .... **LC 65**
See also DLB 31, 101, 252

Berkoff, Steven 1937- .... **CLC 56**
See also CA 104; CANR 72; CBD; CD 5, 6

Berlin, Isaiah 1909-1997 .... **TCLC 105**
See also CA 85-88; 162

Bermant, Chaim (Icyk) 1929-1998 ... **CLC 40**
See also CA 57-60; CANR 6, 31, 57, 105;
CN 2, 3, 4, 5, 6

Bern, Victoria
See Fisher, M(ary) F(rances) K(ennedy)

Bernanos, (Paul Louis) Georges
1888-1948 .... **TCLC 3**
See also CA 104; 130; CANR 94; DLB 72;
EWL 3; GFL 1789 to the Present; RGWL
2, 3

Bernard, April 1956- .... **CLC 59**
See also CA 131; CANR 144

Bernard of Clairvaux 1090-1153 .. **CMLC 71**
See also DLB 208

Berne, Victoria
See Fisher, M(ary) F(rances) K(ennedy)

Bernhard, Thomas 1931-1989 ..... **CLC 3, 32,
61; DC 14; TCLC 165**
See also CA 85-88; 127; CANR 32, 57; CD-
WLB 2; DLB 85, 124; EWL 3; MTCW 1;
RGWL 2, 3

Bernhardt, Sarah (Henriette Rosine)
1844-1923 .... **TCLC 75**
See also CA 157

Bernstein, Charles 1950- .... **CLC 142,**
See also CA 129; CAAS 24; CANR 90; CP
4, 5, 6, 7; DLB 169

Bernstein, Ingrid
See Kirsch, Sarah

Beroul fl. c. 12th cent. - .... **CMLC 75**

Berriault, Gina 1926-1999 .... **CLC 54, 109;
SSC 30**
See also CA 116; 129; 185; CANR 66; DLB
130; SSFS 7,11

Berrigan, Daniel 1921- .... **CLC 4**
See also CA 33-36R, 187; CAAE 187;
CAAS 1; CANR 11, 43, 78; CP 1, 2, 3, 4,
5, 6, 7; DLB 5

Berrigan, Edmund Joseph Michael, Jr.
1934-1983
See Berrigan, Ted
See also CA 61-64; 110; CANR 14, 102

Berrigan, Ted .... **CLC 37**
See Berrigan, Edmund Joseph Michael, Jr.
See also CP 1, 2, 3; DLB 5, 169; WP

Berry, Charles Edward Anderson 1931-
See Berry, Chuck
See also CA 115

Berry, Chuck .... **CLC 17**
See Berry, Charles Edward Anderson

Berry, Jonas
See Ashbery, John (Lawrence)
See also GLL 1

Berry, Wendell (Erdman) 1934- ... **CLC 4, 6,
8, 27, 46; PC 28**
See also AITN 1; AMWS 10; ANW; CA
73-76; CANR 50, 73, 101, 132; CP 1, 2,
3, 4, 5, 6, 7; CSW; DAM POET; DLB 5,
6, 234, 275; MTCW 2; MTFW 2005;
TCLE 1:1

Berryman, John 1914-1972 ... **CLC 1, 2, 3, 4,
6, 8, 10, 13, 25, 62; PC 64**
See also AMW; CA 13-16; 33-36R; CABS
2; CANR 35; CAP 1; CDALB 1941-1968;
CP 1; DAM POET; DLB 48; EWL 3;
MAL 5; MTCW 1, 2; MTFW 2005; PAB;
RGAL 4; WP

Bertolucci, Bernardo 1940- ...... **CLC 16, 157**
See also CA 106; CANR 125

Berton, Pierre (Francis de Marigny)
1920-2004 .... **CLC 104**
See also CA 1-4R; 233; CANR 2, 56, 144;
CPW; DLB 68; SATA 99; SATA-Obit 158

Bertrand, Aloysius 1807-1841 .... **NCLC 31**
See Bertrand, Louis oAloysiusc

Bertrand, Louis oAloysiusc
See Bertrand, Aloysius
See also DLB 217

Bertran de Born c. 1140-1215 .... **CMLC 5**

Besant, Annie (Wood) 1847-1933 ..... **TCLC 9**
See also CA 105; 185

Bessie, Alvah 1904-1985 .... **CLC 23**
See also CA 5-8R; 116; CANR 2, 80; DLB
26

Bestuzhev, Aleksandr Aleksandrovich
1797-1837 .... **NCLC 131**
See also DLB 198

Bethlen, T. D.
See Silverberg, Robert

Beti, Mongo .... **BLC 1; CLC 27**
See Biyidi, Alexandre
See also AFW; CANR 79; DAM MULT;
EWL 3; WLIT 2

Betjeman, John 1906-1984 ...... **CLC 2, 6, 10,
34, 43**
See also BRW 7; CA 9-12R; 112; CANR
33, 56; CDBLB 1945-1960; CP 1, 2, 3;
DA3; DAB; DAM MST, POET; DLB 20;
DLBY 1984; EWL 3; MTCW 1, 2

Bettelheim, Bruno 1903-1990 .... **CLC 79;
TCLC 143**
See also CA 81-84; 131; CANR 23, 61;
DA3; MTCW 1, 2

Betti, Ugo 1892-1953 .... **TCLC 5**
See also CA 104; 155; EWL 3; RGWL 2, 3

Betts, Doris (Waugh) 1932- ..... **CLC 3, 6, 28;
SSC 45**
See also CA 13-16R; CANR 9, 66, 77; CN
6, 7; CSW; DLB 218; DLBY 1982; INT
CANR-9; RGAL 4

Bevan, Alistair
See Roberts, Keith (John Kingston)

Bey, Pilaff
See Douglas, (George) Norman

Bialik, Chaim Nachman
1873-1934 .... **TCLC 25**
See Bialik, Hayyim Nahman
See also CA 170; EWL 3

Bialik, Hayyim Nahman
See Bialik, Chaim Nachman
See also WLIT 6

Bickerstaff, Isaac
See Swift, Jonathan

Bidart, Frank 1939- .... **CLC 33**
See also AMWS 15; CA 140; CANR 106;
CP 7

Bienek, Horst 1930- .... **CLC 7, 11**
See also CA 73-76; DLB 75

Bierce, Ambrose (Gwinett)
1842-1914(?) ..... **SSC 9, 72; TCLC 1, 7,
44; WLC**
See also AAYA 55; AMW; BYA 11; CA
104; 139; CANR 78; CDALB 1865-1917;
DA; DA3; DAC; DAM MST; DLB 11,
12, 23, 71, 74, 186; EWL 3; EXPS; HGG;
LAIT 2; MAL 5; RGAL 4; RGSF 2; SSFS
9; SUFW 1

Biggers, Earl Derr 1884-1933 .... **TCLC 65**
See also CA 108; 153; DLB 306

Billiken, Bud
See Motley, Willard (Francis)

Billings, Josh
See Shaw, Henry Wheeler

Billington, (Lady) Rachel (Mary)
1942- .... **CLC 43**
See also AITN 2; CA 33-36R; CANR 44;
CN 4, 5, 6, 7

Binchy, Maeve 1940- .... **CLC 153**
See also BEST 90:1; BPFB 1; CA 127; 134;
CANR 50, 96, 134; CN 5, 6, 7; CPW;
DA3; DAM POP; DLB 319; INT CA-134;
MTCW 2; MTFW 2005; RHW

Binyon, T(imothy) J(ohn)
1936-2004 .... **CLC 34**
See also CA 111; 232; CANR 28, 140

Bion 335B.C.-245B.C. .... **CMLC 39**

Bioy Casares, Adolfo 1914-1999 ... **CLC 4, 8,
13, 88; HLC 1; SSC 17**
See Casares, Adolfo Bioy; Miranda, Javier;
Sacastru, Martin
See also CA 29-32R; 177; CANR 19, 43,
66; CWW 2; DAM MULT; DLB 113;
EWL 3; HW 1, 2; LAW; MTCW 1, 2;
MTFW 2005

Birch, Allison .... **CLC 65**

Bird, Cordwainer
See Ellison, Harlan (Jay)

Bird, Robert Montgomery
1806-1854 .... **NCLC 1**
See also DLB 202; RGAL 4

Birkerts, Sven 1951- .... **CLC 116**
See also CA 128; 133, 176; CAAE 176;
CAAS 29; INT CA-133

Birney, (Alfred) Earle 1904-1995 .. **CLC 1, 4,
6, 11; PC 52**
See also CA 1-4R; CANR 5, 20; CN 1, 2,
3, 4; CP 1, 2, 3, 4; DAC; DAM MST,
POET; DLB 88; MTCW 1; PFS 8; RGEL
2

Biruni, al 973-1048(?) .... **CMLC 28**

Bishop, Elizabeth 1911-1979 ..... **CLC 1, 4, 9,
13, 15, 32; PC 3, 34; TCLC 121**
See also AMWR 2; AMWS 1; CA 5-8R;
89-92; CABS 2; CANR 26, 61, 108;
CDALB 1968-1988; CP 1, 2, 3; DA;
DA3; DAC; DAM MST, POET; DLB 5,
169; EWL 3; GLL 2; MAL 5; MAWW;
MTCW 1, 2; PAB; PFS 6, 12; RGAL 4;
SATA-Obit 24; TUS; WP

Bishop, John 1935- .... **CLC 10**
See also CA 105

Boker, George Henry 1823-1890 . **NCLC 125**
See also RGAL 4

Boland, Eavan (Aisling) 1944- .. **CLC 40, 67, 113; PC 58**
See also BRWS 5; CA 143, 207; CAAE 207; CANR 61; CP 1, 7; CWP; DAM POET; DLB 40; FW; MTCW 2; MTFW 2005; PFS 12, 22

Boll, Heinrich (Theodor)
See Boell, Heinrich (Theodor)
See also BPFB 1; CDWLB 2; EW 13; EWL 3; RGSF 2; RGWL 2, 3

Bolt, Lee
See Faust, Frederick (Schiller)

Bolt, Robert (Oxton) 1924-1995 ...... **CLC 14; TCLC 175**
See also CA 17-20R; 147; CANR 35, 67; CBD; DAM DRAM; DFS 2; DLB 13, 233; EWL 3; LAIT 1; MTCW 1

Bombal, Maria Luisa 1910-1980 .... **HLCS 1; SSC 37**
See also CA 127; CANR 72; EWL 3; HW 1; LAW; RGSF 2

Bombet, Louis-Alexandre-Cesar
See Stendhal

Bomkauf
See Kaufman, Bob (Garnell)

Bonaventura .... **NCLC 35**
See also DLB 90

Bonaventure 1217(?)-1274 .... **CMLC 79**
See also DLB 115; LMFS 1

Bond, Edward 1934- .... **CLC 4, 6, 13, 23**
See also AAYA 50; BRWS 1; CA 25-28R; CANR 38, 67, 106; CBD; CD 5, 6; DAM DRAM; DFS 3, 8; DLB 13, 310; EWL 3; MTCW 1

Bonham, Frank 1914-1989 .... **CLC 12**
See also AAYA 1; BYA 1, 3; CA 9-12R; CANR 4, 36; JRDA; MAICYA 1, 2; SAAS 3; SATA 1, 49; SATA-Obit 62; TCWW 1, 2; YAW

Bonnefoy, Yves 1923- . **CLC 9, 15, 58; PC 58**
See also CA 85-88; CANR 33, 75, 97, 136; CWW 2; DAM MST, POET; DLB 258; EWL 3; GFL 1789 to the Present; MTCW 1, 2; MTFW 2005

Bonner, Marita .... **HR 1:2**
See Occomy, Marita (Odette) Bonner

Bonnin, Gertrude 1876-1938 .... **NNAL**
See Zitkala-Sa
See also CA 150; DAM MULT

Bontemps, Arna(ud Wendell)
1902-1973 .. **BLC 1; CLC 1, 18; HR 1:2**
See also BW 1; CA 1-4R; 41-44R; CANR 4, 35; CLR 6; CP 1; CWRI 5; DA3; DAM MULT, NOV, POET; DLB 48, 51; JRDA; MAICYA 1, 2; MAL 5; MTCW 1, 2; SATA 2, 44; SATA-Obit 24; WCH; WP

Boot, William
See Stoppard, Tom

Booth, Martin 1944-2004 .... **CLC 13**
See also CA 93-96, 188; 223; CAAE 188; CAAS 2; CANR 92; CP 1, 2, 3, 4

Booth, Philip 1925- .... **CLC 23**
See also CA 5-8R; CANR 5, 88; CP 1, 2, 3, 4, 5, 6, 7; DLBY 1982

Booth, Wayne C(layson) 1921-2005 . **CLC 24**
See also CA 1-4R; CAAS 5; CANR 3, 43, 117; DLB 67

Borchert, Wolfgang 1921-1947 .... **TCLC 5**
See also CA 104; 188; DLB 69, 124; EWL 3

Borel, Petrus 1809-1859 .... **NCLC 41**
See also DLB 119; GFL 1789 to the Present

Borges, Jorge Luis 1899-1986 ... **CLC 1, 2, 3, 4, 6, 8, 9, 10, 13, 19, 44, 48, 83; HLC 1; PC 22, 32; SSC 4, 41; TCLC 109; WLC**
See also AAYA 26; BPFB 1; CA 21-24R; CANR 19, 33, 75, 105, 133; CDWLB 3; DA; DA3; DAB; DAC; DAM MST,

MULT; DLB 113, 283; DLBY 1986; DNFS 1, 2; EWL 3; HW 1, 2; LAW; LMFS 2; MSW; MTCW 1, 2; MTFW 2005; RGSF 2; RGWL 2, 3; SFW 4; SSFS 17; TWA; WLIT 1

Borowski, Tadeusz 1922-1951 .... **SSC 48; TCLC 9**
See also CA 106; 154; CDWLB 4; DLB 215; EWL 3; RGSF 2; RGWL 3; SSFS 13

Borrow, George (Henry)
1803-1881 .... **NCLC 9**
See also DLB 21, 55, 166

Bosch (Gavino), Juan 1909-2001 ..... **HLCS 1**
See also CA 151; 204; DAM MST, MULT; DLB 145; HW 1, 2

Bosman, Herman Charles
1905-1951 .... **TCLC 49**
See Malan, Herman
See also CA 160; DLB 225; RGSF 2

Bosschere, Jean de 1878(?)-1953 ... **TCLC 19**
See also CA 115; 186

Boswell, James 1740-1795 ... **LC 4, 50; WLC**
See also BRW 3; CDBLB 1660-1789; DA; DAB; DAC; DAM MST; DLB 104, 142; TEA; WLIT 3

Bottomley, Gordon 1874-1948 ..... **TCLC 107**
See also CA 120; 192; DLB 10

Bottoms, David 1949- .... **CLC 53**
See also CA 105; CANR 22; CSW; DLB 120; DLBY 1983

Boucicault, Dion 1820-1890 .... **NCLC 41**

Boucolon, Maryse
See Conde, Maryse

Bourdieu, Pierre 1930-2002 .... **CLC 198**
See also CA 130; 204

Bourget, Paul (Charles Joseph)
1852-1935 .... **TCLC 12**
See also CA 107; 196; DLB 123; GFL 1789 to the Present

Bourjaily, Vance (Nye) 1922- .... **CLC 8, 62**
See also CA 1-4R; CAAS 1; CANR 2, 72; CN 1, 2, 3, 4, 5, 6, 7; DLB 2, 143; MAL 5

Bourne, Randolph S(illiman)
1886-1918 .... **TCLC 16**
See also AMW; CA 117; 155; DLB 63; MAL 5

Bova, Ben(jamin William) 1932- ...... **CLC 45**
See also AAYA 16; CA 5-8R; CAAS 18; CANR 11, 56, 94, 111; CLR 3, 96; DLBY 1981; INT CANR-11; MAICYA 1, 2; MTCW 1; SATA 6, 68, 133; SFW 4

Bowen, Elizabeth (Dorothea Cole)
1899-1973 . **CLC 1, 3, 6, 11, 15, 22, 118; SSC 3, 28, 66; TCLC 148**
See also BRWS 2; CA 17-18; 41-44R; CANR 35, 105; CAP 2; CDBLB 1945-1960; CN 1; DA3; DAM NOV; DLB 15, 162; EWL 3; EXPS; FW; HGG; MTCW 1, 2; MTFW 2005; NFS 13; RGSF 2; SSFS 5; SUFW 1; TEA; WLIT 4

Bowering, George 1935- .... **CLC 15, 47**
See also CA 21-24R; CAAS 16; CANR 10; CN 7; CP 1, 2, 3, 4, 5, 6, 7; DLB 53

Bowering, Marilyn R(uthe) 1949- .... **CLC 32**
See also CA 101; CANR 49; CP 4, 5, 6, 7; CWP

Bowers, Edgar 1924-2000 .... **CLC 9**
See also CA 5-8R; 188; CANR 24; CP 1, 2, 3, 4, 5, 6, 7; CSW; DLB 5

Bowers, Mrs. J. Milton 1842-1914
See Bierce, Ambrose (Gwinett)

Bowie, David .... **CLC 17**
See Jones, David Robert

Bowles, Jane (Sydney) 1917-1973 ..... **CLC 3, 68**
See Bowles, Jane Auer
See also CA 19-20; 41-44R; CAP 2; CN 1; MAL 5

Bowles, Jane Auer
See Bowles, Jane (Sydney)
See also EWL 3

Bowles, Paul (Frederick) 1910-1999 . **CLC 1, 2, 19, 53; SSC 3**
See also AMWS 4; CA 1-4R; 186; CAAS 1; CANR 1, 19, 50, 75; CN 1, 2, 3, 4, 5, 6; DA3; DLB 5, 6, 218; EWL 3; MAL 5; MTCW 1, 2; MTFW 2005; RGAL 4; SSFS 17

Bowles, William Lisle 1762-1850 . **NCLC 103**
See also DLB 93

Box, Edgar
See Vidal, (Eugene Luther) Gore
See also GLL 1

Boyd, James 1888-1944 .... **TCLC 115**
See also CA 186; DLB 9; DLBD 16; RGAL 4; RHW

Boyd, Nancy
See Millay, Edna St. Vincent
See also GLL 1

Boyd, Thomas (Alexander)
1898-1935 .... **TCLC 111**
See also CA 111; 183; DLB 9; DLBD 16, 316

Boyd, William (Andrew Murray)
1952- .... **CLC 28, 53, 70**
See also CA 114; 120; CANR 51, 71, 131; CN 4, 5, 6, 7; DLB 231

Boyesen, Hjalmar Hjorth
1848-1895 .... **NCLC 135**
See also DLB 12, 71; DLBD 13; RGAL 4

Boyle, Kay 1902-1992 .... **CLC 1, 5, 19, 58, 121; SSC 5**
See also CA 13-16R; 140; CAAS 1; CANR 29, 61, 110; CN 1, 2, 3, 4, 5; CP 1, 2, 3, 4; DLB 4, 9, 48, 86; DLBY 1993; EWL 3; MAL 5; MTCW 1, 2; MTFW 2005; RGAL 4; RGSF 2; SSFS 10, 13, 14

Boyle, Mark
See Kienzle, William X(avier)

Boyle, Patrick 1905-1982 .... **CLC 19**
See also CA 127

Boyle, T. C.
See Boyle, T(homas) Coraghessan
See also AMWS 8

Boyle, T(homas) Coraghessan
1948- .... **CLC 36, 55, 90; SSC 16**
See Boyle, T. C.
See also AAYA 47; BEST 90:4; BPFB 1; CA 120; CANR 44, 76, 89, 132; CN 6, 7; CPW; DA3; DAM POP; DLB 218, 278; DLBY 1986; EWL 3; MAL 5; MTCW 2; MTFW 2005; SSFS 13, 19

Boz
See Dickens, Charles (John Huffam)

Brackenridge, Hugh Henry
1748-1816 .... **NCLC 7**
See also DLB 11, 37; RGAL 4

Bradbury, Edward P.
See Moorcock, Michael (John)
See also MTCW 2

Bradbury, Malcolm (Stanley)
1932-2000 .... **CLC 32, 61**
See also CA 1-4R; CANR 1, 33, 91, 98, 137; CN 1, 2, 3, 4, 5, 6, 7; CP 1; DAM NOV; DLB 14, 207; EWL 3; MTCW 1, 2; MTFW 2005

Bradbury, Ray (Douglas) 1920- .... **CLC 1, 3, 10, 15, 42, 98; SSC 29, 53; WLC**
See also AAYA 15; AITN 1, 2; AMWS 4; BPFB 1; BYA 4, 5, 11; CA 1-4R; CANR 2, 30, 75, 125; CDALB 1968-1988; CN 1, 2, 3, 4, 5, 6, 7; CPW; DA; DA3; DAB; DAC; DAM MST, NOV, POP; DLB 2, 8;

EXPN; EXPS; HGG; LAIT 3, 5; LATS 1:2; LMFS 2; MAL 5; MTCW 1, 2; MTFW 2005; NFS 1, 22; RGAL 4; RGSF 2; SATA 11, 64, 123; SCFW 1, 2; SFW 4; SSFS 1, 20; SUFW 1, 2; TUS; YAW

Braddon, Mary Elizabeth
1837-1915 .... **TCLC 111**
See also BRWS 8; CA 108; 179; CMW 4; DLB 18, 70, 156; HGG

Bradfield, Scott (Michael) 1955- .... **SSC 65**
See also CA 147; CANR 90; HGG; SUFW 2

Bradford, Gamaliel 1863-1932 .... **TCLC 36**
See also CA 160; DLB 17

Bradford, William 1590-1657 .... **LC 64**
See also DLB 24, 30; RGAL 4

Bradley, David (Henry), Jr. 1950- .... **BLC 1; CLC 23, 118**
See also BW 1, 3; CA 104; CANR 26, 81; CN 4, 5, 6, 7; DAM MULT; DLB 33

Bradley, John Ed(mund, Jr.) 1958- . **CLC 55**
See also CA 139; CANR 99; CN 6, 7; CSW

Bradley, Marion Zimmer
1930-1999 .... **CLC 30**
See Chapman, Lee; Dexter, John; Gardner, Miriam; Ives, Morgan; Rivers, Elfrida
See also AAYA 40; BPFB 1; CA 57-60; 185; CAAS 10; CANR 7, 31, 51, 75, 107; CPW; DA3; DAM POP; DLB 8; FANT; FW; MTCW 1, 2; MTFW 2005; SATA 90, 139; SATA-Obit 116; SFW 4; SUFW 2; YAW

Bradshaw, John 1933- .... **CLC 70**
See also CA 138; CANR 61

Bradstreet, Anne 1612(?)-1672 ...... **LC 4, 30; PC 10**
See also AMWS 1; CDALB 1640-1865; DA; DA3; DAC; DAM MST, POET; DLB 24; EXPP; FW; PFS 6; RGAL 4; TUS; WP

Brady, Joan 1939- .... **CLC 86**
See also CA 141

Bragg, Melvyn 1939- .... **CLC 10**
See also BEST 89:3; CA 57-60; CANR 10, 48, 89; CN 1, 2, 3, 4, 5, 6, 7; DLB 14, 271; RHW

Brahe, Tycho 1546-1601 .... **LC 45**
See also DLB 300

Braine, John (Gerard) 1922-1986 . **CLC 1, 3, 41**
See also CA 1-4R; 120; CANR 1, 33; CD-BLB 1945-1960; CN 1, 2, 3, 4; DLB 15; DLBY 1986; EWL 3; MTCW 1

Braithwaite, William Stanley (Beaumont)
1878-1962 .... **BLC 1; HR 1:2; PC 52**
See also BW 1; CA 125; DAM MULT; DLB 50, 54; MAL 5

Bramah, Ernest 1868-1942 .... **TCLC 72**
See also CA 156; CMW 4; DLB 70; FANT

Brammer, Billy Lee
See Brammer, William

Brammer, William 1929-1978 .... **CLC 31**
See also CA 235; 77-80

Brancati, Vitaliano 1907-1954 .... **TCLC 12**
See also CA 109; DLB 264; EWL 3

Brancato, Robin F(idler) 1936- .... **CLC 35**
See also AAYA 9, 68; BYA 6; CA 69-72; CANR 11, 45; CLR 32; JRDA; MAICYA 2; MAICYAS 1; SAAS 9; SATA 97; WYA; YAW

Brand, Dionne 1953- .... **CLC 192**
See also BW 2; CA 143; CANR 143; CWP

Brand, Max
See Faust, Frederick (Schiller)
See also BPFB 1; TCWW 1, 2

Brand, Millen 1906-1980 .... **CLC 7**
See also CA 21-24R; 97-100; CANR 72

Branden, Barbara .... **CLC 44**
See also CA 148

Brandes, Georg (Morris Cohen)
1842-1927 .... **TCLC 10**
See also CA 105; 189; DLB 300

Brandys, Kazimierz 1916-2000 .... **CLC 62**
See also CA 239; EWL 3

Branley, Franklyn M(ansfield)
1915-2002 .... **CLC 21**
See also CA 33-36R; 207; CANR 14, 39; CLR 13; MAICYA 1, 2; SAAS 16; SATA 4, 68, 136

Brant, Beth (E.) 1941- .... **NNAL**
See also CA 144; FW

Brant, Sebastian 1457-1521 .... **LC 112**
See also DLB 179; RGWL 2, 3

Brathwaite, Edward Kamau
1930- .... **BLCS; CLC 11; PC 56**
See also BW 2, 3; CA 25-28R; CANR 11, 26, 47, 107; CDWLB 3; CP 1, 2, 3, 4, 5, 6, 7; DAM POET; DLB 125; EWL 3

Brathwaite, Kamau
See Brathwaite, Edward Kamau

Brautigan, Richard (Gary)
1935-1984 .... **CLC 1, 3, 5, 9, 12, 34, 42; TCLC 133**
See also BPFB 1; CA 53-56; 113; CANR 34; CN 1, 2, 3; CP 1, 2, 3, 4; DA3; DAM NOV; DLB 2, 5, 206; DLBY 1980, 1984; FANT; MAL 5; MTCW 1; RGAL 4; SATA 56

Brave Bird, Mary .... **NNAL**
See Crow Dog, Mary (Ellen)

Braverman, Kate 1950- .... **CLC 67**
See also CA 89-92; CANR 141

Brecht, (Eugen) Bertolt (Friedrich)
1898-1956 ..... **DC 3; TCLC 1, 6, 13, 35, 169; WLC**
See also CA 104; 133; CANR 62; CDWLB 2; DA; DA3; DAB; DAC; DAM DRAM, MST; DFS 4, 5, 9; DLB 56, 124; EW 11; EWL 3; IDTP; MTCW 1, 2; MTFW 2005; RGWL 2, 3; TWA

Brecht, Eugen Berthold Friedrich
See Brecht, (Eugen) Bertolt (Friedrich)

Bremer, Fredrika 1801-1865 .... **NCLC 11**
See also DLB 254

Brennan, Christopher John
1870-1932 .... **TCLC 17**
See also CA 117; 188; DLB 230; EWL 3

Brennan, Maeve 1917-1993 ... **CLC 5; TCLC 124**
See also CA 81-84; CANR 72, 100

Brenner, Jozef 1887-1919
See Csath, Geza
See also CA 240

Brent, Linda
See Jacobs, Harriet A(nn)

Brentano, Clemens (Maria)
1778-1842 .... **NCLC 1**
See also DLB 90; RGWL 2, 3

Brent of Bin Bin
See Franklin, (Stella Maria Sarah) Miles (Lampe)

Brenton, Howard 1942- .... **CLC 31**
See also CA 69-72; CANR 33, 67; CBD; CD 5, 6; DLB 13; MTCW 1

Breslin, James 1930-
See Breslin, Jimmy
See also CA 73-76; CANR 31, 75, 139; DAM NOV; MTCW 1, 2; MTFW 2005

Breslin, Jimmy .... **CLC 4, 43**
See Breslin, James
See also AITN 1; DLB 185; MTCW 2

Bresson, Robert 1901(?)-1999 .... **CLC 16**
See also CA 110; 187; CANR 49

Breton, Andre 1896-1966 .. **CLC 2, 9, 15, 54; PC 15**
See also CA 19-20; 25-28R; CANR 40, 60; CAP 2; DLB 65, 258; EW 11; EWL 3; GFL 1789 to the Present; LMFS 2; MTCW 1, 2; MTFW 2005; RGWL 2, 3; TWA; WP

Breytenbach, Breyten 1939(?)- .. **CLC 23, 37, 126**
See also CA 113; 129; CANR 61, 122; CWW 2; DAM POET; DLB 225; EWL 3

Bridgers, Sue Ellen 1942- .... **CLC 26**
See also AAYA 8, 49; BYA 7, 8; CA 65-68; CANR 11, 36; CLR 18; DLB 52; JRDA; MAICYA 1, 2; SAAS 1; SATA 22, 90; SATA-Essay 109; WYA; YAW

Bridges, Robert (Seymour)
1844-1930 .... **PC 28; TCLC 1**
See also BRW 6; CA 104; 152; CDBLB 1890-1914; DAM POET; DLB 19, 98

Bridie, James .... **TCLC 3**
See Mavor, Osborne Henry
See also DLB 10; EWL 3

Brin, David 1950- .... **CLC 34**
See also AAYA 21; CA 102; CANR 24, 70, 125, 127; INT CANR-24; SATA 65; SCFW 2; SFW 4

Brink, Andre (Philippus) 1935- . **CLC 18, 36, 106**
See also AFW; BRWS 6; CA 104; CANR 39, 62, 109, 133; CN 4, 5, 6, 7; DLB 225; EWL 3; INT CA-103; LATS 1:2; MTCW 1, 2; MTFW 2005; WLIT 2

Brinsmead, H. F(ay)
See Brinsmead, H(esba) F(ay)

Brinsmead, H. F.
See Brinsmead, H(esba) F(ay)

Brinsmead, H(esba) F(ay) 1922- ...... **CLC 21**
See also CA 21-24R; CANR 10; CLR 47; CWRI 5; MAICYA 1, 2; SAAS 5; SATA 18, 78

Brittain, Vera (Mary) 1893(?)-1970 . **CLC 23**
See also BRWS 10; CA 13-16; 25-28R; CANR 58; CAP 1; DLB 191; FW; MTCW 1, 2

Broch, Hermann 1886-1951 .... **TCLC 20**
See also CA 117; 211; CDWLB 2; DLB 85, 124; EW 10; EWL 3; RGWL 2, 3

Brock, Rose
See Hansen, Joseph
See also GLL 1

Brod, Max 1884-1968 .... **TCLC 115**
See also CA 5-8R; 25-28R; CANR 7; DLB 81; EWL 3

Brodkey, Harold (Roy) 1930-1996 .. **CLC 56; TCLC 123**
See also CA 111; 151; CANR 71; CN 4, 5, 6; DLB 130

Brodsky, Iosif Alexandrovich 1940-1996
See Brodsky, Joseph
See also AITN 1; CA 41-44R; 151; CANR 37, 106; DA3; DAM POET; MTCW 1, 2; MTFW 2005; RGWL 2, 3

Brodsky, Joseph . **CLC 4, 6, 13, 36, 100; PC 9**
See Brodsky, Iosif Alexandrovich
See also AMWS 8; CWW 2; DLB 285; EWL 3; MTCW 1

Brodsky, Michael (Mark) 1948- .... **CLC 19**
See also CA 102; CANR 18, 41, 58; DLB 244

Brodzki, Bella ed. .... **CLC 65**

Brome, Richard 1590(?)-1652 .... **LC 61**
See also BRWS 10; DLB 58

Bromell, Henry 1947- .... **CLC 5**
See also CA 53-56; CANR 9, 115, 116

Bryant, William Cullen 1794-1878 . **NCLC 6, 46; PC 20**
See also AMWS 1; CDALB 1640-1865; DA; DAB; DAC; DAM MST, POET; DLB 3, 43, 59, 189, 250; EXPP; PAB; RGAL 2; TUS

Bryusov, Valery Yakovlevich
1873-1924 .... **TCLC 10**
See also CA 107; 155; EWL 3; SFW 4

Buchan, John 1875-1940 .... **TCLC 41**
See also CA 108; 145; DLB 34, 70, 156; DAM POP; DLB 34, 70, 156; HGG; MSW; MTCW 2; RGEL 2; RHW; YABC 2

Buchanan, George 1506-1582 .... **LC 4**
See also DLB 132

Buchanan, Robert 1841-1901 .... **TCLC 107**
See also CA 179; DLB 18, 35

Buchheim, Lothar-Guenther 1918- .... **CLC 6**
See also CA 85-88

Buchner, (Karl) Georg
1813-1837 .... **NCLC 26, 146**
See also CDWLB 2; DLB 133; EW 6; RGSF 2; RGWL 2, 3; TWA

Buchwald, Art(hur) 1925- .... **CLC 33**
See also AITN 1; CA 5-8R; CANR 21, 67, 107; MTCW 1, 2; SATA 10

Buck, Pearl S(ydenstricker)
1892-1973 .... **CLC 7, 11, 18, 127**
See also AAYA 42; AITN 1; AMWS 2; BPFB 1; CA 1-4R; 41-44R; CANR 1, 34; CDALBS; CN 1; DA; DA3; DAB; DAC; DAM MST, NOV; DLB 9, 102; EWL 3; LAIT 3; MAL 5; MTCW 1, 2; MTFW 2005; RGAL 4; RHW; SATA 1, 25; TUS

Buckler, Ernest 1908-1984 .... **CLC 13**
See also CA 11-12; 114; CAP 1; CCA 1; CN 1, 2, 3; DAC; DAM MST; DLB 68; SATA 47

Buckley, Christopher (Taylor)
1952- .... **CLC 165**
See also CA 139; CANR 119

Buckley, Vincent (Thomas)
1925-1988 .... **CLC 57**
See also CA 101; CP 1, 2, 3, 4; DLB 289

Buckley, William F(rank), Jr. 1925- . **CLC 7, 18, 37**
See also AITN 1; BPFB 1; CA 1-4R; CANR 1, 24, 53, 93, 133; CMW 4; CPW; DA3; DAM POP; DLB 137; DLBY 1980; INT CANR-24; MTCW 1, 2; MTFW 2005; TUS

Buechner, (Carl) Frederick 1926- . **CLC 2, 4, 6, 9**
See also AMWS 12; BPFB 1; CA 13-16R; CANR 11, 39, 64, 114, 138; CN 1, 2, 3, 4, 5, 6, 7; DAM NOV; DLBY 1980; INT CANR-11; MAL 5; MTCW 1, 2; MTFW 2005; TCLE 1:1

Buell, John (Edward) 1927- .... **CLC 10**
See also CA 1-4R; CANR 71; DLB 53

Buero Vallejo, Antonio 1916-2000 ... **CLC 15, 46, 139; DC 18**
See also CA 106; 189; CANR 24, 49, 75; CWW 2; DFS 11; EWL 3; HW 1; MTCW 1, 2

Bufalino, Gesualdo 1920-1996 .... **CLC 74**
See also CA 209; CWW 2; DLB 196

Bugayev, Boris Nikolayevich
1880-1934 .... **PC 11; TCLC 7**
See also Bely, Andrey; Belyi, Andrei
See also CA 104; 165; MTCW 2; MTFW 2005

Bukowski, Charles 1920-1994 ... **CLC 2, 5, 9, 41, 82, 108; PC 18; SSC 45**
See also CA 17-20R; 144; CANR 40, 62, 105; CN 4, 5; CP 1, 2, 3, 4; CPW; DA3; DAM NOV, POET; DLB 5, 130, 169; EWL 3; MAL 5; MTCW 1, 2; MTFW 2005

Bulgakov, Mikhail (Afanas'evich)
1891-1940 ..... **SSC 18; TCLC 2, 16, 159**
See also BPFB 1; CA 105; 152; DAM DRAM, NOV; DLB 272; EWL 3; MTCW 2; MTFW 2005; NFS 8; RGSF 2; RGWL 2, 3; SFW 4; TWA

Bulgya, Alexander Alexandrovich
1901-1956 .... **TCLC 53**
See Fadeev, Aleksandr Aleksandrovich; Fadeev, Alexandr Alexandrovich; Fadeyev, Alexander
See also CA 117; 181

Bullins, Ed 1935- ... **BLC 1; CLC 1, 5, 7; DC 6**
See also BW 2, 3; CA 49-52; CAAS 16; CAD; CANR 24, 46, 73, 134; CD 5, 6; DAM DRAM, MULT; DLB 7, 38, 249; EWL 3; MAL 5; MTCW 1, 2; MTFW 2005; RGAL 4

Bulosan, Carlos 1911-1956 .... **AAL**
See also CA 216; DLB 312; RGAL 4

Bulwer-Lytton, Edward (George Earle Lytton) 1803-1873 .... **NCLC 1, 45**
See also DLB 21; RGEL 2; SFW 4; SUFW 1; TEA

Bunin, Ivan Alexeyevich 1870-1953 ... **SSC 5; TCLC 6**
See also CA 104; DLB 317; EWL 3; RGSF 2; RGWL 2, 3; TWA

Bunting, Basil 1900-1985 ...... **CLC 10, 39, 47**
See also BRWS 7; CA 53-56; 115; CANR 7; CP 1, 2, 3, 4; DAM POET; DLB 20; EWL 3; RGEL 2

Bunuel, Luis 1900-1983 ... **CLC 16, 80; HLC 1**
See also CA 101; 110; CANR 32, 77; DAM MULT; HW 1

Bunyan, John 1628-1688 ..... **LC 4, 69; WLC**
See also BRW 2; BYA 5; CDBLB 1660-1789; DA; DAB; DAC; DAM MST; DLB 39; RGEL 2; TEA; WCH; WLIT 3

Buravsky, Alexandr .... **CLC 59**

Burckhardt, Jacob (Christoph)
1818-1897 .... **NCLC 49**
See also EW 6

Burford, Eleanor
See Hibbert, Eleanor Alice Burford

Burgess, Anthony . **CLC 1, 2, 4, 5, 8, 10, 13, 15, 22, 40, 62, 81, 94**
See Wilson, John (Anthony) Burgess
See also AAYA 25; AITN 1; BRWS 1; CDBLB 1960 to Present; CN 1, 2, 3, 4, 5; DAB; DLB 14, 194, 261; DLBY 1998; EWL 3; RGEL 2; RHW; SFW 4; YAW

Burke, Edmund 1729(?)-1797 .... **LC 7, 36; WLC**
See also BRW 3; DA; DA3; DAB; DAC; DAM MST; DLB 104, 252; RGEL 2; TEA

Burke, Kenneth (Duva) 1897-1993 ... **CLC 2, 24**
See also AMW; CA 5-8R; 143; CANR 39, 74, 136; CN 1, 2; CP 1, 2, 3, 4; DLB 45, 63; EWL 3; MAL 5; MTCW 1, 2; MTFW 2005; RGAL 4

Burke, Leda
See Garnett, David

Burke, Ralph
See Silverberg, Robert

Burke, Thomas 1886-1945 .... **TCLC 63**
See also CA 113; 155; CMW 4; DLB 197

Burney, Fanny 1752-1840 .... **NCLC 12, 54, 107**
See also BRWS 3; DLB 39; FL 1:2; NFS 16; RGEL 2; TEA

Burney, Frances
See Burney, Fanny

Burns, Robert 1759-1796 ... **LC 3, 29, 40; PC 6; WLC**
See also AAYA 51; BRW 3; CDBLB 1789-1832; DA; DA3; DAB; DAC; DAM MST, POET; DLB 109; EXPP; PAB; RGEL 2; TEA; WP

Burns, Tex
See L'Amour, Louis (Dearborn)

Burnshaw, Stanley 1906- .... **CLC 3, 13, 44**
See also CA 9-12R; CP 1, 2, 3, 4, 5, 6, 7; DLB 48; DLBY 1997

Burr, Anne 1937- .... **CLC 6**
See also CA 25-28R

Burroughs, Edgar Rice 1875-1950 . **TCLC 2, 32**
See also AAYA 11; BPFB 1; BYA 4, 9; CA 104; 132; CANR 131; DAM NOV; DLB 8; FANT; MTCW 1, 2; MTFW 2005; RGAL 4; SATA 41; SCFW 1, 2; SFW 4; TCWW 1, 2; TUS; YAW

Burroughs, William S(eward)
1914-1997 .. **CLC 1, 2, 5, 15, 22, 42, 75, 109; TCLC 121; WLC**
See Lee, William; Lee, Willy
See also AAYA 60; AITN 2; AMWS 3; BG 1:2; BPFB 1; CA 9-12R; 160; CANR 20, 52, 104; CN 1, 2, 3, 4, 5, 6; CPW; DA; DA3; DAB; DAC; DAM MST, NOV, POP; DLB 2, 8, 16, 152, 237; DLBY 1981, 1997; EWL 3; HGG; LMFS 2; MAL 5; MTCW 1, 2; MTFW 2005; RGAL 4; SFW 4

Burton, Sir Richard F(rancis)
1821-1890 .... **NCLC 42**
See also DLB 55, 166, 184; SSFS 21

Burton, Robert 1577-1640 .... **LC 74**
See also DLB 151; RGEL 2

Buruma, Ian 1951- .... **CLC 163**
See also CA 128; CANR 65, 141

Busch, Frederick 1941- ... **CLC 7, 10, 18, 47, 166**
See also CA 33-36R; CAAS 1; CANR 45, 73, 92; CN 1, 2, 3, 4, 5, 6, 7; DLB 6, 218

Bush, Barney (Furman) 1946- .... **NNAL**
See also CA 145

Bush, Ronald 1946- .... **CLC 34**
See also CA 136

Bustos, F(rancisco)
See Borges, Jorge Luis

Bustos Domecq, H(onorio)
See Bioy Casares, Adolfo; Borges, Jorge Luis

Butler, Octavia E(stelle) 1947- .. **BLCS; CLC 38, 121**
See also AAYA 18, 48; AFAW 2; AMWS 13; BPFB 1; BW 2, 3; CA 73-76; CANR 12, 24, 38, 73, 145; CLR 65; CN 7; CPW; DA3; DAM MULT, POP; DLB 33; LATS 1:2; MTCW 1, 2; MTFW 2005; NFS 8, 21; SATA 84; SCFW 2; SFW 4; SSFS 6; TCLE 1:1; YAW

Butler, Robert Olen, (Jr.) 1945- ...... **CLC 81, 162**
See also AMWS 12; BPFB 1; CA 112; CANR 66, 138; CN 7; CSW; DAM POP; DLB 173; INT CA-112; MAL 5; MTCW 2; MTFW 2005; SSFS 11

Butler, Samuel 1612-1680 .... **LC 16, 43**
See also DLB 101, 126; RGEL 2

Butler, Samuel 1835-1902 .... **TCLC 1, 33; WLC**
See also BRWS 2; CA 143; CDBLB 1890-1914; DA; DA3; DAB; DAC; DAM MST, NOV; DLB 18, 57, 174; RGEL 2; SFW 4; TEA

Butler, Walter C.
See Faust, Frederick (Schiller)

Canfield, Dorothea F.
See Fisher, Dorothy (Frances) Canfield
Canfield, Dorothea Frances
See Fisher, Dorothy (Frances) Canfield
Canfield, Dorothy
See Fisher, Dorothy (Frances) Canfield
Canin, Ethan 1960- .... **CLC 55; SSC 70**
See also CA 131; 135; MAL 5
Cankar, Ivan 1876-1918 .... **TCLC 105**
See also CDWLB 4; DLB 147; EWL 3
Cannon, Curt
See Hunter, Evan
Cao, Lan 1961- .... **CLC 109**
See also CA 165
Cape, Judith
See Page, P(atricia) K(athleen)
See also CCA 1
Capek, Karel 1890-1938 .... **DC 1; SSC 36;**
TCLC 6, 37; WLC
See also CA 104; 140; CDWLB 4; DA;
DA3; DAB; DAC; DAM DRAM, MST,
NOV; DFS 7, 11; DLB 215; EW 10; EWL
3; MTCW 2; MTFW 2005; RGSF 2;
RGWL 2, 3; SCFW 1, 2; SFW 4
Capote, Truman 1924-1984 . **CLC 1, 3, 8, 13,**
19, 34, 38, 58; SSC 2, 47; TCLC 164;
WLC
See also AAYA 61; AMWS 3; BPFB 1; CA
5-8R; 113; CANR 18, 62; CDALB 1941-
1968; CN 1, 2, 3; CPW; DA; DA3; DAB;
DAC; DAM MST, NOV, POP; DLB 2,
185, 227; DLBY 1980, 1984; EWL 3;
EXPS; GLL 1; LAIT 3; MAL 5; MTCW
1, 2; MTFW 2005; NCFS 2; RGAL 4;
RGSF 2; SATA 91; SSFS 2; TUS
Capra, Frank 1897-1991 .... **CLC 16**
See also AAYA 52; CA 61-64; 135
Caputo, Philip 1941- .... **CLC 32**
See also AAYA 60; CA 73-76; CANR 40,
135; YAW
Caragiale, Ion Luca 1852-1912 ...... **TCLC 76**
See also CA 157
Card, Orson Scott 1951- .... **CLC 44, 47, 50**
See also AAYA 11, 42; BPFB 1; BYA 5, 8;
CA 102; CANR 27, 47, 73, 102, 106, 133;
CPW; DA3; DAM POP; FANT; INT
CANR-27; MTCW 1, 2; MTFW 2005;
NFS 5; SATA 83, 127; SCFW 2; SFW 4;
SUFW 2; YAW
Cardenal, Ernesto 1925- .... **CLC 31, 161;**
HLC 1; PC 22
See also CA 49-52; CANR 2, 32, 66, 138;
CWW 2; DAM MULT, POET; DLB 290;
EWL 3; HW 1, 2; LAWS 1; MTCW 1, 2;
MTFW 2005; RGWL 2, 3
Cardinal, Marie 1929-2001 .... **CLC 189**
See also CA 177; CWW 2; DLB 83; FW
Cardozo, Benjamin N(athan)
1870-1938 .... **TCLC 65**
See also CA 117; 164
Carducci, Giosue (Alessandro Giuseppe)
1835-1907 .... **PC 46; TCLC 32**
See also CA 163; EW 7; RGWL 2, 3
Carew, Thomas 1595(?)-1640 . **LC 13; PC 29**
See also BRW 2; DLB 126; PAB; RGEL 2
Carey, Ernestine Gilbreth 1908- ...... **CLC 17**
See also CA 5-8R; CANR 71; SATA 2
Carey, Peter 1943- .... **CLC 40, 55, 96, 183**
See also CA 123; 127; CANR 53, 76, 117;
CN 4, 5, 6, 7; DLB 289; EWL 3; INT CA-
127; MTCW 1, 2; MTFW 2005; RGSF 2;
SATA 94
Carleton, William 1794-1869 .... **NCLC 3**
See also DLB 159; RGEL 2; RGSF 2
Carlisle, Henry (Coffin) 1926- .... **CLC 33**
See also CA 13-16R; CANR 15, 85
Carlsen, Chris
See Holdstock, Robert P.

Carlson, Ron(ald F.) 1947- .... **CLC 54**
See also CA 105, 189; CAAE 189; CANR
27; DLB 244
Carlyle, Thomas 1795-1881 ..... **NCLC 22, 70**
See also BRW 4; CDBLB 1789-1832; DA;
DAB; DAC; DAM MST; DLB 55, 144,
254; RGEL 2; TEA
Carman, (William) Bliss 1861-1929 ... **PC 34;**
TCLC 7
See also CA 104; 152; DAC; DLB 92;
RGEL 2
Carnegie, Dale 1888-1955 .... **TCLC 53**
See also CA 218
Carossa, Hans 1878-1956 .... **TCLC 48**
See also CA 170; DLB 66; EWL 3
Carpenter, Don(ald Richard)
1931-1995 .... **CLC 41**
See also CA 45-48; 149; CANR 1, 71
Carpenter, Edward 1844-1929 .... **TCLC 88**
See also CA 163; GLL 1
Carpenter, John (Howard) 1948- ... **CLC 161**
See also AAYA 2; CA 134; SATA 58
Carpenter, Johnny
See Carpenter, John (Howard)
Carpentier (y Valmont), Alejo
1904-1980 . **CLC 8, 11, 38, 110; HLC 1;**
SSC 35
See also CA 65-68; 97-100; CANR 11, 70;
CDWLB 3; DAM MULT; DLB 113; EWL
3; HW 1, 2; LAW; LMFS 2; RGSF 2;
RGWL 2, 3; WLIT 1
Carr, Caleb 1955- .... **CLC 86**
See also CA 147; CANR 73, 134; DA3
Carr, Emily 1871-1945 .... **TCLC 32**
See also CA 159; DLB 68; FW; GLL 2
Carr, John Dickson 1906-1977 .... **CLC 3**
See Fairbairn, Roger
See also CA 49-52; 69-72; CANR 3, 33,
60; CMW 4; DLB 306; MSW; MTCW 1,
2
Carr, Philippa
See Hibbert, Eleanor Alice Burford
Carr, Virginia Spencer 1929- .... **CLC 34**
See also CA 61-64; DLB 111
Carrere, Emmanuel 1957- .... **CLC 89**
See also CA 200
Carrier, Roch 1937- .... **CLC 13, 78**
See also CA 130; CANR 61; CCA 1; DAC;
DAM MST; DLB 53; SATA 105
Carroll, James Dennis
See Carroll, Jim
Carroll, James P. 1943(?)- .... **CLC 38**
See also CA 81-84; CANR 73, 139; MTCW
2; MTFW 2005
Carroll, Jim 1951- .... **CLC 35, 143**
See also AAYA 17; CA 45-48; CANR 42,
115; NCFS 5
Carroll, Lewis ..... **NCLC 2, 53, 139; PC 18;**
WLC
See Dodgson, Charles L(utwidge)
See also AAYA 39; BRW 5; BYA 5, 13; CD-
BLB 1832-1890; CLR 2, 18; DLB 18,
163, 178; DLBY 1998; EXPN; EXPP;
FANT; JRDA; LAIT 1; NFS 7; PFS 11;
RGEL 2; SUFW 1; TEA; WCH
Carroll, Paul Vincent 1900-1968 ...... **CLC 10**
See also CA 9-12R; 25-28R; DLB 10; EWL
3; RGEL 2
Carruth, Hayden 1921- ..... **CLC 4, 7, 10, 18,**
84; PC 10
See also CA 9-12R; CANR 4, 38, 59, 110;
CP 1, 2, 3, 4, 5, 6, 7; DLB 5, 165; INT
CANR-4; MTCW 1, 2; MTFW 2005;
SATA 47
Carson, Anne 1950- .... **CLC 185; PC 64**
See also AMWS 12; CA 203; DLB 193;
PFS 18; TCLE 1:1
Carson, Ciaran 1948- .... **CLC 201**
See also CA 112; 153; CANR 113; CP 7

Carson, Rachel
See Carson, Rachel Louise
See also AAYA 49; DLB 275
Carson, Rachel Louise 1907-1964 .... **CLC 71**
See Carson, Rachel
See also AMWS 9; ANW; CA 77-80; CANR
35; DA3; DAM POP; FW; LAIT 4; MAL
5; MTCW 1, 2; MTFW 2005; NCFS 1;
SATA 23
Carter, Angela (Olive) 1940-1992 ...... **CLC 5,**
41, 76; SSC 13, 85; TCLC 139
See also BRWS 3; CA 53-56; 136; CANR
12, 36, 61, 106; CN 3, 4, 5; DA3; DLB
14, 207, 261, 319; EXPS; FANT; FW; GL
2; MTCW 1, 2; MTFW 2005; RGSF 2;
SATA 66; SATA-Obit 70; SFW 4; SSFS
4, 12; SUFW 2; WLIT 4
Carter, Nick
See Smith, Martin Cruz
Carver, Raymond 1938-1988 ..... **CLC 22, 36,**
53, 55, 126; PC 54; SSC 8, 51
See also AMWS 3; BPFB 1; CA
33-36R; 126; CANR 17, 34, 61, 103; CN
4; CPW; DA3; DAM NOV; DLB 130;
DLBY 1984, 1988; EWL 3; MAL 5;
MTCW 1, 2; MTFW 2005; PFS 17;
RGAL 4; RGSF 2; SSFS 3, 6, 12, 13;
TCLE 1:1; TCWW 2; TUS
Cary, Elizabeth, Lady Falkland
1585-1639 .... **LC 30**
Cary, (Arthur) Joyce (Lunel)
1888-1957 .... **TCLC 1, 29**
See also BRW 7; CA 104; 164; CDBLB
1914-1945; DLB 15, 100; EWL 3; MTCW
2; RGEL 2; TEA
Casal, Julian del 1863-1893 .... **NCLC 131**
See also DLB 283; LAW
Casanova, Giacomo
See Casanova de Seingalt, Giovanni Jacopo
See also WLIT 7
Casanova de Seingalt, Giovanni Jacopo
1725-1798 .... **LC 13**
See Casanova, Giacomo
Casares, Adolfo Bioy
See Bioy Casares, Adolfo
See also RGSF 2
Casas, Bartolome de las 1474-1566
See Las Casas, Bartolome de
See also WLIT 1
Casely-Hayford, J(oseph) E(phraim)
1866-1903 .... **BLC 1; TCLC 24**
See also BW 2; CA 123; 152; DAM MULT
Casey, John (Dudley) 1939- .... **CLC 59**
See also BEST 90:2; CA 69-72; CANR 23,
100
Casey, Michael 1947- .... **CLC 2**
See also CA 65-68; CANR 109; CP 2, 3;
DLB 5
Casey, Patrick
See Thurman, Wallace (Henry)
Casey, Warren (Peter) 1935-1988 .... **CLC 12**
See also CA 101; 127; INT CA-101
Casona, Alejandro .... **CLC 49**
See Alvarez, Alejandro Rodriguez
See also EWL 3
Cassavetes, John 1929-1989 .... **CLC 20**
See also CA 85-88; 127; CANR 82
Cassian, Nina 1924- .... **PC 17**
See also CWP; CWW 2
Cassill, R(onald) V(erlin)
1919-2002 .... **CLC 4, 23**
See also CA 9-12R; 208; CAAS 1; CANR
7, 45; CN 1, 2, 3, 4, 5, 6, 7; DLB 6, 218;
DLBY 2002
Cassiodorus, Flavius Magnus c. 490(?)-c.
583(?) .... **CMLC 43**
Cassirer, Ernst 1874-1945 .... **TCLC 61**
See also CA 157

Chapman, John Jay 1862-1933 .... **TCLC 7**
See also AMWS 14; CA 104; 191

Chapman, Lee
See Bradley, Marion Zimmer
See also GLL 1

Chapman, Walker
See Silverberg, Robert

Chappell, Fred (Davis) 1936- ... **CLC 40, 78, 162**
See also CA 5-8R, 198; CAAE 198; CAAS 4; CANR 8, 33, 67, 110; CN 6; CP 7; CSW; DLB 6, 105; HGG

Char, Rene(-Emile) 1907-1988 .... **CLC 9, 11, 14, 55; PC 56**
See also CA 13-16R; 124; CANR 32; DAM POET; DLB 258; EWL 3; GFL 1789 to the Present; MTCW 1, 2; RGWL 2, 3

Charby, Jay
See Ellison, Harlan (Jay)

Chardin, Pierre Teilhard de
See Teilhard de Chardin, (Marie Joseph) Pierre

Chariton fl. 1st cent. (?)- .... **CMLC 49**

Charlemagne 742-814 .... **CMLC 37**

Charles I 1600-1649 .... **LC 13**

Charriere, Isabelle de 1740-1805 .. **NCLC 66**
See also DLB 313

Chartier, Alain c. 1392-1430 .... **LC 94**
See also DLB 208

Chartier, Emile-Auguste
See Alain

Charyn, Jerome 1937- .... **CLC 5, 8, 18**
See also CA 5-8R; CAAS 1; CANR 7, 61, 101; CMW 4; CN 1, 2, 3, 4, 5, 6, 7; DLBY 1983; MTCW 1

Chase, Adam
See Marlowe, Stephen

Chase, Mary (Coyle) 1907-1981 .... **DC 1**
See also CA 77-80; 105; CAD; CWD; DFS 11; DLB 228; SATA 17; SATA-Obit 29

Chase, Mary Ellen 1887-1973 .... **CLC 2; TCLC 124**
See also CA 13-16; 41-44R; CAP 1; SATA 10

Chase, Nicholas
See Hyde, Anthony
See also CCA 1

Chateaubriand, Francois Rene de 1768-1848 .... **NCLC 3, 134**
See also DLB 119; EW 5; GFL 1789 to the Present; RGWL 2, 3; TWA

Chatelet, Gabrielle-Emilie Du
See du Chatelet, Emilie
See also DLB 313

Chatterje, Sarat Chandra 1876-1936(?)
See Chatterji, Saratchandra
See also CA 109

Chatterji, Bankim Chandra 1838-1894 .... **NCLC 19**

Chatterji, Saratchandra .... **TCLC 13**
See Chatterje, Sarat Chandra
See also CA 186; EWL 3

Chatterton, Thomas 1752-1770 .... **LC 3, 54**
See also DAM POET; DLB 109; RGEL 2

Chatwin, (Charles) Bruce 1940-1989 .... **CLC 28, 57, 59**
See also AAYA 4; BEST 90:1; BRWS 4; CA 85-88; 127; CPW; DAM POP; DLB 194, 204; EWL 3; MTFW 2005

Chaucer, Daniel
See Ford, Ford Madox
See also RHW

Chaucer, Geoffrey 1340(?)-1400 .. **LC 17, 56; PC 19, 58; WLCS**
See also BRW 1; BRWC 1; BRWR 2; CD-BLB Before 1660; DA; DA3; DAB; DAC; DAM MST, POET; DLB 146; LAIT 1; PAB; PFS 14; RGEL 2; TEA; WLIT 3; WP

Chavez, Denise (Elia) 1948- .... **HLC 1**
See also CA 131; CANR 56, 81, 137; DAM MULT; DLB 122; FW; HW 1, 2; LLW; MAL 5; MTCW 2; MTFW 2005

Chaviaras, Strates 1935-
See Haviaras, Stratis
See also CA 105

Chayefsky, Paddy .... **CLC 23**
See Chayefsky, Sidney
See also CAD; DLB 7, 44; DLBY 1981; RGAL 4

Chayefsky, Sidney 1923-1981
See Chayefsky, Paddy
See also CA 9-12R; 104; CANR 18; DAM DRAM

Chedid, Andree 1920- .... **CLC 47**
See also CA 145; CANR 95; EWL 3

Cheever, John 1912-1982 ..... **CLC 3, 7, 8, 11, 15, 25, 64; SSC 1, 38, 57; WLC**
See also AAYA 65; AMWS 1; BPFB 1; CA 5-8R; 106; CABS 1; CANR 5, 27, 76; CDALB 1941-1968; CN 1, 2, 3; CPW; DA; DA3; DAB; DAC; DAM MST, NOV, POP; DLB 2, 102, 227; DLBY 1980, 1982; EWL 3; EXPS; INT CANR-5; MAL 5; MTCW 1, 2; MTFW 2005; RGAL 4; RGSF 2; SSFS 2, 14; TUS

Cheever, Susan 1943- .... **CLC 18, 48**
See also CA 103; CANR 27, 51, 92; DLBY 1982; INT CANR-27

Chekhonte, Antosha
See Chekhov, Anton (Pavlovich)

Chekhov, Anton (Pavlovich) 1860-1904 .... **DC 9; SSC 2, 28, 41, 51, 85; TCLC 3, 10, 31, 55, 96, 163; WLC**
See also AAYA 68; BYA 14; CA 104; 124; DA; DA3; DAB; DAC; DAM DRAM, MST; DFS 1, 5, 10, 12; DLB 277; EW 7; EWL 3; EXPS; LAIT 3; LATS 1:1; RGSF 2; RGWL 2, 3; SATA 90; SSFS 5, 13, 14; TWA

Cheney, Lynne V. 1941- .... **CLC 70**
See also CA 89-92; CANR 58, 117; SATA 152

Chernyshevsky, Nikolai Gavrilovich
See Chernyshevsky, Nikolay Gavrilovich
See also DLB 238

Chernyshevsky, Nikolay Gavrilovich 1828-1889 .... **NCLC 1**
See Chernyshevsky, Nikolai Gavrilovich

Cherry, Carolyn Janice 1942-
See Cherryh, C. J.
See also CA 65-68; CANR 10

Cherryh, C. J. .... **CLC 35**
See Cherry, Carolyn Janice
See also AAYA 24; BPFB 1; DLBY 1980; FANT; SATA 93; SCFW 2; SFW 4; YAW

Chesnutt, Charles W(addell) 1858-1932 .... **BLC 1; SSC 7, 54; TCLC 5, 39**
See also AFAW 1, 2; AMWS 14; BW 1, 3; CA 106; 125; CANR 76; DAM MULT; DLB 12, 50, 78; EWL 3; MAL 5; MTCW 1, 2; MTFW 2005; RGAL 4; RGSF 2; SSFS 11

Chester, Alfred 1929(?)-1971 .... **CLC 49**
See also CA 196; 33-36R; DLB 130; MAL 5

Chesterton, G(ilbert) K(eith) 1874-1936 . **PC 28; SSC 1, 46; TCLC 1, 6, 64**
See also AAYA 57; BRW 6; CA 104; 132; CANR 73, 131; CDBLB 1914-1945; CMW 4; DAM NOV, POET; DLB 10, 19, 34, 70, 98, 149, 178; EWL 3; FANT; MSW; MTCW 1, 2; MTFW 2005; RGEL 2; RGSF 2; SATA 27; SUFW 1

Chettle, Henry 1560-1607(?) .... **LC 112**
See also DLB 136; RGEL 2

Chiang, Pin-chin 1904-1986
See Ding Ling
See also CA 118

Chief Joseph 1840-1904 .... **NNAL**
See also CA 152; DA3; DAM MULT

Chief Seattle 1786(?)-1866 .... **NNAL**
See also DA3; DAM MULT

Ch'ien, Chung-shu 1910-1998 .... **CLC 22**
See Qian Zhongshu
See also CA 130; CANR 73; MTCW 1, 2

Chikamatsu Monzaemon 1653-1724 ... **LC 66**
See also RGWL 2, 3

Child, L. Maria
See Child, Lydia Maria

Child, Lydia Maria 1802-1880 .. **NCLC 6, 73**
See also DLB 1, 74, 243; RGAL 4; SATA 67

Child, Mrs.
See Child, Lydia Maria

Child, Philip 1898-1978 .... **CLC 19, 68**
See also CA 13-14; CAP 1; CP 1; DLB 68; RHW; SATA 47

Childers, (Robert) Erskine 1870-1922 .... **TCLC 65**
See also CA 113; 153; DLB 70

Childress, Alice 1920-1994 . **BLC 1; CLC 12, 15, 86, 96; DC 4; TCLC 116**
See also AAYA 8; BW 2, 3; BYA 2; CA 45-48; 146; CAD; CANR 3, 27, 50, 74; CLR 14; CWD; DA3; DAM DRAM, MULT, NOV; DFS 2, 8, 14; DLB 7, 38, 249; JRDA; LAIT 5; MAICYA 1, 2; MAICYAS 1; MAL 5; MTCW 1, 2; MTFW 2005; RGAL 4; SATA 7, 48, 81; TUS; WYA; YAW

Chin, Frank (Chew, Jr.) 1940- .... **AAL; CLC 135; DC 7**
See also CA 33-36R; CAD; CANR 71; CD 5, 6; DAM MULT; DLB 206, 312; LAIT 5; RGAL 4

Chin, Marilyn (Mei Ling) 1955- .... **PC 40**
See also CA 129; CANR 70, 113; CWP; DLB 312

Chislett, (Margaret) Anne 1943- ...... **CLC 34**
See also CA 151

Chitty, Thomas Willes 1926- .... **CLC 11**
See Hinde, Thomas
See also CA 5-8R; CN 7

Chivers, Thomas Holley 1809-1858 .... **NCLC 49**
See also DLB 3, 248; RGAL 4

Choi, Susan 1969- .... **CLC 119**
See also CA 223

Chomette, Rene Lucien 1898-1981
See Clair, Rene
See also CA 103

Chomsky, (Avram) Noam 1928- ..... **CLC 132**
See also CA 17-20R; CANR 28, 62, 110, 132; DA3; DLB 246; MTCW 1, 2; MTFW 2005

Chona, Maria 1845(?)-1936 .... **NNAL**
See also CA 144

Chopin, Kate .... **SSC 8, 68; TCLC 127; WLCS**
See Chopin, Katherine
See also AAYA 33; AMWR 2; AMWS 1; BYA 11, 15; CDALB 1865-1917; DA; DAB; DLB 12, 78; EXPN; EXPS; FL 1:3; FW; LAIT 3; MAL 5; MAWW; NFS 3; RGAL 4; RGSF 2; SSFS 2, 13, 17; TUS

Chopin, Katherine 1851-1904
See Chopin, Kate
See also CA 104; 122; DA3; DAC; DAM MST, NOV

Chretien de Troyes c. 12th cent. - . **CMLC 10**
See also DLB 208; EW 1; RGWL 2, 3; TWA

Christie
See Ichikawa, Kon

DA3; DAM MULT, POET; DLB 5, 41;
EXPP; MAICYA 1, 2; MTCW 1, 2;
MTFW 2005; PFS 1, 14; SATA 20, 69,
128; WP

Clinton, Dirk
See Silverberg, Robert

Clough, Arthur Hugh 1819-1861 .. **NCLC 27,
163**
See also BRW 5; DLB 32; RGEL 2

Clutha, Janet Paterson Frame 1924-2004
See Frame, Janet
See also CA 1-4R; 224; CANR 2, 36, 76,
135; MTCW 1, 2; SATA 119

Clyne, Terence
See Blatty, William Peter

Cobalt, Martin
See Mayne, William (James Carter)

Cobb, Irvin S(hrewsbury)
1876-1944 .... **TCLC 77**
See also CA 175; DLB 11, 25, 86

Cobbett, William 1763-1835 .... **NCLC 49**
See also DLB 43, 107, 158; RGEL 2

Coburn, D(onald) L(ee) 1938- .... **CLC 10**
See also CA 89-92

Cocteau, Jean (Maurice Eugene Clement)
1889-1963 ...... **CLC 1, 8, 15, 16, 43; DC
17; TCLC 119; WLC**
See also CA 25-28; CANR 40; CAP 2; DA;
DA3; DAB; DAC; DAM DRAM, MST,
NOV; DLB 65, 258, 321; EW 10; EWL
3; GFL 1789 to the Present; MTCW 1, 2;
RGWL 2, 3; TWA

Codrescu, Andrei 1946- .... **CLC 46, 121**
See also CA 33-36R; CAAS 19; CANR 13,
34, 53, 76, 125; CN 7; DA3; DAM POET;
MAL 5; MTCW 2; MTFW 2005

Coe, Max
See Bourne, Randolph S(illiman)

Coe, Tucker
See Westlake, Donald E(dwin)

Coen, Ethan 1958- .... **CLC 108**
See also AAYA 54; CA 126; CANR 85

Coen, Joel 1955- .... **CLC 108**
See also AAYA 54; CA 126; CANR 119

The Coen Brothers
See Coen, Ethan; Coen, Joel

Coetzee, J(ohn) M(axwell) 1940- ..... **CLC 23,
33, 66, 117, 161, 162**
See also AAYA 37; AFW; BRWS 6; CA 77-
80; CANR 41, 54, 74, 114, 133; CN 4, 5,
6, 7; DA3; DAM NOV; DLB 225; EWL
3; LMFS 2; MTCW 1, 2; MTFW 2005;
NFS 21; WLIT 2; WWE 1

Coffey, Brian
See Koontz, Dean R.

Coffin, Robert P(eter) Tristram
1892-1955 .... **TCLC 95**
See also CA 123; 169; DLB 45

Cohan, George M(ichael)
1878-1942 .... **TCLC 60**
See also CA 157; DLB 249; RGAL 4

Cohen, Arthur A(llen) 1928-1986 ...... **CLC 7,
31**
See also CA 1-4R; 120; CANR 1, 17, 42;
DLB 28

Cohen, Leonard (Norman) 1934- ...... **CLC 3,
38**
See also CA 21-24R; CANR 14, 69; CN 1,
2, 3, 4, 5, 6, 7; CP 1, 2, 3, 4, 5, 6, 7; DAC;
DAM MST; DLB 53; EWL 3; MTCW 1

Cohen, Matt(hew) 1942-1999 .... **CLC 19**
See also CA 61-64; 187; CAAS 18; CANR
40; CN 1, 2, 3, 4, 5, 6; DAC; DLB 53

Cohen-Solal, Annie 1948- .... **CLC 50**
See also CA 239

Colegate, Isabel 1931- .... **CLC 36**
See also CA 17-20R; CANR 8, 22, 74; CN
4, 5, 6, 7; DLB 14, 231; INT CANR-22;
MTCW 1

Coleman, Emmett
See Reed, Ishmael (Scott)

Coleridge, Hartley 1796-1849 .... **NCLC 90**
See also DLB 96

Coleridge, M. E.
See Coleridge, Mary E(lizabeth)

Coleridge, Mary E(lizabeth)
1861-1907 .... **TCLC 73**
See also CA 116; 166; DLB 19, 98

Coleridge, Samuel Taylor
1772-1834 ...... **NCLC 9, 54, 99, 111; PC
11, 39, 67; WLC**
See also AAYA 66; BRW 4; BRWR 2; BYA
4; CDBLB 1789-1832; DA; DA3; DAB;
DAC; DAM MST, POET; DLB 93, 107;
EXPP; LATS 1:1; LMFS 1; PAB; PFS 4,
5; RGEL 2; TEA; WLIT 3; WP

Coleridge, Sara 1802-1852 .... **NCLC 31**
See also DLB 199

Coles, Don 1928- .... **CLC 46**
See also CA 115; CANR 38; CP 7

Coles, Robert (Martin) 1929- .... **CLC 108**
See also CA 45-48; CANR 3, 32, 66, 70,
135; INT CANR-32; SATA 23

Colette, (Sidonie-Gabrielle)
1873-1954 .... **SSC 10; TCLC 1, 5, 16**
See Willy, Colette
See also CA 104; 131; DA3; DAM NOV;
DLB 65; EW 9; EWL 3; GFL 1789 to the
Present; MTCW 1, 2; MTFW 2005;
RGWL 2, 3; TWA

Collett, (Jacobine) Camilla (Wergeland)
1813-1895 .... **NCLC 22**

Collier, Christopher 1930- .... **CLC 30**
See also AAYA 13; BYA 2; CA 33-36R;
CANR 13, 33, 102; JRDA; MAICYA 1,
2; SATA 16, 70; WYA; YAW 1

Collier, James Lincoln 1928- .... **CLC 30**
See also AAYA 13; BYA 2; CA 9-12R;
CANR 4, 33, 60, 102; CLR 3; DAM POP;
JRDA; MAICYA 1, 2; SAAS 21; SATA 8,
70; WYA; YAW 1

Collier, Jeremy 1650-1726 .... **LC 6**

Collier, John 1901-1980 . **SSC 19; TCLC 127**
See also CA 65-68; 97-100; CANR 10; CN
1, 2; DLB 77, 255; FANT; SUFW 1

Collier, Mary 1690-1762 .... **LC 86**
See also DLB 95

Collingwood, R(obin) G(eorge)
1889(?)-1943 .... **TCLC 67**
See also CA 117; 155; DLB 262

Collins, Billy 1941- .... **PC 68**
See also AAYA 64; CA 151; CANR 92;
MTFW 2005; PFS 18

Collins, Hunt
See Hunter, Evan

Collins, Linda 1931- .... **CLC 44**
See also CA 125

Collins, Tom
See Furphy, Joseph
See also RGEL 2

Collins, (William) Wilkie
1824-1889 .... **NCLC 1, 18, 93**
See also BRWS 6; CDBLB 1832-1890;
CMW 4; DLB 18, 70, 159; GL 2; MSW;
RGEL 2; RGSF 2; SUFW 1; WLIT 4

Collins, William 1721-1759 .... **LC 4, 40**
See also BRW 3; DAM POET; DLB 109;
RGEL 2

Collodi, Carlo .... **NCLC 54**
See Lorenzini, Carlo
See also CLR 5; WCH; WLIT 7

Colman, George
See Glassco, John

Colman, George, the Elder
1732-1794 .... **LC 98**
See also RGEL 2

Colonna, Vittoria 1492-1547 .... **LC 71**
See also RGWL 2, 3

Colt, Winchester Remington
See Hubbard, L(afayette) Ron(ald)

Colter, Cyrus J. 1910-2002 .... **CLC 58**
See also BW 1; CA 65-68; 205; CANR 10,
66; CN 2, 3, 4, 5, 6; DLB 33

Colton, James
See Hansen, Joseph
See also GLL 1

Colum, Padraic 1881-1972 .... **CLC 28**
See also BYA 4; CA 73-76; 33-36R; CANR
35; CLR 36; CP 1; CWRI 5; DLB 19;
MAICYA 1, 2; MTCW 1; RGEL 2; SATA
15; WCH

Colvin, James
See Moorcock, Michael (John)

Colwin, Laurie (E.) 1944-1992 .... **CLC 5, 13,
23, 84**
See also CA 89-92; 139; CANR 20, 46;
DLB 218; DLBY 1980; MTCW 2

Comfort, Alex(ander) 1920-2000 .... **CLC 7**
See also CA 1-4R; 190; CANR 1, 45; CN
1, 2, 3, 4; CP 1, 2, 3, 4, 5, 6, 7; DAM
POP; MTCW 2

Comfort, Montgomery
See Campbell, (John) Ramsey

Compton-Burnett, I(vy)
1892(?)-1969 .... **CLC 1, 3, 10, 15, 34**
See also BRW 7; CA 1-4R; 25-28R; CANR
4; DAM NOV; DLB 36; EWL 3; MTCW
1, 2; RGEL 2

Comstock, Anthony 1844-1915 ...... **TCLC 13**
See also CA 110; 169

Comte, Auguste 1798-1857 .... **NCLC 54**

Conan Doyle, Arthur
See Doyle, Sir Arthur Conan
See also BPFB 1; BYA 4, 5, 11

Conde (Abellan), Carmen
1901-1996 .... **HLCS 1**
See also CA 177; CWW 2; DLB 108; EWL
3; HW 2

Conde, Maryse 1937- ..... **BLCS; CLC 52, 92**
See also BW 2, 3; CA 110; 190; CAAE 190;
CANR 30, 53, 76; CWW 2; DAM MULT;
EWL 3; MTCW 2; MTFW 2005

Condillac, Etienne Bonnot de
1714-1780 .... **LC 26**
See also DLB 313

Condon, Richard (Thomas)
1915-1996 .... **CLC 4, 6, 8, 10, 45, 100**
See also BEST 90:3; BPFB 1; CA 1-4R;
151; CAAS 1; CANR 2, 23; CMW 4; CN
1, 2, 3, 4, 5, 6; DAM NOV; INT CANR-
23; MAL 5; MTCW 1, 2

Condorcet .... **LC 104**
See Condorcet, marquis de Marie-Jean-
Antoine-Nicolas Caritat
See also GFL Beginnings to 1789

**Condorcet, marquis de
Marie-Jean-Antoine-Nicolas Caritat**
1743-1794
See Condorcet
See also DLB 313

Confucius 551B.C.-479B.C. .... **CMLC 19, 65;
WLCS**
See also DA; DA3; DAB; DAC; DAM
MST

Congreve, William 1670-1729 ... **DC 2; LC 5,
21; WLC**
See also BRW 2; CDBLB 1660-1789; DA;
DAB; DAC; DAM DRAM, MST, POET;
DFS 15; DLB 39, 84; RGEL 2; WLIT 3

Conley, Robert J(ackson) 1940- .... **NNAL**
See also CA 41-44R; CANR 15, 34, 45, 96;
DAM MULT; TCWW 2

Connell, Evan S(helby), Jr. 1924- . **CLC 4, 6,
45**
See also AAYA 7; AMWS 14; CA 1-4R;
CAAS 2; CANR 2, 39, 76, 97, 140; CN
1, 2, 3, 4, 5, 6; DAM NOV; DLB 2;
DLBY 1981; MAL 5; MTCW 1, 2;
MTFW 2005

Cox, William Trevor 1928-
 See Trevor, William
 See also CA 9-12R; CANR 4, 37, 55, 76,
  102, 139; DAM NOV; INT CANR-37;
  MTCW 1, 2; MTFW 2005; TEA
Coyne, P. J.
 See Masters, Hilary
Cozzens, James Gould 1903-1978 . **CLC 1, 4,
 11, 92**
 See also AMW; BPFB 1; CA 9-12R; 81-84;
  CANR 19; CDALB 1941-1968; CN 1, 2;
  DLB 9, 294; DLBD 2; DLBY 1984, 1997;
  EWL 3; MAL 5; MTCW 1, 2; MTFW
  2005; RGAL 4
Crabbe, George 1754-1832 .... **NCLC 26, 121**
 See also BRW 3; DLB 93; RGEL 2
Crace, Jim 1946- .... **CLC 157; SSC 61**
 See also CA 128; 135; CANR 55, 70, 123;
  CN 5, 6, 7; DLB 231; INT CA-135
Craddock, Charles Egbert
 See Murfree, Mary Noailles
Craig, A. A.
 See Anderson, Poul (William)
Craik, Mrs.
 See Craik, Dinah Maria (Mulock)
 See also RGEL 2
Craik, Dinah Maria (Mulock)
 1826-1887 .... **NCLC 38**
 See Craik, Mrs.; Mulock, Dinah Maria
 See also DLB 35, 163; MAICYA 1, 2;
  SATA 34
Cram, Ralph Adams 1863-1942 ..... **TCLC 45**
 See also CA 160
Cranch, Christopher Pearse
 1813-1892 .... **NCLC 115**
 See also DLB 1, 42, 243
Crane, (Harold) Hart 1899-1932 .... **PC 3;
 TCLC 2, 5, 80; WLC**
 See also AMW; AMWR 2; CA 104; 127;
  CDALB 1917-1929; DA; DA3; DAB;
  DAC; DAM MST, POET; DLB 4, 48;
  EWL 3; MAL 5; MTCW 1, 2; MTFW
  2005; RGAL 4; TUS
Crane, R(onald) S(almon)
 1886-1967 .... **CLC 27**
 See also CA 85-88; DLB 63
Crane, Stephen (Townley)
 1871-1900 ...... **SSC 7, 56, 70; TCLC 11,
 17, 32; WLC**
 See also AAYA 21; AMW; AMWC 1; BPFB
  1; BYA 3; CA 109; 140; CANR 84;
  CDALB 1865-1917; DA; DA3; DAB;
  DAC; DAM MST, NOV, POET; DLB 12,
  54, 78; EXPN; EXPS; LAIT 2; LMFS 2;
  MAL 5; NFS 4, 20; PFS 9; RGAL 4;
  RGSF 2; SSFS 4; TUS; WYA; YABC 2
Cranmer, Thomas 1489-1556 .... **LC 95**
 See also DLB 132, 213
Cranshaw, Stanley
 See Fisher, Dorothy (Frances) Canfield
Crase, Douglas 1944- .... **CLC 58**
 See also CA 106
Crashaw, Richard 1612(?)-1649 .... **LC 24**
 See also BRW 2; DLB 126; PAB; RGEL 2
Cratinus c. 519B.C.-c. 422B.C. ..... **CMLC 54**
 See also LMFS 1
Craven, Margaret 1901-1980 .... **CLC 17**
 See also BYA 2; CA 103; CCA 1; DAC;
  LAIT 5
Crawford, F(rancis) Marion
 1854-1909 .... **TCLC 10**
 See also CA 107; 168; DLB 71; HGG;
  RGAL 4; SUFW 1
Crawford, Isabella Valancy
 1850-1887 .... **NCLC 12, 127**
 See also DLB 92; RGEL 2
Crayon, Geoffrey
 See Irving, Washington

Creasey, John 1908-1973 .... **CLC 11**
 See Marric, J. J.
 See also CA 5-8R; 41-44R; CANR 8, 59;
  CMW 4; DLB 77; MTCW 1
Crebillon, Claude Prosper Jolyot de (fils)
 1707-1777 .... **LC 1, 28**
 See also DLB 313; GFL Beginnings to 1789
Credo
 See Creasey, John
Credo, Alvaro J. de
 See Prado (Calvo), Pedro
Creeley, Robert (White) 1926-2005 .. **CLC 1,
 2, 4, 8, 11, 15, 36, 78**
 See also AMWS 4; CA 1-4R; 237; CAAS
  10; CANR 23, 43, 89, 137; CP 1, 2, 3, 4,
  5, 6, 7; DA3; DAM POET; DLB 5, 16,
  169; DLBD 17; EWL 3; MAL 5; MTCW
  1, 2; MTFW 2005; PFS 21; RGAL 4; WP
Crenne, Helisenne de 1510-1560 .... **LC 113**
Crevecoeur, Hector St. John de
 See Crevecoeur, Michel Guillaume Jean de
 See also ANW
Crevecoeur, Michel Guillaume Jean de
 1735-1813 .... **NCLC 105**
 See Crevecoeur, Hector St. John de
 See also AMWS 1; DLB 37
Crevel, Rene 1900-1935 .... **TCLC 112**
 See also GLL 2
Crews, Harry (Eugene) 1935- ..... **CLC 6, 23,
 49**
 See also AITN 1; AMWS 11; BPFB 1; CA
  25-28R; CANR 20, 57; CN 3, 4, 5, 6, 7;
  CSW; DA3; DLB 6, 143, 185; MTCW 1,
  2; MTFW 2005; RGAL 4
Crichton, (John) Michael 1942- .... **CLC 2, 6,
 54, 90**
 See also AAYA 10, 49; AITN 2; BPFB 1;
  CA 25-28R; CANR 13, 40, 54, 76, 127;
  CMW 4; CN 2, 3, 6, 7; CPW; DA3; DAM
  NOV, POP; DLB 292; DLBY 1981; INT
  CANR-13; JRDA; MTCW 1, 2; MTFW
  2005; SATA 9, 88; SFW 4; YAW
Crispin, Edmund .... **CLC 22**
 See Montgomery, (Robert) Bruce
 See also DLB 87; MSW
Cristofer, Michael 1945- .... **CLC 28**
 See also CA 110; 152; CAD; CD 5, 6; DAM
  DRAM; DFS 15; DLB 7
Criton
 See Alain
Croce, Benedetto 1866-1952 .... **TCLC 37**
 See also CA 120; 155; EW 8; EWL 3;
  WLIT 7
Crockett, David 1786-1836 .... **NCLC 8**
 See also DLB 3, 11, 183, 248
Crockett, Davy
 See Crockett, David
Crofts, Freeman Wills 1879-1957 .. **TCLC 55**
 See also CA 115; 195; CMW 4; DLB 77;
  MSW
Croker, John Wilson 1780-1857 .... **NCLC 10**
 See also DLB 110
Crommelynck, Fernand 1885-1970 .. **CLC 75**
 See also CA 189; 89-92; EWL 3
Cromwell, Oliver 1599-1658 .... **LC 43**
Cronenberg, David 1943- .... **CLC 143**
 See also CA 138; CCA 1
Cronin, A(rchibald) J(oseph)
 1896-1981 .... **CLC 32**
 See also BPFB 1; CA 1-4R; 102; CANR 5;
  CN 2; DLB 191; SATA 47; SATA-Obit 25
Cross, Amanda
 See Heilbrun, Carolyn G(old)
 See also BPFB 1; CMW; CPW; DLB 306;
  MSW
Crothers, Rachel 1878-1958 .... **TCLC 19**
 See also CA 113; 194; CAD; CWD; DLB
  7, 266; RGAL 4

Croves, Hal
 See Traven, B.
Crow Dog, Mary (Ellen) (?)- .... **CLC 93**
 See Brave Bird, Mary
 See also CA 154
Crowfield, Christopher
 See Stowe, Harriet (Elizabeth) Beecher
Crowley, Aleister .... **TCLC 7**
 See Crowley, Edward Alexander
 See also GLL 1
Crowley, Edward Alexander 1875-1947
 See Crowley, Aleister
 See also CA 104; HGG
Crowley, John 1942- .... **CLC 57**
 See also AAYA 57; BPFB 1; CA 61-64;
  CANR 43, 98, 138; DLBY 1982; FANT;
  MTFW 2005; SATA 65, 140; SFW 4;
  SUFW 2
Crowne, John 1641-1712 .... **LC 104**
 See also DLB 80; RGEL 2
Crud
 See Crumb, R(obert)
Crumarums
 See Crumb, R(obert)
Crumb, R(obert) 1943- .... **CLC 17**
 See also CA 106; CANR 107
Crumbum
 See Crumb, R(obert)
Crumski
 See Crumb, R(obert)
Crum the Bum
 See Crumb, R(obert)
Crunk
 See Crumb, R(obert)
Crustt
 See Crumb, R(obert)
Crutchfield, Les
 See Trumbo, Dalton
Cruz, Victor Hernandez 1949- ... **HLC 1; PC
 37**
 See also BW 2; CA 65-68; CAAS 17;
  CANR 14, 32, 74, 132; CP 1, 2, 3, 4, 5,
  6, 7; DAM MULT, POET; DLB 41; DNFS
  1; EXPP; HW 1, 2; LLW; MTCW 2;
  MTFW 2005; PFS 16; WP
Cryer, Gretchen (Kiger) 1935- .... **CLC 21**
 See also CA 114; 123
Csath, Geza .... **TCLC 13**
 See Brenner, Jozef
 See also CA 111
Cudlip, David R(ockwell) 1933- .... **CLC 34**
 See also CA 177
Cullen, Countee 1903-1946 . **BLC 1; HR 1:2;
 PC 20; TCLC 4, 37; WLCS**
 See also AFAW 2; AMWS 4; BW 1; CA
  108; 124; CDALB 1917-1929; DA; DA3;
  DAC; DAM MST, MULT, POET; DLB 4,
  48, 51; EWL 3; EXPP; LMFS 2; MAL 5;
  MTCW 1, 2; MTFW 2005; PFS 3; RGAL
  4; SATA 18; WP
Culleton, Beatrice 1949- .... **NNAL**
 See also CA 120; CANR 83; DAC
Cum, R.
 See Crumb, R(obert)
Cumberland, Richard
 1732-1811 .... **NCLC 167**
 See also DLB 89; RGEL 2
Cummings, Bruce F(rederick) 1889-1919
 See Barbellion, W. N. P.
 See also CA 123
Cummings, E(dward) E(stlin)
 1894-1962 .. **CLC 1, 3, 8, 12, 15, 68; PC
 5; TCLC 137; WLC**
 See also AAYA 41; AMW; CA 73-76;
  CANR 31; CDALB 1929-1941; DA;
  DA3; DAB; DAC; DAM MST, POET;
  DLB 4, 48; EWL 3; EXPP; MAL 5;
  MTCW 1, 2; MTFW 2005; PAB; PFS 1,
  3, 12, 13, 19; RGAL 4; TUS; WP

Author Index

Davies, Walter C.
See Kornbluth, C(yril) M.
Davies, William Henry 1871-1940 ... **TCLC 5**
See also BRWS 11; CA 104; 179; DLB 19, 174; EWL 3; RGEL 2
Da Vinci, Leonardo 1452-1519 ..... **LC 12, 57, 60**
See also AAYA 40
Davis, Angela (Yvonne) 1944- .... **CLC 77**
See also BW 2, 3; CA 57-60; CANR 10, 81; CSW; DA3; DAM MULT; FW
Davis, B. Lynch
See Bioy Casares, Adolfo; Borges, Jorge Luis
Davis, Frank Marshall 1905-1987 ...... **BLC 1**
See also BW 2, 3; CA 125; 123; CANR 42, 80; DAM MULT; DLB 51
Davis, Gordon
See Hunt, E(verette) Howard, (Jr.)
Davis, H(arold) L(enoir) 1896-1960 . **CLC 49**
See also ANW; CA 178; 89-92; DLB 9, 206; SATA 114; TCWW 1, 2
Davis, Natalie Zemon 1928- .... **CLC 204**
See also CA 53-56; CANR 58, 100
Davis, Rebecca (Blaine) Harding
1831-1910 .... **SSC 38; TCLC 6**
See also CA 104; 179; DLB 74, 239; FW; NFS 14; RGAL 4; TUS
Davis, Richard Harding
1864-1916 .... **TCLC 24**
See also CA 114; 179; DLB 12, 23, 78, 79, 189; DLBD 13; RGAL 4
Davison, Frank Dalby 1893-1970 ..... **CLC 15**
See also CA 217; 116; DLB 260
Davison, Lawrence H.
See Lawrence, D(avid) H(erbert Richards)
Davison, Peter (Hubert) 1928-2004 . **CLC 28**
See also CA 9-12R; 234; CAAS 4; CANR 3, 43, 84; CP 1, 2, 3, 4, 5, 6, 7; DLB 5
Davys, Mary 1674-1732 .... **LC 1, 46**
See also DLB 39
Dawson, (Guy) Fielding (Lewis)
1930-2002 .... **CLC 6**
See also CA 85-88; 202; CANR 108; DLB 130; DLBY 2002
Dawson, Peter
See Faust, Frederick (Schiller)
See also TCWW 1, 2
Day, Clarence (Shepard, Jr.)
1874-1935 .... **TCLC 25**
See also CA 108; 199; DLB 11
Day, John 1574(?)-1640(?) .... **LC 70**
See also DLB 62, 170; RGEL 2
Day, Thomas 1748-1789 .... **LC 1**
See also DLB 39; YABC 1
Day Lewis, C(ecil) 1904-1972 . **CLC 1, 6, 10; PC 11**
See Blake, Nicholas; Lewis, C. Day
See also BRWS 3; CA 13-16; 33-36R; CANR 34; CAP 1; CP 1; CWRI 5; DAM POET; DLB 15, 20; EWL 3; MTCW 1, 2; RGEL 2
Dazai Osamu .... **SSC 41; TCLC 11**
See Tsushima, Shuji
See also CA 164; DLB 182; EWL 3; MJW; RGSF 2; RGWL 2, 3; TWA
de Andrade, Carlos Drummond
See Drummond de Andrade, Carlos
de Andrade, Mario 1892(?)-1945
See Andrade, Mario de
See also CA 178; HW 2
Deane, Norman
See Creasey, John
Deane, Seamus (Francis) 1940- ...... **CLC 122**
See also CA 118; CANR 42
de Beauvoir, Simone (Lucie Ernestine Marie Bertrand)
See Beauvoir, Simone (Lucie Ernestine Marie Bertrand) de

de Beer, P.
See Bosman, Herman Charles
De Botton, Alain 1969- .... **CLC 203**
See also CA 159; CANR 96
de Brissac, Malcolm
See Dickinson, Peter (Malcolm de Brissac)
de Campos, Alvaro
See Pessoa, Fernando (Antonio Nogueira)
de Chardin, Pierre Teilhard
See Teilhard de Chardin, (Marie Joseph) Pierre
de Crenne, Helisenne c. 1510-c.
1560 .... **LC 113**
Dee, John 1527-1608 .... **LC 20**
See also DLB 136, 213
Deer, Sandra 1940- .... **CLC 45**
See also CA 186
De Ferrari, Gabriella 1941- .... **CLC 65**
See also CA 146
de Filippo, Eduardo 1900-1984 ... **TCLC 127**
See also CA 132; 114; EWL 3; MTCW 1; RGWL 2, 3
Defoe, Daniel 1660(?)-1731 .... **LC 1, 42, 108; WLC**
See also AAYA 27; BRW 3; BRWR 1; BYA 4; CDBLB 1660-1789; CLR 61; DA; DA3; DAB; DAC; DAM MST, NOV; DLB 39, 95, 101; JRDA; LAIT 1; LMFS 1; MAICYA 1, 2; NFS 9, 13; RGEL 2; SATA 22; TEA; WCH; WLIT 3
de Gourmont, Remy(-Marie-Charles)
See Gourmont, Remy(-Marie-Charles) de
de Gournay, Marie le Jars
1566-1645 .... **LC 98**
See also FW
de Hartog, Jan 1914-2002 .... **CLC 19**
See also CA 1-4R; 210; CANR 1; DFS 12
de Hostos, E. M.
See Hostos (y Bonilla), Eugenio Maria de
de Hostos, Eugenio M.
See Hostos (y Bonilla), Eugenio Maria de
Deighton, Len .... **CLC 4, 7, 22, 46**
See Deighton, Leonard Cyril
See also AAYA 6; BEST 89:2; BPFB 1; CD-BLB 1960 to Present; CMW 4; CN 1, 2, 3, 4, 5, 6, 7; CPW; DLB 87
Deighton, Leonard Cyril 1929-
See Deighton, Len
See also AAYA 57; CA 9-12R; CANR 19, 33, 68; DA3; DAM NOV, POP; MTCW 1, 2; MTFW 2005
Dekker, Thomas 1572(?)-1632 ..... **DC 12; LC 22**
See also CDBLB Before 1660; DAM DRAM; DLB 62, 172; LMFS 1; RGEL 2
de Laclos, Pierre Ambroise Franois
See Laclos, Pierre-Ambroise Francois
Delacroix, (Ferdinand-Victor-)Eugene
1798-1863 .... **NCLC 133**
See also EW 5
Delafield, E. M. .... **TCLC 61**
See Dashwood, Edmee Elizabeth Monica de la Pasture
See also DLB 34; RHW
de la Mare, Walter (John)
1873-1956 . **SSC 14; TCLC 4, 53; WLC**
See also CA 163; CDBLB 1914-1945; CLR 23; CWRI 5; DA3; DAB; DAC; DAM MST, POET; DLB 19, 153, 162, 255, 284; EWL 3; EXPP; HGG; MAICYA 1, 2; MTCW 2; MTFW 2005; RGEL 2; RGSF 2; SATA 16; SUFW 1; TEA; WCH
de Lamartine, Alphonse (Marie Louis Prat)
See Lamartine, Alphonse (Marie Louis Prat) de
Delaney, Franey
See O'Hara, John (Henry)

Delaney, Shelagh 1939- .... **CLC 29**
See also CA 17-20R; CANR 30, 67; CBD; CD 5, 6; CDBLB 1960 to Present; CWD; DAM DRAM; DFS 7; DLB 13; MTCW 1
Delany, Martin Robison
1812-1885 .... **NCLC 93**
See also DLB 50; RGAL 4
Delany, Mary (Granville Pendarves)
1700-1788 .... **LC 12**
Delany, Samuel R(ay), Jr. 1942- .... **BLC 1; CLC 8, 14, 38, 141**
See also AAYA 24; AFAW 2; BPFB 1; BW 2, 3; CA 81-84; CANR 27, 43, 116; CN 2, 3, 4, 5, 6, 7; DAM MULT; DLB 8, 33; FANT; MAL 5; MTCW 1, 2; RGAL 4; SATA 92; SCFW 1, 2; SFW 4; SUFW 2
De la Ramee, Marie Louise (Ouida)
1839-1908
See Ouida
See also CA 204; SATA 20
de la Roche, Mazo 1879-1961 .... **CLC 14**
See also CA 85-88; CANR 30; DLB 68; RGEL 2; RHW; SATA 64
De La Salle, Innocent
See Hartmann, Sadakichi
de Laureamont, Comte
See Lautreamont
Delbanco, Nicholas (Franklin)
1942- .... **CLC 6, 13, 167**
See also CA 17-20R; 189; CAAE 189; CAAS 2; CANR 29, 55, 116; CN 7; DLB 6, 234
del Castillo, Michel 1933- .... **CLC 38**
See also CA 109; CANR 77
Deledda, Grazia (Cosima)
1875(?)-1936 .... **TCLC 23**
See also CA 123; 205; DLB 264; EWL 3; RGWL 2, 3; WLIT 7
Deleuze, Gilles 1925-1995 .... **TCLC 116**
See also DLB 296
Delgado, Abelardo (Lalo) B(arrientos)
1930-2004 .... **HLC 1**
See also CA 131; 230; CAAS 15; CANR 90; DAM MST, MULT; DLB 82; HW 1, 2
Delibes, Miguel .... **CLC 8, 18**
See Delibes Setien, Miguel
See also DLB 322; EWL 3
Delibes Setien, Miguel 1920-
See Delibes, Miguel
See also CA 45-48; CANR 1, 32; CWW 2; HW 1; MTCW 1
DeLillo, Don 1936- ..... **CLC 8, 10, 13, 27, 39, 54, 76, 143, 210, 213**
See also AMWC 2; AMWS 6; BEST 89:1; BPFB 1; CA 81-84; CANR 21, 76, 92, 133; CN 3, 4, 5, 6, 7; CPW; DA3; DAM NOV, POP; DLB 6, 173; EWL 3; MAL 5; MTCW 1, 2; MTFW 2005; RGAL 4; TUS
de Lisser, H. G.
See De Lisser, H(erbert) G(eorge)
See also DLB 117
De Lisser, H(erbert) G(eorge)
1878-1944 .... **TCLC 12**
See de Lisser, H. G.
See also BW 2; CA 109; 152
Deloire, Pierre
See Peguy, Charles (Pierre)
Deloney, Thomas 1543(?)-1600 .... **LC 41**
See also DLB 167; RGEL 2
Deloria, Ella (Cara) 1889-1971(?) ..... **NNAL**
See also CA 152; DAM MULT; DLB 175
Deloria, Vine (Victor), Jr.
1933-2005 .... **CLC 21, 122; NNAL**
See also CA 53-56; CANR 5, 20, 48, 98; DAM MULT; DLB 175; MTCW 1; SATA 21

del Valle-Inclan, Ramon (Maria)
See Valle-Inclan, Ramon (Maria) del
See also DLB 322

Del Vecchio, John M(ichael) 1947- .. **CLC 29**
See also CA 110; DLBD 9

de Man, Paul (Adolph Michel)
1919-1983 .... **CLC 55**
See also CA 128; 111; CANR 61; DLB 67;
MTCW 1, 2

DeMarinis, Rick 1934- .... **CLC 54**
See also CA 57-60, 184; CAAE 184; CAAS
24; CANR 9, 25, 50; DLB 218; TCWW 2

de Maupassant, (Henri Rene Albert) Guy
See Maupassant, (Henri Rene Albert) Guy
de

Dembry, R. Emmet
See Murfree, Mary Noailles

Demby, William 1922- .... **BLC 1; CLC 53**
See also BW 1, 3; CA 81-84; CANR 81;
DAM MULT; DLB 33

de Menton, Francisco
See Chin, Frank (Chew, Jr.)

Demetrius of Phalerum c.
307B.C.- .... **CMLC 34**

Demijohn, Thom
See Disch, Thomas M(ichael)

De Mille, James 1833-1880 .... **NCLC 123**
See also DLB 99, 251

Deming, Richard 1915-1983
See Queen, Ellery
See also CA 9-12R; CANR 3, 94; SATA 24

Democritus c. 460B.C.-c. 370B.C. . **CMLC 47**

de Montaigne, Michel (Eyquem)
See Montaigne, Michel (Eyquem) de

de Montherlant, Henry (Milon)
See Montherlant, Henry (Milon) de

Demosthenes 384B.C.-322B.C. ...... **CMLC 13**
See also AW 1; DLB 176; RGWL 2, 3

de Musset, (Louis Charles) Alfred
See Musset, (Louis Charles) Alfred de

de Natale, Francine
See Malzberg, Barry N(athaniel)

de Navarre, Marguerite 1492-1549 ... **LC 61;
SSC 85**
See Marguerite d'Angouleme; Marguerite
de Navarre

Denby, Edwin (Orr) 1903-1983 .... **CLC 48**
See also CA 138; 110; CP 1

de Nerval, Gerard
See Nerval, Gerard de

Denham, John 1615-1669 .... **LC 73**
See also DLB 58, 126; RGEL 2

Denis, Julio
See Cortazar, Julio

Denmark, Harrison
See Zelazny, Roger (Joseph)

Dennis, John 1658-1734 .... **LC 11**
See also DLB 101; RGEL 2

Dennis, Nigel (Forbes) 1912-1989 ...... **CLC 8**
See also CA 25-28R; 129; CN 1, 2, 3, 4;
DLB 13, 15, 233; EWL 3; MTCW 1

Dent, Lester 1904-1959 .... **TCLC 72**
See also CA 112; 161; CMW 4; DLB 306;
SFW 4

De Palma, Brian (Russell) 1940- ...... **CLC 20**
See also CA 109

De Quincey, Thomas 1785-1859 ..... **NCLC 4,
87**
See also BRW 4; CDBLB 1789-1832; DLB
110, 144; RGEL 2

Deren, Eleanora 1908(?)-1961
See Deren, Maya
See also CA 192; 111

Deren, Maya .... **CLC 16, 102**
See Deren, Eleanora

Derleth, August (William)
1909-1971 .... **CLC 31**
See also BPFB 1; BYA 9, 10; CA 1-4R; 29-
32R; CANR 4; CMW 4; CN 1; DLB 9;
DLBD 17; HGG; SATA 5; SUFW 1

Der Nister 1884-1950 .... **TCLC 56**
See Nister, Der

de Routisie, Albert
See Aragon, Louis

Derrida, Jacques 1930-2004 .... **CLC 24, 87**
See also CA 124; 127; 232; CANR 76, 98,
133; DLB 242; EWL 3; LMFS 2; MTCW
2; TWA

Derry Down Derry
See Lear, Edward

Dersonnes, Jacques
See Simenon, Georges (Jacques Christian)

Der Stricker c. 1190-c. 1250 .... **CMLC 75**
See also DLB 138

Desai, Anita 1937- .... **CLC 19, 37, 97, 175**
See also BRWS 5; CA 81-84; CANR 33,
53, 95, 133; CN 1, 2, 3, 4, 5, 6, 7; CWRI
5; DA3; DAB; DAM NOV; DLB 271;
DNFS 2; EWL 3; FW; MTCW 1, 2;
MTFW 2005; SATA 63, 126

Desai, Kiran 1971- .... **CLC 119**
See also BYA 16; CA 171; CANR 127

de Saint-Luc, Jean
See Glassco, John

de Saint Roman, Arnaud
See Aragon, Louis

Desbordes-Valmore, Marceline
1786-1859 .... **NCLC 97**
See also DLB 217

Descartes, Rene 1596-1650 .... **LC 20, 35**
See also DLB 268; EW 3; GFL Beginnings
to 1789

Deschamps, Eustache 1340(?)-1404 .. **LC 103**
See also DLB 208

De Sica, Vittorio 1901(?)-1974 .... **CLC 20**
See also CA 117

Desnos, Robert 1900-1945 .... **TCLC 22**
See also CA 121; 151; CANR 107; DLB
258; EWL 3; LMFS 2

Destouches, Louis-Ferdinand
1894-1961 .... **CLC 9, 15**
See Celine, Louis-Ferdinand
See also CA 85-88; CANR 28; MTCW 1

de Tolignac, Gaston
See Griffith, D(avid Lewelyn) W(ark)

Deutsch, Babette 1895-1982 .... **CLC 18**
See also BYA 3; CA 1-4R; 108; CANR 4,
79; CP 1, 2, 3; DLB 45; SATA 1; SATA-
Obit 33

Devenant, William 1606-1649 .... **LC 13**

Devkota, Laxmiprasad 1909-1959 . **TCLC 23**
See also CA 123

De Voto, Bernard (Augustine)
1897-1955 .... **TCLC 29**
See also CA 113; 160; DLB 9, 256; MAL
5; TCWW 1, 2

De Vries, Peter 1910-1993 ..... **CLC 1, 2, 3, 7,
10, 28, 46**
See also CA 17-20R; 142; CANR 41; CN
1, 2, 3, 4, 5; DAM NOV; DLB 6; DLBY
1982; MAL 5; MTCW 1, 2; MTFW 2005

Dewey, John 1859-1952 .... **TCLC 95**
See also CA 114; 170; CANR 144; DLB
246, 270; RGAL 4

Dexter, John
See Bradley, Marion Zimmer
See also GLL 1

Dexter, Martin
See Faust, Frederick (Schiller)

Dexter, Pete 1943- .... **CLC 34, 55**
See also BEST 89:2; CA 127; 131; CANR
129; CPW; DAM POP; INT CA-131;
MAL 5; MTCW 1; MTFW 2005

Diamano, Silmang
See Senghor, Leopold Sedar

Diamond, Neil 1941- .... **CLC 30**
See also CA 108

Diaz del Castillo, Bernal c.
1496-1584 .... **HLCS 1; LC 31**
See also DLB 318; LAW

di Bassetto, Corno
See Shaw, George Bernard

Dick, Philip K(indred) 1928-1982 ... **CLC 10,
30, 72; SSC 57**
See also AAYA 24; BPFB 1; BYA 11; CA
49-52; 106; CANR 2, 16, 132; CN 2, 3;
CPW; DA3; DAM NOV, POP; DLB 8;
MTCW 1, 2; MTFW 2005; NFS 5; SCFW
1, 2; SFW 4

Dickens, Charles (John Huffam)
1812-1870 .... **NCLC 3, 8, 18, 26, 37, 50,
86, 105, 113, 161; SSC 17, 49, 88; WLC**
See also AAYA 23; BRW 5; BRWC 1, 2;
BYA 1, 2, 3, 13, 14; CDBLB 1832-1890;
CLR 95; CMW 4; DA; DA3; DAB; DAC;
DAM MST, NOV; DLB 21, 55, 70, 159,
166; EXPN; GL 2; HGG; JRDA; LAIT 1,
2; LATS 1:1; LMFS 1; MAICYA 1, 2;
NFS 4, 5, 10, 14, 20; RGEL 2; RGSF 2;
SATA 15; SUFW 1; TEA; WCH; WLIT
4; WYA

Dickey, James (Lafayette)
1923-1997 .... **CLC 1, 2, 4, 7, 10, 15, 47,
109; PC 40; TCLC 151**
See also AAYA 50; AITN 1, 2; AMWS 4;
BPFB 1; CA 9-12R; 156; CABS 2; CANR
10, 48, 61, 105; CDALB 1968-1988; CP
1, 2, 3, 4; CPW; CSW; DA3; DAM NOV,
POET, POP; DLB 5, 193; DLBD 7;
DLBY 1982, 1993, 1996, 1997, 1998;
EWL 3; INT CANR-10; MAL 5; MTCW
1, 2; NFS 9; PFS 6, 11; RGAL 4; TUS

Dickey, William 1928-1994 .... **CLC 3, 28**
See also CA 9-12R; 145; CANR 24, 79; CP
1, 2, 3, 4; DLB 5

Dickinson, Charles 1951- .... **CLC 49**
See also CA 128; CANR 141

Dickinson, Emily (Elizabeth)
1830-1886 ... **NCLC 21, 77; PC 1; WLC**
See also AAYA 22; AMW; AMWR 1;
CDALB 1865-1917; DA; DA3; DAB;
DAC; DAM MST, POET; DLB 1, 243;
EXPP; FL 1:3; MAWW; PAB; PFS 1, 2,
3, 4, 5, 6, 8, 10, 11, 13, 16; RGAL 4;
SATA 29; TUS; WP; WYA

Dickinson, Mrs. Herbert Ward
See Phelps, Elizabeth Stuart

Dickinson, Peter (Malcolm de Brissac)
1927- .... **CLC 12, 35**
See also AAYA 9, 49; BYA 5; CA 41-44R;
CANR 31, 58, 88, 134; CLR 29; CMW 4;
DLB 87, 161, 276; JRDA; MAICYA 1, 2;
SATA 5, 62, 95, 150; SFW 4; WYA; YAW

Dickson, Carr
See Carr, John Dickson

Dickson, Carter
See Carr, John Dickson

Diderot, Denis 1713-1784 .... **LC 26, 126**
See also DLB 313; EW 4; GFL Beginnings
to 1789; LMFS 1; RGWL 2, 3

Didion, Joan 1934- . **CLC 1, 3, 8, 14, 32, 129**
See also AITN 1; AMWS 4; CA 5-8R;
CANR 14, 52, 76, 125; CDALB 1968-
1988; CN 2, 3, 4, 5, 6, 7; DA3; DAM
NOV; DLB 2, 173, 185; DLBY 1981,
1986; EWL 3; MAL 5; MAWW; MTCW
1, 2; MTFW 2005; NFS 3; RGAL 4;
TCLE 1:1; TCWW 2; TUS

di Donato, Pietro 1911-1992 .... **TCLC 159**
See also CA 101; 136; DLB 9

Dietrich, Robert
See Hunt, E(verette) Howard, (Jr.)

Edson, Margaret 1961- ...... **CLC 199; DC 24**
See also CA 190; DFS 13; DLB 266
Edson, Russell 1935- .... **CLC 13**
See also CA 33-36R; CANR 115; CP 2, 3, 4, 5, 6, 7; DLB 244; WP
Edwards, Bronwen Elizabeth
See Rose, Wendy
Edwards, G(erald) B(asil)
1899-1976 .... **CLC 25**
See also CA 201; 110
Edwards, Gus 1939- .... **CLC 43**
See also CA 108; INT CA-108
Edwards, Jonathan 1703-1758 .... **LC 7, 54**
See also AMW; DA; DAC; DAM MST; DLB 24, 270; RGAL 4; TUS
Edwards, Sarah Pierpont 1710-1758 .. **LC 87**
See also DLB 200
Efron, Marina Ivanovna Tsvetaeva
See Tsvetaeva (Efron), Marina (Ivanovna)
Egeria fl. 4th cent. - .... **CMLC 70**
Egoyan, Atom 1960- .... **CLC 151**
See also AAYA 63; CA 157
Ehle, John (Marsden, Jr.) 1925- ...... **CLC 27**
See also CA 9-12R; CSW
Ehrenbourg, Ilya (Grigoryevich)
See Ehrenburg, Ilya (Grigoryevich)
Ehrenburg, Ilya (Grigoryevich)
1891-1967 .... **CLC 18, 34, 62**
See Erenburg, Il'ia Grigor'evich
See also CA 102; 25-28R; EWL 3
Ehrenburg, Ilyo (Grigoryevich)
See Ehrenburg, Ilya (Grigoryevich)
Ehrenreich, Barbara 1941- .... **CLC 110**
See also BEST 90:4; CA 73-76; CANR 16, 37, 62, 117; DLB 246; FW; MTCW 1, 2; MTFW 2005
Eich, Gunter
See Eich, Gunter
See also RGWL 2, 3
Eich, Gunter 1907-1972 .... **CLC 15**
See Eich, Gunter
See also CA 111; 93-96; DLB 69, 124; EWL 3
Eichendorff, Joseph 1788-1857 .... **NCLC 8**
See also DLB 90; RGWL 2, 3
Eigner, Larry .... **CLC 9**
See Eigner, Laurence (Joel)
See also CAAS 23; CP 1, 2, 3, 4; DLB 5; WP
Eigner, Laurence (Joel) 1927-1996
See Eigner, Larry
See also CA 9-12R; 151; CANR 6, 84; CP 7; DLB 193
Eilhart von Oberge c. 1140-c.
1195 .... **CMLC 67**
See also DLB 148
Einhard c. 770-840 .... **CMLC 50**
See also DLB 148
Einstein, Albert 1879-1955 .... **TCLC 65**
See also CA 121; 133; MTCW 1, 2
Eiseley, Loren
See Eiseley, Loren Corey
See also DLB 275
Eiseley, Loren Corey 1907-1977 .... **CLC 7**
See Eiseley, Loren
See also AAYA 5; ANW; CA 1-4R; 73-76; CANR 6; DLBD 17
Eisenstadt, Jill 1963- .... **CLC 50**
See also CA 140
Eisenstein, Sergei (Mikhailovich)
1898-1948 .... **TCLC 57**
See also CA 114; 149
Eisner, Simon
See Kornbluth, C(yril) M.
Ekeloef, (Bengt) Gunnar
1907-1968 .... **CLC 27; PC 23**
See Ekelof, (Bengt) Gunnar
See also CA 123; 25-28R; DAM POET

Ekelof, (Bengt) Gunnar 1907-1968
See Ekeloef, (Bengt) Gunnar
See also DLB 259; EW 12; EWL 3
Ekelund, Vilhelm 1880-1949 .... **TCLC 75**
See also CA 189; EWL 3
Ekwensi, C. O. D.
See Ekwensi, Cyprian (Odiatu Duaka)
Ekwensi, Cyprian (Odiatu Duaka)
1921- .... **BLC 1; CLC 4**
See also AFW; BW 2, 3; CA 29-32R; CANR 18, 42, 74, 125; CDWLB 3; CN 1, 2, 3, 4, 5, 6; CWRI 5; DAM MULT; DLB 117; EWL 3; MTCW 1, 2; RGEL 2; SATA 66; WLIT 2
Elaine .... **TCLC 18**
See Leverson, Ada Esther
El Crummo
See Crumb, R(obert)
Elder, Lonne III 1931-1996 ..... **BLC 1; DC 8**
See also BW 1, 3; CA 81-84; 152; CAD; CANR 25; DAM MULT; DLB 7, 38, 44; MAL 5
Eleanor of Aquitaine 1122-1204 ... **CMLC 39**
Elia
See Lamb, Charles
Eliade, Mircea 1907-1986 .... **CLC 19**
See also CA 65-68; 119; CANR 30, 62; CD-WLB 4; DLB 220; EWL 3; MTCW 1; RGWL 3; SFW 4
Eliot, A. D.
See Jewett, (Theodora) Sarah Orne
Eliot, Alice
See Jewett, (Theodora) Sarah Orne
Eliot, Dan
See Silverberg, Robert
Eliot, George 1819-1880 ...... **NCLC 4, 13, 23, 41, 49, 89, 118; PC 20; SSC 72; WLC**
See Evans, Mary Ann
See also BRW 5; BRWC 1, 2; BRWR 2; CDBLB 1832-1890; CN 7; CPW; DA; DA3; DAB; DAC; DAM MST, NOV; DLB 21, 35, 55; FL 1:3; LATS 1:1; LMFS 1; NFS 17, 20; RGEL 2; RGSF 2; SSFS 8; TEA; WLIT 3
Eliot, John 1604-1690 .... **LC 5**
See also DLB 24
Eliot, T(homas) S(tearns)
1888-1965 ...... **CLC 1, 2, 3, 6, 9, 10, 13, 15, 24, 34, 41, 55, 57, 113; PC 5, 31; WLC**
See also AAYA 28; AMW; AMWC 1; AMWR 1; BRW 7; BRWR 2; CA 5-8R; 25-28R; CANR 41; CBD; CDALB 1929-1941; DA; DA3; DAB; DAC; DAM DRAM, MST, POET; DFS 4, 13; DLB 7, 10, 45, 63, 245; DLBY 1988; EWL 3; EXPP; LAIT 3; LATS 1:1; LMFS 2; MAL 5; MTCW 1, 2; MTFW 2005; NCFS 5; PAB; PFS 1, 7, 20; RGAL 4; RGEL 2; TUS; WLIT 4; WP
Elisabeth of Schönau c.
1129-1165 .... **CMLC 82**
Elizabeth 1866-1941 .... **TCLC 41**
Elizabeth I 1533-1603 .... **LC 118**
See also DLB 136
Elkin, Stanley L(awrence)
1930-1995 .. **CLC 4, 6, 9, 14, 27, 51, 91; SSC 12**
See also AMWS 6; BPFB 1; CA 9-12R; 148; CANR 8, 46; CN 1, 2, 3, 4, 5, 6; CPW; DAM NOV, POP; DLB 2, 28, 218, 278; DLBY 1980; EWL 3; INT CANR-8; MAL 5; MTCW 1, 2; MTFW 2005; RGAL 4; TCLE 1:1
Elledge, Scott .... **CLC 34**
Eller, Scott
See Shepard, James R.
Elliott, Don
See Silverberg, Robert

Elliott, George P(aul) 1918-1980 .... **CLC 2**
See also CA 1-4R; 97-100; CANR 2; CN 1, 2; CP 3; DLB 244; MAL 5
Elliott, Janice 1931-1995 .... **CLC 47**
See also CA 13-16R; CANR 8, 29, 84; CN 5, 6, 7; DLB 14; SATA 119
Elliott, Sumner Locke 1917-1991 ..... **CLC 38**
See also CA 5-8R; 134; CANR 2, 21; DLB 289
Elliott, William
See Bradbury, Ray (Douglas)
Ellis, A. E. .... **CLC 7**
Ellis, Alice Thomas .... **CLC 40**
See Haycraft, Anna (Margaret)
See also CN 4, 5, 6; DLB 194
Ellis, Bret Easton 1964- ...... **CLC 39, 71, 117**
See also AAYA 2, 43; CA 118; 123; CANR 51, 74, 126; CN 6, 7; CPW; DA3; DAM POP; DLB 292; HGG; INT CA-123; MTCW 2; MTFW 2005; NFS 11
Ellis, (Henry) Havelock
1859-1939 .... **TCLC 14**
See also CA 109; 169; DLB 190
Ellis, Landon
See Ellison, Harlan (Jay)
Ellis, Trey 1962- .... **CLC 55**
See also CA 146; CANR 92; CN 7
Ellison, Harlan (Jay) 1934- ... **CLC 1, 13, 42, 139; SSC 14**
See also AAYA 29; BPFB 1; BYA 14; CA 5-8R; CANR 5, 46, 115; CPW; DAM POP; DLB 8; HGG; INT CANR-5; MTCW 1, 2; MTFW 2005; SCFW 2; SFW 4; SSFS 13, 14, 15, 21; SUFW 1, 2
Ellison, Ralph (Waldo) 1914-1994 .... **BLC 1; CLC 1, 3, 11, 54, 86, 114; SSC 26, 79; WLC**
See also AAYA 19; AFAW 1, 2; AMWC 2; AMWR 2; AMWS 2; BPFB 1; BW 1, 3; BYA 2; CA 9-12R; 145; CANR 24, 53; CDALB 1941-1968; CN 1, 2, 3, 4, 5; CSW; DA; DA3; DAB; DAC; DAM MST, MULT, NOV; DLB 2, 76, 227; DLBY 1994; EWL 3; EXPN; EXPS; LAIT 4; MAL 5; MTCW 1, 2; MTFW 2005; NCFS 3; NFS 2, 21; RGAL 4; RGSF 2; SSFS 1, 11; YAW
Ellmann, Lucy (Elizabeth) 1956- ..... **CLC 61**
See also CA 128
Ellmann, Richard (David)
1918-1987 .... **CLC 50**
See also BEST 89:2; CA 1-4R; 122; CANR 2, 28, 61; DLB 103; DLBY 1987; MTCW 1, 2; MTFW 2005
Elman, Richard (Martin)
1934-1997 .... **CLC 19**
See also CA 17-20R; 163; CAAS 3; CANR 47; TCLE 1:1
Elron
See Hubbard, L(afayette) Ron(ald)
El Saadawi, Nawal 1931- .... **CLC 196**
See al'Sadaawi, Nawal; Sa'adawi, al-Nawal; Saadawi, Nawal El; Sa'dawi, Nawal al-
See also CA 118; CAAS 11; CANR 44, 92
Eluard, Paul .... **PC 38; TCLC 7, 41**
See Grindel, Eugene
See also EWL 3; GFL 1789 to the Present; RGWL 2, 3
Elyot, Thomas 1490(?)-1546 .... **LC 11**
See also DLB 136; RGEL 2
Elytis, Odysseus 1911-1996 .... **CLC 15, 49, 100; PC 21**
See Alepoudelis, Odysseus
See also CA 102; 151; CANR 94; CWW 2; DAM POET; EW 13; EWL 3; MTCW 1, 2; RGWL 2, 3

Emecheta, (Florence Onye) Buchi
1944- ...... **BLC 2; CLC 14, 48, 128, 214**
See also AAYA 67; AFW; BW 2, 3; CA 81-
84; CANR 27, 81, 126; CDWLB 3; CN
4, 5, 6, 7; CWRI 5; DA3; DAM MULT;
DLB 117; EWL 3; FL 1:5; FW; MTCW
1, 2; MTFW 2005; NFS 12, 14; SATA 66;
WLIT 2

Emerson, Mary Moody
1774-1863 .... **NCLC 66**

Emerson, Ralph Waldo 1803-1882 . **NCLC 1,
38, 98; PC 18; WLC**
See also AAYA 60; AMW; ANW; CDALB
1640-1865; DA; DA3; DAB; DAC; DAM
MST, POET; DLB 1, 59, 73, 183, 223,
270; EXPP; LAIT 2; LMFS 1; NCFS 3;
PFS 4, 17; RGAL 4; TUS; WP

Eminescu, Mihail 1850-1889 .. **NCLC 33, 131**

Empedocles 5th cent. B.C.- .... **CMLC 50**
See also DLB 176

Empson, William 1906-1984 ... **CLC 3, 8, 19,
33, 34**
See also BRWS 2; CA 17-20R; 112; CANR
31, 61; CP 1, 2, 3; DLB 20; EWL 3;
MTCW 1, 2; RGEL 2

Enchi, Fumiko (Ueda) 1905-1986 ..... **CLC 31**
See Enchi Fumiko
See also CA 129; 121; FW; MJW

Enchi Fumiko
See Enchi, Fumiko (Ueda)
See also DLB 182; EWL 3

Ende, Michael (Andreas Helmuth)
1929-1995 .... **CLC 31**
See also BYA 5; CA 118; 124; 149; CANR
36, 110; CLR 14; DLB 75; MAICYA 1,
2; MAICYAS 1; SATA 61, 130; SATA-
Brief 42; SATA-Obit 86

Endo, Shusaku 1923-1996 ..... **CLC 7, 14, 19,
54, 99; SSC 48; TCLC 152**
See Endo Shusaku
See also CA 29-32R; 153; CANR 21, 54,
131; DA3; DAM NOV; MTCW 1, 2;
MTFW 2005; RGSF 2; RGWL 2, 3

Endo Shusaku
See Endo, Shusaku
See also CWW 2; DLB 182; EWL 3

Engel, Marian 1933-1985 .... **CLC 36; TCLC
137**
See also CA 25-28R; CANR 12; CN 2, 3;
DLB 53; FW; INT CANR-12

Engelhardt, Frederick
See Hubbard, L(afayette) Ron(ald)

Engels, Friedrich 1820-1895 .. **NCLC 85, 114**
See also DLB 129; LATS 1:1

Enright, D(ennis) J(oseph)
1920-2002 .... **CLC 4, 8, 31**
See also CA 1-4R; 211; CANR 1, 42, 83;
CN 1, 2; CP 1, 2, 3, 4, 5, 6, 7; DLB 27;
EWL 3; SATA 25; SATA-Obit 140

Ensler, Eve 1953- .... **CLC 212**
See also CA 172; CANR 126

Enzensberger, Hans Magnus
1929- .... **CLC 43; PC 28**
See also CA 116; 119; CANR 103; CWW
2; EWL 3

Ephron, Nora 1941- .... **CLC 17, 31**
See also AAYA 35; AITN 2; CA 65-68;
CANR 12, 39, 83; DFS 22

Epicurus 341B.C.-270B.C. .... **CMLC 21**
See also DLB 176

Epsilon
See Betjeman, John

Epstein, Daniel Mark 1948- .... **CLC 7**
See also CA 49-52; CANR 2, 53, 90

Epstein, Jacob 1956- .... **CLC 19**
See also CA 114

Epstein, Jean 1897-1953 .... **TCLC 92**

Epstein, Joseph 1937- .... **CLC 39, 204**
See also AMWS 14; CA 112; 119; CANR
50, 65, 117

Epstein, Leslie 1938- .... **CLC 27**
See also AMWS 12; CA 73-76, 215; CAAE
215; CANR 23, 69; DLB 299

Equiano, Olaudah 1745(?)-1797 . **BLC 2; LC
16**
See also AFAW 1, 2; CDWLB 3; DAM
MULT; DLB 37, 50; WLIT 2

Erasmus, Desiderius 1469(?)-1536 ..... **LC 16,
93**
See also DLB 136; EW 2; LMFS 1; RGWL
2, 3; TWA

Erdman, Paul E(mil) 1932- .... **CLC 25**
See also AITN 1; CA 61-64; CANR 13, 43,
84

Erdrich, (Karen) Louise 1954- .. **CLC 39, 54,
120, 176; NNAL; PC 52**
See also AAYA 10, 47; AMWS 4; BEST
89:1; BPFB 1; CA 114; CANR 41, 62,
118, 138; CDALBS; CN 5, 6, 7; CP 7;
CPW; CWP; DA3; DAM MULT, NOV,
POP; DLB 152, 175, 206; EWL 3; EXPP;
FL 1:5; LAIT 5; LATS 1:2; MAL 5;
MTCW 1, 2; MTFW 2005; NFS 5; PFS
14; RGAL 4; SATA 94, 141; SSFS 14;
TCWW 2

Erenburg, Ilya (Grigoryevich)
See Ehrenburg, Ilya (Grigoryevich)

Erickson, Stephen Michael 1950-
See Erickson, Steve
See also CA 129; SFW 4

Erickson, Steve .... **CLC 64**
See Erickson, Stephen Michael
See also CANR 60, 68, 136; MTFW 2005;
SUFW 2

Erickson, Walter
See Fast, Howard (Melvin)

Ericson, Walter
See Fast, Howard (Melvin)

Eriksson, Buntel
See Bergman, (Ernst) Ingmar

Eriugena, John Scottus c.
810-877 .... **CMLC 65**
See also DLB 115

Ernaux, Annie 1940- .... **CLC 88, 184**
See also CA 147; CANR 93; MTFW 2005;
NCFS 3, 5

Erskine, John 1879-1951 .... **TCLC 84**
See also CA 112; 159; DLB 9, 102; FANT

Eschenbach, Wolfram von
See Wolfram von Eschenbach
See also RGWL 3

Eseki, Bruno
See Mphahlele, Ezekiel

Esenin, Sergei (Alexandrovich)
1895-1925 .... **TCLC 4**
See Yesenin, Sergey
See also CA 104; RGWL 2, 3

Eshleman, Clayton 1935- .... **CLC 7**
See also CA 33-36R, 212; CAAE 212;
CAAS 6; CANR 93; CP 1, 2, 3, 4, 5, 6,
7; DLB 5

Espriella, Don Manuel Alvarez
See Southey, Robert

Espriu, Salvador 1913-1985 .... **CLC 9**
See also CA 154; 115; DLB 134; EWL 3

Espronceda, Jose de 1808-1842 ..... **NCLC 39**

Esquivel, Laura 1951(?)- ... **CLC 141; HLCS
1**
See also AAYA 29; CA 143; CANR 68, 113;
DA3; DNFS 2; LAIT 3; LMFS 2; MTCW
2; MTFW 2005; NFS 5; WLIT 1

Esse, James
See Stephens, James

Esterbrook, Tom
See Hubbard, L(afayette) Ron(ald)

Estleman, Loren D. 1952- .... **CLC 48**
See also AAYA 27; CA 85-88; CANR 27,
74, 139; CMW 4; CPW; DA3; DAM
NOV, POP; DLB 226; INT CANR-27;
MTCW 1, 2; MTFW 2005; TCWW 1, 2

Etherege, Sir George 1636-1692 . **DC 23; LC
78**
See also BRW 2; DAM DRAM; DLB 80;
PAB; RGEL 2

Euclid 306B.C.-283B.C. .... **CMLC 25**

Eugenides, Jeffrey 1960(?)- .... **CLC 81, 212**
See also AAYA 51; CA 144; CANR 120;
MTFW 2005

Euripides c. 484B.C.-406B.C. .... **CMLC 23,
51; DC 4; WLCS**
See also AW 1; CDWLB 1; DA; DA3;
DAB; DAC; DAM DRAM, MST; DFS 1,
4, 6; DLB 176; LAIT 1; LMFS 1; RGWL
2, 3

Evan, Evin
See Faust, Frederick (Schiller)

Evans, Caradoc 1878-1945 ... **SSC 43; TCLC
85**
See also DLB 162

Evans, Evan
See Faust, Frederick (Schiller)

Evans, Marian
See Eliot, George

Evans, Mary Ann
See Eliot, George
See also NFS 20

Evarts, Esther
See Benson, Sally

Everett, Percival
See Everett, Percival L.
See also CSW

Everett, Percival L. 1956- .... **CLC 57**
See Everett, Percival
See also BW 2; CA 129; CANR 94, 134;
CN 7; MTFW 2005

Everson, R(onald) G(ilmour)
1903-1992 .... **CLC 27**
See also CA 17-20R; CP 1, 2, 3, 4; DLB 88

Everson, William (Oliver)
1912-1994 .... **CLC 1, 5, 14**
See Antoninus, Brother
See also BG 1:2; CA 9-12R; 145; CANR
20; CP 2, 3, 4; DLB 5, 16, 212; MTCW 1

Evtushenko, Evgenii Aleksandrovich
See Yevtushenko, Yevgeny (Alexandrovich)
See also CWW 2; RGWL 2, 3

Ewart, Gavin (Buchanan)
1916-1995 .... **CLC 13, 46**
See also BRWS 7; CA 89-92; 150; CANR
17, 46; CP 1, 2, 3, 4; DLB 40; MTCW 1

Ewers, Hanns Heinz 1871-1943 ..... **TCLC 12**
See also CA 109; 149

Ewing, Frederick R.
See Sturgeon, Theodore (Hamilton)

Exley, Frederick (Earl) 1929-1992 .... **CLC 6,
11**
See also AITN 2; BPFB 1; CA 81-84; 138;
CANR 117; DLB 143; DLBY 1981

Eynhardt, Guillermo
See Quiroga, Horacio (Sylvestre)

Ezekiel, Nissim (Moses) 1924-2004 .. **CLC 61**
See also CA 61-64; 223; CP 1, 2, 3, 4, 5, 6,
7; EWL 3

Ezekiel, Tish O'Dowd 1943- .... **CLC 34**
See also CA 129

Fadeev, Aleksandr Aleksandrovich
See Bulgya, Alexander Alexandrovich
See also DLB 272

Fadeev, Alexandr Alexandrovich
See Bulgya, Alexander Alexandrovich
See also EWL 3

Fadeyev, A.
See Bulgya, Alexander Alexandrovich

Fadeyev, Alexander .... **TCLC 53**
See Bulgya, Alexander Alexandrovich
Fagen, Donald 1948- .... **CLC 26**
Fainzilberg, Ilya Arnoldovich 1897-1937
See Ilf, Ilya
See also CA 120; 165
Fair, Ronald L. 1932- .... **CLC 18**
See also BW 1; CA 69-72; CANR 25; DLB
33
Fairbairn, Roger
See Carr, John Dickson
Fairbairns, Zoe (Ann) 1948- .... **CLC 32**
See also CA 103; CANR 21, 85; CN 4, 5,
6, 7
Fairfield, Flora
See Alcott, Louisa May
Fairman, Paul W. 1916-1977
See Queen, Ellery
See also CA 114; SFW 4
Falco, Gian
See Papini, Giovanni
Falconer, James
See Kirkup, James
Falconer, Kenneth
See Kornbluth, C(yril) M.
Falkland, Samuel
See Heijermans, Herman
Fallaci, Oriana 1930- .... **CLC 11, 110**
See also CA 77-80; CANR 15, 58, 134; FW;
MTCW 1
Faludi, Susan 1959- .... **CLC 140**
See also CA 138; CANR 126; FW; MTCW
2; MTFW 2005; NCFS 3
Faludy, George 1913- .... **CLC 42**
See also CA 21-24R
Faludy, Gyoergy
See Faludy, George
Fanon, Frantz 1925-1961 .... **BLC 2; CLC 74**
See also BW 1; CA 116; 89-92; DAM
MULT; DLB 296; LMFS 2; WLIT 2
Fanshawe, Ann 1625-1680 .... **LC 11**
Fante, John (Thomas) 1911-1983 .... **CLC 60;
SSC 65**
See also AMWS 11; CA 69-72; 109; CANR
23, 104; DLB 130; DLBY 1983
Far, Sui Sin .... **SSC 62**
See Eaton, Edith Maude
See also SSFS 4
Farah, Nuruddin 1945- ...... **BLC 2; CLC 53,
137**
See also AFW; BW 2, 3; CA 106; CANR
81; CDWLB 3; CN 4, 5, 6, 7; DAM
MULT; DLB 125; EWL 3; WLIT 2
Fargue, Leon-Paul 1876(?)-1947 .... **TCLC 11**
See also CA 109; CANR 107; DLB 258;
EWL 3
Farigoule, Louis
See Romains, Jules
Farina, Richard 1936(?)-1966 .... **CLC 9**
See also CA 81-84; 25-28R
Farley, Walter (Lorimer)
1915-1989 .... **CLC 17**
See also AAYA 58; BYA 14; CA 17-20R;
CANR 8, 29, 84; DLB 22; JRDA; MAI-
CYA 1, 2; SATA 2, 43, 132; YAW
Farmer, Philip Jose 1918- .... **CLC 1, 19**
See also AAYA 28; BPFB 1; CA 1-4R;
CANR 4, 35, 111; DLB 8; MTCW 1;
SATA 93; SCFW 1, 2; SFW 4
Farquhar, George 1677-1707 .... **LC 21**
See also BRW 2; DAM DRAM; DLB 84;
RGEL 2
Farrell, J(ames) G(ordon)
1935-1979 .... **CLC 6**
See also CA 73-76; 89-92; CANR 36; CN
1, 2; DLB 14, 271; MTCW 1; RGEL 2;
RHW; WLIT 4

Farrell, James T(homas) 1904-1979 . **CLC 1,
4, 8, 11, 66; SSC 28**
See also AMW; BPFB 1; CA 5-8R; 89-92;
CANR 9, 61; CN 1, 2; DLB 4, 9, 86;
DLBD 2; EWL 3; MAL 5; MTCW 1, 2;
MTFW 2005; RGAL 4
Farrell, Warren (Thomas) 1943- ...... **CLC 70**
See also CA 146; CANR 120
Farren, Richard J.
See Betjeman, John
Farren, Richard M.
See Betjeman, John
Fassbinder, Rainer Werner
1946-1982 .... **CLC 20**
See also CA 93-96; 106; CANR 31
Fast, Howard (Melvin) 1914-2003 .. **CLC 23,
131**
See also AAYA 16; BPFB 1; CA 1-4R, 181;
214; CAAE 181; CAAS 18; CANR 1, 33,
54, 75, 98, 140; CMW 4; CN 1, 2, 3, 4, 5,
6, 7; CPW; DAM NOV; DLB 9; INT
CANR-33; LATS 1:1; MAL 5; MTCW 2;
MTFW 2005; RHW; SATA 7; SATA-
Essay 107; TCWW 1, 2; YAW
Faulcon, Robert
See Holdstock, Robert P.
Faulkner, William (Cuthbert)
1897-1962 .... **CLC 1, 3, 6, 8, 9, 11, 14,
18, 28, 52, 68; SSC 1, 35, 42; TCLC
141; WLC**
See also AAYA 7; AMW; AMWR 1; BPFB
1; BYA 5, 15; CA 81-84; CANR 33;
CDALB 1929-1941; DA; DA3; DAB;
DAC; DAM MST, NOV; DLB 9, 11, 44,
102, 316; DLBD 2; DLBY 1986, 1997;
EWL 3; EXPN; EXPS; GL 2; LAIT 2;
LATS 1:1; LMFS 2; MAL 5; MTCW 1,
2; MTFW 2005; NFS 4, 8, 13; RGAL 4;
RGSF 2; SSFS 2, 5, 6, 12; TUS
Fauset, Jessie Redmon
1882(?)-1961 .. **BLC 2; CLC 19, 54; HR
1:2**
See also AFAW 2; BW 1; CA 109; CANR
83; DAM MULT; DLB 51; FW; LMFS 2;
MAL 5; MAWW
Faust, Frederick (Schiller)
1892-1944 .... **TCLC 49**
See Brand, Max; Dawson, Peter; Frederick,
John
See also CA 108; 152; CANR 143; DAM
POP; DLB 256; TUS
Faust, Irvin 1924- .... **CLC 8**
See also CA 33-36R; CANR 28, 67; CN 1,
2, 3, 4, 5, 6, 7; DLB 2, 28, 218, 278;
DLBY 1980
Faustino, Domingo 1811-1888 ...... **NCLC 123**
Fawkes, Guy
See Benchley, Robert (Charles)
Fearing, Kenneth (Flexner)
1902-1961 .... **CLC 51**
See also CA 93-96; CANR 59; CMW 4;
DLB 9; MAL 5; RGAL 4
Fecamps, Elise
See Creasey, John
Federman, Raymond 1928- .... **CLC 6, 47**
See also CA 17-20R, 208; CAAE 208;
CAAS 8; CANR 10, 43, 83, 108; CN 3,
4, 5, 6; DLBY 1980
Federspiel, J(uerg) F. 1931- .... **CLC 42**
See also CA 146
Feiffer, Jules (Ralph) 1929- ...... **CLC 2, 8, 64**
See also AAYA 3, 62; CA 17-20R; CAD;
CANR 30, 59, 129; CD 5, 6; DAM
DRAM; DLB 7, 44; INT CANR-30;
MTCW 1; SATA 8, 61, 111, 157
Feige, Hermann Albert Otto Maximilian
See Traven, B.
Feinberg, David B. 1956-1994 .... **CLC 59**
See also CA 135; 147

Feinstein, Elaine 1930- .... **CLC 36**
See also CA 69-72; CAAS 1; CANR 31,
68, 121; CN 3, 4, 5, 6, 7; CP 2, 3, 4, 5, 6,
7; CWP; DLB 14, 40; MTCW 1
Feke, Gilbert David .... **CLC 65**
Feldman, Irving (Mordecai) 1928- ..... **CLC 7**
See also CA 1-4R; CANR 1; CP 1, 2, 3, 4,
5, 6, 7; DLB 169; TCLE 1:1
Felix-Tchicaya, Gerald
See Tchicaya, Gerald Felix
Fellini, Federico 1920-1993 .... **CLC 16, 85**
See also CA 65-68; 143; CANR 33
Felltham, Owen 1602(?)-1668 .... **LC 92**
See also DLB 126, 151
Felsen, Henry Gregor 1916-1995 ..... **CLC 17**
See also CA 1-4R; 180; CANR 1; SAAS 2;
SATA 1
Felski, Rita .... **CLC 65**
Fenno, Jack
See Calisher, Hortense
Fenollosa, Ernest (Francisco)
1853-1908 .... **TCLC 91**
Fenton, James Martin 1949- .... **CLC 32, 209**
See also CA 102; CANR 108; CP 2, 3, 4, 5,
6, 7; DLB 40; PFS 11
Ferber, Edna 1887-1968 .... **CLC 18, 93**
See also AITN 1; CA 5-8R; 25-28R; CANR
68, 105; DLB 9, 28, 86, 266; MAL 5;
MTCW 1, 2; MTFW 2005; RGAL 4;
RHW; SATA 7; TCWW 1, 2
Ferdowsi, Abu'l Qasem
940-1020(?) .... **CMLC 43**
See Firdawsi, Abu al-Qasim
See also RGWL 2, 3
Ferguson, Helen
See Kavan, Anna
Ferguson, Niall 1964- .... **CLC 134**
See also CA 190
Ferguson, Samuel 1810-1886 .... **NCLC 33**
See also DLB 32; RGEL 2
Fergusson, Robert 1750-1774 .... **LC 29**
See also DLB 109; RGEL 2
Ferling, Lawrence
See Ferlinghetti, Lawrence (Monsanto)
Ferlinghetti, Lawrence (Monsanto)
1919(?)- .... **CLC 2, 6, 10, 27, 111; PC 1**
See also BG 1:2; CA 5-8R; CAD; CANR 3,
41, 73, 125; CDALB 1941-1968; CP 1, 2,
3, 4, 5, 6, 7; DA3; DAM POET; DLB 5,
16; MAL 5; MTCW 1, 2; MTFW 2005;
RGAL 4; WP
Fern, Fanny
See Parton, Sara Payson Willis
Fernandez, Vicente Garcia Huidobro
See Huidobro Fernandez, Vicente Garcia
Fernandez-Armesto, Felipe .... **CLC 70**
Fernandez de Lizardi, Jose Joaquin
See Lizardi, Jose Joaquin Fernandez de
Ferre, Rosario 1938- ...... **CLC 139; HLCS 1;
SSC 36**
See also CA 131; CANR 55, 81, 134; CWW
2; DLB 145; EWL 3; HW 1, 2; LAWS 1;
MTCW 2; MTFW 2005; WLIT 1
Ferrer, Gabriel (Francisco Victor) Miro
See Miro (Ferrer), Gabriel (Francisco
Victor)
Ferrier, Susan (Edmonstone)
1782-1854 .... **NCLC 8**
See also DLB 116; RGEL 2
Ferrigno, Robert 1948(?)- .... **CLC 65**
See also CA 140; CANR 125
Ferron, Jacques 1921-1985 .... **CLC 94**
See also CA 117; 129; CCA 1; DAC; DLB
60; EWL 3
Feuchtwanger, Lion 1884-1958 .... **TCLC 3**
See also CA 104; 187; DLB 66; EWL 3
Feuerbach, Ludwig 1804-1872 ..... **NCLC 139**
See also DLB 133

Feuillet, Octave 1821-1890 .... **NCLC 45**
See also DLB 192

Feydeau, Georges (Leon Jules Marie)
1862-1921 .... **TCLC 22**
See also CA 113; 152; CANR 84; DAM
DRAM; DLB 192; EWL 3; GFL 1789 to
the Present; RGWL 2, 3

Fichte, Johann Gottlieb
1762-1814 .... **NCLC 62**
See also DLB 90

Ficino, Marsilio 1433-1499 .... **LC 12**
See also LMFS 1

Fiedeler, Hans
See Doeblin, Alfred

Fiedler, Leslie A(aron) 1917-2003 ..... **CLC 4,
13, 24**
See also AMWS 13; CA 9-12R; 212; CANR
7, 63; CN 1, 2, 3, 4, 5, 6; DLB 28, 67;
EWL 3; MAL 5; MTCW 1, 2; RGAL 4;
TUS

Field, Andrew 1938- .... **CLC 44**
See also CA 97-100; CANR 25

Field, Eugene 1850-1895 .... **NCLC 3**
See also DLB 23, 42, 140; DLBD 13; MAI-
CYA 1, 2; RGAL 4; SATA 16

Field, Gans T.
See Wellman, Manly Wade

Field, Michael 1915-1971 .... **TCLC 43**
See also CA 29-32R

Fielding, Helen 1958- .... **CLC 146, 217**
See also AAYA 65; CA 172; CANR 127;
DLB 231; MTFW 2005

Fielding, Henry 1707-1754 .... **LC 1, 46, 85;
WLC**
See also BRW 3; BRWR 1; CDBLB 1660-
1789; DA; DA3; DAB; DAC; DAM
DRAM, MST, NOV; DLB 39, 84, 101;
NFS 18; RGEL 2; TEA; WLIT 3

Fielding, Sarah 1710-1768 .... **LC 1, 44**
See also DLB 39; RGEL 2; TEA

Fields, W. C. 1880-1946 .... **TCLC 80**
See also DLB 44

Fierstein, Harvey (Forbes) 1954- ..... **CLC 33**
See also CA 123; 129; CAD; CD 5, 6;
CPW; DA3; DAM DRAM, POP; DFS 6;
DLB 266; GLL; MAL 5

Figes, Eva 1932- .... **CLC 31**
See also CA 53-56; CANR 4, 44, 83; CN 2,
3, 4, 5, 6, 7; DLB 14, 271; FW

Filippo, Eduardo de
See de Filippo, Eduardo

Finch, Anne 1661-1720 .... **LC 3; PC 21**
See also BRWS 9; DLB 95

Finch, Robert (Duer Claydon)
1900-1995 .... **CLC 18**
See also CA 57-60; CANR 9, 24, 49; CP 1,
2, 3, 4; DLB 88

Findley, Timothy (Irving Frederick)
1930-2002 .... **CLC 27, 102**
See also CA 25-28R; 206; CANR 12, 42,
69, 109; CCA 1; CN 4, 5, 6, 7; DAC;
DAM MST; DLB 53; FANT; RHW

Fink, William
See Mencken, H(enry) L(ouis)

Firbank, Louis 1942-
See Reed, Lou
See also CA 117

Firbank, (Arthur Annesley) Ronald
1886-1926 .... **TCLC 1**
See also BRWS 2; CA 104; 177; DLB 36;
EWL 3; RGEL 2

Firdawsi, Abu al-Qasim
See Ferdowsi, Abu'l Qasem
See also WLIT 6

Fish, Stanley
See Fish, Stanley Eugene

Fish, Stanley E.
See Fish, Stanley Eugene

Fish, Stanley Eugene 1938- .... **CLC 142**
See also CA 112; 132; CANR 90; DLB 67

Fisher, Dorothy (Frances) Canfield
1879-1958 .... **TCLC 87**
See also CA 114; 136; CANR 80; CLR 71;
CWRI 5; DLB 9, 102, 284; MAICYA 1,
2; MAL 5; YABC 1

Fisher, M(ary) F(rances) K(ennedy)
1908-1992 .... **CLC 76, 87**
See also CA 77-80; 138; CANR 44; MTCW
2

Fisher, Roy 1930- .... **CLC 25**
See also CA 81-84; CAAS 10; CANR 16;
CP 1, 2, 3, 4, 5, 6, 7; DLB 40

Fisher, Rudolph 1897-1934 . **BLC 2; HR 1:2;
SSC 25; TCLC 11**
See also BW 1, 3; CA 107; 124; CANR 80;
DAM MULT; DLB 51, 102

Fisher, Vardis (Alvero) 1895-1968 .... **CLC 7;
TCLC 140**
See also CA 5-8R; 25-28R; CANR 68; DLB
9, 206; MAL 5; RGAL 4; TCWW 1, 2

Fiske, Tarleton
See Bloch, Robert (Albert)

Fitch, Clarke
See Sinclair, Upton (Beall)

Fitch, John IV
See Cormier, Robert (Edmund)

Fitzgerald, Captain Hugh
See Baum, L(yman) Frank

FitzGerald, Edward 1809-1883 ...... **NCLC 9,
153**
See also BRW 4; DLB 32; RGEL 2

Fitzgerald, F(rancis) Scott (Key)
1896-1940 ... **SSC 6, 31, 75; TCLC 1, 6,
14, 28, 55, 157; WLC**
See also AAYA 24; AITN 1; AMW; AMWC
2; AMWR 1; BPFB 1; CA 110; 123;
CDALB 1917-1929; DA; DA3; DAB;
DAC; DAM MST, NOV; DLB 4, 9, 86,
219, 273; DLBD 1, 15, 16; DLBY 1981,
1996; EWL 3; EXPN; EXPS; LAIT 3;
MAL 5; MTCW 1, 2; MTFW 2005; NFS
2, 19, 20; RGAL 4; RGSF 2; SSFS 4, 15,
21; TUS

Fitzgerald, Penelope 1916-2000 . **CLC 19, 51,
61, 143**
See also BRWS 5; CA 85-88; 190; CAAS
10; CANR 56, 86, 131; CN 3, 4, 5, 6, 7;
DLB 14, 194; EWL 3; MTCW 2; MTFW
2005

Fitzgerald, Robert (Stuart)
1910-1985 .... **CLC 39**
See also CA 1-4R; 114; CANR 1; CP 1, 2,
3, 4; DLBY 1980; MAL 5

FitzGerald, Robert D(avid)
1902-1987 .... **CLC 19**
See also CA 17-20R; CP 1, 2, 3, 4; DLB
260; RGEL 2

Fitzgerald, Zelda (Sayre)
1900-1948 .... **TCLC 52**
See also AMWS 9; CA 117; 126; DLBY
1984

Flanagan, Thomas (James Bonner)
1923-2002 .... **CLC 25, 52**
See also CA 108; 206; CANR 55; CN 3, 4,
5, 6, 7; DLBY 1980; INT CA-108; MTCW
1; RHW; TCLE 1:1

Flaubert, Gustave 1821-1880 .... **NCLC 2, 10,
19, 62, 66, 135; SSC 11, 60; WLC**
See also DA; DA3; DAB; DAC; DAM
MST, NOV; DLB 119, 301; EW 7; EXPS;
GFL 1789 to the Present; LAIT 2; LMFS
1; NFS 14; RGSF 2; RGWL 2, 3; SSFS
6; TWA

Flavius Josephus
See Josephus, Flavius

Flecker, Herman Elroy
See Flecker, (Herman) James Elroy

Flecker, (Herman) James Elroy
1884-1915 .... **TCLC 43**
See also CA 109; 150; DLB 10, 19; RGEL
2

Fleming, Ian (Lancaster) 1908-1964 . **CLC 3,
30**
See also AAYA 26; BPFB 1; CA 5-8R;
CANR 59; CDBLB 1945-1960; CMW 4;
CPW; DA3; DAM POP; DLB 87, 201;
MSW; MTCW 1, 2; MTFW 2005; RGEL
2; SATA 9; TEA; YAW

Fleming, Thomas (James) 1927- ...... **CLC 37**
See also CA 5-8R; CANR 10, 102; INT
CANR-10; SATA 8

Fletcher, John 1579-1625 .... **DC 6; LC 33**
See also BRW 2; CDBLB Before 1660;
DLB 58; RGEL 2; TEA

Fletcher, John Gould 1886-1950 .... **TCLC 35**
See also CA 107; 167; DLB 4, 45; LMFS
2; MAL 5; RGAL 4

Fleur, Paul
See Pohl, Frederik

Flieg, Helmut
See Heym, Stefan

Flooglebuckle, Al
See Spiegelman, Art

Flora, Fletcher 1914-1969
See Queen, Ellery
See also CA 1-4R; CANR 3, 85

Flying Officer X
See Bates, H(erbert) E(rnest)

Fo, Dario 1926- .... **CLC 32, 109; DC 10**
See also CA 116; 128; CANR 68, 114, 134;
CWW 2; DA3; DAM DRAM; DLBY
1997; EWL 3; MTCW 1, 2; MTFW 2005;
WLIT 7

Fogarty, Jonathan Titulescu Esq.
See Farrell, James T(homas)

Follett, Ken(neth Martin) 1949- .... **CLC 18**
See also AAYA 6, 50; BEST 89:4; BPFB 1;
CA 81-84; CANR 13, 33, 54, 102; CMW
4; CPW; DA3; DAM NOV, POP; DLB
87; DLBY 1981; INT CANR-33; MTCW
1

Fondane, Benjamin 1898-1944 ..... **TCLC 159**

Fontane, Theodor 1819-1898 . **NCLC 26, 163**
See also CDWLB 2; DLB 129; EW 6;
RGWL 2, 3; TWA

Fonte, Moderata 1555-1592 .... **LC 118**

Fontenot, Chester .... **CLC 65**

Fonvizin, Denis Ivanovich
1744(?)-1792 .... **LC 81**
See also DLB 150; RGWL 2, 3

Foote, Horton 1916- .... **CLC 51, 91**
See also CA 73-76; CAD; CANR 34, 51,
110; CD 5, 6; CSW; DA3; DAM DRAM;
DFS 20; DLB 26, 266; EWL 3; INT
CANR-34; MTFW 2005

Foote, Mary Hallock 1847-1938 .. **TCLC 108**
See also DLB 186, 188, 202, 221; TCWW
2

Foote, Samuel 1721-1777 .... **LC 106**
See also DLB 89; RGEL 2

Foote, Shelby 1916-2005 .... **CLC 75**
See also AAYA 40; CA 5-8R; 240; CANR
3, 45, 74, 131; CN 1, 2, 3, 4, 5, 6, 7;
CPW; CSW; DA3; DAM NOV, POP;
DLB 2, 17; MAL 5; MTCW 2; MTFW
2005; RHW

Forbes, Cosmo
See Lewton, Val

Forbes, Esther 1891-1967 .... **CLC 12**
See also AAYA 17; BYA 2; CA 13-14; 25-
28R; CAP 1; CLR 27; DLB 22; JRDA;
MAICYA 1, 2; RHW; SATA 2, 100; YAW

Gelbart, Larry
See Gelbart, Larry (Simon)
See also CAD; CD 5, 6
Gelbart, Larry (Simon) 1928- .... **CLC 21, 61**
See Gelbart, Larry
See also CA 73-76; CANR 45, 94
Gelber, Jack 1932-2003 ...... **CLC 1, 6, 14, 79**
See also CA 1-4R; 216; CAD; CANR 2;
DLB 7, 228; MAL 5
Gellhorn, Martha (Ellis)
1908-1998 .... **CLC 14, 60**
See also CA 77-80; 164; CANR 44; CN 1,
2, 3, 4, 5, 6 7; DLBY 1982, 1998
Genet, Jean 1910-1986 .. **CLC 1, 2, 5, 10, 14,
44, 46; DC 25; TCLC 128**
See also CA 13-16R; CANR 18; DA3;
DAM DRAM; DFS 10; DLB 72, 321;
DLBY 1986; EW 13; EWL 3; GFL 1789
to the Present; GLL 1; LMFS 2; MTCW
1, 2; MTFW 2005; RGWL 2, 3; TWA
Gent, Peter 1942- .... **CLC 29**
See also AITN 1; CA 89-92; DLBY 1982
Gentile, Giovanni 1875-1944 .... **TCLC 96**
See also CA 119
Gentlewoman in New England, A
See Bradstreet, Anne
Gentlewoman in Those Parts, A
See Bradstreet, Anne
Geoffrey of Monmouth c.
1100-1155 .... **CMLC 44**
See also DLB 146; TEA
George, Jean
See George, Jean Craighead
George, Jean Craighead 1919- .... **CLC 35**
See also AAYA 8; BYA 2, 4; CA 5-8R;
CANR 25; CLR 1; 80; DLB 52; JRDA;
MAICYA 1, 2; SATA 2, 68, 124; WYA;
YAW
George, Stefan (Anton) 1868-1933 . **TCLC 2,
14**
See also CA 104; 193; EW 8; EWL 3
Georges, Georges Martin
See Simenon, Georges (Jacques Christian)
Gerald of Wales c. 1146-c. 1223 ... **CMLC 60**
Gerhardi, William Alexander
See Gerhardie, William Alexander
Gerhardie, William Alexander
1895-1977 .... **CLC 5**
See also CA 25-28R; 73-76; CANR 18; CN
1, 2; DLB 36; RGEL 2
Gerson, Jean 1363-1429 .... **LC 77**
See also DLB 208
Gersonides 1288-1344 .... **CMLC 49**
See also DLB 115
Gerstler, Amy 1956- .... **CLC 70**
See also CA 146; CANR 99
Gertler, T. .... **CLC 34**
See also CA 116; 121
Gertsen, Aleksandr Ivanovich
See Herzen, Aleksandr Ivanovich
Ghalib .... **NCLC 39, 78**
See also Ghalib, Asadullah Khan
Ghalib, Asadullah Khan 1797-1869
See Ghalib
See also DAM POET; RGWL 2, 3
Ghelderode, Michel de 1898-1962 ..... **CLC 6,
11; DC 15**
See also CA 85-88; CANR 40, 77; DAM
DRAM; DLB 321; EW 11; EWL 3; TWA
Ghiselin, Brewster 1903-2001 .... **CLC 23**
See also CA 13-16R; CAAS 10; CANR 13;
CP 1, 2, 3, 4, 5, 6, 7
Ghose, Aurabinda 1872-1950 .... **TCLC 63**
See Ghose, Aurobindo
See also CA 163
Ghose, Aurobindo
See Ghose, Aurabinda
See also EWL 3

Ghose, Zulfikar 1935- .... **CLC 42, 200**
See also CA 65-68; CANR 67; CN 1, 2, 3,
4, 5, 6, 7; CP 1, 2, 3, 4, 5, 6, 7; EWL 3
Ghosh, Amitav 1956- .... **CLC 44, 153**
See also CA 147; CANR 80; CN 6, 7;
WWE 1
Giacosa, Giuseppe 1847-1906 .... **TCLC 7**
See also CA 104
Gibb, Lee
See Waterhouse, Keith (Spencer)
Gibbon, Edward 1737-1794 .... **LC 97**
See also BRW 3; DLB 104; RGEL 2
Gibbon, Lewis Grassic .... **TCLC 4**
See Mitchell, James Leslie
See also RGEL 2
Gibbons, Kaye 1960- .... **CLC 50, 88, 145**
See also AAYA 34; AMWS 10; CA 151;
CANR 75, 127; CN 7; CSW; DA3; DAM
POP; DLB 292; MTCW 2; MTFW 2005;
NFS 3; RGAL 4; SATA 117
Gibran, Kahlil 1883-1931 . **PC 9; TCLC 1, 9**
See also CA 104; 150; DA3; DAM POET,
POP; EWL 3; MTCW 2; WLIT 6
Gibran, Khalil
See Gibran, Kahlil
Gibson, Mel 1956- .... **CLC 215**
Gibson, William 1914- .... **CLC 23**
See also CA 9-12R; CAD; CANR 9, 42, 75,
125; CD 5, 6; DA; DAB; DAC; DAM
DRAM, MST; DFS 2; DLB 7; LAIT 2;
MAL 5; MTCW 2; MTFW 2005; SATA
66; YAW
Gibson, William (Ford) 1948- ... **CLC 39, 63,
186, 192; SSC 52**
See also AAYA 12, 59; BPFB 2; CA 126;
133; CANR 52, 90, 106; CN 6, 7; CPW;
DA3; DAM POP; DLB 251; MTCW 2;
MTFW 2005; SCFW 2; SFW 4
Gide, Andre (Paul Guillaume)
1869-1951 ...... **SSC 13; TCLC 5, 12, 36,
177; WLC**
See also CA 104; 124; DA; DA3; DAB;
DAC; DAM MST, NOV; DLB 65, 321;
EW 8; EWL 3; GFL 1789 to the Present;
MTCW 1, 2; MTFW 2005; NFS 21;
RGSF 2; RGWL 2, 3; TWA
Gifford, Barry (Colby) 1946- .... **CLC 34**
See also CA 65-68; CANR 9, 30, 40, 90
Gilbert, Frank
See De Voto, Bernard (Augustine)
Gilbert, W(illiam) S(chwenck)
1836-1911 .... **TCLC 3**
See also CA 104; 173; DAM DRAM, POET;
RGEL 2; SATA 36
Gilbreth, Frank B(unker), Jr.
1911-2001 .... **CLC 17**
See also CA 9-12R; SATA 2
Gilchrist, Ellen (Louise) 1935- .. **CLC 34, 48,
143; SSC 14, 63**
See also BPFB 2; CA 113; 116; CANR 41,
61, 104; CN 4, 5, 6, 7; CPW; CSW; DAM
POP; DLB 130; EWL 3; EXPS; MTCW
1, 2; MTFW 2005; RGAL 4; RGSF 2;
SSFS 9
Giles, Molly 1942- .... **CLC 39**
See also CA 126; CANR 98
Gill, Eric .... **TCLC 85**
See Gill, (Arthur) Eric (Rowton Peter
Joseph)
Gill, (Arthur) Eric (Rowton Peter Joseph)
1882-1940
See Gill, Eric
See also CA 120; DLB 98
Gill, Patrick
See Creasey, John
Gillette, Douglas .... **CLC 70**

Gilliam, Terry (Vance) 1940- .... **CLC 21, 141**
See Monty Python
See also AAYA 19, 59; CA 108; 113; CANR
35; INT CA-113
Gillian, Jerry
See Gilliam, Terry (Vance)
Gilliatt, Penelope (Ann Douglass)
1932-1993 .... **CLC 2, 10, 13, 53**
See also AITN 2; CA 13-16R; 141; CANR
49; CN 1, 2, 3, 4, 5; DLB 14
Gilligan, Carol 1936- .... **CLC 208**
See also CA 142; CANR 121; FW
Gilman, Charlotte (Anna) Perkins (Stetson)
1860-1935 ...... **SSC 13, 62; TCLC 9, 37,
117**
See also AMWS 11; BYA 11; CA 106; 150;
DLB 221; EXPS; FL 1:5; FW; HGG;
LAIT 2; MAWW; MTCW 2; MTFW
2005; RGAL 4; RGSF 2; SFW 4; SSFS 1,
18
Gilmour, David 1946- .... **CLC 35**
Gilpin, William 1724-1804 .... **NCLC 30**
Gilray, J. D.
See Mencken, H(enry) L(ouis)
Gilroy, Frank D(aniel) 1925- .... **CLC 2**
See also CA 81-84; CAD; CANR 32, 64,
86; CD 5, 6; DFS 17; DLB 7
Gilstrap, John 1957(?)- .... **CLC 99**
See also AAYA 67; CA 160; CANR 101
Ginsberg, Allen 1926-1997 .... **CLC 1, 2, 3, 4,
6, 13, 36, 69, 109; PC 4, 47; TCLC
120; WLC**
See also AAYA 33; AITN 1; AMWC 1;
AMWS 2; BG 1:2; CA 1-4R; 157; CANR
2, 41, 63, 95; CDALB 1941-1968; CP 1,
2, 3, 4, 5, 6; DA; DA3; DAB; DAC; DAM
MST, POET; DLB 5, 16, 169, 237; EWL
3; GLL 1; LMFS 2; MAL 5; MTCW 1, 2;
MTFW 2005; PAB; PFS 5; RGAL 4;
TUS; WP
Ginzburg, Eugenia .... **CLC 59**
See Ginzburg, Evgeniia
Ginzburg, Evgeniia 1904-1977
See Ginzburg, Eugenia
See also DLB 302
Ginzburg, Natalia 1916-1991 .... **CLC 5, 11,
54, 70; SSC 65; TCLC 156**
See also CA 85-88; 135; CANR 33; DFS
14; DLB 177; EW 13; EWL 3; MTCW 1,
2; MTFW 2005; RGWL 2, 3
Giono, Jean 1895-1970 .... **CLC 4, 11; TCLC
124**
See also CA 45-48; 29-32R; CANR 2, 35;
DLB 72, 321; EWL 3; GFL 1789 to the
Present; MTCW 1; RGWL 2, 3
Giovanni, Nikki 1943- ...... **BLC 2; CLC 2, 4,
19, 64, 117; PC 19; WLCS**
See also AAYA 22; AITN 1; BW 2, 3; CA
29-32R; CAAS 6; CANR 18, 41, 60, 91,
130; CDALBS; CLR 6, 73; CP 2, 3, 4, 5,
6, 7; CSW; CWP; CWRI 5; DA; DA3;
DAB; DAC; DAM MST, MULT, POET;
DLB 5, 41; EWL 3; EXPP; INT CANR-
18; MAICYA 1, 2; MAL 5; MTCW 1, 2;
MTFW 2005; PFS 17; RGAL 4; SATA
24, 107; TUS; YAW
Giovene, Andrea 1904-1998 .... **CLC 7**
See also CA 85-88
Gippius, Zinaida (Nikolaevna) 1869-1945
See Hippius, Zinaida (Nikolaevna)
See also CA 106; 212
Giraudoux, Jean(-Hippolyte)
1882-1944 .... **TCLC 2, 7**
See also CA 104; 196; DAM DRAM; DLB
65, 321; EW 9; EWL 3; GFL 1789 to the
Present; RGWL 2, 3; TWA
Gironella, Jose Maria (Pous)
1917-2003 .... **CLC 11**
See also CA 101; 212; EWL 3; RGWL 2, 3

Gordon, Caroline 1895-1981 . **CLC 6, 13, 29, 83; SSC 15**
See also AMW; CA 11-12; 103; CANR 36; CAP 1; CN 1, 2; DLB 4, 9, 102; DLBD 17; DLBY 1981; EWL 3; MAL 5; MTCW 1, 2; MTFW 2005; RGAL 4; RGSF 2

Gordon, Charles William 1860-1937
See Connor, Ralph
See also CA 109

Gordon, Mary (Catherine) 1949- .... **CLC 13, 22, 128, 216; SSC 59**
See also AMWS 4; BPFB 2; CA 102; CANR 44, 92; CN 4, 5, 6, 7; DLB 6; DLBY 1981; FW; INT CA-102; MAL 5; MTCW 1

Gordon, N. J.
See Bosman, Herman Charles

Gordon, Sol 1923- .... **CLC 26**
See also CA 53-56; CANR 4; SATA 11

Gordone, Charles 1925-1995 .. **CLC 1, 4; DC 8**
See also BW 1, 3; CA 93-96; 180; 150; CAAE 180; CAD; CANR 55; DAM DRAM; DLB 7; INT CA-93-96; MTCW 1

Gore, Catherine 1800-1861 .... **NCLC 65**
See also DLB 116; RGEL 2

Gorenko, Anna Andreevna
See Akhmatova, Anna

Gorky, Maxim .... **SSC 28; TCLC 8; WLC**
See Peshkov, Alexei Maximovich
See also DAB; DFS 9; DLB 295; EW 8; EWL 3; TWA

Goryan, Sirak
See Saroyan, William

Gosse, Edmund (William)
1849-1928 .... **TCLC 28**
See also CA 117; DLB 57, 144, 184; RGEL 2

Gotlieb, Phyllis (Fay Bloom) 1926- .. **CLC 18**
See also CA 13-16R; CANR 7, 135; CN 7; CP 1, 2, 3, 4; DLB 88, 251; SFW 4

Gottesman, S. D.
See Kornbluth, C(yril) M.; Pohl, Frederik

Gottfried von Strassburg fl. c.
1170-1215 .... **CMLC 10**
See also CDWLB 2; DLB 138; EW 1; RGWL 2, 3

Gotthelf, Jeremias 1797-1854 .... **NCLC 117**
See also DLB 133; RGWL 2, 3

Gottschalk, Laura Riding
See Jackson, Laura (Riding)

Gould, Lois 1932(?)-2002 .... **CLC 4, 10**
See also CA 77-80; 208; CANR 29; MTCW 1

Gould, Stephen Jay 1941-2002 .... **CLC 163**
See also AAYA 26; BEST 90:2; CA 77-80; 205; CANR 10, 27, 56, 75, 125; CPW; INT CANR-27; MTCW 1, 2; MTFW 2005

Gourmont, Remy(-Marie-Charles) de
1858-1915 .... **TCLC 17**
See also CA 109; 150; GFL 1789 to the Present; MTCW 2

Gournay, Marie le Jars de
See de Gournay, Marie le Jars

Govier, Katherine 1948- .... **CLC 51**
See also CA 101; CANR 18, 40, 128; CCA 1

Gower, John c. 1330-1408 .... **LC 76; PC 59**
See also BRW 1; DLB 146; RGEL 2

Goyen, (Charles) William
1915-1983 .... **CLC 5, 8, 14, 40**
See also AITN 2; CA 5-8R; 110; CANR 6, 71; CN 1, 2, 3; DLB 2, 218; DLBY 1983; EWL 3; INT CANR-6; MAL 5

Goytisolo, Juan 1931- .... **CLC 5, 10, 23, 133; HLC 1**
See also CA 85-88; CANR 32, 61, 131; CWW 2; DAM MULT; DLB 322; EWL 3; GLL 2; HW 1, 2; MTCW 1, 2; MTFW 2005

Gozzano, Guido 1883-1916 .... **PC 10**
See also CA 154; DLB 114; EWL 3

Gozzi, (Conte) Carlo 1720-1806 .... **NCLC 23**

Grabbe, Christian Dietrich
1801-1836 .... **NCLC 2**
See also DLB 133; RGWL 2, 3

Grace, Patricia Frances 1937- .... **CLC 56**
See also CA 176; CANR 118; CN 4, 5, 6, 7; EWL 3; RGSF 2

Gracian y Morales, Baltasar
1601-1658 .... **LC 15**

Gracq, Julien .... **CLC 11, 48**
See Poirier, Louis
See also CWW 2; DLB 83; GFL 1789 to the Present

Grade, Chaim 1910-1982 .... **CLC 10**
See also CA 93-96; 107; EWL 3

Graduate of Oxford, A
See Ruskin, John

Grafton, Garth
See Duncan, Sara Jeannette

Grafton, Sue 1940- .... **CLC 163**
See also AAYA 11, 49; BEST 90:3; CA 108; CANR 31, 55, 111, 134; CMW 4; CPW; CSW; DA3; DAM POP; DLB 226; FW; MSW; MTFW 2005

Graham, John
See Phillips, David Graham

Graham, Jorie 1950- .... **CLC 48, 118; PC 59**
See also AAYA 67; CA 111; CANR 63, 118; CP 4, 5, 6, 7; CWP; DLB 120; EWL 3; MTFW 2005; PFS 10, 17; TCLE 1:1

Graham, R(obert) B(ontine) Cunninghame
See Cunninghame Graham, Robert (Gallnigad) Bontine
See also DLB 98, 135, 174; RGEL 2; RGSF 2

Graham, Robert
See Haldeman, Joe (William)

Graham, Tom
See Lewis, (Harry) Sinclair

Graham, W(illiam) S(idney)
1918-1986 .... **CLC 29**
See also BRWS 7; CA 73-76; 118; CP 1, 2, 3, 4; DLB 20; RGEL 2

Graham, Winston (Mawdsley)
1910-2003 .... **CLC 23**
See also CA 49-52; 218; CANR 2, 22, 45, 66; CMW 4; CN 1, 2, 3, 4, 5, 6, 7; DLB 77; RHW

Grahame, Kenneth 1859-1932 ...... **TCLC 64, 136**
See also BYA 5; CA 108; 136; CANR 80; CLR 5; CWRI 5; DA3; DAB; DLB 34, 141, 178; FANT; MAICYA 1, 2; MTCW 2; NFS 20; RGEL 2; SATA 100; TEA; WCH; YABC 1

Granger, Darius John
See Marlowe, Stephen

Granin, Daniil 1918- .... **CLC 59**
See also DLB 302

Granovsky, Timofei Nikolaevich
1813-1855 .... **NCLC 75**
See also DLB 198

Grant, Skeeter
See Spiegelman, Art

Granville-Barker, Harley
1877-1946 .... **TCLC 2**
See Barker, Harley Granville
See also CA 104; 204; DAM DRAM; RGEL 2

Granzotto, Gianni
See Granzotto, Giovanni Battista

Granzotto, Giovanni Battista
1914-1985 .... **CLC 70**
See also CA 166

Grass, Guenter (Wilhelm) 1927- ... **CLC 1, 2, 4, 6, 11, 15, 22, 32, 49, 88, 207; WLC**
See Grass, Gunter (Wilhelm)
See also BPFB 2; CA 13-16R; CANR 20, 75, 93, 133; CDWLB 2; DA; DA3; DAB; DAC; DAM MST, NOV; DLB 75, 124; EW 13; EWL 3; MTCW 1, 2; MTFW 2005; RGWL 2, 3; TWA

Grass, Gunter (Wilhelm)
See Grass, Guenter (Wilhelm)
See also CWW 2

Gratton, Thomas
See Hulme, T(homas) E(rnest)

Grau, Shirley Ann 1929- .... **CLC 4, 9, 146; SSC 15**
See also CA 89-92; CANR 22, 69; CN 1, 2, 3, 4, 5, 6, 7; CSW; DLB 2, 218; INT CA-89-92; CANR-22; MTCW 1

Gravel, Fern
See Hall, James Norman

Graver, Elizabeth 1964- .... **CLC 70**
See also CA 135; CANR 71, 129

Graves, Richard Perceval
1895-1985 .... **CLC 44**
See also CA 65-68; CANR 9, 26, 51

Graves, Robert (von Ranke)
1895-1985 .. **CLC 1, 2, 6, 11, 39, 44, 45; PC 6**
See also BPFB 2; BRW 7; BYA 4; CA 5-8R; 117; CANR 5, 36; CDBLB 1914-1945; CN 1, 2, 3; CP 1, 2, 3, 4; DA3; DAB; DAC; DAM MST, POET; DLB 20, 100, 191; DLBD 18; DLBY 1985; EWL 3; LATS 1:1; MTCW 1, 2; MTFW 2005; NCFS 2; NFS 21; RGEL 2; RHW; SATA 45; TEA

Graves, Valerie
See Bradley, Marion Zimmer

Gray, Alasdair (James) 1934- .... **CLC 41**
See also BRWS 9; CA 126; CANR 47, 69, 106, 140; CN 4, 5, 6, 7; DLB 194, 261, 319; HGG; INT CA-126; MTCW 1, 2; MTFW 2005; RGSF 2; SUFW 2

Gray, Amlin 1946- .... **CLC 29**
See also CA 138

Gray, Francine du Plessix 1930- ..... **CLC 22, 153**
See also BEST 90:3; CA 61-64; CAAS 2; CANR 11, 33, 75, 81; DAM NOV; INT CANR-11; MTCW 1, 2; MTFW 2005

Gray, John (Henry) 1866-1934 ...... **TCLC 19**
See also CA 119; 162; RGEL 2

Gray, John Lee
See Jakes, John (William)

Gray, Simon (James Holliday)
1936- .... **CLC 9, 14, 36**
See also AITN 1; CA 21-24R; CAAS 3; CANR 32, 69; CBD; CD 5, 6; CN 1, 2, 3; DLB 13; EWL 3; MTCW 1; RGEL 2

Gray, Spalding 1941-2004 .... **CLC 49, 112; DC 7**
See also AAYA 62; CA 128; 225; CAD; CANR 74, 138; CD 5, 6; CPW; DAM POP; MTCW 2; MTFW 2005

Gray, Thomas 1716-1771 .... **LC 4, 40; PC 2; WLC**
See also BRW 3; CDBLB 1660-1789; DA; DA3; DAB; DAC; DAM MST; DLB 109; EXPP; PAB; PFS 9; RGEL 2; TEA; WP

Grayson, David
See Baker, Ray Stannard

Grayson, Richard (A.) 1951- .... **CLC 38**
See also CA 85-88; 210; CAAE 210; CANR 14, 31, 57; DLB 234

Guest, Judith (Ann) 1936- .... **CLC 8, 30**
　See also AAYA 7, 66; CA 77-80; CANR
　15, 75, 138; DA3; DAM NOV, POP;
　EXPN; INT CANR-15; LAIT 5; MTCW
　1, 2; MTFW 2005; NFS 1
Guevara, Che .... **CLC 87; HLC 1**
　See Guevara (Serna), Ernesto
Guevara (Serna), Ernesto
　1928-1967 .... **CLC 87; HLC 1**
　See Guevara, Che
　See also CA 127; 111; CANR 56; DAM
　MULT; HW 1
Guicciardini, Francesco 1483-1540 ..... **LC 49**
Guild, Nicholas M. 1944- .... **CLC 33**
　See also CA 93-96
Guillemin, Jacques
　See Sartre, Jean-Paul
Guillen, Jorge 1893-1984 . **CLC 11; HLCS 1;**
　PC 35
　See also CA 89-92; 112; DAM MULT,
　POET; DLB 108; EWL 3; HW 1; RGWL
　2, 3
Guillen, Nicolas (Cristobal)
　1902-1989 .... **BLC 2; CLC 48, 79; HLC**
　1; PC 23
　See also BW 2; CA 116; 125; 129; CANR
　84; DAM MST, MULT, POET; DLB 283;
　EWL 3; HW 1; LAW; RGWL 2, 3; WP
Guillen y Alvarez, Jorge
　See Guillen, Jorge
Guillevic, (Eugene) 1907-1997 .... **CLC 33**
　See also CA 93-96; CWW 2
Guillois
　See Desnos, Robert
Guillois, Valentin
　See Desnos, Robert
Guimaraes Rosa, Joao 1908-1967 .... **HLCS 2**
　See Rosa, Joao Guimaraes
　See also CA 175; LAW; RGSF 2; RGWL 2,
　3
Guiney, Louise Imogen
　1861-1920 .... **TCLC 41**
　See also CA 160; DLB 54; RGAL 4
Guinizelli, Guido c. 1230-1276 ...... **CMLC 49**
　See Guinizzelli, Guido
Guinizzelli, Guido
　See Guinizelli, Guido
　See also WLIT 7
Guiraldes, Ricardo (Guillermo)
　1886-1927 .... **TCLC 39**
　See also CA 131; EWL 3; HW 1; LAW;
　MTCW 1
Gumilev, Nikolai (Stepanovich)
　1886-1921 .... **TCLC 60**
　See Gumilyov, Nikolay Stepanovich
　See also CA 165; DLB 295
Gumilyov, Nikolay Stepanovich
　See Gumilev, Nikolai (Stepanovich)
　See also EWL 3
Gump, P. Q.
　See Card, Orson Scott
Gunesekera, Romesh 1954- .... **CLC 91**
　See also BRWS 10; CA 159; CANR 140;
　CN 6, 7; DLB 267
Gunn, Bill .... **CLC 5**
　See Gunn, William Harrison
　See also DLB 38
Gunn, Thom(son William)
　1929-2004 . **CLC 3, 6, 18, 32, 81; PC 26**
　See also BRWS 4; CA 17-20R; 227; CANR
　9, 33, 116; CDBLB 1960 to Present; CP
　1, 2, 3, 4, 5, 6, 7; DAM POET; DLB 27;
　INT CANR-33; MTCW 1; PFS 9; RGEL
　2
Gunn, William Harrison 1934(?)-1989
　See Gunn, Bill
　See also AITN 1; BW 1, 3; CA 13-16R;
　128; CANR 12, 25, 76

Gunn Allen, Paula
　See Allen, Paula Gunn
Gunnars, Kristjana 1948- .... **CLC 69**
　See also CA 113; CCA 1; CP 7; CWP; DLB
　60
Gunter, Erich
　See Eich, Gunter
Gurdjieff, G(eorgei) I(vanovich)
　1877(?)-1949 .... **TCLC 71**
　See also CA 157
Gurganus, Allan 1947- .... **CLC 70**
　See also BEST 90:1; CA 135; CANR 114;
　CN 6, 7; CPW; CSW; DAM POP; GLL 1
Gurney, A. R.
　See Gurney, A(lbert) R(amsdell), Jr.
　See also DLB 266
Gurney, A(lbert) R(amsdell), Jr.
　1930- .... **CLC 32, 50, 54**
　See Gurney, A. R.
　See also AMWS 5; CA 77-80; CAD; CANR
　32, 64, 121; CD 5, 6; DAM DRAM; EWL
　3
Gurney, Ivor (Bertie) 1890-1937 ... **TCLC 33**
　See also BRW 6; CA 167; DLBY 2002;
　PAB; RGEL 2
Gurney, Peter
　See Gurney, A(lbert) R(amsdell), Jr.
Guro, Elena (Genrikhovna)
　1877-1913 .... **TCLC 56**
　See also DLB 295
Gustafson, James M(oody) 1925- ... **CLC 100**
　See also CA 25-28R; CANR 37
Gustafson, Ralph (Barker)
　1909-1995 .... **CLC 36**
　See also CA 21-24R; CANR 8, 45, 84; CP
　1, 2, 3, 4; DLB 88; RGEL 2
Gut, Gom
　See Simenon, Georges (Jacques Christian)
Guterson, David 1956- .... **CLC 91**
　See also CA 132; CANR 73, 126; CN 7;
　DLB 292; MTCW 2; MTFW 2005; NFS
　13
Guthrie, A(lfred) B(ertram), Jr.
　1901-1991 .... **CLC 23**
　See also CA 57-60; 134; CANR 24; CN 1,
　2, 3; DLB 6, 212; MAL 5; SATA 62;
　SATA-Obit 67; TCWW 1, 2
Guthrie, Isobel
　See Grieve, C(hristopher) M(urray)
Guthrie, Woodrow Wilson 1912-1967
　See Guthrie, Woody
　See also CA 113; 93-96
Guthrie, Woody .... **CLC 35**
　See Guthrie, Woodrow Wilson
　See also DLB 303; LAIT 3
Gutierrez Najera, Manuel
　1859-1895 .... **HLCS 2; NCLC 133**
　See also DLB 290; LAW
Guy, Rosa (Cuthbert) 1925- .... **CLC 26**
　See also AAYA 4, 37; BW 2; CA 17-20R;
　CANR 14, 34, 83; CLR 13; DLB 33;
　DNFS 1; JRDA; MAICYA 1, 2; SATA 14,
　62, 122; YAW
Gwendolyn
　See Bennett, (Enoch) Arnold
H. D. .... **CLC 3, 8, 14, 31, 34, 73; PC 5**
　See Doolittle, Hilda
　See also FL 1:5
H. de V.
　See Buchan, John
Haavikko, Paavo Juhani 1931- .. **CLC 18, 34**
　See also CA 106; CWW 2; EWL 3
Habbema, Koos
　See Heijermans, Herman
Habermas, Juergen 1929- .... **CLC 104**
　See also CA 109; CANR 85; DLB 242
Habermas, Jurgen
　See Habermas, Juergen

Hacker, Marilyn 1942- ...... **CLC 5, 9, 23, 72,**
　91; PC 47
　See also CA 77-80; CANR 68, 129; CP 3,
　4, 5, 6, 7; CWP; DAM POET; DLB 120,
　282; FW; GLL 2; MAL 5; PFS 19
Hadewijch of Antwerp fl. 1250- ... **CMLC 61**
　See also RGWL 3
Hadrian 76-138 .... **CMLC 52**
Haeckel, Ernst Heinrich (Philipp August)
　1834-1919 .... **TCLC 83**
　See also CA 157
Hafiz c. 1326-1389(?) .... **CMLC 34**
　See also RGWL 2, 3; WLIT 6
Hagedorn, Jessica T(arahata)
　1949- .... **CLC 185**
　See also CA 139; CANR 69; CWP; DLB
　312; RGAL 4
Haggard, H(enry) Rider
　1856-1925 .... **TCLC 11**
　See also BRWS 3; BYA 4, 5; CA 108; 148;
　CANR 112; DLB 70, 156, 174, 178;
　FANT; LMFS 1; MTCW 2; RGEL 2;
　RHW; SATA 16; SCFW 1, 2; SFW 4;
　SUFW 1; WLIT 4
Hagiosy, L.
　See Larbaud, Valery (Nicolas)
Hagiwara, Sakutaro 1886-1942 .... **PC 18;**
　TCLC 60
　See Hagiwara Sakutaro
　See also CA 154; RGWL 3
Hagiwara Sakutaro
　See Hagiwara, Sakutaro
　See also EWL 3
Haig, Fenil
　See Ford, Ford Madox
Haig-Brown, Roderick (Langmere)
　1908-1976 .... **CLC 21**
　See also CA 5-8R; 69-72; CANR 4, 38, 83;
　CLR 31; CWRI 5; DLB 88; MAICYA 1,
　2; SATA 12; TCWW 2
Haight, Rip
　See Carpenter, John (Howard)
Hailey, Arthur 1920-2004 .... **CLC 5**
　See also AITN 2; BEST 90:3; BPFB 2; CA
　1-4R; 233; CANR 2, 36, 75; CCA 1; CN
　1, 2, 3, 4, 5, 6, 7; CPW; DAM NOV, POP;
　DLB 88; DLBY 1982; MTCW 1, 2;
　MTFW 2005
Hailey, Elizabeth Forsythe 1938- ..... **CLC 40**
　See also CA 93-96, 188; CAAE 188; CAAS
　1; CANR 15, 48; INT CANR-15
Haines, John (Meade) 1924- .... **CLC 58**
　See also AMWS 12; CA 17-20R; CANR
　13, 34; CP 1, 2, 3, 4; CSW; DLB 5, 212;
　TCLE 1:1
Hakluyt, Richard 1552-1616 .... **LC 31**
　See also DLB 136; RGEL 2
Haldeman, Joe (William) 1943- .... **CLC 61**
　See Graham, Robert
　See also AAYA 38; CA 53-56, 179; CAAE
　179; CAAS 25; CANR 6, 70, 72, 130;
　DLB 8; INT CANR-6; SCFW 2; SFW 4
Hale, Janet Campbell 1947- .... **NNAL**
　See also CA 49-52; CANR 45, 75; DAM
　MULT; DLB 175; MTCW 2; MTFW 2005
Hale, Sarah Josepha (Buell)
　1788-1879 .... **NCLC 75**
　See also DLB 1, 42, 73, 243
Halevy, Elie 1870-1937 .... **TCLC 104**
Haley, Alex(ander Murray Palmer)
　1921-1992 .... **BLC 2; CLC 8, 12, 76;**
　TCLC 147
　See also AAYA 26; BPFB 2; BW 2, 3; CA
　77-80; 136; CANR 61; CDALBS; CPW;
　CSW; DA; DA3; DAB; DAC; DAM MST,
　MULT, POP; DLB 38; LAIT 5; MTCW
　1, 2; NFS 9

Harris, John (Wyndham Parkes Lucas) Beynon 1903-1969
See Wyndham, John
See also CA 102; 89-92; CANR 84; SATA 118; SFW 4

Harris, MacDonald .... **CLC 9**
See Heiney, Donald (William)

Harris, Mark 1922- .... **CLC 19**
See also CA 5-8R; CAAS 3; CANR 2, 55, 83; CN 1, 2, 3, 4, 5, 6, 7; DLB 2; DLBY 1980

Harris, Norman .... **CLC 65**

Harris, (Theodore) Wilson 1921- .... **CLC 25, 159**
See also BRWS 5; BW 2, 3; CA 65-68; CAAS 16; CANR 11, 27, 69, 114; CD-WLB 3; CN 1, 2, 3, 4, 5, 6, 7; CP 1, 2, 3, 4, 5, 6, 7; DLB 117; EWL 3; MTCW 1; RGEL 2

Harrison, Barbara Grizzuti 1934-2002 .... **CLC 144**
See also CA 77-80; 205; CANR 15, 48; INT CANR-15

Harrison, Elizabeth (Allen) Cavanna 1909-2001
See Cavanna, Betty
See also CA 9-12R; 200; CANR 6, 27, 85, 104, 121; MAICYA 2; SATA 142; YAW

Harrison, Harry (Max) 1925- .... **CLC 42**
See also CA 1-4R; CANR 5, 21, 84; DLB 8; SATA 4; SCFW 2; SFW 4

Harrison, James (Thomas) 1937- ...... **CLC 6, 14, 33, 66, 143; SSC 19**
See Harrison, Jim
See also CA 13-16R; CANR 8, 51, 79, 142; DLBY 1982; INT CANR-8

Harrison, Jim
See Harrison, James (Thomas)
See also AMWS 8; CN 5, 6; CP 1, 2, 3, 4, 5, 6, 7; RGAL 4; TCWW 2; TUS

Harrison, Kathryn 1961- .... **CLC 70, 151**
See also CA 144; CANR 68, 122

Harrison, Tony 1937- .... **CLC 43, 129**
See also BRWS 5; CA 65-68; CANR 44, 98; CBD; CD 5, 6; CP 2, 3, 4, 5, 6, 7; DLB 40, 245; MTCW 1; RGEL 2

Harriss, Will(ard Irvin) 1922- .... **CLC 34**
See also CA 111

Hart, Ellis
See Ellison, Harlan (Jay)

Hart, Josephine 1942(?)- .... **CLC 70**
See also CA 138; CANR 70; CPW; DAM POP

Hart, Moss 1904-1961 .... **CLC 66**
See also CA 109; 89-92; CANR 84; DAM DRAM; DFS 1; DLB 7, 266; RGAL 4

Harte, (Francis) Bret(t) 1836(?)-1902 ... **SSC 8, 59; TCLC 1, 25; WLC**
See also AMWS 2; CA 104; 140; CANR 80; CDALB 1865-1917; DA; DA3; DAC; DAM MST; DLB 12, 64, 74, 79, 186; EXPS; LAIT 2; RGAL 4; RGSF 2; SATA 26; SSFS 3; TUS

Hartley, L(eslie) P(oles) 1895-1972 ... **CLC 2, 22**
See also BRWS 7; CA 45-48; 37-40R; CANR 33; CN 1; DLB 15, 139; EWL 3; HGG; MTCW 1, 2; MTFW 2005; RGEL 2; RGSF 2; SUFW 1

Hartman, Geoffrey H. 1929- .... **CLC 27**
See also CA 117; 125; CANR 79; DLB 67

Hartmann, Sadakichi 1869-1944 ... **TCLC 73**
See also CA 157; DLB 54

Hartmann von Aue c. 1170-c. 1210 .... **CMLC 15**
See also CDWLB 2; DLB 138; RGWL 2, 3

Hartog, Jan de
See de Hartog, Jan

Haruf, Kent 1943- .... **CLC 34**
See also AAYA 44; CA 149; CANR 91, 131

Harvey, Caroline
See Trollope, Joanna

Harvey, Gabriel 1550(?)-1631 .... **LC 88**
See also DLB 167, 213, 281

Harwood, Ronald 1934- .... **CLC 32**
See also CA 1-4R; CANR 4, 55; CBD; CD 5, 6; DAM DRAM, MST; DLB 13

Hasegawa Tatsunosuke
See Futabatei, Shimei

Hasek, Jaroslav (Matej Frantisek) 1883-1923 .... **SSC 69; TCLC 4**
See also CA 104; 129; CDWLB 4; DLB 215; EW 9; EWL 3; MTCW 1, 2; RGSF 2; RGWL 2, 3

Hass, Robert 1941- ... **CLC 18, 39, 99; PC 16**
See also AMWS 6; CA 111; CANR 30, 50, 71; CP 3, 4, 5, 6, 7; DLB 105, 206; EWL 3; MAL 5; MTFW 2005; RGAL 4; SATA 94; TCLE 1:1

Hastings, Hudson
See Kuttner, Henry

Hastings, Selina .... **CLC 44**

Hathorne, John 1641-1717 .... **LC 38**

Hatteras, Amelia
See Mencken, H(enry) L(ouis)

Hatteras, Owen .... **TCLC 18**
See Mencken, H(enry) L(ouis); Nathan, George Jean

Hauptmann, Gerhart (Johann Robert) 1862-1946 .... **SSC 37; TCLC 4**
See also CA 104; 153; CDWLB 2; DAM DRAM; DLB 66, 118; EW 8; EWL 3; RGSF 2; RGWL 2, 3; TWA

Havel, Vaclav 1936- ..... **CLC 25, 58, 65, 123; DC 6**
See also CA 104; CANR 36, 63, 124; CD-WLB 4; CWW 2; DA3; DAM DRAM; DFS 10; DLB 232; EWL 3; LMFS 2; MTCW 1, 2; MTFW 2005; RGWL 3

Haviaras, Stratis .... **CLC 33**
See Chaviaras, Strates

Hawes, Stephen 1475(?)-1529(?) .... **LC 17**
See also DLB 132; RGEL 2

Hawkes, John (Clendennin Burne, Jr.) 1925-1998 .. **CLC 1, 2, 3, 4, 7, 9, 14, 15, 27, 49**
See also BPFB 2; CA 1-4R; 167; CANR 2, 47, 64; CN 1, 2, 3, 4, 5, 6; DLB 2, 7, 227; DLBY 1980, 1998; EWL 3; MAL 5; MTCW 1, 2; MTFW 2005; RGAL 4

Hawking, S. W.
See Hawking, Stephen W(illiam)

Hawking, Stephen W(illiam) 1942- . **CLC 63, 105**
See also AAYA 13; BEST 89:1; CA 126; 129; CANR 48, 115; CPW; DA3; MTCW 2; MTFW 2005

Hawkins, Anthony Hope
See Hope, Anthony

Hawthorne, Julian 1846-1934 .... **TCLC 25**
See also CA 165; HGG

Hawthorne, Nathaniel 1804-1864 ... **NCLC 2, 10, 17, 23, 39, 79, 95, 158; SSC 3, 29, 39, 89; WLC**
See also AAYA 18; AMW; AMWC 1; AMWR 1; BPFB 2; BYA 3; CDALB 1640-1865; CLR 103; DA; DA3; DAB; DAC; DAM MST, NOV; DLB 1, 74, 183, 223, 269; EXPN; EXPS; GL 2; HGG; LAIT 1; NFS 1, 20; RGAL 4; RGSF 2; SSFS 1, 7, 11, 15; SUFW 1; TUS; WCH; YABC 2

Hawthorne, Sophia Peabody 1809-1871 .... **NCLC 150**
See also DLB 183, 239

Haxton, Josephine Ayres 1921-
See Douglas, Ellen
See also CA 115; CANR 41, 83

Hayaseca y Eizaguirre, Jorge
See Echegaray (y Eizaguirre), Jose (Maria Waldo)

Hayashi, Fumiko 1904-1951 .... **TCLC 27**
See Hayashi Fumiko
See also CA 161

Hayashi Fumiko
See Hayashi, Fumiko
See also DLB 180; EWL 3

Haycraft, Anna (Margaret) 1932-2005
See Ellis, Alice Thomas
See also CA 122; 237; CANR 90, 141; MTCW 2; MTFW 2005

Hayden, Robert E(arl) 1913-1980 ..... **BLC 2; CLC 5, 9, 14, 37; PC 6**
See also AFAW 1, 2; AMWS 2; BW 1, 3; CA 69-72; 97-100; CABS 2; CANR 24, 75, 82; CDALB 1941-1968; CP 1, 2, 3; DA; DAC; DAM MST, MULT, POET; DLB 5, 76; EWL 3; EXPP; MAL 5; MTCW 1, 2; PFS 1; RGAL 4; SATA 19; SATA-Obit 26; WP

Haydon, Benjamin Robert 1786-1846 .... **NCLC 146**
See also DLB 110

Hayek, F(riedrich) A(ugust von) 1899-1992 .... **TCLC 109**
See also CA 93-96; 137; CANR 20; MTCW 1, 2

Hayford, J(oseph) E(phraim) Casely
See Casely-Hayford, J(oseph) E(phraim)

Hayman, Ronald 1932- .... **CLC 44**
See also CA 25-28R; CANR 18, 50, 88; CD 5, 6; DLB 155

Hayne, Paul Hamilton 1830-1886 . **NCLC 94**
See also DLB 3, 64, 79, 248; RGAL 4

Hays, Mary 1760-1843 .... **NCLC 114**
See also DLB 142, 158; RGEL 2

Haywood, Eliza (Fowler) 1693(?)-1756 .... **LC 1, 44**
See also DLB 39; RGEL 2

Hazlitt, William 1778-1830 ...... **NCLC 29, 82**
See also BRW 4; DLB 110, 158; RGEL 2; TEA

Hazzard, Shirley 1931- .... **CLC 18, 218**
See also CA 9-12R; CANR 4, 70, 127; CN 1, 2, 3, 4, 5, 6, 7; DLB 289; DLBY 1982; MTCW 1

Head, Bessie 1937-1986 ...... **BLC 2; CLC 25, 67; SSC 52**
See also AFW; BW 2, 3; CA 29-32R; 119; CANR 25, 82; CDWLB 3; CN 1, 2, 3, 4; DA3; DAM MULT; DLB 117, 225; EWL 3; EXPS; FL 1:6; FW; MTCW 1, 2; MTFW 2005; RGSF 2; SSFS 5, 13; WLIT 2; WWE 1

Headon, (Nicky) Topper 1956(?)- ..... **CLC 30**

Heaney, Seamus (Justin) 1939- ..... **CLC 5, 7, 14, 25, 37, 74, 91, 171; PC 18; WLCS**
See also AAYA 61; BRWR 1; BRWS 2; CA 85-88; CANR 25, 48, 75, 91, 128; CD-BLB 1960 to Present; CP 1, 2, 3, 4, 5, 6, 7; DA3; DAB; DAM POET; DLB 40; DLBY 1995; EWL 3; EXPP; MTCW 1, 2; MTFW 2005; PAB; PFS 2, 5, 8, 17; RGEL 2; TEA; WLIT 4

Hearn, (Patricio) Lafcadio (Tessima Carlos) 1850-1904 .... **TCLC 9**
See also CA 105; 166; DLB 12, 78, 189; HGG; MAL 5; RGAL 4

Hearne, Samuel 1745-1792 .... **LC 95**
See also DLB 99

Hearne, Vicki 1946-2001 .... **CLC 56**
See also CA 139; 201

Hearon, Shelby 1931- .... **CLC 63**
See also AITN 2; AMWS 8; CA 25-28R;
CANR 18, 48, 103, 146; CSW

Heat-Moon, William Least .... **CLC 29**
See Trogdon, William (Lewis)
See also AAYA 9

Hebbel, Friedrich 1813-1863 . **DC 21; NCLC 43**
See also CDWLB 2; DAM DRAM; DLB
129; EW 6; RGWL 2, 3

Hebert, Anne 1916-2000 .... **CLC 4, 13, 29**
See also CA 85-88; 187; CANR 69, 126;
CCA 1; CWP; CWW 2; DA3; DAC;
DAM MST, POET; DLB 68; EWL 3; GFL
1789 to the Present; MTCW 1, 2; MTFW
2005; PFS 20

Hecht, Anthony (Evan) 1923-2004 .... **CLC 8, 13, 19; PC 70**
See also AMWS 10; CA 9-12R; 232; CANR
6, 108; CP 1, 2, 3, 4, 5, 6, 7; DAM POET;
DLB 5, 169; EWL 3; PFS 6; WP

Hecht, Ben 1894-1964 ..... **CLC 8; TCLC 101**
See also CA 85-88; DFS 9; DLB 7, 9, 25,
26, 28, 86; FANT; IDFW 3, 4; RGAL 4

Hedayat, Sadeq 1903-1951 .... **TCLC 21**
See also CA 120; EWL 3; RGSF 2

Hegel, Georg Wilhelm Friedrich
1770-1831 .... **NCLC 46, 151**
See also DLB 90; TWA

Heidegger, Martin 1889-1976 .... **CLC 24**
See also CA 81-84; 65-68; CANR 34; DLB
296; MTCW 1, 2; MTFW 2005

Heidenstam, (Carl Gustaf) Verner von
1859-1940 .... **TCLC 5**
See also CA 104

Heidi Louise
See Erdrich, (Karen) Louise

Heifner, Jack 1946- .... **CLC 11**
See also CA 105; CANR 47

Heijermans, Herman 1864-1924 .... **TCLC 24**
See also CA 123; EWL 3

Heilbrun, Carolyn G(old)
1926-2003 .... **CLC 25, 173**
See Cross, Amanda
See also CA 45-48; 220; CANR 1, 28, 58,
94; FW

Hein, Christoph 1944- .... **CLC 154**
See also CA 158; CANR 108; CDWLB 2;
CWW 2; DLB 124

Heine, Heinrich 1797-1856 .... **NCLC 4, 54, 147; PC 25**
See also CDWLB 2; DLB 90; EW 5; RGWL
2, 3; TWA

Heinemann, Larry (Curtiss) 1944- .. **CLC 50**
See also CA 110; CAAS 21; CANR 31, 81;
DLBD 9; INT CANR-31

Heiney, Donald (William) 1921-1993
See Harris, MacDonald
See also CA 1-4R; 142; CANR 3, 58; FANT

Heinlein, Robert A(nson) 1907-1988 . **CLC 1, 3, 8, 14, 26, 55; SSC 55**
See also AAYA 17; BPFB 2; BYA 4, 13;
CA 1-4R; 125; CANR 1, 20, 53; CLR 75;
CN 1, 2, 3, 4; CPW; DA3; DAM POP;
DLB 8; EXPS; JRDA; LAIT 5; LMFS 2;
MAICYA 1, 2; MTCW 1, 2; MTFW 2005;
RGAL 4; SATA 9, 69; SATA-Obit 56;
SCFW 1, 2; SFW 4; SSFS 7; YAW

Helforth, John
See Doolittle, Hilda

Heliodorus fl. 3rd cent. - .... **CMLC 52**

Hellenhofferu, Vojtech Kapristian z
See Hasek, Jaroslav (Matej Frantisek)

Heller, Joseph 1923-1999 . **CLC 1, 3, 5, 8, 11, 36, 63; TCLC 131, 151; WLC**
See also AAYA 24; AITN 1; AMWS 4;
BPFB 2; BYA 1; CA 5-8R; 187; CABS 1;
CANR 8, 42, 66, 126; CN 1, 2, 3, 4, 5, 6;
CPW; DA; DA3; DAB; DAC; DAM MST,

NOV, POP; DLB 2, 28, 227; DLBY 1980,
2002; EWL 3; EXPN; INT CANR-8;
LAIT 4; MAL 5; MTCW 1, 2; MTFW
2005; NFS 1; RGAL 4; TUS; YAW

Hellman, Lillian (Florence)
1906-1984 .. **CLC 2, 4, 8, 14, 18, 34, 44, 52; DC 1; TCLC 119**
See also AAYA 47; AITN 1, 2; AMWS 1;
CA 13-16R; 112; CAD; CANR 33; CWD;
DA3; DAM DRAM; DFS 1, 3, 14; DLB
7, 228; DLBY 1984; EWL 3; FL 1:6; FW;
LAIT 3; MAL 5; MAWW; MTCW 1, 2;
MTFW 2005; RGAL 4; TUS

Helprin, Mark 1947- .... **CLC 7, 10, 22, 32**
See also CA 81-84; CANR 47, 64, 124;
CDALBS; CN 7; CPW; DA3; DAM NOV,
POP; DLBY 1985; FANT; MAL 5;
MTCW 1, 2; MTFW 2005; SUFW 2

Helvetius, Claude-Adrien 1715-1771 .. **LC 26**
See also DLB 313

Helyar, Jane Penelope Josephine 1933-
See Poole, Josephine
See also CA 21-24R; CANR 10, 26; CWRI
5; SATA 82, 138; SATA-Essay 138

Hemans, Felicia 1793-1835 ...... **NCLC 29, 71**
See also DLB 96; RGEL 2

Hemingway, Ernest (Miller)
1899-1961 .... **CLC 1, 3, 6, 8, 10, 13, 19, 30, 34, 39, 41, 44, 50, 61, 80; SSC 1, 25, 36, 40, 63; TCLC 115; WLC**
See also AAYA 19; AMW; AMWC 1;
AMWR 1; BPFB 2; BYA 2, 3, 13, 15; CA
77-80; CANR 34; CDALB 1917-1929;
DA; DA3; DAB; DAC; DAM MST, NOV;
DLB 4, 9, 102, 210, 308, 316; DLBD 1,
15, 16; DLBY 1981, 1987, 1996, 1998;
EWL 3; EXPN; EXPS; LAIT 3, 4; LATS
1:1; MAL 5; MTCW 1, 2; MTFW 2005;
NFS 1, 5, 6, 14; RGAL 4; RGSF 2; SSFS
17; TUS; WYA

Hempel, Amy 1951- .... **CLC 39**
See also CA 118; 137; CANR 70; DA3;
DLB 218; EXPS; MTCW 2; MTFW 2005;
SSFS 2

Henderson, F. C.
See Mencken, H(enry) L(ouis)

Henderson, Sylvia
See Ashton-Warner, Sylvia (Constance)

Henderson, Zenna (Chlarson)
1917-1983 .... **SSC 29**
See also CA 1-4R; 133; CANR 1, 84; DLB
8; SATA 5; SFW 4

Henkin, Joshua .... **CLC 119**
See also CA 161

Henley, Beth .... **CLC 23; DC 6, 14**
See Henley, Elizabeth Becker
See also CABS 3; CAD; CD 5, 6; CSW;
CWD; DFS 2; DLBY 1986; FW

Henley, Elizabeth Becker 1952-
See Henley, Beth
See also CA 107; CANR 32, 73, 140; DA3;
DAM DRAM, MST; DFS 21; MTCW 1,
2; MTFW 2005

Henley, William Ernest 1849-1903 .. **TCLC 8**
See also CA 105; 234; DLB 19; RGEL 2

Hennissart, Martha 1929-
See Lathen, Emma
See also CA 85-88; CANR 64

Henry VIII 1491-1547 .... **LC 10**
See also DLB 132

Henry, O. ..... **SSC 5, 49; TCLC 1, 19; WLC**
See Porter, William Sydney
See also AAYA 41; AMWS 2; EXPS; RGAL
4; RGSF 2; SSFS 2, 18; TCWW 1, 2

Henry, Patrick 1736-1799 .... **LC 25**
See also LAIT 1

Henryson, Robert 1430(?)-1506(?) ..... **LC 20, 110; PC 65**
See also BRWS 7; DLB 146; RGEL 2

Henschke, Alfred
See Klabund

Henson, Lance 1944- .... **NNAL**
See also CA 146; DLB 175

Hentoff, Nat(han Irving) 1925- .... **CLC 26**
See also AAYA 4, 42; BYA 6; CA 1-4R;
CAAS 6; CANR 5, 25, 77, 114; CLR 1,
52; INT CANR-25; JRDA; MAICYA 1,
2; SATA 42, 69, 133; SATA-Brief 27;
WYA; YAW

Heppenstall, (John) Rayner
1911-1981 .... **CLC 10**
See also CA 1-4R; 103; CANR 29; CN 1,
2; CP 1, 2, 3; EWL 3

Heraclitus c. 540B.C.-c. 450B.C. ... **CMLC 22**
See also DLB 176

Herbert, Frank (Patrick)
1920-1986 .... **CLC 12, 23, 35, 44, 85**
See also AAYA 21; BPFB 2; BYA 4, 14;
CA 53-56; 118; CANR 5, 43; CDALBS;
CPW; DAM POP; DLB 8; INT CANR-5;
LAIT 5; MTCW 1, 2; MTFW 2005; NFS
17; SATA 9, 37; SATA-Obit 47; SCFW 1,
2; SFW 4; YAW

Herbert, George 1593-1633 . **LC 24, 121; PC 4**
See also BRW 2; BRWR 2; CDBLB Before
1660; DAB; DAM POET; DLB 126;
EXPP; RGEL 2; TEA; WP

Herbert, Zbigniew 1924-1998 ..... **CLC 9, 43; PC 50; TCLC 168**
See also CA 89-92; 169; CANR 36, 74; CD-
WLB 4; CWW 2; DAM POET; DLB 232;
EWL 3; MTCW 1; PFS 22

Herbst, Josephine (Frey)
1897-1969 .... **CLC 34**
See also CA 5-8R; 25-28R; DLB 9

Herder, Johann Gottfried von
1744-1803 .... **NCLC 8**
See also DLB 97; EW 4; TWA

Heredia, Jose Maria 1803-1839 .... **HLCS 2**
See also LAW

Hergesheimer, Joseph 1880-1954 ... **TCLC 11**
See also CA 109; 194; DLB 102, 9; RGAL
4

Herlihy, James Leo 1927-1993 .... **CLC 6**
See also CA 1-4R; 143; CAD; CANR 2;
CN 1, 2, 3, 4, 5

Herman, William
See Bierce, Ambrose (Gwinett)

Hermogenes fl. c. 175- .... **CMLC 6**

Hernandez, Jose 1834-1886 .... **NCLC 17**
See also LAW; RGWL 2, 3; WLIT 1

Herodotus c. 484B.C.-c. 420B.C. .. **CMLC 17**
See also AW 1; CDWLB 1; DLB 176;
RGWL 2, 3; TWA

Herrick, Robert 1591-1674 .... **LC 13; PC 9**
See also BRW 2; BRWC 2; DA; DAB;
DAC; DAM MST, POP; DLB 126; EXPP;
PFS 13; RGAL 4; RGEL 2; TEA; WP

Herring, Guilles
See Somerville, Edith Oenone

Herriot, James 1916-1995 .... **CLC 12**
See Wight, James Alfred
See also AAYA 1, 54; BPFB 2; CA 148;
CANR 40; CLR 80; CPW; DAM POP;
LAIT 3; MAICYA 2; MAICYAS 1;
MTCW 2; SATA 86, 135; TEA; YAW

Herris, Violet
See Hunt, Violet

Herrmann, Dorothy 1941- .... **CLC 44**
See also CA 107

Herrmann, Taffy
See Herrmann, Dorothy

Hersey, John (Richard) 1914-1993 .... **CLC 1, 2, 7, 9, 40, 81, 97**
See also AAYA 29; BPFB 2; CA 17-20R;
140; CANR 33; CDALBS; CN 1, 2, 3, 4,
5; CPW; DAM POP; DLB 6, 185, 278,
299; MAL 5; MTCW 1, 2; MTFW 2005;
SATA 25; SATA-Obit 76; TUS

Herzen, Aleksandr Ivanovich
1812-1870 .... **NCLC 10, 61**
See Herzen, Alexander

Herzen, Alexander
See Herzen, Aleksandr Ivanovich
See also DLB 277

Herzl, Theodor 1860-1904 .... **TCLC 36**
See also CA 168

Herzog, Werner 1942- .... **CLC 16**
See also CA 89-92

Hesiod c. 8th cent. B.C.- .... **CMLC 5**
See also AW 1; DLB 176; RGWL 2, 3

Hesse, Hermann 1877-1962 ... **CLC 1, 2, 3, 6,
   11, 17, 25, 69; SSC 9, 49; TCLC 148;
   WLC**
See also AAYA 43; BPFB 2; CA 17-18;
   CAP 2; CDWLB 2; DA; DA3; DAB;
   DAC; DAM MST, NOV; DLB 66; EW 9;
   EWL 3; EXPN; LAIT 1; MTCW 1, 2;
   MTFW 2005; NFS 6, 15; RGWL 2, 3;
   SATA 50; TWA

Hewes, Cady
See De Voto, Bernard (Augustine)

Heyen, William 1940- .... **CLC 13, 18**
See also CA 33-36R; 220; CAAE 220;
   CAAS 9; CANR 98; CP 3, 4, 5, 6, 7; DLB
   5

Heyerdahl, Thor 1914-2002 .... **CLC 26**
See also CA 5-8R; 207; CANR 5, 22, 66,
   73; LAIT 4; MTCW 1, 2; MTFW 2005;
   SATA 2, 52

Heym, Georg (Theodor Franz Arthur)
1887-1912 .... **TCLC 9**
See also CA 106; 181

Heym, Stefan 1913-2001 .... **CLC 41**
See also CA 9-12R; 203; CANR 4; CWW
   2; DLB 69; EWL 3

Heyse, Paul (Johann Ludwig von)
1830-1914 .... **TCLC 8**
See also CA 104; 209; DLB 129

Heyward, (Edwin) DuBose
1885-1940 .... **HR 1:2; TCLC 59**
See also CA 108; 157; DLB 7, 9, 45, 249;
   MAL 5; SATA 21

Heywood, John 1497(?)-1580(?) .... **LC 65**
See also DLB 136; RGEL 2

Heywood, Thomas 1573(?)-1641 .... **LC 111**
See also DAM DRAM; DLB 62; LMFS 1;
   RGEL 2; TEA

Hibbert, Eleanor Alice Burford
1906-1993 .... **CLC 7**
See Holt, Victoria
See also BEST 90:4; CA 17-20R; 140;
   CANR 9, 28, 59; CMW 4; CPW; DAM
   POP; MTCW 2; MTFW 2005; RHW;
   SATA 2; SATA-Obit 74

Hichens, Robert (Smythe)
1864-1950 .... **TCLC 64**
See also CA 162; DLB 153; HGG; RHW;
   SUFW

Higgins, Aidan 1927- .... **SSC 68**
See also CA 9-12R; CANR 70, 115; CN 1,
   2, 3, 4, 5, 6, 7; DLB 14

Higgins, George V(incent)
1939-1999 .... **CLC 4, 7, 10, 18**
See also BPFB 2; CA 77-80; 186; CAAS 5;
   CANR 17, 51, 89, 96; CMW 4; CN 2, 3,
   4, 5, 6; DLB 2; DLBY 1981, 1998; INT
   CANR-17; MSW; MTCW 1

Higginson, Thomas Wentworth
1823-1911 .... **TCLC 36**
See also CA 162; DLB 1, 64, 243

Higgonet, Margaret ed. .... **CLC 65**

Highet, Helen
See MacInnes, Helen (Clark)

Highsmith, (Mary) Patricia
1921-1995 .... **CLC 2, 4, 14, 42, 102**
See Morgan, Claire
See also AAYA 48; BRWS 5; CA 1-4R; 147;
   CANR 1, 20, 48, 62, 108; CMW 4; CN 1,
   2, 3, 4, 5; CPW; DA3; DAM NOV, POP;
   DLB 306; MSW; MTCW 1, 2; MTFW
   2005

Highwater, Jamake (Mamake)
1942(?)-2001 .... **CLC 12**
See also AAYA 7; BPFB 2; BYA 4; CA 65-
   68; 199; CAAS 7; CANR 10, 34, 84; CLR
   17; CWRI 5; DLB 52; DLBY 1985;
   JRDA; MAICYA 1, 2; SATA 32, 69;
   SATA-Brief 30

Highway, Tomson 1951- ...... **CLC 92; NNAL**
See also CA 151; CANR 75; CCA 1; CD 5,
   6; CN 7; DAC; DAM MULT; DFS 2;
   MTCW 2

Hijuelos, Oscar 1951- .... **CLC 65; HLC 1**
See also AAYA 25; AMWS 8; BEST 90:1;
   CA 123; CANR 50, 75, 125; CPW; DA3;
   DAM MULT, POP; DLB 145; HW 1, 2;
   LLW; MAL 5; MTCW 2; MTFW 2005;
   NFS 17; RGAL 4; WLIT 1

Hikmet, Nazim 1902-1963 .... **CLC 40**
See Nizami of Ganja
See also CA 141; 93-96; EWL 3; WLIT 6

Hildegard von Bingen 1098-1179 . **CMLC 20**
See also DLB 148

Hildesheimer, Wolfgang 1916-1991 .. **CLC 49**
See also CA 101; 135; DLB 69, 124; EWL
   3

Hill, Geoffrey (William) 1932- ...... **CLC 5, 8,
   18, 45**
See also BRWS 5; CA 81-84; CANR 21,
   89; CDBLB 1960 to Present; CP 1, 2, 3,
   4, 5, 6, 7; DAM POET; DLB 40; EWL 3;
   MTCW 1; RGEL 2

Hill, George Roy 1921-2002 .... **CLC 26**
See also CA 110; 122; 213

Hill, John
See Koontz, Dean R.

Hill, Susan (Elizabeth) 1942- ...... **CLC 4, 113**
See also CA 33-36R; CANR 29, 69, 129;
   CN 2, 3, 4, 5, 6, 7; DAB; DAM MST,
   NOV; DLB 14, 139; HGG; MTCW 1;
   RHW

Hillard, Asa G. III .... **CLC 70**

Hillerman, Tony 1925- .... **CLC 62, 170**
See also AAYA 40; BEST 89:1; BPFB 2;
   CA 29-32R; CANR 21, 42, 65, 97, 134;
   CMW 4; CPW; DA3; DAM POP; DLB
   206, 306; MAL 5; MSW; MTCW 2;
   MTFW 2005; RGAL 4; SATA 6; TCWW
   2; YAW

Hillesum, Etty 1914-1943 .... **TCLC 49**
See also CA 137

Hilliard, Noel (Harvey) 1929-1996 ... **CLC 15**
See also CA 9-12R; CANR 7, 69; CN 1, 2,
   3, 4, 5, 6

Hillis, Rick 1956- .... **CLC 66**
See also CA 134

Hilton, James 1900-1954 .... **TCLC 21**
See also CA 108; 169; DLB 34, 77; FANT;
   SATA 34

Hilton, Walter (?)-1396 .... **CMLC 58**
See also DLB 146; RGEL 2

Himes, Chester (Bomar) 1909-1984 .. **BLC 2;
   CLC 2, 4, 7, 18, 58, 108; TCLC 139**
See also AFAW 2; BPFB 2; BW 2; CA 25-
   28R; 114; CANR 22, 89; CMW 4; CN 1,
   2, 3; DAM MULT; DLB 2, 76, 143, 226;
   EWL 3; MAL 5; MSW; MTCW 1, 2;
   MTFW 2005; RGAL 4

Himmelfarb, Gertrude 1922- .... **CLC 202**
See also CA 49-52; CANR 28, 66, 102

Hinde, Thomas .... **CLC 6, 11**
See Chitty, Thomas Willes
See also CN 1, 2, 3, 4, 5, 6; EWL 3

Hine, (William) Daryl 1936- .... **CLC 15**
See also CA 1-4R; CAAS 15; CANR 1, 20;
   CP 1, 2, 3, 4, 5, 6, 7; DLB 60

Hinkson, Katharine Tynan
See Tynan, Katharine

Hinojosa(-Smith), Rolando (R.)
1929- .... **HLC 1**
See Hinojosa-Smith, Rolando
See also CA 131; CAAS 16; CANR 62;
   DAM MULT; DLB 82; HW 1, 2; LLW;
   MTCW 2; MTFW 2005; RGAL 4

Hinton, S(usan) E(loise) 1950- .. **CLC 30, 111**
See also AAYA 2, 33; BPFB 2; BYA 2, 3;
   CA 81-84; CANR 32, 62, 92, 133;
   CDALBS; CLR 3, 23; CPW; DA; DA3;
   DAB; DAC; DAM MST, NOV; JRDA;
   LAIT 5; MAICYA 1, 2; MTCW 1, 2;
   MTFW 2005 !**; NFS 5, 9, 15, 16; SATA
   19, 58, 115, 160; WYA; YAW

Hippius, Zinaida (Nikolaevna) .... **TCLC 9**
See Gippius, Zinaida (Nikolaevna)
See also DLB 295; EWL 3

Hiraoka, Kimitake 1925-1970
See Mishima, Yukio
See also CA 97-100; 29-32R; DA3; DAM
   DRAM; GLL 1; MTCW 1, 2

Hirsch, E(ric) D(onald), Jr. 1928- .... **CLC 79**
See also CA 25-28R; CANR 27, 51; DLB
   67; INT CANR-27; MTCW 1

Hirsch, Edward 1950- .... **CLC 31, 50**
See also CA 104; CANR 20, 42, 102; CP 7;
   DLB 120; PFS 22

Hitchcock, Alfred (Joseph)
1899-1980 .... **CLC 16**
See also AAYA 22; CA 159; 97-100; SATA
   27; SATA-Obit 24

Hitchens, Christopher (Eric)
1949- .... **CLC 157**
See also CA 152; CANR 89

Hitler, Adolf 1889-1945 .... **TCLC 53**
See also CA 117; 147

Hoagland, Edward (Morley) 1932- .. **CLC 28**
See also ANW; CA 1-4R; CANR 2, 31, 57,
   107; CN 1, 2, 3, 4, 5, 6, 7; DLB 6; SATA
   51; TCWW 2

Hoban, Russell (Conwell) 1925- ... **CLC 7, 25**
See also BPFB 2; CA 5-8R; CANR 23, 37,
   66, 114, 138; CLR 3, 69; CN 4, 5, 6, 7;
   CWRI 5; DAM NOV; DLB 52; FANT;
   MAICYA 1, 2; MTCW 1, 2; MTFW 2005;
   SATA 1, 40, 78, 136; SFW 4; SUFW 2;
   TCLE 1:1

Hobbes, Thomas 1588-1679 .... **LC 36**
See also DLB 151, 252, 281; RGEL 2

Hobbs, Perry
See Blackmur, R(ichard) P(almer)

Hobson, Laura Z(ametkin)
1900-1986 .... **CLC 7, 25**
See also BPFB 2; CA 17-20R; 118; CANR
   55; CN 1, 2, 3, 4; DLB 28; SATA 52

Hoccleve, Thomas c. 1368-c. 1437 ...... **LC 75**
See also DLB 146; RGEL 2

Hoch, Edward D(entinger) 1930-
See Queen, Ellery
See also CA 29-32R; CANR 11, 27, 51, 97;
   CMW 4; DLB 306; SFW 4

Hochhuth, Rolf 1931- .... **CLC 4, 11, 18**
See also CA 5-8R; CANR 33, 75, 136;
   CWW 2; DAM DRAM; DLB 124; EWL
   3; MTCW 1, 2; MTFW 2005

Hochman, Sandra 1936- .... **CLC 3, 8**
See also CA 5-8R; CP 1, 2, 3, 4; DLB 5

Hochwaelder, Fritz 1911-1986 .... **CLC 36**
See Hochwalder, Fritz
See also CA 29-32R; 120; CANR 42; DAM
   DRAM; MTCW 1; RGWL 3

Hochwalder, Fritz
See Hochwaelder, Fritz
See also EWL 3; RGWL 2

Ishiguro, Kazuo 1954- . **CLC 27, 56, 59, 110, 219**
See also AAYA 58; BEST 90:2; BPFB 2; BRWS 4; CA 120; CANR 49, 95, 133; CN 5, 6, 7; DA3; DAM NOV; DLB 194; EWL 3; MTCW 1, 2; MTFW 2005; NFS 13; WLIT 4; WWE 1

Ishikawa, Hakuhin
See Ishikawa, Takuboku

Ishikawa, Takuboku 1886(?)-1912 ..... **PC 10; TCLC 15**
See Ishikawa Takuboku
See also CA 113; 153; DAM POET

Iskander, Fazil (Abdulovich) 1929- .. **CLC 47**
See Iskander, Fazil' Abdulevich
See also CA 102; EWL 3

Iskander, Fazil' Abdulevich
See Iskander, Fazil (Abdulovich)
See also DLB 302

Isler, Alan (David) 1934- .... **CLC 91**
See also CA 156; CANR 105

Ivan IV 1530-1584 .... **LC 17**

Ivanov, Vyacheslav Ivanovich 1866-1949 .... **TCLC 33**
See also CA 122; EWL 3

Ivask, Ivar Vidrik 1927-1992 .... **CLC 14**
See also CA 37-40R; 139; CANR 24

Ives, Morgan
See Bradley, Marion Zimmer
See also GLL 1

Izumi Shikibu c. 973-c. 1034 .... **CMLC 33**

J. R. S.
See Gogarty, Oliver St. John

Jabran, Kahlil
See Gibran, Kahlil

Jabran, Khalil
See Gibran, Kahlil

Jackson, Daniel
See Wingrove, David (John)

Jackson, Helen Hunt 1830-1885 .... **NCLC 90**
See also DLB 42, 47, 186, 189; RGAL 4

Jackson, Jesse 1908-1983 .... **CLC 12**
See also BW 1; CA 25-28R; 109; CANR 27; CLR 28; CWRI 5; MAICYA 1, 2; SATA 2, 29; SATA-Obit 48

Jackson, Laura (Riding) 1901-1991 .... **PC 44**
See Riding, Laura
See also CA 65-68; 135; CANR 28, 89; DLB 48

Jackson, Sam
See Trumbo, Dalton

Jackson, Sara
See Wingrove, David (John)

Jackson, Shirley 1919-1965 . **CLC 11, 60, 87; SSC 9, 39; WLC**
See also AAYA 9; AMWS 9; BPFB 2; CA 1-4R; 25-28R; CANR 4, 52; CDALB 1941-1968; DA; DA3; DAC; DAM MST; DLB 6, 234; EXPS; HGG; LAIT 4; MAL 5; MTCW 2; MTFW 2005; RGAL 4; RGSF 2; SATA 2; SSFS 1; SUFW 1, 2

Jacob, (Cyprien-)Max 1876-1944 ..... **TCLC 6**
See also CA 104; 193; DLB 258; EWL 3; GFL 1789 to the Present; GLL 2; RGWL 2, 3

Jacobs, Harriet A(nn) 1813(?)-1897 .... **NCLC 67, 162**
See also AFAW 1, 2; DLB 239; FL 1:3; FW; LAIT 2; RGAL 4

Jacobs, Jim 1942- .... **CLC 12**
See also CA 97-100; INT CA-97-100

Jacobs, W(illiam) W(ymark) 1863-1943 .... **SSC 73; TCLC 22**
See also CA 121; 167; DLB 135; EXPS; HGG; RGEL 2; RGSF 2; SSFS 2; SUFW 1

Jacobsen, Jens Peter 1847-1885 .... **NCLC 34**

Jacobsen, Josephine (Winder) 1908-2003 .... **CLC 48, 102; PC 62**
See also CA 33-36R; 218; CAAS 18; CANR 23, 48; CCA 1; CP 2, 3, 4, 5, 6, 7; DLB 244; PFS 23; TCLE 1:1

Jacobson, Dan 1929- .... **CLC 4, 14**
See also AFW; CA 1-4R; CANR 2, 25, 66; CN 1, 2, 3, 4, 5, 6, 7; DLB 14, 207, 225, 319; EWL 3; MTCW 1; RGSF 2

Jacqueline
See Carpentier (y Valmont), Alejo

Jacques de Vitry c. 1160-1240 ...... **CMLC 63**
See also DLB 208

Jagger, Michael Philip
See Jagger, Mick

Jagger, Mick 1943- .... **CLC 17**
See also CA 239

Jahiz, al- c. 780-c. 869 .... **CMLC 25**
See also DLB 311

Jakes, John (William) 1932- .... **CLC 29**
See also AAYA 32; BEST 89:4; BPFB 2; CA 57-60, 214; CAAE 214; CANR 10, 43, 66, 111, 142; CPW; CSW; DA3; DAM NOV, POP; DLB 278; DLBY 1983; FANT; INT CANR-10; MTCW 1, 2; MTFW 2005; RHW; SATA 62; SFW 4; TCWW 1, 2

James I 1394-1437 .... **LC 20**
See also RGEL 2

James, Andrew
See Kirkup, James

James, C(yril) L(ionel) R(obert) 1901-1989 .... **BLCS; CLC 33**
See also BW 2; CA 117; 125; 128; CANR 62; CN 1, 2, 3, 4; DLB 125; MTCW 1

James, Daniel (Lewis) 1911-1988
See Santiago, Danny
See also CA 174; 125

James, Dynely
See Mayne, William (James Carter)

James, Henry Sr. 1811-1882 .... **NCLC 53**

James, Henry 1843-1916 .... **SSC 8, 32, 47; TCLC 2, 11, 24, 40, 47, 64, 171; WLC**
See also AMW; AMWC 1; AMWR 1; BPFB 2; BRW 6; CA 104; 132; CDALB 1865-1917; DA; DA3; DAB; DAC; DAM MST, NOV; DLB 12, 71, 74, 189; DLBD 13; EWL 3; EXPS; GL 2; HGG; LAIT 2; MAL 5; MTCW 1, 2; MTFW 2005; NFS 12, 16, 19; RGAL 4; RGEL 2; RGSF 2; SSFS 9; SUFW 1; TUS

James, M. R.
See James, Montague (Rhodes)
See also DLB 156, 201

James, Montague (Rhodes) 1862-1936 .... **SSC 16; TCLC 6**
See James, M. R.
See also CA 104; 203; HGG; RGEL 2; RGSF 2; SUFW 1

James, P. D. .... **CLC 18, 46, 122**
See White, Phyllis Dorothy James
See also BEST 90:2; BPFB 2; BRWS 4; CDBLB 1960 to Present; CN 4, 5, 6; DLB 87, 276; DLBD 17; MSW

James, Philip
See Moorcock, Michael (John)

James, Samuel
See Stephens, James

James, Seumas
See Stephens, James

James, Stephen
See Stephens, James

James, William 1842-1910 .... **TCLC 15, 32**
See also AMW; CA 109; 193; DLB 270, 284; MAL 5; NCFS 5; RGAL 4

Jameson, Anna 1794-1860 .... **NCLC 43**
See also DLB 99, 166

Jameson, Fredric (R.) 1934- .... **CLC 142**
See also CA 196; DLB 67; LMFS 2

James VI of Scotland 1566-1625 .... **LC 109**
See also DLB 151, 172

Jami, Nur al-Din 'Abd al-Rahman 1414-1492 .... **LC 9**

Jammes, Francis 1868-1938 .... **TCLC 75**
See also CA 198; EWL 3; GFL 1789 to the Present

Jandl, Ernst 1925-2000 .... **CLC 34**
See also CA 200; EWL 3

Janowitz, Tama 1957- .... **CLC 43, 145**
See also CA 106; CANR 52, 89, 129; CN 5, 6, 7; CPW; DAM POP; DLB 292; MTFW 2005

Japrisot, Sebastien 1931- .... **CLC 90**
See Rossi, Jean-Baptiste
See also CMW 4; NFS 18

Jarrell, Randall 1914-1965 .... **CLC 1, 2, 6, 9, 13, 49; PC 41; TCLC 177**
See also AMW; BYA 5; CA 5-8R; 25-28R; CABS 2; CANR 6, 34; CDALB 1941-1968; CLR 6; CWRI 5; DAM POET; DLB 48, 52; EWL 3; EXPP; MAICYA 1, 2; MAL 5; MTCW 1, 2; PAB; PFS 2; RGAL 4; SATA 7

Jarry, Alfred 1873-1907 .... **SSC 20; TCLC 2, 14, 147**
See also CA 104; 153; DA3; DAM DRAM; DFS 8; DLB 192, 258; EW 9; EWL 3; GFL 1789 to the Present; RGWL 2, 3; TWA

Jarvis, E. K.
See Ellison, Harlan (Jay)

Jawien, Andrzej
See John Paul II, Pope

Jaynes, Roderick
See Coen, Ethan

Jeake, Samuel, Jr.
See Aiken, Conrad (Potter)

Jean Paul 1763-1825 .... **NCLC 7**

Jefferies, (John) Richard 1848-1887 .... **NCLC 47**
See also DLB 98, 141; RGEL 2; SATA 16; SFW 4

Jeffers, (John) Robinson 1887-1962 .. **CLC 2, 3, 11, 15, 54; PC 17; WLC**
See also AMWS 2; CA 85-88; CANR 35; CDALB 1917-1929; DA; DAC; DAM MST, POET; DLB 45, 212; EWL 3; MAL 5; MTCW 1, 2; MTFW 2005; PAB; PFS 3, 4; RGAL 4

Jefferson, Janet
See Mencken, H(enry) L(ouis)

Jefferson, Thomas 1743-1826 . **NCLC 11, 103**
See also AAYA 54; ANW; CDALB 1640-1865; DA3; DLB 31, 183; LAIT 1; RGAL 4

Jeffrey, Francis 1773-1850 .... **NCLC 33**
See Francis, Lord Jeffrey

Jelakowitch, Ivan
See Heijermans, Herman

Jelinek, Elfriede 1946- .... **CLC 169**
See also AAYA 68; CA 154; DLB 85; FW

Jellicoe, (Patricia) Ann 1927- .... **CLC 27**
See also CA 85-88; CBD; CD 5, 6; CWD; CWRI 5; DLB 13, 233; FW

Jelloun, Tahar ben 1944- .... **CLC 180**
See Ben Jelloun, Tahar
See also CA 162; CANR 100

Jemyma
See Holley, Marietta

Jen, Gish .... **AAL; CLC 70, 198**
See Jen, Lillian
See also AMWC 2; CN 7; DLB 312

Jen, Lillian 1955-
See Jen, Gish
See also CA 135; CANR 89, 130

Jenkins, (John) Robin 1912- .... **CLC 52**
See also CA 1-4R; CANR 1, 135; CN 1, 2, 3, 4, 5, 6, 7; DLB 14, 271

Jones, Terence Graham Parry
  1942- .... **CLC 21**
  See Jones, Terry; Monty Python
  See also CA 112; 116; CANR 35, 93; INT
  CA-116; SATA 127
Jones, Terry
  See Jones, Terence Graham Parry
  See also SATA 67; SATA-Brief 51
Jones, Thom (Douglas) 1945(?)- ..... **CLC 81;
  SSC 56**
  See also CA 157; CANR 88; DLB 244
Jong, Erica 1942- .... **CLC 4, 6, 8, 18, 83**
  See also AITN 1; AMWS 5; BEST 90:2;
  BPFB 2; CA 73-76; CANR 26, 52, 75,
  132; CN 3, 4, 5, 6, 7; CP 2, 3, 4, 5, 6, 7;
  CPW; DA3; DAM NOV, POP; DLB 2, 5,
  28, 152; FW; INT CANR-26; MAL 5;
  MTCW 1, 2; MTFW 2005
Jonson, Ben(jamin) 1572(?)-1637 . **DC 4; LC
  6, 33, 110; PC 17; WLC**
  See also BRW 1; BRWC 1; BRWR 1; CD-
  BLB Before 1660; DA; DAB; DAC;
  DAM DRAM, MST, POET; DFS 4, 10;
  DLB 62, 121; LMFS 1; PFS 23; RGEL 2;
  TEA; WLIT 3
Jordan, June (Meyer)
  1936-2002 .. **BLCS; CLC 5, 11, 23, 114;
  PC 38**
  See also AAYA 2, 66; AFAW 1, 2; BW 2,
  3; CA 33-36R; 206; CANR 25, 70, 114;
  CLR 10; CP 3, 4, 5, 6, 7; CWP; DAM
  MULT, POET; DLB 38; GLL 2; LAIT 5;
  MAICYA 1, 2; MTCW 1; SATA 4, 136;
  YAW
Jordan, Neil (Patrick) 1950- .... **CLC 110**
  See also CA 124; 130; CANR 54; CN 4, 5,
  6, 7; GLL 2; INT CA-130
Jordan, Pat(rick M.) 1941- .... **CLC 37**
  See also CA 33-36R; CANR 121
Jorgensen, Ivar
  See Ellison, Harlan (Jay)
Jorgenson, Ivar
  See Silverberg, Robert
Joseph, George Ghevarughese .... **CLC 70**
Josephson, Mary
  See O'Doherty, Brian
Josephus, Flavius c. 37-100 .... **CMLC 13**
  See also AW 2; DLB 176
Josiah Allen's Wife
  See Holley, Marietta
Josipovici, Gabriel (David) 1940- ...... **CLC 6,
  43, 153**
  See also CA 37-40R; 224; CAAE 224;
  CAAS 8; CANR 47, 84; CN 3, 4, 5, 6, 7;
  DLB 14, 319
Joubert, Joseph 1754-1824 .... **NCLC 9**
Jouve, Pierre Jean 1887-1976 .... **CLC 47**
  See also CA 65-68; DLB 258; EWL 3
Jovine, Francesco 1902-1950 .... **TCLC 79**
  See also DLB 264; EWL 3
Joyce, James (Augustine Aloysius)
  1882-1941 .... **DC 16; PC 22; SSC 3, 26,
  44, 64; TCLC 3, 8, 16, 35, 52, 159;
  WLC**
  See also AAYA 42; BRW 7; BRWC 1;
  BRWR 1; BYA 11, 13; CA 104; 126; CD-
  BLB 1914-1945; DA; DA3; DAB; DAC;
  DAM MST, NOV, POET; DLB 10, 19,
  36, 162, 247; EWL 3; EXPN; EXPS;
  LAIT 3; LMFS 1, 2; MTCW 1, 2; MTFW
  2005; NFS 7; RGSF 2; SSFS 1, 19; TEA;
  WLIT 4
Jozsef, Attila 1905-1937 .... **TCLC 22**
  See also CA 116; 230; CDWLB 4; DLB
  215; EWL 3
Juana Ines de la Cruz, Sor
  1651(?)-1695 ...... **HLCS 1; LC 5; PC 24**
  See also DLB 305; FW; LAW; RGWL 2, 3;
  WLIT 1

Juana Inez de La Cruz, Sor
  See Juana Ines de la Cruz, Sor
Judd, Cyril
  See Kornbluth, C(yril) M.; Pohl, Frederik
Juenger, Ernst 1895-1998 .... **CLC 125**
  See Junger, Ernst
  See also CA 101; 167; CANR 21, 47, 106;
  DLB 56
Julian of Norwich 1342(?)-1416(?) . **LC 6, 52**
  See also DLB 146; LMFS 1
Julius Caesar 100B.C.-44B.C.
  See Caesar, Julius
  See also CDWLB 1; DLB 211
Junger, Ernst
  See Juenger, Ernst
  See also CDWLB 2; EWL 3; RGWL 2, 3
Junger, Sebastian 1962- .... **CLC 109**
  See also AAYA 28; CA 165; CANR 130;
  MTFW 2005
Juniper, Alex
  See Hospital, Janette Turner
Junius
  See Luxemburg, Rosa
Junzaburo, Nishiwaki
  See Nishiwaki, Junzaburo
  See also EWL 3
Just, Ward (Swift) 1935- .... **CLC 4, 27**
  See also CA 25-28R; CANR 32, 87; CN 6,
  7; INT CANR-32
Justice, Donald (Rodney)
  1925-2004 .... **CLC 6, 19, 102; PC 64**
  See also AMWS 7; CA 5-8R; 230; CANR
  26, 54, 74, 121, 122; CP 1, 2, 3, 4, 5, 6,
  7; CSW; DAM POET; DLBY 1983; EWL
  3; INT CANR-26; MAL 5; MTCW 2; PFS
  14; TCLE 1:1
Juvenal c. 60-c. 130 .... **CMLC 8**
  See also AW 2; CDWLB 1; DLB 211;
  RGWL 2, 3
Juvenis
  See Bourne, Randolph S(illiman)
K., Alice
  See Knapp, Caroline
Kabakov, Sasha .... **CLC 59**
Kabir 1398(?)-1448(?) .... **LC 109; PC 56**
  See also RGWL 2, 3
Kacew, Romain 1914-1980
  See Gary, Romain
  See also CA 108; 102
Kadare, Ismail 1936- .... **CLC 52, 190**
  See also CA 161; EWL 3; RGWL 3
Kadohata, Cynthia (Lynn)
  1956(?)- .... **CLC 59, 122**
  See also CA 140; CANR 124; SATA 155
Kafka, Franz 1883-1924 ... **SSC 5, 29, 35, 60;
  TCLC 2, 6, 13, 29, 47, 53, 112; WLC**
  See also AAYA 31; BPFB 2; CA 105; 126;
  CDWLB 2; DA; DA3; DAB; DAC; DAM
  MST, NOV; DLB 81; EW 9; EWL 3;
  EXPS; LATS 1:1; LMFS 2; MTCW 1, 2;
  MTFW 2005; NFS 7; RGSF 2; RGWL 2,
  3; SFW 4; SSFS 3, 7, 12; TWA
Kahanovitsch, Pinkhes
  See Der Nister
Kahn, Roger 1927- .... **CLC 30**
  See also CA 25-28R; CANR 44, 69; DLB
  171; SATA 37
Kain, Saul
  See Sassoon, Siegfried (Lorraine)
Kaiser, Georg 1878-1945 .... **TCLC 9**
  See also CA 106; 190; CDWLB 2; DLB
  124; EWL 3; LMFS 2; RGWL 2, 3
Kaledin, Sergei .... **CLC 59**
Kaletski, Alexander 1946- .... **CLC 39**
  See also CA 118; 143
Kalidasa fl. c. 400-455 .... **CMLC 9; PC 22**
  See also RGWL 2, 3

Kallman, Chester (Simon)
  1921-1975 .... **CLC 2**
  See also CA 45-48; 53-56; CANR 3; CP 1,
  2
Kaminsky, Melvin 1926-
  See Brooks, Mel
  See also CA 65-68; CANR 16; DFS 21
Kaminsky, Stuart M(elvin) 1934- ..... **CLC 59**
  See also CA 73-76; CANR 29, 53, 89;
  CMW 4
Kamo no Chomei 1153(?)-1216 .... **CMLC 66**
  See also DLB 203
Kamo no Nagaakira
  See Kamo no Chomei
Kandinsky, Wassily 1866-1944 .... **TCLC 92**
  See also AAYA 64; CA 118; 155
Kane, Francis
  See Robbins, Harold
Kane, Henry 1918-
  See Queen, Ellery
  See also CA 156; CMW 4
Kane, Paul
  See Simon, Paul (Frederick)
Kanin, Garson 1912-1999 .... **CLC 22**
  See also AITN 1; CA 5-8R; 177; CAD;
  CANR 7, 78; DLB 7; IDFW 3, 4
Kaniuk, Yoram 1930- .... **CLC 19**
  See also CA 134; DLB 299
Kant, Immanuel 1724-1804 ..... **NCLC 27, 67**
  See also DLB 94
Kantor, MacKinlay 1904-1977 .... **CLC 7**
  See also CA 61-64; 73-76; CANR 60, 63;
  CN 1, 2; DLB 9, 102; MAL 5; MTCW 2;
  RHW; TCWW 1, 2
Kanze Motokiyo
  See Zeami
Kaplan, David Michael 1946- .... **CLC 50**
  See also CA 187
Kaplan, James 1951- .... **CLC 59**
  See also CA 135; CANR 121
Karadzic, Vuk Stefanovic
  1787-1864 .... **NCLC 115**
  See also CDWLB 4; DLB 147
Karageorge, Michael
  See Anderson, Poul (William)
Karamzin, Nikolai Mikhailovich
  1766-1826 .... **NCLC 3**
  See also DLB 150; RGSF 2
Karapanou, Margarita 1946- .... **CLC 13**
  See also CA 101
Karinthy, Frigyes 1887-1938 .... **TCLC 47**
  See also CA 170; DLB 215; EWL 3
Karl, Frederick R(obert)
  1927-2004 .... **CLC 34**
  See also CA 5-8R; 226; CANR 3, 44, 143
Karr, Mary 1955- .... **CLC 188**
  See also AMWS 11; CA 151; CANR 100;
  MTFW 2005; NCFS 5
Kastel, Warren
  See Silverberg, Robert
Kataev, Evgeny Petrovich 1903-1942
  See Petrov, Evgeny
  See also CA 120
Kataphusin
  See Ruskin, John
Katz, Steve 1935- .... **CLC 47**
  See also CA 25-28R; CAAS 14, 64; CANR
  12; CN 4, 5, 6, 7; DLBY 1983
Kauffman, Janet 1945- .... **CLC 42**
  See also CA 117; CANR 43, 84; DLB 218;
  DLBY 1986
Kaufman, Bob (Garnell) 1925-1986 . **CLC 49**
  See also BG 1:3; BW 1; CA 41-44R; 118;
  CANR 22; CP 1; DLB 16, 41

MST, NOV, POP; DLB 2, 16, 206; EWL
3; EXPN; LAIT 4; MAL 5; MTCW 1, 2;
MTFW 2005; NFS 2; RGAL 4; SATA 66;
SATA-Obit 131; TUS; YAW

Kesselring, Joseph (Otto)
1902-1967 .... **CLC 45**
See also CA 150; DAM DRAM, MST; DFS
20

Kessler, Jascha (Frederick) 1929- ...... **CLC 4**
See also CA 17-20R; CANR 8, 48, 111; CP
1

Kettelkamp, Larry (Dale) 1933- .... **CLC 12**
See also CA 29-32R; CANR 16; SAAS 3;
SATA 2

Key, Ellen (Karolina Sofia)
1849-1926 .... **TCLC 65**
See also DLB 259

Keyber, Conny
See Fielding, Henry

Keyes, Daniel 1927- .... **CLC 80**
See also AAYA 23; BYA 11; CA 17-20R,
181; CAAE 181; CANR 10, 26, 54, 74;
DA; DA3; DAC; DAM MST, NOV;
EXPN; LAIT 4; MTCW 2; MTFW 2005;
NFS 2; SATA 37; SFW 4

Keynes, John Maynard
1883-1946 .... **TCLC 64**
See also CA 114; 162, 163; DLBD 10;
MTCW 2; MTFW 2005

Khanshendel, Chiron
See Rose, Wendy

Khayyam, Omar 1048-1131 ... **CMLC 11; PC
8**
See Omar Khayyam
See also DA3; DAM POET; WLIT 6

Kherdian, David 1931- .... **CLC 6, 9**
See also AAYA 42; CA 21-24R, 192; CAAE
192; CAAS 2; CANR 39, 78; CLR 24;
JRDA; LAIT 3; MAICYA 1, 2; SATA 16,
74; SATA-Essay 125

Khlebnikov, Velimir .... **TCLC 20**
See Khlebnikov, Viktor Vladimirovich
See also DLB 295; EW 10; EWL 3; RGWL
2, 3

Khlebnikov, Viktor Vladimirovich 1885-1922
See Khlebnikov, Velimir
See also CA 117; 217

Khodasevich, Vladislav (Felitsianovich)
1886-1939 .... **TCLC 15**
See also CA 115; DLB 317; EWL 3

Kielland, Alexander Lange
1849-1906 .... **TCLC 5**
See also CA 104

Kiely, Benedict 1919- ... **CLC 23, 43; SSC 58**
See also CA 1-4R; CANR 2, 84; CN 1, 2,
3, 4, 5, 6, 7; DLB 15, 319; TCLE 1:1

Kienzle, William X(avier)
1928-2001 .... **CLC 25**
See also CA 93-96; 203; CAAS 1; CANR
9, 31, 59, 111; CMW 4; DA3; DAM POET;
INT CANR-31; MSW; MTCW 1, 2;
MTFW 2005

Kierkegaard, Soren 1813-1855 ..... **NCLC 34,
78, 125**
See also DLB 300; EW 6; LMFS 2; RGWL
3; TWA

Kieslowski, Krzysztof 1941-1996 .... **CLC 120**
See also CA 147; 151

Killens, John Oliver 1916-1987 .... **CLC 10**
See also BW 2; CA 77-80; 123; CAAS 2;
CANR 26; CN 1, 2, 3, 4; DLB 33; EWL
3

Killigrew, Anne 1660-1685 .... **LC 4, 73**
See also DLB 131

Killigrew, Thomas 1612-1683 .... **LC 57**
See also DLB 58; RGEL 2

Kim
See Simenon, Georges (Jacques Christian)

Kincaid, Jamaica 1949- ...... **BLC 2; CLC 43,
68, 137; SSC 72**
See also AAYA 13, 56; AFAW 2; AMWS 7;
BRWS 7; BW 2, 3; CA 125; CANR 47,
59, 95, 133; CDALBS; CDWLB 3; CLR
63; CN 4, 5, 6, 7; DA3; DAM MULT,
NOV; DLB 157, 227; DNFS 1; EWL 3;
EXPS; FW; LATS 1:2; LMFS 2; MAL 5;
MTCW 2; MTFW 2005; NCFS 1; NFS 3;
SSFS 5, 7; TUS; WWE 1; YAW

King, Francis (Henry) 1923- .... **CLC 8, 53,
145**
See also CA 1-4R; CANR 1, 33, 86; CN 1,
2, 3, 4, 5, 6, 7; DAM NOV; DLB 15, 139;
MTCW 1

King, Kennedy
See Brown, George Douglas

King, Martin Luther, Jr. 1929-1968 . **BLC 2;
CLC 83; WLCS**
See also BW 2, 3; CA 25-28; CANR 27,
44; CAP 2; DA; DA3; DAB; DAC; DAM
MST, MULT; LAIT 5; LATS 1:2; MTCW
1, 2; MTFW 2005; SATA 14

King, Stephen 1947- .... **CLC 12, 26, 37, 61,
113; SSC 17, 55**
See also AAYA 1, 17; AMWS 5; BEST
90:1; BPFB 2; CA 61-64; CANR 1, 30,
52, 76, 119, 134; CN 7; CPW; DA3; DAM
NOV, POP; DLB 143; DLBY 1980; HGG;
JRDA; LAIT 5; MTCW 1, 2; MTFW
2005; RGAL 4; SATA 9, 55, 161; SUFW
1, 2; WYAS 1; YAW

King, Stephen Edwin
See King, Stephen

King, Steve
See King, Stephen

King, Thomas 1943- .... **CLC 89, 171; NNAL**
See also CA 144; CANR 95; CCA 1; CN 6,
7; DAC; DAM MULT; DLB 175; SATA
96

Kingman, Lee .... **CLC 17**
See Natti, (Mary) Lee
See also CWRI 5; SAAS 3; SATA 1, 67

Kingsley, Charles 1819-1875 .... **NCLC 35**
See also CLR 77; DLB 21, 32, 163, 178,
190; FANT; MAICYA 2; MAICYAS 1;
RGEL 2; WCH; YABC 2

Kingsley, Henry 1830-1876 .... **NCLC 107**
See also DLB 21, 230; RGEL 2

Kingsley, Sidney 1906-1995 .... **CLC 44**
See also CA 85-88; 147; CAD; DFS 14, 19;
DLB 7; MAL 5; RGAL 4

Kingsolver, Barbara 1955- .... **CLC 55, 81,
130, 216**
See also AAYA 15; AMWS 7; CA 129; 134;
CANR 60, 96, 133; CDALBS; CN 7;
CPW; CSW; DA3; DAM POP; DLB 206;
INT CA-134; LAIT 5; MTCW 2; MTFW
2005; NFS 5, 10, 12; RGAL 4; TCLE 1:1

Kingston, Maxine (Ting Ting) Hong
1940- .... **AAL; CLC 12, 19, 58, 121;
WLCS**
See also AAYA 8, 55; AMWS 5; BPFB 2;
CA 69-72; CANR 13, 38, 74, 87, 128;
CDALBS; CN 6, 7; DA3; DAM MULT,
NOV; DLB 173, 212, 312; DLBY 1980;
EWL 3; FL 1:6; FW; INT CANR-13;
LAIT 5; MAL 5; MAWW; MTCW 1, 2;
MTFW 2005; NFS 6; RGAL 4; SATA 53;
SSFS 3; TCWW 2

Kinnell, Galway 1927- ..... **CLC 1, 2, 3, 5, 13,
29, 129; PC 26**
See also AMWS 3; CA 9-12R; CANR 10,
34, 66, 116, 138; CP 1, 2, 3, 4, 5, 6, 7;
DLB 5; DLBY 1987; EWL 3; INT CANR-
34; MAL 5; MTCW 1, 2; MTFW 2005;
PAB; PFS 9; RGAL 4; TCLE 1:1; WP

Kinsella, Thomas 1928- .... **CLC 4, 19, 138;
PC 69**
See also BRWS 5; CA 17-20R; CANR 15,
122; CP 1, 2, 3, 4, 5, 6, 7; DLB 27; EWL
3; MTCW 1, 2; MTFW 2005; RGEL 2;
TEA

Kinsella, W(illiam) P(atrick) 1935- . **CLC 27,
43, 166**
See also AAYA 7, 60; BPFB 2; CA 97-100,
222; CAAE 222; CAAS 7; CANR 21, 35,
66, 75, 129; CN 4, 5, 6, 7; CPW; DAC;
DAM NOV, POP; FANT; INT CANR-21;
LAIT 5; MTCW 1, 2; MTFW 2005; NFS
15; RGSF 2

Kinsey, Alfred C(harles)
1894-1956 .... **TCLC 91**
See also CA 115; 170; MTCW 2

Kipling, (Joseph) Rudyard 1865-1936 . **PC 3;
SSC 5, 54; TCLC 8, 17, 167; WLC**
See also AAYA 32; BRW 6; BRWC 1, 2;
BYA 4; CA 105; 120; CANR 33; CDBLB
1890-1914; CLR 39, 65; CWRI 5; DA;
DA3; DAB; DAC; DAM MST, POET;
DLB 19, 34, 141, 156; EWL 3; EXPS;
FANT; LAIT 3; LMFS 1; MAICYA 1, 2;
MTCW 1, 2; MTFW 2005; NFS 21; PFS
22; RGEL 2; RGSF 2; SATA 100; SFW
4; SSFS 8, 21; SUFW 1; TEA; WCH;
WLIT 4; YABC 2

Kircher, Athanasius 1602-1680 .... **LC 121**
See also DLB 164

Kirk, Russell (Amos) 1918-1994 .. **TCLC 119**
See also AITN 1; CA 1-4R; 145; CAAS 9;
CANR 1, 20, 60; HGG; INT CANR-20;
MTCW 1, 2

Kirkham, Dinah
See Card, Orson Scott

Kirkland, Caroline M. 1801-1864 . **NCLC 85**
See also DLB 3, 73, 74, 250, 254; DLBD
13

Kirkup, James 1918- .... **CLC 1**
See also CA 1-4R; CAAS 4; CANR 2; CP
1, 2, 3, 4, 5, 6, 7; DLB 27; SATA 12

Kirkwood, James 1930(?)-1989 .... **CLC 9**
See also AITN 2; CA 1-4R; 128; CANR 6,
40; GLL 2

Kirsch, Sarah 1935- .... **CLC 176**
See also CA 178; CWW 2; DLB 75; EWL
3

Kirshner, Sidney
See Kingsley, Sidney

Kis, Danilo 1935-1989 .... **CLC 57**
See also CA 109; 118; 129; CANR 61; CD-
WLB 4; DLB 181; EWL 3; MTCW 1;
RGSF 2; RGWL 2, 3

Kissinger, Henry A(lfred) 1923- ..... **CLC 137**
See also CA 1-4R; CANR 2, 33, 66, 109;
MTCW 1

Kivi, Aleksis 1834-1872 .... **NCLC 30**

Kizer, Carolyn (Ashley) 1925- ... **CLC 15, 39,
80; PC 66**
See also CA 65-68; CAAS 5; CANR 24,
70, 134; CP 1, 2, 3, 4, 5, 6, 7; CWP; DAM
POET; DLB 5, 169; EWL 3; MAL 5;
MTCW 2; MTFW 2005; PFS 18; TCLE
1:1

Klabund 1890-1928 .... **TCLC 44**
See also CA 162; DLB 66

Klappert, Peter 1942- .... **CLC 57**
See also CA 33-36R; CSW; DLB 5

Klein, A(braham) M(oses)
1909-1972 .... **CLC 19**
See also CA 101; 37-40R; CP 1; DAB;
DAC; DAM MST; DLB 68; EWL 3;
RGEL 2

Klein, Joe
See Klein, Joseph

Klein, Joseph 1946- .... **CLC 154**
See also CA 85-88; CANR 55

Klein, Norma 1938-1989 .... **CLC 30**
See also AAYA 2, 35; BPFB 2; BYA 6, 7,
8; CA 41-44R; 128; CANR 15, 37; CLR
2, 19; INT CANR-15; JRDA; MAICYA
1, 2; SAAS 1; SATA 7, 57; WYA; YAW

Klein, T(heodore) E(ibon) D(onald)
1947- .... **CLC 34**
See also CA 119; CANR 44, 75; HGG

Kleist, Heinrich von 1777-1811 ...... **NCLC 2,
37; SSC 22**
See also CDWLB 2; DAM DRAM; DLB
90; EW 5; RGSF 2; RGWL 2, 3

Klima, Ivan 1931- .... **CLC 56, 172**
See also CA 25-28R; CANR 17, 50, 91;
CDWLB 4; CWW 2; DAM NOV; DLB
232; EWL 3; RGWL 3

Klimentev, Andrei Platonovich
See Klimentov, Andrei Platonovich

Klimentov, Andrei Platonovich
1899-1951 .... **SSC 42; TCLC 14**
See Platonov, Andrei Platonovich; Platonov,
Andrey Platonovich
See also CA 108; 232

Klinger, Friedrich Maximilian von
1752-1831 .... **NCLC 1**
See also DLB 94

Klingsor the Magician
See Hartmann, Sadakichi

Klopstock, Friedrich Gottlieb
1724-1803 .... **NCLC 11**
See also DLB 97; EW 4; RGWL 2, 3

Kluge, Alexander 1932- .... **SSC 61**
See also CA 81-84; DLB 75

Knapp, Caroline 1959-2002 .... **CLC 99**
See also CA 154; 207

Knebel, Fletcher 1911-1993 .... **CLC 14**
See also AITN 1; CA 1-4R; 140; CAAS 3;
CANR 1, 36; CN 1, 2, 3, 4, 5; SATA 36;
SATA-Obit 75

Knickerbocker, Diedrich
See Irving, Washington

Knight, Etheridge 1931-1991 ... **BLC 2; CLC
40; PC 14**
See also BW 1, 3; CA 21-24R; 133; CANR
23, 82; CP 1, 2, 3, 4; DAM POET; DLB
41; MTCW 2; MTFW 2005; RGAL 4;
TCLE 1:1

Knight, Sarah Kemble 1666-1727 .... **LC 7**
See also DLB 24, 200

Knister, Raymond 1899-1932 .... **TCLC 56**
See also CA 186; DLB 68; RGEL 2

Knowles, John 1926-2001 ... **CLC 1, 4, 10, 26**
See also AAYA 10; AMWS 12; BPFB 2;
BYA 3; CA 17-20R; 203; CANR 40, 74,
76, 132; CDALB 1968-1988; CLR 98; CN
1, 2, 3, 4, 5, 6, 7; DA; DAC; DAM MST,
NOV; DLB 6; EXPN; MTCW 1, 2;
MTFW 2005; NFS 2; RGAL 4; SATA 8,
89; SATA-Obit 134; YAW

Knox, Calvin M.
See Silverberg, Robert

Knox, John c. 1505-1572 .... **LC 37**
See also DLB 132

Knye, Cassandra
See Disch, Thomas M(ichael)

Koch, C(hristopher) J(ohn) 1932- .... **CLC 42**
See also CA 127; CANR 84; CN 3, 4, 5, 6,
7; DLB 289

Koch, Christopher
See Koch, C(hristopher) J(ohn)

Koch, Kenneth (Jay) 1925-2002 .... **CLC 5, 8,
44**
See also AMWS 15; CA 1-4R; 207; CAD;
CANR 6, 36, 57, 97, 131; CD 5, 6; CP 1,
2, 3, 4, 5, 6, 7; DAM POET; DLB 5; INT
CANR-36; MAL 5; MTCW 2; MTFW
2005; PFS 20; SATA 65; WP

Kochanowski, Jan 1530-1584 .... **LC 10**
See also RGWL 2, 3

Kock, Charles Paul de 1794-1871 . **NCLC 16**

Koda Rohan
See Koda Shigeyuki

Koda Rohan
See Koda Shigeyuki
See also DLB 180

Koda Shigeyuki 1867-1947 .... **TCLC 22**
See Koda Rohan
See also CA 121; 183

Koestler, Arthur 1905-1983 ... **CLC 1, 3, 6, 8,
15, 33**
See also BRWS 1; CA 1-4R; 109; CANR 1,
33; CDBLB 1945-1960; CN 1, 2, 3;
DLBY 1983; EWL 3; MTCW 1, 2; MTFW
2005; NFS 19; RGEL 2

Kogawa, Joy Nozomi 1935- ...... **CLC 78, 129**
See also AAYA 47; CA 101; CANR 19, 62,
126; CN 6, 7; CP 7; CWP; DAC; DAM
MST, MULT; FW; MTCW 2; MTFW
2005; NFS 3; SATA 99

Kohout, Pavel 1928- .... **CLC 13**
See also CA 45-48; CANR 3

Koizumi, Yakumo
See Hearn, (Patricio) Lafcadio (Tessima
Carlos)

Kolmar, Gertrud 1894-1943 .... **TCLC 40**
See also CA 167; EWL 3

Komunyakaa, Yusef 1947- .. **BLCS; CLC 86,
94, 207; PC 51**
See also AFAW 2; AMWS 13; CA 147;
CANR 83; CP 7; CSW; DLB 120; EWL
3; PFS 5, 20; RGAL 4

Konrad, George
See Konrad, Gyorgy

Konrad, Gyorgy 1933- .... **CLC 4, 10, 73**
See also CA 85-88; CANR 97; CDWLB 4;
CWW 2; DLB 232; EWL 3

Konwicki, Tadeusz 1926- .... **CLC 8, 28, 54,
117**
See also CA 101; CAAS 9; CANR 39, 59;
CWW 2; DLB 232; EWL 3; IDFW 3;
MTCW 1

Koontz, Dean R. 1945- .... **CLC 78, 206**
See also AAYA 9, 31; BEST 89:3, 90:2; CA
108; CANR 19, 36, 52, 95, 138; CMW 4;
CPW; DA3; DAM NOV, POP; DLB 292;
HGG; MTCW 1; MTFW 2005; SATA 92,
165; SFW 4; SUFW 2; YAW

Koontz, Dean Ray
See Koontz, Dean R.

Koontz, Dean Ray
See Koontz, Dean R.

Kopernik, Mikolaj
See Copernicus, Nicolaus

Kopit, Arthur (Lee) 1937- ...... **CLC 1, 18, 33**
See also AITN 1; CA 81-84; CABS 3;
CAD; CD 5, 6; DAM DRAM; DFS 7, 14;
DLB 7; MAL 5; MTCW 1; RGAL 4

Kopitar, Jernej (Bartholomaus)
1780-1844 .... **NCLC 117**

Kops, Bernard 1926- .... **CLC 4**
See also CA 5-8R; CANR 84; CBD; CN 1,
2, 3, 4, 5, 6, 7; CP 1, 2, 3, 4, 5, 6, 7; DLB
13

Kornbluth, C(yril) M. 1923-1958 .... **TCLC 8**
See also CA 105; 160; DLB 8; SCFW 1, 2;
SFW 4

Korolenko, V. G.
See Korolenko, Vladimir Galaktionovich

Korolenko, Vladimir
See Korolenko, Vladimir Galaktionovich

Korolenko, Vladimir G.
See Korolenko, Vladimir Galaktionovich

Korolenko, Vladimir Galaktionovich
1853-1921 .... **TCLC 22**
See also CA 121; DLB 277

Korzybski, Alfred (Habdank Skarbek)
1879-1950 .... **TCLC 61**
See also CA 123; 160

Kosinski, Jerzy (Nikodem)
1933-1991 .... **CLC 1, 2, 3, 6, 10, 15, 53,
70**
See also AMWS 7; BPFB 2; CA 17-20R;
134; CANR 9, 46; CN 1, 2, 3, 4; DA3;
DAM NOV; DLB 2, 299; DLBY 1982;
EWL 3; HGG; MAL 5; MTCW 1, 2;
MTFW 2005; NFS 12; RGAL 4; TUS

Kostelanetz, Richard (Cory) 1940- .. **CLC 28**
See also CA 13-16R; CAAS 8; CANR 38,
77; CN 4, 5, 6; CP 2, 3, 4, 5, 6, 7

Kostrowitzki, Wilhelm Apollinaris de
1880-1918
See Apollinaire, Guillaume
See also CA 104

Kotlowitz, Robert 1924- .... **CLC 4**
See also CA 33-36R; CANR 36

Kotzebue, August (Friedrich Ferdinand) von
1761-1819 .... **NCLC 25**
See also DLB 94

Kotzwinkle, William 1938- ..... **CLC 5, 14, 35**
See also BPFB 2; CA 45-48; CANR 3, 44,
84, 129; CLR 6; CN 7; DLB 173; FANT;
MAICYA 1, 2; SATA 24, 70, 146; SFW
4; SUFW 2; YAW

Kowna, Stancy
See Szymborska, Wislawa

Kozol, Jonathan 1936- .... **CLC 17**
See also AAYA 46; CA 61-64; CANR 16,
45, 96; MTFW 2005

Kozoll, Michael 1940(?)- .... **CLC 35**

Kramer, Kathryn 19(?)- .... **CLC 34**

Kramer, Larry 1935- .... **CLC 42; DC 8**
See also CA 124; 126; CANR 60, 132;
DAM POP; DLB 249; GLL 1

Krasicki, Ignacy 1735-1801 .... **NCLC 8**

Krasinski, Zygmunt 1812-1859 .... **NCLC 4**
See also RGWL 2, 3

Kraus, Karl 1874-1936 .... **TCLC 5**
See also CA 104; 216; DLB 118; EWL 3

Kreve (Mickevicius), Vincas
1882-1954 .... **TCLC 27**
See also CA 170; DLB 220; EWL 3

Kristeva, Julia 1941- .... **CLC 77, 140**
See also CA 154; CANR 99; DLB 242;
EWL 3; FW; LMFS 2

Kristofferson, Kris 1936- .... **CLC 26**
See also CA 104

Krizanc, John 1956- .... **CLC 57**
See also CA 187

Krleza, Miroslav 1893-1981 .... **CLC 8, 114**
See also CA 97-100; 105; CANR 50; CD-
WLB 4; DLB 147; EW 11; RGWL 2, 3

Kroetsch, Robert (Paul) 1927- ... **CLC 5, 23,
57, 132**
See also CA 17-20R; CANR 8, 38; CCA 1;
CN 2, 3, 4, 5, 6, 7; CP 7; DAC; DAM
POET; DLB 53; MTCW 1

Kroetz, Franz
See Kroetz, Franz Xaver

Kroetz, Franz Xaver 1946- .... **CLC 41**
See also CA 130; CANR 142; CWW 2;
EWL 3

Kroker, Arthur (W.) 1945- .... **CLC 77**
See also CA 161

Kroniuk, Lisa
See Berton, Pierre (Francis de Marigny)

Kropotkin, Peter (Aleksieevich)
1842-1921 .... **TCLC 36**
See Kropotkin, Petr Alekseevich
See also CA 119; 219

Kropotkin, Petr Alekseevich
See Kropotkin, Peter (Aleksieevich)
See also DLB 277

Krotkov, Yuri 1917-1981 .... **CLC 19**
See also CA 102

Krumb
See Crumb, R(obert)

Krumgold, Joseph (Quincy)
1908-1980 .... **CLC 12**
See also BYA 1, 2; CA 9-12R; 101; CANR
7; MAICYA 1, 2; SATA 1, 48; SATA-Obit
23; YAW

Krumwitz
See Crumb, R(obert)

Krutch, Joseph Wood 1893-1970 ..... **CLC 24**
See also ANW; CA 1-4R; 25-28R; CANR
4; DLB 63, 206, 275

Krutzch, Gus
See Eliot, T(homas) S(tearns)

Krylov, Ivan Andreevich
1768(?)-1844 .... **NCLC 1**
See also DLB 150

Kubin, Alfred (Leopold Isidor)
1877-1959 .... **TCLC 23**
See also CA 112; 149; CANR 104; DLB 81

Kubrick, Stanley 1928-1999 .... **CLC 16;
TCLC 112**
See also AAYA 30; CA 81-84; 177; CANR
33; DLB 26

Kumin, Maxine (Winokur) 1925- ..... **CLC 5,
13, 28, 164; PC 15**
See also AITN 2; AMWS 4; ANW; CA
1-4R; CAAS 8; CANR 1, 21, 69, 115,
140; CP 2, 3, 4, 5, 6, 7; CWP; DA3; DAM
POET; DLB 5; EWL 3; EXPP; MTCW 1,
2; MTFW 2005; PAB; PFS 18; SATA 12

Kundera, Milan 1929- . **CLC 4, 9, 19, 32, 68,
115, 135; SSC 24**
See also AAYA 2, 62; BPFB 2; CA 85-88;
CANR 19, 52, 74, 144; CDWLB 4; CWW
2; DA3; DAM NOV; DLB 232; EW 13;
EWL 3; MTCW 1, 2; MTFW 2005; NFS
18; RGSF 2; RGWL 3; SSFS 10

Kunene, Mazisi (Raymond) 1930- ... **CLC 85**
See also BW 1, 3; CA 125; CANR 81; CP
1, 7; DLB 117

Kung, Hans .... **CLC 130**
See Kung, Hans

Kung, Hans 1928-
See Kung, Hans
See also CA 53-56; CANR 66, 134; MTCW
1, 2; MTFW 2005

Kunikida Doppo 1869(?)-1908
See Doppo, Kunikida
See also DLB 180; EWL 3

Kunitz, Stanley (Jasspon) 1905- .. **CLC 6, 11,
14, 148; PC 19**
See also AMWS 3; CA 41-44R; CANR 26,
57, 98; CP 1, 2, 3, 4, 5, 6, 7; DA3; DLB
48; INT CANR-26; MAL 5; MTCW 1, 2;
MTFW 2005; PFS 11; RGAL 4

Kunze, Reiner 1933- .... **CLC 10**
See also CA 93-96; CWW 2; DLB 75; EWL
3

Kuprin, Aleksander Ivanovich
1870-1938 .... **TCLC 5**
See Kuprin, Aleksandr Ivanovich; Kuprin,
Alexandr Ivanovich
See also CA 104; 182

Kuprin, Aleksandr Ivanovich
See Kuprin, Aleksander Ivanovich
See also DLB 295

Kuprin, Alexandr Ivanovich
See Kuprin, Aleksander Ivanovich
See also EWL 3

Kureishi, Hanif 1954- .. **CLC 64, 135; DC 26**
See also BRWS 11; CA 139; CANR 113;
CBD; CD 5, 6; CN 6, 7; DLB 194, 245;
GLL 2; IDFW 4; WLIT 4; WWE 1

Kurosawa, Akira 1910-1998 ..... **CLC 16, 119**
See also AAYA 11, 64; CA 101; 170; CANR
46; DAM MULT

Kushner, Tony 1956- .... **CLC 81, 203; DC 10**
See also AAYA 61; AMWS 9; CA 144;
CAD; CANR 74, 130; CD 5, 6; DA3;
DAM DRAM; DFS 5; DLB 228; EWL 3;
GLL 1; LAIT 5; MAL 5; MTCW 2;
MTFW 2005; RGAL 4; SATA 160

Kuttner, Henry 1915-1958 .... **TCLC 10**
See also CA 107; 157; DLB 8; FANT;
SCFW 1, 2; SFW 4

Kutty, Madhavi
See Das, Kamala

Kuzma, Greg 1944- .... **CLC 7**
See also CA 33-36R; CANR 70

Kuzmin, Mikhail (Alekseevich)
1872(?)-1936 .... **TCLC 40**
See also CA 170; DLB 295; EWL 3

Kyd, Thomas 1558-1594 .. **DC 3; LC 22, 125**
See also BRW 1; DAM DRAM; DFS 21;
DLB 62; IDTP; LMFS 1; RGEL 2; TEA;
WLIT 3

Kyprianos, Iossif
See Samarakis, Antonis

L. S.
See Stephen, Sir Leslie

Laȝamon
See Layamon
See also DLB 146

Labe, Louise 1521-1566 .... **LC 120**

Labrunie, Gerard
See Nerval, Gerard de

La Bruyere, Jean de 1645-1696 .... **LC 17**
See also DLB 268; EW 3; GFL Beginnings
to 1789

Lacan, Jacques (Marie Emile)
1901-1981 .... **CLC 75**
See also CA 121; 104; DLB 296; EWL 3;
TWA

Laclos, Pierre-Ambroise Francois
1741-1803 .... **NCLC 4, 87**
See also DLB 313; EW 4; GFL Beginnings
to 1789; RGWL 2, 3

Lacolere, Francois
See Aragon, Louis

La Colere, Francois
See Aragon, Louis

La Deshabilleuse
See Simenon, Georges (Jacques Christian)

Lady Gregory
See Gregory, Lady Isabella Augusta (Persse)

Lady of Quality, A
See Bagnold, Enid

**La Fayette, Marie-(Madelaine Pioche de la
Vergne)** 1634-1693 .... **LC 2**
See Lafayette, Marie-Madeleine
See also GFL Beginnings to 1789; RGWL
2, 3

Lafayette, Marie-Madeleine
See La Fayette, Marie-(Madelaine Pioche
de la Vergne)
See also DLB 268

Lafayette, Rene
See Hubbard, L(afayette) Ron(ald)

La Flesche, Francis 1857(?)-1932 ...... **NNAL**
See also CA 144; CANR 83; DLB 175

La Fontaine, Jean de 1621-1695 .... **LC 50**
See also DLB 268; EW 3; GFL Beginnings
to 1789; MAICYA 1, 2; RGWL 2, 3;
SATA 18

Laforet, Carmen 1921-2004 .... **CLC 219**
See also CWW 2; DLB 322; EWL 3

Laforgue, Jules 1860-1887 . **NCLC 5, 53; PC
14; SSC 20**
See also DLB 217; EW 7; GFL 1789 to the
Present; RGWL 2, 3

Lagerkvist, Paer (Fabian)
1891-1974 ..... **CLC 7, 10, 13, 54; TCLC
144**
See Lagerkvist, Par
See also CA 85-88; 49-52; DA3; DAM
DRAM, NOV; MTCW 1, 2; MTFW 2005;
TWA

Lagerkvist, Par .... **SSC 12**
See Lagerkvist, Paer (Fabian)
See also DLB 259; EW 10; EWL 3; RGSF
2; RGWL 2, 3

Lagerloef, Selma (Ottiliana Lovisa)
.... **TCLC 4, 36**
See Lagerlof, Selma (Ottiliana Lovisa)
See also CA 108; MTCW 2

Lagerlof, Selma (Ottiliana Lovisa)
1858-1940
See Lagerloef, Selma (Ottiliana Lovisa)
See also CA 188; CLR 7; DLB 259; RGWL
2, 3; SATA 15; SSFS 18

La Guma, (Justin) Alex(ander)
1925-1985 . **BLCS; CLC 19; TCLC 140**
See also AFW; BW 1, 3; CA 49-52; 118;
CANR 25, 81; CDWLB 3; CN 1, 2, 3;
CP 1; DAM NOV; DLB 117, 225; EWL
3; MTCW 1, 2; MTFW 2005; WLIT 2;
WWE 1

Laidlaw, A. K.
See Grieve, C(hristopher) M(urray)

Lainez, Manuel Mujica
See Mujica Lainez, Manuel
See also HW 1

Laing, R(onald) D(avid) 1927-1989 . **CLC 95**
See also CA 107; 129; CANR 34; MTCW 1

Laishley, Alex
See Booth, Martin

Lamartine, Alphonse (Marie Louis Prat) de
1790-1869 .... **NCLC 11; PC 16**
See also DAM POET; DLB 217; GFL 1789
to the Present; RGWL 2, 3

Lamb, Charles 1775-1834 ..... **NCLC 10, 113;
WLC**
See also BRW 4; CDBLB 1789-1832; DA;
DAB; DAC; DAM MST; DLB 93, 107,
163; RGEL 2; SATA 17; TEA

Lamb, Lady Caroline 1785-1828 ... **NCLC 38**
See also DLB 116

Lamb, Mary Ann 1764-1847 .... **NCLC 125**
See also DLB 163; SATA 17

Lame Deer 1903(?)-1976 .... **NNAL**
See also CA 69-72

Lamming, George (William) 1927- ... **BLC 2;
CLC 2, 4, 66, 144**
See also BW 2, 3; CA 85-88; CANR 26,
76; CDWLB 3; CN 1, 2, 3, 4, 5, 6, 7; CP
1; DAM MULT; DLB 125; EWL 3;
MTCW 1, 2; MTFW 2005; NFS 15;
RGEL 2

L'Amour, Louis (Dearborn)
1908-1988 .... **CLC 25, 55**
See also AAYA 16; AITN 2; BEST 89:2;
BPFB 2; CA 1-4R; 125; CANR 3, 25, 40;
CPW; DA3; DAM NOV, POP; DLB 206;
DLBY 1980; MTCW 1, 2; MTFW 2005;
RGAL 4; TCWW 1, 2

Lampedusa, Giuseppe (Tomasi) di
.... **TCLC 13**
See Tomasi di Lampedusa, Giuseppe
See also CA 164; EW 11; MTCW 2; MTFW
2005; RGWL 2, 3

Lampman, Archibald 1861-1899 ... **NCLC 25**
See also DLB 92; RGEL 2; TWA

Lancaster, Bruce 1896-1963 .... **CLC 36**
See also CA 9-10; CANR 70; CAP 1; SATA
9

Lanchester, John 1962- .... **CLC 99**
See also CA 194; DLB 267

Landau, Mark Alexandrovich
See Aldanov, Mark (Alexandrovich)

Macaulay, (Emilie) Rose
1881(?)-1958 .... **TCLC 7, 44**
See also CA 104; DLB 36; EWL 3; RGEL
2; RHW

Macaulay, Thomas Babington
1800-1859 .... **NCLC 42**
See also BRW 4; CDBLB 1832-1890; DLB
32, 55; RGEL 2

MacBeth, George (Mann)
1932-1992 .... **CLC 2, 5, 9**
See also CA 25-28R; 136; CANR 61, 66;
CP 1, 2, 3, 4; DLB 40; MTCW 1; PFS 8;
SATA 4; SATA-Obit 70

MacCaig, Norman (Alexander)
1910-1996 .... **CLC 36**
See also BRWS 6; CA 9-12R; CANR 3, 34;
CP 1, 2, 3, 4; DAB; DAM POET; DLB
27; EWL 3; RGEL 2

MacCarthy, Sir (Charles Otto) Desmond
1877-1952 .... **TCLC 36**
See also CA 167

MacDiarmid, Hugh .... **CLC 2, 4, 11, 19, 63;
PC 9**
See Grieve, C(hristopher) M(urray)
See also CDBLB 1945-1960; CP 1, 2; DLB
20; EWL 3; RGEL 2

MacDonald, Anson
See Heinlein, Robert A(nson)

Macdonald, Cynthia 1928- .... **CLC 13, 19**
See also CA 49-52; CANR 4, 44, 146; DLB
105

MacDonald, George 1824-1905 .... **TCLC 9,
113**
See also AAYA 57; BYA 5; CA 106; 137;
CANR 80; CLR 67; DLB 18, 163, 178;
FANT; MAICYA 1, 2; RGEL 2; SATA 33,
100; SFW 4; SUFW; WCH

Macdonald, John
See Millar, Kenneth

MacDonald, John D(ann)
1916-1986 .... **CLC 3, 27, 44**
See also BPFB 2; CA 1-4R; 121; CANR 1,
19, 60; CMW 4; CPW; DAM NOV, POP;
DLB 8, 306; DLBY 1986; MSW; MTCW
1, 2; MTFW 2005; SFW 4

Macdonald, John Ross
See Millar, Kenneth

Macdonald, Ross ..... **CLC 1, 2, 3, 14, 34, 41**
See Millar, Kenneth
See also AMWS 4; BPFB 2; CN 1, 2, 3;
DLBD 6; MSW; RGAL 4

MacDougal, John
See Blish, James (Benjamin)

MacDougal, John
See Blish, James (Benjamin)

MacDowell, John
See Parks, Tim(othy Harold)

MacEwen, Gwendolyn (Margaret)
1941-1987 .... **CLC 13, 55**
See also CA 9-12R; 124; CANR 7, 22; CP
1, 2, 3, 4; DLB 53, 251; SATA 50; SATA-
Obit 55

Macha, Karel Hynek 1810-1846 .... **NCLC 46**

Machado (y Ruiz), Antonio
1875-1939 .... **TCLC 3**
See also CA 104; 174; DLB 108; EW 9;
EWL 3; HW 2; PFS 23; RGWL 2, 3

Machado de Assis, Joaquim Maria
1839-1908 .... **BLC 2; HLCS 2; SSC 24;
TCLC 10**
See also CA 107; 153; CANR 91; DLB 307;
LAW; RGSF 2; RGWL 2, 3; TWA; WLIT
1

Machaut, Guillaume de c.
1300-1377 .... **CMLC 64**
See also DLB 208

Machen, Arthur .... **SSC 20; TCLC 4**
See Jones, Arthur Llewellyn
See also CA 179; DLB 156, 178; RGEL 2;
SUFW 1

Machiavelli, Niccolo 1469-1527 ... **DC 16; LC
8, 36; WLCS**
See also AAYA 58; DA; DAB; DAC; DAM
MST; EW 2; LAIT 1; LMFS 1; NFS 9;
RGWL 2, 3; TWA; WLIT 7

MacInnes, Colin 1914-1976 .... **CLC 4, 23**
See also CA 69-72; 65-68; CANR 21; CN
1, 2; DLB 14; MTCW 1, 2; RGEL 2;
RHW

MacInnes, Helen (Clark)
1907-1985 .... **CLC 27, 39**
See also BPFB 2; CA 1-4R; 117; CANR 1,
28, 58; CMW 4; CN 1, 2; CPW; DAM
POP; DLB 87; MSW; MTCW 1, 2;
MTFW 2005; SATA 22; SATA-Obit 44

Mackay, Mary 1855-1924
See Corelli, Marie
See also CA 118; 177; FANT; RHW

Mackay, Shena 1944- .... **CLC 195**
See also CA 104; CANR 88, 139; DLB 231,
319; MTFW 2005

Mackenzie, Compton (Edward Montague)
1883-1972 .... **CLC 18; TCLC 116**
See also CA 21-22; 37-40R; CAP 2; CN 1;
DLB 34, 100; RGEL 2

Mackenzie, Henry 1745-1831 .... **NCLC 41**
See also DLB 39; RGEL 2

Mackey, Nathaniel (Ernest) 1947- .... **PC 49**
See also CA 153; CANR 114; CP 7; DLB
169

MacKinnon, Catharine A. 1946- .... **CLC 181**
See also CA 128; 132; CANR 73, 140; FW;
MTCW 2; MTFW 2005

Mackintosh, Elizabeth 1896(?)-1952
See Tey, Josephine
See also CA 110; CMW 4

MacLaren, James
See Grieve, C(hristopher) M(urray)

MacLaverty, Bernard 1942- .... **CLC 31**
See also CA 116; 118; CANR 43, 88; CN
5, 6, 7; DLB 267; INT CA-118; RGSF 2

MacLean, Alistair (Stuart)
1922(?)-1987 .... **CLC 3, 13, 50, 63**
See also CA 57-60; 121; CANR 28, 61;
CMW 4; CP 2, 3, 4, 5, 6, 7; CPW; DAM
POP; DLB 276; MTCW 1; SATA 23;
SATA-Obit 50; TCWW 2

Maclean, Norman (Fitzroy)
1902-1990 .... **CLC 78; SSC 13**
See also AMWS 14; CA 102; 132; CANR
49; CPW; DAM POP; DLB 206; TCWW
2

MacLeish, Archibald 1892-1982 ... **CLC 3, 8,
14, 68; PC 47**
See also AMW; CA 9-12R; 106; CAD;
CANR 33, 63; CDALBS; CP 1, 2; DAM
POET; DFS 15; DLB 4, 7, 45; DLBY
1982; EWL 3; EXPP; MAL 5; MTCW 1,
2; MTFW 2005; PAB; PFS 5; RGAL 4;
TUS

MacLennan, (John) Hugh
1907-1990 .... **CLC 2, 14, 92**
See also CA 5-8R; 142; CANR 33; CN 1,
2, 3, 4; DAC; DAM MST; DLB 68; EWL
3; MTCW 1, 2; MTFW 2005; RGEL 2;
TWA

MacLeod, Alistair 1936- .. **CLC 56, 165; SSC
90**
See also CA 123; CCA 1; DAC; DAM
MST; DLB 60; MTCW 2; MTFW 2005;
RGSF 2; TCLE 1:2

Macleod, Fiona
See Sharp, William
See also RGEL 2; SUFW

MacNeice, (Frederick) Louis
1907-1963 .... **CLC 1, 4, 10, 53; PC 61**
See also BRW 7; CA 85-88; CANR 61;
DAB; DAM POET; DLB 10, 20; EWL 3;
MTCW 1, 2; MTFW 2005; RGEL 2

MacNeill, Dand
See Fraser, George MacDonald

Macpherson, James 1736-1796 .... **LC 29**
See Ossian
See also BRWS 8; DLB 109; RGEL 2

Macpherson, (Jean) Jay 1931- .... **CLC 14**
See also CA 5-8R; CANR 90; CP 1, 2, 3, 4,
5, 6, 7; CWP; DLB 53

Macrobius fl. 430- .... **CMLC 48**

MacShane, Frank 1927-1999 .... **CLC 39**
See also CA 9-12R; 186; CANR 3, 33; DLB
111

Macumber, Mari
See Sandoz, Mari(e Susette)

Madach, Imre 1823-1864 .... **NCLC 19**

Madden, (Jerry) David 1933- .... **CLC 5, 15**
See also CA 1-4R; CAAS 3; CANR 4, 45;
CN 3, 4, 5, 6, 7; CSW; DLB 6; MTCW 1

Maddern, Al(an)
See Ellison, Harlan (Jay)

Madhubuti, Haki R. 1942- ... **BLC 2; CLC 6,
73; PC 5**
See Lee, Don L.
See also BW 2, 3; CA 73-76; CANR 24,
51, 73, 139; CP 5, 6, 7; CSW; DAM
MULT, POET; DLB 5, 41; DLBD 8; EWL
3; MAL 5; MTCW 2; MTFW 2005;
RGAL 4

Madison, James 1751-1836 .... **NCLC 126**
See also DLB 37

Maepenn, Hugh
See Kuttner, Henry

Maepenn, K. H.
See Kuttner, Henry

Maeterlinck, Maurice 1862-1949 ..... **TCLC 3**
See also CA 104; 136; CANR 80; DAM
DRAM; DLB 192; EW 8; EWL 3; GFL
1789 to the Present; LMFS 2; RGWL 2,
3; SATA 66; TWA

Maginn, William 1794-1842 .... **NCLC 8**
See also DLB 110, 159

Mahapatra, Jayanta 1928- .... **CLC 33**
See also CA 73-76; CAAS 9; CANR 15,
33, 66, 87; CP 4, 5, 6, 7; DAM MULT

Mahfouz, Naguib (Abdel Aziz Al-Sabilgi)
1911(?)- .... **CLC 153; SSC 66**
See Mahfuz, Najib (Abdel Aziz al-Sabilgi)
See also AAYA 49; BEST 89:2; CA 128;
CANR 55, 101; DA3; DAM NOV;
MTCW 1, 2; MTFW 2005; RGWL 2, 3;
SSFS 9

Mahfuz, Najib (Abdel Aziz al-Sabilgi)
.... **CLC 52, 55**
See Mahfouz, Naguib (Abdel Aziz Al-
Sabilgi)
See also AFW; CWW 2; DLBY 1988; EWL
3; RGSF 2; WLIT 6

Mahon, Derek 1941- .... **CLC 27; PC 60**
See also BRWS 6; CA 113; 128; CANR 88;
CP 1, 2, 3, 4, 5, 6, 7; DLB 40; EWL 3

Maiakovskii, Vladimir
See Mayakovski, Vladimir (Vladimirovich)
See also IDTP; RGWL 2, 3

Mailer, Norman (Kingsley) 1923- . **CLC 1, 2,
3, 4, 5, 8, 11, 14, 28, 39, 74, 111**
See also AAYA 31; AITN 2; AMW; AMWC
2; AMWR 2; BPFB 2; CA 9-12R; CABS
1; CANR 28, 74, 77, 130; CDALB 1968-
1988; CN 1, 2, 3, 4, 5, 6, 7; CPW; DA;
DA3; DAB; DAC; DAM MST, NOV,
POP; DLB 2, 16, 28, 185, 278; DLBD 3;
DLBY 1980, 1983; EWL 3; MAL 5;
MTCW 1, 2; MTFW 2005; NFS 10;
RGAL 4; TUS

Margulies, Donald 1954- .... **CLC 76**
See also AAYA 57; CA 200; CD 6; DFS 13;
DLB 228
Marie de France c. 12th cent. - ..... **CMLC 8;**
PC 22
See also DLB 208; FW; RGWL 2, 3
Marie de l'Incarnation 1599-1672 ...... **LC 10**
Marier, Captain Victor
See Griffith, D(avid Lewelyn) W(ark)
Mariner, Scott
See Pohl, Frederik
Marinetti, Filippo Tommaso
1876-1944 .... **TCLC 10**
See also CA 107; DLB 114, 264; EW 9;
EWL 3; WLIT 7
Marivaux, Pierre Carlet de Chamblain de
1688-1763 .... **DC 7; LC 4, 123**
See also DLB 314; GFL Beginnings to
1789; RGWL 2, 3; TWA
Markandaya, Kamala .... **CLC 8, 38**
See Taylor, Kamala (Purnaiya)
See also BYA 13; CN 1, 2, 3, 4, 5, 6, 7;
EWL 3
Markfield, Wallace (Arthur)
1926-2002 .... **CLC 8**
See also CA 69-72; 208; CAAS 3; CN 1, 2,
3, 4, 5, 6, 7; DLB 2, 28; DLBY 2002
Markham, Edwin 1852-1940 .... **TCLC 47**
See also CA 160; DLB 54, 186; MAL 5;
RGAL 4
Markham, Robert
See Amis, Kingsley (William)
Markoosie .... **NNAL**
See Patsauq, Markoosie
See also CLR 23; DAM MULT
Marks, J.
See Highwater, Jamake (Mamake)
Marks, J
See Highwater, Jamake (Mamake)
Marks-Highwater, J
See Highwater, Jamake (Mamake)
Marks-Highwater, J.
See Highwater, Jamake (Mamake)
Markson, David M(errill) 1927- .... **CLC 67**
See also CA 49-52; CANR 1, 91; CN 5, 6
Marlatt, Daphne (Buckle) 1942- .... **CLC 168**
See also CA 25-28R; CANR 17, 39; CN 6,
7; CP 4, 5, 6, 7; CWP; DLB 60; FW
Marley, Bob .... **CLC 17**
See Marley, Robert Nesta
Marley, Robert Nesta 1945-1981
See Marley, Bob
See also CA 107; 103
Marlowe, Christopher 1564-1593 . **DC 1; LC**
22, 47, 117; PC 57; WLC
See also BRW 1; BRWR 1; CDBLB Before
1660; DA; DA3; DAB; DAC; DAM
DRAM, MST; DFS 1, 5, 13, 21; DLB 62;
EXPP; LMFS 1; PFS 22; RGEL 2; TEA;
WLIT 3
Marlowe, Stephen 1928- .... **CLC 70**
See Queen, Ellery
See also CA 13-16R; CANR 6, 55; CMW
4; SFW 4
Marmion, Shakerley 1603-1639 .... **LC 89**
See also DLB 58; RGEL 2
Marmontel, Jean-Francois 1723-1799 .. **LC 2**
See also DLB 314
Maron, Monika 1941- .... **CLC 165**
See also CA 201
Marquand, John P(hillips)
1893-1960 .... **CLC 2, 10**
See also AMW; BPFB 2; CA 85-88; CANR
73; CMW 4; DLB 9, 102; EWL 3; MAL
5; MTCW 2; RGAL 4
Marques, Rene 1919-1979 .. **CLC 96; HLC 2**
See also CA 97-100; 85-88; CANR 78;
DAM MULT; DLB 305; EWL 3; HW 1,
2; LAW; RGSF 2

Marquez, Gabriel (Jose) Garcia
See Garcia Marquez, Gabriel (Jose)
Marquis, Don(ald Robert Perry)
1878-1937 .... **TCLC 7**
See also CA 104; 166; DLB 11, 25; MAL
5; RGAL 4
Marquis de Sade
See Sade, Donatien Alphonse Francois
Marric, J. J.
See Creasey, John
See also MSW
Marryat, Frederick 1792-1848 .... **NCLC 3**
See also DLB 21, 163; RGEL 2; WCH
Marsden, James
See Creasey, John
Marsh, Edward 1872-1953 .... **TCLC 99**
Marsh, (Edith) Ngaio 1895-1982 .. **CLC 7, 53**
See also CA 9-12R; CANR 6, 58; CMW 4;
CN 1, 2, 3; CPW; DAM POP; DLB 77;
MSW; MTCW 1, 2; RGEL 2; TEA
Marshall, Allen
See Westlake, Donald E(dwin)
Marshall, Garry 1934- .... **CLC 17**
See also AAYA 3; CA 111; SATA 60
Marshall, Paule 1929- .. **BLC 3; CLC 27, 72;**
SSC 3
See also AFAW 1, 2; AMWS 11; BPFB 2;
BW 2, 3; CA 77-80; CANR 25, 73, 129;
CN 1, 2, 3, 4, 5, 6, 7; DA3; DAM MULT;
DLB 33, 157, 227; EWL 3; LATS 1:2;
MAL 5; MTCW 1, 2; MTFW 2005;
RGAL 4; SSFS 15
Marshallik
See Zangwill, Israel
Marsten, Richard
See Hunter, Evan
Marston, John 1576-1634 .... **LC 33**
See also BRW 2; DAM DRAM; DLB 58,
172; RGEL 2
Martel, Yann 1963- .... **CLC 192**
See also AAYA 67; CA 146; CANR 114;
MTFW 2005
Martens, Adolphe-Adhemar
See Ghelderode, Michel de
Martha, Henry
See Harris, Mark
Marti, Jose
See Marti (y Perez), Jose (Julian)
See also DLB 290
Marti (y Perez), Jose (Julian)
1853-1895 .... **HLC 2; NCLC 63**
See Marti, Jose
See also DAM MULT; HW 2; LAW; RGWL
2, 3; WLIT 1
Martial c. 40-c. 104 .... **CMLC 35; PC 10**
See also AW 2; CDWLB 1; DLB 211;
RGWL 2, 3
Martin, Ken
See Hubbard, L(afayette) Ron(ald)
Martin, Richard
See Creasey, John
Martin, Steve 1945- .... **CLC 30, 217**
See also AAYA 53; CA 97-100; CANR 30,
100, 140; DFS 19; MTCW 1; MTFW
2005
Martin, Valerie 1948- .... **CLC 89**
See also BEST 90:2; CA 85-88; CANR 49,
89
Martin, Violet Florence 1862-1915 .. **SSC 56;**
TCLC 51
Martin, Webber
See Silverberg, Robert
Martindale, Patrick Victor
See White, Patrick (Victor Martindale)
Martin du Gard, Roger
1881-1958 .... **TCLC 24**
See also CA 118; CANR 94; DLB 65; EWL
3; GFL 1789 to the Present; RGWL 2, 3

Martineau, Harriet 1802-1876 ...... **NCLC 26,**
137
See also DLB 21, 55, 159, 163, 166, 190;
FW; RGEL 2; YABC 2
Martines, Julia
See O'Faolain, Julia
Martinez, Enrique Gonzalez
See Gonzalez Martinez, Enrique
Martinez, Jacinto Benavente y
See Benavente (y Martinez), Jacinto
Martinez de la Rosa, Francisco de Paula
1787-1862 .... **NCLC 102**
See also TWA
Martinez Ruiz, Jose 1873-1967
See Azorin; Ruiz, Jose Martinez
See also CA 93-96; HW 1
Martinez Sierra, Gregorio
1881-1947 .... **TCLC 6**
See also CA 115; EWL 3
Martinez Sierra, Maria (de la O'LeJarraga)
1874-1974 .... **TCLC 6**
See also CA 115; EWL 3
Martinsen, Martin
See Follett, Ken(neth Martin)
Martinson, Harry (Edmund)
1904-1978 .... **CLC 14**
See also CA 77-80; CANR 34, 130; DLB
259; EWL 3
Martyn, Edward 1859-1923 .... **TCLC 131**
See also CA 179; DLB 10; RGEL 2
Marut, Ret
See Traven, B.
Marut, Robert
See Traven, B.
Marvell, Andrew 1621-1678 .... **LC 4, 43; PC**
10; WLC
See also BRW 2; BRWR 2; CDBLB 1660-
1789; DA; DAB; DAC; DAM MST,
POET; DLB 131; EXPP; PFS 5; RGEL 2;
TEA; WP
Marx, Karl (Heinrich)
1818-1883 .... **NCLC 17, 114**
See also DLB 129; LATS 1:1; TWA
Masaoka, Shiki -1902 .... **TCLC 18**
See Masaoka, Tsunenori
See also RGWL 3
Masaoka, Tsunenori 1867-1902
See Masaoka, Shiki
See also CA 117; 191; TWA
Masefield, John (Edward)
1878-1967 .... **CLC 11, 47**
See also CA 19-20; 25-28R; CANR 33;
CAP 2; CDBLB 1890-1914; DAM POET;
DLB 10, 19, 153, 160; EWL 3; EXPP;
FANT; MTCW 1, 2; PFS 5; RGEL 2;
SATA 19
Maso, Carole (?)- .... **CLC 44**
See also CA 170; CN 7; GLL 2; RGAL 4
Mason, Bobbie Ann 1940- ... **CLC 28, 43, 82,**
154; SSC 4
See also AAYA 5, 42; AMWS 8; BPFB 2;
CA 53-56; CANR 11, 31, 58, 83, 125;
CDALBS; CN 5, 6, 7; CSW; DA3; DLB
173; DLBY 1987; EWL 3; EXPS; INT
CANR-31; MAL 5; MTCW 1, 2; MTFW
2005; NFS 4; RGAL 4; RGSF 2; SSFS 3,
8, 20; TCLE 1:2; YAW
Mason, Ernst
See Pohl, Frederik
Mason, Hunni B.
See Sternheim, (William Adolf) Carl
Mason, Lee W.
See Malzberg, Barry N(athaniel)
Mason, Nick 1945- .... **CLC 35**
Mason, Tally
See Derleth, August (William)
Mass, Anna .... **CLC 59**
Mass, William
See Gibson, William

McCreigh, James
See Pohl, Frederik

McCullers, (Lula) Carson (Smith)
1917-1967 .... **CLC 1, 4, 10, 12, 48, 100; SSC 9, 24; TCLC 155; WLC**
See also AAYA 21; AMW; AMWC 2; BPFB 2; CA 5-8R; 25-28R; CABS 1, 3; CANR 18, 132; CDALB 1941-1968; DA; DA3; DAB; DAC; DAM MST, NOV; DFS 5, 18; DLB 2, 7, 173, 228; EWL 3; EXPS; FW; GLL 1; LAIT 3, 4; MAL 5; MAWW; MTCW 1, 2; MTFW 2005; NFS 6, 13; RGAL 4; RGSF 2; SATA 27; SSFS 5; TUS; YAW

McCulloch, John Tyler
See Burroughs, Edgar Rice

McCullough, Colleen 1937- ...... **CLC 27, 107**
See also AAYA 36; BPFB 2; CA 81-84; CANR 17, 46, 67, 98, 139; CPW; DA3; DAM NOV, POP; MTCW 1, 2; MTFW 2005; RHW

McCunn, Ruthanne Lum 1946- .... **AAL**
See also CA 119; CANR 43, 96; DLB 312; LAIT 2; SATA 63

McDermott, Alice 1953- .... **CLC 90**
See also CA 109; CANR 40, 90, 126; CN 7; DLB 292; MTFW 2005

McElroy, Joseph (Prince) 1930- ... **CLC 5, 47**
See also CA 17-20R; CN 3, 4, 5, 6, 7

McEwan, Ian (Russell) 1948- .... **CLC 13, 66, 169**
See also BEST 90:4; BRWS 4; CA 61-64; CANR 14, 41, 69, 87, 132; CN 3, 4, 5, 6, 7; DAM NOV; DLB 14, 194, 319; HGG; MTCW 1, 2; MTFW 2005; RGSF 2; SUFW 2; TEA

McFadden, David 1940- .... **CLC 48**
See also CA 104; CP 1, 2, 3, 4, 5, 6, 7; DLB 60; INT CA-104

McFarland, Dennis 1950- .... **CLC 65**
See also CA 165; CANR 110

McGahern, John 1934- ... **CLC 5, 9, 48, 156; SSC 17**
See also CA 17-20R; CANR 29, 68, 113; CN 1, 2, 3, 4, 5, 6, 7; DLB 14, 231, 319; MTCW 1

McGinley, Patrick (Anthony) 1937- . **CLC 41**
See also CA 120; 127; CANR 56; INT CA-127

McGinley, Phyllis 1905-1978 .... **CLC 14**
See also CA 9-12R; 77-80; CANR 19; CP 1, 2; CWRI 5; DLB 11, 48; MAL 5; PFS 9, 13; SATA 2, 44; SATA-Obit 24

McGinniss, Joe 1942- .... **CLC 32**
See also AITN 2; BEST 89:2; CA 25-28R; CANR 26, 70; CPW; DLB 185; INT CANR-26

McGivern, Maureen Daly
See Daly, Maureen

McGrath, Patrick 1950- .... **CLC 55**
See also CA 136; CANR 65; CN 5, 6, 7; DLB 231; HGG; SUFW 2

McGrath, Thomas (Matthew)
1916-1990 .... **CLC 28, 59**
See also AMWS 10; CA 9-12R; 132; CANR 6, 33, 95; CP 1, 2, 3, 4; DAM POET; MAL 5; MTCW 1; SATA 41; SATA-Obit 66

McGuane, Thomas (Francis III)
1939- .... **CLC 3, 7, 18, 45, 127**
See also AITN 2; BPFB 2; CA 49-52; CANR 5, 24, 49, 94; CN 2, 3, 4, 5, 6, 7; DLB 2, 212; DLBY 1980; EWL 3; INT CANR-24; MAL 5; MTCW 1; MTFW 2005; TCWW 1, 2

McGuckian, Medbh 1950- .... **CLC 48, 174; PC 27**
See also BRWS 5; CA 143; CP 4, 5, 6, 7; CWP; DAM POET; DLB 40

McHale, Tom 1942(?)-1982 .... **CLC 3, 5**
See also AITN 1; CA 77-80; 106; CN 1, 2, 3

McHugh, Heather 1948- .... **PC 61**
See also CA 69-72; CANR 11, 28, 55, 92; CP 4, 5, 6, 7; CWP

McIlvanney, William 1936- .... **CLC 42**
See also CA 25-28R; CANR 61; CMW 4; DLB 14, 207

McIlwraith, Maureen Mollie Hunter
See Hunter, Mollie
See also SATA 2

McInerney, Jay 1955- .... **CLC 34, 112**
See also AAYA 18; BPFB 2; CA 116; 123; CANR 45, 68, 116; CN 5, 6, 7; CPW; DA3; DAM POP; DLB 292; INT CA-123; MAL 5; MTCW 2; MTFW 2005

McIntyre, Vonda N(eel) 1948- .... **CLC 18**
See also CA 81-84; CANR 17, 34, 69; MTCW 1; SFW 4; YAW

McKay, Claude .... **BLC 3; HR 1:3; PC 2; TCLC 7, 41; WLC**
See McKay, Festus Claudius
See also AFAW 1, 2; AMWS 10; DAB; DLB 4, 45, 51, 117; EWL 3; EXPP; GLL 2; LAIT 3; LMFS 2; MAL 5; PAB; PFS 4; RGAL 4; WP

McKay, Festus Claudius 1889-1948
See McKay, Claude
See also BW 1, 3; CA 104; 124; CANR 73; DA; DAC; DAM MST, MULT, NOV, POET; MTCW 1, 2; MTFW 2005; TUS

McKuen, Rod 1933- .... **CLC 1, 3**
See also AITN 1; CA 41-44R; CANR 40; CP 1

McLoughlin, R. B.
See Mencken, H(enry) L(ouis)

McLuhan, (Herbert) Marshall
1911-1980 .... **CLC 37, 83**
See also CA 9-12R; 102; CANR 12, 34, 61; DLB 88; INT CANR-12; MTCW 1, 2; MTFW 2005

McManus, Declan Patrick Aloysius
See Costello, Elvis

McMillan, Terry (L.) 1951- . **BLCS; CLC 50, 61, 112**
See also AAYA 21; AMWS 13; BPFB 2; BW 2, 3; CA 140; CANR 60, 104, 131; CN 7; CPW; DA3; DAM MULT, NOV, POP; MAL 5; MTCW 2; MTFW 2005; RGAL 4; YAW

McMurtry, Larry 1936- .... **CLC 2, 3, 7, 11, 27, 44, 127**
See also AAYA 15; AITN 2; AMWS 5; BEST 89:2; BPFB 2; CA 5-8R; CANR 19, 43, 64, 103; CDALB 1968-1988; CN 2, 3, 4, 5, 6, 7; CPW; CSW; DA3; DAM NOV, POP; DLB 2, 143, 256; DLBY 1980, 1987; EWL 3; MAL 5; MTCW 1, 2; MTFW 2005; RGAL 4; TCWW 1, 2

McNally, T. M. 1961- .... **CLC 82**

McNally, Terrence 1939- ... **CLC 4, 7, 41, 91; DC 27**
See also AAYA 62; AMWS 13; CA 45-48; CAD; CANR 2, 56, 116; CD 5, 6; DA3; DAM DRAM; DFS 16, 19; DLB 7, 249; EWL 3; GLL 1; MTCW 2; MTFW 2005

McNamer, Deirdre 1950- .... **CLC 70**

McNeal, Tom .... **CLC 119**

McNeile, Herman Cyril 1888-1937
See Sapper
See also CA 184; CMW 4; DLB 77

McNickle, (William) D'Arcy
1904-1977 .... **CLC 89; NNAL**
See also CA 9-12R; 85-88; CANR 5, 45; DAM MULT; DLB 175, 212; RGAL 4; SATA-Obit 22; TCWW 1, 2

McPhee, John (Angus) 1931- .... **CLC 36**
See also AAYA 61; AMWS 3; ANW; BEST 90:1; CA 65-68; CANR 20, 46, 64, 69, 121; CPW; DLB 185, 275; MTCW 1, 2; MTFW 2005; TUS

McPherson, James Alan 1943- . **BLCS; CLC 19, 77**
See also BW 1, 3; CA 25-28R; CAAS 17; CANR 24, 74, 140; CN 3, 4, 5, 6; CSW; DLB 38, 244; EWL 3; MTCW 1, 2; MTFW 2005; RGAL 4; RGSF 2

McPherson, William (Alexander)
1933- .... **CLC 34**
See also CA 69-72; CANR 28; INT CANR-28

McTaggart, J. McT. Ellis
See McTaggart, John McTaggart Ellis

McTaggart, John McTaggart Ellis
1866-1925 .... **TCLC 105**
See also CA 120; DLB 262

Mead, George Herbert 1863-1931 . **TCLC 89**
See also CA 212; DLB 270

Mead, Margaret 1901-1978 .... **CLC 37**
See also AITN 1; CA 1-4R; 81-84; CANR 4; DA3; FW; MTCW 1, 2; SATA-Obit 20

Meaker, Marijane (Agnes) 1927-
See Kerr, M. E.
See also CA 107; CANR 37, 63, 145; INT CA-107; JRDA; MAICYA 1, 2; MAICYAS 1; SATA 20, 61, 99, 160; SATA-Essay 111; YAW

Medoff, Mark (Howard) 1940- .... **CLC 6, 23**
See also AITN 1; CA 53-56; CAD; CANR 5; CD 5, 6; DAM DRAM; DFS 4; DLB 7; INT CANR-5

Medvedev, P. N.
See Bakhtin, Mikhail Mikhailovich

Meged, Aharon
See Megged, Aharon

Meged, Aron
See Megged, Aharon

Megged, Aharon 1920- .... **CLC 9**
See also CA 49-52; CAAS 13; CANR 1, 140; EWL 3

Mehta, Deepa 1950- .... **CLC 208**

Mehta, Gita 1943- .... **CLC 179**
See also CA 225; CN 7; DNFS 2

Mehta, Ved (Parkash) 1934- .... **CLC 37**
See also CA 1-4R; 212; CAAE 212; CANR 2, 23, 69; MTCW 1; MTFW 2005

Melanchthon, Philipp 1497-1560 .... **LC 90**
See also DLB 179

Melanter
See Blackmore, R(ichard) D(oddridge)

Meleager c. 140B.C.-c. 70B.C. ...... **CMLC 53**

Melies, Georges 1861-1938 .... **TCLC 81**

Melikow, Loris
See Hofmannsthal, Hugo von

Melmoth, Sebastian
See Wilde, Oscar (Fingal O'Flahertie Wills)

Melo Neto, Joao Cabral de
See Cabral de Melo Neto, Joao
See also CWW 2; EWL 3

Meltzer, Milton 1915- .... **CLC 26**
See also AAYA 8, 45; BYA 2, 6; CA 13-16R; CANR 38, 92, 107; CLR 13; DLB 61; JRDA; MAICYA 1, 2; SAAS 1; SATA 1, 50, 80, 128; SATA-Essay 124; WYA; YAW

Melville, Herman 1819-1891 ..... **NCLC 3, 12, 29, 45, 49, 91, 93, 123, 157; SSC 1, 17, 46; WLC**
See also AAYA 25; AMW; AMWR 1; CDALB 1640-1865; DA; DA3; DAB; DAC; DAM MST, NOV; DLB 3, 74, 250, 254; EXPN; EXPS; GL 3; LAIT 1, 2; NFS 7, 9; RGAL 4; RGSF 2; SATA 59; SSFS 3; TUS

Members, Mark
    See Powell, Anthony (Dymoke)
Membreno, Alejandro .... CLC 59
Menand, Louis 1952- .... CLC 208
    See also CA 200
Menander c. 342B.C.-c. 293B.C. .... CMLC 9,
    51; DC 3
    See also AW 1; CDWLB 1; DAM DRAM;
    DLB 176; LMFS 1; RGWL 2, 3
Menchu, Rigoberta 1959- .. CLC 160; HLCS
    2
    See also CA 175; CANR 135; DNFS 1;
    WLIT 1
Mencken, H(enry) L(ouis)
    1880-1956 .... TCLC 13
    See also AMW; CA 105; 125; CDALB
    1917-1929; DLB 11, 29, 63, 137, 222;
    EWL 3; MAL 5; MTCW 1, 2; MTFW
    2005; NCFS 4; RGAL 4; TUS
Mendelsohn, Jane 1965- .... CLC 99
    See also CA 154; CANR 94
Mendoza, Inigo Lopez de
    See Santillana, Inigo Lopez de Mendoza,
    Marques de
Menton, Francisco de
    See Chin, Frank (Chew, Jr.)
Mercer, David 1928-1980 .... CLC 5
    See also CA 9-12R; 102; CANR 23; CBD;
    DAM DRAM; DLB 13, 310; MTCW 1;
    RGEL 2
Merchant, Paul
    See Ellison, Harlan (Jay)
Meredith, George 1828-1909 .. PC 60; TCLC
    17, 43
    See also CA 117; 153; CANR 80; CDBLB
    1832-1890; DAM POET; DLB 18, 35, 57,
    159; RGEL 2; TEA
Meredith, William (Morris) 1919- .... CLC 4,
    13, 22, 55; PC 28
    See also CA 9-12R; CAAS 14; CANR 6,
    40, 129; CP 1, 2, 3, 4, 5, 6, 7; DAM
    POET; DLB 5; MAL 5
Merezhkovsky, Dmitrii Sergeevich
    See Merezhkovsky, Dmitry Sergeyevich
    See also DLB 295
Merezhkovsky, Dmitry Sergeevich
    See Merezhkovsky, Dmitry Sergeyevich
    See also EWL 3
Merezhkovsky, Dmitry Sergeyevich
    1865-1941 .... TCLC 29
    See Merezhkovsky, Dmitrii Sergeevich;
    Merezhkovsky, Dmitry Sergeevich
    See also CA 169
Merimee, Prosper 1803-1870 ... NCLC 6, 65;
    SSC 7, 77
    See also DLB 119, 192; EW 6; EXPS; GFL
    1789 to the Present; RGSF 2; RGWL 2,
    3; SSFS 8; SUFW
Merkin, Daphne 1954- .... CLC 44
    See also CA 123
Merleau-Ponty, Maurice
    1908-1961 .... TCLC 156
    See also CA 114; 89-92; DLB 296; GFL
    1789 to the Present
Merlin, Arthur
    See Blish, James (Benjamin)
Mernissi, Fatima 1940- .... CLC 171
    See also CA 152; FW
Merrill, James (Ingram) 1926-1995 .. CLC 2,
    3, 6, 8, 13, 18, 34, 91; PC 28; TCLC
    173
    See also AMWS 3; CA 13-16R; 147; CANR
    10, 49, 63, 108; CP 1, 2, 3, 4; DA3; DAM
    POET; DLB 5, 165; DLBY 1985; EWL 3;
    INT CANR-10; MAL 5; MTCW 1, 2;
    MTFW 2005; PAB; PFS 23; RGAL 4
Merriman, Alex
    See Silverberg, Robert
Merriman, Brian 1747-1805 .... NCLC 70

Merritt, E. B.
    See Waddington, Miriam
Merton, Thomas (James)
    1915-1968 . CLC 1, 3, 11, 34, 83; PC 10
    See also AAYA 61; AMWS 8; CA 5-8R;
    25-28R; CANR 22, 53, 111, 131; DA3;
    DLB 48; DLBY 1981; MAL 5; MTCW 1,
    2; MTFW 2005
Merwin, W(illiam) S(tanley) 1927- ... CLC 1,
    2, 3, 5, 8, 13, 18, 45, 88; PC 45
    See also AMWS 3; CA 13-16R; CANR 15,
    51, 112, 140; CP 1, 2, 3, 4, 5, 6, 7; DA3;
    DAM POET; DLB 5, 169; EWL 3; INT
    CANR-15; MAL 5; MTCW 1, 2; MTFW
    2005; PAB; PFS 5, 15; RGAL 4
Metastasio, Pietro 1698-1782 .... LC 115
    See also RGWL 2, 3
Metcalf, John 1938- .... CLC 37; SSC 43
    See also CA 113; CN 4, 5, 6, 7; DLB 60;
    RGSF 2; TWA
Metcalf, Suzanne
    See Baum, L(yman) Frank
Mew, Charlotte (Mary) 1870-1928 .. TCLC 8
    See also CA 105; 189; DLB 19, 135; RGEL
    2
Mewshaw, Michael 1943- .... CLC 9
    See also CA 53-56; CANR 7, 47; DLBY
    1980
Meyer, Conrad Ferdinand
    1825-1898 .... NCLC 81; SSC 30
    See also DLB 129; EW; RGWL 2, 3
Meyer, Gustav 1868-1932
    See Meyrink, Gustav
    See also CA 117; 190
Meyer, June
    See Jordan, June (Meyer)
Meyer, Lynn
    See Slavitt, David R(ytman)
Meyers, Jeffrey 1939- .... CLC 39
    See also CA 73-76, 186; CAAE 186; CANR
    54, 102; DLB 111
Meynell, Alice (Christina Gertrude
    Thompson) 1847-1922 .... TCLC 6
    See also CA 104; 177; DLB 19, 98; RGEL
    2
Meyrink, Gustav .... TCLC 21
    See Meyer, Gustav
    See also DLB 81; EWL 3
Michaels, Leonard 1933-2003 ..... CLC 6, 25;
    SSC 16
    See also CA 61-64; 216; CANR 21, 62, 119;
    CN 3, 45, 6, 7; DLB 130; MTCW 1;
    TCLE 1:2
Michaux, Henri 1899-1984 .... CLC 8, 19
    See also CA 85-88; 114; DLB 258; EWL 3;
    GFL 1789 to the Present; RGWL 2, 3
Micheaux, Oscar (Devereaux)
    1884-1951 .... TCLC 76
    See also BW 3; CA 174; DLB 50; TCWW
    2
Michelangelo 1475-1564 .... LC 12
    See also AAYA 43
Michelet, Jules 1798-1874 .... NCLC 31
    See also EW 5; GFL 1789 to the Present
Michels, Robert 1876-1936 .... TCLC 88
    See also CA 212
Michener, James A(lbert)
    1907(?)-1997 .. CLC 1, 5, 11, 29, 60, 109
    See also AAYA 27; AITN 1; BEST 90:1;
    BPFB 2; CA 5-8R; 161; CANR 21, 45,
    68; CN 1, 2, 3, 4, 5, 6; CPW; DA3; DAM
    NOV, POP; DLB 6; MAL 5; MTCW 1, 2;
    MTFW 2005; RHW; TCWW 1, 2
Mickiewicz, Adam 1798-1855 . NCLC 3, 101;
    PC 38
    See also EW 5; RGWL 2, 3

Middleton, (John) Christopher
    1926- .... CLC 13
    See also CA 13-16R; CANR 29, 54, 117;
    CP 1, 2, 3, 4, 5, 6, 7; DLB 40
Middleton, Richard (Barham)
    1882-1911 .... TCLC 56
    See also CA 187; DLB 156; HGG
Middleton, Stanley 1919- .... CLC 7, 38
    See also CA 25-28R; CAAS 23; CANR 21,
    46, 81; CN 1, 2, 3, 4, 5, 6, 7; DLB 14
Middleton, Thomas 1580-1627 ...... DC 5; LC
    33, 123
    See also BRW 2; DAM DRAM, MST; DFS
    18, 22; DLB 58; RGEL 2
Migueis, Jose Rodrigues 1901-1980 . CLC 10
    See also DLB 287
Mikszath, Kalman 1847-1910 .... TCLC 31
    See also CA 170
Miles, Jack .... CLC 100
    See also CA 200
Miles, John Russiano
    See Miles, Jack
Miles, Josephine (Louise)
    1911-1985 .... CLC 1, 2, 14, 34, 39
    See also CA 1-4R; 116; CANR 2, 55; CP 1,
    2, 3, 4; DAM POET; DLB 48; MAL 5;
    TCLE 1:2
Militant
    See Sandburg, Carl (August)
Mill, Harriet (Hardy) Taylor
    1807-1858 .... NCLC 102
    See also FW
Mill, John Stuart 1806-1873 .... NCLC 11, 58
    See also CDBLB 1832-1890; DLB 55, 190,
    262; FW 1; RGEL 2; TEA
Millar, Kenneth 1915-1983 .... CLC 14
    See Macdonald, Ross
    See also CA 9-12R; 110; CANR 16, 63,
    107; CMW 4; CPW; DA3; DAM POP;
    DLB 2, 226; DLBD 6; DLBY 1983;
    MTCW 1, 2; MTFW 2005
Millay, E. Vincent
    See Millay, Edna St. Vincent
Millay, Edna St. Vincent 1892-1950 ..... PC 6,
    61; TCLC 4, 49, 169; WLCS
    See Boyd, Nancy
    See also AMW; CA 104; 130; CDALB
    1917-1929; DA; DA3; DAB; DAC; DAM
    MST, POET; DLB 45, 249; EWL 3;
    EXPP; FL 1:6; MAL 5; MAWW; MTCW
    1, 2; MTFW 2005; PAB; PFS 3, 17;
    RGAL 4; TUS; WP
Miller, Arthur 1915-2005 ..... CLC 1, 2, 6, 10,
    15, 26, 47, 78, 179; DC 1; WLC
    See also AAYA 15; AITN 1; AMW; AMWC
    1; CA 1-4R; 236; CABS 3; CAD; CANR
    2, 30, 54, 76, 132; CD 5, 6; CDALB
    1941-1968; DA; DA3; DAB; DAC; DAM
    DRAM, MST; DFS 1, 3, 8; DLB 7, 266;
    EWL 3; LAIT 1, 4; LATS 1:2; MAL 5;
    MTCW 1, 2; MTFW 2005; RGAL 4;
    TUS; WYAS 1
Miller, Henry (Valentine)
    1891-1980 .... CLC 1, 2, 4, 9, 14, 43, 84;
    WLC
    See also AMW; BPFB 2; CA 9-12R; 97-
    100; CANR 33, 64; CDALB 1929-1941;
    CN 1, 2; DA; DA3; DAB; DAC; DAM
    MST, NOV; DLB 4, 9; DLBY 1980; EWL
    3; MAL 5; MTCW 1, 2; MTFW 2005;
    RGAL 4; TUS
Miller, Hugh 1802-1856 .... NCLC 143
    See also DLB 190
Miller, Jason 1939(?)-2001 .... CLC 2
    See also AITN 1; CA 73-76; 197; CAD;
    CANR 130; DFS 12; DLB 7
Miller, Sue 1943- .... CLC 44
    See also AMWS 12; BEST 90:3; CA 139;
    CANR 59, 91, 128; DA3; DAM POP;
    DLB 143

Miller, Walter M(ichael, Jr.)
1923-1996 .... **CLC 4, 30**
See also BPFB 2; CA 85-88; CANR 108;
DLB 8; SCFW 1, 2; SFW 4

Millett, Kate 1934- .... **CLC 67**
See also AITN 1; CA 73-76; CANR 32, 53,
76, 110; DA3; DLB 246; FW; GLL 1;
MTCW 1, 2; MTFW 2005

Millhauser, Steven (Lewis) 1943- .... **CLC 21, 54, 109; SSC 57**
See also CA 110; 111; CANR 63, 114, 133;
CN 6, 7; DA3; DLB 2; FANT; INT CA-
111; MAL 5; MTCW 2; MTFW 2005

Millin, Sarah Gertrude 1889-1968 ... **CLC 49**
See also CA 102; 93-96; DLB 225; EWL 3

Milne, A(lan) A(lexander)
1882-1956 .... **TCLC 6, 88**
See also BRWS 5; CA 104; 133; CLR 1,
26; CMW 4; CWRI 5; DA3; DAB; DAC;
DAM MST; DLB 10, 77, 100, 160; FANT;
MAICYA 1, 2; MTCW 1, 2; MTFW 2005;
RGEL 2; SATA 100; WCH; YABC 1

Milner, Ron(ald) 1938-2004 ..... **BLC 3; CLC 56**
See also AITN 1; BW 1; CA 73-76; 230;
CAD; CANR 24, 81; CD 5, 6; DAM
MULT; DLB 38; MAL 5; MTCW 1

Milnes, Richard Monckton
1809-1885 .... **NCLC 61**
See also DLB 32, 184

Milosz, Czeslaw 1911-2004 .... **CLC 5, 11, 22, 31, 56, 82; PC 8; WLCS**
See also AAYA 62; CA 81-84; 230; CANR
23, 51, 91, 126; CDWLB 4; CWW 2;
DA3; DAM MST, POET; DLB 215; EW
13; EWL 3; MTCW 1, 2; MTFW 2005;
PFS 16; RGWL 2, 3

Milton, John 1608-1674 ..... **LC 9, 43, 92; PC 19, 29; WLC**
See also AAYA 65; BRW 2; BRWR 2; CD-
BLB 1660-1789; DA; DA3; DAB; DAC;
DAM MST, POET; DLB 131, 151, 281;
EFS 1; EXPP; LAIT 1; PAB; PFS 3, 17;
RGEL 2; TEA; WLIT 3; WP

Min, Anchee 1957- .... **CLC 86**
See also CA 146; CANR 94, 137; MTFW
2005

Minehaha, Cornelius
See Wedekind, (Benjamin) Frank(lin)

Miner, Valerie 1947- .... **CLC 40**
See also CA 97-100; CANR 59; FW; GLL
2

Minimo, Duca
See D'Annunzio, Gabriele

Minot, Susan (Anderson) 1956- ...... **CLC 44, 159**
See also AMWS 6; CA 134; CANR 118;
CN 6, 7

Minus, Ed 1938- .... **CLC 39**
See also CA 185

Mirabai 1498(?)-1550(?) .... **PC 48**

Miranda, Javier
See Bioy Casares, Adolfo
See also CWW 2

Mirbeau, Octave 1848-1917 .... **TCLC 55**
See also CA 216; DLB 123, 192; GFL 1789
to the Present

Mirikitani, Janice 1942- .... **AAL**
See also CA 211; DLB 312; RGAL 4

Mirk, John (?)-c. 1414 .... **LC 105**
See also DLB 146

Miro (Ferrer), Gabriel (Francisco Victor)
1879-1930 .... **TCLC 5**
See also CA 104; 185; DLB 322; EWL 3

Misharin, Alexandr .... **CLC 59**

Mishima, Yukio ... **CLC 2, 4, 6, 9, 27; DC 1; SSC 4; TCLC 161**
See Hiraoka, Kimitake
See also AAYA 50; BPFB 2; GLL 1; MJW;
RGSF 2; RGWL 2, 3; SSFS 5, 12

Mistral, Frederic 1830-1914 .... **TCLC 51**
See also CA 122; 213; GFL 1789 to the
Present

Mistral, Gabriela
See Godoy Alcayaga, Lucila
See also DLB 283; DNFS 1; EWL 3; LAW;
RGWL 2, 3; WP

Mistry, Rohinton 1952- ... **CLC 71, 196; SSC 73**
See also BRWS 10; CA 141; CANR 86,
114; CCA 1; CN 6, 7; DAC; SSFS 6

Mitchell, Clyde
See Ellison, Harlan (Jay)

Mitchell, Emerson Blackhorse Barney
1945- .... **NNAL**
See also CA 45-48

Mitchell, James Leslie 1901-1935
See Gibbon, Lewis Grassic
See also CA 104; 188; DLB 15

Mitchell, Joni 1943- .... **CLC 12**
See also CA 112; CCA 1

Mitchell, Joseph (Quincy)
1908-1996 .... **CLC 98**
See also CA 77-80; 152; CANR 69; CN 1,
2, 3, 4, 5, 6; CSW; DLB 185; DLBY 1996

Mitchell, Margaret (Munnerlyn)
1900-1949 .... **TCLC 11, 170**
See also AAYA 23; BPFB 2; BYA 1; CA
109; 125; CANR 55, 94; CDALBS; DA3;
DAM NOV, POP; DLB 9; LAIT 2; MAL
5; MTCW 1, 2; MTFW 2005; NFS 9;
RGAL 4; RHW; TUS; WYAS 1; YAW

Mitchell, Peggy
See Mitchell, Margaret (Munnerlyn)

Mitchell, S(ilas) Weir 1829-1914 .... **TCLC 36**
See also CA 165; DLB 202; RGAL 4

Mitchell, W(illiam) O(rmond)
1914-1998 .... **CLC 25**
See also CA 77-80; 165; CANR 15, 43; CN
1, 2, 3, 4, 5, 6; DAC; DAM MST; DLB
88; TCLE 1:2

Mitchell, William (Lendrum)
1879-1936 .... **TCLC 81**
See also CA 213

Mitford, Mary Russell 1787-1855 ... **NCLC 4**
See also DLB 110, 116; RGEL 2

Mitford, Nancy 1904-1973 .... **CLC 44**
See also BRWS 10; CA 9-12R; CN 1; DLB
191; RGEL 2

Miyamoto, (Chujo) Yuriko
1899-1951 .... **TCLC 37**
See Miyamoto Yuriko
See also CA 170, 174

Miyamoto Yuriko
See Miyamoto, (Chujo) Yuriko
See also DLB 180

Miyazawa, Kenji 1896-1933 .... **TCLC 76**
See Miyazawa Kenji
See also CA 157; RGWL 3

Miyazawa Kenji
See Miyazawa, Kenji
See also EWL 3

Mizoguchi, Kenji 1898-1956 .... **TCLC 72**
See also CA 167

Mo, Timothy (Peter) 1950- .... **CLC 46, 134**
See also CA 117; CANR 128; CN 5, 6, 7;
DLB 194; MTCW 1; WLIT 4; WWE 1

Modarressi, Taghi (M.) 1931-1997 ... **CLC 44**
See also CA 121; 134; INT CA-134

Modiano, Patrick (Jean) 1945- .... **CLC 18, 218**
See also CA 85-88; CANR 17, 40, 115;
CWW 2; DLB 83, 299; EWL 3

Mofolo, Thomas (Mokopu)
1875(?)-1948 .... **BLC 3; TCLC 22**
See also AFW; CA 121; 153; CANR 83;
DAM MULT; DLB 225; EWL 3; MTCW
2; MTFW 2005; WLIT 2

Mohr, Nicholasa 1938- .... **CLC 12; HLC 2**
See also AAYA 8, 46; CA 49-52; CANR 1,
32, 64; CLR 22; DAM MULT; DLB 145;
HW 1, 2; JRDA; LAIT 5; LLW; MAICYA
2; MAICYAS 1; RGAL 4; SAAS 8; SATA
8, 97; SATA-Essay 113; WYA; YAW

Moi, Toril 1953- .... **CLC 172**
See also CA 154; CANR 102; FW

Mojtabai, A(nn) G(race) 1938- ..... **CLC 5, 9, 15, 29**
See also CA 85-88; CANR 88

Moliere 1622-1673 ..... **DC 13; LC 10, 28, 64, 125; WLC**
See also DA; DA3; DAB; DAC; DAM
DRAM, MST; DFS 13, 18, 20; DLB 268;
EW 3; GFL Beginnings to 1789; LATS
1:1; RGWL 2, 3; TWA

Molin, Charles
See Mayne, William (James Carter)

Molnar, Ferenc 1878-1952 .... **TCLC 20**
See also CA 109; 153; CANR 83; CDWLB
4; DAM DRAM; DLB 215; EWL 3;
RGWL 2, 3

Momaday, N(avarre) Scott 1934- ...... **CLC 2, 19, 85, 95, 160; NNAL; PC 25; WLCS**
See also AAYA 11, 64; AMWS 4; ANW;
BPFB 2; BYA 12; CA 25-28R; CANR 14,
34, 68, 134; CDALBS; CN 2, 3, 4, 5, 6,
7; CPW; DA; DA3; DAB; DAC; DAM
MST, MULT, NOV, POP; DLB 143, 175,
256; EWL 3; EXPP; INT CANR-14;
LAIT 4; LATS 1:2; MAL 5; MTCW 1, 2;
MTFW 2005; NFS 10; PFS 2, 11; RGAL
4; SATA 48; SATA-Brief 30; TCWW 1,
2; WP; YAW

Monette, Paul 1945-1995 .... **CLC 82**
See also AMWS 10; CA 139; 147; CN 6;
GLL 1

Monroe, Harriet 1860-1936 .... **TCLC 12**
See also CA 109; 204; DLB 54, 91

Monroe, Lyle
See Heinlein, Robert A(nson)

Montagu, Elizabeth 1720-1800 .... **NCLC 7, 117**
See also FW

Montagu, Mary (Pierrepont) Wortley
1689-1762 .... **LC 9, 57; PC 16**
See also DLB 95, 101; FL 1:1; RGEL 2

Montagu, W. H.
See Coleridge, Samuel Taylor

Montague, John (Patrick) 1929- ..... **CLC 13, 46**
See also CA 9-12R; CANR 9, 69, 121; CP
1, 2, 3, 4, 5, 6, 7; DLB 40; EWL 3;
MTCW 1; PFS 12; RGEL 2; TCLE 1:2

Montaigne, Michel (Eyquem) de
1533-1592 .... **LC 8, 105; WLC**
See also DA; DAB; DAC; DAM MST; EW
2; GFL Beginnings to 1789; LMFS 1;
RGWL 2, 3; TWA

Montale, Eugenio 1896-1981 ... **CLC 7, 9, 18; PC 13**
See also CA 17-20R; 104; CANR 30; DLB
114; EW 11; EWL 3; MTCW 1; PFS 22;
RGWL 2, 3; TWA; WLIT 7

Montesquieu, Charles-Louis de Secondat
1689-1755 .... **LC 7, 69**
See also DLB 314; EW 3; GFL Beginnings
to 1789; TWA

Montessori, Maria 1870-1952 ...... **TCLC 103**
See also CA 115; 147

Montgomery, (Robert) Bruce 1921(?)-1978
See Crispin, Edmund
See also CA 179; 104; CMW 4

Mortimer, Penelope (Ruth)
1918-1999 .... **CLC 5**
See also CA 57-60; 187; CANR 45, 88; CN
1, 2, 3, 4, 5, 6

Mortimer, Sir John
See Mortimer, John (Clifford)

Morton, Anthony
See Creasey, John

Morton, Thomas 1579(?)-1647(?) .... **LC 72**
See also DLB 24; RGEL 2

Mosca, Gaetano 1858-1941 .... **TCLC 75**

Moses, Daniel David 1952- .... **NNAL**
See also CA 186

Mosher, Howard Frank 1943- .... **CLC 62**
See also CA 139; CANR 65, 115

Mosley, Nicholas 1923- .... **CLC 43, 70**
See also CA 69-72; CANR 41, 60, 108; CN
1, 2, 3, 4, 5, 6, 7; DLB 14, 207

Mosley, Walter 1952- .... **BLCS; CLC 97, 184**
See also AAYA 57; AMWS 13; BPFB 2;
BW 2; CA 142; CANR 57, 92, 136; CMW
4; CN 7; CPW; DA3; DAM MULT, POP;
DLB 306; MSW; MTCW 2; MTFW 2005

Moss, Howard 1922-1987 . **CLC 7, 14, 45, 50**
See also CA 1-4R; 123; CANR 1, 44; CP 1,
2, 3, 4; DAM POET; DLB 5

Mossgiel, Rab
See Burns, Robert

Motion, Andrew (Peter) 1952- .... **CLC 47**
See also BRWS 7; CA 146; CANR 90, 142;
CP 4, 5, 6, 7; DLB 40; MTFW 2005

Motley, Willard (Francis)
1909-1965 .... **CLC 18**
See also BW 1; CA 117; 106; CANR 88;
DLB 76, 143

Motoori, Norinaga 1730-1801 .... **NCLC 45**

Mott, Michael (Charles Alston)
1930- .... **CLC 15, 34**
See also CA 5-8R; CAAS 7; CANR 7, 29

Mountain Wolf Woman 1884-1960 . **CLC 92;
NNAL**
See also CA 144; CANR 90

Moure, Erin 1955- .... **CLC 88**
See also CA 113; CP 7; CWP; DLB 60

Mourning Dove 1885(?)-1936 .... **NNAL**
See also CA 144; CANR 90; DAM MULT;
DLB 175, 221

Mowat, Farley (McGill) 1921- .... **CLC 26**
See also AAYA 1, 50; BYA 2; CA 1-4R;
CANR 4, 24, 42, 68, 108; CLR 20; CPW;
DAC; DAM MST; DLB 68; INT CANR-
24; JRDA; MAICYA 1, 2; MTCW 1, 2;
MTFW 2005; SATA 3, 55; YAW

Mowatt, Anna Cora 1819-1870 ..... **NCLC 74**
See also RGAL 4

Moyers, Bill 1934- .... **CLC 74**
See also AITN 2; CA 61-64; CANR 31, 52

Mphahlele, Es'kia
See Mphahlele, Ezekiel
See also AFW; CDWLB 3; CN 4, 5, 6; DLB
125, 225; RGSF 2; SSFS 11

Mphahlele, Ezekiel 1919- ... **BLC 3; CLC 25,
133**
See also Mphahlele, Es'kia
See also BW 2, 3; CA 81-84; CANR 26,
76; CN 1, 2, 3; DA3; DAM MULT; EWL
3; MTCW 2; MTFW 2005; SATA 119

Mqhayi, S(amuel) E(dward) K(rune Loliwe)
1875-1945 .... **BLC 3; TCLC 25**
See also CA 153; CANR 87; DAM MULT

Mrozek, Slawomir 1930- .... **CLC 3, 13**
See also CA 13-16R; CAAS 10; CANR 29;
CDWLB 4; CWW 2; DLB 232; EWL 3;
MTCW 1

Mrs. Belloc-Lowndes
See Lowndes, Marie Adelaide (Belloc)

Mrs. Fairstar
See Horne, Richard Henry Hengist

M'Taggart, John M'Taggart Ellis
See McTaggart, John McTaggart Ellis

Mtwa, Percy (?)- .... **CLC 47**
See also CD 6

Mueller, Lisel 1924- .... **CLC 13, 51; PC 33**
See also CA 93-96; CP 7; DLB 105; PFS 9,
13

Muggeridge, Malcolm (Thomas)
1903-1990 .... **TCLC 120**
See also AITN 1; CA 101; CANR 33, 63;
MTCW 1, 2

Muhammad 570-632 .... **WLCS**
See also DA; DAB; DAC; DAM MST;
DLB 311

Muir, Edwin 1887-1959 . **PC 49; TCLC 2, 87**
See Moore, Edward
See also BRWS 6; CA 104; 193; DLB 20,
100, 191; EWL 3; RGEL 2

Muir, John 1838-1914 .... **TCLC 28**
See also AMWS 9; ANW; CA 165; DLB
186, 275

Mujica Lainez, Manuel 1910-1984 ... **CLC 31**
See Lainez, Manuel Mujica
See also CA 81-84; 112; CANR 32; EWL
3; HW 1

Mukherjee, Bharati 1940- ..... **AAL; CLC 53,
115; SSC 38**
See also AAYA 46; BEST 89:2; CA 107,
232; CAAE 232; CANR 45, 72, 128; CN
5, 6, 7; DAM NOV; DLB 60, 218; DNFS
1, 2; EWL 3; FW; MAL 5; MTCW 1, 2;
MTFW 2005; RGAL 4; RGSF 2; SSFS 7;
TUS; WWE 1

Muldoon, Paul 1951- .... **CLC 32, 72, 166**
See also BRWS 4; CA 113; 129; CANR 52,
91; CP 2, 3, 4, 5, 6, 7; DAM POET; DLB
40; INT CA-129; PFS 7, 22; TCLE 1:2

Mulisch, Harry (Kurt Victor)
1927- .... **CLC 42**
See also CA 9-12R; CANR 6, 26, 56, 110;
CWW 2; DLB 299; EWL 3

Mull, Martin 1943- .... **CLC 17**
See also CA 105

Muller, Wilhelm .... **NCLC 73**

Mulock, Dinah Maria
See Craik, Dinah Maria (Mulock)
See also RGEL 2

Multatuli 1820-1887 .... **NCLC 165**
See also RGWL 2, 3

Munday, Anthony 1560-1633 .... **LC 87**
See also DLB 62, 172; RGEL 2

Munford, Robert 1737(?)-1783 .... **LC 5**
See also DLB 31

Mungo, Raymond 1946- .... **CLC 72**
See also CA 49-52; CANR 2

Munro, Alice (Anne) 1931- .... **CLC 6, 10, 19,
50, 95, 222; SSC 3; WLCS**
See also AITN 2; BPFB 2; CA 33-36R;
CANR 33, 53, 75, 114; CCA 1; CN 1, 2,
3, 4, 5, 6, 7; DA3; DAC; DAM MST,
NOV; DLB 53; EWL 3; MTCW 1, 2;
MTFW 2005; RGEL 2; RGSF 2; SATA
29; SSFS 5, 13, 19; TCLE 1:2; WWE 1

Munro, H(ector) H(ugh) 1870-1916 .... **WLC**
See Saki
See also AAYA 56; CA 104; 130; CANR
104; CDBLB 1890-1914; DA; DA3;
DAB; DAC; DAM MST, NOV; DLB 34,
162; EXPS; MTCW 1, 2; MTFW 2005;
RGEL 2; SSFS 15

Murakami, Haruki 1949- .... **CLC 150**
See Murakami Haruki
See also CA 165; CANR 102, 146; MJW;
RGWL 3; SFW 4

Murakami Haruki
See Murakami, Haruki
See also CWW 2; DLB 182; EWL 3

Murasaki, Lady
See Murasaki Shikibu

Murasaki Shikibu 978(?)-1026(?) .. **CMLC 1,
79**
See also EFS 2; LATS 1:1; RGWL 2, 3

Murdoch, (Jean) Iris 1919-1999 ... **CLC 1, 2,
3, 4, 6, 8, 11, 15, 22, 31, 51; TCLC 171**
See also BRWS 1; CA 13-16R; 179; CANR
8, 43, 68, 103, 142; CBD; CDBLB 1960
to Present; CN 1, 2, 3, 4, 5, 6; CWD;
DA3; DAB; DAC; DAM MST, NOV;
DLB 14, 194, 233; EWL 3; INT CANR-8;
MTCW 1, 2; MTFW 2005; NFS 18;
RGEL 2; TCLE 1:2; TEA; WLIT 4

Murfree, Mary Noailles 1850-1922 .. **SSC 22;
TCLC 135**
See also CA 122; 176; DLB 12, 74; RGAL
4

Murnau, Friedrich Wilhelm
See Plumpe, Friedrich Wilhelm

Murphy, Richard 1927- .... **CLC 41**
See also BRWS 5; CA 29-32R; CP 1, 2, 3,
4, 5, 6, 7; DLB 40; EWL 3

Murphy, Sylvia 1937- .... **CLC 34**
See also CA 121

Murphy, Thomas (Bernard) 1935- ... **CLC 51**
See Murphy, Tom
See also CA 101

Murphy, Tom
See Murphy, Thomas (Bernard)
See also DLB 310

Murray, Albert L. 1916- .... **CLC 73**
See also BW 2; CA 49-52; CANR 26, 52,
78; CN 7; CSW; DLB 38; MTFW 2005

Murray, James Augustus Henry
1837-1915 .... **TCLC 117**

Murray, Judith Sargent
1751-1820 .... **NCLC 63**
See also DLB 37, 200

Murray, Les(lie Allan) 1938- .... **CLC 40**
See also BRWS 7; CA 21-24R; CANR 11,
27, 56, 103; CP 1, 2, 3, 4, 5, 6, 7; DAM
POET; DLB 289; DLBY 2001; EWL 3;
RGEL 2

Murry, J. Middleton
See Murry, John Middleton

Murry, John Middleton
1889-1957 .... **TCLC 16**
See also CA 118; 217; DLB 149

Musgrave, Susan 1951- .... **CLC 13, 54**
See also CA 69-72; CANR 45, 84; CCA 1;
CP 2, 3, 4, 5, 6, 7; CWP

Musil, Robert (Edler von)
1880-1942 .... **SSC 18; TCLC 12, 68**
See also CA 109; CANR 55, 84; CDWLB
2; DLB 81, 124; EW 9; EWL 3; MTCW
2; RGSF 2; RGWL 2, 3

Muske, Carol .... **CLC 90**
See Muske-Dukes, Carol (Anne)

Muske-Dukes, Carol (Anne) 1945-
See Muske, Carol
See also CA 65-68, 203; CAAE 203; CANR
32, 70; CWP

Musset, (Louis Charles) Alfred de
1810-1857 .... **DC 27; NCLC 7, 150**
See also DLB 192, 217; EW 6; GFL 1789
to the Present; RGWL 2, 3; TWA

Mussolini, Benito (Amilcare Andrea)
1883-1945 .... **TCLC 96**
See also CA 116

Mutanabbi, Al-
See al-Mutanabbi, Ahmad ibn al-Husayn
Abu al-Tayyib al-Jufi al-Kindi
See also WLIT 6

My Brother's Brother
See Chekhov, Anton (Pavlovich)

Myers, L(eopold) H(amilton)
1881-1944 .... **TCLC 59**
See also CA 157; DLB 15; EWL 3; RGEL
2

Ni Chuilleanain, Eilean 1942- .... **PC 34**
    See also CA 126; CANR 53, 83; CP 7;
    CWP; DLB 40
Nicolas, F. R. E.
    See Freeling, Nicolas
Niedecker, Lorine 1903-1970 ..... **CLC 10, 42;**
        PC 42
    See also CA 25-28; CAP 2; DAM POET;
    DLB 48
Nietzsche, Friedrich (Wilhelm)
        1844-1900 .... **TCLC 10, 18, 55**
    See also CA 107; 121; CDWLB 2; DLB
    129; EW 7; RGWL 2, 3; TWA
Nievo, Ippolito 1831-1861 .... **NCLC 22**
Nightingale, Anne Redmon 1943-
    See Redmon, Anne
    See also CA 103
Nightingale, Florence 1820-1910 ... **TCLC 85**
    See also CA 188; DLB 166
Nijo Yoshimoto 1320-1388 .... **CMLC 49**
    See also DLB 203
Nik. T. O.
    See Annensky, Innokenty (Fyodorovich)
Nin, Anais 1903-1977 ..... **CLC 1, 4, 8, 11, 14,**
        60, 127; SSC 10
    See also AITN 2; AMWS 10; BPFB 2; CA
    13-16R; 69-72; CANR 22, 53; CN 1, 2;
    DAM NOV, POP; DLB 2, 4, 152; EWL
    3; GLL 2; MAL 5; MAWW; MTCW 1, 2;
    MTFW 2005; RGAL 4; RGSF 2
Nisbet, Robert A(lexander)
        1913-1996 .... **TCLC 117**
    See also CA 25-28R; 153; CANR 17; INT
    CANR-17
Nishida, Kitaro 1870-1945 .... **TCLC 83**
Nishiwaki, Junzaburo 1894-1982 .... **PC 15**
    See Junzaburo, Nishiwaki
    See also CA 194; 107; MJW; RGWL 3
Nissenson, Hugh 1933- .... **CLC 4, 9**
    See also CA 17-20R; CANR 27, 108; CN
    5, 6; DLB 28
Nister, Der
    See Der Nister
    See also EWL 3
Niven, Larry .... **CLC 8**
    See Niven, Laurence Van Cott
    See also AAYA 27; BPFB 2; BYA 10; DLB
    8; SCFW 1, 2
Niven, Laurence Van Cott 1938-
    See Niven, Larry
    See also CA 21-24R, 207; CAAE 207;
    CAAS 12; CANR 14, 44, 66, 113; CPW;
    DAM POP; MTCW 1, 2; SATA 95; SFW
    4
Nixon, Agnes Eckhardt 1927- .... **CLC 21**
    See also CA 110
Nizan, Paul 1905-1940 .... **TCLC 40**
    See also CA 161; DLB 72; EWL 3; GFL
    1789 to the Present
Nkosi, Lewis 1936- .... **BLC 3; CLC 45**
    See also BW 1, 3; CA 65-68; CANR 27,
    81; CBD; CD 5, 6; DAM MULT; DLB
    157, 225; WWE 1
Nodier, (Jean) Charles (Emmanuel)
        1780-1844 .... **NCLC 19**
    See also DLB 119; GFL 1789 to the Present
Noguchi, Yone 1875-1947 .... **TCLC 80**
Nolan, Christopher 1965- .... **CLC 58**
    See also CA 111; CANR 88
Noon, Jeff 1957- .... **CLC 91**
    See also CA 148; CANR 83; DLB 267;
    SFW 4
Norden, Charles
    See Durrell, Lawrence (George)
Nordhoff, Charles Bernard
        1887-1947 .... **TCLC 23**
    See also CA 108; 211; DLB 9; LAIT 1;
    RHW 1; SATA 23

Norfolk, Lawrence 1963- .... **CLC 76**
    See also CA 144; CANR 85; CN 6, 7; DLB
    267
Norman, Marsha (Williams) 1947- . **CLC 28,**
        186; DC 8
    See also CA 105; CABS 3; CAD; CANR
    41, 131; CD 5, 6; CSW; CWD; DAM
    DRAM; DFS 2; DLB 266; DLBY 1984;
    FW; MAL 5
Normyx
    See Douglas, (George) Norman
Norris, (Benjamin) Frank(lin, Jr.)
        1870-1902 .... **SSC 28; TCLC 24, 155**
    See also AAYA 57; AMW; AMWC 2; BPFB
    2; CA 110; 160; CDALB 1865-1917; DLB
    12, 71, 186; LMFS 2; NFS 12; RGAL 4;
    TCWW 1, 2; TUS
Norris, Leslie 1921- .... **CLC 14**
    See also CA 11-12; CANR 14, 117; CAP 1;
    CP 1, 2, 3, 4, 5, 6, 7; DLB 27, 256
North, Andrew
    See Norton, Andre
North, Anthony
    See Koontz, Dean R.
North, Captain George
    See Stevenson, Robert Louis (Balfour)
North, Captain George
    See Stevenson, Robert Louis (Balfour)
North, Milou
    See Erdrich, (Karen) Louise
Northrup, B. A.
    See Hubbard, L(afayette) Ron(ald)
North Staffs
    See Hulme, T(homas) E(rnest)
Northup, Solomon 1808-1863 ...... **NCLC 105**
Norton, Alice Mary
    See Norton, Andre
    See also MAICYA 1; SATA 1, 43
Norton, Andre 1912-2005 .... **CLC 12**
    See Norton, Alice Mary
    See also AAYA 14; BPFB 2; BYA 4, 10,
    12; CA 1-4R; 237; CANR 68; CLR 50;
    DLB 8, 52; JRDA; MAICYA 2; MTCW
    1; SATA 91; SUFW 1, 2; YAW
Norton, Caroline 1808-1877 .... **NCLC 47**
    See also DLB 21, 159, 199
Norway, Nevil Shute 1899-1960
    See Shute, Nevil
    See also CA 102; 93-96; CANR 85; MTCW
    2
Norwid, Cyprian Kamil
        1821-1883 .... **NCLC 17**
    See also RGWL 3
Nosille, Nabrah
    See Ellison, Harlan (Jay)
Nossack, Hans Erich 1901-1978 .... **CLC 6**
    See also CA 93-96; 85-88; DLB 69; EWL 3
Nostradamus 1503-1566 .... **LC 27**
Nosu, Chuji
    See Ozu, Yasujiro
Notenburg, Eleanora (Genrikhovna) von
    See Guro, Elena (Genrikhovna)
Nova, Craig 1945- .... **CLC 7, 31**
    See also CA 45-48; CANR 2, 53, 127
Novak, Joseph
    See Kosinski, Jerzy (Nikodem)
Novalis 1772-1801 .... **NCLC 13**
    See also CDWLB 2; DLB 90; EW 5; RGWL
    2, 3
Novick, Peter 1934- .... **CLC 164**
    See also CA 188
Novis, Emile
    See Weil, Simone (Adolphine)
Nowlan, Alden (Albert) 1933-1983 ... **CLC 15**
    See also CA 9-12R; CANR 5; CP 1, 2, 3;
    DAC; DAM MST; DLB 53; PFS 12

Noyes, Alfred 1880-1958 ...... **PC 27; TCLC 7**
    See also CA 104; 188; DLB 20; EXPP;
    FANT; PFS 4; RGEL 2
Nugent, Richard Bruce
        1906(?)-1987 .... **HR 1:3**
    See also BW 1; CA 125; DLB 51; GLL 2
Nunn, Kem .... **CLC 34**
    See also CA 159
Nussbaum, Martha Craven 1947- .. **CLC 203**
    See also CA 134; CANR 102
Nwapa, Flora (Nwanzuruaha)
        1931-1993 .... **BLCS; CLC 133**
    See also BW 2; CA 143; CANR 83; CD-
    WLB 3; CWRI 5; DLB 125; EWL 3;
    WLIT 2
Nye, Robert 1939- .... **CLC 13, 42**
    See also BRWS 10; CA 33-36R; CANR 29,
    67, 107; CN 1, 2, 3, 4, 5, 6, 7; CP 1, 2, 3,
    4, 5, 6, 7; CWRI 5; DAM NOV; DLB 14,
    271; FANT; HGG; MTCW 1; RHW;
    SATA 6
Nyro, Laura 1947-1997 .... **CLC 17**
    See also CA 194
Oates, Joyce Carol 1938- .. **CLC 1, 2, 3, 6, 9,**
        11, 15, 19, 33, 52, 108, 134; SSC 6, 70;
        WLC
    See also AAYA 15, 52; AITN 1; AMWS 2;
    BEST 89:2; BPFB 2; BYA 11; CA 5-8R;
    CANR 25, 45, 74, 113, 129; CDALB
    1968-1988; CN 1, 2, 3, 4, 5, 6, 7; CP 7;
    CPW; CWP; DA; DA3; DAB; DAC;
    DAM MST, NOV, POP; DLB 2, 5, 130;
    DLBY 1981; EWL 3; EXPS; FL 1:6; FW;
    GL 3; HGG; INT CANR-25; LAIT 4;
    MAL 5; MAWW; MTCW 1, 2; MTFW
    2005; NFS 8; RGAL 4; RGSF 2; SATA
    159; SSFS 1, 8, 17; SUFW 2; TUS
O'Brian, E. G.
    See Clarke, Arthur C(harles)
O'Brian, Patrick 1914-2000 .... **CLC 152**
    See also AAYA 55; CA 144; 187; CANR
    74; CPW; MTCW 2; MTFW 2005; RHW
O'Brien, Darcy 1939-1998 .... **CLC 11**
    See also CA 21-24R; 167; CANR 8, 59
O'Brien, Edna 1932- ..... **CLC 3, 5, 8, 13, 36,**
        65, 116; SSC 10, 77
    See also BRWS 5; CA 1-4R; CANR 6, 41,
    65, 102; CDBLB 1960 to Present; CN 1,
    2, 3, 4, 5, 6, 7; DA3; DAM NOV; DLB
    14, 231, 319; EWL 3; FW; MTCW 1, 2;
    MTFW 2005; RGSF 2; WLIT 4
O'Brien, Fitz-James 1828-1862 .... **NCLC 21**
    See also DLB 74; RGAL 4; SUFW
O'Brien, Flann .... **CLC 1, 4, 5, 7, 10, 47**
    See O Nuallain, Brian
    See also BRWS 2; DLB 231; EWL 3;
    RGEL 2
O'Brien, Richard 1942- .... **CLC 17**
    See also CA 124
O'Brien, (William) Tim(othy) 1946- . **CLC 7,**
        19, 40, 103, 211; SSC 74
    See also AAYA 16; AMWS 5; CA 85-88;
    CANR 40, 58, 133; CDALBS; CN 5, 6,
    7; CPW; DA3; DAM POP; DLB 152;
    DLBD 9; DLBY 1980; LATS 1:2; MAL
    5; MTCW 2; MTFW 2005; RGAL 4;
    SSFS 5, 15; TCLE 1:2
Obstfelder, Sigbjoern 1866-1900 .... **TCLC 23**
    See also CA 123
O'Casey, Sean 1880-1964 .... **CLC 1, 5, 9, 11,**
        15, 88; DC 12; WLCS
    See also BRW 7; CA 89-92; CANR 62;
    CBD; CDBLB 1914-1945; DA3; DAB;
    DAC; DAM DRAM, MST; DFS 19; DLB
    10; EWL 3; MTCW 1, 2; MTFW 2005;
    RGEL 2; TEA; WLIT 4
O'Cathasaigh, Sean
    See O'Casey, Sean
Occom, Samson 1723-1792 .... **LC 60; NNAL**
    See also DLB 175

Ortega y Gasset, Jose 1883-1955 ...... **HLC 2; TCLC 9**
See also CA 106; 130; DAM MULT; EW 9; EWL 3; HW 1, 2; MTCW 1, 2; MTFW 2005

Ortese, Anna Maria 1914-1998 .... **CLC 89**
See also DLB 177; EWL 3

Ortiz, Simon J(oseph) 1941- ... **CLC 45, 208; NNAL; PC 17**
See also AMWS 4; CA 134; CANR 69, 118; CP 3, 4, 5, 6, 7; DAM MULT, POET; DLB 120, 175, 256; EXPP; MAL 5; PFS 4, 16; RGAL 4; TCWW 2

Orton, Joe ...... **CLC 4, 13, 43; DC 3; TCLC 157**
See Orton, John Kingsley
See also BRWS 5; CBD; CDBLB 1960 to Present; DFS 3, 6; DLB 13, 310; GLL 1; RGEL 2; TEA; WLIT 4

Orton, John Kingsley 1933-1967
See Orton, Joe
See also CA 85-88; CANR 35, 66; DAM DRAM; MTCW 1, 2; MTFW 2005

Orwell, George ...... **SSC 68; TCLC 2, 6, 15, 31, 51, 128, 129; WLC**
See Blair, Eric (Arthur)
See also BPFB 3; BRW 7; BYA 5; CDBLB 1945-1960; CLR 68; DAB; DLB 15, 98, 195, 255; EWL 3; EXPN; LAIT 4, 5; LATS 1:1; NFS 3, 7; RGEL 2; SCFW 1, 2; SFW 4; SSFS 4; TEA; WLIT 4; YAW

Osborne, David
See Silverberg, Robert

Osborne, George
See Silverberg, Robert

Osborne, John (James) 1929-1994 .... **CLC 1, 2, 5, 11, 45; TCLC 153; WLC**
See also BRWS 1; CA 13-16R; 147; CANR 21, 56; CBD; CDBLB 1945-1960; DA; DAB; DAC; DAM DRAM, MST; DFS 4, 19; DLB 13; EWL 3; MTCW 1, 2; MTFW 2005; RGEL 2

Osborne, Lawrence 1958- .... **CLC 50**
See also CA 189

Osbourne, Lloyd 1868-1947 .... **TCLC 93**

Osgood, Frances Sargent
1811-1850 .... **NCLC 141**
See also DLB 250

Oshima, Nagisa 1932- .... **CLC 20**
See also CA 116; 121; CANR 78

Oskison, John Milton
1874-1947 .... **NNAL; TCLC 35**
See also CA 144; CANR 84; DAM MULT; DLB 175

Ossian c. 3rd cent. - .... **CMLC 28**
See Macpherson, James

Ossoli, Sarah Margaret (Fuller)
1810-1850 .... **NCLC 5, 50**
See Fuller, Margaret; Fuller, Sarah Margaret
See also CDALB 1640-1865; FW; LMFS 1; SATA 25

Ostriker, Alicia (Suskin) 1937- .... **CLC 132**
See also CA 25-28R; CAAS 24; CANR 10, 30, 62, 99; CWP; DLB 120; EXPP; PFS 19

Ostrovsky, Aleksandr Nikolaevich
See Ostrovsky, Alexander
See also DLB 277

Ostrovsky, Alexander 1823-1886 .. **NCLC 30, 57**
See Ostrovsky, Aleksandr Nikolaevich

Otero, Blas de 1916-1979 .... **CLC 11**
See also CA 89-92; DLB 134; EWL 3

O'Trigger, Sir Lucius
See Horne, Richard Henry Hengist

Otto, Rudolf 1869-1937 .... **TCLC 85**

Otto, Whitney 1955- .... **CLC 70**
See also CA 140; CANR 120

Otway, Thomas 1652-1685 ... **DC 24; LC 106**
See also DAM DRAM; DLB 80; RGEL 2

Ouida .... **TCLC 43**
See De la Ramee, Marie Louise (Ouida)
See also DLB 18, 156; RGEL 2

Ouologuem, Yambo 1940- .... **CLC 146**
See also CA 111; 176

Ousmane, Sembene 1923- ... **BLC 3; CLC 66**
See Sembene, Ousmane
See also BW 1, 3; CA 117; 125; CANR 81; CWW 2; MTCW 1

Ovid 43B.C.-17 .... **CMLC 7; PC 2**
See also AW 2; CDWLB 1; DA3; DAM POET; DLB 211; PFS 22; RGWL 2, 3; WP

Owen, Hugh
See Faust, Frederick (Schiller)

Owen, Wilfred (Edward Salter)
1893-1918 ... **PC 19; TCLC 5, 27; WLC**
See also BRW 6; CA 104; 141; CDBLB 1914-1945; DA; DAB; DAC; DAM MST, POET; DLB 20; EWL 3; EXPP; MTCW 2; MTFW 2005; PFS 10; RGEL 2; WLIT 4

Owens, Louis (Dean) 1948-2002 .... **NNAL**
See also CA 137; 179; 207; CAAE 179; CAAS 24; CANR 71

Owens, Rochelle 1936- .... **CLC 8**
See also CA 17-20R; CAAS 2; CAD; CANR 39; CD 5, 6; CP 1, 2, 3, 4, 5, 6, 7; CWD; CWP

Oz, Amos 1939- ...... **CLC 5, 8, 11, 27, 33, 54; SSC 66**
See also CA 53-56; CANR 27, 47, 65, 113, 138; CWW 2; DAM NOV; EWL 3; MTCW 1, 2; MTFW 2005; RGSF 2; RGWL 3; WLIT 6

Ozick, Cynthia 1928- .... **CLC 3, 7, 28, 62, 155; SSC 15, 60**
See also AMWS 5; BEST 90:1; CA 17-20R; CANR 23, 58, 116; CN 3, 4, 5, 6, 7; CPW; DA3; DAM NOV, POP; DLB 28, 152, 299; DLBY 1982; EWL 3; EXPS; INT CANR-23; MAL 5; MTCW 1, 2; MTFW 2005; RGAL 4; RGSF 2; SSFS 3, 12

Ozu, Yasujiro 1903-1963 .... **CLC 16**
See also CA 112

Pabst, G. W. 1885-1967 .... **TCLC 127**

Pacheco, C.
See Pessoa, Fernando (Antonio Nogueira)

Pacheco, Jose Emilio 1939- .... **HLC 2**
See also CA 111; 131; CANR 65; CWW 2; DAM MULT; DLB 290; EWL 3; HW 1, 2; RGSF 2

Pa Chin .... **CLC 18**
See Li Fei-kan
See also EWL 3

Pack, Robert 1929- .... **CLC 13**
See also CA 1-4R; CANR 3, 44, 82; CP 1, 2, 3, 4, 5, 6, 7; DLB 5; SATA 118

Padgett, Lewis
See Kuttner, Henry

Padilla (Lorenzo), Heberto
1932-2000 .... **CLC 38**
See also AITN 1; CA 123; 131; 189; CWW 2; EWL 3; HW 1

Page, James Patrick 1944-
See Page, Jimmy
See also CA 204

Page, Jimmy 1944- .... **CLC 12**
See Page, James Patrick

Page, Louise 1955- .... **CLC 40**
See also CA 140; CANR 76; CBD; CD 5, 6; CWD; DLB 233

Page, P(atricia) K(athleen) 1916- ...... **CLC 7, 18; PC 12**
See Cape, Judith
See also CA 53-56; CANR 4, 22, 65; CP 1, 2, 3, 4, 5, 6, 7; DAC; DAM MST; DLB 68; MTCW 1; RGEL 2

Page, Stanton
See Fuller, Henry Blake

Page, Stanton
See Fuller, Henry Blake

Page, Thomas Nelson 1853-1922 .... **SSC 23**
See also CA 118; 177; DLB 12, 78; DLBD 13; RGAL 4

Pagels, Elaine Hiesey 1943- .... **CLC 104**
See also CA 45-48; CANR 2, 24, 51; FW; NCFS 4

Paget, Violet 1856-1935
See Lee, Vernon
See also CA 104; 166; GLL 1; HGG

Paget-Lowe, Henry
See Lovecraft, H(oward) P(hillips)

Paglia, Camille (Anna) 1947- .... **CLC 68**
See also CA 140; CANR 72, 139; CPW; FW; GLL 2; MTCW 2; MTFW 2005

Paige, Richard
See Koontz, Dean R.

Paine, Thomas 1737-1809 .... **NCLC 62**
See also AMWS 1; CDALB 1640-1865; DLB 31, 43, 73, 158; LAIT 1; RGAL 4; RGEL 2; TUS

Pakenham, Antonia
See Fraser, Antonia (Pakenham)

Palamas, Costis
See Palamas, Kostes

Palamas, Kostes 1859-1943 .... **TCLC 5**
See Palamas, Kostis
See also CA 105; 190; RGWL 2, 3

Palamas, Kostis
See Palamas, Kostes
See also EWL 3

Palazzeschi, Aldo 1885-1974 .... **CLC 11**
See also CA 89-92; 53-56; DLB 114, 264; EWL 3

Pales Matos, Luis 1898-1959 .... **HLCS 2**
See Pales Matos, Luis
See also DLB 290; HW 1; LAW

Paley, Grace 1922- .. **CLC 4, 6, 37, 140; SSC 8**
See also AMWS 6; CA 25-28R; CANR 13, 46, 74, 118; CN 2, 3, 4, 5, 6, 7; CPW; DA3; DAM POP; DLB 28, 218; EWL 3; EXPS; FW; INT CANR-13; MAL 5; MAWW; MTCW 1, 2; MTFW 2005; RGAL 4; RGSF 2; SSFS 3, 20

Palin, Michael (Edward) 1943- .... **CLC 21**
See Monty Python
See also CA 107; CANR 35, 109; SATA 67

Palliser, Charles 1947- .... **CLC 65**
See also CA 136; CANR 76; CN 5, 6, 7

Palma, Ricardo 1833-1919 .... **TCLC 29**
See also CA 168; LAW

Pamuk, Orhan 1952- .... **CLC 185**
See also CA 142; CANR 75, 127; CWW 2; WLIT 6

Pancake, Breece Dexter 1952-1979
See Pancake, Breece D'J
See also CA 123; 109

Pancake, Breece D'J .... **CLC 29; SSC 61**
See Pancake, Breece Dexter
See also DLB 130

Panchenko, Nikolai .... **CLC 59**

Pankhurst, Emmeline (Goulden)
1858-1928 .... **TCLC 100**
See also CA 116; FW

Panko, Rudy
See Gogol, Nikolai (Vasilyevich)

Papadiamantis, Alexandros
1851-1911 .... **TCLC 29**
See also CA 168; EWL 3

Papadiamantopoulos, Johannes 1856-1910
  See Moreas, Jean
  See also CA 117
Papini, Giovanni 1881-1956 .... **TCLC 22**
  See also CA 121; 180; DLB 264
Paracelsus 1493-1541 .... **LC 14**
  See also DLB 179
Parasol, Peter
  See Stevens, Wallace
Pardo Bazan, Emilia 1851-1921 .... **SSC 30**
  See also EWL 3; FW; RGSF 2; RGWL 2, 3
Pareto, Vilfredo 1848-1923 .... **TCLC 69**
  See also CA 175
Paretsky, Sara 1947- .... **CLC 135**
  See also AAYA 30; BEST 90:3; CA 125;
  129; CANR 59, 95; CMW 4; CPW; DA3;
  DAM POP; DLB 306; INT CA-129;
  MSW; RGAL 4
Parfenie, Maria
  See Codrescu, Andrei
Parini, Jay (Lee) 1948- .... **CLC 54, 133**
  See also CA 97-100, 229; CAAE 229;
  CAAS 16; CANR 32, 87
Park, Jordan
  See Kornbluth, C(yril) M.; Pohl, Frederik
Park, Robert E(zra) 1864-1944 ..... **TCLC 73**
  See also CA 122; 165
Parker, Bert
  See Ellison, Harlan (Jay)
Parker, Dorothy (Rothschild)
  1893-1967 . **CLC 15, 68; PC 28; SSC 2;**
  TCLC 143
  See also AMWS 9; CA 19-20; 25-28R; CAP
  2; DA3; DAM POET; DLB 11, 45, 86;
  EXPP; FW; MAL 5; MAWW; MTCW 1,
  2; MTFW 2005; PFS 18; RGAL 4; RGSF
  2; TUS
Parker, Robert B(rown) 1932- .... **CLC 27**
  See also AAYA 28; BEST 89:4; BPFB 3;
  CA 49-52; CANR 1, 26, 52, 89, 128;
  CMW 4; CPW; DAM NOV, POP; DLB
  306; INT CANR-26; MSW; MTCW 1;
  MTFW 2005
Parkin, Frank 1940- .... **CLC 43**
  See also CA 147
Parkman, Francis, Jr. 1823-1893 .. **NCLC 12**
  See also AMWS 2; DLB 1, 30, 183, 186,
  235; RGAL 4
Parks, Gordon (Alexander Buchanan)
  1912- .... **BLC 3; CLC 1, 16**
  See also AAYA 36; AITN 2; BW 2, 3; CA
  41-44R; CANR 26, 66, 145; DA3; DAM
  MULT; DLB 33; MTCW 2; MTFW 2005;
  SATA 8, 108
Parks, Suzan-Lori 1964(?)- .... **DC 23**
  See also AAYA 55; CA 201; CAD; CD 5,
  6; CWD; DFS 22; RGAL 4
Parks, Tim(othy Harold) 1954- ...... **CLC 147**
  See also CA 126; 131; CANR 77, 144; CN
  7; DLB 231; INT CA-131
Parmenides c. 515B.C.-c.
  450B.C. .... **CMLC 22**
  See also DLB 176
Parnell, Thomas 1679-1718 .... **LC 3**
  See also DLB 95; RGEL 2
Parr, Catherine c. 1513(?)-1548 .... **LC 86**
  See also DLB 136
Parra, Nicanor 1914- ... **CLC 2, 102; HLC 2;**
  PC 39
  See also CA 85-88; CANR 32; CWW 2;
  DAM MULT; DLB 283; EWL 3; HW 1;
  LAW; MTCW 1
Parra Sanojo, Ana Teresa de la
  1890-1936 .... **HLCS 2**
  See de la Parra, (Ana) Teresa (Sonojo)
  See also LAW
Parrish, Mary Frances
  See Fisher, M(ary) F(rances) K(ennedy)

Parshchikov, Aleksei 1954- .... **CLC 59**
  See Parshchikov, Aleksei Maksimovich
Parshchikov, Aleksei Maksimovich
  See Parshchikov, Aleksei
  See also DLB 285
Parson, Professor
  See Coleridge, Samuel Taylor
Parson Lot
  See Kingsley, Charles
Parton, Sara Payson Willis
  1811-1872 .... **NCLC 86**
  See also DLB 43, 74, 239
Partridge, Anthony
  See Oppenheim, E(dward) Phillips
Pascal, Blaise 1623-1662 .... **LC 35**
  See also DLB 268; EW 3; GFL Beginnings
  to 1789; RGWL 2, 3; TWA
Pascoli, Giovanni 1855-1912 .... **TCLC 45**
  See also CA 170; EW 7; EWL 3
Pasolini, Pier Paolo 1922-1975 .. **CLC 20, 37,**
  106; PC 17
  See also CA 93-96; 61-64; CANR 63; DLB
  128, 177; EWL 3; MTCW 1; RGWL 2, 3
Pasquini
  See Silone, Ignazio
Pastan, Linda (Olenik) 1932- .... **CLC 27**
  See also CA 61-64; CANR 18, 40, 61, 113;
  CP 3, 4, 5, 6, 7; CSW; CWP; DAM
  POET; DLB 5; PFS 8
Pasternak, Boris (Leonidovich)
  1890-1960 ...... **CLC 7, 10, 18, 63; PC 6;**
  SSC 31; WLC
  See also BPFB 3; CA 127; 116; DA; DA3;
  DAB; DAC; DAM MST, NOV, POET;
  DLB 302; EW 10; MTCW 1, 2; MTFW
  2005; RGSF 2; RGWL 2, 3; TWA; WP
Patchen, Kenneth 1911-1972 .... **CLC 1, 2, 18**
  See also BG 1:3; CA 1-4R; 33-36R; CANR
  3, 35; CN 1; CP 1; DAM POET; DLB 16,
  48; EWL 3; MAL 5; MTCW 1; RGAL 4
Pater, Walter (Horatio) 1839-1894 . **NCLC 7,**
  90, 159
  See also BRW 5; CDBLB 1832-1890; DLB
  57, 156; RGEL 2; TEA
Paterson, A(ndrew) B(arton)
  1864-1941 .... **TCLC 32**
  See also CA 155; DLB 230; RGEL 2; SATA
  97
Paterson, Banjo
  See Paterson, A(ndrew) B(arton)
Paterson, Katherine (Womeldorf)
  1932- .... **CLC 12, 30**
  See also AAYA 1, 31; BYA 1, 2, 7; CA 21-
  24R; CANR 28, 59, 111; CLR 7, 50;
  CWRI 5; DLB 52; JRDA; LAIT 4; MAI-
  CYA 1, 2; MAICYAS 1; MTCW 1; SATA
  13, 53, 92, 133; WYA; YAW
Patmore, Coventry Kersey Dighton
  1823-1896 .... **NCLC 9; PC 59**
  See also DLB 35, 98; RGEL 2; TEA
Paton, Alan (Stewart) 1903-1988 ...... **CLC 4,**
  10, 25, 55, 106; TCLC 165; WLC
  See also AAYA 26; AFW; BPFB 3; BRWS
  2; BYA 1; CA 13-16; 125; CANR 22;
  CAP 1; CN 1, 2, 3, 4; DA; DA3; DAB;
  DAC; DAM MST, NOV; DLB 225;
  DLBD 17; EWL 3; EXPN; LAIT 4;
  MTCW 1, 2; MTFW 2005; NFS 3, 12;
  RGEL 2; SATA 11; SATA-Obit 56; TWA;
  WLIT 2; WWE 1
Paton Walsh, Gillian 1937- .... **CLC 35**
  See Paton Walsh, Jill; Walsh, Jill Paton
  See also AAYA 11; CANR 38, 83; CLR 2,
  65; DLB 161; JRDA; MAICYA 1, 2;
  SAAS 3; SATA 4, 72, 109; YAW
Paton Walsh, Jill
  See Paton Walsh, Gillian
  See also AAYA 47; BYA 1, 8

Patterson, (Horace) Orlando (Lloyd)
  1940- .... **BLCS**
  See also BW 1; CA 65-68; CANR 27, 84;
  CN 1, 2, 3, 4, 5, 6
Patton, George S(mith), Jr.
  1885-1945 .... **TCLC 79**
  See also CA 189
Paulding, James Kirke 1778-1860 ... **NCLC 2**
  See also DLB 3, 59, 74, 250; RGAL 4
Paulin, Thomas Neilson 1949-
  See Paulin, Tom
  See also CA 123; 128; CANR 98
Paulin, Tom .... **CLC 37, 177**
  See Paulin, Thomas Neilson
  See also CP 3, 4, 5, 6, 7; DLB 40
Pausanias c. 1st cent. - .... **CMLC 36**
Paustovsky, Konstantin (Georgievich)
  1892-1968 .... **CLC 40**
  See also CA 93-96; 25-28R; DLB 272;
  EWL 3
Pavese, Cesare 1908-1950 .... **PC 13; SSC 19;**
  TCLC 3
  See also CA 104; 169; DLB 128, 177; EW
  12; EWL 3; PFS 20; RGSF 2; RGWL 2,
  3; TWA; WLIT 7
Pavic, Milorad 1929- .... **CLC 60**
  See also CA 136; CDWLB 4; CWW 2; DLB
  181; EWL 3; RGWL 3
Pavlov, Ivan Petrovich 1849-1936 . **TCLC 91**
  See also CA 118; 180
Pavlova, Karolina Karlovna
  1807-1893 .... **NCLC 138**
  See also DLB 205
Payne, Alan
  See Jakes, John (William)
Payne, Rachel Ann
  See Jakes, John (William)
Paz, Gil
  See Lugones, Leopoldo
Paz, Octavio 1914-1998 . **CLC 3, 4, 6, 10, 19,**
  51, 65, 119; HLC 2; PC 1, 48; WLC
  See also AAYA 50; CA 73-76; 165; CANR
  32, 65, 104; CWW 2; DA; DA3; DAB;
  DAC; DAM MST, MULT, POET; DLB
  290; DLBY 1990, 1998; DNFS 1; EWL
  3; HW 1, 2; LAW; LAWS 1; MTCW 1, 2;
  MTFW 2005; PFS 18; RGWL 2, 3; SSFS
  13; TWA; WLIT 1
p'Bitek, Okot 1931-1982 .... **BLC 3; CLC 96;**
  TCLC 149
  See also AFW; BW 2, 3; CA 124; 107;
  CANR 82; CP 1, 2, 3; DAM MULT; DLB
  125; EWL 3; MTCW 1, 2; MTFW 2005;
  RGEL 2; WLIT 2
Peabody, Elizabeth Palmer
  1804-1894 .... **NCLC 169**
  See also DLB 1, 223
Peacham, Henry 1578-1644(?) .... **LC 119**
  See also DLB 151
Peacock, Molly 1947- .... **CLC 60**
  See also CA 103; CAAS 21; CANR 52, 84;
  CP 7; CWP; DLB 120, 282
Peacock, Thomas Love
  1785-1866 .... **NCLC 22**
  See also BRW 4; DLB 96, 116; RGEL 2;
  RGSF 2
Peake, Mervyn 1911-1968 .... **CLC 7, 54**
  See also CA 5-8R; 25-28R; CANR 3; DLB
  15, 160, 255; FANT; MTCW 1; RGEL 2;
  SATA 23; SFW 4
Pearce, Philippa
  See Christie, Philippa
  See also CA 5-8R; CANR 4, 109; CWRI 5;
  FANT; MAICYA 2
Pearl, Eric
  See Elman, Richard (Martin)
Pearson, T(homas) R(eid) 1956- .... **CLC 39**
  See also CA 120; 130; CANR 97; CSW;
  INT CA-130

Peck, Dale 1967- .... **CLC 81**
See also CA 146; CANR 72, 127; GLL 2

Peck, John (Frederick) 1941- .... **CLC 3**
See also CA 49-52; CANR 3, 100; CP 4, 5, 6, 7

Peck, Richard (Wayne) 1934- .... **CLC 21**
See also AAYA 1, 24; BYA 1, 6, 8, 11; CA 85-88; CANR 19, 38, 129; CLR 15; INT CANR-19; JRDA; MAICYA 1, 2; SAAS 2; SATA 18, 55, 97, 110, 158; SATA-Essay 110; WYA; YAW

Peck, Robert Newton 1928- .... **CLC 17**
See also AAYA 3, 43; BYA 1, 6; CA 81-84, 182; CAAE 182; CANR 31, 63, 127; CLR 45; DA; DAC; DAM MST; JRDA; LAIT 3; MAICYA 1, 2; SAAS 1; SATA 21, 62, 111, 156; SATA-Essay 108; WYA; YAW

Peckinpah, (David) Sam(uel)
1925-1984 .... **CLC 20**
See also CA 109; 114; CANR 82

Pedersen, Knut 1859-1952
See Hamsun, Knut
See also CA 104; 119; CANR 63; MTCW 1, 2

Peele, George 1556-1596 .... **DC 27; LC 115**
See also BRW 1; DLB 62, 167; RGEL 2

Peeslake, Gaffer
See Durrell, Lawrence (George)

Peguy, Charles (Pierre)
1873-1914 .... **TCLC 10**
See also CA 107; 193; DLB 258; EWL 3; GFL 1789 to the Present

Peirce, Charles Sanders
1839-1914 .... **TCLC 81**
See also CA 194; DLB 270

Pellicer, Carlos 1897(?)-1977 .... **HLCS 2**
See also CA 153; 69-72; DLB 290; EWL 3; HW 1

Pena, Ramon del Valle y
See Valle-Inclan, Ramon (Maria) del

Pendennis, Arthur Esquir
See Thackeray, William Makepeace

Penn, Arthur
See Matthews, (James) Brander

Penn, William 1644-1718 .... **LC 25**
See also DLB 24

PEPECE
See Prado (Calvo), Pedro

Pepys, Samuel 1633-1703 ... **LC 11, 58; WLC**
See also BRW 2; CDBLB 1660-1789; DA; DA3; DAB; DAC; DAM MST; DLB 101, 213; NCFS 4; RGEL 2; TEA; WLIT 3

Percy, Thomas 1729-1811 .... **NCLC 95**
See also DLB 104

Percy, Walker 1916-1990 .... **CLC 2, 3, 6, 8, 14, 18, 47, 65**
See also AMWS 3; BPFB 3; CA 1-4R; 131; CANR 1, 23, 64; CN 1, 2, 3, 4; CPW; CSW; DA3; DAM NOV, POP; DLB 2; DLBY 1980, 1990; EWL 3; MAL 5; MTCW 1, 2; MTFW 2005; RGAL 4; TUS

Percy, William Alexander
1885-1942 .... **TCLC 84**
See also CA 163; MTCW 2

Perec, Georges 1936-1982 .... **CLC 56, 116**
See also CA 141; DLB 83, 299; EWL 3; GFL 1789 to the Present; RGWL 3

Pereda (y Sanchez de Porrua), Jose Maria de 1833-1906 .... **TCLC 16**
See also CA 117

Pereda y Porrua, Jose Maria de
See Pereda (y Sanchez de Porrua), Jose Maria de

Peregoy, George Weems
See Mencken, H(enry) L(ouis)

Perelman, S(idney) J(oseph)
1904-1979 .. **CLC 3, 5, 9, 15, 23, 44, 49; SSC 32**
See also AITN 1, 2; BPFB 3; CA 73-76; 89-92; CANR 18; DAM DRAM; DLB 11, 44; MTCW 1, 2; MTFW 2005; RGAL 4

Peret, Benjamin 1899-1959 .... **PC 33; TCLC 20**
See also CA 117; 186; GFL 1789 to the Present

Peretz, Isaac Leib
See Peretz, Isaac Loeb
See also CA 201

Peretz, Isaac Loeb 1851(?)-1915 ...... **SSC 26; TCLC 16**
See Peretz, Isaac Leib
See also CA 109

Peretz, Yitzkhok Leibush
See Peretz, Isaac Loeb

Perez Galdos, Benito 1843-1920 ..... **HLCS 2; TCLC 27**
See Galdos, Benito Perez
See also CA 125; 153; EWL 3; HW 1; RGWL 2, 3

Peri Rossi, Cristina 1941- .. **CLC 156; HLCS 2**
See also CA 131; CANR 59, 81; CWW 2; DLB 145, 290; EWL 3; HW 1, 2

Perlata
See Peret, Benjamin

Perloff, Marjorie G(abrielle)
1931- .... **CLC 137**
See also CA 57-60; CANR 7, 22, 49, 104

Perrault, Charles 1628-1703 .... **LC 2, 56**
See also BYA 4; CLR 79; DLB 268; GFL Beginnings to 1789; MAICYA 1, 2; RGWL 2, 3; SATA 25; WCH

Perry, Anne 1938- .... **CLC 126**
See also CA 101; CANR 22, 50, 84; CMW 4; CN 6, 7; CPW; DLB 276

Perry, Brighton
See Sherwood, Robert E(mmet)

Perse, St.-John
See Leger, (Marie-Rene Auguste) Alexis Saint-Leger

Perse, Saint-John
See Leger, (Marie-Rene Auguste) Alexis Saint-Leger
See also DLB 258; RGWL 3

Persius 34-62 .... **CMLC 74**
See also AW 2; DLB 211; RGWL 2, 3

Perutz, Leo(pold) 1882-1957 .... **TCLC 60**
See also CA 147; DLB 81

Peseenz, Tulio F.
See Lopez y Fuentes, Gregorio

Pesetsky, Bette 1932- .... **CLC 28**
See also CA 133; DLB 130

Peshkov, Alexei Maximovich 1868-1936
See Gorky, Maxim
See also CA 105; 141; CANR 83; DA; DAC; DAM DRAM, MST, NOV; MTCW 2; MTFW 2005

Pessoa, Fernando (Antonio Nogueira)
1888-1935 ..... **HLC 2; PC 20; TCLC 27**
See also CA 125; 183; DAM MULT; DLB 287; EW 10; EWL 3; RGWL 2, 3; WP

Peterkin, Julia Mood 1880-1961 ...... **CLC 31**
See also CA 102; DLB 9

Peters, Joan K(aren) 1945- .... **CLC 39**
See also CA 158; CANR 109

Peters, Robert L(ouis) 1924- .... **CLC 7**
See also CA 13-16R; CAAS 8; CP 1, 7; DLB 105

Petofi, Sandor 1823-1849 .... **NCLC 21**
See also RGWL 2, 3

Petrakis, Harry Mark 1923- .... **CLC 3**
See also CA 9-12R; CANR 4, 30, 85; CN 1, 2, 3, 4, 5, 6, 7

Petrarch 1304-1374 .... **CMLC 20; PC 8**
See also DA3; DAM POET; EW 2; LMFS 1; RGWL 2, 3; WLIT 7

Petronius c. 20-66 .... **CMLC 34**
See also AW 2; CDWLB 1; DLB 211; RGWL 2, 3

Petrov, Evgeny .... **TCLC 21**
See Kataev, Evgeny Petrovich

Petry, Ann (Lane) 1908-1997 .. **CLC 1, 7, 18; TCLC 112**
See also AFAW 1, 2; BPFB 3; BW 1, 3; BYA 2; CA 5-8R; 157; CAAS 6; CANR 4, 46; CLR 12; CN 1, 2, 3, 4, 5, 6; DLB 76; EWL 3; JRDA; LAIT 1; MAICYA 1, 2; MAICYAS 1; MTCW 1; RGAL 4; SATA 5; SATA-Obit 94; TUS

Petursson, Halligrimur 1614-1674 .... **LC 8**

Peychinovich
See Vazov, Ivan (Minchov)

Phaedrus c. 15B.C.-c. 50 .... **CMLC 25**
See also DLB 211

Phelps (Ward), Elizabeth Stuart
See Phelps, Elizabeth Stuart
See also FW

Phelps, Elizabeth Stuart
1844-1911 .... **TCLC 113**
See Phelps (Ward), Elizabeth Stuart
See also DLB 74

Philips, Katherine 1632-1664 . **LC 30; PC 40**
See also DLB 131; RGEL 2

Philipson, Morris H. 1926- .... **CLC 53**
See also CA 1-4R; CANR 4

Phillips, Caryl 1958- .... **BLCS; CLC 96**
See also BRWS 5; BW 2; CA 141; CANR 63, 104, 140; CBD; CD 5, 6; CN 5, 6, 7; DA3; DAM MULT; DLB 157; EWL 3; MTCW 2; MTFW 2005; WLIT 4; WWE 1

Phillips, David Graham
1867-1911 .... **TCLC 44**
See also CA 108; 176; DLB 9, 12, 303; RGAL 4

Phillips, Jack
See Sandburg, Carl (August)

Phillips, Jayne Anne 1952- .... **CLC 15, 33, 139; SSC 16**
See also AAYA 57; BPFB 3; CA 101; CANR 24, 50, 96; CN 4, 5, 6, 7; CSW; DLBY 1980; INT CANR-24; MTCW 1, 2; MTFW 2005; RGAL 4; RGSF 2; SSFS 4

Phillips, Richard
See Dick, Philip K(indred)

Phillips, Robert (Schaeffer) 1938- .... **CLC 28**
See also CA 17-20R; CAAS 13; CANR 8; DLB 105

Phillips, Ward
See Lovecraft, H(oward) P(hillips)

Philostratus, Flavius c. 179-c.
244 .... **CMLC 62**

Piccolo, Lucio 1901-1969 .... **CLC 13**
See also CA 97-100; DLB 114; EWL 3

Pickthall, Marjorie L(owry) C(hristie)
1883-1922 .... **TCLC 21**
See also CA 107; DLB 92

Pico della Mirandola, Giovanni
1463-1494 .... **LC 15**
See also LMFS 1

Piercy, Marge 1936- .... **CLC 3, 6, 14, 18, 27, 62, 128; PC 29**
See also BPFB 3; CA 21-24R, 187; CAAE 187; CAAS 1; CANR 13, 43, 66, 111; CN 3, 4, 5, 6, 7; CP 1, 2, 3, 4, 5, 6, 7; CWP; DLB 120, 227; EXPP; FW; MAL 5; MTCW 1, 2; MTFW 2005; PFS 9, 22; SFW 4

Piers, Robert
See Anthony, Piers

Prishvin, Mikhail 1873-1954 .... **TCLC 75**
See Prishvin, Mikhail Mikhailovich
Prishvin, Mikhail Mikhailovich
See Prishvin, Mikhail
See also DLB 272; EWL 3
Pritchard, William H(arrison)
1932- .... **CLC 34**
See also CA 65-68; CANR 23, 95; DLB 111
Pritchett, V(ictor) S(awdon)
1900-1997 ... **CLC 5, 13, 15, 41; SSC 14**
See also BPFB 3; BRWS 3; CA 61-64; 157; CANR 31, 63; CN 1, 2, 3, 4, 5, 6; DA3; DAM NOV; DLB 15, 139; EWL 3; MTCW 1, 2; MTFW 2005; RGEL 2; RGSF 2; TEA
Private 19022
See Manning, Frederic
Probst, Mark 1925- .... **CLC 59**
See also CA 130
Procaccino, Michael
See Cristofer, Michael
Proclus c. 412-485 .... **CMLC 81**
Prokosch, Frederic 1908-1989 ...... **CLC 4, 48**
See also CA 73-76; 128; CANR 82; CN 1, 2, 3, 4; CP 1, 2, 3, 4; DLB 48; MTCW 2
Propertius, Sextus c. 50B.C.-c.
16B.C. .... **CMLC 32**
See also AW 2; CDWLB 1; DLB 211; RGWL 2, 3
Prophet, The
See Dreiser, Theodore (Herman Albert)
Prose, Francine 1947- .... **CLC 45**
See also CA 109; 112; CANR 46, 95, 132; DLB 234; MTFW 2005; SATA 101, 149
Proudhon
See Cunha, Euclides (Rodrigues Pimenta) da
Proulx, Annie
See Proulx, E. Annie
Proulx, E. Annie 1935- .... **CLC 81, 158**
See also AMWS 7; BPFB 3; CA 145; CANR 65, 110; CN 6, 7; CPW 1; DA3; DAM POP; MAL 5; MTCW 2; MTFW 2005; SSFS 18
Proulx, Edna Annie
See Proulx, E. Annie
Proust, (Valentin-Louis-George-Eugene)
Marcel 1871-1922 ..... **SSC 75; TCLC 7, 13, 33; WLC**
See also AAYA 58; BPFB 3; CA 104; 120; CANR 110; DA; DA3; DAB; DAC; DAM MST, NOV; DLB 65; EW 8; EWL 3; GFL 1789 to the Present; MTCW 1, 2; MTFW 2005; RGWL 2, 3; TWA
Prowler, Harley
See Masters, Edgar Lee
Prudentius, Aurelius Clemens 348-c.
405 .... **CMLC 78**
See also EW 1; RGWL 2, 3
Prus, Boleslaw 1845-1912 .... **TCLC 48**
See also RGWL 2, 3
Pryor, Richard (Franklin Lenox Thomas)
1940-2005 .... **CLC 26**
See also CA 122; 152
Przybyszewski, Stanislaw
1868-1927 .... **TCLC 36**
See also CA 160; DLB 66; EWL 3
Pteleon
See Grieve, C(hristopher) M(urray)
See also DAM POET
Puckett, Lute
See Masters, Edgar Lee
Puig, Manuel 1932-1990 .... **CLC 3, 5, 10, 28, 65, 133; HLC 2**
See also BPFB 3; CA 45-48; CANR 2, 32, 63; CDWLB 3; DA3; DAM MULT; DLB 113; DNFS 1; EWL 3; GLL 1; HW 1, 2; LAW; MTCW 1, 2; MTFW 2005; RGWL 2, 3; TWA; WLIT 1

Pulitzer, Joseph 1847-1911 .... **TCLC 76**
See also CA 114; DLB 23
Purchas, Samuel 1577(?)-1626 .... **LC 70**
See also DLB 151
Purdy, A(lfred) W(ellington)
1918-2000 .... **CLC 3, 6, 14, 50**
See also CA 81-84; 189; CAAS 17; CANR 42, 66; CP 1, 2, 3, 4, 5, 6, 7; DAC; DAM MST, POET; DLB 88; PFS 5; RGEL 2
Purdy, James (Amos) 1923- .... **CLC 2, 4, 10, 28, 52**
See also AMWS 7; CA 33-36R; CAAS 1; CANR 19, 51, 132; CN 1, 2, 3, 4, 5, 6, 7; DLB 2, 218; EWL 3; INT CANR-19; MAL 5; MTCW 1; RGAL 4
Pure, Simon
See Swinnerton, Frank Arthur
Pushkin, Aleksandr Sergeevich
See Pushkin, Alexander (Sergeyevich)
See also DLB 205
Pushkin, Alexander (Sergeyevich)
1799-1837 .... **NCLC 3, 27, 83; PC 10; SSC 27, 55; WLC**
See Pushkin, Aleksandr Sergeevich
See also DA; DA3; DAB; DAC; DAM DRAM, MST, POET; EW 5; EXPS; RGSF 2; RGWL 2, 3; SATA 61; SSFS 9; TWA
P'u Sung-ling 1640-1715 .... **LC 49; SSC 31**
Putnam, Arthur Lee
See Alger, Horatio, Jr.
Puttenham, George 1529(?)-1590 ...... **LC 116**
See also DLB 281
Puzo, Mario 1920-1999 .... **CLC 1, 2, 6, 36, 107**
See also BPFB 3; CA 65-68; 185; CANR 4, 42, 65, 99, 131; CN 1, 2, 3, 4, 5, 6; CPW; DA3; DAM NOV, POP; DLB 6; MTCW 1, 2; MTFW 2005; NFS 16; RGAL 4
Pygge, Edward
See Barnes, Julian (Patrick)
Pyle, Ernest Taylor 1900-1945
See Pyle, Ernie
See also CA 115; 160
Pyle, Ernie .... **TCLC 75**
See Pyle, Ernest Taylor
See also DLB 29; MTCW 2
Pyle, Howard 1853-1911 .... **TCLC 81**
See also AAYA 57; BYA 2, 4; CA 109; 137; CLR 22; DLB 42, 188; DLBD 13; LAIT 1; MAICYA 1, 2; SATA 16, 100; WCH; YAW
Pym, Barbara (Mary Crampton)
1913-1980 .... **CLC 13, 19, 37, 111**
See also BPFB 3; BRWS 2; CA 13-14; 97-100; CANR 13, 34; CAP 1; DLB 14, 207; DLBY 1987; EWL 3; MTCW 1, 2; MTFW 2005; RGEL 2; TEA
Pynchon, Thomas (Ruggles, Jr.)
1937- ...... **CLC 2, 3, 6, 9, 11, 18, 33, 62, 72, 123, 192, 213; SSC 14, 84; WLC**
See also AMWS 2; BEST 90:2; BPFB 3; CA 17-20R; CANR 22, 46, 73, 142; CN 1, 2, 3, 4, 5, 6, 7; CPW 1; DA; DA3; DAB; DAC; DAM MST, NOV, POP; DLB 2, 173; EWL 3; MAL 5; MTCW 1, 2; MTFW 2005; RGAL 4; SFW 4; TCLE 1:2; TUS
Pythagoras c. 582B.C.-c. 507B.C. . **CMLC 22**
See also DLB 176

Q
See Quiller-Couch, Sir Arthur (Thomas)
Qian, Chongzhu
See Ch'ien, Chung-shu
Qian, Sima 145B.C.-c. 89B.C. .... **CMLC 72**
Qian Zhongshu
See Ch'ien, Chung-shu
See also CWW 2
Qroll
See Dagerman, Stig (Halvard)

Quarles, Francis 1592-1644 .... **LC 117**
See also DLB 126; RGEL 2
Quarrington, Paul (Lewis) 1953- ..... **CLC 65**
See also CA 129; CANR 62, 95
Quasimodo, Salvatore 1901-1968 .... **CLC 10; PC 47**
See also CA 13-16; 25-28R; CAP 1; DLB 114; EW 12; EWL 3; MTCW 1; RGWL 2, 3
Quatermass, Martin
See Carpenter, John (Howard)
Quay, Stephen 1947- .... **CLC 95**
See also CA 189
Quay, Timothy 1947- .... **CLC 95**
See also CA 189
Queen, Ellery .... **CLC 3, 11**
See Dannay, Frederic; Davidson, Avram (James); Deming, Richard; Fairman, Paul W.; Flora, Fletcher; Hoch, Edward D(entinger); Kane, Henry; Lee, Manfred B(ennington); Marlowe, Stephen; Powell, (Oval) Talmage; Sheldon, Walter J(ames); Sturgeon, Theodore (Hamilton); Tracy, Don(ald Fiske); Vance, John Holbrook
See also BPFB 3; CMW 4; MSW; RGAL 4
Queen, Ellery, Jr.
See Dannay, Frederic; Lee, Manfred B(ennington)
Queneau, Raymond 1903-1976 ..... **CLC 2, 5, 10, 42**
See also CA 77-80; 69-72; CANR 32; DLB 72, 258; EW 12; EWL 3; GFL 1789 to the Present; MTCW 1, 2; RGWL 2, 3
Quevedo, Francisco de 1580-1645 .... **LC 23**
Quiller-Couch, Sir Arthur (Thomas)
1863-1944 .... **TCLC 53**
See also CA 118; 166; DLB 135, 153, 190; HGG; RGEL 2; SUFW 1
Quin, Ann (Marie) 1936-1973 .... **CLC 6**
See also CA 9-12R; 45-48; CN 1; DLB 14, 231
Quincey, Thomas de
See De Quincey, Thomas
Quindlen, Anna 1953- .... **CLC 191**
See also AAYA 35; CA 138; CANR 73, 126; DA3; DLB 292; MTCW 2; MTFW 2005
Quinn, Martin
See Smith, Martin Cruz
Quinn, Peter 1947- .... **CLC 91**
See also CA 197
Quinn, Simon
See Smith, Martin Cruz
Quintana, Leroy V. 1944- ...... **HLC 2; PC 36**
See also CA 131; CANR 65, 139; DAM MULT; DLB 82; HW 1, 2
Quintilian c. 40-c. 100 .... **CMLC 77**
See also AW 2; DLB 211; RGWL 2, 3
Quintillian 0035-0100 .... **CMLC 77**
Quiroga, Horacio (Sylvestre)
1878-1937 ... **HLC 2; SSC 89; TCLC 20**
See also CA 117; 131; DAM MULT; EWL 3; HW 1; LAW; MTCW 1; RGSF 2; WLIT 1
Quoirez, Francoise 1935-2004 .... **CLC 9**
See Sagan, Francoise
See also CA 49-52; 231; CANR 6, 39, 73; MTCW 1, 2; MTFW 2005; TWA
Raabe, Wilhelm (Karl) 1831-1910 . **TCLC 45**
See also CA 167; DLB 129
Rabe, David (William) 1940- .. **CLC 4, 8, 33, 200; DC 16**
See also CA 85-88; CABS 3; CAD; CANR 59, 129; CD 5, 6; DAM DRAM; DFS 3, 8, 13; DLB 7, 228; EWL 3; MAL 5
Rabelais, Francois 1494-1553 .... **LC 5, 60; WLC**
See also DA; DAB; DAC; DAM MST; EW 2; GFL Beginnings to 1789; LMFS 1; RGWL 2, 3; TWA

Remarque, Erich Maria 1898-1970 . **CLC 21**
See also AAYA 27; BPFB 3; CA 77-80; 29-32R; CDWLB 2; DA; DA3; DAB; DAC; DAM MST, NOV; DLB 56; EWL 3; EXPN; LAIT 3; MTCW 1, 2; MTFW 2005; NFS 4; RGWL 2, 3

Remington, Frederic S(ackrider)
1861-1909 .... **TCLC 89**
See also CA 108; 169; DLB 12, 186, 188; SATA 41; TCWW 2

Remizov, A.
See Remizov, Aleksei (Mikhailovich)

Remizov, A. M.
See Remizov, Aleksei (Mikhailovich)

Remizov, Aleksei (Mikhailovich)
1877-1957 .... **TCLC 27**
See Remizov, Alexey Mikhaylovich
See also CA 125; 133; DLB 295

Remizov, Alexey Mikhaylovich
See Remizov, Aleksei (Mikhailovich)
See also EWL 3

Renan, Joseph Ernest 1823-1892 . **NCLC 26, 145**
See also GFL 1789 to the Present

Renard, Jules(-Pierre) 1864-1910 .. **TCLC 17**
See also CA 117; 202; GFL 1789 to the Present

Renart, Jean fl. c. early 13th cent. .... **CMLC 83**

Renault, Mary .... **CLC 3, 11, 17**
See Challans, Mary
See also BPFB 3; BYA 2; CN 1, 2, 3; DLBY 1983; EWL 3; GLL 1; LAIT 1; RGEL 2; RHW

Rendell, Ruth (Barbara) 1930- .. **CLC 28, 48**
See Vine, Barbara
See also BPFB 3; BRWS 9; CA 109; CANR 32, 52, 74, 127; CN 5, 6, 7; CPW; DAM POP; DLB 87, 276; INT CANR-32; MSW; MTCW 1, 2; MTFW 2005

Renoir, Jean 1894-1979 .... **CLC 20**
See also CA 129; 85-88

Resnais, Alain 1922- .... **CLC 16**

Revard, Carter (Curtis) 1931- .... **NNAL**
See also CA 144; CANR 81; PFS 5

Reverdy, Pierre 1889-1960 .... **CLC 53**
See also CA 97-100; 89-92; DLB 258; EWL 3; GFL 1789 to the Present

Rexroth, Kenneth 1905-1982 .... **CLC 1, 2, 6, 11, 22, 49, 112; PC 20**
See also BG 1:3; CA 5-8R; 107; CANR 14, 34, 63; CDALB 1941-1968; CP 1, 2, 3; DAM POET; DLB 16, 48, 165, 212; DLBY 1982; EWL 3; INT CANR-14; MAL 5; MTCW 1, 2; MTFW 2005; RGAL 4

Reyes, Alfonso 1889-1959 .... **HLCS 2; TCLC 33**
See also CA 131; EWL 3; HW 1; LAW

Reyes y Basoalto, Ricardo Eliecer Neftali
See Neruda, Pablo

Reymont, Wladyslaw (Stanislaw)
1868(?)-1925 .... **TCLC 5**
See also CA 104; EWL 3

Reynolds, John Hamilton
1794-1852 .... **NCLC 146**
See also DLB 96

Reynolds, Jonathan 1942- .... **CLC 6, 38**
See also CA 65-68; CANR 28

Reynolds, Joshua 1723-1792 .... **LC 15**
See also DLB 104

Reynolds, Michael S(hane)
1937-2000 .... **CLC 44**
See also CA 65-68; 189; CANR 9, 89, 97

Reznikoff, Charles 1894-1976 .... **CLC 9**
See also AMWS 14; CA 33-36; 61-64; CAP 2; CP 1, 2; DLB 28, 45; WP

Rezzori (d'Arezzo), Gregor von
1914-1998 .... **CLC 25**
See also CA 122; 136; 167

Rhine, Richard
See Silverstein, Alvin; Silverstein, Virginia B(arbara Opshelor)

Rhodes, Eugene Manlove
1869-1934 .... **TCLC 53**
See also CA 198; DLB 256; TCWW 1, 2

R'hoone, Lord
See Balzac, Honore de

Rhys, Jean 1890-1979 .... **CLC 2, 4, 6, 14, 19, 51, 124; SSC 21, 76**
See also BRWS 2; CA 25-28R; 85-88; CANR 35, 62; CDBLB 1945-1960; CDWLB 3; CN 1, 2; DA3; DAM NOV; DLB 36, 117, 162; DNFS 2; EWL 3; LATS 1:1; MTCW 1, 2; MTFW 2005; NFS 19; RGEL 2; RGSF 2; RHW; TEA; WWE 1

Ribeiro, Darcy 1922-1997 .... **CLC 34**
See also CA 33-36R; 156; EWL 3

Ribeiro, Joao Ubaldo (Osorio Pimentel)
1941- .... **CLC 10, 67**
See also CA 81-84; CWW 2; EWL 3

Ribman, Ronald (Burt) 1932- .... **CLC 7**
See also CA 21-24R; CAD; CANR 46, 80; CD 5, 6

Ricci, Nino (Pio) 1959- .... **CLC 70**
See also CA 137; CANR 130; CCA 1

Rice, Anne 1941- .... **CLC 41, 128**
See Rampling, Anne
See also AAYA 9, 53; AMWS 7; BEST 89:2; BPFB 3; CA 65-68; CANR 12, 36, 53, 74, 100, 133; CN 6, 7; CPW; CSW; DA3; DAM POP; DLB 292; GL 3; GLL 2; HGG; MTCW 1, 2; MTFW 2005; SUFW 2; YAW

Rice, Elmer (Leopold) 1892-1967 ...... **CLC 7, 49**
See Reizenstein, Elmer Leopold
See also CA 21-22; 25-28R; CAP 2; DAM DRAM; DFS 12; DLB 4, 7; IDTP; MAL 5; MTCW 1, 2; RGAL 4

Rice, Tim(othy Miles Bindon)
1944- .... **CLC 21**
See also CA 103; CANR 46; DFS 7

Rich, Adrienne (Cecile) 1929- ... **CLC 3, 6, 7, 11, 18, 36, 73, 76, 125; PC 5**
See also AMWR 2; AMWS 1; CA 9-12R; CANR 20, 53, 74, 128; CDALBS; CP 1, 2, 3, 4, 5, 6, 7; CSW; CWP; DA3; DAM POET; DLB 5, 67; EWL 3; EXPP; FL 1:6; FW; MAL 5; MAWW; MTCW 1, 2; MTFW 2005; PAB; PFS 15; RGAL 4; WP

Rich, Barbara
See Graves, Robert (von Ranke)

Rich, Robert
See Trumbo, Dalton

Richard, Keith .... **CLC 17**
See Richards, Keith

Richards, David Adams 1950- .... **CLC 59**
See also CA 93-96; CANR 60, 110; CN 7; DAC; DLB 53; TCLE 1:2

Richards, I(vor) A(rmstrong)
1893-1979 .... **CLC 14, 24**
See also BRWS 2; CA 41-44R; 89-92; CANR 34, 74; CP 1, 2; DLB 27; EWL 3; MTCW 2; RGEL 2

Richards, Keith 1943-
See Richard, Keith
See also CA 107; CANR 77

Richardson, Anne
See Roiphe, Anne (Richardson)

Richardson, Dorothy Miller
1873-1957 .... **TCLC 3**
See also CA 104; 192; DLB 36; EWL 3; FW; RGEL 2

Richardson (Robertson), Ethel Florence Lindesay 1870-1946
See Richardson, Henry Handel
See also CA 105; 190; DLB 230; RHW

Richardson, Henry Handel .... **TCLC 4**
See Richardson (Robertson), Ethel Florence Lindesay
See also DLB 197; EWL 3; RGEL 2; RGSF 2

Richardson, John 1796-1852 .... **NCLC 55**
See also CCA 1; DAC; DLB 99

Richardson, Samuel 1689-1761 ...... **LC 1, 44; WLC**
See also BRW 3; CDBLB 1660-1789; DA; DAB; DAC; DAM MST, NOV; DLB 39; RGEL 2; TEA; WLIT 3

Richardson, Willis 1889-1977 .... **HR 1:3**
See also BW 1; CA 124; DLB 51; SATA 60

Richler, Mordecai 1931-2001 .... **CLC 3, 5, 9, 13, 18, 46, 70, 185**
See also AITN 1; CA 65-68; 201; CANR 31, 62, 111; CCA 1; CLR 17; CN 1, 2, 3, 4, 5, 7; CWRI 5; DAC; DAM MST, NOV; DLB 53; EWL 3; MAICYA 1, 2; MTCW 1, 2; MTFW 2005; RGEL 2; SATA 44, 98; SATA-Brief 27; TWA

Richter, Conrad (Michael)
1890-1968 .... **CLC 30**
See also AAYA 21; BYA 2; CA 5-8R; 25-28R; CANR 23; DLB 9, 212; LAIT 1; MAL 5; MTCW 1, 2; MTFW 2005; RGAL 4; SATA 3; TCWW 1, 2; TUS; YAW

Ricostranza, Tom
See Ellis, Trey

Riddell, Charlotte 1832-1906 .... **TCLC 40**
See Riddell, Mrs. J. H.
See also CA 165; DLB 156

Riddell, Mrs. J. H.
See Riddell, Charlotte
See also HGG; SUFW

Ridge, John Rollin 1827-1867 ...... **NCLC 82; NNAL**
See also CA 144; DAM MULT; DLB 175

Ridgeway, Jason
See Marlowe, Stephen

Ridgway, Keith 1965- .... **CLC 119**
See also CA 172; CANR 144

Riding, Laura .... **CLC 3, 7**
See Jackson, Laura (Riding)
See also CP 1, 2, 3, 4; RGAL 4

Riefenstahl, Berta Helene Amalia 1902-2003
See Riefenstahl, Leni
See also CA 108; 220

Riefenstahl, Leni .... **CLC 16, 190**
See Riefenstahl, Berta Helene Amalia

Riffe, Ernest
See Bergman, (Ernst) Ingmar

Riggs, (Rolla) Lynn
1899-1954 .... **NNAL; TCLC 56**
See also CA 144; DAM MULT; DLB 175

Riis, Jacob A(ugust) 1849-1914 ..... **TCLC 80**
See also CA 113; 168; DLB 23

Riley, James Whitcomb 1849-1916 .... **PC 48; TCLC 51**
See also CA 118; 137; DAM POET; MAICYA 1, 2; RGAL 4; SATA 17

Riley, Tex
See Creasey, John

Rilke, Rainer Maria 1875-1926 .... **PC 2; TCLC 1, 6, 19**
See also CA 104; 132; CANR 62, 99; CDWLB 2; DA3; DAM POET; DLB 81; EW 9; EWL 3; MTCW 1, 2; MTFW 2005; PFS 19; RGWL 2, 3; TWA; WP

Runyon, (Alfred) Damon
1884(?)-1946 .... **TCLC 10**
See also CA 107; 165; DLB 11, 86, 171;
MAL 5; MTCW 2; RGAL 4
Rush, Norman 1933- .... **CLC 44**
See also CA 121; 126; CANR 130; INT CA-
126
Rushdie, (Ahmed) Salman 1947- .... **CLC 23,**
31, 55, 100, 191; SSC 83; WLCS
See also AAYA 65; BEST 89:3; BPFB 3;
BRWS 4; CA 108; 111; CANR 33, 56,
108, 133; CN 4, 5, 6, 7; CPW 1; DA3;
DAB; DAC; DAM MST, NOV, POP;
DLB 194; EWL 3; FANT; INT CA-111;
LATS 1:2; LMFS 2; MTCW 1, 2; MTFW
2005; NFS 22; RGEL 2; RGSF 2; TEA;
WLIT 4
Rushforth, Peter (Scott) 1945- .... **CLC 19**
See also CA 101
Ruskin, John 1819-1900 .... **TCLC 63**
See also BRW 5; BYA 5; CA 114; 129; CD-
BLB 1832-1890; DLB 55, 163, 190;
RGEL 2; SATA 24; TEA; WCH
Russ, Joanna 1937- .... **CLC 15**
See also BPFB 3; CA 25-28; CANR 11, 31,
65; CN 4, 5, 6, 7; DLB 8; FW; GLL 1;
MTCW 1; SCFW 1, 2; SFW 4
Russ, Richard Patrick
See O'Brian, Patrick
Russell, George William 1867-1935
See A.E.; Baker, Jean H.
See also BRWS 8; CA 104; 153; CDBLB
1890-1914; DAM POET; EWL 3; RGEL
2
Russell, Jeffrey Burton 1934- .... **CLC 70**
See also CA 25-28R; CANR 11, 28, 52
Russell, (Henry) Ken(neth Alfred)
1927- .... **CLC 16**
See also CA 105
Russell, William Martin 1947-
See Russell, Willy
See also CA 164; CANR 107
Russell, Willy .... **CLC 60**
See Russell, William Martin
See also CBD; CD 5, 6; DLB 233
Russo, Richard 1949- .... **CLC 181**
See also AMWS 12; CA 127; 133; CANR
87, 114
Rutherford, Mark .... **TCLC 25**
See White, William Hale
See also DLB 18; RGEL 2
Ruyslinck, Ward .... **CLC 14**
See Belser, Reimond Karel Maria de
Ryan, Cornelius (John) 1920-1974 ..... **CLC 7**
See also CA 69-72; 53-56; CANR 38
Ryan, Michael 1946- .... **CLC 65**
See also CA 49-52; CANR 109; DLBY
1982
Ryan, Tim
See Dent, Lester
Rybakov, Anatoli (Naumovich)
1911-1998 .... **CLC 23, 53**
See Rybakov, Anatolii (Naumovich)
See also CA 126; 135; 172; SATA 79;
SATA-Obit 108
Rybakov, Anatolii (Naumovich)
See Rybakov, Anatoli (Naumovich)
See also DLB 302
Ryder, Jonathan
See Ludlum, Robert
Ryga, George 1932-1987 .... **CLC 14**
See also CA 101; 124; CANR 43, 90; CCA
1; DAC; DAM MST; DLB 60
S. H.
See Hartmann, Sadakichi
S. S.
See Sassoon, Siegfried (Lorraine)

Sa'adawi, al- Nawal
See El Saadawi, Nawal
See also AFW; EWL 3
Saadawi, Nawal El
See El Saadawi, Nawal
See also WLIT 2
Saba, Umberto 1883-1957 .... **TCLC 33**
See also CA 144; CANR 79; DLB 114;
EWL 3; RGWL 2, 3
Sabatini, Rafael 1875-1950 .... **TCLC 47**
See also BPFB 3; CA 162; RHW
Sabato, Ernesto (R.) 1911- .... **CLC 10, 23;**
HLC 2
See also CA 97-100; CANR 32, 65; CD-
WLB 3; CWW 2; DAM MULT; DLB 145;
EWL 3; HW 1, 2; LAW; MTCW 1, 2;
MTFW 2005
Sa-Carneiro, Mario de 1890-1916 . **TCLC 83**
See also DLB 287; EWL 3
Sacastru, Martin
See Bioy Casares, Adolfo
See also CWW 2
Sacher-Masoch, Leopold von
1836(?)-1895 .... **NCLC 31**
Sachs, Hans 1494-1576 .... **LC 95**
See also CDWLB 2; DLB 179; RGWL 2, 3
Sachs, Marilyn 1927- .... **CLC 35**
See also AAYA 2; BYA 6; CA 17-20R;
CANR 13, 47; CLR 2; JRDA; MAICYA
1, 2; SAAS 2; SATA 3, 68, 164; SATA-
Essay 110; WYA; YAW
Sachs, Marilyn Stickle
See Sachs, Marilyn
Sachs, Nelly 1891-1970 .... **CLC 14, 98**
See also CA 17-18; 25-28R; CANR 87;
CAP 2; EWL 3; MTCW 2; MTFW 2005;
PFS 20; RGWL 2, 3
Sackler, Howard (Oliver)
1929-1982 .... **CLC 14**
See also CA 61-64; 108; CAD; CANR 30;
DFS 15; DLB 7
Sacks, Oliver (Wolf) 1933- .... **CLC 67, 202**
See also CA 53-56; CANR 28, 50, 76;
CPW; DA3; INT CANR-28; MTCW 1, 2;
MTFW 2005
Sackville, Thomas 1536-1608 .... **LC 98**
See also DAM DRAM; DLB 62, 132;
RGEL 2
Sadakichi
See Hartmann, Sadakichi
Sa'dawi, Nawal al-
See El Saadawi, Nawal
See also CWW 2
Sade, Donatien Alphonse Francois
1740-1814 .... **NCLC 3, 47**
See also DLB 314; EW 4; GFL Beginnings
to 1789; RGWL 2, 3
Sade, Marquis de
See Sade, Donatien Alphonse Francois
Sadoff, Ira 1945- .... **CLC 9**
See also CA 53-56; CANR 5, 21, 109; DLB
120
Saetone
See Camus, Albert
Safire, William 1929- .... **CLC 10**
See also CA 17-20R; CANR 31, 54, 91
Sagan, Carl (Edward) 1934-1996 .... **CLC 30,**
112
See also AAYA 2, 62; CA 25-28R; 155;
CANR 11, 36, 74; CPW; DA3; MTCW 1,
2; MTFW 2005; SATA 58; SATA-Obit 94
Sagan, Francoise .... **CLC 3, 6, 9, 17, 36**
See Quoirez, Francoise
See also CWW 2; DLB 83; EWL 3; GFL
1789 to the Present; MTCW 2
Sahgal, Nayantara (Pandit) 1927- .... **CLC 41**
See also CA 9-12R; CANR 11, 88; CN 1,
2, 3, 4, 5, 6, 7

Said, Edward W. 1935-2003 .... **CLC 123**
See also CA 21-24R; 220; CANR 45, 74,
107, 131; DLB 67; MTCW 2; MTFW
2005
Saint, H(arry) F. 1941- .... **CLC 50**
See also CA 127
St. Aubin de Teran, Lisa 1953-
See Teran, Lisa St. Aubin de
See also CA 118; 126; CN 6, 7; INT CA-
126
Saint Birgitta of Sweden c.
1303-1373 .... **CMLC 24**
Saint Gregory of Nazianzus
329-389 .... **CMLC 82**
Sainte-Beuve, Charles Augustin
1804-1869 .... **NCLC 5**
See also DLB 217; EW 6; GFL 1789 to the
Present
Saint-Exupery, Antoine (Jean Baptiste
Marie Roger) de 1900-1944 .... **TCLC 2,**
56, 169; WLC
See also AAYA 63; BPFB 3; BYA 3; CA
108; 132; CLR 10; DA3; DAM NOV;
DLB 72; EW 12; EWL 3; GFL 1789 to
the Present; LAIT 3; MAICYA 1, 2;
MTCW 1, 2; MTFW 2005; RGWL 2, 3;
SATA 20; TWA
St. John, David
See Hunt, E(verette) Howard, (Jr.)
St. John, J. Hector
See Crevecoeur, Michel Guillaume Jean de
Saint-John Perse
See Leger, (Marie-Rene Auguste) Alexis
Saint-Leger
See also EW 10; EWL 3; GFL 1789 to the
Present; RGWL 2
Saintsbury, George (Edward Bateman)
1845-1933 .... **TCLC 31**
See also CA 160; DLB 57, 149
Sait Faik .... **TCLC 23**
See Abasiyanik, Sait Faik
Saki .... **SSC 12; TCLC 3**
See Munro, H(ector) H(ugh)
See also BRWS 6; BYA 11; LAIT 2; RGEL
2; SSFS 1; SUFW
Sala, George Augustus 1828-1895 . **NCLC 46**
Saladin 1138-1193 .... **CMLC 38**
Salama, Hannu 1936- .... **CLC 18**
See also EWL 3
Salamanca, J(ack) R(ichard) 1922- .. **CLC 4,**
15
See also CA 25-28R, 193; CAAE 193
Salas, Floyd Francis 1931- .... **HLC 2**
See also CA 119; CAAS 27; CANR 44, 75,
93; DAM MULT; DLB 82; HW 1, 2;
MTCW 2; MTFW 2005
Sale, J. Kirkpatrick
See Sale, Kirkpatrick
Sale, Kirkpatrick 1937- .... **CLC 68**
See also CA 13-16R; CANR 10
Salinas, Luis Omar 1937- ... **CLC 90; HLC 2**
See also AMWS 13; CA 131; CANR 81;
DAM MULT; DLB 82; HW 1, 2
Salinas (y Serrano), Pedro
1891(?)-1951 .... **TCLC 17**
See also CA 117; DLB 134; EWL 3
Salinger, J(erome) D(avid) 1919- .. **CLC 1, 3,**
8, 12, 55, 56, 138; SSC 2, 28, 65; WLC
See also AAYA 2, 36; AMW; AMWC 1;
BPFB 3; CA 5-8R; CANR 39, 129;
CDALB 1941-1968; CLR 18; CN 1, 2, 3,
4, 5, 6, 7; CPW 1; DA; DA3; DAB; DAC;
DAM MST, NOV, POP; DLB 2, 102, 173;
EWL 3; EXPN; LAIT 4; MAICYA 1, 2;
MAL 5; MTCW 1, 2; MTFW 2005; NFS
1; RGAL 4; RGSF 2; SATA 67; SSFS 17;
TUS; WYA; YAW
Salisbury, John
See Caute, (John) David

Scarlett, Susan
　See Streatfeild, (Mary) Noel
Scarron 1847-1910
　See Mikszath, Kalman
Scarron, Paul 1610-1660 .... **LC 116**
　See also GFL Beginnings to 1789; RGWL
　2, 3
Schaeffer, Susan Fromberg 1941- ..... **CLC 6,
　11, 22**
　See also CA 49-52; CANR 18, 65; CN 4, 5,
　6, 7; DLB 28, 299; MTCW 1, 2; MTFW
　2005; SATA 22
Schama, Simon (Michael) 1945- ..... **CLC 150**
　See also BEST 89:4; CA 105; CANR 39,
　91
Schary, Jill
　See Robinson, Jill
Schell, Jonathan 1943- .... **CLC 35**
　See also CA 73-76; CANR 12, 117
Schelling, Friedrich Wilhelm Joseph von
　1775-1854 .... **NCLC 30**
　See also DLB 90
Scherer, Jean-Marie Maurice 1920-
　See Rohmer, Eric
　See also CA 110
Schevill, James (Erwin) 1920- .... **CLC 7**
　See also CA 5-8R; CAAS 12; CAD; CD 5,
　6; CP 1, 2, 3, 4
Schiller, Friedrich von 1759-1805 ...... **DC 12;
　NCLC 39, 69**
　See also CDWLB 2; DAM DRAM; DLB
　94; EW 5; RGWL 2, 3; TWA
Schisgal, Murray (Joseph) 1926- .... **CLC 6**
　See also CA 21-24R; CAD; CANR 48, 86;
　CD 5, 6; MAL 5
Schlee, Ann 1934- .... **CLC 35**
　See also CA 101; CANR 29, 88; SATA 44;
　SATA-Brief 36
Schlegel, August Wilhelm von
　1767-1845 .... **NCLC 15, 142**
　See also DLB 94; RGWL 2, 3
Schlegel, Friedrich 1772-1829 .... **NCLC 45**
　See also DLB 90; EW 5; RGWL 2, 3; TWA
Schlegel, Johann Elias (von)
　1719(?)-1749 .... **LC 5**
Schleiermacher, Friedrich
　1768-1834 .... **NCLC 107**
　See also DLB 90
Schlesinger, Arthur M(eier), Jr.
　1917- .... **CLC 84**
　See also AITN 1; CA 1-4R; CANR 1, 28,
　58, 105; DLB 17; INT CANR-28; MTCW
　1, 2; SATA 61
Schlink, Bernhard 1944- .... **CLC 174**
　See also CA 163; CANR 116
Schmidt, Arno (Otto) 1914-1979 ...... **CLC 56**
　See also CA 128; 109; DLB 69; EWL 3
Schmitz, Aron Hector 1861-1928
　See Svevo, Italo
　See also CA 104; 122; MTCW 1
Schnackenberg, Gjertrud (Cecelia)
　1953- .... **CLC 40; PC 45**
　See also AMWS 15; CA 116; CANR 100;
　CP 7; CWP; DLB 120, 282; PFS 13
Schneider, Leonard Alfred 1925-1966
　See Bruce, Lenny
　See also CA 89-92
Schnitzler, Arthur 1862-1931 ..... **DC 17; SSC
　15, 61; TCLC 4**
　See also CA 104; CDWLB 2; DLB 81, 118;
　EW 8; EWL 3; RGSF 2; RGWL 2, 3
Schoenberg, Arnold Franz Walter
　1874-1951 .... **TCLC 75**
　See also CA 109; 188
Schonberg, Arnold
　See Schoenberg, Arnold Franz Walter
Schopenhauer, Arthur 1788-1860 . **NCLC 51,
　157**
　See also DLB 90; EW 5

Schor, Sandra (M.) 1932(?)-1990 ..... **CLC 65**
　See also CA 132
Schorer, Mark 1908-1977 .... **CLC 9**
　See also CA 5-8R; 73-76; CANR 7; CN 1,
　2; DLB 103
Schrader, Paul (Joseph) 1946- . **CLC 26, 212**
　See also CA 37-40R; CANR 41; DLB 44
Schreber, Daniel 1842-1911 .... **TCLC 123**
Schreiner, Olive (Emilie Albertina)
　1855-1920 .... **TCLC 9**
　See also AFW; BRWS 2; CA 105; 154;
　DLB 18, 156, 190, 225; EWL 3; FW;
　RGEL 2; TWA; WLIT 2; WWE 1
Schulberg, Budd (Wilson) 1914- .. **CLC 7, 48**
　See also BPFB 3; CA 25-28R; CANR 19,
　87; CN 1, 2, 3, 4, 5, 6, 7; DLB 6, 26, 28;
　DLBY 1981, 2001; MAL 5
Schulman, Arnold
　See Trumbo, Dalton
Schulz, Bruno 1892-1942 .. **SSC 13; TCLC 5,
　51**
　See also CA 115; 123; CANR 86; CDWLB
　4; DLB 215; EWL 3; MTCW 2; MTFW
　2005; RGSF 2; RGWL 2, 3
Schulz, Charles M. 1922-2000 .... **CLC 12**
　See also AAYA 39; CA 9-12R; 187; CANR
　6, 132; INT CANR-6; MTFW 2005;
　SATA 10; SATA-Obit 118
Schulz, Charles Monroe
　See Schulz, Charles M.
Schumacher, E(rnst) F(riedrich)
　1911-1977 .... **CLC 80**
　See also CA 81-84; 73-76; CANR 34, 85
Schumann, Robert 1810-1856 ...... **NCLC 143**
Schuyler, George Samuel 1895-1977 . **HR 1:3**
　See also BW 2; CA 81-84; 73-76; CANR
　42; DLB 29, 51
Schuyler, James Marcus 1923-1991 .. **CLC 5,
　23**
　See also CA 101; 134; CP 1, 2, 3, 4; DAM
　POET; DLB 5, 169; EWL 3; INT CA-101;
　MAL 5; WP
Schwartz, Delmore (David)
　1913-1966 ... **CLC 2, 4, 10, 45, 87; PC 8**
　See also AMWS 2; CA 17-18; 25-28R;
　CANR 35; CAP 2; DLB 28, 48; EWL 3;
　MAL 5; MTCW 1, 2; MTFW 2005; PAB;
　RGAL 4; TUS
Schwartz, Ernst
　See Ozu, Yasujiro
Schwartz, John Burnham 1965- .... **CLC 59**
　See also CA 132; CANR 116
Schwartz, Lynne Sharon 1939- .... **CLC 31**
　See also CA 103; CANR 44, 89; DLB 218;
　MTCW 2; MTFW 2005
Schwartz, Muriel A.
　See Eliot, T(homas) S(tearns)
Schwarz-Bart, Andre 1928- .... **CLC 2, 4**
　See also CA 89-92; CANR 109; DLB 299
Schwarz-Bart, Simone 1938- . **BLCS; CLC 7**
　See also BW 2; CA 97-100; CANR 117;
　EWL 3
Schwerner, Armand 1927-1999 .... **PC 42**
　See also CA 9-12R; 179; CANR 50, 85; CP
　2, 3, 4; DLB 165
**Schwitters, Kurt (Hermann Edward Karl
　Julius)** 1887-1948 .... **TCLC 95**
　See also CA 158
Schwob, Marcel (Mayer Andre)
　1867-1905 .... **TCLC 20**
　See also CA 117; 168; DLB 123; GFL 1789
　to the Present
Sciascia, Leonardo 1921-1989 .. **CLC 8, 9, 41**
　See also CA 85-88; 130; CANR 35; DLB
　177; EWL 3; MTCW 1; RGWL 2, 3

Scoppettone, Sandra 1936- .... **CLC 26**
　See Early, Jack
　See also AAYA 11, 65; BYA 8; CA 5-8R;
　CANR 41, 73; GLL 1; MAICYA 2; MAI-
　CYAS 1; SATA 9, 92; WYA; YAW
Scorsese, Martin 1942- .... **CLC 20, 89, 207**
　See also AAYA 38; CA 110; 114; CANR
　46, 85
Scotland, Jay
　See Jakes, John (William)
Scott, Duncan Campbell
　1862-1947 .... **TCLC 6**
　See also CA 104; 153; DAC; DLB 92;
　RGEL 2
Scott, Evelyn 1893-1963 .... **CLC 43**
　See also CA 104; 112; CANR 64; DLB 9,
　48; RHW
Scott, F(rancis) R(eginald)
　1899-1985 .... **CLC 22**
　See also CA 101; 114; CANR 87; CP 1, 2,
　3, 4; DLB 88; INT CA-101; RGEL 2
Scott, Frank
　See Scott, F(rancis) R(eginald)
Scott, Joan .... **CLC 65**
Scott, Joanna 1960- .... **CLC 50**
　See also CA 126; CANR 53, 92
Scott, Paul (Mark) 1920-1978 ...... **CLC 9, 60**
　See also BRWS 1; CA 81-84; 77-80; CANR
　33; CN 1, 2; DLB 14, 207; EWL 3;
　MTCW 1; RGEL 2; RHW; WWE 1
Scott, Ridley 1937- .... **CLC 183**
　See also AAYA 13, 43
Scott, Sarah 1723-1795 .... **LC 44**
　See also DLB 39
Scott, Sir Walter 1771-1832 .... **NCLC 15, 69,
　110; PC 13; SSC 32; WLC**
　See also AAYA 22; BRW 4; BYA 2; CD-
　BLB 1789-1832; DA; DAB; DAC; DAM
　MST, NOV, POET; DLB 93, 107, 116,
　144, 159; GL 3; HGG; LAIT 1; RGEL 2;
　RGSF 2; SSFS 10; SUFW 1; TEA; WLIT
　3; YABC 2
Scribe, (Augustin) Eugene 1791-1861 . **DC 5;
　NCLC 16**
　See also DAM DRAM; DLB 192; GFL
　1789 to the Present; RGWL 2, 3
Scrum, R.
　See Crumb, R(obert)
Scudery, Georges de 1601-1667 .... **LC 75**
　See also GFL Beginnings to 1789
Scudery, Madeleine de 1607-1701 .. **LC 2, 58**
　See also DLB 268; GFL Beginnings to 1789
Scum
　See Crumb, R(obert)
Scumbag, Little Bobby
　See Crumb, R(obert)
Seabrook, John
　See Hubbard, L(afayette) Ron(ald)
Seacole, Mary Jane Grant
　1805-1881 .... **NCLC 147**
　See also DLB 166
Sealy, I(rwin) Allan 1951- .... **CLC 55**
　See also CA 136; CN 6, 7
Search, Alexander
　See Pessoa, Fernando (Antonio Nogueira)
Sebald, W(infried) G(eorg)
　1944-2001 .... **CLC 194**
　See also BRWS 8; CA 159; 202; CANR 98;
　MTFW 2005
Sebastian, Lee
　See Silverberg, Robert
Sebastian Owl
　See Thompson, Hunter S(tockton)
Sebestyen, Igen
　See Sebestyen, Ouida
Sebestyen, Ouida 1924- .... **CLC 30**
　See also AAYA 8; BYA 7; CA 107; CANR
　40, 114; CLR 17; JRDA; MAICYA 1, 2;
　SAAS 10; SATA 39, 140; WYA; YAW

Shaw, Irwin 1913-1984 .... **CLC 7, 23, 34**
    See also AITN 1; BPFB 3; CA 13-16R; 112;
    CANR 21; CDALB 1941-1968; CN 1, 2,
    3; CPW; DAM DRAM, POP; DLB 6,
    102; DLBY 1984; MAL 5; MTCW 1, 21;
    MTFW 2005
Shaw, Robert (Archibald)
    1927-1978 .... **CLC 5**
    See also AITN 1; CA 1-4R; 81-84; CANR
    4; CN 1, 2; DLB 13, 14
Shaw, T. E.
    See Lawrence, T(homas) E(dward)
Shawn, Wallace 1943- .... **CLC 41**
    See also CA 112; CAD; CD 5, 6; DLB 266
Shchedrin, N.
    See Saltykov, Mikhail Evgrafovich
Shea, Lisa 1953- .... **CLC 86**
    See also CA 147
Sheed, Wilfrid (John Joseph) 1930- . **CLC 2,
    4, 10, 53**
    See also CA 65-68; CANR 30, 66; CN 1, 2,
    3, 4, 5, 6, 7; DLB 6; MAL 5; MTCW 1,
    2; MTFW 2005
Sheehy, Gail 1937- .... **CLC 171**
    See also CA 49-52; CANR 1, 33, 55, 92;
    CPW; MTCW 1
Sheldon, Alice Hastings Bradley
    1915(?)-1987
    See Tiptree, James, Jr.
    See also CA 108; 122; CANR 34; INT CA-
    108; MTCW 1
Sheldon, John
    See Bloch, Robert (Albert)
Sheldon, Walter J(ames) 1917-1996
    See Queen, Ellery
    See also AITN 1; CA 25-28R; CANR 10
Shelley, Mary Wollstonecraft (Godwin)
    1797-1851 ...... **NCLC 14, 59, 103; WLC**
    See also AAYA 20; BPFB 3; BRW 3;
    BRWC 2; BRWS 3; BYA 5; CDBLB
    1789-1832; DA; DA3; DAB; DAC; DAM
    MST, NOV; DLB 110, 116, 159, 178;
    EXPN; FL 1:3; GL 3; HGG; LAIT 1;
    LMFS 1, 2; NFS 1; RGEL 2; SATA 29;
    SCFW 1, 2; SFW 4; TEA; WLIT 3
Shelley, Percy Bysshe 1792-1822 .. **NCLC 18,
    93, 143; PC 14, 67; WLC**
    See also AAYA 61; BRW 4; BRWR 1; CD-
    BLB 1789-1832; DA; DA3; DAB; DAC;
    DAM MST, POET; DLB 96, 110, 158;
    EXPP; LMFS 1; PAB; PFS 2; RGEL 2;
    TEA; WLIT 3; WP
Shepard, James R. .... **CLC 36**
    See also CA 137; CANR 59, 104; SATA 90,
    164
Shepard, Jim
    See Shepard, James R.
Shepard, Lucius 1947- .... **CLC 34**
    See also CA 128; 141; CANR 81, 124;
    HGG; SCFW 2; SFW 4; SUFW 2
Shepard, Sam 1943- .... **CLC 4, 6, 17, 34, 41,
    44, 169; DC 5**
    See also AAYA 1, 58; AMWS 3; CA 69-72;
    CABS 3; CAD; CANR 22, 120, 140; CD
    5, 6; DA3; DAM DRAM; DFS 3, 6, 7,
    14; DLB 7, 212; EWL 3; IDFW 3, 4;
    MAL 5; MTCW 1, 2; MTFW 2005;
    RGAL 4
Shepherd, Jean Parker
    1921-1999 .... **TCLC 177**
    See also AITN 2; CA 77-80, 187
Shepherd, Michael
    See Ludlum, Robert
Sherburne, Zoa (Lillian Morin)
    1912-1995 .... **CLC 30**
    See also AAYA 13; CA 1-4R; 176; CANR
    3, 37; MAICYA 1, 2; SAAS 18; SATA 3;
    YAW
Sheridan, Frances 1724-1766 .... **LC 7**
    See also DLB 39, 84

Sheridan, Richard Brinsley
    1751-1816 .... **DC 1; NCLC 5, 91; WLC**
    See also BRW 3; CDBLB 1660-1789; DA;
    DAB; DAC; DAM DRAM, MST; DFS
    15; DLB 89; WLIT 3
Sherman, Jonathan Marc 1968- .... **CLC 55**
    See also CA 230
Sherman, Martin 1941(?)- .... **CLC 19**
    See also CA 116; 123; CAD; CANR 86;
    CD 5, 6; DFS 20; DLB 228; GLL 1; IDTP
Sherwin, Judith Johnson
    See Johnson, Judith (Emlyn)
    See also CANR 85; CP 2, 3, 4; CWP
Sherwood, Frances 1940- .... **CLC 81**
    See also CA 146, 220; CAAE 220
Sherwood, Robert E(mmet)
    1896-1955 .... **TCLC 3**
    See also CA 104; 153; CANR 86; DAM
    DRAM; DFS 11, 15, 17; DLB 7, 26, 249;
    IDFW 3, 4; MAL 5; RGAL 4
Shestov, Lev 1866-1938 .... **TCLC 56**
Shevchenko, Taras 1814-1861 .... **NCLC 54**
Shiel, M(atthew) P(hipps)
    1865-1947 .... **TCLC 8**
    See Holmes, Gordon
    See also CA 106; 160; DLB 153; HGG;
    MTCW 2; MTFW 2005; SCFW 1, 2;
    SFW 4; SUFW
Shields, Carol (Ann) 1935-2003 ...... **CLC 91,
    113, 193**
    See also AMWS 7; CA 81-84; 218; CANR
    51, 74, 98, 133; CCA 1; CN 6, 7; CPW;
    DA3; DAC; MTCW 2; MTFW 2005
Shields, David (Jonathan) 1956- ...... **CLC 97**
    See also CA 124; CANR 48, 99, 112
Shiga, Naoya 1883-1971 .... **CLC 33; SSC 23;
    TCLC 172**
    See Shiga Naoya
    See also CA 101; 33-36R; MJW; RGWL 3
Shiga Naoya
    See Shiga, Naoya
    See also DLB 180; EWL 3; RGWL 3
Shilts, Randy 1951-1994 .... **CLC 85**
    See also AAYA 19; CA 115; 127; 144;
    CANR 45; DA3; GLL 1; INT CA-127;
    MTCW 2; MTFW 2005
Shimazaki, Haruki 1872-1943
    See Shimazaki Toson
    See also CA 105; 134; CANR 84; RGWL 3
Shimazaki Toson .... **TCLC 5**
    See Shimazaki, Haruki
    See also DLB 180; EWL 3
Shirley, James 1596-1666 .... **DC 25; LC 96**
    See also DLB 58; RGEL 2
Sholokhov, Mikhail (Aleksandrovich)
    1905-1984 .... **CLC 7, 15**
    See also CA 101; 112; DLB 272; EWL 3;
    MTCW 1, 2; MTFW 2005; RGWL 2, 3;
    SATA-Obit 36
Shone, Patric
    See Hanley, James
Showalter, Elaine 1941- .... **CLC 169**
    See also CA 57-60; CANR 58, 106; DLB
    67; FW; GLL 2
Shreve, Susan
    See Shreve, Susan Richards
Shreve, Susan Richards 1939- .... **CLC 23**
    See also CA 49-52; CANR 5, 38, 54;
    69, 100; MAICYA 1, 2; SATA 46, 95, 152;
    SATA-Brief 41
Shue, Larry 1946-1985 .... **CLC 52**
    See also CA 145; 117; DAM DRAM; DFS
    7
Shu-Jen, Chou 1881-1936
    See Lu Hsun
    See also CA 104
Shulman, Alix Kates 1932- .... **CLC 2, 10**
    See also CA 29-32R; CANR 43; FW; SATA
    7

Shuster, Joe 1914-1992 .... **CLC 21**
    See also AAYA 50
Shute, Nevil .... **CLC 30**
    See Norway, Nevil Shute
    See also BPFB 3; DLB 255; NFS 9; RHW;
    SFW 4
Shuttle, Penelope (Diane) 1947- .... **CLC 7**
    See also CA 93-96; CANR 39, 84, 92, 108;
    CP 3, 4, 5, 6, 7; CWP; DLB 14, 40
Shvarts, Elena 1948- .... **PC 50**
    See also CA 147
Sidhwa, Bapsi
    See Sidhwa, Bapsy (N.)
    See also CN 6, 7
Sidhwa, Bapsy (N.) 1938- .... **CLC 168**
    See Sidhwa, Bapsi
    See also CA 108; CANR 25, 57; FW
Sidney, Mary 1561-1621 .... **LC 19, 39**
    See Sidney Herbert, Mary
Sidney, Sir Philip 1554-1586 . **LC 19, 39; PC
    32**
    See also BRW 1; BRWR 2; CDBLB Before
    1660; DA; DA3; DAB; DAC; DAM MST,
    POET; DLB 167; EXPP; PAB; RGEL 2;
    TEA; WP
Sidney Herbert, Mary
    See Sidney, Mary
    See also DLB 167
Siegel, Jerome 1914-1996 .... **CLC 21**
    See Siegel, Jerry
    See also CA 116; 169; 151
Siegel, Jerry
    See Siegel, Jerome
    See also AAYA 50
Sienkiewicz, Henryk (Adam Alexander Pius)
    1846-1916 .... **TCLC 3**
    See also CA 104; 134; CANR 84; EWL 3;
    RGSF 2; RGWL 2, 3
Sierra, Gregorio Martinez
    See Martinez Sierra, Gregorio
Sierra, Maria (de la O'LeJarraga) Martinez
    See Martinez Sierra, Maria (de la
    O'LeJarraga)
Sigal, Clancy 1926- .... **CLC 7**
    See also CA 1-4R; CANR 85; CN 1, 2, 3,
    4, 5, 6, 7
Siger of Brabant 1240(?)-1284(?) . **CMLC 69**
    See also DLB 115
Sigourney, Lydia H.
    See Sigourney, Lydia Howard (Huntley)
    See also DLB 73, 183
Sigourney, Lydia Howard (Huntley)
    1791-1865 .... **NCLC 21, 87**
    See Sigourney, Lydia H.; Sigourney, Lydia
    Huntley
    See also DLB 1
Sigourney, Lydia Huntley
    See Sigourney, Lydia Howard (Huntley)
    See also DLB 42, 239, 243
Siguenza y Gongora, Carlos de
    1645-1700 .... **HLCS 2; LC 8**
    See also LAW
Sigurjonsson, Johann
    See Sigurjonsson, Johann
Sigurjonsson, Johann 1880-1919 ... **TCLC 27**
    See also CA 170; DLB 293; EWL 3
Sikelianos, Angelos 1884-1951 .... **PC 29;
    TCLC 39**
    See also EWL 3; RGWL 2, 3
Silkin, Jon 1930-1997 .... **CLC 2, 6, 43**
    See also CA 5-8R; CAAS 5; CANR 89; CP
    1, 2, 3, 4, 5, 6; DLB 27
Silko, Leslie (Marmon) 1948- .... **CLC 23, 74,
    114, 211; NNAL; SSC 37, 66; WLCS**
    See also AAYA 14; AMWS 4; ANW; BYA
    12; CA 115; 122; CANR 45, 65, 118; CN
    4, 5, 6, 7; CP 4, 5, 6, 7; CPW 1; CWP;
    DA; DA3; DAC; DAM MST, MULT,
    POP; DLB 143, 175, 256, 275; EWL 3;

Skvorecky, Josef (Vaclav) 1924- ...... **CLC 15, 39, 69, 152**
See also CA 61-64; CAAS 1; CANR 10, 34, 63, 108; CDWLB 4; CWW 2; DA3; DAC; DAM NOV; DLB 232; EWL 3; MTCW 1, 2; MTFW 2005

Slade, Bernard 1930- .... **CLC 11, 46**
See Newbound, Bernard Slade
See also CAAS 9; CCA 1; CD 6; DLB 53

Slaughter, Carolyn 1946- .... **CLC 56**
See also CA 85-88; CANR 85; CN 5, 6, 7

Slaughter, Frank G(ill) 1908-2001 ... **CLC 29**
See also AITN 2; CA 5-8R; 197; CANR 5, 85; INT CANR-5; RHW

Slavitt, David R(ytman) 1935- ..... **CLC 5, 14**
See also CA 21-24R; CAAS 3; CANR 41, 83; CN 1, 2; CP 1, 2, 3, 4, 5, 6, 7; DLB 5, 6

Slesinger, Tess 1905-1945 .... **TCLC 10**
See also CA 107; 199; DLB 102

Slessor, Kenneth 1901-1971 .... **CLC 14**
See also CA 102; 89-92; DLB 260; RGEL 2

Slowacki, Juliusz 1809-1849 .... **NCLC 15**
See also RGWL 3

Smart, Christopher 1722-1771 . **LC 3; PC 13**
See also DAM POET; DLB 109; RGEL 2

Smart, Elizabeth 1913-1986 .... **CLC 54**
See also CA 81-84; 118; CN 4; DLB 88

Smiley, Jane (Graves) 1949- ...... **CLC 53, 76, 144**
See also AAYA 66; AMWS 6; BPFB 3; CA 104; CANR 30, 50, 74, 96; CN 6, 7; CPW 1; DA3; DAM POP; DLB 227, 234; EWL 3; INT CANR-30; MAL 5; MTFW 2005; SSFS 19

Smith, A(rthur) J(ames) M(arshall) 1902-1980 .... **CLC 15**
See also CA 1-4R; 102; CANR 4; CP 1, 2, 3; DAC; DLB 88; RGEL 2

Smith, Adam 1723(?)-1790 .... **LC 36**
See also DLB 104, 252; RGEL 2

Smith, Alexander 1829-1867 .... **NCLC 59**
See also DLB 32, 55

Smith, Anna Deavere 1950- .... **CLC 86**
See also CA 133; CANR 103; CD 5, 6; DFS 2, 22

Smith, Betty (Wehner) 1904-1972 .... **CLC 19**
See also BPFB 3; BYA 3; CA 5-8R; 33-36R; DLBY 1982; LAIT 3; RGAL 4; SATA 6

Smith, Charlotte (Turner) 1749-1806 .... **NCLC 23, 115**
See also DLB 39, 109; RGEL 2; TEA

Smith, Clark Ashton 1893-1961 .... **CLC 43**
See also CA 143; CANR 81; FANT; HGG; MTCW 2; SCFW 1, 2; SFW 4; SUFW

Smith, Dave .... **CLC 22, 42**
See Smith, David (Jeddie)
See also CAAS 7; CP 3, 4, 5, 6, 7; DLB 5

Smith, David (Jeddie) 1942-
See Smith, Dave
See also CA 49-52; CANR 1, 59, 120; CSW; DAM POET

Smith, Florence Margaret 1902-1971
See Smith, Stevie
See also CA 17-18; 29-32R; CANR 35; CAP 2; DAM POET; MTCW 1, 2; TEA

Smith, Iain Crichton 1928-1998 .... **CLC 64**
See also BRWS 9; CA 21-24R; 171; CN 1, 2, 3, 4, 5, 6; CP 1, 2, 3, 4; DLB 40, 139, 319; RGSF 2

Smith, John 1580(?)-1631 .... **LC 9**
See also DLB 24, 30; TUS

Smith, Johnston
See Crane, Stephen (Townley)

Smith, Joseph, Jr. 1805-1844 .... **NCLC 53**

Smith, Lee 1944- .... **CLC 25, 73**
See also CA 114; 119; CANR 46, 118; CN 7; CSW; DLB 143; DLBY 1983; EWL 3; INT CA-119; RGAL 4

Smith, Martin
See Smith, Martin Cruz

Smith, Martin Cruz 1942- .. **CLC 25; NNAL**
See also BEST 89:4; BPFB 3; CA 85-88; CANR 6, 23, 43, 65, 119; CMW 4; CPW; DAM MULT, POP; HGG; INT CANR-23; MTCW 2; MTFW 2005; RGAL 4

Smith, Patti 1946- .... **CLC 12**
See also CA 93-96; CANR 63

Smith, Pauline (Urmson) 1882-1959 .... **TCLC 25**
See also DLB 225; EWL 3

Smith, Rosamond
See Oates, Joyce Carol

Smith, Sheila Kaye
See Kaye-Smith, Sheila

Smith, Stevie .... **CLC 3, 8, 25, 44; PC 12**
See Smith, Florence Margaret
See also BRWS 2; CP 1; DLB 20; EWL 3; PAB; PFS 3; RGEL 2

Smith, Wilbur (Addison) 1933- .... **CLC 33**
See also CA 13-16R; CANR 7, 46, 66, 134; CPW; MTCW 1, 2; MTFW 2005

Smith, William Jay 1918- .... **CLC 6**
See also AMWS 13; CA 5-8R; CANR 44, 106; CP 1, 2, 3, 4, 5, 6, 7; CSW; CWRI 5; DLB 5; MAICYA 1, 2; SAAS 22; SATA 2, 68, 154; SATA-Essay 154; TCLE 1:2

Smith, Woodrow Wilson
See Kuttner, Henry

Smith, Zadie 1976- .... **CLC 158**
See also AAYA 50; CA 193; MTFW 2005

Smolenskin, Peretz 1842-1885 .... **NCLC 30**

Smollett, Tobias (George) 1721-1771 ... **LC 2, 46**
See also BRW 3; CDBLB 1660-1789; DLB 39, 104; RGEL 2; TEA

Snodgrass, W(illiam) D(e Witt) 1926- .... **CLC 2, 6, 10, 18, 68**
See also AMWS 6; CA 1-4R; CANR 6, 36, 65, 85; CP 1, 2, 3, 4, 5, 6, 7; DAM POET; DLB 5; MAL 5; MTCW 1, 2; MTFW 2005; RGAL 4; TCLE 1:2

Snorri Sturluson 1179-1241 .... **CMLC 56**
See also RGWL 2, 3

Snow, C(harles) P(ercy) 1905-1980 ... **CLC 1, 4, 6, 9, 13, 19**
See also BRW 7; CA 5-8R; 101; CANR 28; CDBLB 1945-1960; CN 1, 2; DAM NOV; DLB 15, 77; DLBD 17; EWL 3; MTCW 1, 2; MTFW 2005; RGEL 2; TEA

Snow, Frances Compton
See Adams, Henry (Brooks)

Snyder, Gary (Sherman) 1930- . **CLC 1, 2, 5, 9, 32, 120; PC 21**
See also AMWS 8; ANW; BG 1:3; CA 17-20R; CANR 30, 60, 125; CP 1, 2, 3, 4, 5, 6, 7; DA3; DAM POET; DLB 5, 16, 165, 212, 237, 275; EWL 3; MAL 5; MTCW 2; MTFW 2005; PFS 9, 19; RGAL 4; WP

Snyder, Zilpha Keatley 1927- .... **CLC 17**
See also AAYA 15; BYA 1; CA 9-12R; CANR 38; CLR 31; JRDA; MAICYA 1, 2; SAAS 2; SATA 1, 28, 75, 110, 163; SATA-Essay 112, 163; YAW

Soares, Bernardo
See Pessoa, Fernando (Antonio Nogueira)

Sobh, A.
See Shamlu, Ahmad

Sobh, Alef
See Shamlu, Ahmad

Sobol, Joshua 1939- .... **CLC 60**
See Sobol, Yehoshua
See also CA 200

Sobol, Yehoshua 1939-
See Sobol, Joshua
See also CWW 2

Socrates 470B.C.-399B.C. .... **CMLC 27**

Soderberg, Hjalmar 1869-1941 ...... **TCLC 39**
See also DLB 259; EWL 3; RGSF 2

Soderbergh, Steven 1963- .... **CLC 154**
See also AAYA 43

Sodergran, Edith (Irene) 1892-1923
See Soedergran, Edith (Irene)
See also CA 202; DLB 259; EW 11; EWL 3; RGWL 2, 3

Soedergran, Edith (Irene) 1892-1923 .... **TCLC 31**
See Sodergran, Edith (Irene)

Softly, Edgar
See Lovecraft, H(oward) P(hillips)

Softly, Edward
See Lovecraft, H(oward) P(hillips)

Sokolov, Alexander V(sevolodovich) 1943-
See Sokolov, Sasha
See also CA 73-76

Sokolov, Raymond 1941- .... **CLC 7**
See also CA 85-88

Sokolov, Sasha .... **CLC 59**
See Sokolov, Alexander V(sevolodovich)
See also CWW 2; DLB 285; EWL 3; RGWL 2, 3

Solo, Jay
See Ellison, Harlan (Jay)

Sologub, Fyodor .... **TCLC 9**
See Teternikov, Fyodor Kuzmich
See also EWL 3

Solomons, Ikey Esquir
See Thackeray, William Makepeace

Solomos, Dionysios 1798-1857 .... **NCLC 15**

Solwoska, Mara
See French, Marilyn

Solzhenitsyn, Aleksandr I(sayevich) 1918- .. **CLC 1, 2, 4, 7, 9, 10, 18, 26, 34, 78, 134; SSC 32; WLC**
See Solzhenitsyn, Aleksandr Isaevich
See also AAYA 49; AITN 1; BPFB 3; CA 69-72; CANR 40, 65, 116; DA; DA3; DAB; DAC; DAM MST, NOV; DLB 302; EW 13; EXPS; LAIT 4; MTCW 1, 2; MTFW 2005; NFS 6; RGSF 2; RGWL 2, 3; SSFS 9; TWA

Solzhenitsyn, Aleksandr Isaevich
See Solzhenitsyn, Aleksandr I(sayevich)
See also CWW 2; EWL 3

Somers, Jane
See Lessing, Doris (May)

Somerville, Edith Oenone 1858-1949 .... **SSC 56; TCLC 51**
See also CA 196; DLB 135; RGEL 2; RGSF 2

Somerville & Ross
See Martin, Violet Florence; Somerville, Edith Oenone

Sommer, Scott 1951- .... **CLC 25**
See also CA 106

Sommers, Christina Hoff 1950- ...... **CLC 197**
See also CA 153; CANR 95

Sondheim, Stephen (Joshua) 1930- . **CLC 30, 39, 147; DC 22**
See also AAYA 11, 66; CA 103; CANR 47, 67, 125; DAM DRAM; LAIT 4

Sone, Monica 1919- .... **AAL**
See also DLB 312

Song, Cathy 1955- .... **AAL; PC 21**
See also CA 154; CANR 118; CWP; DLB 169, 312; EXPP; FW; PFS 5

Stapledon, (William) Olaf
  1886-1950 .... **TCLC 22**
    See also CA 111; 162; DLB 15, 255; SCFW
    1, 2; SFW 4
Starbuck, George (Edwin)
  1931-1996 .... **CLC 53**
    See also CA 21-24R; 153; CANR 23; CP 1,
    2, 3, 4; DAM POET
Stark, Richard
    See Westlake, Donald E(dwin)
Staunton, Schuyler
    See Baum, L(yman) Frank
Stead, Christina (Ellen) 1902-1983 ... **CLC 2,
  5, 8, 32, 80**
    See also BRWS 4; CA 13-16R; 109; CANR
    33, 40; CN 1, 2, 3; DLB 260; EWL 3;
    FW; MTCW 1, 2; MTFW 2005; RGEL 2;
    RGSF 2; WWE 1
Stead, William Thomas
  1849-1912 .... **TCLC 48**
    See also CA 167
Stebnitsky, M.
    See Leskov, Nikolai (Semyonovich)
Steele, Richard 1672-1729 .... **LC 18**
    See also BRW 3; CDBLB 1660-1789; DLB
    84, 101; RGEL 2; WLIT 3
Steele, Timothy (Reid) 1948- .... **CLC 45**
    See also CA 93-96; CANR 16, 50, 92; CP
    7; DLB 120, 282
Steffens, (Joseph) Lincoln
  1866-1936 .... **TCLC 20**
    See also CA 117; 198; DLB 303; MAL 5
Stegner, Wallace (Earle) 1909-1993 .. **CLC 9,
  49, 81; SSC 27**
    See also AITN 1; AMWS 4; ANW; BEST
    90:3; BPFB 3; CA 1-4R; 141; CAAS 9;
    CANR 1, 21, 46; CN 1, 2, 3, 4, 5; DAM
    NOV; DLB 9, 206, 275; DLBY 1993;
    EWL 3; MAL 5; MTCW 1, 2; MTFW
    2005; RGAL 4; TCWW 1, 2; TUS
Stein, Gertrude 1874-1946 .... **DC 19; PC 18;
  SSC 42; TCLC 1, 6, 28, 48; WLC**
    See also AAYA 64; AMW; AMWC 2; CA
    104; 132; CANR 108; CDALB 1917-
    1929; DA; DA3; DAB; DAC; DAM MST,
    NOV, POET; DLB 4, 54, 86, 228; DLBD
    15; EWL 3; EXPS; FL 1:6; GLL 1; MAL
    5; MAWW; MTCW 1, 2; MTFW 2005;
    NCFS 4; RGAL 4; RGSF 2; SSFS 5;
    TUS; WP
Steinbeck, John (Ernst) 1902-1968 ... **CLC 1,
  5, 9, 13, 21, 34, 45, 75, 124; SSC 11, 37,
  77; TCLC 135; WLC**
    See also AAYA 12; AMW; BPFB 3; BYA 2,
    3, 13; CA 1-4R; 25-28R; CANR 1, 35;
    CDALB 1929-1941; DA; DA3; DAB;
    DAC; DAM DRAM, MST, NOV; DLB 7,
    9, 212, 275, 309; DLBD 2; EWL 3;
    EXPS; LAIT 3; MAL 5; MTCW 1, 2;
    MTFW 2005; NFS 1, 5, 7, 17, 19; RGAL
    4; RGSF 2; RHW; SATA 9; SSFS 3, 6;
    TCWW 1, 2; TUS; WYA; YAW
Steinem, Gloria 1934- .... **CLC 63**
    See also CA 53-56; CANR 28, 51, 139;
    DLB 246; FW; MTCW 1, 2; MTFW 2005
Steiner, George 1929- .... **CLC 24, 221**
    See also CA 73-76; CANR 31, 67, 108;
    DAM NOV; DLB 67, 299; EWL 3;
    MTCW 1, 2; MTFW 2005; SATA 62
Steiner, K. Leslie
    See Delany, Samuel R(ay), Jr.
Steiner, Rudolf 1861-1925 .... **TCLC 13**
    See also CA 107
Stendhal 1783-1842 .. **NCLC 23, 46; SSC 27;
  WLC**
    See also DA; DA3; DAB; DAC; DAM
    MST, NOV; DLB 119; EW 5; GFL 1789
    to the Present; RGWL 2, 3; TWA
Stephen, Adeline Virginia
    See Woolf, (Adeline) Virginia

Stephen, Sir Leslie 1832-1904 .... **TCLC 23**
    See also BRW 5; CA 123; DLB 57, 144,
    190
Stephen, Sir Leslie
    See Stephen, Sir Leslie
Stephen, Virginia
    See Woolf, (Adeline) Virginia
Stephens, James 1882(?)-1950 .... **SSC 50;
  TCLC 4**
    See also CA 104; 192; DLB 19, 153, 162;
    EWL 3; FANT; RGEL 2; SUFW
Stephens, Reed
    See Donaldson, Stephen R(eeder)
Stephenson, Neal 1959- .... **CLC 220**
    See also AAYA 38; CA 122; CANR 88, 138;
    CN 7; MTCW 2005; SFW 4
Steptoe, Lydia
    See Barnes, Djuna
    See also GLL 1
Sterchi, Beat 1949- .... **CLC 65**
    See also CA 203
Sterling, Brett
    See Bradbury, Ray (Douglas); Hamilton,
    Edmond
Sterling, Bruce 1954- .... **CLC 72**
    See also CA 119; CANR 44, 135; CN 7;
    MTFW 2005; SCFW 2; SFW 4
Sterling, George 1869-1926 .... **TCLC 20**
    See also CA 117; 165; DLB 54
Stern, Gerald 1925- .... **CLC 40, 100**
    See also AMWS 9; CA 81-84; CANR 28,
    94; CP 3, 4, 5, 6, 7; DLB 105; RGAL 4
Stern, Richard (Gustave) 1928- ... **CLC 4, 39**
    See also CA 1-4R; CANR 1, 25, 52, 120;
    CN 1, 2, 3, 4, 5, 6, 7; DLB 218; DLBY
    1987; INT CANR-25
Sternberg, Josef von 1894-1969 .... **CLC 20**
    See also CA 81-84
Sterne, Laurence 1713-1768 .... **LC 2, 48;
  WLC**
    See also BRW 3; BRWC 1; CDBLB 1660-
    1789; DA; DAB; DAC; DAM MST, NOV;
    DLB 39; RGEL 2; TEA
Sternheim, (William Adolf) Carl
  1878-1942 .... **TCLC 8**
    See also CA 105; 193; DLB 56, 118; EWL
    3; IDTP; RGWL 2, 3
Stevens, Margaret Dean
    See Aldrich, Bess Streeter
Stevens, Mark 1951- .... **CLC 34**
    See also CA 122
Stevens, Wallace 1879-1955 . **PC 6; TCLC 3,
  12, 45; WLC**
    See also AMW; AMWR 1; CA 104; 124;
    CDALB 1929-1941; DA; DA3; DAB;
    DAC; DAM MST, POET; DLB 54; EWL
    3; EXPP; MAL 5; MTCW 1, 2; PAB; PFS
    13, 16; RGAL 4; TUS; WP
Stevenson, Anne (Katharine) 1933- .. **CLC 7,
  33**
    See also BRWS 6; CA 17-20R; CAAS 9;
    CANR 9, 33, 123; CP 3, 4, 5, 6, 7; CWP;
    DLB 40; MTCW 1; RHW
Stevenson, Robert Louis (Balfour)
  1850-1894 ...... **NCLC 5, 14, 63; SSC 11,
  51; WLC**
    See also AAYA 24; BPFB 3; BRW 5;
    BRWC 1; BRWR 1; BYA 1, 2, 4, 13; CD-
    BLB 1890-1914; CLR 10, 11; DA; DA3;
    DAB; DAC; DAM MST, NOV; DLB 18,
    57, 141, 156, 174; DLBD 13; GL 3; HGG;
    JRDA; LAIT 1, 3; MAICYA 1, 2; NFS
    11, 20; RGEL 2; RGSF 2; SATA 100;
    SUFW; TEA; WCH; WLIT 4; WYA;
    YABC 2; YAW

Stewart, J(ohn) I(nnes) M(ackintosh)
  1906-1994 .... **CLC 7, 14, 32**
    See Innes, Michael
    See also CA 85-88; 147; CAAS 3; CANR
    47; CMW 4; CN 1, 2, 3, 4, 5; MTCW 1,
    2
Stewart, Mary (Florence Elinor)
  1916- .... **CLC 7, 35, 117**
    See also AAYA 29; BPFB 3; CA 1-4R;
    CANR 1, 59, 130; CMW 4; CPW; DAB;
    FANT; RHW; SATA 12; YAW
Stewart, Mary Rainbow
    See Stewart, Mary (Florence Elinor)
Stifle, June
    See Campbell, Maria
Stifter, Adalbert 1805-1868 .. **NCLC 41; SSC
  28**
    See also CDWLB 2; DLB 133; RGSF 2;
    RGWL 2, 3
Still, James 1906-2001 .... **CLC 49**
    See also CA 65-68; 195; CAAS 17; CANR
    10, 26; CSW; DLB 9; DLBY 01; SATA
    29; SATA-Obit 127
Sting 1951-
    See Sumner, Gordon Matthew
    See also CA 167
Stirling, Arthur
    See Sinclair, Upton (Beall)
Stitt, Milan 1941- .... **CLC 29**
    See also CA 69-72
Stockton, Francis Richard 1834-1902
    See Stockton, Frank R.
    See also AAYA 68; CA 108; 137; MAICYA
    1, 2; SATA 44; SFW 4
Stockton, Frank R. .... **TCLC 47**
    See Stockton, Francis Richard
    See also BYA 4, 13; DLB 42, 74; DLBD
    13; EXPS; SATA-Brief 32; SSFS 3;
    SUFW; WCH
Stoddard, Charles
    See Kuttner, Henry
Stoker, Abraham 1847-1912
    See Stoker, Bram
    See also CA 105; 150; DA; DA3; DAC;
    DAM MST, NOV; HGG; MTFW 2005;
    SATA 29
Stoker, Bram . **SSC 62; TCLC 8, 144; WLC**
    See Stoker, Abraham
    See also AAYA 23; BPFB 3; BRWS 3; BYA
    5; CDBLB 1890-1914; DAB; DLB 304;
    GL 3; LATS 1:1; NFS 18; RGEL 2;
    SUFW; TEA; WLIT 4
Stolz, Mary (Slattery) 1920- .... **CLC 12**
    See also AAYA 8; AITN 1; CA 5-8R;
    CANR 13, 41, 112; JRDA; MAICYA 1,
    2; SAAS 3; SATA 10, 71, 133; YAW
Stone, Irving 1903-1989 .... **CLC 7**
    See also AITN 1; BPFB 3; CA 1-4R; 129;
    CAAS 3; CANR 1, 23; CN 1, 2, 3, 4;
    CPW; DA3; DAM POP; INT CANR-23;
    MTCW 1, 2; MTFW 2005; RHW; SATA
    3; SATA-Obit 64
Stone, Oliver (William) 1946- .... **CLC 73**
    See also AAYA 15, 64; CA 110; CANR 55,
    125
Stone, Robert (Anthony) 1937- ... **CLC 5, 23,
  42, 175**
    See also AMWS 5; BPFB 3; CA 85-88;
    CANR 23, 66, 95; CN 4, 5, 6, 7; DLB
    152; EWL 3; INT CANR-23; MAL 5;
    MTCW 1; MTFW 2005
Stone, Ruth 1915- .... **PC 53**
    See also CA 45-48; CANR 2, 91; CP 7;
    CSW; DLB 105; PFS 19
Stone, Zachary
    See Follett, Ken(neth Martin)

Suzuki, Teitaro
See Suzuki, Daisetz Teitaro

Svevo, Italo .... **SSC 25; TCLC 2, 35**
See Schmitz, Aron Hector
See also DLB 264; EW 8; EWL 3; RGWL 2, 3; WLIT 7

Swados, Elizabeth (A.) 1951- .... **CLC 12**
See also CA 97-100; CANR 49; INT CA-97-100

Swados, Harvey 1920-1972 .... **CLC 5**
See also CA 5-8R; 37-40R; CANR 6; CN 1; DLB 2; MAL 5

Swan, Gladys 1934- .... **CLC 69**
See also CA 101; CANR 17, 39; TCLE 1:2

Swanson, Logan
See Matheson, Richard (Burton)

Swarthout, Glendon (Fred)
1918-1992 .... **CLC 35**
See also AAYA 55; CA 1-4R; 139; CANR 1, 47; CN 1, 2, 3, 4, 5; LAIT 5; SATA 26; TCWW 1, 2; YAW

Swedenborg, Emanuel 1688-1772 ..... **LC 105**

Sweet, Sarah C.
See Jewett, (Theodora) Sarah Orne

Swenson, May 1919-1989 ...... **CLC 4, 14, 61, 106; PC 14**
See also AMWS 4; CA 5-8R; 130; CANR 36, 61, 131; CP 1, 2, 3, 4; DA; DAB; DAC; DAM MST, POET; DLB 5; EXPP; GLL 2; MAL 5; MTCW 1, 2; MTFW 2005; PFS 16; SATA 15; WP

Swift, Augustus
See Lovecraft, H(oward) P(hillips)

Swift, Graham (Colin) 1949- ...... **CLC 41, 88**
See also BRWC 2; BRWS 5; CA 117; 122; CANR 46, 71, 128; CN 4, 5, 6, 7; DLB 194; MTCW 2; MTFW 2005; NFS 18; RGSF 2

Swift, Jonathan 1667-1745 ..... **LC 1, 42, 101; PC 9; WLC**
See also AAYA 41; BRW 3; BRWC 1; BRWR 1; BYA 5, 14; CDBLB 1660-1789; CLR 53; DA; DA3; DAB; DAC; DAM MST, NOV, POET; DLB 39, 95, 101; EXPN; LAIT 1; NFS 6; RGEL 2; SATA 19; TEA; WCH; WLIT 3

Swinburne, Algernon Charles
1837-1909 ... **PC 24; TCLC 8, 36; WLC**
See also BRW 5; CA 105; 140; CDBLB 1832-1890; DA; DA3; DAB; DAC; DAM MST, POET; DLB 35, 57; PAB; RGEL 2; TEA

Swinfen, Ann .... **CLC 34**
See also CA 202

Swinnerton, Frank (Arthur)
1884-1982 .... **CLC 31**
See also CA 202; 108; CN 1, 2, 3; DLB 34

Swinnerton, Frank Arthur
1884-1982 .... **CLC 31**
See also CA 108; DLB 34

Swithen, John
See King, Stephen

Sylvia
See Ashton-Warner, Sylvia (Constance)

Symmes, Robert Edward
See Duncan, Robert (Edward)

Symonds, John Addington
1840-1893 .... **NCLC 34**
See also DLB 57, 144

Symons, Arthur 1865-1945 .... **TCLC 11**
See also CA 107; 189; DLB 19, 57, 149; RGEL 2

Symons, Julian (Gustave)
1912-1994 .... **CLC 2, 14, 32**
See also CA 49-52; 147; CAAS 3; CANR 3, 33, 59; CMW 4; CN 1, 2, 3, 4, 5; CP 1, 3, 4; DLB 87, 155; DLBY 1992; MSW; MTCW 1

Synge, (Edmund) J(ohn) M(illington)
1871-1909 .... **DC 2; TCLC 6, 37**
See also BRW 6; BRWR 1; CA 104; 141; CDBLB 1890-1914; DAM DRAM; DFS 18; DLB 10, 19; EWL 3; RGEL 2; TEA; WLIT 4

Syruc, J.
See Milosz, Czeslaw

Szirtes, George 1948- .... **CLC 46; PC 51**
See also CA 109; CANR 27, 61, 117; CP 4, 5, 6, 7

Szymborska, Wislawa 1923- ... **CLC 99, 190; PC 44**
See also CA 154; CANR 91, 133; CDWLB 4; CWP; CWW 2; DA3; DLB 232; DLBY 1996; EWL 3; MTCW 2; MTFW 2005; PFS 15; RGWL 3

T. O., Nik
See Annensky, Innokenty (Fyodorovich)

Tabori, George 1914- .... **CLC 19**
See also CA 49-52; CANR 4, 69; CBD; CD 5, 6; DLB 245

Tacitus c. 55-c. 117 .... **CMLC 56**
See also AW 2; CDWLB 1; DLB 211; RGWL 2, 3

Tagore, Rabindranath 1861-1941 .... **PC 8; SSC 48; TCLC 3, 53**
See also CA 104; 120; DA3; DAM DRAM, POET; EWL 3; MTCW 1, 2; MTFW 2005; PFS 18; RGEL 2; RGSF 2; RGWL 2, 3; TWA

Taine, Hippolyte Adolphe
1828-1893 .... **NCLC 15**
See also EW 7; GFL 1789 to the Present

Talayesva, Don C. 1890-(?) .... **NNAL**

Talese, Gay 1932- .... **CLC 37**
See also AITN 1; CA 1-4R; CANR 9, 58, 137; DLB 185; INT CANR-9; MTCW 1, 2; MTFW 2005

Tallent, Elizabeth (Ann) 1954- .... **CLC 45**
See also CA 117; CANR 72; DLB 130

Tallmountain, Mary 1918-1997 .... **NNAL**
See also CA 146; 161; DLB 193

Tally, Ted 1952- .... **CLC 42**
See also CA 120; 124; CAD; CANR 125; CD 5, 6; INT CA-124

Talvik, Heiti 1904-1947 .... **TCLC 87**
See also EWL 3

Tamayo y Baus, Manuel
1829-1898 .... **NCLC 1**

Tammsaare, A(nton) H(ansen)
1878-1940 .... **TCLC 27**
See also CA 164; CDWLB 4; DLB 220; EWL 3

Tam'si, Tchicaya U
See Tchicaya, Gerald Felix

Tan, Amy (Ruth) 1952- . **AAL; CLC 59, 120, 151**
See also AAYA 9, 48; AMWS 10; BEST 89:3; BPFB 3; CA 136; CANR 54, 105, 132; CDALBS; CN 6, 7; CPW 1; DA3; DAM MULT, NOV, POP; DLB 173, 312; EXPN; FL 1:6; FW; LAIT 3, 5; MAL 5; MTCW 2; MTFW 2005; NFS 1, 13, 16; RGAL 4; SATA 75; SSFS 9; YAW

Tandem, Felix
See Spitteler, Carl (Friedrich Georg)

Tanizaki, Jun'ichiro 1886-1965 ... **CLC 8, 14, 28; SSC 21**
See Tanizaki Jun'ichiro
See also CA 93-96; 25-28R; MJW; MTCW 2; MTFW 2005; RGSF 2; RGWL 2

Tanizaki Jun'ichiro
See Tanizaki, Jun'ichiro
See also DLB 180; EWL 3

Tannen, Deborah F(rances) 1945- .. **CLC 206**
See also CA 118; CANR 95

Tanner, William
See Amis, Kingsley (William)

Tao Lao
See Storni, Alfonsina

Tapahonso, Luci 1953- .... **NNAL; PC 65**
See also CA 145; CANR 72, 127; DLB 175

Tarantino, Quentin (Jerome)
1963- .... **CLC 125**
See also AAYA 58; CA 171; CANR 125

Tarassoff, Lev
See Troyat, Henri

Tarbell, Ida M(inerva) 1857-1944 . **TCLC 40**
See also CA 122; 181; DLB 47

Tarkington, (Newton) Booth
1869-1946 .... **TCLC 9**
See also BPFB 3; BYA 3; CA 110; 143; CWRI 5; DLB 9, 102; MAL 5; MTCW 2; RGAL 4; SATA 17

Tarkovskii, Andrei Arsen'evich
See Tarkovsky, Andrei (Arsenyevich)

Tarkovsky, Andrei (Arsenyevich)
1932-1986 .... **CLC 75**
See also CA 127

Tartt, Donna 1964(?)- .... **CLC 76**
See also AAYA 56; CA 142; CANR 135; MTFW 2005

Tasso, Torquato 1544-1595 .... **LC 5, 94**
See also EFS 2; EW 2; RGWL 2, 3; WLIT 7

Tate, (John Orley) Allen 1899-1979 .. **CLC 2, 4, 6, 9, 11, 14, 24; PC 50**
See also AMW; CA 5-8R; 85-88; CANR 32, 108; CN 1, 2; CP 1, 2; DLB 4, 45, 63; DLBD 17; EWL 3; MAL 5; MTCW 1, 2; MTFW 2005; RGAL 4; RHW

Tate, Ellalice
See Hibbert, Eleanor Alice Burford

Tate, James (Vincent) 1943- ..... **CLC 2, 6, 25**
See also CA 21-24R; CANR 29, 57, 114; CP 1, 2, 3, 4, 5, 6, 7; DLB 5, 169; EWL 3; PFS 10, 15; RGAL 4; WP

Tate, Nahum 1652(?)-1715 .... **LC 109**
See also DLB 80; RGEL 2

Tauler, Johannes c. 1300-1361 ...... **CMLC 37**
See also DLB 179; LMFS 1

Tavel, Ronald 1940- .... **CLC 6**
See also CA 21-24R; CAD; CANR 33; CD 5, 6

Taviani, Paolo 1931- .... **CLC 70**
See also CA 153

Taylor, Bayard 1825-1878 .... **NCLC 89**
See also DLB 3, 189, 250, 254; RGAL 4

Taylor, C(ecil) P(hilip) 1929-1981 .... **CLC 27**
See also CA 25-28R; 105; CANR 47; CBD

Taylor, Edward 1642(?)-1729 . **LC 11; PC 63**
See also AMW; DA; DAB; DAC; DAM MST, POET; DLB 24; EXPP; RGAL 4; TUS

Taylor, Eleanor Ross 1920- .... **CLC 5**
See also CA 81-84; CANR 70

Taylor, Elizabeth 1912-1975 ..... **CLC 2, 4, 29**
See also CA 13-16R; CANR 9, 70; CN 1, 2; DLB 139; MTCW 1; RGEL 2; SATA 13

Taylor, Frederick Winslow
1856-1915 .... **TCLC 76**
See also CA 188

Taylor, Henry (Splawn) 1942- .... **CLC 44**
See also CA 33-36R; CAAS 7; CANR 31; CP 7; DLB 5; PFS 10

Taylor, Kamala (Purnaiya) 1924-2004
See Markandaya, Kamala
See also CA 77-80; 227; MTFW 2005; NFS 13

Taylor, Mildred D(elois) 1943- .... **CLC 21**
See also AAYA 10, 47; BW 1; BYA 3, 8; CA 85-88; CANR 25, 115, 136; CLR 9, 59, 90; CSW; DLB 52; JRDA; LAIT 3; MAICYA 1, 2; MTFW 2005; SAAS 5; SATA 135; WYA; YAW

3; HW 1, 2; LAIT 5; LATS 1:2; LAW;
LAWS 1; MTCW 1, 2; MTFW 2005;
RGWL 2; SSFS 14; TWA; WLIT 1

Varnhagen von Ense, Rahel
1771-1833 .... **NCLC 130**
See also DLB 90

Vasari, Giorgio 1511-1574 .... **LC 114**

Vasiliu, George
See Bacovia, George

Vasiliu, Gheorghe
See Bacovia, George
See also CA 123; 189

Vassa, Gustavus
See Equiano, Olaudah

Vassilikos, Vassilis 1933- .... **CLC 4, 8**
See also CA 81-84; CANR 75; EWL 3

Vaughan, Henry 1621-1695 .... **LC 27**
See also BRW 2; DLB 131; PAB; RGEL 2

Vaughn, Stephanie .... **CLC 62**

Vazov, Ivan (Minchov) 1850-1921 . **TCLC 25**
See also CA 121; 167; CDWLB 4; DLB
147

Veblen, Thorstein B(unde)
1857-1929 .... **TCLC 31**
See also AMWS 1; CA 115; 165; DLB 246;
MAL 5

Vega, Lope de 1562-1635 ... **HLCS 2; LC 23,
119**
See also EW 2; RGWL 2, 3

Vendler, Helen (Hennessy) 1933- ... **CLC 138**
See also CA 41-44R; CANR 25, 72, 136;
MTCW 1, 2; MTFW 2005

Venison, Alfred
See Pound, Ezra (Weston Loomis)

Ventsel, Elena Sergeevna 1907-2002
See Grekova, I.
See also CA 154

Verdi, Marie de
See Mencken, H(enry) L(ouis)

Verdu, Matilde
See Cela, Camilo Jose

Verga, Giovanni (Carmelo)
1840-1922 .... **SSC 21, 87; TCLC 3**
See also CA 104; 123; CANR 101; EW 7;
EWL 3; RGSF 2; RGWL 2, 3; WLIT 7

Vergil 70B.C.-19B.C. ... **CMLC 9, 40; PC 12;
WLCS**
See Virgil
See also AW 2; DA; DA3; DAB; DAC;
DAM MST, POET; EFS 1; LMFS 1

Vergil, Polydore c. 1470-1555 .... **LC 108**
See also DLB 132

Verhaeren, Emile (Adolphe Gustave)
1855-1916 .... **TCLC 12**
See also CA 109; EWL 3; GFL 1789 to the
Present

Verlaine, Paul (Marie) 1844-1896 .. **NCLC 2,
51; PC 2, 32**
See also DAM POET; DLB 217; EW 7;
GFL 1789 to the Present; LMFS 2; RGWL
2, 3; TWA

Verne, Jules (Gabriel) 1828-1905 ... **TCLC 6,
52**
See also AAYA 16; BYA 4; CA 110; 131;
CLR 88; DA3; DLB 123; GFL 1789 to
the Present; JRDA; LAIT 2; LMFS 2;
MAICYA 1, 2; MTFW 2005; RGWL 2, 3;
SATA 21; SCFW 1, 2; SFW 4; TWA;
WCH

Verus, Marcus Annius
See Aurelius, Marcus

Very, Jones 1813-1880 .... **NCLC 9**
See also DLB 1, 243; RGAL 4

Vesaas, Tarjei 1897-1970 .... **CLC 48**
See also CA 190; 29-32R; DLB 297; EW
11; EWL 3; RGWL 3

Vialis, Gaston
See Simenon, Georges (Jacques Christian)

Vian, Boris 1920-1959(?) .... **TCLC 9**
See also CA 106; 164; CANR 111; DLB
72, 321; EWL 3; GFL 1789 to the Present;
MTCW 2; RGWL 2, 3

Viaud, (Louis Marie) Julien 1850-1923
See Loti, Pierre
See also CA 107

Vicar, Henry
See Felsen, Henry Gregor

Vicente, Gil 1465-c. 1536 .... **LC 99**
See also DLB 318; IDTP; RGWL 2, 3

Vicker, Angus
See Felsen, Henry Gregor

Vidal, (Eugene Luther) Gore 1925- .. **CLC 2,
4, 6, 8, 10, 22, 33, 72, 142**
See Box, Edgar
See also AAYA 64; AITN 1; AMWS 4;
BEST 90:2; BPFB 3; CA 5-8R; CAD;
CANR 13, 45, 65, 100, 132; CD 5, 6;
CDALBS; CN 1, 2, 3, 4, 5, 6, 7; CPW;
DA3; DAM NOV, POP; DFS 2; DLB 6,
152; EWL 3; INT CANR-13; MAL 5;
MTCW 1, 2; MTFW 2005; RGAL 4;
RHW; TUS

Viereck, Peter (Robert Edwin)
1916- .... **CLC 4; PC 27**
See also CA 1-4R; CANR 1, 47; CP 1, 2, 3,
4, 5, 6, 7; DLB 5; MAL 5; PFS 9, 14

Vigny, Alfred (Victor) de
1797-1863 .... **NCLC 7, 102; PC 26**
See also DAM POET; DLB 119, 192, 217;
EW 5; GFL 1789 to the Present; RGWL
2, 3

Vilakazi, Benedict Wallet
1906-1947 .... **TCLC 37**
See also CA 168

Villa, Jose Garcia 1908-1997 ... **AAL; PC 22,
TCLC 176**
See also CA 25-28R; CANR 12, 118; CP 1,
2, 3, 4; DLB 312; EWL 3; EXPP

Villard, Oswald Garrison
1872-1949 .... **TCLC 160**
See also CA 113; 162; DLB 25, 91

Villarreal, Jose Antonio 1924- .... **HLC 2**
See also CA 133; CANR 93; DAM MULT;
DLB 82; HW 1; LAIT 4; RGAL 4

Villaurrutia, Xavier 1903-1950 .... **TCLC 80**
See also CA 192; EWL 3; HW 1; LAW

Villaverde, Cirilo 1812-1894 .... **NCLC 121**
See also LAW

Villehardouin, Geoffroi de
1150(?)-1218(?) .... **CMLC 38**

Villiers, George 1628-1687 .... **LC 107**
See also DLB 80; RGEL 2

**Villiers de l'Isle Adam, Jean Marie Mathias
Philippe Auguste** 1838-1889 ... **NCLC 3;
SSC 14**
See also DLB 123, 192; GFL 1789 to the
Present; RGSF 2

Villon, Francois 1431-1463(?) . **LC 62; PC 13**
See also DLB 208; EW 2; RGWL 2, 3;
TWA

Vine, Barbara .... **CLC 50**
See Rendell, Ruth (Barbara)
See also BEST 90:4

Vinge, Joan (Carol) D(ennison)
1948- .... **CLC 30; SSC 24**
See also AAYA 32; BPFB 3; CA 93-96;
CANR 72; SATA 36, 113; SFW 4; YAW

Viola, Herman J(oseph) 1938- .... **CLC 70**
See also CA 61-64; CANR 8, 23, 48, 91;
SATA 126

Violis, G.
See Simenon, Georges (Jacques Christian)

Viramontes, Helena Maria 1954- ..... **HLCS 2**
See also CA 159; DLB 122; HW 2; LLW

Virgil
See Vergil
See also CDWLB 1; DLB 211; LAIT 1;
RGWL 2, 3; WP

Visconti, Luchino 1906-1976 .... **CLC 16**
See also CA 81-84; 65-68; CANR 39

Vitry, Jacques de
See Jacques de Vitry

Vittorini, Elio 1908-1966 .... **CLC 6, 9, 14**
See also CA 133; 25-28R; DLB 264; EW
12; EWL 3; RGWL 2, 3

Vivekananda, Swami 1863-1902 .... **TCLC 88**

Vizenor, Gerald Robert 1934- .... **CLC 103;
NNAL**
See also CA 13-16R, 205; CAAE 205;
CAAS 22; CANR 5, 21, 44, 67; DAM
MULT; DLB 175, 227; MTCW 2; MTFW
2005; TCWW 2

Vizinczey, Stephen 1933- .... **CLC 40**
See also CA 128; CCA 1; INT CA-128

Vliet, R(ussell) G(ordon)
1929-1984 .... **CLC 22**
See also CA 37-40R; 112; CANR 18; CP 2,
3

Vogau, Boris Andreyevich 1894-1938
See Pilnyak, Boris
See also CA 123; 218

Vogel, Paula A(nne) 1951- ... **CLC 76; DC 19**
See also CA 108; CAD; CANR 119, 140;
CD 5, 6; CWD; DFS 14; MTFW 2005;
RGAL 4

Voigt, Cynthia 1942- .... **CLC 30**
See also AAYA 3, 30; BYA 1, 3, 6, 7, 8;
CA 106; CANR 18, 37, 40, 94, 145; CLR
13, 48; INT CANR-18; JRDA; LAIT 5;
MAICYA 1, 2; MAICYAS 1; MTFW
2005; SATA 48, 79, 116, 160; SATA-Brief
33; WYA; YAW

Voigt, Ellen Bryant 1943- .... **CLC 54**
See also CA 69-72; CANR 11, 29, 55, 115;
CP 7; CSW; CWP; DLB 120; PFS 23

Voinovich, Vladimir (Nikolaevich)
1932- .... **CLC 10, 49, 147**
See also CA 81-84; CAAS 12; CANR 33,
67; CWW 2; DLB 302; MTCW 1

Vollmann, William T. 1959- .... **CLC 89**
See also CA 134; CANR 67, 116; CN 7;
CPW; DA3; DAM NOV, POP; MTCW 2;
MTFW 2005

Voloshinov, V. N.
See Bakhtin, Mikhail Mikhailovich

Voltaire 1694-1778 . **LC 14, 79, 110; SSC 12;
WLC**
See also BYA 13; DA; DA3; DAB; DAC;
DAM DRAM, MST; DLB 314; EW 4;
GFL Beginnings to 1789; LATS 1:1;
LMFS 1; NFS 7; RGWL 2, 3; TWA

von Aschendrof, Baron Ignatz
See Ford, Ford Madox

von Chamisso, Adelbert
See Chamisso, Adelbert von

von Daeniken, Erich 1935- .... **CLC 30**
See also AITN 1; CA 37-40R; CANR 17,
44

von Daniken, Erich
See von Daeniken, Erich

von Hartmann, Eduard
1842-1906 .... **TCLC 96**

von Hayek, Friedrich August
See Hayek, F(riedrich) A(ugust von)

von Heidenstam, (Carl Gustaf) Verner
See Heidenstam, (Carl Gustaf) Verner von

von Heyse, Paul (Johann Ludwig)
See Heyse, Paul (Johann Ludwig von)

von Hofmannsthal, Hugo
See Hofmannsthal, Hugo von

von Horvath, Odon
See von Horvath, Odon

von Horvath, Odon
See von Horvath, Odon

von Horvath, Odon 1901-1938 .... **TCLC 45**
See von Horvath, Oedoen
See also CA 118; 194; DLB 85, 124; RGWL
2, 3

von Horvath, Oedoen
See von Horvath, Odon
See also CA 184

von Kleist, Heinrich
See Kleist, Heinrich von

**von Liliencron, (Friedrich Adolf Axel)
Detlev**
See Liliencron, (Friedrich Adolf Axel) De-
tlev von

Vonnegut, Kurt, Jr. 1922- . **CLC 1, 2, 3, 4, 5,
8, 12, 22, 40, 60, 111, 212; SSC 8;
WLC**
See also AAYA 6, 44; AITN 1; AMWS 2;
BEST 90:4; BPFB 3; BYA 3, 14; CA
1-4R; CANR 1, 25, 49, 75, 92; CDALB
1968-1988; CN 1, 2, 3, 4, 5, 6, 7; CPW 1;
DA; DA3; DAB; DAC; DAM MST, NOV,
POP; DLB 2, 8, 152; DLBD 3; DLBY
1980; EWL 3; EXPN; EXPS; LAIT 4;
LMFS 2; MAL 5; MTCW 1, 2; MTFW
2005; NFS 3; RGAL 4; SCFW; SFW 4;
SSFS 5; TUS; YAW

Von Rachen, Kurt
See Hubbard, L(afayette) Ron(ald)

von Rezzori (d'Arezzo), Gregor
See Rezzori (d'Arezzo), Gregor von

von Sternberg, Josef
See Sternberg, Josef von

Vorster, Gordon 1924- .... **CLC 34**
See also CA 133

Vosce, Trudie
See Ozick, Cynthia

Voznesensky, Andrei (Andreievich)
1933- .... **CLC 1, 15, 57**
See Voznesensky, Andrey
See also CA 89-92; CANR 37; CWW 2;
DAM POET; MTCW 1

Voznesensky, Andrey
See Voznesensky, Andrei (Andreievich)
See also EWL 3

Wace, Robert c. 1100-c. 1175 .... **CMLC 55**
See also DLB 146

Waddington, Miriam 1917-2004 .... **CLC 28**
See also CA 21-24R; 225; CANR 12, 30;
CCA 1; CP 1, 2, 3, 4, 5, 6, 7; DLB 68

Wagman, Fredrica 1937- .... **CLC 7**
See also CA 97-100; INT CA-97-100

Wagner, Linda W.
See Wagner-Martin, Linda (C.)

Wagner, Linda Welshimer
See Wagner-Martin, Linda (C.)

Wagner, Richard 1813-1883 ..... **NCLC 9, 119**
See also DLB 129; EW 6

Wagner-Martin, Linda (C.) 1936- .... **CLC 50**
See also CA 159; CANR 135

Wagoner, David (Russell) 1926- .... **CLC 3, 5,
15; PC 33**
See also AMWS 9; CA 1-4R; CAAS 3;
CANR 2, 71; CN 1, 2, 3, 4, 5, 6, 7; CP 1,
2, 3, 4, 5, 6, 7; DLB 5, 256; SATA 14;
TCWW 1, 2

Wah, Fred(erick James) 1939- .... **CLC 44**
See also CA 107; 141; CP 1, 7; DLB 60

Wahloo, Per 1926-1975 .... **CLC 7**
See also BPFB 3; CA 61-64; CANR 73;
CMW 4; MSW

Wahloo, Peter
See Wahloo, Per

Wain, John (Barrington) 1925-1994 . **CLC 2,
11, 15, 46**
See also CA 5-8R; 145; CAAS 4; CANR
23, 54; CDBLB 1960 to Present; CN 1, 2,
3, 4, 5; CP 1, 2, 3, 4; DLB 15, 27, 139,
155; EWL 3; MTCW 1, 2; MTFW 2005

Wajda, Andrzej 1926- .... **CLC 16, 219**
See also CA 102

Wakefield, Dan 1932- .... **CLC 7**
See also CA 21-24R; 211; CAAE 211;
CAAS 7; CN 4, 5, 6, 7

Wakefield, Herbert Russell
1888-1965 .... **TCLC 120**
See also CA 5-8R; CANR 77; HGG; SUFW

Wakoski, Diane 1937- ...... **CLC 2, 4, 7, 9, 11,
40; PC 15**
See also CA 13-16R, 216; CAAE 216;
CAAS 1; CANR 9, 60, 106; CP 1, 2, 3, 4,
5, 6, 7; CWP; DAM POET; DLB 5; INT
CANR-9; MAL 5; MTCW 2; MTFW
2005

Wakoski-Sherbell, Diane
See Wakoski, Diane

Walcott, Derek (Alton) 1930- ... **BLC 3; CLC
2, 4, 9, 14, 25, 42, 67, 76, 160; DC 7;
PC 46**
See also BW 2; CA 89-92; CANR 26, 47,
75, 80, 130; CBD; CD 5, 6; CDWLB 3;
CP 1, 2, 3, 4, 5, 6, 7; DA3; DAB; DAC;
DAM MST, MULT, POET; DLB 117;
DLBY 1981; DNFS 1; EFS 1; EWL 3;
LMFS 2; MTCW 1, 2; MTFW 2005; PFS
6; RGEL 2; TWA; WWE 1

Waldman, Anne (Lesley) 1945- .... **CLC 7**
See also BG 1:3; CA 37-40R; CAAS 17;
CANR 34, 69, 116; CP 1, 2, 3, 4, 5, 6, 7;
CWP; DLB 16

Waldo, E. Hunter
See Sturgeon, Theodore (Hamilton)

Waldo, Edward Hamilton
See Sturgeon, Theodore (Hamilton)

Walker, Alice (Malsenior) 1944- .... **BLC 3;
CLC 5, 6, 9, 19, 27, 46, 58, 103, 167;
PC 30; SSC 5; WLCS**
See also AAYA 3, 33; AFAW 1, 2; AMWS
3; BEST 89:4; BPFB 3; BW 2, 3; CA 37-
40R; CANR 9, 27, 49, 66, 82, 131;
CDALB 1968-1988; CN 4, 5, 6, 7; CPW;
CSW; DA; DA3; DAC; DAM MST,
MULT, NOV, POET, POP; DLB 6, 33,
143; EWL 3; EXPN; EXPS; FL 1:6; FW;
INT CANR-27; LAIT 3; MAL 5; MAWW;
MTCW 1, 2; MTFW 2005; NFS 5; RGAL
4; RGSF 2; SATA 31; SSFS 2, 11; TUS;
YAW

Walker, David Harry 1911-1992 ...... **CLC 14**
See also CA 1-4R; 137; CANR 1; CN 1, 2;
CWRI 5; SATA 8; SATA-Obit 71

Walker, Edward Joseph 1934-2004
See Walker, Ted
See also CA 21-24R; 226; CANR 12, 28,
53

Walker, George F(rederick) 1947- .. **CLC 44,
61**
See also CA 103; CANR 21, 43, 59; CD 5,
6; DAB; DAC; DAM MST; DLB 60

Walker, Joseph A. 1935-2003 .... **CLC 19**
See also BW 1, 3; CA 89-92; CAD; CANR
26, 143; CD 5, 6; DAM DRAM, MST;
DFS 12; DLB 38

Walker, Margaret (Abigail)
1915-1998 .... **BLC; CLC 1, 6; PC 20;
TCLC 129**
See also AFAW 1, 2; BW 2, 3; CA 73-76;
172; CANR 26, 54, 76, 136; CN 1, 2, 3,
4, 5, 6; CP 1, 2, 3, 4; CSW; DAM MULT;
DLB 76, 152; EXPP; FW; MAL 5;
MTCW 1, 2; MTFW 2005; RGAL 4;
RHW

Walker, Ted .... **CLC 13**
See Walker, Edward Joseph
See also CP 1, 2, 3, 4, 5, 6, 7; DLB 40

Wallace, David Foster 1962- ... **CLC 50, 114;
SSC 68**
See also AAYA 50; AMWS 10; CA 132;
CANR 59, 133; CN 7; DA3; MTCW 2;
MTFW 2005

Wallace, Dexter
See Masters, Edgar Lee

Wallace, (Richard Horatio) Edgar
1875-1932 .... **TCLC 57**
See also CA 115; 218; CMW 4; DLB 70;
MSW; RGEL 2

Wallace, Irving 1916-1990 .... **CLC 7, 13**
See also AITN 1; BPFB 3; CA 1-4R; 132;
CAAS 1; CANR 1, 27; CPW; DAM NOV,
POP; INT CANR-27; MTCW 1, 2

Wallant, Edward Lewis 1926-1962 ... **CLC 5,
10**
See also CA 1-4R; CANR 22; DLB 2, 28,
143, 299; EWL 3; MAL 5; MTCW 1, 2;
RGAL 4

Wallas, Graham 1858-1932 .... **TCLC 91**

Waller, Edmund 1606-1687 .... **LC 86**
See also BRW 2; DAM POET; DLB 126;
PAB; RGEL 2

Walley, Byron
See Card, Orson Scott

Walpole, Horace 1717-1797 .... **LC 2, 49**
See also BRW 3; DLB 39, 104, 213; GL 3;
HGG; LMFS 1; RGEL 2; SUFW 1; TEA

Walpole, Hugh (Seymour)
1884-1941 .... **TCLC 5**
See also CA 104; 165; DLB 34; HGG;
MTCW 2; RGEL 2; RHW

Walrond, Eric (Derwent) 1898-1966 . **HR 1:3**
See also BW 1; CA 125; DLB 51

Walser, Martin 1927- .... **CLC 27, 183**
See also CA 57-60; CANR 8, 46, 145;
CWW 2; DLB 75, 124; EWL 3

Walser, Robert 1878-1956 ..... **SSC 20; TCLC
18**
See also CA 118; 165; CANR 100; DLB
66; EWL 3

Walsh, Gillian Paton
See Paton Walsh, Gillian

Walsh, Jill Paton .... **CLC 35**
See Paton Walsh, Gillian
See also CLR 2, 65; WYA

Walter, Villiam Christian
See Andersen, Hans Christian

Walters, Anna L(ee) 1946- .... **NNAL**
See also CA 73-76

Walther von der Vogelweide c.
1170-1228 .... **CMLC 56**

Walton, Izaak 1593-1683 .... **LC 72**
See also BRW 2; CDBLB Before 1660;
DLB 151, 213; RGEL 2

Wambaugh, Joseph (Aloysius), Jr.
1937- .... **CLC 3, 18**
See also AITN 1; BEST 89:3; BPFB 3; CA
33-36R; CANR 42, 65, 115; CMW 4;
CPW 1; DA3; DAM NOV, POP; DLB 6;
DLBY 1983; MSW; MTCW 1, 2

Wang Wei 699(?)-761(?) .... **PC 18**
See also TWA

Warburton, William 1698-1779 .... **LC 97**
See also DLB 104

Ward, Arthur Henry Sarsfield 1883-1959
See Rohmer, Sax
See also CA 108; 173; CMW 4; HGG

Ward, Douglas Turner 1930- .... **CLC 19**
See also BW 1; CA 81-84; CAD; CANR
27; CD 5, 6; DLB 7, 38

Ward, E. D.
See Lucas, E(dward) V(errall)

Wellman, John McDowell 1945-
See Wellman, Mac
See also CA 166; CD 5

Wellman, Mac .... **CLC 65**
See Wellman, John McDowell; Wellman,
John McDowell
See also CAD; CD 6; RGAL 4

Wellman, Manly Wade 1903-1986 ... **CLC 49**
See also CA 1-4R; 118; CANR 6, 16, 44;
FANT; SATA 6; SATA-Obit 47; SFW 4;
SUFW

Wells, Carolyn 1869(?)-1942 .... **TCLC 35**
See also CA 113; 185; CMW 4; DLB 11

Wells, H(erbert) G(eorge) 1866-1946 . **SSC 6,
70; TCLC 6, 12, 19, 133; WLC**
See also AAYA 18; BPFB 3; BRW 6; CA
110; 121; CDBLB 1914-1945; CLR 64;
DA; DA3; DAB; DAC; DAM MST, NOV;
DLB 34, 70, 156, 178; EWL 3; EXPS;
HGG; LAIT 3; LMFS 2; MTCW 1, 2;
MTFW 2005; NFS 17, 20; RGEL 2;
RGSF 2; SATA 20; SCFW 1, 2; SFW 4;
SSFS 3; SUFW; TEA; WCH; WLIT 4;
YAW

Wells, Rosemary 1943- .... **CLC 12**
See also AAYA 13; BYA 7, 8; CA 85-88;
CANR 48, 120; CLR 16, 69; CWRI 5;
MAICYA 1, 2; SAAS 1; SATA 18, 69,
114, 156; YAW

Wells-Barnett, Ida B(ell)
1862-1931 .... **TCLC 125**
See also CA 182; DLB 23, 221

Welsh, Irvine 1958- .... **CLC 144**
See also CA 173; CANR 146; CN 7; DLB
271

Welty, Eudora (Alice) 1909-2001 .. **CLC 1, 2,
5, 14, 22, 33, 105, 220; SSC 1, 27, 51;
WLC**
See also AAYA 48; AMW; AMWR 1; BPFB
3; CA 9-12R; 199; CABS 1; CANR 32,
65, 128; CDALB 1941-1968; CN 1, 2, 3,
4, 5, 6, 7; CSW; DA; DA3; DAB; DAC;
DAM MST, NOV; DLB 2, 102, 143;
DLBD 12; DLBY 1987, 2001; EWL 3;
EXPS; HGG; LAIT 3; MAL 5; MAWW;
MTCW 1, 2; MTFW 2005; NFS 13, 15;
RGAL 4; RGSF 2; RHW; SSFS 2, 10;
TUS

Wen I-to 1899-1946 .... **TCLC 28**
See also EWL 3

Wentworth, Robert
See Hamilton, Edmond

Werfel, Franz (Viktor) 1890-1945 ... **TCLC 8**
See also CA 104; 161; DLB 81, 124; EWL
3; RGWL 2, 3

Wergeland, Henrik Arnold
1808-1845 .... **NCLC 5**

Wersba, Barbara 1932- .... **CLC 30**
See also AAYA 2, 30; BYA 6, 12, 13; CA
29-32R, 182; CAAE 182; CANR 16, 38;
CLR 3, 78; DLB 52; JRDA; MAICYA 1,
2; SAAS 2; SATA 1, 58; SATA-Essay 103;
WYA; YAW

Wertmueller, Lina 1928- .... **CLC 16**
See also CA 97-100; CANR 39, 78

Wescott, Glenway 1901-1987 .. **CLC 13; SSC
35**
See also CA 13-16R; 121; CANR 23, 70;
CN 1, 2, 3, 4; DLB 4, 9, 102; MAL 5;
RGAL 4

Wesker, Arnold 1932- .... **CLC 3, 5, 42**
See also CA 1-4R; CAAS 7; CANR 1, 33;
CBD; CD 5, 6; CDBLB 1960 to Present;
DAB; DAM DRAM; DLB 13, 310, 319;
EWL 3; MTCW 1; RGEL 2; TEA

Wesley, John 1703-1791 .... **LC 88**
See also DLB 104

Wesley, Richard (Errol) 1945- .... **CLC 7**
See also BW 1; CA 57-60; CAD; CANR
27; CD 5, 6; DLB 38

Wessel, Johan Herman 1742-1785 .... **LC 7**
See also DLB 300

West, Anthony (Panther)
1914-1987 .... **CLC 50**
See also CA 45-48; 124; CANR 3, 19; CN
1, 2, 3, 4; DLB 15

West, C. P.
See Wodehouse, P(elham) G(renville)

West, Cornel (Ronald) 1953- .... **BLCS; CLC
134**
See also CA 144; CANR 91; DLB 246

West, Delno C(loyde), Jr. 1936- .... **CLC 70**
See also CA 57-60

West, Dorothy 1907-1998 ...... **HR 1:3; TCLC
108**
See also BW 2; CA 143; 169; DLB 76

West, (Mary) Jessamyn 1902-1984 ... **CLC 7,
17**
See also CA 9-12R; 112; CANR 27; CN 1,
2, 3; DLB 6; DLBY 1984; MTCW 1, 2;
RGAL 4; RHW; SATA-Obit 37; TCWW
2; TUS; YAW

West, Morris L(anglo) 1916-1999 ..... **CLC 6,
33**
See also BPFB 3; CA 5-8R; 187; CANR
24, 49, 64; CN 1, 2, 3, 4, 5, 6; CPW; DLB
289; MTCW 1, 2; MTFW 2005

West, Nathanael 1903-1940 .. **SSC 16; TCLC
1, 14, 44**
See also AMW; AMWR 2; BPFB 3; CA
104; 125; CDALB 1929-1941; DA3; DLB
4, 9, 28; EWL 3; MAL 5; MTCW 1, 2;
MTFW 2005; NFS 16; RGAL 4; TUS

West, Owen
See Koontz, Dean R.

West, Paul 1930- .... **CLC 7, 14, 96**
See also CA 13-16R; CAAS 7; CANR 22,
53, 76, 89, 136; CN 1, 2, 3, 4, 5, 6, 7;
DLB 14; INT CANR-22; MTCW 2;
MTFW 2005

West, Rebecca 1892-1983 ... **CLC 7, 9, 31, 50**
See also BPFB 3; BRWS 3; CA 5-8R; 109;
CANR 19; CN 1, 2, 3; DLB 36; DLBY
1983; EWL 3; FW; MTCW 1, 2; MTFW
2005; NCFS 4; RGEL 2; TEA

Westall, Robert (Atkinson)
1929-1993 .... **CLC 17**
See also AAYA 12; BYA 2, 6, 7, 8, 9, 15;
CA 69-72; 141; CANR 18, 68; CLR 13;
FANT; JRDA; MAICYA 1, 2; MAICYAS
1; SAAS 2; SATA 23, 69; SATA-Obit 75;
WYA; YAW

Westermarck, Edward 1862-1939 . **TCLC 87**

Westlake, Donald E(dwin) 1933- . **CLC 7, 33**
See also BPFB 3; CA 17-20R; CAAS 13;
CANR 16, 44, 65, 94, 137; CMW 4;
CPW; DAM POP; INT CANR-16; MSW;
MTCW 2; MTFW 2005

Westmacott, Mary
See Christie, Agatha (Mary Clarissa)

Weston, Allen
See Norton, Andre

Wetcheek, J. L.
See Feuchtwanger, Lion

Wetering, Janwillem van de
See van de Wetering, Janwillem

Wetherald, Agnes Ethelwyn
1857-1940 .... **TCLC 81**
See also CA 202; DLB 99

Wetherell, Elizabeth
See Warner, Susan (Bogert)

Whale, James 1889-1957 .... **TCLC 63**

Whalen, Philip (Glenn) 1923-2002 .... **CLC 6,
29**
See also BG 1:3; CA 9-12R; 209; CANR 5,
39; CP 1, 2, 3, 4, 5, 6, 7; DLB 16; WP

Wharton, Edith (Newbold Jones)
1862-1937 ... **SSC 6, 84; TCLC 3, 9, 27,
53, 129, 149; WLC**
See also AAYA 25; AMW; AMWC 2;
AMWR 1; BPFB 3; CA 104; 132; CDALB
1865-1917; DA; DA3; DAB; DAC; DAM
MST, NOV; DLB 4, 9, 12, 78, 189; DLBD
13; EWL 3; EXPS; FL 1:6; GL 3; HGG;
LAIT 2, 3; LATS 1:1; MAL 5; MAWW;
MTCW 1, 2; MTFW 2005; NFS 5, 11,
15, 20; RGAL 4; RGSF 2; RHW; SSFS 6,
7; SUFW; TUS

Wharton, James
See Mencken, H(enry) L(ouis)

Wharton, William (a pseudonym)
1925- .... **CLC 18, 37**
See also CA 93-96; CN 4, 5, 6, 7; DLBY
1980; INT CA-93-96

Wheatley (Peters), Phillis
1753(?)-1784 ... **BLC 3; LC 3, 50; PC 3;
WLC**
See also AFAW 1, 2; CDALB 1640-1865;
DA; DA3; DAC; DAM MST, MULT,
POET; DLB 31, 50; EXPP; FL 1:1; PFS
13; RGAL 4

Wheelock, John Hall 1886-1978 .... **CLC 14**
See also CA 13-16R; 77-80; CANR 14; CP
1, 2; DLB 45; MAL 5

Whim-Wham
See Curnow, (Thomas) Allen (Monro)

White, Babington
See Braddon, Mary Elizabeth

White, E(lwyn) B(rooks)
1899-1985 .... **CLC 10, 34, 39**
See also AAYA 62; AITN 2; AMWS 1; CA
13-16R; 116; CANR 16, 37; CDALBS;
CLR 1, 21; CPW; DA3; DAM POP; DLB
11, 22; EWL 3; FANT; MAICYA 1, 2;
MAL 5; MTCW 1, 2; MTFW 2005; NCFS
5; RGAL 4; SATA 2, 29, 100; SATA-Obit
44; TUS

White, Edmund (Valentine III)
1940- .... **CLC 27, 110**
See also AAYA 7; CA 45-48; CANR 3, 19,
36, 62, 107, 133; CN 5, 6, 7; DA3; DAM
POP; DLB 227; MTCW 1, 2; MTFW
2005

White, Hayden V. 1928- .... **CLC 148**
See also CA 128; CANR 135; DLB 246

White, Patrick (Victor Martindale)
1912-1990 ...... **CLC 3, 4, 5, 7, 9, 18, 65,
69; SSC 39; TCLC 176**
See also BRWS 1; CA 81-84; 132; CANR
43; CN 1, 2, 3, 4; DLB 260; EWL 3;
MTCW 1; RGEL 2; RGSF 2; RHW;
TWA; WWE 1

White, Phyllis Dorothy James 1920-
See James, P. D.
See also CA 21-24R; CANR 17, 43, 65,
112; CMW 4; CN 7; CPW; DA3; DAM
POP; MTCW 1, 2; MTFW 2005; TEA

White, T(erence) H(anbury)
1906-1964 .... **CLC 30**
See also AAYA 22; BPFB 3; BYA 4, 5; CA
73-76; CANR 37; DLB 160; FANT;
JRDA; LAIT 1; MAICYA 1, 2; RGEL 2;
SATA 12; SUFW 1; YAW

White, Terence de Vere 1912-1994 ... **CLC 49**
See also CA 49-52; 145; CANR 3

White, Walter
See White, Walter F(rancis)

White, Walter F(rancis) 1893-1955 ... **BLC 3;
HR 1:3; TCLC 15**
See also BW 1; CA 115; 124; DAM MULT;
DLB 51

White, William Hale 1831-1913
See Rutherford, Mark
See also CA 121; 189

POET; DLB 4, 16, 54, 86; EWL 3; EXPP;
MAL 5; MTCW 1, 2; MTFW 2005; NCFS
4; PAB; PFS 1, 6, 11; RGAL 4; RGSF 2;
TUS; WP

Williamson, David (Keith) 1942- ..... **CLC 56**
See also CA 103; CANR 41; CD 5, 6; DLB
289

Williamson, Ellen Douglas 1905-1984
See Douglas, Ellen
See also CA 17-20R; 114; CANR 39

Williamson, Jack .... **CLC 29**
See Williamson, John Stewart
See also CAAS 8; DLB 8; SCFW 1, 2

Williamson, John Stewart 1908-
See Williamson, Jack
See also CA 17-20R; CANR 23, 70; SFW 4

Willie, Frederick
See Lovecraft, H(oward) P(hillips)

Willingham, Calder (Baynard, Jr.)
1922-1995 .... **CLC 5, 51**
See also CA 5-8R; 147; CANR 3; CN 1, 2,
3, 4, 5; CSW; DLB 2, 44; IDFW 3, 4;
MTCW 1

Willis, Charles
See Clarke, Arthur C(harles)

Willy
See Colette, (Sidonie-Gabrielle)

Willy, Colette
See Colette, (Sidonie-Gabrielle)
See also GLL 1

Wilmot, John 1647-1680 .... **LC 75; PC 66**
See Rochester
See also BRW 2; DLB 131; PAB

Wilson, A(ndrew) N(orman) 1950- .. **CLC 33**
See also BRWS 6; CA 112; 122; CN 4, 5,
6, 7; DLB 14, 155, 194; MTCW 2

Wilson, Angus (Frank Johnstone)
1913-1991 . **CLC 2, 3, 5, 25, 34; SSC 21**
See also BRWS 1; CA 5-8R; 134; CANR
21; CN 1, 2, 3, 4; DLB 15, 139, 155;
EWL 3; MTCW 1, 2; MTFW 2005; RGEL
2; RGSF 2

Wilson, August 1945-2005 .. **BLC 3; CLC 39,**
50, 63, 118, 222; DC 2; WLCS
See also AAYA 16; AFAW 2; AMWS 8; BW
2, 3; CA 115; 122; CAD; CANR 42, 54,
76, 128; CD 5, 6; DA; DA3; DAB; DAC;
DAM DRAM, MST, MULT; DFS 3, 7,
15, 17; DLB 228; EWL 3; LAIT 4; LATS
1:2; MAL 5; MTCW 1, 2; MTFW 2005;
RGAL 4

Wilson, Brian 1942- .... **CLC 12**

Wilson, Colin (Henry) 1931- .... **CLC 3, 14**
See also CA 1-4R; CAAS 5; CANR 1, 22,
33, 77; CMW 4; CN 1, 2, 3, 4, 5, 6; DLB
14, 194; HGG; MTCW 1; SFW 4

Wilson, Dirk
See Pohl, Frederik

Wilson, Edmund 1895-1972 .. **CLC 1, 2, 3, 8,**
24
See also AMW; CA 1-4R; 37-40R; CANR
1, 46, 110; CN 1; DLB 63; EWL 3; MAL
5; MTCW 1, 2; MTFW 2005; RGAL 4;
TUS

Wilson, Ethel Davis (Bryant)
1888(?)-1980 .... **CLC 13**
See also CA 102; CN 1, 2; DAC; DAM
POET; DLB 68; MTCW 1; RGEL 2

Wilson, Harriet
See Wilson, Harriet E. Adams
See also DLB 239

Wilson, Harriet E.
See Wilson, Harriet E. Adams
See also DLB 243

Wilson, Harriet E. Adams
1827(?)-1863(?) .... **BLC 3; NCLC 78**
See Wilson, Harriet; Wilson, Harriet E.
See also DAM MULT; DLB 50

Wilson, John 1785-1854 .... **NCLC 5**

Wilson, John (Anthony) Burgess 1917-1993
See Burgess, Anthony
See also CA 1-4R; 143; CANR 2, 46; DA3;
DAC; DAM NOV; MTCW 1, 2; MTFW
2005; NFS 15; TEA

Wilson, Lanford 1937- .. **CLC 7, 14, 36, 197;**
DC 19
See also CA 17-20R; CABS 3; CAD; CANR
45, 96; CD 5, 6; DAM DRAM; DFS 4, 9,
12, 16, 20; DLB 7; EWL 3; MAL 5; TUS

Wilson, Robert M. 1941- .... **CLC 7, 9**
See also CA 49-52; CAD; CANR 2, 41; CD
5, 6; MTCW 1

Wilson, Robert McLiam 1964- .... **CLC 59**
See also CA 132; DLB 267

Wilson, Sloan 1920-2003 .... **CLC 32**
See also CA 1-4R; 216; CANR 1, 44; CN
1, 2, 3, 4, 5, 6

Wilson, Snoo 1948- .... **CLC 33**
See also CA 69-72; CBD; CD 5, 6

Wilson, William S(mith) 1932- .... **CLC 49**
See also CA 81-84

Wilson, (Thomas) Woodrow
1856-1924 .... **TCLC 79**
See also CA 166; DLB 47

Wilson and Warnke eds. .... **CLC 65**

Winchilsea, Anne (Kingsmill) Finch
1661-1720
See Finch, Anne
See also RGEL 2

Windham, Basil
See Wodehouse, P(elham) G(renville)

Wingrove, David (John) 1954- .... **CLC 68**
See also CA 133; SFW 4

Winnemucca, Sarah 1844-1891 .... **NCLC 79;**
NNAL
See also DAM MULT; DLB 175; RGAL 4

Winstanley, Gerrard 1609-1676 .... **LC 52**

Wintergreen, Jane
See Duncan, Sara Jeannette

Winters, Arthur Yvor
See Winters, Yvor

Winters, Janet Lewis .... **CLC 41**
See Lewis, Janet
See also DLBY 1987

Winters, Yvor 1900-1968 .... **CLC 4, 8, 32**
See also AMWS 2; CA 11-12; 25-28R; CAP
1; DLB 48; EWL 3; MAL 5; MTCW 1;
RGAL 4

Winterson, Jeanette 1959- .... **CLC 64, 158**
See also BRWS 4; CA 136; CANR 58, 116;
CN 5, 6, 7; CPW; DA3; DAM POP; DLB
207, 261; FANT; FW; GLL 1; MTCW 2;
MTFW 2005; RHW

Winthrop, John 1588-1649 .... **LC 31, 107**
See also DLB 24, 30

Wirth, Louis 1897-1952 .... **TCLC 92**
See also CA 210

Wiseman, Frederick 1930- .... **CLC 20**
See also CA 159

Wister, Owen 1860-1938 .... **TCLC 21**
See also BPFB 3; CA 108; 162; DLB 9, 78,
186; RGAL 4; SATA 62; TCWW 1, 2

Wither, George 1588-1667 .... **LC 96**
See also DLB 121; RGEL 2

Witkacy
See Witkiewicz, Stanisław Ignacy

Witkiewicz, Stanisław Ignacy
1885-1939 .... **TCLC 8**
See also CA 105; 162; CDWLB 4; DLB
215; EW 10; EWL 3; RGWL 2, 3; SFW 4

Wittgenstein, Ludwig (Josef Johann)
1889-1951 .... **TCLC 59**
See also CA 113; 164; DLB 262; MTCW 2

Wittig, Monique 1935-2003 .... **CLC 22**
See also CA 116; 135; 212; CANR 143;
CWW 2; DLB 83; EWL 3; FW; GLL 1

Wittlin, Jozef 1896-1976 .... **CLC 25**
See also CA 49-52; 65-68; CANR 3; EWL
3

Wodehouse, P(elham) G(renville)
1881-1975 . **CLC 1, 2, 5, 10, 22; SSC 2;**
TCLC 108
See also AAYA 65; AITN 2; BRWS 3; CA
45-48; 57-60; CANR 3, 33; CDBLB
1914-1945; CN 1, 2; CPW 1; DA3; DAB;
DAC; DAM NOV; DLB 34, 162; EWL 3;
MTCW 1, 2; MTFW 2005; RGEL 2;
RGSF 2; SATA 22; SSFS 10

Woiwode, L.
See Woiwode, Larry (Alfred)

Woiwode, Larry (Alfred) 1941- ... **CLC 6, 10**
See also CA 73-76; CANR 16, 94; CN 3, 4,
5, 6, 7; DLB 6; INT CANR-16

Wojciechowska, Maia (Teresa)
1927-2002 .... **CLC 26**
See also AAYA 8, 46; BYA 3; CA 9-12R;
183; 209; CAAE 183; CANR 4, 41; CLR
1; JRDA; MAICYA 1, 2; SAAS 1; SATA
1, 28, 83; SATA-Essay 104; SATA-Obit
134; YAW

Wojtyla, Karol (Jozef)
See John Paul II, Pope

Wojtyla, Karol (Josef)
See John Paul II, Pope

Wolf, Christa 1929- .... **CLC 14, 29, 58, 150**
See also CA 85-88; CANR 45, 123; CD-
WLB 2; CWW 2; DLB 75; EWL 3; FW;
MTCW 1; RGWL 2, 3; SSFS 14

Wolf, Naomi 1962- .... **CLC 157**
See also CA 141; CANR 110; FW; MTFW
2005

Wolfe, Gene 1931- .... **CLC 25**
See also AAYA 35; CA 57-60; CAAS 9;
CANR 6, 32, 60; CPW; DAM POP; DLB
8; FANT; MTCW 2; MTFW 2005; SATA
118, 165; SCFW 2; SFW 4; SUFW 2

Wolfe, Gene Rodman
See Wolfe, Gene

Wolfe, George C. 1954- .... **BLCS; CLC 49**
See also CA 149; CAD; CD 5, 6

Wolfe, Thomas (Clayton)
1900-1938 ...... **SSC 33; TCLC 4, 13, 29,**
61; WLC
See also AMW; BPFB 3; CA 104; 132;
CANR 102; CDALB 1929-1941; DA;
DA3; DAB; DAC; DAM MST, NOV;
DLB 9, 102, 229; DLBD 2, 16; DLBY
1985, 1997; EWL 3; MAL 5; MTCW 1,
2; NFS 18; RGAL 4; SSFS 18; TUS

Wolfe, Thomas Kennerly, Jr.
1931- .... **CLC 147**
See Wolfe, Tom
See also CA 13-16R; CANR 9, 33, 70, 104;
DA3; DAM POP; DLB 185; EWL 3; INT
CANR-9; MTCW 1, 2; MTFW 2005; TUS

Wolfe, Tom ...... **CLC 1, 2, 9, 15, 35, 51**
See Wolfe, Thomas Kennerly, Jr.
See also AAYA 8, 67; AITN 2; AMWS 3;
BEST 89:1; BPFB 3; CN 5, 6, 7; CPW;
CSW; DLB 152; LAIT 5; RGAL 4

Wolff, Geoffrey (Ansell) 1937- .... **CLC 41**
See also CA 29-32R; CANR 29, 43, 78

Wolff, Sonia
See Levitin, Sonia (Wolff)

Wolff, Tobias (Jonathan Ansell)
1945- .... **CLC 39, 64, 172; SSC 63**
See also AAYA 16; AMWS 7; BEST 90:2;
BYA 12; CA 114; 117; CAAS 22; CANR
54, 76, 96; CN 5, 6, 7; CSW; DA3; DLB
130; EWL 3; INT CA-117; MTCW 2;
MTFW 2005; RGAL 4; RGSF 2; SSFS 4,
11

Wolfram von Eschenbach c. 1170-c.
1220 .... **CMLC 5**
See Eschenbach, Wolfram von
See also CDWLB 2; DLB 138; EW 1;
RGWL 2

Wolitzer, Hilma 1930- .... **CLC 17**
See also CA 65-68; CANR 18, 40; INT
CANR-18; SATA 31; YAW

Wollstonecraft, Mary 1759-1797 .... **LC 5, 50,
90**
See also BRWS 3; CDBLB 1789-1832;
DLB 39, 104, 158, 252; FL 1:1; FW;
LAIT 1; RGEL 2; TEA; WLIT 3

Wonder, Stevie .... **CLC 12**
See Morris, Steveland Judkins

Wong, Jade Snow 1922- .... **CLC 17**
See also CA 109; CANR 91; SATA 112

Woodberry, George Edward
1855-1930 .... **TCLC 73**
See also CA 165; DLB 71, 103

Woodcott, Keith
See Brunner, John (Kilian Houston)

Woodruff, Robert W.
See Mencken, H(enry) L(ouis)

Woolf, (Adeline) Virginia 1882-1941 .. **SSC 7,
79; TCLC 1, 5, 20, 43, 56, 101, 123,
128; WLC**
See also AAYA 44; BPFB 3; BRW 7;
BRWC 2; BRWR 1; CA 104; 130; CANR
64, 132; CDBLB 1914-1945; DA; DA3;
DAB; DAC; DAM MST, NOV; DLB 36,
100, 162; DLBD 10; EWL 3; EXPS; FL
1:6; FW; LAIT 3; LATS 1:1; LMFS 2;
MTCW 1, 2; MTFW 2005; NCFS 2; NFS
8, 12; RGEL 2; RGSF 2; SSFS 4, 12;
TEA; WLIT 4

Woollcott, Alexander (Humphreys)
1887-1943 .... **TCLC 5**
See also CA 105; 161; DLB 29

Woolrich, Cornell .... **CLC 77**
See Hopley-Woolrich, Cornell George
See also MSW

Woolson, Constance Fenimore
1840-1894 .... **NCLC 82; SSC 90**
See also DLB 12, 74, 189, 221; RGAL 4

Wordsworth, Dorothy 1771-1855 . **NCLC 25,
138**
See also DLB 107

Wordsworth, William 1770-1850 .. **NCLC 12,
38, 111; PC 4, 67; WLC**
See also BRW 4; BRWC 1; CDBLB 1789-
1832; DA; DA3; DAB; DAC; DAM MST,
POET; DLB 93, 107; EXPP; LATS 1:1;
LMFS 1; PAB; PFS 2; RGEL 2; TEA;
WLIT 3; WP

Wotton, Sir Henry 1568-1639 .... **LC 68**
See also DLB 121; RGEL 2

Wouk, Herman 1915- .... **CLC 1, 9, 38**
See also BPFB 2, 3; CA 5-8R; CANR 6,
33, 67, 146; CDALBS; CN 1, 2, 3, 4, 5,
6; CPW; DA3; DAM NOV, POP; DLBY
1982; INT CANR-6; LAIT 4; MAL 5;
MTCW 1, 2; MTFW 2005; NFS 7; TUS

Wright, Charles (Penzel, Jr.) 1935- .. **CLC 6,
13, 28, 119, 146**
See also AMWS 5; CA 29-32R; CAAS 7;
CANR 23, 36, 62, 88, 135; CP 3, 4, 5, 6,
7; DLB 165; DLBY 1982; EWL 3;
MTCW 1, 2; MTFW 2005; PFS 10

Wright, Charles Stevenson 1932- ..... **BLC 3;
CLC 49**
See also BW 1; CA 9-12R; CANR 26; CN
1, 2, 3, 4, 5, 6, 7; DAM MULT, POET;
DLB 33

Wright, Frances 1795-1852 .... **NCLC 74**
See also DLB 73

Wright, Frank Lloyd 1867-1959 .... **TCLC 95**
See also AAYA 33; CA 174

Wright, Jack R.
See Harris, Mark

Wright, James (Arlington)
1927-1980 .... **CLC 3, 5, 10, 28; PC 36**
See also AITN 2; AMWS 3; CA 49-52; 97-
100; CANR 4, 34, 64; CDALBS; CP 1, 2;
DAM POET; DLB 5, 169; EWL 3; EXPP;
MAL 5; MTCW 1, 2; MTFW 2005; PFS
7, 8; RGAL 4; TUS; WP

Wright, Judith (Arundell)
1915-2000 .... **CLC 11, 53; PC 14**
See also CA 13-16R; 188; CANR 31, 76,
93; CP 1, 2, 3, 4, 5, 6, 7; CWP; DLB 260;
EWL 3; MTCW 1, 2; MTFW 2005; PFS
8; RGEL 2; SATA 14; SATA-Obit 121

Wright, L(aurali) R. 1939- .... **CLC 44**
See also CA 138; CMW 4

Wright, Richard (Nathaniel)
1908-1960 ... **BLC 3; CLC 1, 3, 4, 9, 14,
21, 48, 74; SSC 2; TCLC 136; WLC**
See also AAYA 5, 42; AFAW 1, 2; AMW;
BPFB 3; BW 1; BYA 2; CA 108; CANR
64; CDALB 1929-1941; DA; DA3; DAB;
DAC; DAM MST, MULT, NOV; DLB 76,
102; DLBD 2; EWL 3; EXPN; LAIT 3,
4; MAL 5; MTCW 1, 2; MTFW 2005;
NCFS 1; NFS 1, 7; RGAL 4; RGSF 2;
SSFS 3, 9, 15, 20; TUS; YAW

Wright, Richard B(ruce) 1937- .... **CLC 6**
See also CA 85-88; CANR 120; DLB 53

Wright, Rick 1945- .... **CLC 35**

Wright, Rowland
See Wells, Carolyn

Wright, Stephen 1946- .... **CLC 33**
See also CA 237

Wright, Willard Huntington 1888-1939
See Van Dine, S. S.
See also CA 115; 189; CMW 4; DLBD 16

Wright, William 1930- .... **CLC 44**
See also CA 53-56; CANR 7, 23

Wroth, Lady Mary 1587-1653(?) .... **LC 30;
PC 38**
See also DLB 121

Wu Ch'eng-en 1500(?)-1582(?) .... **LC 7**

Wu Ching-tzu 1701-1754 .... **LC 2**

Wulfstan c. 10th cent. -1023 .... **CMLC 59**

Wurlitzer, Rudolph 1938(?)- .... **CLC 2, 4, 15**
See also CA 85-88; CN 4, 5, 6, 7; DLB 173

Wyatt, Sir Thomas c. 1503-1542 . **LC 70; PC
27**
See also BRW 1; DLB 132; EXPP; RGEL
2; TEA

Wycherley, William 1640-1716 .... **LC 8, 21,
102**
See also BRW 2; CDBLB 1660-1789; DAM
DRAM; DLB 80; RGEL 2

Wyclif, John c. 1330-1384 .... **CMLC 70**
See also DLB 146

Wylie, Elinor (Morton Hoyt)
1885-1928 .... **PC 23; TCLC 8**
See also AMWS 1; CA 105; 162; DLB 9,
45; EXPP; MAL 5; RGAL 4

Wylie, Philip (Gordon) 1902-1971 ... **CLC 43**
See also CA 21-22; 33-36R; CAP 2; CN 1;
DLB 9; SFW 4

Wyndham, John .... **CLC 19**
See Harris, John (Wyndham Parkes Lucas)
Beynon
See also DLB 255; SCFW 1, 2

Wyss, Johann David Von
1743-1818 .... **NCLC 10**
See also CLR 92; JRDA; MAICYA 1, 2;
SATA 29; SATA-Brief 27

Xenophon c. 430B.C.-c. 354B.C. ... **CMLC 17**
See also AW 1; DLB 176; RGWL 2, 3

Xingjian, Gao 1940-
See Gao Xingjian
See also CA 193; DFS 21; RGWL 3

Yakamochi 718-785 .... **CMLC 45; PC 48**

Yakumo Koizumi
See Hearn, (Patricio) Lafcadio (Tessima
Carlos)

Yamada, Mitsuye (May) 1923- .... **PC 44**
See also CA 77-80

Yamamoto, Hisaye 1921- .... **AAL; SSC 34**
See also CA 214; DAM MULT; DLB 312;
LAIT 4; SSFS 14

Yamauchi, Wakako 1924- .... **AAL**
See also CA 214; DLB 312

Yanez, Jose Donoso
See Donoso (Yanez), Jose

Yanovsky, Basile S.
See Yanovsky, V(assily) S(emenovich)

Yanovsky, V(assily) S(emenovich)
1906-1989 .... **CLC 2, 18**
See also CA 97-100; 129

Yates, Richard 1926-1992 .... **CLC 7, 8, 23**
See also AMWS 11; CA 5-8R; 139; CANR
10, 43; CN 1, 2, 3, 4, 5; DLB 2, 234;
DLBY 1981, 1992; INT CANR-10

Yau, John 1950- .... **PC 61**
See also CA 154; CANR 89; CP 4, 5, 6, 7;
DLB 234, 312

Yeats, W. B.
See Yeats, William Butler

Yeats, William Butler 1865-1939 . **PC 20, 51;
TCLC 1, 11, 18, 31, 93, 116; WLC**
See also AAYA 48; BRW 6; BRWR 1; CA
104; 127; CANR 45; CDBLB 1890-1914;
DA; DA3; DAB; DAC; DAM DRAM,
MST, POET; DLB 10, 19, 98, 156; EWL
3; EXPP; MTCW 1, 2; MTFW 2005;
NCFS 3; PAB; PFS 1, 2, 5, 7, 13, 15;
RGEL 2; TEA; WLIT 4; WP

Yehoshua, A(braham) B. 1936- .. **CLC 13, 31**
See also CA 33-36R; CANR 43, 90, 145;
CWW 2; EWL 3; RGSF 2; RGWL 3;
WLIT 6

Yellow Bird
See Ridge, John Rollin

Yep, Laurence Michael 1948- .... **CLC 35**
See also AAYA 5, 31; BYA 7; CA 49-52;
CANR 1, 46, 92; CLR 3, 17, 54; DLB 52,
312; FANT; JRDA; MAICYA 1, 2; MAI-
CYAS 1; SATA 7, 69, 123; WYA; YAW

Yerby, Frank G(arvin) 1916-1991 ..... **BLC 3;
CLC 1, 7, 22**
See also BPFB 3; BW 1, 3; CA 9-12R; 136;
CANR 16, 52; CN 1, 2, 3, 4, 5; DAM
MULT; DLB 76; INT CANR-16; MTCW
1; RGAL 4; RHW

Yesenin, Sergei Alexandrovich
See Esenin, Sergei (Alexandrovich)

Yesenin, Sergey
See Esenin, Sergei (Alexandrovich)
See also EWL 3

Yevtushenko, Yevgeny (Alexandrovich)
1933- ...... **CLC 1, 3, 13, 26, 51, 126; PC
40**
See Evtushenko, Evgenii Aleksandrovich
See also CA 81-84; CANR 33, 54; DAM
POET; EWL 3; MTCW 1

Yezierska, Anzia 1885(?)-1970 .... **CLC 46**
See also CA 126; 89-92; DLB 28, 221; FW;
MTCW 1; RGAL 4; SSFS 15

Yglesias, Helen 1915- .... **CLC 7, 22**
See also CA 37-40R; CAAS 20; CANR 15,
65, 95; CN 4, 5, 6, 7; INT CANR-15;
MTCW 1

Yokomitsu, Riichi 1898-1947 .... **TCLC 47**
See also CA 170; EWL 3

Yonge, Charlotte (Mary)
1823-1901 .... **TCLC 48**
See also CA 109; 163; DLB 18, 163; RGEL
2; SATA 17; WCH

York, Jeremy
See Creasey, John

York, Simon
See Heinlein, Robert A(nson)
Yorke, Henry Vincent 1905-1974 ..... **CLC 13**
See Green, Henry
See also CA 85-88; 49-52
Yosano Akiko 1878-1942 .... **PC 11; TCLC 59**
See also CA 161; EWL 3; RGWL 3
Yoshimoto, Banana .... **CLC 84**
See Yoshimoto, Mahoko
See also AAYA 50; NFS 7
Yoshimoto, Mahoko 1964-
See Yoshimoto, Banana
See also CA 144; CANR 98; SSFS 16
Young, Al(bert James) 1939- .. **BLC 3; CLC 19**
See also BW 2, 3; CA 29-32R; CANR 26, 65, 109; CN 2, 3, 4, 5, 6, 7; CP 1, 2, 3, 4, 5, 6, 7; DAM MULT; DLB 33
Young, Andrew (John) 1885-1971 ...... **CLC 5**
See also CA 5-8R; CANR 7, 29; CP 1; RGEL 2
Young, Collier
See Bloch, Robert (Albert)
Young, Edward 1683-1765 .... **LC 3, 40**
See also DLB 95; RGEL 2
Young, Marguerite (Vivian)
1909-1995 .... **CLC 82**
See also CA 13-16; 150; CAP 1; CN 1, 2, 3, 4, 5, 6
Young, Neil 1945- .... **CLC 17**
See also CA 110; CCA 1
Young Bear, Ray A. 1950- ... **CLC 94; NNAL**
See also CA 146; DAM MULT; DLB 175; MAL 5
Yourcenar, Marguerite 1903-1987 ... **CLC 19, 38, 50, 87**
See also BPFB 3; CA 69-72; CANR 23, 60, 93; DAM NOV; DLB 72; DLBY 1988; EW 12; EWL 3; GFL 1789 to the Present; GLL 1; MTCW 1, 2; MTFW 2005; RGWL 2, 3
Yuan, Chu 340(?)B.C.-278(?)B.C. . **CMLC 36**
Yurick, Sol 1925- .... **CLC 6**
See also CA 13-16R; CANR 25; CN 1, 2, 3, 4, 5, 6, 7; MAL 5
Zabolotsky, Nikolai Alekseevich
1903-1958 .... **TCLC 52**
See Zabolotsky, Nikolay Alekseevich
See also CA 116; 164
Zabolotsky, Nikolay Alekseevich
See Zabolotsky, Nikolai Alekseevich
See also EWL 3
Zagajewski, Adam 1945- .... **PC 27**
See also CA 186; DLB 232; EWL 3
Zalygin, Sergei -2000 .... **CLC 59**
Zalygin, Sergei (Pavlovich)
1913-2000 .... **CLC 59**
See also DLB 302

Zamiatin, Evgenii
See Zamyatin, Evgeny Ivanovich
See also RGSF 2; RGWL 2, 3
Zamiatin, Evgenii Ivanovich
See Zamyatin, Evgeny Ivanovich
See also DLB 272
Zamiatin, Yevgenii
See Zamyatin, Evgeny Ivanovich
Zamora, Bernice (B. Ortiz) 1938- .. **CLC 89; HLC 2**
See also CA 151; CANR 80; DAM MULT; DLB 82; HW 1, 2
Zamyatin, Evgeny Ivanovich
1884-1937 .... **SSC 89; TCLC 8, 37**
See Zamiatin, Evgenii; Zamiatin, Evgenii Ivanovich; Zamyatin, Yevgeny Ivanovich
See also CA 105; 166; SFW 4
Zamyatin, Yevgeny Ivanovich
See Zamyatin, Evgeny Ivanovich
See also EW 10; EWL 3
Zangwill, Israel 1864-1926 ... **SSC 44; TCLC 16**
See also CA 109; 167; CMW 4; DLB 10, 135, 197; RGEL 2
Zanzotto, Andrea 1921- .... **PC 65**
See also CA 208; CWW 2; DLB 128; EWL 3
Zappa, Francis Vincent, Jr. 1940-1993
See Zappa, Frank
See also CA 108; 143; CANR 57
Zappa, Frank .... **CLC 17**
See Zappa, Francis Vincent, Jr.
Zaturenska, Marya 1902-1982 ..... **CLC 6, 11**
See also CA 13-16R; 105; CANR 22; CP 1, 2, 3
Zayas y Sotomayor, Maria de 1590-c. 1661 .... **LC 102**
See also RGSF 2
Zeami 1363-1443 .... **DC 7; LC 86**
See also DLB 203; RGWL 2, 3
Zelazny, Roger (Joseph) 1937-1995 . **CLC 21**
See also AAYA 7, 68; BPFB 3; CA 21-24R; 148; CANR 26, 60; CN 6; DLB 8; FANT; MTCW 1, 2; MTFW 2005; SATA 57; SATA-Brief 39; SCFW 1, 2; SFW 4; SUFW 1, 2
Zhang Ailing
See Chang, Eileen
See also CWW 2; RGSF 2
Zhdanov, Andrei Alexandrovich
1896-1948 .... **TCLC 18**
See also CA 117; 167
Zhukovsky, Vasilii Andreevich
See Zhukovsky, Vasily (Andreevich)
See also DLB 205
Zhukovsky, Vasily (Andreevich)
1783-1852 .... **NCLC 35**
See Zhukovsky, Vasilii Andreevich
Ziegenhagen, Eric .... **CLC 55**

Zimmer, Jill Schary
See Robinson, Jill
Zimmerman, Robert
See Dylan, Bob
Zindel, Paul 1936-2003 ...... **CLC 6, 26; DC 5**
See also AAYA 2, 37; BYA 2, 3, 8, 11, 14; CA 73-76; 213; CAD; CANR 31, 65, 108; CD 5, 6; CDALBS; CLR 3, 45, 85; DA; DA3; DAB; DAC; DAM DRAM, MST, NOV; DFS 12; DLB 7, 52; JRDA; LAIT 5; MAICYA 1, 2; MTCW 1, 2; MTFW 2005; NFS 14; SATA 16, 58, 102; SATA-Obit 142; WYA; YAW
Zinn, Howard 1922- .... **CLC 199**
See also CA 1-4R; CANR 2, 33, 90
Zinov'Ev, A. A.
See Zinoviev, Alexander (Aleksandrovich)
Zinov'ev, Aleksandr (Aleksandrovich)
See Zinoviev, Alexander (Aleksandrovich)
See also DLB 302
Zinoviev, Alexander (Aleksandrovich)
1922- .... **CLC 19**
See Zinov'ev, Aleksandr (Aleksandrovich)
See also CA 116; 133; CAAS 10
Zizek, Slavoj 1949- .... **CLC 188**
See also CA 201; MTFW 2005
Zoilus
See Lovecraft, H(oward) P(hillips)
Zola, Emile (Edouard Charles Antoine)
1840-1902 ...... **TCLC 1, 6, 21, 41; WLC**
See also CA 104; 138; DA; DA3; DAB; DAC; DAM MST, NOV; DLB 123; EW 7; GFL 1789 to the Present; IDTP; LMFS 1, 2; RGWL 2; TWA
Zoline, Pamela 1941- .... **CLC 62**
See also CA 161; SFW 4
Zoroaster 628(?)B.C.-551(?)B.C. .. **CMLC 40**
Zorrilla y Moral, Jose 1817-1893 .... **NCLC 6**
Zoshchenko, Mikhail (Mikhailovich)
1895-1958 .... **SSC 15; TCLC 15**
See also CA 115; 160; EWL 3; RGSF 2; RGWL 3
Zuckmayer, Carl 1896-1977 .... **CLC 18**
See also CA 69-72; DLB 56, 124; EWL 3; RGWL 2, 3
Zuk, Georges
See Skelton, Robin
See also CCA 1
Zukofsky, Louis 1904-1978 ... **CLC 1, 2, 4, 7, 11, 18; PC 11**
See also AMWS 3; CA 9-12R; 77-80; CANR 39; CP 1, 2; DAM POET; DLB 5, 165; EWL 3; MAL 5; MTCW 1; RGAL 4
Zweig, Paul 1935-1984 .... **CLC 34, 42**
See also CA 85-88; 113
Zweig, Stefan 1881-1942 .... **TCLC 17**
See also CA 112; 170; DLB 81, 118; EWL 3
Zwingli, Huldreich 1484-1531 .... **LC 37**
See also DLB 179

Literary Criticism Series
Cumulative Topic Index

This index lists all topic entries in Thompson Gale's *Children's Literature Review* (CLR), *Classical and Medieval Literature Criticism* (CMLC), *Contemporary Literary Criticism* (CLC), *Drama Criticism* (DC), *Literature Criticism from 1400 to 1800* (LC), *Nineteenth-Century Literature Criticism* (NCLC), *Short Story Criticism* (SSC), and *Twentieth-Century Literary Criticism* (TCLC). The index also lists topic entries in the Gale Critical Companion Collection, which includes the following publications: *The Beat Generation* (BG), *Feminism in Literature* (FL), *Gothic Literature* (GL), and *Harlem Renaissance* (HR).

Topic Index

Topic Index

NCLC Cumulative Nationality Index

NCLC-169 Title Index

ISBN 0-7876-8653-0

90000